SPORTS AND GAMES

Spreadsheet Modeling and Applications
Essentials of Practical Management Science

Spreadsheet Modeling and Applications

Essentials of Practical Management Science

S. Christian Albright

Kelley School of Business, Indiana University

Wayne L. Winston

Kelley School of Business, Indiana University

With Cases by

Mark Broadie

Graduate School of Business, Columbia University

Lawrence L. Lapin

San Jose State University

William D. Whisler

California State University, Hayward

THOMSON
SOUTH-WESTERN

Australia · Brazil · Canada · Mexico · Singapore · Spain · United Kingdom · United States

THOMSON
SOUTH-WESTERN

Spreadsheet Modeling and Applications: Essentials of Practical Management Science

S. Christian Albright and Wayne L. Winston

With Cases by
Mark Broadie, Lawrence L. Lapin, and William D. Whisler

VP/Editorial Director:
Jack W. Calhoun

Publisher:
Curt Hinrichs

Developmental Editor:
Cheryll Linthicum

Assistant Editor:
Ann Day

Senior Editorial Assistant:
Katherine Brayton

Technology Project Manager:
Burke Taft

Marketing Manager:
Tom Ziolkowski

Marketing Assistant:
Jessica Bothwell

Advertising Project Manager:
Nathaniel Bergson-Michelson

Project Manager, Editorial Production:
Sandra Craig

Creative Director:
Rob Hugel

Print/Media Buyer:
Karen Hunt

Permissions Editor:
Sommy Ko

Production:
Susan Reiland

Text Design:
Tani Hasegawa

Photo Research:
Stephen Forsling

Copy Editor:
Christine Levesque

Illustrator:
Lori Heckelman

Cover Design:
Joan Greenfield

Cover Illustration:
Todd Damen

Cover Printer:
Phoenix Color Corp

Compositor:
ATLIS Graphics

Printer:
Quebecor World
Dubuque, IA

Library of Congress Control Number:
2004102060

For more information about our products, contact us at:

Thomson Learning Academic Resource Center

1-800-423-0563

Thomson Higher Education
5191 Natorp Boulevard
Mason, OH 45040
USA

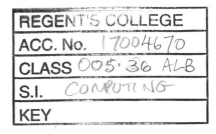

About the Authors

S. Christian Albright got his B.S. degree in Mathematics from Stanford in 1968 and his Ph.D. degree in Operations Research from Stanford in 1972. Since then he has been teaching in the Operations & Decision Technologies Department in the Kelley School of Business at Indiana University. He has taught courses in management science, computer simulation, and statistics to all levels of business students: undergraduates, MBAs, and doctoral students. He also teaches regular courses on database analysis to the Army. He has published over 20 articles in leading operations research journals in the area of applied probability, and he has authored several books, including the spreadsheet-based "trilogy" *Practical Management Science, Data Analysis and Decision Making,* and *Data Analysis for Managers.* Recently, he jointly developed *StatTools,* a statistical add-in for Excel, with the Palisade Corporation. His current interests are in spreadsheet modeling and the development of VBA applications in Excel, as well as Web programming with Microsoft's .NET technology.

On the personal side, Chris has been married to his wonderful wife Mary for 33 years. They have one son, Sam, who is currently working in New York City in the music business and plays saxophone with Davy Jones (from the Monkees) on a regular basis. Chris has many interests outside the academic area. They include activities with his family (especially traveling with Mary), going to cultural events at Indiana University, playing golf and tennis, running and power walking, and reading. And although he earns his livelihood from statistics and management science, his *real* passion is for playing classical music on the piano.

Wayne L. Winston is Professor of Operations & Decision Technologies in the Kelley School of Business at Indiana University, where he has taught since 1975. Wayne received his B.S. degree in Mathematics from MIT and his Ph.D. degree in Operations Research from Yale. He has written the successful textbooks *Operations Research: Applications and Algorithms, Mathematical Programming: Applications and Algorithms, Simulation Modeling Using @RISK, Data Analysis and Decision Making,* and *Financial Models Using Simulation and Optimization.* Wayne has published over 20 articles in leading journals and has won many teaching awards, including the schoolwide MBA award four times. He has taught classes at Microsoft, GM, Ford, Eli Lilly, Bristol-Myers Squibb, Arthur Andersen, Roche, PriceWaterhouseCoopers, and NCR. His current interest is in showing how spreadsheet models can be used to solve business problems in all disciplines, particularly in finance and marketing.

Wayne enjoys swimming and basketball, and his passion for trivia won him an appearance several years ago on the television game show *Jeopardy,* where he won two games. He is married to the lovely and talented Vivian. They have two children, Gregory and Jennifer.

To Mary, my wonderful wife, best friend, and constant companion

And to Bryn, the new Corgi in the family who keeps us both young   S.C.A.

To my wonderful family

Vivian, Jennifer, and Gregory   W.L.W.

Brief Contents

Contents

4 Linear Programming Models 115

5 Network Models 185

6 Optimization Models with Integer Variables 245

Preface

Spreadsheet Modeling and Applications (SMA) provides a spreadsheet-based, example-driven approach to the essential topics of management science. Our goal in writing this text is to illustrate the broad range of applications and show how they can be modeled and analyzed using Microsoft Excel. We believe that our approach mirrors the way in which problems are solved by professionals by emphasizing proven problem-solving methods and decision making based upon them. Management science is a quantitative science that can be inherently difficult for some students. However, we have made every effort in this text to present the concepts in an accessible manner without unnecessary mathematics or theory. We are confident that after reading this book and working its problems, you will have acquired valuable skills that will help you in your future coursework and your careers.

Spreadsheet Modeling and Applications is an outgrowth of our *Practical Management Science* (PMS) book, now in its second edition. Our initial objective in writing PMS was to reverse negative attitudes about the course by making the subject relevant to students. We did this by emphasizing modeling skills that students could appreciate and take with them into their careers. We have been very gratified by the success of that book. It has done a lot to meet our initial objectives in our own courses. We are especially pleased to hear about the success of the book at many other colleges and universities around the world. The latest information is that over 200 schools are using the book in the United States alone. However, as the spreadsheet approach has become more widely adopted, we have learned better pedagogical methods for teaching it in the classroom.

Much has changed since the first edition of PMS was published in 1996, and we believe that these changes are for the better. We have learned a lot about the "best practices" of spreadsheet modeling to promote clarity and communication. We have also developed better ways of teaching the materials, and we better understand where students tend to have difficulty with the concepts. A primary objective of this text is to illustrate and apply these pedagogical methods to make the subject more easily understood. We hope that this will help foster even better spreadsheet modeling practices among students, instructors, and, eventually, business professionals. In addition, we have eliminated a few of the more advanced topics found in PMS from the current book, thereby making it an "essentials" version that can be more easily covered in a one-semester course. Also, we have had the opportunity to teach this material at several organizations, including Eli Lilly, Price Waterhouse Coopers, General Motors, Microsoft, Intel, and the Army. Our experience with these organizations has further enhanced the realism of the models included in this book.

Why We Wrote This Book

Our initial objectives in writing SMA were very simple. We wanted to make management science relevant and practical to a wide body of students and professionals. We also wanted to make the book accessible to instructors who view our PMS book as too advanced (or too long) for their students. Nevertheless, our basic philosophy is the same as it has been in PMS, as described by the following goals:

- **Teach By Example.** We believe that the best way to learn modeling concepts is by working through examples and plenty of problems. This active learning approach is not new, but we believe this book has more fully developed the approach than any book in the field. The feedback we have received from many PMS users has confirmed the success of this pedagogical approach for management science, and we continue with it here.

- **Teach Modeling and Not Just Models.** We believe that the previous emphasis on algebraic formulations and memorization of models simply does not work, except possibly in technically advanced courses. Our experience indicates that the majority of students gain more insight into the power of management science by developing skills in spreadsheet modeling. Throughout the book, we stress the logic associated with model development, and we discuss the solutions in this context. In addition, we try to build a "bridge" from the verbal statement of the problem to the eventual spreadsheet model by listing and discussing the inputs, outputs, decision variables, and constraints that need to be considered. This is particularly relevant in the optimization chapters.

- **Provide Numerous Problems and Cases.** While all textbooks contain problem sets for students to practice, we have spent an enormous amount of time crafting the problems and cases contained in this book. These include over 250 new problems and cases that were not in PMS. There are four types of problems: Skill-Building Problems, Skill-Extending Problems, Modeling Problems, and Cases. We have attempted to grade these problems carefully within each section and at the ends of chapters. Selected worked-out solutions to problems featuring a colored box around the problem number are available for students in the Student Solutions Manual, available at your bookstore. Solutions for all of the problems and cases are provided to adopting instructors. In addition, shell files (templates) are available for most of the problems (again, to adopting instructors). The shell files contain the basic structure of the problems with the relevant formulas omitted. By adding or omitting hints in individual solutions, instructors can tailor these shell files for their own purposes.

- **Integrate Modeling with Finance, Marketing, and Operations Management.** We integrate modeling into all functional areas of business. This is an important feature because the majority of business students at many schools major in finance and marketing. Competing textbooks tend to emphasize operations-management-related examples. Although these examples are important and many are included in this book, the application of modeling to problems in finance and marketing is too important to ignore. Throughout the book, we use real examples from all functional areas of business to illustrate the power of spreadsheet modeling to all of these areas. At our school, this has led to the development of special team-taught advanced electives in finance and marketing that build upon the content in this book. The inside front cover of the book illustrates the integrative applications contained in the book.

A New AACSB Mandate

Before 1991, a course in management science was virtually required for all business schools by the AACSB, the business school accreditation organization. Then in 1991, the AACSB overhauled its accreditation system and eliminated this requirement. This was at a time when management science courses in business schools were viewed by many people as irrelevant, primarily because they were being taught as a math course. However, with the move toward spreadsheet modeling, interest in management science has increased and has, in part, led AACSB to reverse itself. In 2003, the AACSB now includes the statement, "Normally, the curriculum management process will result in undergraduate and masters programs that will include learning experiences in such management-specific knowledge and skill areas as: . . . Statistical data analysis and management science as they support decision-making processes throughout an organization." (For more about this mandate, consult the August 2003 issue of *ORMS Today* or at www.aacsb.edu.)

We cannot predict how business schools will respond to this new mandate, or even how many are currently in compliance, but we are very gratified that the mandate has been passed. It certainly strengthens our case that the material in this book is important and worthy of study by *all* business students. This book is not about abstract mathematical models; it is about real-world decision making, supported by spreadsheet analysis, and it is within the grasp of all business people. The AACSB evidently agrees.

Important New Features of the Book

Our experience over the past few years has taught us much about teaching a spreadsheet-based course in management science, and we have incorporated many suggestions from users of PMS to create the current book. Our original thought was to do a simple cut-and-paste on PMS: cut the more difficult examples, problems, and even chapters to arrive at an "essentials" book. However, we ended up going much farther than this. While many of the same topics, examples, and problems from PMS are retained here, we have made extensive changes throughout the book. Relative to PMS, our goal in SMA has been to *simplify, clarify,* and *enlighten.* The following is a list of important features, where asterisks denote items that were not present at all in PMS:

- **Improved Spreadsheet Readability and Documentation.** Many professionals we have taught instinctively document their spreadsheet models for the purpose of sharing them with colleagues or communicating them in presentations and reports. We believe this is an essential element of good spreadsheet modeling, and the current book does much more to emphasize this. To achieve this goal of better readability and documentation, we have reworked many of the examples in the chapters, adding labels, textboxes, and other documenting features, and we have incorporated our habits in all new examples. This is especially important because the book continues to be example-oriented.

- ***Example Objectives.** Following the statement of each example, we provide a short statement of the objectives, both business-concept and spreadsheet-oriented, to be addressed by that example.

- ***Where Do the Numbers Come From?** We now include a "Where Do the Numbers Come From?" section in each example, in which we specify where a company or individual might find the required input data.

- ***Tables of Key Variables and Constraints.** We realize that it is difficult for many students to translate a "story problem" into a spreadsheet model. This is particularly true for the optimization models in Chapters 3–7. At the very least, students need to identify input variables, output variables, decision variables, and the constraints. Therefore, in all of the examples in the optimization chapters, we begin the solution by listing all of the variables and constraints in a table. We believe this type of table, along with the thought process required to create it, should help students bridge the gap from the problem statement to the spreadsheet model.

- **Greater Emphasis on Insights and Decision Making.** We were sometimes criticized by PMS users for solving a problem and then immediately going on to the next example, without examining the solution itself. We now try to provide insights into the solutions—why they turn out as they do—and we spend more time discussing possible sensitivity analyses. In the optimization chapters, we continue to use our SolverTable add-in to provide easy-to-interpret sensitivity reports. However, we also discuss Solver's Sensitivity Reports in more detail than in PMS. We realize that many instructors like to use Solver's reports, so we explain when they are applicable, what their outputs mean, and how they compare to SolverTable results.

- ***Margin notes.** We supply many notes in the margins to help the students learn and study the material.

- ***Boxed-in Definitions, Formulas.** We display the really important definitions, and occasionally formulas, in boxes. These are designed to make it easier for students to study the material.

- ***Summaries of Key Terms.** At the end of each chapter, we include lists of Key Management Science Terms and Key Excel Terms.

- **Range Names.** We continue to make frequent use of range names. After all, the formula =SUMPRODUCT(Flows,UnitCosts) is much easier to read (and grade) than =SUMPRODUCT(C15:C30,E15:E30). Although the use of range names is undoubtedly a great habit, one that is mandated by many organizations, it can be time-consuming to name the ranges in the first place. Therefore, we illustrate a very useful shortcut for creating range names, using available labels in adjacent rows or columns. We also explain how to create a list of all named ranges for documentation purposes.

- **Color Coding.** As in *Practical Management Science,* the accompanying Excel example files contain color-coding that helps clarify the models. (This color-coding is illustrated in Chapters 3 and 4.) All input cells are in a blue border and shaded, all decision variable cells (changing cells for Solver models) are in a red border, all random cells (for the simulation chapters) are in a dashed green border, and the target cell for optimization models is in a double-black border. The designation of input cells, whether in a blue border with shading or by some other means, is particularly important. When you look at someone else's model, you should immediately be able to tell which cells are the inputs and which are calculated from them.

- **New Problems.** Many of the more difficult problems from PMS have been deleted, and the problems have been reorganized. The problems that now follow the various sections are mostly new problems. (There are about 250 such new problems. All other problems have been moved to the "end-of-chapter" sections.) These new problems extend the example(s) discussed in the preceding sections. We believe instructors and students will appreciate these new problems. Because many are based on already-solved examples, students do not need to start from scratch; they need only modify existing models. This allows students to do exactly what they will need to do in many real-world studies: add functionality or extensions to existing models.

- **New Modeling Approach to Project Scheduling.** Project scheduling, discussed in Chapters 5 and 10, is a difficult problem to model, particularly if we want to incorporate "crashing." Although it is probably impossible to develop a model that satisfies everyone—there are some strong opinions on how project scheduling *should* be modeled—we believe we now finally have it right. Our approach is in line with the traditional approach to project scheduling, and it is consistent throughout Chapters 5 and 10.

- **More Discussion of Input Probability Distributions in Simulation.** Our experience indicates that the biggest problem for students in spreadsheet simulation is an understanding of input probability distributions: Why should they use one distribution rather than another, and what are the implications of using one over another? We have provided much more discussion of these issues in Chapter 9, the introductory simulation chapter, and we have taken full advantage of the previously overlooked (and extremely easy-to-use) software package, RISKview, that accompanies the book.

The DecisionTools Suite Software

We are very excited about offering the Student Edition of DecisionTools suite that is packaged with new copies of the book. The commercial value of the DecisionTools software exceeds $1000 if purchased directly. This software is for students only and will function for two years. Students who elect to purchase a used copy of this text may purchase the DecisionTools software separately. Professionals may use the software for 30 days but will need to contact the software vendors directly to obtain licensed versions. The following software is included:

- Palisade's **DecisionTools™ Suite,** including the award-winning **@Risk, PrecisionTree, BestFit, TopRank,** and **RISKview.** This software is not available with any competing textbook (except PMS). The @RISK and RISKview add-ins are used extensively for simulation in Chapters 9 and 10. The PrecisionTree add-in is used for decision making under uncertainty in Chapter 8. For more information about the Palisade Corporation and the DecisionTools Suite, visit Palisade's Web site at www.palisade.com.

- Also from Palisade Corporation is **StatTools™,** an Excel add-in for data analysis. (Formerly known as StatPro, the Palisade version has the same basic functionality as StatPro, but it incorporates a friendlier and more compact user interface.) The StatTools add-in is featured in Chapter 12, where we discuss regression and forecasting. It performs many useful statistical operations, from creating simple charts and calculating basic summary measures to more complex techniques such as regression and forecasting. Much of StatTools is not necessary for this book, but the regression and forecasting tools are very useful in the final chapter.

Contents of the Book's CD

The CD-ROM included in the text contains the book-specific software, example and data files, and an Excel Tutorial. To make sensitivity analysis useful and intuitive, we provide **SolverTable,** developed by one of the authors. SolverTable provides sensitivity output that is easy to interpret. It works much like Excel's data tables. You specify one or two input cells, a range of values for these cells that you want to test, and one or more output cells that you want to keep track of. Then SolverTable runs Solver repeatedly with your varying inputs and reports the corresponding outputs. It is the most intuitive way we have found of conducting sensitivity analysis in optimization models, and students can learn it almost immediately.

The CD-ROM also contains the **Excel workbooks** that are used in the examples. For most of the examples, there are two versions: a "template" with the input data only and a finished version. The CD-ROM also includes the data files required for a number of problems and cases. We also mention that there are a number of problems denoted with a color box in the chapters. Solutions to these problems are available to students in the Student Solutions Manual. These solutions are *not* included on the CD-ROM that accompanies the book and must be purchased separately from Duxbury.

Finally, the CD-ROM contains an interactive Word file, **ExcelTutorial.doc,** that gets you up to speed in many basic Excel tools. It can be used by Excel beginners to learn about such things as VLookup functions and data tables, and it can be used by experienced Excel users to improve their efficiency in carrying out common tasks.

Ancillary Materials

Besides the CD-ROM that accompanies this text, the following materials are available to qualified adopters:

- **Instructor's Suite CD-ROM.** The Instructor's Suite CD contains the Instructor's Solutions Manual in Microsoft Excel, Test Bank in Microsoft Word, and Microsoft PowerPoint slides. These are provided to help the adopter teach from the book.

- **Student Solutions Manual.** The Student Solutions Manual contains the solutions to selected problems. Problems with a colored box have solutions included in the Student Solutions Manual. This Manual consists of Microsoft Excel screenshots, visually showing the student the solutions to the problems.

Acknowledgments

This book has gone through several stages of reviews, and it is a much better product because of them. The majority of the reviewers' suggestions were very good ones, and we have attempted to incorporate them. Thanks go to Timothy Anderson, Portland State University; William Christian, James Madison University; Abe Feinberg, California State University, Northridge; Roger Grinde, University of New Hampshire; Tom Grossman, University of Calgary; Mehran Hojati, University of Saskatchewan; Harvey Iglarsh, Georgetown University; Jason Merrick, Virginia Commonwealth University; Prakash Mirchandani, University of Pittsburgh; James Morris, University of Wisconsin-Madison; Alysse Morton, Westminster College; Danny Myers, Bowling Green State University; Steve Nahmias, Santa Clara University; Gary Reeves, University of South Carolina; Thomas Schriber, University of Michigan; Don Simmons, Ithaca College; and Thomas Whalen, Georgia State University. We extend thanks as well to the accuracy checker, Anand Paul, University of Florida.

We would also like to thank two special people. First, we want to thank our editor Curt Hinrichs for continuing to be the guiding light on this project. Throughout the development of PMS and now this book, Curt has kept up incredible enthusiasm for the spreadsheet approach to teaching management science. He is truly a visionary in this area, and his ideas have shaped much of what we have done here. If the new edition continues to be a success, it is due in large part to Curt's efforts. We also want to thank our production editor, Susan Reiland. She has been wonderful to work with. Any management science book is bound to contain a lot of details, and one based on spreadsheets has even more details. Trying to get all of these details correct is a difficult task—to say the least—and Susan has had the patience and the perfectionist attitude to help us "get it right."

Other team members we would like to acknowledge are Katherine Brayton, senior editorial assistant; Cheryll Linthicum, development editor; Ann Day, assistant editor; Burke Taft, technology project manager; Tom Ziolkowski, marketing manager; Jessica Bothwell, marketing assistant; and Sandra Craig, editorial production project manager.

We would also enjoy hearing from you—we can be reached by e-mail. And please visit either of the following Web sites for more information and occasional updates: www.indiana.edu/~mgtsci or http://swlearning.com.

S. Christian Albright
albright@indiana.edu

Wayne L. Winston
winston@indiana.edu

Introduction to Modeling

© EyeWire

ALGORITHMS SOLVE COMPLEX REAL-WORLD PROBLEMS

As you embark on your study of management science, you might question the usefulness of quantitative methods to the "real world." A front-page article in the December 31, 1997, edition of *USA Today* entitled "Higher Math Delivers Formula for Success" provides some convincing evidence of the applicability of the methods you will be learning. The subheading of the article, "Businesses turn to algorithms to solve complex problems," says it all. Today's business problems tend to be very complex. In the past, many managers and executives used a "seat of the pants" approach to solve problems—that is, they used their business experience, their intuition, and some thoughtful guesswork to obtain solutions. But common sense and intuition go only so far in the solution of the complex problems businesses now face. This is where management science models—and the algorithms mentioned in the title of the article—are so useful. When the methods in this book are implemented in user-friendly computer software packages and are then applied to complex problems, the results can be amazing. Robert Cross, whose company, DFI Aeronomics, sells algorithm-based systems to airlines, states it succinctly: "It's like taking raw information and spinning money out of it."

The power of the methods in this book is that they are applicable to so many problems and environments. The article mentions the following "success stories" where management science has been applied; others will be discussed throughout this book. (1) United Airlines installed one of DFI's systems, which cost between $10 million and $20 million. United expects the system to add $50 million to $100 million *annually* to its revenues. (2) The Gap clothing chain uses management science to determine exactly how many employees should staff each store during the Christmas rush. (3) Management science has helped medical researchers test potentially dangerous drugs on fewer people with better results. (4) IBM obtained a $93 million contract to build a computer system for the Department of Energy that would do a once-impossible task: make exact real-time models of atomic blasts. It won the contract—and convinced the DOE that its system was cost-effective—only by developing management science models that would cut the processing time by half. (5) Hotels, airlines, and television broadcasters all use management science to implement a new method called "yield management." In this method, different prices are charged to different customers, depending on their willingness to pay. The effect is that more customers are attracted, and revenues increase.

The article concludes by stating that Microsoft's Excel spreadsheet software has a built-in optimization program called Solver. This is a key statement. Many of the algorithms that enable the successes discussed in the article are very complex mathematically. They are well beyond the grasp of the typical user, including most readers of this book. However, users no longer need to understand all of the details behind the algorithms. They need only to know (1) how to model business problems so that appropriate algorithms can be applied and (2) how to apply these algorithms with user-friendly software. We will see in Chapters 3–7 how to apply Excel's Solver to a variety of complex problems. You will not learn the intricacies of how Solver does its optimization, but you *will* learn how to use Solver very productively. The same statement applies to the other methods discussed in this book. You might not understand exactly what is happening in the computer's "black box" as it performs its calculations, but you will learn how to become very effective problem solvers by taking advantage of powerful software. ■

1.1 INTRODUCTION

The purpose of this book is to expose you to a variety of problems that have been solved successfully with management science methods and to give you experience in modeling these problems in the Excel spreadsheet package. The subject of management science has evolved for over 50 years and is now a mature field within the broad category of applied mathematics. Our intent in this book is to emphasize both the applied and mathematical aspects of management science. Beginning in this chapter and continuing throughout the rest of the book, we will discuss many successful management science applications, where teams of highly trained people have implemented solutions to the problems faced by major companies and have saved these companies millions of dollars. Many airlines and oil companies, for example, could hardly operate as they do today without the support of management science. In this book we will lead you through the solution procedure of many interesting and realistic problems, and you will experience firsthand what is required to solve these problems successfully. We recognize that most of you are not highly trained in mathematics. Therefore, we will utilize spreadsheets to solve problems. This makes the quantitative analysis much more understandable and intuitive.

The key to virtually every management science application is a **mathematical model**. In simple terms, a mathematical model is a quantitative representation of a real problem. This representation might be phrased in terms of mathematical expressions (equations and inequalities) or as a series of interrelated cells in a spreadsheet. We prefer the latter, especially for teaching purposes, and we will concentrate primarily on spreadsheet models in this book. However, in either case the purpose of a mathematical model is to represent the essence of a problem in a concise form. This has several advantages. First, it enables an analyst to understand the problem better. In particular, it helps to define the scope of the problem, the possible solutions, and the data requirements. Second, it allows the analyst to employ a variety of the mathematical solution procedures that have been developed over the past half-century. These solution procedures are often very computer intensive, but with today's cheap and abundant computing power, they are usually possible. Finally, the modeling process itself, if it is done correctly, often helps to "sell" the solution to the people who must work with the system that is eventually implemented.

In this chapter we will introduce the concept of a mathematical model with a relatively simple example. Then we will discuss the difference between modeling and a collection of models, and we will describe a seven-step model-building process that should be followed—in essence if not in strict conformance—in all management science applications. Next, we will describe a successful application of management science. For this application, we will illustrate how the seven-step model-building process was followed. Finally, we will discuss why the study of management science is valuable, not only to large corporations, but also to students like you who are about to enter the business world.

1.2 A WAITING-LINE EXAMPLE

As indicated earlier, a mathematical model is a set of mathematical relationships that represent, or approximate, a real situation. Some models simply describe a situation. Such models are called **descriptive** models. Other models suggest a desirable course of action. Such models are called **prescriptive**, or **optimization**, models. To get us started, we discuss the following simple example of a mathematical model. It begins as a descriptive model, but we then expand it to an optimization model.

Consider a 7-Eleven store with a single cash register. The manager of the store suspects that customers might be waiting too long in line at the checkout register and that these excessive waiting times could be hurting business. Customers who have to wait a long time might not come back, and potential customers who see a long line might not enter the store at all. Therefore, the manager wants to build a mathematical model to help understand the problem. The manager wants to build a model that reflects the current situation at the store but will also be able to improve the current situation.

A Descriptive Model

This example is a typical waiting line, or **queueing**, problem. (Such problems are discussed in detail in Chapter 11.) The manager first wants to build a model that reflects the *current* situation at the store. Later he will alter the model to predict what might make the situation better. To describe the current situation, the manager realizes that there are two important *inputs* to the problem: (1) the arrival rate of potential customers to the store and (2) the rate at which customers can be served by the single cashier. It is intuitively clear that as the arrival rate increases or the service rate decreases, the waiting line will tend to increase and each customer will tend to wait longer in line. In addition, it is likely that more potential customers will decide not to enter at all. It is common to refer to these latter quantities (length of waiting line, time in line per customer, fraction of customers who don't enter) as *outputs*. The manager believes he has some understanding of the relationship between the inputs and the outputs, but he is not at all sure how to *quantify* the relationship between them.

This is where a mathematical model is useful. By making several simplifying assumptions about the nature of the arrival and service process at the store (as will be discussed in Chapter 11), we can relate the inputs to the outputs. In some cases, when the model is sufficiently simple, we can write an *equation* for an output in terms of the inputs. For example, in one of the simplest queueing models, if we let A be the arrival rate of customers per minute, S be the service rate of customers per minute, and W be the average time a typical customer waits in line (assuming that all potential customers enter the store), then the following relationship can be derived mathematically:

$$W = \frac{A}{S(S - A)}$$

This relationship is intuitive in one sense. It correctly predicts that as the service rate S increases, the average waiting time W will decrease, and as the arrival rate A increases, the average waiting time W will increase. Also, if the arrival rate is just barely less than the service rate—that is, $S - A$ is positive but very small—the average waiting time will become quite large. (This model requires the arrival rate to be *less than* the service rate; otherwise, the equation for W makes no sense.)

In many other models there is no such "closed-form" relationship between inputs and outputs (or if there is, it is too complex for the level of this book). Nevertheless, there may still be a mathematical procedure for calculating outputs from inputs, and it may be possible to implement this procedure in Excel. This is the case for the 7-Eleven problem. Again, by making certain simplifying assumptions, including the assumption that potential customers will not enter if there are already N customers in the store, we can develop a spreadsheet model of the situation at the store.

Before presenting it, however, we discuss how the manager can obtain the inputs he needs for the spreadsheet model. There are actually three inputs: the arrival rate A, the service rate S, and the maximum number in the store, labeled N. The first two of these can be measured with a stopwatch. For example, the manager can request an employee to measure the times between customer arrivals. Let's say the employee does this for several hours, and the average time between arrivals is observed to be 2 minutes. Then the arrival rate can be estimated as $A = 1/2 = 0.5$ (1 customer every 2 minutes). Similarly, the employee can record the times it takes the cashier to serve successive customers. If the average of these times (taken over many customers) is, say, 2.5 minutes, then the service rate can be estimated as $S = 1/2.5 = 0.4$ (1 customer every 2.5 minutes). Finally, if the manager notices that potential customers tend to take their business elsewhere when there are 5 customers in the store, then he can let $N = 5$. (Note that A is allowed to be greater than S when N is a finite value.)

These input estimates can now be entered in the spreadsheet model shown in Figure 1.1. (See the file **QueueingExample.xls**.) Don't worry about the details of this spreadsheet—they will be covered in Chapter 11. Just trust us that the formulas built into this spreadsheet reflect an adequate approximation of the 7-Eleven store's situation. For now, the important thing is that this model allows the manager to enter any values for the inputs in cells B4–B6 and observe the resulting outputs in cells B9–B13. The input values in Figure 1.1 represent the store's current input values. These values indicate that on average there are slightly more than 2 customers waiting in line, an average customer waits slightly more than 6 minutes in line, and about 27% of all potential customers do not enter the store at all (due to the perception that waiting times will be long).

Figure 1.1

Descriptive Queueing Model for 7-Eleven Store

	A	B
1	Descriptive queueing model for 7-Eleven	
2		
3	Inputs	
4	Arrival rate (customers per minute)	0.5
5	Service rate (customers per minute)	0.4
6	Maximum customers (before others go elsewhere)	5
7		
8	Outputs	
9	Average number in system	3.13
10	Average number in queue	2.22
11	Average time (minutes) in system	8.59
12	Average time (minutes) in queue	6.09
13	Percentage of potential arrivals who don't enter	27.1%

The information in Figure 1.1 may not be all that useful to the manager. After all, he probably already has a sense of how long waiting times are and how many customers are being lost. The power of the model is that it allows the manager to ask many what-if questions. For example, what if he could somehow speed up the cashier, say, from 2.5 minutes per customer to 1.8 minutes per customer? He might guess that since the average service time has decreased by 28%, all of the outputs should also decrease by 28%. Is this the case? Evidently not, as shown in Figure 1.2. The average queue length decreases to 1.41, a 36% decrease; the average waiting time in the queue decreases to 3.22, a 47% decrease; and the percentage of customers who do not enter decreases to 12.6%, a 54% decrease.

Figure 1.2

Queueing Model with a Faster Service Rate

	A	B
1	Descriptive queueing model for 7-Eleven	
2		
3	Inputs	
4	Arrival rate (customers per minute)	0.5
5	Service rate (customers per minute)	0.556
6	Maximum customers (before others go elsewhere)	5
7		
8	Outputs	
9	Average number in system	2.19
10	Average number in queue	1.41
11	Average time (minutes) in system	5.02
12	Average time (minutes) in queue	3.22
13	Percentage of potential arrivals who don't enter	12.6%

To illustrate an even more extreme change, suppose the manager could cut the service time in half, from 2.5 minutes to 1.25 minutes. The spreadsheet in Figure 1.3 (page 6) shows that the average number in line decreases to 0.69, a 69% decrease from the original value; the average waiting time in queue decreases to 1.42, a 77% decrease; and the percentage of customers who do not enter decreases to 3.8%, a whopping 86% decrease. The important lesson to be learned from the spreadsheet model is that as the manager increases the service rate, the output measures improve more than he might have expected.

Figure 1.3

Queueing Model
with an Even Faster
Service Rate

	A	B
1	Descriptive queueing model for 7-Eleven	
2		
3	Inputs	
4	Arrival rate (customers per minute)	0.5
5	Service rate (customers per minute)	0.8
6	Maximum customers (before others go elsewhere)	5
7		
8	Outputs	
9	Average number in system	1.29
10	Average number in queue	0.69
11	Average time (minutes) in system	2.67
12	Average time (minutes) in queue	1.42
13	Percentage of potential arrivals who don't enter	3.8%

In reality, the manager would attempt to validate the spreadsheet model before trusting its answers to these what-if questions. At the very least, the manager should examine whether the assumptions are reasonable. For example, one assumption is that the arrival rate remains *constant* for the time period under discussion. If the manager intends to use this model—with the *same* input parameters—during periods of time when the arrival rate varies quite a lot (such as peak lunchtime traffic followed by slack times in the early afternoon), then he is almost certainly asking for trouble.

Besides determining whether the assumptions are reasonable, the manager can also check the outputs predicted by the model when the current inputs are used. For example, Figure 1.1 predicts that the average time a customer waits in line is approximately 6 minutes. At this point, the manager could ask his employee to use a stopwatch again to time customers' waiting times. If they average close to 6 minutes, then the manager can put more confidence in the model. However, if they average much more or much less than 6 minutes, then the manager probably needs to search for a new model.

An Optimization Model

As the model stands so far, it fails to reflect any *economic* information, such as the cost of speeding up service, the cost of making customers wait in line, or the cost of losing customers. Given the spreadsheet model developed previously, however, it is relatively straightforward to incorporate economic information and then make rational choices.

For example, if the manager could hire a second person to help the first cashier and thereby decrease the average service time from 2.5 to 1.8 minutes, then the model in Figure 1.2 becomes relevant. Alternatively, if the manager could lease a new model of cash register that would decrease the service time from 2.5 to 1.25 minutes, then the model in Figure 1.3 becomes relevant. However, there are costs and benefits from both of these possible changes. In an optimization model, we would quantify these costs and benefits and choose the decision that minimizes the expected net cost. We will not pursue the details here, but we will examine a similar optimization model in Chapter 11. Indeed, we will examine a variety of optimization models throughout much of the book.

1.3 MODELING VERSUS MODELS

Management science, at least as it has been taught in most traditional courses, has evolved as a collection of mathematical models. These include various linear programming models (the transportation model, the diet model, the shortest route model, and many others), inventory models, queueing models, and so on. Much time has been devoted to teaching (and learning) the intricacies of these particular models as an end in itself. Management science *practitioners*, on the other hand, have justifiably criticized this emphasis on specific models. They argue that the majority of real-world problems that can be solved by management science methods cannot be neatly classified as one of the handful of models typically included in a management science textbook. In other words, there is often no "off-the-shelf" model that can be used, without modification, to solve a company's real problem.

Fortunately, this emphasis on specific models has been changing in the past decade, and our goal in this book is to continue this change. Specifically, we plan to stress *modeling*, not models. Although the distinction between modeling and models is probably difficult to grasp at this point, it will become clearer as you proceed through the book. Learning specific models is generally more of a memorization process, and possibly learning how to "trick" other problems into looking like the models you have learned. Modeling, on the other hand, is a *process*, where we abstract the essence of a real problem into a model, spreadsheet or otherwise. We do not try to shoehorn each problem into one of a small number of well-studied models. Instead, we treat each problem on its own merits and model it appropriately, using whatever logical, analytical, or spreadsheet skills we have at our disposal—and, of course, drawing analogies from previous models we have built whenever they are relevant.

1.4 THE SEVEN-STEP MODELING PROCESS

The discussion of the queueing model in Section 1.2 presented some of the basic principles of management science modeling. In this section we will further expand on these ideas by characterizing the modeling process as the following seven-step procedure.

Step 1: Problem Definition

The management scientist first defines the organization's problem. Defining the problem includes specifying the organization's objectives and the parts of the organization that must be studied before the problem can be solved. In our simple queueing model the organization's problem was how to minimize the expected net cost associated with the operation of the store's cash register.

Step 2: Data Collection

After defining the problem, the analyst collects data to estimate the value of parameters that affect the organization's problem. These estimates are used to develop a mathematical model (step 3) of the organization's problem and predict solutions (step 4). In the 7-Eleven queueing example, the manager needs to observe the arrivals and the checkout process to estimate the arrival rate A and the service rate S.

Step 3: Model Development

In the third step the analyst develops a model of the problem. In this book we will describe many methods that can be used to model systems.[1] Models such as the equation for W, where we use an equation to relate inputs such as A and S to outputs such as W, are called **analytic models**. Most realistic applications are so complex, however, that an analytic model does not exist or is too complex to work with. For example, if the 7-Eleven store had more than one register and customers were allowed to join any line or jump from one line to another, there would be no tractable analytic model—no equation or system of

---

[1]All of these models can generically be called **mathematical models**. However, because we will implement them in spreadsheets, we generally refer to them as **spreadsheet models**.

equations—that could be used to determine W from knowledge of A, S, and the number of lines. When no tractable analytic model exists, we often rely instead on a **simulation model**, which enables us to approximate the behavior of the actual system. We will discuss simulation models in Chapters 9 and 10.

Step 4: Model Verification

The management scientist now tries to determine whether the model developed in the previous step is an accurate representation of reality. A first step in determining how well the model fits reality is to check whether the model is valid for the current situation. As discussed previously, to validate the equation for the waiting time W, the manager might observe actual customer waiting times for several hours. As we have already seen, the equation for W predicts that when $A = 0.5$ and $S = 0.4$, the average customer spends 6.09 minutes in line. Now suppose the manager observes that 120 customers spend a total of 750 minutes in line. This indicates an average of $750/120 = 6.25$ minutes in line per customer. Because 6.25 is reasonably close to 6.09, the manager's observations would appear to lend credibility to the model. In contrast, if the 120 customers had spent 1200 minutes total in line, for an average of 10 minutes per customer, this would not agree very well with the model's prediction of 6.09 minutes, and we would doubt the validity of the model.

Step 5: Optimization and Decision Making

Given a model and a set of possible decisions, the analyst must now choose the decision that best meets the organization's objectives. We briefly discussed an optimization model for the 7-Eleven example, and we will discuss many others throughout the book.

Step 6: Model Communication to Management

In this step the analyst presents the model and the recommendations from the previous step to the organization. In some situations the analyst might present several alternatives and let the organization choose the one that best meets its needs.

Step 7: Model Implementation

If the organization has accepted the validity and usefulness of the study, the analyst then helps to implement its recommendations. The implemented system must be monitored constantly (and updated dynamically as the environment changes) to ensure that the model enables the organization to meet its objectives.

Flowchart of Procedure

The flowchart in Figure 1.4 illustrates this seven-step process. As the arrows pointing down and to the left indicate, there is room for feedback in the process. For example, at various steps the analyst might realize that the current model is not capturing some key aspects of the real problem. In this case the analyst might need to revise the problem definition or develop a new model.

Figure 1.4   Flowchart for Seven-Step Process

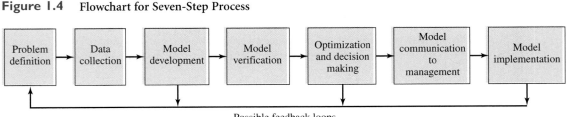

Possible feedback loops

Discussion of the Seven Steps

We now discuss the seven modeling steps in more detail.

Step 1: Problem Definition

Typically, a management science model is commissioned when an organization believes it has a problem. Perhaps the company is losing money, perhaps its market share is declining, perhaps its customers are waiting too long for service—any number of problems might be evident. The organization (which we will refer to as the client) calls in a management scientist (the analyst) to help solve this problem. In such cases the problem has probably already been defined by the client, and the client hires the analyst to solve *this particular problem*.

As Miser (1993) and Volkema (1995) point out, however, the analyst should do some investigating before accepting the client's claim that the problem is already well defined. Failure to do so could mean solving the wrong problem and wasting valuable time and energy.

For example, Miser cites the experience of an analyst who was hired by the military to investigate overly long turnaround times between fighter planes landing and taking off again to rejoin the battle. The military (the client) was convinced that the problem was caused by inefficient ground crews—if they were sped up, turnaround times would presumably decrease. The analyst nearly accepted this statement of the problem and was about to do classical time-and-motion studies on the ground crew to pinpoint the source of their inefficiency. However, by snooping around, he found that the problem lay elsewhere. It seems that the trucks that refueled the planes were frequently late, which in turn was due to the inefficient way they were refilled from storage tanks at another location. Once this latter problem was solved—and its solution was embarrassingly simple—the turnaround times decreased to an acceptable level without any changes on the part of the ground crews. If the analyst had accepted the client's statement of the problem, the *real* problem might never have been located or solved.

The moral of this story is clear: If an analyst defines a problem incorrectly or too narrowly, the best solution to the real problem might never emerge. In his article, Volkema (1995) advocates spending as much time thinking about the problem and defining it properly as modeling and solving it. This is undoubtedly good advice, especially in real-world applications where problem boundaries are often difficult to define.

Step 2: Data Collection

This crucial step in the modeling process is often the most tedious. All organizations keep track of various data on their operations, but these data are often not in the form the analyst requires. In addition, data are often stored in different places throughout the organization and in all kinds of formats. Therefore, one of the analyst's first jobs is to gather exactly the right data and put the data into the appropriate form required by the model. This typically requires asking questions of key people (such as the accountants) throughout the organization, studying existing organizational databases, and performing time-consuming observational studies of the organization's processes. In short, it often entails a lot of leg work.

In this book, as in most management science textbooks, we tend to shield you from this data-collection process by supplying the appropriate data to formulate and solve a model. Although this makes the overall modeling process seem easier than it really is, it is simply not practical in most class settings to have students go out to companies and gather data. (In many cases it would not even be allowed for proprietary reasons.) Nevertheless, we provide some insights with "Where Do the Numbers Come From?" sections. If nothing else, these sections remind you that in real applications, someone has to gather the necessary inputs.

Step 3: Model Development

This step (along with step 5) is where the analyst brings his or her special skills into play. After defining the client's problem and gathering the necessary data, the analyst must develop a model of the problem. Several properties are desirable for a good model. First, it should represent the client's real problem accurately. If it uses a linear (straight-line) function for costs when the real cost function is highly nonlinear (curved), the recommendations of the model could be very misleading. Similarly, if it ignores an important constraint such as an upper bound on capacity, its recommendations might not be possible to implement.

On the other hand, the model should be as simple as possible. Most good models (where "good" really means *useful*) capture the essence of the problem without getting bogged down in minor details. They should be *approximations* of the real world, not mirror images in every last detail. Overly complex models are often of little practical use. First, overly complex models are sometimes too difficult to solve with the solution algorithms available. Second, complex models tend to be incomprehensible to clients. After all, if a client cannot understand a thing about a model, the chances are not too good that the model's recommendations will ever be implemented. Therefore, a good model should achieve the right balance between being too simplistic and too complex.

Step 4: Model Verification

This step is particularly important in real management science applications. A client is much more likely to accept an analyst's model if the analyst can provide some type of verification. This verification might take several forms. For example, the analyst could use the model with the company's current values of the *input* parameters. If the model's outputs are then in line with the *outputs* currently observed by the client, the analyst has at least shown that the model can duplicate the current situation.

A second way to verify a model is to enter a number of sets of input parameters (even if they are not the company's current inputs) and see whether the outputs from the model are *reasonable*. One common approach is to use extreme values of the inputs to see whether the outputs behave as they should. For example, for the 7-Eleven queueing model we could enter an extremely large service rate or a service rate just barely above the arrival rate in the equation for W. In the first case we would expect the average waiting time to approach 0, whereas in the latter case we would expect it to become very large. You can use the equation for W to verify that this is exactly what happens. Therefore, we have another piece of evidence that this model is reasonable.

What if we enter certain inputs in the model, and the model's outputs are *not* as expected? There could be two causes. First, the model could simply be a poor representation of the actual situation. In this case it is up to the analyst to refine the model until it lines up more accurately with reality. Second, it is possible that the model is fine but our intuition is not very good. That is, when asked what we think would happen if the inputs were set equal to certain values, we might provide totally wrong predictions. In this case the fault lies with us, not the model. Sometimes, good models prove that people's ability to predict outcomes in complex environments is lacking. In such cases, the verification step becomes harder because of "political" reasons.

Step 5: Optimization and Decision Making

Once the problem has been defined, the data have been collected, and the model has been formulated and verified, it is time to use the model to recommend decisions or strategies. In the majority of management science models, this requires the optimization of an objective, such as maximizing profit or minimizing cost.

The optimization phase is typically the most difficult phase from a mathematical standpoint. Indeed, much of the management science literature (mostly from academics) has focused on complex solution algorithms for various classes of models. Fortunately for us, this research has led to a number of solution algorithms—and computer packages that implement these algorithms—that can be used to solve real problems. The most famous of these is the simplex algorithm. This algorithm, which has been implemented by many commercial software packages (including Excel's Solver), is used on a daily basis to solve linear programming optimization models for many companies. (We will take advantage of the simplex method in Chapters 3–5.)

Not all solution procedures find the optimal solution to a problem. Many models are too large or too complex to be solved exactly. Therefore, many complex problems use **heuristic** methods to locate "good" solutions. A heuristic is a solution method that is guided by common sense, intuition, and trial and error to achieve a good, but probably not optimal, solution. Some heuristics are "quick and dirty," whereas others are quite sophisticated. As models become larger and more complex, good heuristics are sometimes the best that can be achieved—and frequently they are perfectly adequate.

Step 6: Model Communication to Management

Sooner or later, an analyst must communicate a model and its recommendations to the client. To appreciate this step, you must appreciate the large gap that typically exists between the technical analyst and the managers of organizations. Managers know their business, but they often do not understand much about mathematics and mathematical models—even spreadsheet implementations of these models. The burden is therefore on the analyst to present the model in terms that nonmathematical people can understand; otherwise, a perfectly good model might never see the light of day.

The best strategy for successful presentation is to involve key people in the organization, including top executives, in the project *from the beginning*. If these people have been working with the analyst, helping to supply appropriate data and helping the analyst to understand the way the organization really works, they are much more likely to accept the eventual model. Step 6, therefore, should really occur throughout the modeling process, not just toward the end.

The analyst should also try to make the model as intuitive and as user-friendly as possible. Clients appreciate menu-driven systems with plenty of graphics. They also appreciate the ability to ask what-if questions and obtain answers quickly, in a form that is easy to understand. This is one reason for developing *spreadsheet* models. Although not all models can be developed on spreadsheets, due to size and/or complexity, we believe the spreadsheet approach in this book is an excellent choice whenever possible because most business people are comfortable with spreadsheets. Spreadsheet packages support the use of graphics, customized menus and toolbars, data tables and other tools for what-if analyses, and even macros (that can be made transparent to the users) for running complex programs.

Step 7: Model Implementation

A real management science application is not complete until it has been implemented. A successful implementation can occur only when step 6 has been accomplished. That is, the analyst must demonstrate the model to the client, and the client must be convinced that the model adds real value and can be used by the people who will have to use it. For this reason, the analyst's job is not really complete until the system is up and running on a daily basis. To achieve a successful implementation, it is not just sufficient for upper management to accept the model; the people who will run it every day must also be thoroughly trained in its use. At the very least, they should understand how to enter appropriate inputs, run what-if analyses, and interpret the model's outputs correctly. If they conclude that the model is more trouble than it's worth, they might simply refuse to use it, and the whole exercise will have been a waste of time.

It is interesting to observe how many successful management science applications take a life of their own after the initial implementation. Once an organization sees the benefits of a useful model—and of management science in general—it is likely to expand the model or create new models for uses beyond those originally intended. Knowing that this is often the case, the best analysts design models that can be expanded. They try to anticipate problems the organization might face besides the current problem. Also, they stay in contact with the organization after the initial implementation, just in case the organization needs guidance in expanding the scope of the model.

This discussion of the seven-step modeling process has taken an optimistic point of view. We have assumed that a successful study will employ these seven steps, in approximately this chronological order, and everything will go smoothly. It does not always work out this way. Numerous potential applications are never implemented even though the *technical* aspects of the models are perfectly correct. The most frequent cause is probably a failure to communicate. The analyst builds a complex mathematical model, but the people in the organization don't understand how it works and hence are reluctant to use it. Also, company politics can be a model's downfall, especially if the model recommends a course of action that top management simply does not want to follow—for whatever reasons.

Even for applications that are eventually implemented, the analyst might not proceed through the seven steps exactly as described in this section. He or she might backtrack considerably throughout the process. For example, based on a tentative definition of the problem, a model is built and demonstrated to management. Management says that the model is impressive, but it doesn't really solve the company's problem. Therefore, the analyst goes back to step 1, redefines the problem, and builds a new model (or modifies the original model). In this way, the analyst might generate several iterations of some or all of the seven steps before the project is considered complete.

1.5 A SUCCESSFUL MANAGEMENT SCIENCE APPLICATION

In this section we discuss one particular successful management science application at GE Capital. We provide a detailed (but nonquantitative) description of this application, and we tie our discussion of this application to the seven-step model-building process discussed in the previous section.

GE Capital

GE Capital, a subsidiary of the General Electric Company's financial services business, provides credit card service to 50 million accounts. The average total outstanding balance exceeds $12 billion. GE Capital, led by Makuch et al. (1992), developed the PAYMENT system to reduce delinquent accounts and the cost of collecting from delinquent accounts.

Step 1: Problem Definition

At any time, GE Capital has over $1 billion in delinquent accounts. The company spends $100 million annually processing these accounts. Each day employees contact over 200,000 delinquent credit cardholders with letters, taped phone messages, or live phone calls. However, prior to the study, there was no real scientific basis for the methods used to collect on various types of accounts. For example, GE Capital had no idea whether an account 2 months overdue should receive a taped phone message, a live phone call, some combination of these, or no contact at all. The company's goal was to reduce delinquent accounts and the cost of processing these accounts, but it was not sure how to accomplish this goal. Therefore, GE Capital's retail financial services component, together with management scientists and statisticians from GE's corporate research and development group, analyzed the problem and eventually developed a model called PAYMENT. The purpose of this model was to assign the most cost-effective collection methods to delinquent accounts.

Step 2: Data Collection

The key data requirements for modeling delinquent accounts are delinquency movement matrices (DMMs). A DMM shows how the probability of the payment on a delinquent account depends on the collection action taken (no action, live phone call, taped message, or letter), the size of the unpaid balance, and the account's performance score. (The higher the performance score associated with a delinquent account, the more likely the account is to be collected.) For example, if a $250 account is 2 months delinquent, has a high performance score, and is contacted with a phone message, then certain events might occur with certain probabilities. The events and the probabilities listed in Table 1.1 illustrate one possibility. The key is to estimate these probabilities for each possible collection action and each type of account.

Table 1.1   Sample DMM Entries

Event	Probability
Account completely paid off	0.30
One month is paid off	0.40
Nothing is paid off	0.30

Fortunately, because GE Capital had millions of delinquent accounts, plenty of data was available to estimate the DMMs accurately. To illustrate, suppose there are 1000 2-month delinquent accounts, each with balances under $300 and a high performance score. Also, suppose that each of these is contacted with a phone message. If 300 of these accounts are completely paid off by the next month, then an estimate of the probability of an account being completely paid off by next month is 0.30 (= 300/1000). By collecting the necessary data to estimate similar probabilities for all account types and collection actions, GE Capital finally had the basis for seeing which collection strategies were most cost-effective.

Step 3: Model Development

After collecting the required data and expressing it in the form of DMMs, the company needed to discover which collections worked best in which situations. Specifically, the analysts wanted to maximize the expected delinquent accounts collected during the following 6 months. However, they realized that this is a *dynamic* decision problem.

For example, one strategy is called "creaming." In this strategy, most collection resources are concentrated on live phone calls to the delinquent accounts classified as most likely to pay up—the best customers. This creaming strategy is attractive because it is likely to generate short-term cash flows from these customers. However, it has two negative aspects. First, it is likely to cause a loss of goodwill among the best customers. Second, it gains nothing in the long run from the customers who are most likely to default on their payments. Therefore, the analysts developed the PAYMENT model to find the best *decision strategy*, a contingency plan for each type of customer that specifies which collection strategy to use at each stage of the account's delinquency. There are also constraints in the PAYMENT model to ensure that available resources are not overused.

Step 4: Model Verification

A key aspect of GE Capital's problem is uncertainty. When the PAYMENT model specifies the collection method to use for a certain type of account, it implies that the probability of collecting on this account with this collection method is relatively high. However, there is still a chance that the collection method will fail. With this high degree of uncertainty, it is difficult to convince skeptics that the model will work as advertised until it has been demonstrated in an actual environment.

This is exactly what GE Capital did. It piloted the PAYMENT model on a $62 million portfolio for a single department store chain. To see the real effect of PAYMENT's recommended strategies, the pilot study used manager-recommended strategies for some accounts and PAYMENT-recommended strategies for others. They referred to this as the "champion" versus the "challenger." The challenger (PAYMENT) strategies were the clear winners, with an average monthly improvement of $185,000 over the champion strategies during a 5-month period. In addition, because the PAYMENT strategies included more "no contact" actions—don't bother the customer this month—they led to lower collection costs and greater customer goodwill. This demonstration was very convincing. In no time, other account managers wanted to take advantage of PAYMENT.

Step 5: Optimization and Decision Making

As described in step 3, the output from the PAYMENT model is a contingency plan. The model uses a very complex optimization scheme, along with the DMMs from step 2, to decide what collection strategy to use for each type of delinquent account at each month of its delinquency. At the end of each month, after the appropriate collection methods have been used and the results (actual payments) have been observed, the model then uses the status of each account to recommend the collection method for the next month. In this way, the model is used dynamically through time.

Step 6: Model Communication to Management

In general, the analyst communicates the model to the client in step 6. In this application, however, the management science team members were GE's own people—they came from GE Capital and the GE corporate research and development group. Throughout the model-building process, the team of analysts strived to understand the requirements of the collection managers and staff—the end users—and tried to involve them in shaping the final system. This early and continual involvement, plus the impressive performance of PAYMENT in the pilot study, made it easy to "sell" the model to the people who would have to use it.

Step 7: Model Implementation

After the pilot study, PAYMENT was applied to the $4.6 billion Montgomery Ward department store portfolio with 18 million accounts. Compared to the collection results from a year earlier, PAYMENT increased collections by $1.6 million per month, or over $19 million per year. Since then, PAYMENT has been applied to virtually all of GE Capital's accounts, with similar success. Overall, GE Capital estimates that PAYMENT has increased collections by $37 million per year and uses less resources than previous strategies. Since the original study, the model has been expanded in several directions. For example, the original model assumed that collection resources, such as the amount available for live phone calls, were fixed. The model has since been expanded to treat these resource levels as decision variables in a more encompassing optimization model.

1.6 WHY STUDY MANAGEMENT SCIENCE?

After reading the previous section, you should be convinced that management science is an important area and that highly trained analysts are needed to solve the large and complex problems faced by the business world. However, unless you are one of the relatively few students who intends to become a management science professional, you are probably wondering why you need to study management science. This is a legitimate concern. Indeed, for many years students and business professionals criticized management science courses because they were irrelevant to the majority of students who were required to take them. Looking back, it is difficult to argue with these critics. Typical management courses were centered primarily around a collection of very specific models and, worse, a collection of mind-numbing mathematical solution techniques.

Two forces have helped to turn this around. First, the many vocal critics have motivated many of us to examine our course materials and teaching methods. Certain topics have been eliminated and replaced by material that is more relevant and interesting to students. The second force is the emergence of powerful personal computers (PCs) and the accompanying easy-to-use software, especially spreadsheets. With the availability of computers to do the number crunching, there is no need—except in very advanced courses—to delve into the mathematical details of the solution techniques. We can delegate this task to computers, and we can use the time formerly spent on such details to develop valuable modeling skills.

Our intent in this book is to teach a general approach to the model-building process. Furthermore, we believe that the spreadsheet approach is the best way to do this, and that it appeals to the largest audience. We have been teaching our own courses with this spreadsheet modeling approach for several years—to a wide range of business students—and we have received very few complaints about irrelevance. Indeed, many students have stated openly that this is one of the most valuable business courses they have ever taken. The following are some of the reasons for this new-found relevance.

Development of Logical Modeling Skills

The modeling approach emphasized throughout this book is an important way to think about problems in general, not just the specific problems we discuss. This approach forces you to think logically. You must discover how given data can be used (or, as in some of the "modeling" problems, which data are necessary), you must determine the elements of the problem that you can control (the "decision variables"), and you must determine how the elements of the problem are logically related. Students realize that these logical thinking skills will be valuable in their careers, regardless of the specific careers they choose.

Development of Quantitative Skills

Management science is admittedly built around *quantitative* skills—it deals primarily with numbers and relationships between numbers. Some critics object that not everything in the real world can be reduced to numbers, but as one of our reviewers correctly pointed out, "a great deal that is of importance can." As you work through the many models in this book, your quantitative skills will be sharpened immensely. In a business world driven increasingly by numbers, quantitative skills are an obvious asset.

Development of Spreadsheet Skills

When you enter this course, your spreadsheet abilities might not be very good. By the time you finish this course, however, we can promise you that you will be a proficient spreadsheet user. We deliberately chose the spreadsheet package Excel, which is arguably the most widely used package (other than word-processing packages) in the business world today. Many of our students have told us that the facility they gained in Excel was worth the price of the course.

This is not just a course in spreadsheet fundamentals and neat tricks, although you will undoubtedly pick up a few useful tricks along the way. A great spreadsheet package—and we strongly believe that Excel is the greatest spreadsheet package written to date—gives you complete control over your model. You can apply spreadsheets to an endless variety of problems. Spreadsheets give you the flexibility to work in a way that suits *your* style best, and spreadsheets present results (and often catch errors) almost immediately. As you succeed with relatively easy problems, your confidence will build, and before long you will be able to tackle more difficult problems successfully. In short, spreadsheets enable everyone, not just technical people, to develop and use their quantitative skills.

Development of Intuition

Management science modeling helps you to develop your intuition, and it also indicates where intuition alone sometimes fails. When you confront a problem, you often make an educated guess at the solution. If the problem is sufficiently complex, as many of the problems in this book are, this guess will frequently be wide of the mark. In this sense the study of management science can be a humbling experience—you find that your unaided intuition is often not very good. However, by studying many models and examining their solutions, you can sharpen your intuition considerably.

This is sometimes called the "Aha!" effect. All of a sudden, you see why a certain solution is best. The chances are that when you originally thought about the problem, you forgot to consider an important constraint or a key relationship, and this caused the poor initial guess. Presumably, the more problems you analyze, the better you become at recognizing the critical elements of new problems. Experienced management scientists tend to have excellent intuition—that is, the ability to see through to the essence of a problem almost immediately. However, they are not born with this talent. It comes through the kind of analysis you will be performing as you work through this book.

1.7 SOFTWARE INCLUDED IN THIS BOOK

Very few business problems are small enough to be solved with pencil and paper. They require powerful software. The software included in this book, together with Microsoft® Excel, provides you with a powerful software combination. It is software that is being used—and will continue to be used—by leading companies all over the world to solve large, complex problems. We firmly believe that the experience you obtain with this software, through working the examples and problems in the book, will give you a key competitive advantage in the marketplace.

It all begins with Excel. All of the quantitative methods that we discuss are implemented in Excel. Excel is *the* most heavily used spreadsheet package on the market, and there is every reason to believe that this state will persist for at least several years. Most companies use Excel, most employees and most students have been trained in Excel, and Excel is a *very* powerful, flexible, and easy-to-use package.

Although Excel has a huge set of tools for performing quantitative analysis, we have included additional software with this book (available on the accompanying CD-ROM) that makes Excel even more powerful. We discuss these briefly here and in much more depth in the specific chapters where they apply. Throughout the text, you will see where each of these add-ins is used, as denoted by the icon next to each description.

Palisade Software

The Palisade Corporation has developed several powerful add-ins for Excel in a Decision Tools Suite that we have included in this book. The packages in this suite are slightly scaled-down educational versions of commercial software packages used widely in the business world. We describe them briefly here.

@RISK

The @RISK add-in is extremely useful for the development and analysis of spreadsheet simulation models, discussed in Chapters 9 and 10. First, it provides a number of probability functions that enable us to build uncertainty explicitly into Excel models. Then when we run a simulation, @RISK automatically keeps track of any outputs we select, it displays the results in a number of tabular and graphical forms, and it enables us to perform sensitivity analysis, so that we can see which inputs have the most effect on the outputs.

PrecisionTree®

The PrecisionTree add-in is used in Chapter 8 to analyze decision problems with uncertainty. The primary tool for performing this type of analysis is a decision tree. Decision trees are inherently graphical, and they have always been difficult to implement in spreadsheets, which are based on rows and columns. However, PrecisionTree does this in a very clever and intuitive way. Equally important, once the basic decision tree has been built, PrecisionTree makes it easy for us to perform sensitivity analysis on the model inputs.

RISKview®

RISKview is a software package that complements @RISK. A number of probability distributions are available with @RISK that can be used as inputs for simulation models. RISKview allows us to examine these probability distributions with an extremely user-friendly graphical interface.[2]

StatTools®

StatTools is a statistics add-in that enhances the statistical capabilities of Excel. Excel's built-in statistical tools are rather limited. It has several functions such as AVERAGE and STDEV for summarizing data, and it also includes the Analysis ToolPak, an add-in that was developed by a third party. However, these tools are not sufficiently powerful or flexible for the "heavy-duty" statistical analysis that is sometimes required. StatTools provides a collection of tools that help to fill the gap. Admittedly, this is not a *statistics* book, but we will use StatTools briefly in Chapter 12.

BestFit®

BestFit is used to determine the most appropriate probability distribution for a spreadsheet model when we have data on some uncertain quantity. For example, if we have historical

---

[2]RISKview and BestFit were originally developed by Palisade as stand-alone software packages (not Excel add-ins), and they are still provided in this form. However, the current version of @RISK incorporates the functionality of RISKview and BestFit.

weekly demands for some product, then BestFit allows us to "fit" several potential probability distributions to the data, and it ranks these according to goodness-of-fit. We will not use BestFit in this book, but it is included on the CD-ROM.

TopRank®

TopRank is a nonsimulation "what-if" tool. We start with any spreadsheet model, where a set of inputs are used, together with spreadsheet formulas, to produce one or more outputs. TopRank then allows us to perform sensitivity analysis to see which inputs have the largest effects on the outputs. For example, it might tell us which affects after-tax profit the most: the tax rate, the risk-free rate for investing, the inflation rate, or the price charged by a competitor. We will not use TopRank in this book, but it is included on the CD-ROM.

SolverTable

The final add-in, called SolverTable, was developed by one of the authors. It complements Solver's ability to perform sensitivity analysis on the optimization models discussed in Chapters 3–7.

Together with Excel and the add-ins included in this book, you have a wealth of software at your disposal. The examples and step-by-step instructions throughout this book will help you to become a power user of this software. This takes plenty of practice and a willingness to experiment, but it is certainly within your grasp. When you are finished, we will not be surprised if you rate improved software skills as the most valuable thing you have learned from this book.

1.8 CONCLUSION

In this chapter we have introduced the field of management science and the process of mathematical modeling. To provide a more concrete understanding of these concepts, we described a simple queueing model and chronicled one very successful management science application. We also emphasized a seven-step model-building process that begins with problem definition and proceeds through final implementation. Finally, we discussed why the study of management science is a valuable experience, even if you do not intend to pursue a professional career in this field. Now it is time to launch Excel, roll up your sleeves, and get started!

Introduction to Spreadsheet Modeling

© Artville

ANALYSIS OF HIV/AIDS

Many of management science's most successful applications are in traditional functional areas of business, including operations management, logistics, finance, and marketing. Indeed, we will analyze many such applications in this book. However, another area where management science has had a strong influence over the past decade has been the analysis of the worldwide HIV/AIDS epidemic. Not only have theoretical models been developed, but even more important, they have been *applied* to help understand the epidemic and reduce its spread. To highlight the importance of management science modeling in this area, an entire special issue (May–June 1998) of *Interfaces*, the journal that reports successful management science applications, was devoted to HIV/AIDS models. We will discuss some of the highlights here, just so that you can get an idea of what management science has to offer in this important area.

Kahn et al. (1998) provide an overview of the problem. They discuss how governments, public-health agencies, and health-care providers must determine how best to allocate scarce resources for HIV treatment and prevention among different programs and populations. They discuss in some depth how management science models have influenced, and will continue to influence, AIDS policy decisions. Other articles in the issue discuss more specific problems. Caulkins et al. (1998) analyze whether the distribution of difficult-to-reuse syringes would reduce the spread of HIV among injection drug users. Based on their model, they conclude that the extra expense of these types of syringes would not be worth the marginal benefit they might provide.

Paltiel and Freedberg (1998) investigate the costs and benefits of developing and administering treatments for cytomegalovirus (CMV), an infection to which HIV carriers are increasingly exposed. (Retinitis, CMV's most common manifestation, is associated with blindness and sometimes death.) Their model suggests that the costs compare unfavorably with alternative uses of scarce resources. Owens et al. (1998) analyze the effect of women's relapse to high-risk sexual and needle-sharing behavior on the costs and benefits of a voluntary program to screen women of childbearing age for HIV. They find, for example, that the effect of relapse to high-risk behaviors on screening program costs and benefits can be substantial, suggesting that behavioral interventions that produce sustained reductions in risk behavior, even if expensive, could be cost-saving.

The important point is that these articles (and others not mentioned here) base their results on rigorous management science models of the HIV/AIDS phenomenon. In addition, they are backed up with real data. They are not simply opinions of the authors. ■

2.1 INTRODUCTION

This book is all about spreadsheet modeling. By the time we are finished, we will have covered some reasonably complex—and realistic—models. We will also have transformed many of you into Excel "power" users. However, from our experience in teaching this material, there is a danger of our starting too quickly or assuming too much background on the part of the reader. For practice in getting up to speed with basic Excel features, we have included an Excel tutorial in the CD-ROM that accompanies this book. (See the file **ExcelTutorial.doc**.) You can work through this tutorial at your own speed and cover the topics you need help with. Even if you have used Excel extensively, we urge you to give this tutorial a look. You might be surprised how some of our tips can improve your productivity.

Second, we have written this chapter to provide an introduction to Excel modeling. This chapter will illustrate some interesting and relatively simple models, and we will take you through the modeling process. As we do so, we will cover some of the less well-known, but particularly helpful, Excel tools that are available. These include data tables, Goal Seek, lookup tables, and auditing commands. Keep in mind, however, that our objective is not the same as that of the many "how-to" Excel books on the market. Specifically, we are not teaching Excel just for the sake of its many interesting features. Rather, we plan to *use* these features to provide insight into solving real business problems. In short, we regard Excel as a problem-solving tool, not an end in itself.

2.2 BASIC SPREADSHEET MODELING: CONCEPTS AND BEST PRACTICES

Most mathematical models, including spreadsheet models, involve **inputs**, **decision variables**, and **outputs**. The model inputs are given values that are fixed, at least for the pur-

Some inputs, such as demand in this example, contain a considerable degree of uncertainty. In some cases, such as Example 2.4, we will model this uncertainty explicitly.

poses of the model. The decision variables are values that a decision maker has control over. The model outputs are the ultimate values of interest; they are determined by the inputs and decision variables. A typical example is the following. Suppose a manager must place an order for a certain seasonal product. This product will go out of date fairly soon, so this is the only order that will be made for the product. The inputs are then the fixed cost of the order, the unit variable cost of each item ordered, the price charged for each item sold, the "salvage" value for each item, if any, left in inventory after the product has gone out of date, and the demand for the product. The decision variable is the number of items to order. Finally, the main output is the profit (or loss) from the product. We might also break this "main" output into the outputs that contribute to it: the total ordering cost, the revenue from sales, and the salvage value from any leftover items. We will certainly have to calculate these outputs to obtain profit.

Spreadsheet modeling is the process of entering the inputs and decision variables into a spreadsheet and then relating them appropriately, by means of formulas, to obtain the outputs. Once we have done this, we can then proceed in several directions. We might want to perform a sensitivity analysis to see how one or more outputs change as selected inputs or decision variables change. We might want to find the values of the decision variable(s) that minimize or maximize a particular output, possibly subject to certain constraints. We might also want to create charts that show graphically how certain parameters of the model are related.

We will illustrate these operations with several examples in this chapter. Indeed, getting all of the spreadsheet logic correct and producing useful results is a big part of the battle. However, we want to go further—we want to stress good spreadsheet modeling *practices*. The chances are that you will not be developing spreadsheet models for your own use. You will probably be sharing these with colleagues or even a boss (or an instructor). The point is that other people will probably be reading and trying to make sense out of your spreadsheet models. Therefore, it is imperative that you construct your spreadsheet models with *readability* in mind. Several features that can improve readability include:

- A clear, logical layout to the overall model
- Separation of different parts of a model, possibly across multiple worksheets
- Clear headings for different sections of the model and for all inputs, decision variables, and outputs
- Liberal use of range names
- Liberal use of boldface, italics, larger font size, coloring, indentation, and other formatting features
- Liberal use of cell comments
- Liberal use of text boxes for assumptions, lists, or any explanations

Obviously, the formulas and logic in any spreadsheet model must be correct, and this is what we will emphasize throughout this book. However, correctness will not take you very far if no one can understand what you have done. Much of the power of spreadsheets derives from their flexibility. When you open a blank spreadsheet, it is like a big blank canvas waiting for you to insert useful data and formulas. Practically anything is allowed. However, this power can be abused if you do not have an overall plan as to what should go where. So we urge you to plan ahead, before diving in. And if your plan does not look good once you start filling in the spreadsheet, do not hesitate to revise your plan.

The following example illustrates the process of building a spreadsheet model according to the guidelines we have described. We build this model in stages. In the first stage we build a model that is correct, but not very readable. At each subsequent stage, we modify the model to make it more readable. You do not need to go through each of these stages explicitly when you build your own models. Indeed, you should strive for the final stage right away, at least after you get used to the modeling process. We show the various stages here simply for contrast.

EXAMPLE	**2.1 ORDERING NCAA T-SHIRTS**

It is March, and the annual NCAA Basketball Tournament is down to the final 4 teams. Randy Kitchell is a t-shirt vendor who plans to order t-shirts with the names of the final 4 teams from a manufacturer and then sell them to the fans. The fixed cost of any order is $750, the variable cost per t-shirt to Randy is $6, and Randy's selling price is $10. However, this price will be charged only until a week after the tournament. After that time, Randy figures that interest in the t-shirts will be low, so he plans to sell all remaining t-shirts, if any, at $4 apiece. His best guess is that demand for the t-shirts during the full-price period will be 1500. He is thinking about ordering 1400 t-shirts, but he wants to build a spreadsheet model that will let him experiment with the uncertain demand and his order quantity. How should he proceed?

Objective   To build a spreadsheet model in a series of stages, all stages being correct but each stage being more readable and flexible than the previous stages.

Solution

The logic behind the model is simple. If demand is greater than the order quantity, Randy will sell all of the t-shirts ordered for $10 apiece. However, if demand is less than the order quantity, Randy will sell as many t-shirts as are demanded at the $10 price and all leftovers at the $4 price. We will implement this logic in Excel with an IF function.

A first attempt at a spreadsheet model appears in Figure 2.1. (See the file **TShirtSales.xls**, where we have built each stage on a separate worksheet.) We enter a possible demand in cell B3, a possible order quantity in cell B4, and then calculate the profit with the formula

=-750-6*B4+IF(B3>B4,10*B4,10*B3+4*(B4-B3))

This formula subtracts the fixed and variable costs and then adds the revenue, according to the logic we just described.'

→ **EXCEL FUNCTION:** *IF*
Excel's IF function is probably already familiar to you, but it is too important not to discuss. It has the syntax **=IF(condition,resultIfTrue,resultIfFalse)**. *The* condition *is any expression that is either true or false. The two expressions* resultIfTrue *and* resultIfFalse *can be any expressions you would enter in a cell: numbers, text, or other Excel functions (including other IF functions). Note that if either expression is text, it must be enclosed in double quotes, such as*

=IF(Score>=90,"A","B").

Finally, Condition *can be complex combinations of conditions, using the keywords AND or OR. Then the syntax is, for example,*

=IF(AND(Score1<60,Score2<60),"Fail","Pass"). ■

Figure 2.1

Base Model

	A	B
1	NCAA t-shirt sales	
2		
3	Demand	1500
4	Order	1400
5	Profit	4850

This model is entirely correct, but it is not very readable or flexible. It breaks a rule that you should strive never to break—it "hard codes" input values into the profit formula. A spreadsheet model should never include input numbers in formulas. Instead, it should include *references* to these inputs, which should be stored in separate cells. A remedy appears in Figure 2.2. Here, the inputs have been entered in the range B3:B6, and the profit formula in cell B10 has been changed to

=-B3-B4*B9+IF(B8>B9,B5*B9,10*B8+B6*(B9-B8))

This is exactly the same formula as before, but it is now more flexible. If an input changes, the profit recalculates automatically. Most importantly, the inputs are no longer "buried" in the formula.

Figure 2.2

Model with Input
Cells

	A	B
1	NCAA t-shirt sales	
2		
3	Fixed order cost	$750
4	Variable cost	$6
5	Selling price	$10
6	Discount price	$4
7		
8	Demand	1500
9	Order	1400
10	Profit	$4,850

Still, the profit formula is not very readable as it stands. We can make it more readable by using range names. We will explain the mechanics of range names in detail later in this chapter. For now, we simply show the results of using range names for cells B3, B4, B5, B6, B8, and B9 in Figure 2.3. This model looks exactly like the previous model, but the formula in cell B10 is now

=-Fixed_order_cost-Variable_cost*Order+IF(Demand>Order,
Selling_price*Order,Selling_price*Demand+Salvage_value*(Order-Demand))

This formula is admittedly more long-winded, but it is certainly easier to read.

Figure 2.3

Model with Range
Names in Profit
Formula

	A	B	C	D	E	F
1	NCAA t-shirt sales					
2						
3	Fixed order cost	$750		Range names used		
4	Variable cost	$6		Demand	='Model 3'!$B$8	
5	Selling price	$10		Discount_price	='Model 3'!$B$6	
6	Discount price	$4		Fixed_order_cost	='Model 3'!$B$3	
7				Order	='Model 3'!$B$9	
8	Demand	1500		Selling_price	='Model 3'!$B$5	
9	Order	1400		Variable_cost	='Model 3'!$B$4	
10	Profit	$4,850				

Randy might like to have profit broken down into various costs and revenues, rather one single profit cell. We do this in Figure 2.4. The formulas in cells B12, B13, B15, and B16 are straightforward and will not be repeated here. Then we accumulate these to get profit in cell B17 with the formula

=-(B12+B13)+(B15+B16)

Of course, range names could be used for these intermediate output cells, but it is probably more work than it is worth. You must always use some judgment when deciding how many range names to use.

Figure 2.4

Model with Intermediate Outputs

	A	B	C	D	E	F
1	**NCAA t-shirt sales**					
2						
3	Fixed order cost	$750		**Range names used**		
4	Variable cost	$6		Demand	='Model 4'!$B$8	
5	Selling price	$10		Discount_price	='Model 4'!$B$6	
6	Discount price	$4		Fixed_order_cost	='Model 4'!$B$3	
7				Order	='Model 4'!$B$9	
8	Demand	1500		Selling_price	='Model 4'!$B$5	
9	Order	1400		Variable_cost	='Model 4'!$B$4	
10						
11	Costs					
12	Fixed cost	$750				
13	Variable costs	$8,400				
14	Revenues					
15	Full-price shirts	$14,000				
16	Discount-price shirts	$0				
17	Profit	$4,850				

If Randy's assistant is presented with this model, how does she know at a glance which cells are inputs or decision variables or outputs? Labels and/or color coding can help a lot to distinguish these types. We use a blue/red/black color-coding style that we will discuss later in this chapter. We have applied this color coding in Figure 2.5, along with descriptive labels in boldface. The blue cells at the top are input cells, the red cell in the middle is a decision variable, and the black cell at the bottom is the main output.[1] There is nothing sacred about this convention. You should feel free to adopt your own, but you should adopt a style and use it as consistently as possible.

---

[1]Since the colors blue and red are indistinguishable in this book, we shade the blue cells.

Figure 2.5

Model with
Category Labels and
Color Coding

	A	B	C	D	E	F
1	**NCAA t-shirt sales**					
2						
3	Input variables			**Range names used**		
4	Fixed order cost	$750		Demand	='Model 5'!$B$10	
5	Variable cost	$6		Discount_price	='Model 5'!$B$7	
6	Selling price	$10		Fixed_order_cost	='Model 5'!$B$4	
7	Discount price	$4		Order	='Model 5'!$B$13	
8				Selling_price	='Model 5'!$B$6	
9	**Uncertain variable**			Variable_cost	='Model 5'!$B$5	
10	Demand	1500				
11						
12	**Decision variable**					
13	Order	1400				
14						
15	**Output variables**					
16	Costs					
17	Fixed cost	$750				
18	Variable costs	$8,400				
19	**Revenues**					
20	Full-price shirts	$14,000				
21	Discount-price shirts	$0				
22	Profit	$4,850				

The model in Figure 2.5 is still not the last word on this problem. As we will illustrate in later examples in this chapter, we could create data tables to see how sensitive profit is to the inputs, the demand, and the order quantity. We could also create charts to show any numerical results graphically. But for now, we will stop here. Looking back, we hope you agree that the model in Figure 2.5 is much more readable and flexible than the original model in Figure 2.1. ∎

Because we place such emphasis on good spreadsheet style, we have included an appendix to this chapter that discusses a few tools for editing and documenting your spreadsheet models. We recommend that you use these tools right away. They will be very useful as you progress through the book.

We strongly believe in example-based learning. We think we can teach better, and you can learn better, if we cover modeling concepts and spreadsheet features in the context of examples rather than in the abstract. Therefore, we will proceed directly to examples for the rest of this chapter. As we discuss these examples, we will introduce several important modeling concepts (such as sensitivity analysis), several important Excel features (such as data tables), and even some important business concepts (such as net present value).We will also continue to discuss good spreadsheet practices—why we do something in a certain way. To get the most from these examples, you should follow along at your own PC, starting with a blank spreadsheet. It is one thing to read about spreadsheet modeling; it is quite another to *do* it!

2.3 COST PROJECTIONS

We begin with a very simple example, where a company wants to project its costs of producing its products, given that material and labor costs are likely to increase through time. We will build a simple model and then use Excel's charting capabilities to obtain a graphical image of projected costs.

2.2 PROJECTING THE COSTS OF BOOKSHELVES AT WOODWORKS

The Woodworks Company produces a variety of custom-designed wood furniture for its customers. One favorite item is a bookshelf, made from either cherry or oak. The company knows that wood prices and labor costs are likely to increase in the future. Table 2.1 shows the number of board-feet and labor hours required for a bookshelf, the current costs per board-foot and labor hour, and the anticipated annual increases in these costs. (The top row indicates that either type of bookshelf requires 30 board-feet of wood and 16 hours of labor.) Build a spreadsheet model that allows the company to experiment with the growth rates in wood and labor costs so that a manager can see, both numerically and graphically, how the costs of the bookshelves will vary in the next few years.

Table 2.1   Input Data for Manufacturing a Bookshelf

Resource	Cherry	Oak	Labor
Required per bookshelf	30	30	16
Current unit cost	$7.30	$4.30	$18.50
Anticipated annual cost increase	4.2%	2.1%	1.5%

Business Objectives[2]   To build a model that allows Woodworks to see, numerically and graphically, how its costs of manufacturing bookshelves will increase in the future, and to allow the company to answer what-if questions with this model.

Excel Objectives   To learn good spreadsheet practices, to enable copying formulas with the careful use of relative and absolute addresses, and to create line charts from multiple series of data.

Solution

We believe it is useful to list the key variables in a table before developing the actual spreadsheet model, and we will continue to do this in future examples. (See Table 2.2.) This practice forces us to examine the roles of the variables—which are inputs, which are decision variables, and which are outputs. Although the variables and their roles are fairly clear for this example, future examples will require more thought.

Table 2.2   Key Variables for the Bookshelf Manufacturing Example

Input variables	Wood and labor requirements per bookshelf, current unit costs of wood and labor, anticipated annual increases in unit costs
Output variables	Projected unit costs of wood and labor, projected total bookshelf costs

The reasoning behind the model is straightforward. We first project the unit costs for wood and labor into the future. Then for any year, we multiply the unit costs by the required numbers of board-feet and labor hours per bookshelf. Finally, we add the wood and labor costs to obtain the total cost of a bookshelf.

---

[2]In later chapters we will simply list the "Objective" of each example. However, because this chapter has been designed to enhance basic spreadsheet skills, we will separate the business objectives from the Excel objectives.

DEVELOPING THE SPREADSHEET MODEL

Our spreadsheet model appears in Figure 2.6 and in the file **BookshelfCost.xls**.[3] We developed it with the following steps.

Figure 2.6 Bookshelf Cost Model

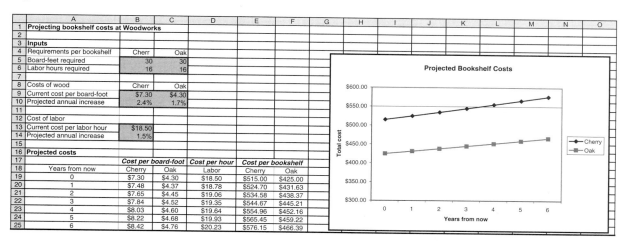

	A	B	C	D	E	F	G
1	Projecting bookshelf costs at Woodworks						
2							
3	**Inputs**						
4	Requirements per bookshelf	Cherr	Oak				
5	Board-feet required	30	30				
6	Labor hours required	16	16				
7							
8	Costs of wood	Cherr	Oak				
9	Current cost per board-foot	$7.30	$4.30				
10	Projected annual increase	2.4%	1.7%				
11							
12	Cost of labor						
13	Current cost per labor hour	$18.50					
14	Projected annual increase	1.5%					
15							
16	**Projected costs**						
17		Cost per board-foot		Cost per hour	Cost per bookshelf		
18	Years from now	Cherry	Oak	Labor	Cherry	Oak	
19	0	$7.30	$4.30	$18.50	$515.00	$425.00	
20	1	$7.48	$4.37	$18.78	$524.70	$431.63	
21	2	$7.65	$4.45	$19.06	$534.58	$438.37	
22	3	$7.84	$4.52	$19.35	$544.67	$445.21	
23	4	$8.03	$4.60	$19.64	$554.96	$452.16	
24	5	$8.22	$4.68	$19.93	$565.45	$459.22	
25	6	$8.42	$4.76	$20.23	$576.15	$466.39	

Always enter input values in "input cells" and then refer to them in Excel formulas. Do not bury input numbers in formulas!

1 Inputs. It is usually a good idea to enter the inputs for a model in the upper left corner of a worksheet. We have done this in the shaded ranges in Figure 2.6, using the data from Table 2.1. We have used our standard convention of enclosing inputs—the numbers from the statement of the problem—in a blue border and shading these cells. You can develop your own convention, but we believe strongly that the input cells should be distinguished in some way. Note that we have grouped the inputs logically, and we have explained them with appropriate labels. You should always document your spreadsheet model with informational labels. Also, note that by entering inputs explicitly in their own "input cells," we can *refer* to them later with Excel formulas.

2 Design output table. Think ahead of time how you want to structure your outputs. We decided to create a table where there is a row for every year in the future (year 0 corresponds to the current year), there are three columns for projected unit costs (columns B–D), and there are two columns for projected total bookshelf costs (columns E–F). The headings reflect this design. Of course, this is not the only possible design, but it works well. The important point is that you should have *some* logical design in mind before diving in.

3 Projected unit costs of wood. The dollar values in the range B19:F25 are all calculated from Excel formulas. Although the logic in this example is straightforward, it is still important to have a strategy in mind before you enter formulas. In particular, you should design your spreadsheet so that you can enter a *single* formula and then copy it whenever possible. This saves work and it avoids errors. For the costs per board-foot in columns B and C, enter the formula

=B9

[3]The CD-ROM accompanying this book includes templates and completed files for all examples in this book. However, especially in this chapter, we suggest that you start with a blank spreadsheet and follow our step-by-step instructions on your own.

in cell B19 and copy it to cell C19. Then enter the general formula

=B19*(1+B$10)

in cell B20 and copy it to the range B20:C25. We assume you know the rules for absolute and relative addresses (dollar sign for absolute, no dollar sign for relative), but it takes some planning to use these so that copying is possible. Make sure you understand why we made row 10 absolute but column B relative.

→ **EXCEL TIP:** *Relative and Absolute Addresses in Formulas*

Relative and absolute addresses are used in Excel formulas to facilitate copying. A dollar sign next to a column or row address indicates that the address is absolute and will not change when copying. The lack of a dollar sign indicates that the address is relative and will change when copying. Once you select a cell in a formula, you can press the F4 key repeatedly to cycle through the relative/absolute possibilities, for example, =B4 (both column and row relative), =$B$4 (both column and row absolute), =B$4 (column relative, row absolute), and =$B4 (column absolute, row relative). ∎

4 **Projected unit labor costs.** To calculate projected hourly labor costs, enter the formula

=B13

in cell D19. Then enter the formula

=D19*(1+B$14)

in cell D20 and copy it down column D.

5 **Projected bookshelf costs.** Each bookshelf cost is the sum of its wood and labor costs. By a careful use of absolute and relative addresses, we can enter a single formula for these costs—for all years and for both types of wood. To do this, enter the formula

=B$5*B19+B$6*$D19

in cell E19 and copy it to the range E19:F25. The idea here is that the units of wood and labor per bookshelf are always in rows 5 and 6, and the projected unit labor cost is always in column D, but all other references should be relative to allow copying.

6 **Chart.** To produce the graph of total costs through time, highlight the range E19:F25 and click on Excel's Chart Wizard button. This leads you through a sequence of steps. We will illustrate what we did to get the graph in Figure 2.6, but you should experiment with the possibilities—and Excel gives you many possibilities! In the first step, we selected a Line chart of the default type. In the second step, we clicked on the Series tab. The resulting dialog box initially appears as in Figure 2.7. We modified it to appear as in Figure 2.8. (This makes the legend more understandable, by giving names to the two series, and it provides values for the horizontal axis.) In the third step, we clicked on the Titles tab and provided titles for the chart and the axes. In the fourth and final step, we accepted the default (to keep the chart on the same sheet as the model). The vertical scale on the resulting chart went from $0 to $700, meaning that the lines for both series were up near the top of the chart. Therefore, we rescaled this axis. To do so, we right-clicked on the vertical axis, selected the Format Axis menu item from the resulting menu, clicked on the Scale tab, and changed the minimum from 0 to 300.[4]

---

[4]To explain all of Excel's charting options would require a chapter in itself. We believe experimentation is the best way to learn how to create Excel charts and modify them, so we invite you to experiment.

Figure 2.7

Default Series
Dialog Box

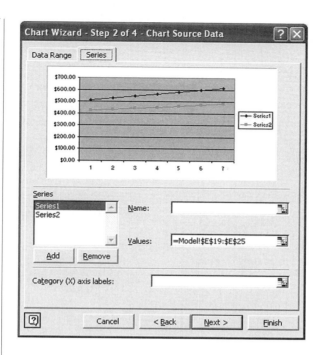

Figure 2.8

Series Dialog Box
After Modifications

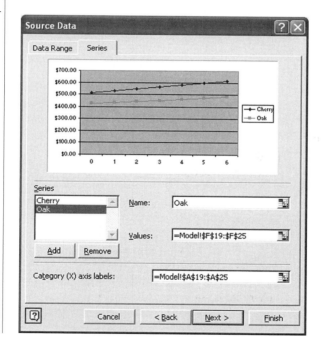

Using the Model for What-If Questions

The model in Figure 2.6 can now be used to answer any what-if questions Woodworks might want to ask. In fact, many models are built exactly for this purpose: to permit experimenting with various scenarios. The important point is that the model has been built in such a way that a manager can enter any desired values in the input cells, and all of the outputs, including the chart, will update automatically. As a simple example, if the annual percentage increases for wood costs are twice as high as Woodworks anticipated, we can enter these higher values in row 10 and immediately see the effect, as shown in Figure 2.9. By comparing bookshelf costs in this scenario to those in the original scenario, we see that the projected cost in year 6 for cherry bookshelves, for example, increases by about 6.5%, from \$576.15 to \$613.80.

Figure 2.9   Effect of Higher Increases in Wood Costs

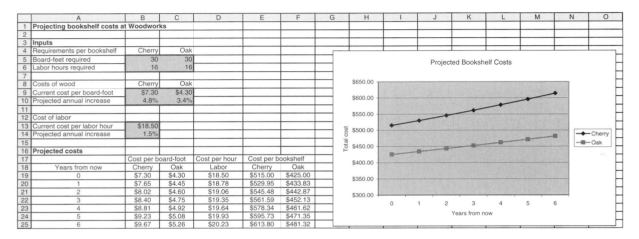

We hope you realize by now why burying input numbers inside Excel formulas is such a bad practice—and we hope you will not do it yourself! For example, if we had buried the annual increases of wood costs from row 10 in the formulas in columns B and C, imagine how difficult it would be to answer the what-if question in the previous paragraph. We would first have to find, and then change, all of the numbers in the formulas. This is a lot of work, but even worse, it is likely to lead to errors. ■

2.4 BREAKEVEN ANALYSIS

Many business problems require us to find the appropriate level of some activity. This might be the level that maximizes profit (or minimizes cost), or it might be the level that allows a company to break even—no profit, no loss. We will discuss a typical breakeven analysis in the following example.

EXAMPLE   **2.3 BREAKEVEN ANALYSIS AT GREAT THREADS**

The Great Threads Company sells hand-knit sweaters. The company is planning to print a catalog of its products and undertake a direct mail campaign. The cost of printing the catalog is \$20,000 plus \$0.10 per catalog. The cost of mailing each catalog (including postage, order forms, and buying of names from a mail-order database) is \$0.15. In addition, the company will include direct reply envelopes in its mailings. It incurs $0.20 in extra costs for each direct mail envelope that is used by a respondent. The average size of a customer order is $40, and the company's variable cost per order (due primarily to labor and material costs) averages about 80% of the order's value—that is, $32. The company plans to mail 100,000 catalogs. It wants to develop a spreadsheet model to answer the following questions:

1. How does a change in the response rate affect profit?
2. For what response rate does the company break even?
3. If the company estimates a response rate of 3%, should it proceed with the mailing?
4. How does the presence of uncertainty affect the usefulness of the model?

Business Objectives   To create a model to determine the company's profit, and to see how sensitive the profit is to the response rate from the mailing.

Excel Objectives   To learn how to work with range names, to learn how to answer what-if questions with one-way data tables, to introduce Excel's Goal Seek tool, and to learn how to document and audit Excel models with cell comments and the auditing toolbar.

Solution

The key variables appear in Table 2.3. Note that we have designated all variables as input variables, decision variables, or output variables. Furthermore, there is typically a single "bottom line" output variable, in this case, profit, that is of most concern. (In the next few chapters, we will refer to it as the "target" variable.) Therefore, we distinguish this key output variable from the other output variables that we calculate along the way.

Table 2.3	Key Variables in Great Threads Problem
Input variables	Various unit costs, average order size, response rate
Decision variable	Number mailed
Key output variable	Profit
Other output variables	Number of responses, revenue and cost totals

The logic for converting inputs and the decision variable into outputs is quite straightforward. Once we do this, we will investigate how the response rate affects the profit with a sensitivity analysis.

The completed spreadsheet model appears in Figure 2.10 on page 32. (See the file **BreakevenAnalysis.xls**.) First, note the clear layout of the model. The input cells are outlined (in blue on a color screen) and shaded, they are separated from the outputs, there are boldfaced headings, several headings are indented, numbers are formatted appropriately, and there is a list to the right that spells out all range names we have used. (See the Excel Tip on how to create this list.) Also, following the convention we will continue to use throughout the book, the decision variable (number mailed) is enclosed in a red border, and the bottom-line output (profit) is enclosed in a double-line black border.

Adopt some layout and formatting conventions, even if they differ from ours, to make your spreadsheets readable and easy to follow.

Figure 2.10 Great Threads Model

	A	B	C	D	E	F	G	H	I
1	Great Threads direct mail model								
2									
3	Catalog inputs			Model of responses			Range names used		
4	Fixed cost of printing	$20,000		Response rate	8%		Average_order	=Sheet1!$B$11	
5	Variable cost of printing mailing	$0.25		Number of responses	8000		Fixed_cost_of_printing	=Sheet1!$B$4	
6							Number_mailed	=Sheet1!$B$8	
7	Decision variable			Model of revenue, costs, and profit			Number_of_responses	=Sheet1!$E$5	
8	Number mailed	100000		Total Revenue	$320,000		Profit	=Sheet1!$E$13	
9				Fixed cost of printing	$20,000		Response_rate	=Sheet1!$E$4	
10	Order inputs			Total variable cost of printing mailing	$25,000		Total_cost	=Sheet1!$E$12	
11	Average order	$40		Total variable cost of orders	$257,600		Total_revenue	=Sheet1!$E$8	
12	Variable cost per order	$32.20		Total cost	$302,600		Variable_cost_of_printing_mailing	=Sheet1!$B$5	
13				Profit	$17,400		Variable_cost_per_order	=Sheet1!$B$12	

→ **EXCEL TIP:** *Creating Range Names*

To create a range name for a range of cells (which could be a single cell), highlight the cell(s), click in the Name Box just to the left of the Formula Bar, and type a range name. Alternatively, if there is a column of labels next to the cells to be range-named, we can use these labels as the range names. To do this, highlight the labels and the cells to be named (for example, A4:B5 in Figure 2.10), select the Insert/Name/Create menu item, and make sure the appropriate box in the resulting dialog box (see Figure 2.11) is checked. The labels in our example are to the left of the cells to be named, so we check the Left column box. This is a very quick way to create range names, and we did it for all range names in the example. In fact, by keeping your finger on the Ctrl key, you can select multiple ranges. Once all of your ranges are selected, you can sometimes create all of your range-names in one step. Note that if a label contains any "illegal" range-name characters, such as a space, the illegal characters are converted to underscores. ■

Figure 2.11

Range Name Create
Dialog Box

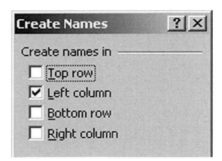

→ **EXCEL TIP:** *Pasting Range Names*

It is often useful to include a list of the range names in your spreadsheet. To do this, select a cell (such as cell G4 in Figure 2.10). Then select the Insert/Name/Paste menu item and click on the Paste List button. You will get a list of all range names and their cell addresses. However, if you change any of these range names (delete one, for example), the paste list will not update automatically. You will have to create it again. ■

DEVELOPING THE SPREADSHEET MODEL

To create this model, proceed through the following steps.

❶ **Headings and range names.** Obviously, we have named a lot of cells, more than you might want to name, but you will see their value when we create formulas. In general, we strongly support range names, but we caution you not to go overboard. You can waste a lot of time naming ranges that do not *really* need to be named. Of course, you can use the Insert/Name/Create option we described previously to speed up the process.[5]

The appendix to this chapter discusses how you can easily implement our color border conventions.

② **Values of input variables and the decision variable.** Enter these values and format them appropriately. As usual, we have used our blue/red/black color-coding scheme. Note that we have designated the number mailed as a *decision* variable, not as an input variable (and we have enclosed it in a red, not a blue, border). This is because the company gets to choose the value of this variable. Finally, note that we have combined some of the values in the statement of the problem. For example, the $32.20 in cell B12 is really 80% of the $40 average order size, plus the $0.20 per return envelope. To document this process, we entered comments in a few cells, as shown in Figure 2.12.

Figure 2.12 Cell Comments in Model

	A	B	C	D	E	F	G	H	I
1	Great Threads direct mail model								
2									
3	Catalog inputs			Model of responses		Trial value, will do sensitivity analysis on	sed		
4	Fixed cost of printing	$20,000			8%		Average_order	=Model!$B$11	
5	Variable cost of printing mailing	$0.25	Includes $0.10 for printing and $0.15 for mailing each catalog	nses	8000		Fixed_cost_of_printing	=Model!$B$4	
6							Number_mailed	=Model!$B$8	
7	Decision variable			Model of revenue, costs, and profit			Number_of_responses	=Model!$E$5	
8	Number mailed	100000		Total Revenue	$320,000		Profit	=Model!$E$13	
9				Fixed cost of printing	$20,000		Response_rate	=Model!$E$4	
10	Order inputs			Total variable cost of printing mailing	$25,000		Total_cost	=Model!$E$12	
11	Average order	$40	Includes 80% of the average	f orders	$257,600		Total_Revenue	=Model!$E$8	
12	Variable cost per order	$32.20	$40 order size, plus $0.20 per return envelope		$302,600		Variable_cost_of_printing_mailing	=Model!$B$5	
13					$17,400		Variable_cost_per_order	=Model!$B$12	

→ EXCEL TIP: *Inserting Cell Comments*

Inserting comments in cells is a great way to document your spreadsheet models without making the spreadsheet too cluttered. To enter a comment in a cell, right-click on the cell, select the Insert Comment item, and type your comment. This creates a little red mark in the cell, indicating a comment, and you can see the comment by resting the mouse pointer over the cell. When a cell contains a comment, you can edit or delete the comment by right-clicking on the cell and selecting the appropriate item. If you want all of the cell comments to be visible (for example, in a printout as in Figure 2.12), select the Tools/Options menu item, click on the View tab, and select the Comment & Indicator option. Note that the Indicator Only option is the default. ■

③ **Model the responses.** We have not specified the response rate to the mailing, so enter *any* reasonable value, such as 8%, in the Response_rate cell—we will perform sensitivity on this value later on. Then enter the formula

=Number_mailed*Response_rate

in cell E5. (Do you see the advantage of range names?)

④ **Model the revenue, costs, and profits.** Enter the formula

=Number_of_responses*Average_order

in cell E8, enter the formulas

=Fixed_cost_of_printing
=Variable_cost_of_printing_mailing*Number_mailed

---

[5]We learned of one company that does not allow any formulas in its corporate spreadsheets to include cell references; they must all reference range names. This is pretty extreme, but that company's formulas are certainly easy to read!

and

=Number_of_responses*Variable_cost_per_order

in cells E9, E10, and E11, enter the formula

=SUM(E9:E11)

in cell E12, and enter the formula

=Total_revenue-Total_cost

in cell E13. These formulas should all be self-explanatory, especially because of the range names we have used.

Forming a One-Way Data Table

Data tables are also called what-if tables. They let us see what happens to selected outputs if selected inputs change.

Now that a basic model has been created, we can answer the questions posed by the company. For question 1, we form a one-way data table to show how profit varies with the response rate. This data table appears in Figure 2.13. We will use data tables often, so make sure you understand how to create them. We will walk you through the procedure once or twice, but from then on, you will be on your own. First, enter a sequence of trial values of the response rate in column A, and enter a "link" to profit in cell B17 with the formula **=Profit**. We have shaded this cell for emphasis, but this is not really necessary. (In general, other outputs could be part of the table, and they would be placed in columns C, D, and so on. There would be a link to each output in row 17.) Finally, highlight the entire table range, A17:B27, and select the Data/Table menu item to bring up the dialog box in Figure 2.14. It should be filled in as shown to indicate that the only input, Response_rate, is listed along a column. (You can enter either a range name or a cell address in this dialog box.)

Figure 2.13 Data Table for Profit

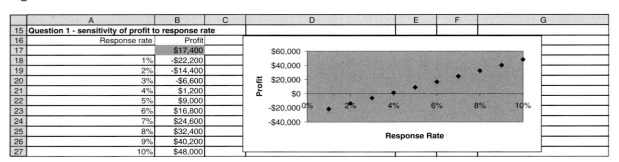

Figure 2.14
Data Table Dialog Box

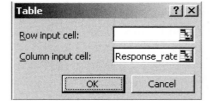

When you click on OK, Excel substitutes each response rate value in the table into the Response_rate cell, recalculates profit, and reports it in the table. For a final touch, we have created a scatterplot (or in Excel's terminology, an X-Y chart) of the values in the data table. (This is straightforward. Highlight the A18:B27 range, click on the Chart Wizard button, select an XY plot of the default type, and click on Finish. Then you can fix it up by adding titles, removing the legend, and so on to suit your taste.)

A one-way data table allows us to see how one or more output variables vary as a single input variable varies over a selected range of values. These input values can be arranged vertically in a column or horizontally in a row. We will explain only the former, since it is probably the most common. To create the table, enter the input values in a column range, such as A18:A27 of Figure 2.13, and enter links to one or more output cells in columns to the right and one row above the inputs, as in cell B17 of Figure 2.13. Then highlight the entire table, beginning with the upper left blank cell (A17 in the figure), select the Data/Table menu item, and fill in the resulting dialog box as in Figure 2.14, leaving the Row Input cell blank and using the cell where the original value of the input variable lives as the Column Input cell. When you click on OK, each value in the left column of the table is substituted into the column input cell, the spreadsheet recalculates, and the resulting value of the output is placed in the table. Also, if you click anywhere in the body of the table (B18:B27 in the figure), you will see that Excel has entered the =TABLE function to remind you that a data table lives here. ■

As the chart indicates, profit increases in a linear manner as response rate varies. More specifically, each 1% increase in the response rate increases profit by $7800. Here is the reasoning. Each 1% increase in response rate results in 100,000(0.01) = 1000 more orders. Each order yields a revenue of $40, on average, but incurs a variable cost of $32.20. The net gain in profit is $7.80 per order, or $7800 for 1000 orders.

The purpose of the Goal Seek tool is to solve one equation in one unknown. Here, we find the response rate that makes profit equal to 0.

USING GOAL SEEK

From the data table, we see that profit changes from negative to positive when the response rate is somewhere between 5% and 6%. Question 2 asks for the exact breakeven point. This could be found by trial and error, but it is easier to find with Excel's Goal Seek tool. Essentially, Goal Seek is useful for solving a *single* equation in a *single* unknown. Here, the equation is **Profit=0**, and the single unknown is the response rate. In Excel terminology, the unknown is called the **changing cell** because we are allowed to change it to make the equation true. To implement Goal Seek, select the Tools/Goal Seek menu item and fill in the resulting dialog box as shown in Figure 2.15. (Range names or cell addresses can be used in the top and bottom boxes, but a *number* must be entered in the middle box.) After you click on OK, the ResponseRate and Profit cells have values 5.77% and $0. In words, if the response rate is 5.77%, Great Threads breaks even. If the response rate is greater than 5.77%, the company makes money; if it is less than 5.77%, the company loses money. Of course, this assumes that the company indeed mails 100,000 catalogs. If it sent more or fewer catalogs, the breakeven response rate would change.

Figure 2.15
Goal Seek Dialog
Box

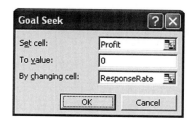

→ **EXCEL TOOL:** *Goal Seek*

The purpose of the Goal Seek tool is to solve one equation in one unknown. Specifically, it allows you to vary a single input cell to force a single output cell to a selected value. To use it, use the Tools/Goal Seek menu item and fill in the resulting dialog box in Figure 2.15. In the Set cell box enter a reference to the output cell, in the To value box enter the numeric value you want the output cell to equal, and in the By changing cell box enter a reference to the input cell. Note that Goal Seek sometimes stops when the Set cell is close, but not exactly equal to, the desired value. To improve Goal Seek's accuracy, select the Tools/Options menu item and click on the Calculation tab. Then check the Iteration box and reduce Maximum change to any desired level of precision. We chose a precision level of 0.000001. For this level of precision, Goal Seek searches until profit is within 0.000001 of the desired value, $0. ■

Limitations of the Model

Question 3 asks whether the company should proceed with the mailing if the response rate is only 3%. From the data table (see Figure 2.13), the apparent answer is "no" because profit is negative. However, like many companies, we are taking the short-term view with this reasoning. We should realize that many customers who respond to direct mail will *reorder* in the future. The company nets $7.80 per order. If each of the respondents ordered two more times, say, the company would earn 3000($7.80)(2) = $46,800 more than appears in the model, and profit would then be positive. The moral is that we must look at the long-term impact of our decisions. However, if we want to incorporate the long term explicitly into the model, we must build a more complex model.

Later chapters, especially Chapters 8–10, deal explicitly with uncertainty.

Finally, question 4 asks about the impact of uncertainty in the model. We would be kidding ourselves to think that all model inputs are known with certainty. For example, the size of an order is not always $40—it might range, say, from $10 to $100. When there is a high degree of uncertainty about model inputs, it makes little sense to talk about *the* profit level or *the* breakeven response rate. It makes much more sense to talk about the *probability* that profit will have a certain value or the *probability* that the company will break even. We will illustrate how this can be done in the following example, and we will see many more such examples in Chapters 8–10.

Using the Auditing Tool

The model in this example is fairly small and simple. Even so, it is useful to illustrate a little-known Excel feature to see how all of the parts fit together. This is the Auditing tool, available from the Auditing toolbar (also available from the Tools menu). See Figure 2.16. Actually, this toolbar is not even on the list of toolbars you see when you select the View/Toolbars menu item (or right-click on any visible toolbar), but you can find it as follows. Select the Tools/Customize menu item, and click on the Toolbars tab. Now the Auditing toolbar *is* on the list, so you can check its box to make it visible. You might even decide to keep it visible *all* the time.

Figure 2.16

Auditing Toolbar

The second and fourth buttons from the left (Trace Precedents and Trace Dependents) are probably the most useful buttons on this toolbar. To see which formulas have direct links to the NumResponses cell, select this cell and click on the Trace Dependents button.

The Auditing toolbar is indispensable for untangling the logic in a spreadsheet, especially one that someone else developed!

Arrows are drawn to each cell that directly depends on the number of responses, as shown in Figure 2.17. Alternatively, to see which cells are used to create the formula in the Total_revenue cell, select this cell and click on the Trace Precedents button. Now you will see that the Average_order and Number_of_responses cells were used directly to calculate revenue, as shown in Figure 2.18. Using these two buttons, you can trace your logic (or someone else's logic) as far backward or forward as you like. When you are finished, just click on the Remove All Arrows button (sixth from the left).

Figure 2.17

Dependents of Number_of_ responses Cell

	A	B	C	D	E
1	Great Threads direct mail model				
2					
3	Catalog inputs			Model of responses	
4	Fixed cost of printing	$20,000		Response rate	8%
5	Variable cost of printing mailing	$0.25		Number of responses	8000
6					
7	Decision variable			Model of revenue, costs, and profit	
8	Number mailed	100000		Total Revenue	$320,000
9				Fixed cost of printing	$20,000
10	Order inputs			Total variable cost of printing mailing	$25,000
11	Average order	$40		Total variable cost of orders	$257,600
12	Variable cost per order	$32.20		Total cost	$302,600
13				Profit	$17,400

Figure 2.18

Precedents of Total_revenue Cell

	A	B	C	D	E
1	Great Threads direct mail model				
2					
3	Catalog inputs			Model of responses	
4	Fixed cost of printing	$20,000		Response rate	8%
5	Variable cost of printing mailing	$0.25		Number of responses	8000
6					
7	Decision variable			Model of revenue, costs, and profit	
8	Number mailed	100000		Total Revenue	$320,000
9				Fixed cost of printing	$20,000
10	Order inputs			Total variable cost of printing mailing	$25,000
11	Average order	$40		Total variable cost of orders	$257,600
12	Variable cost per order	$32.20		Total cost	$302,600
13				Profit	$17,400

→ **EXCEL TOOL:** *Auditing Toolbar*

The auditing toolbar allows you to see dependents of a selected cell (which cells have formulas that reference this cell) or precedents of a given cell (which cells are referenced in this cell's formula). In fact, you can even see dependents or precedents that reside on a different worksheet. In this case, the auditing arrows appear as dashed lines and point to a small spreadsheet icon. By double-clicking on the dashed line, you can see a list of dependents or precedents on other worksheets. These tools are especially useful for understanding how someone else's spreadsheet works. To make this toolbar visible, select the Tools/Customize menu item, click on the Toolbars tab, and check the Formula Auditing item in the list. ■

You can place charts on the same sheet as the underlying data or on separate chart sheets. The choice is a matter of personal preference.

Is the spreadsheet layout in Figure 2.12 the best possible layout? This question is probably not too crucial for this model because this model is so small. However, we have put all of the inputs together (usually a good practice), and we have put all of the outputs together in a logical order. You might want to put the answers to questions 1 and 2 on separate sheets, but with such a small model, it is arguably better to keep everything on a single sheet. We generally use separate sheets only when things start getting bigger and more complex. One final issue is placement of the chart. As you might know, the last step of the Chart Wizard allows you to select whether you want to place the chart on the worksheet ("floating" above the cells) or on a separate chart sheet that has no rows or columns. This choice depends on your personal preference—neither choice is necessarily better than the other—but for this small model, we believe once again that it is better to keep everything on a single sheet.

Finally, could we have chosen the number mailed, rather than the response rate, as the basis for a sensitivity analysis? We certainly could have. When we run a sensitivity analysis, we typically base it on an uncertain input variable, such as the response rate, or a decision variable that the decision maker has direct influence over. ■

PROBLEMS

Solutions for problems whose numbers appear within a color box can be found in the Student Solutions Manual. Order your copy today at http://e-catalog.thomsonlearning.com/110/ by using ISBN 0-534-39687-9.

Skill-Building Problems

1. In the Great Threads model, the range E9:E11 does not have a range name. Open your completed Excel file and name this range Costs. Then look at the formula in cell E12. It does *not* automatically use the new range name. Modify it so that it does. Then click on cell G4 and paste the new list of range names over the previous list.

2. The sensitivity analysis in the Great Threads example was on the response rate. Suppose now that the response rate is *known* to be 8%, and the company wants to do a sensitivity analysis on the number mailed. After all, this is a variable under direct control of the company. Create a one-way data table, and a corresponding X-Y chart, of profit versus the number mailed, where the number mailed varies from 80,000 to 150,000 in increments of 10,000. Does it appear,

from the results you see here, that there is an "optimal" number to mail, from all possible values, that will maximize profit? Write a concise memo to management about your results.

3. Continuing the previous problem, use Goal Seek for *each* value of number mailed (once for 80,000, once for 90,000, and so on). For each, find the response rate that allows the company to break even. Then chart these values, where the number mailed is on the horizontal axis and the breakeven response rate is on the vertical axis. Explain the behavior in this chart in a brief memo to management.

Skill-Extending Problem

4. As the Great Threads problem is now modeled, if all inputs remain fixed except for the number mailed, profit will increase indefinitely as the number mailed increases. This hardly seems realistic—the company could become infinitely rich! Discuss realistic ways to modify the model so that this unrealistic behavior would be eliminated.

2.5 ORDERING WITH QUANTITY DISCOUNTS AND DEMAND UNCERTAINTY

In the following example we again attempt to find the appropriate level of some activity: how much of a product to order when customer demand for the product is uncertain. Two important features of this example are the presence of quantity discounts and the explicit use of probabilities to model uncertain demand. (Except for these features, the problem is very similar to the one discussed in Example 2.1.)

<table>
<tr><td>EXAMPLE</td><td>2.4 ORDERING WITH QUANTITY DISCOUNTS AT SAM'S BOOKSTORE</td></tr>
</table>

Sam's Bookstore, with many locations across the United States, places orders for all of the latest books and then distributes them to its individual bookstores. Sam's needs a model to help it order the appropriate number of any title. For example, Sam's plans to order a popular new hardback novel, which it will sell for $30. It can purchase any number of this book from the publisher, but due to quantity discounts, the unit cost for all books it orders depends on the number ordered. Specifically, if the number ordered is less than 1000, the unit cost is $24. After each 1000, the unit cost drops: to $23 for at least 1000 copies, to $22.25 for at least 2000, to $21.75 for at least 3000, and to $21.30 (the lowest possible unit cost) for at least 4000. For example, if Sam's orders 2500 books, its total cost is $22.25(2500) = $55,625. Sam's is very uncertain about the demand for this book—it estimates that demand could be anywhere from 500 to 4500. Also, as with most hardback novels, this one will eventually come out in paperback. Therefore, if Sam's has any hardbacks left when the paperback comes out, it will put them on sale for $10, at which price it believes all leftovers will be sold. How many copies of this hardback novel should Sam's order from the publisher?

Business Objectives   To create a model to determine the company's profit, given fixed values of demand and the order quantity, and then to model the demand uncertainty explicitly and to choose the expected profit maximizing ("best") order quantity.

Excel Objectives   To learn how to build in complex logic with IF formulas, to get online help about Excel functions with the f_x button, to learn how to use lookup functions, to see how two-way data tables allow us to answer more extensive what-if questions, and to introduce Excel's SUMPRODUCT function.

Solution

The key variables for this model appear in Table 2.4. Our primary modeling tasks are (1) to show how any combination of demand and order quantity determines the number of units sold, both at the regular price and at the leftover sale price, and (2) to calculate the total ordering cost for any order quantity. Once we accomplish these tasks, we will model the uncertainty of demand explicitly, and we will then choose the "best" order quantity.

Table 2.4   Key Variables for Sam's Bookstore Problem

Input variables	Unit prices, table of unit costs specifying quantity discount structure
Uncertain variable	Demand
Decision variable	Order quantity
Key output variable	Profit
Other output variables	Units sold at each price, revenue and cost totals

We will first develop a spreadsheet model to calculate Sam's profit for any order quantity and any possible demand. Then we will perform a sensitivity analysis to see how profit depends on these two quantities. Finally, we will indicate one possible method Sam's might use to choose the "best" order quantity.

Whenever we use the term trial value for an input or a decision variable, you can be fairly sure that we will follow up with a data table or (in later chapters) by running Solver to optimize.

DEVELOPING THE SPREADSHEET MODEL

The profit model appears in Figure 2.19. (See the file **QuantityDiscounts.xls**.) Note that the order quantity and demand in the Order_quantity and Demand cells are "trial" values. (We put comments in these cells to remind ourselves of this.) We can put any values in these cells, just to test the logic of the model. The Order_quantity cell is enclosed in a red border because the company can choose its value. In contrast, we enclose the Demand cell in a dashed green border. We will use this convention here and in future chapters to indicate that an input value is uncertain and is being treated explicitly as such. Also, note how we have used a table to indicate the quantity discounts cost structure. Use the following steps to build the model.

Figure 2.19 Sam's Profit Model

	A	B	C	D	E	F	G	H	I	J
1	Ordering decision with quantity discounts									
2										
3	Inputs			Quantity discount structure				Range names used:		
4	Unit cost - see table to right			At least	Unit cost			Cost	=Model!$B$18	
5	Regular price	$30		0	$24.00			CostLookup	=Model!$D$5:$E$9	
6	Leftover price	$10		1000	$23.00			Demand	=Model!$B$12	
7				2000	$22.25			Leftover_price	=Model!$B$6	
8	Decision variable			3000	$21.75			Order_quantity	=Model!$B$9	
9	Order quantity	2500		4000	$21.30			Probabilities	=Model!$B$35:$J$35	
10								Profit	=Model!$B$19	
11	Uncertain quantity							Regular_price	=Model!$B$5	
12	Demand	2000						Revenue	=Model!$B$17	
13								Units_sold_at_leftover_price	=Model!$B$16	
14	Profit model							Units_sold_at_regular_price	=Model!$B$15	
15	Units sold at regular price	2000								
16	Units sold at leftover price	500								
17	Revenue	$65,000								
18	Cost	$55,625								
19	Profit	$9,375								

1 Inputs and range names. Enter all inputs and name the ranges as indicated in columns H and I. Note that we used the Insert/Name/Create shortcut to name all ranges except for CostLookup and Probabilities. For these latter two, we highlighted the ranges and entered the names in the Name Box—the "manual" method. (Why the difference? To use the Insert/Name/Create shortcut, you must have appropriate labels in adjacent cells. Sometimes this is simply not convenient.)

2 Revenues. The company can sell only what it has, and it will sell any leftovers at the discounted sale price. Therefore, enter the formulas

=MIN(Order_quantity,Demand)
=IF(Order_quantity >Demand, Order_quantity -Demand,0)

and

=Units_sold_at_regular_price*Regular_price+Units_sold_at_leftover_price*Leftover_price

in cells B15, B16, and B17. The logic in the first two of these cells is necessary to account correctly for the cases when the order quantity is greater than demand and when it is less than or equal to demand. Note that we could use the following equivalent alternative to the IF function:

=MAX(Order_quantity-Demand,0).

→ **EXCEL TOOL: f_x Button**

If you want to learn more about how an Excel function operates, use the f_x button. This is called the "Insert Function" button, although some people call it the "Function Wizard." If you have already entered a function, such as an IF function, in a cell and then click on the f_x button, you will get help on this function. If you select an empty cell and then click on the f_x button, you can choose a function to get help on.[6] ∎

3 Total ordering cost. Depending on the order quantity, we find the appropriate unit cost from the unit cost table and multiply it by the order quantity to obtain the total ordering cost. This could be accomplished with a complex nested IF formula, but a much better way is to use the VLOOKUP function. Specifically, enter the formula

=VLOOKUP(Order_quantity,CostLookup,2)*Order_quantity

in cell B18. The VLOOKUP part of this formula says to compare the order quantity to the first (leftmost) column of the table in the CostLookup range and return the corresponding value in the second column (because the last argument is 2). In general, there are two important things to remember about lookup tables: (1) The leftmost column is always the column used for comparison, and (2) the entries in this column must be arranged in increasing order from top to bottom.

→ **EXCEL FUNCTION: *VLOOKUP***

The VLOOKUP function acts like a tax table, where you look up the tax corresponding to your adjusted gross income from a table of incomes and taxes. To use it, first create a vertical lookup table, with values to use for comparison listed in the left column of the table in increasing order and corresponding output values in as many columns to the right as you like. (See the CostLookup range in Figure 2.19 for an example.) Then the VLOOKUP function typically takes three arguments: the value you want to compare to the values in the left column, the lookup table range, and index of the column you want the returned value to come from, where the index of the left column is 1, the index of the next column is 2, and so on. (See online help for an optional fourth argument.) Here, "compare" means to scan down the leftmost column of the table and find the last entry less than or equal to the first argument. There is also an HLOOKUP function. It works exactly the same way, except that the lookup table is constructed from rows, not columns. ∎

4 Profit. Calculate the profit with the formula

=Revenue-Cost

Two-Way Data Table

The next step is to create a two-way data table for profit as a function of the order quantity and demand. This appears in Figure 2.20. To create this table, first enter a link to the profit by entering the formula **=Profit** in cell A22, and enter possible order quantities and possible demands in column A and row 22, respectively. (We used the same values for both order quantity and demand, from 500 to 4500 in increments of 500. This is not necessary—we could let demand change in increments of 100 or even 1, for instance—but it is reasonable. Perhaps Sam's is required by the publisher to order in multiples of 500.) Then select the Data/Table menu item, and enter the Demand cell as the Row Input cell and the Order_quantity cell as the Column Input cell. (See Figure 2.21.)

A two-way data table allows you to see how a single output varies as two inputs vary simultaneously.

---

[6] If the f_x button isn't on any of your toolbars, select the Tools/Customize menu item, click on the Commands tab, and select the Insert category in the left pane. Then scroll down in the right pane for the f_x button, drag it up to an existing toolbar, and close the Customize window. If you then close Excel and open it again, the f_x button will still be there.

Figure 2.20 Profit as a Function of Order Quantity and Demand

	A	B	C	D	E	F	G	H	I	J
21	Data table of profit as a function of order quantity (along side) and demand (along top)									
22	$9,375	500	1000	1500	2000	2500	3000	3500	4000	4500
23	500	$3,000	$3,000	$3,000	$3,000	$3,000	$3,000	$3,000	$3,000	$3,000
24	1000	-$3,000	$7,000	$7,000	$7,000	$7,000	$7,000	$7,000	$7,000	$7,000
25	1500	-$9,500	$500	$10,500	$10,500	$10,500	$10,500	$10,500	$10,500	$10,500
26	2000	-$14,500	-$4,500	$5,500	$15,500	$15,500	$15,500	$15,500	$15,500	$15,500
27	2500	-$20,625	-$10,625	-$625	$9,375	$19,375	$19,375	$19,375	$19,375	$19,375
28	3000	-$25,250	-$15,250	-$5,250	$4,750	$14,750	$24,750	$24,750	$24,750	$24,750
29	3500	-$31,125	-$21,125	-$11,125	-$1,125	$8,875	$18,875	$28,875	$28,875	$28,875
30	4000	-$35,200	-$25,200	-$15,200	-$5,200	$4,800	$14,800	$24,800	$34,800	$34,800
31	4500	-$40,850	-$30,850	-$20,850	-$10,850	-$850	$9,150	$19,150	$29,150	$39,150

Figure 2.21

Dialog Box for Two-Way Data Table

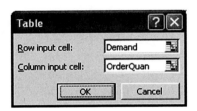

→ **EXCEL TOOL:** *Two-Way Data Table*

A two-way data table allows us to see how a single output cell varies as we vary two input cells. (Unlike a one-way data table, only a single output cell can be chosen.) To create this type of table, enter a reference to the output cell in the top left corner of the table, enter possible values of the two inputs below and to the right of this corner cell, and highlight the entire table. Then select the Data/Table command, and enter references to the cells where the original two input variables live. The Row Input cell corresponds to the values along the top row of the table, and Column Input cell corresponds to the values along the left column of the table. When you click on OK, Excel substitutes each pair of input values into these two input cells, recalculates the spreadsheet, and enters the corresponding output value in the table. By clicking on any cell in the body of the table, you will see that Excel also enters the function =TABLE to remind you that the cell is part of a data table. ■

The resulting data table shows that profit depends heavily on both order quantity and demand, and (by scanning across rows) how higher demands lead to larger profits. But it is still far from clear which order quantity Sam's should select. Remember that Sam's has complete control over the order quantity (it can choose the *row* of the data table), but it has no direct control over demand (it cannot choose the column).

The ordering decision depends not only on which demands are *possible*, but on which demands are *likely* to occur. The usual way to express this information is with a set of probabilities that sum to 1. Suppose Sam's estimates these as the values in row 35 of Figure 2.22. These are probably based on other similar books it has sold in the past. We see that the most likely demands are 2000 and 2500, with other values on both sides less likely. We can use these probabilities to find an *expected* profit for each order quantity. This expected profit is a weighted average of the profits in any row in the data table, using the probabilities as the weights. The easiest way to do this is to enter the formula

=SUMPRODUCT(B23:J23,Probabilities)

This is actually a preview of decision making under uncertainty. To calculate an expected profit, we multiply each profit by its probability and add the products. We will cover this topic in depth in Chapter 8.

in cell B38 and copy it down to cell B46. We also create a bar chart of these expected profits, as shown in Figure 2.22. (Excel's Chart Wizard refers to these as "column charts." The height of each bar is the expected profit for that particular order quantity.)

Figure 2.22 Comparison of Expected Profits

	A	B	C	D	E	F	G	H	I	J	K	L
33	Model of expected demands											
34	Demand	500	1000	1500	2000	2500	3000	3500	4000	4500		
35	Probability	0.025	0.05	0.15	0.25	0.25	0.15	0.07	0.04	0.015		
36												
37	Order quantity	Expected profit					Sum of probabilities -->			1		
38	500	$3,000										
39	1000	$6,750										
40	1500	$9,500										
41	2000	$12,250		Order 2000 to								
42	2500	$11,375		maximize the								
43	3000	$9,500		expected profit.								
44	3500	$4,875										
45	4000	$1,350										
46	4500	-$4,150										
47												
48												
49												
50												
51												
52												
53												

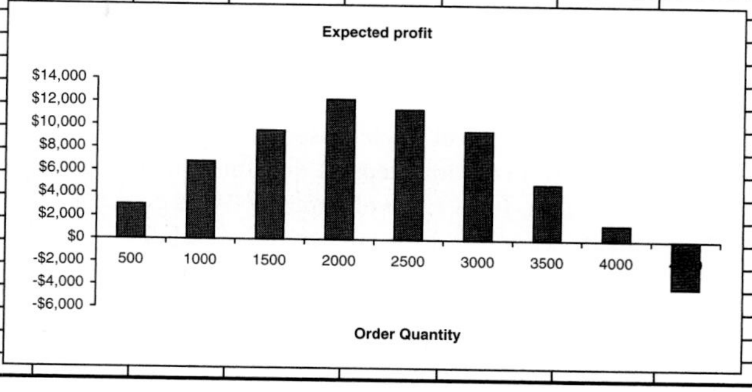

→ **EXCEL FUNCTION:** *SUMPRODUCT*
The SUMPRODUCT function takes two range arguments, which must be exactly the same size and shape, and it sums the products of the corresponding values in these two ranges. For example, the formula **=SUMPRODUCT(A10:B11,E12:F13)** *is a shortcut for a formula involving the sum of 4 products:* **=A10*E12+A11*E13+B10*F12+B11*F13**. *It is an extremely useful function, especially when the ranges involved are large, and we will use it repeatedly throughout this book. (Actually, the SUMPRODUCT function can have more than two range arguments, all of the same size and shape, but the most common use of SUMPRODUCT is when there are just two ranges involved.)* ■

The largest of the expected profits, $12,250, corresponds to an order quantity of 2000, so we would recommend that Sam's order 2000 copies of the book. This does not guarantee that Sam's will make a profit of $12,250—the actual profit depends on the eventual demand—but it represents a reasonable way to proceed in the face of uncertain demand. We will say much more about making decisions under uncertainty and the expected value criterion in Chapter 8. ■

PROBLEMS

Skill-Building Problems

5. The spreadsheet model for Sam's Bookstore contains a two-way data table for profit versus order quantity and demand. Experiment with Excel's chart types to create a chart that shows this information graphically in an intuitive format. (Choose the format you would choose if you were giving a presentation to your boss.)

6. In some ordering problems like the one for Sam's Bookstore, whenever demand exceeds existing inventory, the excess demand is not lost but is filled by expedited orders—at a premium cost to the company. Change Sam's model to reflect this behavior. Assume that the unit cost of expediting is $40, well above the highest "regular" unit cost.

7. In the Sam's Bookstore problem the quantity discount structure is such that *all* of the units ordered have the same unit cost. For example, if the order quantity is 2500, then each unit costs $22.25. Sometimes the quantity discount structure is such that the unit cost for the first so many items is one value, the unit cost for the next so many units is a slightly lower value, and so on. Modify the model so that the Sam's pays $24 for units 1 to 1500, $23 for units 1501 to 2500, and $22 for units 2501 and above. For example, the total cost for an order quantity of 2750 is 1500(24)+1000(23)+250(22). (*Hint:* Use IF functions, not VLOOKUP.)

Skill-Extending Problems

8. The current spreadsheet model essentially finds the expected profit in several steps. It first finds the profit in cell B16 for a *fixed* value of demand. Then it uses a data table to find the profit for each of several demands, and finally it uses SUMPRODUCT to find the expected profit. Modify the model so that expected profit is found directly, without a data table. To do this, change row 11 so that instead of a single demand, there is a list of possible demands, those cur-

rently in row 34. Then insert a new row below row 11 that lists the probabilities of these demands. Next, in the rows below the Profit Model label, calculate the units sold, revenue, cost, and profit for *each* demand. For example, the quantities in column C will be for the second possible demand. Finally, use SUMPRODUCT to calculate *expected* profit below the Profit row.

9. Continuing Problem 6, create a two-way data table for expected profit with order quantity along the side and unit expediting cost along the top. Allow the order quantity to vary from 500 to 4500 in increments of 500, and allow the unit expediting cost to vary from $36 to $45 in increments of $1. Each column of this table will allow you to choose a "best" order quantity for a given unit expediting cost. How does this best order quantity change as the unit expediting cost increases? Write up your results in a concise memo to management. (*Hint:* You will have to modify the existing spreadsheet model so that there is a cell for expected profit that changes automatically when you change either the order quantity or the unit expediting cost. See the previous problem for guidelines.)

2.6 DECISIONS INVOLVING THE TIME VALUE OF MONEY

In many business situations, cash flows are received at different points in time, and a company must determine a course of action that maximizes the "value" of cash flows. Here are some examples:

- Should a company buy a more expensive machine that lasts for 10 years or a less expensive machine that lasts for 5 years?
- What level of plant capacity is best for the next 20 years?
- A company must market one of several midsize cars. Which car should it market?

To make decisions when cash flows are received at different points in time, we need to understand that the later a dollar is received, the less valuable the dollar is. For example, suppose we can invest money at a 10% annual interest rate. Then $1.00 received now is essentially equivalent to $1.10 a year from now. The reason is that if we have $1.00 now, we can invest it and gain $0.10 in interest in one year. If we let $r = 0.10$ be the interest rate (expressed as a decimal), we can write this as

$$\$1.00 \text{ now} = \$1.10 \text{ a year from now} = \$1.00(1 + r) \qquad (2.1)$$

Dividing both sides of equation (2.1) by $1 + r$, we can rewrite it as

$$\$1.00 \times 1/(1 + r) \text{ now} = \$1.00 \text{ a year from now} \qquad (2.2)$$

The value $1/(1 + r)$ in equation (2.2) is called the **discount factor**, and it is always less than 1. The quantity on the left, which evaluates to $0.909 for $r = 0.10$, is called the **present value** of $1.00 received a year from now. The idea is that if we had $0.909 now, we could invest it at 10% and have it grow to $1.00 in a year.

In general, if money can be invested at annual rate r compounded each year, then $1 received t years from now has the same value as $1/(1 + r)^t$ dollars received today—that is, the $1 is discounted by the discount factor raised to the t power. If we multiply a cash flow received t years from now by $1/(1 + r)^t$ to obtain its present value, then the total of these present values over all years is called the **net present value (NPV)** of our cash flows. Basic financial theory tells us that projects with positive NPVs increase the value of the company, whereas projects with negative NPVs decrease the value of the company.

The rate r (usually called the **discount rate**) used by major corporations generally comes from some version of the **capital asset pricing model**. Most companies use a discount rate ranging from 10% to 20%. The following example illustrates how spreadsheet models and the time value of money can be used to make complex business decisions.

> The **discount factor** is 1 divided by (1 plus the **discount rate**). To discount a cash flow that occurs t years from now, multiply it by the discount factor raised to the t power. The **NPV** is the sum of all discounted cash flows.

<table>
<tr><td>EXAMPLE</td><td>2.5 CALCULATING NPV AT ACRON</td></tr>
</table>

Acron is a large drug company. At the current time, the beginning of year 0, Acron is trying to decide whether one of its new drugs, Niagra, is worth pursuing. Niagra is in the final stages of development and will be ready to enter the market in year 1. The final cost of development, to be incurred at the beginning of year 1, is $9.3 million. Acron estimates that the demand for Niagra will gradually grow and then decline over its useful lifetime of 20 years. Specifically, the company expects its gross margin (revenue minus cost) to be $1.2 million in year 1, then to increase at an annual rate of 10% through year 8, and finally to decrease at an annual rate of 5% through year 20. Acron wants to develop a spreadsheet model of its 20-year cash flows, assuming its cash flows, other than the initial development cost, are incurred at the *ends* of the respective years.[7] Using an annual discount rate of 12% for the purpose of calculating NPV, the drug company wants to answer the following questions:

1. Is the drug worth pursuing, or should Acron abandon it now and not incur the $9.3 million development cost?
2. How do changes in the model inputs change the answer to question 1?
3. How realistic is the model?

Business Objectives   To develop a model that calculates the NPV of Acron's cash flows, to use this model to determine whether the drug should be developed further and then marketed, and to see how sensitive the answer to this question is to model parameters.

Excel Objectives   To illustrate efficient selection and copying of large ranges and to learn Excel's NPV function.

Solution

The key variables in Acron's problem appear in Table 2.5. The first two rows contain the inputs stated in the problem. We have made a judgment call as to which of these are known with some certainty and which are uncertain. Although we will not do it here in this chapter, a thorough study of Acron's problem would treat this uncertainty explicitly, probably

---

[7]To simplify the model, we will ignore taxes.

with simulation. For now, we will accept the values given in the statement of the problem and leave the simulation for a later chapter.

Table 2.5	Key Variables for Acron's Problem
Input variables	Development cost, first year gross margin, rate of increase during early years, years of growth, rate of decrease in later years, discount rate
Key output variable	NPV
Other calculated variables	Yearly gross margins

The model of Acron's cash flows appears in Figure 2.23. As with many financial spreadsheet models that extend over a multiyear period, we enter "typical" formulas in the first year or two and then copy this logic across to all years. For copying purposes, however, it is useful to divide the screen horizontally into two panes so that we can see the first and last years, as shown in the figure. To do this, click on the "separator" just to the right of the horizontal scrollbar at the bottom of the screen and drag it to the left. (There is a similar separator just above the vertical scrollbar for dividing the screen vertically.)

Figure 2.23 Acron's Model of 20-Year NPV

	A	B	C	D	E	F	G	H	S	T	U
1	Calculating NPV at Acron										
2											
3	Inputs			Range names used:							
4	Development cost	9.3		Development_cost		=Model!$B$4					
5	Gross margin year 1	1.2		Discount_rate		=Model!$B$9					
6	Rate of increase	10%		Gross_margin_year_1		=Model!$B$5					
7	Increase through year	8		Gross_margins		=Model!$B$13:$U$13					
8	Rate of decrease	5%		Increase_through_year	=Model!$B$7						
9	Discount rate	12%		Rate_of_decrease		=Model!$B$8					
10				Rate_of_increase		=Model!$B$6					
11	Cash flows										
12	End of year	1	2	3	4	5	6	7	18	19	20
13	Gross margins	1.2000	1.3200	1.4520	1.5972	1.7569	1.9326	2.1259	1.4001	1.3301	1.2636
14											
15	NPV	3.3003									

→ EXCEL TIP: *Splitting the Screen*
To split the screen horizontally, drag the separator just to the right of the bottom scrollbar to the left. To split the screen vertically, drag the separator just above the right scrollbar downward. Drag either separator back to its original position to remove the split. ■

DEVELOPING THE SPREADSHEET MODEL

To create the model, complete the following steps. (See the file **CalculatingNPV.xls**.)

❶ **Inputs and range names.** Enter the given input data in the shaded cells, and name the ranges as shown. As usual, note that the range names for cells B4–B9 can be created all at once with the Insert/Names/Create shortcut, as can the range name for row 13. In the latter case, we highlight the whole range A13:U13 and then use the Insert/Names/Create menu item.

❷ **Cash flows.** Start by entering the formula

=B5

in cell B13 for the year 1 gross margin. Then enter the general formula

=IF(C12<=Increase_through_year,B13*(1+Rate_of_increase),B13*(1-Rate_of_decrease))

in cell C13 and copy it across to cell U13 to calculate the other yearly gross margins. Note how this IF function checks the year index in row 12 to see whether sales are still increasing or have started to decrease. Of course, by using the (range-named) input cells in this formula, we can change any of these inputs in cells B6–B8, and the calculated cells will automatically update. This is a *much* better practice than embedding the numbers in the formula itself.

→ EXCEL TIP: *Efficient Selection*

An easy way to select a large range, assuming that the first and last cells of the range are visible, is to select the first cell and then, with your finger on the Shift key, select the last cell. (And don't forget that you can split the screen horizontally and/or vertically to make these first and last cells visible.) This selects the entire range and is easier than scrolling.[8] ∎

→ EXCEL TIP: *Efficient Copying with Ctrl-Enter*

An easy way to copy a formula to a range is to select the range (as in the preceding Excel tip), type the formula, and press Ctrl-Enter (both keys at once). Once you get used to this shortcut, you'll use it all the time. ∎

③ Net present value. The NPV is based on the sequence of cash flows in row 13. From our general discussion of NPV, to discount everything back to the beginning of year 1, the value in cell B13 should be multiplied by $1/(1 + r)^1$, the value in cell C13 should be multiplied by $1/(1 + r)^2$, and so on, and these quantities should be summed to obtain the NPV. (Here, $r = 0.12$ is the discount rate.) Fortunately, however, Excel has a built-in NPV function to accomplish this calculation. To use it, enter the formula

=-Development_cost+NPV(Discount_rate,Gross_margins)

in the NPV cell. The NPV function takes two arguments: the discount rate and a range of cash flows. Furthermore, it assumes that the first cell in this range is the cash flow at the *end* of year 1, the second cell is the cash flow at the end of year 2, and so on. This explains why we subtracted the development cost *outside* of the NPV function—it is incurred at the *beginning* of year 1. In general, any cash flow incurred at the beginning of year 1 must be placed outside of the NPV function.

To get some understanding of NPV, note that the *sum* of the cash flows in row 13 is slightly more than $34.14 million, but the NPV (aside from the development cost) is only about $12.60 million. This is because values farther into the future are discounted so heavily. At the extreme, the $1.2636 million cash flow in year 20 is equivalent to only $1.2636[1/(1 + 0.12)^{20}] = \$0.131$ million now!

→ EXCEL FUNCTION: *NPV*

The stream of cash flows in the NPV function must occur at the ends of year 1, year 2, and so on. If the timing is irregular, you must discount "manually"; the NPV function will not work properly.

The NPV function takes two arguments, the discount rate (entered as a decimal, such as 0.12 for 12%) and a stream of cash flows. It is assumed that these cash flows occur in consecutive years, starting at the end of year 1. If there is an initial cash flow at the beginning of year 1, such as an initial investment, it should be entered outside of the NPV function. (Note that there is there is also an XNPV function that has three arguments: a discount rate, a series of cash flows, and a series of dates when the cash flows occur. Because these dates do not have to be equally spaced through time, this function is considerably more flexible than the NPV function. To use it, the Analysis Toolpak add-in that ships with Excel must be loaded. We will

---

[8]We include other tips like this for increasing your efficiency in the **ExcelTutorial.doc** file on the accompanying CD-ROM.

not use the XNPV function in this book, but you can learn more about it in Excel's online help.) ∎

Deciding Whether to Continue with the Drug

NPV calculations are typically used to see whether a certain plan should be undertaken. If the NPV is positive, the plan is worth pursuing. If the NPV is negative, then the company should look for other ways of investing its money. We see from Figure 2.23 that the NPV for this drug is positive, over $3 million.[9] Therefore, if Acron is comfortable with its predictions of future cash flows, it should continue with the development and marketing of the drug. However, it might first want to see how sensitive the NPV is to changes in the sales predictions. After all, these predictions are intelligent guesses at best.

One possible sensitivity analysis appears in Figure 2.24. Here we build a one-way data table to see how the NPV changes when the number of years of increase (the input in cell B7) changes. Again, the important question is whether the NPV stays positive. It certainly does when the input variable is greater than its current value of 8. However, if sales start decreasing soon enough—that is, if the value in B7 is 3 or less—then the NPV turns negative. This should probably not concern Acron, since its best guess for the years of increase is considerably greater than 3.

Figure 2.24

Sensitivity of NPV to Years of Sales Increase

	A	B	C
17	Sensitivity to years of increase (cell B7)		
18		3.3003	
19	3	-0.7190	
20	4	0.1374	
21	5	0.9687	
22	6	1.7739	
23	7	2.5516	
24	8	3.3003	
25	9	4.0181	
26	10	4.7027	

Another possibility is to see how long *and* how good the good years are. To do this, we create the two-way data table shown in Figure 2.25, where cell B6 is the row input cell and cell B7 is the column input cell. Now we see that if sales increase through year 6, all reasonable yearly increases result in a positive NPV. However, if sales increase only through year 5, say, then a low enough yearly increase can produce a negative NPV. Acron might want to step back and estimate how likely these "bad" scenarios are before proceeding with the drug.

Figure 2.25

Sensitivity of NPV to Years of Increase and Yearly Increase

	A	B	C	D	E	F	G
28	Sensitivity to rate of increase in early years (cell B6) and years of increase (cell B7)						
29	3.3003	5%	6%	7%	8%	9%	10%
30	3	-1.3405	-1.2184	-1.0951	-0.9708	-0.8454	-0.7190
31	4	-0.8203	-0.6352	-0.4469	-0.2554	-0.0606	0.1374
32	5	-0.3383	-0.0897	0.1652	0.4265	0.6943	0.9687
33	6	0.1074	0.4195	0.7419	1.0750	1.4189	1.7739
34	7	0.5182	0.8934	1.2838	1.6899	2.1123	2.5516
35	8	0.8958	1.3330	1.7912	2.2711	2.7738	3.3003
36	9	1.2413	1.7392	2.2643	2.8182	3.4023	4.0181
37	10	1.5559	2.1125	2.7033	3.3306	3.9963	4.7027

[9]You might wonder why we didn't discount back to the beginning of the current year, year 0, instead of year 1. This is a fairly arbitrary decision on our part. To discount back to year 0, we would simply divide our NPV by 1.12. The important point, however, is that this would have no bearing on Acron's decision: A positive NPV would stay positive, and a negative NPV would stay negative.

Limitations of the Model

Probably the major flaw in this model is that we have ignored uncertainty. It is clear that future cash flows are highly uncertain, due mainly to uncertain demand for the drug. We will discuss how to incorporate uncertainty into this type of model when we discuss simulation in Chapters 9 and 10. Aside from this uncertainty, there are almost always ways to make *any* model more realistic—at the cost of increased complexity. For example, we could model the impact of competition on Niagra's profitability. Alternatively, we could allow Acron to treat its prices as decision variables. However, this might influence the likelihood of competition entering the market, which would certainly complicate the model. The point is that this model is only a start. When millions of dollars are at stake, a more thorough analysis is certainly warranted. ■

PROBLEMS

Skill-Building Problems

10. Modify Acron's model so that development lasts for an extra year. Specifically, assume that development costs of $7.2 million and $2.1 million are incurred at the beginnings of years 1 and 2, and then the sales in the current model occur one year later, that is, from year 2 until year 21. Again, calculate the NPV discounted back to the beginning of year 1, and perform the same sensitivity analyses. Comment on the effects of this change in timing.

11. Modify Acron's model so that sales increase, then stay steady, and finally decrease. Specifically, assume that the gross margin is $1.2 million in year 1, then increases by 10% annually through year 6, then stays constant through year 10, and finally decreases by 5% annually through year 20. Perform a sensitivity analysis with a two-way data table to see how NPV varies with the length of the increase period (currently 6 years) and the length of the constant period (currently 4 years). Comment on whether Acron should pursue the drug, given your results.

12. Create a one-way data table in the Acron model to see how the NPV varies with discount rate, which is allowed to vary from 8% to 18% in increments of 0.5%. Explain intuitively why the results go in the direction they go—that is, the NPV decreases as the discount rate increases. Should Acron pursue the drug for all of these discount rates?

Skill-Extending Problems

13. The NPV function automatically discounts each of the cash flows and sums the discounted values. Verify that it does this correctly for Acron's model by calculating the NPV the "long way." That is, discount each cash flow and then sum these discounted values. Use Excel formulas to do this, but don't use the NPV function. (*Hint:* Remember that the discounted value of $1 received t years from now is $1/(1 + r)^t$ dollars today.)

14. In a situation such as Acron's, where there is a one-time cost followed by a sequence of cash flows, the **internal rate of return**, or IRR, is the discount rate that makes the NPV equal to 0. The idea is that if the discount rate is greater than the IRR, the company will not pursue the project, whereas if the discount rate is less than the IRR, the project is financially attractive.
   a. Use Excel's Goal Seek tool to find the IRR for the Acron model.
   b. Excel also has an IRR function. Look it up in online help to see how it works, and then use it on Acron's model. Of course, you should get the same IRR as in part **a**.
   c. Verify that the NPV is negative when the discount rate is slightly greater than the IRR, and that it is positive when the discount rate is slightly less than the IRR.

15. We claimed that there is also an XNPV function that can calculate NPV for any (possibly irregular) series of cash flows. Look this function up in Excel's online help. Then use it to set up a spreadsheet model that finds the NPV of the following series: a payment of $25,000 today (assumed to be June 15, 2003), and cash inflows of $10,000 on March 1, 2004, $15,000 on September 15, 2004, $8000 on January 20, 2005, $20,000 on April 1, 2005, and $10,000 on May 15, 2005. Discount these back to "today" using a discount rate of 12%. (*Note:* To use the XNPV function, Excel's Analysis ToolPak must be added in. To ensure this, select the Tools/Add-Ins menu item, and make sure the Analysis ToolPak is checked.)

2.7 CONCLUSION

The examples in this chapter have provided a glimpse of things to come in later chapters. We have illustrated the spreadsheet modeling approach to realistic business problems, we have discussed how to design spreadsheet models for readability, and we have illustrated some of Excel's powerful tools, particularly data tables. In addition, at least three important themes have emerged from these examples: relating inputs and decision variables to outputs by means of appropriate formulas, optimization (finding a "best" order quantity), and the role of uncertainty (uncertain response rate or demand). Although we have not yet learned the tools to explore these themes fully, we will do so before long. Indeed, these themes will occupy us for most of the rest of this book.

Summary of Key Management Science Terms

Term	Explanation	Page
Model inputs	The numeric values that are "givens" in any problem statement	20
Decision variables	The variables a decision maker has control over to effect better solutions	20
Model outputs	The numeric values that result from combinations of inputs and decision variables through the use of logical formulas	20
Net present value	The current worth of a stream of cash flows that occur in the future	45
Discount rate	Interest rate used for discounting future cash flows to get the net present value	45

Summary of Key Excel Terms

Term	Explanation	Excel	Page
IF function	Useful for implementing logic	=IF(*condition,resultIfTrue, resultIfFalse*)	22
Relative, absolute cell addresses	Useful for copying formulas; absolute row or column stays fixed, relative row or column "moves"	A1 (relative), $A1 or A$1 (mixed), $A$1 (absolute); press F4 to cycle through possibilities	28
Range names	Useful for making formulas more meaningful	Type name in "Name" box, or use Insert/Name/Define menu item	32
Pasting range names	Provides a list of all range names in the current workbook	Use Insert/Name/Paste menu item	32
Cell comments	Useful for documenting contents of the cell	Right-click on cell, select Insert Comment menu item	33
One-way data table	Shows how one or more outputs vary as a single input varies	Use Data/Table menu item	35
Goal Seek	Solves one equation in one unknown	Use Tools/Goal Seek menu item	36

Auditing toolbar	Useful for checking which cells are related to other cells through formulas	Use Tools/Customize menu item, select Formula Auditing from Toolbars tab	37
f_x button	Useful for getting help on Excel functions	On Standard toolbar (by default)	40
VLOOKUP function	Useful for finding a particular value based on a comparison	=VLOOKUP (*valueToCompare, lookupTable, columnToReturn*)	41
Two-way data table	Shows how a single output varies as two inputs vary	Use Data/Table menu item	42
SUMPRODUCT function	Calculates the sum of products of values in two (or more) similar-sized ranges	=SUMPRODUCT (*range1,range2*)	43
Splitting screen	Useful for separating the screen horizontally and/or vertically	Use screen splitters at top and right of scrollbars	46
NPV function	Calculates NPV of a stream of cash flows at the ends of consecutive years, starting in year 1	=NPV (*discountRate,cashFlows*)	47
Efficient selection	Useful for selecting a large rectangular range	Pressing Shift-key, click on upper left and bottom right cells of range	47
Efficient copying	Shortcut for copying a formula to a range	Select range, enter formula, and press Ctrl-Enter	47

PROBLEMS

Skill-Building Problems

16. Julie James is opening a lemonade stand. She believes the fixed cost per week of running the stand is $50.00. Her best guess is that she can sell 300 cups per week at $0.50 per cup. The variable cost of producing a cup of lemonade is $0.20.
   a. Given her other assumptions, what level of sales volume will enable Julie to break even?
   b. Given her other assumptions, discuss how a change in sales volume affects profit.
   c. Given her other assumptions, discuss how a change in sales volume and variable cost jointly affect profit.
   d. Use Excel's auditing tool to show which cells in your spreadsheet affect profit directly.

17. We are thinking of opening a Broadway play, *I Love You, You're Mediocre, Now Get Better!* It will cost $5 million to develop the show. There are eight shows per week, and we project the show will run for 100 weeks. It costs $1000 to open the theatre each night. Tickets sell for $50.00, and we earn an average of $1.50 profit per ticket holder from concessions. The theatre holds 800, and we expect 80% of the seats to be full.
   a. Given our other assumptions, how many weeks will the play have to run for us to earn a 100% return on the play's development cost?
   b. Given our other assumptions, how does an increase in the percentage of seats full affect profit?
   c. Given our other assumptions, determine how a joint change in the average ticket price and number of weeks the play runs influence profit.
   d. Use Excel's auditing tool to show which cells in the spreadsheet are directly affected by the percentage of seats full.

18. We are thinking of opening a small copy shop. It costs us $5000 to rent a copier for a year. It costs us $0.03 per copy to operate the copier. Other fixed costs of running the store amount to $400 per month. We charge an average of $0.10 per copy. We are open 365 days per year. Each copier can make up to 100,000 copies per year.

   a. For 1–5 copiers rented and daily demands of 500, 1000, 1500, and 2000 copies per day, compute annual profit. That is, compute annual profit for *each* of these combinations of copiers rented and daily demand.

   b. If we rent three copiers, what daily demand for copies will allow us to break even?

   c. Graph profit as a function of the number of copiers for a daily demand of 500 copies; for a daily demand of 2000 copies. Interpret your graphs.

19. Georgia Mcbeal is trying to save for her retirement. She believes she can earn 10% on average each year on her retirement fund. Assume that at the beginning of each of the next 40 years, Georgia will allocate x dollars to her retirement fund. If at the beginning of a year Georgia has y dollars in her fund, by the end of the year, it will grow to $1.1y$ dollars. How much should Georgia allocate to her retirement fund each year to ensure that she will have $1 million at the end of 40 years? What key factors are being ignored in our analysis of the amount saved for retirement?

20. Dataware is trying to determine whether to give a $10 rebate, to cut the price $6, or to have no price change on a software product. Currently, 40,000 units of the product are sold each week for $45. The variable cost of the product is $5. The most likely case appears to be that a $10 rebate will increase sales 30% and half of all people will claim the rebate. For the price cut, the most likely case is that sales will increase 20%.

   a. Given all other assumptions, what increase in sales from the rebate would make the rebate and price cut equally desirable?

   b. Dataware does not really know the increase in sales that will result from a rebate or price cut. However, it is quite sure that the rebate will increase sales by between 15% and 40% and that the price cut will increase sales by between 10% and 30%. Perform a sensitivity analysis that could be used to help determine Dataware's course of action.

21. Assume that the number of units sold of a product is given by $100 - 0.5P + 26\sqrt{A}$, where P is the price (in dollars) charged for product and A is the amount spent on advertising (in thousands of dollars). Each unit of the product costs $5 to produce. What combination of price and advertising will maximize profit? (*Hint:* Use a data table.)

22. The yield of a chemical reaction is defined as the ratio (expressed as a percentage) of usable output to the amount of raw material input. Suppose the yield of a chemical reaction is found to depend on the length of time the process is run and the temperature at which the process is run. The yield can be expressed as follows:

$$\text{Yield} = 90.79 - 1.095x_1 - 1.045x_2$$
$$-2.781x_1^2 - 2.524x_2^2 - 0.775x_1x_2$$

   a. Here $x_1 = $ (Temperature $- 125$)/10 and $x_2 = $ (Time $- 300$)/30, where temperature is measured in degrees Fahrenheit and time is measured in seconds. Find the temperature and time settings that maximize the yield of this process. (*Hint:* Use a data table.)

23. A bond is currently selling for $1040. It pays the amounts listed in the file **P02_23.xls** at the end of the next 6 years. The yield of the bond is the interest rate that would make the NPV of the bond's payments equal to the bond's price. Use Excel's Goal Seek tool to find the yield of the bond.

24. Assume the demand for the drug Wozac during the current year is 50,000, and assume demand will grow at 5% a year. If we build a plant that can produce x units of Wozac per year, it will cost us $16x$. Each unit of Wozac is sold for $3. Each unit of Wozac produced incurs a variable production cost of $0.20. It costs $0.40 per year to operate a unit of capacity. Determine how large a Wozac plant to build to maximize expected profit over the next 10 years.

25. Consider a project with the following cash flows: year 1, $-$400; year 2, $200; year 3, $600; year 4, $-$900; year 5, $1000; year 6, $250; year 7, $230. Assume a discount rate of 15% per year.

   a. Compute the project's NPV if cash flows occur at the ends of the respective years.

   b. Compute the project's NPV if cash flows occur at the beginnings of the respective years.

   c. Compute the project's NPV if cash flows occur at the middles of the respective years.

26. The payback of a project is the number of years it takes before the project's total cash flow is positive. Payback ignores the time value of money. It is interesting, however, to see how differing assumptions on project growth impact payback. Suppose, for example, that a project requires a $300 million investment at year 0 (right now). The project yields cash flows for 10 years, and the year 1 cash flow will be between $30 million and $100 million. The annual cash flow growth will be between 5% and 25% per year. (Assume that this growth is the *same* each year.) Use a data table to see how the project payback depends on the year 1 cash flow and the cash flow growth rate.

27. A software company is considering translating its program into French. Each unit of the program sells for $50 and incurs a variable cost of $10 to produce. Currently the size of the market for the product is 300,000 units per year and the English version of the software has a 30% share of the market. The company estimates that the market size will grow by 10% a year for the next 5 years, and at 5% per year after that. It will cost the company $6 million to create a French version of the program. The translation will increase its market share to 40%. Given a 10-year planning horizon, for what discount rates is it profitable to create the French version of the software?

Skill-Extending Problems

28. We are entering the widget business. It costs $500,000, payable in year 1, to develop a prototype. This cost can be depreciated on a straight-line basis during years 1–5. Each widget sells for $40 and incurs a variable cost of $20. During year 1 the market size is 100,000, and the market is growing at 10% per year. We believe we will attain a 30% market share. Profits are taxed at 40%, but there are no taxes on *negative* profits.
   a. Given our other assumptions, what market share is needed to ensure a total free cash flow (FCF) of $0 over years 1–5? *Note:* FCF during a year equals after-tax profits plus depreciation minus fixed costs (if any).
   b. Explain how an increase in market share changes profit.
   c. Explain how an increase in market size growth changes profit.
   d. Use Excel's auditing tool to show how the market growth assumption influences your spreadsheet.

29. Suppose we are borrowing $25,000 and making monthly payments with 1% interest. Show that the monthly payments should equal $556.11. The key relationships are that for any month t

(Ending month t balance)

   = (Ending month $t - 1$ balance)

      − ((Monthly payment) − (Month t interest))

(Month t interest)

   = (Beginning month t balance)

      × (Monthly interest rate)

Of course, the ending month 60 balance must equal 0.

30. You are thinking of starting Peaco, which will produce Peakbabies, a product that competes with Ty's Beanie Babies. In year 0 (right now) you will incur costs of $4 million to build a plant. In year 1 you expect to sell 80,000 Peakbabies for a unit price of $25.

The price of $25 will remain unchanged through years 1–5. Unit sales are expected to grow by the same percentage (g) each year. During years 1–5 Peaco incurs two types of costs: variable costs and SG&A (selling, general, and administrative) costs. Each year variable costs equal half of revenue. During year 1, SG&A costs equal 40% of revenue. This percentage is assumed to drop 2% per year, so during year 2, SG&A costs will equal 38% of revenue, and so on. Peaco's goal is to have profits for years 0–5 sum to 0 (ignoring the time value of money). This will ensure that the $4 million investment in year 0 is "paid back" by the end of year 5. What annual percentage growth rate g does Peaco require to "pay back" the plant cost by the end of year 5?

31. Suppose the demand (in thousands) for a toaster is given by $100p^{-2}$, where p is the price in dollars charged for the toaster.
   a. If the variable cost of producing a toaster is $10, what price will maximize profit?
   b. The elasticity of demand is defined as the percentage change in demand created by a 1% change in price. Show that the demand for toasters appears to have constant elasticity of demand. Would this be true if the demand for toasters were linear in price?

32. How could you determine a discount rate that makes two projects have the same NPV?

33. The internal rate of return (IRR) is the discount rate r that makes a project have an NPV of $0. You can find IRR in Excel with the built-in IRR function, using the syntax =IRR(range of cash flows). However, it can be tricky. In fact, if the IRR is not near 10%, this function might not find an answer and you will get an error message. Then you must try the syntax =IRR(range of cash flows, guess), where "guess" is your best guess for the IRR. It is best to try a range of guesses (say, −90% to 100%). Find the IRR of the project described in Problem 25.

34. A project does not necessarily have a unique IRR. (Refer to the previous problem for more information on IRR.) Show that a project with the following cash flows has two IRRs: year 1, −$20; year 2, $82; year 3, −$60; year 4, $2. (*Note:* It can be shown that if the cash flow of a project changes sign only once, the project is guaranteed to have a unique IRR.)

35. How could you use Goal Seek to find a project's IRR? (Refer to Problem 33 for more information on IRR.)

**TIPS FOR EDITING AND
DOCUMENTING SPREADSHEETS**

We have stressed the importance of editing and documenting your spreadsheet models. The following tips will make it much easier to do so.

Format Appropriately

Appropriate formatting can make a spreadsheet model much easier to read. To boldface, for example, select one or more cells and click on the **B** button on the Formatting toolbar (or press Ctrl-b). Similarly, to italicize, indent, increase or decrease the number of decimal places, right-justify, or perform other common formatting tasks, use the buttons on the Formatting toolbar. (See Figure 2.26.) If by any chance the Formatting toolbar is not visible on your screen, you can make it visible by choosing the View/Toolbars menu item and checking the Formatting item.

Figure 2.26

Excel Formatting
Toolbar

Use Range Names

It takes time to name ranges, but it can make formulas much easier to read and understand. To enter a range name, highlight any cell or range of cells and enter a name for the range in the Name Box (just to the left of the formula bar). If you want to edit or delete range names, you must do so from the Insert/Name/Define menu item. Here are some other things you can do from the Insert/Name menu item.

- Once you have named some ranges, you might want a list of them in your spreadsheet. To obtain such a list, place the cursor at the top of the range where you want the list to be placed, select the Insert/Name/Paste menu item, and click on the Paste List button.

- Suppose you have labels such as FixedCost, VarCost, Revenue, and Profit in the range A3:A6, with their values next to them in column B. If you want to name the cells in column B with the labels in column A, highlight the range A3:B6, select the Insert/Name/Create menu item, and make sure the Left Column box is checked. This creates the range names you want.

- If you have a formula such as =SUM(A10:A20) and then name the range A10:A20 as Costs, say, the formula will *not* change automatically to =SUM(Costs). However, you can make it adapt to your new range name by using the Insert/Name/Apply menu item.

- Sometimes you might want to use the *same* range name, such as TotalCost, on multiple worksheets of a workbook. For example, you might want TotalCost to refer to cell B26 in Sheet1 and to cell C59 in Sheet2. This is trickier than you might think. We refer you to our Web site www.indiana.edu/~mgtsci (scroll down the first page) for a discussion on how to do this.

Use Text Boxes

Text boxes are very useful for documenting your work. To enter an explanation or any other text into a text box, make sure the Drawing toolbar is visible (select the View/Toolbars menu item and check the Drawing item to make it visible), click on the Text Box button and drag a box, and start typing.

Use Cell Comments

Cell comments provide another good way to document your work. To enter a comment in a cell, select the cell and right-click. This brings up the dialog box in Figure 2.27 (which is also useful for tasks other than entering comments). Click on the Insert Comment item to enter a comment. If there is already a comment in the cell, this menu will contain Edit Comment and Delete Comment items. The cells with comments should have small red triangles in their corners. If they don't, select the Tools/Options menu item, click on the View tab, and make sure the Comment Indicator Only button is selected.

Figure 2.27

Popup Dialog Box for Cells or Ranges

Modify Toolbars

You might think you are stuck with the built-in Excel toolbars, but you are not. Try the following. Select the Tools/Customize menu item, and click on the Commands tab. Under the various categories, you will see a lot of built-in toolbar buttons that come with Excel. Click on any of these to see a short description of the button's functionality. If you see any you like, you can drag them up to an existing toolbar—*any* toolbar. They will stay there until you open Customize again and drag them off. In fact, once Customize is open, you can drag *any* toolbar buttons off existing toolbars to get rid of them. Why clutter up toolbars with buttons you never use!

This is just the beginning. You might not want to become a programmer, but you can improve your productivity immensely without any real programming at all. Suppose you want to perform a task such as putting a blue border around a selected range and shading it gray. This is not difficult, but if you need to do it repeatedly, it becomes a real bother. Take a look at the file **BorderMacros.doc** on the accompanying CD-ROM for step-by-step instructions on how to set up your own toolbar with this type of functionality.

Other Tips

Finally, we urge you once again to open the **ExcelTutorial.doc** file on the accompanying CD-ROM and work through it. It includes a number of techniques that will make you a better and more efficient Excel user.

Introduction to Optimization Modeling

© Royalty-free/Corbis

DIET MODELS

One of the many classic applications of linear programming is the "diet problem." This problem appears as a prototype linear programming example in almost all management science (MS) textbooks. Basically, it involves finding a group of foods—a diet—that meets all daily nutritional requirements at minimum cost. The problem is important in many real settings, as outlined by Lancaster (1992). A number of versions of this model have actually been used by institutions such as hospitals, nursing homes, schools, prisons, and other food-systems operations. In many of these applications, the computer-generated menus have provided a 10% to 30% cost savings, the nutritional requirements are guaranteed (in contrast to menus generated by traditional, non-MS methods), and, surprisingly, the acceptance of the menus by consumers has been very high.

This problem provides a good example of how to distinguish between good models and poor models. In the simplified diet problems in most textbooks, it is easy to develop a model that satisfies the conditions of low cost and minimal daily nutritional requirements but the resulting diet is so bland (or weird) that no one would eat it. The trick is to incorporate suitable "constraints" (mathematical equations or inequalities) that rule out unappetizing menus. For example, the applications cited in Lancaster (1992) obtained more acceptable diets in one of two ways. Either they included a separation constraint (such as requiring at least three days between successive servings of mashed potatoes) or a frequency constraint (such as requiring that mashed potatoes be served at most three times per week). By adding enough of these types of constraints, they obtained menus that people were quite willing to eat.

A related article by Dantzig (1990) illustrates the humorous side of the problem. When Dantzig (one of the founders of linear programming) was developing his famous solution technique for linear programming in the late 1940s, he decided to use it to solve his *own* diet problem, one that would prescribe what he would actually eat each day. Even he was surprised by the outcome. His first solution called for various amounts of "normal" foods, plus 500 gallons of vinegar—he had forgotten a constraint! So he reformulated the problem, and his next solution called for 200 bouillon cubes per day. Still not (too) discouraged, he reformulated the problem with an upper limit on bouillon cubes, and his resulting solution called for two pounds of bran per day. After an upper limit on bran was imposed, his next diet called for two pounds of blackstrap molasses. By this time, he started to get the point: It is possible to generate a low-cost, nutritional, and tasty diet using management science techniques, but it is not as easy as it appears! ■

3.1 INTRODUCTION

In this chapter we introduce spreadsheet optimization, one of the most powerful and flexible methods of quantitative analysis. The specific type of optimization we will discuss here is **linear programming** (LP). LP is used in all types of organizations, often on a daily basis, to solve a wide variety of problems. These include problems in labor scheduling, inventory management, selection of advertising media, bond trading, management of cash flows, operation of an electrical utility's hydroelectric system, routing of delivery vehicles, blending in oil refineries, hospital staffing, and many others. The goal of this chapter is to introduce the basic elements of LP: the types of problems it can solve, how LP problems can be modeled in Excel, and how Excel's powerful Solver add-in can be used to find optimal solutions. Then in the next several chapters we will examine a variety of LP applications, and we will also look at applications of integer and nonlinear programming, two important extensions of LP.

3.2 INTRODUCTION TO OPTIMIZATION

Before we discuss the details of LP modeling, it is useful to discuss optimization in general. All optimization problems have several elements in common. They all have **decision variables**, the variables whose values the decision maker is allowed to choose. Either directly or indirectly, the values of these variables determine such outputs as total cost, revenue, and profit. Essentially, they are the variables a company or organization must know to function properly; they determine everything else. All optimization problems have an **objective function** (**objective**, for short) whose value is to be optimized—maximized or minimized.[1] Finally, most optimization problems have **constraints** that must be satisfied. These are usually physical, logical, or economic restrictions that are due to the nature of the problem. In searching for the values of the decision variables that optimize the objective, we are allowed to choose only those values that satisfy all of the constraints.

Excel uses its own terminology for optimization, and we will use it throughout the book. Excel refers to the decision variables as the **changing cells**. As we will see, these cells must contain *numbers* that are allowed to change freely; they are *not* allowed to contain formulas. Excel refers to the objective as the **target cell**. There can be only one target cell, which could contain profit, total cost, total distance traveled, or others, and it must be related through formulas to the changing cells. When the changing cells change, the target cell should change accordingly.

> The **changing cells** contain the values of the decision variables.
>
> The **target cell** contains the objective to be minimized or maximized.
>
> The **constraints** impose restrictions on the values in the changing cells.

Finally, there must be appropriate cells and cell formulas that allow us to operationalize the constraints. For example, there might be a constraint that says the amount of labor used is no more than the amount of labor available. In this case there must be cells for each of these two quantities, and typically at least one of them (probably the amount of labor used) will be related through formulas to the changing cells. Constraints can come in a variety of forms. One very common form is **nonnegativity**. This type of constraint states that changing cells must have nonnegative (zero or positive) values. We usually include nonnegativity constraints for physical reasons. For example, it is impossible to produce a negative number of automobiles.

> **Nonnegativity** constraints imply that changing cells must contain nonnegative values.

Typically, most of our effort goes into the model development step.

There are basically two steps in solving an optimization problem. The first step is the **model development** step. Here we decide what the decision variables are, what the objective is, which constraints are required, and how everything fits together. If we are developing an algebraic model, we must derive the correct algebraic expressions. If we are developing a spreadsheet model, the main focus of this book, we must relate all variables with appropriate cell formulas. In particular, we must ensure that our model contains formulas for relating the changing cells to the target cell and that it contains formulas for operationalizing the constraints. This model development step, as we will see, is where most of our effort will go.

The second step in any optimization model is to **optimize**. This means that we must systematically choose the values of the decision variables that make the objective as large (for maximization) or small (for minimization) as possible and cause all of the constraints to be satisfied. A bit of terminology is useful here. Any set of values of the decision variables that satisfies all of the constraints is called a **feasible solution**. The set of all feasible solutions is called the **feasible region**. In contrast, an **infeasible solution** is a solution where at least one constraint is not satisfied. We must rule out infeasible solutions. We want the feasible solution that provides the *best* value—minimum for a minimization problem, maximum for a maximization problem—of the objective. This solution is called the **optimal solution**.

---

[1]Actually, some optimization models are "multicriteria" models, where we try to optimize several objectives simultaneously. However, we will not discuss multicriteria models in this book.

> A **feasible solution** is a solution that satisfies all of the constraints.
>
> The **feasible region** is the set of all feasible solutions.
>
> An **infeasible solution** violates at least one of the constraints.
>
> The **optimal solution** is the feasible solution that optimizes the objective.

*An **algorithm** is basically a "plan of attack." It is a prescription for carrying out the steps required to achieve some goal, such as finding an optimal solution. An algorithm is typically translated into a computer program that does the work.*

Although most of our effort typically goes into the model development step, much of the published research in optimization has gone into the optimization step. Algorithms have been devised for searching through the feasible region to find the optimal solution. One such algorithm is called the **simplex method**. It is suitable for linear models. There are other more complex algorithms suitable for other types of models (those with integer decision variables and/or nonlinearities).

Fortunately, in this book we do not need to discuss the details of these algorithms. They have been programmed into the Solver add-in that is part of Excel. All we need to do is develop the model and then tell Solver what the target cell is, what the changing cells are, what the constraints are, and what type of model (linear, integer, or nonlinear) we have. Solver then goes to work, finding the best feasible solution with the most suitable algorithm. You should appreciate that if we used a trial and error procedure, even a clever and fast one, it could take us hours, weeks, or even years to complete. However, by using the appropriate algorithm, Solver typically finds the optimal solution in a matter of seconds.

Before concluding this discussion, we mention that there is really a *third* step in the optimization process: **sensitivity analysis**. We typically choose the most likely values of input variables, such as unit costs, forecasted demands, and resource availabilities, and then find the optimal solution for these particular input values. This provides a single "answer." However, in any realistic setting, it is wishful thinking to believe that all of the input values we use are exactly correct. Therefore, it is useful—indeed, mandatory in most applied studies—to follow up the optimization step with a lot of "what-if" questions. What if the unit costs increased by 5%? What if forecasted demands were 10% lower? What if resource availabilities could be increased by 20%? What effects would such changes have on the optimal solution? This type of sensitivity analysis can be done in an informal manner or it can be highly structured. We will say a lot about sensitivity analysis in later examples. Fortunately, as with the optimization step itself, good software allows us to obtain answers to a lot of what-if questions quickly and easily.

3.3 A TWO-VARIABLE MODEL

We will begin with a very simple two-variable problem that is essentially a version of the diet problem discussed at the beginning of this chapter. We will see how to model this problem algebraically and then how to model it in Excel. We will also see how to find its optimal solution with Excel's Solver add-in. Next, because it contains only two decision variables, we will see how it can be solved graphically. Although this graphical solution is not practical for most realistic problems, it provides useful insights into general optimization models. Finally, we will ask a number of what-if questions about the completed model.

EXAMPLE	**3.1 PLANNING DESSERTS**

Maggie Stewart loves desserts, but due to weight and cholesterol concerns, she has decided that she must plan her desserts carefully. There are two possible desserts she is considering: snack bars and ice cream. After reading the nutrition labels on the snack bar and ice cream packages, she learns that each "serving" of snack bar weighs 37 grams and contains 120 calories and 5 grams of fat. Each serving of ice cream weighs 65 grams and contains 160 calories and 10 grams of fat. Maggie will allow herself no more than 450 calories and 25 grams of fat in her daily desserts, but because she loves desserts so much, she requires at least 120 grams of dessert per day. Also, she assigns a "taste index" to each gram of each dessert, where 0 is the lowest and 100 is the highest. She assigns a taste index of 95 to ice cream and 85 to snack bars (since she prefers ice cream to snack bars). What should her daily dessert plan be to stay within her constraints and maximize the total taste index of her dessert?

Objective   To use linear programming to find the tastiest combination of desserts that stays within Maggie's constraints.

Solution

Tables such as this serve as a bridge between the problem statement and the ultimate spreadsheet (or algebraic) model.

In all optimization models we are given a variety of numbers—the inputs—and we are asked to make some decisions that optimize an objective, while satisfying some constraints. We will summarize this information in a table, as shown in Table 3.1. We believe it is a good idea to create such a table, before diving into the modeling details. In particular, you always need to identify the appropriate decision variables, the appropriate objective, and the constraints, and you should always think about the relationships between them. Without a clear idea of these elements, it is almost impossible to develop a correct algebraic or spreadsheet model.

Table 3.1   Variables and Constraints for Dessert Model

Input variables	Ingredients (calories, fat) per serving, serving sizes, taste indexes, maximum allowed daily ingredients, minimum required daily grams
Decision variables (changing cells)	Daily servings of each dessert consumed
Objective (target cell)	Total taste index
Other calculated variables	Daily ingredients consumed, daily grams consumed
Constraints	Daily ingredients consumed ≤ Maximum allowed Daily grams consumed ≥ Minimum required

It is important to decide on a convenient unit of measurement and then be consistent in its use.

We make two comments about these variables. First, it is probably clear that the decision variables must be the daily amounts of the desserts consumed, but why do we choose *servings* rather than *grams*? The answer is that it doesn't really matter. Because we know the number of grams per serving of each dessert, it is simple to convert from servings to grams or vice versa. Choosing the unit of measurement is a common problem in modeling. It doesn't usually matter which unit of measurement we select, so long as we are consistent. Second, note that Maggie assigns a taste index of 85 to each gram of snack bar and 95 to each gram of ice cream. If she consumes, say, 50 grams of snack bar and 100 grams of ice cream, it seems reasonable that a measure of her total "taste satisfaction" is 50(85) + 100(95). This is how we define the total taste index, and it is the objective we will attempt to maximize.

An Algebraic Model

In the traditional algebraic solution method, we first identify the decision variables.[2] In this small problem they are the numbers of servings of each dessert to consume daily. We

---

[2]This is not a book about algebraic models; our main focus is on *spreadsheet* modeling. However, we will present algebraic models of the examples in this chapter, just for comparison with the spreadsheet models.

label these x_1 and x_2, although any other labels would do. Next, we write expressions for the total taste index and the constraints in terms of the x's. Finally, because only nonnegative amounts can be consumed, we add explicit constraints to ensure that the x's are nonnegative. The resulting algebraic model is

$$\text{Maximize } 37(85)x_1 + 65(95)x_2$$

$$\text{subject to:}$$

$$120x_1 + 160x_2 \leq 450$$

$$5x_1 + 10x_2 \leq 25$$

$$37x_1 + 65x_2 \geq 120$$

$$x_1, x_2 \geq 0$$

To understand this model, consider the objective first. Each serving of snack bar weighs 37 grams, and each of these grams contributes 85 "points" to the total taste index. If x_1 servings of snack bar are consumed, they will contribute $37(85)x_1$ points to the total taste index. A similar calculation holds for ice cream. We then sum the contributions from snack bars and ice cream to obtain the total taste index.

The constraints are similar. For example, each serving of snack bar contains 120 calories and 5 grams of fat. These explain the $120x_1$ and $5x_1$ terms in the top two constraints (the calorie and fat constraints). We add these to the similar terms for ice cream to the left-hand sides of these constraints. Then the right-hand sides of these constraints are the given maximum daily allowances. The third constraint (minimal daily requirement of calories) follows similarly. Finally, we can't consume negative amounts of either dessert, so we include nonnegativity constraints on x_1 and x_2.

Many commercial optimization packages require, as input, an algebraic model of a problem. If you ever use one of these packages, you will be required to think algebraically.

For many years all LP problems were modeled this way in textbooks. This was because many commercial LP computer packages are written to accept LP problems in essentially this format. In the past decade, however, a more intuitive method of expressing LP problems has emerged. This method takes advantage of the power and flexibility of spreadsheets. Actually, LP problems could always be *modeled* on spreadsheets, but now with the addition of Solver add-ins, spreadsheets have the ability to *solve*—that is, optimize—LP problems as well. Specifically, Microsoft® Excel, Lotus® 1-2-3®, and Corel® Quattro® Pro all have built-in Solvers, and there is an LP add-in called What's Best! that can be used with all three. We will use Excel's Solver for all examples in this book.[3]

A Graphical Solution

When there are only two decision variables in an LP model, as there are in the dessert model, we can solve the problem graphically. Although this solution approach is not practical in most realistic optimization models—where there are many more than two decision variables—the graphical procedure we illustrate here still yields important insights.

This graphical approach works only for problems with two decision variables.

In general, if the two decision variables are labeled x_1 and x_2, then we express the constraints and the objective in terms of x_1 and x_2, we graph the constraints to find the feasible region [the set of all pairs (x_1, x_2) satisfying the constraints, where x_1 is on the horizontal axis and x_2 is on the vertical axis], and we then move the objective through the feasible region until it is optimized.

To do this for the dessert problem in Example 3.1, note that the constraint on calories can be expressed as $120x_1 + 160x_2 \leq 450$. To graph this, we consider the associated equality (replacing $\leq$ with $=$) and find where the associated line crosses the axes. Specifically, when $x_1 = 0$, then $x_2 = 450/160 = 2.81$, and when $x_2 = 0$, then $x_1 = 450/120 = 3.75$.

---

[3]This Solver add-in is built into Microsoft Excel, but it has been developed by a third-party software company, Frontline Systems. We provide more information about Solver software offered by Frontline in the appendix to this chapter.

Recall from algebra that any line of the form $ax_1 + bx_2 = c$ has slope $-a/b$. This is because it can be put into the slope–intercept form $x_2 = c/b - (a/b)x_1$.

This provides the line labeled "calories constraint" in Figure 3.1. It has slope $-120/160 = -0.75$. The set of all points that satisfy the calories constraint includes the points on this line plus the points below it, as indicated by the arrow drawn from the line. (We know that the feasible points are *below* the line because the point $(0, 0)$ is obviously below the line, and $(0, 0)$ clearly satisfies the calories constraint.) Similarly, we can graph the fat constraint and the grams constraint, as shown in the figure. The points that satisfy all three of these constraints and are nonnegative comprise the feasible region, which is shaded in the figure.

Figure 3.1

Graphical Solution for Dessert Problem

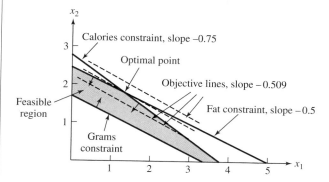

To see which feasible point maximizes the objective, we draw a sequence of lines where, for each, the objective is a constant. One such typical line is of the form $37(85)x_1 + 67(95)x_2 = c$, where c is a constant. Any such line has slope $-[37(85)]/[67(95)] = -0.509$, regardless of the value of c. This line is slightly steeper than the constraint line for fat, and it is not as steep as the constraint line for calories. We want to move a line with this slope up and to the right, making c larger, until it just barely touches the feasible region. The last feasible point that it touches is the optimal point.

Several lines with slope -0.509 are shown in Figure 3.1. The one farthest up and to the right is the one with the largest total taste index. The associated optimal point is clearly the point where the calories and fat lines intersect. We will eventually find (from Solver) that this point is $(1.25, 1.875)$, but even if we didn't have the Solver add-in, we could find the coordinates of this point by solving two equations (the ones for calories and fat) in two unknowns.

Although limited in use, the graphical approach yields the important insight that the optimal solution to any LP model is a corner point of a polygon. This limits the search for the optimal solution and makes the simplex method possible.

Again, the graphical procedure illustrated here can be used only for the simplest of LP models, those with two decision variables. However, the type of behavior pictured in Figure 3.1 generalizes to *all* LP problems. In general, all feasible regions are (the multidimensional versions of) solid polygons. That is, they are bounded by straight lines (actually, "hyperplanes") that intersect at several "corner points." (There are 5 corner points in Figure 3.1, 4 of which are on the axes.) When we push the objective line (again, really a hyperplane) as far as possible toward better values, the last feasible point it touches is one of the corner points. The actual corner point it last touches is determined by the slopes of the objective and constraint lines. Because there are only a finite number of corner points, we must search only among this finite set, not the infinite number of points in the entire feasible region.[4] This insight is largely responsible for the efficiency of the simplex method for solving LP problems.

---

[4]This is not entirely true. If the objective line is exactly parallel to one of the constraint lines, there can be **multiple optimal solutions**—a whole line segment of optimal solutions. Even in this case, however, at least one of the optimal solutions is a corner point.

A Spreadsheet Model

We now turn our focus to spreadsheet modeling. There are many ways to develop an LP spreadsheet model. Everyone has his or her own preferences for arranging the data in the various cells. We will not give any exact prescriptions, but we will present enough examples to help you develop good habits. The common elements in all LP spreadsheet models are the inputs, changing cells, target cell, and constraints.

Inputs. All numerical **inputs**—that is, all numeric data given in the statement of the problem—must appear somewhere in the spreadsheet. As discussed in Chapter 2, our convention is to enclose all inputs in a blue border with shading. We also try to put most of the inputs in the upper left section of the spreadsheet. However, we sometimes violate this latter convention when certain inputs fit more naturally somewhere else.

Changing cells. Instead of using variable names, such as x's, spreadsheet models use a set of designated cells for the decision variables. The values in these cells can be changed to optimize the objective. Excel calls these cells the **changing cells**. To designate them clearly, our convention is to enclose the changing cells in a red border.

Target (objective) cell. One cell, called the **target cell**, contains the value of the objective. Solver systematically varies the values in the changing cells to optimize the value in the target cell. Our convention is to enclose the target cell in a double-line black border.[5]

> *Our coloring conventions*
> Use a blue border around input cells, and shade these cells.
> Use a red border around changing cells.
> Use a double-line black border around the target cell.

Constraints. Excel does not show the constraints directly on the spreadsheet. Instead, we specify constraints in a Solver dialog box, to be discussed shortly. For example, we might designate a set of related constraints by

B15:D15<=B16:D16

This implies three separate constraints. The value in B15 must be less than or equal to the value in B16, the value in C15 must be less than or equal to the value in C16, and the value in D15 must be less than or equal to the value in D16. We will always assign range names to the ranges that appear in the constraints. Then a typical constraint might be specified as

Ingredients_consumed<=Ingredients_allowed

This is much easier to read and understand.

Nonnegativity. Normally, we want the decision variables—that is, the values in the changing cells—to be nonnegative. These constraints do not need to be written explicitly; we simply check an option in a Solver dialog box to indicate that we want nonnegative changing cells. Note, however, that if we want to constrain any *other* cells to be nonnegative, we need to specify these constraints explicitly.

Overview of the Solution Process

As we discussed previously, the complete solution of a problem involves three stages. In the model development stage we enter all of the inputs, trial values for the changing cells,

---

[5]Our red/blue/black color scheme shows up very effectively on a color monitor. The shading (for input cells) and double-line border (for the target cell) are used for clarification on the printed page.

and formulas relating these in a spreadsheet. This stage is the most crucial because it is here that all of the "ingredients" of the model are included and related appropriately. In particular, the spreadsheet *must* include a formula that relates the objective to the changing cells, either directly or indirectly, so that if the values in the changing cells vary, the objective value varies accordingly. Similarly, the spreadsheet must include formulas for the various constraints (usually their left-hand sides) that are related directly or indirectly to the changing cells.

After the model is developed, we can proceed to the second stage—invoking Solver. At this point, we formally designate the objective cell, the changing cells, the constraints, and selected options, and we tell Solver to find the *optimal* solution. If the first stage has been done correctly, the second stage is usually very straightforward.

The third stage is sensitivity analysis. Here we see how the optimal solution changes (if at all) as we vary selected inputs. This often gives us important insights about how the model works.

We now carry out this procedure for the dessert problem in Example 3.1.

DEVELOPING THE SPREADSHEET MODEL

The spreadsheet model appears in Figure 3.2. (See the file **DessertPlanning.xls**.) To develop this model, use the following steps.

Figure 3.2
Spreadsheet Model for Dessert Problem

	A	B	C	D	E	F	G	H
1	Planning desserts							
2								
3	Ingredients (per serving) of each dessert					Range names used:		
4		Snack bar	Ice cream			Dessert_Plan	=Model!$B$16:$C$16	
5	Calories	120	160			Grams_consumed	=Model!$B$25	
6	Fat (grams)	5	10			Grams_required	=Model!$D$25	
7						Ingredients_allowed	=Model!$D$20:$D$21	
8	Grams per serving	37	65			Ingredients_consumed	=Model!$B$20:$B$21	
9						Total_taste_index	=Model!$B$27	
10	Taste index of each dessert (on a 100-point scale, per gram)							
11		Snack bar	Ice cream					
12		85	95					
13								
14	Dessert plan (servings per day)							
15		Snack bar	Ice cream					
16		1.5	2.0					
17								
18	Constraints on calories and fat (per day)							
19		Consumed		Allowed				
20	Calories	500	<=	450				
21	Fat (grams)	27.5	<=	25				
22								
23	Constraint on total grams of dessert per day							
24		Consumed		Required				
25		185.5	>=	120				
26								
27	Total taste index	17067.5						

❶ Inputs. Enter all of the inputs from the statement of the problem in the shaded cells as shown. Note that in later examples we will often include a brief discussion on Where Do the Numbers Come From. For this problem it is easy to get the numbers. The inputs in rows 5, 6, and 8 are printed on the packages of most foods, and the other inputs are Maggie's preferences.

❷ Range names. Create the range names shown in columns F and G. Our convention is to enter "enough" range names but not to go overboard. Specifically, we enter enough range names so that the setup in the Solver dialog box, to be explained shortly, is entirely in terms of range names. Of course, you can add more range names if you like. And, of course, you can use the Insert/Name/Create shortcut we discussed in the previous chapter to speed up the range-naming process.

At this stage it is pointless to try to "outguess" the optimal solution. Any values in the changing cells will suffice.

❸ Changing cells. Enter any two values for the changing cells in the Dessert_plan range. *Any* trial values can be used initially; Solver will eventually find the *optimal* values. Note that the two values shown in Figure 3.2 cannot be optimal because they are not feasible—they contain more calories and fat than are allowed. However, we do not need to worry about satisfying constraints at this point; Solver will take care of this later on.

❹ Ingredients consumed. To operationalize the calorie and fat constraints, we must calculate the amounts consumed by the dessert plan. To do this, enter the formula

=SUMPRODUCT(B5:C5,Dessert_Plan)

in cell B20 for calories and copy it to cell B21 for fat. This formula is a shortcut for the "written out" formula

=B5*B16+C5*C16

The "linear" in linear programming is all about sums of products. Therefore, the SUMPRODUCT function is natural and should be used whenever possible.

As we discussed in Chapter 2, the SUMPRODUCT function is very useful in spreadsheet models, especially LP models, and we will see it often. Here, it multiplies the amount of calories per serving by the number of servings for each dessert and then sums such products over the two desserts. When there are only two products in the sum, as in this example, the SUMPRODUCT formula is not really simpler to enter than the "written out" formula. However, imagine that there are 50 desserts. Then the SUMPRODUCT formula becomes *much* simpler to enter (and read). For this reason, we will use it whenever possible. Note that each range in this function, B5:C5 and Dessert_Plan, is a one-row, two-column range. It is important in the SUMPRODUCT function that the two ranges be exactly the same size and shape.

❺ Grams consumed. Similarly, we must calculate the total number of grams of dessert consumed daily. To do this, enter the formula

=SUMPRODUCT(B8:C8,Dessert_Plan)

in cell B25. Each product in this SUMPRODUCT is grams per serving times number of servings; hence, its units are grams.

❻ Total taste index. To calculate the total taste index, enter the formula

=SUMPRODUCT(B12:C12,B8:C8,Dessert_Plan)

Although the SUMPRODUCT function usually takes two range arguments, it can take three or more, provided they all have the same size and shape.

in cell B27. This formula shows that the SUMPRODUCT function can use three ranges (or more), provided that they are all exactly the same size and shape. Three are required here because we need to multiply taste points per gram time grams per serving times number of servings. Again, this formula is equivalent to the "written out" formula

=B12*B8*B16+C12*C8*C16

Experimenting with Possible Solutions

The next step is to specify the changing cells, the target cell, and the constraints in a Solver dialog box and then instruct Solver to find the optimal solution. However, before we do this, it is instructive to try a few guesses in the changing cells. There are two reasons for doing so. First, by entering different sets of values in the changing cells, you can confirm that the formulas in the other cells are working correctly. Second, this experimentation might help you to develop a better understanding of the model.

For example, Maggie prefers the taste of ice cream to snack bars, so you might guess that her dessert plan will consist of ice cream only. If so, she should consume as much ice cream as will fit into her constraints on calories and fat. You can check that this is 2.5 servings per day, as shown in Figure 3.3. With this plan, she could eat more calories, but she can't eat any more fat. Is this plan optimal? It turns out that it isn't, as we will see shortly, but this fact is not obvious. By the way, if Maggie decided to go entirely with snack bars and no ice cream, you can check that she could then consume 3.75 servings, which would exhaust her calorie allowance, but not her fat allowance, and would provide a total taste index of 11,793.75. Because this is well less than the total taste index for the plan with ice cream only, it certainly cannot be optimal.

Figure 3.3

Best Plan with Ice Cream Only

	A	B	C	D	E	F	G	H
1	Planning desserts							
2								
3	Ingredients (per serving) of each dessert					Range names used:		
4		Snack bar	Ice cream			Dessert_Plan	=Model!$B$16:$C$16	
5	Calories	120	160			Grams_consumed	=Model!$B$25	
6	Fat (grams)	5	10			Grams_required	=Model!$D$25	
7						Ingredients_allowed	=Model!$D$20:$D$21	
8	Grams per serving	37	65			Ingredients_consumed	=Model!$B$20:$B$21	
9						Total_taste_index	=Model!$B$27	
10	Taste index of each dessert (on a 100-point scale, per gram)							
11		Snack bar	Ice cream					
12		85	95					
13								
14	Dessert plan (servings per day)							
15		Snack bar	Ice cream					
16		0	2.5					
17								
18	Constraints on calories and fat (per day)							
19		Consumed		Allowed				
20	Calories	400	<=	450				
21	Fat (grams)	25	<=	25				
22								
23	Constraint on total grams of dessert per day							
24		Consumed		Required				
25		162.5	>=	120				
26								
27	Total taste index	15437.5						

You can continue to try different values in the changing cells, attempting to get as large a total taste index as possible while staying within the constraints. Even for this small model with only two changing cells, it is not easy! You can only imagine how much more difficult it would be if there were hundreds or even thousands of changing cells and many constraints. This is why we need software such as Excel's Solver. It uses a quick and efficient algorithm to search through all feasible solutions and eventually find the optimal solution. Fortunately, it is quite easy to use, as we now explain.

USING SOLVER

To invoke Excel's Solver, select the Tools/Solver menu item. (If there is no such menu item on your PC, see the appendix to this chapter.) The dialog box in Figure 3.4 (page 68) appears. It has three important sections that you must fill in: the target cell, the changing cells, and the constraints. For the dessert problem, we can fill these in by typing cell references or we can point, click, and drag the appropriate ranges in the usual way. Better yet, if there are any named ranges, we can use these range names instead of cell addresses. In fact, for reasons of readability, our convention is to use *only* range names, not cell addresses, in this dialog box.

→ EXCEL TIP: *Range Names in Solver Dialog Box*
Our usual procedure is to use the mouse to select the relevant ranges for the Solver dialog box. Fortunately, if these ranges have already been named, then the range names will automatically replace the cell addresses. ■

Figure 3.4

Solver Dialog Box
for Dessert Model

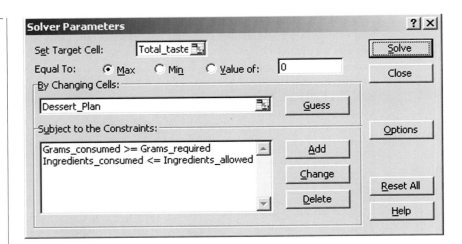

① **Objective.** Select the Total_taste_index cell as the target cell, and click on the Max option.

② **Changing cells.** Select the Dessert_Plan range (the numbers of daily servings of each dessert) as the changing cells.

③ **Constraints.** Click on the Add button to bring up the dialog box in Figure 3.5. Here you specify a typical constraint by entering a cell reference or range name on the left, the type of constraint from the dropdown list in the middle, and a cell reference, range name, or numeric value on the right. Use this dialog box to enter the constraint

Ingredients_consumed<=Ingredients_allowed

(*Note*: You can type these range names into the dialog box, or you can drag them in the usual way. If you drag them, the cell addresses will eventually change into range names if range names exist.) Then click on the Add button and enter the constraint

Grams_consumed>=Grams_required

Then click on OK to get back to the Solver dialog box. The first constraint says to consume no more calories and fat than are allowed. The second constraint says to consume at least as many grams as are required.

Figure 3.5

Add Constraint
Dialog Box

→ **EXCEL TIP:** *Inequality and Equality Labels in Spreadsheet Models*
The <= signs in cells C20:C21 and the >= sign in cell C25 (see Figure 3.2 or Figure 3.3) are not a necessary part of the Excel model. They are entered simply as labels in the spreadsheet and do not substitute for entering the constraints in the Add Constraint dialog box. However, they help to document the model, so we include them in all of the examples. In fact, we try to plan our spreadsheet models so that the two sides of a constraint are in nearby cells, with "gutter" cells in between where we can attach a label like <=, >=, or =. This convention tends to make the resulting spreadsheet models much more readable. ∎

Checking the Assume Non-Negative box ensures only that the changing cells, not any other cells, will be nonnegative.

4 Nonnegativity. Because negative quantities of dessert make no sense, we must tell Solver *explicitly* to make the changing cells nonnegative. To do this, click on the Options button in Figure 3.4 and check the Assume Non-Negative box in the resulting dialog box. (See Figure 3.6.) This automatically ensures that *all* changing cells are nonnegative.

Figure 3.6
Solver Options
Dialog Box

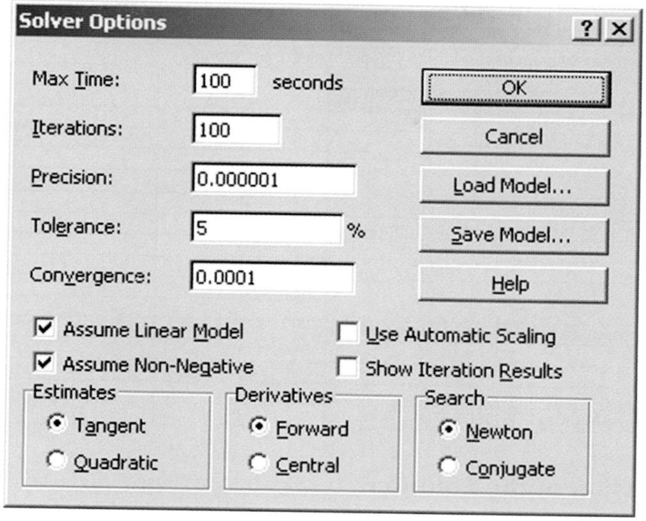

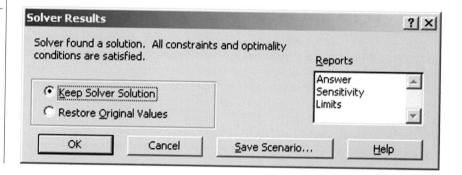

5 Linear model. There is one last step before clicking on the Solve button. As we stated previously, Solver uses one of several numerical algorithms to solve various types of models. The models discussed in this chapter are all *linear* models. (We will discuss the properties of linear models shortly.) Linear models can be solved most efficiently by the simplex method. To instruct Solver to use this method, you must check the Assume Linear Model in the Solver options dialog box shown in Figure 3.6.

6 Optimize. Click on the Solve button in the dialog box in Figure 3.4. At this point, Solver does its work. It searches through a number of possible solutions until it finds the optimal solution. (You can watch the progress on the lower left of the screen, although for small models the process is almost instantaneous.) When it finishes, it displays the message in Figure 3.7. You can then instruct it to return the values in the changing cells to their original (probably nonoptimal) values or retain the optimal values found by Solver. In most cases you will choose the latter. For now, click on the OK button to keep the Solver solution. You should see the solution shown in Figure 3.8 (page 70).

→ **SOLVER TIP:** *Messages from Solver*
Actually, the message in Figure 3.7 is the one we hope for. However, in some cases Solver is not able to find an optimal solution, in which case one of several other messages will appear. We will discuss some of these later in this chapter. ■

Figure 3.7
Solver Message That
Optimal Solution
Has Been Found

Figure 3.8

Optimal Solution
for Dessert Model

	A	B	C	D	E	F	G	H
1	Planning desserts							
2								
3	Ingredients (per serving) of each dessert					Range names used:		
4		Snack bar	Ice cream			Dessert_Plan	=Model!$B$16:$C$16	
5	Calories	120	160			Grams_consumed	=Model!$B$25	
6	Fat (grams)	5	10			Grams_required	=Model!$D$25	
7						Ingredients_allowed	=Model!$D$20:$D$21	
8	Grams per serving	37	65			Ingredients_consumed	=Model!$B$20:$B$21	
9						Total_taste_index	=Model!$B$27	
10	Taste index of each dessert (on a 100-point scale, per gram)							
11		Snack bar	Ice cream					
12		85	95					
13								
14	Dessert plan (servings per day)							
15		Snack bar	Ice cream					
16		1.25	1.875					
17								
18	Constraints on calories and fat (per day)							
19		Consumed		Allowed				
20	Calories	450	<=	450				
21	Fat (grams)	25	<=	25				
22								
23	Constraint on total grams of dessert per day							
24		Consumed		Required				
25		168.125	>=	120				
26								
27	Total taste index	15509.375						

Discussion of the Solution

*In reality, Maggie
would probably vary
this so that she
averaged these
quantities over time.*

This solution says that Maggie should consume 1.25 servings of snack bars and 1.875 servings of ice cream per day. This plan leaves no room for any more calories or fat, and it more than satisfies her requirement of 120 dessert grams per day. It provides a total taste index that is slightly more than the plan with ice cream only in Figure 3.3. In fact, we now know that *no* plan can provide a total taste index larger than this one—that is, without violating at least one of the constraints.

The solution in Figure 3.8 is typical of solutions to optimization models in the following sense. Of all the inequality constraints, some are satisfied exactly and others are not. In this solution the calorie and fat constraints are met exactly. We say that they are **binding**. However, the constraint on grams is **nonbinding**. The number of grams consumed is *greater than* the number required. The difference is called **slack**.[6] You can think of the binding constraints as "bottlenecks." They are the constraints that prevent the objective from being improved. If it were not for constraints on calories and fat, Maggie could obtain an even higher total taste index. ∎

An inequality constraint is **binding** if the solution makes it an equality. Otherwise, it is **nonbinding**, and the positive difference between the two sides of the constraint is called the **slack**.

3.4 SENSITIVITY ANALYSIS

Now that we have solved Maggie's dessert problem, it might appear that we are finished. But in real LP applications the solution to a *single* model is hardly ever the end of the analysis. It is almost always useful to perform a sensitivity analysis to see how (or if) the optimal solution changes as we change one or more inputs. We will illustrate systematic

---

[6]Some analysts use the term *slack* only for ≤ constraints and use the term **surplus** for ≥ constraints. We will refer to each of these as slack—the absolute difference between the two sides of the constraint.

ways of doing so in this section. Actually, we will discuss two approaches. The first uses an optional sensitivity report that Solver offers. The second uses an add-in called SolverTable that we have developed.

Solver's Sensitivity Report

When you run Solver, the dialog box in Figure 3.7 offers you the option to obtain a sensitivity report.[7] This report is based on a well-established theory of sensitivity analysis in optimization models, especially LP models. This theory was developed around algebraic models that are arranged in a "standardized" format. Essentially, all such algebraic models look alike, so the same type of sensitivity report applies to all of them. Specifically, they have an objective function of the form $c_1x_1 + \cdots + c_nx_n$, where n is the number of decision variables, the c's are constants, and the x's are the decision variables, and each constraint can be put in the form $a_1x_1 + \cdots + a_nx_n \leq b$, $a_1x_1 + \cdots + a_nx_n \geq b$, or $a_1x_1 + \cdots + a_nx_n = b$, where the a's and b are constants. Solver's sensitivity report performs two types of sensitivity analysis: (1) on the coefficients of the objective, the c's, and (2) on the right-hand sides of the constraints, the b's.

We illustrate the typical analysis by looking at the sensitivity report for Maggie's dessert planning model in Example 3.1. For convenience, we repeat the algebraic model here, and we repeat the spreadsheet model in Figure 3.9.

$$\text{Maximize } 37(85)x_1 + 65(95)x_2$$

subject to:

$$120x_1 + 160x_2 \leq 450$$
$$5x_1 + 10x_2 \leq 25$$
$$37x_1 + 65x_2 \geq 120$$
$$x_1, x_2 \geq 0$$

Figure 3.9

Dessert Model with Optimal Solution

---

[7]It also offers Answer and Limits reports. We don't find these particularly useful, and we will not discuss them here.

This time, when we run Solver, we ask for a sensitivity report in Solver's final dialog box. (See Figure 3.7.) This creates the sensitivity report on a new worksheet, as shown in Figure 3.10.[8] It contains two sections. The top section is for sensitivity to changes in the two coefficients, 37(85) = 3145 and 65(95) = 6175, of the decision variables in the objective function. Each row in this section indicates how the optimal solution will change if we change one of these coefficients. The bottom section is for the sensitivity to changes in the right-hand sides, 450, 25, and 120, of the constraints. Each row of this section indicates how the optimal solution will change if we change one of these right-hand sides. (Note that the constraint on grams consumed is listed first, not last as in our spreadsheet model. We're not sure why.)

Figure 3.10

Solver's Sensitivity Report for Dessert Model

	A	B	C	D	E	F	G	H
1		Microsoft Excel 10.0 Sensitivity Report						
2		Worksheet: [DessertPlanning.xls]Model						
3		Report Created: 1/6/2003 11:45:53 AM						
4								
5								
6		Adjustable Cells						
7				Final	Reduced	Objective	Allowable	Allowable
8		Cell	Name	Value	Cost	Coefficient	Increase	Decrease
9		$B$16	Snack bar	1.25	0	3145	1486.25	57.5
10		$C$16	Ice cream	1.875	0.000	6175	115	1981.666667
11								
12		Constraints						
13				Final	Shadow	Constraint	Allowable	Allowable
14		Cell	Name	Value	Price	R.H. Side	Increase	Decrease
15		$B$25	Grams_consumed	168.125	0	120	48.125	1E+30
16		$B$20	Calories Consumed	450	1.4375	450	150	50
17		$B$21	Fat (grams) Consumed	25	594.5	25	3.125	6.25

Now let's look at the specific numbers and their interpretation. In the first row of the top section, the *allowable decrease* and *allowable increase* indicate how much the coefficient of snack bars in the objective, currently 3145, could change before the optimal dessert plan would change. If the coefficient of snack bars stays within this allowable range, the optimal dessert plan—the values in the changing cells—will not change at all. However, outside of these limits the optimal mix between snack bars and ice cream might change.

To see what this implies, change the value in cell B12 from 85 to 84. Then the coefficient of snack bars decreases by 37, from 37(85) to 37(84). This change is within the allowable decrease of 57.5. If you rerun Solver, you will obtain the *same* values in the changing cells, although the objective value will decrease. Next, change the value in cell B12 to 83. This time, the coefficient of snack bars decreases by 74 from its original value, from 37(85) to 37(83). This change is outside the allowable decrease, so the solution might change. If you rerun Solver, you will indeed see a change—*no* snack bars are now in the optimal solution.

The *reduced costs* in the second column indicate, in general, how much the objective coefficient of a decision variable that is currently 0—that is, not in the optimal solution—must change before that variable will become positive. These reduced costs are always 0 if the corresponding decision variables are already positive, as they are in the original example. However, when we change the value in cell B12 to 83, as above, and rerun Solver, snack bars drop out of the optimal solution, and the new sensitivity report appears as in Figure 3.11. Now the reduced cost is −16.5. This implies that the coefficient of snack bars must be increased by 16.5 before snack bars will enter the optimal mix.

---

[8]If your table looks different from ours, make sure you have checked Assume Linear Model. Otherwise, Solver uses a nonlinear algorithm and produces a different type of sensitivity report.

Figure 3.11

Sensitivity Table for
Revised Model

	A	B	C	D	E	F	G	H
1		Microsoft Excel 10.0 Sensitivity Report						
2		Worksheet: [DessertPlanning.xls]Model						
3		Report Created: 1/6/2003 11:58:33 AM						
4								
5								
6	Adjustable Cells							
7				Final	Reduced	Objective	Allowable	Allowable
8		Cell	Name	Value	Cost	Coefficient	Increase	Decrease
9		$B$16	Snack bar	0	-16.5	3071	16.5	1E+30
10		$C$16	Ice cream	2.500	0.000	6175	1E+30	33
11								
12	Constraints							
13				Final	Shadow	Constraint	Allowable	Allowable
14		Cell	Name	Value	Price	R.H. Side	Increase	Decrease
15		$B$25	Grams_consumed	162.5	0	120	42.5	1E+30
16		$B$20	Calories Consumed	400	0	450	1E+30	50
17		$B$21	Fat (grams) Consumed	25	617.5	25	3.125	6.538461538

The **reduced cost** for any decision variable not currently in the optimal solution indicates how much better that coefficient must be before that variable will enter at a positive level. The reduced cost for any variable already in the optimal solution is automatically 0.[9]

We now turn to the bottom section of the report in Figure 3.10. Each row in this section corresponds to a constraint. To have this part of the report make economic sense, the model should be developed as we have done here, where the right-hand side of each constraint is a numeric constant (not a formula). For example, the right-hand side of the calories constraint is 450, the maximum allowable calories. Then the report indicates how much these right-hand side constants can change before the optimal solution changes. To understand this more fully, we need the concept of shadow prices. A **shadow price** indicates the amount of change in the objective when a right-hand-side constant changes.

The term **shadow price** is an economic term. It indicates the change in the optimal value of the objective function when the right-hand side of some constraint changes by a given amount.

The shadow prices are reported for each constraint. For example, the shadow price for the calorie constraint is 1.4375. This means that if the right-hand side of the calorie constraint increases by 1 calorie, from 450 to 451, the optimal value of the objective will increase by 1.4375 units. It works in the other direction as well. If the right-hand side of the calorie constraint *decreases* by 1 calorie, from 450 to 449, the optimal value of the objective will decrease by 1.4375 units. However, as we continue to increase or decrease the right-hand side, this 1.4375 change in the objective might not continue. This is where the reported allowable decrease and allowable increase are relevant. As long as the right-hand side increases or decreases within its allowable limits, the same shadow price of 1.4375 will still apply. Beyond these limits, however, a different shadow price will probably apply.

You can prove this for yourself. First, increase the right-hand side of the calorie constraint by 150, from 450 to 600, and rerun Solver. You will see that the objective indeed increases by 1.4375(150), from 15,509.375 to 15,725. Now increase this right-hand side from 600 to 601 and rerun Solver. You will observe that the objective doesn't increase at all. This means that the shadow price beyond 600 is *less than* 1.4375; in fact, it is 0. This is typical. When a right-hand side is increased beyond its allowable increase, the new

---

[9]As we will see in Example 3.2, this is not quite true. If there are upper bound constraints on certain decision variables, the reduced costs for these variables have a slightly different interpretation.

shadow price is typically less than the original shadow price (although it doesn't typically fall to 0, as in this example).

The idea is that a constraint "costs us" by keeping the objective from being better than we would like. A shadow price indicates how much we would be willing to pay (in units of the objective function) to "relax" a constraint. In this example, we would be willing to pay 1.4375 taste index units to increase the right-hand side of the calorie constraint by 1 calorie. This is because such a change would increase the objective by 1.4375 units. But beyond a certain point—150 calories, in this example—further relaxation of the calorie constraint does us no good, and we are not willing to pay for any further increases.

The constraint on grams consumed is slightly different. It has a shadow price of 0. This always occurs in a nonbinding constraint, which makes sense. If we change the right-hand side of this constraint from 120 to 121, nothing at all will happen to the optimal dessert plan and its objective value; there will just be one gram less slack in this constraint. However, the allowable increase of 48.125 indicates that something *will* change when the right-hand side reaches 168.125. At this point, the constraint becomes binding—the grams consumed equals the grams required—and beyond this, the optimal dessert plan will start to change. By the way, the allowable decrease for this constraint, shown as 1+E30, means that it is essentially infinite. We can decrease the right-hand side of this constraint below 120 as much as we like, and absolutely nothing will change in the optimal solution.

The SolverTable Add-In

Solver's sensitivity report is almost impossible to unravel for some models. In these cases SolverTable is preferable because of its easily interpreted results.

The reason we can interpret Solver's sensitivity report for the dessert model in a fairly natural way is that our spreadsheet model is almost a direct translation of a standard algebraic model. Unfortunately, given the flexibility of spreadsheets, this is not always the case. We have seen many perfectly good spreadsheet models—and have developed many ourselves—that are structured quite differently from their standard algebraic-model counterparts. In these cases, we have found Solver's sensitivity report to be more confusing than useful. Therefore, we developed an Excel add-in called SolverTable. SolverTable allows us to ask sensitivity questions about *any* of the input variables, not just coefficients of the objective and right-hand sides, and it provides straightforward answers.

The SolverTable add-in is contained on the CD that comes with this book.[10] To install it, simply run the Setup program on this CD-ROM and make sure the SolverTable option is selected. You can then check that it is installed by selecting the Tools/Add-Ins menu item in Excel. There should be a SolverTable item in the resulting list of add-ins. To actually add SolverTable—that is, to load it into memory—just check the SolverTable box in this list. To unload it from memory, just uncheck the box.

The SolverTable add-in was developed to mimic Excel's built-in Data Table feature. Recall that data tables allow you to vary one or two inputs in a spreadsheet model and see instantaneously how selected outputs change. SolverTable is similar except that it runs Solver for every new input (or pair of inputs). There are two ways it can be used.

1. **One-way table.** A one-way table means that there is a *single* input cell and *any number* of output cells. That is, there can be a single output cell or multiple output cells.

2. **Two-way table.** A two-way table means that there are *two* input cells and one or more outputs. (You might recall that an Excel two-way data table allows only *one* output. The SolverTable add-in allows more than one. It creates a separate table for each output as a function of the two inputs.)

---

[10]It is also on the authors' Web site at www.indiana.edu/~mgtsci. This Web site will contain any possible updates to SolverTable.

We illustrate some of the possibilities for the dessert example. Specifically, we check how sensitive the optimal dessert plan and total taste index are to (1) changes in the number of calories per serving of snack bars and (2) the number of daily dessert calories allowed. Then we check how sensitive the optimal objective value is to simultaneous changes in the taste indexes of snack bars and ice cream.

We chose the input range from 60 to 140 in increments of 10 fairly arbitrarily. You can choose any desired range of input values.

We assume that the dessert model has been formulated and optimized, as shown in Figure 3.8, and that the SolverTable add-in has been loaded. Then the solution to question 1 is shown in Figure 3.12. To obtain this output (the part in the range A30:D39), we use the Data/SolverTable menu item, select a one-way table in the first dialog box, and fill in the second dialog box as shown in Figure 3.13. (Note that ranges can be entered as cell addresses or range names. Also, multiple ranges in the Outputs box should be separated by commas.)

Figure 3.12

Sensitivity to Calories per Serving of Snack Bars

	A	B	C	D
29	Sensitivity to calories per serving of snack bars			
30		$B$16	$C$16	$B$27
31	60	5	0.000	15725
32	70	5	0.000	15725
33	80	5	0.000	15725
34	90	5	0.000	15725
35	100	2.5	1.250	15581.25
36	110	1.6666667	1.667	15533.33
37	120	1.25	1.875	15509.38
38	130	1	2.000	15495
39	140	0.8333333	2.083	15485.42

Figure 3.13

SolverTable Dialog Box for One-Way Table

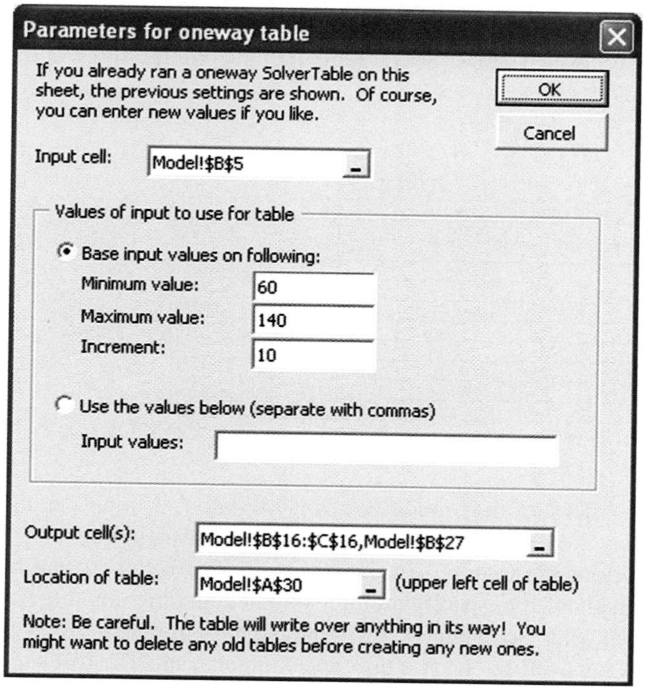

Parameters for oneway table

If you already ran a oneway SolverTable on this sheet, the previous settings are shown. Of course, you can enter new values if you like.

OK

Cancel

Input cell: Model!$B$5

Values of input to use for table

⦿ Base input values on following:

Minimum value: 60

Maximum value: 140

Increment: 10

○ Use the values below (separate with commas)

Input values:

Output cell(s): Model!$B$16:$C$16,Model!$B$27

Location of table: Model!$A$30 (upper left cell of table)

Note: Be careful. The table will write over anything in its way! You might want to delete any old tables before creating any new ones.

→ **EXCEL TIP:** *Selecting Multiple Ranges*

If you need to select multiple output ranges, the trick is to keep your finger on the Ctrl key as you drag the ranges. This automatically enters the separating comma(s) for you. The same trick works for selecting multiple changing cell ranges in Solver's dialog box. ■

When you click on OK, Solver solves a separate optimization problem for each of the 9 rows of the table and then reports the requested outputs (servings consumed and total taste index) in the table. It can take a while, depending on the speed of your computer, but everything is automatic. However, if you want to update this table—by using new calorie values in column A, for example—you must repeat the procedure. SolverTable enters comments (indicated by the small red triangles) in several cells to help you interpret the output.

The outputs in this table show that as the calories per serving of snack bars increase, the optimal dessert plan is initially to eat snack bars only, and it stays this way for a while. But beyond 90 calories per serving, the optimal plan gradually uses fewer snack bars and starts using ice cream. Beyond some point—somewhere above 140 calories per serving—the optimal plan probably uses no snack bars at all. (This point could be found with another SolverTable run, using a different input range.) Also, note that as calories per serving increase beyond 90, the optimal total taste index in column D continually decreases. This makes sense. As one ingredient increases in calories, the total calorie limit dictates that not as much dessert can be eaten, so the total taste index decreases.

The answer to question 2 appears in Figure 3.14. It is formed through the same dialog box as in Figure 3.13, except that the input variable is now in cell D20, which we allow to vary from 400 to 600 calories in increments of 25 calories. Now we see that as the total calorie allowance increases, the optimal dessert plan uses more snack bars and less ice cream, and the total taste index increases. In fact, we calculate this latter increase in column E. (We do this manually, not with SolverTable. For example, the formula in cell E44 is **=D44−D43**.) We see that, at least for this input range, the objective increases by the *same* amount, 35.9375, for each 25-calorie increase in the daily calorie allowance. Alternatively, the *per unit* change, 1.4375 (=35.9375/25), is the same shadow price we saw previously. In this sense, SolverTable outputs can reinforce outputs from Solver's sensitivity report.

Figure 3.14

Sensitivity to Daily Calorie Allowance

	A	B	C	D	E
41	Sensitivity to calories allowed				
42		$B$16	$C$16	$B$27	Increase
43	400	0	2.500	15437.5	
44	425	0.625	2.188	15473.44	35.9375
45	450	1.25	1.875	15509.38	35.9375
46	475	1.875	1.563	15545.31	35.9375
47	500	2.5	1.250	15581.25	35.9375
48	525	3.125	0.938	15617.19	35.9375
49	550	3.75	0.625	15653.13	35.9375
50	575	4.375	0.313	15689.06	35.9375
51	600	5	0.000	15725	35.9375

The final sensitivity questions ask us to vary two inputs simultaneously. This requires a two-way SolverTable. The resulting output appears in Figure 3.15 and is produced by the dialog settings in Figure 3.16. Here we specify two inputs and two input ranges, and we are again allowed to specify multiple output cells. An output table is generated for *each* of the output cells. For example, the top table in Figure 3.15 shows how the optimal servings of snack bars vary as the two taste index inputs vary. The results, especially in the two top tables, are probably not very surprising. When the taste index of either dessert increases, we tend to use more of it in the optimal dessert plan.

Figure 3.15

Sensitivity to Taste
Indexes of Both
Desserts

	A	B	C	D	E	F	G
53	Sensitivity to taste indexes of snack bars and ice cream						
54	$B$16	70	75	80	85	90	95
55	60	0	0	0	0	0	0
56	65	1.25	0	0	0	0	0
57	70	1.25	1.25	0	0	0	0
58	75	1.25	1.25	1.25	1.25	0	0
59	80	1.25	1.25	1.25	1.25	1.25	0
60	85	1.25	1.25	1.25	1.25	1.25	1.25
61	90	1.25	1.25	1.25	1.25	1.25	1.25
62	95	3.75	1.25	1.25	1.25	1.25	1.25
63							
64	$C$16	70	75	80	85	90	95
65	60	2.500	2.500	2.500	2.500	2.500	2.500
66	65	1.875	2.500	2.500	2.500	2.500	2.500
67	70	1.875	1.875	2.500	2.500	2.500	2.500
68	75	1.875	1.875	1.875	1.875	2.500	2.500
69	80	1.875	1.875	1.875	1.875	1.875	2.500
70	85	1.875	1.875	1.875	1.875	1.875	1.875
71	90	1.875	1.875	1.875	1.875	1.875	1.875
72	95	0.000	1.875	1.875	1.875	1.875	1.875
73							
74	$B$27	70	75	80	85	90	95
75	60	11375	12187.5	13000	13812.5	14625	15437.5
76	65	11537.5	12187.5	13000	13812.5	14625	15437.5
77	70	11768.75	12378.125	13000	13812.5	14625	15437.5
78	75	12000	12609.375	13218.75	13828.13	14625	15437.5
79	80	12231.25	12840.625	13450	14059.38	14668.75	15437.5
80	85	12462.5	13071.875	13681.25	14290.63	14900	15509.38
81	90	12693.75	13303.125	13912.5	14521.88	15131.25	15740.63
82	95	13181.25	13534.375	14143.75	14753.13	15362.5	15971.88

Figure 3.16

SolverTable Dialog
Box for Two-Way
Table

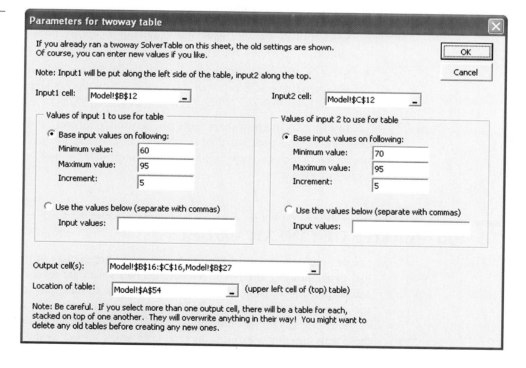

It is always possible to run a sensitivity analysis by changing inputs manually in the spreadsheet model and rerunning Solver. The advantages of the SolverTable add-in, however, are that it enables you to perform a *systematic* sensitivity analysis for any selected inputs and outputs, and it keeps track of the results in a table. We will see other applications of this useful add-in later in this chapter and in subsequent chapters.

Comparison of Solver's Sensitivity Report and SolverTable

Sensitivity analysis in optimization models is extremely important, so it is important that you understand the pros and cons of the two tools we have discussed in this section. Here are some points to keep in mind.

- Solver's sensitivity report focuses only on the coefficients of the objective and the right-hand sides of the constraints. SolverTable allows you to vary *any* of the inputs.

- Solver's sensitivity report provides very useful information through its reduced costs, shadow prices, and allowable increases and decreases. This same information can be obtained with SolverTable, but it requires a bit more work and some experimentation with the appropriate input ranges.

- Solver's sensitivity report is based on changing only one objective coefficient or one right-hand side at a time. We will see that this one-at-a-time restriction prevents us from answering certain questions directly. SolverTable is much more flexible in this respect.

- Solver's sensitivity report is based on a well-established mathematical theory of sensitivity analysis in linear programming. If you lack this mathematical background—as many users do—the outputs can be difficult to understand, especially for somewhat "nonstandard" spreadsheet formulations. In contrast, SolverTable's outputs are straightforward. You vary one or two inputs and see directly how the optimal solution changes.

- Solver's sensitivity report is not even available for integer-constrained models, and its interpretation for nonlinear models is more difficult than for linear models. SolverTable's outputs have the same interpretation for any type of optimization model.

- Solver's sensitivity report comes with Excel. SolverTable is a separate add-in that is not included with Excel—but it is included with this book and is freely available from the authors' Web site at http://www.indiana.edu/~mgtsci.

In summary, each of these tools can be used to answer certain questions. We tend to favor SolverTable because of its flexibility, but in the optimization examples in this chapter and later chapters, we will illustrate both tools to show how they can each provide useful information.

3.5 PROPERTIES OF LINEAR MODELS

Linear programming is an important subset of a larger class of models called **mathematical programming models**.[11] All such models select the levels of various activities that can be performed, subject to a set of constraints, to maximize or minimize an objective such as total profit or total cost. In Maggie's dessert example, the activities are the amounts of the two desserts consumed daily, and the purpose of the model is to find the levels of these activities that maximize the total taste index subject to specified constraints.

---

[11]The word *programming* in linear programming or mathematical programming has nothing to do with computer programming. It originated with the British term *programme*, which is essentially a plan or a schedule of operations.

In terms of this general setup—selecting the optimal levels of activities—there are three important properties that LP models possess that distinguish them from general mathematical programming models: **proportionality**, **additivity**, and **divisibility**. We discuss these properties briefly in this section.

Proportionality

Proportionality means that if the level of any activity is multiplied by a constant factor, then the contribution of this activity to the objective, or to any of the constraints in which the activity is involved, is multiplied by the same factor. For example, suppose that the consumption of snack bars is cut from its optimal value of 1.25 (see Figure 3.8) to 0.625—that is, it is multiplied by 0.5. Then the amounts of calories, fat, and grams contributed to the dessert plan by snack bars are all cut in half, and the total taste index contributed by snack bars is also cut in half.

Proportionality is probably a perfectly valid assumption in the dessert model, but it is often violated in certain types of models. For example, in various *blending* models used by petroleum companies, chemical outputs vary in a nonlinear manner as chemical inputs are varied. If a chemical input is doubled, say, the resulting chemical output is not necessarily doubled. This type of behavior violates the proportionality property, and it takes us into the realm of *nonlinear* optimization, which we will discuss in Chapter 7.

Additivity

The additivity property implies that the sum of the contributions from the various activities to a particular constraint equals the total contribution to that constraint. For example, if the two types of dessert contribute, respectively, 180 and 320 calories (as in Figure 3.2), then the total number of calories in the plan is the *sum* of these amounts, 500 calories. Similarly, the additivity property applies to the objective. That is, the value of the objective is the *sum* of the contributions from the various activities. The additivity property implies that the contribution of any decision variable to the objective or to any constraint is *independent* of the levels of the other decision variables.

Divisibility

The divisibility property simply means that we allow both integer and noninteger levels of the activities. In the dessert example, it turned out that the optimal values in the changing cells are nonintegers: 1.25 and 1.875. Because of the divisibility property, we allow such values in LP models. In some problems, however, they do not make physical sense. For example, if we are deciding how many refrigerators to produce, it makes no sense to make 47.53 refrigerators. If we want the levels of some activities to be integer values, there are two possible approaches: (1) We can solve the LP model without integer constraints, and if the solution turns out to have noninteger values, we can attempt to round them to integer values, or (2) we can explicitly constrain certain changing cells to contain integer values. The latter approach, however, takes us into the realm of *integer programming*, which we will study in Chapter 6.

Discussion of the Linear Properties

The previous discussion of these three properties, especially proportionality and additivity, is a bit abstract. How can you recognize whether a model satisfies proportionality and additivity? This is easy if the model is described algebraically. In this case the objective must be of the form

$$a_1x_1 + a_2x_2 + \cdots + a_nx_n$$

where n is the number of decision variables, the a's are constants, and the x's are decision variables. This expression is called a *linear combination* of the x's. Also, each constraint must be equivalent to a form where the left-hand side is a linear combination of the x's and the right-hand side is a constant. For example, the following is a typical linear constraint:

$$3x_1 + 7x_2 - 2x_3 \leq 50$$

It is not quite so easy to recognize proportionality and additivity—or the lack of them—in a spreadsheet model because the logic of the model can be embedded in a series of cell formulas. However, the ideas are the same. First, the target cell must ultimately (possibly through a series of formulas in intervening cells) be a sum of products of constants and changing cells, where a "constant" is defined by the fact that it does not depend on changing cells. Second, each side of each constraint must ultimately be either a constant or a sum of products of constants and changing cells. Sometimes it is easier to recognize when a model is *not* linear. Two particular situations that lead to nonlinear models are when (1) there are products or quotients of expressions involving changing cells and (2) there are nonlinear functions, such as squares, square roots, or logarithms, of changing cells. These are typically easy to spot, and they guarantee that the model is nonlinear.

Real-life problems are almost never exactly linear. However, a linear approximation often yields very useful results.

Whenever we model a real problem, we usually make some simplifying assumptions. This is certainly the case with LP models. The world is frequently *not* linear, which means that an entirely realistic model will typically violate some or all of the three properties we just discussed. However, numerous successful applications of LP have demonstrated the usefulness of linear models, even if they are only *approximations* of reality. If we suspect that the violations are serious enough to invalidate a linear model, then we should use an integer or nonlinear model, as we will illustrate in Chapters 6 and 7.

In terms of Excel's Solver, if the model is linear—that is, if it satisfies the proportionality, additivity, and divisibility properties—then we should check the Assume Linear Model box that appears in the Solver Options dialog box. Then Solver will use the simplex method, a very efficient method for a linear model, to solve the problem. Actually, we can check the Assume Linear Model box even if the divisibility property is violated—that is, for linear models with integer-constrained variables—but Solver will use a method other than the simplex method in its solution procedure.

Linear Models and Scaling[12]

In some cases you might be sure that a model is linear, but when you check the Assume Linear Model box and then solve, you get a Solver message that "the conditions for Assume Linear Model are not satisfied." This can indicate a logical error in your formulation, so that at least one of the proportionality, additivity, and divisibility conditions is indeed not satisfied. However, it can also indicate that Solver erroneously *thinks* the linearity conditions are not satisfied, which is typically due to roundoff error in its calculations—not any error on your part. If the latter occurs and you are convinced that the model is correct, you can try *not* checking the Assume Linear Model box to see whether that works. If it does not, you should consult your instructor. It is possible that the nonlinear algorithm employed by Solver when this box is not checked simply cannot find the solution to your problem.

[12]This section might seem overly technical. However, when you develop a model that you are sure is linear, and Solver then tells you it doesn't satisfy the linear conditions, you will appreciate this section.

In any case, it always helps to have a *well-scaled* model. In a well-scaled model, all of the numbers are roughly the same magnitude. If the model contains some very large numbers—100,000 or more, say—and some very small numbers—0.001 or less, say—it is *poorly scaled* for the methods used by Solver, and roundoff error is far more likely to be an issue, not only in Solver's test for linearity conditions but in all of its algorithms.

If you believe your model is poorly scaled, there are two possible remedies. The first is to check the Use Automatic Scaling box in the Solver Options dialog box (see Figure 3.6). This might help and it might not; we have had mixed success. (Frontline Systems, the company that developed Solver, has told us that the only drawback to checking this box is that the solution procedure can take more time.) The second option is to redefine the units in which the various quantities are defined. For example, if we had originally defined our changing cells in the dessert model as the number of *grams* consumed, we might decide later to rescale to the number of *servings* consumed. (In fact, this is partly why we chose number of *servings* in the first place, although scaling doesn't really cause any difficulties in this small problem.)

3.6 INFEASIBILITY AND UNBOUNDEDNESS

In this section we discuss two of the things that can go wrong when we invoke Solver. Both of these might indicate that there is a mistake in the model. Therefore, because mistakes are common in LP models, you should be aware of the error messages you might encounter.

Infeasibility

The first problem is infeasibility. Recall that a solution is *feasible* if it satisfies all of the constraints. Among all of the feasible solutions, we are looking for the one that optimizes the objective. However, it is possible that there are no feasible solutions to the model. There are generally two reasons for this: (1) There is a mistake in the model (an input was entered incorrectly, such as a $\geq$ instead of a $\leq$) or (2) the problem has been so constrained that there are no solutions left! In the former case, a careful check of the model should find the error. In the latter case, the analyst might need to change, or even eliminate, some of the constraints.

A perfectly reasonable model can have no feasible solutions because of too many constraints.

To show how an infeasible problem could occur, suppose in Maggie's dessert problem that we change the required daily grams of dessert from 120 to 200 (and leave everything else unchanged). If Solver is then used, the message in Figure 3.17 appears, indicating that Solver cannot find a feasible solution. The reason is clear: There is no way, given the constraints on daily allowances of calories and fat, that Maggie can find a dessert plan with at least 200 grams. Her only choice is to relax at least one of the constraints: increase the daily allowances of calories and/or fat, or decrease the required daily grams of dessert. In general, there is no foolproof way to find the problem when a "no feasible solution" message appears. Careful checking and rethinking are required.

Figure 3.17

Solver Dialog Box Indicating No Feasible Solution

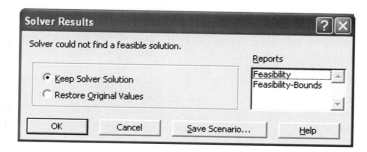

Unboundedness

A second type of problem is **unboundedness**. In this case, the model has been formulated in such a way that the objective is unbounded—that is, it can be made as large (or as small, for minimization problems) as we like. If this occurs, we have probably entered a wrong input or forgotten some constraints. To see how this could occur in the dessert problem, suppose that we enter daily allowance constraints on calories and fat with $\geq$ instead of $\leq$. Now there is no upper bound on how much of each dessert Maggie can consume (at least not in the model!). If we make this change in the model and then use Solver, the message in Figure 3.18 appears, stating that the target cell does not converge. In other words, the total taste index can grow without bound.

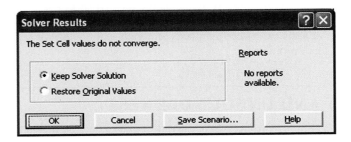

Comparison of Infeasibility and Unboundedness

Except in very rare situations, if Solver informs you that your model is unbounded, you have made an error.

Infeasibility and unboundedness are quite different in a practical sense. It is quite possible for a reasonable model to have no feasible solutions. For example, the marketing department might impose several constraints, the production department might add some more, the engineering department might add even more, and so on. Together, they might constrain the problem so much that there are no feasible solutions left. The only way out is to change or eliminate some of the constraints. An unboundedness problem is quite different. There is no way a realistic model can have an unbounded solution. If you get the message in Figure 3.18, then you must have made a mistake: You entered an input incorrectly, you omitted one or more constraints, or there is a logical error in your model.

PROBLEMS

Solutions for problems whose numbers appear within a color box can be found in the Student Solutions Manual. Order your copy today at http://e-catalog.thomsonlearning.com/110/ by using ISBN 0-534-39687-9.

Skill-Building Problems

1. Other sensitivity analyses besides those discussed could be performed on Maggie's dessert model. Use SolverTable to perform each of the following. In each case keep track of the values in the changing cells and the target cell, and discuss your findings.
   a. Let the fat per serving of snack bars vary from 1 to 7 grams in increments of 1 gram.
   b. Let the calories per serving of ice cream vary from 140 to 200 in increments of 5.

   c. Let the total daily gram requirement vary from 100 to 200 in increments of 10.
   d. Let the calorie and fat daily allowances vary simultaneously, with the calorie allowance varying from 300 to 500 in increments of 50, and the fat allowance varying from 20 to 40 in increments of 5.

2. In Maggie's dessert problem, assume there is another possible dessert, in addition to snack bars and ice cream, that Maggie can consider: oatmeal raisin cookies. Each cookie, which is considered a "serving," weighs 43 grams and contains 140 calories and 6 grams of fat. Maggie likes these cookies almost as much as ice cream, and she gives each gram a taste index of 90. Modify the spreadsheet model to include

this new dessert, and use Solver to find the optimal dessert plan.

3. Continuing the previous problem, perform a sensitivity analysis on the taste index of the cookies. Let this index vary from 60 to 100 in increments of 5, and keep track of the values in the changing cells and the target cell. Discuss your findings.

4. We stated that changing cells in the dessert model could be measured in servings or in grams. Modify the spreadsheet model so that they are measured in grams, and use Solver to find the optimal solution. Discuss how the solution to this modified model is different from the solution we found; discuss how they are the same.

5. Use the graphical solution of Maggie's dessert problem to determine all values of the right-hand side of the total daily gram requirement that make the model infeasible—that is, it has no feasible solutions.

6. There are 5 corner points in the feasible region for the dessert problem. We identified the coordinates of one of them: (1.25, 1.875). Identify the coordinates of the others. If we vary the taste index values in row 12 of the spreadsheet model, is it possible for each of these corner points to become an optimal solution? Why or why not?

Skill-Extending Problems

7. The graphical solution to the dessert problem indicates why the optimal solution contains both snack bars and ice cream: It is because the slope of the total taste index line is *between* the slopes of the two constraint lines for calories and fat. With this in mind, consider changes in the taste index of snack bars, which is currently 85. How large would this have to be for Maggie to consume all snack bars and no ice cream? How small would it have to be for Maggie to consume all ice cream and no snack bars? Answer in terms of slopes and which corner points would become optimal.

8. The SolverTable add-in can be used for "less obvious" sensitivity analyses. Suppose in the dessert model that we want to vary both of the calories per serving values in row 5, but we want them to stay in the same ratio, 4 to 3. We want calories per serving of snack bars to vary from 100 to 140 in increments of 5, and we want to keep track of the values in the changing cells and the target cell. Modify the model slightly so that this analysis can be performed with a *one-way* SolverTable.

9. Consider the graphical solution to the dessert problem. Now imagine that another constraint—*any* constraint—is added. Which of the following three things are possible: (1) feasible region shrinks; (2) feasible region stays the same; (3) feasible region expands? Which of the following three things are possible: (1) optimal value in target cell decreases; (2) optimal value in target cell stays the same; (3) optimal value in target cell increases? Explain your answers. Do they hold just for this particular model, or do they hold in general?

3.7 A PRODUCT MIX MODEL

The problem we will examine in this section is often considered the prototype LP problem. The basic problem is to select the optimal mix of products to produce to maximize profit. We will refer to it as a *product mix* problem.

EXAMPLE	3.2 PRODUCING FRAMES AT MONET

The Monet Company produces four types of picture frames, which we label 1, 2, 3, and 4. The four types of frames differ with respect to size, shape, and materials used. Each type requires a certain amount of skilled labor, metal, and glass, as shown in Table 3.2 (page 84). This table also lists the unit selling price Monet charges for each type of frame. During the coming week, Monet can purchase up to 4000 hours of skilled labor, 6000 ounces of metal, and 10,000 ounces of glass. The unit costs are $8.00 per labor hour, $0.50 per ounce of metal, and $0.75 per ounce of glass. Also, market constraints are such that it is impossible to sell more than 1000 type 1 frames, 2000 type 2 frames, 500 type 3 frames, and 1000 type 4 frames, and Monet does not want to keep any frames in inventory at the end of the week. What should the company do to maximize its profit for this week?

Table 3.2 Data for Monet Picture Frame Example

	Frame 1	Frame 2	Frame 3	Frame 4
Skilled labor	2	1	3	2
Metal	4	2	1	2
Glass	6	2	1	2
Selling price	$28.50	$12.50	$29.25	$21.50

Objective To use LP to find the mix of frames to produce that maximizes profit and stays within the resource availability and maximum sales constraints.

WHERE DO THE NUMBERS COME FROM?

Textbooks typically state a problem, including a number of input values, and proceed directly to a solution—without saying where these input values might come from. However, finding the correct input values can sometimes be the most difficult step in a real-world situation. (Recall that finding the necessary data was step 2 of the overall modeling process, as discussed in Chapter 1.) There are a variety of inputs in Monet's problem, some easy to find and others more difficult. Here are some ideas on how they might be obtained.

- The unit costs in cells B4:B6 should be easy to obtain. (See Figure 3.19 on page 86.) These are the going rates for these resources. We might mention, however, that the $8 per hour labor rate is probably a regular-time rate. If Monet wants to consider overtime hours, then the overtime rate (and labor hour availability during overtime) would be necessary, and the model would need to be modified.

- The resource usages in the range B9:E11, often called *technological coefficients*, should be available from the production department. These people know how much of each resource it takes to make the various types of frames.

- The unit selling prices in row 12 have actually been *chosen* by Monet's management, probably in response to market pressures and the company's own costs. In reality, they would be chosen based on production costs and market pressures.

- The maximum sales values in row 18 are probably forecasts from the marketing department. These people have some sense of how much they can sell, based on current outstanding orders, historical data, and the unit prices they plan to charge.

- The labor hour availability in cell D21 is probably based on the current workforce size and possibly on new workers who could be hired in the short run. It is likely that the other resource availabilities in cells D22 and D23 are the amounts available from the regular suppliers, whereas any additional quantities would require prohibitively expensive expediting costs.

Solution

Table 3.3 lists the variables and constraints for this model. We must choose the number of frames of each type to produce, which cannot be larger than the maximum we can sell. This choice determines the amounts of resources used and all revenues and costs. We must also ensure that no more resources are used than are available.

Table 3.3 Variables and Constraints for Product Mix Model

Input variables	Unit costs of resources (labor, glass, metal), resources used per frame of each type, unit selling prices of frames, maximum sales of frames, availabilities of resources
Decision variables (changing cells)	Numbers of frames of various types to produce
Objective (target cell)	Profit
Other calculated variables	Amounts of resources used, revenues, costs
Constraints	Frames produced ≤ Maximum sales Amounts of resources used ≤ Amounts available

An Algebraic Model

To model this problem algebraically, we let x_1, x_2, x_3, and x_4 represent the numbers of frames of types 1, 2, 3, and 4 to produce. Next, we write total profit and the constraints in terms of the x's. Finally, since only nonnegative amounts can be produced, we add explicit constraints to ensure that the x's are nonnegative. The resulting algebraic model is shown here:

$$\text{Maximize } 6x_1 + 2x_2 + 4x_3 + 3x_4 \quad \text{(profit objective)}$$

subject to:

$$2x_1 + x_2 + 3x_3 + 2x_4 \leq 4000 \quad \text{(labor constraint)}$$
$$4x_1 + 2x_2 + x_3 + 2x_4 \leq 6000 \quad \text{(metal constraint)}$$
$$6x_1 + 2x_2 + x_3 + 2x_4 \leq 10{,}000 \quad \text{(glass constraint)}$$
$$x_1 \leq 1000 \quad \text{(frame 1 sales constraint)}$$
$$x_2 \leq 2000 \quad \text{(frame 2 sales constraint)}$$
$$x_3 \leq 500 \quad \text{(frame 3 sales constraint)}$$
$$x_4 \leq 1000 \quad \text{(frame 4 sales constraint)}$$
$$x_1, x_2, x_3, x_4 \geq 0 \quad \text{(nonnegativity constraints)}$$

To understand this model, consider the profit objective first. The profit from x_1 frames of type 1 is $6x_1$ because each frame contributes \$6 to profit. This \$6 is calculated as the unit selling price minus the cost of the inputs that go into a single type 1 frame:

$$\text{Unit profit for type 1 frame} = 28.50 - [2(8.00) + 4(0.50) + 6(0.75)] = \$6$$

Profits for the other three types of frames are obtained similarly. Their unit profits are \$2.00, \$4.00, and \$3.00, respectively. Then the total profit is the sum of the profits from the four products.

Next, consider the skilled labor constraint. The right-hand side, 4000, is the number of hours available. On the left-hand side, each type 1 frame uses 2 hours of labor, so x_1 units require $2x_1$ hours of labor. Similar statements hold for the other three products, and the total number of labor hours used is the sum over the four products. Then the constraint states that the number of hours used cannot exceed the number of hours available. The constraints for metal and glass are similar. Finally, the maximum sales constraints and the nonnegativity constraints put upper and lower limits on the quantities that can be produced.

Again, many LP software packages would accept this algebraic model exactly as we have stated it. However, because we are focusing on spreadsheet models, we now turn to a spreadsheet model of Monet's problem.

Note how the expressions in the model are sums of terms like $2x_1$. This makes the model linear. It also accounts for the widespread use of the SUMPRODUCT function in spreadsheet LP models.

DEVELOPING THE SPREADSHEET MODEL

The spreadsheet in Figure 3.19 illustrates the solution procedure for Monet's product mix problem. (See the file **ProductMix.xls**.) The first stage is to develop the spreadsheet model step by step.

Figure 3.19

An Initial Solution for Product Mix Model

	A	B	C	D	E	F	G	H	I
1	Product mix model								
2									
3	Input data						Range names used:		
4	Hourly wage rate	$8.00					Frames_produced	=Model!$B$16:$E$16	
5	Cost per oz of metal	$0.50					Maximum_sales	=Model!$B$18:$E$18	
6	Cost per oz of glass	$0.75					Profit	=Model!$F$32	
7							Resources_available	=Model!$D$21:$D$23	
8	Frame type	1	2	3	4		Resources_used	=Model!$B$21:$B$23	
9	Labor hours per frame	2	1	3	2				
10	Metal (oz.) per frame	4	2	1	2				
11	Glass (oz.) per frame	6	2	1	2				
12	Unit selling price	$28.50	$12.50	$29.25	$21.50				
13									
14	Production plan								
15	Frame type	1	2	3	4				
16	Frames produced	500	800	400	1500				
17		<=	<=	<=	<=				
18	Maximum sales	1000	2000	500	1000				
19									
20	Resource constraints	Used		Available					
21	Labor hours	6000	<=	4000					
22	Metal (oz.)	7000	<=	6000					
23	Glass (oz.)	8000	<=	10000					
24									
25	Revenue, cost summary								
26	Frame type	1	2	3	4	Totals			
27	Revenue	$14,250	$10,000	$11,700	$32,250	$68,200			
28	Costs of inputs								
29	Labor	$8,000	$6,400	$9,600	$24,000	$48,000			
30	Metal	$1,000	$800	$200	$1,500	$3,500			
31	Glass	$2,250	$1,200	$300	$2,250	$6,000			
32	Profit	$3,000	$1,600	$1,600	$4,500	$10,700			

1 Inputs. Enter the various inputs in the shaded ranges. Again, remember that our convention is to shade all input cells (and enclose them in a blue border). Enter only *numbers*, not formulas, in input cells. They should always be numbers directly from the problem statement.

2 Range names. Name the ranges we have indicated. According to our convention, we have again named enough ranges so that the Solver dialog box contains only range names, no cell addresses. Of course, you can name additional ranges if you like.

3 Changing cells. Enter *any* four values in the Frames_produced range. This range contains the changing cells. You do *not* have to enter the values shown in Figure 3.19. Any trial values can be used initially; Solver will eventually find the *optimal* values. Note that the four values shown in Figure 3.19 cannot be optimal because they do not satisfy all of the constraints. Specifically, this plan uses more labor hours and metal than are available, and it produces more type 4 frames than can be sold. However, we do not need to worry about satisfying constraints at this point; Solver will take care of this later.

4 Resources used. Enter the formula

=SUMPRODUCT(B9:E9,Frames_produced)

in cell B21 and copy it to the rest of the Resources_used range. These formulas calculate the units of labor, metal, and glass used by the current product mix. We see again how useful the SUMPRODUCT function is in LP models. Here it says to multiply each value in the range B9:E9 by the corresponding value in the Frames_produced range and then sum these products.

→ **EXCEL TIP:** *Copying formulas with range names*
When you enter a range name in an Excel formula and then copy it, the range name reference acts like an absolute reference. ■

⑤ Revenues, costs, and profits. The area from row 25 down shows the summary of monetary values. Actually, all we need is the total profit in cell F32, but it is useful to calculate the revenues and costs associated with each product. To obtain the revenues, enter the formula

=B12*B16

in cell B27 and copy this to the range C27:E27. For the costs, enter the formula

=$B4*B$16*B9

in cell B29 and copy this to the range B29:E31. (Note how the mixed absolute and relative references enable copying to the entire range.) Then calculate profits for each product by entering the formula

=B27-SUM(B29:B31)

in cell B32 and copy this to the range C32:E32. Finally, calculate the totals in column F by summing across each row with the SUM function. (The cost sums in column F are easy to understand. For example, the $32,000 labor cost in cell F29 is the 4000 labor hours used multiplied by the unit $8 cost per labor hour.)

Experimenting with Other Solutions

Before going any further, you might want to experiment with other values in the changing cells. For example, here is one reasonable strategy. Because frame 1 has the highest profit margin ($6) and its market constraint permits at most 1000 frames, enter 1000 in cell B16. Note that none of the resources are yet used up completely. Therefore, we can make some type 3 frames, the type with the next highest profit margin. Because the type 3 market constraint permits at most 500 frames, enter 500 in cell D16. There is still some availability of each resource. This allows us to make some type 4 frames, the type with the next largest profit margin. However, the most we can make is 250 type 4 frames, because at this point we completely exhaust the available labor hours. The resulting solution appears in Figure 3.20 (page 88). Its corresponding profit is $8750.

Figure 3.20

Another Possible Solution for Product Mix Model

	A	B	C	D	E	F	G	H	I
1	**Product mix model**								
2									
3	**Input data**						**Range names used:**		
4	Hourly wage rate	$8.00					Frames_produced	=Model!$B$16:$E$16	
5	Cost per oz of metal	$0.50					Maximum_sales	=Model!$B$18:$E$18	
6	Cost per oz of glass	$0.75					Profit	=Model!$F$32	
7							Resources_available	=Model!$D$21:$D$23	
8	Frame type	1	2	3	4		Resources_used	=Model!$B$21:$B$23	
9	Labor hours per frame	2	1	3	2				
10	Metal (oz.) per frame	4	2	1	2				
11	Glass (oz.) per frame	6	2	1	2				
12	Unit selling price	$28.50	$12.50	$29.25	$21.50				
13									
14	**Production plan**								
15	Frame type	1	2	3	4				
16	Frames produced	1000	0	500	250				
17		<=	<=	<=	<=				
18	Maximum sales	1000	2000	500	1000				
19									
20	**Resource constraints**	Used		Available					
21	Labor hours	4000	<=	4000					
22	Metal (oz.)	5000	<=	6000					
23	Glass (oz.)	7000	<=	10000					
24									
25	**Revenue, cost summary**								
26	Frame type	1	2	3	4	Totals			
27	Revenue	$28,500	$0	$14,625	$5,375	$48,500			
28	Costs of inputs								
29	Labor	$16,000	$0	$12,000	$4,000	$32,000			
30	Metal	$2,000	$0	$250	$250	$2,500			
31	Glass	$4,500	$0	$375	$375	$5,250			
32	Profit	$6,000	$0	$2,000	$750	$8,750			

This type of "greedy" analysis—produce in the decreasing order of profit margins—is easy and intuitive. Unfortunately, as we have seen, it is not guaranteed to produce an optimal solution.

We have now produced as much as possible of the three frame types with the three highest profit margins. Does this guarantee that this solution is the best possible product mix? Unfortunately, it does not! The solution in Figure 3.20 is *not* optimal. In this small model it is difficult to guess the optimal solution, even when we use a relatively intelligent trial-and-error procedure. The problem is that a frame type with a high profit margin can use up a lot of the resources and preclude other profitable frames from being produced. Therefore, we turn to Solver to eliminate the guesswork and find the *real* optimal solution.

USING SOLVER

To use Solver, select the Tools/Solver menu item, and fill it in as shown in Figure 3.21. (Again, note that we have named enough ranges so that only range names appear in this dialog box.) Also, click on the Options button, and check the Assume Linear Model and Assume Non-Negative boxes, as in Figure 3.6. This is because the model is indeed linear, and we do not want to allow negative numbers of frames to be produced.

Figure 3.21
Solver Dialog Box for Product Mix Model

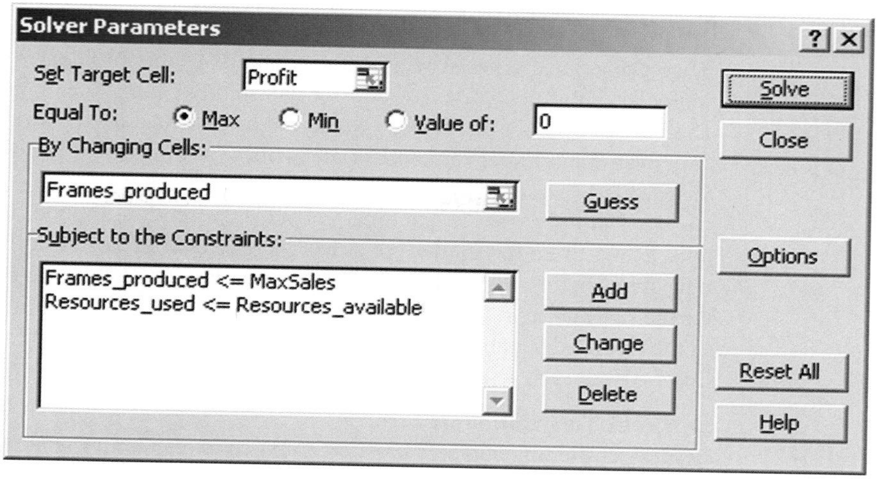

Figure 3.22
Optimal Solution for Product Mix Model

You typically gain insights into a solution by checking which constraints are binding and which contain slack.

Discussion of the Solution

When you click on Solve, you will obtain the optimal solution shown in Figure 3.22. The optimal plan is to produce 1000 type 1 frames, 800 type 2 frames, 400 type 3 frames, and no type 4 frames. This is close to the production plan from Figure 3.20, but the current plan earns $450 more profit. Also, it uses all of the available labor hours and metal, but only 8000 of the 10,000 available ounces of glass. Finally, in terms of maximum sales, the optimal plan could produce more of frame types 2, 3, and 4 (if there were more skilled labor and/or metal available). This is typical of an LP solution. Some of the constraints are met exactly—they are binding—whereas others contain a certain amount of slack. The binding constraints are the ones that prevent Monet from earning an even higher profit.

	A	B	C	D	E	F	G	H	I
1	**Product mix model**								
2									
3	**Input data**						Range names used:		
4	Hourly wage rate	$8.00					Frames_produced	=Model!$B$16:$E$16	
5	Cost per oz of metal	$0.50					Maximum_sales	=Model!$B$18:$E$18	
6	Cost per oz of glass	$0.75					Profit	=Model!$F$32	
7							Resources_available	=Model!$D$21:$D$23	
8	Frame type	1	2	3	4		Resources_usec	=Model!$B$21:$B$23	
9	Labor hours per frame	2	1	3	2				
10	Metal (oz.) per frame	4	2	1	2				
11	Glass (oz.) per frame	6	2	1	2				
12	Unit selling price	$28.50	$12.50	$29.25	$21.50				
13									
14	**Production plan**								
15	Frame type	1	2	3	4				
16	Frames produced	1000	800	400	0				
17		<=	<=	<=	<=				
18	Maximum sales	1000	2000	500	1000				
19									
20	**Resource constraints**	Used		Available					
21	Labor hours	4000	<=	4000					
22	Metal (oz.)	6000	<=	6000					
23	Glass (oz.)	8000	<=	10000					
24									
25	**Revenue, cost summary**								
26	Frame type	1	2	3	4	Totals			
27	Revenue	$28,500	$10,000	$11,700	$0	$50,200			
28	Costs of inputs								
29	Labor	$16,000	$6,400	$9,600	$0	$32,000			
30	Metal	$2,000	$800	$200	$0	$3,000			
31	Glass	$4,500	$1,200	$300	$0	$6,000			
32	Profit	$6,000	$1,600	$1,600	$0	$9,200			

Sensitivity Analysis

If we want to experiment with different inputs to this problem—the unit revenues or resource availabilities, for example—we can simply change the inputs and then rerun Solver. The second time we use Solver, we do not have to specify the target and changing cells or the constraints. Excel remembers all of these settings, and it saves them when we save the file.

As a simple what-if example, consider the modified model in Figure 3.23. Here the unit selling price for frame type 4 has increased from $21.50 to $26.50, and all other inputs are as before. By making type 4 frames more profitable, we might expect them to enter the optimal mix. This is exactly what happens. The new optimal plan (the one shown in the figure) discontinues production of frame types 2 and 3 and instead calls for production of 1000 type 4 frames. This solution increases the total profit to $14,000.

→ **Excel Tip:** *Roundoff Error*
Because of the way numbers are stored and calculated on a computer, the optimal values in the changing cells and elsewhere can contain small roundoff errors. For example, the value that really appeared in cell E16 (in Figure 3.23) on our PC was 8.731E-09, a very small number (0.000000008731). For all practical purposes, this number can be treated as 0, and we have formatted it as such in the spreadsheet. ∎

Figure 3.23

Optimal Solution for Product Mix Model with a New Input

	A	B	C	D	E	F	G	H	I
1	Product mix model								
2									
3	Input data						Range names used:		
4	Hourly wage rate	$8.00					Frames_produced	=Model!$B$16:$E$16	
5	Cost per oz of metal	$0.50					Maximum_sales	=Model!$B$18:$E$18	
6	Cost per oz of glass	$0.75					Profit	=Model!$F$32	
7							Resources_available	=Model!$D$21:$D$23	
8	Frame type	1	2	3	4		Resources_usec	=Model!$B$21:$B$23	
9	Labor hours per frame	2	1	3	2				
10	Metal (oz.) per frame	4	2	1	2				
11	Glass (oz.) per frame	6	2	1	2				
12	Unit selling price	$28.50	$12.50	$29.25	$26.50				
13									
14	Production plan								
15	Frame type	1	2	3	4				
16	Frames produced	1000	0	0	1000				
17		<=	<=	<=	<=				
18	Maximum sales	1000	2000	500	1000				
19									
20	Resource constraints	Used		Available					
21	Labor hours	4000	<=	4000					
22	Metal (oz.)	6000	<=	6000					
23	Glass (oz.)	8000	<=	10000					
24									
25	Revenue, cost summary								
26	Frame type	1	2	3	4	Totals			
27	Revenue	$28,500	$0	$0	$26,500	$55,000			
28	Costs of inputs								
29	Labor	$16,000	$0	$0	$16,000	$32,000			
30	Metal	$2,000	$0	$0	$1,000	$3,000			
31	Glass	$4,500	$0	$0	$1,500	$6,000			
32	Profit	$6,000	$0	$0	$8,000	$14,000			

We can also use SolverTable to perform a more systematic sensitivity analysis on one or more input variables. One possibility appears in Figure 3.24, where we allow the number of available labor hours to vary from 2500 to 5000 in increments of 250, and we keep track of the optimal product mix and profit. There are several ways to interpret the output from this sensitivity analysis. First, we can look at columns B–E to see how the product mix changes as more labor hours become available. For example, frames of type 4 are finally produced when 4500 labor hours are available, and frames of type 2 are discontinued in the final row. Second, we can see how extra labor hours add to the total profit. We show this numerically in column G, where each value is the increase in profit from the previous row. (We created column G manually; it is not part of the SolverTable output.) Note exactly what this increased profit means. For example, when labor hours increase from 2500 to 2750, the model requires that we *pay* $8 apiece for these extra hours (if we use them). But the *net* effect is that profit increases by $500. In other words, the labor cost increases by $2000 [=$8(250)], but this is more than offset by the increase in revenue that comes from having the extra labor hours.

Figure 3.24

Sensitivity of Optimal Solution to Labor Hours

	A	B	C	D	E	F	G
34	Sensitivity of optimal solution to number of labor hours						
35			Frames produced				
36	Labor hours	1	2	3	4	Total profit	Increase
37		$B$16	$C$16	$D$16	$E$16	$F$32	
38	2500	1000	500	0	0	$7,000	
39	2750	1000	750	0	0	$7,500	$500
40	3000	1000	1000	0	0	$8,000	$500
41	3250	1000	950	100	0	$8,300	$300
42	3500	1000	900	200	0	$8,600	$300
43	3750	1000	850	300	0	$8,900	$300
44	4000	1000	800	400	0	$9,200	$300
45	4250	1000	750	500	0	$9,500	$300
46	4500	1000	500	500	250	$9,750	$250
47	4750	1000	250	500	500	$10,000	$250
48	5000	1000	0	500	750	$10,250	$250

As column G illustrates, it is worthwhile to obtain extra labor hours, even though we have to pay for them, because profit increases. However, the increase in profit per extra labor hour—the *shadow price* of labor hours—is not constant. We see that it decreases as more labor hours are already owned. An extra 250 labor hours first results in $500 more profit, then $300, and then only $250. This is typical of shadow prices for scarce resources in LP models, where each extra unit of a resource is worth *at most* as much as the previous unit.

We can also chart the optimal profit values in column F (or any other quantities from a SolverTable output). The line chart in Figure 3.25 illustrates how the shadow price (slope of the line) decreases as more labor hours are already owned. (The first decrease in slope is perceptible; the second is hard to see in the chart, but it *is* there.)

Figure 3.25

Sensitivity of Optimal Profit to Labor Hours

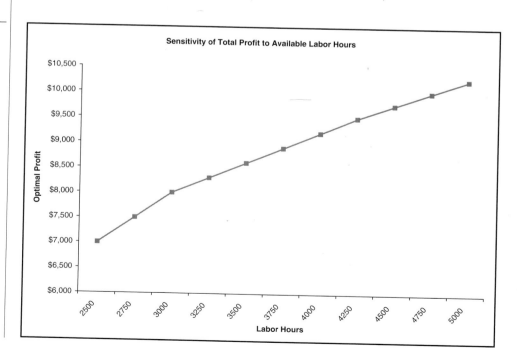

The reduced cost for a variable with an upper constraint can be nonzero if that variable is currently at its upper bound.

Finally, we can gain additional insight from Solver's sensitivity report, shown in Figure 3.26. This report contains a twist we did not see in the diet example. Now there are two types of constraints: upper bounds on the changing cells (the maximum sales constraints) and resource availability constraints. Solver treats the upper bound constraints differently from "normal" constraints in this report. First, it doesn't include rows for the upper bound constraints in the bottom section of the report. Second, in the top part of the report, a reduced cost can be nonzero even for a variable that is in the solution, provided that this variable is at its upper bound. Specifically, Monet is producing as many type 1 frames, 1000, as it is allowed to produce. The reduced cost of 2 means that the profit margin on type 1 frames must *decrease* by at least $2 before the company will produce less than 1000 of these frames.

Figure 3.26

Solver's Sensitivity Report

	A	B	C	D	E	F	G	H
1		Microsoft Excel 10.0 Sensitivity Report						
2		Worksheet: [ProductMix.xls]Model						
3		Report Created: 1/6/2003 2:01:33 PM						
4								
5								
6		Adjustable Cells						
7				Final	Reduced	Objective	Allowable	Allowable
8		Cell	Name	Value	Cost	Coefficient	Increase	Decrease
9		$B$16	Frames produced	1000	2.0	6	1E+30	2
10		$C$16	Frames produced	800	0.0	2	1	0.25
11		$D$16	Frames produced	400	0.0	4	2	0.5
12		$E$16	Frames produced	0	-0.2	3	0.2	1E+30
13								
14		Constraints						
15				Final	Shadow	Constraint	Allowable	Allowable
16		Cell	Name	Value	Price	R.H. Side	Increase	Decrease
17		$B$21	Labor hours Used	4000	1.2	4000	250	1000
18		$B$22	Metal (oz.) Used	6000	0.4	6000	2000	500
19		$B$23	Glass (oz.) Used	8000	0.0	10000	1E+30	2000

In contrast, the reduced cost of -0.2 for type 4 frames implies that the profit margin on these frames would have to increase by at least $0.20 before the company would include them in its optimal mix (since they are currently *not* included).

Finally, there are positive shadow prices on labor hours and metal, the two resources that are being used to capacity. The company's profit would increase by $1.20 for every extra labor hour and by $0.40 for every extra ounce of metal—but only up to the allowable increases shown in the report. ∎

PROBLEMS

Skill-Building Problems

10. Modify Monet's product mix model so that there is no maximum sales constraint. (This is easy to do in the Solver dialog box. Just highlight the constraint and click on the Delete button.) Does this make the problem unbounded? Does it change the optimal solution at all? Explain its effect.

11. In the product mix model it makes sense to change the maximum sales constraint to a "minimum sales" constraint, simply by changing the direction of the inequality. Then the input values in row 18 might be considered customer demands that must be met. Make this change and rerun Solver. What do you find? What

do you find if you run Solver again, this time making the values in row 18 half their current values?

12. Use SolverTable to run a sensitivity analysis on the cost per ounce of metal in the product mix model. Let this unit cost vary from $0.30 to $1.30 in increments of $0.20, and keep track of the values in the changing cells and the target cell. Discuss what happens to the optimal product mix. Also, does each 20-cent increase in the cost of metal result in the *same* decrease in profit?

13. Create a two-way SolverTable for the product mix model, where Profit is the only output and the two inputs are the hourly cost of labor and the total labor hours available. Let the former vary from $6 to $10 in increments of $1, and let the latter vary from 3000 to 7000 in increments of 500. Discuss the changes in profit you see as you look across the various rows of the table. Discuss the changes in profit you see as you look down the various columns of the table.

14. In the current solution to the product mix model, type 4 frames are not produced at all. This is due, at least in part, to the low unit selling price of type 4 frames. Use SolverTable appropriately to determine how large this unit selling price would have to be before type 4 frames would be included in the optimal product mix.

Skill-Expanding Problems

15. Suppose we want to increase *all three* of the resource availabilities in the product mix model simultaneously by the same factor. We want this factor to vary from 0.8 to 2.0 in increments of 0.1. For example, if this factor is 1.0, we get the current model, whereas if the factor is 2.0, the resource availabilities become 8000, 12,000, and 20,000. Modify the spreadsheet model

slightly so that this sensitivity analysis can be performed with a *one-way* SolverTable, using the factor as the single input. Keep track of the values in the changing cells and the target cell. Discuss the results.

16. Some analysts complain that spreadsheet models are difficult to resize. We'll let you be the judge of this. Suppose the current product mix problem is changed so that there is an extra resource, plastic, and two additional frame types, 5 and 6. What additional data are required? What modifications are necessary in the spreadsheet model (including range name changes)? Make up values for any extra required data and incorporate these into a modified spreadsheet model. (You might want to try inserting new columns in the *middle* of your range, rather than inserting them at the end. See if you can discover why the former is more efficient.) Then optimize with Solver. Do you conclude that it is easy to resize a spreadsheet model? (By the way, it turns out that algebraic models are typically *much* easier to resize.)

3.8 A MULTIPERIOD PRODUCTION MODEL

The dessert and product mix examples illustrate typical LP models. However, LP models come in many forms. For variety, we will now illustrate a quite different type of problem that can also be solved with LP. (In the next few chapters we will illustrate many other examples, linear and otherwise.) The distinguishing feature of the following problem is that it relates decisions made during several time periods. This type of problem occurs when a company must make a decision now that will have ramifications in the future. The company does not want to focus completely on the near future and forget about the long run.

| EXAMPLE | 3.3 PRODUCING FOOTBALLS AT PIGSKIN |

The Pigskin Company produces footballs. Pigskin must decide how many footballs to produce each month. The company has decided to use a 6-month planning horizon. The forecasted demands for the next 6 months are 10,000, 15,000, 30,000, 35,000, 25,000, and 10,000. Pigskin wants to meet these demands on time, knowing that it currently has 5000 footballs in inventory and that it can use a given month's production to help meet the demand for that month. (For simplicity, we assume that production occurs during the month, and demand occurs at the end of the month.) During each month there is enough production capacity to produce up to 30,000 footballs, and there is enough storage capacity to store up to 10,000 footballs at the end of the month, after demand has occurred. The forecasted production costs per football for the next 6 months are $12.50, $12.55, $12.70, $12.80, $12.85, and $12.95, respectively. The holding cost per football held in inventory at the end of any month is figured at 5% of the production cost for that month. (This cost includes the cost of storage and also the cost of money tied up in inventory.) The selling price for footballs is not considered relevant to the production decision because Pigskin will satisfy all customer demand exactly when it occurs—at whatever the selling price is. Therefore, Pigskin wants to determine the production schedule that minimizes the total production and holding costs.

Objective To use LP to find the production schedule that meets demand on time and minimizes total production and inventory holding costs.

WHERE DO THE NUMBERS COME FROM?

The input values for this problem are not all easy to find. Here are some thoughts on where they might be obtained. (See Figure 3.27 on page 96.)

- The initial inventory in cell B4 should be available from the company's database system or from a physical count.

- The unit production costs in row 8 would probably be estimated in two steps. First, the company might ask its cost accountants to estimate the current unit production cost. Then it could examine historical trends in costs to estimate inflation factors for future months.

- The holding cost percentage in cell B5 is typically difficult to determine. Depending on the type of inventory being held, this cost can include storage and handling, rent, property taxes, insurance, spoilage, and obsolescence. It can also include capital costs—the cost of money that could be used for other investments.

- The demands in row 18 are probably forecasts made by the marketing department. They might be "seat-of-the-pants" forecasts, or they might be the result of a formal quantitative forecasting procedure. (We discuss such procedures in Chapter 12.) Of course, if there are already some orders on the books for future months, then these are included in the demand figures.

- The production and storage capacities in rows 14 and 22 are probably supplied by the production department. They are based on the size of the workforce, the available machinery, availability of raw materials, and physical space.

Solution

The variables and constraints for this model are listed in Table 3.4. As we will see when we develop the spreadsheet model, there are two keys to relating these variables. First, the months cannot be treated independently. This is because the ending inventory in one month is the beginning inventory for the next month. Second, to ensure that demand is satisfied on time, we must ensure that the amount on hand after production in each month is at least as large as the demand for that month.

Table 3.4   Variables and Constraints for Production/Inventory Planning Model

Input variables	Initial inventory, unit holding cost, unit production costs, forecasted demands, production and storage capacities
Decision variables (changing cells)	Monthly production quantities
Objective (target cell)	Total cost
Other calculated variables	Units on hand after production, ending inventories, monthly production and inventory holding costs
Constraints	Units on hand after production $\geq$ Demand (each month) Units produced $\leq$ Production capacity (each month) Ending inventory $\leq$ Storage capacity (each month)

When we model this type of problem, we must be very specific about the *timing* of events. In fact, depending on the assumptions we make, there can be a variety of potential models. For example, when does the demand for footballs in a given month occur: at the beginning of the month, at the end of the month, or continually throughout the month? The same question can be asked about production in a given month. The answers to these two questions indicate how much of the production in a given month can be used to help satisfy the demand in that month. Also, are the maximum storage constraint and the holding cost based on the *ending* inventory in a month, the *average* amount of inventory in a month, or the *maximum* inventory in a month? Each of these possibilities is reasonable and could be implemented.

To simplify the model, we will assume that (1) all production occurs at the beginning of the month, (2) all demand occurs *after* production, so that all units produced in a month can be used to satisfy that month's demand, and (3) the storage constraint and the holding cost are based on *ending* inventory for a given month. (You are asked in the problems to modify these assumptions.)

An Algebraic Model

In the traditional algebraic model, the decision variables are the production quantities for the 6 months, labeled P_1 through P_6. It is also convenient to let I_1 through I_6 be the corresponding end-of-month inventories (after demand has occurred).[13] For example, I_3 is the number of footballs left over at the end of month 3. Therefore, the obvious constraints are on production and inventory storage capacities: $P_j \leq 300$ and $I_j \leq 100$ for each month j, $1 \leq j \leq 6$. (From here on, to minimize the number of zeros shown, we will express all quantities in *hundreds* of footballs.)

In addition to these constraints, we need "balance" constraints that relate the P's and I's. In any month the inventory from the previous month plus the current production equals the current demand plus leftover inventory. If D_j is the forecasted demand for month j, then the balance equation for month j is

$$I_{j-1} + P_j = D_j + I_j$$

The balance equation for month 1 uses the known beginning inventory, 50, for the previous inventory (the I_{j-1} term). By putting all variables (P's and I's) on the left and all known values on the right (a standard LP convention), we can write these balance constraints as

$$P_1 - I_1 = 100 - 50$$
$$I_1 + P_2 - I_2 = 150$$
$$I_2 + P_3 - I_3 = 300$$
$$I_3 + P_4 - I_4 = 350$$
$$I_4 + P_5 - I_5 = 250$$
$$I_5 + P_6 - I_6 = 100$$

(3.1)

As usual, we also impose nonnegativity constraints: all P's and I's must be nonnegative.

What about meeting demand on time? This requires that, in each month, the inventory from the preceding month plus the current production must be at least as large as the current demand. But take a look, for example, at the balance equation for month 3. By rearranging it slightly, we can write it as

$$I_3 = I_2 + P_3 - 300$$

Now, the nonnegativity constraint on I_3 implies that the right side of this equation, $I_2 + P_3 - 300$, is also nonnegative. But this implies that demand in month 3 is covered—the

---

[13]This example illustrates a subtle difference between algebraic and spreadsheet models. It is often convenient in algebraic models to define "decision variables," in this case the I's, that are really determined by other decision variables, in this case the P's. In spreadsheet models, however, we typically define the changing cells as the smallest set of variables that really must be chosen—in this case the production quantities. Then we calculate values that are determined by these changing cells, such as the ending inventory levels, with spreadsheet formulas.

beginning inventory in month 3 plus month 3 production is at least 300. Therefore, the nonnegativity constraints on the I's *automatically* guarantee that all demands will be met on time, and no other constraints are needed. Alternatively, we could write directly that $I_2 + P_3 \geq 300$. In words, the amount on hand after production in month 3 must be at least as large as the demand in month 3. We will take advantage of this interpretation in the spreadsheet model.

Finally, the objective we want to minimize is the sum of production and holding costs. It is the sum of unit production costs multiplied by P's, plus unit holding costs multiplied by I's.

DEVELOPING THE SPREADSHEET MODEL

The spreadsheet model of Pigskin's production problem is given in Figure 3.27. (See the file **ProductionScheduling.xls**.) The main feature that distinguishes this model from the product mix model is that some of the constraints, namely, the balance equations (3.1), are built into the spreadsheet itself by means of formulas. This means that the only changing cells are the production quantities. The ending inventories shown in row 20 are *determined* by the production quantities and equations (3.1). As we see, the decision variables in an algebraic model (the P's and I's) are not *necessarily* the same as the changing cells in an equivalent spreadsheet model. (The only changing cells in our spreadsheet model correspond to the P's.)

To develop the spreadsheet model in Figure 3.27, proceed as follows.

Figure 3.27 Nonoptimal Solution to Pigskin's Production Model

	A	B	C	D	E	F	G	H	I	J	K
1	Multiperiod production model										
2											
3	Input data								Range names used:		
4	Initial inventory (100s)	50							Demand	=Model!$B$18:$G$18	
5	Holding cost as % of prod cost	5%							Ending_inventory	=Model!$B$20:$G$20	
6									On_hand_after_production	=Model!$B$16:$G$16	
7	Month	1	2	3	4	5	6		Production_capacity	=Model!$B$14:$G$14	
8	Production cost/unit	$12.50	$12.55	$12.70	$12.80	$12.85	$12.95		Storage_capacity	=Model!$B$22:$G$22	
9									Total_cost	=Model!$H$28	
10	Production plan (all quantities are in 100s of footballs)								Units_produced	=Model!$B$12:$G$12	
11	Month	1	2	3	4	5	6				
12	Units produced	150	150	300	300	250	100				
13		<=	<=	<=	<=	<=	<=				
14	Production capacity	300	300	300	300	300	300				
15											
16	On hand after production	200	250	400	400	300	150				
17		>=	>=	>=	>=	>=	>=				
18	Demand	100	150	300	350	250	100				
19											
20	Ending inventory	100	100	100	50	50	50				
21		<=	<=	<=	<=	<=	<=				
22	Storage capacity	100	100	100	100	100	100				
23											
24	Summary of costs (all costs are in hundreds of dollars)										
25	Month	1	2	3	4	5	6	Totals			
26	Production costs	$1,875.00	$1,882.50	$3,810.00	$3,840.00	$3,212.50	$1,295.00	$15,915.00			
27	Holding costs	$62.50	$62.75	$63.50	$32.00	$32.13	$32.38	$285.25			
28	Totals	$1,937.50	$1,945.25	$3,873.50	$3,872.00	$3,244.63	$1,327.38	$16,200.25			

① **Inputs.** Enter the inputs in the shaded ranges. Again, these are all entered as *numbers* straight from the problem statement. (Unlike some spreadsheet modelers who prefer to put all inputs in the upper left corner of the spreadsheet, we have entered the inputs wherever they fit most naturally. Of course, this takes some planning before diving in.)

② **Name ranges.** Name the ranges indicated. Note that all but one of these (Total_cost) can be named easily with the Insert/Name/Create shortcut, using the labels in column A.

③ Production quantities. Enter *any* values in the range Units_produced as production quantities. As always, you can enter values that you believe are good, maybe even optimal. This is not crucial, however, because Solver will eventually find the *optimal* production quantities.

④ On-hand inventory. Enter the formula

=B4+B12

in cell B16. This calculates the first month's on-hand inventory after production (but before demand). Then enter the "typical" formula

=B20+C12

for on-hand inventory after production in month 2 in cell C16 and copy it across row 16.

⑤ Ending inventories. Enter the formula

=B16-B18

for ending inventory in cell B20 and copy it across row 20. This formula calculates ending inventory in the current month as on-hand inventory before demand minus the demand in that month.

⑥ Production and holding costs. Enter the formula

=B8*B12

in cell B26 and copy it across to cell G26 to calculate the monthly production costs. Then enter the formula

=$B$5*B8*B20

in cell B27 and copy it across to cell G27 to calculate the monthly holding costs. Note that these are based on monthly ending inventories. Finally, calculate the cost totals in column H by summing with the SUM function.

In multiperiod problems, we often need one formula for the first period and a slightly different formula for all other periods.

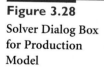

USING SOLVER

To use Solver, fill out the main dialog box as shown in Figure 3.28. The logic behind the constraints is straightforward. All we have to guarantee is that (1) the production quantities do not exceed the production capacities, (2) the on-hand inventories after production are at least as large as demands, and (3) ending inventories do not exceed storage capacities. We also need to check the Assume Linear Model and Assume Non-Negative options, and than click on Solve.

Figure 3.28
Solver Dialog Box for Production Model

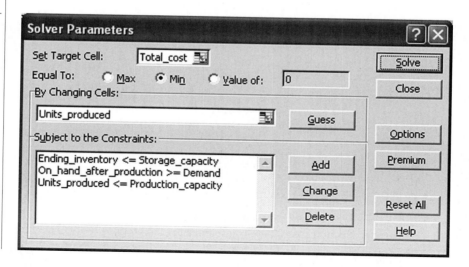

Discussion of the Solution

The optimal solution from Solver appears in Figure 3.29. This solution is also represented graphically in Figure 3.30. We can interpret the solution by comparing production quantities with demands. (Remember that all spreadsheet quantities are in units of 100 footballs.) In month 1 Pigskin should produce just enough to meet month 1 demand (taking into account the initial inventory of 5000). In month 2 it should produce 5000 more footballs than month 2 demand, and then in month 3 it should produce just enough to meet month 3 demand, while still carrying the extra 5000 footballs in inventory from month 2 production. In month 4 Pigskin should finally use these 5000 footballs, along with the maximum production amount, 30,000, to meet month 4 demand. Then in months 5 and 6 it should produce exactly enough to meet these months' demands. The total cost is $1,535,563, most of which is production cost. (This total cost is expressed in actual dollars. The value in the spreadsheet is in hundreds of dollars.)

Figure 3.29   Optimal Solution for the Production Model

	A	B	C	D	E	F	G	H	I	J	K
1	Multiperiod production model										
2									Range names used:		
3	Input data								Demand	=Model!$B$18:$G$18	
4	Initial inventory (100s)	50							Ending_inventory	=Model!$B$20:$G$20	
5	Holding cost as % of prod cost	5%							On_hand_after_production	=Model!$B$16:$G$16	
6									Production_capacity	=Model!$B$14:$G$14	
7	Month	1	2	3	4	5	6		Storage_capacity	=Model!$B$22:$G$22	
8	Production cost/unit	$12.50	$12.55	$12.70	$12.80	$12.85	$12.95		Total_cost	=Model!$H$28	
9									Units_produced	=Model!$B$12:$G$12	
10	Production plan (all quantities are in 100s of footballs)										
11	Month	1	2	3	4	5	6				
12	Units produced	50	200	300	300	250	100				
13		<=	<=	<=	<=	<=	<=				
14	Production capacity	300	300	300	300	300	300				
15											
16	On hand after production	100	200	350	350	250	100				
17		>=	>=	>=	>=	>=	>=				
18	Demand	100	150	300	350	250	100				
19											
20	Ending inventory	0	50	50	0	0	0				
21		<=	<=	<=	<=	<=	<=				
22	Storage capacity	100	100	100	100	100	100				
23											
24	Summary of costs (all costs are in hundreds of dollars)										
25	Month	1	2	3	4	5	6	Totals			
26	Production costs	$625.00	$2,510.00	$3,810.00	$3,840.00	$3,212.50	$1,295.00	$15,292.50			
27	Holding costs	$0.00	$31.38	$31.75	$0.00	$0.00	$0.00	$63.13			
28	Totals	$625.00	$2,541.38	$3,841.75	$3,840.00	$3,212.50	$1,295.00	$15,355.63			

Figure 3.30

Graphical Representation of Optimal Production Schedule

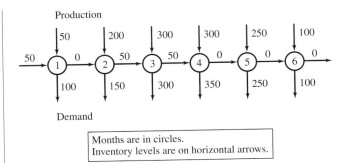

Months are in circles.
Inventory levels are on horizontal arrows.

Could you have guessed this optimal solution? Upon reflection, it makes perfect sense. Because the monthly holding costs are large relative to the differences in monthly production costs, there is little incentive to produce footballs before they are needed to take

You can often improve your intuition by trying to reason why Solver's solution is indeed optimal.

advantage of a "cheap" production month. Therefore, the Pigskin Company produces footballs in the month when they are needed—when this is possible. The only exception to this rule is the 20,000 footballs produced during month 2 when only 15,000 are needed. The extra 5000 footballs produced in month 2 are needed, however, to meet month 4 demand of 35,000, because month 3 production capacity is used entirely to meet month 3 demand. Thus month 3 capacity is not available to meet month 4 demand, and 5000 units of month 2 capacity are used to meet month 4 demand.

Sensitivity Analysis

If you want SolverTable to keep track of a quantity that is not in your model, you need to create it with an appropriate formula in a new cell.

We can use SolverTable to perform a number of interesting sensitivity analyses. We illustrate two possibilities. First, note that the most inventory ever carried at the end of a month is 50 (5000 footballs), although the storage capacity each month is 100. Perhaps this is because the holding cost percentage, 5%, is fairly large. Would more ending inventory be carried if this holding cost percentage were lower? Or would even less be carried if it were higher? We can check this with the SolverTable output shown in Figure 3.31. Now the single input cell is cell B5, and the *single* output we keep track of is the maximum ending inventory ever held, which we calculate in cell B31 with the formula

=MAX(Ending_inventory)

As we see, only when the holding cost percentage decreases to 1% do we hit the storage capacity limit. (From this output we cannot tell which month or how many months the ending inventory will be at this upper limit.) On the other side, even when the holding cost percentage reaches 10%, we still continue to hold a maximum ending inventory of 50.

Figure 3.31
Sensitivity of Maximum Ending Inventory to Holding Cost Percentage

	A	B	C	D	E	F
30	**Sensitivity of maximum amount of ending inventory to holding cost percentage**					
31	Output formula	50				
32						
33	Holding cost percentage	MaxEndInv				
34		$B$31				
35	1%	100				
36	2%	50				
37	3%	50				
38	4%	50				
39	5%	50				
40	6%	50				
41	7%	50				
42	8%	50				
43	9%	50				
44	10%	50				

A second possible sensitivity analysis is suggested by the way the optimal production schedule would probably be implemented. The optimal solution to Pigskin's model specifies the production level for each of the next 6 months. In reality, however, the company might implement the model's recommendation only for the *first* month. Then at the beginning of the second month, it will gather new forecasts for the *next* 6 months, months 2 through 7, solve a new 6-month model, and again implement the model's recommendation for the first of these months, month 2. If the company continues in this manner, we say that it is following a 6-month **rolling planning horizon**.

The question, then, is whether the assumed demands (really, forecasts) toward the end of the planning horizon have much effect on the optimal production quantity in month 1. We would hope not, because these forecasts could be quite inaccurate. The two-way Solver table in Figure 3.32 (page 100) shows how the optimal month 1 production quantity varies with the forecasted demands in months 5 and 6. As we see, if the forecasted months 5 and 6 demands remain fairly small, the optimal month 1 production quantity remains at 50. This is good news. It means that the optimal production quantity in month 1 is fairly insensitive to the possibly inaccurate forecasts for months 5 and 6.

Figure 3.32

Sensitivity of
Month 1
Production to
Demands in
Months 5 and 6

	A	B	C	D	E
46	Sensitivity of month 1 production quantity to demands in months 5 and 6				
47	Month 5 demand is along side, month 6 demand is along top				
48	$B$12	100	200	300	
49	100	50	50	50	
50	200	50	50	50	
51	300	50	50	50	

Solver's sensitivity report for this model appears in Figure 3.33. The bottom part of this report is fairly straightforward to interpret. The first 6 rows are for sensitivity to changes in the storage capacity, whereas the last 6 are for sensitivity to changes in the demands. (There are no rows for the production capacity constraints because these are simple upper bound constraints on the decision variables. Recall that Solver's sensitivity report handles this type of constraint differently from "normal" constraints.) In contrast, the top part of the report is very difficult to unravel. This is because the objective coefficients of the decision variables are each based on *multiple* inputs. (Each is a combination of unit production costs and the holding cost percentage.) Therefore, if we want to know how the solution will change if we change a single unit production cost or the holding cost percentage, this report will not answer our question, at least not easily. This is one case where we believe sensitivity analysis with SolverTable is more straightforward and intuitive. It allows us to change *any* of the model's inputs and directly see the effects on the solution.

Figure 3.33

Solver's Sensitivity
Report for
Production Model

	A	B	C	D	E	F	G	H
1		Microsoft Excel 10.0 Sensitivity Report						
2		Worksheet: [ProductionScheduling.xls]Model						
3		Report Created: 2/15/2003 7:43:45 PM						
4								
5								
6	Adjustable Cells							
7				Final	Reduced	Objective	Allowable	Allowable
8		Cell	Name	Value	Cost	Coefficient	Increase	Decrease
9		$B$12	Units produced	50	0	16.3175	1E+30	0.575
10		$C$12	Units produced	200	0	15.7425	0.575	0.4775
11		$D$12	Units produced	300	-0.4775	15.265	0.4775	1E+30
12		$E$12	Units produced	300	-1.0125	14.73	1.0125	1E+30
13		$F$12	Units produced	250	0	14.14	1.6025	0.5425
14		$G$12	Units produced	100	0	13.5975	0.5425	13.5975
15								
16	Constraints							
17				Final	Shadow	Constraint	Allowable	Allowable
18		Cell	Name	Value	Price	R.H. Side	Increase	Decrease
19		$B$20	Ending inventory >=	0	0	100	1E+30	100
20		$C$20	Ending inventory >=	50	0	100	1E+30	50
21		$D$20	Ending inventory >=	50	0	100	1E+30	50
22		$E$20	Ending inventory >=	0	0	100	1E+30	100
23		$F$20	Ending inventory >=	0	0	100	1E+30	100
24		$G$20	Ending inventory >=	0	0	100	1E+30	100
25		$B$16	On hand after production <=	100	0.575	100	100	50
26		$C$16	On hand after production <=	200	0	150	50	1E+30
27		$D$16	On hand after production <=	350	0	300	50	1E+30
28		$E$16	On hand after production <=	350	1.6025	350	50	50
29		$F$16	On hand after production <=	250	0.5425	250	50	200
30		$G$16	On hand after production <=	100	13.5975	100	100	100

MODELING ISSUES

We assume that Pigskin uses a 6-month planning horizon. Why 6 months? In multiperiod models such as this, the company has to make forecasts about the future, such as the level of customer demand. Therefore, the length of the planning horizon is usually the length of time for which the company can make reasonably accurate forecasts. Here, Pigskin evidently believes that it can forecast up to 6 months from now, so it uses a 6-month planning horizon. ∎

PROBLEMS

Skill-Building Problems

17. Can you guess the results of a sensitivity analysis on the initial inventory in the Pigskin model? See if your guess is correct by using SolverTable and allowing the initial inventory to vary from 0 to 100 in increments of 10. (These are in 100s of footballs.) Keep track of the values in the changing cells and the target cell.

18. Modify the Pigskin model so that there are 8 months in the planning horizon. You can make up reasonable values for any extra required data. Don't forget to modify range names. Then modify the model again so that there are only 4 months in the planning horizon. Do either of these modifications change the optimal production quantity in month 1?

19. As indicated by the algebraic formulation of the Pigskin model, there is no real need to calculate inventory on hand after production and constrain it to be greater than or equal to demand. An alternative is to calculate ending inventory directly and constrain it to be nonnegative. Modify the current spreadsheet model to do this. (Delete rows 16 and 17, and calculate ending inventory appropriately. Then add an *explicit* nonnegativity constraint on ending inventory.)

20. In one modification of the Pigskin problem, the maximum storage constraint and the holding cost are based on the *average* inventory (not ending inventory) for a given month, where the average inventory is defined as the sum of beginning inventory and ending inventory, divided by 2, and beginning inventory is before production or demand. Modify the Pigskin model with this new assumption, and use Solver to find the optimal solution. How does this change the optimal production schedule? How does it change the optimal total cost?

Skill-Extending Problems

21. Modify the Pigskin spreadsheet model so that except for month 6, demand need not be met on time. The only requirement is that all demand be met eventually by the end of month 6. How does this change the optimal production schedule? How does it change the optimal total cost?

22. Modify the Pigskin spreadsheet model so that demand in any of the first 5 months must be met no later than a month late, whereas demand in month 6 must be met on time. For example, the demand in month 3 can be met partly in month 3 and partly in month 4. How does this change the optimal production schedule? How does it change the optimal total cost?

23. Modify the Pigskin spreadsheet model in the following way. Assume that the timing of demand and production are such that only 70% of the production in a given month can be used to satisfy the demand in that month. The other 30% occurs too late in that month and must be carried as inventory to help satisfy demand in later months. How does this change the optimal production schedule? How does it change the optimal total cost? Then use SolverTable to see how the optimal production schedule and optimal cost vary as the percentage of production usable for this month's demand (now 70%) is allowed to vary from 20% to 100% in increments of 10%.

3.9 A COMPARISON OF ALGEBRAIC AND SPREADSHEET MODELS

To this point we have seen three algebraic optimization models and three corresponding spreadsheet models. How do they differ? If you review the first two examples in this chapter, the diet and product mix examples, we believe you will agree that (1) the algebraic models are quite straightforward and (2) the spreadsheet models are almost direct translations into Excel of the algebraic models. In particular, each algebraic model has a set of x's that corresponds to the changing cell range in the spreadsheet model. In addition, each objective and each left-hand side of each constraint in the spreadsheet model corresponds to a linear expression involving x's in the algebraic model.

However, the Pigskin production planning model is quite different. The spreadsheet model includes one set of changing cells, the production quantities, and everything else is related to these through spreadsheet formulas. In contrast, the algebraic model has *two* sets of variables, the P's for the production quantities and the I's for the ending inventories, and together these comprise the "decision variables." These two sets of variables must then be related algebraically, and this is done through a series of "balance equations."

This is a typical situation in algebraic models, where one set of variables (the production quantities) corresponds to the *real* decision variables, whereas other sets of variables, along with extra equations, must be introduced to get the logic straight. We believe—and this belief is reinforced by many years of teaching experience—that this extra level of abstraction makes algebraic models much more difficult for typical users to develop and comprehend. It is the primary reason we have decided to focus almost exclusively on spreadsheet models in this book.

3.10 A DECISION SUPPORT SYSTEM

If your job is to develop an LP spreadsheet model to solve a problem such as Pigskin's production problem, then you will be considered the "expert" in LP. Many people who need to use such models, however, are *not* experts. They might understand the basic ideas behind LP and the types of problems it is intended to solve, but they will not know the details. In this case it is useful to provide these users with a **decision support system** (DSS) that can help them solve problems without having to worry about technical details.

We will not teach you in this book how to build a full-scale DSS, but we will show you what a typical DSS looks like and what it can do.[14] (We will consider only DSSs built around spreadsheets. There are many other platforms for developing DSSs that we will not consider.) Basically, a spreadsheet-based DSS contains a spreadsheet model of a problem, such as the one in Figure 3.27. However, users will probably never even see this model. Instead, they see a "front end" and a "back end." The front end allows them to select input values for their particular problem. The user interface for this front end can include several features, such as buttons, dialog boxes, toolbars, and menus—the things we are used to seeing in Windows applications. The back end then produces a report that explains the optimal policy in nontechnical terms.

We illustrate a DSS for a slight variation of the Pigskin problem in the file **DecisionSupport.xls**. This file has three sheets. When you open the file, you see the Explanation sheet. (See Figure 3.34.) It contains two buttons, one for setting up the problem (getting the user's inputs) and one for solving the problem (running Solver). When you press the Set Up Problem button, you are asked for a series of inputs: the initial inventory, the number of months in the planning horizon, the forecasted demands for each month, and others. An example appears in Figure 3.35, where you must enter information about the holding costs. These input boxes should be self-explanatory, so that all you need to do is enter the values you want to try. After you have entered all of these inputs, you can take a look at the Formulation sheet. This sheet contains a spreadsheet model similar to the one we saw previously in Figure 3.29, but with the inputs you just entered.

---

[14]For readers interested in learning more about spreadsheet DSSs, Albright has written the book *VBA for Modelers*. It contains a primer on the VBA language, and then it presents many applications and instructions for creating DSSs with VBA.

Figure 3.34 Explanation Sheet for DSS

Pigskin Planning Problem

This application solves a multiperiod production scheduling model similar to Example 3 in the chapter. The only differences are that (1) the number of periods in the planning horizon can be any number from 3 to 12, and (2) the unit production cost is assumed to grow by a constant percentage from one period to the next. To run the application, click on the left button to enter inputs. Then click on the right button to run the Solver and obtain a solution report.

| Set Up Problem | Find Optimal Solution |

Figure 3.35

Input Dialog Box for Holding Cost Percentage

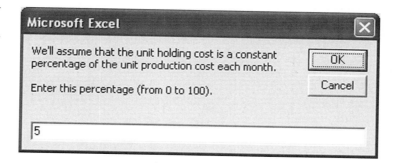

Microsoft Excel

We'll assume that the unit holding cost is a constant percentage of the unit production cost each month.

Enter this percentage (from 0 to 100).

OK Cancel

5

Now go back to the Explanation sheet and press the Find Optimal Solution button. This automatically sets up the Solver dialog box and runs Solver. There are two possibilities. First, it is possible that there is no feasible solution to the problem with the inputs you entered. In this case you will see a message to this effect, as in Figure 3.36. In most cases, however, the problem will have a feasible solution. In this case you will see the Report sheet, which summarizes the optimal solution in nontechnical terms. An example appears in Figure 3.37, which presents the solution for a 4-month planning horizon.

Figure 3.36

No Solution Message

No solution

⚠ The Solver couldn't find a solution. Try a different set of inputs.

OK

Figure 3.37

Report Sheet for DSS

Monthly schedule (scroll down to see more)

Month 1

Units		Dollars	
Start with	50		
Produce	150	Production cost	$1,875.00
Demand is	150		
End with	50	Holding cost	$31.25

Month 2

Units		Dollars	
Start with	50		
Produce	300	Production cost	$3,787.50
Demand is	350		
End with	0	Holding cost	$0.00

Month 3

Units		Dollars	
Start with	0		
Produce	200	Production cost	$2,550.26
Demand is	200		
End with	0	Holding cost	$0.00

Month 4

Units		Dollars	
Start with	0		
Produce	150	Production cost	$1,931.82
Demand is	150		
End with	0	Holding cost	$0.00

After studying this report, you can then click on the Solve Another Problem button, which takes you back to the Explanation sheet so that you can solve a new problem. All of this is done automatically with Excel macros. These macros use Microsoft's Visual Basic for Applications (VBA) programming language to automate various tasks. We will not explain any of the details of this language, but you are encouraged to look at the code in the Visual Basic Editor to get some sense of what it is doing. (Press Alt-F11 to get into the Visual Basic Editor.) In most professional applications, nontechnical people need only to enter inputs and look at reports. Therefore, the Formulation sheet and programming code would most likely be hidden and protected from end users.

3.11 CONCLUSION

This chapter has provided a good start to LP modeling—and to optimization modeling in general. We have learned how to develop three basic LP spreadsheet models, how to use Solver to find their optimal solutions, and how to perform sensitivity analyses with Solver's sensitivity reports or with the SolverTable add-in. We have also learned how to recognize whether a mathematical programming model satisfies the linear assumptions. In the next few chapters we will discuss a variety of other optimization models, but the three basic steps of model development, Solver optimization, and sensitivity analysis will remain the same.

Summary of Key Management Science Terms

Term	Explanation	Page
Linear programming model	An optimization model with a linear objective and linear constraints	58
Objective	The value, such as profit, to be optimized in an optimization model	58
Constraints	Conditions that must be satisfied in an optimization model	59
Nonnegativity constraints	Constraints that require the decision variables to be nonnegative, usually for physical reasons	59
Feasible solution	A solution that satisfies all of the constraints	59
Feasible region	The set of all feasible solutions	59
Optimal solution	The feasible solution that has the best value of the objective	59
Simplex method	An efficient algorithm for finding the optimal solution in a linear programming model	60
Sensitivity analysis	Seeing how the optimal solution changes as various input values change	60
Algebraic model	A model that expresses the constraints and the objective algebraically	61
Spreadsheet model	A model that uses spreadsheet formulas to express the logic of the model	62
Graphical solution	Shows the constraints and objective graphically so that the optimal solution can be identified; useful only when there are 2 decision variables	62
Binding constraint	A constraint that holds as an equality	70
Nonbinding constraint, slack	A constraint where there is a difference, called the slack, between the two sides of the inequality	70
Reduced cost	Amount the objective coefficient of a variable currently equal to 0 must change before it is optimal for that variable to be positive	73
Shadow price	The change in the objective for a change in the right-hand side of a constraint; used to see how we'd pay for more of a scarce resource	73
Mathematical programming model	Any optimization model, whether linear, integer, or nonlinear	78
Proportionality, additivity, divisibility	Properties of optimization model that result in a linear programming model	79
Infeasibility	Condition where a model has no feasible solutions	81
Unboundedness	Condition where there is no limit to the objective; always a sign of an error in the model	82
Decision support system	User-friendly system where an end-user can enter inputs to a model and see outputs, but need not be concerned with technical details	102

Summary of Key Excel Terms

Term	Explanation	Excel	Page
Changing cells	Cells that contain the values of the decision variables	Specify in Solver dialog box	64
Target cell	Cell that contains the value of the objective	Specify in Solver dialog box	64
Solver	Add-in that ships with Excel for performing optimization	Use Tools/Solver menu item	67
Solver's sensitivity report	Report available from Solver that shows sensitivity to objective coefficients and right-hand sides of constraints	Available in Solver dialog box right after Solver runs	71
SolverTable add-in	Add-in that performs sensitivity analysis to any inputs and reports results similar to an Excel data table	Use Data/SolverTable menu item	74
Selecting multiple ranges	Useful when changing cells, e.g., are in noncontiguous ranges	Pressing Ctrl key, drag ranges, one after the other	75

PROBLEMS

Skill-Building Problems

24. Leary Chemical manufactures three chemicals: A, B, and C. These chemicals are produced via two production processes: 1 and 2. Running process 1 for an hour costs $4 and yields 3 units of A, 1 unit of B, and 1 unit of C. Running process 2 for an hour costs $1 and yields 1 unit of A and 1 unit of B. To meet customer demands, at least 10 units of A, 5 units of B, and 3 units of C must be produced daily.

    a. Use Solver to determine a daily production plan that minimizes the cost of meeting Leary's daily demands.

    b. Confirm graphically that the daily production plan from part **a** minimizes the cost of meeting Leary's daily demands.

25. Starting with the optimal solution to the previous problem, use SolverTable to see what happens to the decision variables and the total cost when the hourly processing cost for process 2 increases in increments of $0.50. How large must this cost increase be before the decision variables change? What happens when it continues to increase beyond this point?

26. Furnco manufactures desks and chairs. Each desk uses 4 units of wood, and each chair uses 3 units of wood.

A desk contributes $40 to profit, and a chair contributes $25. Marketing restrictions require that the number of chairs produced be at least twice the number of desks produced. There are 20 units of wood available.

    a. Use Solver to maximize Furnco's profit.

    b. Confirm graphically that the solution in part **a** maximizes Furnco's profit.

27. Starting with the optimal solution to the previous problem, use SolverTable to see what happens to the decision variables and the total profit when the availability of wood varies from 10 to 30 in 1-unit increments. Based on your findings, how much would Furnco be willing to pay for each extra unit of wood over its current 20 units? How much profit would Furnco lose if it lost any of its current 20 units?

28. A farmer in Iowa owns 45 acres of land. He is going to plant each acre with wheat or corn. Each acre planted with wheat yields $200 profit, requires 3 workers, and requires 2 tons of fertilizer; each with corn yields $300 profit, requires 2 workers, and requires 4 tons of fertilizer. One hundred workers and 120 tons of fertilizer are available.

    a. Use Solver to help the farmer maximize the profit from his land.

b. Confirm graphically that the solution from part **a** maximizes the farmer's profit from his land.

29. Starting with the optimal solution to the previous problem, use SolverTable to see what happens to the decision variables and the total profit when the availability of fertilizer varies from 20 tons to 220 tons in 10-ton increments.

   a. When does the farmer discontinue producing wheat? When does he discontinue producing corn?

   b. How does the profit change for each 10-ton increment? Make this more obvious by creating a line chart of profit (vertical axis) versus fertilizer availability.

30. A customer requires during the next 4 months, respectively, 50, 65, 100, and 70 units of a commodity, and no backlogging is allowed (that is, the customer's requirements must be met on time). Production costs are $5, $8, $4, and $7 per unit during these months. The storage cost from one month to the next is $2 per unit (assessed on ending inventory). It is estimated that each unit on hand at the end of month 4 can be sold for $6. Determine how to minimize the net cost incurred in meeting the demands for the next 4 months.

31. Starting with the optimal solution to the previous problem, use SolverTable to see what happens to the decision variables and the total cost when the initial inventory varies from 0 (the implied value in the previous problem) to 100 in 10-unit increments. How much lower would the total cost be if the company started with 10 units in inventory, rather than none? Would this same cost decrease occur for *every* 10-unit increase in initial inventory?

32. A company faces the following demands during the next 3 weeks: week 1, 20 units; week 2, 10 units; week 3, 15 units. The unit production costs during each week are as follows: week 1, $13; week 2, $14; week 3, $15. A holding cost of $2 per unit is assessed against each week's ending inventory. At the beginning of week 1, the company has 5 units on hand. In reality, not all goods produced during a month can be used to meet the current month's demand. To model this fact, we assume that only half of the goods produced during a week can be used to meet the current week's demands. Determine how to minimize the cost of meeting the demand for the next 3 weeks.

33. Revise the model for the previous problem so that the demands are of the form $D_t + k\Delta_t$, where D_t is the original demand (from the previous problem) in month t, k is a factor, and Δ_t is an amount of change in month t demand. (The Greek symbol Δ is typically used to indicate change.) Formulate the model in such a way that you can use SolverTable to analyze changes in the amounts produced and the total cost when k varies from 0 to 10 in 1-unit increments, for any fixed values of the Δ_t's. For example, try this

when $\Delta_1 = 2$, $\Delta_2 = 5$, and $\Delta_3 = 3$. Describe the behavior you observe in the table. Can you find any "reasonable" Δ_t's that induce *positive* production levels in week 3?

34. Bloomington Brewery produces beer and ale. Beer sells for $5 per barrel, and ale sells for $2 per barrel. Producing a barrel of beer requires 5 pounds of corn and 2 pounds of hops. Producing a barrel of ale requires 2 pounds of corn and 1 pound of hops. The brewery has 60 pounds of corn and 25 pounds of hops.

   a. Use Solver to maximize Bloomington Brewery's revenue.

   b. Confirm graphically that the solution in part **a** maximizes Bloomington Brewery's revenue.

35. Starting with the optimal solution to the previous problem, use SolverTable to either substantiate or refute the following statements: The availability of corn can decrease by any amount (up to 60 pounds), and each unit decrease will cost Bloomington Brewery the same amount in terms of lost revenue. On the other hand, increases in the availability of corn do *not* have a constant effect on total revenue; the first few extra units have a larger effect than subsequent units.

36. For a telephone survey, a marketing research group needs to contact at least 150 wives, 120 husbands, 100 single adult males, and 110 single adult females. It costs $2 to make a daytime call and (because of higher labor costs) $5 to make an evening call. The file **P03_36.xls** lists the results that can be expected. For example, 30% of all daytime calls are answered by a wife, and 15% of all evening calls are answered by a single male. Because of a limited staff, at most half of all phone calls can be evening calls. Determine how to minimize the cost of completing the survey.

37. Starting with the optimal solution to the previous problem, use the SolverTable add-in to investigate changes in the unit cost of either type of call. Specifically, investigate changes in the cost of a daytime call, with the cost of an evening call fixed, to see when (if ever) *only* daytime calls or *only* evening calls will be made. Then repeat the analysis by changing the cost of an evening call and keeping the cost of a daytime call fixed.

38. Woodco manufactures tables and chairs. Each table and chair must be made entirely out of oak or entirely out of pine. A total of 150 board feet of oak and 210 board feet of pine are available. A table requires either 17 board feet of oak or 30 board feet of pine, and a chair requires either 5 board feet of oak or 13 board feet of pine. Each table can be sold for $40, and each chair for $15. Determine how Woodco can maximize its revenue.

39. Referring to the previous problem, suppose you want to investigate the effects of simultaneous changes in

the selling prices of the products. Specifically, you want to see what happens to the total revenue when the selling prices of oak products change by a factor $1 + k_1$ and the selling prices of pine products change by a factor $1 + k_2$. Revise your model from the previous problem so that you can use SolverTable to investigate changes in total revenue as k_1 and k_2 both vary from -0.3 to 0.3 in increments of 0.1. Would you conclude that total revenue changes *linearly* within this range?

40. Alden Enterprises produces two products. Each product can be produced on either of two machines. The time (in hours) required to produce each product on each machine is listed in the file **P03_40.xls**. Each month, 500 hours of time are available on each machine. Each month, customers are willing to buy up to the quantities of each product at the prices also given in the file **P03_40.xls**. The company's goal is to maximize the revenue obtained from selling units during the next 2 months. Determine how it can meet this goal. Assume that Alden will not produce any units in either month that it cannot sell in that month.

41. Referring to the previous problem, suppose Alden wants to see what will happen if customer demands for each product in each month simultaneously change by a factor $1 + k$. Revise the model so that you can use SolverTable to investigate the effect of this change on total revenue as k varies from -0.3 to 0.3 in increments of 0.1. Does revenue change in a linear manner over this range? Can you explain intuitively why it changes in the way it does?

42. There are three factories on the Momiss River: 1, 2, and 3. Each emits two types of pollutants, labeled P_1 and P_2, into the river. If the waste from each factory is processed, the pollution in the river can be reduced. It costs $15 to process a ton of factory 1 waste, and each ton processed reduces the amount of P_1 by 0.10 ton and the amount of P_2 by 0.45 ton. It costs $10 to process a ton of factory 2 waste, and each ton processed will reduce the amount of P_1 by 0.20 ton and the amount of P_2 by 0.25 ton. It costs $20 to process a ton of factory 3 waste, and each ton processed will reduce the amount of P_1 by 0.40 ton and the amount of P_2 by 0.30 ton. The state wants to reduce the amount of P_1 in the river by at least 30 tons and the amount of P_2 by at least 40 tons.
  a. Use Solver to determine how to minimize the cost of reducing pollution by the desired amounts.
  b. Are the LP assumptions (proportionality, additivity, divisibility) reasonable in this problem?

43. Referring to the previous problem, suppose you want to investigate the effects of increases in the minimal reductions required by the state. Specifically, you want to see what happens to the amounts of waste processed at the three factories and the total cost if

both requirements (currently 30 and 40 tons, respectively) are increased by the *same* percentage. Revise your model so that you can use the SolverTable add-in to investigate these changes when the percentage increase varies from 10% to 100% in increments of 10%. Do the amounts processed at the three factories and the total cost change in a linear manner?

Skill-Extending Problems

44. Truckco manufactures two types of trucks, types 1 and 2. Each truck must go through the painting shop and the assembly shop. If the painting shop were completely devoted to painting type 1 trucks, 800 per day could be painted, whereas if the painting shop were completely devoted to painting type 2 trucks, 700 per day could be painted. If the assembly shop were completely devoted to assembling truck 1 engines, 1500 per day could be assembled, and if the assembly shop were completely devoted to assembling truck 2 engines, 1200 per day could be assembled. It is possible, however, to paint *both* types of trucks in the painting shop. Similarly, it is possible to assemble both types in the assembly shop. Each type 1 truck contributes $300 to profit; each type 2 truck contributes $500. Use Solver to maximize Truckco's profit. (*Hint*: One approach, but not the only approach, is to try a graphical procedure first and then deduce the constraints from the graph.)

45. U.S. Labs manufactures mechanical heart valves from the heart valves of pigs. Different heart operations require valves of different sizes. U.S. Labs purchases pig valves from three different suppliers. The cost and size mix of the valves purchased from each supplier are given in the file **P03_45.xls**. Each month, U.S. Labs places an order with each supplier. At least 500 large, 300 medium, and 300 small valves must be purchased each month. Because of the limited availability of pig valves, at most 500 valves per month can be purchased from each supplier. Use Solver to determine how U.S. Labs can minimize the cost of acquiring the needed valves.

46. Referring to the previous problem, suppose U.S. Labs wants to investigate the effect on total cost of increasing its minimal purchase requirements each month. Specifically, it wants to see how total cost changes as the minimal purchase requirements of large, medium, and small valves all increase from their values in the previous problem by the *same* percentage. Revise your model so that SolverTable can be used to investigate these changes when the percentage increase varies from 2% to 20% in increments of 2%. Explain intuitively what happens when this percentage is at least 16%.

47. Sailco Corporation must determine how many sailboats to produce during each of the next four quarters.

The demand during each of the next four quarters is as follows: first quarter, 40 sailboats; second quarter, 60 sailboats; third quarter, 75 sailboats; fourth quarter, 25 sailboats. Sailco must meet demands on time. At the beginning of the first quarter, Sailco has an inventory of 10 sailboats. At the beginning of each quarter, Sailco must decide how many sailboats to produce during that quarter. For simplicity, we assume that sailboats manufactured during a quarter can be used to meet demand for that quarter. During each quarter, Sailco can produce up to 40 sailboats with regular-time labor at a total cost of $400 per sailboat. By having employees work overtime during a quarter, Sailco can produce additional sailboats with overtime labor at a total cost of $450 per sailboat. At the end of each quarter (after production has occurred and the current quarter's demand has been satisfied), a holding cost of $20 per sailboat is incurred. Determine a production schedule to minimize the sum of production and inventory holding costs during the next four quarters.

48. Referring to the previous problem, suppose Sailco wants to see whether any changes in the $20 holding cost per sailboat could induce the company to carry more or less inventory. Revise your model so that SolverTable can be used to investigate the effects on ending inventory during the 4-month interval of systematic changes in the unit holding cost. (Assume that even though the unit holding cost changes, it is still constant over the 4-month interval.) Are there any (nonnegative) unit holding costs that would induce Sailco to hold *more* inventory than it holds when the holding cost is $20? Are there any unit holding costs that would induce Sailco to hold *less* inventory than it holds when the holding cost is $20?

49. During the next 2 months General Cars must meet (on time) the following demands for trucks and cars: month 1, 400 trucks and 800 cars; month 2, 300 trucks and 300 cars. During each month at most 1000 vehicles can be produced. Each truck uses 2 tons of steel, and each car uses 1 ton of steel. During month 1, steel costs $400 per ton; during month 2, steel costs $600 per ton. At most 2500 tons of steel can be purchased each month. (Steel can be used only during the month in which it is purchased.) At the beginning of month 1, 100 trucks and 200 cars are in the inventory. At the end of each month, a holding cost of $150 per vehicle is assessed. Each car gets 20 mpg, and each truck gets 10 mpg. During each month, the vehicles produced by the company must average at least 16 mpg. Determine how to meet the demand and mileage requirements at minimum total cost.

50. Referring to the previous problem, check how sensitive the total cost is to the 16 mpg requirement by using SolverTable. Specifically, let this requirement vary from 14 mpg to 18 mpg in increments of 0.25 mpg, and write a short report of your results. In your report,

explain intuitively what happens when the requirement is greater than 17 mpg.

51. The Deckers Clothing Company produces shirts and pants. Each shirt requires 2 square yards of cloth, and each pair of pants requires 3 square yards of cloth. During the next 2 months the following demands for shirts and pants must be met (on time): month 1, 1000 shirts and 1500 pairs of pants; month 2, 1200 shirts and 1400 pairs of pants. During each month the following resources are available: month 1, 9000 square yards of cloth; month 2, 6000 square yards of cloth. (Cloth that is available during month 1 and is not used can be used during month 2.) During each month it costs $4 to make an article of clothing with regular-time labor and $8 with overtime labor. During each month a total of at most 2500 articles of clothing can be produced with regular-time labor, and an unlimited number of articles of clothing can be produced with overtime labor. At the end of each month, a holding cost of $3 per article of clothing is assessed. Determine how to meet demands for the next 2 months (on time) at minimum cost. Assume that, at the beginning of month 1, 100 shirts and 200 pairs of pants are available.

52. Referring to the previous problem, use SolverTable to investigate the effect on total cost of two *simultaneous* changes. The first change is to allow the ratio of overtime to regular time production cost (currently $8/$4 = 2) to decrease from 20% to 80% in increments of 20%, while keeping the regular time cost at $4. The second change is to allow the production capacity *each* month (currently 2500) to decrease from 10% to 50% in increments of 10%. The idea here is that less regular time capacity is available, but overtime is becoming relatively cheaper. Is the net effect on total cost positive or negative?

53. Each year, Comfy Shoes faces demands (which must be met on time) for pairs of shoes as shown in the file **P03_53.xls**. Employees work three consecutive quarters and then receive one quarter off. For example, a worker might work during quarters 3 and 4 of one year and quarter 1 of the next year. During a quarter in which an employee works, he or she can produce up to 500 pairs of shoes. Each worker is paid $5000 per quarter. At the end of each quarter, a holding cost of $10 per pair of shoes is assessed. Determine how to minimize the cost per year (labor plus holding) of meeting the demands for shoes. To simplify matters, assume that at the end of each year, the ending inventory is 0. (*Hint:* You may assume that a given worker will get the *same* quarter off during each year.)

54. Referring to the previous problem, suppose Comfy Shoes can pay a flat fee for a training program that will increase the productivity of all of its workers. Use SolverTable to see how much the company would be willing to pay for a training program that increases worker productivity from 500 pairs of shoes per quarter to P pairs of shoes per quarter, where P varies from 525 to 700 in increments of 25.

55. A company must meet (on time) the following demands: quarter 1, 3000 units; quarter 2, 2000 units; quarter 3, 4000 units. Each quarter, up to 2700 units can be produced with regular-time labor, at a cost of $40 per unit. During each quarter, an unlimited number of units can be produced with overtime labor, at a cost of $60 per unit. Of all units produced, 20% are unsuitable and cannot be used to meet demand. Also, at the end of each quarter, 10% of all units on hand spoil and cannot be used to meet any future demands. After each quarter's demand is satisfied and spoilage is accounted for, a cost of $15 per unit is assessed against the quarter's ending inventory. Determine how to minimize the total cost of meeting the demands of the next 3 quarters. Assume that 1000 usable units are available at the beginning of quarter 1.

56. Referring to the previous problem, the company wants to know how much money it would be worth to decrease the percentage of unsuitable items and/or the percentage of items that spoil. Write a short report that provides relevant information. Base your report on three uses of SolverTable: (1) where the percentage of unsuitable items decreases and the percentage of items that spoil stays at 10%; (2) where the percentage of unsuitable items stays at 20% and the percentage of items that spoil decreases; and (3) where both percentages decrease. Does the sum of the separate effects on total cost from the first two tables equal the combined effect from the third table? Include an answer to this question in your report.

57. A pharmaceutical company manufactures two drugs at Los Angeles and Indianapolis. The cost of manufacturing a pound of each drug depends on the location, as indicated in the file **P03_57.xls**. The machine time (in hours) required to produce a pound of each drug at each city is also shown in this table. The company must produce at least 1000 pounds per week of drug 1 and at least 2000 pounds per week of drug 2. It has 500 hours per week of machine time at Indianapolis and 400 hours per week at Los Angeles.

   a. Determine how the company can minimize the cost of producing the required drugs.
   b. Use SolverTable to determine how much the company would be willing to pay to purchase a combination of A extra hours of machine time at Indianapolis and B extra hours of machine time at Los Angeles, where A and B can be any positive multiples of 10 up to 50.

58. A company manufactures two products on two machines. The number of hours of machine time and labor depends on the machine and product as shown in the file **P03_58.xls**. The cost of producing a unit of each product depends on which machine produces it. These unit costs also appear in the file **P03_58.xls**. There are 200 hours available on each of the two machines, and there are 400 labor hours available. This month at least 200 units of product 1 and at least 240 units of product 2 must be produced. Also, at least half of the product 1 requirement must be produced on machine 1, and at least half of the product 2 requirement must be made on machine 2.

   a. Determine how the company can minimize the cost of meeting this month's requirements.
   b. Use SolverTable to see how much the "at least half" requirements are costing the company. Do this by changing *both* of these requirements from "at least half" to "at least x percent," where x can be any multiple of 5% from 0% to 50%.

APPENDIX **INFORMATION ON SOLVERS**

Microsoft Office (or Excel) ships with a built-in version of Solver. This version and all other versions of Solver have been developed by Frontline Systems, not Microsoft. When you install Office (or Excel), you have the option of installing or not installing Solver. In most cases, a "typical" install should install Solver. To check whether Solver is installed on your system, open Excel and select the Tools/Add-Ins menu item. If there is a Solver item in the list, then Solver has been installed. (To actually add it in, make sure this item is checked.) Otherwise, you need to run the Office Setup program with the Add/Remove feature to install Solver.

The built-in version of Solver is able to solve most problems you are likely to encounter. However, it does have one limitation you should be aware of. It allows only 200 changing cells. This might sound like plenty, but many real-world problems go well beyond 200 changing cells. If you want to solve larger problems, you will need to purchase one of Frontline's commercial versions of Solver.

Shelby Shelving is a small company that manufactures two types of shelves for grocery stores. Model S is the standard model, and model LX is a heavy-duty model. Shelves are manufactured in three major steps: stamping, forming, and assembly. In the stamping stage, a large machine is used to stamp, i.e., cut, standard sheets of metal into appropriate sizes. In the forming stage, another machine bends the metal into shape. Assembly involves joining the parts with a combination of soldering and riveting. Shelby's stamping and forming machines work on both models of shelves. Separate assembly departments are used for the final stage of production.

The file **Shelby.xls** contains relevant data for Shelby. (See Figure 3.38.) The hours required on each machine for each unit of product are shown in the range B5:C6 of the Accounting Data sheet. For example, the production of one model S shelf requires 0.25 hour on the forming machine. Both the stamping and forming machines can operate for 800 hours each month. The model S assembly department has a monthly capacity of 1900 units. The model LX assembly department has a monthly capacity of only 1400 units. Currently Shelby is producing and selling 400 units of model S and 1400 units of model LX per month.

Model S shelves are sold for $1800, and model LX shelves are sold for $2100. Shelby's operation is fairly small in the industry, and management at Shelby believes it cannot raise prices beyond these levels because of the competition. However, the marketing department feels that Shelby can sell as much as it can produce at these prices. The costs of production are summarized in the Accounting Data sheet. As usual, values in blue borders are given, whereas other values are calculated from these.

Management at Shelby just met to discuss next month's operating plan. Although the shelves are selling well, the overall profitability of the company is a concern. The plant's engineer suggested that the current production of model S shelves be cut back. According to him, "Model S shelves are sold for $1800 per unit, but our costs are $1839. Even though we're only selling 400 units a month, we're losing money on each one. We should decrease production of model S." The controller disagreed. He said that the problem was the model S assembly department trying to absorb a large overhead with a small production volume. "The model S units are making a contribution to overhead. Even though production doesn't cover all of the fixed costs, we'd be worse off with lower production."

Figure 3.38 Accounting Data for Shelby

A	B	C	D	E	F	G	H	I
1 Shelby Shelving Data for Current Production Schedule								
2								
3 Machine requirements (hours per unit)					Given monthly overhead cost data			
4	Model S	Model LX	Available			Fixed	Variable S	Variable LX
5 Stamping	0.3	0.3	800		Stamping	$125,000	$80	$90
6 Forming	0.25	0.5	800		Forming	$95,000	$120	$170
7					Model S Assembly	$80,000	$165	$0
8	Model S	Model LX			Model LX Assembly	$85,000	$0	$185
9 Current monthly production	400	1400						
10								
11 Hours spent in departments					Standard costs of the shelves -- based on the current production levels			
12	Model S	Model LX	Totals			Model S	Model LX	
13 Stamping	120	420	540		Direct materials	$1,000	$1,200	
14 Forming	100	700	800		Direct labor:			
15					Stamping	$35	$35	
16 Percentages of time spent in departments					Forming	$60	$90	
17	Model S	Model LX			Assembly	$80	$85	
18 Stamping	22.2%	77.8%			Total direct labor	$175	$210	
19 Forming	12.5%	87.5%			Overhead allocation			
20					Stamping	$149	$159	
21 Unit selling price	$1,800	$2,100			Forming	$150	$229	
22					Assembly	$365	$246	
23 Assembly capacity	1900	1400			Total overhead	$664	$635	
					Total cost	$1,839	$2,045	

Your job is to complete the formulation of an LP model on the LP sheet (of the **Shelby.xls** file), then run Solver, and finally make a recommendation to Shelby management, with a short verbal argument supporting the engineer or the controller.

Notes on Accounting Data Calculations

The fixed overhead is distributed using activity-based costing principles. For example, at current production levels, the forming machine spends 100 hours on model S shelves and 700 hours on model LX shelves. The forming machine is used 800 hours of the month, of which 12.5% of the time is spent on model S shelves and 87.5% is spent on model LX shelves. The $95,000 of fixed overhead in the forming department is distributed as $11,875 ($= 95,000 \times 0.125$) to model S shelves and $83,125 ($= 95,000 \times 0.875$) to model LX shelves. The fixed overhead per unit of output is allocated as $29.69 ($= 11,875/400$) for model S and $59.38 ($= 83,125/1400$) for model LX. In the calculation of the standard overhead cost, the fixed and variable costs are added together, so that the overhead cost for the forming department allocated to a model S shelf is $149.69 ($= 29.69 + 120$, shown rounded up to 150). Similarly, the overhead cost for the forming department allocated to a model LX shelf is $229.38 ($= 59.38 + 170$, shown rounded down to 229). ∎

After graduating from business school, George Clark went to work for a Big Six accounting firm in San Francisco. Since his hobby has always been wine making, when he had the opportunity a few years later he purchased 5 acres plus an option to buy 35 additional acres of land in Sonoma Valley in Northern California. He plans eventually to grow grapes on that land and make wine with them. George knows that this is a big undertaking and that it will require more capital than he has at the present. However, he figures that, if he persists, he will be able to leave accounting and live full-time from his winery earnings by the time he is 40.

Since wine making is capital-intensive and since growing commercial-quality grapes with a full yield of 5 tons per acre takes at least 8 years, George is planning to start small. This is necessitated by both his lack of capital and his inexperience in wine making on a large scale, although he has long made wine at home. His plan is first to plant the grapes on his land to get the vines started. Then he needs to set up a small trailer where he can live on weekends while he installs the irrigation system and does the required work to the vines, such as pruning and fertilizing. To help maintain a positive cash flow during the first few years, he also plans to buy grapes from other nearby growers so he can make his own label wine. He proposes to market it through a small tasting room that he will build on his land and keep open on weekends during the spring–summer season.

To begin, George is going to use $10,000 in savings to finance the initial purchase of grapes from which he will make his first batch of wine. He is also thinking about going to the Bank of Sonoma and asking for a loan. He knows that, if he goes to the bank, the loan officer will ask for a business plan; so he is trying to pull together some numbers for himself first. This way he will have a rough notion of the profitability and cash flows associated with his ideas before he develops a formal plan with a pro forma income statement and balance sheet. He has decided to make the preliminary planning horizon 2 years and would like to estimate the profit over that

period. His most immediate task is to decide how much of the $10,000 should be allocated to purchasing grapes for the first year and how much to purchasing grapes for the second year. In addition, each year he must decide how much he should allocate to purchasing grapes to make his favorite Petite Sirah and how much to purchasing grapes to make the more popular Sauvignon Blanc that seems to have been capturing the attention of a wider market during the last few years in California.

In the first year, each bottle of Petite Sirah requires $0.80 worth of grapes and each bottle of Sauvignon Blanc uses $0.70 worth of grapes. For the second year, the costs of the grapes per bottle are $0.75 and $0.85, respectively.

George anticipates that his Petite Sirah will sell for $8.00 a bottle in the first year and for $8.25 in the second year, while his Sauvignon Blanc's price remains the same in both years at $7.00 a bottle.

Besides the decisions about the amounts of grapes purchased in the 2 years, George must make estimates of the sales levels for the two wines during the 2 years. The local wine-making association has told him that marketing is the key to success in any wine business; generally, demand is directly proportional to the amount of effort spent on marketing. Thus, since George cannot afford to do any market research about sales levels due to his lack of capital, he is pondering how much money he should spend to promote each wine each year. The wine-making association has given him a rule of thumb that relates estimated demand to the amount of money spent on advertising. For instance, they estimate that, for each dollar spent in the first year promoting the Petite Sirah, a demand for five bottles will be created; and for each dollar spent in the second year, a demand for six bottles will result. Similarly, for each dollar spent on advertising for the Sauvignon Blanc in the first year, up to eight bottles can be sold; and for each dollar spent in the second year, up to ten bottles can be sold.

The initial funds for the advertising will come from the $10,000 savings. Assume that the cash earned from wine sales in the first year is available in the second year.

A personal concern George has is that he maintain a proper balance of wine products so that

[15]This case was written by William D. Whisler, California State University, Hayward.

he will be well positioned to expand his marketing capabilities when he moves to the winery and makes it his full-time job. Thus, in his mind it is important to ensure that the number of bottles of Petite Sirah sold each year falls in the range between 40% and 70% of the overall number of bottles sold.

Questions

1. George needs help to decide how many grapes to buy, how much money to spend on advertising, how many bottles of wine to sell, and how much profit he can expect to earn over the two-year period. Develop a spreadsheet LP model to help him.

2. Solve the linear programming model formulated in Question 1.

The following questions should be attempted only after Questions 1 and 2 have been answered correctly.

3. After showing the business plan to the Bank of Sonoma, George learns that the loan officer is concerned about the market prices used in estimating the profits; recently it has been forecasted that Chile and Australia will be flooding the market with high-quality, low-priced white wines over the next couple of years. In particular, the loan officer estimates that the price used for the Sauvignon Blanc in the second year is highly speculative and realistically might be only half the price George calculated. Thus, the bank is nervous about lending the money because of the big effect such a decrease in price might have on estimated profits. What do you think?

4. Another comment the loan officer of the Bank of Sonoma has after reviewing the business plan is: "I see that you do have an allowance in your calculations for the carryover of inventory of unsold wine from the first year to the second year, but you do not have any cost associated with this. All companies must charge something for holding inventory, so you should redo your plans to allow for this." If the holding charges are $0.10 per bottle per year, how much, if any, does George's plan change?

5. The president of the local grape growers' association mentions to George that there is likely to be

a strike soon over the unionization of the grape workers (currently they are not represented by any union). This means that the costs of the grapes might go up by anywhere from 50% to 100%. How might this affect George's plan?

6. Before taking his business plan to the bank, George had it reviewed by a colleague at the accounting firm where he works. Although his friend was excited about the plan and its prospects, he was dismayed to learn that George had not used present value in determining his profit. "George, you are an accountant and must know that money has a time value; and although you are only doing a 2-year planning problem, it still is important to calculate the present value profit." George replies, "Yes, I know all about present value. For big investments over long time periods, it is important to consider. But in this case, for a small investment and only a 2-year time period, it really doesn't matter." Who is correct, George or his colleague? Why? Use an 8% discount factor in answering this question. Does the answer change if a 6% or 10% discount rate is used? Use a spreadsheet to determine the coefficients of the objective function for the different discount rates.

7. Suppose that the Bank of Sonoma is so excited about the prospects of George's wine-growing business that they offer to lend him an extra $10,000 at their best small business rate—28% plus a 10% compensating balance.[16] Should he accept the bank's offer? Why or why not?

8. Suppose that the rule of thumb George was given by the local wine-making association is incorrect. Assume that the number of bottles of Petite Sirah sold in the first and second years is at most four for each dollar spent on advertising. And likewise for the Sauvignon Blanc, assume that it can be at most only five in years one and two.

9. How much could profits be increased if George's personal concerns (that Petite Sirah sales should account for between 40% and 70% of overall sales) are ignored? ■

---

[16]The compensating balance requirement means that only $9,000 of the $10,000 loan is available to George; the remaining $1,000 remains with the bank.

Linear Programming Models

© Digital Vision/Photodisc

GLASS MANUFACTURING AT LIBBEY-OWENS-FORD

As we saw in the previous chapter, linear programming (LP) can be used for product mix decisions and inventory planning. This was the case at Libbey-Owens-Ford (LOF), a large plate glass company with 9000 employees and annual sales of $900 million. In the article "Integrated Production, Distribution, and Inventory Planning at Libbey-Owens-Ford," Martin, Dent, and Eckhart (1993) describe the process of building and implementing a large-scale LP model of the plate glass production and distribution process at LOF. The model (named FLAGPOL for *FLAt Glass Products Optimization ModeL*) deals with four manufacturing plants, over 200 separate glass products, and over 40 demand centers in a 12-month planning horizon. The development of the model took over 2 years, but resulted in annual savings of over $2 million.

The production of plate glass is an involved manufacturing process. The glass is produced in large batches, each batch producing a certain color or tint of glass. The batches are large because the time required to change from one tint to another is very long (on the order of 2 to 4 days). Therefore, production occurs in cycles of approximately 10 months, and a particular tint is produced only once during a cycle. Given these long cycles, inventory planning is crucial. The production quantity of a particular tint in a cycle must be large enough to cover orders, both planned and forecasted, for a long period of time. Another complication is the cutting process. The glass is produced in long "ribbons" that can be cut to various dimensions. If the cuts are made during the production processing, yields tend to be higher than if they are made off-line, after processing. However, off-line cuts are sometimes necessary when orders arrive for nonstandard dimensions of glass.

The management at LOF decided that the complexity of the entire process necessitated a management science model. Therefore, the company appointed a task force to develop an LP model of the process. Since the task force included staff members from finance, marketing, MIS, materials management, transportation, production planning, and representatives from the plants, the scope of the resulting model became very broad. The first step was to develop the database that would support the model. This was a major undertaking since data were required on market demand and selling prices, freight rates, production rates and yields, manufacturing costs, inventory levels, and interplant rail schedules. Once these data were available, the FLAGPOL model was built, tested, and finally implemented. The implementation process itself took about 9 months. During this time, several changes to the original model were required. For example, the company realized that differences in the cost accounting systems of the various plants needed to be addressed. Also, the model's reports were redesigned to make them more useful and comprehensible to the eventual users.

Now that FLAGPOL is fully implemented, it is run 10 to 20 times each month for short-run tactical plans, as well as for longer-range strategic decisions. At the tactical level, the model recommends how much of each product to produce at each plant each month, how much of each product to ship between plants each month, how much of each product to cut off-line at each plant each month, and how much inventory of each product to hold at each plant each month. At the strategic level, FLAGPOL has been used to address such issues as (1) planning the transition from a two-plant operation to a four-plant operation, (2) introducing new products or eliminating existing products from plants, (3) developing schedules for major construction and plant maintenance, and (4) analyzing possible locations and sizing for new facilities. Management at LOF now considers FLAGPOL an integrated part of the company's planning process. It helps the company to reduce costs, increase profits, and enhance overall customer service. ■

4.1 INTRODUCTION

In a recent survey of Fortune 500 firms, 85% of those responding said that they used linear programming. In this chapter we will discuss some of the LP models that are most often applied to real-world applications. In the chapter's examples, you will discover how to build optimization models to

- purchase television ads
- schedule postal workers
- create an aggregate labor and production plan at a shoe company
- create a blending plan to transform crude oils into end products

- plan production of interdependent products at a drug company
- choose an investment strategy at a financial investment company
- manage a pension fund

There are two basic goals in this chapter. The first is to illustrate some of the many real applications that can take advantage of LP. You will see that these applications cover a wide range. The second goal is to increase your facility in modeling LP problems on a spreadsheet. We will present a few principles that will help you model a wide variety of problems. The best way to learn, however, is to see many examples and work through numerous problems. In short, mastering the art of LP spreadsheet modeling takes hard work and practice. You will have plenty of opportunity to do each with the material in this chapter.

Before continuing, we remind you that all of the models in this chapter are *linear* models, as described in the previous chapter. This means that the target cell is ultimately (possibly through a series of formulas in intervening cells) a sum of products of constants and changing cells, where a "constant" is defined by the fact that it does not depend on changing cells. Similarly, each side of each constraint is either a constant or a sum of products of constants and changing cells. Also, each changing cell (except in a few cases where we specify otherwise) is allowed to contain a continuous range of values, not just integer values. These properties allow us to check the Assume Linear Model option in Solver, which in turn allows Solver to use its very efficient simplex method to find the optimal solution.[1]

4.2 ADVERTISING MODELS

Many companies spend enormous amounts of money to advertise their products. They want to ensure that they are spending their money wisely. Typically, they want to reach large numbers of various groups of potential customers and keep their advertising costs as low as possible. The following example illustrates a simple model—and a reasonable extension of this model—for a company that purchases television ads.

EXAMPLE 4.1 PURCHASING TELEVISION ADS

The General Flakes Company sells a brand of low-fat breakfast cereal that appeals to people of all age groups and both genders. The company advertises this cereal in a variety of 30-second television ads, and these ads can be placed in a variety of television shows. The ads in different shows vary by cost—some 30-second slots are much more expensive than others—and by the types of viewers they are likely to reach. The company has segmented the potential viewers into six mutually exclusive categories: males age 18 to 35, males age 36 to 55, males over 55, females age 18 to 35, females age 36 to 55, and females over 55. A rating service can supply data on the numbers of viewers in each of these categories who will watch a 30-second ad on any particular television show. Each such viewer is called an *exposure*. The company has determined the required number of exposures it wants to obtain for each of the groups. It wants to know how many ads to place on each of several television shows to obtain these required exposures at minimum cost. The data on costs per ad, numbers of exposures per ad, and minimal required exposures are listed in Table 4.1 (page 118), where numbers of exposures are expressed in millions, and costs are in thousands of dollars. What should the company do?

This list is a small subset of shows from which a company could choose, but it is a good representation of the types of shows favored by various age groups and genders.

---

[1]In the special cases where we impose integer constraints on some changing cells, we can still check the Assume Linear Model box. However, Solver uses another algorithm, not the simplex method, to optimize when there are integer-constrained changing cells.

Table 4.1 Data for Advertising Problem

Viewer Group/TV Show	Friends	Monday Night Football	Malcolm in the Middle	Sports Center	TRL Live (MTV)	Lifetime Evening Movie	CNN	JAG	Minimal Required Exposures
Men 18–35	6	6	5	0.5	0.7	0.1	0.1	1	60
Men 36–55	3	5	2	0.5	0.2	0.1	0.2	2	60
Men >55	1	3	0	0.3	0	0	0.3	4	28
Women 18–35	9	1	4	0.1	0.9	0.6	0.1	1	60
Women 36–55	4	1	2	0.1	0.1	1.3	0.2	3	60
Women >55	2	1	0	0	0	0.4	0.3	4	28
Cost per Ad	160	100	80	9	13	15	8	85	

Objective   To develop an LP spreadsheet model that relates the numbers of ads on various television shows to the exposures to various viewer groups, and to use Solver to find the minimum cost advertising strategy that meets minimum exposure constraints.

WHERE DO THE NUMBERS COME FROM?

The data for this problem would probably be straightforward to obtain, as suggested here:

- The advertising costs per ad are the going rates for 30-second slots for the various types of shows.

- The exposures per ad on the various shows are typically supplied by the media planning departments of advertising agencies. (However, see the Modeling Issue at the end of this example.)

- The required numbers of exposures are probably determined internally by the company. Their marketing department knows whom they want to sell their cereal to, and they probably have some sense of the numbers of exposures they should obtain for their general level of advertising.

Solution

This problem is straightforward to model. As indicated in Table 4.2, we need to decide on the number of ads to place on each television show. This determines the total advertising cost, which we want to minimize, and the total number of exposures to each viewer group. The only constraint, other than nonnegativity, is that there must be at least the required number of exposures for each group.

Table 4.2 Variables and Constraints for Advertising Model

Input variables	Cost per ad, exposures per ad, minimal required exposures
Decision variables (changing cells)	Numbers of ads to place on various types of shows
Objective (target cell)	Total advertising cost
Other calculated variables	Total exposures to each viewer group
Constraints	Actual exposures ≥ Required exposures

Comparison to Product Mix Model

Before continuing, it is worth noting that this model is essentially the opposite of the product mix model in the previous chapter. There we tried to make the values of the decision variables (numbers of frames to produce) as large as possible so as to make a large profit. The constraints on resource availability restricted us from making these values as large as we would like. In contrast, we now want to make the values of the decision variables as *small* as possible so as to minimize cost. This time, the constraints on required exposures prevent us from making these values as *small* as we would like. These two prototype LP models—maximizing profit subject to "less than or equal to" constraints, and minimizing cost subject to "greater than or equal to" constraints—are certainly not the only types of LP models that exist, but they are very common.

DEVELOPING THE SPREADSHEET MODEL

The spreadsheet model for the advertising problem appears in Figure 4.1.[2] (See the file **Advertising1.xls**.) It can be created with the following steps.

Figure 4.1 Optimal Solution for Advertising Model

Note: All monetary values are in $1000s, and all exposures to ads are in millions of exposures.

	A	B	C	D	E	F	G	H	I
1	Advertising model								
2									
3	Inputs								
4	Exposures to various groups per ad								
5		Friends	MNF	Malcolm in Middle	Sports Center	TRL Live	Lifetime movie	CNN	JAG
6	Men 18-35	6	6	5	0.5	0.7	0.1	0.1	1
7	Men 36-55	3	5	2	0.5	0.2	0.1	0.2	2
8	Men >55	1	3	0	0.3	0	0	0.3	4
9	Women 18-35	9	1	4	0.1	0.9	0.6	0.1	1
10	Women 36-55	4	1	2	0.1	0.1	1.3	0.2	3
11	Women >55	2	1	0	0	0	0.4	0.3	4
12	Total viewers	25	17	13	1.5	1.9	2.5	1.2	15
13									
14	Cost per ad	160	100	80	9	13	15	8	85
15	Cost per million exposures	6.400	5.882	6.154	6.000	6.842	6.000	6.667	5.667
16									
17	Advertising plan								
18		Friends	MNF	Malcolm in Middle	Sports Center	TRL Live	Lifetime movie	CNN	JAG
19	Number ads purchased	4.070	0.000	0.000	79.888	0.000	20.837	0.000	2.881
20									
21	Constraints on numbers of exposures								
22		Actual exposures		Required exposures			Range names used:		
23	Men 18-35	69.328	>=	60			Actual_exposures	=Model!$B$23:$B$28	
24	Men 36-55	60.000	>=	60			Number_ads_purchased	=Model!$B$19:$I$19	
25	Men >55	39.562	>=	28			Required_exposures	=Model!$D$23:$D$28	
26	Women 18-35	60.000	>=	60			Total_cost	=Model!$B$31	
27	Women 36-55	60.000	>=	60					
28	Women >55	28.000	>=	28					
29									
30	Objective to minimize								
31	Total cost	$1,927.629							

---

1 **Input values and range names.** Enter the inputs from Table 4.1 in the shaded ranges, and name the ranges as shown.

→ **EXCEL TIP: *Range Name Shortcut***
We've said it before, but we'll say it once again. Whenever possible, use "nice" labels such as in cells A19 and B22. Then you can take advantage of these labels, along with the Insert/Name/Create shortcut, to name as many desired ranges as possible. In fact, we usually try to highlight several ranges, so that we can create several range names at once, and then use the Alt-i, n, c keystroke sequence to select the Insert/Name/Create menu item. Try it out. It can be a real time saver over "manual" range naming. ■

2 **Ads purchased.** Enter *any* values in the Number_ads_purchased range. These are the only changing cells for this model.

---

[2]From here on, to save space we will typically show only the *optimal* solution. However, remember that when you develop a spreadsheet optimization model, you can enter *any* values in the changing cells initially. Solver will eventually find the optimal solution.

③ Exposures obtained. The numbers of ads purchased determine the numbers of exposures to the various viewer groups. To calculate these exposures, enter the formula

=SUMPRODUCT(B6:I6,Number_ads_purchased)

in cell B23 and copy it down to cell B28.

④ Total cost. The numbers of ads purchased also determine the total cost of advertising. Calculate this cost in cell B31 with the formula

=SUMPRODUCT(B14:I14,Number_ads_purchased)

USING SOLVER

The main Solver dialog box appears in Figure 4.2. After filling it out as shown and checking the usual Assume Linear Model and Assume Non-Negative options, click on the Solve button to obtain the solution in Figure 4.1.

Figure 4.2

Solver Dialog Box for Advertising Model

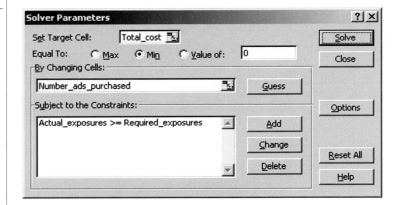

Discussion of the Solution

The optimal solution is probably not the one you would have guessed. With a set of ads that cost very different amounts and reach very different mixes of viewers, it is difficult to guess the optimal strategy. For comparison, however, we calculated the total number of viewers from each type of ad in row 12, and we divided the costs in row 14 by the numbers of viewers in row 12 to obtain the costs per million viewers in row 15. You might expect the ads with low costs per million viewers to be chosen most frequently. However, this is not necessarily the case. For example, Monday Night Football (MNF) has the second-lowest cost per million viewers, but the optimal solution includes no ads for this show.

Sensitivity Analysis

Solver's sensitivity report, shown in Figure 4.3, is enlightening for this solution. Here is a sample of the information it provides.

Figure 4.3 Sensitivity Report for Advertising Model

	A	B	C	D	E	F	G	H
1		Microsoft Excel 10.0 Sensitivity Report						
2		Worksheet: [Advertising1.xls]Model						
3		Report Created: 1/7/2003 1:13:54 PM						
4								
5								
6		Adjustable Cells						
7				Final	Reduced	Objective	Allowable	Allowable
8		Cell	Name	Value	Cost	Coefficient	Increase	Decrease
9		$B$19	Number ads purchased Friends	4.070	0.000	160	11.11702128	64.41176471
10		$C$19	Number ads purchased MNF	0.000	1.377	100	1E+30	1.377266388
11		$D$19	Number ads purchased Malcolm in Middle	0.000	5.467	80	1E+30	5.467224547
12		$E$19	Number ads purchased Sports Center	79.888	0.000	9	0.157245223	6.716216216
13		$F$19	Number ads purchased TRL Live	0.000	1.312	13	1E+30	1.311715481
14		$G$19	Number ads purchased Lifetime movie	20.837	0.000	15	7.259259259	1.994949495
15		$H$19	Number ads purchased CNN	0.000	0.709	8	1E+30	0.708856346
16		$I$19	Number ads purchased JAG	2.881	0.000	85	4.498861048	20
17								
18		Constraints						
19				Final	Shadow	Constraint	Allowable	Allowable
20		Cell	Name	Value	Price	R.H. Side	Increase	Decrease
21		$B$23	Men 18-35 Actual exposures	69.328	0.000	60	9.327754533	1E+30
22		$B$24	Men 36-55 Actual exposures	60.000	15.474	60	124.5	9.982089552
23		$B$25	Men >55 Actual exposures	39.562	0.000	28	11.56206416	1E+30
24		$B$26	Women 18-35 Actual exposures	60.000	9.163	60	54.18300654	19.9047619
25		$B$27	Women 36-55 Actual exposures	60.000	3.466	60	37.56363636	18.44444444
26		$B$28	Women >55 Actual exposures	28.000	8.623	28	30.18181818	9.412300683

- The company is not currently purchasing any ads on Malcolm in the Middle. The reduced cost for this show implies that the cost per ad would have to decrease by at least 5.467 ($5467) before it would be optimal to purchase any ads on this show.

- The company is currently purchasing almost 80 ads on Sports Center. The allowable increase and decrease for this show indicate how much the cost per ad would have to change before the optimal number of ads on the show would change. For example, if the price per ad increased above 9 + 0.157 ($9157), the company would purchase fewer than 80 ads. How many fewer? We would need to rerun Solver to know.

- The constraint on exposures to men in the 36–55 age range has the largest shadow price, 15.474. If the company relaxed this constraint to require only 59 million exposures, it would save $15,474 in total advertising cost. On the other side, if the company required 61 million exposures to this group, rather than 60 million, its cost would increase by $15,474.

A Dual-Objective Extension of the Model

We refer to this as a dual-objective optimization model. Typically, the two objectives are pulling in different directions, as they are here.

This advertising model can be extended in a very natural way. General Flakes really has two competing objectives: (1) obtain as many exposures as possible, and (2) keep the total advertising cost as low as possible. In the original model we decided to minimize total cost and constrain the exposures to be at least as large as a required level. An alternative is to maximize the total number of excess exposures and put a budget constraint on total cost. Here, "excess exposures" are those above the minimal required level.

To implement this alternative, only minor modifications to the original model are necessary, as shown in Figure 4.4 (page 122). (See the file **Advertising2.xls**.) We did this with the following steps.

Figure 4.4   Spreadsheet Model for Extension to Advertising Problem

	A	B	C	D	E	F	G	H	I	J
1	Two-objective advertising model									
2				Note: All monetary values are in $1000s, and all						
3	Inputs			exposures to ads are in millions of exposures.						
4	Exposures to various groups per ad									
5		Friends	MNF	Malcolm in Middle	Sports Center	TRL Live	Lifetime movie	CNN	JAG	
6	Men 18-35	6	6	5	0.5	0.7	0.1	0.1	1	
7	Men 36-55	3	5	2	0.5	0.2	0.1	0.2	2	
8	Men >55	1	3	0	0.3	0	0	0.3	4	
9	Women 18-35	9	1	4	0.1	0.9	0.6	0.1	1	
10	Women 36-55	4	1	2	0.1	0.1	1.3	0.2	3	
11	Women >55	2	1	0	0	0	0.4	0.3	4	
12	Total viewers	25	17	13	1.5	1.9	2.5	1.2	15	
13										
14	Cost per ad	160	100	80	9	13	15	8	85	
15	Cost per million exposures	6.400	5.882	6.154	6.000	6.842	6.000	6.667	5.667	
16										
17	Advertising plan									
18		Friends	MNF	Malcolm in Middle	Sports Center	TRL Live	Lifetime movie	CNN	JAG	
19	Number ads purchased	0.000	6.047	9.953	0.000	0.000	16.744	0.000	4.093	
20										
21	Constraints on numbers of exposures									
22		Actual exposures		Required exposures		Excess exposures		Range names used:		
23	Men 18-35	91.814	>=	60		31.814		Actual_exposures	=Model!$B$23:$B$28	
24	Men 36-55	60.000	>=	60		0.000		Budget	=Model!$D$32	
25	Men >55	34.512	>=	28		6.512		Excess_exposures	=Model!$F$23:$F$28	
26	Women 18-35	60.000	>=	60		0.000		Number_ads_purchased	=Model!$B$19:$I$19	
27	Women 36-55	60.000	>=	60		0.000		Required_exposures	=Model!$D$23:$D$28	
28	Women >55	29.116	>=	28		1.116		Total_cost	=Model!$B$32	
29								Total_excess_exposures	=Model!$B$35	
30	Budget constrain on total cost									
31		Total cost		Budget						
32		$2,000	<=	$2,000						
33										
34	Objective to maximize									
35	Total excess exposures	39.442								

① Excess exposures. For each viewer group, calculate the number of excess exposures by entering the formula

=B23-D23

in cell F23 and copying it down. Then sum these in cell B35 with the SUM function. This cell becomes the new target cell to maximize.

② Budget constraint. Calculate the total cost exactly as before, but now constrain it to be less than or equal to a given budget in cell D32.

③ Solver Dialog Box. Modify the Solver dialog box as shown in Figure 4.5.

Figure 4.5
Modified Solver
Dialog Box for
Extension to
Advertising Problem

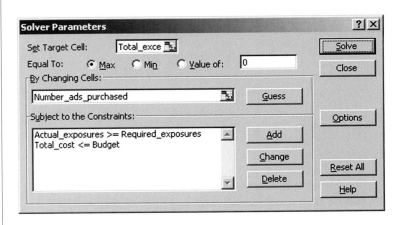

At this point, you are probably wondering where the budget of $2 million in Figure 4.4 comes from. This requires some explanation of our solution strategy in this extension of the original model. Our basic assumption is that the company has two objectives: It wants to maximize total excess exposures *and* minimize total cost. Unfortunately, it is impossible to do both of these because they are pulling in different directions. Whenever we have a multiple-objective problem such as this, we typically use one of the objectives as the target cell and constrain the other(s). Here, we are asking how many excess exposures we can get for a given budget. There is no natural budget to use, and it makes perfect sense to ask questions such as these: How many exposures can we get for $1.9 million? How many can we get for $2.0 million? How many can we get for $2.1 million?

For two-objective models, we optimize one objective and put a constraint on the other. Then we can use SolverTable to vary the right-hand side of this constraint. The result is a "trade-off curve."

Fortunately, SolverTable is the precise tool we need to answer all of these questions in one step. We develop the model as in Figure 4.4, using *any* budget such as $2.0 million in cell D32, and we use Solver in the usual way. Then we run a one-way SolverTable, allowing the budget to vary over some desired range and keeping track of selected output variables. Typical results appear in Figure 4.6, which are based on the SolverTable settings in Figure 4.7. We see that for low budget levels, the problem is infeasible—there is no way with this budget to obtain the minimal required exposures. Above a certain budget level, the problem becomes feasible, and the optimal solutions are shown. As the budget increases, the company can clearly obtain larger numbers of excess exposures, but the optimal advertising strategy in columns B–I changes in a fairly unpredictable way.

Figure 4.6 Sensitivity of Optimal Solution to Advertising Budget

	Friends	MNF	Malcolm in Middle	Sports Center	TRL Live	Lifetime movie	CNN	JAG	Total excess exposures
	$B$19	$C$19	$D$19	$E$19	$F$19	$G$19	$H$19	$I$19	$B$35
1800	Not feasible								
1850	Not feasible								
1900	Not feasible								
1950	2.449	0.000	4.092	69.388	0.000	17.755	0.000	4.000	26.888
2000	0.000	6.047	9.953	0.000	0.000	16.744	0.000	4.093	39.442
2050	0.000	5.116	10.384	0.000	0.000	11.860	0.000	6.233	49.105
2100	0.000	4.186	10.814	0.000	0.000	6.977	0.000	8.372	58.767
2150	0.000	3.256	11.244	0.000	0.000	2.093	0.000	10.512	68.430
2200	0.000	2.609	11.304	0.000	0.000	0.000	0.000	12.174	77.913
2250	0.000	2.174	11.087	0.000	0.000	0.000	0.000	13.478	87.261
2300	0.000	1.739	10.870	0.000	0.000	0.000	0.000	14.783	96.609
2350	0.000	1.304	10.652	0.000	0.000	0.000	0.000	16.087	105.957
2400	0.000	0.870	10.435	0.000	0.000	0.000	0.000	17.391	115.304
2450	0.000	0.435	10.217	0.000	0.000	0.000	0.000	18.696	124.652
2500	0.000	0.000	10.000	0.000	0.000	0.000	0.000	20.000	134.000

Figure 4.7

SolverTable Settings for Sensitivity Analysis

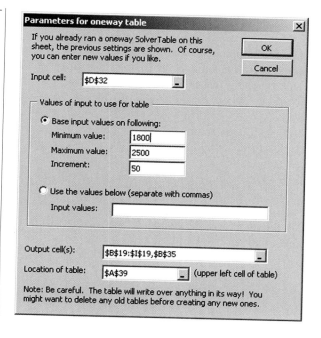

Parameters for oneway table

If you already ran a oneway SolverTable on this sheet, the previous settings are shown. Of course, you can enter new values if you like.

OK

Cancel

Input cell: $D$32

Values of input to use for table

● Base input values on following:

Minimum value: 1800

Maximum value: 2500

Increment: 50

○ Use the values below (separate with commas)

Input values:

Output cell(s): $B$19:$I$19,$B$35

Location of table: $A$39 (upper left cell of table)

Note: Be careful. The table will write over anything in its way! You might want to delete any old tables before creating any new ones.

The results of this sensitivity analysis can be shown graphically in a "trade-off curve," as in Figure 4.8. To create this, we highlight the numbers in columns A and J of Figure 4.6 (from row 43 down) and use the Chart Wizard to create an X-Y chart of the type with the "dots connected." This chart illustrates the rather obvious fact that when the company is allowed to spend more on advertising, it can obtain more total excess exposures.

Figure 4.8

Trade-Off Curve
Between Total
Excess Exposures
and Total Cost

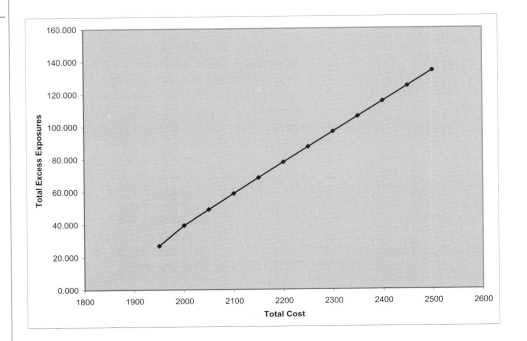

Using Integer Constraints

The two advertising models to this point have allowed noninteger values in the changing cells. In reality, this is not allowed; the company cannot purchase, say, 4.07 ads on Friends. It must purchase integer numbers of ads. Given this, your first instinct is probably to round the optimal values in the changing cells to the nearest integers to obtain the optimal integer solution. Unfortunately, this can have unpredictable results. First, the rounded solution might not be feasible. Second, even if it is feasible, it might not be the *optimal* integer solution.

Use the "int" option in the Solver constraint dialog box to constrain changing cells to be integers.

Although we will spend an entire chapter (Chapter 6) on special types of *integer programming models*—those with integer constraints on at least some of the changing cells—we can preview the topic here. In fact, from a user's standpoint, there isn't much to it. To force the changing cells to have integer values, you simply add another constraint in the Solver dialog box, as shown in Figure 4.9. In the left text box, select the changing cell range. In the middle text box, select "int" (for integer). The right text box is then essentially irrelevant; it automatically contains the word Integer. When you eventually click on Solve, you get the optimal integer solution shown in Figure 4.10.

Figure 4.9

Specifying an Integer Constraint

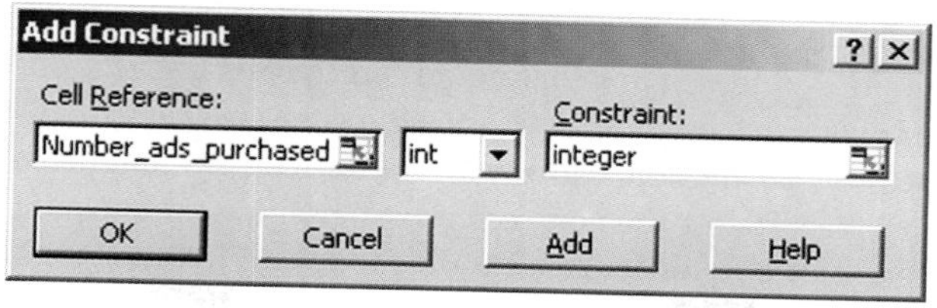

Figure 4.10 Optimal Integer Solution to Advertising Problem

Note: All monetary values are in $1000s, and all exposures to ads are in millions of exposures.

	A	B	C	D	E	F	G	H	I
1	Advertising model								
2									
3	Inputs								
4	Exposures to various groups per ad								
5		Friends	MNF	Malcolm in Middle	Sports Center	TRL Live	Lifetime movie	CNN	JAG
6	Men 18-35	6	6	5	0.5	0.7	0.1	0.1	1
7	Men 36-55	3	5	2	0.5	0.2	0.1	0.2	2
8	Men >55	1	3	0	0.3	0	0	0.3	4
9	Women 18-35	9	1	4	0.1	0.9	0.6	0.1	1
10	Women 36-55	4	1	2	0.1	0.1	1.3	0.2	3
11	Women >55	2	1	0	0	0	0.4	0.3	4
12	Total viewers	25	17	13	1.5	1.9	2.5	1.2	15
13									
14	Cost per ad	160	100	80	9	13	15	8	85
15	Cost per million exposures	6.400	5.882	6.154	6.000	6.842	6.000	6.667	5.667
16									
17	Advertising plan								
18		Friends	MNF	Malcolm in Middle	Sports Center	TRL Live	Lifetime movie	CNN	JAG
19	Number ads purchased	4	3	0	53	0	23	1	2
20									
21	Constraints on numbers of exposures								
22		Actual exposures		Required exposures			Range names used:		
23	Men 18-35	72.900	>=	60			Actual_exposures	=Model!$B$23:$B$28	
24	Men 36-55	60.000	>=	60			Number_ads_purchased	=Model!$B$19:$I$19	
25	Men >55	37.200	>=	28			Required_exposures	=Model!$D$23:$D$28	
26	Women 18-35	60.200	>=	60			Total_cost	=Model!$B$31	
27	Women 36-55	60.400	>=	60					
28	Women >55	28.500	>=	28					
29									
30	Objective to minimize								
31	Total cost	$1,940.000							

We make the following three comments about this integer solution.

- The total cost in the target cell is now worse (larger) than before. This illustrates the general rule that when *any* additional constraints are imposed, including integer constraints, the objective can only get worse or remain the same; it can never get better.

- The optimal integer solution is *not* the rounded noninteger solution. In fact, it isn't even close. (Compare the before and after MNF and Sports Center values, for example.) As we said, rounding noninteger solutions sometimes works, and sometimes it doesn't. It is always safer to use Solver with explicit integer constraints.

It is easy to specify integer constraints in the Solver dialog box. Be aware, however, that Solver must typically do a lot more work to solve problems with integer constraints.

- You should be aware that when there are integer constraints, Solver uses an algorithm that is significantly different from the simplex method. (It is called *branch and bound*.) Integer-constrained models are typically *much* harder to solve than models without any integer constraints. Although this small model still solves in a fraction of a second, larger integer models can take *minutes* or even *hours* of solution time.

MODELING ISSUES

There is one glaring weakness in our advertising model, at least for realistic applications. Perhaps you have spotted it. This is the problem of double-counting. Suppose a company runs 3 ads for the same product on a Monday Night Football telecast. Also, let's suppose that the rating service claims that an ad will reach, say, 6 million men age 18–35. How many *total* exposures do these 3 ads reach for this viewer group? Our model claims that it reaches 3(6) = 18 million. However, the "effective" number of exposures is probably much lower than 18, for the simple reason that the *same* men are watching all 3 ads.

Unfortunately, most marketing models, including this one, are inherently nonlinear.

This presents two difficulties for the modeler. First, it is probably quite difficult to estimate the effective number of exposures to any viewer group when an ad is run multiple times on the same show. Second, even if a company can obtain such estimates, it faces a nonlinear model, as discussed in Chapter 7. This is because the proportionality assumption of LP no longer holds. Specifically, each extra ad on a given show reaches a decreasing number of "new" exposures. We will revisit this model in Chapter 7. ∎

PROBLEMS

Solutions for problems whose numbers appear within a color box can be found in the Student Solutions Manual. Order your copy today at http://e-catalog.thomsonlearning.com/110/ by using ISBN 0-534-39687-9.

Skill-Building Problems

1. Suppose, as a matter of corporate policy, that General Flakes decides not to advertise on the Lifetime channel. Modify the original advertising model appropriately and find the new optimal solution. How much has it cost the company to make this policy decision?

2. In addition to the constraints already in the (original) advertising model, suppose General Flakes also wants to obtain at least 180 million exposures to men and at least 160 million exposures to women. Does the current optimal solution satisfy these constraints? If not, modify the model as necessary, and rerun Solver to find the new optimal solution.

3. Suppose, in addition to the shows already listed, General Flakes wants to open the possibility of purchasing ads on the "Good Morning America" show on ABC. Make up any reasonable input data you need to include this possibility in the (original) model, and find the optimal solution.

4. Suppose that General Flakes decides that it shouldn't place any more than 10 ads on any given show. Mod-

ify the (original) advertising model appropriately to incorporate this constraint, and then reoptimize (with integer constraints on the numbers of ads). Finally, run SolverTable to see how sensitive the optimal solution is to the maximum number of ads per show allowed. You can decide on a reasonable range for the sensitivity analysis.

Skill-Extending Problems

5. In the two-objective advertising model, we put a budget constraint on the total advertising cost and then maximized the total number of excess exposures. Do it the opposite way, reversing the roles of the two objectives. That is, model it so that you put a lower limit on the total number of excess exposures and minimize the total advertising cost. Then run a sensitivity analysis on this lower limit, and create a trade-off curve from the results of the sensitivity analysis.

6. Suppose we consider *three* objectives, not just two: the total advertising cost, the total number of excess exposures to men, and the total number of excess exposures to women. Continuing the approach suggested in the previous problem, how might you proceed? Take it as far as you can, including a sensitivity analysis and a trade-off curve.

4.3 STATIC WORKFORCE SCHEDULING MODELS

Many organizations must determine how to schedule employees to provide adequate service. The following example illustrates how LP can be used to schedule employees.

4.2 POSTAL EMPLOYEE SCHEDULING

A post office requires different numbers of full-time employees on different days of the week. The number of full-time employees required each day is given in Table 4.3. Union rules state that each full-time employee must work 5 consecutive days and then receive 2 days off. For example, an employee who works Monday to Friday must be off on Saturday and Sunday. The post office wants to meet its daily requirements using only full-time employees. Its objective is to minimize the number of full-time employees that must be hired.

Table 4.3   Employee Requirements for Post Office

Day of Week	Minimum Number of Employees Required
Monday	17
Tuesday	13
Wednesday	15
Thursday	19
Friday	14
Saturday	16
Sunday	11

Objective   To develop an LP spreadsheet model that relates 5-day shift schedules to daily numbers of employees available, and to use Solver on this model to find a schedule that uses the fewest number of employees and meets all daily workforce requirements.

In real employee scheduling problems much of the work involves forecasting and queueing analysis to obtain worker requirements. This must be done before any schedule optimizing can be accomplished.

WHERE DO THE NUMBERS COME FROM?

The only inputs we need for this problem are the minimum employee requirements in Table 4.3, but these are not necessarily easy to obtain. They would probably be obtained through a combination of two quantitative techniques we will discuss in later chapters: forecasting (Chapter 12) and queueing analysis (Chapter 11). The postal office would first use historical data to forecast customer and mail arrival patterns throughout a typical week. It would then use queueing analysis to translate these arrival patterns into worker requirements on a daily basis. Actually, we have kept the problem relatively simple by considering only *daily* requirements. In a realistic setting, the organization might forecast worker requirements on an hourly or even a 15-minute basis.

Solution

The variables and constraints for this problem appear in Table 4.4. The trickiest part is identifying the appropriate decision variables. Many people believe the decision variables should be the numbers of employees working on the various days of the week. Clearly, we need to know these values. However, it is not enough to specify, say, that 18 employees are working on Monday. The problem is that we don't know when these 18 employees start their 5-day shifts. Without this knowledge, it is impossible to implement the 5-consecutive-day, 2-day-off requirement. (If you don't believe this, try developing your own model with the "wrong" decision variables. You will eventually reach a dead end.)

The key to this model is choosing the correct changing cells.

   The trick is to define the decision variables as the numbers of employees working each of the 7 possible 5-day shifts. For example, we need to know the number of employees who work Monday through Friday. By knowing the values of these decision variables, we can calculate the other output variables we need. For example, the number working on

Thursday is the total of those who begin their 5-day shifts on Sunday, Monday, Tuesday, Wednesday, and Thursday.

Table 4.4 **Variables and Constraints for Postal Scheduling Problem**

Input variables	Minimum required number of workers each day
Decision variables (changing cells)	Number of employees working each of the 5-day shifts (defined by their first day of work)
Objective (target cell)	Total number of employees on the payroll
Other calculated variables	Number of employees working each day
Constraints	Employees working $\geq$ Employees required

Note that this is a "wrap-around" problem. We assume that the daily requirements in Table 4.3 and the worker schedules continue week after week. So, for example, if we find that 8 employees are assigned to the Thursday–Monday shift, then these employees always wrap around from one week to the next on their 5-day shift.

DEVELOPING THE SPREADSHEET MODEL

The spreadsheet model for this problem is shown in Figure 4.11. (See the file **Worker-Scheduling.xls**.) To form this spreadsheet, proceed as follows.

Figure 4.11   Postal Scheduling Model with Optimal Solution

	A	B	C	D	E	F	G	H	I	J	K	L
1	Post Office scheduling model											
2										Range names used:		
3	Decision variables: number of employees starting their five-day shift on various days									Employees_available	=Model!$B$23:$H$23	
4	Mon	6.33								Employees_required	=Model!$B$25:$H$25	
5	Tue	5.00								Employees_starting	=Model!$B$4:$B$10	
6	Wed	0.33								Total_employees	=Model!$B$28	
7	Thu	7.33										
8	Fri	0.00										
9	Sat	3.33										
10	Sun	0.00										
11												
12	Result of decisions: number of employees working on various days (along top) who started their shift on various days (along side)											
13		Mon	Tue	Wed	Thu	Fri	Sat	Sun				
14	Mon	6.33	6.33	6.33	6.33	6.33						
15	Tue		5.00	5.00	5.00	5.00	5.00					
16	Wed			0.33	0.33	0.33	0.33	0.33				
17	Thu	7.33			7.33	7.33	7.33	7.33				
18	Fri	0.00	0.00			0.00	0.00	0.00				
19	Sat	3.33	3.33	3.33			3.33	3.33				
20	Sun	0.00	0.00	0.00	0.00			0.00				
21												
22	Constraint on worker availabilities											
23	Employees available	17.00	14.67	15.00	19.00	19.00	16.00	11.00				
24		>=	>=	>=	>=	>=	>=	>=				
25	Employees required	17	13	15	19	14	16	11				
26												
27	Objective to maximize											
28	Total employees	22.33										

---

① Inputs and range names. Enter the number of employees needed on each day of the week (from Table 4.3) in the shaded range, and create the range names shown.

② Employees beginning each day. Enter *any* trial values for the number of employees beginning work on each day of the week in the Employees_starting range. These beginning days determine the possible 5-day shifts. For example, the employees in cell B4 work Monday through Friday.

③ Employees on hand each day. The key to this solution is to realize that the numbers in the Employees_starting range—the changing cells—do not represent the number of workers who will show up each day. As an example, the number in B4 who start on Monday work Monday–Friday. Therefore, enter the formula

=$B$4

in cell B14 and copy it across to cell F14. Proceed similarly for rows 15–20, being careful to take "wrap arounds" into account. For example, the workers starting on Thursday work Thursday–Sunday, plus Monday. Then calculate the total number who show up on each day by entering the formula

=SUM(B14:B20)

in cell B23 and copying it across to cell H23.

→ EXCEL TIP: *Ctrl-Enter Shortcut*

*We've mentioned this before, but we'll mention it again. You will enter a "typical" formula into a cell and then copy it many times throughout this book. To do this efficiently, highlight the entire range, here B23:H23. Then enter the typical formula, here =**SUM(B14:B20)**, and press **Ctrl-Enter**. This has the same effect as copying, but it is quicker.* ■

④ Total employees. Calculate the total number of employees in cell B28 with the formula

=SUM(Employees_starting)

Note that there is no double-counting in this sum. For example, the employees in cells B4 and B5 are *not* the same people.

At this point, you might want to try experimenting with the numbers in the changing cell range to see whether you can "guess" an optimal solution (without looking at Figure 4.11). It is not that easy! Each worker who starts on a given day works the next 4 days as well, so when you find a solution that meets the minimal requirements for the various days, you usually have a few more workers available on some days than are needed.

USING SOLVER

Invoke Solver and fill out its main dialog box as shown in Figure 4.12. Also, check the Assume Linear Model and Assume Non-Negativity options in the Options dialog box.

Figure 4.12

Solver Dialog Box for Postal Model

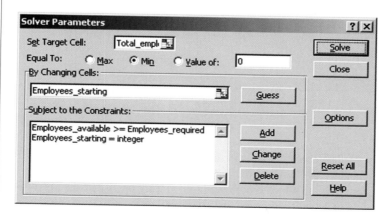

Discussion of the Solution

The optimal solution shown in Figure 4.11 has one drawback: It requires the number of employees starting work on some days to be a fraction. Because part-time employees are not allowed, this solution is unrealistic. However, as we discussed in Example 4.1, it is simple to add integer constraints on the changing cells. We fill in a new constraint as shown in Figure 4.13 and then reoptimize. This produces the optimal integer solution shown in Figure 4.14.

Figure 4.13

Solver Dialog Box with Integer Constraint

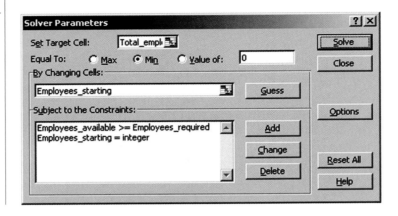

Figure 4.14 Optimal Integer Solution to Postal Scheduling Model

	A	B	C	D	E	F	G	H	I	J	K	L
1	Post Office scheduling model											
2												
3	Decision variables: number of employees starting their five-day shift on various days									Range names used:		
4	Mon	6								Employees_available	=Model!$B$23:$H$23	
5	Tue	6								Employees_required	=Model!$B$25:$H$25	
6	Wed	0								Employees_starting	=Model!$B$4:$B$10	
7	Thu	7								Total_employees	=Model!$B$28	
8	Fri	0										
9	Sat	4										
10	Sun	0										
11												
12	Result of decisions: number of employees working on various days (along top) who started their shift on various days (along side)											
13		Mon	Tue	Wed	Thu	Fri	Sat	Sun				
14	Mon	6	6	6	6	6						
15	Tue		6	6	6	6	6					
16	Wed			0	0	0	0	0				
17	Thu	7			7	7	7	7				
18	Fri	0	0			0	0	0				
19	Sat	4	4	4			4	4				
20	Sun	0	0	0	0			0				
21												
22	Constraint on worker availabilities											
23	Employees available	17	16	16	19	19	17	11				
24		>=	>=	>=	>=	>=	>=	>=				
25	Employees required	17	13	15	19	14	16	11				
26												
27	Objective to maximize											
28	Total employees	23										

The changing cells in the optimal solution indicate the numbers of workers who start their 5-day shifts on the various days. We can then look at the *columns* of the B14:H20 range to see which employees are working on any given day. This optimal solution is typical in scheduling problems. Due to a labor constraint—each employee must work 5 consecutive days and then have 2 days off—it is typically impossible to meet the minimum employee requirements exactly. To ensure that there are enough employees available on busy days, it is often necessary to have more than enough on hand on light days.

Another interesting aspect of this problem is that if you solve this problem on your own PC, you might get a *different* schedule that is still optimal—that is, it still uses a total of 23 employees and meets all constraints. This is a case of **multiple optimal solutions** and is not at all uncommon in LP problems. In fact, it is typically good news for a manager, who can then choose among the optimal solutions using other, possibly nonquantitative criteria.[3]

Multiple optimal solutions have different values in the changing cells, but they all have the same objective value.

Technical Note: Solver Tolerance Setting

Set Solver's Tolerance to 0 to ensure that you get the optimal integer solution. Be aware, however, that this can incur significant extra computing time for larger models.

One technical comment about integer constraints concerns Solver's **Tolerance** setting. The idea is as follows. As Solver searches for the best integer solution, it is often able to find a "good" solution fairly quickly, but it often has to spend a lot of time finding slightly better solutions. A *nonzero* tolerance setting allows it to quit early. The default tolerance setting is 0.05. This means that if Solver finds a feasible solution that is guaranteed to have an objective value no more than 5% from the optimal value, it will quit and report this "good" solution (which might even be the *optimal* solution). Therefore, if you keep this default tolerance value, your integer solutions will sometimes not be optimal, but they will be close. If you want to ensure that you get an optimal solution, you can change the Solver tolerance value to 0. (For the standard Solver that accompanies Excel, this setting is directly under the Solver Options. If you happen to use the Premium Solver, you can find the setting by clicking on the Solver Options button, then on the Integer Options button.)

Sensitivity Analysis

To run some sensitivity analyses with SolverTable, you need to modify the original model slightly to incorporate the effect of the input being varied.

The most obvious type of sensitivity analysis involves examining how the work schedule and the total number of employees change as the number of employees required each day changes. Suppose the number of employees needed on each day of the week increases by 2, 4, or 6. How does this change the total number of employees needed? We can answer this by using SolverTable, but we first have to alter the model slightly, as shown in Figure 4.15 (page 132). The problem is that we want to increase *each* of the daily minimal required values by the same amount. Therefore, we move the original requirements up to row 12, enter a trial value for the extra number required per day in cell K12, enter the formula **=B12+$K$12** in cell B27, and then copy this formula across to cell H27. Now we can use the one-way SolverTable option, using the Extra cell as the single input, letting it vary from 0 to 6 in increments of 2, and specifying the Total_employees cell as the single output cell.

---

[3]It is usually difficult to tell whether there are multiple optimal solutions. You typically discover this by rerunning Solver from different starting solutions.

Figure 4.15   Sensitivity Analysis for Postal Model

	A	B	C	D	E	F	G	H	I	J	K	L
1	Post Office scheduling model											
2												
3	Decision variables: number of employees starting their five-day shift on various days									Range names used:		
4	Mon	2								Employees_available	=Model!$B$25:$H$25	
5	Tue	2								Employees_required	=Model!$B$27:$H$27	
6	Wed	2								Employees_starting	=Model!$B$4:$B$10	
7	Thu	8								Total_employees	=Model!$B$30	
8	Fri	0										
9	Sat	4										
10	Sun	5										
11												
12	Employees required (original values)	17	13	15	19	14	16	11		Extra required each day	0	
13												
14	Result of decisions: number of employees working on various days (along top) who started their shift on various days (along side)											
15		Mon	Tue	Wed	Thu	Fri	Sat	Sun				
16	Mon	2	2	2	2	2						
17	Tue		2	2	2	2	2					
18	Wed			2	2	2	2	2				
19	Thu	8			8	8	8	8				
20	Fri	0	0			0	0	0				
21	Sat	4	4	4			4	4				
22	Sun	5	5	5	5			5				
23												
24	Constraint on worker availabilities											
25	Employees available	19	13	15	19	14	16	19				
26		>=	>=	>=	>=	>=	>=	>=				
27	Employees required	17	13	15	19	14	16	11				
28												
29	Objective to maximize											
30	Total employees	23										
31												
32	Sensitivity of total employees to extra required per day											
33			$B$30									
34		0	23									
35		2	25									
36		4	28									
37		6	31									

The results appear in rows 34–37 of Figure 4.15. When the requirement increases by 2 each day, only 2 extra employees are necessary (scheduled appropriately). However, when the requirement increases by 4 each day, *more* than 4 extra employees are necessary. The same is true when the requirement increases by 6 each day. This might surprise you at first, but there is an intuitive explanation: Each extra worker works only 5 days of the week.

Note that we did not use Solver's sensitivity report here for two reasons. First, Solver does not offer a sensitivity report for models with integer constraints. Second, even if we deleted the integer constraints, Solver's sensitivity report is not suited for questions about *multiple* input changes, as we have asked here. It is used primarily for questions about one-at-a-time changes to inputs, such as a change to a *specific* day's worker requirement. In this sense, SolverTable is a more flexible tool. ■

MODELING ISSUES

1. The postal employee scheduling example is called a *static* scheduling model, because we assume that the post office faces the same situation each week. In reality, demands change over time, workers take vacations in the summer, and so on, so the post office does not face the same situation each week. *Dynamic* scheduling models are discussed in the next section.

Heuristic solutions are often close to optimal, but they are never guaranteed to be optimal.

2. If you wanted to develop a weekly scheduling model for a supermarket or a fast-food restaurant, the number of variables could be very large and optimization software such as Solver might have difficulty finding an exact solution. In such cases, **heuristic** methods (essentially clever trial-and-error algorithms) can often be used to find a good solution to the problem. Love and Hoey (1990) indicate how this can be done for a particular staff scheduling example.

3. Our model can easily be expanded to handle part-time employees, the use of overtime, and alternative objectives such as maximizing the number of weekend days off received by employees. You can explore such extensions in the problems. ■

Encoder Scheduling at Ohio National Bank

Krajewski, Ritzman, and McKenzie (1980) use linear programming to schedule clerks who process checks at Ohio National Bank. Their model determines the minimum cost combination of part-time employees, full-time employees, and overtime labor needed to complete the processing of the checks received each day by the end of the workday (10 P.M.). The major input to their model is a forecast of the number of checks arriving at the bank each hour. This forecast is generated with a multiple regression model. The major output of the LP is a work schedule. For example, the LP might suggest that 2 full-time employees work daily from 11 A.M. to 8 P.M., 33 part-time employees work every day from 1 P.M. to 6 P.M., and 27 part-time employees work from 6 P.M. to 10 P.M. on Monday, Tuesday, and Friday.

The LP approach to scheduling encoder clerks saved an estimated $80,000 per year in labor costs. The LP approach also resulted in faster processing of the checks. Before LP was used to schedule encoder clerks, the day's checks were rarely processed by the end of the day, whereas after LP was used, the day's checks were processed by the end of the day 98% of the time! ■

PROBLEMS

Skill-Building Problems

7. Modify the post office model so that employees are paid $10 per hour on weekdays and $15 per hour on weekends. Change the objective so that you now minimize the weekly payroll. (You can assume that each employee works 8 hours per day.) Is the previous optimal solution still optimal?

8. How much influence can the worker requirements for one, two, or three days have on the weekly schedule in the post office example? You are asked to explore this in the following questions.

a. Let Monday's requirements change from 17 to 25 in increments of 1. Use SolverTable to see how the total number of employees changes.

b. Suppose the Monday and Tuesday requirements can each, independently of one another, increase from 1 to 8 in increments of 1. Use a two-way SolverTable to see how the total number of employees changes.

c. Suppose the Monday, Tuesday, and Wednesday requirements each increase by the *same* amount, where this increase can be from 1 to 8 in increments of 1. Use a one-way SolverTable to investigate how the total number of employees changes.

9. In the post office example, suppose that each fulltime employee works 8 hours per day. Thus, Monday's requirement of 17 workers can be viewed as a requirement of 8(17) = 136 hours. The post office can meet its daily labor requirements by using both full-time and part-time employees. During each week a full-time employee works 8 hours a day for 5 consecutive days, and a part-time employee works 4 hours a day for 5 consecutive days. A full-time employee costs the post office $15 per hour, whereas a part-time employee (with reduced fringe benefits) costs the post office only $10 per hour. Union requirements limit part-time labor to 25% of weekly labor requirements.

a. Modify the model as necessary, and then use Solver to minimize the post office's weekly labor costs.

b. Use SolverTable to determine how a change in the part-time labor limitation (currently 25%) influences the optimal solution.

Skill-Extending Problems

10. In the post office example, suppose the employees want more flexibility in their schedules. They want to be allowed to work 5 consecutive days followed by

2 days off *or* to work 3 consecutive days followed by a day off followed by 2 consecutive days followed by another day off. Modify the original model (with integer constraints) to allow this flexibility. Might this be a good deal for management as well as labor? Explain.

11. In the post office example, suppose that the post office can force employees to work 1 day of overtime each week on the day immediately following this 5-day shift. For example, an employee whose regular shift is Monday to Friday can also be required to work on Saturday. Each employee is paid $100 a day for each of the first 5 days worked during a week and $124 for the overtime day (if any). Determine how the post office can minimize the cost of meeting its weekly work requirements.

12. Suppose the post office has 25 full-time employees and is not allowed to hire or fire any of them. Determine a schedule that maximizes the number of weekend days off received by these employees.

4.4 AGGREGATE PLANNING MODELS

In this section we extend the production planning model discussed in Example 3.3 of the previous chapter to include a situation where the number of workers available influences the possible production levels. We allow the workforce level to be modified each period through the hiring and firing of workers. Such models, where we determine workforce levels and production schedules for a multiperiod time horizon, are called **aggregate planning** models. There are many aggregate planning models we could develop, depending on the detailed assumptions we make. We will consider a fairly simple version and then ask you to modify it in the problems.

EXAMPLE | 4.3 WORKER AND PRODUCTION PLANNING AT SURESTEP

During the next 4 months the SureStep Company must meet (on time) the following demands for pairs of shoes: 3000 in month 1; 5000 in month 2; 2000 in month 3; and 1000 in month 4. At the beginning of month 1, 500 pairs of shoes are on hand, and SureStep has 100 workers. A worker is paid $1500 per month. Each worker can work up to 160 hours a month before he or she receives overtime. A worker can work up to 20 hours of overtime per month and is paid $13 per hour for overtime labor. It takes 4 hours of labor and $15 of raw material to produce a pair of shoes. At the beginning of each month, workers can be hired or fired. Each hired worker costs $1600, and each fired worker costs $2000. At the end of each month, a holding cost of $3 per pair of shoes left in inventory is incurred. Production in a given month can be used to meet that month's demand. SureStep wants to use LP to determine its optimal production schedule and labor policy.

Objective To develop an LP spreadsheet model that relates workforce and production decisions to monthly costs, and to use Solver to find the minimum cost solution that meets forecasted demands on time and stays with limits on overtime hours and production capacity.

WHERE DO THE NUMBERS COME FROM?

There are a number of required inputs for a this type of problem. Some, including initial inventory, holding costs, and demands, are similar to requirements for Example 3.3 in the previous chapter, so we won't discuss them again here. Others might be obtained as follows:

- The data on the current number of workers, the regular hours per worker per month, the regular hourly wage rates, and the overtime hourly rate, should be well known. The maximum number of overtime hours per worker per month is probably either the result of a policy decision by management or a clause in the workers' contracts.

- The costs for hiring and firing a worker are not trivial. The hiring cost includes training costs and the cost of decreased productivity due to the fact that a new worker must learn the job (the "learning curve" effect). The firing cost includes severance costs and costs due to loss of morale. Neither the hiring nor the firing cost would be simple to estimate accurately, but the human resources department should be able to estimate their values.

- The unit production cost is a combination of two inputs, the raw material cost per pair of shoes and the labor hours per pair of shoes. The raw material cost is the going rate from the supplier(s). The labor hours per pair of shoes represents the "production function"—the average labor required to produce a unit of the product. The operations managers should be able to supply this number.

Solution

The key to this model is choosing the correct changing cells—the decision variables that determine all outputs.

The variables and constraints for this aggregate planning model are listed in Table 4.5. As we see, there are a lot of variables to keep track of. In fact, the most difficult aspect of modeling this problem is knowing which variables the company gets to choose—the decision variables—and which variables are *determined* by these decisions. It should be clear that the company gets to choose the number of workers to hire and fire and the number of shoes to produce. Also, because management sets only an upper limit on overtime hours, it gets to decide how many overtime hours to use within this limit. But once it decides the values of these variables, everything else is determined. We will show how these are determined through detailed cell formulas, but you should mentally go through the list of "Other output variables" in the table and deduce how they are determined by the decision variables. Also, you should also convince yourself that the three constraints we have listed are the ones, and the only ones, that are required.

Table 4.5	Variables and Constraints for Aggregate Planning Problem
Input variables	Initial inventory of shoes, initial number of workers, number and wage rate of regular hours, maximum number and wage rate of overtime hours, hiring and firing costs, data for unit production and holding costs, forecasted demands
Decision variables (changing cells)	Monthly values for number of workers hired and fired, number of shoes produced, and overtime hours used
Objective (target cell)	Total cost
Other calculated variables	Monthly values for workers on hand before and after hiring/firing, regular hours available, maximum overtime hours available, total production hours available, production capacity, inventory on hand after production, ending inventory, and various costs
Constraints	Overtime labor hours used ≤ Maximum overtime hours allowed Production ≤ Capacity Inventory on hand after production ≥ Demand

DEVELOPING THE SPREADSHEET MODEL

The spreadsheet model appears in Figure 4.16 (page 136). (See the file **AggregatePlanning1.xls**.) It can be developed as follows.

Figure 4.16 SureStep Aggregate Planning Model

	A	B	C	D	E	F	G	H	I
1	SureStep aggregate planning model								
2									
3	**Input data**						Range names used:		
4	Initial inventory of shoes	500					Forecasted_demand	=Model!$B$36:$E$36	
5	Initial number of workers	100					Inventory_after_production	=Model!$B$34:$E$34	
6	Regular hours/worker/month	160					Maximum_overtime_labor_hours_available	=Model!$B$25:$E$25	
7	Maximum overtime hours/worker/month	20					Overtime_labor_hours_used	=Model!$B$23:$E$23	
8	Hiring cost/worker	$1,600					Production_capacity	=Model!$B$32:$E$32	
9	Firing cost/worker	$2,000					Shoes_produced	=Model!$B$30:$E$30	
10	Regular wages/worker/month	$1,500					Total_cost	=Model!$F$46	
11	Overtime wage rate/hour	$13					Workers_fired	=Model!$B$19:$E$19	
12	Labor hours/pair of shoes	4					Workers_hired	=Model!$B$18:$E$18	
13	Raw material cost/pair of shoes	$15							
14	Holding cost/pair of shoes in inventory/month	$3							
15									
16	**Worker plan**	Month 1	Month 2	Month 3	Month 4				
17	Workers from previous month	100	94	93	50				
18	Workers hired	0	0	0	0				
19	Workers fired	6	1	43	0				
20	Workers available after hiring and firing	94	93	50	50				
21							Notes: We originally omitted integer constraints on		
22	Regular-time hours available	15040	14880	8000	8000		workers hired and fired, and Solver found a noninteger		
23	Overtime labor hours used	0	80	0	0		solution with no problems. Then we added these integer		
24		<=	<=	<=	<=		constraints and Solver reported "no feasible solution."		
25	Maximum overtime labor hours available	1880	1860	1000	1000		So we tried checking the Automatic Scaling in Solver's		
26							Options dialog box, and we got the solution shown here.		
27	Total hours for production	15040	14960	8000	8000				
28									
29	**Production plan**	Month 1	Month 2	Month 3	Month 4				
30	Shoes produced	3760	3740	2000	1000				
31		<=	<=	<=	<=				
32	Production capacity	3760	3740	2000	2000				
33									
34	Inventory after production	4260	5000	2000	1000				
35		>=	>=	>=	>=				
36	Forecasted demand	3000	5000	2000	1000				
37	Ending inventory	1260	0	0	0				
38									
39	**Monetary outputs**	Month 1	Month 2	Month 3	Month 4	Totals			
40	Hiring cost	$0	$0	$0	$0	$0			
41	Firing cost	$12,000	$2,000	$86,000	$0	$100,000			
42	Regular-time wages	$141,000	$139,500	$75,000	$75,000	$430,500			
43	Overtime wages	$0	$1,040	$0	$0	$1,040			
44	Raw material cost	$56,400	$56,100	$30,000	$15,000	$157,500			
45	Holding cost	$3,780	$0	$0	$0	$3,780			
46	Totals	$213,180	$198,640	$191,000	$90,000	$692,820	Objective to minimize		

1 **Inputs and range names.** Enter the input data in the range B4:B14 and the Forecasted_demand range. Also, create the range names listed. (As usual, we took great advantage of the Insert/Name/Create shortcut.)

2 **Production, hiring and firing plan.** Enter *any* trial values for the number of pairs of shoes produced each month, the overtime hours used each month, the workers hired each month, and the workers fired each month. These four ranges, in rows 18, 19, 23, and 30, comprise the changing cells.

This is common in multiperiod problems. We usually have to relate a beginning value in one period to an ending value from the previous period.

3 **Workers available each month.** In cell B17 enter the initial number of workers available with the formula

=B5

Because the number of workers available at the beginning of any other month (before hiring and firing) is equal to the number of workers from the previous month, enter the formula

=B20

in cell C17 and copy it to the range D17:E17. Then in cell B20 calculate the number of workers available in month 1 (after hiring and firing) with the formula

=B17+B18-B19

and copy this formula to the range C20:E20 for months 2 through 4.

④ Overtime capacity. Because each available worker can work up to 20 hours of overtime in a month, enter the formula

=$B$7*B20

in cell B25 and copy it to the range C25:E25.

⑤ Production capacity. Because each worker can work 160 regular-time hours per month, calculate the regular-time hours available in month 1 in cell B22 with the formula

=$B$6*B20

In Example 3.3 from the previous chapter, production capacities were given inputs. Now they are based on the size of the workforce, which itself is a decision variable.

and copy it to the range C22:E22 for the other months. Then calculate the total hours available for production in cell B27 with the formula

=SUM(B22:B23)

and copy it to the range C27:E27 for the other months. Finally, because it takes 4 hours of labor to make a pair of shoes, calculate the production capacity in month 1 by entering the formula

=B27/$B$12

in cell B32 and copy it to the range C32:E32.

⑥ Inventory each month. Calculate the inventory after production in month 1 (which is available to meet month 1 demand) by entering the formula

=B4+B30

in cell B34. For any other month, the inventory after production is the previous month's ending inventory plus that month's production, so enter the formula

=B37+C30

in cell C34 and copy it to the range D34:E34. Then calculate the month 1 ending inventory in cell B37 with the formula

=B34-B36

and copy it to the range C37:E37.

⑦ Monthly costs. Calculate the various costs shown in rows 40 through 45 for month 1 by entering the formulas

=$B$8*B18
=$B$9*B19
=$B$10*B20
=$B$11*B23
=$B$13*B30
=$B$14*B37

in cells B40 through B45. Then copy the range B40:B45 to the range C40:E45 to calculate these costs for the other months.

⑧ Totals. In row 46 and column F, use the SUM function to calculate cost totals, with the value in F46 being the overall total cost.

→ EXCEL TIP: *Calculating Row and Column Sums Quickly*

A common operation in spreadsheet models is to calculate row and column sums for a rectangular range, as we did for costs in step 8. There is a very quick way to do this. Highlight the row and column where the sums will go (remember to press the Ctrl key to highlight nonadjacent ranges) and click on the summation (Σ) toolbar button. This enters all of the sums automatically. It even calculates the "grand sum" in the corner (cell F46 in the example) if you highlight this cell. ■

USING SOLVER

The Solver dialog box should be filled in as shown in Figure 4.17. Note that the changing cells include four separate named ranges. To enter these in the dialog box, drag the four ranges, keeping your finger on the Ctrl key. (Alternatively, you can drag a range, type comma, drag a second range, type another comma, and so on.) As usual, you should also check the Assume Linear Model and Assume Non-Negative options before optimizing.

Figure 4.17

Solver Dialog Box for SureStep Model

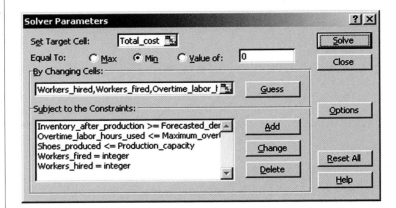

Note that we entered integer constraints on the numbers hired and fired. We could also constrain the numbers of shoes produced to be integers. However, integer constraints typically require longer solution times. Therefore, it is often best to omit such constraints, especially when the optimal values are fairly large, such as the production quantities in this model. If the solution then has noninteger values, we can usually round them to integers for a solution that is at least close to the optimal integer solution.

Discussion of the Solution

The optimal solution is given in Figure 4.16. Observe that SureStep should never hire any workers, and it should fire 6 workers in month 1, 1 worker in month 2, and 43 workers in month 3. Eighty hours of overtime are used, but only in month 2. The company produces over 3700 pairs of shoes during each of the first 2 months, 2000 pairs in month 3, and 1000 pairs in month 4. A total cost of $692,820 is incurred. The model will recommend overtime hours only when regular-time production capacity is exhausted. This is because overtime labor is more expensive.

Because integer constraints make a model harder to solve, use them sparingly—only when they are really needed.

Again, we would probably not force the number of pairs of shoes produced each month to be an integer. It makes little difference whether the company produces 3760 or 3761 pairs of shoes during a month, and forcing each month's shoe production to be an integer can greatly increase the time the computer needs to find an optimal solution. On the other hand, it is somewhat more important to ensure that the number of workers hired and fired each month is an integer, given the small numbers of workers involved.

Finally, if you want to ensure that Solver finds the optimal solution in a problem where some or all of the changing cells must be integers, it is a good idea to go into Options (in the Solver dialog box) and set the tolerance to 0. Otherwise, Solver might stop when it finds a solution that is *close* to optimal.

Sensitivity Analysis

There are many sensitivity analyses we could perform on this final SureStep model. We illustrate one of them with SolverTable, where we see how the overtime hours used and the total cost vary with the overtime wage rate.[4] The results appear in Figure 4.18. As we see, when wage rate is really low, we use considerably more overtime hours, whereas when it is sufficiently large, we use no overtime hours. It is not surprising that the company uses much more overtime when the overtime rate is $7 or $9 per hour. The *regular*-time wage rate is $9.375 per hour ($=1500/160$). Of course, it is not likely that the company would pay *less* per hour for overtime than for regular time!

Figure 4.18

Sensitivity to
Overtime Wage Rate

	A	B	C	D	E
48	Sensitivity of overtime hours used and total cost to overtime wage rate				
49		$B$23	$C$23	$D$23	$E$23
50	7	1620	1660	0	0
51	9	80	1760	0	0
52	11	0	80	0	0
53	13	0	80	0	0
54	15	0	80	0	0
55	17	0	80	0	0
56	19	0	0	0	0
57	21	0	0	0	0

The Rolling Planning Horizon Approach

In reality, an aggregate planning model is usually implemented via a rolling planning horizon. To illustrate, we assume that SureStep works with a 4-month planning horizon. To implement the SureStep model in the rolling planning horizon context, we view the "demands" as forecasts and solve a 4-month model with these forecasts. However, we implement only the month 1 production and work scheduling recommendation. Thus (assuming that the numbers of workers hired and fired in a month must be integers and that shortages are not allowed) SureStep should hire no workers, fire 6 workers, and produce 3760 pairs of shoes with regular-time labor in month 1. Next, we observe month 1's actual demand. Suppose it is 2950. Then SureStep begins month 2 with 1310 ($= 4260 - 2950$) pairs of shoes and 94 workers. We would now enter 1310 in cell B4 and 94 in cell B5 (referring to Figure 4.16). Then we would replace the demands in the Demand range with the updated forecasts for the *next* 4 months. Finally, we would rerun Solver and use the production levels and hiring and firing recommendations in column B as the production level and workforce policy for month 2.

Model with Backlogging Allowed[5]

The term backlogging *means that the customer's demand will be met at a later date. The term* backordering *means the same thing.*

In many situations, backlogging of demand is allowed—that is, customer demand can be met later than it occurs. We now show how to modify the SureStep model to include the option of backlogging demand. We assume that at the end of each month a cost of $20 is incurred for each unit of demand that remains unsatisfied at the end of the month. This is easily modeled by allowing a month's ending inventory to be negative. For example, if month 1's ending inventory is -10, a shortage cost of $200 (and no holding cost) is incurred. To ensure that SureStep produces any shoes at all, we constrain month 4's ending inventory to be nonnegative. This implies that all demand is *eventually* satisfied by the end of the 4-month planning horizon. We now need to modify the monthly cost computations to incorporate costs due to shortages.

[4]As we mentioned in Example 4.2, Solver's sensitivity report isn't even available here because of the integer constraints.
[5]This extension of the model is more advanced and can be omitted without loss of continuity.

There are actually several modeling approaches to this backlogging problem. We show the most natural approach in Figure 4.19. (See the file **AggregatePlanning2.xls**.) To begin, we enter the per-unit monthly shortage cost in cell B15. (We inserted a new row for this cost input.) Note in row 38 how the ending inventory in months 1–3 can be positive (leftovers) or negative (shortages). We can account correctly for the resulting costs with IF functions in rows 46 and 47. For holding costs, enter the formula

=IF(B38>0,$B$14*B38,0)

in cell B46 and copy it across. For shortage costs, enter the formula

=IF(B38<0,-$B$15*B38,0)

in cell B47 and copy it across. (The minus sign makes this a *positive* cost.)

Figure 4.19   Nonlinear SureStep Model with Backlogging Using IF Functions

	A	B	C	D	E	F	G	H	I
1	SureStep aggregate planning model with backlogging: a nonsmooth model Solver might not handle correctly								
2									
3	Input data						Range names used:		
4	Initial inventory of shoes	500					Forecasted_demand_4		=Model!$E$37
5	Initial number of workers	100					Inventory_after_production_4		=Model!$E$35
6	Regular hours/worker/month	160					Maximum_overtime_labor_hours_available		=Model!$B$26:$E$26
7	Maximum overtime hours/worker/month	20					Overtime_labor_hours_used		=Model!$B$24:$E$24
8	Hiring cost/worker	$1,600					Production_capacity		=Model!$B$33:$E$33
9	Firing cost/worker	$2,000					Shoes_produced		=Model!$B$31:$E$31
10	Regular wages/worker/month	$1,500					Total_cost		=Model!$F$48
11	Overtime wage rate/hour	$13					Workers_fired		=Model!$B$20:$E$20
12	Labor hours/pair of shoes	4					Workers_hired		=Model!$B$19:$E$19
13	Raw material cost/pair of shoes	$15							
14	Holding cost/pair of shoes in inventory/month	$3							
15	Shortage cost/pair of shoes/month	$20							
16									
17	Worker plan	Month 1	Month 2	Month 3	Month 4				
18	Workers from previous month	100	94	93	38				
19	Workers hired	0	0	0	0				
20	Workers fired	6	1	55	0				
21	Workers available after hiring and firing	94	93	38	38				
22									
23	Regular-time hours available	15040	14880	6080	6080				
24	Overtime labor hours used	0	0	0	0				
25		<=	<=	<=	<=				
26	Maximum overtime labor hours available	1880	1860	760	760				
27									
28	Total hours for production	15040	14880	6080	6080				
29									
30	Production plan	Month 1	Month 2	Month 3	Month 4				
31	Shoes produced	3760	3720	1520	1500				
32		<=	<=	<=	<=				
33	Production capacity	3760	3720	1520	1520				
34									
35	Inventory after production	4260	4980	1500	1000				
36					>=				
37	Forecasted demand	3000	5000	2000	1000				
38	Ending inventory	1260	-20	-500	0				
39									
40	Monetary outputs	Month 1	Month 2	Month 3	Month 4	Totals	Note that we use IF functions in rows		
41	Hiring cost	$0	$0	$0	$0	$0	46 and 47 to capture the holding and		
42	Firing cost	$12,000	$2,000	$110,000	$0	$124,000	shortage costs. These IF functions		
43	Regular-time wages	$141,000	$139,500	$57,000	$57,000	$394,500	make the model nonlinear (and		
44	Overtime wages	$0	$0	$0	$0	$0	"nonsmooth"), and Solver can't		
45	Raw material cost	$56,400	$55,800	$22,800	$22,500	$157,500	handle these functions in a		
46	Holding cost	$3,780	$0	$0	$0	$3,780	predictable manner. We just got lucky		
47	Shortage cost	$0	$400	$10,000	$0	$10,400			
48	Totals	$213,180	$197,700	$199,800	$79,500	$690,180	← Objective to minimize		

IF functions involving changing cells make a model nonlinear.

Although these formulas accurately compute holding and shortage costs, the IF functions make the target cell a *nonlinear* function of the changing cells, and we must use Solver's GRG nonlinear algorithm, as indicated in Figure 4.20, where the Assume Linear Model box is *not* checked.[6] (How do you know the model is nonlinear? Although there is

---

[6]GRG stands for generalized reduced gradient. This is a technical term for the mathematical algorithm used.

a mathematical reason, it is easier to try running Solver with the Assume Linear Model box checked. Solver will then *inform* you that the model is not linear.)

We ran Solver with this setup from a variety of initial solutions in the changing cells, and it always found the solution shown in Figure 4.19. It turns out that this is indeed the optimal solution, but we were lucky. When certain functions, including IF, MIN, MAX, and ABS, are used to relate the target cell to the changing cells, the resulting model becomes not only nonlinear but "nonsmooth." Essentially, nonsmooth functions can have sharp edges or discontinuities. Solver's GRG nonlinear algorithm can handle "smooth" nonlinearities, as we will see in Chapter 7, but it has trouble with nonsmooth functions. Sometimes it gets lucky, as it did here, and other times it finds a nonoptimal solution that is not even close to the optimal solution. For example, we changed the unit shortage cost from $20 to $40 and reran Solver. Starting from a solution where all changing cells contain 0, Solver stopped at a solution with total cost $725,360, even though the optimal solution has total cost $692,820. In other words, we weren't so lucky on this problem.

The moral is that you should avoid these nonsmooth functions in optimization models if at all possible. If you *do* use them, as we have done here, then you should run Solver several times, starting from different initial solutions. There is still absolutely no guarantee that you will get the optimal solution, but you will get more evidence of how Solver is progressing.

→ **SOLVER TIP:** *Nonsmooth Functions*
There is nothing inherently wrong with using IF, MIN, MAX, ABS, and other nonsmooth functions in spreadsheet optimization models. The only problem is that Solver cannot handle these functions in a predictable manner. ■

There are sometimes alternatives to using IF, MIN, MAX, and ABS functions that make a model linear. Unfortunately, these alternatives are often far from intuitive, and we will not cover them here. (If you are interested, we have included the "linearized" version of the backlogging model in the file **AggregatePlanning3.xls**.) Alternatively, nonsmooth functions can be handled with a totally different kind of algorithm, called a **genetic algorithm**, and Frontline's Premium Solver includes an Evolutionary Solver that implements a genetic algorithm. However, we will not cover genetic algorithms in this book. ■

1. Silver et al. (1998) recommend that when demand is seasonal, the planning horizon should extend beyond the next seasonal peak.

2. Beyond a certain point, the cost of using extra hours of overtime labor increases because workers become less efficient. We haven't modeled this type of behavior because it would make the model nonlinear. ■

ADDITIONAL APPLICATIONS

Multiproduct Production Scheduling at Owens-Corning Fiberglass

Oliff and Burch (1985) developed an aggregate planning LP model that is used to schedule production of fiberglass products at Owens-Corning Fiberglass. Their model minimizes the sum of direct payroll costs, overtime costs, hiring and firing costs, and inventory holding costs. They also take into account (using integer programming; see Chapter 6) the cost due to lost production time that is incurred when a machine changes from making one product to making a different product. Their model has saved Owens-Corning over $100,000 per year. ■

PROBLEMS

Skill-Building Problems

13. Extend SureStep's original (no backlogging) aggregate planning model from 4 to 6 months. Try several different values for demands in months 5 and 6, and run Solver for each. Is your optimal solution for the *first* 4 months the same as the one in the book?

14. The current solution to SureStep's no-backlogging aggregate planning model does quite a lot of firing. Run a one-way SolverTable with the firing cost as the input variable and the numbers fired as the outputs. Let the firing cost increase from its current value to double that value in increments of $400. Do high firing costs eventually induce the company to fire fewer workers?

15. SureStep is currently getting 160 regular-time hours from each worker per month. This is actually calculated from 8 hours per day times 20 days per week. For this, they are paid $9.375 per hour (=1500/160). Suppose workers can change their contract so that they only have to work 7.5 hours per day regular time—everything above this becomes overtime—and their regular-time wage rate increases to $10 per hour. They will still work 20 days per month. Will this change the optimal no-backlogging solution?

16. Suppose SureStep could begin a machinery upgrade and training program to increase its worker productivity. This program would result in the following values of labor hours per pair of shoes over the next 4 months: 4, 3.9, 3.8, and 3.8. How much would this new program be worth to SureStep, at least for this 4-month planning horizon with no backlogging? How might you evaluate the program's worth *beyond* the next 4 months?

Skill-Extending Problems

17. In the current no-backlogging problem SureStep doesn't hire any workers, and it uses almost no overtime. This is evidently because of low demand. Change the demands to 6000, 8000, 5000, and 3000, and reoptimize. Is there now hiring and overtime? With this new demand pattern, explore the trade-off between hiring and overtime by running a two-way SolverTable. As inputs, use the hiring cost per worker and the maximum overtime hours allowed per worker per month, varied as you see fit. As outputs, use the total number of workers hired over the 4 months and the total number of overtime hours used over the 4 months. Write up your results in a short memo to SureStep management.

18. In the SureStep no-backlogging problem, change the demands so that they become 6000, 8000, 5000, 3000. Also, change the problem slightly so that newly hired workers take 6 hours to produce a pair of shoes during their first month of employment. After that, they take only 4 hours per pair of shoes. Modify the model appropriately, and use Solver to find the optimal solution.

19. We saw that the "natural" way to model SureStep's backlogging model, with IF functions, leads to a non-smooth model that Solver has difficulty handling. There is another version of the problem that is also difficult for Solver. Suppose SureStep wants to meet all demand on time (no backlogging), but it wants to keep its employment level as constant across time as possible. To induce this, it charges a cost of $1000 each month on the absolute difference between the beginning number of workers and the number after hiring and firing—that is, the absolute difference between the values in rows 17 and 20 of the original spreadsheet model. Implement this extra cost in the model in the "natural" way, using the ABS function. Using demands of 6000, 8000, 5000, and 3000, see how well Solver does in trying to solve this non-smooth model. Try several initial solutions, and see whether Solver gets the same optimal solution from each of them.

4.5 BLENDING MODELS

In many situations various inputs must be blended together to produce desired outputs. In many of these situations linear programming can find the optimal combination of outputs as well as the "mix" of inputs that are used to produce the desired outputs. Some examples of blending problems are given in Table 4.6.

Table 4.6 Examples of Blending Problems

Inputs	Outputs
Meat, filler, water	Different types of sausage
Various types of oil	Heating oil, gasolines, aviation fuels
Carbon, iron, molybdenum	Different types of steel
Different types of pulp	Different kinds of recycled paper

The following example illustrates how to model a typical blending problem in a spreadsheet. Although this example is small relative to blending problems in real applications, we think you will agree that it is fairly complex. If you are able to guess the optimal solution, your intuition is much better than ours!

EXAMPLE | **4.4 BLENDING AT CHANDLER OIL**

Chandler Oil has 5000 barrels of crude oil 1 and 10,000 barrels of crude oil 2 available. Chandler sells gasoline and heating oil. These products are produced by blending together the two crude oils. Each barrel of crude oil 1 has a "quality level" of 10 and each barrel of crude oil 2 has a quality level of 5.[7] Gasoline must have an average quality level of at least 8, whereas heating oil must have an average quality level of at least 6. Gasoline sells for $25 per barrel, and heating oil sells for $20 per barrel. We assume that demand for heating oil and gasoline is unlimited, so that all of Chandler's production can be sold. Chandler wants to maximize its revenue from selling gasoline and heating oil.

Objective   To develop an LP spreadsheet model that relates a detailed blending plan to relevant quantities on crude oil inputs and gasoline/heating oil outputs, and to use Solver to find the revenue-maximizing plan that meets quality constraints and stays within limits on crude oil availabilities.

---

[7]To avoid getting into an overly technical discussion, we use the generic term *quality level*. In real oil blending, qualities of interest might be octane rating, viscosity, and others.

WHERE DO THE NUMBERS COME FROM?

Most of the inputs for this problem should be easy to obtain.

- The selling prices for outputs are dictated by market pressures.
- The availabilities of inputs are based on crude supplies from the suppliers.
- The quality levels of crude oils are known from chemical analysis, whereas the required quality levels for outputs are specified by Chandler, probably in response to competitive pressures.

Solution

In typical blending problems, the correct decision variables are the amounts of each input blended into each output.

The variables and constraints required for this blending model are listed in Table 4.7. The key to a successful model of this problem is the selection of the appropriate decision variables. Many people, when asked what decision variables should be used, specify the amounts of the two crude oils used and the amounts of the two products produced. However, this is not enough! The problem is that this information doesn't tell Chandler how to *make* the outputs from the inputs. What we need instead is a blending plan: how much of each input to use in the production of a barrel of each output. Once you understand that this blending plan is the basic decision, then all other output variables follow in a straightforward manner.

Table 4.7 Variables and Constraints for Blending Model

Input variables	Unit selling prices, availabilities of inputs, quality levels of inputs, required quality levels of outputs
Decision variables (changing cells)	Barrels of each input used to produce each output
Objective (target cell)	Revenue from selling gasoline and heating oil
Other calculated variables	Barrels of inputs used, barrels of outputs produced (and sold), quality obtained and quality required for outputs
Constraints	Barrels of inputs used ≤ Barrels available Quality of outputs obtained ≥ Quality required

A secondary, but very important, issue in typical blending problems is how to implement the "quality" constraints. [The constraints here are in terms of quality. In other blending problems they are often expressed in terms of percentages of some ingredient(s). For example, a typical quality constraint might be that some output can contain no more than 2% sulfur. Such constraints are typical of blending problems.] When we explain how to develop the spreadsheet model, we will discuss the preferred way to implement quality constraints.

DEVELOPING THE SPREADSHEET MODEL

The spreadsheet model for this problem appears in Figure 4.21. (See the file **Blending.xls**.) To set it up, proceed as follows.

Figure 4.21 Chandler Oil Blending Model

	A	B	C	D	E	F	G	H
1	Chandler blending model							
2								
3	Monetary inputs	Gasoline	Heating oil			Range names used:		
4	Selling price/barrel	$25.00	$20.00			Barrels_available	=Model!$F$16:$F$17	
5						Barrels_used	=Model!$D$16:$D$17	
6	Quality level per barrel of crudes					Blending_plan	=Model!$B$16:$C$17	
7	Crude oil 1	10				Quality_points_obtained	=Model!$B$22:$C$22	
8	Crude oil 2	5				Quality_points_required	=Model!$B$24:$C$24	
9						Revenue	=Model!$B$27	
10	Required quality level per barrel of product							
11		Gasoline	Heating oil					
12		8	6					
13								
14	Blending plan (barrels of crudes in each product)							
15		Gasoline	Heating oil	Barrels used				
16	Crude oil 1	3000	2000	5000	<=	Barrels available		
17	Crude oil 2	2000	8000	10000	<=	5000		
18	Barrels sold	5000	10000			10000		
19								
20	Constraints on quality							
21		Gasoline	Heating oil					
22	Quality points obtained	40000	60000					
23		>=	>=					
24	Quality points required	40000	60000					
25								
26	Objective to maximize							
27	Revenue	$325,000						

1 Inputs and range names. Enter the unit selling prices, quality levels for inputs, required quality levels for outputs, and availabilities of inputs in the shaded ranges. Then name the ranges as indicated.

2 Inputs blended into each output. As we discussed, the quantities Chandler must specify are the barrels of each input used to produce each output. Therefore, enter *any* trial values for these quantities in the Blending_plan range. For example, the value in cell B16 is the amount of crude oil 1 used to make gasoline and the value in cell C16 is the amount of crude oil 1 used to make heating oil. The Blending_plan range contains the changing cells.

3 Inputs used and outputs sold. We need to calculate the row sums (in column D) and column sums (in row 18) of the Blending_plan range. According to the Excel tip from the previous example, there is a quick way to do this. In case you missed that tip, just highlight both the row and column where the sums will go (highlight one, then hold down the Ctrl key and highlight the other), and click on the Summation (Σ) button on the main Excel toolbar. This creates SUM formulas in each highlighted cell.

4 Quality achieved. Keeping track of the quality level of gasoline and heating oil in the Quality_points_obtained range is tricky. Begin by calculating for each output the number of "quality points" (QP) in the inputs used to produce this output:

$$\text{QP in gasoline} = 10 \text{ (Oil 1 in gasoline)} + 5 \text{ (Oil 2 in gasoline)}$$

$$\text{QP in heating oil} = 10 \text{ (Oil 1 in heating oil)} + 5 \text{ (Oil 2 in heating oil)}$$

For the gasoline produced to have a quality level of at least 8, we must have

$$\text{QP in gasoline} \geq 8 \text{ (Gasoline sold)} \tag{4.1}$$

For the heating oil produced to have a quality level of at least 6, we must have

$$\text{QP in heating oil} \geq 6 \text{ (Heating oil sold)} \tag{4.2}$$

To implement inequalities (4.1) and (4.2), calculate the QP for gasoline in cell B22 with the formula

=SUMPRODUCT(B16:B17, $B$7:$B$8)

Then copy this formula to cell C22 to generate the QP for heating oil.

5 **Quality required.** Calculate the required quality points for gasoline and heating oil in cells B24 and C24. Specifically, determine the required quality points for gasoline in cell B24 with the formula

=B12*B18

Then copy this formula to cell C24 for heating oil.

6 **Revenue.** Calculate the total revenue in cell B27 with the formula

=SUMPRODUCT(B4:C4,$B$18:$C$18)

USING SOLVER

To solve Chandler's problem with Solver, fill out the main Solver dialog box as shown in Figure 4.22. As usual, check the Assume Linear Model and Assume Non-Negative options before optimizing. You should obtain the optimal solution shown in Figure 4.21.

Figure 4.22

Solver Dialog Box for Blending Model

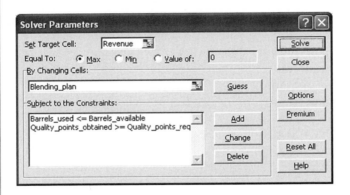

Discussion of the Solution

The optimal solution implies that Chandler should make 5000 barrels of gasoline with 3000 barrels of crude oil 1 and 2000 barrels of crude oil 2. The company should also make 10,000 barrels of heating oil with 2000 barrels of crude oil 1 and 8000 barrels of crude oil 2. With this blend, Chandler will obtain a revenue of $325,000. As stated previously, we believe this problem is sufficiently complex to defy intuition. Clearly, gasoline is more profitable per barrel than heating oil, but given the crude availability and the quality constraints, it turns out that Chandler should sell twice as much heating oil as gasoline. This would have been very difficult to guess ahead of time.

Sensitivity Analysis

We perform two typical sensitivity analyses on the Chandler blending model. In each, we see how revenue and the amounts of the outputs produced (and sold) vary. In the first analysis, we use the unit selling price of gasoline as the input and let it vary from $20 to $80 in increments of $5. The SolverTable results appear in Figure 4.23. Two things are of interest. First, as the price of gasoline increases, Chandler produces more gasoline and less heating oil, exactly as we would expect. Second, the revenue always increases, as the changes in column E indicate.

Figure 4.23

Sensitivity to the Selling Price of Gasoline

	A	B	C	D	E
29	Sensitivity of outputs sold and revenue to the selling price of gasoline				
30	Price of gasoline	Gasoline	Heating oil	Revenue	
31		$B$18	$C$18	$B$27	Increase
32	20	5000	10000	$300,000	
33	25	5000	10000	$325,000	$25,000
34	30	5000	10000	$350,000	$25,000
35	35	5000	10000	$375,000	$25,000
36	40	5000	10000	$400,000	$25,000
37	45	5000	10000	$425,000	$25,000
38	50	5000	10000	$450,000	$25,000
39	55	5000	10000	$475,000	$25,000
40	60	8333	0	$500,000	$25,000
41	65	8333	0	$541,667	$41,667
42	70	8333	0	$583,333	$41,667
43	75	8333	0	$625,000	$41,667
44	80	8333	0	$666,667	$41,667

In the second sensitivity analysis we vary the availability of crude 1 from 2000 barrels to 20,000 barrels in increments of 1000 barrels. The resulting SolverTable output appears in Figure 4.24. These results make sense if we analyze them carefully. First, the revenue increases, but at a decreasing rate, as more crude 1 is available. This is a common occurrence in LP models. As more of a resource is made available, revenue can only increase or remain the same, but each extra unit of the resource produces less (or at least no more) revenue than the previous unit. Second, the amount of gasoline produced increases, whereas the amount of heating oil produced decreases. Here is the reason. Crude 1 has a higher quality than crude 2, and gasoline requires higher quality. Gasoline also sells for a higher price. Therefore, as more crude 1 is available, Chandler can produce more gasoline, receive more revenue, and still meet quality standards.

Figure 4.24

Sensitivity to the Availability of Crude 1

	A	B	C	D	E
46	Sensitivity of outputs sold and revenue to the availability of crude 1				
47	Availability of crude 1	Gasoline	Heating oil	Revenue	
48		$B$18	$C$18	$B$27	Increase
49	2000	0	10000	$200,000	
50	3000	1000	12000	$265,000	$65,000
51	4000	3000	11000	$295,000	$30,000
52	5000	5000	10000	$325,000	$30,000
53	6000	7000	9000	$355,000	$30,000
54	7000	9000	8000	$385,000	$30,000
55	8000	11000	7000	$415,000	$30,000
56	9000	13000	6000	$445,000	$30,000
57	10000	15000	5000	$475,000	$30,000
58	11000	17000	4000	$505,000	$30,000
59	12000	19000	3000	$535,000	$30,000
60	13000	21000	2000	$565,000	$30,000
61	14000	23000	1000	$595,000	$30,000
62	15000	25000	0	$625,000	$30,000
63	16000	26000	0	$650,000	$25,000
64	17000	27000	0	$675,000	$25,000
65	18000	28000	0	$700,000	$25,000
66	19000	29000	0	$725,000	$25,000
67	20000	30000	0	$750,000	$25,000

Could we also answer these sensitivity questions with Solver's sensitivity report, shown in Figure 4.25 (page 148)? Consider the sensitivity to the change in the price of gasoline. The first and third rows of the top table in this report are for sensitivity to the objective coefficients of decision variables involving gasoline. The problem is that when we change the price of gasoline, we automatically change *both* of these coefficients. The reason is that we sum these two decision variables to calculate the amount of gasoline sold, which we then multiply by the unit price of gasoline in the objective. However, Solver's sensitivity report is valid only for one-at-a-time coefficient changes. Therefore, it cannot answer our question.

Figure 4.25

Sensitivity Report
for Blending Model

	A	B	C	D	E	F	G	H
1		Microsoft Excel 10.0 Sensitivity Report						
2		Worksheet: [Blending.xls]Model						
3		Report Created: 6/25/2003 1:17:32 PM						
4								
5								
6		Adjustable Cells						
7				Final	Reduced	Objective	Allowable	Allowable
8		Cell	Name	Value	Cost	Coefficient	Increase	Decrease
9		$B$16	Crude oil 1 Gasoline	3000	0.0	25	58.33	8.33
10		$C$16	Crude oil 1 Heating oil	2000	0.0	20	8.33	58.33
11		$B$17	Crude oil 2 Gasoline	2000	0.0	25	87.50	6.25
12		$C$17	Crude oil 2 Heating oil	8000	0.0	20	6.25	14.58
13								
14		Constraints						
15				Final	Shadow	Constraint	Allowable	Allowable
16		Cell	Name	Value	Price	R.H. Side	Increase	Decrease
17		$D$16	Crude oil 1 Barrels used	5000	30.0	5000	10000	2500
18		$D$17	Crude oil 2 Barrels used	10000	17.5	10000	10000	6666.67
19		$B$22	Quality points obtained Gasoline	40000	-2.5	0	5000	20000
20		$C$22	Quality points obtained Heating oil	60000	-2.5	0	10000	6666.67

In contrast, the first row of the bottom table in Figure 4.25 complements the SolverTable sensitivity analysis on the availability of crude 1. It shows that if the availability increases by no more than 10,000 barrels or decreases by no more than 2500 barrels, then the shadow price stays at $30 per barrel—that is, the same $30,000 increase in profit per 1000 barrels we saw in Figure 4.24. Beyond that range, the sensitivity report indicates only that the shadow price will change. The SolverTable results indicate *how* it changes. For example, when crude 1 availability increases beyond 15,000 barrels, the SolverTable results indicate that the shadow price decreases to $25 per barrel.

A Caution About Blending Constraints

Before concluding this example, we should discuss why our model is linear. The key is our implementation of the quality constraints, as shown in inequalities (4.1) and (4.2). To keep a model linear, each side of an inequality constraint must be a constant, the product of a constant and a variable, or a sum of such products. If we implement the quality constraints as in inequalities (4.1) and (4.2), we indeed get linear constraints. However, it is arguably more natural to rewrite this type of constraint by dividing through by the amount sold. For example, the modified gasoline constraint would be

$$\frac{\text{QP in gasoline}}{\text{Gasoline sold}} \geq 8 \tag{4.3}$$

Blending models usually have various "quality" constraints, often expressed as required percentages of various ingredients. To keep these models linear (and avoid dividing by 0), it is important to clear denominators.

Although this form of the constraint is perfectly valid—and is possibly more natural to many users—it suffers from two drawbacks. First, it makes the model nonlinear. This is because the left-hand side is no longer a sum of products; it involves a quotient. We prefer linear models whenever possible. Second, suppose it turned out that Chandler's optimal solution called for *no* gasoline at all. Then we would be dividing by 0 in inequality (4.3), and this would cause an error in Excel. Because of these two drawbacks, the moral is to clear denominators in all such blending constraints. ■

MODELING ISSUES

In reality, a company using a blending model would run the model periodically (each day, say) and set production on the basis of the current inventory of inputs and the current forecasts of demands and prices. Then the forecasts and the input levels would be updated, and the model would be run again to determine the next day's production. ■

Blending at Texaco

Texaco [see DeWitt et al. (1989)] uses a nonlinear programming model (OMEGA) to plan and schedule its blending applications. Their model is nonlinear because blend volatilities and octanes are nonlinear functions of the amount of each input used to produce a particular gasoline.

Blending in the Oil Industry

Many oil companies use LP to optimize their refinery operations. Magoulas and Marinos-Kouris (1988) discuss one such blending model that has been used to maximize a refinery's profit. ■

PROBLEMS

Skill-Building Problems

20. Use SolverTable in Chandler's blending model to see whether, by increasing the selling price of gasoline, you can get an optimal solution that produces only gasoline, no heating oil. Then use SolverTable again to see whether, by increasing the selling price of heating oil, you can get an optimal solution that produces only heating oil, no gasoline.

21. Use SolverTable in Chandler's blending model to find the shadow price of crude oil 1—that is, the amount Chandler would be willing to spend to acquire more crude oil 1. Does this shadow price change as Chandler keeps getting more of crude oil 1? Answer the same questions for crude oil 2.

22. How sensitive is the optimal solution (barrels of each output sold and profit) to the required quality points? Answer this by running a two-way SolverTable with these three outputs. You can choose the values of the two inputs to vary.

23. In Chandler's blending model suppose there is a chemical ingredient, which we'll call CI, that both gasoline and heating oil need. At least 3% of every barrel of gasoline must be CI, and at least 5% of every barrel of heating oil must be CI. Suppose that 4% of all crude oil 1 is CI and 6% of all crude oil 2 is CI. Modify the model to incorporate the constraints on

CI, and then optimize. Don't forget to clear denominators.

24. As we have formulated Chandler's blending model, a barrel of any input results in a barrel of output. However, in a real blending problem there can be losses. Suppose a barrel of input results in only a fraction of a barrel of output. Specifically, each barrel of either crude oil used for gasoline results in only 0.95 barrel of gasoline, and each barrel of either crude used for heating oil results in only 0.97 barrel of heating oil. Modify the model to incorporate these losses, and reoptimize.

Skill-Extending Problem

25. We warned you about clearing denominators in the quality constraints. This problem indicates what happens if you don't do so.
   a. Implement the quality constraints as indicated in inequality (4.3) of the text. Then run Solver with Assume Linear Model checked. What happens? What if you uncheck the Assume Linear Model option?
   b. Repeat part **a**, but increase the selling price of heating oil to $40 per barrel. What happens now? Does it matter whether you check or uncheck the Assume Linear Model option? Why?

4.6 PRODUCTION PROCESS MODELS

Linear programming is often used to determine the optimal method of operating a production process. In particular, many oil refineries use LP to manage their production operations. The models are often characterized by the fact that some of the products produced are *inputs* to the production of other products. The following example is typical.

4.5 DRUG PRODUCTION AT REPCO

Repco produces three drugs, A, B, and C, and can sell these drugs in unlimited quantities at unit prices $8, $70, and $100, respectively. Producing a unit of drug A requires 1 hour of labor. Producing a unit of drug B requires 2 hours of labor and 2 units of drug A. Producing 1 unit of drug C requires 3 hours of labor and 1 unit of drug B. Any drug A that is used to produce drug B cannot be sold separately, and any drug B that is used to produce drug C cannot be sold separately. A total of 4000 hours of labor are available. Repco wants to use LP to maximize its sales revenue.

Objective To develop an LP spreadsheet model that relates production decisions to amounts required for production and amounts available for selling, and to use Solver to maximize sales revenue, subject to staying within a limit on labor hours.

WHERE DO THE NUMBERS COME FROM?

The inputs for this problem should be easy to obtain.

■ The company sets its selling prices, which are probably dictated by the market.

■ The available labor hours are based on the size of the current workforce assigned to production of these drugs. These might be flexible quantities, depending on whether workers could be diverted from other duties to work on these drugs and whether new labor could be hired.

■ The labor and drug usage inputs for producing the various drugs are probably well known, based on productivity levels and chemical requirements.

Solution

We follow the principle that the decision variables should be the smallest set of variables that determines everything else. Once the company decides how much of each drug to produce, there is really nothing left to decide.

The variables and constraints required to model this problem are listed in Table 4.8. The key to the model is understanding which variables can be chosen—the decision variables—and which variables are determined by this choice. It is probably clear that Repco must decide how much of each drug to produce. However, it might not be clear why the amounts used for production of other drugs and the amounts sold are *not* decision variables. The idea is that as soon as Repco decides to produce, say, 10 units of drug B, it automatically knows that it must produce at least 20 units of drug A. In fact, it cannot decide to produce just *any* quantities of the three drugs. For example, it couldn't decide to produce 10 units of drug B and only 15 units of drug A. Therefore, the drugs required for production of other drugs put automatic constraints on the production quantities. Of course, any drugs left over, that is, not used in production of other drugs, will be sold.

Table 4.8   Variables and Constraints for Production Process Model

Input variables	Labor inputs to drug production, drugs required for production of other drugs, selling prices of drugs, labor hours available
Decision variables (changing cells)	Units of drugs to produce
Objective (target cell)	Revenue from sales
Other calculated variables	Units of drugs used to make other drugs, units of drugs left over to sell
Constraints	Drugs produced ≥ Drugs required for production of other drugs Labor hours used ≤ Labor hours available

DEVELOPING THE SPREADSHEET MODEL

The key to the spreadsheet model is that everything produced must be used in some way. Either it must be used as an input to the production of some other drug, or it is sold. Therefore, we have the following "balance" equation for each product:

$$\text{Amount produced} = \text{Amount used to produce other drugs} + \text{Amount sold} \quad \textbf{(4.4)}$$

We implement this balance equation in three steps:

1. Specify the amounts produced in changing cells.

2. Calculate the amounts used to produce other drugs based on the way the production process works.

3. Calculate the amounts sold from equation (4.4) by subtraction. Then we impose a constraint that equation (4.4) must be satisfied.

The spreadsheet model for Repco appears in Figure 4.26. (See the file **Production-Process.xls**.) To proceed, carry out the following steps.

Figure 4.26 Repco Production Process Model

	A	B	C	D	E	F	G	H	I	J
1	Repco production process model									
2										
3	Inputs used (along side) to make one unit of product (along top)					Range names used:				
4		Drug A	Drug B	Drug C		Hours_available	=Model!$D$23			
5	Labor hours	1	2	3		Hours_used	=Model!$B$23			
6						Revenue_from_sales	=Model!$B$25			
7	Drug A	0	2	0		Units_produced	=Model!$B$16:$D$16			
8	Drug B	0	0	1		Units_sold	=Model!$B$19:$D$19			
9	Drug C	0	0	0		Units_used_in_production	=Model!$B$18:$D$18			
10										
11	Unit selling prices	Drug A	Drug B	Drug C						
12		$8	$70	$100						
13										
14	Production and sales plan					Units of products used (along side) to make products (along top)				
15		Drug A	Drug B	Drug C				Drug A	Drug B	Drug C	Total used
16	Units produced	2000	1000	0			Drug A	0	2000	0	2000
17		>=	>=	>=			Drug B	0	0	0	0
18	Units used in production	2000	0	0			Drug C	0	0	0	0
19	Units sold	0	1000	0							
20										
21	Labor hour constraint										
22		Hours used		Hours available						
23		4000	<=	4000						
24										
25	Revenue from sales	$70,000	← Objective to maximize							

1 **Inputs and range names.** Enter the inputs in the shaded ranges. For example, the 2 in cell C7 indicates that 2 units of drug A are needed to produce each unit of drug B, and the 0's in this range indicate which drugs are not needed to produce other drugs. (Note, however, the 0 in cell D7, which might be misleading. Drug A is required to make drug B, and drug B is required to make drug C. Therefore, drug A is required indirectly to make drug C. However, this indirect effect is accounted for by the values in cells C7 and D8, and the 0 in cell D7 is appropriate.) Then create the range names indicated.

2 **Units produced.** Enter *any* trial values for the number of units produced in the Units_produced range. This range contains the only changing cells.

3 **Units used to make other products.** In the range G16:I18, calculate the total number of units of each product that are used to produce other products. Begin by calculating the amount of A used to produce A in cell G16 with the formula

=B7*B$16

and copy this formula to the range G16:I18 for the other combinations of products. For example, in the solution shown, 10 units of drug B are produced, so 20 units of drug A are required, as calculated in cell H16. Then calculate the row totals in column J with the SUM function. It is then convenient to "transfer" these sums in column J to the B18:D18 range. This is easy, using Excel's TRANSPOSE function, which creates a row from a column or vice versa. To do so, highlight the B18:D18 range, type the formula

=TRANSPOSE(J16:J18)

and press Ctrl-Shift-Enter (all three keys at once).

→ EXCEL FUNCTION: *TRANSPOSE and Other Array Functions*

*The TRANSPOSE function is useful for linking a row to a column or vice versa. It has the syntax =**TRANSPOSE(Range)**. To implement it, highlight the row or column range where the results will go, type the formula, and press Ctrl-Shift-Enter. This function is one of several array functions in Excel, which means that it fills up an entire range, not just a single cell, all at once. All array formulas require you to highlight the entire range where the results will go, type the formula, and then press Ctrl-Shift-Enter. Once you do this, you will notice curly brackets around the formula in the formula bar. You should not actually type these curly brackets. They simply indicate the presence of an array function.* ∎

4 **Units sold.** Referring to equation (4.4), we can determine the units sold of each drug by subtraction. Specifically, enter the formula

=B16-B18

in cell B19 and copy it to the range C19:D19.

5 **Labor hours used.** Calculate the total number of labor hours used in cell B23 with the formula

=SUMPRODUCT(B5:D5,Units_produced)

6 **Total revenue.** Calculate Repco's revenue from sales in cell B25 with the formula

=SUMPRODUCT(B12:D12,Units_sold)

USING SOLVER

To use Solver to maximize Repco's revenue, fill in the main Solver dialog box as shown in Figure 4.27. As usual, check the Assume Linear Model and Assume Non-Negative options before optimizing. Note that we have constrained the drugs produced to be greater than or equal to the drugs used in production of other drugs. An equivalent alternative is to constrain the units sold to be nonnegative.

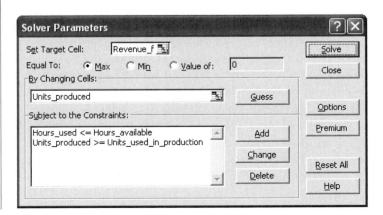

Figure 4.27

Solver Dialog Box for Repco Model

Discussion of the Solution

The optimal solution in Figure 4.26 indicates that Repco obtains a revenue of $70,000 by producing 2000 units of drug A, all of which are used to produce 1000 units of drug B. All units of drug B produced are sold. Even though drug C has the highest selling price, Repco produces none of drug C, evidently because of the large labor requirement for drug C.

Sensitivity Analysis

We saw that drug C is not produced at all, even though its selling price is by far the highest. How high would this selling price have to be to induce Repco to produce any of drug C? We use SolverTable to answer this, using drug C selling price as the input variable, letting it vary from $100 to $200 in increments of $10, and keeping track of the total revenue, the units produced of each drug, and the units used (row 18) of each drug. The results are given in Figure 4.28.

Figure 4.28   Sensitivity to Selling Price of Drug C

	A	B	C	D	E	F	G	H
28	Sensitivity of revenue, units produced, and units used as inputs to drug C selling price							
29	Drug C selling price	A produced	B produced	C produced	A used		B used	C used	Revenue
30		$B$16	$C$16	$D$16	$B$18		$C$18	$D$18	$B$25
31	100	2000.0	1000.0	0.0	2000.0	0	.0	0.0	$70,000
32	110	2000.0	1000.0	0.0	2000.0	0	.0	0.0	$70,000
33	120	2000.0	1000.0	0.0	2000.0	0	.0	0.0	$70,000
34	130	1142.9	571.4	571.4	1142.9		571.4	0.0	$74,286
35	140	1142.9	571.4	571.4	1142.9		571.4	0.0	$80,000
36	150	1142.9	571.4	571.4	1142.9		571.4	0.0	$85,714
37	160	1142.9	571.4	571.4	1142.9		571.4	0.0	$91,429
38	170	1142.9	571.4	571.4	1142.9		571.4	0.0	$97,143
39	180	1142.9	571.4	571.4	1142.9		571.4	0.0	$102,857
40	190	1142.9	571.4	571.4	1142.9		571.4	0.0	$108,571
41	200	1142.9	571.4	571.4	1142.9		571.4	0.0	$114,286

As we see, until the drug C selling price reaches $130, Repco uses the same solution as before.[8] However, when it increases to $130 and beyond, 571.4 units of drug C are produced. This in turn requires 571.4 units of drug B, which requires 1142.9 units of drug A, but only drug C is actually sold. Of course, Repco would like to produce even more of drug C (which would require more production of drugs A and B), but the labor hour constraint does not allow it. Therefore, further increases in the selling price of drug C have no effect on the solution—other than increasing revenue.

Because available labor imposes an upper limit on the production of drug C, even when it is very profitable, it is interesting to see what happens when the selling price of drug C *and* the labor hours available both increase. Here we use a two-way SolverTable, selecting selling price of drug C and labor hour availability as the two inputs with reasonable values, and selecting the amount produced of drug C as the single output. The results from SolverTable appear in Figure 4.29 (page 154).

[8]If you obtain Solver's sensitivity report, you will see that the change actually occurs when the price of drug C reaches $122.50. Our SolverTable grid of prices is too coarse to detect this exact changeover point.

Figure 4.29 Sensitivity to Price of Drug C and Labor Hour Availability

	A	B	C	D	E	F	G	H
43	Sensitivity of amount of C produced to selling price of C (along side) and labor hour availability (along top							
44	$D$16	4000	5000	6000	7000	8000	9000	10000
45	100	0.0	0.0	0.0	0.0	0.0	0.0	0.0
46	110	0.0	0.0	0.0	0.0	0.0	0.0	0.0
47	120	0.0	0.0	0.0	0.0	0.0	0.0	0.0
48	130	571.4	714.3	857.1	1000.0	1142.9	1285.7	1428.6
49	140	571.4	714.3	857.1	1000.0	1142.9	1285.7	1428.6
50	150	571.4	714.3	857.1	1000.0	1142.9	1285.7	1428.6
51	160	571.4	714.3	857.1	1000.0	1142.9	1285.7	1428.6
52	170	571.4	714.3	857.1	1000.0	1142.9	1285.7	1428.6
53	180	571.4	714.3	857.1	1000.0	1142.9	1285.7	1428.6
54	190	571.4	714.3	857.1	1000.0	1142.9	1285.7	1428.6
55	200	571.4	714.3	857.1	1000.0	1142.9	1285.7	1428.6

This table again shows that no drug C is produced, regardless of labor hour availability, until the selling price of drug C reaches $130. (Of course, the actual breakpoint might be *between* $120 and $130. We can't tell from the grid of input values used in the table.) The effect of increases in labor hour availability is to let Repco produce more of drug C. Specifically, Repco will produce as much of drug C as possible, given that 1 unit of drug B, and hence 2 units of drug A, are required for each unit of drug C.

Before leaving this example, we provide further insight into the sensitivity behavior in Figure 4.28. Specifically, why should Repco start producing drug C when its unit selling price increases to some value between $120 and $130? We can provide a straightforward answer to this question because there is a *single* resource constraint, the labor hour constraint. (The analysis would be significantly more complicated with multiple resources.)

As this analysis illustrates, we can sometimes—but not always—gain an intuitive understanding of the information obtained by SolverTable.

Consider the production of 1 unit of drug B. It requires 2 labor hours plus 2 units of drug A, each of which requires 1 labor hour, for a total of 4 labor hours, and it returns $70 in revenue. Therefore, revenue per labor hour when producing drug B is $17.50. To be eligible as a "winner," drug C has to beat this. Note that each unit of drug C requires 7 labor hours (3 for itself and 4 for the unit of drug B it requires). To beat the $17.50 revenue per labor hour of drug B, the unit selling price of drug C must be at least $122.50 [= 17.50(7)]. If its selling price is below this, for example, $121, Repco will sell all drug B and no drug C. If its selling price is above this, for example, $127, Repco will sell all drug C and no drug B. ■

ADDITIONAL APPLICATIONS

Production Process Modeling for a Creamery

Sullivan and Secrest (1985) developed a linear programming model to aid Dairyman's Cooperative Creamery Association in its production of dairy products. Each day their program took as input the amount of available raw milk and cream. As an output, the LP told the creamery how much sour cream, raw milk, buttermilk, and cottage cheese to produce. The problem was complicated by the relationships between the products. For example, if cottage cheese is produced, then whey is produced as a by-product. Then the whey is used to produce cream, which is used in other products. The model has increased the creamery's profit by $48,000 per year. ■

PROBLEMS

Skill-Building Problems

26. Run a one-way sensitivity analysis on the optimal solution to the unit selling price of drug A in the Repco problem. If this price is high enough, will Repco start selling drug A, in addition to producing it? Then run a similar one-way sensitivity analysis on the optimal solution to the price of drug B? If this price gets low enough, what happens to the optimal solution?

27. We claimed in the Repco model that we could either constrain the units produced to be greater than or equal to the units used by production or the units sold to be nonnegative. We chose the former. Modify the model to implement the latter (deleting the former), and verify that you get the same optimal solution.

28. Suppose that there is a fourth drug, drug D, that Repco can produce and sell. Each unit of drug D requires 4 labor hours, 1 unit of drug A, and 1 unit of drug C to produce, and it sells for $150 per unit. Modify the current model to incorporate drug D, and

reoptimize. If drug D isn't produced in the optimal solution, use sensitivity analysis to see how much higher its selling price would have to be before Repco would produce it. If drug D is produced in the optimal solution, use sensitivity analysis to see how much lower its selling price would have to be before Repco would stop producing it.

Skill-Extending Problem

29. In a production process model such as Repco's, there are certain inputs that make no sense in the "usage" table (the range B7:D9 of our model). For example, suppose that, in addition to current usages, each unit of drug A requires 1 unit of drug C. Why does this result in a nonsensical problem? What happens if you run Solver on it anyway? What happens if you run Solver on it after adding a constraint that the sum of the units produced (over all three drugs) must be at least 1?

4.7 FINANCIAL MODELS

The majority of optimization examples described in management science textbooks are in the area of operations: scheduling, blending, logistics, aggregate planning, and others. This is probably warranted, because many of the most successful management science applications in the real world have been in these areas. However, optimization and other management science methods have also been applied successfully in a number of financial areas, and they deserve recognition. We will discuss several of these applications throughout this book. In this section we begin the discussion with two typical applications of LP in finance. The first involves investment strategy. The second involves pension fund management.

EXAMPLE | **4.6 FINDING AN OPTIMAL INVESTMENT STRATEGY AT BARNEY-JONES**

At the present time, the beginning of year 1, the Barney-Jones Investment Corporation has $100,000 to invest for the next 4 years. There are five possible investments, labeled A–E. The timing of cash outflows and cash inflows for these investments is somewhat irregular. For example, to take part in investment A, cash must be invested at the beginning of year 1, and for every dollar invested, there are returns of $0.50 and $1.00 at the beginnings of years 2 and 3. Similar information for the other investments are as follows, where all returns are per dollar invested:

- Investment B: Invest at the beginning of year 2, receive returns of $0.50 and $1.00 at the beginnings of years 3 and 4

- Investment C: Invest at the beginning of year 1, receive return of $1.20 at the beginning of year 2

- Investment D: Invest at the beginning of year 4, receive return of $1.90 at the beginning of year 5

- Investment E: Invest at the beginning of year 3, receive return of $1.50 at the beginning of year 4

We assume that any amounts can be invested in these strategies and that the returns are the same for each dollar invested. However, to create a diversified portfolio, Barney-Jones decides to limit the amount put into any investment to $75,000. The company wants an investment strategy that maximizes the amount of cash on hand at the beginning of year 5. At the beginning of any year, it can invest only cash on hand, which includes returns from previous investments. Any cash not invested in any year can be put in a short-term money market account that earns 3% annually.

Objective To develop an LP spreadsheet model that relates investment decisions to total ending cash, and to use Solver to find the strategy that maximizes ending cash and invests no more than a given amount in any one investment.

WHERE DO THE NUMBERS COME FROM?

There is no mystery here. We assume that the terms of each investment are spelled out, so that Barney-Jones knows exactly when money must be invested and what the amounts and timing of returns will be. Of course, this would not be the case for many real-world investments, such as money put into the stock market, where considerable uncertainty is involved. We will consider one such example of investing with uncertainty when we study portfolio optimization in Chapter 7.

Solution

There are often multiple equivalent ways to state a constraint. You can choose the one that is most natural for you.

The variables and constraints for this investment model are listed in Table 4.9. On the surface, this problem looks to be very straightforward. We must decide how much to invest in the available investments at the beginning of each year, and we can use only the cash available. If you try modeling this problem without our help, however, we suspect that you will have some difficulty. It took us a few tries to get a "nice" model, one that is easy to read and one that generalizes to other similar investment problems. By the way, the second constraint in the table can be expressed in two ways. It can be expressed as shown, where the cash on hand *after* investing is nonnegative, or it can be expressed as "cash on hand at the beginning of any year must be greater than or equal to cash invested that year." These are equivalent. The one you choose is a matter of taste.

Table 4.9 Variables and Constraints for Investment Model

Input variables	Timing of investments and returns, initial cash, maximum amount allowed in any investment, money market rate on cash
Decision variables (changing cells)	Amounts to invest in investments
Objective (target cell)	Ending cash at the beginning of year 5
Other calculated variables	Cash available at the beginning of years 2–4
Constraints	Amount in any investment ≤ Maximum amount per investment Cash on hand after investing each year ≥ 0

DEVELOPING THE SPREADSHEET MODEL

The spreadsheet model for this investment problem appears in Figure 4.30. (See the file **Investing.xls**.) To set up this spreadsheet, proceed as follows.

Figure 4.30 Spreadsheet Model for Investment Problem

	A	B	C	D	E	F	G	H
1	Investments with irregular timing of returns							
2								
3	Inputs						Range names used	
4	Initial amount to invest	$100,000					Cash_after_investing	=Model!$E$32:$E$35
5	Maximum per investment	$75,000					Dollars_invested	=Model!$B$26:$F$26
6	Interest rate on cash	3%					Final_cash	=Model!$B$38
7							Maximum_per_investment	=Model!$B$28:$F$28
8	Cash outlays on investments (all incurred at beginning of year)							
9		Investment						
10	Year	A	B	C	D	E		
11	1	$1.00	$0.00	$1.00	$0.00	$0.00		
12	2	$0.00	$1.00	$0.00	$0.00	$0.00		
13	3	$0.00	$0.00	$0.00	$0.00	$1.00		
14	4	$0.00	$0.00	$0.00	$1.00	$0.00		
15								
16	Cash returns from investments (all incurred at beginning of year)							
17		Investment						
18	Year	A	B	C	D	E		
19	1	$0.00	$0.00	$0.00	$0.00	$0.00		
20	2	$0.50	$0.00	$1.20	$0.00	$0.00		
21	3	$1.00	$0.50	$0.00	$0.00	$0.00		
22	4	$0.00	$1.00	$0.00	$0.00	$1.50		
23	5	$0.00	$0.00	$0.00	$1.90	$0.00		
24								
25	Investment decisions							
26	Dollars invested	$64,286	$75,000	$35,714	$75,000	$75,000		
27		<=	<=	<=	<=	<=		
28	Maximum per investment	$75,000	$75,000	$75,000	$75,000	$75,000		
29								
30	Constraints on cash balance							
31	Year	Beginning cash	Returns from investments	Cash invested	Cash after investing			
32	1	$100,000	$0	$100,000	$0	>=		0
33	2	$0	$75,000	$75,000	-$0	>=		0
34	3	-$0	$101,786	$75,000	$26,786	>=		0
35	4	$27,589	$187,500	$75,000	$140,089	>=		0
36	5	$144,292	$142,500					
37								
38	Final cash	$286,792	◄———	Objective to maximize: final cash at beginning of year 5				

❶ Inputs and range names. As usual, enter the given inputs in the shaded ranges and name the ranges indicated. Pay particular attention to the two shaded tables. This is probably the first model we have encountered where model development is affected significantly by the way we enter the inputs, specifically, the information about the investments. We suggest separating cash outflows from cash inflows, as shown in the two ranges B11:F14 and B19:F23. The top table indicates when we invest, where a 0 indicates no possible investment, and a 1 indicates a dollar of investment. The bottom table then indicates the amounts and timing of returns per dollar invested.

❷ Investment amounts. Enter *any* trial values in the Dollars_invested range. This range contains the changing cells. Also put a link to the maximum investment amount per investment by entering the formula

=$B$5

in cell B28 and copying it across.

❸ Cash balances and flows. The key to the model is the section in rows 32–36. For each year, we need to calculate the beginning cash held from the previous year, the returns from investments that are due in that year, the investments made in that year, and cash balance after investments. Begin by entering the initial cash in cell B32 with the formula

=B4

Moving across, calculate the return due in year 1 in cell C32 with the formula

=SUMPRODUCT(B19:F19,Dollars_invested)

Note how the two input tables at the top of the spreadsheet allow us to use, and copy, the SUMPRODUCT function for cash outflows and inflows. Careful spreadsheet planning can often greatly simplify the necessary formulas.

Admittedly, no returns come due in year 1, but this formula can be copied down column C for other years. Next, calculate the total amount invested in year 1 in cell D32 with the formula

=SUMPRODUCT(B11:F11,Dollars_invested)

Now find the cash balance after investing in year 1 in cell E32 with the formula

=B32+C32-D32

The only other required formula is the formula for the cash available at the beginning of year 2. Because any cash not invested earns 3% interest, enter the formula

=E32*(1+$B$6)

in cell B33. This formula, along with those in cells C32, D32, and E32, can now be copied down. (The 0's in column G are entered manually to remind us of the nonnegativity constraint on cash after investing.)

Always look at the Solver solution for signs of implausibility. This can often lead you to an error in your model.

④ Ending cash. The ending cash at the beginning of year 5 is sum of the amount in the money market and any returns that come due in year 5. Calculate this sum with the formula

=SUM(B36:C36)

in cell B38. (*Note:* Here is the type of error to watch out for. We originally failed to calculate the return in cell C36 and mistakenly used the beginning cash in cell B36 as the target cell. We realized our error when the optimal solution called for no money in investment D, which is clearly an attractive investment. The moral is that you can often catch errors by looking at the *plausibility* of your optimal solution.)

Review of the Model

Take a careful look at this model and how it has been set up. There are undoubtedly many alternative ways to model this problem, but the attractive feature of our model is the way the tables of inflows and outflows in rows 11–14 and 19–23 allow us to copy formulas for returns and investment amounts in columns C and D of rows 32–35. In fact, this same model setup, with only minor modifications, will work for *any* set of investments, regardless of the timing of investments and their returns. This is a quality you should strive for in your own spreadsheet models: generalizability.

USING SOLVER

To find the optimal investment strategy, fill in the main Solver dialog box as shown in Figure 4.31, check the Assume Linear Model and Assume Non-Negative options, and optimize. Note that the explicit nonnegativity constraint in Figure 4.31 is necessary, even though we check the Assume Non-Negative option. Again, this is because the Assume Non-Negative option covers only the changing cells. If we want other output cells to be nonnegative, we must add such constraints explicitly.

Figure 4.31

Solver Dialog Box
for Investment
Model

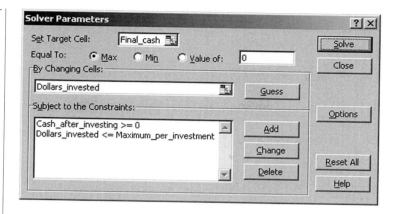

Discussion of the Results

The optimal solution appears in Figure 4.30. Let's follow the cash. The company spends all of its cash in year 1 on the two available investments, A and C ($64,286 in A, $35,714 in C). A total of $75,000 in returns from these investments is available in year 2, and all of this is invested in investment B. (The minus signs in cells E33 and B34 are due to round-off error. The values in these cells are very small negative numbers, but they are equal to 0 for all practical purposes.) At the beginning of year 3, a total of $101,786 is available from investment A and B returns, and $75,000 of this invested in investment E. This leaves $26,786 for the money market, which grows to $27,589 at the beginning of year 4. In addition, returns totaling $187,500 from investments B and E come due in year 4. Of this total cash of $215,089, $75,000 is invested in investment D, and the rest, $140,089, is put in the money market. The return from investment D, $142,500, plus the money available from the money market, $144,292, equals the final cash in the target cell, $286,792.

Sensitivity Analysis

Constraints always have the potential to "penalize" the objective to some extent. SolverTable is a perfect tool for finding the magnitude of this penalty.

A close look at the optimal solution in Figure 4.30 indicates that Barney-Jones is really "penalizing" itself by imposing a maximum of $75,000 per investment. This upper limit is forcing the company to put cash into the money market fund, despite this fund's low rate of return. Therefore, a natural sensitivity analysis is to see how the optimal solution changes as this maximum value changes. We performed this sensitivity analysis with a one-way SolverTable, shown in Figure 4.32 (page 160).[9] It uses the maximum in cell B5 as the input cell, varied from $75,000 to $225,000 in increments of $25,000, and keeps track of the optimal changing cells and target cell. As we see, the final cash (column G) grows steadily as we allow the maximum investment amount to increase. This is because the company can take greater advantage of the attractive investments and put less in the money market.

---

[9]Because Solver's sensitivity reports do not help answer our specific sensitivity questions in this example or the next example, we will discuss only the SolverTable results.

Figure 4.32 Sensitivity of Optimal Solution to Maximum Investment Amount

	A	B	C	D	E	F	G
40	Sensitivity of optimal solution to maximum per investment						
41		$B$26	$C$26	$D$26	$E$26	$F$26	$B$38
42	75000	$64,286	$75,000	$35,714	$75,000	$75,000	$285,118
43	100000	$61,538	$76,923	$38,462	$100,000	$100,000	$319,462
44	125000	$100,000	$50,000	$0	$125,000	$125,000	$352,250
45	150000	$100,000	$50,000	$0	$150,000	$125,000	$374,250
46	175000	$100,000	$50,000	$0	$175,000	$125,000	$396,250
47	200000	$100,000	$50,000	$0	$200,000	$125,000	$418,250
48	225000	$100,000	$50,000	$0	$225,000	$125,000	$440,250

To perform sensitivity on an output variable not calculated explicitly in your spreadsheet model, calculate it in some unused portion of the spreadsheet before running SolverTable.

We go one step further with the two-way SolverTable in Figure 4.33. Here we allow both the maximum investment amount and the money market rate to vary, and we keep track of the maximum amount ever put in the money market. Because this latter amount is not calculated in the spreadsheet model, we calculate it with the formula **=MAX(Cash_after_investing)** in cell B51 and then use it as the output cell for SolverTable. In every case, even with a large maximum investment amount and a low money market rate, the company puts *some* money in the money market. The reason is simple. Even when the maximum investment amount is $225,000, the company evidently has more cash than this to invest at some point (probably at the beginning of year 4). Therefore, it will have to put some of it in the money market. ■

Figure 4.33 Sensitivity of Maximum in Money Market to Two Inputs

	A	B	C	D	E	F	G	H
51	Maximum in money market	$140,089	←	Extra output for use in sensitivity analysis below				
52								
53	Sensitivity of maximum placed in money market to interest rate on cash and maximum per investment							
54	$B$51	75000	100000	125000	150000	175000	200000	225000
55	0.5%	$139,420	$126,923	$112,500	$87,500	$62,500	$37,500	$12,500
56	1.0%	$139,554	$126,923	$112,500	$87,500	$62,500	$37,500	$12,500
57	1.5%	$139,688	$126,923	$112,500	$87,500	$62,500	$37,500	$12,500
58	2.0%	$139,821	$126,923	$112,500	$87,500	$62,500	$37,500	$12,500
59	2.5%	$139,955	$126,923	$112,500	$87,500	$62,500	$37,500	$12,500
60	3.0%	$140,089	$126,923	$112,500	$87,500	$62,500	$37,500	$12,500
61	3.5%	$140,223	$126,923	$112,500	$87,500	$62,500	$37,500	$12,500
62	4.0%	$140,357	$126,923	$112,500	$87,500	$62,500	$37,500	$12,500
63	4.5%	$140,491	$126,923	$112,500	$87,500	$62,500	$37,500	$12,500

The following example illustrates a common situation where fixed payments are due in the future and current funds must be allocated and invested so that their returns are sufficient to make the payments. We put this in a pension fund context.

EXAMPLE 4.7 MANAGING A PENSION FUND AT ARMCO

James Judson is the financial manager in charge of the company pension fund at Armco Incorporated. James knows that the fund must be sufficient to make the payments listed in Table 4.10. Each payment must be made on the first day of each year. James is going to finance these payments by purchasing bonds. It is currently January 1, 2003, and three bonds are available for immediate purchase. The prices and coupons for the bonds are as follows. (All coupon payments are received on Jaunary 1 and arrive in time to meet cash demands for the date on which they arrive.)

- Bond 1 costs $980 and yields a $60 coupon in the years 2004–2007 and a $1060 payment on maturity in the year 2008.

- Bond 2 costs $970 and yields a $65 coupon in the years 2004–2013 and a $1065 payment on maturity in the year 2014.

- Bond 3 costs $1050 and yields a $75 coupon in the years 2004–2016 and a $1075 payment on maturity in the year 2017.

James must decide how much cash to allocate (from company coffers) to meet the initial $11,000 payment and buy enough bonds to make future payments. He knows that any excess cash on hand can earn an annual rate of 4% in a fixed-rate account. How should he proceed?

Table 4.10   Payments for Pension Problem

Year	Payment	Year	Payment	Year	Payment
2003	$11,000	2008	$18,000	2013	$25,000
2004	$12,000	2009	$20,000	2014	$30,000
2005	$14,000	2010	$21,000	2015	$31,000
2006	$15,000	2011	$22,000	2016	$31,000
2007	$16,000	2012	$24,000	2017	$31,000

Objective   To develop an LP spreadsheet model that relates initial allocation of money and bond purchases to future cash availabilities, and to use Solver to minimize the initialize allocation of money required to meet all future pension fund payments.

WHERE DO THE NUMBERS COME FROM?

As in the previous financial example, the inputs are fairly easy to obtain. A pension fund has known liabilities that must be met in future years, and information on bonds and fixed-rate accounts is widely available.

Solution

Although it doesn't occur very often, it is perfectly acceptable to make the target cell one of the changing cells. In fact, this is the key to the current model.

The variables and constraints required for this pension fund model are listed in Table 4.11 (page 162). When modeling this problem, we see a new twist that involves the money James must allocate in 2003 for his funding problem. It is clear that he must decide how many bonds of each type to purchase in 2003 (note that no bonds are purchased *after* 2003), but he must also decide how much money to allocate from company coffers. This allocated money has to cover the initial pension payment in 2003 *and* the bond purchases. In addition, James wants to find the *minimum* allocation that will suffice. Therefore, this initial allocation serves two roles in the model. It is a decision variable *and* it is the objective we want to minimize. In terms of spreadsheet modeling, it is perfectly acceptable to make the target cell one of the changing cells, and we do so here. You might not see this in many models—because the objective typically involves a linear combination of several decision variables—but it is occasionally the most natural way to proceed.

Table 4.11 Variables and Constraints for Pension Model

Input variables	Pension payments, information on bonds, fixed interest rate on cash
Decision variables (changing cells)	Money to allocate in 2003, numbers of bonds to purchase in 2003
Object (target cell)	Money to allocate in 2003 (minimize)
Other calculated variables	Cash available to meet pension payments each year
Constraints	Cash available for payments ≥ Payment amounts

DEVELOPING THE SPREADSHEET MODEL

The completed spreadsheet model is shown in Figure 4.34. (See the file **PensionFund-Mgt.xls**.) You can create it with the following steps.

Figure 4.34 Spreadsheet Model for Pension Fund Management

	A	B	C	D	E	F	G	H	I	J	K	L	M	N	O	P
1	Pension fund management															
2																
3	Costs (in 2003) and income (in other years) from bonds															
4	Year	2003	2004	2005	2006	2007	2008	2009	2010	2011	2012	2013	2014	2015	2016	2017
5	Bond 1	$980	$60	$60	$60	$60	$1,060									
6	Bond 2	$970	$65	$65	$65	$65	$65	$65	$65	$65	$65	$65	$1,065			
7	Bond 3	$1,050	$75	$75	$75	$75	$75	$75	$75	$75	$75	$75	$75	$75	$75	$1,075
8																
9	Interest rate	4%														
10																
11	Number of bonds (allowing fractional values) to purchase in 2003															
12	Bond 1	73.69														
13	Bond 2	77.21														
14	Bond 3	28.84														
15																
16	Money allocated	$197,768														
17																
18	Constraints to meet payments															
19	Year	2003	2004	2005	2006	2007	2008	2009	2010	2011	2012	2013	2014	2015	2016	2017
20	Amount available	$20,376	$21,354	$21,332	$19,228	$16,000	$85,298	$77,171	$66,639	$54,646	$41,133	$25,000	$84,390	$58,728	$31,000	$31,000
21		>=	>=	>=	>=	>=	>=	>=	>=	>=	>=	>=	>=	>=	>=	>=
22	Amount required	$11,000	$12,000	$14,000	$15,000	$16,000	$18,000	$20,000	$21,000	$22,000	$24,000	$25,000	$30,000	$31,000	$31,000	$31,000
23																
24	Range names used:															
25	Amount_available	=Model!$B$20:$P$20														
26	Amount_required	=Model!$B$22:$P$22														
27	Bonds_purchased	=Model!$B$12:$B$14														
28	Money_allocated	=Model!$B$16														

Objective to minimize, also a changing cell (← arrow pointing to cell B16)

The value in cell B16 is the money allocated to make the 2003 payment and buy bonds in 2003. It is both a changing cell and the target cell to minimize; hence the "combination" type border.

---

1 Inputs and range names. Enter the given data in the shaded cells and name the ranges as indicated. Note that we have entered the bond costs in the range B5:B7 as *positive* quantities. Some financial analysts might prefer that they be entered as negative numbers, indicating outflows. It doesn't really matter, however, as long as we are careful with spreadsheet formulas later on.

Always document your spreadsheet conventions as clearly as possible.

2 Money allocated and bonds purchased. As we discussed previously, the money allocated in 2003 and the numbers of bonds purchased are both decision variables, so enter *any* values for these in the Money_allocated and Bonds_purchased ranges. Note that we had to modify our color-coding convention for the Money_allocated cell. Because it is both a changing cell and the target cell, we enclosed it in a double-line red border. (This convention is certainly not standard, so we also documented the change with a text box explanation.)

3 Cash available to make payments. In 2003, the only cash available is the money initially allocated minus cash used to purchase bonds. Calculate this quantity in cell B20 with the formula

=Money_allocated-SUMPRODUCT(Bonds_purchased,B5:B7)

For all other years, the cash available comes from two sources: excess cash invested at the fixed interest rate the year before and payments from bonds. Calculate this quantity for 2004 in cell C20 with the formula

=(B20-B22)*(1+$B$9)+SUMPRODUCT(Bonds_purchased,C5:C7)

and copy it across row 20 for the other years.

As you see, this model is fairly straightforward to develop once you understand the role of the amount allocated in cell B16. However, we have often given this problem as an assignment to our students, and many fail to deal correctly with the amount allocated. (They usually forget to make it a changing cell.) So make sure you understand what we have done, and why we have done it this way.

USING SOLVER

The main Solver dialog box should be filled out as shown in Figure 4.35. As usual, the Assume Linear Model and Assume Non-Negative options should be checked before optimizing. Once again, notice that the Money_allocated cell is both the target cell and one of the changing cells.

Figure 4.35
Solver Dialog Box
for Pension Model

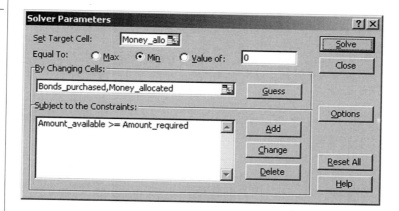

Discussion of the Solution

The optimal solution appears in Figure 4.34. You might argue that the numbers of bonds purchased should be constrained to integer values. We tried this and the optimal solution changed very little: The optimal numbers of bonds to purchase changed to 74, 79, and 27, and the optimal money to allocate increased to $197,887. With this integer solution, shown in Figure 4.36, James sets aside $197,887 initially. Any less than this would not work—he couldn't make enough from bonds to meet future pension payments. All but $20,387 of this (see cell B20) is spent on bonds, and of the $20,387, $11,000 is used to make the 2003 pension payment. After this, the amounts in row 20, which are always sufficient to make the payments in row 22, are composed of returns from bonds and cash, with interest, from the previous year. Even more so than in previous examples, we see no way to "guess" this optimal solution. The timing of bond returns and the irregular pension payments make a spreadsheet optimization model an absolute necessity.

Figure 4.36 Optimal Integer Solution for Pension Model

	A	B	C	D	E	F	G	H	I	J	K	L	M	N	O	P
1	Pension fund management															
2																
3	Costs (in 2003) and income (in other years) from bonds															
4	Year	2003	2004	2005	2006	2007	2008	2009	2010	2011	2012	2013	2014	2015	2016	2017
5	Bond 1	$980	$60	$60	$60	$60	$1,060									
6	Bond 2	$970	$65	$65	$65	$65	$65	$65	$65	$65	$65	$1,065				
7	Bond 3	$1,050	$75	$75	$75	$75	$75	$75	$75	$75	$75	$75	$75	$75	$75	$1,075
8																
9	Interest rate	4%														
10																
11	Number of bonds (allowing fractional values) to purchase in 2003															
12	Bond 1	74.00														
13	Bond 2	79.00														
14	Bond 3	27.00														
15																
16	Money allocated	$197,887	← Objective to minimize, also a changing cell													
17																
18	Constraints to meet payments															
19	Year	2003	2004	2005	2006	2007	2008	2009	2010	2011	2012	2013	2014	2015	2016	2017
20	Amount available	$20,387	$21,363	$21,337	$19,231	$16,000	$85,600	$77,464	$66,923	$54,919	$41,396	$25,252	$86,422	$60,704	$32,917	$31,019
21		>=	>=	>=	>=	>=	>=	>=	>=	>=	>=	>=	>=	>=	>=	>=
22	Amount required	$11,000	$12,000	$14,000	$15,000	$16,000	$18,000	$20,000	$21,000	$22,000	$24,000	$25,000	$30,000	$31,000	$31,000	$31,000
23																
24	Range names used:															
25	Amount_available	=Model!$B$20:$P$20														
26	Amount_required	=Model!$B$22:$P$22														
27	Bonds_purchased	=Model!$B$12:$B$14														
28	Money_allocated	=Model!$B$16														

The value in cell B16 is the money allocated to make the 2003 payment and buy bonds in 2003. It is both a changing cell and the target cell to minimize; hence the "combination" type border.

Sensitivity Analysis

Since the bond information and pension payments are evidently fixed, we see only one promising direction for sensitivity analysis: on the fixed interest rate in cell B9. We tried this, allowing this rate to vary from 2% to 6% in increments of 0.5%, and we kept track of the optimal changing cells, including the target cell. The results appear in Figure 4.37. They indicate that as the interest rate increases, James can get by with fewer bonds of types 1 and 2, and he can allocate less money for the problem. The reason is that he is making more interest on excess cash.

Figure 4.37
Sensitivity to Fixed Interest Rate

	A	B	C	D	E
30	Sensitivity to interest rate				
31		$B$12	$B$13	$B$14	$B$16
32	2.0%	77.12	78.71	28.84	$202,010
33	2.5%	76.24	78.33	28.84	$200,930
34	3.0%	75.37	77.95	28.84	$199,863
35	3.5%	74.53	77.58	28.84	$198,809
36	4.0%	73.69	77.21	28.84	$197,768
37	4.5%	72.88	76.84	28.84	$196,741
38	5.0%	72.09	76.49	28.84	$195,727
39	5.5%	71.30	76.13	28.84	$194,725
40	6.0%	70.54	75.78	28.84	$193,737

ADDITIONAL APPLICATIONS

Using LP to Optimize Bond Portfolios

Many Wall Street firms buy and sell bonds. Rohn (1987) developed a bond selection model that maximizes profit from bond purchases and sales subject to constraints that minimize the firm's risk exposure. The method used to model this situation is closely related to the method we used to model the Barney-Jones problem. (See Problem 47 for a simplified version of this model.)

PROBLEMS

Skill-Building Problems

30. Modify the Barney-Jones investment problem so that there is a minimum amount that must be put into any investment, although this minimum can vary by investment. For example, the minimum amount for investment A might be $0, whereas the minimum amount for investment D might be $50,000. These minimum amounts should be inputs; you can make up any values you like. Run Solver on your modified model.

31. In the Barney-Jones investment problem, increase the maximum amount allowed in any investment to $150,000. Then run a one-way sensitivity analysis to the money market rate on cash. Capture one output variable: the maximum amount of cash ever put in the money market. You can choose any reasonable range for varying the money market rate.

32. We claimed that our model for Barney-Jones is generalizable. Try generalizing it to the case where there are two more potential investments, F and G. Investment F requires a cash outlay in year 2 and returns $0.50 in *each* of the next 4 years. Investment G requires a cash outlay in year 3 and returns $0.75 in each of years 5, 6, and 7. Modify the model as necessary, making the objective the final cash after year 7.

33. In our Barney-Jones spreadsheet model we ran investments across columns and years down rows. Many financial analysts seem to prefer the opposite. Modify the spreadsheet model so that years go across columns and investments go down rows. Run Solver to ensure that your modified model is correct! (We suggest three possible ways to do this, and you can experiment to see which you prefer. First, you could basically start over on a blank worksheet. Second, you could use the Edit/Copy and then Edit/Paste Special with the Transpose option. Third, you could use Excel's TRANSPOSE function.)

34. In the pension fund problem, suppose there is a fourth bond, bond 4. Its unit cost in 2003 is $1020, it returns coupons of $70 in years 2004–2009 and a payment of $1070 in 2010. Modify the model to incorporate this extra bond, and reoptimize. Does the solution change—that is, should James purchase any of bond 4?

35. In the pension fund problem, suppose there is an upper limit of 60 on the number of bonds of any particular type that can be purchased. Modify the model to incorporate this extra constraint and then reoptimize. How much more money does James need to allocate initially?

36. In the pension fund problem, suppose James has been asked to see how the optimal solution will change if the required payments in years 2010–2017 all increase by the same percentage, where this percentage could be anywhere from 5% to 25%. Use an appropriate one-way SolverTable to help him out, and write a memo describing the results.

37. Our pension fund model is streamlined, perhaps too much. It does all of the calculations concerning cash flows in row 20. James decides he would like to "break these out" into several rows of calculations: Beginning cash (for 2003, this is the amount allocated; for other years, it is the unused cash, plus interest, from the previous year), Amount spent on bonds (positive in 2003 only), Amount received from bonds (positive for years 2004–2017 only), Cash available for making pension fund payments, and (below the Amount required row) Cash left over (amount invested in the fixed interest rate). Modify the model by inserting these rows, enter the appropriate formulas, and run Solver. You should obtain the same result, but you get more detailed information.

Skill-Extending Problems

38. Suppose the investments in the Barney-Jones problem sometimes require cash outlays in more than one year. For example, a $1 investment in investment B might require $0.25 to be spent in year 1 and $0.75 to be spent in year 2. Does our model easily accommodate such investments? Try it with some cash outlay data you make up, run Solver, and interpret your results.

39. In the pension fund problem, we know that if the amount of money initially is *less* than the amount found by Solver, then James will not be able to meet all of the pension fund payments. Use the current model to demonstrate that this is true. To do so, enter a value less than the optimal value into cell B16. Then run Solver, but remove the Money_allocated cell as a changing cell and as the target cell. (If there is no target cell, Solver simply tries to find a solution that satisfies all of the constraints.) What do you find?

40. Continuing the previous problem in a slightly different direction, continue to use the Money_allocated cell as a changing cell, and add a constraint that it must be less than or equal to any value, such as $195,000, that is less than its current optimal value. With this constraint, James will again not be able to meet all of the pension fund payments. Create a new target cell to minimize the total amount of payments not met. The easiest way to do this is with IF functions. Unfortunately, this makes the model nonsmooth, and Solver might have trouble finding the optimal solution. Try it and see.

4.8 CONCLUSION

In this chapter we have developed LP spreadsheet models of many diverse situations. There is no standard procedure that can be used to attack all problems. However, there are several keys to most spreadsheet models, as follows:

- Determine the changing cells, the cells that contain the values of the decision variables. These cells should contain the values the decision maker has direct control over, and they should determine all other outputs, either directly or indirectly. For example, in blending problems the changing cells should contain the amount of each input used to produce each output; in employee scheduling problems the changing cells should contain the number of employees who work each possible 5-day shift.

- Set up the spreadsheet so that you can easily compute what you wish to maximize or minimize (usually profit or cost). For example, in the aggregate planning model a good way to compute total cost is to compute the monthly cost of operation in each row.

- Set up the spreadsheet so that the relationships between the cells in the spreadsheet and the problem constraints are readily apparent. For example, in the post office scheduling example, it is convenient to calculate the number of employees working each day of the week near the number of employees needed for each day of the week.

- Make your spreadsheet readable. Use descriptive labels, use range names liberally, use cell comments and text boxes for explanations, and think about your model layout before you dive in. This might not be too important for small, straightforward models, but it is crucial for large, complex models. Just remember that *other* people are likely to be examining your spreadsheet models.

- LP models tend to fall into categories, but they are definitely not all alike. For example, a problem might involve a combination of the ideas discussed in the inventory scheduling, blending, and production process examples of this chapter. Each new model presents new challenges, and you must be flexible and imaginative to meet these challenges. It takes practice and perseverance.

Summary of Key Management Science Terms

Term	Explanation	Page
Dual-objective model	Model with two competing objectives; usual strategy is to constrain one of them and optimize the other	121
Integer constraints	Constraints that limit (some) changing cells to integer values	124
Multiple optimal solutions	Case where several solutions have the same optimal value of the objective	131
Heuristic	An "educated guess" solution, not guaranteed to be optimal but usually quick and easy to obtain	132
Nonsmooth problems	Nonlinear models with "sharp edges" or discontinuities that make them very difficult to solve	141

Summary of Key Excel Terms

Term	Explanation	Excel	Page
Range name shortcut	Quick way to create range names, using labels in adjacent cells	Use Insert/Name/Create menu item	119
Solver integer constraints	Constraints on changing cells forcing them to be integers	Specify in Add Constraint dialog box with Solver	124
Row, column sums shortcut	Quick way of getting row and/or column sums from a table	Highlight row under table and column to right of table, click on Σ Excel toolbar button	137
Nonsmooth functions with Solver	Avoid use of functions such as IF, MIN, MAX, and ABS in Solver models; Solver can't handle them predictably		141
TRANSPOSE function	Useful function for transferring column range to row range, or vice versa	Highlight result range, type =TRANSPOSE(*range*), press Ctrl-Shift-Enter	152
Array functions	Excel functions such as TRANSPOSE that fill a whole range at once	Highlight result range, type formula, press Ctrl-Shift-Enter	152

PROBLEMS

Skill-Building Problems

41. During each 4-hour period, the Smalltown police force requires the following number of on-duty police officers: 8 from midnight to 4 A.M.; 7 from 4 A.M. to 8 A.M.; 6 from 8 A.M. to noon; 6 from noon to 4 P.M.; 5 from 4 P.M. to 8 P.M.; and 4 from 8 P.M. to midnight. Each police officer works 2 consecutive 4-hour shifts.
   a. Determine how to minimize the number of police officers needed to meet Smalltown's daily requirements.
   b. Use SolverTable to see how the number of police officers changes as the number of officers needed from midnight to 4 A.M. changes.

42. A bus company believes that it will need the following numbers of bus drivers during each of the next 5 years: 60 drivers in year 1; 70 drivers in year 2; 50 drivers in year 3; 65 drivers in year 4; 75 drivers in year 5. At the beginning of each year, the bus company must decide how many drivers to hire or fire. It costs $4000 to hire a driver and $2000 to fire a driver. A driver's salary is $10,000 per year. At the beginning of year 1 the company has 50 drivers. A driver hired at the beginning of a year can be used to meet the current year's requirements and is paid full salary for the current year.
   a. Determine how to minimize the bus company's salary, hiring, and firing costs over the next 5 years.
   b. Use SolverTable to determine how the total number hired, total number fired, and total cost change as the unit hiring and firing costs *each* increase by the same percentage.

43. Shoemakers of America forecasts the following demand for the next 6 months: 5000 pairs in month 1; 6000 pairs in month 2; 5000 pairs in month 3; 9000 pairs in month 4; 6000 pairs in month 5; 5000 pairs in month 6. It takes a shoemaker 15 minutes to produce a pair of shoes. Each shoemaker works 150 hours per month plus up to 40 hours per month of overtime. A shoemaker is paid a regular salary of $2000 per month plus $50 per hour for overtime. At the beginning of each month, Shoemakers can either hire or fire workers. It costs the company $1500 to hire a worker and $1900 to fire a worker. The monthly holding cost per pair of shoes is 3% of the cost of producing a pair of shoes with regular-time labor. The raw materials in a pair of shoes cost $10. At the beginning of month 1, Shoemakers has 13 workers. Determine how to minimize the cost of meeting (on time) the demands of the next 6 months.

44. NewAge Pharmaceuticals produces the drug NasaMist from four chemicals. Today, the company must produce 1000 pounds of the drug. The three active ingredients in NasaMist are A, B, and C. By weight, at least 8% of NasaMist must consist of A, at least 4% of B, and at least 2% of C. The cost per pound of each chemical and the amount of each active ingredient in 1 pound of each chemical are given in the file **P04_44.xls**. It is necessary that at least 100 pounds of chemical 2 be used.
   a. Determine the cheapest way of producing today's batch of NasaMist.
   b. Use SolverTable to see how much the percentage of requirement of A is really costing NewAge. Let the percentage required vary from 6% to 12%.

45. You have decided to enter the candy business. You are considering producing two types of candies: Slugger candy and Easy Out candy, both of which consist solely of sugar, nuts, and chocolate. At present you have in stock 10,000 ounces of sugar, 2000 ounces of nuts, and 3000 ounces of chocolate. The mixture used to make Easy Out candy must contain at least 20% nuts. The mixture used to make Slugger candy must contain at least 10% nuts and 10% chocolate. Each ounce of Easy Out candy can be sold for $0.50, and each ounce of Slugger candy for $0.40.
   a. Determine how you can maximize your revenue from candy sales.
   b. Use SolverTable to determine how changes in the price of Easy Out change the optimal solution.
   c. Use SolverTable to determine how changes in the amount of available sugar change the optimal solution.

46. Sunblessed Juice Company sells bags of oranges and cartons of orange juice. Sunblessed grades oranges on a scale of 1 (poor) to 10 (excellent). At present, Sunblessed has 100,000 pounds of grade 9 oranges and 120,000 pounds of grade 6 oranges on hand. The average quality of oranges sold in bags must be at least 7, and the average quality of the oranges used to produce orange juice must be at least 8. Each pound of oranges that is used for juice yields a revenue of $1.50 and incurs a variable cost (consisting of labor costs, variable overhead costs, inventory costs, and so on) of $1.05. Each pound of oranges sold in bags yields a revenue of $1.50 and incurs a variable cost of $0.70.
   a. Determine how Sunblessed can maximize its profit.

   b. Use SolverTable to determine how a change in the cost per bag of oranges changes the optimal solution.
   c. Use SolverTable to determine how a change in the amount of grade 9 oranges available affects the optimal solution.
   d. Use SolverTable to determine how a change in the required average quality required for juice changes the optimal solution.

47. A bank is attempting to determine where its assets should be invested during the current year. At present, $500,000 is available for investment in bonds, home loans, auto loans, and personal loans. The annual rates of return on each type of investment are known to be the following: bonds, 10%; home loans, 16%; auto loans, 13%; personal loans, 20%. To ensure that the bank's portfolio is not too risky, the bank's investment manager has placed the following three restrictions on the bank's portfolio:

   ■ The amount invested in personal loans cannot exceed the amount invested in bonds.

   ■ The amount invested in home loans cannot exceed the amount invested in auto loans.

   ■ No more than 25% of the total amount invested can be in personal loans.

   Help the bank maximize the annual return on its investment portfolio.

48. Young MBA Erica Cudahy can invest up to $1000 in stocks and loans. Each dollar invested in stocks yields $0.10 profit, and each dollar invested in a loan yields $0.15 profit. At least 30% of all money invested must be in stocks, and at least $400 must be in loans. Determine how Erica can maximize the profit earned on her investments.

49. Bullco blends silicon and nitrogen to produce two types of fertilizers. Fertilizer 1 must be at least 40% nitrogen and sells for $70 per pound. Fertilizer 2 must be at least 70% silicon and sells for $40 per pound. Bullco can purchase up to 8000 pounds of nitrogen at $15 per pound and up to 10,000 pounds of silicon at $10 per pound.
   a. Assuming that all fertilizer produced can be sold, determine how Bullco can maximize its profit.
   b. Use SolverTable to explore the effect on profit of changing the minimum percentage of nitrogen required in fertilizer 1.
   c. Suppose the availabilities of nitrogen and silicon both increase by the same percentage from their current values. Use SolverTable to explore the effect of this change on profit.

50. Eli Daisy uses chemicals 1 and 2 to produce two drugs. Drug 1 must be at least 70% chemical 1, and

drug 2 must be at least 60% chemical 2. Up to 4000 ounces of drug 1 can be sold at $6 per ounce; up to 3000 ounces of drug 2 can be sold at $5 per ounce. Up to 4500 ounces of chemical 1 can be purchased at $6 per ounce, and up to 4000 ounces of chemical 2 can be purchased at $4 per ounce. Determine how to maximize Daisy's profit.

51. Hiland's TV-Radio Store must determine how many TVs and radios to keep in stock. A TV requires 10 square feet of floor space, whereas a radio requires 4 square feet; 5000 square feet of floor space is available. A TV sale results in an $80 profit, and a radio earns a profit of $20. The store stocks only TVs and radios. Marketing requirements dictate that at least 60% of all appliances in stock be radios. Finally, a TV ties up $200 in capital, and a radio $50. Hiland wants to have at most $60,000 worth of capital tied up at any time.
   a. Determine how to maximize Hiland's profit.
   b. Use SolverTable to explore how much profit the minimum percentage of radio requirement is costing Hiland's.
   c. Use SolverTable to explore how much profit the upper limit on capital being tied up is costing Hiland's.

52. Linear programming models are used by many Wall Street firms to select a desirable bond portfolio. The following is a simplified version of such a model. Solodrex is considering investing in four bonds; $1 million is available for investment. The expected annual return, the worst-case annual return on each bond, and the "duration" of each bond are given in the file **P04_52.xls**. (The duration of a bond is a measure of the bond's sensitivity to interest rates.) Solodrex wants to maximize the expected return from its bond investments, subject to three constraints:

   ■ The worst-case return of the bond portfolio must be at least 8%.

   ■ The average duration of the portfolio must be at most 6. For example, a portfolio that invests $600,000 in bond 1 and $400,000 in bond 4 has an average duration of [600,000(3) + 400,000(9)]/1,000,000 = 5.4

   ■ Because of diversification requirements, at most 40% of the total amount invested can be invested in a single bond.

   Determine how Solodrex can maximize the expected return on its investment.

53. Coalco produces coal at three mines and ships it to four customers. The cost per ton of producing coal, the ash and sulfur content (per ton) of the coal, and the production capacity (in tons) for each mine are given in the file **P04_53.xls**. The number of tons of coal demanded by each customer is also listed in this same file. The cost (in dollars) of shipping a ton of coal from a mine to each customer is also provided. The amount of coal shipped to each customer must contain at most 6% ash and at most 3.5% sulfur. Show Coalco how to minimize the cost of meeting customer demands.

54. Furnco manufactures tables and chairs. A table requires 40 board feet of wood, and a chair requires 30 board feet of wood. Wood can be purchased at a cost of $1 per board foot, and 40,000 board feet of wood are available for purchase. It takes 2 hours of skilled labor to manufacture an unfinished table or an unfinished chair. Three more hours of skilled labor will turn an unfinished table into a finished table, and 2 more hours of skilled labor will turn an unfinished chair into a finished chair. A total of 6000 hours of skilled labor is available (and have already been paid for). All furniture produced can be sold at the following unit prices: an unfinished table, $70; a finished table, $140; an unfinished chair, $60; a finished chair, $110.
   a. Determine how to maximize Furnco's profit from manufacturing tables and chairs.
   b. Use a two-way SolverTable to see how the numbers of unfinished products (both chairs and tables) sold depend on the selling prices of these unfinished products. Of course, neither unfinished selling price should be as large as the corresponding finished selling price.

55. A company produces three products, A, B, and C, and can sell these products in unlimited quantities at the following unit prices: A, $10; B, $56; C, $100. Producing a unit of A requires 1 hour of labor; a unit of B, 2 hours of labor plus 2 units of A; and a unit of C, 3 hours of labor plus 1 unit of B. Any A that is used to produce B cannot be sold. Similarly, any B that is used to produce C cannot be sold. A total of 40 hours of labor is available. Determine how to maximize the company's revenue.

56. Abotte Products produces three products, A, B, and C. The company can sell up to 300 pounds of each product at the following prices (per pound): product A, $10; product B, $12; product C, $20. Abotte purchases raw material at $5 per pound. Each pound of raw material can be used to produce either 1 pound of A or 1 pound of B. For a cost of $3 per pound processed, product A can be converted to 0.6 pound of product B and 0.4 pound of product C. For a cost of $2 per pound processed, product B can be converted to 0.8 pound of product C. Determine how Abotte can maximize its profit.

57. Moneyco has $100,000 to invest at time 1 (the beginning of year 1). The cash flows associated with the five available investments are listed in the file **P04_57.xls**. For example, every dollar invested in A in

year 1 yields $1.40 in year 4. In addition to these investments, Moneyco can invest as much money each year as it wants in CDs, which pay 6% interest. The company wants to maximize its available cash in year 4. Assuming it can put no more than $500 in any investment, develop an LP model to help Moneyco achieve its goal.

58. At the beginning of year 1, you have $10,000. Investments A and B are available; their cash flows are shown in the file **P04_58.xls**. Assume that any money not invested in A or B earns interest at an annual rate of 8%.
   a. Determine how to maximize your cash on hand in year 4.
   b. Use SolverTable to determine how a change in the year 3 yield for investment A changes the optimal solution to the problem.
   c. Use SolverTable to determine how a change in the yield of investment B changes the optimal solution to the problem.

59. You now have $10,000, and the following investment plans are available to you during the next 3 years:

   ■ Investment A: Every dollar invested now yields $0.10 a year from now and $1.30 3 years from now.

   ■ Investment B: Every dollar invested now yields $0.20 a year from now and $1.10 2 years from now.

   ■ Investment C: Every dollar invested a year from now yields $1.50 3 years from now.

   During each year, you can place uninvested cash in money market funds that yield 6% interest per year. However, you can invest at most $5000 in any one of plans A, B, or C. Determine how to maximize your cash on hand 3 years from now.

60. Sunco processes oil into aviation fuel and heating oil. It costs $40 to purchase each 1000 barrels of oil, which is then distilled and yields 500 barrels of aviation fuel and 500 barrels of heating oil. Output from the distillation can be sold directly or processed in the catalytic cracker. If sold after distillation without further processing, aviation fuel sells for $60 per 1000 barrels, and heating oil sells for $40 per 1000 barrels. It takes 1 hour to process 1000 barrels of aviation fuel in the catalytic cracker, and these 1000 barrels can be sold for $130. It takes 45 minutes to process 1000 barrels of heating oil in the cracker, and these 1000 barrels can be sold for $90. Each day at most 20,000 barrels of oil can be purchased, and 8 hours of cracker time are available. Determine how to maximize Sunco's profit.

61. All steel manufactured by Steelco must meet the following requirements: between 3.2% and 3.5% carbon;

between 1.8% and 2.5% silicon; between 0.9% and 1.2% nickel; tensile strength of at least 45,000 pounds per square inch (psi). Steelco manufactures steel by combining two alloys. The cost and properties of each alloy are given in the file **P04_61.xls**. Assume that the tensile strength of a mixture of the two alloys can be determined by averaging the tensile strength of the alloys that are mixed together. For example, a 1-ton mixture that is 40% alloy 1 and 60% alloy 2 has a tensile strength of $0.4(42,000) + 0.6(50,000)$. Determine how to minimize the cost of producing a ton of steel.

62. Steelco manufactures two types of steel at three different steel mills. During a given month, each steel mill has 200 hours of blast furnace time available. Because of differences in the furnaces at each mill, the time and cost to produce a ton of steel differ for each mill, as listed in the file **P04_62.xls**. Each month Steelco must manufacture at least 500 tons of steel 1 and 600 tons of steel 2. Determine how Steelco can minimize the cost of manufacturing the desired steel.

63. Based on Heady and Egbert (1964). Walnut Orchard has two farms that grow wheat and corn. Because of differing soil conditions, there are differences in the yields and costs of growing crops on the two farms. The yields and costs are listed in the file **P04_63.xls**. Each farm has 100 acres available for cultivation; 11,000 bushels of wheat and 7000 bushels of corn must be grown.
   a. Determine a planting plan that will minimize the cost of meeting these requirements.
   b. Use SolverTable to see how the total cost changes if the requirements for wheat and corn both change by the *same* percentage, where this percentage change can be as low as −50% or as high as +50%.

64. Candy Kane Cosmetics (CKC) produces Leslie Perfume, which requires chemicals and labor. Two production processes are available. Process 1 transforms 1 unit of labor and 2 units of chemicals into 3 ounces of perfume. Process 2 transforms 2 units of labor and 3 units of chemicals into 5 ounces of perfume. It costs CKC $3 to purchase a unit of labor and $2 to purchase a unit of chemicals. Each year up to 20,000 units of labor and 35,000 units of chemicals can be purchased. In the absence of advertising, CKC believes it can sell 1000 ounces of perfume. To stimulate demand for Leslie, CKC can hire the lovely model Jenny Nelson. Jenny is paid $100 per hour. Each hour Jenny works for the company is estimated to increase the demand for Leslie Perfume by 200 ounces. Each ounce of Leslie Perfume sells for $5. Determine how CKC can maximize its profit.

65. Sunco Oil has refineries in Los Angeles and Chicago. The Los Angeles refinery can refine up to 2 million barrels of oil per year, and the Chicago refinery up to

3 million. Once refined, oil is shipped to two distribution points, Houston and New York City. Sunco estimates that each distribution point can sell up to 5 million barrels per year. Because of differences in shipping and refining costs, the profit earned (in dollars) per million barrels of oil shipped depends on where the oil was refined and on the point of distribution. This information is listed in the file **P04_65.xls**. Sunco is considering expanding the capacity of each refinery. Each million barrels of annual refining capacity that is added will cost $120,000 for the Los Angeles refinery and $150,000 for the Chicago refinery. Determine how Sunco can maximize its profit (including expansion costs) over a 10-year period.

66. Feedco produces two types of cattle feed, both consisting totally of wheat and alfalfa. Feed 1 must contain at least 80% wheat, and feed 2 must contain at least 60% alfalfa. Feed 1 sells for $1.50 per pound, and feed 2 sells for $1.30 per pound. Feedco can purchase up to 1000 pounds of wheat at $0.50 per pound and up to 800 pounds of alfalfa at $0.40 per pound. Demand for each type of feed is unlimited. Determine how to maximize Feedco's profit.

67. Carrington Oil produces gas 1 and gas 2 from two types of crude oil: crude 1 and crude 2. Gas 1 is allowed to contain up to 4% impurities, and gas 2 is allowed to contain up to 3% impurities. Gas 1 sells for $8 per barrel, whereas gas 2 sells for $12 per barrel. Up to 4200 barrels of gas 1 and up to 4300 barrels of gas 2 can be sold. The cost per barrel of each crude, their availability, and the level of impurities in each crude are listed in the file **P04_67.xls**. Before blending the crude oil into gas, any amount of each crude can be "purified" for a cost of $0.50 per barrel. Purification eliminates half of the impurities in the crude oil.
   a. Determine how to maximize profit.
   b. Use SolverTable to determine how an increase in the availability of crude 1 affects the optimal profit.
   c. Use SolverTable to determine how an increase in the availability of crude 2 affects the optimal profit.
   d. Use SolverTable to determine how a change in the profitability of gas 2 changes profitability and the types of gas produced.

68. A company produces two products: A and B. Product A sells for $11 per unit and product B sells for $23 per unit. To produce a unit of product A requires 2 hours on assembly line 1 and 1 unit of raw material. To produce a unit of product B requires 2 units of raw material, 1 unit of A, and 2 hours on assembly line 2. There are 1300 hours of time available on line 1 and 500 hours on line 2. A unit of raw material can be bought (for $5 a unit) or produced (at no cost) by using 2 hours of time on line 1.

   a. Determine how to maximize profit.
   b. The company will stop buying raw material when the price of raw material exceeds what value? (Use SolverTable.)

Skill-Extending Problems

69. During the next 4 quarters, Dorian Auto must meet (on time) the following demands for cars: 4000 in quarter 1; 2000 in quarter 2; 5000 in quarter 3; 1000 in quarter 4. At the beginning of quarter 1, there are 300 autos in stock. The company has the capacity to produce at most 3000 cars per quarter. At the beginning of each quarter, the company can change production capacity. It costs $100 to increase quarterly production capacity by one unit. For example, it would cost $10,000 to increase capacity from 3000 to 3100. It also costs $50 per quarter to maintain each unit of production capacity (even if it is unused during the current quarter). The variable cost of producing a car is $2000. A holding cost of $150 per car is assessed against each quarter's ending inventory. It is required, that at the end of quarter 4, plant capacity must be at least 4000 cars.
   a. Determine how to minimize the total cost incurred during the next 4 quarters.
   b. Use SolverTable to determine how much the total cost increases as the required capacity at the end of quarter 4 increases (from its current value of 4000).

70. The Internal Revenue Service (IRS) has determined that during each of the next 12 months it will need the numbers of supercomputers given in the file **P04_70.xls**. To meet these requirements, the IRS rents supercomputers for a period of 1, 2, or 3 months. It costs $100 to rent a supercomputer for 1 month, $180 for 2 months, and $250 for 3 months. At the beginning of month 1, the IRS has no supercomputers.
   a. Determine the rental plan that meets the requirements for the next 12 months at minimum cost. You can assume that fractional rentals are allowed. Thus, if your solution says to rent 140.6 computers for one month, you can round this up to 141 or down to 140 without much effect on the total cost.
   b. Suppose the monthly requirement increases anywhere from 10% to 50% each month. (Assume that whatever the percentage increase is, it is the *same* each month.) Use SolverTable to see whether the total rental cost increases by this same percentage.

71. You own a wheat warehouse with a capacity of 20,000 bushels. At the beginning of month 1, you have 6000 bushels of wheat. Each month wheat can be bought and sold at the prices per 1000 bushels listed in the file **P04_71.xls**. The sequence of events during each month is as follows:

- You observe your initial stock of wheat.

- You can sell any amount of wheat up to your initial stock at the current month's selling price.

- You can buy as much wheat as you want, subject to the limitation of warehouse size.

    a. Determine how to maximize the profit earned over the next 10 months.

    b. Use SolverTable to determine how a change in the capacity of the warehouse affects the optimal solution.

    c. Use SolverTable to determine how simultaneous changes in the buying and selling price for month 6 affect the optimal solution.

72. The risk index of an investment can be obtained by taking the absolute values of percentage changes in the value of the investment for each year and averaging them. Suppose you are trying to determine what percentage of your money you should invest in T-bills, gold, and stocks. The file **P04_72.xls** lists the annual returns (percentage changes in value) for these investments for the years 1968–1988. Let the risk index of a portfolio be the weighted average of the risk indices of these investments, where the weights are the fractions of the portfolio assigned to the investments. Suppose that the amount of each investment must be between 20% and 50% of the total invested. You would like the risk index of your portfolio to equal 0.15, and your goal is to maximize the expected return on your portfolio, subject to the stated constraints. Determine the maximum expected return on your portfolio, subject to the stated constraints. Use the average return earned by each investment during the years 1968–1988 as your estimate of expected return.

73. Based on Magoulas and Marinos-Kouris (1988). Oilco produces two products: regular and premium gasoline. Each product contains 0.15 gram of lead per liter. The two products are produced from these six inputs: reformate, fluid catalytic cracker gasoline (FCG), isomerate (ISO), polymer (POL), MTBE, and butane (BUT). Each input has four attributes: research octane number (RON), RVP, ASTM volatility at 70 degrees Celsius, and ASTM volatility at 130 degrees Celsius. The attributes and daily availability (in liters) of each input are listed in the file **P04_73.xls**. The requirements for each output are also listed in this file. The daily demand (in thousands of liters) for each product must be met, but more can be produced if desired. The RON and ASTM requirements are minimums; the RVP requirement is a maximum. Regular gasoline sells for $0.2949 per liter, premium gasoline for $0.3143. Before each product is ready for sale, 0.15 gram per liter of lead must be removed. The cost of removing 0.1 gram per liter is $0.085. At most 38% of each type of gasoline can consist of FCG. How can Oilco maximize its daily profit?

74. Capsule Drugs manufactures two drugs, 1 and 2. The drugs are produced by blending two chemicals, 1 and 2. By weight, drug 1 must contain at least 65% chemical 1, and drug 2 must contain at least 55% chemical 1. Drug 1 sells for $6 per ounce, and drug 2 sells for $4 per ounce. Chemicals 1 and 2 can be produced by one of two production processes. Running process 1 for an hour requires 7 ounces of raw material and 2 hours skilled labor, and it yields 3 ounces of each chemical. Running process 2 for an hour requires 5 ounces of raw material and 3 hours of skilled labor, and it yields 3 ounces of chemical 1 and 1 ounce of chemical 2. A total of 120 hours of skilled labor and 100 ounces of raw material are available. Determine how to maximize Capsule's sales revenues.

75. Molecular Products produces 3 chemicals, B, C, and D. The company begins by purchasing chemical A for a cost of $6 per 100 liters. For an additional cost of $3 and the use of 3 hours of skilled labor, 100 liters of A can be transformed into 40 liters of C and 60 liters of B. Chemical C can either be sold or processed further. It costs $1 and 1 hour of skilled labor to process 100 liters of C into 60 liters of D and 40 liters of B. For each chemical the selling price per 100 liters and the maximum amount (in 100s of liters) that can be sold are listed in the file **P04_75.xls**. A maximum of 200 labor hours is available. Determine how Molecular can maximize its profit.

76. Bexter Labs produces three products: A, B, and C. Bexter can sell up to 30 units of product A, up to 20 units of product B, and up to 20 units of product C. Each unit of product C uses 2 units of A and 3 units of B and incurs $5 in processing costs. Products A and B are produced from either raw material 1 or raw material 2. It costs $6 to purchase and process 1 unit of raw material 1. Each processed unit of raw material 1 yields 2 units of A and 3 units of B. It costs $3 to purchase and process a unit of raw material 2. Each processed unit of raw material 2 yields 1 unit of A and 2 units of B. The unit prices for the products are: A, $5; B, $4; C, $25. The quality levels of each product are: A, 8; B, 7; C, 6. The average quality level of the units sold must be at least 7. Determine how to maximize Bexter's profit.

77. Mondo Motorcycles is determining its production schedule for the next 4 quarters. Demands for motorcycles are forecasted to be 40 in quarter 1; 70 in quarter 2; 50 in quarter 3; 20 in quarter 4. Mondo incurs four types of costs, as described here:

- It costs Mondo $400 to manufacture each motorcycle.

- At the end of each quarter, a holding cost of $100 per motorcycle left in inventory is incurred.

- Increasing production from one quarter to the next incurs costs for training employees. It is estimated that a cost of $700 per motorcycle is incurred if production is increased from one quarter to the next.

- Decreasing production from one quarter to the next incurs costs for severance pay, decreasing morale, and so forth. It is estimated that a cost of $600 per motorcycle is incurred if production is decreased from one quarter to the next.

All demands must be met on time, and a quarter's production can be used to meet demand for the current quarter (as well as future quarters). During the quarter immediately preceding quarter 1, 50 Mondos were produced. Assume that at the beginning of quarter 1, no Mondos are in inventory.

a. Determine how to minimize Mondo's total cost during the next 4 quarters.

b. Use SolverTable to determine how Mondo's optimal production schedule would be affected by a change in the cost of increasing production from one quarter to the next.

c. Use SolverTable to determine how Mondo's optimal production schedule would be affected by a change in the cost of decreasing production from one quarter to the next.

78. Carco has a $150,000 advertising budget. To increase its automobile sales, the firm is considering advertising in newspapers and on television. The more Carco uses a particular medium, the less effective each additional ad is. The file **P04_78.xls** lists the number of new customers reached by each ad. Each newspaper ad costs $1000, and each television ad costs $10,000. At most 30 newspaper ads and 15 television ads can be placed. How can Carco maximize the number of new customers created by advertising?

79. Broker Sonya Wong is currently trying to maximize her profit in the bond market. Four bonds are available for purchase and sale at the bid and ask prices shown in the file **P04_79.xls**. Sonya can buy up to 1000 units of each bond at the ask price or sell up to 1000 units of each bond at the bid price. During each of the next 3 years, the person who sells a bond will pay the owner of the bond the cash payments listed in the file **P04_79.xls**. Sonya's goal is to maximize her revenue from selling bonds minus her payment for buying bonds, subject to the constraint that after each year's payments are received, her current cash position (due only to cash payments from bonds and not purchases or sales of bonds) is nonnegative. Note that her current cash position can depend on past coupons and that cash accumulated at the end of each year earns 11.111% annual interest. Determine how to maximize net profit from buying and selling bonds, subject to the constraints previously described. Why

do you think we limit the number of units of each bond that can be bought or sold?

80. Pear produces low-budget cars. Each car is sold for $790. The raw material in a car costs $600. Labor time and robot time are needed to produce cars. A worker can do the needed labor on at most 100 cars per month and a robot can complete the needed work on at most 200 cars per month. Initially Pear has 4 workers. Each worker receives a monthly salary of $6000. It costs $2500 to hire a worker and $1000 to fire a worker. Hired workers are fully productive during the month they are hired. Robots must be bought at the beginning of month 1 at a cost of $15,000 per robot. The (assumed known) demand for cars is listed in the file **P04_80.xls**. At the end of each month Pear incurs a holding cost of $50 per car. How can Pear maximize the profit earned during the next 6 months?

81. The ZapCon Company is considering investing in three projects. If it fully invests in a project, the realized cash flows (in millions of dollars) will be as listed in the file **P04_81.xls**. For example, project 1 requires a cash outflow of $3 million today and returns $5.5 million 3 years from now. Today ZapCon has $2 million in cash. At each time point (0, 0.5, 1, 1.5, 2, and 2.5 years from today), the company can, if desired, borrow up to $2 million at 3.5% (per 6 months) interest. Leftover cash earns 3% (per 6 months) interest. For example, if after borrowing and investing at time 0, ZapCon has $1 million, it would receive $30,000 in interest at time 0.5 year. The company's goal is to maximize cash on hand after cash flows 3 years from now are accounted for. What investment and borrowing strategy should it use? Assume that the company can invest in a fraction of a project. For example, if it invests in 0.5 of project 3, it has, for example, cash outflows of $-$1 million at times 0 and 0.5.

82. You are a CFA (chartered financial analyst). An overextended client has come to you because she needs help paying off her credit card bills. She owes the amounts on her credit cards listed in the file **P04_82.xls**. The client is willing to allocate up to $5000 per month to pay off these credit cards. All cards must be paid off within 36 months. The client's goal is to minimize the total of all her payments. To solve this problem, you must understand how interest on a loan works. To illustrate, suppose the client pays $5000 on Saks during month 1. Then her Saks balance at the beginning of month 2 is $20,000 - [5000 - 0.005(20,000)]$. This follows because she incurs $0.005(20,000)$ in interest charges on her Saks card during month 1. Help the client solve her problem. Once you have solved this problem, give an intuitive explanation of the solution found by Solver.

83. Aluminaca produces 100-foot-long, 200-foot-long, and 300-foot-long ingots for customers. This week's demand for ingots is listed in the file **P04_83.xls**. Aluminaca has four furnaces in which ingots can be produced. During 1 week each furnace can be operated for 50 hours. Because ingots are produced by cutting up long strips of aluminum, longer ingots take less time to produce than shorter ingots. If a furnace is devoted completely to producing one type of ingot, the number it can produce in 1 week is listed in the file **P04_83.xls**. For example, furnace 1 could produce 350 300-foot ingots per week. The material in an ingot costs $10 per foot. A customer who wants a 100-foot or 200-foot ingot will accept an ingot of that length or longer. How can Aluminaca minimize the material costs incurred in meeting required weekly demands?

84. Each day Eastinghouse produces capacitors during three shifts: 8 A.M. to 4 P.M., 4 P.M. to midnight, and midnight to 8 A.M. The hourly salary paid to the employees on each shift, the price charged for each capacitor made during each shift, and the number of defects in each capacitor produced during a given shift are listed in the file **P04_84.xls**. The company can employ up to 25 workers, and each worker can be assigned to one of the three shifts. A worker produces 10 capacitors during a shift, but due to machinery limitations, no more than 10 workers can be assigned to any shift. Each capacitor produced can be sold, but the average number of defects per capacitor for the day's production cannot exceed 3. Determine how Eastinghouse can maximize its daily profit.

85. During the next 3 months, Airco must meet (on time) the following demands for air conditioners: month 1, 300; month 2, 400; month 3, 500. Air conditioners can be produced in either New York or Los Angeles. It takes 1.5 hours of skilled labor to produce an air conditioner in Los Angeles, and 2 hours in New York. It costs $400 to produce an air conditioner in Los Angeles, and $350 in New York. During each month each city has 420 hours of skilled labor available. It costs $100 to hold an air conditioner in inventory for a month. At the beginning of month 1, Airco has 200 air conditioners in stock. Determine how Airco can minimize the cost of meeting air conditioner demands for the next 3 months.

86. Gotham City National Bank is open Monday through Friday from 9 A.M. to 5 P.M. From past experience, the bank knows that it needs the numbers of tellers listed in the file **P04_86.xls**. Gotham City Bank hires two types of tellers. Full-time tellers work 9 A.M. to 5 P.M. 5 days a week, with 1 hour off each day for lunch. The bank determines when a full-time employee takes his or her lunch hour, but each teller must go between noon and 1 P.M. or between 1 P.M. and 2 P.M. Full-time employees are paid (including fringe benefits) $8

per hour, which includes payment for lunch hour. The bank can also hire part-time tellers. Each part-time teller must work exactly 3 consecutive hours each day. A part-time teller is paid $5 per hour and receives no fringe benefits. To maintain adequate quality of service, the bank has decided that at most 5 part-time tellers can be hired. Determine how to meet the bank's teller requirements at minimum cost.

87. Based on Rothstein (1973). The Springfield City Police Department employs 30 police officers. Each officer works 5 days per week. The crime rate fluctuates with the day of the week, so the number of police officers required each day depends on the day of the week, as follows: Saturday, 28; Sunday, 18; Monday, 18; Tuesday, 24; Wednesday, 25; Thursday, 16; Friday, 21. The police department wants to schedule police officers to minimize the number whose days off are *not* consecutive. Determine how to accomplish this goal.

88. Based on Charnes and Cooper (1955). Alex Cornby makes his living buying and selling corn. On January 1 he has 50 tons of corn and $1000. On the first day of each month Alex can buy corn at the following prices per ton: January, $300; February, $350; March, $400; April, $500. On the last day of each month, Alex can sell corn at the following prices per ton: January, $250; February, $400; March, $350; April, $550. Alex stores his corn in a warehouse that can hold at most 100 tons of corn. He must be able to pay cash for all corn at the time of purchase. Determine how Alex can maximize his cash on hand at the end of April.

89. City 1 produces 500 tons of waste per day, and city 2 produces 400 tons of waste per day. Waste must be incinerated at incinerator 1 or 2, and each incinerator can process up to 500 tons of waste per day. The cost to incinerate waste is $40 per ton at incinerator 1 and $30 per ton at incinerator 2. Incineration reduces each ton of waste to 0.2 ton of debris, which must be dumped at one of two landfills. Each landfill can receive at most 200 tons of debris per day. It costs $3 per mile to transport a ton of material (either debris or waste). Distances (in miles) between locations are listed in the file **P04_89.xls**. Determine how to minimize the total cost of disposing of the waste from both cities.

90. Based on Smith (1965). Silicon Valley Corporation (Silvco) manufactures transistors. An important aspect of the manufacture of transistors is the melting of the element germanium (a major component of a transistor) in a furnace. Unfortunately, the melting process yields germanium of highly variable quality. Two methods can be used to melt germanium. Method 1 costs $50 per transistor, and method 2 costs $70 per transistor. The qualities of germanium obtained by

methods 1 and 2 are listed in the file **P04_90.xls**. Silvco can refire melted germanium in an attempt to improve its quality. It costs $25 to refire the melted germanium for one transistor. The results of the refiring process are also listed in the file **P04_90.xls**. For example, if grade 3 germanium is refired, half of the resulting germanium will be grade 3 and the other half will be grade 4. Silvco has sufficient furnace capacity to melt or refire germanium for at most 20,000 transistors per month. Silvco's monthly demands are for 1000 grade 4 transistors, 2000 grade 3 transistors, 3000 grade 2 transistors, and 3000 grade 1 transistors. Determine how to minimize the cost of producing the needed transistors.

91. The Wild Turkey Company produces two types of turkey cutlets for sale to fast-food restaurants. Each type of cutlet consists of white meat and dark meat. Cutlet 1 sells for $4 per pound and must consist of at least 70% white meat. Cutlet 2 sells for $3 per pound and must consist of at least 60% white meat. At most 50 pounds of cutlet 1 and 30 pounds of cutlet 2 can be sold. The two types of turkey used to manufacture the cutlets are purchased from the GobbleGobble Turkey Farm. Each type 1 turkey costs $10 and yields 5 pounds of white meat and 2 pounds of dark meat. Each type 2 turkey costs $8 and yields 3 pounds of white meat and 3 pounds of dark meat. Determine how to maximize Wild Turkey's profit.

92. The production line employees at Grummins Engine work 4 days a week, 10 hours a day. Each day of the week, the following minimum numbers of line employees are needed: Monday through Friday, 7 employees; Saturday and Sunday, 3 employees. Grummins employs 11 line employees. Determine how to maximize the number of consecutive days off received by these employees. For example, a worker who gets Sunday, Monday, and Wednesday off receives 2 consecutive days off.

93. Based on Lanzenauer et al. (1987). To process income tax forms, the Internal Revenue Service (IRS) first sends each form through the data preparation (DP) department, where information is coded for computer entry. Then the form is sent to data entry (DE), where it is entered into the computer. During the next 3 weeks, the following numbers of forms will arrive: week 1, 40,000; week 2, 30,000; week 3, 60,000. All employees work 40 hours per week and are paid $500 per week. Data preparation of a form requires 15 minutes, and data entry of a form requires 10 minutes. Each week an employee is assigned to either data entry or data preparation. The IRS must complete processing all forms by the end of week 5 and wants to minimize the cost of accomplishing this goal. Assume that all workers are full-time employees and that the IRS will have the same number of employees each week. Assume that all employees are capable of performing data preparation and data entry. Determine how many workers should be working and how the workers should allocate their hours during the next 5 weeks.

94. Based on Robichek et al. (1965). The Korvair Department Store has $100,000 in available cash. At the beginning of each of the next 6 months, Korvair will receive revenues and pay bills as listed in the file **P04_94.xls**. It is clear that Korvair will have a short-term cash flow problem until the store receives revenues from the Christmas shopping season. To solve this problem, Korvair must borrow money. At the beginning of July, the company takes out a 6-month loan. Any money borrowed for a 6-month period must be paid back at the end of December along with 9% interest (early payback does not reduce the total interest of the loan). Korvair can also meet cash needs through month-to-month borrowing. Any money borrowed for a 1-month period incurs an interest cost of 4% per month. Determine how Korvair can minimize the cost of paying its bills on time.

95. Mackk Engine produces diesel trucks. New government emission standards have dictated that the average pollution emissions of all trucks produced in the next 3 years cannot exceed 10 grams per truck. Mackk produces two types of trucks. Each type 1 truck sells for $20,000, costs $15,000 to manufacture, and emits 15 grams of pollution. Each type 2 truck sells for $17,000, costs $14,000 to manufacture, and emits 5 grams of pollution. Production capacity limits total truck production during each year to at most 320 trucks. The maximum numbers of each truck type that can be sold during each of the next 3 years are listed in the file **P04_95.xls**. Demand can be met from previous production or the current year's production. It costs $2000 to hold one truck (of any type) in inventory for 1 year. Determine how Mackk can maximize its profit during the next 3 years.

96. Each hour from 10 A.M. to 7 P.M., Bank One receives checks and must process them. Its goal is to process all checks the same day they are received. The bank has 13 check processing machines, each of which can process up to 500 checks per hour. It takes one worker to operate each machine. Bank One hires both full-time and part-time workers. Full-time workers work 10 A.M. to 6 P.M., 11 A.M. to 7 P.M., or noon to 8 P.M. and are paid $160 per day. Part-time workers work either 2 P.M. to 7 P.M. or 3 P.M. to 8 P.M. and are paid $75 per day. The numbers of checks received each hour are listed in the file **P04_96.xls**. In the interest of maintaining continuity, Bank One believes that it must have at least 3 full-time workers under contract. Develop a work schedule that processes all checks by 8 P.M. and minimizes daily labor costs.

Modeling Problems

97. You have been assigned to develop a model that can be used to schedule employees at a local fast-food restaurant. Assume that computer technology has advanced to the point where very large problems can be solved on a PC at the restaurant.

    a. What data would you collect as inputs to your model?

    b. Describe in words several appropriate objective functions for your model.

    c. Describe in words the constraints needed for your model.

98. You have been assigned to develop a model that can be used to schedule the nurses working in a maternity ward.

    a. What data would you collect as inputs to your model?

    b. Describe in words several appropriate objective functions for your model.

    c. Describe in words the constraints needed for your model.

99. Keefer Paper produces recycled paper from paper purchased from local offices and universities. The company sells three grades of paper: high-brightness paper, medium-brightness paper, and low-brightness paper. The high-brightness paper must have a brightness level of at least 90, the medium-brightness paper must have a brightness level of between 80 and 90, and the low-brightness paper must have a brightness level no greater than 80. Discuss how Keefer might use a blending model to maximize its profit.

100. In this chapter we give you the cost of producing a product and other inputs that are used in the analysis. Do you think that it is easy for most companies to determine the cost of producing a product? What difficulties might arise?

101. Discuss how the aggregate planning model could be extended to handle a company that produces several products on several types of machines. What information would you need to model this type of problem?

102. A large CPA firm currently has 100 junior staff members and 20 partners. In the long run—say, 20 years from now—the firm would like to consist of 130 junior staff members and 20 partners. During a given year, 10% of all partners and 30% of all junior staff members leave the firm. The firm can control the number of hires each year and the fraction of junior employees who are promoted to partner each year. Can you develop a personnel strategy that would meet the CPA firm's goals?

Saudi Arabia is a kingdom in the Middle East with an area of 865,000 square miles; it occupies about four-fifths of the Arabian Peninsula. It has a population of about 10 million, and its capital is Riyadh. It is a Muslim and an Arab state that is generally recognized as being formed in 1927 when Ibn Sa'ud united the country and was acknowledged as the sovereign independent ruler. Summer heat is intense in the interior, reaching 124°F, but it is dry and tolerable in contrast to coastal regions and some highlands, which have high humidity during the summer. Winters (December through February) are cool, with the coldest weather occurring at high altitudes and in the far north. A minimum temperature recorded at at-Turayf in 1950 was 10°F, and it was accompanied by several inches of snow and an inch of ice on ponds. Average winter temperatures are 74°F at Jidda and 58°F at Riyadh, which has an annual precipitation of $2\frac{1}{2}$–3 inches.

After oil was discovered in Bahrain in 1932, many companies turned to Saudi Arabia and started exploring. Thus in 1937, the American Arabian Oil Company, Inc. (AMARCO), was formed as a joint venture between Standard Oil Company of California (SOCAL) and the Government of Saudi Arabia to explore, produce, and market any petroleum found in the country. The year before, a geologist from SOCAL had discovered a small quantity of oil in the Eastern Province at Dammam Dome, on which the oil company town of Dhahran is now built. It was just beginning to be developed when another discovery was made—of what was to prove to be the largest oil field in the world. Called the Ghamar field, it would start Saudi Arabia on the road to becoming a highly developed country in just a generation. Located about 50 miles inland from the western shores of the Persian Gulf, the Ghamar field is a structural accumulation along 140 miles of a north–south anticline. The productive area covers approximately 900 square miles and the vertical oil column is about 1,300 feet. It is generally considered to have recoverable reserves of about 75 billion barrels of oil. Total proven reserves in Saudi Arabia are estimated at more than 500 billion barrels, enough for more than a hundred years of production.

Since 1950 Saudi Arabia has experienced greater and more rapid changes than it had in the several preceding centuries. For example, during this time, as skilled nationals became available, more and more of the exploration, drilling, refining, and other production activities came under the control of the country. SOCAL was left primarily with the marketing and transportation functions outside the country.

During the 1960s, AMARCO increased its profitability substantially by hiring Dr. George Dantzig, then of the University of California, as a consultant. He supervised the development and implementation of linear programming models to optimize the production of different types of crude oils, their refining, and the marketing of some of their principal products. As a result of this effort, an operations research (OR) department was started in the company with the responsibility of continuing to review the firm's operations to find other areas where costs might be decreased or profits increased by applications of OR.

Now attention is being focused on another aspect of one of the company's small California refinery operations: the production of three types of aviation gasoline from the Saudi Arabian crude oil available. Recently the marketing of petroleum products to the airline industry has become a rather substantial portion of AMARCO's business. The situation is pictured in Figure 4.38 (page 178). As the figure indicates, the three aviation gasolines, A, B, and C, are made by blending four feedstocks: Alkylate, Catalytic Cracked Gasoline, Straight Run Gasoline, and Isopentane.

In Table 4.12, TEL stands for tetraethyl lead, which is measured in units of milliliters per gallon (ml/gal). Thus, a TEL of 0.5 means that there is 0.5 milliliter of tetraethyl lead per gallon of feed stock. Table 4.12 shows that TEL does influence the octane number but does not influence the Reid Vapor Pressure.

Each type of aviation gasoline has a maximum permissible Reid Vapor Pressure of 7. Aviation gasoline A has a TEL level of 0.5 ml/gal and has a minimum octane number of 80. The TEL level of aviation gasolines B and C is 4 ml/gal, but the former has a minimum octane number of 91, whereas the latter has a minimum of 100.

[10]This case was written by William D. Whisler, California State University, Hayward.

Assume that all feedstocks going into aviation gasoline A are leaded at a TEL level of 0.5 ml/gal and that those going into aviation gasolines B and C are leaded at a TEL level of 4 ml/gal. Table 4.13 gives the aviation gasoline data. A final condition is that marketing requires that the amount of aviation gas A produced be at least as great as the amount of aviation gas B.

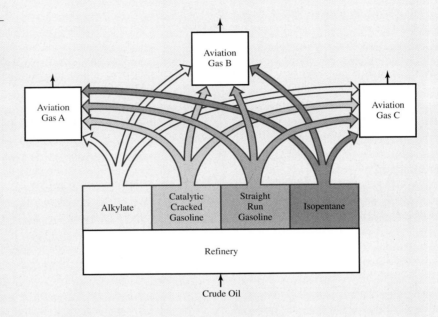

Figure 4.38

The Production of Aviation Gasoline

Table 4.12   Stock Availabilities[a]

| Characteristic | | Feedstock | | |
	Alkylate	Catalytic Cracked Gasoline	Straight Run Gasoline	Isopentane
Reid Vapor Pressure	5	8	4	20
Octane Number				
If TEL is 0.5	94	83	74	95
If TEL is 4.0	107.5	93	87	108
Available (Bbl/day)	14,000	13,000	14,000	11,000
Value ($/Bbl)	17.00	14.50	13.50	14.00

[a]Some of the data in this case have been adapted from Walter W. Garvin, *Introduction to Linear Programming* (New York: McGraw-Hill, 1960), Chapter 5.

Table 4.13   Aviation Gasoline Data

| Characteristic | Aviation Gasoline | | |
	A	B	C
Minimum requirements (Bbl/day)	12,000	13,000	12,000
Price ($/Bbl)	15.00	16.00	16.50

Questions

1. AMARCO's planners want to determine how the three grades of aviation gasoline should be blended from the available input streams so that the specifications are met and the income is maximized. Develop an LP spreadsheet model of the company's problem.

2. Solve the linear programming model formulated in Question 1.

The following questions should be attempted only after Questions 1 and 2 have been answered correctly.

3. Suppose that a potential supply shortage of Saudi Arabian petroleum products exists in the near future due to possible damage to AMARCO's oil production facilities from Iraqi attacks. This could cause the prices of the three types of aviation gasolines to double (while the values of the stocks remain the same, since they are currently on hand). How would this affect the refinery's operations? If, after current stocks are exhausted, additional quantities must be obtained at values double those given in Table 4.12, how might AMARCO's plans be affected?

4. Suppose that because of the new Iraqi crisis the supply of alkylate is decreased by 1,800 bbl/day, catalytic cracked gas is decreased by 2,000 bbl/day, and straight run gasoline is decreased by 5,000 bbl/day. How does this affect AMARCO's operations?

5. AMARCO is considering trying to fill the aviation gasoline shortage created by the new Iraqi crisis by increasing its own production. If additional quantities of alkylate, catalytic cracked gasoline, straight run gasoline, and isopentane are available, should they be processed? If so, how much of them should be processed, and how do their values affect the situation?

6. Due to the uncertainty about both the U.S. economy and the world economy resulting from the Iraqi crisis, AMARCO's economists are considering doing a new market research study to reestimate the minimum requirement forecasts. With the economy continually weakening, it is felt that demand will decrease, possibly drastically, in the future. However, since such marketing research is expensive, management is wondering whether it would be worthwhile. That is, do changes in the minimum requirements have a significant effect on AMARCO's operations? What is the change in profit from an increase or a decrease in the minimum requirements? Over what ranges of demand do these profit changes apply?

7. Suppose that the Middle East crisis ends and a flood of oil fills the marketplace, causing the prices of aviation gasoline to drop to $10.00, $11.00, and $11.50, respectively, for A, B, and C. How would this affect the company's plans?

8. Suppose that the U.S. government is considering mandating the elimination of lead from aviation gasoline in order to decrease air pollution. This law would be based on new technology that allows jet engines to burn unleaded gasoline efficiently at any octane level. Thus, there would no longer be any need for constraints on octane level. How would such a new law affect AMARCO?

9. The Environmental Protection Agency is proposing regulations to decrease air pollution. It plans to improve the quality of aviation gasolines by decreasing the requirement on Reid Vapor Pressure from 7 to 6. Management is concerned about this regulation and wonders how it might affect AMARCO's profitability. Analyze and make a recommendation.

10. The Marketing Department indicates that AMARCO will be able to increase its share of the market substantially with a new contract being negotiated with a new customer. The difficulty is that this contract will require that the amount of aviation gas A plus the amount of B must be at least as great as the amount of C produced. Since aviation gasolines A and B are least profitable of the three, this could cause a big decrease in profit for the company. However, marketing indicates that this is a short-run view, because the "large" increase in market share with the concomitant long-run profit increases will more than offset the "temporary small decrease" in profits because of the additional restriction. What do you recommend? Why? ■

American Office Systems, Inc., was established by the late R. J. Miller, Sr., in 1939. It started as an office supply story in Mountain View, California, and expanded slowly over the years into the manufacture of small office equipment, overhead projectors, and bookkeeping machines. In the 1950s computers started eroding its market for bookkeeping machines, so the company diversified into the copy machine market. However, it never captured a large market share because bigger firms like Xerox, Canon, Sharp, and A. B. Dick were so firmly entrenched.

A couple of years ago American Office Systems' engineering staff developed an adapter that links a standard copy machine to personal computers, allowing a copy machine to be used as a laser printer, scanner, and fax. The adapters show great promise for both home and office use. However, the company is not well known by either the financial community or the copy machine market, principally due to its small size and rather lackluster record, so it could secure only $15 million in initial financial backing for the adapters. The $15 million was used to finance the construction of a small production facility and of administrative offices in 1994, and in 1995 production and sales began. Two versions of the adapter exist, one for IBM-compatible computers and one for Macintosh computers. The former sells for $175 and the latter for $200.

At the beginning of December 1995, Dr. R. J. Miller, II, President, convened a meeting about the coming year's plans for the adapters. Rob Olsen, Vice President of Production, argued that production facilities should be expanded: "Until we have sufficient capacity to produce the adapters," he said, "there is no use advertising." Sue Williams, Director of Marketing, replied, "On the contrary, without any demand for the adapters, there is no reason to produce them. We need to focus on advertising first." J. T. Howell, the Comptroller, pointed out that Mr. Olsen and Mrs. Williams were talking about the situation as if it only involved a decision between production and marketing: "Yes, funds need to be allocated between production and advertising. However, more important than both is the cash flow difficulty that the company has been experiencing. As you know, it was only yesterday that, finally, I was able to secure a $750,000 line of credit for the coming year from Citibank. I might add that it is at a very favorable interest rate of 16%. This will partially solve our cash flow problems and it will have a big effect on both production and advertising decisions. In addition, there are financial and accounting factors that must be allowed for in any decision about the adapters." Mr. Olsen interjected, "Wow, this is more complicated than I anticipated originally. Before we make a decision, I think we ought to use some modern management science techniques to be sure that all the relevant factors are considered. Last week I hired Carlos Garcia from Stanford. He has a Master's Degree in Operations Research. I think this would be a good project for him." However, Mrs. Williams said that she thinks that an executive, judgmental decision would be much better. "Let's not get carried away with any of the quantitative mumbo-jumbo that Rob is always suggesting. Besides, his studies always take too much time and are so technical that no one can understand them. We need a decision by the end of next week." After listening to the discussion, Dr. Miller decided to appoint an executive action team to study the problem and make a recommendation of next week's meeting. "Rob and Sue, I want both of you to document your arguments in more detail. J. T., be more precise with your comments about the cash flow, accounting, and financial problems. And, by the way Rob, have Carlos look into a model to see if it might produce some insights."

Most of the $15 million initial financing was used to build a five-story building in Mountain View, south of San Francisco. Although currently only about 90% complete, it is being used. The first floor contains the production and shipping facilities plus a small storage area. A larger warehouse, already owned by the company, is located across the street. The other four floors of the building are for the engineering department (second floor), a research lab (third floor), and administration (top two floors). The production facility operates two shifts per day and has a production capacity of 30 IBM adapters and 10

[11]This case was written by William D. Whisler, California State University, Hayward.

Macintosh adapters per hour. Mr. Olsen uses 20 production days per month in his planning. Usually there are a few more, but these are reserved for maintenance and repairs. The last stage of the initial construction will be finished by the beginning of the fourth quarter, making the building 100% finished. This will increase the production capacity rates by 10%.

Mr. Howell normally does the company's financial planning monthly and he assumes that cash flows associated with all current operating expenses, sales revenues (taking collections into account), advertising costs, loans from the line of credit, investments of excess cash in short-term government securities, and so forth, occur at the end of the corresponding month. Because he needs information for the meeting next week, however, he decides to do a rough plan on a quarterly basis. This means that all the above-mentioned cash flows, etc., will be assumed to occur at the end of the quarter. After the meeting, when more time is available, the plan will be expanded to a monthly basis. To get started, one of his senior financial analysts prepares the list of quarterly fixed operating expenses shown in Table 4.14. In addition, the accounting department calculates that the variable costs of the adapters are $100 each for the IBM version and $110 each for the Macintosh version.

Table 4.14	Quarterly Fixed Operating Expenses
Expense	**Cost**
Administrative expense	$1,500,000
Fixed manufacturing costs	750,000
Sales agents' salaries	750,000
Depreciation	100,000

At present, American Office Systems is experiencing a cash flow squeeze due to the large cash requirements of the startup of the adapter production, advertising, and sales costs. If excess cash is available in any quarter, however, Mr. Howell says that the company policy is to invest it in short-term government securities, such as treasury bills. He estimates that during the coming year these investments will yield a return of 6%.

Mr. Olsen asks Mr. Garcia to look into the production and inventory aspects of the situation first, since this area was his specialty at Stanford. Then he says that he wants him to think about a programming model that might integrate all components of the problem—production, sales, advertising, inventory, accounting, and finance. A mixed-integer programming model appears to be the most appropriate; however, he asks Mr. Garcia to use linear programming as an approximation due to the time limitations and Mrs. Williams's concern about his ideas always being too technical. "There will be more time after next week's meeting to refine the model," he says.

After discussions with Mr. Olsen and Mrs. Williams, Mr. Garcia feels that something needs to be done to help the company handle the uncertainty surrounding future sales of the adapters. He points out that it is impossible to guarantee that the company will never be out of stock. However, it is possible to decrease shortages so that any difficulties associated with them would be small and they would not cause major disruptions or additional management problems, such as excess time and cost spent expediting orders, and so forth. Thus, Mr. Garcia formulates an inventory model. To be able to solve the model he has to check the inventory levels of the adapters currently on hand in the warehouse. From these quantities he calculates that there will be 10,000 IBM and 5,000 Macintosh adapters on hand at the beginning of 1996. Based on the results of the model, he recommends that a simple rule of thumb be used: production plus the end-of-period inventory for the adapters should be at least 10% larger than the estimated sales for the next period. This would be a safety cushion to help prevent shortages of the adapters. In addition, to provide a smooth transition to 1997, the inventory level plus production at the end of the fourth quarter of 1996 should be at least twice the maximum expected sales for that quarter. Mr. Garcia says that using these rules of thumb will minimize annual inventory costs. When explaining the inventory model to Mr. Olsen, Mr. Garcia emphasizes the importance of including inventory carrying costs as part of any analysis, even though such costs frequently are not out-of-pocket. He says that his analysis of data provided by the accounting department yielded a 1% per month inventory carry cost, and this is what he used in his model.

Sales during the first year (1995) for the adapters are shown in Table 4.15. Next year's sales are uncertain. One reason for the uncertainty is that they depend on the advertising done. To begin the analysis, Mrs. Williams asks her marketing research analyst, Debra Lu, to estimate the maximum sales levels for the coming four quarters if no advertising is done. Since last year's sales of both models showed a steady increase throughout the year, Ms. Lu projects a continuation of the trend. She forecasts that the company will be able to sell any number of adapters up to the maximum expected sales amounts shown in Table 4.15.

Table 4.15   1995 Adapter Sales and Maximum Expected 1996 Sales

| | 1995 Sales | | 1996 Maximum Expected Sales | |
Quarter	IBM Adapters	Macintosh Adapters	IBM Adapters	Macintosh Adapters
1	5,000	1,000	9,000	1,800
2	6,000	1,200	10,000	2,000
3	7,000	1,400	11,000	2,200
4	8,000	1,600	12,000	2,400

Dr. Miller suggests that advertising in magazines such as *PC World* and *Home Office* will increase consumer awareness of both the company and adapters. The next day, Mrs. Williams has a meeting with several staff members of a San Francisco advertising agency. They show her recommendations for two types of ads (one for the IBM adapters and one for the Macintosh adapters), give her cost information, and the estimated effectiveness of an advertising campaign. Armed with this information and some data from Ms. Lu, Mrs. Williams prepares a brief report for Dr. Miller setting out her reasons for thinking that each $10 spent on advertising will sell an additional IBM adapter; the same relationship holds true for the Macintosh adapter.

Based on an analysis of 1995 sales and accounts receivable, the accounting department determines that collection experience is as shown in Table 4.16. For example, 75% of the IBM adapters sold in a quarter are paid for during the quarter, 20% are paid for during the following quarter, and 3% are paid for during the third quarter. The remaining 2% are written off and sold to a collection agency for $0.50 on the dollar.

Table 4.16   Collections

Quarter	IBM Adapters	Macintosh Adapters
1	0.75	0.80
2	0.20	0.11
3	0.03	0.05

Questions

1. Suppose that you are Mr. Garcia. Develop an LP spreadsheet model of the situation to help the executive action team make a decision about how to allocate funds between production and advertising such that all the cash flow, financial, accounting, marketing, inventory, and production considerations are taken into account and American Office Systems' profits are maximized. Use the data collected and the estimates made by the members of the executive action team.

2. Solve the linear programming model formulated in Question 1.

The executive action team has assembled to reconsider the plans for the adapters for the coming year. Mr. Garcia, who developed the linear programming model, concludes his presentation by saying, "As everyone can see, the model gives the optimal solution that maximizes profits. Since I have incorporated the estimates and assumptions that all of you made, clearly it is the best solution. No other alternative can give a higher profit." Even Mrs. Williams, who initially was skeptical of using quantitative models for making executive-level decisions, is impressed and indicates that she will go along with the results.

Dr. Miller says, "Good work, Carlos! This is a complex problem but your presentation made it all seem so simple. However, remember that those figures you used were based on estimates made by all of us. Some were little better than guesses. What happens if they are wrong? In other words, your presentation has helped me get a handle on the problem we are facing, and I know that models are useful where hard, accurate, data exist. However, with all the uncertainty in our situation and the many rough estimates made, it seems to me that I will still have to make a judgment call when it comes down to making a final decision. Also, there has been a new development. J. T. tells me that we might be able to get another $1 million line of credit from a Bahamian bank. It will take a while to work out the details and maybe it will cost us a little. I am wondering if it is worth it. What would we do with the $1 million if we got it?" T. J. responds, "We really need the $1 million. But it is a drop in the bucket. My analysis shows that we really need another $8 million line of credit."

Analyze, as Mr. Garcia is going to do, the effect of uncertainty and errors on the results of Questions 1 and 2 by answering the following questions. They should be attempted only after Questions 1 and 2 have been answered correctly.

3. One area where assumptions were made is adapter price.
   a. What happens if the prices for the adapters are a little weak and they decrease to $173 for the IBM version and $198 for the Macintosh version? Does this make any difference?
   b. What about decreases to $172 and $197, respectively, for the IBM and Macintosh versions? Explain the answers in terms that Dr. Miller will understand.
   c. Suppose that American Office Systems can increase the price of the adapters to $180 and $205. How would this affect the original solution?

4. Another potential variable is adapter production cost.
   a. Suppose that an error was made in determining the costs of the adapters and that they really should have been $102 for the IBM version and $112 for the Macintosh version. What is the effect of this error?
   b. What about costs of $105 and $115? Explain the answers in terms that Dr. Miller will understand.

5. Mr. Howell notes that one of the contributing factors to American Office Systems' cash squeeze is the slow collection of accounts receivable. He

is considering adopting a new collection procedure recommended by a consulting company. It will cost $100,000 and will change the collection rates to those given in Table 4.17.
   a. Analyze the effect of this new collection policy and make a recommendation to Mr. Howell about whether to implement the new procedure. As before, any accounts receivable not collected by the end of the third quarter will be sold to a collection agency for $0.50 on the dollar.
   b. Mr. Howell wonders whether switching to selling adapters for all cash is worth the effort. This would ameliorate the cash squeeze because it would eliminate not only the slow collections but also the use of the collection agency for accounts that remain unpaid after 9 months. It would cost about $90,000 more than at present to implement the all-cash policy because the accounting system would need to be modified and personnel would have to be retrained. Analyze this possibility and make a recommendation to Mr. Howell.

Table 4.17 New Collections

Quarter	IBM Adapters	Macintosh Adapters
1	0.90	0.92
2	0.07	0.03
3	0.01	0.01

6. Yet another variable is advertising effectiveness.
   a. Suppose that Mrs. Williams overestimated the effectiveness of advertising. It now appears that $100 is needed to increase sales by one adapter. How will this affect the original solution? Explain the answer in terms that Dr. Miller will understand.
   b. What happens if the required advertising outlay is $12.50 per additional adapter sold?

7. Suppose that the line of credit from Citibank that Mr. Howell thought he had arranged did not work out because of the poor financial situation of the company. The company can obtain one for

the same amount from a small local bank; however, the interest rate is much higher, 24%. Analyze how this change affects American Office Systems.

8. The safety cushion for inventory is subject to revision.

    a. Suppose that Mr. Garcia finds a bug in his original inventory model. Correcting it results in a safety cushion of 15% instead of the 10% he suggested previously. Determine whether this is important.

    b. What if the error were 20%? Explain the answers in terms that Dr. Miller will understand.

9. Production capacity is scheduled to increase by 10% in the fourth quarter.

    a. Suppose that Dr. Miller is advised by the construction company that the work will not be finished until the following year. How will this delay affect the company's plans?

    b. In addition to the delay in part (a), suppose that an accident in the production facility damages some of the equipment so that the capacity is decreased by 10% in the fourth quar-

ter. Analyze how this will affect the original solution.

10. Mrs. Williams is worried about the accuracy of Ms. Lu's 1996 maximum expected sales forecasts. If errors in these forecasts have a big effect on the company profits, she is thinking about hiring a San Francisco marketing research firm to do a more detailed analysis. They would charge $50,000 for a study. Help Mrs. Williams by analyzing what would happen if Ms. Lu's forecasts are in error by $\pm 1,000$ for IBM adapters and ± 200 for Macintosh adapters each quarter. Should she hire the marketing research firm?

11. a. To determine whether the extra $1 million line of credit is needed, analyze its effect on the original solution given in Question 2.

    b. To fully understand the ramifications of the extra $1,000,000 line of credit, redo (1) Question 3b, (2) Question 4b, (3) Question 6a, and (4) Question 8b. Summarize your results.

    c. What about Mr. Howell's claim that an extra $8,000,000 line of credit is necessary? Use that adjustment and redo Question 6a. ∎

Network Models

Illustration/Lisa Torri

DEC GLOBAL SUPPLY CHAIN MANAGEMENT

Many of the models in this chapter can be characterized as logistics problems—that is, problems of finding the least expensive way to transport products from their origin to their destination. In addition, real logistics problems are often coupled with manufacturing or plant location decisions; a company must decide where to locate its manufacturing plants and what products to produce at each plant. Computer manufacturer Digital Equipment Corporation (DEC) faced such a problem, as reported by Arntzen et al. (1995) in "Global Supply Chain Management at Digital Equipment Corporation." DEC faces a huge global manufacturing and distribution problem with its wide range of products (mainframe computers, minicomputers, PCs, and many types of computer parts and peripherals). The company must decide where (or whether) to manufacture these products and how to get them to its customers around the world in the most economical manner.

Until the late 1980s DEC specialized primarily in mainframes and minicomputers, using a manufacturing and distribution system that had proved very successful for over 20 years. But as PCs revolutionized the industry, DEC realized that it had to change—quickly and radically—if it wanted to remain a thriving company. The company had too many plants and too much overhead. In addition, too many groups within DEC were making decisions without central coordination. In 1989 the company began to redesign its supply and delivery network and to reengineer its manufacturing and logistics processes. A key step in these corporate changes was the development of the Global Supply Chain Model (GSCM), an extremely complex linear programming model.[1] Since that time, DEC has used GSCM to perform thousands of optimizations in scores of studies.

The typical models run with GSCM are huge. They generally contain from 2000 to 6000 constraints and from 5000 to 20,000 decision variables. (They are *not* suitable for spreadsheets!) The objective typically minimizes total cost, where total cost includes production costs, inventory holding costs, facility material handling costs, taxes, facility fixed charges, production line fixed costs, transportation costs, and duty costs.

The constraints include customer demand requirements, "balance" constraints for production and inventory, limits on the weight of products through the facilities, production capacities, and storage capacities. Also, the models become even more complicated because of multiple products, multiple time periods (planning for four consecutive quarters, for example), and the complexities of international trade. Nevertheless, by taking advantage of the special structure of these models and the advanced software that is now available, DEC is able to solve these models routinely.

To illustrate, DEC ran a large study during 1992 to determine the optimal supply chain design for all of DEC's manufacturing. The study recommended an 18-month plan to restructure the manufacturing infrastructure completely to cut costs. Specifically, the quarter-by-quarter implementation plan called for the number of worldwide plants to be reduced from 33 to 12 and for the three basic customer regions (Pacific Rim, Americas, and Europe) to be served primarily by plants within their own regions. This 18-month plan has since been implemented. By spring 1994 implementation of the plan led to a decrease of $167 million in manufacturing costs (with another $160 million by June 1995) and a decrease of over $200 million in logistics costs. This is quite impressive considering that the number of units manufactured and shipped increased dramatically during this same time period. ■

5.1 INTRODUCTION

Many important optimization models have a natural graphical network representation. In this chapter we will consider several specific examples of network models. There are several reasons for distinguishing network models from other LP models.

- The network structure of these models allows us to represent them graphically in a way that is intuitive to users. We can then use this graphical representation as an aid in the spreadsheet model formulation. Indeed, for a book at this level, the best argument for singling out network problems for special consideration is the fact that they can be represented graphically.

- Many companies have real problems, often extremely large, that can be represented as network models. Indeed, many of the best management science success stories have

---

[1]The GSCM is actually more than an LP model; it is a mixed-integer model with 0–1 (binary) variables for the plant location decisions. We will study problems with binary variables in the next chapter.

involved large network models. For example, Delta Airlines recently developed a network model to schedule its entire fleet of passenger airplanes.

■ Specialized solution techniques have been developed specifically for network models. Although we will not discuss the details of these solution techniques—and they are *not* implemented in Excel's Solver—they are important in real-world applications because they allow companies to solve huge problems that could not be solved by the usual LP algorithms.

5.2 TRANSPORTATION MODELS

In many situations a company produces products at locations called **origins** and ships these products to customer locations called **destinations**. Typically, each origin has a limited amount that it can ship, and each customer destination must receive a required quantity of the product. Spreadsheet optimization models can be used to determine the minimum-cost shipping method for satisfying customer demands.

For now we assume that the only possible shipments are those directly from an origin to a destination. That is, no shipments between origins or between destinations are possible. This problem has been studied extensively in management science. In fact, it was one of the first management science models developed, over a half century ago. It is generally called the **transportation problem**. The following is a typical example of a small transportation problem.

EXAMPLE | 5.1 SHIPPING CARS FROM PLANTS TO REGIONS OF THE COUNTRY

The Grand Prix Automobile Company manufactures automobiles in three plants and then ships them to four regions of the country. The plants can supply the amounts listed in the right column of Table 5.1. The customer demands by region are listed in the bottom row of this table, and the unit costs of shipping an automobile from each plant to each region are listed in the middle of the table. Grand Prix wants to find the lowest-cost shipping plan for meeting the demands of the four regions without exceeding the capacities of the plants.

Table 5.1	Input Data for Grand Prix Example				
	Region 1	Region 2	Region 3	Region 4	Capacity
Plant 1	131	218	266	120	450
Plant 2	250	116	263	278	600
Plant 3	178	132	122	180	500
Demand	450	200	300	300	

Objective To develop a spreadsheet optimization model that finds the least-cost way of shipping the automobiles from plants to regions that stays within plant capacities and meets regional demands.

WHERE DO THE NUMBERS COME FROM?

A typical transportation problem requires three sets of numbers: capacities (or supplies), demands (or requirements), and unit shipping (and possibly production) costs. We discuss each of these next.

- The capacities indicate the most each plant can supply in a given amount of time—a month, say—under current operating conditions. In some cases it might be possible to increase the "base" capacities, by using overtime, for example. In such cases we could modify the model to determine the amounts of additional capacity to use (and pay for).

- The customer demands are typically estimated from some type of forecasting model (as discussed in Chapter 12). The forecasts are often based on historical customer demand data.

- The unit shipping costs come from a transportation cost analysis—how much does it really cost to send a single automobile from any plant to any region? This is not an easy question to answer, and it requires an analysis of the best *mode* of transportation (railroad, ship, or truck, say). However, companies typically have the required data. Actually, the unit "shipping" cost can also include the unit production cost at each plant. However, if this cost is the same across all plants, as we are tacitly assuming here, it can be omitted from the model.

Solution

The variables and constraints required for this model are listed in Table 5.2. We must know the amounts sent out of the plants and the amounts sent to the regions. However, these aggregate quantities are not directly the decision variables. The company must decide exactly the number of autos to send from each plant to each region—a shipping plan.

Table 5.2   Variables and Constraints for Transportation Model

Input variables	Plant capacities, regional demands, unit shipping costs
Decision variables (changing cells)	Number of autos sent from each plant to each region
Objective (target cell)	Total shipping cost
Other calculated variables	Number sent out of each plant, number sent to each region
Constraints	Number sent out of each plant ≤ Plant capacity
	Number sent to each region ≥ Region demand

Representing as a Network Model

In a transportation problem all flows go from left to right— from origins to destinations. We will see more complex network structures in Section 5.4.

The common feature of models in this chapter is that they can be represented graphically, as in Figure 5.1.

A network diagram of this model appears in Figure 5.1. This diagram is typical of network models. It consists of nodes and arcs. A **node**, indicated by a circle, generally represents a geographical location. In this case the nodes on the left correspond to plants, and the nodes on the right correspond to regions. An **arc**, indicated by an arrow, generally represents a route for getting a product from one node to another. Here, the arcs all go from a plant node to a region node—from left to right.

The problem data fit nicely on such a diagram. The capacities are placed next to the plant nodes, the demands are placed next to the region nodes, and the unit shipping costs are placed on the arcs. The decision variables are usually called **flows**. They represent the amounts shipped on the various arcs. Sometimes (although not in this problem), there are upper limits on the flows on some or all of the arcs. These upper limits are called **arc capacities**, and they can also be shown on the diagram.[2]

---

[2]There can even be *lower* limits, other than 0, on certain flows, but we won't consider any such models here.

Figure 5.1

Network
Representation of
Grand Prix Problem

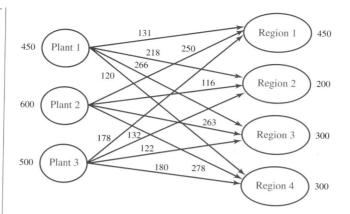

DEVELOPING THE SPREADSHEET MODEL

The spreadsheet model appears in Figure 5.2. (See the file **Transport1.xls**.) To develop this model, perform the following steps.

Figure 5.2 Grand Prix Transportation Model

	A	B	C	D	E	F	G	H	I	J	K	L
1	Grand Prix transportation model											
2												
3	Unit shipping costs								Range names used:			
4			To						Capacity	=Model!$I$13:$I$15		
5			Region 1	Region 2	Region 3	Region 4			Demand	=Model!$C$18:$F$18		
6	From	Plant 1	$131	$218	$266	$120			Shipping_plan	=Model!$C$13:$F$15		
7		Plant 2	$250	$116	$263	$278			Total_cost	=Model!$B$21		
8		Plant 3	$178	$132	$122	$180			Total_received	=Model!$C$16:$F$16		
9									Total_shipped	=Model!$G$13:$G$15		
10	Shipping plan, and constraints on supply and demand											
11			To									
12			Region 1	Region 2	Region 3	Region 4	Total shipped			Capacity		
13	From	Plant 1	150	0	0	300	450	<=		450		
14		Plant 2	100	200	0	0	300	<=		600		
15		Plant 3	200	0	300	0	500	<=		500		
16		Total received	450	200	300	300						
17			>=	>=	>=	>=						
18		Demand	450	200	300	300						
19												
20	Objective to minimize											
21	Total cost	$176,050										

1 Inputs.[3] Enter the unit shipping costs, plant capacities, and region demands in the shaded ranges.

2 Shipping plan. Enter *any* trial values for the shipments from plants to regions in the Shipping_plan range. These are the changing cells. Note that we model this as a rectangular range with exactly the same shape as the range where the unit shipping costs are entered. This is natural, and it simplifies the formulas in the following steps.

3 Numbers shipped from plants. We need to calculate the amount shipped out of each plant with row sums in the range G13:G15. To do this most easily, highlight this range and click on the summation (Σ) toolbar button.

[3]From here on, we won't remind you about creating range names, but we will continue to list our suggested range names on the spreadsheet.

4 **Amounts received by regions.** We also need to calculate the amount shipped to each region with column sums in the range C16:F16. Again, do this by highlighting the range and clicking on the summation button.

5 **Total shipping cost.** Calculate the total cost of shipping power from the plants to the regions in the Total_cost cell with the formula

=SUMPRODUCT(C6:F8,Shipping_plan)

This formula sums all products of unit shipping costs and amounts shipped. We see the benefit of placing unit shipping costs and amounts shipped in similar-size rectangular ranges—we can then use the SUMPRODUCT function.

USING SOLVER

Invoke Solver with the settings shown in Figure 5.3. As usual, check the Assume Linear Model and Assume Non-Negative options before optimizing.

Figure 5.3

Solver Dialog Box for Transportation Model

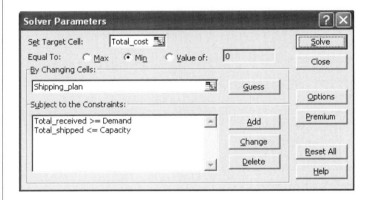

Discussion of the Solution

It is typical in transportation models, especially large models, that only a relatively few of the possible routes are used.

The Solver solution appears in Figure 5.2 and is illustrated graphically in Figure 5.4. The company incurs a total shipping cost of $176,050 by using the shipments listed in Figure 5.4. Except for the six routes shown, no other routes are used. Most of the shipments occur on the low-cost routes, but this is not always the case. For example, the route from plant 2 to region 1 is relatively expensive, and it *is* used. On the other hand, the route from plant 3 to region 2 is relatively cheap, but it is *not* used. A good shipping plan tries to use cheap routes, but it is constrained by capacities and demands.

Figure 5.4

Graphical Representation of Optimal Solution

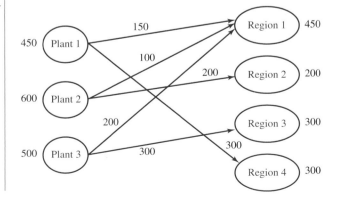

Note that the available capacity is not all used. The reason is that total capacity is 1550, whereas total demand is only 1250. Even though we constrained the demand constraints to be of the "≥" type, there is clearly no reason to send the regions *more* than the regions request because it only increases shipping costs. Therefore, we send them the minimal amounts they request and no more. In fact, we could have expressed the demand constraints as "=" constraints, and we would have obtained exactly the same solution.

Sensitivity Analysis

There are many sensitivity analyses we could perform on the basic transportation model. For example, we could vary any one of the unit shipping costs, capacities, or demands. The effect of any such change in a single input is captured nicely in Solver's sensitivity report, shown in Figure 5.5. The top part indicates the effects of changes in the unit shipping costs. The results here are typical. For all routes with positive flows, the corresponding reduced cost is 0, whereas for all routes not currently being used, the reduced cost indicates how much less the unit shipping cost would have to be before the company would start shipping along it. For example, if the unit shipping cost from plant 2 to region 3 decreased by more than $69, then this route would become attractive.

Figure 5.5

Solver's Sensitivity Report for Transportation Model

	A	B	C	D	E	F	G	H
1	Microsoft Excel 10.0 Sensitivity Report							
2	Worksheet: [Transport1.xls]Model							
3	Report Created: 2/16/2003 5:05:07 PM							
4								
5								
6	Adjustable Cells							
7				Final	Reduced	Objective	Allowable	Allowable
8		Cell	Name	Value	Cost	Coefficient	Increase	Decrease
9		$C$13	Plant 1 Region 1	150	0	131	119	13
10		$D$13	Plant 1 Region 2	0	221	218	1E+30	221
11		$E$13	Plant 1 Region 3	0	191	266	1E+30	191
12		$F$13	Plant 1 Region 4	300	0	120	13	239
13		$C$14	Plant 2 Region 1	100	0	250	39	72
14		$D$14	Plant 2 Region 2	200	0	116	88	116
15		$E$14	Plant 2 Region 3	0	69	263	1E+30	69
16		$F$14	Plant 2 Region 4	0	39	278	1E+30	39
17		$C$15	Plant 3 Region 1	200	0	178	13	69
18		$D$15	Plant 3 Region 2	0	88	132	1E+30	88
19		$E$15	Plant 3 Region 3	300	0	122	69	194
20		$F$15	Plant 3 Region 4	0	13	180	1E+30	13
21								
22	Constraints							
23				Final	Shadow	Constraint	Allowable	Allowable
24		Cell	Name	Value	Price	R.H. Side	Increase	Decrease
25		$C$16	Total received Region 1	450	250	450	300	100
26		$D$16	Total received Region 2	200	116	200	300	200
27		$E$16	Total received Region 3	300	194	300	200	100
28		$F$16	Total received Region 4	300	239	300	150	100
29		$G$13	Plant 1 Total shipped	450	-119	450	100	150
30		$G$14	Plant 2 Total shipped	300	0	600	1E+30	300
31		$G$15	Plant 3 Total shipped	500	-72	500	100	200

The bottom part of this report is useful because of its shadow prices. For example, we know that plants 1 and 3 are shipping all of their capacity, so the company would benefit from having more capacity at these plants. In particular, the report indicates that each extra unit of capacity at plant 1 is worth $119, and each extra unit of capacity at plant 3 is worth $72. However, because the allowable increase for each of these is 100, we know that after an increase in capacity of 100 at either plant, further increases will probably be worth *less* than the stated shadow prices.

One interesting analysis that cannot be performed with Solver's sensitivity report is to keep shipping costs and capacities constant and allow *all* of the demands to change by a certain percentage (positive or negative). To perform this analysis, we use SolverTable, with the varying percentage as the single input. Then we can keep track of the total cost and any particular amounts shipped of interest. The key to doing this correctly is to modify the model slightly before running SolverTable. The appropriate modifications appear in Figure 5.6. (See the file **Transport2.xls**.) Now we store the original demands in row 10, we enter a percent increase in cell I10, and we enter *formulas* in the Demand range in row 20. For example, the formula in cell C20 is **=C10*(1+$I$10)**. Then we run SolverTable with cell I10 as the single input cell, allowing it to vary from -20% to 40% in increments of 5%, and we keep track of total cost. As the table shows, the total shipping cost increases at an increasing rate as the demands increase. However, at some point the problem becomes infeasible. As soon as the total demand is greater than the total capacity, it is impossible to meet all demand.

Figure 5.6   Sensitivity Analysis to Percentage Changes in All Demands

	A	B	C	D	E	F	G	H	I	J	K	L
1	Grand Prix transportation model with sensitivity analysis											
2												
3	Unit shipping costs											
4			To									
5			Region 1	Region 2	Region 3	Region 4						
6	From	Plant 1	$131	$218	$266	$120						
7		Plant 2	$250	$116	$263	$278						
8		Plant 3	$178	$132	$122	$180						
9												
10	Original demands		450	200	300	300		% change	0%	←	Input for SolverTable	
11												
12	Shipping plan, and constraints on supply and demand											
13			To									
14			Region 1	Region 2	Region 3	Region 4	Total shipped		Capacity			
15	From	Plant 1	150	0	0	300	450	<=	450			
16		Plant 2	100	200	0	0	300	<=	600			
17		Plant 3	200	0	300	0	500	<=	500			
18		Total received	450	200	300	300						
19			>=	>=	>=	>=						
20		Demand	450	200	300	300						
21												
22	Objective to minimize											
23	Total cost	$176,050										
24												
25	Sensitivity of total cost to percentage change in each of the demands											
26			$B$23	Increase								
27	-20%	$130,850										
28	-15%	$140,350	$9,500									
29	-10%	$149,850	$9,500									
30	-5%	$162,770	$12,920									
31	0%	$176,050	$13,280									
32	5%	$189,330	$13,280									
33	10%	$202,610	$13,280									
34	15%	$215,890	$13,280									
35	20%	$229,170	$13,280									
36	25%	Not feasible										
37	30%	Not feasible										

An Alternative Model

The transportation model in Figure 5.2 is a very natural one. If we consider the graphical representation in Figure 5.1, we note that all arcs go from left to right, that is, from plants to regions. Therefore, the rectangular range of shipments allows us to calculate shipments out of plants as row sums and shipments into regions as column sums. In anticipation of later models in this chapter, however, where the graphical network can be more complex, we present an alternative model of the transportation problem. (See the file **Transport3.xls**.)

First, it is useful to introduce some additional network terminology. We already defined flows as the amounts shipped on the various arcs. The direction of the arcs indicates which way the flows are allowed to travel. An arc pointed into a node is called an **inflow**, whereas an arrow pointed out of a node is called an **outflow**. In the basic transportation model, all outflows originate from suppliers, and all inflows go toward demanders. However, general networks can have both inflows and outflows for *any* given node.

Although this model is possibly less natural than the original model, it generalizes much better to other network models in this chapter.

With this general structure in mind, the typical network model has one changing cell per arc. It indicates how much (if any) to send along that arc in the direction of the arrow. Therefore, it is often useful to model network problems by listing all of the arcs and their corresponding flows in one long list. Then we can deal with constraints in a separate section of the spreadsheet. Specifically, for each node in the network, there is a **flow balance constraint**. These flow balance constraints for the basic transportation model are simply the supply and demand constraints we have already discussed, but they can be more general for other network models, as we will discuss in later sections.

The alternative model of the Grand Prix problem appears in Figure 5.7. In the range A5:C16, we manually enter the plant and region indexes and the associated unit shipping costs. Each row in this range corresponds to an arc in the network. For example, row 12 corresponds to the arc from plant 2 to region 4, with unit shipping cost $278. Then we create a column of changing cells for the flows in column D. (If there were arc capacities, we would place them to the right of the flows, as we will illustrate in later examples.)

Figure 5.7 Alternative Model of Transportation Problem

	A	B	C	D	E	F	G	H	I	J	K	L	M	N
1	Midwest Electric transportation model: a more general network formulation													
2														
3	Network structure and flows					Flow balance constraints					Range names used:			
4	Origin	Destination	Unit cost	Flow		Capacity constraints					Capacity	=Model!$I$6:$I$8		
5	1	1	131	150		Plant	Outflow		Capacity		Demand	=Model!$I$12:$I$15		
6	1	2	218	0		1	450	<=	450		Destination	=Model!$B$5:$B$16		
7	1	3	266	0		2	300	<=	600		Flow	=Model!$D$5:$D$16		
8	1	4	120	300		3	500	<=	500		Inflow	=Model!$G$12:$G$15		
9	2	1	250	100							Origin	=Model!$A$5:$A$16		
10	2	2	116	200		Demand constraints					Outflow	=Model!$G$6:$G$8		
11	2	3	263	0		Region	Inflow		Demand		Total_Cost	=Model!$B$19		
12	2	4	278	0		1	450	>=	450					
13	3	1	178	200		2	200	>=	200					
14	3	2	132	0		3	300	>=	300					
15	3	3	122	300		4	300	>=	300					
16	3	4	180	0										
17														
18	Objective to minimize													
19	Total Cost		$176,050											

The flow balance constraints are conceptually straightforward. Each cell in the Outflow and Inflow ranges in column G contains the appropriate sum of flows. For example, cell G6, the outflow from plant 1, represents the sum of cells D5 through D8, whereas cell G12, the inflow to plant 1, represents the sum of cells D5, D9, and D13. Fortunately, there is an *easy* way to enter these summation formulas.[4] We use Excel's built-in SUMIF function, in the form =SUMIF(*CompareRange,Criteria,SumRange*). For example, the formula in cell G6 is

=SUMIF(Origin,F6,Flow)

This formula compares the plant number in cell F6 to the Origin range in column A and sums all flows where they are equal—that is, it sums all flows out of plant 1. By copying this formula down to cell G8, we obtain the flows out of the other plants. For flows into regions, we enter the similar formula

=SUMIF(Destination,F12,Flow)

[4]Try entering these formulas manually, even for a 3 × 4 transportation model, and you will see why we use the SUMIF function!

in cell G12 to sum all flows into region 1, and we copy it down to cell G15 for flows into the other regions. In general, the SUMIF function finds all cells in the first argument that satisfy the criterion in the second argument and then sums the corresponding cells in the third argument. It is a *very* handy function, especially for network modeling.

→ **EXCEL FUNCTION:** *SUMIF*
*The SUMIF function is useful for summing values in a certain range if cells in a related range satisfy given conditions. It has the syntax =**SUMIF(compareRange,criterion,sumRange)**, where* compareRange *and* sumRange *are similar-size ranges. This formula checks each cell in* compareRange *to see whether it satisfies the criterion. If it does, it adds the corresponding value in* sumRange *to the overall sum. For example,* =**SUMIF(A12:A23,1,D12:D23)** *sums all values in the range D12:D23 where the corresponding cell in the range A12:A23 has the value 1.* ■

This use of the SUMIF function, along with the list of origins, destinations, unit costs, and flows in columns A–D, is the key to the network formulation. From there on, the model is straightforward. We calculate the total cost as the SUMPRODUCT of unit costs and flows, and we set up the Solver dialog box as in Figure 5.8.

Figure 5.8

Solver Dialog Box for Alternative Transportation Model

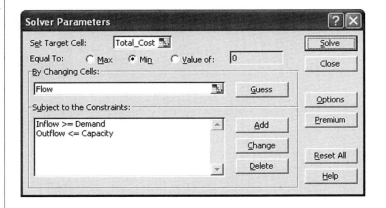

The alternative network model not only accommodates more general networks, but it is more efficient in that it has the fewest number of changing cells.

We will see several similar formulations throughout this chapter. To a certain extent, this makes all network models look alike. There is an additional benefit from this model formulation. Suppose that, for whatever reason, flows from certain plants to certain regions are not allowed. (Maybe no roads exist.) It is not easy to disallow such routes in the original model. The usual trick is to allow the "disallowed" routes but to impose extremely large unit shipping costs on them. This works, but it is wasteful because it adds changing cells that do not really belong in the model. However, the alternative network model simply omits arcs that are not allowed. For example, if the route from plant 2 to city 4 is not allowed, we simply omit the data in the range A12:D12. This creates a model with exactly as many changing cells as allowable arcs. This additional benefit can be very valuable when the number of potential arcs in the network is huge—even though the vast majority of them are disallowed—and this is exactly the situation in most large network models.

We do not necessarily recommend this more general network model for simple transportation problems. In fact, we believe it is less natural than the original model in Figure 5.2. However, it paves the way for the more complex network problems discussed later in this chapter. ■

MODELING ISSUES

Depending on how you treat the demand constraints, you can get several varieties of the basic transportation model.

1. The customer demands in typical transportation problems can be handled in one of two ways. First, we can think of these forecasted demands as *minimal* requirements that must be sent to the customers. This is how we treated regional demands here. For example, we constrained the amount shipped to region 1 to be *at least* 450. Alternatively, we could consider the demands as *maximal* sales quantities, the most each region can sell. Then we would constrain the amounts sent to the regions to be less than or equal to the forecasted demands. Whether we express the demand constraints as "≥" or "≤" (or even "=") constraints depends on the context of the problem—do the dealers need at least this many, do they need exactly this many, or can they sell only this many?

2. If all the supplies and demands for a transportation problem are integers, then the optimal Solver solution automatically has integer-valued shipments. We do *not* have to add explicit integer constraints. This is a very important benefit. It allows us to use the "fast" simplex method rather than much slower branch and bound algorithms.

3. Shipping costs are often nonlinear (and nonsmooth) due to quantity discounts. For example, if it costs $3 per item to ship up to 100 items between locations and $2 per item for each additional item, the proportionality assumption of LP is violated and the transportation models we have developed are nonlinear. Shipping problems that involve quantity discounts are generally quite difficult to solve.

4. Excel's Solver uses the simplex method to solve transportation problems. There is a streamlined version of the simplex method, called the **transportation simplex method**, that is much more efficient than the ordinary simplex method for transportation problems. Large transportation problems are usually solved with the transportation simplex method. See Winston (2003) for a discussion of the transportation simplex method. ∎

It is fairly easy to extend the basic Grand Prix transportation model, even when the cost structure is considerably more complex. We illustrate one such extension in the following example.

EXAMPLE | **5.2 PRODUCTION AND SHIPMENT OF AUTOMOBILES WITH VARYING TAX RATES**

We again consider Grand Prix's problem of shipping automobiles from three plants to four regions. However, we extend the problem in two directions. First, we assume that Grand Prix not only ships the autos, but it manufactures them at the plants and sells them in the various regions. Second, we assume that this problem takes place in an international context. The effect is that the unit production costs vary by plant, the unit selling prices vary by region, and the tax rates on profits vary according to the plant at which the autos are produced (regardless of where they are sold). The capacities of the plants, the demands of the regions, and the unit shipping costs are the same as before, in Table 5.1. In addition, the unit production costs and tax rates are given in Table 5.3 (page 196), and the unit selling prices in Table 5.4. For example, if plant 1 produces an auto and ships it to region 2, where it is sold, the profit before taxes is $20,520 − $14,350 − $218 = $5,952. This is taxed at plant 1's rate of 30%, so the after-tax profit is $5,952(1 − 0.3) = $4,166.40. The company now needs to find a production and shipping plan that maximizes its after-tax profit.

Table 5.3 Plant Production Costs and Tax Rates for Grand Prix Problem

Plant	Unit Production Cost	Tax Rate
1	$14,350	30%
2	$16,270	35%
3	$16,940	22%

Table 5.4 Selling Prices in Regions

Region	Unit Selling Price
1	$19,290
2	$20,520
3	$17,570
4	$18,320

Objective   To extend the previous Grand Prix transportation model to take into account varying production costs, selling prices, and tax rates.

WHERE DO THE NUMBERS COME FROM?

We leave it to the cost accountants to derive the numbers in Table 5.3 and Table 5.4. This is no easy task, particularly in an international setting, but the numbers are certainly available.

Solution

In addition to the variables required for the original transportation model in Example 5.1, we require one extra set of calculations. In particular, we need the after-tax profit per automobile produced in a given plant and sold in a given region. Once we find these unit after-tax profits, it is straightforward to calculate the total after-tax profit from any production/shipping plan, and this becomes the objective we want to maximize. The details are explained here.

DEVELOPING THE SPREADSHEET MODEL

The completed spreadsheet model appears in Figure 5.9. (See the file **Transport4.xls**.) Because the only differences from the previous example are in the monetary section, from row 25 down, we need only the following two steps to extend the model in Figure 5.2.

Figure 5.9 Spreadsheet Model for Extended Grand Prix Problem

	A	B	C	D	E	F	G	H	I	J	K	L	M	N
1	Grand Prix transportation model with taxes													
2														
3	Input data													
4	Unit shipping costs (shipping only)										Range names used:			
5			To								After_tax_profit	=Model!$B$31		
6			Region 1	Region 2	Region 3	Region 4		Plant data			Capacity	=Model!$I$16:$I$18		
7	From	Plant 1	$131	$218	$266	$120		Unit cost	Tax rate		Demand	=Model!$C$21:$F$21		
8		Plant 2	$250	$116	$263	$278		$14,350	30%		Shipping_plan	=Model!$C$16:$F$18		
9		Plant 3	$178	$132	$122	$180		$16,270	35%		Total_received	=Model!$C$19:$F$19		
10								$16,940	22%		Total_shipped	=Model!$G$16:$G$18		
11	Unit selling prices at regions		$19,290	$20,520	$17,570	$18,320								
12														
13	Shipping plan, and constraints on supply and demand													
14			To											
15			Region 1	Region 2	Region 3	Region 4	Total shipped				Capacity			
16	From	Plant 1	450	0	0	0	450	<=			450			
17		Plant 2	0	0	300	300	600	<=			600			
18		Plant 3	0	500	0	0	500	<=			500			
19		Total received	450	500	300	300								
20			>=	>=	>=	>=								
21		Demand	450	200	300	300								
22														
23	Monetary outputs													
24	After-tax profit per unit produced in given plant and sold in given region													
25			Region 1	Region 2	Region 3	Region 4								
26		Plant 1	$3,366.30	$4,166.40	$2,067.80	$2,695.00								
27		Plant 2	$1,800.50	$2,687.10	$674.05	$1,151.80								
28		Plant 3	$1,694.16	$2,689.44	$396.24	$936.00								
29														
30	Objective to maximize													
31	After-tax profit	$3,407,310												

This is another example of how the careful planning of spreadsheet layout simplifies the development of the model.

1 **Unit after-tax profits.** The after-tax profit is the unit selling price minus the production cost minus the shipping cost, all multiplied by 1 minus the tax rate. Calculate this for the plant 1, region 1 combination in cell C26 with the formula

=(C$11-$H7-C7)*(1-$I7)

and copy it to the range C26:F28 for the other combinations. Note how we are able to use a single formula to fill this entire range. This takes careful modeling (entering the plant production cost and tax rate data in columns, and the region selling price data in a row) and appropriate use of absolute and relative addresses.

2 **Total after-tax profit.** Calculate the total after-tax profit in cell B31 with the formula

=SUMPRODUCT(C26:F28,Shipping_plan)

USING SOLVER

The Solver setup is practically the same as before, as shown in Figure 5.10. However, don't forget to check the Maximize option—you do not want to *minimize* after-tax profit!

Figure 5.10

Solver Dialog Box for Extended Grand Prix Model

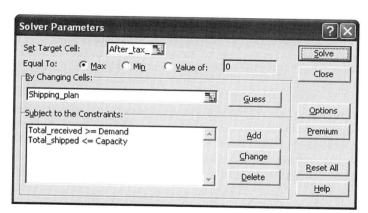

Discussion of the Solution

The optimal solution shown in Figure 5.9 uses only four of the possible twelve routes, and, surprisingly, these are not the four routes with the largest unit after-tax profits. In fact, the route with the largest after-tax profit, from plant 1 to region 2, is not used at all. Basically, the reason for this is that if we used this route to its fullest extent, then we would have to satisfy region 1's demand from plant 2 or 3, and both of these routes have very low unit after-tax profits. Of course, Solver figures this out for us.

Note also that the demand constraints cannot now be changed to "=" constraints. In the previous example there was no incentive to use all plant capacity, but now there is. The selling prices are large enough that every automobile sale adds to after-tax profit, so the company sells as many as it can. Of course, this raises the question of how many automobiles each region can *really* sell. It might be more realistic to keep the lower bounds on sales (the current demand constraints) but to impose upper limits on sales as well. We ask you to explore this in one of the problems. ■

PROBLEMS

Solutions for problems whose numbers appear within a color box can be found in the Student Solutions Manual. Order your copy today at http://e-catalog.thomsonlearning.com/110/ by using ISBN 0-534-39687-9.

Skill-Building Problems

1. In the original Grand Prix example, the total capacity of the three plants is 1550, well above the total customer demand. Would it help to have 100 more units of capacity at plant 1? What is the most Grand Prix would be willing to pay for this extra capacity? Answer the same questions for plant 2; for plant 3. Explain why extra capacity can be valuable even though the company already has more total capacity than it requires.

2. The optimal solution to the original Grand Prix problem indicates that with a unit shipping cost of $132, the route from plant 3 to region 2 is evidently too expensive—no autos are shipped along this route. Use SolverTable to see how much this unit shipping cost would have to be reduced before some autos would be shipped along this route.

3. Suppose in the original Grand Prix example that the routes from plant 2 to region 1 and from plant 3 to region 3 are not allowed. (Perhaps there are no railroad lines for these routes.) How would you modify the original model (Figure 5.2) to rule out these routes? How would you modify the alternative model (Figure 5.7) to do so? Discuss the pros and cons of these two approaches.

4. In the Grand Prix example with varying tax rates, the optimal solution more than satisfies customer demands. Modify the model so that regions have not only lower limits on the amounts they require, but upper limits on the amounts they can sell. Assume these upper limits are 50 autos above the required lower limits. For example, the lower and upper limits for region 1 are 450 and 500. Modify the model and find the optimal solution. How does it differ from the solution without upper limits?

5. In the Grand Prix example with varying tax rates, the optimal solution uses all available plant capacity, and it more than satisfies customer demands. Will this always be the case? Experiment with the unit selling prices and/or tax rates to see whether the company ever uses less than its total capacity.

Skill-Extending Problems

6. Here is a problem to challenge your intuition. In the original Grand Prix example, reduce the capacity of plant 2 to 300. Then the total capacity is equal to the total demand. Reoptimize the model. You should find that the optimal solution uses all capacity and exactly meets all demands with a total cost of $176,050. Now increase the capacity of plant 1 and the demand at region 2 by 1 automobile each, and optimize again. What happens to the optimal total cost? How can you explain this "more for less" paradox?

7. Continuing the previous problem, suppose we want to see how much extra capacity and extra demand we can add to plant 1 and region 2 (the same amount to each) before the total shipping cost stops decreasing and starts *increasing*. Use SolverTable appropriately to find out. (You will probably need to use some trial and error on the range of input values.) Can you explain intuitively what causes the total cost to stop decreasing and start increasing?

8. Modify the original Grand Prix example as follows. Increase the demands at the regions by 200 each, so that total demand is well above total plant capacity. However, now interpret these "demands" as "maximum sales," the most each region can accommodate, and change the "demand" constraints to become "≤" constraints, not "≥" constraints. How does the optimal solution change? Does it make realistic sense? If not, how might you change the model to obtain a realistic solution?

9. Modify the original Grand Prix example as follows. Increase the demands at the regions by 200 each, so that total demand is well above total plant capacity.

This means that some demands cannot be supplied. Suppose there is a unit "penalty" cost at each region for not supplying an automobile. Let these unit penalty costs be $600, $750, $625, and $550 for the four regions. Develop a model to minimize the sum of shipping costs and penalty costs for unsatisfied demands. (*Hint*: This requires a trick. Introduce a fourth plant with plenty of capacity, and set its "unit shipping costs" to the regions equal to the unit penalty costs. Then interpret an auto shipped from this fictitious plant to a region as a unit of demand not satisfied.)

5.3 ASSIGNMENT MODELS

In this section we examine a class of network models called **assignment models**. Assignment models are used to assign, on a one-to-one basis, members of one set to members of another set in a least-cost (or least-time) manner. The prototype assignment model is the assignment of machines to jobs. For example, suppose there are 4 jobs and 5 machines. Every pairing of a machine and a job has a given job completion time. The problem is to assign the machines to the jobs so that the total time to complete all jobs is minimized.

Assignment models are special cases of transportation models where all flows are 0 or 1.

To see how this is a network problem, recall the transportation problem of sending goods from suppliers to customers. Now think of the machines as the suppliers, the jobs as the customers, and the assignment times as the unit shipping costs. The capacity of any machine represents the most jobs it can handle. The "demand" of any job is the number of times it must be done, usually 1. Finally, there is an arc from every machine to every job it can handle, and the allowable flows on these arcs are all 0 or 1—a particular machine is either paired with a particular job (a flow of 1) or it isn't (a flow of 0). Therefore, we can formulate this assignment problem *exactly* like we formulated the Grand Prix transportation problem in Example 5.1 by using the appropriate input values.

An example of this model appears in Figures 5.11 and 5.12. (See the file **Assignment.xls**.) Here, we see that there are four jobs that must be completed by five machines. Machines 1, 3, and 5 can handle at most one job apiece, whereas machines 2 and 4 can handle two jobs apiece. The spreadsheet model in Figure 5.12 is identical to the transportation model we discussed previously, except with different inputs. The only minor difference, as indicated in the Solver dialog box in Figure 5.13, is that we make the demand constraints "=" constraints, because we want each job to be completed exactly once.

Figure 5.11

Network Representation of Assignment of Machines to Jobs

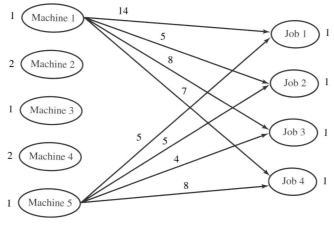

Note: Similar arcs exist out of machines 2, 3, and 4.

Figure 5.12 Spreadsheet Model of Assignment Problem

	A	B	C	D	E	F	G	H	I	J	K	L
1	Assignment of jobs to machines											
2												
3	Times to perform jobs on various machines								Range names used:			
4			Job						Assignments	=Model!$C$15:$F$19		
5			1	2	3	4			Jobs_on_machine	=Model!$G$15:$G$19		
6	Machine	1	14	5	8	7			Machine_capacity	=Model!$I$15:$I$19		
7		2	2	12	6	5			Machines_on_job	=Model!$C$20:$F$20		
8		3	7	8	3	9			Total_time	=Model!$B$25		
9		4	2	4	6	10						
10		5	5	5	4	8						
11												
12	Assignments, and constraints on machine capacities and job completion requirements											
13			Job									
14			1	2	3	4	Jobs on machine		Machine capacity			
15	Machine	1	0	0	0	0	0	<=	1			
16		2	0	0	0	1	1	<=	2			
17		3	0	0	1	0	1	<=	1			
18		4	1	1	0	0	2	<=	2			
19		5	0	0	0	0	0	<=	1			
20		Machines on job	1	1	1	1						
21			=	=	=	=						
22		Required	1	1	1	1						
23												
24	Objective to minimize											
25	Total time	14										

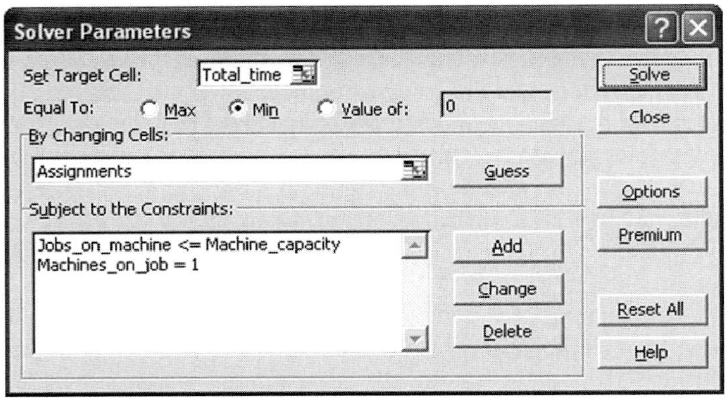

Figure 5.13

Solver Dialog Box for Assignment Model

The optimal solution in Figure 5.12 indicates, by the 1's and 0's in the changing cells, which machines are assigned to which jobs. Specifically, machine 2 is assigned to job 4, machine 3 is assigned to job 3, machine 4 is assigned to jobs 1 and 2, and machines 1 and 5 are not assigned to any jobs. With this optimal assignment, it takes 14 time units to complete all jobs.

We examine a somewhat different and less obvious type of assignment problem in the following example.

EXAMPLE | **5.3 ASSIGNING SCHOOL BUSES TO ROUTES AT SPRING VIEW**

The city of Spring View is taking bids from six bus companies on the eight routes that must be driven in the surrounding school district. Each company enters a bid on how much it will charge to drive selected routes, although not all companies bid on all routes. The data are listed in Table 5.5. (If a company does not bid on a route, the corresponding cell is blank.) The city must decide which companies to assign to which routes with the specifications that (1) if a company does not bid on a route, it cannot be assigned to that route, (2) exactly one company must be assigned to each route, and (3) a company can be assigned to at most two routes. The objective is to minimize the total cost of covering all routes.

Table 5.5 Bids on Bus Routes

Company	Route 1	Route 2	Route 3	Route 4	Route 5	Route 6	Route 7	Route 8
1		8200	7800	5400		3900		
2	7800	8200		6300		3300	4900	
3		4800				4400	5600	3600
4			8000	5000	6800		6700	4200
5	7200	6400		3900	6400	2800		3000
6	7000	5800	7500	4500	5600		6000	4200

Objective   To use a network model to assign companies to bus routes so that each route is covered at minimum cost to the city and no company is assigned to more than two routes.

WHERE DO THE NUMBERS COME FROM?

This is straightforward. The companies involved make the bids, and the city probably decides that it is not physically possible (or safe) for any company to handle more than two routes.

Solution

The variables and constraints for this model are given in Table 5.6. As in the machine-to-job assignment model in Figure 5.12, the changing cells will all contain 0's or 1's. The 1's will indicate which assignments are made.

Table 5.6   Variables and Constraints for Assignment Model

Input variables	Bids for routes, maximum number of bus routes per company
Decision variables (changing cells)	Assignments of companies to bus routes
Objective (target cell)	Total cost
Other calculated variables	Number of bus routes assigned to each company, number of companies assigned to each bus route
Constraints	Bus routes assigned to each company ≤ Maximum routes per company Companies assigned to each bus route = 1

All arcs go from company nodes to bus route nodes, and the allowable flows are all 0 or 1.

   We model this problem in the "network" way. Although we won't show the rather large network, you can imagine nodes for the bus companies on the left, nodes for the bus routes on the right, and all arrows going from left to right. All flows are 0 or 1—a company is either assigned to a bus route or it isn't. The constraint that a company can be assigned to at most two bus routes is handled by constraining the outflow from any company node to be at most 2. To ensure that each bus route is covered by exactly one company, we constrain the inflow to each bus route node to be 1.

Because this is essentially a transportation model (with some disallowed arcs, the ones where a company doesn't bid on a route), we could mimic the transportation models in Figure 5.2 and Figure 5.12, or we could mimic the more general formulation in Figure 5.7. For efficiency, we do the latter. This actually has two advantages. It doesn't force us to include changing cells for disallowed assignments, and it gets us ready for the more general network model in the next section.

The model appears in Figure 5.14. (See the file **BusRoutes.xls**.) Because this model is so similar to the Grand Prix transportation model in Figure 5.7, we will not repeat all of the details here. The key steps are as follows. (For help on the SUMIF function, revisit the discussion of the alternative model in Example 5.1.)

Figure 5.14 Bus Route Assignment Model

	A	B	C	D	E	F	G	H	I	J	K	L/M	N
1	Assignment of bus companies to routes												
2													
3	Input data										Range names used:		
4	Maximum routes per company	2									Companies_assigned	=Model!$I$25:$I$32	
5											Cost	=Model!$C$17:$C$47	
6	Network setup, flows, and arc capacity constraints					Flow balance constraints					Destination	=Model!$B$17:$B$47	
7	Origin	Destination	Cost	Flow		Company	Routes assigned		Maximum allowed		Flow	=Model!$D$17:$D$47	
8	1	2	8200	0		1	1	<=	2		Maximum_allowed	=Model!$K$17:$K$22	
9	1	3	7800	1		2	2	<=	2		Origin	=Model!$A$17:$A$47	
10	1	4	5400	0		3	1	<=	2		Routes_assigned	=Model!$I$17:$I$22	
11	1	6	3900	0		4	0	<=	2		Total_cost	=Model!$B$50	
12	2	1	7800	0		5	2	<=	2				
13	2	2	8200	0		6	2	<=	2				
14	2	4	6300	0									
15	2	6	3300	1		Route	Companies assigned		Required				
16	2	7	4900	1		1	1	=	1				
17	3	2	4800	1		2	1	=	1				
18	3	6	4400	0		3	1	=	1				
19	3	7	5600	0		4	1	=	1				
20	3	8	3600	0		5	1	=	1				
21	4	3	8000	0		6	1	=	1				
22	4	4	5000	0		7	1	=	1				
23	4	5	6800	0		8	1	=	1				
24	4	7	6700	0									
25	4	8	4200	0									
26	5	1	7200	0									
27	5	2	6400	0									
28	5	4	3900	1									
29	5	5	6400	0									
30	5	6	2800	0									
31	5	8	3000	1									
32	6	1	7000	1									
33	6	2	5800	0									
34	6	3	7500	0									
35	6	4	4500	0									
36	6	5	5600	1									
37	6	7	6000	0									
38	6	8	4200	0									
39													
40	Objective to minimize												
41	Total cost	40300											

① Arc lists. The list of arcs (company–bus route pairs) in rows 8–38 corresponds to the nonblank cells in Table 5.5. There is no point in including arcs that correspond to disallowed assignments. We enter these arcs manually, referring to Table 5.5.

② Inputs. Enter the costs from the (nonblank) cells in Table 5.5 in the range C8:C38. Also, enter the maximum number of routes per company in cell B4.

③ Assignments. Enter *any* values in the Flow range. Although these will eventually be 0's and 1's to indicate which assignments are made, any values can be used initially. Solver will eventually find the optimal values.

④ Inflows and outflows. In column G, we require *outflows* (numbers of routes assigned) for company nodes and *inflows* (numbers of companies assigned) for bus route nodes. To calculate these, enter the formulas

=SUMIF(Origin,F8,Flow)

and

=SUMIF(Destination,F16,Flow)

in cells G8 and G16, and copy them down their respective ranges.

5 **Requirements on flows.** Enter a link to cell B4 in each cell of the range I8:I13. This will be used to prevent any company from being assigned to more than 2 routes. Also, enter 1 in each cell of the range I16:I23 to reflect the fact that each route must be assigned to exactly one company.

6 **Total cost.** Calculate the total cost to the city in cell B41 with the formula

=SUMPRODUCT(Cost,Flow)

USING SOLVER

The Solver setup should appear as in Figure 5.15. As usual, check the Assume Linear Model and Assume Non-Negative options before optimizing.

Figure 5.15

Solver Dialog Box for Bus Route Assignment Model

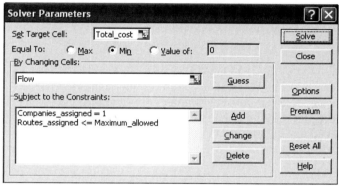

Discussion of the Solution

The optimal solution in Figure 5.14 indicates that the city should make the following assignments: company 1 covers bus route 3, company 2 covers bus routes 6 and 7, company 3 covers bus route 2, company 5 covers bus routes 4 and 8, and company 6 covers bus routes 1 and 5. The total cost to the city of this assignment is $40,300. Note that company 4 is not assigned to any bus routes. After all, there is no constraint that every company must be assigned to at least one bus route, and company 4 is evidently underbid by at least one company for all bus routes. If the city wanted to require that *all* companies be assigned to at least one bus route, we would simply put a *lower* bound of 1 on all of the outflows from the company nodes (in rows 8–13). Of course, this would probably increase the total cost to the city.

Sensitivity Analysis

One interesting sensitivity analysis is to see what effect the upper bound constraint on the maximum routes has on the total cost. Presumably, if we allow more bus routes per company (assuming this is physically possible for the companies), the companies who tend to bid lowest will be assigned to the bulk of the bus routes, and the total cost will probably decrease. Using SolverTable, the analysis itself is straightforward, with no modifications to the model necessary. We specify cell B4 as the single input cell, allow it to vary, say, from 1 to 7 in increments of 1, and keep track of total cost. The resulting output appears in Figure 5.16 (page 204).

Figure 5.16

Sensitivity to the
Maximum Number
of Routes

	A	B	C	D	E	F	G
43	Sensitivity of total cost to maximum routes per company						
44		$B$41					
45	1	Not feasible		The first problem is clearly infeasible because			
46	2	40300		there are only 6 companies and there are 8 routes.			
47	3	39500		There is a cost savings from being allowed to			
48	4	39500		assign 3 (rather than 2) routes to a company, but			
49	5	39500		there is no incentive to assign more than 3 routes			
50	6	39500		to any company.			
51	7	39500					

We see first that if each company can be assigned to only one route, there is no feasible solution. But this is clear: There are eight routes to cover and only six companies! For larger values of the maximum routes allowed, the total cost begins to decrease, but only until this input value reaches 3. From that point, the city achieves no additional flexibility by allowing companies to travel more routes. Evidently, there is no single company or pair of companies who are consistently underbidding all others. ■

ADDITIONAL APPLICATIONS

Assigning Managers at Heery International

LeBlanc et al. (2000) used an optimization model to assign managers to construction projects for Heery International. Heery contracts with the state of Tennessee for projects such as hospitals, office buildings, state park facilities (hotels and cabins), higher-education facilities (libraries, classrooms, and dormitories), armories and prisons. The assignment model is used for problems with up to 114 projects and seven managers. As a result of the model, Heery has managed its projects without replacing a manager who resigned and has reduced travel costs. ■

PROBLEMS

Skill-Building Problems

10. Modify the machine-to-job assignment model under the assumption that we require only 3 of the 4 jobs to be completed. In other words, 1 of the 4 jobs does not have to be assigned to any machine. What is the new optimal solution?

11. One possible solution method for the machine-to-job assignment problem is the following heuristic procedure. Assign the machine to job 1 that completes job 1 quickest. Then assign the machine to job 2 that, among all machines that still have some capacity, completes job 2 quickest. Keep going until a machine has been assigned to all jobs. Does this heuristic procedure yield the optimal solution for this problem? If it does, see whether you can change the job times so that the heuristic does *not* yield the optimal solution.

12. In the machine-to-job assignment problem, the current capacities of the machines are 1, 2, 1, 2, and 1. If you could increase one of these capacities by 1, which would you increase? Why?

13. Modify the bus route assignment model, assuming that company 1 decides to place bids on routes 7 and 8 (in addition to its current bids on other routes). The bids on these two routes are $5200 and $3300. Does the optimal solution change?

14. We modeled the bus route assignment problem with the alternative form of the transportation model (as in Figure 5.7). Model it instead with the "standard" form (as in Figure 5.2). Discuss the pros and cons of these two approaches for this particular example.

Skill-Extending Problems

15. In the optimal solution to the machine-to-job assignment problem, jobs 1 and 2 are both assigned to machine 4. Suppose we impose the restriction that jobs 1 and 2 must be assigned to *different* machines. Change the model to accommodate this restriction and find the new optimal solution.

16. In the optimal solution to the machine-to-job assignment problem, jobs 3 and 4 are assigned to different machines. Suppose we impose the restriction that these jobs must be assigned to the *same* machine. Change the model to accommodate this restriction and find the new optimal solution.

17. In the optimal solution to the bus route assignment problem, company 2 is assigned to bus routes 6 and 7. Suppose these two routes are far enough apart that it is infeasible for one company to service both of them. Change the model to accommodate this restriction and find the new optimal solution.

18. When we (the authors) originally developed the bus route assignment model, we included an arc capacity constraint: Flow ≤ 1. After giving this further thought, we deleted this constraint as being redundant. Why could we do this? Specifically, why can't one or more of the flows found by Solver be greater than 1? (*Hint*: Think in terms of flows out of and into the nodes in the network diagram.)

5.4 MINIMUM COST NETWORK FLOW MODELS

The objective of many real-world network models is to ship goods from one set of locations to another set of locations at minimum cost, subject to various constraints. There are many variations of these models. The simplest models include a single product that must be shipped via one mode of transportation (truck, for example) in a particular period of time. More complex models—and much larger ones—can include multiple products, multiple modes of transportation, and/or multiple time periods. We will refer to this general class of problems as **minimum cost network flow** problems. We will discuss several examples of such problems in this section.

Basically, the general minimum cost network flow problem is like the transportation problem except for two possible differences. First, arc capacities are often imposed on some or all of the arcs. These become simple upper bound constraints in the model. Second and more significant, there can be inflows *and* outflows associated with any node. Nodes are generally categorized as **suppliers**, **demanders**, and **transshipment points**. A supplier is a location that starts with a certain supply (or possibly a capacity for supplying). A demander is the opposite; it requires a certain amount to end up there. A transshipment point is a location where goods simply pass through.

The best way to think of these categories is in terms of **net inflow** and **net outflow**. The net inflow for any node is defined as total inflow minus total outflow for that node. The net outflow is the negative of this, total outflow minus total inflow. Then a supplier is a node with positive net outflow, a demander is a node with positive net inflow, and a transshipment point is a node with net outflow (and net inflow) equal to 0. It is important to realize that inflows are sometimes allowed to suppliers, but their *net* outflows must be positive. Similarly, outflows from demanders are sometimes allowed, but their *net* inflows must be positive. For example, if Cincinnati and Memphis are manufacturers (suppliers) and Dallas and Phoenix are retail locations (demanders), then it is possible that flow could go from Cincinnati to Memphis to Dallas to Phoenix.

There are typically two types of constraints in minimum cost network flow models (other than nonnegativity of flows). The first type represents the arc capacity constraints, which are simple upper bounds on the arc flows. The second type represents the flow balance constraints, one for each node. For a supplier, this constraint is typically of the form **Net Outflow = Original Supply** or possibly **Net Outflow <= Capacity**. For a demander, it is typically of the form **Net Inflow >= Demand** or possibly **Net Inflow = Demand**. For a transshipment point, it is of the form **Net Inflow = 0** (which is equivalent to **Net Outflow = 0**, whichever you prefer).

If we represent the network graphically, then it is easy to "see" these constraints. We simply examine the flows on the arrows leading into and out of the various nodes. We illustrate the typical situation in the following example.

5.4 PRODUCING AND SHIPPING TOMATO PRODUCTS AT REDBRAND

The RedBrand Company produces a tomato product at three plants. This product can be shipped directly to the company's two customers or it can first be shipped to the company's two warehouses and then to the customers. Figure 5.17 is a network representation of RedBrand's problem. Nodes 1, 2, and 3 represent the plants (these are the suppliers, denoted by S), nodes 4 and 5 represent the warehouses (these are the transshipment points, denoted by T), and nodes 6 and 7 represent the customers (these are the demanders, denoted by D). Note that we allow the possibility of some shipments among plants, among warehouses, and among customers. Also, some arcs have arrows on both ends. This means that flow is allowed in either direction.

Figure 5.17

Graphical Representation of RedBrand Logistics Model

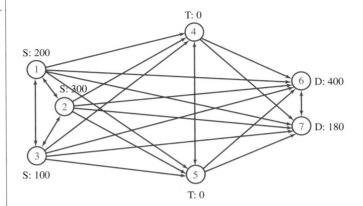

The cost of producing the product is the same at each plant, so RedBrand is concerned with minimizing the total shipping cost incurred in meeting customer demands. The production capacity of each plant (in tons per year) and the demand of each customer are shown in Figure 5.17. For example, plant 1 (node 1) has a capacity of 200, and customer 1 (node 6) has a demand of 400. In addition, the cost (in thousands of dollars) of shipping a ton of the product between each pair of locations is listed in Table 5.7, where a blank indicates that RedBrand cannot ship along that arc. We also assume that at most 200 tons of the product can be shipped between any two nodes. This is the common arc capacity. RedBrand wants to determine a minimum-cost shipping schedule.

Table 5.7   Shipping Costs for RedBrand Example

	To node						
	1	2	3	4	5	6	7
From node 1		5.0	3.0	5.0	5.0	20.0	20.0
2	9.0		9.0	1.0	1.0	8.0	15.0
3	0.4	8.0		1.0	0.5	10.0	12.0
4					1.2	2.0	12.0
5				0.8		2.0	12.0
6							1.0
7						7.0	

Objective   To find the minimum-cost way to ship the tomato product from suppliers to customers, possibly through warehouses, so that customer demands are met and supplier capacities are not exceeded.

The network configuration itself would come from geographical considerations—which routes are physically possible (or sensible) and which are not. The numbers themselves would be derived as in the Grand Prix automobile example. (See Example 5.1 for further discussion.)

Solution

Other than arc capacity constraints, the only constraints are flow balance constraints.

The variables and constraints for RedBrand's model are listed in Table 5.8. The key to the model is handling the flow balance constraints. We will see exactly how to implement these when we give step-by-step instructions for developing the spreadsheet model. However, it is not enough, say, to specify that the flow out of plant 2 is less than or equal to the capacity of plant 2. The reason is that there might also be flow *into* plant 2 (from another plant). Therefore, the correct flow balance constraint for plant 2 is that the flow out of it must be less than or equal to its capacity plus any flow into it. Equivalently, the *net* flow out of plant 2 must be less than or equal to its capacity.

Table 5.8 Variables and Constraints for RedBrand Logistics Model

Input variables	Plant capacities, customer demands, unit shipping costs on allowable arcs, common arc capacity
Decision variables (changing cells)	Shipments on allowed arcs
Objective (target cell)	Total cost
Other calculated variables	Flows into and out of nodes
Constraints	Flow on each arc ≤ Common arc capacity
	Flow balance at each node

DEVELOPING THE SPREADSHEET MODEL

To set up the spreadsheet model, proceed as follows. (See Figure 5.18 and the file **RedBrand1.xls**. Also, refer to the network in Figure 5.17.)

Figure 5.18 Spreadsheet Model for RedBrand Problem

	A	B	C	D	E	F	G	H	I	J	K	L	M	N	O	P
1	RedBrand shipping model															
2																
3	Inputs															
4	Common arc capacity	150											Range names used:			
5													Arc_Capacity	=Model!$F$19:$F$44		
6	Network structure, flows, and arc capacity constraints												Customer_demand	=Model!$K$31:$K$32		
7	Origin	Destination	Unit Cost	Flow		Arc Capacity		Node balance constraints					Customer_net_inflow	=Model!$I$31:$I$32		
8	1	2	5	0	<=	150		Plant constraints					Destination	=Model!$B$19:$B$44		
9	1	3	3	150	<=	150		Node	Plant net outflow		Plant capacity		Flow	=Model!$D$19:$D$44		
10	1	4	5	30	<=	150		1	180	<=	200		Origin	=Model!$A$19:$A$44		
11	1	5	5	0	<=	150		2	300	<=	300		Plant_capacity	=Model!$K$20:$K$22		
12	1	6	20	0	<=	150		3	100	<=	100		Plant_net_outflow	=Model!$I$20:$I$22		
13	1	7	20	0	<=	150							Total_cost	=Model!$B$47		
14	2	1	9	0	<=	150		Warehouse constraints					Unit_Cost	=Model!$C$19:$C$44		
15	2	3	9	0	<=	150		Node	Warehouse net outflow		Required		Warehouse_net_outflow	=Model!$I$26:$I$27		
16	2	4	1	120	<=	150		4	0	=	0					
17	2	5	1	30	<=	150		5	0	=	0					
18	2	6	8	150	<=	150										
19	2	7	15	0	<=	150		Customer constraints								
20	3	1	0.4	0	<=	150		Node	Customer net inflow		Customer demand					
21	3	2	8	0	<=	150		6	400	>=	400					
22	3	4	1	0	<=	150		7	180	>=	180					
23	3	5	0.5	120	<=	150										
24	3	6	10	100	<=	150										
25	3	7	12	30	<=	150										
26	4	5	1.2	0	<=	150										
27	4	6	2	150	<=	150										
28	4	7	12	0	<=	150										
29	5	4	0.8	0	<=	150										
30	5	6	2	150	<=	150										
31	5	7	12	0	<=	150										
32	6	7	1	150	<=	150										
33	7	6		0	<=	150										
34																
35	Objective to minimize															
36	Total cost	$4,120														

① **Origins and destinations.** Enter the node numbers (1 to 7) for the origins and destinations of the various arcs in the range A8:B33. Note that the disallowed arcs are not entered in this list.

② **Input data.** Enter the unit shipping costs (in thousands of dollars), the common arc capacity, the plant capacities, and the customer demands in the shaded ranges. Again, only the nonblank entries in Table 5.7 are used to fill up the column of unit shipping costs.

③ **Flows on arcs.** Enter *any* initial values for the flows in the range D8:D33. These are the changing cells.

④ **Arc capacities.** To indicate a common arc capacity for all arcs, enter the formula

=$B$4

in cell F8 and copy it down column F.

We generally prefer positive numbers on right-hand sides of constraints. This is why we calculate net outflows for plants and net inflows for customers.

⑤ **Flow balance constraints.** Nodes 1, 2, and 3 are supply nodes, nodes 4 and 5 are transshipment points, and nodes 6 and 7 are demand nodes. Therefore, set up the left sides of the flow balance constraints appropriately for these three cases. Specifically, enter the net *outflow* for node 1 in cell I9 with the formula

=SUMIF(Origin,H9,Flow)-SUMIF(Destination,H9,Flow)

and copy it down to cell I11. This formula subtracts flows into node 1 from flows out of node 1 to obtain net outflow for node 1. Next, copy this *same* formula to cells I15 and I16 for the warehouses. (Remember that for transshipment nodes, the left side of the constraint can be net outflow *or* net inflow, whichever you prefer. The reason is that if net outflow is 0, then net inflow must also be 0.) Finally, enter the net *inflow* for node 6 in cell I20 with the formula

=SUMIF(Destination,H20,Flow)-SUMIF(Origin,H20,Flow)

and copy it to cell I21. This formula subtracts flows out of node 6 from flows into node 6 to obtain the net inflow for node 6.

⑥ **Total shipping cost.** Calculate the total shipping cost (in thousands of dollars) in cell B36 with the formula

=SUMPRODUCT(Unit_cost,Flow)

USING SOLVER

The Solver dialog box should be set up as in Figure 5.19. We want to minimize total shipping costs, subject to the three types of flow balance constraints and the arc capacity constraints.

Figure 5.19
Solver Dialog Box for RedBrand Model

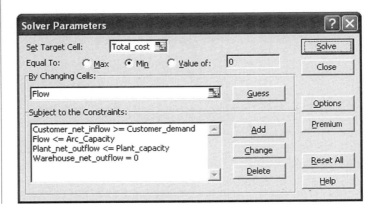

Discussion of the Solution

The optimal solution in Figure 5.18 indicates that RedBrand's customer demand can be satisfied with a shipping cost of $3,260,000. This solution appears graphically in Figure 5.20. Note in particular that plant 1 produces 180 tons (under capacity) and ships it all to plant 3, not directly to warehouses or customers. Also, note that all shipments from the warehouses go directly to customer 1. Then customer 1 ships 180 tons to customer 2. We purposely chose unit shipping costs (probably unrealistic ones) to produce this type of behavior, just to show that it *can* occur. As you can see, the costs of shipping from plant 1 directly to warehouses or customers are relatively large compared to the cost of shipping directly to plant 3. Similarly, the costs of shipping from plants or warehouses directly to customer 2 are prohibitive. Therefore, RedBrand should ship to customer 1 and let customer 1 forward some of its shipment to customer 2.

Figure 5.20

Optimal Flows for RedBrand Example

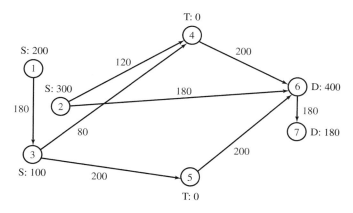

Sensitivity Analysis

How much effect does the arc capacity have on the optimal solution? Currently, we see that three of the arcs with positive flow are at the arc capacity of 200. We can use SolverTable to see how sensitive this number and the total cost are to the arc capacity.[5] In this case the single input cell for SolverTable is cell B4, which we vary from 150 to 300 in increments of 25. We keep track of two outputs: total cost and the number of arcs at arc capacity. As before, if we want to keep track of an output that does not already exist, we create it with an appropriate formula in a new cell before running SolverTable. This is shown in Figure 5.21. The formula in cell B39 is **=COUNTIF(Flow,B4)**. This formula counts the arcs with flow equal to arc capacity.

Figure 5.21

Sensitivity to Arc Capacity

	A	B	C	D	E
38	Additional output variable (for sensitivity analysis)				
39	Arcs at capacity	5			
40					
41	Sensitivity of total cost and arcs at capacity to arc capacity				
42		$B$36	$B$39		
43	150	$4,120	6		
44	175	$3,643	6		
45	200	$3,260	3		
46	225	$2,998	3		
47	250	$2,735	3		
48	275	$2,473	3		
49	300	$2,320	2		

[5]Note that Solver's sensitivity report would not answer our question. This report is useful only for one-at-a-time changes in inputs, and here we are simultaneously changing the upper limit for *each* flow. However, this report (its bottom section) could be useful to assess the effects of changes in plant capacities or customer demands.

→ **EXCEL FUNCTION:** *COUNTIF*

*The COUNTIF counts the number of values in a given range that satisfy some criterion. The syntax is =**COUNTIF(range,criterion)**. For example, the formula =**COUNTIF(D8:D33,150)** counts the number of cells in the range D8:D33 that contain the value 150. This formula could also be entered as =**COUNTIF(D8:D33,"=150")**. Similarly, the formula =**COUNTIF(D8:D33,">=100")** would count the number of cells in this range with values greater than or equal to 100.* ∎

The SolverTable output is what we would expect. As the arc capacity decreases, more flows bump up against it, and the total cost increases. But even when the arc capacity is increased to 300, two flows are constrained by it. In this sense, even this large an arc capacity costs RedBrand money.

Variations of the Model

There are endless variations of this basic minimum cost network flow model, corresponding to the many types of real-world shipping problems.

There are many variations of the RedBrand shipping problem that can be handled by a network formulation. We briefly consider two possible variations. First, suppose that Red-Brand ships two products along the given network. We assume that the unit shipping costs are the same for both products (although this assumption could easily be relaxed), but the arc capacity, which we now change to 300, represents the maximum flow of *both* products that can flow on any arc. In this sense, the two products are competing for arc capacity. Each plant has a separate production capacity for each product, and each customer has a separate demand for each product.

The spreadsheet model for this variation appears in Figure 5.22. (See the file **RedBrand2.xls**.) Very little in the original model must be changed. We need to (1) have two columns of changing cells (columns D and E), (2) apply the previous logic to both products separately in the flow balance constraints, and (3) apply the arc capacities to the *total* flows in column F (which are the sums of flows in columns D and E). The modified Solver dialog box is shown in Figure 5.23. Note that we have range-named blocks of cells for the flow balance constraints. For example, the ranges K9:L11 and N9:O11 are named Plant_net_outflow and Plant_capacity. Then we can use these entire blocks to specify the capacity constraints for both products with the single entry **Plant_net_outflow <=Plant_capacity** in the Solver dialog box. This is another example of planning the spreadsheet layout so that the resulting model is as efficient and readable as possible.

Figure 5.22   RedBrand Model with Two Products

	A	B	C	D	E	F	G	H	I	J	K	L	M	N	O
1	RedBrand shipping model with two products competing for arc capacity														
2															
3	Inputs														
4	Common arc capacity	300													
5															
6	Network structure, flows, and arc capacity constraints							Node balance constraints							
7	Origin	Destination	Unit Cost	Flow product 1	Flow product 2	Total flow		Arc Capacity		Plant constraints					
8		1	2	5	0	0	0	<=	300		Node	Net outflow product 1	Net outflow product 2		Capacity product 1	Capacity product 2
9		1	3	3	160	140	300	<=	300		1	180	140	<=	200	200
10		1	4	5	20	0	20	<=	300		2	300	100	<=	300	100
11		1	5	5	0	0	0	<=	300		3	100	100	<=	100	100
12		1	6	20	0	0	0	<=	300							
13		1	7	20	0	0	0	<=	300		Warehouse constraints					
14		2	1	9	0	0	0	<=	300		Node	Net outflow product 1	Net outflow product 2		Required product 1	Required product 2
15		2	3	9	0	0	0	<=	300		4	0	0	=	0	0
16		2	4	1	100	0	100	<=	300		5	0	0	=	0	0
17		2	5	1	0	0	0	<=	300							
18		2	6	8	200	100	300	<=	300		Customer constraints					
19		2	7	15	0	0	0	<=	300		Node	Net inflow product 1	Net inflow product 2		Demand product 1	Demand product 2
20		3	1	0.4	0	0	0	<=	300		6	400	200	>=	400	200
21		3	2	8	0	0	0	<=	300		7	180	140	>=	180	140
22		3	4	1	0	180	180	<=	300							
23		3	5	0.5	240	60	300	<=	300							
24		3	6	10	0	0	0	<=	300							
25		3	7	12	20	0	20	<=	300							
26		4	5	1.2	0	0	0	<=	300							
27		4	6	2	120	180	300	<=	300							
28		4	7	12	0	0	0	<=	300							
29		5	4	0.8	0	0	0	<=	300							
30		5	6	2	240	60	300	<=	300							
31		5	7	12	0	0	0	<=	300							
32		6	7	1	160	140	300	<=	300							
33		7	6	7	0	0	0	<=	300							
34															
35	Objective to minimize														
36	Total cost	$5,570													

Figure 5.23
Solver Dialog Box
for Two-Product
Model

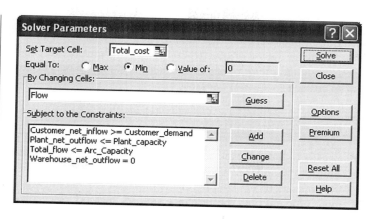

A second variation of the model is appropriate for perishable goods, such as fruit. (See the file **RedBrand3.xls**.) We again assume that there is a single product, but some percentage of the product that is shipped to warehouses perishes and cannot be sent to customers. This means that the total inflow to a warehouse is *greater than* the total outflow from the warehouse. We model this behavior as shown in Figure 5.24. (The corresponding Solver dialog box, not shown here, is the same as in the original RedBrand model.) The "shrinkage factor" in cell B5, the percentage that does *not* spoil in the warehouses, becomes a new input. It is then incorporated into the warehouse flow balance constraints by entering the formula

=SUMIF(Origin,H16,Flow)-$B$5*SUMIF(Destination,H16,Flow)

in cell I16 and copying to cell I17. This formula says that what goes out (the first term) is 90% of what goes in. The other 10% perishes. Of course, shrinkage results in a larger total cost—about 20% larger—than in the original RedBrand model.

Figure 5.24   RedBrand Model with Shrinkage

	A	B	C	D	E	F	G	H	I	J	K
1	RedBrand shipping model with shrinkage at warehouses										
2											
3	Inputs										
4	Common arc capacity	150									
5	Shrinkage factor	90%									
6											
7	Network formulation							Node balance constraints			
8		Origin	Destination	Unit Cost	Flow		Arc Capacity	Plant constraints			
9		1	2	5	0	<=	150	Node	Plant net outflow		Plant capacity
10		1	3	3	150	<=	150	1	200	<=	200
11		1	4	5	0	<=	150	2	300	<=	300
12		1	5	5	50	<=	150	3	100	<=	100
13		1	6	20	0	<=	150				
14		1	7	20	0	<=	150	Warehouse constraints			
15		2	1	9	0	<=	150	Node	Warehouse net outflow		Required
16		2	3	9	0	<=	150	4	0	=	0
17		2	4	1	33	<=	150	5	0	=	0
18		2	5	1	117	<=	150				
19		2	6	8	150	<=	150				
20		2	7	15	0	<=	150	Customer constraints			
21		3	1	0.4	0	<=	150	Node	Customer net inflow		Customer demand
22		3	2	8	0	<=	150	6	400	>=	400
23		3	4	1	0	<=	150	7	180	>=	180
24		3	5	0.5	0	<=	150				
25		3	6	10	150	<=	150				
26		3	7	12	100	<=	150				
27		4	5	1.2	0	<=	150				
28		4	6	2	30	<=	150				
29		4	7	12	0	<=	150				
30		5	4	0.8	0	<=	150				
31		5	6	2	150	<=	150				
32		5	7	12	0	<=	150				
33		6	7	1	80	<=	150				
34		7	6	7	0	<=	150				
35											
36	Objective to minimize										
37	Total cost	$5,190									

Interestingly, however, some units are still sent to both warehouses, and the entire capacity of all plants is now used. Finally, you can check that a feasible solution exists even for a shrinkage factor of 0% (where everything sent to warehouses disappears). As you might guess, the solution then is to send everything directly from plants to customers—at a steep cost. ■

MODELING ISSUES

1. Excel's Solver uses the simplex method to solve network flow models. However, the simplex method can be simplified dramatically for these types of models. The simplified version of the simplex method, called the **network simplex method**, is much more efficient than the ordinary simplex method. Specialized computer codes have been written to implement the network simplex method, and all large network flow problems are solved by using the network simplex method. This is fortunate because real network models can be extremely large. See Winston (2003) for a discussion of this method.

2. If the given supplies and demands for the nodes are integers and all arc capacities are integers, then the network flow model always has an optimal solution with all integer flows. Again, this is very fortunate for large problems—we get integer solutions "for free" without having to use an integer programming algorithm. Note, however, that this "integers for free" benefit is guaranteed only for the "basic" network flow model, as in the original RedBrand model. When we modify the model, by adding a shrinkage factor, say, the optimal solution is no longer guaranteed to be integer-valued. ■

ADDITIONAL APPLICATIONS

Distribution in Nu-kote International's Network

LeBlanc et al. (2002) used a linear programming transportation model like the one in Section 5.3 to analyze distribution in Nu-kote International's network of vendors, manufacturing plants, warehouses, and customers. Nu-kote, a manufacturer of inkjet, laser, and toner cartridges, saves approximately $1 million annually as a result of this model. The LP has nearly 6,000 variables and 2,500 constraints. Total time available for data collection and model development and verification was limited to only six weeks. It is a tribute to the efficiency and user-friendliness of Microsoft Excel that all of this was completed within this time frame. ■

PROBLEMS

Skill-Building Problems

19. In the original RedBrand problem, suppose the plants cannot ship to each other and the customers cannot ship to each other. Modify the model appropriately, and reoptimize. How much does the total cost increase because of these disallowed routes?

20. Modify the original RedBrand problem so that all flows must be from plants to warehouses and from warehouses to customers. Disallow all other arcs.

How much does this restriction cost RedBrand, relative to the original optimal shipping cost?

21. In the original RedBrand problem, the costs for shipping from plants or warehouses to customer 2 were purposely made high so that it would be optimal to ship to customer 1 and then let customer 1 ship to customer 2. Use SolverTable appropriately to do the following. Decrease the unit shipping costs from plants and warehouses to customer 1, all by the same amount, until it is no longer optimal for customer 1 to ship to customer 2. Describe what happens to the optimal shipping plan at this point.

22. In the original RedBrand problem we assume a constant arc capacity, the same for all allowable arcs. Modify the model so that each arc has its own arc capacity. You can make up the required arc capacities.

23. Continuing the previous problem, make the problem even more general by allowing upper bounds (arc capacities) *and* lower bounds for the flows on the allowable arcs. Some of the upper bounds can be very large numbers, effectively indicating that there is no arc capacity for these arcs, and the lower bounds can be 0 or positive. If they are positive, then they indicate that some positive flow must occur on these arcs. Modify the model appropriately to handle these upper and lower bounds. You can make up the required bounds.

24. Expand the RedBrand two-product spreadsheet model so that there are now three products competing for the arc capacity. You can make up the required input data.

25. In the RedBrand two-product problem, we assumed that the unit shipping costs are the same for both products. Modify the spreadsheet model so that each product has its own unit shipping costs. You can assume that the original unit shipping costs apply to product 1, and you can make up new unit shipping costs for product 2.

Skill-Extending Problems

26. How difficult is it to expand the original RedBrand model? Answer this by adding a new plant, two new warehouses, and three new customers, and modify the spreadsheet model appropriately. You can make up the required input data.

27. In the RedBrand problem with shrinkage, change the assumptions. Now instead of assuming that there is some shrinkage at the warehouses, assume that there is shrinkage in delivery along each route. Specifically, assume that a certain percentage of the units sent along each arc perish in transit—from faulty refrigeration, say—and this percentage can differ from one arc to another. Modify the model appropriately to take this type of behavior into account. You can make up the shrinkage factors, and you can assume that arc capacities apply to the amounts originally shipped, not to the amounts after shrinkage. (Make sure your input data permit a *feasible* solution. After all, if there is too much shrinkage, it will be impossible to meet demands with available plant capacity. Increase the plant capacities if necessary.)

28. Consider a modification of the original RedBrand problem where there are N plants, M warehouses, and L customers. Assume that the only allowable arcs are from plants to warehouses and from warehouses to customers. If *all* such arcs are allowable—all plants can ship to all warehouses and all warehouses can ship to all customers—how many changing cells are in the spreadsheet model? Keeping in mind that Excel's Solver can handle at most 200 changing cells, give some combinations of N, M, and L that will just barely stay within Solver's limit.

29. Continuing the previous problem, develop a sample model with your own choices of N, M, and L that barely stay within Solver's limit. You can make up any input data. The important point here is the layout and formulas of the spreadsheet model.

5.5 SHORTEST PATH MODELS

In many applications it is important to find the shortest path between two points in a network. Sometimes this problem occurs in a geographical context where, for example, we might want to find the shortest path on interstate freeways from Seattle to Miami. Surprisingly, there are other problems that do not look like shortest path problems but can be modeled in the same way. We will look at one possibility in this section when we find an optimal schedule for replacing equipment.

It is always useful in management science to recognize that one problem can be modeled as a special case of another more general (and well understood) model. This saves us from having to "reinvent the wheel" on every new problem.

The typical shortest path problem is a special case of the minimum cost network flow problem from the previous section. To see why this is the case, suppose that we want to find the shortest path between node 1 and node N in a network. To find this shortest path we create a network flow model where the supply for node 1 is 1 and the demand for node N is 1. All other nodes are transshipment nodes. If there is an arc joining two nodes in the network, the "shipping cost" is equal to the length of the arc. The "flow" through each arc in the network (in the optimal solution) is either 1 or 0, depending on whether the shortest path includes the arc. No arc capacities are required in the model. The value of the objective is then equal to the sum of the distances of the arcs involved in the path.

Geographical Shortest Path Models

The following example illustrates the shortest path model in the context of a geographic network.

5.5 Shortest Walk Across the State

Maude Jenkins, a 90-year old woman, is planning to walk across the state, west to east, to gain support for a political cause she favors.[6] She wants to travel the shortest distance to get from city 1 to city 10, using the arcs (roads) shown in Figure 5.25. The numbers on the arcs are miles. Arcs with double-headed arrows indicate that travel is possible in both directions (and the distance is the same in both directions). What route should Maude take?

Figure 5.25
Network for
Shortest Path
Problem

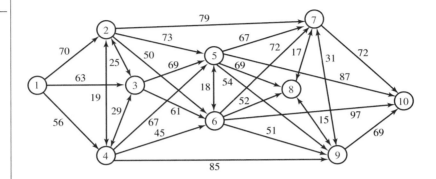

Objective   To specialize the general network flow model so that we can find a shortest path from node 1 to node 10 for Maude's trip across the state.

WHERE DO THE NUMBERS COME FROM?

The distances on the arcs are presumably listed on state maps for the roads Maude is considering. Note, however, that in shortest path problems such as this, the objective is sometimes total *cost*, not distance. Although the cost of an arc might be proportional to its distance, it might not be. For example, a steep uphill route might be more "costly" than a flat stretch of similar length. In such cases, the arc costs would be a bit more difficult to obtain.

The "distances" in shortest path models are sometimes costs.

Solution

The variables and constraints for this model are listed in Table 5.9. This network model is exactly like the general minimum cost network flow model in the previous section. All we need to specify is that node 1 has a supply of 1 (you can think of it as Maude herself), node 10 has a demand of 1, and all other nodes are transshipment nodes.

---

[6]Far-fetched? This is based on a real 90-year-old woman who reportedly decided to walk across the *country*. We assume she finished!

Table 5.9	Variables and Constraints for Maude's Shortest Path Model
Input variables	Network structure and arc distances
Decision variables (changing cells)	Flows on arcs (1 if arc is used, 0 otherwise)
Objective (target cell)	Total distance
Other calculated variables	Flows into and out of arcs
Constraints	Flow balance at each node

DEVELOPING THE SPREADSHEET MODEL

The completed model and associated Solver dialog box appear in Figures 5.26 and 5.27. (See the file **ShortestPath.xls**.) Because this is so similar to the general minimum cost network flow model, we will omit most of the details. However, the following points are important.

Figure 5.26 Shortest Path Model

	A	B	C	D	E	F	G	H	I	J	K	L	M	N
1	Shortest path model													
2														
3	Network structure and flows					Flow balance constraints					Range names used:			
4	Origin	Destination	Distance	Flow		Node	Net outflow		Required net outflow		Destination	=Model!$B$5:$B$39		
5	1	2	70	0		1	1	=	1		Distance	=Model!$C$5:$C$39		
6	1	3	63	0		2	0	=	0		Flow	=Model!$D$5:$D$39		
7	1	4	56	1		3	0	=	0		Net_outflow	=Model!$G$5:$G$14		
8	2	3	25	0		4	0	=	0		Origin	=Model!$A$5:$A$39		
9	2	4	19	0		5	0	=	0		Required_net_outflow	=Model!$I$5:$I$14		
10	2	5	73	0		6	0	=	0		Total_distance	=Model!$B$42		
11	2	6	50	0		7	0	=	0					
12	2	7	79	0		8	0	=	0					
13	3	2	25	0		9	0	=	0					
14	3	4	29	0		10	-1	=	-1					
15	3	5	69	0										
16	3	6	61	0										
17	4	2	19	0										
18	4	3	29	0										
19	4	5	67	0										
20	4	6	45	1										
21	4	9	85	0										
22	5	6	18	0										
23	5	7	67	0										
24	5	8	69	0										
25	5	9	54	0										
26	5	10	87	0										
27	6	5	18	0										
28	6	7	72	0										
29	6	8	52	0										
30	6	9	51	0										
31	6	10	97	1										
32	7	8	17	0										
33	7	9	31	0										
34	7	10	72	0										
35	8	7	17	0										
36	8	9	15	0										
37	9	7	31	0										
38	9	8	15	0										
39	9	10	69	0										
40														
41	Objective to minimize													
42	Total distance	198												

Figure 5.27
Solver Dialog Box for Shortest Path Model

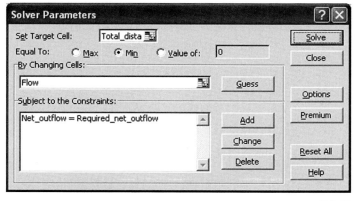

① **Arc list.** There is an arc listed in columns A and B for each arc in the graphical network. If the arc goes in both directions, it is listed twice (2 to 4 and 4 to 2, for example) with the same distance in both directions.

② **Net outflows.** We list all types of nodes in a single block in the flow balance constraint section. Node 1 is a supplier with a supply of 1, and it has only outflows. Similarly, node 10 is a demander with demand 1, and it has only inflows. The intermediate nodes are all transshipment nodes. We can treat all of the nodes similarly by calculating the net *outflow* from each. To do so, enter the formula

=SUMIF(Origin,F5,Flow)-SUMIF(Destination,F5,Flow)

in cell G5 and copy it down for the other nodes. For node 1, this net outflow is really just the outflow, so it should be 1. For node 10, this net outflow is really just the *negative* of the inflow, so it should be −1. For all intermediate nodes, the net outflow should be 0. This explains the required values in column I.

③ **Total distance.** The objective to minimize is total distance, calculated in cell B42 with the formula

=SUMPRODUCT(Distance,Flow)

Discussion of the Solution

Once Solver finds the optimal flows, which are 0's and 1's, it is easy to identify the shortest path—we just "follow the 1's." According to Figure 5.26, Maude first goes from node 1 to node 4 (see row 7), then she goes from node 4 to node 6 (see row 20), and finally she goes from node 6 to node 10 (see row 31). Using this route from 1 to 10, Maude must walk 198 miles, the sum of the distances on the three arcs she traverses.

Make sure you understand exactly how this model works. There are really two parts: the total distance and the balance of inflows and outflows. For any solution of 0's and 1's in the Flow column, the SUMPRODUCT for total distance simply "picks up" the distances in column C corresponding to the arcs traversed. This accurately reflects the total distance Maude walks.

All flows in a shortest path model are either 0 or 1; a route is either used or it isn't.

For flow balance, consider any intermediate node. If Maude's route goes through it, such as with node 6, then the two SUMIF functions in column G for this node will both evaluate to 1—that is, one of the arcs leading into node 6 will have a flow of 1, and one of the arcs leading out of node 6 will have a flow of 1. On the other hand, if Maude's route doesn't go through the node, such as with node 3, then the two SUMIF functions for this node will both evaluate to 0—no flow in and no flow out. Finally, the flow balance constraints for nodes 1 and 10 ensure that exactly one arc leading out of node 1 will have a flow of 1, and exactly one arc leading into node 10 will have a flow of 1. ■

Equipment Replacement Models[7]

Although shortest path problems often involve traveling through a network, this is not always the case. For example, when should you trade your car in for a new car? As a car gets older, the maintenance cost per year increases and it might become worthwhile to buy a new car. If your goal is to minimize the average annual cost of owning a car (ignoring the time value of money), then it is possible to set up a shortest path representation of this problem. Actually, the method we discuss can be used in any situation where equipment replacement is an issue. Of course, many people trade in a car because they like the "feel" of a new car. We will not model this aspect of the problem; we will consider only the fi-

---

[7]This section is somewhat more complex and can be omitted without any loss of continuity.

nancial aspects. The following is an example of how equipment replacement can be modeled as a shortest path problem.

EXAMPLE | **5.6 EQUIPMENT REPLACEMENT AT VANBUREN METALS**

VanBuren Metals is a manufacturing company that uses many large machines to work on metals. These machines require frequent maintenance because of wear and tear, and VanBuren finds that it is sometimes advantageous, from a cost standpoint, to replace machines rather than continue to maintain them. For one particular class of machines, the company has estimated the quarterly costs of maintenance, the salvage value from re-selling an old machine, and the cost to purchase a new machine.[8] We assume that the maintenance cost and the salvage value depend on the *age* of the current machine (at the beginning of the quarter). However, we assume that the maintenance costs, the salvage values, and the purchase cost do *not* depend on time. In other words, we assume no inflation. Specifically, we assume the following:

- The purchase cost of a new machine is always $3530.

- The maintenance cost of a machine in its first quarter of use is $100. For each succeeding quarter, the maintenance cost increases by $65. This reflects the fact that machines require more maintenance as they age.

- The salvage value of a machine after one quarter of use is $1530. After each succeeding quarter of use, the salvage value decreases by $110.

VanBuren would like to devise a strategy for purchasing machines over the next 5 years. As a matter of policy, the company never sells a machine that is less than 1 year old, and it never keeps a machine that is more than 3 years old. Also, the machine in use at the beginning of the current quarter is brand new.

Objective   To find the optimal replacement strategy by modeling the problem as an equivalent shortest path problem.

WHERE DO THE NUMBERS COME FROM?

In general, a company would gather historical data on maintenance costs and salvage values for similar machines and fit appropriate curves to the data (probably using regression, as discussed in Chapter 12).

Solution

The variables and constraints required for this machine replacement model appear in Table 5.10 (page 218). We claimed that this problem can be modeled as a shortest path model, which is probably far from obvious. There are two keys to understanding why this is possible: (1) the meaning of nodes and arcs, and (2) the calculation of costs on arcs. After you understand this, the modeling details are *exactly* as in the previous example.

---

[8]One issue in these types of models is the time period to use. We will assume that VanBuren uses quarters. Therefore, the only times it considers purchasing new machines are beginnings of quarters.

Table 5.10   Variables and Constraints for the Equipment Replacement Model

Input variables	Purchase cost, maintenance costs as a function of age, salvage values as a function of age
Decision variables (changing cells)	Flows on arcs (1 if arc is used, 0 otherwise), which determine the replacement schedule
Objective (target cell)	Total (net) cost
Other output cells	Flows into and out of arcs
Constraints	Flow balance at each node

The network is constructed as follows. There is a node for each quarter, including the current quarter and the quarter exactly 5 years (20 quarters) from now. (Remember that VanBuren wants a 5-year planning horizon.) We label these nodes 1 through 21, where node 1 is the current quarter, node 2 is the next quarter, and so on. There is an arc from each node to each *later* node that is at least 4 quarters ahead but no more than 12 quarters ahead. (This is because VanBuren never sells a machine less than 1 year old, and never keeps a machine more than 3 years.) Several of these arcs are shown in Figure 5.28. (Many nodes and arcs do *not* appear in this figure.)

Figure 5.28

Selected Nodes and Arcs for Machine Replacement Network

An arc from any node to a later node corresponds to keeping a machine for a certain period of time and then trading it in for a new machine.

Consider the arc from node 9 to node 17, for example. "Using" this arc on the shortest path—that is, putting a flow of 1 on it—corresponds to starting with a new machine in quarter 9, keeping it for 8 quarters, and selling it and purchasing another new machine at the beginning of quarter 17. An entire strategy for the 5-year period is a string of such arcs. For example, with the path 1–9–17–21, VanBuren keeps the first machine for 8 quarters, trades it in for a second machine at the beginning of quarter 9, keeps the second machine for 8 quarters, trades it in for a third machine at the beginning of quarter 17, keeps the third machine for 4 quarters, and finally trades it in for a fourth machine at the beginning of quarter 21.

An arc cost is a sum of maintenance costs minus a salvage value plus the cost of a new machine.

Given the meaning of the arcs, the calculation of arc costs is a matter of careful bookkeeping. Again, consider the arc from node 9 to node 17. The cost on this arc is the total maintenance cost for this machine during the 8 quarters it is kept, minus the salvage value of an 8-quarter-old machine sold in quarter 17, plus the cost of the replacement machine purchased at the beginning of quarter 17. The total maintenance cost for this machine is the maintenance cost of a machine in its first quarter of use, plus the maintenance cost of a machine in its second quarter of use, plus the maintenance cost of a machine in its third quarter of use, and so on. The first of these is $100, the second is $165, the third is $230, and so on for the 8 quarters it is kept. The sum of these 8 costs is $2620. The salvage value at the end of quarter 17 is $1530 − 7($110) = $760, and the cost of the replacement machine is $3530. Therefore, the (net) cost on this arc is $2620 − $760 + $3530 = $5390.

DEVELOPING THE SPREADSHEET MODEL

The information about arcs in the spreadsheet model is given in Figure 5.29, where rows 27–124 have been hidden. (See the file **MachineReplacement.xls**.) This part of the model can be completed with the following steps.

Figure 5.29 Arc Information in Machine Replacement Model

	A	B	C	D	E	F	G	H	I	J	K	L	M	N	O	P	Q	R	S
1	**Machine replacement model - shortest path formulation**																		
2																			
3	**Inputs**			**Range names used:**															
4	Purchase cost	3530		Destination	=Model!$B$14:$B$130														
5	Maintenance cost			Flow	=Model!$S$14:$S$130														
6	In first quarter	100		Net_outflow	=Model!$V$14:$V$34														
7	Increase per quarter	65		Origin	=Model!$A$14:$A$130														
8	Salvage value			Required	=Model!$X$14:$X$34														
9	After one quarter	1530		Total_cost	=Model!$V$36														
10	Decrease per quarter	110																	
11																			
12	**Network arcs**			**Maintenance costs in quarter of use:**															
13	Origin	Destination	Quarters to keep	1	2	3	4	5	6	7	8	9	10	11	12	Salvage value	Purchase cost	Total cost	Flow
14	1	5	4	100	165	230	295	0	0	0	0	0	0	0	0	1200	3530	3120	0
15	1	6	5	100	165	230	295	360	0	0	0	0	0	0	0	1090	3530	3590	0
16	1	7	6	100	165	230	295	360	425	0	0	0	0	0	0	980	3530	4125	1
17	1	8	7	100	165	230	295	360	425	490	0	0	0	0	0	870	3530	4725	0
18	1	9	8	100	165	230	295	360	425	490	555	0	0	0	0	760	3530	5390	0
19	1	10	9	100	165	230	295	360	425	490	555	620	0	0	0	650	3530	6120	0
20	1	11	10	100	165	230	295	360	425	490	555	620	685	0	0	540	3530	6915	0
21	1	12	11	100	165	230	295	360	425	490	555	620	685	750	0	430	3530	7775	0
22	1	13	12	100	165	230	295	360	425	490	555	620	685	750	815	320	3530	8700	0
23	2	6	4	100	165	230	295	0	0	0	0	0	0	0	0	1200	3530	3120	0
24	2	7	5	100	165	230	295	360	0	0	0	0	0	0	0	1090	3530	3590	0
25	2	8	6	100	165	230	295	360	425	0	0	0	0	0	0	980	3530	4125	0
26	2	9	7	100	165	230	295	360	425	490	0	0	0	0	0	870	3530	4725	0
125	15	19	4	100	165	230	295	0	0	0	0	0	0	0	0	1200	3530	3120	0
126	15	20	5	100	165	230	295	360	0	0	0	0	0	0	0	1090	3530	3590	0
127	15	21	6	100	165	230	295	360	425	0	0	0	0	0	0	980	3530	4125	0
128	16	20	4	100	165	230	295	0	0	0	0	0	0	0	0	1200	3530	3120	0
129	16	21	5	100	165	230	295	360	0	0	0	0	0	0	0	1090	3530	3590	0
130	17	21	4	100	165	230	295	0	0	0	0	0	0	0	0	1200	3530	3120	0

1 Inputs. Enter the inputs for the purchase cost, maintenance costs, and salvage values in the shaded ranges.

The allowable arcs are determined by the company's trade-in policy.

2 Arcs. In the bottom section, columns A and B indicate the arcs in the network. Enter these "origins" and "destinations" manually. Just make sure that the difference between them is at least 4 and no greater than 12 (because of the company's trade-in policy). Also, make sure that the origin is at least 1 and the destination is no more than 21.

3 Quarters to keep. Calculate the differences between the values in columns B and A in column C. These differences indicate how many quarters the machine is kept for each arc.

4 Maintenance costs. Calculate the quarterly maintenance costs in columns D through O. First, you need to realize why there are so many columns. The maintenance cost for any arc is the *total* maintenance cost for a machine until it is traded in. Because the company can keep a machine for up to 12 quarters, we need 12 columns. For example, for the arc from 1 to 5 in row 14, cell D14 contains the maintenance cost in the first quarter of this period, cell E14 contains the maintenance cost in the second quarter of this period, and so on. Fortunately, you can calculate all of these maintenance costs at once by entering the formula

=IF(D$13>$C14,0,$B$6+$B$7*(D$13-1))

in cell D14 and copying it to the range D14:O130. The IF function ensures that no maintenance costs for this machine are incurred unless the machine is still in use.

Careful planning of the spreadsheet layout is important here. The reference numbers in row 13 allow us to incorporate age in the formulas.

Pay particular attention to the way age is incorporated in this formula. The reference numbers in the range D13:O13 indicate the quarter of use, 1–12. For example, consider the situation in cell F24. A new machine was purchased in quarter 2 and is now in its third quarter of use. Therefore, its maintenance cost is \$100 + 2(\$65) = \$230.

5 Salvage values. In a similar way, calculate the salvage values in column P by entering the formula

=$B$9-$B$10*(C14-1)

in cell P14 and copying down column P. For example, the salvage value in row 24 is for a machine that is sold after its fifth year of use. This is $1530 − 4($110) = $1090.

6 **Purchase cost.** The purchase cost of a new machine never changes, so put an absolute link to cell B4 in cell Q14, and copy it down column Q.

7 **Total arc costs.** Calculate the total costs on the arcs as total maintenance cost minus salvage value plus purchase cost. To do this, enter the formula

=SUM(D14:O14)-P14+Q14

in cell R14, and copy it down column R.

8 **Flows.** Enter *any* flows on the arcs in column S. As usual, Solver will eventually find flows that are equal to 0 or 1.

USING SOLVER

From this point, the model is developed *exactly* as in the shortest path model in Example 5.5, with node 1 as the "origin" node and node 21 as the "destination" node. We create the flow balance constraints, calculate the total network cost, and use Solver exactly as before, so we will not repeat the details here. (See Figure 5.30.)

Figure 5.30

Constraints and
Objective for
Machine
Replacement Model

	U	V	W	X
12	**Flow balance constraints**			
13	Node	Net outflow		Required
14	1	1	=	1
15	2	0	=	0
16	3	0	=	0
17	4	0	=	0
18	5	0	=	0
19	6	0	=	0
20	7	0	=	0
21	8	0	=	0
22	9	0	=	0
23	10	0	=	0
24	11	0	=	0
25	12	0	=	0
26	13	0	=	0
27	14	0	=	0
28	15	0	=	0
29	16	0	=	0
30	17	0	=	0
31	18	0	=	0
32	19	0	=	0
33	20	0	=	0
34	21	-1	=	-1
35				
36	Total cost	$13,575		

Discussion of the Solution

Once we use Solver to find the shortest path, we can follow the 1's in the Flow range to identify the optimal equipment replacement policy. Although not all of the rows appear in Figure 5.29, you can check in the **MachineReplacement.xls** file that only three arcs have a flow of 1: arcs 1–7, 7–14, and 14–21. This solution indicates that VanBuren should keep the current machine for 6 quarters, trade it in for a new machine at the beginning of quarter 7, keep the second machine for 7 quarters, trade it in for a new machine at the beginning of quarter 14, keep the third machine for 7 quarters, and finally trade it in for a new machine at the beginning of quarter 21. The total (net) cost of this strategy is $13,575.

Although Solver finds the minimum-cost replacement strategy, this might be a good time for you to try your own strategy, just to make sure you understand how the network works. For example, see if you can enter the appropriate flows for the strategy that replaces in quarters 6, 11, 17, and 21. Your flows should automatically satisfy the flow balance constraints, and your total cost should be $14,425. Of course, this is a suboptimal solution; its cost is larger than the minimum cost we found with Solver. ■

MODELING ISSUES

1. There is no inflation in this model, so that monetary values do not increase through time. Inflation could certainly be built in, but we would need to estimate exactly how inflation affects the costs and salvage values, and we would have to build this behavior into the spreadsheet formulas in the model.

2. As the model now stands, VanBuren is *forced* to resell the current machine and purchase a new one at the end of the 5-year period. This is because the cost of every arc leading into the last node, node 21, includes a salvage value *and* a purchase cost. This feature of the model is not as bad as it might seem. *Every* path from node 1 to node 21 includes the purchase cost in quarter 21, so this cost has no effect on which path is best. The effect of including the salvage value in arcs into node 21 is to penalize strategies that end with old machines after 5 years. Regardless of how we model the problem, we probably *ought* to penalize such strategies in some way. In addition, VanBuren will probably use a rolling planning horizon—that is, it will implement only short-term decisions from the model. The way we model the end of the 5-year horizon should have little effect on these early decisions. ■

ADDITIONAL APPLICATIONS

Replacing Vehicles at Phillips Petroleum Company

Waddell (1983) used the shortest path model to help Phillips Petroleum Company schedule replacement of individual highway tractors, cars, and trucks. The model allowed for the possibility of leasing vehicles, as well as purchasing them. Replacement of vehicles was allowed at 3-month intervals. The goal was to find a vehicle replacement policy that would minimize discounted costs over a planning horizon of 20 years. The following costs were included in the model:

- maintenance and operating costs such as fuel, oil, salaries of repair personnel, and so on
- leasing cost for leased vehicles
- purchase cost for purchased vehicles
- state license fees and road taxes
- cost of purchasing vehicle
- savings due to investment tax credits and investment depreciation

When the model was applied to cars and trucks, vehicles were grouped according to their age, odometer mileage, and function. It is estimated that the equipment replacement model saved Phillips $90,000 annually when applied to tractors alone. ■

Skill-Building Problems

30. In Maude's shortest path problem, suppose all arcs in the current network from higher-numbered nodes to lower-numbered nodes, such as from node 6 to node 5, are disallowed. Modify the spreadsheet model and find the shortest path from node 1 to node 10. Is it the same as before? Should you have known the answer to this question before making any changes to the original model? Explain.

31. In Maude's shortest path problem, suppose all arcs in the network are "double-arrowed," that is, Maude can travel along each arc (with the same distance) in either direction. Modify the spreadsheet model appropriately. Is her optimal solution still the same?

32. Continuing the previous problem, suppose again that all arcs go in either direction, but suppose Maude's objective is to find the shortest path from node 1 to node 7 (not node 10). Modify the spreadsheet model appropriately and solve.

33. How difficult is it to add nodes and arcs to an existing shortest path model? Answer by adding a new node, node 11, to Maude's network. Assume that node 11 is at the top of the network, geographically, with double-arrowed arcs joining it to nodes 2, 5, and 7 with distances 45, 22, and 10. Assume that Maude's objective is still to get from node 1 to node 10. Does the new optimal solution go through node 11?

34. In the VanBuren machine replacement problem, we assumed that the maintenance cost and salvage values are *linear* functions of age. Suppose instead that the maintenance cost increases by 50% each quarter and that the salvage value decreases by 10% each quarter.

Rework the model with these assumptions. What is the optimal replacement schedule?

35. In the VanBuren machine replacement problem, the company's current policy is to keep a machine at least 4 quarters but no more than 12 quarters. Suppose this policy is instead to keep a machine at least 5 quarters but no more than 10 quarters. Modify the spreadsheet model appropriately. Is the new optimal solution the same as before?

36. In the VanBuren machine replacement problem, the company's current policy is to keep a machine at least 4 quarters but no more than 12 quarters. Suppose instead that the company imposes no upper limit on how long it will keep a machine; its only policy requirement is that a machine must be kept at least 4 quarters. Modify the spreadsheet model appropriately. Is the new optimal solution the same as before?

Skill-Extending Problems

37. In the VanBuren machine replacement problem, suppose the company starts with a machine that is 8 quarters old at the beginning of the first quarter. Modify the model appropriately, keeping in mind that this initial machine must be sold no more than 4 quarters from now.

38. We illustrated how a machine replacement problem can be modeled as a shortest path problem. This is probably not the approach most people would think of when they first see a machine replacement problem. In fact, most people would probably never think in terms of a network. How would *you* model the problem? Does your approach result in an LP model?

5.6 PROJECT SCHEDULING MODELS

Network models can be used to help schedule large, complex projects that consist of many activities. If the time to finish each activity is known with certainty, then we can determine the length of time required to complete a project. If the activity times are not known with certainty, then simulation (see Chapter 10) can be used to find the probability distribution of the time needed to complete a project.

The methods in this section have been used successfully in many real-world applications, including the following:

- scheduling construction projects such as office buildings, highways, and swimming pools
- scheduling the movement of a 400-bed hospital from Portland, Oregon, to a suburban location
- developing a countdown and "hold" procedure for space flights

- installing a new computer system
- designing and marketing a new product
- completing a corporate merger
- building a ship

To proceed, we need a list of the activities that comprise the project. The project is complete when all of the activities have been completed. Each activity has a set of activities called its **immediate predecessors** that must be completed before the activity begins. It also has a set of activities called its **immediate successors** that cannot start until it has finished. (The word *immediate* is sometimes omitted.) A project network diagram is usually used to represent the precedence relationships among activities. There are two types of diagrams that do this, **activity-on-node** (AON) networks and **activity-on-arc** (AOA) networks, and proponents of each type have rather strong feelings. We favor AON networks because we believe they are more intuitive, so we will not discuss AOA networks in this book.

In the AON representation of a project, there is a node for each activity. Then there is an arc from node *i* to node *j* if node *i* is an immediate predecessor of node *j*. To illustrate this, consider a project that consists of five activities, labeled A, B, C, D, and E. Activities A and B can start immediately. Activity C cannot start until activity B is finished, activity D cannot start until activity A is finished, and activity E cannot start until activities A and C are both finished. The project is finished when all activities are finished.

AON networks use nodes for activities and arcs to indicate precedence relationships.

We indicate the precedence relationships in Table 5.11 and the AON network in Figure 5.31. Table 5.11 also includes activity times, also called **durations**, for each activity. In an AON network, these durations are placed next to the nodes. In addition, there is typically a *Start* node and a *Finish* node in the diagram. These simply indicate the start and the finish of the project. Note that activity E illustrates what we mean by the term *immediate* predecessor. Clearly, activity B is also a predecessor of activity E—it must be finished before activity E can start—but it is not an *immediate* predecessor because it will be finished before another predecessor of activity E, activity C, can even begin.

Table 5.11   Data for Five-Activity Project

Node	Immediate Predecessor(s)	Immediate Successor(s)	Duration
A	None	D, E	7
B	None	C	10
C	B	E	3
D	A	None	12
E	A, C	None	6

Figure 5.31

AON Network for Five-Activity Project

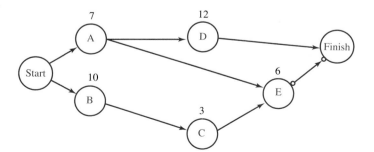

The rules for drawing an AON network are as follows:

- Include a node for each activity and place its duration next to the node.
- Include an arc from node i to node j only if node i is an immediate predecessor of node j.
- Include a Start and a Finish node with zero durations. There is an arc from the Start node to each node that has no predecessors. These activities can all start immediately. There is an arc into the Finish node from each node that has no successors. When all of these activities have been finished, the project is finished.

Two problems are typically analyzed in project scheduling. In the first, which we discuss in this subsection, we find the time to complete the project and locate the "bottleneck" activities. In the second, to be discussed in the next subsection, we try to find cost-efficient ways to complete the project within a given deadline. In each of these problems, a key concept is a "bottleneck" activity, called a **critical** activity. This is an activity that prevents the project from being completed any sooner. More precisely, a critical activity is an activity such that, if its duration increases, the time to complete the project necessarily increases. The set of critical activities is called the **critical path**. The critical path is important for practical reasons. It identifies the activities that we should attempt to expedite, because this will have a beneficial effect on the overall project time. In contrast, if an activity is *not* on the critical path, then speeding it up will not have any beneficial effect on the overall project time.

An activity is **critical** if, by increasing its duration, the time to complete the project increases. The **critical path** is the set of critical activities.

There are several ways to model project scheduling. The way we have selected is called the "traditional" approach because of its widespread use in the project scheduling field. It does *not* use Solver. This has the advantage that it allows us to simulate projects with *random* durations in a natural way, as we illustrate in Chapter 10.

We first require some basic insights. Let ES_j be the earliest time activity j can start, and let EF_j be the earliest time activity j can finish. Clearly, the earliest an activity can finish is the earliest time it can start plus its duration. Therefore, if d_j is the duration of activity j, we have

$$EF_j = ES_j + d_j \tag{5.1}$$

Now, if activity i is an immediate predecessor of activity j, then activity j cannot start until activity i finishes. In fact, activity j cannot start until *all* of its predecessors have finished, so the earliest time activity j can start is the *maximum* of the earliest finish times of its immediate predecessors:

$$ES_j = \max(EF_i) \tag{5.2}$$

Here, the maximum is over all immediate predecessors i of activity j.

We will use equations (5.1) and (5.2) to find the earliest start times and earliest finish times of all activities, beginning with the fact that the earliest start time for the Start node is 0—it can start right away. A by-product of these calculations is that we automatically obtain the project completion time. It is the earliest start time of the Finish node:

$$\text{Project completion time} = ES_{\text{Finish node}} \tag{5.3}$$

The reason is that as soon as we reach the Finish node, the entire project is complete.

To find the critical activities and the critical path, we need two other equations. Let LS_j and LF_j be the latest time activity j can start and the latest time it can finish *without in-*

creasing the project completion time. Again, it is clear that we have, analogous to equation (5.1),

$$LS_j = LF_j - d_j \qquad (5.4)$$

(We write the equation in this form because we will find LF_j first and then use it to find LS_j.)

Now suppose activity j is an immediate successor of activity i. Then activity i must be finished before activity j can start. In fact, a bit of thought should convince you that the latest time activity i can finish is the *minimum* of the latest start times of all its successors:

$$LF_i = \min(LS_j) \qquad (5.5)$$

Here, the minimum is over all immediate successors j of activity i. For example, suppose activity F has two successors, G and H, and we somehow find that the latest start times for G and H are 26 and 30. In this case, the "bottleneck," at least for this part of the network, is activity G. The latest it can start without delaying the project is 26; activity H can start later. Therefore, activity G's predecessor, activity F, has to be finished no later than time 26.

We will use equations (5.4) and (5.5) to calculate the latest start and latest finish times for all activities, beginning with the fact that the latest finish time for the Finish node is the project completion time. (Make sure you see why this is true.) Then we will calculate the **slack** of each activity j as the difference between the latest start time and the earliest start time of activity j:

$$\text{Slack of activity } j = LS_j - ES_j \qquad (5.6)$$

The idea behind slack is very simple. If an activity has any positive slack, then this activity has some room to maneuver—it could start a bit later without delaying the project. In fact, its duration could increase by the amount of its slack without delaying the project. However, if an activity has zero slack, then any increase in its duration will necessarily delay the project. Therefore, the critical path consists of activities with zero slack.

The **earliest start time** and **earliest finish time** for any activity are the earliest the activity could start or finish, given precedence relationships and durations. The **latest start time** and **latest finish time** for any activity are the latest the activity could start or finish without delaying the project as a whole. The **slack** of any activity is the amount of time the activity could be delayed beyond its earliest start time without delaying the project as a whole. An activity is critical only if its slack is 0.

The following example illustrates how to implement this method.

EXAMPLE	**5.7 BUILDING A NEW ROOM**

The lists of activities and their immediate predecessors in such a table are enough to determine the list of immediate successors. Try listing the successors on your own.

Tom Lingley, an independent contractor, has agreed to build a new room on an existing house. He plans to begin work on Monday morning, June 1. The main concern is when he will complete the project, given that he works only on weekdays. The work proceeds in stages, labeled A through J, as summarized in Table 5.12 (page 226). Figure 5.32 is the corresponding AON diagram. Three of these activities, E, F, and G, will be done by separate independent subcontractors. Lingley wants to know how long the project will take to complete, given the activity times (durations) in the table. He also wants to identify the critical activities.

Table 5.12 Data on Room-Building Activities

Description	Activity	Immediate Predecessor(s)	Immediate Successor(s)	Duration (days)
Prepare foundation	A	None	B	4
Put up frame	B	A	D, I	4
Order custom windows	C	None	I	11
Erect outside walls	D	B	E, F, G	3
Do electrical wiring	E	D	H	4
Do plumbing	F	D	H	3
Put in duct work	G	D	H	4
Hang dry wall	H	E, F, G	J	3
Install windows	I	B, C	None	1
Paint and clean up	J	H	None	2

Figure 5.32

AON Diagram for
Room-Building
Project

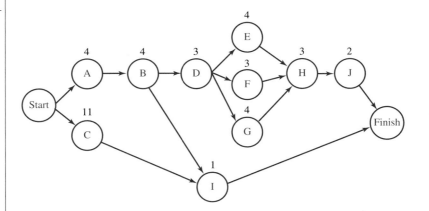

Objective To develop a spreadsheet model of the room-building project so that we can calculate the time required to complete the project and identify the critical activities.

WHERE DO THE NUMBERS COME FROM?

An experienced builder would have no problem obtaining the data in the first four columns of Table 5.12. He would know what needs to be done, and in which order. However, the data in the last column, the durations, are probably guesses at best. There is usually uncertainty regarding activity times, due to workers not showing up, bad weather, out-of-stock parts, and so on. We will ignore this uncertainty here, but we will deal with it explicitly in Chapter 10, when we discuss simulation.

Solution

The traditional approach used to find the critical activities and the project completion time does not require Solver.

To implement the method, we use equations (5.1) and (5.2) to find the earliest start and finish times of all activities, equation (5.3) to find the project completion time, equations (5.4) and (5.5) to find the latest start and finish times, and finally equation (5.6) to find the slacks and hence the critical activities.

DEVELOPING THE SPREADSHEET MODEL

The completed spreadsheet model is shown in Figure 5.33. (See the file **ProjectScheduling.xls**.) It can be developed with the following steps.

Figure 5.33 Spreadsheet Model of Room-Building Project

	A	B	C	D	E	F
1	Room construction project - finding critical path (without Solver)					
2						
3	Data on activity network					
4	Activity	Label	Predecessors	Successors	Duration	
5	Dummy Start node	Start	None	A,C	0	
6	Prepare foundation	A	Start	B	4	
7	Put up frame	B	A	D,I	4	
8	Order custom windows	C	Start	I	11	
9	Erect outside walls	D	B	E,F,G	3	
10	Do electrical wiring	E	D	H	4	
11	Do plumbing	F	D	H	3	
12	Put in duct work	G	D	H	4	
13	Hang dry wall	H	E,F,G	J	3	
14	Install windows	I	B,C	Finish	1	
15	Paint and clean up	J	H	Finish	2	
16	Dummy Finish node	Finish	I,J	None	0	
17						
18	Activity start and finish times					
19	Activity	Earliest start time	Earliest finish time	Latest finish time	Latest start time	Slack
20	Start	0	0	0	0	
21	A	0	4	4	0	0
22	B	4	8	8	4	0
23	C	0	11	19	8	8
24	D	8	11	11	8	0
25	E	11	15	15	11	0
26	F	11	14	15	12	1
27	G	11	15	15	11	0
28	H	15	18	18	15	0
29	I	11	20	20	19	8
30	J	18	20	20	18	0
31	Finish	20	20	20	20	
32						
33	Project completion time	20				

Note (cells G22–I30): Activities with 0 slack are on critical, i.e., they are on the critical path. This example illustrates that there can be two critical paths (a tie) on the AON network: A-B-D-E-H-J and A-B-D-G-H-J. The durations of the non-critical activities, C, G, and I, could be increased slightly without affecting the project completion time.

Each earliest start time is the maximum of the earliest finish times of all predecessors.

① Input data. Enter the predecessors, successors, and durations in the shaded range. Note how we have entered data for the Start and Finish nodes in rows 5 and 16.

② Earliest start and finish times. Here we implement equations (5.1) and (5.2). To implement equation (5.1), enter the formula

=B20+E5

in cell C20 and copy it down to cell C31. To implement equation (5.2), begin by entering 0 in cell B20. This is because the Start node can begin immediately. Then every other earliest start time is the *maximum* of the earliest finish times of its predecessors. Unfortunately, there is no way to enter a single formula and copy it down. We need to specialize each formula to each activity's particular predecessors. For example, the formulas for activities D and H, in cells D24 and D28, are

=C22

and

=MAX(C25:C27)

This is because activity D has a single predecessor, whereas activity H has three predecessors. The other formulas in column B are similar.

③ Project completion time. The project completion time is given in equation (5.3) as the earliest start time of the Finish node. We record it in cell B33 with the formula

=B31

Each latest finish time is the minimum of the latest start times of all successors.

④ Latest start and finish times. Next, we implement equations (5.4) and (5.5). To implement equation (5.4), enter the formula

=D20-E5

in cell E20 and copy it down to cell E31. To implement equation (5.5), begin by entering the formula

=B33

in cells D31. By definition, the latest the Finish node can start (or finish, since it has 0 duration) is the project completion time. For the other activities, we use equation (5.5) to calculate the latest finish times. Again, there is no way to copy one formula to all cells; it depends on each activity's particular successors. For example, the formulas for activities D and G, in cells D24 and D27, are

=MIN(E25:E27)

and

=E28

This is because activity D has three successors, whereas activity G has only a single successor. The other formulas in column D are similar.

5 **Slacks.** Using equation (5.6), enter the formula

=E20-B20

in cell F20 and copy it down to cell F31 to calculate the slacks.

Discussion of the Solution

The solution in Figure 5.33 indicates that the room can be completed in 20 days—but no less—if the various activities are started within their earliest and latest start time ranges. Given that the project begins on Monday, June 1, and work occurs only on weekdays, this implies the project will be complete at the end of Friday, June 26. We see, for example, that activity B, which is critical, *must* start at time 4. However, activity C, which is noncritical, can start at any time from 0 to 8. The critical activities are the ones with zero slack: A, B, D, E, G, H, and J. Referring to the AON network in Figure 5.32, we see that there are actually two critical paths from Start to Finish: A–B–D–E–H–J and A–B–D–G–H–J. (This is because the "parallel" activities E and G have identical durations.) If any of the activities on either path is delayed, the project completion time will necessarily increase.

To convince yourself of the difference between critical and noncritical activities, try increasing the duration any critical activity such as activity D by 1 day. You will see that the project completion time increases by 1 day as well. However, try increasing the duration of any noncritical activity such as activity C by any amount up to its slack. You will see that the project completion time does not increase at all.

A Gantt chart shows the time line of the project.

This solution can be depicted best with a **Gantt chart**, as shown in Figure 5.34. This popular type of chart is essentially a time line of when activities start and finish. For example, the horizontal bar for electrical wiring indicates that this activity starts 11 days from now and is completed 4 days later. (Keep in mind that the current time is day 0.) From the bars farthest to the right, we see that the project is indeed completed 20 days from now. We created this Gantt chart, using the data shown in Figure 5.35, as explained in the following Excel Tip.

Figure 5.34 Gantt Chart for Room-Building Project

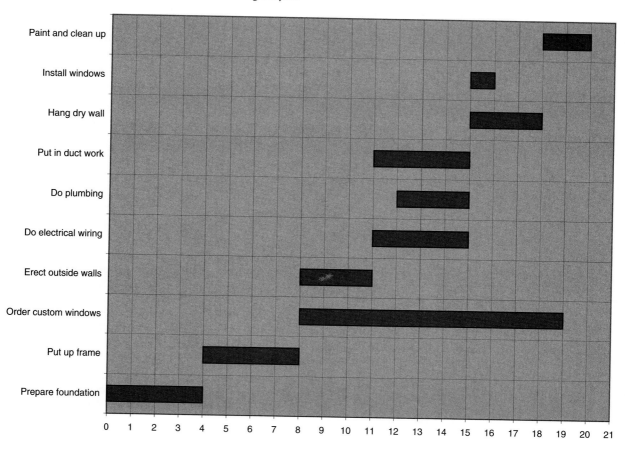

Figure 5.35 Data for Gantt Chart

	A	B	C	D	E	F	G	H
35	**Data for Gantt chart**							
36	Activity	Start time	Duration					
37	Prepare foundation	0	4					
38	Put up frame	4	4					
39	Order custom windows	8	11					
40	Erect outside walls	8	3	The non-critical activities can have start times				
41	Do electrical wiring	11	4	anywhere within their earliest to latest start				
42	Do plumbing	12	3	time ranges. There is no such flexibility for the				
43	Put in duct work	11	4	critical activities.				
44	Hang dry wall	15	3					
45	Install windows	15	1					
46	Paint and clean up	18	2					

→ **EXCEL TIP: *Creating a Gantt Chart***
To create a Gantt chart as in Figure 5.34, enter the data in Figure 5.35—the names of the activities, their start times, and their durations—in a 3-column range. Highlight this range, click on the Chart Wizard, and select a stacked horizontal bar chart (the second subtype in the Bar category). You can accept the rest of the default settings in the Chart Wizard, except to get rid of the legend. The resulting chart will have two adjacent bars for each activity, one on the left for the start time and one on the right for the duration. Right-click on one of the start time bars and select Format Data Series. Then change the border to None and the area

The bars in the Gantt chart for noncritical activities can be adjusted slightly. The bars for critical activities are fixed.

color to None. This effectively hides the start time bars and shows only the appropriately placed duration bars. ∎

According to this Excel Tip, we require start times and durations. We could use any start times within the earliest and latest start time ranges. In fact, you can try your own values in column B of Figure 5.35 to see how the Gantt chart changes. However, remember that you have choices only for the noncritical activities, C, F, and I. The start times for the critical activities cannot be changed without increasing the overall project time. ∎

Crashing the Activities

The objective in many project scheduling analyses is to find a minimum-cost method of reducing activity times to meet a deadline. The term *crashing the activities* is often used to mean reducing the activity times. Of course, it typically costs money to crash activities—hiring extra workers, using extra equipment, using overtime, and so on—so the problem becomes one of crashing just the right activities in just the right amounts to meet a deadline at minimum cost. We now illustrate how Solver can be used to solve this problem.

EXAMPLE	5.7 (CONTINUED) MEETING A DEADLINE FOR FINISHING A NEW ROOM

From the previous discussion of the room-building project, Tom Lingley knows that if the room construction activities continue to take as long as listed in Table 5.12, the entire project will take 20 working days to complete. Unfortunately, he is under pressure to finish the job in 15 working days—that is, by the end of Friday, June 19. He estimates that each activity could be crashed by a certain amount at a certain cost. Specifically, he estimates the cost per day of activity time reduction and the maximum possible days of reduction for each activity, as shown in Table 5.13. For example, activity A's duration could be reduced from 4 days to 3 days at cost $150, or it could be reduced from 4 days to 2 days at cost $300. (It is even possible to have a fractional reduction, such as from 4 days to 2.5 days at cost $225.) How can Tom meet the June 19 deadline at minimum cost?

Table 5.13 Crashing Inputs

Activity	Cost per Day	Maximum Reduction
A	150	2
B	160	2
C	80	4
D	80	1
E	160	2
F	150	1
G	130	2
H	100	1
I	70	0.5
J	100	1

Objective   To use a Solver model to decide how much to crash each activity so that the deadline is met at minimum cost.

WHERE DO THE NUMBERS COME FROM?

The numbers in Table 5.13 are not necessarily easy to obtain. The contractor probably has some idea of the minimum possible time to perform any activity, regardless of the amount spent. For example, hanging drywall takes a minimal amount of time, regardless of how many people are working on it. He probably also has a good idea of what it would take to expedite any activity—extra workers, for example—and the corresponding cost.

Solution

The required Solver model follows almost immediately from the project scheduling Solver model in Figure 5.33 discussed previously. We need to make only a few changes, as summarized in the following list and in Table 5.14.

- There are extra changing cells, which indicate how much crashing to do.
- There are two extra constraints: we cannot crash by more than the allowable limits, and we must meet the deadline.
- The objective is now to minimize the crashing costs. The project length is no longer the objective; it is part of the deadline constraint.

Table 5.14 Variables and Constraints for Crashing Model

Input variables	Activity durations (before crashing), precedence relationships, crashing data, deadline
Decision variables (changing cells)	Crashing amounts of activities
Objective (target cell)	Total crashing cost
Other calculated variables	Project length
Constraints	Precedence constraints (as in previous Solver model)
	Crashing amount of activity $\leq$ Maximum reduction of activity
	Project length $\leq$ Deadline

DEVELOPING THE SPREADSHEET MODEL

The spreadsheet model is shown in Figure 5.36 (page 232). (See the Crashing sheet in the **ProjectScheduling.xls** file.) Because much of this model is identical to the previous project scheduling model, we will discuss only the modifications.

Figure 5.36 Crashing Spreadsheet Model

	A	B	C	D	E	F	G	H	I	J	K	L
1	Room construction project - crashing to meet a deadline											
2												
3	Data on activity network						Crashing section					
4	Activity	Label	Predecessors	Successors		Duration	Original duration	Crash amount		Max crash		Cost per day
5	Dummy Start node	Start	None	A,C		0						
6	Prepare foundation	A	Start	B		2	4	2	<=	2		$150
7	Put up frame	B	A	D,I		4	4	0	<=	2		$160
8	Order custom windows	C	Start	I		11	11	0	<=	4		$80
9	Erect outside walls	D	B	E,F,G		2	3	1	<=	1		$80
10	Do electrical wiring	E	D	H		4	4	0	<=	2		$160
11	Do plumbing	F	D	H		3	3	0	<=	1		$150
12	Put in duct work	G	D	H		4	4	0	<=	2		$130
13	Hang dry wall	H	E,F,G	J		2	3	1	<=	1		$100
14	Install windows	I	B,C	Finish		1	1	0	<=	0.5		$70
15	Paint and clean up	J	H	Finish		1	2	1	<=	1		$100
16	Dummy Finish node	Finish	I,J	None		0						
17												
18	Activity start and finish times											
19	Activity	Earliest start time	Earliest finish time	Latest finish time	Latest start time	Slack						
20	Start	0	0	0	0							
21	A	0	2	2	0	0						
22	B	2	6	6	2	0						
23	C	0	11	14	3	3						
24	D	6	8	8	6	0						
25	E	8	12	12	8	0						
26	F	8	11	12	9	1						
27	G	8	12	12	8	0						
28	H	12	14	14	12	0						
29	I	11	12	15	14	3						
30	J	14	15	15	14	0						
31	Finish	15	15	15	15							
32							Range names used:					
33	Deadline constraint						Crash_amount	=Crashing!$H$6:$H$15				
34		Project time		Deadline			Crashing_cost	=Crashing!$B$37				
35		15	<=	15			Deadline	=Crashing!$D$35				
36							Max_crash	=Crashing!$J$6:$J$15				
37	Crashing cost	$580					Project_time	=Crashing!$B$35				

Activities with 0 slack are on critical, i.e., they are on the critical path. This example illustrates that there can be two critical paths (a tie) on the AON network: A-B-D-E-H-J and A-B-D-G-H-J. The durations of the noncritical activities, C, F, and I, could be increased slightly without affecting the project completion time.

❶ Input data. There are three extra inputs: the per day crashing costs, the upper limits on crashing, and the deadline. Enter these in the shaded ranges.

❷ Reductions. There are changing cells in column H for the reductions in activity durations. Enter *any* initial values for these.

❸ Durations. Calculate the durations *after* crashing in column E by subtracting the reductions in column H from the original durations, which have been moved to column G.

❹ Crashing cost. To calculate the total cost of crashing, enter the formula

=SUMPRODUCT(Crash_amount,L6:L15)

in cell B37.

USING SOLVER

The Solver dialog box appears in Figure 5.37. As usual, you should check the Assume Non-Negative option, but *not* the Assume Linear Model, before optimizing. We have introduced a subtle nonlinearity into this model that would be easy to miss. For any crashing amounts in the changing cells, the new durations are calculated in column E, and these are used to calculate the project completion time, using the same logic for earliest start and finish times as before. (Actually, we don't really require the latest start and finish times. They are used only to calculate the slacks.)

Figure 5.37

Solver Dialog Box for Crashing Model

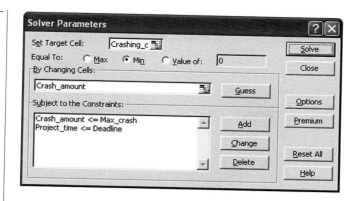

The problem is that some of the formulas in the earliest start time column use the MAX function, and this introduces nonlinearity into the model. In fact, it makes the model *nonsmooth*—the same problem we discussed with IF functions in the backlogging aggregate planning model in Chapter 4. So you should be aware that Solver is not totally reliable for this version of the model. (There is a linear version of the crashing model available, and we have included it for your convenience in the file **ProjectCrashing.xls**. However, we decided to stick with a single model, even if it does sometimes cause problems for Solver. In our experience, this model *has* obtained the correct solution in almost every situation.)

Discussion of the Solution

According to the optimal solution in Figure 5.36, Tom should reduce activity A's duration by 2 days, and he should reduce the durations of activities D, H, and J by 1 day each. The total cost of this strategy is $580, and it allows him to complete the project in the required 15 days. Note that none of the originally noncritical activities is crashed. These activities were not bottlenecks in the first place, so it doesn't make much sense to crash these activities. ■

MODELING ISSUES

1. The crashing cost functions we have used are *linear* in the amount of reduction—each day of reduction (for a given activity) costs the same amount. This is probably unrealistic. Each extra day of reduction typically costs *more* than the previous day. However, if we can specify the nonlinear relationship between amount of reduction and cost (probably by estimating it from historical data), then Solver's nonlinear algorithms are able to solve the problem with very little modification to the model. Alternatively, there might only be discrete crashing opportunities available. For example, there might be two types of equipment we could purchase to reduce some activity's duration, each involving a certain cost and leading to a certain reduction. This kind of discrete choice can be handled with binary (0–1) variables, the topic of the next chapter.

2. This introductory account of project scheduling barely scratches the surface. The topic can become very complex, and various versions of it are used routinely by many companies. Indeed, entire software packages such as Microsoft Project are devoted entirely to this topic. We will not pursue it any further here, but we will briefly discuss project scheduling with uncertain activity times when we discuss simulation in Chapter 10. ■

PROBLEMS

Skill-Building Problems

39. Use a one-way data table to see how sensitive the project completion time in Tom Lingley's room-building project is to the duration of activity H (hanging dry wall). Let the duration vary from 2 to 8 days in increments of 0.5 day. (*Note*: By now you are probably used to using SolverTable for sensitivity analysis. However, when there is no Solver optimization model, you can use Excel data tables instead.)

40. Use a two-way data table to see how sensitive the project completion time in Tom Lingley's room-building project is to the duration of activities E and F (electrical wiring and plumbing). Let the durations of each of these activities vary from 2 to 6 days in increments of 0.5 day.

41. In Tom Lingley's room-building project, he is currently subcontracting the electrical wiring, plumbing, and duct work. This explains why these three activities can be performed simultaneously. Suppose instead that Tom plans to do the first two of these by himself, and he can work on only one activity at a time—electrical wiring and then plumbing. Modify the critical path model appropriately. How much does the project completion time increase? What is the new critical path?

42. Continuing the previous problem, where electrical wiring must be done *before* plumbing, suppose Tom must complete the project within a deadline of 17 days. Assume the crashing data are the same as before. What should he do?

43. How difficult is it to add new activities to an existing project scheduling model? Answer this question by assuming Tom Lingley must also install bookshelves in the room, and these can be installed only after the drywall has been hung. It typically takes to 2.5 days to install the bookshelves. However, he has been instructed to make these bookshelves from a special type of wood, which must be custom ordered. He can place the order right away, and it is likely to take 10 working days to arrive. In addition, he has been instructed to install a wet bar in the room. This cannot be started until the plumbing and electrical wiring are finished, and this wet bar takes an estimated 3.5 days to finish. Find the new project completion time. Does the critical path change because of the new activities?

Skill-Extending Problems

44. We stated that when you construct the data (start times and durations) for building a Gantt chart, you can use *any* start times within the earliest to latest start time ranges. It follows that you should be able to enter *random* values within these ranges, so try the following. It turns out that the Excel formula **=LoVal+(HiVal−LoVal)*RAND()** generates a random number between LoVal and HiVal. Here, LoVal and HiVal are two given values, with LoVal ≤ HiVal. Use this formula, with appropriate values of LoVal and HiVal, in column B of Figure 5.35. Then activate the Gantt chart sheet and press the recalc (F9) key repeatedly. Each time you press this key, you get new random numbers. Explain the behavior you see.

45. In Tom Lingley's room-building problem, we first found that the noncritical activities are C, G, and I. Then when we crashed the project to meet a deadline, we found that these noncritical activities were not crashed. Will this always be the case—that is, is it always best to crash only critical activities? Experiment with the deadline and the crashing data to explore this question.

5.7 CONCLUSION

In this chapter we have discussed a number of management science problems that can be formulated as network models. Often these problems are of a logistics nature—shipping goods from one set of locations to another. However, we have also seen that problems that do not involve shipping or traveling along a physical network can sometimes be formulated as network models. Examples include the bus route assignment and machine replacement problems.

There are at least two advantages to formulating a problem as a network model. First, although Excel's Solver doesn't employ them, fast special-purpose algorithms exist for various forms of network models. These enable companies to solve extremely large problems that might not be solvable with ordinary LP algorithms. Second, the graphical representation of network models often makes them easier to visualize. Once a problem can be visualized graphically, it is often simpler to model (in a spreadsheet or otherwise) and ultimately to optimize.

Summary of Key Management Science Terms

Term	Explanation	Page
Network models	Class of optimization models that can be represented graphically as a network; typically (but not always) involves shipping goods from one set of locations to another at minimum cost	186
Nodes	Points in a network representation; often correspond to locations	188
Arcs	Arrows in a network representation; often correspond to routes connecting locations	188
Flows	Decision variables that represent the amounts sent along arcs	188
Arc capacities	Upper bounds on flows on some or all arcs	188
Flow balance constraints	Constraints that force the amount sent into a node to equal the amount sent out, except possibly for amounts that start out or end up at the node	193
Transshipment point	A node where nothing starts out or ends up; flow into equals flow out of	205
Shortest path models	Network models where the goal is to get from an "origin" node to a "destination" node at minimal cost (or distance)	213
Project scheduling models	Models for analyzing projects composed of several activities, especially when there are precedence relations among the activities	222
Activity-on-node diagram	A graphical representation of a project, where nodes represent activities and arcs represent precedence relationships	223
Critical path, critical activities	The "bottleneck" path through a project; includes the critical activities, those that cannot be delayed without delaying the project as a whole	224
Gantt chart	A diagram showing the time line of activities in a project	228
Crashing	Reducing selected activity times (at a cost) to meet a deadline	230

Summary of Key Excel Terms

Term	Explanation	Excel	Page
SUMIF function	Sums values in one range corresponding to cells in a related range that satisfy a criterion	=SUMIF(*compareRange, criterion,sumRange*)	194
COUNTIF function	Counts values in one range that satisfy a criterion	=COUNTIF(*range,criterion*)	210

PROBLEMS

Skill-Building Problems

46. The 7th National Bank has two check processing sites. Site 1 can process 10,000 checks per day, and site 2 can process 6000 checks per day. The bank processes three types of checks: vendor, salary, and personal. The processing cost per check depends on the site, as listed in the file **P05_46.xls**. Each day 5000 checks of each type must be processed. Determine how to minimize the daily cost of processing checks.

47. The government is auctioning off oil leases at two sites: 1 and 2. At each site 100,000 acres of land are to be auctioned. Cliff Ewing, Blake Barnes, and Alexis Pickens are bidding for the oil. Government rules state that no bidder can receive more than 40% of the land being auctioned. Cliff has bid $1000 per acre for site 1 land and $2000 per acre for site 2 land. Blake has bid $900 per acre for site 1 land and $2200 per acre for site 2 land. Alexis has bid $1100 per acre for site 1 land and $1900 per acre for site 2 land.
  a. Determine how to maximize the government's revenue.
  b. Use SolverTable to see how changes in the government's rule on 40% of all land being auctioned affect the optimal revenue. Why can the optimal revenue not decrease if this percentage required increases? Why can the optimal revenue not increase if this percentage required decreases?

48. The Amorco Oil Company controls two oil fields. Field 1 can produce up to 40 million barrels of oil per day, and field 2 can produce up to 50 million barrels of oil per day. At field 1 it costs $3 to extract and refine a barrel of oil; at field 2 the cost is $2. Amorco sells oil to two countries: United Kingdom and Japan. The shipping costs per barrel are shown in the file **P05_48.xls**. Each day the United Kingdom is willing to buy up to 40 million barrels at $6 per barrel, and Japan is willing to buy up to 30 million barrels at $6.50 per barrel. Determine how to maximize Amorco's profit.

49. Touche Young has three auditors. Each can work up to 160 hours during the next month, during which time three projects must be completed. Project 1 takes 130 hours, project 2 takes 140 hours, and project 3 takes 160 hours. The amount per hour that can be billed for assigning each auditor to each project is given in the file **P05_49.xls**. Determine how to maximize total billings during the next month.

50. Five employees are available to perform four jobs. The time it takes each person to perform each job is given in the file **P05_50.xls**. Determine the assignment of employees to jobs that minimizes the total time required to perform the four jobs. (A dash indicates that a person cannot do that particular job.)

51. Based on Machol (1970). Doc Councilman is putting together a relay team for the 400-meter relay. Each swimmer must swim 100 meters of breaststroke, backstroke, butterfly, or freestyle, and each swimmer can swim only one race. Doc believes that each swimmer will attain the times given in the file **P05_51.xls**. To minimize the team's time for the race, which swimmers should swim which strokes?

52. A company is taking bids on four construction jobs. Three contractors have placed bids on the jobs. Their bids (in thousands of dollars) are given in the file **P05_52.xls**. (A dash indicates that the contractor did not bid on the given job.) Contractor 1 can do only one job, but contractors 2 and 3 can each do up to two jobs. Determine the minimum cost assignment of contractors to jobs.

53. Widgetco manufactures widgets at two factories, one in Memphis and one in Denver. The Memphis factory can produce up to 150 widgets per day, and the Denver factory can produce up to 200 widgets per day. Widgets are shipped by air to customers in Los Angeles and Boston. The customers in each city require 130 widgets per day. Because of the deregulation of air fares, Widgetco believes that it might be cheaper to first fly some widgets to New York or Chicago and then fly them to their final destinations. The costs of flying a widget are shown in the file **P05_53.xls**.
  a. Determine how to minimize the total cost of shipping the required widgets to the customers.
  b. Suppose the capacities of both factories are reduced in increments of 10 widgets per day. Use SolverTable to see how much the common reduction can be before the total cost increases; before there is no feasible solution.

54. General Ford produces cars in Los Angeles and Detroit and has a warehouse in Atlanta. The company supplies cars to customers in Houston and Tampa. The costs of shipping a car between various points are listed in the file **P05_54.xls**, where a dash means that a shipment is not allowed. Los Angeles can produce up to 1100 cars, and Detroit can produce up to 2900 cars. Houston must receive 2400 cars, and Tampa must receive 1500 cars.
  a. Determine how to minimize the cost of meeting demands in Houston and Tampa.
  b. Modify the answer to part **a** if shipments between Los Angeles and Detroit are not allowed.
  c. Modify the answer to part **a** if shipments between Houston and Tampa are allowed at a cost of $5 per car.

55. Sunco Oil produces oil at two wells. Well 1 can produce up to 150,000 barrels per day, and well 2 can produce up to 200,000 barrels per day. It is possible to ship oil directly from the wells to Sunco's customers in Los Angeles and New York. Alternatively, Sunco could transport oil to the ports of Mobile and Galveston and then ship it by tanker to New York or Los Angeles. Los Angeles requires 160,000 barrels per day, and New York requires 140,000 barrels per day. The costs of shipping 1000 barrels between various locations are shown in the file **P05_55.xls**, where a dash indicates shipments that are not allowed. Determine how to minimize the transport costs in meeting the oil demands of Los Angeles and New York.

56. Nash Auto has two plants, two warehouses, and three customers. The locations of these are as follows: The plants are in Detroit and Atlanta, the warehouses are in Denver and New York, and the customers are in Los Angeles, Chicago, and Philadelphia. Cars are produced at plants, then shipped to warehouses, and finally shipped to customers. Detroit can produce 150 cars per week, and Atlanta can produce 100 cars per week. Los Angeles requires 80 cars per week, Chicago requires 70, and Philadelphia requires 60. It costs $10,000 to produce a car at each plant. The costs of shipping a car between various cities are listed in the file **P05_56.xls**. Assume that during a week, at most 50 cars can be shipped from a warehouse to any particular city. Determine how to meet Nash's weekly demands at minimum cost.

57. Fordco produces cars in Detroit and Dallas. The Detroit plant can produce up to 6500 cars, and the Dallas plant can produce up to 6000 cars. Producing a car costs $2000 in Detroit and $1800 in Dallas. Cars must be shipped to three cities. City 1 must receive 5000 cars, city 2 must receive 4000 cars, and city 3 must receive 3000 cars. The costs of shipping a car from each plant to each city are given in the file **P05_57.xls**. At most 2700 cars can be sent from a given plant to a given city. Determine how to minimize the cost of meeting all demands.

58. Each year Data Corporal produces up to 400 computers in Boston and up to 300 computers in Raleigh. Los Angeles customers must receive 400 computers, and 300 computers must be supplied to Austin customers. Producing a computer costs $800 in Boston and $900 in Raleigh. Computers are transported by plane and can be sent through Chicago. The costs of sending a computer between pairs of cities are shown in the file **P05_58.xls**.

   a. Determine how to minimize the total (production plus distribution) cost of meeting Data Corporal's annual demand.

   b. How would you modify the model in part **a** if at most 200 units could be shipped through Chicago?

59. Suppose it costs $10,000 to purchase a new car. The annual operating cost and resale value of a used car are shown in the file **P05_59.xls**. Assume that you presently have a new car. Determine a replacement policy that minimizes your net costs of owning and operating a car for the next 6 years.

60. It costs $40 to buy a telephone from the department store. Assume that I can keep a telephone for at most 5 years and that the estimated maintenance cost each year of operation is as follows: year 1, $20; year 2, $30; year 3, $40; year 4, $60; year 5, $70. I have just purchased a new telephone. Assuming that a telephone has no salvage value, determine the strategy that minimizes the total cost of purchasing and operating a telephone for the next 6 years.

61. At the beginning of year 1, a new machine must be purchased. The cost of maintaining a machine, depending on its age, is given in the file **P05_61.xls**. The cost of purchasing a machine at the beginning of each year is given in this same file. There is no trade-in value when a machine is replaced. The goal is to minimize the total (purchase plus maintenance) cost of having a machine for 5 years. Determine the years in which a new machine should be purchased.

62. There are three school districts in the town of Busville. The numbers of black and white students in each district are shown in the file **P05_62.xls**. The Supreme Court requires the schools in Busville to be racially balanced. Thus, each school must have exactly 300 students, and each school must have the same number of black students. The distances between districts are also shown in the file **P05_62.xls**. Determine how to minimize the total distance that students must be bused while still satisfying the Supreme Court's requirements. Assume that a student who remains in his or her own district does not need to be bused.

63. Delko is considering hiring people for four types of jobs. The company would like to hire the number of people listed in the file **P05_63.xls** for each type of job. Delko can hire four types of people. Each type is qualified to perform two types of jobs, as shown in this same file. A total of 20 type 1, 30 type 2, 40 type 3, and 20 type 4 people have applied for jobs. Determine how Delko can maximize the number of employees assigned to suitable jobs, assuming that each person can be assigned to at most one job. (*Hint*: Set this up as a transportation model where the "supplies" are the applicants.)

64. A truck must travel from New York to Los Angeles. As shown in Figure 5.38 (page 238), several routes are available. The number associated with each arc is the number of gallons of fuel required by the truck to traverse the arc. Determine the route from New York to Los Angeles that uses the minimum amount of gas.

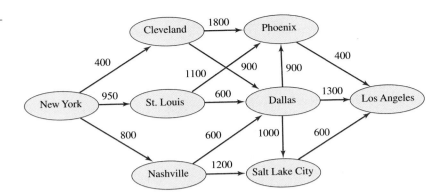

Figure 5.38
Network for Truck Problem

65. Before a new product can be introduced at Jiffyco, the activities shown in the file **P05_65.xls** must be completed, where all times are in weeks.
  a. Draw the AON project network and determine a critical path and the minimum number of weeks required before the new product can be introduced.
  b. The duration of each activity can be reduced by up to 2 weeks at the following cost per week: A, $80; B, $60; C, $30; D, $60; E, $40; F, $30; G, $20. (Assume that activity H cannot be crashed.) Determine how to minimize the cost of getting the product into the stores by Christmas, assuming that it is now 12 weeks until Christmas.

66. A company has a project that consists of 11 activities, described in the file **P05_66.xls**. Draw an AON project network and then find the critical path and the minimum number of days required to complete this project. Also, create the associated Gantt chart.

67. The promoters of a rock concert in Indianapolis must perform the tasks shown in the file **P05_67.xls** before the concert can be held. (All durations are in days.)
  a. Draw the AON project network.
  b. Find the critical path and the minimum number of days needed to prepare for the concert.
  c. Create the associated Gantt chart.

68. Consider the (simplified) list of activities and predecessors that are involved in building a house, as listed in the file **P05_68.xls**.
  a. Draw an AON project network and find the critical path and the minimum number of days needed to build the house. Also, create the associated Gantt chart.
  b. Suppose that by hiring additional workers, the duration of each activity can be reduced. The costs per day of reducing the duration of the activities are also given in the file **P05_68.xls**. Use LP to find the strategy that minimizes the cost of completing the project within 20 days.

69. Horizon Cable is about to expand its cable TV offerings in Smalltown by adding MTV and other exciting stations. The activities listed in the file **P05_69.xls**

must be completed before the service expansion can be completed. Draw the AON project network and find the critical path and the minimum number of weeks needed to complete the project. Also, create the associated Gantt chart.

70. A company is planning to manufacture a product that consists of three parts (A, B, and C). The company anticipates that it will take 5 weeks to design the three parts and determine the way in which these parts must be assembled to make the final product. Then the company estimates that it will take 4 weeks to make part A, 5 weeks to make part B, and 3 weeks to make part C. The company must test part A after it is completed, and this takes 2 weeks. The assembly line process will then proceed as follows: assemble parts A and B (2 weeks) and then attach part C (1 week). Then the final product must undergo 1 week of testing.
  a. Draw the AON project network.
  b. Find the critical path and the minimum amount of time needed to complete the project.
  c. Create the associated Gantt chart.

71. When an accounting firm audits a corporation, the first phase of the audit involves obtaining knowledge of the business. This phase of the audit requires the activities listed in the file **P05_71.xls**.
  a. Draw the AON project network and determine the critical path and the minimum number of days needed to complete the first phase of the audit. Also, create the associated Gantt chart.
  b. Assume that the first phase must be completed within 30 days. The duration of each activity can be reduced by incurring the costs listed in the file **P05_71.xls**. Use LP to find the strategy that minimizes the cost of meeting this deadline.

Skill-Extending Problems

72. Allied Freight supplies goods to three customers, who each require 30 units. The company has two warehouses. In warehouse 1, 40 units are available, and in warehouse 2, 30 units are available. The costs of shipping one unit from each warehouse to each customer are shown in the file **P05_72.xls**. There is a penalty for each unsatisfied customer unit of demand—with customer 1 a penalty cost of $90 is incurred; with customer 2, $80; and with customer 3, $110.

a. Determine how to minimize the sum of penalty and shipping costs.

b. Use SolverTable to see how a change in the unit penalty cost of customer 3 affects the optimal cost.

c. Use SolverTable to see how a change in the capacity of warehouse 2 affects the optimal cost.

73. Referring to the previous problem, suppose that Allied Freight can purchase and ship extra units to either warehouse for a total cost of $100 per unit and that all customer demand must be met. Determine how to minimize the sum of purchasing and shipping costs.

74. Based on Glover and Klingman (1977). The government has many computer files that must be merged frequently. For example, consider the Survey of Current Income (SCI) and the Consumer Price Service (CPS) files, which keep track of family income and family size. The breakdown of records in each file is given in the file **P05_74.xls**. SCI and CPS files contain other pieces of data, but the only variables common to the two files are income and family size. Suppose that the SCI and CPS files must be merged to create a file that will be used for an important analysis of government policy. How should the files be merged? We would like to lose as little information as possible in merging the records. For example, merging an SCI record for a family with income $25,000 and family size 2 with a CPS record for a family with income $26,000 and family size 2 results in a smaller loss of information than if an SCI record for a family with income $25,000 and family size 2 is merged with a CPS record for a family with income $29,000 and family size 3. Let the "cost" of merging an SCI record with a CPS record be $|I_{SCI} - I_{CPS}| + |FS_{SCI} - FS_{CPS}|$ where I_{SCI} and I_{CPS} are the incomes from the SCI and CPS records, and FS_{SCI} and FS_{CPS} are the family sizes. Determine the least expensive way to merge the SCI and CPS records.

75. Based on Evans (1984). Currently, State University can store 200 files on hard disk, 100 files in computer memory, and 300 files on tape. Users want to store 300 word-processing files, 100 packaged-program files, and 100 data files. Each month a typical word-processing file is accessed eight times; a typical packaged-program file, four times; and a typical data file, two times. When a file is accessed, the time it takes for the file to be retrieved depends on the type of file and on the storage medium. The times are listed in the file **P05_75.xls**. The goal is to minimize the total time per month that users spend accessing their files. Determine where files should be stored.

76. Bloomington has two hospitals. Hospital 1 has four ambulances, and hospital 2 has two ambulances. Ambulance service is deemed adequate if there is only a 10% chance that no ambulance will be available when an ambulance call is received by a hospital. The average length of an ambulance service call is 20 minutes. Given this information, queueing theory tells us that hospital 1 can be assigned up to 4.9 calls per hour and that hospital 2 can be assigned up to 1.5 calls per hour. Bloomington has been divided into 12 districts. The average number of calls per hour emanating from each district is given in the file **P05_76.xls**. This file also shows the travel time (in minutes) needed to travel from each district to each hospital. The objective is to minimize the average travel time needed to respond to a call. Determine the proper assignment of districts to hospitals. (*Hint*: Be careful about defining the supply points!)

77. In Problem 55, assume that before being shipped to Los Angeles or New York, all oil produced at the wells must be refined at either Galveston or Mobile. To refine 1000 barrels of oil costs $12 at Mobile and $10 at Galveston. Assuming that both Mobile and Galveston have infinite refinery capacity, determine how to minimize the daily cost of transporting and refining the oil requirements of Los Angeles and New York.

78. Rework the previous problem under the assumption that Galveston has a refinery capacity of 150,000 barrels per day and Mobile has a refinery capacity of 180,000 barrels per day.

79. Oilco has oil fields in San Diego and Los Angeles. The San Diego field can produce up to 500,000 barrels per day, and the Los Angeles field can produce up to 400,000 barrels per day. Oil is sent from the fields to a refinery, either in Dallas or in Houston. (Assume that each refinery has unlimited capacity.) To refine 100,000 barrels costs $700 at Dallas and $900 at Houston. Refined oil is shipped to customers in Chicago and New York. Chicago customers require 400,000 barrels per day, and New York customers require 300,000 barrels per day. The costs of shipping 100,000 barrels of oil (refined or unrefined) between cities are shown in the file **P05_79.xls**.

a. Determine how to minimize the total cost of meeting all demands.

b. If each refinery had a capacity of 380,000 barrels per day, how would you modify the model in part **a**?

80. At present there are 500 long-distance calls that must be routed from New York to Los Angeles (L.A.) and 400 calls that must be routed from Philadelphia to L.A. On route to L.A. from Philadelphia or New York, calls are sent through Indianapolis or Cleveland, then through Dallas or Denver, and finally to L.A. The number of calls that can be routed between any pair of cities is shown in the file **P05_80.xls**. The phone company wants to know how many of the 500 + 400 = 900 calls originating in New York and Philadelphia can be routed to L.A. Set this up as a minimum cost network flow model—that is, specify the nodes, arcs, shipping costs, and arc capacities. Then solve it.

81. Eight students need to be assigned to four dorm rooms at Faber College. Based on "incompatibility measurements," the cost incurred for any pair of students rooming together is shown in the file **P05_81.xls**. How should the students be assigned to the four rooms to minimize the total incompatibility cost?

82. Based on Ravindran (1971). A library must build shelving to shelve 200 4-inch-high books, 100 8-inch-high books, and 80 12-inch-high books. Each book is 0.5 inch thick. The library has several ways to store the books. For example, an 8-inch-high shelf can be built to store all books of height less than or equal to 8 inches, and a 12-inch-high shelf can be built for the 12-inch books. Alternatively, a 12-inch-high shelf can be built to store all books. The library believes it costs $2300 to build a shelf and that a cost of $5 per square inch is incurred for book storage. (Assume that the area required to store a book is given by the height of the storage area multiplied by the book's thickness.) Determine how to shelve the books at minimum cost. (*Hint*: Create nodes 0, 4, 8, and 12, and make the cost associated with the arc joining nodes i and j equal to the total cost of shelving all books of height greater than i and less than or equal to j on a single shelf.)

83. In the original RedBrand problem (Example 5.4), suppose that the company could add up to 100 tons of capacity, in increments of 10 tons, to any *single* plant. Use SolverTable to determine the yearly savings in cost from having extra capacity at the various plants. Assume that the capacity will cost $28,000 per ton right now. Also, assume that the annual cost savings from having the extra capacity will extend over 10 years, and that the total 10-year savings will be discounted at an annual 10% interest rate. How much extra capacity should the company purchase, and which plant should be expanded? (*Hint*: Use the PV function to find the present value of the total cost saving over the 10-year period. You can assume that the costs occur at the *ends* of the respective years.)

84. Based on Jacobs (1954). The Carter Caterer Company must have the following number of clean napkins available at the beginning of each of the next 4 days: day 1, 1500; day 2, 1200; day 3, 1800; day 4, 600. After being used, a napkin can be cleaned by one of two methods: fast service or slow service. Fast service costs 10 cents per napkin, and a napkin cleaned via fast service is available for use the day after it is last used. Slow service costs 6 cents per napkin, and these napkins can be reused 2 days after they are last used. New napkins can be purchased for a cost of 20 cents per napkin. Determine how to minimize the cost of meeting the demand for napkins during the next 4 days. (*Note*: There are at least two possible modeling approaches, one network and one nonnetwork. See if you can model it each way.)

85. Kellwood, a company that produces a single product, has three plants and four customers. The three plants will produce 3000, 5000, and 5000 units, respectively, during the next time period. Kellwood has made a commitment to sell 4000 units to customer 1, 3000 units to customer 2, and at least 3000 units to customer 3. Both customers 3 and 4 also want to buy as many of the remaining units as possible. The profit associated with shipping a unit from each plant to each customer is given in the file **P05_85.xls**. Determine how to maximize Kellwood's profit.

86. I have put four valuable paintings up for sale. Four customers are bidding for the paintings. Customer 1 is willing to buy two paintings, but each other customer is willing to purchase at most one painting. The prices that each customer is willing to pay are given in the file **P05_86.xls**. Determine how to maximize the total revenue received from the sale of the paintings.

87. Powerhouse produces capacitors at three locations: Los Angeles, Chicago, and New York. Capacitors are shipped from these locations to public utilities in five regions of the country: northeast (NE), northwest (NW), midwest (MW), southeast (SE), and southwest (SW). The cost of producing and shipping a capacitor from each plant to each region of the country is given in the file **P05_87.xls**. Each plant has an annual production capacity of 100,000 capacitors. Each year, each region of the country must receive the following number of capacitors: NE, 55,000; NW, 50,000; MW, 60,000; SE, 60,000; SW, 45,000. Powerhouse believes that shipping costs are too high, and it is therefore considering building one or two more production plants. Possible sites are Atlanta and Houston. The costs of producing a capacitor and shipping it to each region of the country are also given in the file **P05_87.xls**. It costs $3 million (in current dollars) to build a new plant, and operating each plant incurs a fixed cost (in addition to variable shipping and production costs) of $50,000 per year. A plant at Atlanta or Houston will have the capacity to produce 100,000 capacitors per year. Assume that future demand patterns and production costs will remain unchanged. If costs are discounted at a rate of 12% per year, how can Powerhouse minimize the net present value (NPV) of all costs associated with meeting current and future demands?

88. Based on Hansen and Wendell (1982). During the month of July, Pittsburgh resident Bill Fly must make four round-trip flights between Pittsburgh and

Chicago. The dates of the trips are shown in the file **P05_88.xls**. Bill must purchase four round-trip tickets. Without a discounted fare, a round-trip ticket between Pittsburgh and Chicago costs $500. If Bill's stay in a city includes a weekend, he gets a 20% discount on the round-trip fare. If his stay in a city is at least 21 days, he receives a 35% discount, and if his stay is more than 10 days, he receives a 30% discount. However, at most one discount can be applied toward the purchase of any ticket. Determine how to minimize the total cost of purchasing the four round-trip tickets. (*Hint*: It might be beneficial to pair one half of one round-trip ticket number with half of another round-trip ticket.)

89. Three professors must be assigned to teach six sections of finance. Each professor must teach two sections of finance, and each has ranked the six time periods during which finance is taught, as shown in the file **P05_89.xls**. A ranking of 10 means that the professor wants to teach at that time, and a ranking of 1 means that he or she does not want to teach at that time. Determine an assignment of professors to sections that maximizes the total satisfaction of the professors.

90. Based on Denardo et al. (1988). Three fires have just broken out in New York. Fires 1 and 2 each require two fire engines, and fire 3 requires three fire engines. The "cost" of responding to each fire depends on the time at which the fire engines arrive. Let t_{ij} be the time in minutes when the engine j arrives at fire i (if it is dispatched to that location). Then the cost of responding to each fire is as follows: fire 1, $6t_{11} + 4t_{12}$; fire 2, $7t_{21} + 3t_{22}$; fire 3, $9t_{31} + 8t_{32} + 5t_{33}$. There are three fire companies that can respond to the three fires. Company 1 has three engines available, and companies 2 and 3 each have two engines available. The time (in minutes) it takes an engine to travel from each company to each fire is shown in the file **P05_90.xls**.

a. Determine how to minimize the cost associated with assigning the fire engines. (*Hint*: A network with seven destination nodes is necessary.)

b. Would the formulation in part **a** still be valid if the cost of fire 1 were $4t_{11} + 6t_{12}$?

Modeling Problems

91. A company produces several products at several different plants. The products are then shipped to two warehouses for storage and are finally shipped to one of many customers. How would you use a network flow model to help the company reduce its production and distribution costs? Pay particular attention to discussing the data you would need to implement a network flow model.

92. You want to start a campus business to match compatible male and female students for dating. How would you use the models in this chapter to help you run your business?

93. You have been assigned to ensure that each high school in the Indianapolis area is racially balanced. Explain how you would use a network model to help attain this goal.

International Textile Company, Ltd., is a Hong Kong–based firm that distributes textiles worldwide. The company is owned by the Lao family. Present plans are to remain in Hong Kong through the transition in governments. Should the People's Republic of China continue its economic renaissance, the company hopes to use its current base to expand operations to the mainland. International Textile has mills in the Bahamas, Hong Kong, Korea, Nigeria, and Venezuela, each weaving fabrics out of two or more raw fibers: cotton, polyester, and/or silk. The mills service eight company distribution centers located near the customers' geographical centers of activity.

Since transportation costs historically have been less than 10% of total expenses, management has paid little attention to extracting savings through judicious routing of shipments. Ching Lao is returning from the United States, where he has just completed his bachelor's degree in marketing. He believes that each year he can save International Textile hundreds of thousands of dollars—perhaps millions—just by better routing of fabrics from mills to distribution centers. One glaring example of poor routing is the current assignment of fabric output to the Mexico City distribution center from Nigeria instead of from Venezuela, less than a third the distance. Similarly, the Manila center now gets most of its textiles from Nigeria and Venezuela, although the mills in Hong Kong itself are much closer.

Of course, the cost of shipping a bolt of cloth does not depend on distance alone. Table 5.15 provides the actual costs supplied to Mr. Lao from company headquarters. Distribution center demands are seasonal, so a new shipment plan must be made each month. Table 5.16 provides the fabric requirements for the month of March. International Textile's mills have varying capacities for producing the various types of cloth. Table 5.17 provides the quantities that apply during March.

Table 5.15   Shipping Cost Data (dollars per bolt)

	Distribution Center							
Mill	Los Angeles	Chicago	London	Mexico City	Manila	Rome	Tokyo	New York
Bahamas	2	2	3	3	7	4	7	1
Hong Kong	6	7	8	10	2	9	4	8
Korea	5	6	8	11	4	9	1	7
Nigeria	14	12	6	9	11	7	5	10
Venezuela	4	3	5	1	9	6	11	4

Table 5.16   Fabric Demands for March (bolts)

	Distribution Center							
Fabric	Los Angeles	Chicago	London	Mexico City	Manila	Rome	Tokyo	New York
Cotton	500	800	900	900	800	100	200	700
Polyester	1,000	2,000	3,000	1,500	400	700	900	2,500
Silk	100	100	200	50	400	200	700	200

[10]This case was written by Lawrence L. Lapin, San Jose State University.

Table 5.17

Table 5.17 March Production Capacities (bolts)

Mill	Cotton	Polyester	Silk
		Production Capacity	
Bahamas	1,000	3,000	0
Hong Kong	2,000	2,500	1,000
Korea	1,000	3,500	500
Nigeria	2,000	0	0
Venezuela	1,000	2,000	0

Mr. Lao wants to schedule production and shipments in such a way that the most costly customers are shorted when there is insufficient capacity and the least-efficient plants operate at less than full capacity when demand falls below maximum production capacity.

You have been retained by International to assist Mr. Lao.

Questions

1. Find the optimal March shipment schedule and its total transportation cost for each of the following:
   a. cotton
   b. polyester cloth
   c. silk

2. The company will be opening a silk-making department in the Nigeria mill. Although it will not be completed for several months, a current capacity of 1,000 bolts for that fabric might be used during March for an added one-time cost of $2,000. Find the new optimal shipment schedule and the total cost for that fabric. Should the Nigeria mill process silk in March?

3. Mr. Lao learns that changes might have to be made to the March plans. If a new customer is obtained, the cotton demand in Manila and in Mexico City will increase by 10% each. Meanwhile, a big New York customer might cut back, which would reduce polyester demand 10% in both New York and Chicago. Find the contingent optimal schedules and total costs (a) for cotton and (b) for polyester.

4. International Textile loses a profit of $10 for each bolt of cotton it falls short of meeting the distribution center's demand. For polyester, the loss is $20 per bolt; for silk, it is a whopping $50 per bolt. By running the mills on overtime, the company can produce additional bolts at the additional costs shown in Table 5.18. Using only the original data from Tables 5.15–5.17 and the information in Table 5.18, determine new production schedules to maximize overall profit for successively (a) cotton, (b) polyester, and (c) silk. Which fabrics and locations involve overtime production, and what are the overtime quantities?

5. Without making any calculations, offer Mr. Lao other suggestions for reducing costs of transportion.

Table 5.18 Overtime Production Costs

Mill	Cotton	Polyester	Silk
		Cost per Bolt	
Bahamas	$10	$10	N.A.
Hong Kong	15	12	$25
Korea	5	8	22
Nigeria	6	N.A.	N.A.
Venezuela	7	6	N.A.

Optimization Models with Integer Variables

© Photodisc

KLM AIRCRAFT MAINTENANCE

As we discussed in Chapter 4, many management science applications deal with workforce scheduling. These problems can be extremely complex and frequently require an integer programming approach to handle a variety of constraints. As an example, Dijkstra et al. (1994) report the use of integer programming in their article "Planning the Size and Organization of KLM's Aircraft Maintenance Personnel." KLM Royal Dutch Airlines, the major Dutch carrier since 1919, owns (as of 1993) about 90 aircraft of eight different types. To guarantee safety, KLM carries out high-quality aircraft maintenance, both on its own aircraft and on aircraft belonging to about 30 other carriers, according to fairly strict schedules. Maintenance standards require KLM engineers to perform routine maintenance between flights and major inspections after a certain number of flight hours. The company employs about 400 maintenance engineers, many of whom are highly skilled for their demanding jobs. Each of these highly skilled engineers is licensed to work on at most two types of aircraft (B737s and B747s, for example) and at most one particular skill (mechanical, electrical, or radio operations). For this reason the engineers operate in nearly identical teams of about 20 engineers each, so that each team has the capabilities required to service all aircraft.

The workload varies considerably across days of the week and within a given day. To respond to this workload in a timely manner, it is important for KLM to determine the composition of its maintenance teams and to schedule these teams optimally. KLM realized that its workforce scheduling problem was too complex for "manual" analysis and therefore employed a management science team.

The team built a decision support system (DSS) to help KLM solve its maintenance scheduling problem. The DSS includes a database module, an analysis module, and a graphical user interface. In simple terms, the database module gathers all of the necessary data about flight timetables, required maintenance, required skill levels, and other necessary information. It then feeds these data into the analysis module, which uses integer programming to either (1) minimize the size of the maintenance teams subject to meeting a specified service level or (2) maximize the service level subject to the composition of existing teams. Because both of these problems result in large and difficult integer programming models, good approximations have been developed to yield near-optimal results. The graphical user interface then allows the users to see the results of the analysis and ask a number of what-if questions.

The managers at KLM have been quite satisfied with the DSS. They consider it a valuable tool for analyzing both strategic and tactical problems, and they have advocated expanding its use into other departments of KLM such as the helicopter department. ∎

6.1 INTRODUCTION

In this chapter we see how many complex problems can be modeled using 0–1 variables and other variables that are forced to assume integer values. A **0–1 variable** is a decision variable that must equal 0 or 1. Usually a 0–1 variable corresponds to an activity that either is or is not undertaken. If the 0–1 variable corresponding to the activity equals 1, then the activity is undertaken; if it equals 0, the activity is not undertaken. A 0–1 variable is often called a **binary variable**.

Optimization models in which some or all of the variables must be integers are known as **integer programming** (IP) models. In this chapter we illustrate many of the tricks of the trade that are needed to formulate IP models of complex situations. You should be aware that a spreadsheet Solver typically has a much harder time solving an IP problem than an LP problem. In fact, a spreadsheet Solver is sometimes unable to solve an IP problem, even if the IP problem has an optimal solution. The reason is that these problems are inherently difficult to solve, no matter what software package is used. However, as we will see in this chapter, our ability to *model* complex problems increases tremendously when we are able to use binary variables.

IP models come in many forms. We saw examples in Chapter 4 where the decision variables were naturally integer-valued. For example, when scheduling postal workers (Example 4.2), it is natural to require the numbers of workers to be integers. In examples like this, where we do not want certain decision variables to have fractional values, the problems are basically LP models with integer constraints added at the last minute. In many such examples, if we ignored the integer constraints, optimized with Solver, and then rounded to the nearest integers, the chances are that the resulting integer solution would be close to optimal—although there are admittedly times when the rounded solution is not so good.

The "integer" models in Chapter 4 are not the types of IP models we will discuss in this chapter. Indeed, if it were simply a matter of adding integer constraints to decision variables such as the numbers of workers, we would not have included this chapter at all. However, there are many inherently *nonlinear* problems that can be transformed into linear models with the use of binary variables. These are the types of models we will discuss here.[1] As we will see, the clever use of binary variables allows us to solve many interesting and difficult problems that LP algorithms are incapable of solving.

Except for binary constraints on some changing cells, all of the models in this chapter are linear.

It is important to point out that all of the models we will develop in this chapter are, aside from binary changing cells, *linear* models. As in previous chapters, this means that if we look at the target cell, it is ultimately a sum of products of constants and changing cells. The same goes for both sides of all constraints. In other words, the models in this chapter will *look* much like the models in the previous three chapters, the only difference being that some of the changing cells are now constrained to be binary. Although the basic algorithm that Solver uses for such models is fundamentally different—because of the binary variables—it still helps that the models are linear. They would present even more of a challenge to Solver if they were nonlinear.

6.2 OVERVIEW OF OPTIMIZATION WITH INTEGER VARIABLES

When Excel's Solver solves a linear model without integer constraints, it uses a very efficient algorithm, the simplex method, to perform the optimization. As we discussed briefly in Chapter 3, this method examines the "corner" points of the feasible region and returns the best corner point as the optimal solution. The simplex method is efficient because it typically examines only a very small fraction of the hundreds, thousands, or even millions of possible corner points before determining the best corner point.

The branch and bound algorithm is a general approach to searching through all of the possibly millions of solutions in an efficient manner.

The main difference between LP and IP models is that LP models allow fractional values such as 0.137 and 5.3246 for the changing cells, whereas IP models allow only integer values for integer-constrained changing cells. In fact, if changing cells are constrained to be binary, then the only allowable values are 0 and 1. This suggests that IP models are easier to solve. After all, there are many fewer integer values in a given region than there are continuous values, so searching through the integers should be quicker—especially if their only possible values are 0 and 1. However, it turns out that IP models are *much* more difficult to solve than LP models, primarily because we cannot rely on the simplex method. Although several solution methods have been suggested by researchers—and new methods for specialized problems are still being developed—the solution procedure used by Solver is called **branch and bound**. Although we will not go into the details of the algorithms, we will discuss briefly what Solver is doing. This way you can appreciate some of the difficulties with IP models, and you might also understand some of the messages you see in the status bar as Solver performs its optimization.

Branch and Bound Algorithm

Consider a model with 100 changing cells, all constrained to be binary. Because there are only two values for each binary variable, 0 and 1, there are at most 2^{100} feasible solutions, and many of these might be infeasible because they do not satisfy other constraints. Unfortunately, 2^{100} is an *extremely* large number, so it would take even a very fast computer a long time to check each one of them. Therefore, the naive method of **complete**

---

[1]This is not quite true for the first example, which gets us off to a relatively easy start, but it is true of all the other examples in this chapter.

enumeration of all possible solutions—look at each solution and select the best—is usually impractical. However, it might be practical to use **implicit enumeration**. This approach examines only a fraction of all 2^{100} potential solutions, hopefully a very small fraction, and in doing so, it guarantees that solutions not examined have no chance of being optimal. To see how this works, suppose we find a feasible solution with a profit of $500. If we can somehow guarantee that each solution in a particular subset of solutions has profit *less* than $500, then we can ignore this entire subset because it cannot possibly contain the profit-maximizing solution.

This general idea is the essence of the branch and bound method used by Solver in IP models. The "branching" part means that the algorithm systematically searches through the set of all feasible integer solutions, creating branches—that is, subsets—of solutions as it goes. For example, if x_1 is a binary variable, one branch might have $x_1 = 0$ and another branch might have $x_1 = 1$. Then if x_2 is another binary variable, two branches might be created off the $x_1 = 0$ branch—one with $x_2 = 0$ and one with $x_2 = 1$. By forming enough branches, we can eventually search all possible integer solutions. However, the details of the branch and bound algorithm are beyond the scope of this book.

The Solver Tolerance Setting

In the Solver Options dialog box there is a **Tolerance** setting. This setting is relevant for integer-constrained models. Excel's default tolerance is 5%. To explain the Tolerance option, we must first define the **LP relaxation** of an IP model. This is the same model as the IP model, except that all integer constraints are omitted. In particular, cells that are originally constrained to be binary are allowed, under the LP relaxation, to have *any* fractional values between 0 and 1. The LP relaxation is easy to solve (using the simplex method), and it provides a bound for the IP model. For example, consider a maximization problem where the optimal solution to the LP relaxation has an optimal objective value of $48,214. Then we know that the optimal objective for the original integer-constrained problem can be no larger than $48,214, so that this value represents an upper bound for the original problem.

A tolerance setting of 5% means that Solver will stop as soon as it finds a feasible (integer) solution to the IP model that is within 5% of the current upper bound. Initially, the optimal objective value of the LP relaxation serves as the upper bound. As Solver proceeds to find solutions that satisfy the integer constraints, it keeps updating the upper bound. The exact details need not concern us. The important point is that when Solver stops, it guarantees an integer solution that is within at least 5% of the "true" optimal integer solution.

The implication is that if we set the tolerance to 0%, Solver will (in theory) run until it finds the *optimal* integer solution. So why don't we always use a tolerance setting of 0%? The reason is that for many IP models, especially large models, it can take Solver a long time to find the optimal solution (or guarantee that the best solution found so far *is* optimal). On the other hand, a solution that is *close* to optimal—within 5%, say—can often be found quickly. This explains why Frontline Systems, the developer of Solver, chose the default tolerance setting of 5%.

> *To guarantee an optimal integer solution, change the Solver tolerance setting to 0%. The disadvantage of this approach is that Solver might run considerably longer on large models.*

We used a tolerance of 0% for all of the models in this chapter, simply to guarantee an optimal solution. Therefore, if you use the default tolerance of 5%, you *might* get a solution that is slightly worse than ours.

6.3 CAPITAL BUDGETING MODELS

Perhaps the simplest binary IP model is the following capital budgeting example. It illustrates the "go–no go" nature of many IP models.

EXAMPLE **6.1** **SELECTING INVESTMENTS AT TATHAM**

The Tatham Company is considering seven investments. The cash required for each investment and the net present value (NPV) each investment adds to the firm are listed in Table 6.1. The cash available for investment is $15,000. Tatham wants to find the investment policy that maximizes its NPV. The crucial assumption here is that if Tatham wishes to take part in any of these investments, it must go "all the way." It cannot, for example, go halfway in investment 1 by investing $2500 and realizing an NPV of $8000. In fact, if partial investments were allowed, we wouldn't need IP; we could use LP.

Table 6.1 Data for Capital Budgeting Example

Investment	Cash Required	NPV
1	$5,000	$16,000
2	$2,500	$8,000
3	$3,500	$10,000
4	$6,000	$19,500
5	$7,000	$22,000
6	$4,500	$12,000
7	$3,000	$7,500

Objective To use binary IP to find the set of investments that stays within budget and maximizes total NPV.

WHERE DO THE NUMBERS COME FROM?

The initial required cash and the available budget are easy to obtain. It is undoubtedly harder to obtain the NPV for each investment. Here we require a time sequence of anticipated cash inflows from the investments, and we need a discount factor. We might even use simulation to estimate these NPVs. In any case, estimation of the required NPVs would definitely put the financial analysts to work.

Solution

The variables and constraints required for this model are listed in Table 6.2. The most important part is that the decision variables must be binary, where a 1 means an investment is undertaken and a 0 means it is not. These variables cannot have fractional values such as 0.5, because we do not allow partial investments—the company has to go all the way or not at all. Note in this table that we specify the binary restriction in the second row, not the last row. We will do this throughout this chapter. However, when we set up the Solver dialog box, we will add explicit binary constraints in the constraints section.

Table 6.2 Variables and Constraints for Capital Budgeting Model

Input variables	Initial cash required for investments, NPVs from investments, budget
Decision variables (changing cells)	Whether to invest (binary variables)
Objective (target cell)	Total NPV
Other calculated variables	Total initial cash required
Constraints	Total initial cash required ≤ Budget

DEVELOPING THE SPREADSHEET MODEL

To form the spreadsheet model, which is shown in Figure 6.1, proceed as follows. (See the file **CapitalBudgeting1.xls**.)

Figure 6.1   Capital Budgeting Model

	A	B	C	D	E	F	G	H	I	J	K	L	M	N
1	Tatham capital budgeting model													
2														
3	Input data on potential investments										Range names used:			
4	Investment	1	2	3	4	5	6	7			Amount_invested	=Model!$B$14		
5	Investment cost	$5,000	$2,500	$3,500	$6,000	$7,000	$4,500	$3,000			Budget	=Model!$D$14		
6	NPV	$16,000	$8,000	$10,000	$19,500	$22,000	$12,000	$7,500			Investment_levels	=Model!$B$10:$H$10		
7	NPV per investment dollar	3.20	3.20	2.86	3.25	3.14	2.67	2.50			Total_NPV	=Model!$B$17		
8														
9	Decisions: whether to inves													
10	Investment levels	1	1	0	0	1	0	0						
11														
12	Budget constraint													
13		Amount invested		Budget										
14		$14,500	<=	$15,000										
15														
16	Objective to maximiz													
17	Total NPV	$46,000												

A SUMPRODUCT formula, where one of the ranges comprises 0's and 1's, really just sums the values in the other range that "match up" with the 1's.

❶ Inputs. Enter the initial cash requirements, the NPVs, and the budget in the shaded ranges.

❷ 0–1 values for investments. Enter *any* trial 0–1 values for the investments in the Investment_levels range. Actually, you can even enter fractional values such as 0.5 in these cells. The Solver constraints will eventually force them to be 0 or 1.

❸ Cash invested. Calculate the total cash invested in cell B14 with the formula

=SUMPRODUCT(B5:H5,Investment_levels)

Note that this formula "picks up" the costs *only* for those investments with 0–1 variables equal to 1. To see this, think how the SUMPRODUCT function works when one of its ranges is a range of 0's and 1's. It effectively sums the cells in the other range corresponding to the 1's.

❹ NPV contribution. Calculate the NPV contributed by the investments in cell B17 with the formula

=SUMPRODUCT(B6:H6,Investment_levels)

Again, this picks up only the NPVs of the investments with 0–1 variables equal to 1.

Excel's Solver makes it easy to specify binary constraints, just by clicking on the "bin" option.

USING SOLVER

The Solver dialog box appears in Figure 6.2. We want to maximize the total NPV, subject to staying within the budget. However, we also need to *constrain* the changing cells to be 0–1. Fortunately, Solver makes this simple, as shown in the dialog box in Figure 6.3. We add a constraint with Investments in the left box and choose the "bin" option in the middle box. The "binary" in the right box is then added automatically. Note that if *all* changing cells are binary, we do not need to check Solver's Assume Non-Negative option (because 0 and 1 are certainly nonnegative), but we should still check the Assume Linear Model option if the model is linear, as it is here.[2]

---

[2]All of the models in this chapter satisfy two of the three linearity assumptions in Chapter 3, proportionality and additivity. Even though they clearly violate the third assumption, divisibility, which precludes integer constraints, they are still considered linear by Solver. Therefore, we gain efficiency by checking the Assume Linear Model option.

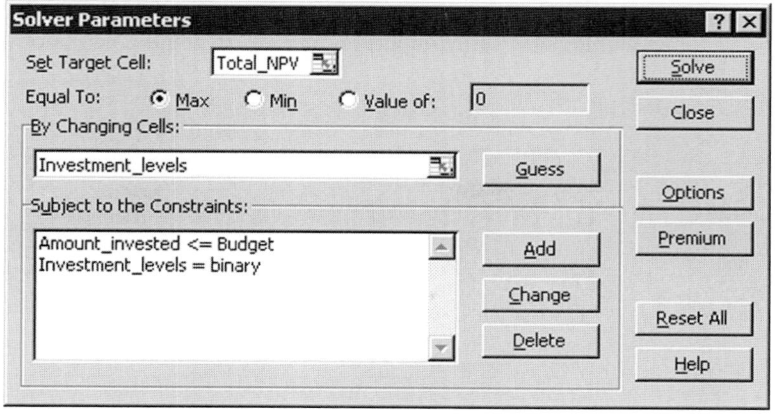

Figure 6.2

Solver Dialog Box for Capital Budgeting Model

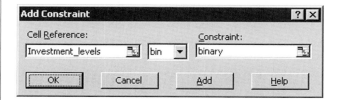

Figure 6.3

Specifying a Binary Constraint

Discussion of the Solution

The optimal solution in Figure 6.1 indicates that Tatham can obtain a maximum NPV of $46,000 by selecting investments 1, 2, and 5. These three investments consume only $14,500 of the available budget, with $500 left over. However, this $500 is not enough—because of the "investing all the way" requirement—to invest in any of the remaining investments.

If we rank Tatham's investments on the basis of NPV per dollar invested (see row 7 of Figure 6.1), the ranking from best to worst is 4, 1, 2, 5, 3, 6, 7. Using your economic intuition, you might expect the investments to be chosen in this order—until the budget runs out. However, the optimal solution does not do this. It selects the second, third, and fourth-best investments, but it ignores the best. To understand why it does this, imagine investing in the order from best to worst, according to row 7, until the budget allows no more. By the time you have invested in investments 4, 1, and 2, you will have consumed $13,500 of the budget, and the remainder, $1500, is not sufficient to invest in any of the rest. This strategy provides an NPV of only $43,500. A smarter strategy, the optimal solution from Solver, gains you an extra $2500 in NPV.

Sensitivity Analysis

SolverTable can be used on models with binary variables exactly as we have used it in previous models.[3] Here we see how the total NPV varies as the budget increases. We select the Budget cell as the single input cell, allow it to vary from $15,000 to $25,000 in increments of $1000, and keep track of the total NPV, the amount of the budget used, and the binary variables. The results are given in Figure 6.4 (page 252). Clearly, Tatham can achieve a larger NPV with a larger budget, but as the numbers and the chart show, each extra $1000 of budget does *not* have the same effect on total NPV. The first $1000 increase to the budget adds $3500 to total NPV, the next two $1000 increases add $4000 each, the next two $1000 increases add $2000 each, and so on. Note also how the selected

---

[3]As we mentioned in Chapter 4, Solver's sensitivity report is not even available for models with integer constraints. There is a good reason for this—the mathematical theory behind the report changes significantly when variables are constrained to be integers.

investments vary quite a lot as the budget increases. This somewhat strange behavior is due to the "lumpiness" of the inputs and the all-or-nothing nature of the problem.

Figure 6.4 Sensitivity to Budget

	A	B	C	D	E	F	G	H	I	J
19	Sensitivity of total NPV, amount invested, and investments to budget									
20	Budget	Total NPV	Amt invested	Invest1	Invest2	Invest3	Invest4	Invest5	Invest6	Invest7
21		$B$17	$B$14	$B$10	$C$10	$D$10	$E$10	$F$10	$G$10	$H$10
22	15000	$46,000	$14,500	1	1	0	0	1	0	0
23	16000	$49,500	$16,000	0	0	0	1	1	0	1
24	17000	$53,500	$17,000	1	1	1	1	0	0	0
25	18000	$57,500	$18,000	1	0	0	1	1	0	0
26	19000	$59,500	$19,000	0	1	1	1	1	0	0
27	20000	$61,500	$20,000	1	1	1	1	0	0	1
28	21000	$65,500	$20,500	1	1	0	1	1	0	0
29	22000	$67,500	$21,500	1	0	1	1	1	0	0
30	23000	$69,500	$22,500	1	0	0	1	1	1	0
31	24000	$75,500	$24,000	1	1	1	1	1	0	0
32	25000	$77,500	$25,000	1	1	0	1	1	1	0

Total NPV versus Budget

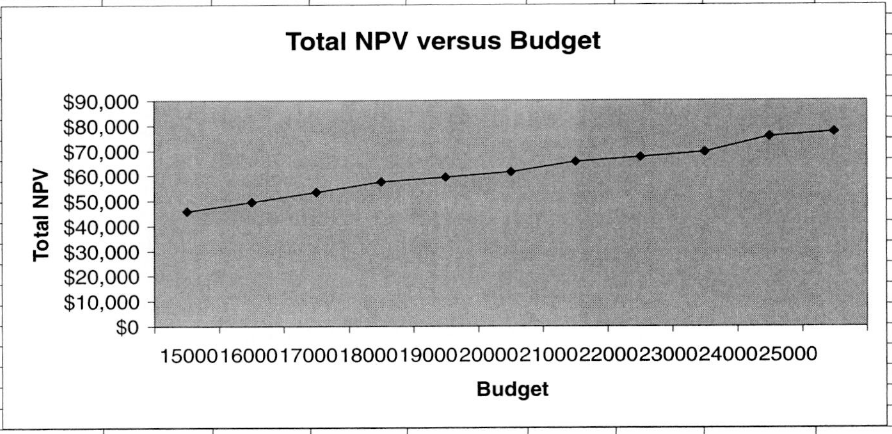

Effect of Solver Tolerance Setting

When the Tolerance setting is 5% instead of 0%, Solver's solution might not be optimal, but it will be close.

To illustrate the effect of the Solver Tolerance setting, compare the SolverTable results in Figure 6.5 with those in Figure 6.4. Each is for the Tatham capital budgeting model, but Figure 6.5 uses Solver's default tolerance of 5%, whereas Figure 6.4 uses a tolerance of 0%. The four shaded cells in Figure 6.5 indicate *lower* total NPVs than the corresponding cells in Figure 6.4. In these four cases, Solver stopped short of finding the true optimal solutions because it found solutions within the 5% tolerance and then quit.

Figure 6.5 Results with Tolerance at 5%

	A	B	C	D	E	F	G	H	I	J
19	Sensitivity of total NPV, amount invested, and investments to budget									
20	Budget	Total NPV	Amt invested	Invest1	Invest2	Invest3	Invest4	Invest5	Invest6	Invest7
21		$B$17	$B$14	$B$10	$C$10	$D$10	$E$10	$F$10	$G$10	$H$10
22	15000	$45,500	$15,000	1	0	0	0	1	0	1
23	16000	$49,500	$15,500	0	1	0	1	1	0	0
24	17000	$53,500	$17,000	1	1	1	1	0	0	0
25	18000	$57,500	$18,000	1	0	0	1	1	0	0
26	19000	$59,500	$19,000	0	1	1	1	1	0	0
27	20000	$60,000	$20,000	1	0	1	0	1	1	0
28	21000	$65,500	$20,500	1	1	0	1	1	0	0
29	22000	$65,500	$20,500	1	1	0	1	1	0	0
30	23000	$68,000	$22,500	1	1	1	0	1	1	0
31	24000	$75,500	$24,000	1	1	1	1	1	0	0
32	25000	$77,500	$25,000	1	1	0	1	1	1	0

1. The following modifications of the capital budgeting example can be handled easily. You are asked to explore similar modifications in the problems.
   - Suppose that at most two projects can be selected. In this case we add a constraint that the sum of the 0–1 variables for the investments is less than or equal to 2. This constraint will be satisfied if 0, 1, or 2 investments are chosen, but it will be violated if 3 or more investments are chosen.
   - Suppose that if investment 2 is selected, then investment 1 must also be selected. In this case we add a constraint saying that the 0–1 variable for investment 1 is greater than or equal to the 0–1 variable for investment 2. This constraint rules out the one possibility that is not allowed—where investment 2 is selected but investment 1 is not.
   - Suppose that either investment 1 or investment 3 (or both) *must* be selected. In this case we add a constraint that the sum of the 0–1 variables for investments 1 and 3 must be greater than or equal to 1. This rules out the one possibility that is not allowed—where both of these 0–1 variables are 0, so that neither investment is selected.

2. Capital budgeting models with multiple periods can also be handled. Figure 6.6 shows one possibility. (See the **CapitalBudgeting2.xls** file.) The costs in rows 5 and 6 are *both* incurred if any given investment is selected. Now there are two budget constraints, one in each year, but otherwise the model is exactly as before. Note that some investments could have a cost of 0 in year 1 and a positive cost in year 2. This would effectively mean that these investments are undertaken in year 2 rather than year 1. Also, it would be easy to modify the model to incorporate costs in years 3, 4, and so on.

Figure 6.6 A Two-Period Capital Budgeting Model

	A	B	C	D	E	F	G	H	I	J	K	L	M
1	Tatham two-period capital budgeting model												
2													
3	Input data on potential investments												
4	Investment	1	2	3	4	5	6	7		Range names used:			
5	Year 1 cost	$5,000	$2,500	$3,500	$6,500	$7,000	$4,500	$3,000		Amount_invested	=Model!$B$14:$B$15		
6	Year 2 cost	$2,000	$1,500	$2,000	$0	$500	$1,500	$0		Budget	=Model!$D$14:$D$15		
7	NPV	$16,000	$8,000	$10,000	$20,000	$22,000	$12,000	$8,000		Investment_levels	=Model!$B$10:$H$10		
8										Total_NPV	=Model!$B$18		
9	Decisions: whether to invest												
10	Investment levels	1	1	0	1	0	0	0					
11													
12	Budget constraints												
13		Amount invested		Budget									
14		$14,000	<=	$14,000									
15		$3,500	<=	$4,500									
16													
17	Objective to maximize												
18	Total NPV	$44,000											

3. If Tatham could choose a *fractional* amount of an investment, then we could maximize its NPV by deleting the binary constraint. The optimal solution to the resulting LP model has a total NPV of $48,714. All of investments 1, 2, and 4, and 0.214 of investment 5 are chosen.[4] Note that there is no way to round the changing cell values from this LP solution to obtain the optimal IP solution. Sometimes the solution to an IP model *without* the integer constraints bears little resemblance to the optimal IP solution.

---

[4]If you try this with the **CapitalBudgeting1.xls** file, delete the binary constraint, but don't forget to constrain the Investment_levels range to be nonnegative and less than or equal to 1.

4. Any IP involving 0–1 variables with only one constraint is called a **knapsack problem**. Think of the problem faced by a hiker going on an overnight hike. For example, imagine that the hiker's knapsack can hold only 14 pounds, and she must choose which of several available items to take on the hike. The benefit derived from each item is analogous to the NPV of each project, and the weight of each item is analogous to the cash required by each investment. The single constraint is analogous to the budget constraint—that is, only 14 pounds can fit in the knapsack. In a knapsack problem the goal is to get the most value in the knapsack without overloading it. ■

ADDITIONAL APPLICATIONS

Integer Programming at Monsanto

Monsanto [see Boykin (1985)] used an IP model to determine the settings of its chemical reactors that minimize the annual cost of meeting customer demands. The model is credited with saving Monsanto between $1 and $3 million annually. The model contained a 0–1 variable for each possible setting of each reactor. ■

PROBLEMS

Solutions for problems whose numbers appear within a color box can be found in the Student Solutions Manual. Order your copy today at http://e-catalog.thomsonlearning.com/110/ by using ISBN 0-534-39687-9.

Skill-Building Problems

1. Solve the following modifications of the capital budgeting model in Figure 6.1. (Solve each part independently of the others.)
   a. Suppose that at most two of projects 1–5 can be selected.
   b. Suppose that if investment 1 is selected, then investment 3 must also be selected.
   c. Suppose that at least one of investments 6 and 7 *must* be selected.
   d. Suppose that investment 2 can be selected only if *both* investments 1 and 3 are selected.

2. In the capital budgeting model in Figure 6.1, we supplied the NPV for each investment. Suppose instead that you are given only the streams of cash inflows from each investment shown in the file **P06_02.xls**. This file also shows the cash requirements and the budget. You can assume that (1) all cash outflows occur at the beginning of year 1, (2) all cash inflows occur at the ends of their respective years, and (3) the company uses a 10% discount rate for calculating its NPVs. Which investments should the company make?

3. Solve the previous problem using the input data in the file **P06_03.xls**.

4. Solve Problem 2 with the extra assumption that the investments can be grouped naturally as follows: 1–4, 5–8, 9–12, 13–16, and 17–20.
   a. Find the optimal investments when at most one investment from each group can be selected.
   b. Find the optimal investments when at least one investment from each group must be selected. (If the budget isn't large enough to permit this, increase the budget to a larger value.)

5. In the capital budgeting model in Figure 6.1, investment 4 has the largest ratio of NPV to cash requirement, but it is not selected in the optimal solution. How much NPV will be lost if Tatham is *forced* to select investment 4? Answer by solving a suitably modified model.

6. As it currently stands, investment 7 in the capital budgeting model in Figure 6.1 has the lowest ratio of NPV to cash requirement, 2.5. Keeping this same ratio, can you change the cash requirement and NPV for investment 7 in such a way that it *is* selected in the optimal solution? Does this lead to any general insights? Explain.

7. Expand the capital budgeting model in Figure 6.1 so that there are now 20 possible investments. You can make up the data on cash requirements, NPVs, and the budget. However, use the following guidelines:
   ■ The cash requirements and NPVs for the various investments can vary widely, but the ratio of NPV to cash requirement should be between 2.5 and 3.5 for each investment.

- The budget should be such that somewhere between 5 and 10 of the investments can be selected.

8. Suppose in the capital budgeting model in Figure 6.1 that each investment requires $2000 during year 2 and only $5000 is available for investment during year 2.
  a. Assuming that available money uninvested at the end of year 1 cannot be used during year 2, what combination of investments maximizes NPV?
  b. Suppose that any uninvested money at the end of year 1 is available for investment in year 2. Does your answer to part **a** change?

Skill-Extending Problems

9. The models in this chapter are often called *combinatorial* models because each solution is a combination of the various 0's and 1's, and there are only a finite number of such combinations. For the capital budget-ing model in Figure 6.1, there are 7 investments, so there are $2^7 = 128$ possible solutions (some of which are infeasible). This is a fairly large number, but not *too* large. Solve the model *without* Solver by listing all 128 solutions. For each, calculate the total cash requirement and total NPV for the model. Then manu-ally choose the one that stays within the budget and has the largest NPV.

10. Make up an example, as described in Problem 7, with 20 possible investments. However, do it so the ratios of NPV to cash requirement are in a very tight range, from 3 to 3.2. Then use Solver to find the optimal so-lution when the Solver tolerance is set to its default value of 5%, and record the solution. Next, solve again with the tolerance set to 0. Do you get the same solution? Try this on a few more instances of the model, where you keep tinkering with the inputs. The question is whether the tolerance matters in these types of "close call" problems.

6.4 FIXED-COST MODELS

In many situations a fixed cost is incurred if an activity is undertaken at any *positive* level. This cost is independent of the level of the activity and is known as a **fixed cost** (or **fixed charge**). Here are three examples of fixed costs:

- The construction of a warehouse incurs a fixed cost that is the same whether the ware-house is built with a low or a high capacity level.

- A cash withdrawal from a bank incurs a fixed cost, independent of the size of the withdrawal.

- A machine that is used to produce several products must be set up for the production of each product. Regardless of how many units of a product the company produces, it incurs the same fixed cost (lost production due to the setup time) for producing the product.

In these examples a fixed cost is incurred if an activity is undertaken at any positive level, whereas no fixed cost is incurred if the activity is not undertaken at all. Although it might not be obvious, this feature makes the problem inherently *nonlinear*, which means that a straightforward application of LP is not possible. However, a clever use of 0–1 vari-ables can result in a model with linear constraints and a linear objective.

Unless we use binary variables to handle the logic, fixed-cost models are nonlinear and quite difficult to solve.

It is important to realize that, compared to the previous capital budgeting model and the integer-constrained models in Chapter 4, the type of model we discuss here and throughout the rest of this chapter is inherently different. We do not simply create an LP model and then add integer constraints. Instead, we use 0–1 variables to *model the logic*. In this particular section the logic is that if a certain activity is done at any *positive* level, then a fixed cost is incurred, whereas no fixed cost is incurred if the activity is not done at all. Your first instinct might be to handle such logic in Excel with IF functions. However, Solver cannot handle IF functions predictably. This is not really a weakness of Solver. These types of problems are inherently difficult. Fortunately, Solver *is* able to handle lin-ear models with binary variables, so this is the approach we will take. By using 0–1 vari-ables appropriately, we are able to solve a whole new class of difficult problems. The fol-lowing example is typical.

EXAMPLE | **6.2 TEXTILE MANUFACTURING AT GREAT THREADS**

The Great Threads Company is capable of manufacturing shirts, shorts, pants, skirts, and jackets. Each type of clothing requires that Great Threads have the appropriate type of machinery available. The machinery needed to manufacture each type of clothing must be rented at the weekly rates shown in Table 6.3. This table also lists the amounts of cloth and labor required per unit of clothing, as well as the sales price and the unit variable cost for each type of clothing. There are 4000 labor hours and 4500 square yards (sq yd) of cloth available in a given week. The company wants to find a solution that maximizes its weekly profit.

Table 6.3 Data for Great Threads Example

	Rental Cost	Labor Hours	Cloth (sq yd)	Sales Price	Unit Variable Cost
Shirts	$1500	2.0	3.0	$35	$20
Shorts	$1200	1.0	2.5	$40	$10
Pants	$1600	6.0	4.0	$65	$25
Skirts	$1500	4.0	4.5	$70	$30
Jackets	$1600	8.0	5.5	$110	$35

Objective To develop a linear model with binary variables that can be used to maximize the company's profit, correctly accounting for fixed costs and staying within resource availabilities.

WHERE DO THE NUMBERS COME FROM?

Except for the fixed costs, this is the same basic problem as the product mix problem (Example 3.2) in Chapter 3. Therefore, the same discussion there about input variables applies here. As for the fixed costs, these would simply be the given rental rates for the machinery.

Solution

Fixed costs imply that the proportionality assumption of linear models no longer holds.

The variables and constraints required for this model are listed in Table 6.4. We first note that the cost of producing x shirts during a week is 0 if $x = 0$, but it is $1500 + 20x$ if $x > 0$. This cost structure violates the proportionality assumption (discussed in Chapter 3) that is needed for a linear model. If proportionality were satisfied, then the cost of making, say, 10 shirts would be double the cost of making 5 shirts. However, because of the fixed cost, the total cost of making 5 shirts is $1600, and the cost of making 10 shirts is only $1700. This violation of proportionality requires us to resort to 0–1 variables to obtain a *linear* model. These 0–1 variables will allow us to model the fixed costs correctly, as explained in detail here.

Table 6.4 Variables and Constraints for Fixed-Cost Model

Input variables	Fixed rental costs, resource usages (labor hours, cloth) per unit of clothing, sales prices, unit variable costs, resource availabilities
Decision variables (changing cells)	Whether to produce any of each clothing (binary), how much of each clothing to produce
Objective (target cell)	Profit
Other calculated variables	Resources used, upper limits on amounts to produce, total revenue, total variable cost, total fixed cost
Constraints	Amount produced ≤ Logical upper limit (capacity) Resources used ≤ Resources available

DEVELOPING THE SPREADSHEET MODEL

The spreadsheet model, shown in Figure 6.7, can now be formulated as follows. (See the file **FixedCostMfg.xls**.)

Figure 6.7 Fixed-Cost Clothing Model

	A	B	C	D	E	F	G	H	I	J	K	L
1	Great Threads fixed cost clothing model											
2												
3	Input data on products											
4									Range names used:			
5	Labor hours/unit	Shirts	Shorts	Pants	Skirts	Jackets			Logical_upper_limit	=Model!$B$18:$F$18		
6	Cloth (sq. yd.)/unit	2	1	6	4	8			Produce_any?	=Model!$B$14:$F$14		
7		3	2.5	4	4.5	5.5			Profit	=Model!$B$29		
8	Selling price/unit	$35	$40	$65	$70	$110			Resource_available	=Model!$D$22:$D$23		
9	Variable cost/unit	$20	$10	$25	$30	$35			Resource_used	=Model!$B$22:$B$23		
10	Fixed cost for equipment	$1,500	$1,200	$1,600	$1,500	$1,600			Units_produced	=Model!$B$16:$F$16		
11												
12	Production plan, constraints on capacity											
13		Shirts	Shorts	Pants	Skirts	Jackets						
14	Produce any?	0	1	0	0	1						
15												
16	Units produced	0	965.52	0	0	379.31						
17		<=	<=	<=	<=	<=						
18	Logical upper limit	0.00	1800.00	0.00	0.00	500.00						
19												
20	Constraints on resources											
21		Resource used		Available								
22	Labor hours	4000.00	<=	4000								
23	Cloth	4500.00	<=	4500								
24												
25	Monetary outputs											
26	Revenue	$80,345										
27	Variable cost	$22,931										
28	Fixed cost for equipment	$2,800										
29	Profit	$54,614	←	Objective to maximize								

① Inputs. Enter the given inputs in the shaded ranges.

② Binary values for clothing types. Enter *any* trial values for the 0–1 variables for the various clothing types in the Produce_any? range. For example, if you enter a 1 in cell C14, you are implying that *some* shorts are produced. More importantly, you are implying that the machinery for making shorts will be rented and its fixed cost will be incurred.

③ Production quantities. Enter *any* trial values for the numbers of the various clothing types produced in the Units_produced range. At this point you could enter "illegal" values, such as 0 in cell B14 and a positive value in cell B16. We say this is illegal because it implies that the company produces some shirts but avoids the fixed cost of the machinery for shirts. However, Solver will eventually disallow such illegal combinations.

④ Labor and cloth used. In cell B22 enter the formula

=SUMPRODUCT(B5:F5,Units_produced)

to calculate total labor hours, and copy this to cell B23 for cloth.

⑤ Effective capacities. Now we come to the tricky part of the formulation. We need to ensure that if any of a given type of clothing is produced, then its 0–1 variable equals 1. This ensures that the model incurs the fixed cost of renting the machine for this type of clothing. We could easily implement these constraints with IF statements. For example, to implement the constraint for shirts, we could enter the following formula in cell B14:

=IF(B16>0,1,0)

However, Excel's Solver is unable to deal with IF functions predictably. Therefore, we instead model the fixed-cost constraints as follows:

$$\text{Shirts produced} \leq \text{Maximum capacity} \times (0\text{–}1 \text{ variable for shirts}) \quad \textbf{(6.1)}$$

There are similar inequalities for the other types of clothing.

The effect of binary variables is to force the model to incur the fixed costs if positive production levels are used.

Here is the logic behind inequality (6.1). If the 0–1 variable for shirts is 0, then the right-hand side of the inequality is 0, which means that the left side must be 0—no shirts can be produced. That is, if the 0–1 variable for shirts is 0, so that no fixed cost for shirts is incurred, then inequality (6.1) does not allow Great Threads to "cheat" and produce a positive number of shirts. On the other hand, if the 0–1 variable for shirts is 1, then the inequality is certainly true and is essentially redundant. It simply states that the number of shirts produced must be no greater than the *maximum* number that could be produced. Inequality (6.1) rules out the one case we want it to rule out—namely, that Great Threads produces shirts but avoids the fixed cost.

To implement inequality (6.1), we need a maximum capacity—an upper limit on the number of shirts that *could* be produced. To obtain this, suppose the company puts all of its resources into producing shirts. Then the number of shirts that can be produced is limited by the smaller of

$$\frac{\text{Available labor hours}}{\text{Labor hours per shirt}}$$

and

$$\frac{\text{Available square yards of cloth}}{\text{Square yards of cloth per shirt}}$$

The point of these ratios is to provide an upper limit on production of any product when no "natural" upper limit is available.

Therefore, the smaller of these—the most limiting—can be used as the maximum needed in inequality (6.1).

To implement this logic, calculate the "effective capacity" for shirts in cell B18 with the formula

=B14*MIN($D$22/B5,$D$23/B6)

Then copy this formula to the range C16:F16 for the other types of clothing.[5] By the way, this MIN formula causes no problems for Solver because it does not involve *changing* cells, only input cells.

6 **Monetary values.** Calculate the total sales revenue and the total variable cost by entering the formula

=SUMPRODUCT(B8:F8,Units_produced)

in cell B26 and copying it to cell B27. Then calculate the total fixed cost in cell B28 with the formula

=SUMPRODUCT(B10:F10,Produce_any?)

Note that this formula picks up the fixed costs only for those products with 0–1 variables equal to 1. Finally, calculate the total profit in cell B29 with the formula

=B26-B27-B28

USING SOLVER

The Solver dialog box is shown in Figure 6.8. We maximize profit, subject to using no more labor hours or cloth than are available, and we ensure that production is less than or equal to "effective" capacity. The key is that this effective capacity is 0 if we decide to pro-

---

[5]Why not set the upper limit on shirts equal to a huge number like 1,000,000? The reason is that Solver works most efficiently when the upper limit is as "tight"—that is, as low—as possible. A tighter upper limit means fewer potential feasible solutions for Solver to search through.

duce none of a given type of clothing. As usual, check the Assume Linear Model and Assume Non-Negative boxes under Solver options, and set the tolerance to 0.

Figure 6.8

Solver Dialog Box for Fixed-Cost Model

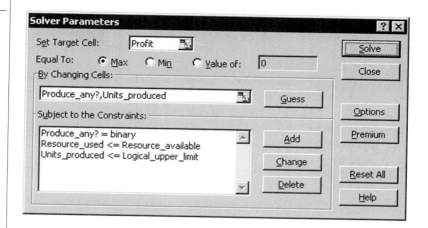

Although Solver finds the optimal solution automatically, you should understand the effect of the logical upper bound constraint on production. It rules out a solution such as the one shown in Figure 6.9. This solution calls for a positive production level of pants but does not incur the fixed cost of the pants equipment. The logical upper bound constraint rules this out because it prevents a positive value in row 16 if the corresponding binary value in row 14 is 0. In other words, if the company wants to produce some pants, then the constraint in inequality (6.1) will force the associated binary variable to be 1, thus incurring the fixed cost for pants.

Figure 6.9 An Illegal (and Nonoptimal) Solution

	A	B	C	D	E	F	G	H	I	J	K	L
1	Great Threads fixed cost clothing model											
2												
3	Input data on products											
4									Range names used:			
5	Labor hours/unit	Shirts	Shorts	Pants	Skirts	Jackets			Logical_upper_limit	=Model!$B$18:$F$18		
		2	1	6	4	8			Produce_any?	=Model!$B$14:$F$14		
6	Cloth (sq. yd.)/unit	3	2.5	4	4.5	5.5			Profit	=Model!$B$29		
7									Resource_available	=Model!$D$22:$D$23		
8	Selling price/unit	$35	$40	$65	$70	$110			Resource_used	=Model!$B$22:$B$23		
9	Variable cost/unit	$20	$10	$25	$30	$35			Units_produced	=Model!$B$16:$F$16		
10	Fixed cost for equipment	$1,500	$1,200	$1,600	$1,500	$1,600						
11												
12	Production plan, constraints on capacity											
13		Shirts	Shorts	Pants	Skirts	Jackets						
14	Produce any?	0	1	0	1	1						
15												
16	Units produced	0	965.52	450	0	379.31						
17		<=	<=	<=	<=	<=						
18	Logical upper limit	0.00	1800.00	0.00	1000.00	500.00						
19												
20	Constraints on resources											
21		Resource used		Available								
22	Labor hours	6700.00	<=	4000								
23	Cloth	6300.00	<=	4500								
24												
25	Monetary outputs											
26	Revenue	$109,595										
27	Variable cost	$34,181										
28	Fixed cost for equipment	$4,300										
29	Profit	$71,114	◄———	Objective to maximize								

There is no point to setting a binary variable equal to 1—and Solver will never do it—unless there is positive production of that product.

Note that inequality (6.1) does *not* rule out the situation we see for skirts, where the binary value is 1 and the production level is 0. However, Solver will never choose this type of solution as optimal. Solver recognizes that the binary value in this case can be changed to 0, so that no skirt equipment is rented and its fixed cost is not incurred.

Discussion of the Solution

The optimal solution appears in Figure 6.7. It indicates that Great Threads should produce about 966 shorts and 379 jackets, but no shirts, pants, or skirts. The total profit is $54,614. Note that the 0–1 variables for shirts, pants, and skirts are all 0, which forces production of these products to be 0. However, the 0–1 variables for shorts and jackets, the products that are produced, are 1. This ensures that the fixed cost of producing shorts and jackets is included in the total cost.

It might be helpful to think of this solution as occurring in two stages. In the first stage Solver determines which products to produce—in this case, shorts and jackets only. Then in the second stage, Solver figures out how *many* shorts and jackets to produce. If you know that the company plans to produce shorts and jackets only, you could then ignore the fixed costs and determine the best production quantities with the same product mix model discussed in Example 3.2 of Chapter 3. Of course, these two stages—deciding which products to produce and how many of each to produce—are interrelated, and Solver considers both of them in its solution process.

Because of fixed costs, the optimal solution might call for only a small subset of products to be produced. Only extra "side" constraints can force more products to be produced.

The Great Threads management might not be very excited about producing shorts and jackets only. Suppose the company wants to ensure that at least three types of clothing are produced at positive levels. One approach is to add another constraint—namely, that the sum of the 0–1 values in row 14 is greater than or equal to 3. You can check, however, that when this constraint is added and Solver is rerun, the 0–1 variable for skirts becomes 1, but no skirts are produced! Shorts and jackets are more profitable than skirts, so only shorts and jackets are produced. (See Figure 6.10.) The new constraint forces Great Threads to rent an extra piece of machinery (for skirts), but it doesn't force the company to use it. To force the company to produce some skirts, we would also need to add a constraint on the value in E16, such as E16>=100. Any of these additional constraints will cost Great Threads money, but if, as a matter of policy, the company wants to produce more than two types of clothing, this is its only option.

Figure 6.10   Great Threads Model with Extra Constraint

	A	B	C	D	E	F	G	H	I	J	K	L
1	Great Threads fixed cost clothing model											
2												
3	Input data on products								Range names used:			
4		Shirts	Shorts	Pants	Skirts	Jackets			Logical_upper_limit	=Model!$B$18:$F$18		
5	Labor hours/unit	2	1	6	4	8			Produce_any?	=Model!$B$14:$F$14		
6	Cloth (sq. yd.)/unit	3	2.5	4	4.5	5.5			Profit	=Model!$B$29		
7									Resource_available	=Model!$D$22:$D$23		
8	Selling price/unit	$35	$40	$65	$70	$110			Resource_used	=Model!$B$22:$B$23		
9	Variable cost/unit	$20	$10	$25	$30	$35			Units_produced	=Model!$B$16:$F$16		
10	Fixed cost for equipment	$1,500	$1,200	$1,600	$1,500	$1,600						
11												
12	Production plan, constraints on capacity											
13		Shirts	Shorts	Pants	Skirts	Jackets	Sum			Required		
14	Produce any?	0	1	0	1	1	3	>=		3		
15												
16	Units produced	0	965.52	0	0	379.31						
17		<=	<=	<=	<=	<=						
18	Logical upper limit	0.00	1800.00	0.00	1000.00	500.00						
19												
20	Constraints on resources											
21		Resource used		Available								
22	Labor hours	4000.00	<=	4000								
23	Cloth	4500.00	<=	4500								
24												
25	Monetary outputs											
26	Revenue	$80,345										
27	Variable cost	$22,931										
28	Fixed cost for equipment	$4,300										
29	Profit	$53,114	←	Objective to maximize								

Sensitivity Analysis

Because the optimal solution currently calls for only shorts and jackets to be produced, an interesting sensitivity analysis is to see how much "incentive" is required for other products to be produced. One way to check this is to increase the sales price for a nonproduced product such as skirts in a one-way SolverTable. We did this, keeping track of all binary variables and profit, with the results shown in Figure 6.11. When the sales price for skirts is $85 or less, the company continues to produce only shorts and jackets. However, when the sales price is $90 or greater, the company stops producing shorts and jackets and produces *only* skirts. You can check that the optimal production quantity of skirts is 1000 when the sales price of skirts is any value $90 or above. The only reason that the profits in Figure 6.11 increase from row 37 down is that the revenues from these 1000 skirts increase.

Figure 6.11

Sensitivity of Binary Variables to Unit Revenues of Shorts and Pants

	A	B	C	D	E	F	G
31	Sensitivity of binary variables and profit to unit revenue from skirts						
32		$B$14	$C$14	$D$14	$E$14	$F$14	$B$29
33	70	0	1	0	0	1	$54,614
34	75	0	1	0	0	1	$54,614
35	80	0	1	0	0	1	$54,614
36	85	0	1	0	0	1	$54,614
37	90	0	0	0	1	0	$58,500
38	95	0	0	0	1	0	$63,500
39	100	0	0	0	1	0	$68,500

A Model with IF Functions

In case you are still not convinced that the binary variable approach is required, and you think IF functions could be used instead, take a look at the file **FixedCostMfg_IF.xls**. The resulting model *looks* the same as in Figure 6.8, but it incorporates the following changes:

- We no longer use the binary range as part of the changing cells range. Instead, we enter the formula **=IF(B16>0,1,0)** in cell B14 and copy it across to cell F14. Logically, this probably appears more natural. If a production quantity is positive, then a 1 is entered in row 14, which means that the fixed cost is incurred.

- We model the effective capacities in row 18 with IF functions. Specifically, we enter the formula **=IF(B16>0,MIN($D$22/B5,$D$23/B6),0)** in cell B18 and copy it across to cell F18.

- We change the Solver dialog box so that it appears as in Figure 6.12. The Produce_any? range is not part of the changing cells range, and there is no binary constraint. We also uncheck the Assume Linear Model box in Solver's options because the IF functions make the model nonlinear.

Figure 6.12

Solver Dialog Box When IF Functions Are Used

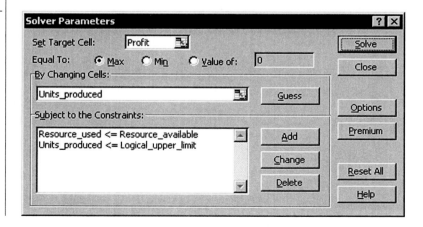

You can try modeling the logic with IF functions, but, depending on the initial values in the changing cells, Solver might get the wrong solution.

When we ran Solver on this modified model, we found inconsistent results, depending on the initial production quantities entered in row 16. For example, when we entered initial values all equal to 0, the Solver solution was exactly that—all 0's. Of course, this solution is *terrible* because it leads to a profit of $0. However, when we entered initial production quantities all equal to 100, Solver found the correct optimal solution, the same as in Figure 6.7. Was this just lucky? To check, we tried another initial solution, where the production quantities for shorts and jackets were 0, and the production quantities for shirts, pants, and skirts were all 500. In this case Solver found a solution where only skirts are produced. Of course, we know this is not optimal.

The moral is that the IF-function approach is not the way to go. Its success depends strongly on the initial values we enter in the changing cells, and this requires us to make very good guesses. The binary approach ensures that we get the correct solution. ∎

The following example is similar to the Great Threads example in that there is a fixed cost for any positive level of production of a given product. However, there is an additional requirement that if the company produces *any* of a given product, then (possibly for economies of scale) it must produce at least some minimal level such as 1000. This is a typical example of a problem with **either–or constraints**: The company's level of production must either be 0 or at least 1000. We see how the use of binary variables allows us to model the either–or constraints in a linear manner.

EXAMPLE 6.3 MANUFACTURING AT DORIAN AUTO

Dorian Auto is considering manufacturing three types of cars—compact, midsize, and large—and two types of minivans—midsize and large. The resources required and the profit contributions yielded by each type of vehicle are shown in Table 6.5. At present, 6500 tons of steel and 65,000 hours of labor are available. If any vehicles of a given type are produced, production of that type of vehicle will be economically feasible only if at least a minimal number of that type are produced. These minimal numbers are also listed in Table 6.5. Dorian wants to find a production schedule that maximizes its profit.

Table 6.5 Data for Dorian Car Example

Vehicle Type	Compact Car	Midsize Car	Large Car	Midsize Minivan	Large Minivan
Steel (tons)/unit	1.5	3	5	6	8
Labor hours/unit	30	25	40	45	55
Minimum production (if any)	1000	1000	1000	200	200
Profit contribution/unit	$2,000	$2,500	$3,000	$5,500	$7,000

Objective To use a binary model to determine which types of vehicles to produce (above their minimal requirements), and in what quantities, to maximize profit.

WHERE DO THE NUMBERS COME FROM?

This is basically a product mix problem, similar to the one in Example 3.2 of Chapter 3. Therefore, the same comments about inputs discussed there apply here as well. The only new inputs in this problem are the minimal production quantities. These might be policy decisions determined by Dorian—management sees no reason to produce midsize minivans unless it can produce at least 200 of them, say—but these policy decisions are undoubtedly based on costs. Presumably, the fixed costs of product design, manufacturing, and marketing are prohibitive unless a minimal number of any vehicle type is produced.

Solution

The variables and constraints for the Dorian model are listed in Table 6.6. It is clear that Dorian must decide how many of each type of vehicle to produce. However, it must also decide which types to produce at all. Of course, once it decides to produce small minivans, say, then it must produce at least 200 of them. The constraints include the usual resource availability constraints. In addition, there are lower and upper limits on the production quantities of any vehicle type. The lower limit is 0 or the minimal production quantity, depending on whether that vehicle type is produced. The upper limit is similar to the upper limit in the Great Thread's fixed-cost model in the previous example. That is, it is either 0, if the vehicle type is not produced at all, or it is some suitable large number. As in Example 6.2, this large number is the number of that type of vehicle that could be produced if *all* of the steel and labor hours were devoted to it alone.

Table 6.6   Variables and Constraints for Dorian Manufacturing Model

Input variables	Resources (steel and labor hours) consumed by each vehicle type, profit contribution for each vehicle type, minimal production quantity for each vehicle type, resource availabilities
Decision variables (changing cells)	Whether to produce any of each vehicle type (binary), units produced of each vehicle type
Objective (target cell)	Profit
Other calculated variables	Logical lower and upper bounds on production quantities, resources used
Constraints	Production quantities ≥ Logical lower bounds Production quantities ≤ Logical upper bounds Resources used ≤ Resources available

DEVELOPING THE SPREADSHEET MODEL

The example can be modeled with the following steps. (See Figure 6.13 and the file **EitherOrManufacturing.xls**.)

Figure 6.13   Dorian Auto Production Model

	A	B	C	D	E	F	G	H	I	J	K
1	Dorian Auto production model with either-or constraints										
2											
3	**Inputs**										
4	Vehicle type	Compact car	Midsize car	Large car	Midsize minivan	Large minivan		**Range names used:**			
5	Steel (tons)/unit	1.5	3	5	6	8		Logical_capacity	=Model!$B$19:$F$19		
6	Labor hours/unit	30	25	40	45	55		Minimum_production	=Model!$B$15:$F$15		
7	Minimum production (if any)	1000	1000	1000	200	200		Produce_at_least_minimum?	=Model!$B$13:$F$13		
8								Profit	=Model!$B$27		
9	Profit contribution/unit	$2,000	$2,500	$3,000	$5,500	$7,000		Resource_available	=Model!$D$23:$D$24		
10								Resource_used	=Model!$B$23:$B$24		
11	**Production plan and bounds on production quantities**							Units_produced	=Model!$B$17:$F$17		
12	Type of car	Compact car	Midsize car	Large car	Midsize minivan	Large minivan					
13	Produce at least minimum?	1	0	0	1	1					
14											
15	Minimum production	1000	0	0	200	200					
16		<=	<=	<=	<=	<=					
17	Units produced	1000	0	0	200	473					
18		<=	<=	<=	<=	<=					
19	Logical capacity	2167	0	0	1083	813					
20											
21	**Constraints on resources**										
22		Resource used		Resource available							
23	Steel	6482	<=	6500							
24	Labor hours	65000	<=	65000							
25											
26	**Objective to maximize**										
27	Profit	$6,409,091									

1 **Inputs.** Enter the input data in the shaded ranges.

2 **Number of vehicles produced.** Enter *any* trial values for the number of vehicles of each type produced in the Units_produced range.

3 **Binary variables for minimum production.** Enter *any* trial 0–1 values in the Produce_at_least_minimum? range. If a value in this range is 1, it means that Dorian must produce at least the minimum number of the corresponding vehicle type. A value of 0 in this range means that Dorian does not produce any of the corresponding vehicle type.

4 **Lower limits on production.** The either–or constraints are implemented with the binary variables in row 13 and the inequalities indicated in rows 15–19. To obtain the lower limits on production, enter the formula

=B7*B13

in cell B15 and copy it across row 15. This lower limit implies that if the binary variable in row 13 is 1, then Dorian must produce at least the minimum number of that vehicle type. However, if the binary variable is 0, then the lower bound in row 15 is 0 and is essentially redundant—it just says that production must be nonnegative.

5 **Upper limits on production.** To obtain upper limits on production, enter the formula

B13*MIN($D$23/B5,$D$24/B6)

in cell B19 and copy it across row 19. Note that the MIN term in this formula is the maximum number of compact cars Dorian could make if it devoted *all* of its resources to compact cars. (A similar upper limit was used in the Great Threads model in Example 6.2.) If the binary variable in row 13 is 1, this upper limit is essentially redundant—production can never be greater than this in any case. But if the binary variable is 0, then this upper limit is 0, which prevents Dorian from making any vehicles of this type.

To summarize the lower and upper limits, if the binary variable is 1, the production limits become

Minimum production required ≤ Production ≤ Maximum production possible

On the other hand, if the binary variable is 0, the limits become

0 ≤ Production ≤ 0

The trick is in getting the constraints to allow what we want to allow, but to disallow "illegal" solutions.

Of course, these latter inequalities imply that production is 0. Exactly one of these cases must hold for each car type, so they successfully implement the either–or constraints. These lower and upper limits are the key to the model.

6 **Steel and labor used.** Calculate the tons of steel and number of labor hours used in the Resources_used range by entering the formula

=SUMPRODUCT(B5:F5,Units_produced)

in cell B23 and copying it to cell B24.

7 **Profit.** Calculate the profit in cell B27 with the formula

=SUMPRODUCT(B9:F9,Units_produced)

USING SOLVER

The completed Solver dialog box should look like the one in Figure 6.14. The objective is to maximize profit, the changing cells are the production quantities and the binary variables, and the constraints specify the production limits and resource availabilities. Note that we do not constrain the production quantities to be integers, although you could try doing so. Extra integer constraints only make the model more difficult to optimize, and if the optimal number of some vehicle type turns out to be 472.7, say, it is probably all right to round this up to 473.

Figure 6.14
Solver Dialog Box for Dorian Production Model

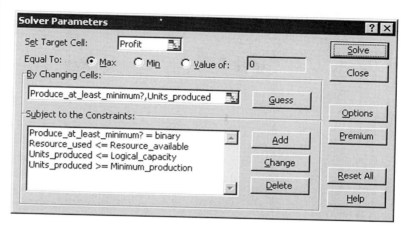

Discussion of the Solution

The optimal solution in Figure 6.13 indicates, by the 0 values in row 13, that Dorian should not produce any midsize or large cars. The number of 1's in this row, however, indicates that Dorian *must* produce at least the minimum number, 1000, of compact cars and the minimum number, 200, of each type of minivan. More specifically, the company should produce just enough compact cars and midsize minivans to meet the minimal production quantities. These vehicle types are relatively profitable, given the resources they use. However, they are evidently not as profitable as large minivans. The company should make as many of these as it can, after producing the compact cars and midsize minivans, until it runs out of labor hours.

This solution is certainly not intuitive. (For example, if large minivans are so profitable, why doesn't the company produce all large minivans and nothing else? Do you see why?) Also, this solution appears to be very sensitive to the inputs. Although we will not present any formal sensitivity analyses with SolverTable, we urge you to try different values for the minimal production quantities, the unit profit contributions, and/or the resource availabilities. We found that even small changes in these can yield a quite different optimal production policy. For example, you can check that if the availability of steel decreases to 600 tons, only compact cars and midsize minivans should be produced, both above their minimal levels, and *no* large minivans should be produced! ■

ADDITIONAL APPLICATIONS

Locating Distribution Centers

When Dow Consumer Products (a manufacturer of food-care products) acquired the Texize home-care product lines of Morton Thiokol in 1985 to form DowBrands, Inc., the distribution channels of the two organizations remained, for the most part, separate. Each had its own district and regional distribution centers for storing and then shipping products to the customer regions. This led to possible inefficiencies in a business where keeping logistics costs low is the key to survival. Robinson et al. (1993), acting as consultants for DowBrands, modeled the problem as a fixed-cost network problem—which distribution centers to keep open and which routes to use to satisfy which customers with which products. The study was highly successful and convinced DowBrands to close a significant number of distribution centers to reduce costs.

Locating Out-of-State Audit Offices

To increase the collection of state taxes from companies doing business in Texas, the state's auditors must often travel out of state. To reduce the cost associated with these trips, the state of Texas decided to locate auditors at several locations throughout the country. Fitzsimmons and Allen (1983) used a fixed-cost model to help the state of Texas locate out-of-state audit offices. ■

PROBLEMS

Skill-Building Problems

11. How difficult is it to expand the Great Threads model to accommodate another type of clothing? Answer by assuming that the company can also produce sweatshirts. The rental cost for sweatshirt equipment is $1100, the variable cost per unit and the selling price are $15 and $45, respectively, and each sweatshirt requires 1 labor hour and 3.5 square yards of cloth.

12. Referring to the previous problem, if it is optimal for the company to produce sweatshirts, use SolverTable to see how much larger the fixed cost of sweatshirt machinery would have to be before the company would *not* produce any sweatshirts. However, if the solution to the previous problem calls for no sweatshirts to be produced, use SolverTable to see how much lower the fixed cost of sweatshirt machinery would have to be before the company would start producing sweatshirts.

13. In the Great Threads model, we didn't constrain the production quantities in row 16 to be integers, arguing that any fractional values could be safely rounded to integers. See whether this is true. Constrain these quantities to be integers and then run Solver. Are the optimal integer values the same as the rounded fractional values in Figure 6.7?

14. In the optimal solution to the Great Threads model, the labor hour and cloth constraints are both binding—the company is using all it has.
  a. Use SolverTable to see what happens to the optimal solution when the amount of available cloth increases from its current value. (You can choose the range of input values to use.) Capture all of the changing cells, the labor hours and cloth used, and the profit as outputs in the table. The real issue here is whether the company can profitably use more cloth when it is already constrained by labor hours.
  b. Repeat part **a**, but reverse the roles of labor hours and cloth. That is, use the available labor hours as the input for SolverTable.

15. In the optimal solution to the Great Threads model, no pants are produced. Suppose Great Threads has an order for 300 pairs of pants that *must* be produced. Modify the model appropriately and use Solver to find the new optimal solution. (Is it enough to put a lower bound of 300 on the production quantity in cell D16? Will this automatically force the binary value in cell C14 to be 1? Explain.) How much profit does the company lose because of having to produce pants?

16. In the Dorian production model, the optimal solution calls for the minimum number of compact cars and midsize minivans to be produced, but for *more* than the minimum number of large minivans to be produced. If the large minivans are evidently that profitable, why doesn't Dorian discontinue making compact cars and midsize minivans and instead produce even more large minivans?

17. The optimal solution to the Dorian production model appears to be quite sensitive to the model inputs. For each of the following inputs, create a one-way SolverTable that captures all changing cells and the target cell as outputs. You can choose the ranges of these inputs to make the results "interesting." Comment on your results.
  a. The steel available
  b. The labor hours available
  c. The unit profit contribution of large minivans
  d. The minimum production level (currently 200) of large minivans
  e. The minimum production level (currently 1000) of compact cars

18. As the Dorian production model is currently stated, there is a minimum production level for each vehicle type; if this type is produced at all, its production quantity must be at least this minimum. Suppose that for large minivans, there is also a *maximum* production level of 400. If large minivans are produced, the production level must be from 200 to 400. Modify the model as necessary and use Solver to find the new optimal solution. How do you know that the current optimal solution will not be optimal for the modified model?

19. If Solver could handle IF functions correctly, how would you use them in the Dorian production example to create an arguably more "natural" model—without binary variables? Run Solver on your modified model. Do you get the correct solution? (*Note:* You'll have to uncheck the Assume Linear Model box.)

Skill-Extending Problems

20. In the Great Threads model, we found an upper bound on production of any clothing type by calculating the amount that could be produced if *all* of the resources were devoted to this clothing type.
   a. What if we instead used a very large value such as 1,000,000 for this upper bound? Try it and see whether you get the same optimal solution.
   b. Explain why *any* such upper bound is required. Exactly what role does it play in the model, as we have formulated it?

21. In the file **FixedCostMfg_IF.xls**, we illustrated one way to model the Great Threads problem with IF functions, and we saw that this approach didn't work. Try a slightly different approach here. Eliminate the binary variables in row 14 altogether, and eliminate the upper bounds in row 18 and the corresponding upper bound constraints in the Solver dialog box. (The only constraints will now be the resource availability constraints.) However, use IF functions to calculate the total fixed cost of renting equipment, so that if the amount of any clothing type is positive, then its fixed cost will be added to the total fixed cost. Is Solver able to handle this model? Does it depend on the initial values in the changing cells? (Don't forget to uncheck the Assume Linear Model box.)

22. In the Dorian production model, suppose that the production quantity of compact cars must either be less than or equal to 100 (a small batch) or greater than or equal to 1000 (a large batch). The same statements hold for the other vehicle types as well, except that the small and large batch limits for both sizes of minivans are 50 and 200. Modify the model appropriately and use Solver to find the optimal solution.

23. Suppose in the Dorian production model that there are no minimum production limits on the individual vehicle types. However, there are minimum production limits on *all* cars and on *all* minivans. Specifically, if Dorian produces *any* cars, regardless of size, it must produce at least 1500 cars total. Similarly, if the company produces *any* minivans, it must produce at least 1000 minivans total. Modify the model appropriately and use Solver to find the optimal solution.

6.5 SET-COVERING AND LOCATION-ASSIGNMENT MODELS

Many companies have geographically dispersed customers that they must service in some way. To do this, they create service center facilities at selected locations and then assign each customer to one of the service centers. Various costs are incurred, including (1) fixed costs of locating service centers in particular locations, (2) operating costs, depending on the service centers' locations, and (3) transportation costs, depending on the distances between customers and their assigned service centers. In this section we illustrate several examples of this basic problem.

We first examine a particular type of location model called a **set-covering** model. In a set-covering model, each member of a given set (set 1) must be "covered" by an acceptable member of another set (set 2). The objective in a set-covering problem is to minimize the number of members in set 2 that are needed to cover all of the members in set 1. For example, set 1 might consist of all cities in a county and set 2 might consist of the cities where a fire station is located. A fire station "covers" a city if the fire station is located, say, within 10 minutes of the city. The goal is to minimize the number of fire stations needed to cover all cities. Set-covering models have been applied to areas as diverse as airline crew scheduling, truck dispatching, political redistricting, and capital investment. The following example presents a typical set-covering model.

EXAMPLE | **6.4 HUB LOCATION AT WESTERN AIRLINES**

Western Airlines has decided that it wants to design a "hub" system in the United States. Each hub is used for connecting flights to and from cities within 1000 miles of the hub. Western runs flights among the following cities: Atlanta, Boston, Chicago,

Denver, Houston, Los Angeles, New Orleans, New York, Pittsburgh, Salt Lake City, San Francisco, and Seattle. The company wants to determine the smallest number of hubs it will need to cover all of these cities, where a city is "covered" if it is within 1000 miles of at least one hub. Table 6.7 lists which cities are within 1000 miles of other cities.

Table 6.7   Data for Western Set-Covering Example

	Cities Within 1000 Miles
Atlanta (AT)	AT, CH, HO, NO, NY, PI
Boston (BO)	BO, NY, PI
Chicago (CH)	AT, CH, NY, NO, PI
Denver (DE)	DE, SL
Houston (HO)	AT, HO, NO
Los Angeles (LA)	LA, SL, SF
New Orleans (NO)	AT, CH, HO, NO
New York (NY)	AT, BO, CH, NY, PI
Pittsburgh (PI)	AT, BO, CH, NY, PI
Salt Lake City (SL)	DE, LA, SL, SF, SE
San Francisco (SF)	LA, SL, SF, SE
Seattle (SE)	SL, SF, SE

Objective   To develop a binary model to find the minimum number of hub locations that can cover all cities.

WHERE DO THE NUMBERS COME FROM?

Western has evidently made a policy decision that its hubs will cover only cities within a 1000-mile radius. Then the cities covered by any hub location can be found from a map. (In a later sensitivity analysis, we will explore how the solution changes when we allow the coverage distance to vary.)

Solution

The variables and constraints for this set-covering model are listed in Table 6.8. The model is straightforward. We use a binary variable for each city to indicate whether a hub is located there. Then we calculate the number of hubs that cover each city and require it to be at least 1. There are no monetary costs in this version of the problem. We simply minimize the number of hubs.

Table 6.8   Variables and Constraints for Set-Covering Model

Input variables	Cities within 1000 miles of one another
Decision variables (changing cells)	Locations of hubs (binary)
Objective (target cell)	Number of hubs
Other calculated variables	Number of hubs covering each city
Constraints	Number of hubs covering a city $\geq$ 1

The spreadsheet model for Western is shown in Figure 6.15. (See the file **LocatingHubs1.xls**.) It can be developed as follows.

Figure 6.15 Airline Hub Set-Covering Model

	A	B	C	D	E	F	G	H	I	J	K	L	M	N	O	P	Q
1	Western Airlines hub location model																
2																	
3	Input data: which cities are covered by which potential hubs																
4		Potential hub													Range names used:		
5	City	AT	BO	CH	DE	HO	LA	NO	NY	PI	SL	SF	SE		Hubs_covered_by	=Model!$B$25:$B$36	
6	AT	1	0	1	0	1	0	1	1	1	0	0	0		Total_hubs	=Model!$B$39	
7	BO	0	1	0	0	0	0	0	1	1	0	0	0		Used_as_hub?	=Model!$B$21:$M$21	
8	CH	1	0	1	0	0	0	1	1	1	0	0	0				
9	DE	0	0	0	1	0	0	0	0	0	1	0	0				
10	HO	1	0	0	0	1	0	0	0	0	1	0	0				
11	LA	0	0	0	0	0	1	0	0	0	0	1	0				
12	NO	1	0	1	0	1	0	1	0	0	0	1	0				
13	NY	1	1	1	0	0	0	1	0	1	0	0	0				
14	PI	1	1	1	0	0	0	0	1	1	0	0	0				
15	SL	0	0	0	1	0	1	0	0	1	1	0	0				
16	SF	0	0	0	0	0	1	0	0	0	1	1	1				
17	SE	0	0	0	0	0	0	0	0	0	1	1	1				
18																	
19	Decisions: which cities to use as hubs																
20			AT	BO	CH	DE	HO	LA	NO	NY	PI	SL	SF	SE			
21	Used as hub?	0	0	0	0	1	0	0	1	0	1	0	0				
22																	
23	Constraints that each city must be covered by at least one hub																
24	City	Hubs covered by		Required													
25	AT	2	>=	1													
26	BO	1	>=	1													
27	CH	1	>=	1													
28	DE	1	>=	1													
29	HO	1	>=	1													
30	LA	1	>=	1													
31	NO	1	>=	1													
32	NY	1	>=	1													
33	PI	1	>=	1													
34	SL	1	>=	1													
35	SF	1	>=	1													
36	SE	1	>=	1													
37																	
38	Objective to minimize																
39	Total hubs	3															

Note that there are multiple optimal solutions to this model, all of which require a total of 3 hubs You might get a different solution from the one shown here.

❶ Inputs. Enter the information from Table 6.7 in the shaded range. A 1 in a cell indicates that the column city covers the row city, whereas a 0 indicates that the column city does not cover the row city. For example, the three 1's in row 7 indicate that Boston, New York, and Pittsburgh are the only cities within 1000 miles of Boston.

❷ 0–1 values for hub locations. Enter *any* trial values of 0's or 1's in the Used_as_hub? range to indicate which cities are used as hubs. These are the changing cells.

❸ Cities covered by hubs. We now determine the number of hubs that cover each city. Specifically, calculate the total number of hubs within 1000 miles of Atlanta in cell B25 with the formula

=SUMPRODUCT(B6:M6,Used_as_hub?)

A SUMPRODUCT of two 0–1 ranges just finds the number of "matches" of 1's in the two ranges. Here it calculates the number of hubs that cover a given city.

For any 0–1 values in the changing-cells range, this formula "picks up" the number of hubs that cover Atlanta. Then copy this to the rest of the Hubs_covered_by range. Note that a value in the Hubs_covered_by range can be 2 or greater. This indicates that a city is within 1000 miles of multiple hubs.

❹ Number of hubs. Calculate the total number of hubs used in cell B39 with the formula

=SUM(Used_as_hub?)

The Solver dialog box should appear as in Figure 6.16. We minimize the total number of hubs, subject to covering each city by at least one hub and ensuring that the changing cells are binary. As usual, the Assume Linear Model option should be checked.

Figure 6.16

Solver Dialog Box for Set-Covering Model

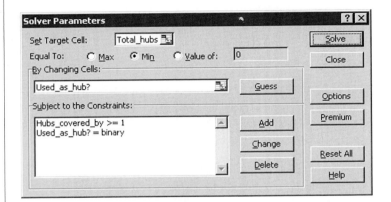

Discussion of the Solution

Figure 6.17 is a graphical representation of the optimal solution, where the double ovals indicate hub locations and the large circles indicate ranges covered by the hubs. (These large circles are not drawn to scale. In reality, they should be circles of radius 1000 miles centered at the hubs.) Three hubs—in Houston, New York, and Salt Lake City—are needed.[6] Would you have guessed this? The Houston hub covers Houston, Atlanta, and New Orleans. The New York hub covers Atlanta, Pittsburgh, Boston, New York, and Chicago. The Salt Lake City hub covers Denver, Los Angeles, Salt Lake City, San Francisco, and Seattle. Note that Atlanta is the only city covered by two hubs; it can be serviced by New York or Houston.

Figure 6.17

Graphical Solution to Set-Covering Model

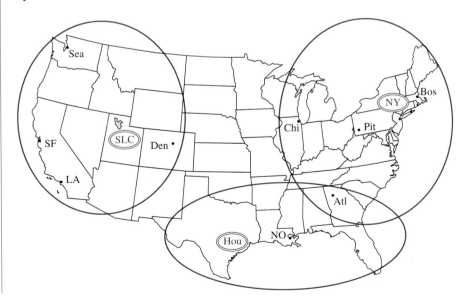

---

[6]There are multiple optimal solutions for this model, all requiring three hubs, so you might obtain a different solution from ours.

Sensitivity Analysis

An interesting sensitivity analysis for Western's problem is to see how the solution is affected by the mile limit. Currently, a hub can service all cities within 1000 miles. What if the limit were 800 or 1200 miles, say? To answer this question, we must first collect data on actual distances among all of the cities. Once we have a matrix of these distances, we can build the 0–1 matrix, corresponding to the range B6:M17 in Figure 6.15, with IF functions. The modified model appears in Figure 6.18. (See the file **LocatingHubs2.xls**.) The typical formula in B24 is **=IF(B8<=$B$4,1,0)**, which is then copied to the rest of the

---

Figure 6.18 Sensitivity to Mile Limit

	A	B	C	D	E	F	G	H	I	J	K	L	M
1	Western Airlines hub location model with distances												
2													
3	Input data												
4	Mile limit	1000											
5													
6	Distance from each city to each other city												
7		AT	BO	CH	DE	HO	LA	NO	NY	PI	SL	SF	SE
8	AT	0	1037	674	1398	789	2182	479	841	687	1878	2496	2618
9	BO	1037	0	1005	1949	1804	2979	1507	222	574	2343	3095	2976
10	CH	674	1005	0	1008	1067	2054	912	802	452	1390	2142	2013
11	DE	1398	1949	1008	0	1019	1059	1273	1771	1411	504	1235	1307
12	HO	789	1804	1067	1019	0	1538	356	1608	1313	1438	1912	2274
13	LA	2182	2979	2054	1059	1538	0	1883	2786	2426	715	379	1131
14	NO	479	1507	912	1273	356	1883	0	1311	1070	1738	2249	2574
15	NY	841	222	802	1771	1608	2786	1311	0	368	2182	2934	2815
16	PI	687	574	452	1411	1313	2426	1070	368	0	1826	2578	2465
17	SL	1878	2343	1390	504	1438	715	1738	2182	1826	0	752	836
18	SF	2496	3095	2142	1235	1912	379	2249	2934	2578	752	0	808
19	SE	2618	2976	2013	1307	2274	1131	2574	2815	2465	836	808	0
20													
21	Which cities are covered by which potential hubs with this mile limit												
22		Potential hub											
23	City	AT	BO	CH	DE	HO	LA	NO	NY	PI	SL	SF	SE
24	AT	1	0	1	0	1	0	1	1	1	0	0	0
25	BO	0	1	0	0	0	0	0	1	1	0	0	0
26	CH	1	0	1	0	0	0	1	1	1	0	0	0
27	DE	0	0	0	1	0	0	0	0	0	1	0	0
28	HO	1	0	0	0	1	0	1	0	0	0	0	0
29	LA	0	0	0	0	0	1	0	0	0	1	1	0
30	NO	1	0	1	0	1	0	1	0	0	0	0	0
31	NY	1	1	1	0	0	0	1	1	1	0	0	0
32	PI	1	1	1	0	0	0	1	1	1	0	0	0
33	SL	0	0	0	1	0	1	0	0	0	1	1	1
34	SF	0	0	0	1	0	1	0	0	0	1	1	1
35	SE	0	0	0	0	0	1	0	0	0	1	1	1
36													
37	Decisions: which cities to use as hubs												
38		AT	BO	CH	DE	HO	LA	NO	NY	PI	SL	SF	SE
39	Used as hub?	0	0	0	0	1	0	0	1	0	1	0	0
40													
41	Constraints that each city must be covered by at least one hub												
42	City	Hubs covered by		Required									
43	AT	2	>=	1									
44	BO	1	>=	1									
45	CH	1	>=	1									
46	DE	1	>=	1									
47	HO	1	>=	1									
48	LA	1	>=	1									
49	NO	1	>=	1									
50	NY	1	>=	1									
51	PI	1	>=	1									
52	SL	1	>=	1									
53	SF	1	>=	1									
54	SE	1	>=	1									
55													
56	Objective to minimize												
57	Total hubs	3											

Note: There are multiple optimal solutions to these problems, so don't be surprised if you don't get exactly the same hub locations as shown here.

	A	B	C	D	E	F	G	H	I	J	K	L	M	N
59	Sensitivity of total hubs and their locations to the mile limit													
60	Mile limit	AT	BO	CH	DE	HO	LA	NO	NY	PI	SL	SF	SE	Total
61		$B$39	$C$39	$D$39	$E$39	$F$39	$G$39	$H$39	$I$39	$J$39	$K$39	$L$39	$M$39	$B$57
62	800	1	1	0	0	0	0	0	0	0	1	0	1	4
63	900	0	0	0	1	0	1	0	1	0	1	0	0	4
64	1000	0	1	0	0	0	1	0	0	1	0	0	3
65	1100	0	0	1	0	0	0	0	0	0	1	0	2
66	1200	0	0	1	0	0	0	0	0	0	0	1	2

Range names used:

Hubs_covered_by	=Model!$B$43:$B$54
Total_hubs	=Model!$B$57
Used_as_hub?	=Model!$B$39:$M$39

B24:M35 range.[7] We then run SolverTable, selecting cell B4 as the single input cell, letting it vary from 800 to 1200 in increments of 100, and keeping track of where the hubs are located and the number of hubs. The SolverTable results at the bottom show the effect of the mile limit. When this limit is lowered to 800 miles, 4 hubs are required, but when it is increased to 1100 or 1200, only 2 hubs are required. By the way, the solution shown for the 1000-mile limit is different from the previous solution in Figure 6.15, but it still requires 3 hubs. ■

Station Staffing at Pan Am

Like many other airlines, Pan Am has used management science to determine optimal staffing levels for its support staff (for ticket counters, baggage loading and unloading, mechanical maintenance, and so on). Schindler and Semmel (1993) describe how Pan Am used a set-covering model to determine flexible shifts of full-time and part-time personnel in the United States, Central and South America, and Europe. The model allowed the company to reduce its deployment of staff by up to 11% in work-hour requirements and suggested how existing staff could be used more efficiently. ■

The following example is similar to a set-covering model, but it also has an assignment component.

EXAMPLE | **6.5 LOCATING AND ASSIGNING SERVICE CENTERS AT UNITED COPIERS**

United Copiers sells copy machines to customers in 11 cities throughout the country. It also services these machines as needed. The company wants to set up service centers in three of these cities. Once United Copiers chooses the location of the service centers, it must assign customers in each city to one of the service centers. For example, if it decides to locate a service center in New York and then assigns its Boston customers to the New York service center, a service representative from New York will travel from Boston when services there are required. The distances (in miles) between the cities are listed in Table 6.9. The estimated annual numbers of trips to the various customers are listed in Table 6.10. What should United Copiers do to minimize the total annual distance traveled by its service representatives?

[7]We have warned you about using IF functions in Solver models. However, the current use affects only the *inputs* to the problem, not quantities that depend on the changing cells. Therefore, it causes no problems.

Table 6.9 Distances for Service Center Example

	Boston	Chicago	Dallas	Denver	LA	Miami	NY	Phoenix	Pittsburgh	SF	Seattle
Boston	0	983	1815	1991	3036	1539	213	2664	792	2385	2612
Chicago	983	0	1205	1050	2112	1390	840	1729	457	2212	2052
Dallas	1815	1205	0	801	1425	1332	1604	1027	1237	1765	2404
Denver	1991	1050	801	0	1174	2041	1780	836	1411	1765	2404
LA	3036	2112	1425	1174	0	2757	2825	398	2456	403	1373
Miami	1539	1390	1332	2041	2757	0	1258	2359	1250	3097	1909
NY	213	840	1604	1780	2825	1258	0	2442	386	3036	3389
Phoenix	2664	1729	1027	836	398	2359	2442	0	2073	800	2900
Pittsburgh	792	457	1237	1411	2456	1250	386	2073	0	2653	1482
SF	2385	2212	1765	1765	403	3097	3036	800	2653	0	2517
Seattle	2612	2052	2404	1373	1909	3389	2900	1482	2517	817	0

Table 6.10 Estimated Numbers of Annual Trips to Customers

Boston	Chicago	Dallas	Denver	LA	Miami	NY	Phoenix	Pittsburgh	SF	Seattle
885	760	1124	708	1224	1152	1560	1222	856	1443	612

Objective   To develop a linear model, using binary variables, that determines the locations of service centers, and then assigns customers to these service centers, to minimize total annual distance traveled.

WHERE DO THE NUMBERS COME FROM?

The distances come directly from a map. The numbers of annual trips could be estimated in several ways. For example, the company could multiply the number of customers in each city by the estimated number of trips required per year per customer. However, this might overestimate the total number of trips because a single trip could service multiple customers. More likely, the company would estimate the numbers of trips in Table 6.10 directly from historical records. Finally, the number of service centers to use, in this case three, is probably a policy decision based on cost. However, this number is an obvious candidate for sensitivity analysis.

Solution

If we already knew where the service centers were located, then this would just be an assignment problem of the type we discussed in the previous chapter.

The variables and constraints for this location-assignment model are listed in Table 6.11 (page 274). The keys to this model are the binary decision variables and the logical constraints. For each city, we use a binary variable to indicate whether a service center is located there. Also, for each pair of cities, we use a binary variable to indicate whether a service center in the first city is assigned to the customer in the second city. Using these binary variables, the first two constraints in the table are straightforward: Three cities should include service centers, and each city should be assigned to exactly one service center. The last constraint in the table is less obvious. It states that a customer can be assigned to a service center location only if this location has a service center. For example, if no service center is located in Pittsburgh (its binary variable is 0), then no customers can be assigned to a service center in Pittsburgh.

Table 6.11 Variables and Constraints for Service Center Model

Input variables	Distances between cities, annual number of trips to each city, number of service centers to locate
Decision variables (changing cells)	Whether each city includes a service center (binary), whether a city is assigned to a particular service center (binary)
Objective (target cell)	Total distance traveled annually
Other calculated variables	Number of service center locations chosen, number of service centers assigned to each customer, total distance traveled to each customer
Constraints	Number of service center locations chosen = 3 Number of service centers assigned to each customer = 1 Binary variable for assignment ≤ Binary variable for service center

DEVELOPING THE SPREADSHEET MODEL

The spreadsheet can be developed with the following steps. (See Figure 6.19 and the file **LocatingServiceCenters1.xls**.)

Figure 6.19 Spreadsheet Model for Service Center Problem

	A	B	C	D	E	F	G	H	I	J	K	L	M	N	O	P	Q
1	Locating service centers and assigning service centers to customers																
2														Range names used:			
3	Distances between cities													Allowed	=Model!$O$19		
4		Boston	Chicago	Dallas	Denver	Los Angeles	Miami	New York	Phoenix	Pittsburgh	San Francisc o	Seattle		Assignments	=Model!$B$23:$L$33		
5	Boston	0	983	1815	1991	3036	1539	213	2664	792	2385	2612		Included?	=Model!$B$19:$L$19		
6	Chicago	983	0	1205	1050	2112	1390	840	1729	457	2212	2052		Included?_copies	=Model!$B$35:$L$45		
7	Dallas	1815	1205	0	801	1425	1332	1604	1027	1237	1765	2404		Locations_assigned_to	=Model!$M$23:$M$33		
8	Denver	1991	1050	801	0	1174	2041	1780	836	1411	1765	1373		Total_distance	=Model!$B$62		
9	Los Angeles	3036	2112	1425	1174	0	2757	2825	398	2456	403	1909		Total_service_centers	=Model!$M$19		
10	Miami	1539	1390	1332	2041	2757	0	1258	2359	1250	3097	3389					
11	New York	213	840	1604	1780	2825	1258	0	2442	386	3036	2900					
12	Phoenix	2664	1729	1027	836	398	2359	2442	0	2073	800	1482					
13	Pittsburgh	792	457	1237	1411	2456	1250	386	2073	0	2653	2517					
14	San Francisco	2385	2212	1765	1765	403	3097	3036	800	2653	0	817					
15	Seattle	2612	2052	2404	1373	1909	3389	2900	1482	2517	817	0					
16																	
17	Locations of service centers																
18		Boston	Chicago	Dallas	Denver	Los Angeles	Miami	New York	Phoenix	Pittsburgh	San Francisc o	Seattle	Total service centers			Allowed	
19	Included?	0	0	1	0	0	1	0	0	1	0		3		<=	3	
20																	
21	Assignments (1 if customers along side are serviced by service center along top, 0 otherwise																
22		Boston	Chicago	Dallas	Denver	Los Angeles	Miami	New York	Phoenix	Pittsburgh	San Francisc o	Seattle	Locations assigned to			Required	
23	Boston	0	0	0	0	0	0	1	0	0	0	0	1	=	1		
24	Chicago	0	0	0	0	0	0	1	0	0	0	0	1	=	1		
25	Dallas	0	0	1	0	0	0	0	0	0	0	0	1	=	1		
26	Denver	0	0	1	0	0	0	0	0	0	0	0	1	=	1		
27	Los Angeles	0	0	0	0	0	0	0	0	0	1	0	1	=	1		
28	Miami	0	0	0	0	0	1	0	0	0	0	0	1	=	1		
29	New York	0	0	0	0	0	0	1	0	0	0	0	1	=	1		
30	Phoenix	0	0	0	0	0	0	0	0	0	1	0	1	=	1		
31	Pittsburgh	0	0	0	0	0	0	1	0	0	0	0	1	=	1		
32	San Francisco	0	0	0	0	0	0	0	0	0	1	0	1	=	1		
33	Seattle	0	0	0	0	0	0	0	0	0	1	0	1	=	1		
34		<=	<=	<=	<=	<=	<=	<=	<=	<=	<=	<=					
35	Copies of "Included?" row	0	0	1	0	0	1	0	0	1	0			The logical constraint			
36		0	0	1	0	0	1	0	0	1	0			is that a customer			
37		0	0	1	0	0	1	0	0	1	0			cannot be assigned			
38		0	0	1	0	0	1	0	0	1	0			to a service center			
39		0	0	1	0	0	1	0	0	1	0			unless that service			
40		0	0	1	0	0	1	0	0	1	0			center exists.			
41		0	0	1	0	0	1	0	0	1	0						
42		0	0	1	0	0	1	0	0	1	0						
43		0	0	1	0	0	1	0	0	1	0						
44		0	0	1	0	0	1	0	0	1	0						
45		0	0	1	0	0	1	0	0	1	0						
46																	
47	Numbers of annual trips to customers, and total distances (1000s of miles) traveled annually to customers																
48		Annual trips	Total distance														
49	Boston	885	189														
50	Chicago	760	638														
51	Dallas	1124	0														
52	Denver	708	567														
53	Los Angeles	1224	493		These distances are 0 because the												
54	Miami	1152	1449		optimal solution locates service												
55	New York	1560	0		centers in these cities.												
56	Phoenix	1222	978														
57	Pittsburgh	856	330														
58	San Francisco	1443	0														
59	Seattle	612	500														
60																	
61	Objective to minimize (1000s of miles)																
62	Total distance	5,145															

1 Inputs. Enter the given data in the shaded ranges.

2 Service center location decisions. Enter *any* trial 0–1 values in the Included? range. For example, a 1 in cell D19 means that there is a service center located in Dallas, whereas a 0 in cell E19 means that there is no service center located in Denver.

3 **Assignment decisions.** Enter *any* 0–1 trial values In the Assignments range. For example, a 1 in cell D26 means that Denver is serviced by the center in Dallas, whereas a 0 in cell D27 means that Los Angeles is not serviced by the center in Dallas. At this point, you might ask what these mean if there *is* no service center in Dallas. This is where the logical constraints are necessary, as explained subsequently. For now, we simply state that if there is a 1 in some column of the Assignments range, then the corresponding city *will* eventually include a service center.

4 **Number of service centers.** Calculate the number of service centers with the formula

=SUM(Included?)

in cell M19. This just sums 0's and 1's, so it equals the number of 1's.

5 **Number of service centers assigned to each city.** Calculate the number of service centers assigned to each city with row sums in the Number_assigned_to range in column M. That is, enter the formula

=SUM(B23:L23)

in cell M23 and copy it to down to cell M33. We will eventually constrain these row sums to 1 to ensure that exactly one service center is assigned to each city.

6 **Total annual distances.** Calculate the total annual distance traveled (in 1000s of miles) to each city by entering the formula

=B49*SUMPRODUCT(B5:L5,B23:L23)/1000

in cell C49 for Boston and copying it down to cell C59 for the other cities. Note that this SUMPRODUCT includes a row of distances from Boston and a row of assignments to customers in Boston. We know, however, that this row of assignments will eventually include only a *single* 1—only a single service center will be assigned to customers in Boston. Therefore, this SUMPRODUCT will be the distance between Boston and the service center assigned to Boston. Then we multiply it by the annual trips to Boston (cell B49) to obtain the total annual distance traveled to Boston, and we divide by 1000 to convert to thousands of miles.

7 **Copies of 0–1 variables.** We need to ensure that only existing service locations can be assigned to customers. Essentially, *each* row of the Assignments range must be less than or equal to the Included? range. For example, if there is a 0 for Denver in the Included? range, there cannot be a 1 in any cell of the Denver column of the Assignments range. The best way to implement this constraint is to make 11 copies of the Included? range right below the Assignments range. To do this, enter the formula

=B$19

in cell B35 and copy it to the range B35:L45. We will eventually constrain the Assignment range to be less than or equal to this "copy" range.

8 **Total annual distance traveled.** Calculate the total distance traveled annually (in 1000s of miles) in cell B62 with the formula

=SUM(C49:C59)

USING SOLVER

The completed Solver dialog box is shown in Figure 6.20 (page 276). We also check the Assume Linear Model option and set the Solver tolerance to 0%. (There is no need to check the Assume Non-Negative option because all changing cells are binary and hence

---

Always be careful to convert to appropriate units of measurement, if necessary. A factor such as 100 or 1000 in a formula is often evidence of a measurement conversion.

nonnegative.) It is important to understand the first constraint in the list: Assignments <= Included?_copies. Because all cells in these ranges are binary, the constraint effectively says that if an Assignment cell is 1, then the corresponding Included?_copies cell must also be 1. For example, if an assignment is made of the Denver customer to the Dallas service center, so that cell D26 contains 1, then the copy of the Dallas service center binary in cell D38 must be 1. But this means that the original Dallas service center binary in cell D19 must be 1, which means we have to locate a service center in Dallas. This is exactly the behavior we want the model to enforce.

Figure 6.20

Solver Dialog Box for Service Center Model

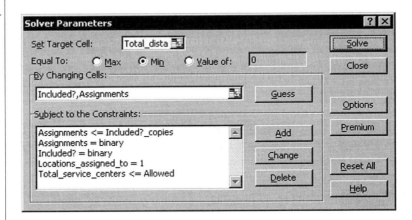

Discussion of the Solution

The optimal solution in Figure 6.19 indicates that United Copiers should locate service centers in Dallas, New York, and San Francisco. Of course, each of these will service the customers in its own city. In addition, the Dallas center will service customers in Denver, the New York center will service customers in Boston, Chicago, Miami, and Pittsburgh, and the San Francisco center will service customers in Los Angeles, Phoenix, and Seattle. The total distance traveled annually is slightly over 5.1 million miles.

Solver Message

When we solved this model, we obtained the Solver message in Figure 6.21. This message can easily occur with reasonably large IP models. It means that the Solver algorithm has already done a lot of calculations but is still not finished. Our recommendation is to click on the Continue button. Alternatively, you can change Solver's default maximum number of iterations, under its Options dialog box, from 100 to a larger number such as 500 before you run Solver.

Figure 6.21

Maximum Iteration Limit Message from Solver

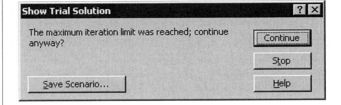

Sensitivity Analysis

A natural sensitivity analysis is to see how the service center locations and the total annual distance change as we vary the number of required service centers. This is straightforward with SolverTable. We use cell O19 as the single input cell, vary it from 1 to 11 in increments of 1, and keep track of the binary values in row 19 and the target cell. The results are shown in Figure 6.22. As we see, service centers are typically located in Dallas, New York, and San Francisco, but not always. In particular, if only one service center is allowed, it should be located in Dallas, but if two service centers are allowed, they should be located in New York and Phoenix. Of course, as we create more service centers, less traveling is required. At the extreme, if there a service center in every city, the required traveling distance is 0!

Figure 6.22 Sensitivity to Number of Service Centers Allowed

	A	B	C	D	E	F	G	H	I	J	K	L	M
64	Sensitivity of location binaries and total distance to number of service center locations												
65		$B$19	$C$19	$D$19	$E$19	$F$19	$G$19	$H$19	$I$19	$J$19	$K$19	$L$19	$B$62
66	1	0	0	1	0	0	0	0	0	0	0	0	15,202
67	2	0	0	0	0	0	0	1	1	0	0	0	6,901
68	3	0	0	1	0	0	0	1	1	0	0	0	5,145
69	4	0	0	1	0	0	0	1	0	0	1	0	3,695
70	5	0	0	0	0	1	1	1	0	0	1	0	2,711
71	6	0	1	1	0	1	1	1	0	0	1	0	2,072
72	7	0	1	1	1	1	1	1	0	0	1	0	1,505
73	8	0	1	1	1	1	1	1	0	0	1	1	1,005
74	9	0	1	1	1	1	1	1	1	0	1	1	519
75	10	0	1	1	1	1	1	1	1	0	1	1	189
76	11	1	1	1	1	1	1	1	1	1	1	1	0

MODELING ISSUES

To ensure that no city is serviced by a center that does not exist, we created several copies of the Included? row and then constrained that the Assignments range be less than or equal to the copy block. There is at least one other way to model this logical constraint. If we calculate the column sums of the Assignments range, each such sum represents the number of cities assigned to a certain service center. This number is certainly no greater than 11, the number of cities total, and it must logically be 0 if the service center doesn't exist. Therefore, an upper limit on each column sum is 11 multiplied by the corresponding service center binary value.

In binary IP models, the way a constraint is modeled can have a large effect on solution times. Even if two constraints are equivalent in a logical sense, one can lead to a much quicker solution than the other.

The resulting model is shown in Figure 6.23 (page 278). (See the file **LocatingServiceCenters2.xls**.) Each value in row 34 is a column sum of the binary values above it, and each value in row 36 is 11 multiplied by the corresponding binary value in row 19. This is a perfectly valid way of modeling this constraint. If a service center is not opened, then the corresponding column sum is forced to be 0. If a service center is opened, then the corresponding column must not exceed 11—no real constraint since there are only 11 cities. However, if you run Solver on this version of the model—or worse yet, if you run SolverTable on it—you will notice that it takes considerably more time to solve. There is a technical reason for this that is beyond the level of this book. However, it points out that not all IP models are "equal." Some models might *look* just as good as others, but they can take Solver considerably more time to solve. Unfortunately, it is difficult to know which models are "efficient" and which are less efficient. ∎

Figure 6.23   An Alternative Way to Model the Logical Constraint

Locating service centers and assigning service centers to customers - an alternative way of modeling the logical constraint

Distances between cities

	Boston	Chicago	Dallas	Denver	Los Angeles	Miami	New York	Phoenix	Pittsburgh	San Francisco	Seattle
Boston	0	983	1815	1991	3036	1539	213	2664	792	2385	2612
Chicago	983	0	1205	1050	2112	1390	840	1729	457	2212	2052
Dallas	1815	1205	0	801	1425	1332	1604	1027	1237	1765	2404
Denver	1991	1050	801	0	1174	2041	1780	836	1411	1765	1373
Los Angeles	3036	2112	1425	1174	0	2757	2825	398	2456	403	1909
Miami	1539	1390	1332	2041	2757	0	1258	2359	1250	3097	3389
New York	213	840	1604	1780	2825	1258	0	2442	386	3036	2900
Phoenix	2664	1729	1027	836	398	2359	2442	0	2073	800	1482
Pittsburgh	792	457	1237	1411	2456	1250	386	2073	0	2653	2517
San Francisco	2385	2212	1765	1765	403	3097	3036	800	2653	0	817
Seattle	2612	2052	2404	1373	1909	3389	2900	1482	2517	817	0

Range names used:

Assignments	=Model!$B$23:$L$33
Centers_allowed	=Model!$O$19
Included?	=Model!$B$19:$L$19
Locations_assigned_to	=Model!$M$23:$M$33
Logical_capacity	=Model!$B$36:$L$36
Number_serviced_by	=Model!$B$34:$L$34
Service_centers	=Model!$M$19
Total_distance	=Model!$B$53

Locations of service centers

	Boston	Chicago	Dallas	Denver	Los Angeles	Miami	New York	Phoenix	Pittsburgh	San Francisco	Seattle	Service centers		Centers allowed
Included?	0	0	1	0	0	0	1	0	0	1	0	3	<=	3

Assignments (1 if customers along side are serviced by service center along top, 0 otherwise)

	Boston	Chicago	Dallas	Denver	Los Angeles	Miami	New York	Phoenix	Pittsburgh	San Francisco	Seattle	Locations assigned to		Required
Boston	0	0	0	0	0	0	1	0	0	0	0	1	=	1
Chicago	0	0	0	0	0	0	1	0	0	0	0	1	=	1
Dallas	0	0	1	0	0	0	0	0	0	0	0	1	=	1
Denver	0	0	1	0	0	0	0	0	0	0	0	1	=	1
Los Angeles	0	0	0	0	0	0	0	0	0	1	0	1	=	1
Miami	0	0	0	0	0	0	1	0	0	0	0	1	=	1
New York	0	0	0	0	0	0	1	0	0	0	0	1	=	1
Phoenix	0	0	0	0	0	0	0	0	0	1	0	1	=	1
Pittsburgh	0	0	0	0	0	0	1	0	0	0	0	1	=	1
San Francisco	0	0	0	0	0	0	0	0	0	1	0	1	=	1
Seattle	0	0	0	0	0	0	0	0	0	1	0	1	=	1
Number serviced by	0	0	2	0	0	0	5	0	0	4	0			
	<=	<=	<=	<=	<=	<=	<=	<=	<=	<=	<=			
Logical capacity	0	0	11	0	0	0	11	0	0	11	0			

Numbers of annual trips to customers, and total distances (1000s of miles) traveled annually to customer

	Annual trips	Total distance
Boston	885	189
Chicago	760	638
Dallas	1124	0
Denver	708	567
Los Angeles	1224	493
Miami	1152	1449
New York	1560	0
Phoenix	1222	978
Pittsburgh	856	330
San Francisco	1443	0
Seattle	612	500

These distances are 0 because the optimal solution locates service centers in these cities.

Objective to minimize (1000s of miles)

Total distance	5145

The final example in this section is structurally similar to the service center location model, but it arises in a slightly different business context.[8]

EXAMPLE

6.6 MANUFACTURING AND DISTRIBUTING FERTILIZER AT GREEN GRASS

Like the previous example, this example is basically a fixed-cost location–assignment model. However, one difference here is that not all customers need to be assigned.

The Green Grass Company manufactures and distributes a fertilizer product. The company sells its product to high-volume customers in various U.S. cities where it has manufacturing plants, but it can decide to operate only some of these plants in any given month. There is a fixed monthly cost of $60,000 for operating any plant, there is a plant capacity of 2500 pounds per month for any operating plant, and there is a production cost of $10.25 per pound at any operating plant. Once the product is manufactured, it is shipped to customers at a rate of $0.02 per pound per mile. The cities and the distances between them are listed in Table 6.12. The customers submit order sizes and price bids to Green Grass, as listed in Table 6.13. For example, the customer in Boston requires an order of 1430 pounds this month and is willing to pay $75,740 for it. Green Grass can decide to fill this order or not. If not, we assume that the customer will take its business to another company. For the current month, Green Grass must decide which plants to operate and which customers to service from which operating plants to maximize its monthly profit.

---

[8]This example is based on a real problem one of the authors was asked to solve during a consulting experience with a major U.S. manufacturing company.

Table 6.12 Distances Between Cities for Green Grass Example

	Boston	Chicago	Dallas	Denver	LA	Miami	NY	Phoenix
Boston	0	983	1815	1991	3036	1539	213	2664
Chicago	983	0	1205	1050	2112	1390	840	1729
Dallas	1815	1205	0	801	1425	1332	1604	1027
Denver	1991	1050	801	0	1174	2065	1780	836
LA	3036	2112	1425	1174	0	2757	2825	398
Miami	1539	1390	1332	2065	2757	0	1258	2359
NY	213	840	1604	1780	2825	1258	0	2442
Phoenix	2664	1729	1027	836	398	2359	2442	0

Table 6.13 Orders and Price Bids for Green Grass Example

	Quantity	Price
Boston	1430	$75,740
Chicago	870	$44,370
Dallas	770	$46,320
Denver	1140	$87,780
LA	700	$43,850
Miami	830	$21,000
NY	1230	$74,850
Phoenix	1070	$83,980

Objective To develop a binary model to help Green Grass decide which manufacturing plants to operate and which customer orders to fill from which operating plants.

WHERE DO THE NUMBERS COME FROM?

The distances in Table 6.12 are well known, and the customers would supply the data in Table 6.13. Cost accountants would supply the fixed cost of operating a plant, the variable production cost per pound, and the unit shipping cost per mile. However, such values should be available.

Solution

The variables and constraints for the Green Grass model are listed in Table 6.14 (page 280). As in the previous example, there are two sets of binary variables. The first set indicates which plants are open for operation. The second set indicates which customers are supplied by which plants. The first constraint in the table ensures that no customer will be supplied by more than one plant. However, it allows the possibility that the customer will not be supplied by *any* Green Grass plant. The second constraint ensures that no plant will produce and ship more than its "logical capacity." This logical capacity is 0 if the plant is not opened at all, and it is the 2500-pound limit if the plant is opened. With these changing cells and constraints, we see which plants to open and which customers to supply from which open plants to maximize profit.

Table 6.14 Variables and Constraints for Green Grass Model

Input variables	Fixed cost of operating a plant, production cost per pound, shipping cost per pound per mile, plant capacities, distance matrix, customer order sizes and price bids
Decision variables (changing cells)	Which plants to open (binary), which customers to supply from which open plants (binary)
Objective (target cell)	Monthly profit
Other calculated variables	Pounds shipped out of each plant, logical capacity of each plant, number of plants shipping to each customer, revenue minus production and shipping cost for each plant/customer pair, total fixed plant cost
Constraints	Plants supplying each customer ≤ 1 Pounds shipped out of each plant ≤ Logical plant capacity

DEVELOPING THE SPREADSHEET MODEL

The spreadsheet model appears in Figure 6.24. (See the file **FixedCostTransportation.xls**.) It can be developed with the following steps.

Figure 6.24 Green Grass Production/Shipping Model

	A	B	C	D	E	F	G	H	I	J	K	L	M	N
1	Fixed cost logistics model with customer bids for orders										Range names used:			
2											Assignments	=Model!$B$26:$I$33		
3	Inputs										Logical_capacity	=Model!$B$36:$I$36		
4	Production cost per pound	$10.25									Number_serviced_by	=Model!$J$26:$J$33		
5	Shipping cost per pound per mile	$0.02									Open?	=Model!$B$22:$I$22		
6	Monthly plant fixed cost	$60,000									Pounds_shipped_out_of	=Model!$B$34:$I$34		
7	Plant capacity (pounds)	2500									Total_monthly_profit	=Model!$B$51		
8														
9	Distance matrix										Quantities required and prices bid by customers			
10		Boston	Chicago	Dallas	Denver	LA	Miami	NY	Phoenix			Quantity	Price	
11	Boston	0	983	1815	1991	3036	1539	213	2664		Boston	1430	$75,740	
12	Chicago	983	0	1205	1050	2112	1390	840	1729		Chicago	870	$44,370	
13	Dallas	1815	1205	0	801	1425	1332	1604	1027		Dallas	770	$46,320	
14	Denver	1991	1050	801	0	1174	2065	1780	836		Denver	1140	$87,780	
15	LA	3036	2112	1425	1174	0	2757	2825	398		LA	700	$43,850	
16	Miami	1539	1390	1332	2065	2757	0	1258	2359		Miami	830	$21,000	
17	NY	213	840	1604	1780	2825	1258	0	2442		NY	1230	$74,850	
18	Phoenix	2664	1729	1027	836	398	2359	2442	0		Phoenix	1070	$83,980	
19														
20	Which plants to open													
21		Boston	Chicago	Dallas	Denver	LA	Miami	NY	Phoenix					
22	Open?	1	0	0	1	0	0	1	1					
23														
24	Which customers (along side) to ship to from which plants (along top)													
25		Boston	Chicago	Dallas	Denver	LA	Miami	NY	Phoenix	Number supplied by		Allowed		
26	Boston	1	0	0	0	0	0	0	0	1	<=	1		
27	Chicago	0	0	0	0	0	0	1	0	1	<=	1		
28	Dallas	0	0	0	1	0	0	0	0	1	<=	1		
29	Denver	0	0	0	1	0	0	0	0	1	<=	1		
30	LA	0	0	0	0	0	0	0	1	1	<=	1		
31	Miami	0	0	0	0	0	0	0	0	0	<=	1		
32	NY	0	0	0	0	0	0	1	0	1	<=	1		
33	Phoenix	0	0	0	0	0	0	0	1	1	<=	1		
34	Pounds shipped out of	1430	0	0	1910	0	0	2100	1770					
35		<=	<=	<=	<=	<=	<=	<=	<=					
36	Logical capacity	2500	0	0	2500	0	0	2500	2500					
37														
38	Monetary outputs													
39	Matrix of revenue minus sum of production and shipping cost for each customer (along side) and plant (along top) pair													
40		Boston	Chicago	Dallas	Denver	LA	Miami	NY	Phoenix					
41	Boston	$61,083	$0	$0	$0	$0	$0	$0	$0					
42	Chicago	$0	$0	$0	$0	$0	$0	$20,837	$0					
43	Dallas	$0	$0	$0	$26,092	$0	$0	$0	$0					
44	Denver	$0	$0	$0	$0	$76,095	$0	$0	$0					
45	LA	$0	$0	$0	$0	$0	$0	$0	$31,103					
46	Miami	$0	$0	$0	$0	$0	$0	$0	$0					
47	NY	$0	$0	$0	$0	$0	$0	$62,243	$0					
48	Phoenix	$0	$0	$0	$0	$0	$0	$0	$73,013					
49														
50	Monthly fixed cost	$240,000												
51	Total monthly profit	$110,464												

1 **Inputs.** Enter the inputs in the shaded ranges.

2 **Plant opening decisions.** Enter *any* set of 0's and 1's in the Open? range. These changing cells indicate which plants to open.

3 **Assignment decisions.** Enter *any* set of 0's and 1's in the Assignments range. Each changing cell in this range indicates whether a particular plant supplies a particular customer.

4 **Plants supplying customers.** Each customer can be supplied by at most one plant. To see how many plants are supplying each customer, create row sums of the Assignments range. That is, enter the formula

=SUM(B26:I26)

in cell J26 and copy it down to cell J33. Each such sum is just the number of 1's in that row of the Assignments range.

5 **Amounts produced at plants.** We assume that if a plant is assigned to supply any customer, its production for that customer will equal the customer's order requirement. This allows us to calculate the total produced (and shipped out) for each plant, given the 0–1 assignments. To implement this idea, enter the formula

=SUMPRODUCT(B26:B33,$L$11:$L$18)

in cell B34 for the first plant and copy it across row 34 for the other plants.

6 **Logical plant capacities.** If a plant is not open, its capacity is 0. If it is open, its capacity is 2500. To calculate these effective plant capacities, enter the formula

=$B$7*B22

in cell B36 for the first plant, and copy it across row 36 for the other plants. The binary value in this formula reduces effective capacity to 0 or keeps it at 2500. (Note that the logic used here is very similar to the logic in the Great Threads fixed-cost model in Example 6.2. The only difference is that we now have a "natural" capacity, 2500, in case the plant is opened. In the Great Threads example, we had to calculate a suitable upper limit on production.)

7 **Revenues and variable costs.** If any particular plant–customer assignment is made, we can calculate the revenue minus production and shipping costs for satisfying that customer's order from that plant. To calculate these, enter the formula

=B26*($M11-$L11*($B$4+$B$5*B11))

in cell B41 and copy it to the range B41:I48. The first term in this formula is the binary assignment variable. If it is 0, no revenues or costs are incurred on this route because the route isn't used. However, if this binary value is 1, then the formula subtracts costs from revenue. (Be careful to check the measurement units in these types of calculations. The production cost is pounds multiplied by cost per pound. The shipping cost is pounds multiplied by miles multiplied by cost per pound per mile.)

8 **Fixed costs.** Each 1 in the Open? range adds a fixed cost. To calculate the total fixed cost, enter the formula

=B6*SUM(Open?)

in cell B50. This is the number of open plants multiplied by the fixed cost per plant.

9 **Monthly profit.** Calculate the monthly profit in cell B51 with the formula

=SUM(B41:I48)-B50

USING SOLVER

The Solver dialog box should be filled out as in Figure 6.25. As usual, you should check the Assume Linear Model option, but you do not need to check the Assume Non-Negative option because all changing cells are constrained to be binary, hence nonnegative. In words, we want to choose the binary values for plant openings and customer assignments to maximize profit. We must ensure that each plant produces 0 (if it is not open) or no more than its capacity (if it is open). Also, we ensure that each customer's demand is satisfied by at most one plant. Of course, this allows the possibility that a customer's demand will not be satisfied by Green Grass at all.

Figure 6.25

Solver Dialog Box
for Green Grass
Model

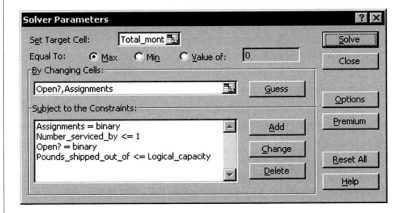

Discussion of the Solution

The optimal solution in Figure 6.24 indicates that the company should open four plants: Boston (to supply the Boston customer), Denver (to supply the Denver and Dallas customers), New York (to supply the New York and Chicago customers), and Phoenix (to supply the Phoenix and Los Angeles customers). In addition, the model indicates that Green Grass should not supply the Miami customer at all. You can see the main reason for this if you calculate the ratio of order size to price bid for each customer. Miami's ratio is well below the others. Therefore, it is evidently not profitable to supply the Miami customer.

Sensitivity Analysis

One possible sensitivity analysis is to see how much larger Miami's price bid would need to be before Green Grass would supply it. We tried this, varying Miami's price bid and keeping track of the row sum in cell J31 that indicates whether Miami is supplied. The results (after some trial and error to find the "interesting" price bid range) appear in Figure 6.26. When the Miami price bid increases to some value between $31,000 and $32,000, it becomes profitable to supply Miami. (You can check, by rerunning Solver, that Miami will then be supplied by New York.)

Figure 6.26

Sensitivity to
Miami's Price Bid

	A	B	C	D	E
53	Sensitivity of whether Miami is supplied to Miami's bid price				
54		$J$31			
55	28000	0			
56	29000	0			
57	30000	0			
58	31000	0			
59	32000	1			
60	33000	1			
61	34000	1			
62	35000	1			

Another possible sensitivity analysis is on the common plant capacity, currently 2500 pounds. The optimal solution in Figure 6.24 indicates that capacity is not currently a constraining factor. Four of the plants are open, and all of them are operating well under capacity. Therefore, an *increase* in the common capacity will have absolutely no effect, and a slight *decrease* (down to 2100, the highest plant production) will also have no effect. However, any decrease below 2100 should have an effect. We explore this in Figure 6.27, where we vary the common plant capacity and keep track of the optimal total fixed cost and profit. As we see, if the capacity is below 2100, the total profit decreases. However, the total fixed cost remains constant, at least for this range of capacities. This implies that all of these solutions keep four plants open. How does the optimal solution change? Although the results in Figure 6.27 do not provide the answer, you can rerun Solver with any of these capacities to find out. It turns out that the *same* four plants stay open but supply fewer customers. For example, when the common capacity is 1500 or 1750, the four plants supply *only* the customers in their respective cities.

Figure 6.27

Sensitivity to Common Plant Capacity

	A	B	C	D	E	F
64	Sensitivity of total fixed cost and profit to common plant capacity					
65		$B$50	$B$51			
66	1500	$240,000	$32,433			
67	1750	$240,000	$32,433			
68	2000	$240,000	$89,628			
69	2250	$240,000	$110,464			
70	2500	$240,000	$110,464			

If you run these sensitivity analyses with SolverTable, you will immediately notice the longer computing times. These are *difficult* problems, even for Solver, and you will not get the immediate solutions you have gotten in previous models. Each problem has 2^{72} possible binary solutions (because there are 72 binary changing cells), and this is an enormous number of potential solutions for Solver to sort through with its branch and bound algorithm. Although a binary model of this type and size are still well within Solver's capabilities, this example should convince you that not all management science optimization models are easy to solve! ■

MODELING ISSUES

1. We have assumed that all possible plant locations are in the same cities as the customers. This is certainly not required. We could have any number of customers at one set of locations and any other number of plant locations at another set of locations. As long as we know the distance from each plant to each customer, the model would hardly change at all.

2. We have assumed that the inputs in the range B4:B7 (see Figure 6.24) are constant, the same for each plant or plant–customer pair. This is also not required. If these inputs differ across plants or plant–customer pairs, more input values must be estimated by the cost accountants, but modifications to the model itself are minimal.

3. We currently assume that the plants in the various locations are already built, and it is just a matter of which to open each month. Suppose instead that the company is expanding and must decide where (or whether) to build *new* plants. Then there would be a one-time fixed cost of building each new plant, in addition to the fixed cost of opening an existing plant that we saw in the example. Unfortunately, it is not a trivial matter to combine these costs. The fixed cost of building must be amortized over some period of time so that it can be combined correctly with *monthly* revenues and costs. ■

PROBLEMS

Skill-Building Problems

24. In the original Western set-covering model in Figure 6.15, we assumed that each city must be covered by at least one hub. Suppose that for added flexibility in flight routing, Western requires that each city must be covered by at least two hubs. How do the model and optimal solution change?

25. In the original Western set-covering model in Figure 6.15, we used the number of hubs as the objective to minimize. Suppose instead that there is a fixed cost of locating a hub in any city, where these fixed costs can possibly vary across cities. Make up some reasonable fixed costs, modify the model appropriately, and use Solver to find the solution that minimizes the sum of fixed costs.

26. Set-covering models such as the original Western model in Figure 6.15 often have multiple optimal solutions. See how many alternative optimal solutions you can find. Of course, each must use three hubs because we know this is optimal. (*Hint*: Use various initial values in the changing cells and then run Solver repeatedly.)[9]

27. How hard is it to expand a set-covering model to accommodate new cities? Answer this by modifying the model in Figure 6.18. (See the file **LocatingHubs2.xls**.) Add several cities that must be served: Memphis, Dallas, Tucson, Philadelphia, Cleveland, and Buffalo. You can look up the distances from these cities to each other and to the other cities in a reference book (or on the Web), or you can make up approximate distances.
  a. Modify the model appropriately, assuming that these new cities must be covered *and* are candidates for hub locations.
  b. Modify the model appropriately, assuming that these new cities must be covered but are *not* candidates for hub locations.

28. In the United Copiers service center model in Example 6.5, we assumed that the potential locations of service centers are the same as existing customer locations. Change the model so that the customer locations are the ones given, but the only potential service center locations are in Memphis, Houston, Cleveland, Buffalo, Minneapolis, St. Louis, and Kansas City. You can look up the distances from these cities to the customer cities in a reference book (or on the Web), or you can make up approximate distances. Use Solver to find the optimal solution.

29. In the United Copiers service center model, we used total distance traveled as the objective to minimize. Suppose in addition that there is an annual fixed cost of locating a service center in any city, where this fixed cost can vary across cities. There is also a cost per mile of traveling. Modify the current model to make total annual cost the objective to minimize. You can make up reasonable fixed costs and unit traveling costs.

30. In the Green Grass shipping model, we assumed that certain inputs (see the range B4:B7 in Figure 6.24) are the same for all plants or plant/customer combinations. Change this so that the unit production cost, the monthly fixed cost, and the monthly capacity can vary by plant, and the unit shipping cost can vary by plant–customer combination. (You can make up data that vary around the values in the B4:B7 range.) Use Solver to find the new optimal solution.

31. In the optimal solution to the Green Grass shipping model, the Miami customer's order is not satisfied. Suppose that Green Grass decides, as a matter of policy, to satisfy *each* customer's order (at the customer's bid price). How much profit will the company lose from this policy decision?

32. In the Green Grass shipping model, use SolverTable to perform a sensitivity analysis on the fixed cost of opening a plant, letting it vary over some reasonable range that extends below and above the current value of $60,000. Keep track of enough outputs so that you can see the effect on the plants that are opened and the customers whose orders are satisfied, as well as on the total profit. Summarize your findings in words.

Skill-Extending Problems

33. In the United Copiers service center model, we assumed that a customer is serviced totally by a single service center. Suppose it is possible for a customer to be serviced partly by multiple service centers. For example, the customer in Denver could get half of its service from Dallas and the other half from San Francisco. In this case, we assume that half of Denver's annual trips would be made from Dallas reps and half by San Francisco reps. Modify the model appropriately and then solve it with Solver. How do you interpret the optimal solution? (*Hint*: Allow the changing cells in the Assignments range to be fractional values between 0 and 1.)

[9]One of our colleagues at Indiana University, Vic Cabot, now deceased, worked for years trying to develop a general algorithm (other than trial and error) for finding *all* alternative optimal solutions to optimization models. It turns out that this is a very difficult problem—and one that Vic never totally solved.

34. In the Green Grass shipping model, we currently assume that if a customer's order is satisfied, it must be satisfied from a *single* plant. Suppose instead that it can be satisfied from more than one plant. For example, if the company decides to satisfy Dallas's order, it could ship part of this order from Denver and part from Phoenix (or some other combination of open plants). Continue to assume, however, that the company must satisfy either *all* or *none* of each customer's order. Modify the model appropriately and use Solver to solve it. Does the solution change?

35. In the Green Grass shipping model, we assumed that the plants are already built, so that in each month the only decision is whether to open particular plants (at a monthly fixed cost). Consider instead a general location–shipping model of this type where the plants are not yet built. The company must first decide where to build plants and then how much to produce at the plants and which customers to service from them. The problem is that the building costs are "one-time" costs, whereas other costs are monthly. How can you reconcile these two types of costs? What should you use as an objective to minimize? Illustrate your procedure on the Green Grass example, where the plant opening fixed costs are ignored—we assume that all plants that are built will remain open—but building costs (which you can make up) are given.

6.6 CONCLUSION

Three important points emerge from this chapter.

- A wide variety of important problems can be modeled as IP problems with binary variables. These can generally be identified as problems where at least some of the "activities" (such as making a particular investment, opening a particular plant, supplying a customer from a particular plant, and so on) must be done or not done; there is no in-between. Regular LP models cannot handle these problems; IP models with binary variables are required.

- Some IP models are simply LP models with integer constraints on the variables. For example, we might impose that constraint that the number of refrigerators produced is an integer. These problems can often be solved by solving the associated LP model and then rounding the solution to integer values. Although there is no guarantee that the rounded solution is optimal, it is often close enough. In contrast, the problems discussed in this chapter introduce binary decision variables that specify whether an activity is done. If we ignore the binary constraints and only constrain these variables to be *between* 0 and 1, it is generally impossible to find the optimal solution by rounding.

- The solution approach required for IP problems, especially those with 0–1 variables, is inherently more difficult than the simplex method for LP problems. The relatively small examples in this chapter might give the impression that a spreadsheet Solver can handle IP models just as easily as it handles LP models, but this is definitely not the case. In fact, even with the most sophisticated IP computer codes on the most powerful computers, there are IP problems—from real applications—that defy solution.

Summary of Key Management Science Terms

Term	Explanation	Page
Integer programming models	Optimization models where some or all of the decision variables are constrained to have integer values	246
Binary variables	Variables constrained to have values 1 or 0; usually used to indicate that an activity is undertaken or not	246
Branch and bound algorithm	A general algorithm for searching through all integer solutions in an integer programming model	247

(continued)

Term	Explanation	Page
Fixed-cost models	Difficult-to-solve models where certain costs are fixed at some positive level if an activity is undertaken at any level, and are 0 otherwise	255
Either–or constraints	Constraints where one of mutually exclusive conditions must be satisfied	262
Set-covering models	Models where members of one set (such as ambulances) must be located so that they "cover" members of another set (such as city districts)	267
Location models	Models where items (such as branch offices) must be located so as to provide required services at minimal cost	272

Summary of Key Excel Terms

Term	Explanation	Excel	Page
Solver tolerance setting	Setting that specifies whether Solver will stop at a near-optimal integer solution or will continue to optimality	Specify under Solver Options (default 5% doesn't guarantee optimality; 0% does)	248

PROBLEMS

Skill-Building Problems

36. Four projects are available for investment. The projects require the cash flows and yield the net present values (in millions) shown in the file **P06_36.xls**. If $6 million is available now for investment, find the investment plan that maximizes NPV.

37. You are given a group of possible investment projects for your company's capital. For each project you are given the NPV the project would add to the firm, as well as the cash outflow required by each project during each year. Given the information in the file **P06_37.xls**, determine the investments that maximize the firm's NPV. The firm has 30 million dollars available during each of the next 5 years. All numbers are in millions of dollars.

38. I am moving from New Jersey to Indiana and have rented a truck that can haul up to 1100 cubic feet of furniture. The volume and value of each item I am considering moving on the truck are given in the file **P06_38.xls**. Which items should I bring to Indiana?

39. NASA must determine how many of three types of objects to bring on board the space shuttle. The weight and benefit of each of the items are given in the file **P06_39.xls**. If the space shuttle can carry up to 26 pounds of items 1 through 3, which items should be taken on the space shuttle?

40. Coach Night is trying to choose the starting lineup for the basketball team. The team consists of seven play- ers who have been rated on a scale of 1 (poor) to 3 (excellent) according to their ballhandling, shooting, rebounding, and defensive abilities. The positions that each player is allowed to play and the players' abili- ties are listed in the file **P06_40.xls**. The five-player starting lineup must satisfy the following restrictions:

- At least four members must be able to play guard (G), at least two members must be able to play for- ward (F), and at least one member must be able to play center (C).
- The average ballhandling, shooting, and rebound- ing level of the starting lineup must each be at least 1.8.
- Either player 2 or player 3 (or both) must start. Given these constraints, Coach Night wants to maxi- mize the total defensive ability of the starting team. Use Solver to determine his starting team.

41. To graduate from Southeastern University with a ma- jor in operations research (OR), a student must com- plete at least two math courses, at least two OR courses, and at least two computer courses. Some courses can be used to fulfill more than one require- ment: Calculus can fulfill the math requirement; Op- erations Research can fulfill the math and OR require- ments; Data Structures can fulfill the computer and math requirements; Business Statistics can fulfill the math and OR requirements; Computer Simulation can fulfill the OR and computer requirements; Introduc- tion to Computer Programming can fulfill the computer requirement; and Forecasting can fulfill the OR and math requirements. Some courses are prerequisites for others: Calculus is a prerequisite for Business Statistics; Introduction to Computer Programming is a prerequisite for Computer Simulation and for Data Structures; and Business Statistics is a prerequisite for Forecasting. Determine how to minimize the number of courses needed to satisfy the major requirements. (*Hint*: Since Calculus is a prerequisite for Business Statistics, for example, you will need a constraint that ensures that the changing cell for Calculus is greater than or equal to the changing cell for Business Statistics.)

42. Based on Bean et al. (1987). Boris Milkem's firm owns six assets. The expected selling price (in millions of dollars) for each asset is given in the file **P06_42.xls**. For example, if asset 1 is sold in year 2, the firm receives $20 million. To maintain a regular cash flow, Milkem must sell at least $20 million of assets during year 1, at least $30 million worth during year 2, and at least $35 million worth during year 3. Determine how Milkem can maximize his total revenue from assets sold during the next 3 years. In implementing this model, how might the idea of a rolling planning horizon be used?

43. The Cubs are trying to determine which of the following free-agent pitchers should be signed: Rick Sutcliffe (RS), Bruce Sutter (BS), Dennis Eckersley (DE), Steve Trout (ST), or Tim Stoddard (TS). (Feel free to substitute your own set of players for these "old" guys!) The cost of signing each pitcher and the predicted number of victories each pitcher will add to the Cubs are listed in the file **P06_43.xls**. The Cubs want to sign the pitchers who will add the most victories to the team. Determine who the Cubs should sign based on the following restrictions:
- At most $12 million can be spent.
- At most two right-handed pitchers can be signed.
- The Cubs cannot sign both BS and RS.

44. Based on Sonderman and Abrahamson (1985). In treating a brain tumor with radiation, physicians want the maximum amount of radiation possible to bombard the tissue containing the tumors. The constraint is, however, that there is a maximum amount of radiation that normal tissue can handle without suffering tissue damage. Physicians must therefore decide how to aim the radiation so as to maximize the radiation that hits the tumor tissue subject to the constraint of not damaging the normal tissue. As a simple example of this situation, suppose there are six types of radiation beams (beams differ in where they are aimed and their intensity) that can be aimed at a tumor. The region containing the tumor has been divided into six regions: three regions contain tumors and three contain normal tissue. The amount of radiation delivered

to each region by each type of beam is shown in the file **P06_44.xls**. If each region of normal tissue can handle at most 60 units of radiation, which beams should be used to maximize the total amount of radiation received by the tumors?

45. Because of excessive pollution on the Momiss River, the state of Momiss is going to build some pollution control stations. Three sites (1, 2, and 3) are under consideration. Momiss is interested in controlling the pollution levels of two pollutants (1 and 2). The state legislature requires that at least 80,000 tons of pollutant 1 and at least 50,000 tons of pollutant 2 be removed from the river. The relevant data for this problem are shown in the file **P06_45.xls**. (The last two columns indicate the number of tons of pollutants removed per ton treated.)
   a. Determine how to minimize the cost of meeting the state legislature's goals.
   b. Use SolverTable to analyze how a change in the requirement for pollutant 1 changes the optimal solution. Do the same for pollutant 2.

46. A manufacturer can sell product 1 at a profit of $2 per unit and product 2 at a profit of $5 per unit. Three units of raw material are needed to manufacture one unit of product 1, and six units of raw material are needed to manufacture one unit of product 2. A total of 120 units of raw material are available. If any product 1 is produced, a setup cost of $10 is incurred; if any product 2 is produced, a setup cost of $20 is incurred.
   a. Determine how to maximize the manufacturer's profit.
   b. Use SolverTable to analyze how a change in the setup cost for product 1 affects the optimal solution. Do the same for the setup cost for product 2.

47. A company is considering opening warehouses in four cities: New York, Los Angeles, Chicago, and Atlanta. Each warehouse can ship 100 units per week. The weekly fixed cost of keeping each warehouse open is $400 for New York, $500 for Los Angeles, $300 for Chicago, and $150 for Atlanta. Region 1 of the country requires 80 units per week, region 2 requires 70 units per week, and region 3 requires 40 units per week. The costs (including production and shipping costs) of sending one unit from a plant to a region are shown in the file **P06_47.xls**. The company wants to meet weekly demands at minimum cost, subject to the preceding information and the following restrictions:
- If the New York warehouse is opened, then the Los Angeles warehouse must be opened.
- At most two warehouses can be opened.
- Either the Atlanta or the Los Angeles warehouse must be opened.

48. Glueco produces three types of glue on two different production lines. Each line can be utilized by up to seven workers at a time. Workers are paid $500 per week on production line 1 and $900 per week on production line 2. For a week of production it costs $1000 to set up production line 1 and $2000 to set up production line 2. During a week on a production line each worker produces the number of units of glue shown in the file **P06_48.xls**. Each week at least 120 units of glue 1, at least 150 units of glue 2, and at least 200 units of glue 3 must be produced. Determine how to minimize the total cost of meeting weekly demands.

49. Fruit Computer produces two types of computers: Pear computers and Apricot computers. The relevant data are given in the file **P06_49.xls**. The equipment cost is a fixed cost; it is incurred if any of this type of computer is produced. A total of 3000 chips and 1200 hours of labor are available.
  a. Determine how Fruit can maximize its profit.
  b. Use SolverTable to analyze the effect on the optimal solution of a change in the selling price of Pear computers. Do the same for the selling price of Apricot computers.

50. Consider the Pigskin example (Example 3.3) from Chapter 3. Find Pigskin's optimal production policy if, in addition to the given production and holding costs, there is a fixed cost of $1000 during any month in which there is positive production. Assume now that maximum storage capacity is 200 footballs.

51. A product can be produced on four different machines. Each machine has a fixed setup cost, variable production cost per unit processed, and a production capacity, given in the file **P06_51.xls**. A total of 2000 units of the product must be produced. Determine how to minimize the total cost.

52. Bookco Publishers is considering publishing five textbooks. The maximum number of copies of each textbook that can be sold, the variable cost of producing each textbook, the selling price of each textbook, and the fixed cost of a production run for each book are given in the file **P06_52.xls**. For example, producing 2000 copies of book 1 brings in a revenue of $(2000)(50) = \$100,000$ but costs $80,000 + 25(2000) = \$130,000$.
  a. Determine how Bookco can maximize its profit if it can produce at most 10,000 books.
  b. Use SolverTable to analyze the effect on the optimal solution of a change in the demand for book 1. Repeat for the demands for the other books.

53. Comquat owns four production plants at which personal computers are produced. Comquat can sell up to 20,000 computers per year at a price of $3500 per computer. For each plant, the production capacity, the production cost per computer, and the fixed cost of operating a plant for a year are given in the file

P06_53.xls. Determine how Comquat can maximize its yearly profit from computer production.

54. Eastinghouse sells air conditioners. The annual demand for air conditioners in each region of the country is as follows: East, 100,000; South, 150,000; Midwest, 110,000; West, 90,000. Eastinghouse is considering building its air conditioners in four different cities: New York, Atlanta, Chicago, and Los Angeles. The cost of producing an air conditioner in a city and shipping it to a region of the country is given in the file **P06_54.xls**. Any factory can produce up to 150,000 air conditioners per year. The annual fixed cost of operating a factory in each city is also given in the file **P06_54.xls**. At least 50,000 units of the Midwest demand for air conditioners must come from New York and at least 50,000 units of the Midwest demand must come from Atlanta. Determine how Eastinghouse can minimize the annual cost of meeting demand for air conditioners.

55. During the next five periods, the demands listed in the file **P06_55.xls** must be met on time. At the beginning of period 1, the inventory level is 0. During each period when production occurs, a setup cost of $250 and a per-unit production cost of $2 are incurred. At the end of each period, a per-unit holding cost of $1 is incurred. Determine the cost-minimizing production schedule.

56. Ford has four automobile plants. Each is capable of producing the Taurus, Lincoln, or Escort, but it can produce only one of these cars. The fixed cost of operating each plant for a year and the variable cost of producing a car of each type at each plant are given in the file **P06_56.xls**. Ford faces the following restrictions:
  ■ Each plant can produce only one type of car.
  ■ The total production of each type of car must be at a single plant. For example, if any Tauruses are made at plant 1, then all Tauruses must be made there.
  ■ Each year Ford must produce 5 million of each type of car.
  a. Determine how to minimize the annual cost of producing these cars.
  b. Use SolverTable to see how a change in the demand for a type of car changes the optimal solution. Do this separately for each type of car.
  c. Use SolverTable to see how the optimal solution is affected by a change in the variable cost of producing a Lincoln.

57. At a machine tool plant, five jobs must be completed each day. The time it takes to do each job depends on the machine used to do the job. If a machine is used at all, there is a setup time required. The relevant times (in minutes) are given in the file **P06_57.xls**.

a. Determine how to minimize the sum of the setup and machine operation times needed to complete all jobs.

b. Use SolverTable to see how a change in the setup time for machine 4 changes the optimal solution.

c. Use SolverTable to see how a change in the required time for machine 1 to complete job 3 changes the optimal solution.

58. Heinsco produces tomato sauce at five different plants. The tomato sauce is then shipped to one of three warehouses, where it is stored until it is shipped to one of the company's four customers. All of the inputs for the problem are given in the file **P06_58.xls**, as follows:

   ■ The plant capacities (in tons)
   ■ The cost per ton of producing tomato sauce at each plant and shipping it to each warehouse
   ■ The cost of shipping a ton of sauce from each warehouse to each customer
   ■ The customer requirements (in tons) of sauce
   ■ The fixed annual cost of operating each plant and warehouse

   Heinsco must decide which plants and warehouses to open, and which routes from plants to warehouses and from warehouses to customers to use. All customer demand must be met. A given customer's demand can be met from more than one warehouse, and a given plant can ship to more than one warehouse.

   a. Determine the minimum-cost method for meeting customer demands.

   b. Use SolverTable to see how a change in the capacity of plant 1 affects the total cost.

   c. Use SolverTable to see how a change in the customer 2 demand affects the total cost.

59. Suppose in the previous problem that each customer's demand must be met from a *single* warehouse. Solve the problem with this restriction.

60. Based on Walker (1974). The Smalltown Fire Department currently has seven conventional ladder companies and seven alarm boxes. The two closest ladder companies to each alarm box are listed in the file **P06_60.xls**. The town council wants to maximize the number of conventional ladder companies that can be replaced with "tower" ladder companies. Unfortunately, political considerations dictate that a conventional company can be replaced only if, after replacement, at least one of the two closest companies to each alarm box is still a conventional company. Determine how to maximize the number of conventional companies that can be replaced by tower companies.

61. At Blair General Hospital, six types of surgical operations are performed. The types of operations each surgeon is qualified to perform (indicated by an X) are listed in the file **P06_61.xls**. Suppose that surgeons 1 and 2 dislike each other and cannot be on duty at the same time. Determine the minimum number of surgeons required so that the hospital can perform all types of surgery.

62. State University must purchase 1100 computers from three vendors. Vendor 1 charges $500 per computer plus a total delivery charge of $5000. Vendor 2 charges $350 per computer plus a total delivery charge of $4000. Vendor 3 charges $250 per computer plus a total delivery charge of $6000. Vendor 1 will sell the university at most 500 computers, vendor 2, at most 900, and vendor 3, at most 400. The minimum order from a vendor is 200 computers. Determine how to minimize the cost of purchasing the needed computers.

63. Eastinghouse ships 12,000 capacitors per month to its customers. The capacitors can be produced at three different plants. The production capacity, fixed monthly cost of operation, and variable cost of producing a capacitor at each plant are given in the file **P06_63.xls**. The fixed cost for a plant is incurred only if the plant is used to make any capacitors. If a plant is used at all, at least 3000 capacitors per month must be produced at the plant. Determine how to minimize the company's monthly costs of meeting its customers' demands.

64. Based on Liggett (1973). A court decision has stated that the enrollment of each high school in Metropolis must be at least 20% black. The numbers of black and white high school students in each of the city's five school districts are shown in the file **P06_64.xls**. The distance (in miles) that a student in each district must travel to each high school is also shown in the file **P06_64.xls**. School board policy requires that all students in a given district must attend the same school. Assuming that each school must have an enrollment of at least 150 students, determine how to minimize the total distance that Metropolis students must travel to high school.

65. Based on Westerberg, Bjorklund, and Hultman (1977). Newcor's steel mill has received an order for 25 tons of steel. The steel must be 5% carbon and 5% molybdenum by weight. The steel is manufactured by combining three types of metal: steel ingots, scrap steel, and alloys. Four individual steel ingots are available. At most, one of each can be purchased. The weight (in tons), cost per ton, and the carbon and molybdenum content of each ingot are given in the file **P06_65.xls**. Three types of alloys can be purchased. The cost per ton and chemical makeup of each alloy are also given in the file **P06_65.xls**. Steel scrap can be purchased at a cost of $100 per ton. Steel scrap contains 3% carbon and 9% molybdenum. Determine how Newcor can minimize the cost of filling its order.

66. Based on Boykin (1985). Chemco annually produces 359 million pounds of the chemical maleic anhydride.

A total of four reactors are available to produce maleic anhydride. Each reactor can be run on one of three settings. The cost (in thousands of dollars) and pounds produced (in millions) annually for each reactor and each setting are given in the file **P06_66.xls**. A reactor can be run on only one setting for the entire year. Determine how Chemco can minimize the cost of meeting its annual demand for maleic anhydride.

67. Based on Zangwill (1992). Hallco runs a day shift and a night shift. Regardless of the number of units produced, the only production cost during a shift is a setup cost. It costs $8000 to run the day shift and $4500 to run the night shift. Demand for the next two days is as follows: day 1, 2000; night 1, 3000; day 2, 2000; night 2, 3000. It costs $1 per unit to hold a unit in inventory for a shift.
   a. Determine a production schedule that minimizes the sum of setup and inventory costs. All demand must be met on time. (*Note*: Not all shifts have to be run.)
   b. After listening to a seminar on the virtues of the Japanese theory of production, Hallco has cut the setup cost of its day shift to $1000 per shift and the setup cost of its night shift to $3500 per shift. Now determine a production schedule that minimizes the sum of setup and inventory costs. All demand must be met on time. Show that the decrease in setup costs has actually raised the average inventory level. Is this reasonable?

68. Based on Fitzsimmons and Allen (1983). The State of Texas frequently audits companies doing business in Texas. Since these companies often have headquarters located outside the state, auditors must be sent to out-of-state locations. Each year, auditors must make 500 trips to cities in the Northeast, 400 trips to cities in the Midwest, 300 trips to cities in the West, and 400 trips to cities in the South. Texas is considering basing auditors in Chicago, New York, Atlanta, and Los Angeles. The annual cost of basing auditors in any city is $100,000. The cost of sending an auditor from any of these cities to a given region of the country is given in the file **P06_68.xls**. Determine how to minimize the annual cost of conducting out-of-state audits.

Skill-Extending Problems

69. You have been assigned to arrange the songs on the cassette version of Madonna's latest album. (Feel free to substitute your own favorite rock star for Madonna!) A cassette tape has two sides (1 and 2). The songs on each side of the cassette must total between 14 and 16 minutes in length. The length and type of each song are given in the file **P06_69.xls**. The assignment of songs to the tape must satisfy the following conditions:

- Each side must have exactly two ballads.
- Side 1 must have at least three hit songs.
- Either song 5 or song 6 must be on side 1.

Determine whether there is an arrangement of songs satisfying these restrictions. (*Hint*: You do not need a target cell when using Solver. In the Solver dialog box, just leave the Target Cell box empty.)

70. Cousin Bruzie of radio station WABC schedules radio commercials in 60-second blocks. This hour, the station has sold commercial time for commercials of 15, 16, 20, 25, 30, 35, 40, and 50 seconds. Determine the minimum number of 60-second blocks of commercials that must be scheduled to fit in all the current hour's commercials. (*Hint*: Certainly no more than eight blocks of time are needed.)

71. Based on Bean et al. (1988). Simon's Mall has 10,000 square feet of space to rent and wants to determine the types of stores that should occupy the mall. The minimum number and maximum number of each type of store (along with the square footage of each type) are given in the file **P06_71.xls**. The annual profit made by each type of store depends on how many stores of that type are in the mall. This dependence is also given in the file **P06_71.xls** (where all profits are in units of $10,000). For example, if there are two department stores in the mall, each department store will earn $210,000 profit per year. Each store pays 5% of its annual profit as rent to Simon's. Determine how Simon can maximize its rental income from the mall.

72. Indiana University's Business School has two rooms that seat 50 students, one room that seats 100 students, and one room that seats 150 students. Classes are held 5 hours a day. At present, the four types of requests for rooms are listed in the file **P06_72.xls**. The business school must decide how many requests of each type to assign to each type of room. Suppose that classes that cannot be assigned to a business school room are assigned to another campus building. Determine how to assign classes so as to minimize the number of hours students spend each week outside the business building.

73. Based on Efroymson and Ray (1966). Breadco Bakeries is a new bakery chain that sells bread to customers throughout the state of Indiana. Breadco is considering building bakeries in three locations: Evansville, Indianapolis, and South Bend. Each bakery can bake up to 900,000 loaves of bread each year. The cost of building a bakery at each site is $5 million in Evansville, $4 million in Indianapolis, and $4.5 million in South Bend. To simplify the problem, we assume that Breadco has only three customers. Their demands each year are 700,000 loaves (customer 1); 400,000 loaves (customer 2); and 300,000 loaves (customer 3). The total cost of baking and shipping a load of bread to a customer is given in the file

P06_73.xls. Assume that future shipping and production costs are discounted at a rate of 12% per year. Assume that once built, a bakery lasts forever. How would you minimize Breadco's total cost of meeting demand, present and future? (*Note*: Although your model is actually linear, the Excel Solver might report that "the conditions for Assume Linear Model are not satisfied" if you do not scale your changing cells and costs in "natural" units, as discussed in Chapter 3. For example, costs can be expressed in units of $1 million or $100,000, and annual shipments can be expressed in units of 100,000 loaves.)

74. On Monday morning you have $3000 in cash on hand. For the next seven days the following cash requirements must be met: Monday, $5000; Tuesday, $6000; Wednesday, $9000; Thursday, $2000; Friday, $7000; Saturday, $2000; Sunday, $3000. At the beginning of each day you must decide how much money (if any) to withdraw from the bank. It costs $10 to make a withdrawal of any size. You believe that the opportunity cost of having $1 of cash on hand for a year is $0.20. Assume that opportunity costs are incurred on each day's ending balance. Determine how much money you should withdraw from the bank during each of the next seven days.

75. Based on Eaton et al. (1985). Gotham City has been divided into eight districts. The time (in minutes) it takes an ambulance to travel from one district to another is shown in the file **P06_75.xls**. The population of each district (in thousands) is as follows: district 1, 40; district 2, 30; district 3, 35; district 4, 20; district 5, 15; district 6, 50; district 7, 45; district 8, 60. Suppose Gotham City has n ambulance locations. Determine the locations of ambulances that maximize the number of people who live within two minutes of an ambulance. Do this separately for $n = 1$; $n = 2$; $n = 3$; $n = 4$. (*Hint*: Set it up so that SolverTable can solve all four problems simultaneously.)

76. Arthur Ross, Inc., must complete many corporate tax returns during the period February 15 to April 15. This year the company must begin and complete the five jobs shown in the file **P06_76.xls** during this 8-week period. Arthur Ross employs four full-time accountants who normally work 40 hours per week. If necessary, however, they can work up to 20 hours of overtime per week for which they are paid $100 per hour. Determine how Arthur Ross can minimize the overtime cost incurred in completing all jobs by April 15.

77. Based on Muckstadt and Wilson (1968). PSI believes it will need the amounts of generating capacity (in millions of kwh) shown in the file **P06_77.xls** during the next 5 years. The company has a choice of building (and then operating) power plants with the capacities (in millions of kwh) and costs (in millions of dollars) also shown in the file **P06_77.xls**. Determine how to minimize the total cost of meeting PSI's generating capacity requirements for the next 5 years.

78. Houseco Developers is considering erecting three office buildings. The time (in years) required to complete each of them and the number of workers required to be on the job at all times are shown in the file **P06_78.xls**. Once a building is completed, it brings in the following amount of rent per year: building 1, $50,000; building 2, $30,000; building 3, $40,000. Houseco faces the following constraints:
   - During each year 60 workers are available.
   - At most one building can be started during any year.
   - Building 2 must be completed by the end of year 4.

   Determine the maximum total rent that can be earned by Houseco by the end of year 4.

79. Four trucks are available to deliver milk to five grocery stores. The capacity and daily operating cost of each truck are shown in the file **P06_79.xls**. The demand of each grocery store can be supplied by only one truck, but a truck can deliver to more than one grocery. The daily demands of each grocery are as follows: grocery 1, 100 gallons; grocery 2, 200 gallons; grocery 3, 300 gallons; grocery 4, 500 gallons; grocery 5, 800 gallons. Determine how to minimize the daily cost of meeting the demands of the five groceries.

80. A county is going to build two hospitals. There are nine cities in which the hospitals can be built. The number of hospital visits per year made by people in each city and the x-y coordinates of each city are listed in the file **P06_80.xls**. The county's goal is to minimize the total distance that patients must travel to hospitals. Where should it locate the hospitals? (*Hint*: You will need to determine the distance between each pair of cities. An easy way to do this is with lookup tables.)

81. It is currently the beginning of 2003. Gotham City is trying to sell municipal bonds to support improvements in recreational facilities and highways. The face values (in thousands of dollars) of the bonds and the due dates at which principal comes due are listed in the file **P06_81.xls**. (The due dates are the *beginnings* of the years listed.) The Gold and Silver Company (GS) wants to underwrite Gotham City's bonds. A proposal to Gotham for underwriting this issue consists of the following: (1) an interest rate, 3%, 4%, 5%, 6%, or 7%, for each bond, where coupons are paid annually, and (2) an up-front premium paid by GS to Gotham City. GS has determined the set of fair prices (in thousands of dollars) for the bonds listed in the file **P06_81.xls**. For example, if GS underwrites bond 2 maturing in 2001 at 5%, it would charge Gotham City $444,000 for that bond. GS is constrained to use at most three different interest rates.

GS wants to make a profit of at least $46,000, where its profit is equal to the sale price of the bonds minus the face value of the bonds minus the premium GS pays to Gotham City. To maximize the chance that GS will get Gotham City's business, GS wants to minimize the total cost of the bond issue to Gotham City, which is equal to the total interest on the bonds minus the premium paid by GS. For example, if the year 2000 bond (bond 1) is issued at a 4% rate, then Gotham City must pay 2 years of coupon interest: $2(0.04)(\$700,000) = \$56,000$. What assignment of interest rates to each bond and up-front premiums ensure that GS will make the desired profit (assuming it gets the contract) and maximize the chance of GS getting Gotham City's business?

82. Based on Spencer et al. (1990). When you lease 800 phone numbers from AT&T for telemarketing, AT&T uses an optimization model to tell you where you should locate calling centers to minimize your operating costs over a 10-year horizon. To illustrate the model, suppose you are considering seven calling center locations: Boston, New York, Charlotte, Dallas, Chicago, Los Angeles, and Omaha. You know the average cost (in dollars) incurred if a telemarketing call is made from any these cities to any region of the country. You also know the hourly wage that you must pay workers in each city. This information is listed in the file **P06_82.xls**. Assume that an average call requires 4 minutes of labor. You make calls 250 days per year, and the average number of calls made per day to each region of the country is also listed in the file **P06_82.xls**. The cost (in millions of dollars) of building a calling center in each possible location is also listed in the file **P06_82.xls**. Each calling center can make up to 5000 calls per day. Given this information, how can you minimize the discounted cost (at 10% per year) of running the telemarketing operation for 10 years? Assume all wage and calling costs are paid at the *ends* of the respective years.

83. Consider the following puzzle. You are to select four three-letter "words" from the following list: DBA DEG ADI FFD GHI BCD FDF BAI. For each word you earn a score equal to the position of the word's third letter in the alphabet. For example, DBA earns a score of 1, DEG earns a score of 7, and so on. Your goal is to choose the four words that maximize your total score, subject to the following constraint: The sum of the positions in the alphabet for the first letters of the four words chosen must be at least as large as the sum of the positions in the alphabet for the second letters of the words chosen. Use Solver to solve this problem.

Modeling Problems

84. Suppose that you want to divide a state containing 12 cities into five congressional districts. How might you use IP to assign cities to districts?

85. The Wanderers Insurance Company has hired you to determine the number of sales divisions into which the country should be divided. Each division will need a president, a vice president, and a divisional staff. The time needed to call on a client will depend on the distance of the salesperson from the client. Discuss how you would determine the optimal number of sales divisions and the allocation of the company's salesforce to the various divisions.

86. Ten different types of brownies are sold. You are thinking of developing a new brownie for sale. Brownies are rated on the basis of five qualities: price, chocolate flavor, chewiness, sweetness, and ease of preparation. You want to group the ten brownies on the market into three clusters. Each cluster should contain brownies that are relatively similar.
    a. Why would this be useful to you?
    b. How would you do it?

87. Telco, a national telemarketing firm, usually picks a number of sites around the country from which to make its calls. As a service, AD&D's telecommunication marketing department wants to help Telco choose the number and location of its sites. How can integer programming be used to approach this problem?

This case deals with strategic planning issues for a large company. The main issue is planning the company's production capacity for the coming year. At issue is the overall level of capacity and the type of capacity—for example, the degree of *flexibility* in the manufacturing system. The main tool used to aid the company's planning process in GMC is a mixed integer programming (MIP) model. A *mixed* integer program has both integer and continuous variables.

Problem Statement

The Giant Motor Company (GMC) produces three lines of cars for the domestic (U.S.) market: Lyras, Libras, and Hydras. The Lyra is a relatively inexpensive subcompact car that appeals mainly to first-time car owners and to households using it as a second car for commuting. The Libra is a sporty compact car that is sleeker, faster, and roomier than the Lyra. Without any options, the Libra costs slightly more than the Lyra; additional options increase the price further. The Hydra is the luxury car of the GMC line. It is significantly more expensive than the Lyra and Libra, and it has the highest profit margin of the three cars.

Retooling Options for Capacity Expansion

Currently GMC has three manufacturing plants in the United States. Each plant is dedicated to producing a single line of cars. In its planning for the coming year, GMC is considering the retooling of its Lyra and/or Libra plants. Retooling either plant would represent a major expense for the company. The retooled plants would have significantly increased production capacities. Although having greater *fixed* costs, the retooled plants would be more efficient and have lower *marginal* production costs—that is, higher *marginal* profit contributions. In addition, the retooled plants would be *flexible*—they would have the capability of producing more than one line of cars.

The characteristics of the current plants and the retooled plants are given in Table 6.15. The retooled Lyra and Libra plants are prefaced by the word *new*. The fixed costs and capacities in Table 6.15 are given on an annual basis. A dash in the profit margin section indicates that the plant cannot manufacture that line of car. For example, the new Lyra plant would be capable of producing both Lyras and Libras but not Hydras. The new Libra plant would be capable of producing any of the three lines of cars. Note, however, that the new Libra plant has a slightly lower profit margin for producing Hydras than the Hydra plant. The flexible new Libra plant is capable of producing the luxury Hydra model but is not quite as efficient as the current Hydra plant that is dedicated to Hydra production.

Table 6.15 Plant Characteristics

	Lyra	Libra	Hydra	New Lyra	New Libra
Capacity (in 1000s)	1000	800	900	1600	1800
Fixed cost (in $millions)	2000	2000	2600	3400	3700
Profit Margin by Car Line (in $1000s)					
Lyra	2	—	—	2.5	2.3
Libra	—	3	—	3.0	3.5
Hydra	—	—	5	—	4.8

The fixed costs are annual costs that are incurred by GMC independent of the number of cars that are produced by the plant. For the current plant configurations, the fixed costs include property taxes, insurance, payments on the loan that was taken out to construct the plant, and so on. If a plant is retooled, the fixed costs will include the previous fixed costs plus the additional cost of the renovation. The additional renovation cost will be an annual cost representing the cost of the renovation amortized over a long period.

Demand for GMC Cars

Short-term demand forecasts have been very reliable in the past and are expected to be reliable in the future. The demand for GMC cars for the coming year is given in Table 6.16.

Table 6.16   **Demand for GMC Cars**

	Demand (in 1000s)
Lyra	1400
Libra	1100
Hydra	800

A quick comparison of plant capacities and demands in Table 6.15 and Table 6.16 indicates that GMC is faced with insufficient capacity. Partially offsetting the lack of capacity is the phenomenon of **demand diversion**. If a potential car buyer walks into a GMC dealer showroom wanting to buy a Lyra but the dealer is out of stock, frequently the salesperson can convince the customer to purchase the better Libra car, which is in stock. Unsatisfied demand for the Lyra is said to be *diverted* to the Libra. Only rarely in this situation can the salesperson convince the customer to switch to the luxury Hydra model.

From past experience, GMC estimates that 30% of unsatisfied demand for Lyras is diverted to demand for Libras and 5% to demand for Hydras.

Similarly, 10% of unsatisfied demand for Libras is diverted to demand for Hydras. For example, if the demand for Lyras is 1,400,000 cars, then the unsatisfied demand will be 400,000 if no capacity is added. Out of this unsatisfied demand, 120,000 (= 400,000 × 0.3) will materialize as demand for Libras, and 20,000 (= 400,000 × 0.05) will materialize as demand for Hydras. Similarly, if the demand for Libras is 1,220,000 cars (1,100,000 original demand plus 120,000 demand diverted from Lyras), then the unsatisfied demand for Lyras would be 420,000 if no capacity is added. Out of this unsatisfied demand, 42,000 (= 420,000 × 0.1) will materialize as demand for Hydras. All other unsatisfied demand is lost to competitors. The pattern of demand diversion is summarized in Table 6.17.

Table 6.17   **Demand Diversion Matrix**

	Lyra	Libra	Hydra
Lyra	NA	0.3	0.05
Libra	0	NA	0.10
Hydra	0	0.0	NA

Question

GMC wants to decide whether to retool the Lyra and Libra plants. In addition, GMC wants to determine its production plan at each plant in the coming year. Based on the previous data, formulate a mixed integer programming model for solving GMC's production planning–capacity expansion problem for the coming year. ■

Nonlinear Optimization Models

© Photodisc

GASOLINE BLENDING AT TEXACO

Since the 1950s oil companies have been among the most dedicated users of management science methods, particularly mathematical programming models. They often run optimization models on a daily basis and consider them absolutely indispensable to their operations. DeWitt et al. (1989) describe one company's experiences in the article "OMEGA: An Improved Gasoline Blending System for Texaco." Texaco began using computerized blending models in many of its refineries in the 1960s. By the early 1980s, however, the company realized that these models were not being used routinely by all of its refineries, partly because the optimization routines themselves did not always work correctly. Therefore, a fresh analysis began and culminated in OMEGA, a decision support system that combines data acquisition with nonlinear optimization and presents the blending technicians at Texaco's refineries with graphical descriptions of the results. Texaco estimates (somewhat conservatively) that OMEGA has increased profits up to 30%, which translates to more than $30 million annually.

Generally, Texaco develops aggregated plans at a fairly broad level for medium-range decisions. For example, it creates a monthly operating plan for the entire downstream operation of a regional subdivision of the company. At this broad level of planning, the company makes enough simplifying assumptions to permit the use of linear programming for the blending portion of the model. However, for the short-term day-to-day scheduling of blending at the refineries, linear programming is unable to capture the complex chemical relationships between inputs and outputs. Therefore a nonlinear model is required.

The cause of the complexity of the problem is that Texaco uses various grades of crude oil, refines them into intermediate stocks with particular chemical properties, and finally blends these stocks into required blends of gasoline (such as the regular unleaded and super unleaded we buy at the gas station). Sometimes as many as 15 stocks are used to blend up to eight blends. The qualities of the blends are determined by the qualities of the stocks. Typical stock qualities include percentage of sulfur, octane indices, percentage of aromatics, lead content, and others. There are a number of equations that translate these stock qualities into blend qualities. Of particular importance are blend volatilities and octanes, both of which are related to input stock qualities by *nonlinear* equations. These nonlinear equations require Texaco to employ nonlinear programming. The resulting nonlinear models must take into account constraints on the availabilities of the stocks, the technical requirements on the various blends (such as the maximum percentage of lead allowed), and market considerations. The nonlinear optimizer within OMEGA has been able to perform the optimization quickly and accurately, with the performance results noted previously.

An interesting aspect of the DeWitt article is its discussion of Texaco's experience with nonlinear optimizers. Until OMEGA, Texaco used a nonlinear optimization package that gave rather inconsistent results. Not only was it very slow, but it sometimes failed to provide *any* feasible solution to the problem, and it sometimes stopped at *different* solutions, depending on which initial solution was used. (Based on your experience with Excel's Solver in previous chapters, imagine how you would feel if you and your classmates all used the same spreadsheet model but all got different answers because of different initial trial values. You wouldn't have much faith in the Solver!) This was simply the state of the art at the time—nonlinear optimizers were far from perfect. Fortunately, advances have been made, and the nonlinear optimizer currently used by OMEGA does not suffer from these early problems. ■

7.1 INTRODUCTION

In many complex optimization problems the objective and/or the constraints are nonlinear functions of the decision variables. Such optimization problems are called **nonlinear programming** (NLP) problems. In this chapter we will discuss a variety of interesting problems with inherent nonlinearities, from product pricing to portfolio optimization to rating sports teams.

There are several reasons why a model can become nonlinear, including the following:

- There are nonconstant returns to scale, which means that the effect of some input on some output is nonlinear. For example, consider the effect of advertising on sales. There might be a saturation effect, so that beyond some level, extra advertising dollars have very little effect on sales—much less than the effect of initial advertising dollars. This violates the proportionality assumption of linear models discussed in Chapter 3.

- In pricing models, where we try to maximize revenue (or profit), revenue is price multiplied by quantity sold, and price is typically the decision variable. Because quantity sold is related to price, through a demand function, revenue is really price multiplied by a function of price, and this product is a nonlinear function of price. For example, even if the demand function is linear in price, the product of price and demand will be quadratic in price because it includes a squared price term.

- We often try to find the model that best "fits" observed data. To measure the goodness of the fit, we typically sum the squared differences between the observed values and the model's predicted values. Then we attempt to minimize this sum of squared differences. The squaring introduces nonlinearity.

- In one of the most used financial models, the portfolio optimization model, we try to invest in various securities so that we have high return and low risk. The risk is typically measured as the variance (or standard deviation) of the portfolio, and it is inherently a nonlinear function of the decision variables (the investment amounts).

Nonlinear models are often more realistic than linear models, but they are also more difficult to solve.

As these examples illustrate, we do not need to look very far to find nonlinear models in the real world. In fact, it is probably more accurate to state that truly *linear* models are hard to find. The real world often behaves in a nonlinear manner, so that when we model a problem with LP, we are typically making one or more approximations. By allowing nonlinearities in our models, we can often create more realistic models. Unfortunately, this comes at a price—nonlinear optimization models are more difficult to analyze and solve.

7.2 BASIC IDEAS OF NONLINEAR OPTIMIZATION

When we solve an LP problem with Solver, we can guarantee that the Solver solution is optimal. When we solve an NLP problem, however, it is sometimes possible that Solver will obtain a *suboptimal* solution. For example, if we use Solver to maximize the function in Figure 7.1, it might have difficulty. For the function graphed in this figure, points *A* and *C* are called **local maxima** because the function is larger at *A* and *C* than at nearby points. However, only point *A* actually maximizes the function; it is called the **global maximum**. The problem is that Solver can get "stuck" near point *C*, concluding that *C* maximizes the function, and not find point *A*. Similarly, points *B* and *D* are **local minima** because the function has a lower value at *B* and *D* than at nearby points. However, only point *D* is a **global minimum**. If you ask Solver to *minimize* this function, it might conclude—incorrectly—that point *B* is optimal.

A **local** optimum is better than all nearby points. A **global** optimum is the best point in the entire feasible region. For some NLP problems, Solver can get stuck at a local optimum and never find the global optimum.

Figure 7.1

Function with Local Maxima and Minima

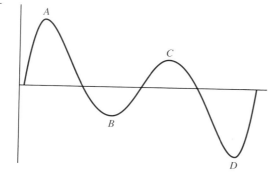

Convex and Concave Functions

Fortunately, there are certain types of NLPs that Solver is guaranteed to solve correctly. To describe these NLPs, we need to define **convex** and **concave** functions. A function of one variable is *convex* in a region if its slope (rate of change) in that region is always nondecreasing. Equivalently, a function of one variable is convex if a line drawn connecting two points on the curve never lies below the curve.[1] Figures 7.2 and 7.3 illustrate two examples of convex functions. In Figure 7.2 the function first decreases and then increases, but the slope is always increasing, first becoming less and less negative and then becoming more and more positive. In contrast, the function in Figure 7.3 is always decreasing, but again the slope is constantly increasing: It is becoming less and less negative.

A function is **convex** if its slope is always nondecreasing.

A function is **concave** if its slope is always nonincreasing.

Figure 7.2

A Convex Function with a Global Minimum

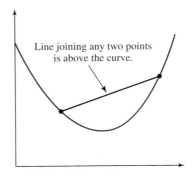

Line joining any two points is above the curve.

Figure 7.3

A Decreasing Convex Function

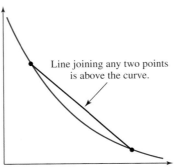

Line joining any two points is above the curve.

The following are common examples of convex functions, although they are by no means the *only* functions that are convex:

$$y = cx^a, \text{ where } a \geq 1, c \geq 0, \text{ and } x \geq 0$$
$$y = ce^x, \text{ where } c \geq 0$$

Similarly, a function of one variable is *concave* in a region if its slope is always nonincreasing. Equivalently, a function of one variable is concave if a line drawn connecting two points on the curve never lies above the curve. Figures 7.4 and 7.5 illustrate typical concave functions. The first has a global maximum and the second is increasing, but the slopes of both are constantly decreasing.

---

[1]For functions of several variables, the precise definition of convexity is more difficult to state. However, the geometric idea of convexity given here will suffice for this book.

Figure 7.4

A Concave Function
with a Global
Maximum

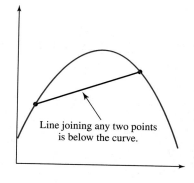

Line joining any two points
is below the curve.

Figure 7.5

An Increasing
Concave Function

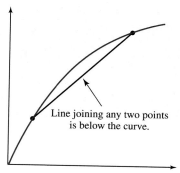

Line joining any two points
is below the curve.

The following are common examples of concave functions, where $\ln(x)$ is the natural logarithm of x:

$$y = c \ln(x), \text{ where } c \geq 0 \text{ and } x > 0$$
$$y = cx^a, \text{ where } 0 < a \leq 1, c \geq 0, \text{ and } x \geq 0$$

A linear function ($y = ax + b$) is both convex and concave. This is because the slope of a linear function is constant.

A more intuitive way to think about convex and concave functions is as follows. Imagine that you are walking up a hill. If you are on a stretch where the hill keeps getting steeper every step you take, you are on the *convex* part of the hill. If it keeps getting less steep, then you are on the *concave* part of the hill. Alternatively, if you are walking down a hill and it is getting less steep with every step you take, you are on the *convex* part of the hill; if it is getting steeper, you are on the *concave* part. In either case (walking uphill or downhill), if the steepness is not changing, you are on the linear part of the hill, which means it is both convex and concave.[2]

It can be shown that the sum of convex functions is convex and the sum of concave functions is concave. Also, if you multiply any convex function by a positive constant, the result is still convex, and if you multiply any concave function by a positive constant, the result is still concave. However, if you multiply a convex function by a *negative* constant, the result is concave, and if you multiply a concave function by a negative constant, the result is convex.

[2]As still one more way of distinguishing convex and concave functions, it might be helpful to think of convex functions as those that "hold water" (see Figure 7.2) and concave functions as those that don't hold water (see Figure 7.4).

Problems That Solvers Always Solve Correctly

Unfortunately, the conditions listed here are often difficult to check without a solid background in calculus.

As Figure 7.2 suggests, Solver will perform well for a minimization problem if the objective function is convex. This is because convex functions cannot have any local minima that are not global minima. Similarly, Figure 7.4 suggests that Solver will perform well for a maximization problem if the objective function is concave. These statements can be generalized to the situation where there are many decision variables and constraints. In fact, if the following conditions hold, then Solver is guaranteed to find the global minimum or global maximum if it exists.[3] (There are actually more general conditions than these, but the conditions stated here will suffice.)

Conditions for Maximization Problems

Solver is guaranteed to find the global maximum (if it exists) if

1. the objective function is concave or the logarithm of the objective function is concave, and

2. the constraints are linear.

Conditions for Minimization Problems

Solver is guaranteed to find the global minimum (if it exists) if

1. the objective function is convex, and

2. the constraints are linear.

Therefore, if the constraints are linear, we need only check for the appropriate concavity or convexity of the objective to assure that Solver will find the optimal solution (instead of a local but nonglobal optimum).

When the Assumptions Do Not Hold

There are many problems for which the conditions outlined previously do not hold or cannot be verified. Because we are then not sure whether Solver's solution is the optimal solution, the best strategy is to (1) try several possible starting values for the changing cells, (2) run Solver from each of these, and (3) take the best solution Solver finds.

For example, consider the following NLP:

$$\text{Maximize } (x - 1)(x - 2)(x - 3)(x - 4)(x - 5) \qquad \textbf{(7.1)}$$

$$\text{Subject to:}$$

$$x \geq 1 \text{ and } x \leq 5$$

When an objective function has multiple local optima, the solution Solver finds can depend on the starting solution in the changing cells.

This is the function shown in Figure 7.1, where the graph extends from $x = 1$ to $x = 5$. Obviously, this function equals 0 when x equals 1, 2, 3, 4, or 5. (Just substitute any of these values for x into the function.) From the graph we see that the global maximum is between $x = 1$ and $x = 2$, but that there is a local maximum between $x = 3$ and $x = 4$. The spreadsheet in Figure 7.6 shows the results of using Solver to solve this problem. In columns A and B we show what happened when the starting value in the changing cell was $x = 1.5$. Solver eventually found $x = 1.355567$ with a corresponding objective value of 3.631432. (The objective in cell B11 is the product of the five numbers above it, and the constraints are B5≤5 and B5≥1.) However, given the identical setup in columns D and E, but with a starting value of $x = 3.5$, Solver found the local maximum $x = 3.543912$ and its corresponding objective value of 1.418697. This second solution is not the correct solution to

---

[3]The following discussion assumes that your spreadsheet contains no IF, MAX, MIN, or ABS statements that depend on changing cells. Current-generation spreadsheet Solvers are not equipped to deal with these functions, and errors often occur if they are present.

the problem in equation (7.1), but Solver found it because of an "unlucky" starting value of x.

Figure 7.6

Function with Local and Global Maxima

	A	B	C	D	E
1	Function with local and global maxima				
2					
3	The function is: y=(x-1)(x-2)(x-3)(x-4)(x-5)				
4					
5	x	1.355567		x	3.543912
6	x-1	0.355567		x-1	2.543912
7	x-2	-0.644433		x-2	1.543912
8	x-3	-1.644433		x-3	0.543912
9	x-4	-2.644433		x-4	-0.456088
10	x-5	-3.644433		x-5	-1.456088
11	Product	3.631432		Product	1.418697

In general, if you try several starting combinations for the changing cells and Solver obtains the same optimal solution in all cases, you can be fairly confident—but still not absolutely sure—that you have found the optimal solution to the NLP. On the other hand, if you try different starting values for the changing cells and obtain several different solutions, then the best you can do is keep the "best" solution you have found.

7.3 PRICING MODELS

Setting prices on products and services is becoming a critical decision for many companies. A good example is pricing of hotel rooms and airline tickets. To many airline customers, ticket pricing appears to be madness on the part of the airlines (how can it cost less to fly thousands of miles to London than to fly a couple of hundred miles within the United States?), but there is some method to the madness. In this section we will examine some pricing problems that can be modeled as NLPs.

EXAMPLE | 7.1 PRICING DECISIONS AT MADISON

The Madison Company manufactures and retails a certain product. The company wants to determine the price that maximizes its profit from this product. The unit cost of producing and marketing the product is $50. Madison will certainly charge at least $50 for the product to ensure that it makes *some* profit. However, there is a very competitive market for this product, so that Madison's demand will fall sharply as it increases its price. How should the company proceed?[4]

Objective To use a demand function in a nonlinear model to find the price that maximizes the company's profit.

WHERE DO THE NUMBERS COME FROM?

Cost accountants should be able to supply the unit cost. Historical data on demands and prices of the product will be needed to estimate the demand function, as discussed subsequently.

---

[4]This example and the next two are based on Dolan and Simon (1996).

Solution

The variables and constraints for this model are listed in Table 7.1. The unit price drives everything. Through a demand function, price determines demand, and these combine to determine the revenue, cost, and profit. (We assume the company produces only what it can sell—that is, it observes its demand and then produces exactly this much.) The only constraint is that the company doesn't want to charge a price less than its unit cost.

Table 7.1 Variables and Constraints for Madison's Pricing Model

Input variables	Unit cost, demand function (or points on demand function)
Decision variables (changing cells)	Unit price to charge
Objective (target cell)	Profit
Other output variables	Revenue, cost
Constraints	Unit price ≥ Unit cost

More specifically, if Madison charges P dollars per unit, then its profit will be $(P - 50)D$, where D is the number of units demanded. The problem, however, is that D depends on P. As the price P increases, the demand D decreases. Therefore, the first step is to estimate how D varies with P—that is, we have to estimate the demand function. In fact, this is the first step in almost all pricing problems. We will illustrate two possibilities: a *linear* demand function of the form $D = a - bP$, and a *constant elasticity* demand function of the form $D = aP^b$.

Estimating the Demand Function

The elasticity of demand measures the sensitivity of demand to changes in price.

You might recall from microeconomics that the *elasticity* of demand is the percentage change in demand caused by a 1% increase in price. The larger the (magnitude of) elasticity is, the more demand reacts to price changes. The advantage of the constant elasticity demand function is that the elasticity remains constant over all points on the demand curve. For example, the elasticity of demand is the same when price is $60 as when price is $70. Actually, the exponent b is approximately equal to this constant elasticity. For example, if $b = -2.5$, then demand will decrease by about 2.5% if price increases by 1%. In contrast, the elasticity *changes* for different price levels if the demand function is linear. Nevertheless, both forms of demand functions are commonly used in economic models, and we could use either in our pricing model.

Regardless of the *form* of the demand function, the parameters of the function (a and b) must be estimated before any price optimization can be performed. This can be done with Excel trendlines. (We will discuss trendlines in more detail in Chapter 12.) Suppose that Madison can estimate two points on the demand curve. (At least two are required. More than two could be used in the same way.) Specifically, suppose the company estimates demand to be 400 units when price equals $70 and 300 units when price equals $80. Then we create an X-Y chart of demand versus price from these two points, select either chart, and use Excel's Chart/Add Trendline menu item with the option to list the equation of the trendline on the chart. For a linear demand curve, we select the Linear trendline option, and for the constant elasticity demand curve, we select the Power trendline option. (The relevant dialog box appears in Figure 7.7. To find the option to list the equation on the chart, click on the Options tab.)

Figure 7.7

Excel's Trendline
Dialog Box

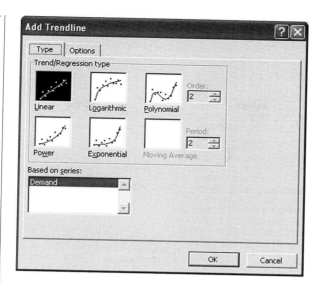

The results are presented in Figure 7.8, where we show both the linear estimate and constant elasticity estimate. (When you do this, the constant for the constant elasticity curve might appear as 4E+06. To get more significant digits, just click on the equation and then use the Format menu and the Number tab to format the number appropriately.) We can use either of these trendline equations as an of estimate the demand function for the pricing model.

Figure 7.8 Determining Parameters of Demand Functions

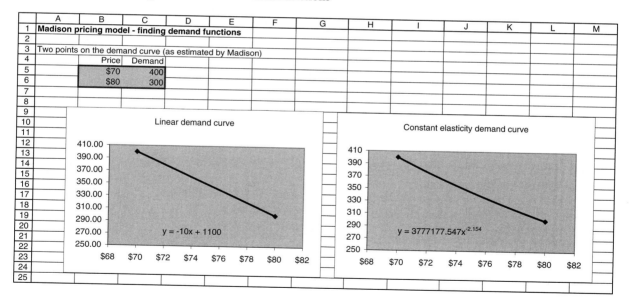

DEVELOPING THE SPREADSHEET MODEL

Given a demand function, the pricing decision is straightforward, as shown in Figure 7.9 (page 304). (See the file **Pricing1.xls**.) Here we have used the constant elasticity demand curve. (The model for linear demand is similar. The **Pricing1.xls** file illustrates both cases.) The model requires the following steps.

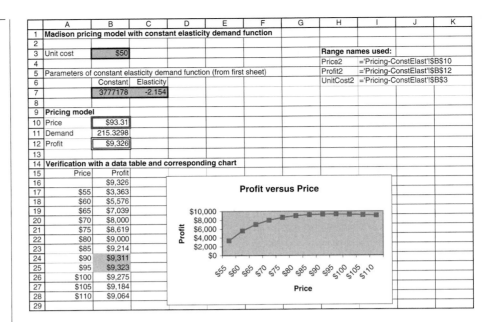

Figure 7.9

Pricing Model with Constant Elasticity Demand

	A	B	C	D	E	F	G	H	I	J	K
1	Madison pricing model with constant elasticity demand function										
2											
3	Unit cost	$50						Range names used:			
4								Price2	='Pricing-ConstElast'!$B$10		
5	Parameters of constant elasticity demand function (from first sheet)							Profit2	='Pricing-ConstElast'!$B$12		
6		Constant	Elasticity					UnitCost2	='Pricing-ConstElast'!$B$3		
7		3777178	-2.154								
8											
9	Pricing model										
10	Price	$93.31									
11	Demand	215.3298									
12	Profit	$9,326									
13											
14	Verification with a data table and corresponding chart										
15	Price	Profit									
16		$9,326									
17	$55	$3,363									
18	$60	$5,576									
19	$65	$7,039									
20	$70	$8,000									
21	$75	$8,619									
22	$80	$9,000									
23	$85	$9,214									
24	$90	$9,311									
25	$95	$9,323									
26	$100	$9,275									
27	$105	$9,184									
28	$110	$9,064									
29											

① Inputs. The inputs for this model are the unit cost and the parameters of the demand function found previously. Enter them as shown.

② Price. Enter any trial value for price. It will be the single changing cell.

③ Demand. Calculate the corresponding demand from the demand function by entering the formula

=B7*Price2^C7

in cell B11. (To minimize range name conflicts, we used the names Price1, UnitCost1, and Profit1 for the linear demand model, and we used Price2, UnitCost2, and Profit2 for the constant elasticity model.)

④ Profit. Calculate the profit as unit contribution (price minus unit cost) multiplied by demand with the formula

=(Price2-UnitCost2)*B11

in cell B12.

If you check the Assume Linear Model box for any model in this chapter, you will get an error message. This is because Solver automatically recognizes that these models are nonlinear.

USING SOLVER

The relevant Solver dialog box is shown in Figure 7.10. We maximize profit subject to the constraint that price must be at least as large as unit cost, with price as the only decision variable. However, we do *not* check the Assume Linear Model box under Solver options. This model is nonlinear for two reasons. First, the demand function is nonlinear in price because price is raised to a power. But even if the demand function were linear, profit would still be nonlinear. The reason is that it involves the *product* of price and demand, and demand is a function of price. This nonlinearity can be seen easily with the data table and corresponding chart in Figure 7.9. These show how profit varies with price—the relationship is clearly nonlinear. Profit increases to a maximum, then declines slowly. (This type of data table and chart are useful in nonlinear models with a *single* changing cell. They show exactly how the objective changes as the changing cell changes. We will employ these in other nonlinear examples whenever possible.)

Figure 7.10

Solver Dialog Box
for Pricing Model

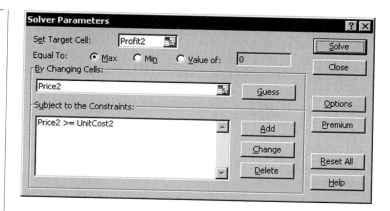

Discussion of the Solution

*Pricing problems are
inherently nonlinear,
and the trade-off
between selling a lot
of units at a low price
and selling fewer units
at a higher price is
difficult to make.*

It is usually not easy to guess the optimal price in this type of model. As the company increases its price, it makes more money on each unit sold, but it sells fewer units. Therefore, the trade-off is always between selling a few relatively high-priced units and selling a lot of relatively low-priced units. Complicating the matter is the fact that as price increases, total cost decreases (because fewer units are demanded). In the present case we see from the graph in Figure 7.9 that profit increases fairly quickly as price goes from $55 to about $85. After this point, profit is almost unaffected by price (at least for the range of prices shown), and any price from $85 to about $110 will result in a profit within $200 of the optimal profit. Of course, Solver does better than this; it provides us with the *optimal* price, $93.31.

Is the Solver Solution Optimal?

There is no guarantee in general that profit is a concave function for all possible inputs to this model. However, the graph in Figure 7.9 indicates that it *is* concave for the particular inputs we have used and that the Solver solution is indeed optimal (because there are no local maxima that aren't global maxima).

Sensitivity Analysis

From an economic point of view, it should be interesting to see how the profit-maximizing price varies with the elasticity of the demand function. To do this, we use SolverTable with the elasticity in cell C7 as the single input cell, allowing it to vary from -2.4 to -1.8 in increments of 0.1.[5] (Note that when the range of input values is negative, the one with the largest magnitude must be entered first in the SolverTable dialog box.) The results are shown in Figure 7.11 (page 306). When the demand is most elastic (at the top of the table), increases in price have a greater effect on demand. Therefore, the company should not set the price as high in this case. Interestingly, when demand is least elastic, the company should not only charge a higher price, but this price will result in a much higher profit. Would you have guessed this?

---

[5]Solver *does* provide a sensitivity report for nonlinear models. However, the mathematical theory behind this report is significantly more complex than for linear models, so we will present the more straightforward SolverTable outputs in this chapter.

Figure 7.11

Sensitivity to
Elasticity of
Demand

	A	B	C	D
31	Sensitivity of optimal solution to elasticity			
32		Price	Demand	Profit
33		$B$10	$B$11	$B$12
34	-2.4	$85.71	86.66	$3,095
35	-2.3	$88.46	125.79	$4,838
36	-2.2	$91.67	182.10	$7,587
37	-2.1	$95.45	262.78	$11,945
38	-2.0	$100.00	377.72	$18,886
39	-1.9	$105.56	540.20	$30,011
40	-1.8	$112.50	767.53	$47,970

EXAMPLE **7.2 PRICING WITH EXCHANGE RATE CONSIDERATIONS AT MADISON**

We continue Example 7.1, but we now assume that Madison manufactures its product in the United States and sells it in the United Kingdom (UK). Given the prevailing exchange rate in dollars per pound, Madison wants to determine the price in pounds it should charge in the UK so that its profit in dollars is maximized. The company also wants to see how the optimal price and the optimal profit depend on exchange rate fluctuations.

Objective   To use a nonlinear model to find the price in pounds that maximizes the profit in dollars.

WHERE DO THE NUMBERS COME FROM?

The only new input in this model is the exchange rate, and it is readily available. For example, you can find exchange rates at http://www.oanda.com/convert/classic.

Solution

The model is shown in Figure 7.12. (See the file **Pricing2.xls**.) It is very similar to the previous model, so we will highlight only the new features. The exchange rate in cell B4 indicates the number of dollars required to purchase one pound. For example, with an exchange rate of 1.56, it takes $1.56 to purchase one pound. Alternatively, 1/1.56 = 0.641 £ is required to purchase one dollar. As this exchange rate decreases, we say that the dollar gets stronger; as it increases, the dollar gets weaker. Note that we *divide* by the exchange rate to convert dollars to pounds, and we *multiply* by the exchange rate to convert pounds to dollars. With this in mind, the model development is straightforward.

Figure 7.12

Pricing Model in a
Foreign Market

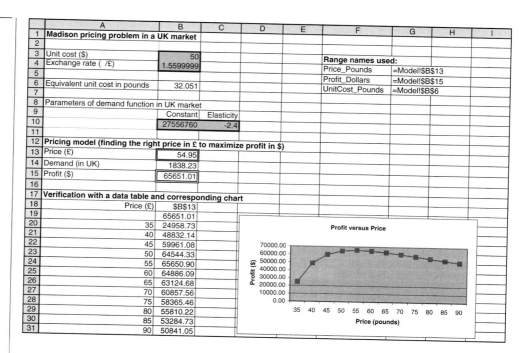

DEVELOPING THE SPREADSHEET MODEL

The following steps are required.

1 Inputs. The inputs are the unit cost (in dollars), the exchange rate, and the parameters of the company's demand function for the UK market. These latter values would need to be estimated exactly as we discussed in the previous example. We chose "reasonable" values for this example, as shown in row 10.

2 Unit cost in pounds. Although Madison's unit cost occurs in the United States and is expressed in dollars, it is convenient to express it in pounds. Do this in cell B6 with the formula

=B3/B4

(Actually, we calculate this so that we can form a constraint on the price: the unit price in pounds must be no less than the unit cost in pounds.)

3 Price, demand. As in the previous example, enter any price in cell B13 (which is now in pounds), and calculate the demand in cell B14 from the demand function with the formula

=B10*Price_Pounds^C10

4 Profit. The profit should be in dollars, so enter the formula

=(Price_Pounds*B4-B3)*B14

in cell B15. Note that the unit cost is already in dollars, but the UK price must be converted to dollars.

USING SOLVER

The Solver dialog box (not shown here) is set up exactly as in Figure 7.10, except that the constraint on price is now Price_Pounds≥UnitCost_Pounds, so that pounds are compared to pounds. In fact, the specification of this constraint is the only place where the value in cell B6 enters the model.

Discussion of the Solution

The optimal solution, with an exchange rate of 1.56, says that Madison should charge 54.95 £ per unit in the UK. This will create demand for about 1828 units. Each of these will cost $50 to produce, and the dollar revenue from each of them will be 54.95(1.56), or $85.71. The resulting profit in dollars will be approximately $65,651. The graph in Figure 7.12, created from a data table of profit versus price, shows how profit declines on either side of the optimal price.

Is the Solver Solution Optimal?

As in the previous example, the objective is not necessarily a concave function of price for all possible values of the input parameters. However, the graph in Figure 7.12 indicates that it is concave for our particular input parameters and that the Solver solution is indeed optimal.

Sensitivity Analysis

What happens when the dollar gets stronger or weaker? We use SolverTable with exchange rate as the single input, allowing it to vary from 1.30 to 1.80 in increments of 0.05, and we keep track of price, demand, and profit. The results in Figure 7.13 indicate that, as the dollar strengthens (the exchange rate decreases), Madison charges more in pounds for the product, but it obtains a lower profit. The opposite is true when the dollar weakens. Are these results in line with your economic intuition? Note that when the dollar strengthens, pounds are not worth as much to an American company. Therefore, when we convert the pound revenue to dollars in the profit cell, the profit tends to decrease. But in this case, why does the optimal price in pounds *increase*? We'll say no more here—except that this should be a good question for class discussion.

Figure 7.13

Sensitivity of the Optimal Solution to the Exchange Rate

	A	B	C	D
33	Sensitivity of price, demand, and profit to exchange rate			
34		$B$13	$B$14	$B$15
35	1.30	65.93	1186.76	42384.44
36	1.35	63.49	1299.28	46402.71
37	1.40	61.22	1417.78	50634.87
38	1.45	59.11	1542.35	55084.01
39	1.50	57.14	1673.09	59753.24
40	1.55	55.30	1810.07	64645.52
41	1.60	53.57	1953.39	69763.83
42	1.65	51.95	2103.11	75111.06
43	1.70	50.42	2259.32	80690.01
44	1.75	48.98	2422.10	86503.51
45	1.80	47.62	2591.52	92554.26

Many products create tie-ins to other products. For example, if you own a men's clothing store, you should recognize that when a person buys a suit, he often buys a shirt or a tie. Failure to take this into account will cause you to price your suits too high—and lose potential sales of shirts and ties. The following example illustrates the idea.

EXAMPLE | **7.3 PRICING SUITS AT SULLIVAN'S**

Sullivan's is a retailer of upscale men's clothing. Suits cost Sullivan's $320. The current price of suits to customers is $350, which leads to annual sales of 300 suits. The elasticity of the demand for men's suits is estimated to be -2.5, and it is assumed to be constant over the relevant price range. Each purchase of a suit leads to an average of 2 shirts and 1.5 ties being sold. Each shirt contributes $25 to profit and each tie contributes $15 to profit. Determine a profit-maximizing price for suits.

Objective   To use a nonlinear model to price men's suits optimally, taking into account the purchases of shirts and ties that typically accompany purchases of suits.

WHERE DO THE NUMBERS COME FROM?

The dollar figures could be supplied by a cost accountant. The elasticity of demand would be estimated from historical data on demands and prices, as discussed in Example 7.1. Finally, the average numbers of shirts and ties sold with suit purchases would be available from historical data, assuming the company keeps track of such complementary purchases.

Solution

The variables and constraints for this pricing model are listed in Table 7.2. As in the previous two examples, we must first determine the demand function for suits. Although this could be a linear function or some other form, we will again assume a constant elasticity function of the form $D = aP^b$, where the exponent b is the elasticity. The solution from this point is practically the same as the solution to Example 7.1 except for the profit function. Each suit sold also generates demand for 2 shirts and 1.5 ties (on average), which contributes $2(25) + 1.5(15)$ extra dollars in profit. Therefore, it makes sense that the profit-maximizing price for suits will be *lower* than in the absence of shirts and ties—the company wants to generate more demand for suits so that it can reap the benefits from shirts and ties. The only constraint is that the price of suits should be at least as large as the unit cost of suits. (Is this constraint really necessary? We will discuss this question next.)

Table 7.2	Variables and Constraints for Suit Pricing Model
Input variables	Unit cost of suit, current price of suit, current demand for suits, elasticity of demand, ties and shirts purchased per suit, unit profits from a tie and a shirt
Decision variables (changing cells)	Price to charge for a suit
Objective (target cell)	Total profit
Other output variables	Constant in demand function, demand for suits, profit from suits alone, profit from ties and shirts
Constraints	Price of suit ≥ Unit cost of suit (necessary?)

DEVELOPING THE SPREADSHEET MODEL

The spreadsheet solution appears in Figure 7.14 (page 310). (See the file **Pricing3.xls**.) Instead of solving a single model, we will actually solve two: the one stated previously and one where we ignore shirts and ties. This way we can gauge the effect that shirts and ties have on the optimal price of suits. We could set this up as two distinct models, but a clever use of SolverTable allows us to treat both cases in a single model. The details are as follows.

Figure 7.14 Pricing Model with Complementary Products

	A	B	C	D	E	F	G	H	I	J
1	Pricing complementary products									
2										
3	Suits			Complementary products				Range names used:		
4	Current price	$350			Ties	Shirts		Price	=Model!$B$13	
5	Current demand	300		Units sold per suit	1.5	2		Profit	=Model!$B$15	
6	Unit cost	$320		Profit per unit	$15	$25		UnitCost	=Model!$B$6	
7										
8	Demand function			Sensitivity factor for units sold per suit						
9	Constant	687,529,545			1					
10	Elasticity	-2.5								
11										
12	Decision taking complementary products into account									
13	Price	$412.50								
14	Demand	198.9								
15	Profit from suits only	$18,402								
16	Profit from shirts and ties	$14,423								
17	Total profit	$32,826								
18										
19	Verification with a data table and corresponding chart									
20		Price	Profit							
21			$32,826							
22		380	$32,363							
23		390	$32,617							
24		400	$32,765							
25		410	$32,824							
26		420	$32,806							
27		430	$32,725							
28		440	$32,590							
29		450	$32,410							
30		460	$32,193							
31		470	$31,943							
32		480	$31,667							
33										
34	Sensitivity of price, demand, profit to sensitivity factor									
35			$B$13	$B$14		$B$15	$B$16	$B$17			
36		0	$533.33	104.7		$22,328	$0	$22,328			
37		0.5	$472.92	141.4		$21,616	$5,124	$26,741			
38		1	$412.50	198.9		$18,402	$14,423	$32,826			
39		1.5	$352.08	295.6		$9,483	$32,145	$41,628			
40		2	$320.00	375.3		$0	$54,423	$54,423			

Profit versus Price chart (Price 380–480 on x-axis, Profit $31,000–$33,000 on y-axis).

When sensitivity factor is 0, it is as if complementary products are ignored.

❶ **Inputs.** Enter all inputs in the shaded regions.

❷ **Constant for demand function.** The demand function is of the form $D = aP^b$. We can find the constant a from the current demand and price for suits: $300 = a(350^{-2.5})$, so that $a = 300/350^{-2.5}$. Therefore, calculate this constant a in cell B9 with the formula

=B5/B4^B10

As this example illustrates, a clever use of SolverTable sometimes enables us to solve multiple problems at once.

❸ **Sensitivity factor.** We will treat both cases, when shirts and ties are ignored and when they are not, by using SolverTable with a "sensitivity factor" as the input cell. When this factor is 0, the complementary products are ignored; when it is positive, they are taken into consideration. Enter 1 in the sensitivity factor cell E9 for now. In general, this factor determines the average number of shirts and ties purchased with the purchase of a suit— we multiply this factor by the values in the E5:F5 range. When this factor is 1, we get the values in the statement of the problem. When it is 0, no shirts and ties are purchased with a suit.

❹ **Price, demand.** Enter *any* price in cell B13, and calculate the corresponding demand for suits in cell B14 with the formula

=B9*B13^B10

❺ **Profits.** The total profit is the profit from suits alone, plus the extra profit from shirts and ties that are purchased along with suits. Calculate the first of these in cell B15 with the formula

=(Price-Unit cost)*B14

and calculate the second in cell B16 with the formula

=E9*SUMPRODUCT(E5:F5,E6:F6)*B14

Then sum them to get the total profit in cell B17. Note that the sensitivity factor in cell E9 scales the extra profit, depending on how many ties and shirts per suit are sold. If the value in cell E9 is 0, then no shirts and ties are sold; if this value is 1, then the numbers of shirts and ties stated in the problem are sold.

USING SOLVER

The Solver setup, not shown here, is the same as in Example 7.1. We maximize profit, with the price of suits as the only changing cell, and we constrain this price to be at least as large as the unit cost of suits.

Discussion of the Solution

The solution in Figure 7.14 uses a sensitivity factor of 1 in cell E9, which means that every suit sale is accompanied (on average) by the sale of 2 shirts and 1.5 ties. This induces the company to keep the suit price relatively low, at $412.50, so that it can sell a lot of suits and therefore a lot of ties and shirts. In fact, we see that the total profit is nearly evenly divided between the profit from suits and the profit from shirts and ties.

The potential sales of complementary products induces a company to price its main product lower than if there were no complementary products.

To see the effect of complementary products, we then run SolverTable with cell E9 as the single input cell, varied, say, from 0 to 2.5 (or any other upper limit you like) in increments of 0.5, and keep track of price, demand, and profit. (Again, see Figure 7.14.) The SolverTable results show that when the company ignores shirts and ties (or, equivalently, suits do not generate any demand for shirts and ties), the optimal price is set high, at $533.33. However, as more ties and shirts are purchased by purchasers of suits, the optimal price of suits decreases fairly dramatically. As we would imagine, as more shirts and ties are purchased with suits, the company makes more profit—*if* it takes shirts and ties into account and prices suits properly. Interestingly, if the sensitivity factor increases to 2, so that customers on average buy 3 ties and 4 shirts with every suit, then the company sets its price so that it just breaks even on suits and makes all of its profit on ties and shirts. (If you are skeptical of this result, read the "Is the Constraint Needed?" section that follows.)

For the situation in the problem statement, how much profit does the company lose if it ignores shirts and ties? You can answer this by entering $533.33 in the Price cell, keeping the sensitivity factor equal to 1. If you do so, you will find that profit decreases from $32,826 to $29,916, a drop of about 9%. This is the penalty of pricing in a nonoptimal manner.

Is the Solver Solution Optimal?

As in the preceding two examples, the graph in Figure 7.14, formed from a data table of profit versus price, indicates that the Solver solution is indeed optimal—there are no local maxima.

Is the Constraint Needed?

In pricing models we hardly think twice before constraining the price to be at least as large as the unit cost. However, it might make sense to price a product *below* cost if sales of this product lead to sales—and profits—from other products. Therefore, we deleted the constraint on price in the example and reran SolverTable. The results appear in Figure 7.15 (page 312). The only change is in row 25, where the sensitivity factor is 2. We now price the suits below cost, just to sell more shirts and ties. In fact, the only reason we priced to break even in this row before was the constraint—we didn't allow a price below the unit cost. When we allow this behavior, the profit increases from its earlier value of $54,423 to $55,210.

Figure 7.15 Solution with Pricing Below Cost Allowed

	A	B	C	D	E	F	G	H	I	J
19	Sensitivity of price, demand, profit to sensitivity factor									
20		$B$13	$B$14	$B$15	$B$16	$B$17				
21	0	$533.33	104.7	$22,328	$0	$22,328				
22	0.5	$472.92	141.4	$21,616	$5,124	$26,741		Pricing below cost is indeed optimal in this last row.		
23	1	$412.50	198.9	$18,402	$14,423	$32,826				
24	1.5	$352.08	295.6	$9,483	$32,145	$41,628	←			
25	2	$291.67	473.2	-$13,408	$68,619	$55,210				

Automobile and appliance dealers who profit from maintenance contracts would probably increase their profits significantly if they factored the profits from the maintenance agreements into the determination of prices of their major products. That is, we suspect that the prices of their major products are set too high—not from the customers' standpoint but from the dealers'. Probably the ultimate "tie-in" reduction in price is the fact that many companies now give software away for free. They are hoping, of course, that the receiver of free software will later buy the "tie-in" product, which is the upgrade. ■

In many situations there are peak-load and off-peak demands for a product. In such a situation it might be optimal for a producer to charge a larger price for peak-load service than for off-peak service. The following example illustrates this situation.

EXAMPLE

7.4 PEAK-LOAD PRICING AT FLORIDA POWER AND LIGHT

Florida Power and Light (FPL) faces demands during both peak-load and off-peak times. FPL must determine the price per kilowatt hour (kwh) to charge during both peak-load and off-peak periods. The daily demand for power during each period (in kwh) is related to price as follows:

$$D_p = 60 - 0.5P_p + 0.1P_o \qquad (7.2)$$

$$D_o = 40 - P_o + 0.1P_p \qquad (7.3)$$

The positive coefficients of prices in these demand equations indicate the "substitute" behavior. A larger price for one product will induce customers to demand more of the other.

Here, D_p and P_p are demand and price during peak-load times, whereas D_o and P_o are demand and price during off-peak times. Note that we are now using *linear* demand functions, not the constant elasticity demand functions from the previous examples. (We do this for the sake of variety. The model would not differ substantially if we used constant elasticity demand functions.) Also, note from the signs of the coefficients that an increase in the peak-load price decreases the demand for power during the peak-load period but *increases* the demand for power during the off-peak period. Similarly, an increase in the price for the off-peak period decreases the demand for the off-peak period but *increases* the demand for the peak-load period. In economic terms, this implies that peak-load power and off-peak power are *substitutes* for one another. In addition, it costs FPL $10 per day to maintain 1 kwh of capacity. The company wants to determine a pricing strategy and a capacity level that maximize its daily profit.

Objective To use a nonlinear model to determine prices and capacity when there are two different daily usage patterns, peak-load and off-peak.

WHERE DO THE NUMBERS COME FROM?

As usual, a cost accountant should be able to estimate the unit cost of capacity. The real difficulty here would be to estimate the demand functions in equations (7.2) and (7.3). This would require either sufficient historical data on prices and demands (for both peak-load and off-peak periods) or educated guesses from management.

Solution

The capacity must be at least as large as the peak-load and off-peak demands. Actually, there is no incentive for it to be larger than the maximum of these two demands.

The variables and constraints for this model are listed in Table 7.3. The company must decide on two prices, and it must determine the amount of capacity to maintain. Because this capacity level, once determined, is relevant for peak-load and off-peak periods, it must be large enough to meet demands for both periods. This is the reasoning behind the constraint.

Table 7.3   Variables and Constraints for Peak-Load Pricing Model

Input variables	Parameters of demand functions, unit cost of capacity
Decision variables (changing cells)	Peak-load and off-peak prices, capacity
Objective (target cell)	Profit
Other output variables	Peak-load and off-peak demands, revenue, cost of capacity
Constraints	Demands ≤ Capacity

Due to the relationships between the demand and price variables, it is not at all obvious what FPL should do. The pricing decisions determine demand, and larger demand requires larger capacity, which costs money. In addition, revenue is price multiplied by demand, so it is not clear whether price should be low or high to increase revenue.

DEVELOPING THE SPREADSHEET MODEL

The spreadsheet model appears in Figure 7.16. (See the file **Pricing4.xls**.) It can be developed as follows.

Figure 7.16   Peak-Load Pricing Model

	A	B	C	D	E	F	G	H	I
1	Florida Power & Light peak-load pricing model								
2									
3	**Input data**								
4	Coefficients of demand functions					Range names used:			
5		Constant	Peak price	Off-peak price		Capacity	=PeakLoad!$B$15		
6	Peak-load demand	60	-0.5	0.1		Common_Capacity	=PeakLoad!$B$21:$C$21		
7	Off-peak demand	40	0.1	-1		Demands	=PeakLoad!$B$19:$C$19		
8						Prices	=PeakLoad!$B$13:$C$13		
9	Cost of capacity/kwh	$10				Profit	=PeakLoad!$B$26		
10									
11	**Decisions**								
12		Peak-load	Off-peak						
13	Prices	$70.31	$26.53						
14									
15	Capacity	27.50							
16									
17	**Constraints on demand**								
18		Peak-load	Off-peak						
19	Demand	27.50	20.50						
20		<=	<=						
21	Capacity	27.50	27.50						
22									
23	**Monetary summary**								
24	Revenue	$2,477.30							
25	Cost of capacity	$275.00							
26	Profit	$2,202.30							

1 **Inputs.** Enter the parameters of the demand functions and the cost of capacity in the shaded ranges.

2 **Prices and capacity level.** Enter *any* trial prices (per kwh) for peak-load and off-peak power in the Prices range, and enter *any* trial value for the capacity level in the Capacity cell. These are the three values FPL has control over, so they become the changing cells.

3 **Demands.** Calculate the demand for the peak-load period by substituting into equation (7.2). That is, enter the formula

=B6+SUMPRODUCT(Prices,C6:D6)

in cell B19. Similarly, enter the formula

=B7+SUMPRODUCT(Prices,C7:D7)

in cell C19 for the off-peak demand.

4 **Copy capacity.** To indicate the capacity constraints, enter the formula

=Capacity

in cells B21 and C21. The reason for creating these links is that we want the two demand cells in row 19 to be paired with two capacity cells in row 21, so that we can specify the Solver constraints appropriately. (Solver doesn't allow us to have a "two versus one" constraint like B19:C19 <= B15.)

5 **Monetary values.** Calculate the daily revenue, cost of capacity, and profit in the corresponding cells with the formulas

=SUMPRODUCT(Demands,Prices)

=Capacity*B9

and

=B24-B25

USING SOLVER

The Solver dialog box should be filled in as in Figure 7.17. We maximize profit by setting appropriate prices and capacity, and we ensure that demand never exceeds the capacity. Logically, we should also check Solver's Assume Non-Negative box (prices and capacity cannot be negative), but we should *not* check the Assume Linear Model box. Again, this is because we are multiplying prices by demands, which are functions of prices, so that profit is a nonlinear function of the prices.

Figure 7.17
Solver Dialog Box
for Peak-Load
Pricing Model

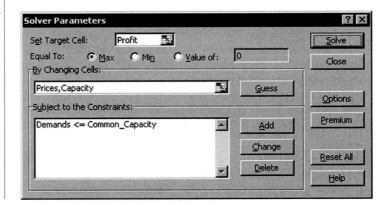

Discussion of the Solution

The Solver solution in Figure 7.16 indicates that FPL should charge $70.31 per kwh during the peak-load period and $26.53 during the off-peak-load period. These prices generate demands of 27.5 (peak-load) and 20.5 (off-peak), so that a capacity of 27.5 kwh is required. The cost of this capacity is $275. When this is subtracted from the revenue of $2477.30, the daily profit becomes $2202.30.

Varying the changing cells slightly from their optimal values sometimes provides insight into the optimal solution.

To gain some insight into this solution, consider what happens if FPL changes the peak-load price slightly from its optimal value of $70.31. If FPL decreases the price to $70, say, you can check that the peak-load demand increases to 27.65 and the off-peak demand decreases to 20.47. The net effect is that revenue increases slightly, to $2478.78. However, the peak-load demand is now greater than capacity, so FPL must increase its capacity from 27.50 to 27.65. This costs an extra $1.50, which more than offsets the increase in revenue. A similar chain of effects occurs if FPL increases the peak price to $71. In this case, peak-load demand decreases, off-peak demand increases, and total revenue decreases. Although FPL can get by with lower capacity, the net effect is slightly less profit. Fortunately, Solver evaluates all of these trade-offs for us when it finds the optimal solution.

Is the Solver Solution Optimal?

All of the constraints in this example are linear, so they certainly meet the assumptions for a maximization problem. Also, it can be shown that the objective (daily profit) is a concave function of peak-load price, off-peak price, and capacity level—although this is far from obvious. (It requires calculus to verify.) Algebraically, this objective function is called **quadratic**, meaning that it is a sum of linear terms (such as P_p), squared terms (such as P_p^2), and cross-product terms (such as $P_p P_o$). Not all quadratic functions are concave, but there is a test to check whether a given quadratic function is concave. We will not cover the details of this test, but we assure you that the quadratic function for this example passes the test. Therefore, the assumptions for a maximization problem are satisfied, and the Solver solution is guaranteed to be optimal.

Sensitivity Analysis

To gain even more insight, we use SolverTable to see the effects of changing the unit cost of capacity, which we allow to vary from $5 to $15 in increments of $1. The results appear in Figure 7.18. They indicate that as the cost of capacity increases, the peak-load price increases, the off-peak price stays constant, the amount of capacity decreases, and profit decreases. The latter two effects are probably intuitive, but we challenge you to explain the effects on price. In particular, why does the peak-load price *increase*, and why doesn't the off-peak price increase as well?

Figure 7.18
Sensitivity to Cost of Capacity

	A	B	C	D	E
28	Sensitivity of changing cells and profit to cost of capacity				
29		$B$13	$C$13	$B$15	$B$26
30	5	$67.81	$26.53	28.75	$2,342.92
31	6	$68.31	$26.53	28.50	$2,314.30
32	7	$68.81	$26.53	28.25	$2,285.92
33	8	$69.31	$26.53	28.00	$2,257.80
34	9	$69.81	$26.53	27.75	$2,229.92
35	10	$70.31	$26.53	27.50	$2,202.30
36	11	$70.81	$26.53	27.25	$2,174.92
37	12	$71.31	$26.53	27.00	$2,147.80
38	13	$71.81	$26.53	26.75	$2,120.92
39	14	$72.31	$26.53	26.50	$2,094.30
40	15	$72.81	$26.53	26.25	$2,067.92

PROBLEMS

Solutions for problems whose numbers appear within a color box can be found in the Student Solutions Manual. Order your copy today at http://e-catalog.thomsonlearning.com/110/ by using ISBN 0-534-39687-9.

Skill-Building Problems

1. In Example 7.1 we assumed that two points on the demand curve were given. (See Figure 7.8.) Suppose three additional points are estimated by Madison: (1) demand of 460 when price is $65, (2) demand of 355 when price is $75, and (3) demand of 275 when price is $85. With these new points and the original two points, estimate and interpret the best-fitting linear demand curve; the best-fitting constant elasticity demand curve.

2. Continuing the previous problem, calculate the mean absolute percentage error (MAPE) for each of the two fits, linear and constant elasticity, where each MAPE is the average of the absolute percentage errors for the five points. On the basis of MAPE, which curve provides the better fit?

3. In the pricing model in Example 7.1 with the constant elasticity demand function, the assumption is that all units demanded are sold. Suppose the company has the capacity to produce only 200 units. If demand is less than capacity, all of demand will be sold. If demand is greater than or equal to capacity, only 200 units will be sold. Use Solver to find the optimal price and the corresponding profit. Then use SolverTable to see how sensitive these answers are to the production capacity, letting it vary from 170 to 230 in increments of 10. Discuss your findings relative to the original solution in Example 7.1. In other words, what is the effect of capacity on the optimal price and profit?

4. Continuing the previous problem, create a two-way data table similar to the one-way data table in Figure 7.9. This time, however, allow price to vary down a column and allow the capacity to vary across a row. Each cell of the data table should capture the corresponding profit. Explain how the values in the data table confirm the findings from SolverTable in the previous problem.

5. Continuing Problem 3 in a slightly different direction, create a two-way SolverTable, where the inputs are the elasticity and the production capacity, and the outputs are the optimal price and the optimal profit. (This will actually create two tables, one for each output.) Discuss your findings.

6. Change the exchange rate model in Example 7.2 slightly so that the company is now a UK manufacturing company producing for a U.S. market. Assume that the unit cost is now 75 £, the demand function has the same parameters as before (although the price for this demand function is now in dollars), and the exchange rate is the same as before. Your Solver solution should now specify the optimal price to charge in dollars and the optimal profit in £.

7. In the exchange rate model in Example 7.2, suppose the company continues to manufacture its product in the United States, but now it sells its product in the United States, the United Kingdom, and possibly other countries. The company can independently set its price in each country where it sells. For example, the price could be $150 in the United States and 110 £ in the United Kingdom. You can assume that the demand function in each country is of the constant elasticity form, each with its own parameters. The question is whether the company can use Solver *independently* in each country to find the optimal price in this country. (You should be able to answer this question without actually running any Solver model(s), but you might want to experiment, just to verify your reasoning.)

8. In the exchange rate model in Example 7.2, we found that the optimal unit revenue, when converted to dollars, is $85.71. Now change the problem so that the company is selling in Japan, not the United Kingdom. Assume that the exchange rate is 0.00821 ($/¥) and that the constant in the demand function is 161,423,232,300, but everything else, including the elasticity of the demand function, remains the same. What is the optimal price in yen? What is the optimal unit revenue when converted to dollars? Is it still $85.71? Do you have an intuitive explanation for this?

9. In the complementary-product pricing model in Example 7.3, the elasticity of demand for suits is currently −2.5. Use SolverTable to see how the optimal price of suits and the optimal profit vary as the elasticity varies from −1.8 to −2.7 in increments of 0.1. Are the results intuitive? Explain.

10. In the complementary-product pricing model in Example 7.3, the SolverTable in Figure 7.15 indicates that the company can sometimes increase overall profit by selling suits below cost. How far might this behavior continue? Answer by extending the SolverTable to larger values of the sensitivity factor, so that more and more shirts and ties are being purchased per suit. Does there appear to be a lower limit on the price that should be charged for suits? Might it reach a point where the company *gives* them away? (Of course, this would require an unrealistic purchase of shirts and ties, but is it mathematically possible?)

11. In the peak-load pricing model in Example 7.4, the demand functions have positive and negative coefficients of prices. The negative coefficients indicate that as the price of a product increases, demand for *that* product decreases. The positive coefficients indicate that as the price of a product increases, demand for the *other* product increases.

a. Increase the magnitudes of the negative coefficients from -0.5 and -1 to -0.7 and -1.2, and then rerun Solver. Are the changes in the optimal solution intuitive? Explain.

b. Increase the magnitudes of the positive coefficients from 0.1 and 0.1 to 0.3 and 0.3, and then rerun Solver. Are the changes in the optimal solution intuitive? Explain.

c. Make the changes in parts **a** and **b** simultaneously, and then rerun Solver. What happens now?

12. In the peak-load pricing model in Example 7.4, we assumed that the capacity level is a decision variable. Assume now that capacity has already been set at 30 kwh. (Note that the cost of capacity is now a sunk cost, so it is irrelevant to the decision problem.) Change the model appropriately and run Solver. Then use SolverTable to see how sensitive the optimal solution is to the capacity level, letting it vary over some relevant range. Does it appear that the optimal prices will be set so that demand will always equal capacity for at least one of the two periods of the day?

Skill-Extending Problems

13. Continuing Problem 7, suppose the company is selling in the United States, the United Kingdom, and Japan. Assume the unit production cost is $50 and the exchange rates are 1.56 ($/£) and 0.00821 ($/¥). Each country has its own constant elasticity demand function. The parameters for the United States are 19,200,000 and -2, the parameters for the United Kingdom are 10,933,620 and -2.2, and the parameters for Japan are 15,003,380,400 and -1.9. The company has a production capacity of 3000. Therefore, the company can sell only as many units, in total, to all three countries as it can produce.

a. Develop a spreadsheet model that determines the prices the company should charge and the numbers of units it should sell in each of the three countries to maximize its total profit in dollars. (Note that if its total demand is greater than capacity, it will

have to decide how much to sell in each country. Therefore, the amounts to sell become changing cells.)

b. When the capacity is 3000, is all of this capacity used? Answer the same question if the capacity is increased to 4000.

c. Discuss the customer behavior that might result from the solution to the model in part **a**. If the company sets its price in one country relatively low compared to its price in another country, what might customers do?

14. In the complementary-product pricing model in Example 7.3, we have assumed that the profit per unit from shirts and ties is given. Presumably this is because the prices of these products have already been set. Change the model so that the company must determine the prices of shirts and ties, as well the price of suits. Assume that the unit costs of shirts and ties are, respectively, $20 and $15. Continue to assume that, on average, 2 shirts and 1.5 ties are sold along with every suit (regardless of the prices of shirts and ties), but that shirts and ties have their own separate demand functions. These demands are for shirts and ties purchased separately from suit purchases. Assume constant elasticity demand functions for shirts and ties with parameters 288,500 and -1.7 (shirts), and 75,460 and -1.6 (ties). Assume the same unit cost and demand function for suits as in Example 7.3.

a. How much should the company charge for suits, shirts, and ties to maximize the profit from all three products?

b. The assumption that customers will always buy, on average, the *same* number of shirts and ties per suit purchase, regardless of the prices of shirts and ties, is questionable. How might you change this assumption, and change your model from part **a** accordingly, to make it more realistic?

15. Continuing the previous problem (the model in part **a**) one step further, assume that shirts and ties are also complementary. Specifically, assume that each time a shirt is purchased (and is *not* accompanied by a suit purchase), 1.3 ties, on average and regardless of the price of ties, are also purchased. Modify the model from part **a** of the previous problem to find the prices of suits, shirts, and ties to maximize overall profit.

7.4 ADVERTISING RESPONSE AND SELECTION MODELS

In Chapter 4 we discussed an advertising allocation model (Example 4.1), where the problem was basically to decide how many ads to place on various television shows to reach the required number of viewers. One assumption of that model was that the "advertising response"—that is, the number of exposures—is *linear* in the number of ads. This means that if one ad gains, say, 1 million exposures, then 10 ads will gain 10 million exposures.

This is a questionable assumption at best. It is more likely that there is a decreasing marginal effect at work, where each extra ad gains *fewer* exposures than the previous ad. In fact, there might even be a saturation effect, where there is an upper limit on the number of exposures possible and, after sufficiently many ads, this saturation level will nearly be reached.

In this section we will look at two related examples. In the first example we will see how a company might use historical data to estimate its advertising response function—the number of exposures it gains from a given number of ads. This is itself a nonlinear optimization model. Then we will use this type of advertising response function in the second example to solve a nonlinear version of the advertising selection problem from Chapter 4. Because the advertising response functions are nonlinear, the advertising selection problem is also nonlinear.

| EXAMPLE | **7.5 ESTIMATING AN ADVERTISING RESPONSE FUNCTION** |

Recall that the General Flakes Company from Example 4.1 of Chapter 4 sells a brand of low-fat breakfast cereal that appeals to people of all age groups and genders. The company has advertised this product in various media for a number of years, and it has accumulated data on its advertising effectiveness. For example, it has tracked the number of exposures to young men from ads placed on a particular television show for five different time periods. In each of these time periods, a different number of ads was used. Specifically, the numbers of ads were 1, 8, 20, 50, and 100. The corresponding numbers of exposures (in millions) were 4.7, 22.1, 48.7, 90.3, and 130.5. What type of nonlinear response function might "fit" these data well?

Objective To use nonlinear optimization to find the response function (from a given class of functions) that best fits the historical data.

WHERE DO THE NUMBERS COME FROM?

The question here is how the company measures the number of exposures a given number of ads has achieved. But what does the company mean by "exposures?" If one person sees the same ad 10 times, does this result in 10 exposures? Is it the same thing as 10 people seeing the same ad once each? Although we defer to the marketing experts here, we believe one person seeing the same ad 10 times results in fewer "exposures" than 10 people seeing the same ad once each. However the marketing experts decide to count "exposures," it should then lead to the decreasing marginal effects we have built into this example.

Solution

The chart in Figure 7.19 is an X-Y plot of the historical data (with the dots connected). It clearly indicates a nonlinear pattern, where extra ads have less effect than the first few ads. There are many mathematical functions that have this basic shape, and we could use any of them. However, we will settle here for one of the simplest, a function of the form

$$f(n) = a(1 - e^{-bn}) \tag{7.4}$$

The function in equation (7.4) is only one of several nonlinear functions that exhibits the type of behavior (increasing at a decreasing rate) that we want.

Here, n is the number of ads placed, $f(n)$ is the resulting number of exposures, a and b are constants to estimate, and e is the special number approximately equal to 2.718. This function has some nice properties: (1) it is 0 when $n = 0$; (2) it increases at a decreasing rate when $b > 0$; and (3) it increases to a as n gets large. This latter property is the saturation effect we mentioned previously. The only question, then, is which values of a and b to use to match the historical data in Figure 7.19 as well as possible.

Figure 7.19   Graph of Historical Data

Historical Data

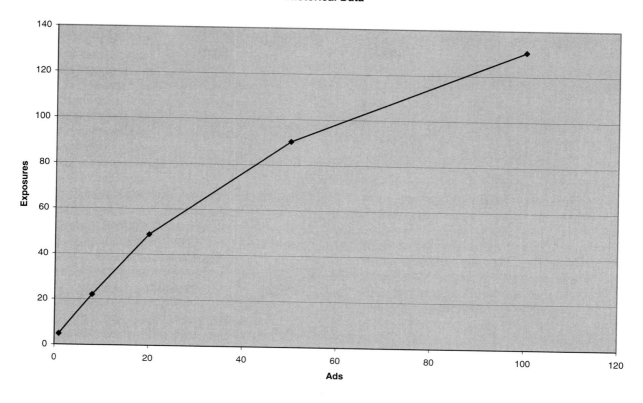

The squared differences in the goodness-of-fit measure make this a nonlinear model.

To do this, we use a standard estimation procedure. Although the spreadsheet details will be given shortly, it is worth discussing the idea behind this procedure first. Using the model in equation (7.4) with *any* values of a and b, we predict the number of exposures we would obtain for 1, 8, 20, 50, or 100 ads. Then we compare these to the actual exposures observed, using a "goodness-of-fit" measure. The specific goodness-of-fit measure we will use is the sum of squared differences between actual and predicted exposures. This measure has been used most frequently in estimation problems, so we will continue to use it here. Specifically, we will use Solver to find the constants a and b that minimize the sum of squared prediction errors. Of course, the *squares* make this a nonlinear optimization model.

DEVELOPING THE SPREADSHEET MODEL

The completed spreadsheet model is shown in Figure 7.20 (page 320). (See the file **AdvertisingResponse.xls**.) It can be created with the following steps.

Figure 7.20 Estimation of Response Function

	A	B	C	D	E	F	G	H	I	J
1	Fitting an advertising response curve									
2										
3	Parameters of response curve					Range names used:				
4	Constant	155.03				Parameters	=Model!$B$4:$B$5			
5	Coefficient in exponent	0.0181				RMSE	=Model!$D$14			
6										
7	Historical data									
8	Ads	Exposures	Predicted	Squared error						
9	1	4.7	2.787	3.660						
10	8	22.1	20.942	1.341						
11	20	48.7	47.172	2.334						
12	50	90.3	92.440	4.580						
13	100	130.5	129.761	0.547						
14				1.579	←	Root mean squared error, objective to minimize				

1 **Inputs.** Enter the historical data in the shaded region. There are no other inputs.

2 **Parameters of response function.** Enter *any* values for the constants *a* and *b* of the advertising response function in cells B4 and B5. These become the changing cells.

3 **Predicted exposures.** Use equation (7.4), with the values of *a* and *b* in cells B4 and B5, to calculate the predicted number of exposures for each number of ads. To do this, enter the formula

=$B$4*(1-EXP(-$B$5*A9))

in cell C9, and copy it down to cell C13.

4 **Squared errors.** Calculate the squared difference between actual and predicted exposures by entering the formula

=(B9-C9)^2

in cell D9 and copying it down to cell D13.

RMSE is the square root of the average of the squared errors.

5 **Objective to minimize.** We said previously that we will minimize the sum of squared errors. Actually, this is equivalent to minimizing the "root mean squared error" (RMSE), which is the *square root* of the average of the squared errors. We will use RMSE as the objective to minimize, so enter the formula

=SQRT(AVERAGE(D9:D13))

in cell D14. (One reason to use RMSE as the objective, rather than the sum of squared errors, is that it is a smaller number and is less likely to give Solver numerical problems. In any case, we should get the same solution either way. Besides, RMSE has historically been a popular measure to minimize.)

USING SOLVER

In an unconstrained optimization model, there are no infeasible points—all points qualify. We simply need to search for the point with the best objective value.

This is a particularly simple Solver setup. As Figure 7.21 indicates, we minimize RMSE, using cells B4 and B5 (jointly range-named Parameters) as the changing cells. There are no constraints, not even nonnegativity constraints.[6] An optimization model with no constraints is called an **unconstrained model**.

[6]Actually, by the increasing nature of the historical data and the form of the response function in equation (7.4), we expect *a* and *b* to be positive, but it is not necessary to *constrain* them to be nonnegative.

Figure 7.21

Solver Dialog Box for Estimation Problem

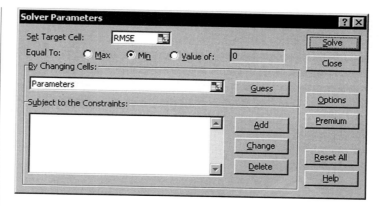

Discussion of the Solution

The Solver solution in Figure 7.20 indicates that when we use $a = 155.03$ and $b = 0.0181$ in equation (7.4), we get the best possible fit to the historical data. A glance at the Actual and Predicted columns in rows 9–13 indicates that this fit is indeed quite good. We can then see what this version of equation (7.4) looks like, as well as the number of exposures it would predict for other numbers of ads. We do this numerically and graphically in Figure 7.22. For example, the formula in cell B21 is **=$B$4*(1-EXP(-$B$5*A21))**, which is copied down. We then plot the values in columns A and B to obtain the curve in the figure. As we see, the response function increases at a decreasing rate, and it approaches $a = 155.03$ as the number of ads gets large.

Figure 7.22 Estimated Response Function

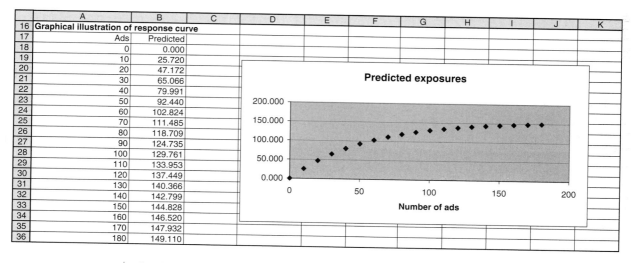

	A	B	C
16	**Graphical illustration of response curve**		
17	Ads	Predicted	
18	0	0.000	
19	10	25.720	
20	20	47.172	
21	30	65.066	
22	40	79.991	
23	50	92.440	
24	60	102.824	
25	70	111.485	
26	80	118.709	
27	90	124.735	
28	100	129.761	
29	110	133.953	
30	120	137.449	
31	130	140.366	
32	140	142.799	
33	150	144.828	
34	160	146.520	
35	170	147.932	
36	180	149.110	

Is the Solver Solution Optimal?

In some nonlinear models such as this one, Solver finds the optimal solution only if the starting solution is reasonably close to the optimal solution.

It is difficult to verify whether RMSE is a concave function of the two parameters a and b—even for mathematicians who are calculus whizzes! Therefore, the best approach is to try several starting solutions in cells B4 and B5 and see whether Solver converges to the *same* solution in each case. We tried this, and it works—unless the starting solution is way off. For example, if the starting solution has 200 and 0.1 in cells B4 and B5, Solver finds the solution in Figure 7.20. However, if the starting solution has 0 and 0 in these cells, Solver stops at a very different solution. In fact, it *stays* at this 0–0 solution. This is typical of many nonlinear optimization models. Unless the starting solution is "reasonably close" to the optimal solution, Solver can go to a completely wrong solution. ∎

MODELING ISSUES

We used the popular sum-of-squared-errors measure (or its RMSE equivalent) to find the best-fitting response function. Another possibility is to use the sum (or average) of the *absolute* errors. Still another possibility is to use the *maximum* of the absolute errors. All of these have been used in estimation problems, and all of them lead to nonlinear optimization models. They typically lead to similar, but not necessarily identical, solutions. We used the sum-of-squared-errors measure because it has historically been the most frequently used measure and because it leads to a "smooth" nonlinear model—the kind that Solver handles best. ∎

Now that we see how a company might estimate the advertising response function for any type of ad to any group of customers, we use this type of response function in an advertising selection model.

EXAMPLE | 7.6 ADVERTISING SELECTION WITH NONLINEAR RESPONSE FUNCTIONS

In this model each customer group has its own nonlinear advertising response function to each television show.

In this example we revisit the problem faced by the General Flakes Company in Example 4.1 of Chapter 4. The company must decide how many ads to place on each of several television shows to meet exposure constraints for each of six groups of customers. (We refer you to Figure 7.23 and the file **AdvertisingSelection.xls** for the specific inputs.) The difference now is that each combination of television show and customer group has its own advertising response function of the form in equation (7.4). That is, there are constants *a* and *b* of the response function for *each* such combination. (These constants appear in rows 5–10 and 14–19 of the file.) The company wants to find the selection of ads that minimizes its total cost of meeting all exposure requirements.

Objective   To use a nonlinear model to find a minimum-cost way of meeting all exposure requirements.

WHERE DO THE NUMBERS COME FROM?

We already discussed where many of the inputs come from in Example 4.1 of Chapter 4. The new inputs, the parameters of the various response functions, would come from fitting response functions, exactly as we did in the previous example, for each combination of television show and customer group. Of course, this assumes the company has enough historical data to carry out this procedure. The numbers we have used are for illustration only, although they are "reasonable."

Solution

The variables and constraints for this model are listed in Table 7.4. Except for the new inputs from the advertising response functions, this table is exactly like the table for Example 4.1 of Chapter 4.

Table 7.4 Variables and Constraints for Advertising Model

Input variables	Cost per ad, minimal required exposures, parameters of advertising response functions
Decision variables (changing cells)	Numbers of ads to place on various types of shows
Objective (target cell)	Total advertising cost
Other output variables	Total exposures to each viewer group
Constraints	Actual exposures ≥ Required exposures

DEVELOPING THE SPREADSHEET MODEL

The spreadsheet model is shown in Figure 7.23 and the file **AdvertisingSelection.xls**. It can be developed with the following steps.

Figure 7.23 Spreadsheet Model for Advertising Selection

	A	B	C	D	E	F	G	H	I
1	Advertising model with nonlinear response functions								
2						Note: All monetary values are in $1000s, and all exposures to ads are in millions of exposures.			
3	Constant in advertising response function for various groups for different shows								
4		Friends	MNF	Malcolm in Middle	Sports Center	TRL Live	Lifetime movie	CNN	JAG
5	Men 18-35	93.061	116.808	84.772	43.647	26.711	11.99	11.793	11.323
6	Men 36-55	61.129	76.527	61.528	47.749	19.655	10.281	9.982	21.759
7	Men >55	33.376	57.84	9.913	30.075	10.751	11.51	22.218	28.121
8	Women 18-35	105.803	40.113	66.998	22.101	42.451	29.403	8.236	8.93
9	Women 36-55	71.784	26.534	46.146	16.151	34.609	24.276	10.426	22.849
10	Women >55	56.828	17.209	8.887	9.101	8.46	31.149	23.105	40.672
11									
12	Coefficient of exponent in advertising response function for various groups for different shows								
13		Friends	MNF	Malcolm in Middle	Sports Center	TRL Live	Lifetime movie	CNN	JAG
14	Men 18-35	0.029	0.055	0.093	0.071	0.087	0.038	0.029	0.080
15	Men 36-55	0.084	0.050	0.085	0.094	0.018	0.090	0.054	0.070
16	Men >55	0.071	0.068	0.077	0.027	0.039	0.051	0.013	0.036
17	Women 18-35	0.035	0.063	0.069	0.074	0.060	0.012	0.039	0.026
18	Women 36-55	0.089	0.057	0.061	0.055	0.014	0.022	0.046	0.040
19	Women >55	0.010	0.033	0.078	0.078	0.035	0.050	0.072	0.030
20									
21	Cost per ad	160	100	80	9	13	15	8	85
22									
23	Advertising plan								
24		Friends	MNF	Malcolm in Middle	Sports Center	TRL Live	Lifetime movie	CNN	JAG
25	Number ads purchased	3.847	0.000	3.539	22.679	19.531	10.349	16.275	0.000
26									
27	Exposures to each group from each show								
28		Friends	MNF	Malcolm in Middle	Sports Center	TRL Live	Lifetime movie	CNN	JAG
29	Men 18-35	9.823	0.000	23.776	34.925	21.828	3.898	4.437	0.000
30	Men 36-55	16.879	0.000	15.985	42.085	5.826	6.230	5.837	0.000
31	Men >55	7.977	0.000	2.365	13.772	5.732	4.720	4.237	0.000
32	Women 18-35	13.327	0.000	14.517	17.975	29.300	3.434	3.870	0.000
33	Women 36-55	20.811	0.000	8.961	11.511	8.280	4.943	5.494	0.000
34	Women >55	2.144	0.000	2.144	7.549	4.189	12.583	15.947	0.000
35									
36	Constraints on numbers of exposures								
37		Actual exposures		Required exposures		Range names used:			
38	Men 18-35	98.686	>=	60		Actual_exposures	=Sheet1!$B$38:$B$43		
39	Men 36-55	92.842	>=	60		Number_ads_purchased	=Sheet1!$B$25:$I$25		
40	Men >55	38.802	>=	28		Required_exposures	=Sheet1!$D$38:$D$43		
41	Women 18-35	82.424	>=	60		Total_cost	=Sheet1!$B$46		
42	Women 36-55	60.000	>=	60					
43	Women >55	44.557	>=	28					
44									
45	Objective to minimize								
46	Total cost	$1,642.069							

① Inputs. Enter the inputs in the shaded cells. These include the parameters of the advertising response functions in rows 5–10 and 14–19. Again, we made up these inputs, but they would typically be estimated from historical data.

② Ads purchased. Enter *any* trial values of the numbers of ads purchased for the various shows in row 25. These cells become the changing cells.

3 **Exposures from each show to each group.** Use the advertising response functions to calculate the numbers of exposures to each customer group from each show. To do this, enter the formula

=B5*(1-EXP(-B14*B$25))

in cell B29 and copy it to the range B29:I34. Note that row 25 must be kept absolute for copying to work correctly. This is because the numbers of ads are always in row 25.

4 **Total exposures to each group.** Calculate the numbers of exposures to each group by entering the formula

=SUM(B29:I29)

in cell B38 and copying it down to cell B43. This formula sums over exposures from the various television shows.

5 **Total cost.** Calculate the total cost of advertising in cell B46 with the formula

=SUMPRODUCT(B21:I21,Number_ads_purchased)

USING SOLVER

Integer constraints can be added, but they do not affect the optimal solution to a great extent.

The Solver dialog box is straightforward to complete, as illustrated in Figure 7.24. Just remember to check the Assume Non-Negative box under Solver options, but do *not* check the Assume Linear Model box. The nonlinear advertising response functions make the model nonlinear. Note that we could also constrain the changing cells to be integers. This would make the model more difficult for Solver to solve, but it would also make the solution more realistic. (However, you can check that it doesn't change the optimal solution by much.)

Figure 7.24

Solver Dialog Box for Advertising Selection Model

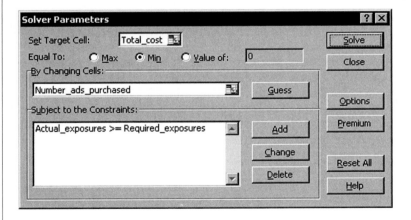

Discussion of the Solution

First, note that the constants in rows 5–10 of the advertising response functions indicate the maximum numbers of exposures possible to each group from each show. The constants in rows 14–19 indicate how fast the response functions approach these maximum limits: When one of these constants increases, fewer ads are needed to approach the saturation level. Together, these two sets of constants indicate which types of ads are most effective to the various customer groups. Solver uses this information in its intricate algorithm to decide how many ads to place on each show. Perhaps surprisingly, no ads are placed on "Monday Night Football," although many exposures to men under 55 would be achieved from these ads. Evidently these ads are too expensive, and exposures to men in these groups can be achieved with cheaper ads on other shows. Note also that the women in the 36–55 group are evidently the "bottleneck" group. (Check the differences between the two sides of the exposure constraints.) To achieve the required exposures for this group, many more ads are required than are needed to achieve the required exposures to the other groups.

Is the Solver Solution Optimal?

It can be shown (with calculus) that this model satisfies the conditions necessary to ensure that there is a single local minimum. Therefore, we know that the Solver solution is indeed optimal. If you didn't know this, however, you could try running Solver several times, each from a different starting solution in row 25. You should find that they all converge to the solution in Figure 7.23.

Sensitivity Analysis

An interesting sensitivity analysis for this nonlinear model is to see how the optimal cost varies if we change all of the required exposures by the *same* percentage. In a linear model, if we did this (and there were no other constraints to worry about), the optimal cost would change by the same percentage. This is due to the proportionality property of linear models. For example, if we increased the right-hand sides of all constraints by 10%, we would expect the optimal cost to increase by 10% in a linear model. However, this is not true in a nonlinear model, as Figure 7.25 indicates. Here we changed the model slightly so that we can vary the single percentage in cell F44. (The original required exposures are now in column F, and the formula in cell D38 is **=F38*(1+$F$44)**, which is copied down.)

Figure 7.25 Sensitivity of Total Cost to Percentage Change in Exposures Required

	A	B	C	D	E	F
36	Constraints on numbers of exposures					
37		Actual exposures		Required exposures		Originally required
38	Men 18-35	98.686	>=	60		60
39	Men 36-55	92.842	>=	60		60
40	Men >55	38.802	>=	28		28
41	Women 18-35	82.424	>=	60		60
42	Women 36-55	60.000	>=	60		60
43	Women >55	44.557	>=	28		28
44					Percentage change	0%
45	Objective to minimize					
46	Total cost	$1,642.069				
47						
48	Sensitivity of total cost to percentage change in all required exposures					
49		$B$46	Percentage increase			
50	0%	$1,642.070				
51	10%	$1,858.230	13.2%			
52	20%	$2,084.050	26.9%			
53	30%	$2,320.420	41.3%			
54	40%	$2,568.390	56.4%			
55	50%	$2,829.140	72.3%			

We then used SolverTable to see how sensitive the total cost is to the percentage increase in the required exposures to each group. The percentage increases in total cost, relative to the original cost, are calculated manually (not with SolverTable) in column C. As we see, because of the decreasing marginal effect of extra ads, it takes larger percentage increases in cost to achieve a given percentage increase in exposures. For example, if we need 40% more exposures to each group, we require a 56.4% increase in total cost. This illustrates in a very real way a possible consequence of nonlinearity. ■

PROBLEMS

Skill-Building Problems

16. In estimating the advertising response function in Example 7.5, we indicated that the sum of squared prediction errors *or* RMSE could be used as the objective, and we used RMSE. Try using the sum of squared prediction errors instead. Does Solver find the same solution as in the example? Try running Solver several times, each time from a different starting solution in the changing cells, and report what happens.

17. The best-fitting advertising response function in Example 7.5 fits the observed data. This is because we rigged the observed data to fall close to a curve of the form in equation (7.4). See what happens when one of the observed points is an outlier—that is, it doesn't fit the pattern of the others.
   a. Specifically, change the number of exposures corresponding to 50 ads from 90.3 to 125, and then rerun Solver. Do you get essentially the same response function as before, or does this one outlier exert a large influence on the estimated response function?
   b. Repeat part **a**, but now change the number of exposures corresponding to 50 ads from 90.3 to 55.

18. In judging the fit of the estimated response function in Example 7.5, we could use MAD instead of RMSE. Here, MAD stands for mean absolute deviation, and it is defined to be the average of the *absolute* prediction errors.
   a. When you run Solver with MAD as your objective, do you get approximately the same estimated response function as with RMSE?
   b. Repeat part **a**, but do it with the outliers in parts **a** and **b** of the previous problem.

19. As we mentioned, the advertising response function in equation (7.4) is only one of several nonlinear functions we could have used to get the same "increasing at a decreasing rate" behavior we want in Example 7.5. Another possibility is the function $f(n) = an^b$, where a and b are again constants to be determined. Using the same data as in Example 7.5 and RMSE as the fitting criterion, find the best fit to this type of function. In terms of RMSE, which function appears to fit the data better, the one here or the one in the example? Can you spot any qualitative difference between the two types of functions?

20. Starting with the solution to the advertising selection problem in Example 7.6, suppose the company, for whatever reason, cannot place ads on "Sports Center." Make the appropriate changes in the model and rerun Solver. Comment on the changes to the changing cells. Then comment on the change to the total cost. In particular, explain how the total cost could change so dramatically in the direction it changed.

21. The preceding problem indicates how fewer alternatives can cause total cost to increase. This problem indicates the opposite. Starting with the solution to the advertising selection problem in Example 7.6, add a new show, "The View," that appeals primarily to women. Use the following constants and coefficients of exponents for the response functions to the various customer groups for this show: 5, 7, 10, 15, 35, 35 (constants); and 0.03, 0.03, 0.03, 0.08, 0.08, 0.08 (coefficients of exponents). Assume that each ad on "The View" costs $10,000. Make the appropriate changes in the model and rerun Solver. Comment on the changes to the changing cells. Then comment on the change to the total cost. In particular, explain how the total cost could change so dramatically in the direction it changed.

22. In the solution to the advertising selection model in Example 7.6, we indicated that the women 36–55 group is a "bottleneck" in the sense that the company needs to spend a lot more than it would otherwise have to just to meet the constraint for this group. Form a SolverTable to see how much this group's exposure constraint is costing the company. Vary the required exposures to this group from 30 to 60 in increments of 5, and keep track of the total advertising cost. Comment on your results.

Skill-Extending Problem

23. In Example 7.5, we implied that each of the five observations was from one period of time, such as a particular week. Suppose instead that each is an *average* over several weeks. For example, the 4.7 million exposures corresponding to 1 ad might really be an average over 15 different weeks where 1 ad was shown in each of these weeks. Similarly, the 90.3 million exposures corresponding to 50 ads might really be an average over only 3 different weeks where 50 ads were shown in each of these weeks. If the observations are really averages over *different* numbers of weeks, then simply summing the squared prediction errors doesn't seem appropriate. For example, it seems more appropriate that an average over 15 weeks should get 5 times as much weight as an average over only 3 weeks. Assume the five observations in the example are really averages over 15, 10, 4, 3, and 1 weeks, respectively. Devise an appropriate "fitting" function, to replace sum of squared errors or RMSE, and use it to find the best fit.

7.5 FACILITY LOCATION MODELS

Suppose you need to find a location for a facility such as a warehouse, a tool crib in a factory, or a fire station. Your goal is to locate the facility so as to minimize the total distance that must be traveled to provide required services. Facility location problems such as these can usually be set up as NLP models. The following example is typical.

EXAMPLE | **7.7 WAREHOUSE LOCATION AT LAFFERTY**

The Lafferty Company wants to locate a warehouse from which it will ship products to four customers. The location (in the x–y plane) of the four customers and the number of shipments per year needed by each customer are given in Table 7.5. (All locations are in miles, relative to the point $x = 0$ and $y = 0$.) A single warehouse must be used to service all of the customers. Lafferty wants to determine the location of the warehouse that minimizes the total distance traveled from the warehouse to the customers.

Table 7.5 Data for Lafferty Example

Customer	x-coordinate	y-coordinate	Shipments per Year
1	5	10	200
2	10	5	150
3	0	12	200
4	12	0	300

Objective   To find the warehouse location, using NLP, that minimizes the total annual distance traveled from the warehouse to the customers.

WHERE DO THE NUMBERS COME FROM?

The data for this problem are self-explanatory. Of course, at the time the model is solved, the annual shipments for the various customers are probably forecasts.

Solution

The variables and constraints for this model are listed in Table 7.6. As we see, there are no constraints in this model, not even nonnegativity. We can locate the warehouse at *any x–y* coordinate.

Table 7.6   Variables and Constraints for Warehouse Location Problem

Input variables	Customer coordinates, annual customer shipments
Decision variables (changing cells)	Coordinates of warehouse location
Objective (target cell)	Total annual distance traveled to the customers from the warehouse
Other output variables	Distances from customers to warehouse
Constraints	None

DEVELOPING THE SPREADSHEET MODEL

To develop the spreadsheet model, use the following steps. (See Figure 7.26 and the file **WarehouseLocation.xls.**)

Figure 7.26 Facility Location Model

	A	B	C	D	E	F	G	H	I
1	Lafferty facility location model								
2									
3	Customer data						Range names used:		
4		X-coordinate	Y-coordinate		Annual shipments		Location	=Model!$B$11:$C$11	
5	Customer 1	5	10		200		TotDistance	=Model!$B$19	
6	Customer 2	10	5		150				
7	Customer 3	0	12		200				
8	Customer 4	12	0		300				
9									
10	Warehouse location	X-coordinate	Y-coordinate						
11		9.315	5.029						
12									
13	Customer distances from warehouse								
14	Customer 1	6.583							
15	Customer 2	0.686							
16	Customer 3	11.635							
17	Customer 4	5.701							
18									
19	Total annual distance	5456.540							
20									
21	Testing optimality								
22	Is this solution optimal? Test it yourself. Click on the left button to generate a "random" set of starting values for								
23	the changing cells. Then click on the right button to run Solver. Does it always take you to the same solution?								
24									
25		Generate random values			Run Solver				
26									
27									

1 **Inputs.** Enter the given customer data in the shaded ranges.

2 **Coordinates of warehouse.** Enter *any* trial values in Location range for the *x–y* coordinates of the warehouse.

3 **Distances from warehouse to customers.** Calculate the distances from the warehouse to the customers in the range B14:B17. To do so, recall from the Pythagorean theorem that the (straight-line) distance between the two points (a, b) and (c, d) is $\sqrt{(c - a)^2 + (d - b)^2}$. Therefore, enter the formula

=SQRT(SUMXMY2(B5:C5,Location))

in cell B14 and copy it down to cell B17.

→ **EXCEL FUNCTION:** *SUMXMY2*

Microsoft realized that we often want to sum squared differences between two ranges, so it provided the Excel function SUMXMY2 (read "sum of x minus y squared"). This function uses the syntax **=SUMXMY2(xRange,yRange)**. *For our example it is equivalent to the longer form* **(B5-$B$11)^2+(C5-$C$11)^2**. *Of course, we take the square root of it to get distance.* ∎

4 **Total annual distance.** The total annual distance traveled from the warehouse to meet the demands of all customers is the sum over all customers of the distance from the warehouse to the customer multiplied by the annual shipments for the customer. Therefore, calculate the total annual distance traveled in cell B19 with the formula

=SUMPRODUCT(E5:E8,B14:B17)

USING SOLVER

This Solver setup for this model is shown in Figure 7.27. All we need to specify is that TotDistance should be minimized and the Location range contains the changing cells. There are no constraints, not even nonnegativity constraints. Also, because of the squares in the straight-line distance formula, this model is nonlinear, so the Assume Linear Model option should *not* be checked.

Figure 7.27

Solver Dialog Box for Warehouse Location Model

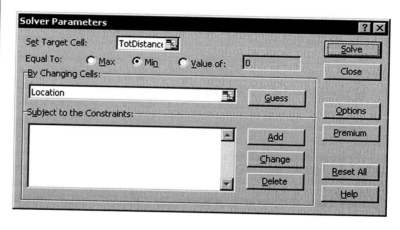

Discussion of the Solution

The Solver solution in Figure 7.26 is represented graphically in Figure 7.28. The warehouse should be located at $x = 9.31$ and $y = 5.03$. Each year a total of 5456.54 miles will be traveled annually from the warehouse to the customers. This solution represents a compromise. On the one hand, Lafferty would like to position the facility near customer 4 because the most trips are made to customer 4. However, because customer 4 is reasonably far from the other customers, the warehouse is located in a more central position.

Figure 7.28

Graph of Solution to Warehouse Location Example

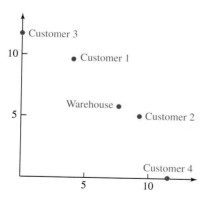

Sensitivity Analysis

As the numer of shipments to any customer increases, the optimal warehouse location gets closer to that customer.

One possible sensitivity analysis is to see how the optimal location of the warehouse changes as the annual number of shipments to any particular customer increases. We did this for customer 4 in Figure 7.29 (page 330). We ran SolverTable with the number of shipments to customer 4 (cell E8) as the single input cell, allowing it to vary from 300 to 700 in increments of 50, and we kept track of the total annual distance and the warehouse location coordinates. As expected, the total annual distance increases as the annual shipments to customer 4 increase. Also, the warehouse gradually gets closer to customer 4. In fact, when the annual shipments to customer 4 are 600 or above, the optimal location for the warehouse is *at* customer 4.

Figure 7.29

Sensitivity Analysis for Warehouse Location

	A	B	C	D	E	F
28	Sensitivity of total distance and warehouse coordinates to shipments to customer					
29		$B$19	$B$11	$C$11		
30	300	5456.540	9.314	5.029		
31	350	5732.969	9.634	4.877		
32	400	6000.839	9.690	4.762		
33	450	6260.753	9.680	4.510		
34	500	6501.694	9.788	3.846		
35	550	6646.106	11.787	0.266		
36	600	6643.199	12.000	0.000		
37	650	6643.198	12.000	0.000		
38	700	6643.198	12.000	0.000		

Is the Solver Solution Optimal?

The Lafferty model has no constraints. Therefore, we know that the Solver will find an optimal solution if the objective is a convex function of the coordinates of the warehouse. It can be shown (with some difficulty) that the annual distance traveled is indeed a convex function of the coordinates of the warehouse. Therefore, we know that the Solver solution is optimal.

The buttons in this file let you experiment with randomly generated starting values in the changing cells.

However, what if you do not know whether the objective is a convex function of the coordinates? Then the best strategy is to try different starting solutions in the Location range, run the Solver on each of them, and see whether they all take you to the same solution. In fact, we have made this easy for you in the **WarehouseLocation.xls** file. (Again see Figure 7.26.) We have written two short macros that are automated by clicking buttons. You can click on the left button to randomly generate a new starting location in the changing cells. Then you can click on the right button to run Solver. You should find that they always take you to the same solution.[7] ■

MODELING ISSUES

1. The straight-line distance function we used in the Lafferty example is relevant if the company is shipping by air. However, if it is shipping by road, we must take into account that most roads are built in a north–south or east–west direction. Then the relevant distance between points (a, b) and (c, d) is $|a - c| + |b - d|$ (the sum of the absolute differences), and this objective should be used in place of the square root objective. Because of absolute values, it is *still* nonlinear.

2. Besides assuming straight-line distance, we made two other assumptions in the Lafferty example: (1) exactly one warehouse will be built, and (2) this warehouse can be built *anywhere*. In real-world facility location problems, it might be necessary to modify these assumptions. First, it might be possible to build several warehouses. Second, the *possible* locations might be restricted to a certain subset of geographical locations. And third, the distances from all potential warehouse locations to customers might be given by a distance matrix, rather than calculated from some formula. In this situation, an IP model with binary variables would be more suitable. There would be a 0–1 variable for each potential warehouse location (either build there or don't) and a 0–1 variable for each warehouse–customer pair (either supply that customer from that warehouse or don't). We ask you to model such a version of the warehouse location problem in one of the following problems. ■

---

[7]If you would like to write similar macros for other NLP models, it is fairly easy. With the **WarehouseLocation.xls** file open, press the Alt-F11 key combination to see the Visual Basic screen. The code for the macros is in the Module sheet for this file. Except for the line indicated in the code and the range name of the changing cells, these macros can be used for other problems with no changes.

Skill-Building Problems

24. Modify the warehouse location model so that there is an extra customer. This customer has 250 shipments per year. Try placing this new customer at various locations (see Figure 7.28 for guidance). For example, try placing the customer way up to the right, or way down to the left, or near a current customer, etc. For each such location, find the optimal warehouse location. Discuss the effect of this new customer and its location on the optimal warehouse location.

25. Modify the warehouse location model so that customers always travel in horizontal or vertical directions. For example, this means that if a customer's coordinates are (5, 10) and a warehouse is located at (7, 7), then the traveling distance is $|5 - 7| + |10 - 7| = 5$.

26. Use SolverTable in the warehouse location model to see the effect on the optimal solution of moving one customer farther and farther away from the others. Specifically, let customer 1's coordinates be of the form $(5c, 10c)$, where the factor c is allowed to vary from 1 to 10 in increments of 1. Keep track of the changing cells and the target cell.

Skill-Extending Problem

27. Modify the warehouse location model as suggested in the second Modeling Issue on page 330. Specifically, assume that there are the same four customers with the same annual shipments. However, there are now only two possible warehouse locations, each with distances to the various customers. (These distances, along with other inputs, are in the file **P07_27.xls**.) The company can build either or both of these warehouses. The cost to build a warehouse is $50,000. (You can assume that this cost has been annualized. That is, the company incurs a building cost that is equivalent to $50,000 per year.) If only one warehouse is built, it will ship to all customers. However, if both warehouses are built, then the company must decide which warehouse will ship to each customer. There is a traveling cost of $1 per mile.

a. Develop an appropriate model to minimize total annual cost, and then use Solver to optimize it. Is this model an NLP or an IP model (or both)?

b. Use SolverTable with a single input, the traveling cost per mile, to see how large this cost must be before the company builds both warehouses rather than just one.

7.6 MODELS FOR RATING SPORTS TEAMS

Sports fans always wonder which team is best in a given sport. Was USC, LSU, or Oklahoma number 1 during the 2003 NCAA football season? You might be surprised to learn that Solver can be used to rate sports teams. We examine one method for doing this in the following example.

EXAMPLE | **7.8 RATING NFL TEAMS**[8]

We obtained the results of the 248 regular-season NFL games from the 2001 season and entered the data into a spreadsheet, shown at the bottom of Figure 7.30 on page 332 (see the file **NFL2001Ratings.xls**). (Some of these results are hidden in Figure 7.30 to conserve space.) The teams are indexed 1–31, as shown at the top of the sheet. For example, team 1 is Arizona, team 2 is Atlanta, and so on. The first game entered (row 46) was team 17 (Minnesota) versus team 5 (Carolina), played at Minnesota. Carolina won the game by a score of 24 to 13, and the point spread (home team score minus visitor team

---

[8]The procedure used in this example is practically identical to the procedure used by the nationally syndicated Jeff Sagarin to rate various sports teams. You can see his ratings at www.usatoday.com/sports/sagarin.htm.

score) is calculated in column F. A positive point spread in column F means that the home team won; a negative point spread indicates that the visiting team won. Our goal is to determine a set of ratings for the 31 NFL teams that most accurately predicts the actual outcomes of the games played.

Figure 7.30   NFL Ratings Model

	A	B	C	D	E	F	G	H
1	Rating NFL teams in 2001							
2								
3	Ratings of teams				Range names used:			
4	Index	Team name	Rating		Actual_average	=Model!$B$41		
5	1	Arizona Cardinals	80.84		Home_team_advantage	=Model!$B$37		
6	2	Atlanta Falcons	80.31		Nominal_average	=Model!$D$41		
7	3	Baltimore Ravens	88.21		Rating	=Model!$C$5:$C$35		
8	4	Buffalo Bills	75.48		Sum_squared_errors	=Model!$H$39		
9	5	Carolina Panthers	76.05					
10	6	Chicago Bears	92.91					
11	7	Cincinnatti Bengals	81.48					
12	8	Cleveland Browns	84.20					
13	9	Dallas Cowboys	79.02					
14	10	Denver Broncos	84.53					
15	11	Detroit Lions	77.79					
16	12	Green Bay Packers	91.63					
17	13	Indianapolis Colts	81.23					
18	14	Jacksonville Jaguars	85.85					
19	15	Kansas City Chiefs	83.84					
20	16	Miami Dolphins	87.72					
21	17	Minnesota Vikings	80.27					
22	18	New England Patriots	89.33					
23	19	New Orleans Saints	80.18					
24	20	New York Giants	83.21					
25	21	New York Jets	85.83					
26	22	Oakland Raiders	88.62					
27	23	Philadelphia Eagles	92.73					
28	24	Pittsburgh Steelers	92.35					
29	25	St. Louis Rams	98.35					
30	26	San Diego Chargers	84.73					
31	27	San Francisco 49ers	91.84					
32	28	Seattle Seahawks	83.13					
33	29	Tampa Bay Buccanee	89.03					
34	30	Tennessee Titans	82.95					
35	31	Washington Redskins	81.35					
36								
37	Home team advantage	2.01						
38							Objective to minimize	
39	Constraint on average rating (any nominal value could be used)						Sum squared error	33085.63
40		Actual average		Nominal average				
41		85.0	=	8 5				
42								
43	Estimation model							
44		Results of games					Model predictions and errors	
45		Home team index	Visiting team index	Home team score	Away team score	Point spread	Predicted spread	Squared error
46		17	5	13	24	-11	6.2236	296.6510
47		3	6	17	6	11	-2.6950	187.5533
291		22	21	22	24	-2	4.8038	46.2918
292		24	8	28	7	21	10.1586	117.5359
293		3	17	19	3	16	9.9468	36.6410

Objective   To use NLP to find the ratings that best predict the actual point spreads observed.

WHERE DO THE NUMBERS COME FROM?

For us sports fans, thank heavens for the Web. The results of NFL games, as well as NBA, MLB, and other sporting games, can be found on a number of Web sites. Check out www.sportingnews.com, for example. To see much more about sports ratings, go to Jeff Sagarin's page at www.usatoday.com/sports/sagarin.htm. Of course, if you are an avid sports fan, you probably already know the good Web sites!

Solution

We first need to explain the methodology we will use to rate teams. Suppose that a team plays at home against another team. Then our prediction for the point spread of the game (home team score minus visitor team score) is:

Predicted point spread

$$= \text{Home team rating} - \text{Visitor team rating} + \text{Home team advantage}$$

The home team advantage is the number of points extra for the home team because of the psychological (or physical) advantage of playing on its home field. Football experts claim that this home team advantage in the NFL is about 3 points. However, we will estimate it, as well as the ratings.

We define the prediction error to be:

$$\text{Prediction error} = \text{Actual point spread} - \text{Predicted point spread}$$

The ratings are chosen so that the predicted point spreads match up as well as possible with the actual point spreads.

We will determine ratings that minimize the sum of squared prediction errors.[9] To get a unique answer to the problem, we need to "normalize" the ratings—that is, fix the average rating at some nominal value. Because the well-known Sagarin ratings use a nominal value in the mid-80s, we will use a nominal value of 85. (Any nominal value could be used to produce exactly the same *relative* ratings.) Then what do ratings of, say, 82 and 91 really mean? They mean that if two teams with these ratings played each other on a neutral field, the higher rated team would be predicted to win by 9 points.

DEVELOPING THE SPREADSHEET MODEL

To produce the model in Figure 7.30, proceed as follows.

1 Input game data. If you want to determine the ratings for another NFL (or NBA or MLB) season, you will have to get the data from the Web. (We are fortunate to have an inside contact—Winston's best friend is Jeff Sagarin!)

2 Changing cells. Enter *any* value for the home field advantage and the 31 team ratings in the Home_team_advantage and Rating ranges. These comprise the changing cells. Note that it would be possible to use a "given" value for the home team advantage, such as 3, but we will let Solver choose the home team advantage that best fits the data.

3 Average rating. Enter the nominal average rating in cell D41, and average the ratings in cell B41 with the formula

=AVERAGE(Rating)

4 Actual point spreads. Enter the actual point spreads in column F as differences between columns D and E.

The VLOOKUP functions let us find the ratings to use for the predicted point spread.

5 Predictions. We have entered the data on games played by referring to the team index numbers. This allows us to use lookup functions to predict the point spreads. To do this, enter the formula

=Home_team_advantage+VLOOKUP(B46,$A$5:$C$35,3)-VLOOKUP(C46,$A$5:$C$35,3)

in cell G46 for the first game, and copy it down column G for the rest of the games. The VLOOKUP functions simply look up the ratings of the home and visiting teams.

---

[9]Why *squared* errors? Admittedly, we could minimize the sum of the *absolute* prediction errors, but minimizing the sum of squared errors has a long tradition in statistics.

6 Prediction errors. We want to minimize the sum of squared prediction errors. Therefore, enter the formula

=(F46-G46)^2

in cell H46, copy it down, and then sum the squared errors in cell H39.

USING SOLVER

The completed Solver dialog box should look like Figure 7.31. We find the ratings and home field advantage that minimize the sum of squared prediction errors. The only constraint is to make the ratings average to the nominal rating. Because of the *squared* errors, this is a nonlinear model, so the Assume Linear Model option should not be checked. Also, there is no need to check the Assume Non-Negative option.

Figure 7.31
Solver Dialog Box for NFL Ratings Model

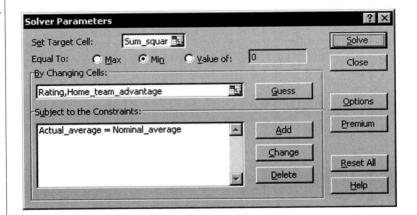

Discussion of the Solution

The solution in Figure 7.30 shows that a home team advantage of 2.01 provides the best fit, at least for the 2001 season. To provide a better picture of the ratings, we have sorted them from best to worst in Figure 7.32. You might recall that New England won the Super Bowl, beating St. Louis. The ratings ranked St. Louis number 1 and New England about 9-point underdogs (based on regular-season games only). The ratings support the playoff picture. As we indicate with color in the file, 11 of the 12 highest-rated teams went to the playoffs. Jacksonville, rated 12th, did not go to the playoffs. The 12th playoff team was the New York Jets, rated 13th.

Figure 7.32
Sorted NFL Ratings

	A	B	C	D	E	F	G
1	Sorted from best to worst						
2							
3	Team name	Rating					
4	St. Louis Rams	98.35	←	Loser in Super Bowl			
5	Chicago Bears	92.91					
6	Philadelphia Eagles	92.73		Other playoff teams shown in green			
7	Pittsburgh Steelers	92.35					
8	San Francisco 49ers	91.84					
9	Green Bay Packers	91.63					
10	New England Patriots	89.33	←	Eventual Super Bowl champion!			
11	Tampa Bay Buccaneers	89.03					
12	Oakland Raiders	88.62					
13	Baltimore Ravens	88.21					
14	Miami Dolphins	87.72					
15	Jacksonville Jaguars	85.85					
16	New York Jets	85.83					
17	San Diego Chargers	84.73					
18	Denver Broncos	84.53					
19	Cleveland Browns	84.20					
20	Kansas City Chiefs	83.84					
21	New York Giants	83.21					
22	Seattle Seahawks	83.13					
23	Tennessee Titans	82.95					
24	Cincinnatti Bengals	81.48					
25	Washington Redskins	81.35					
26	Indianapolis Colts	81.23					
27	Arizona Cardinals	80.84					
28	Atlanta Falcons	80.31					
29	Minnesota Vikings	80.27					
30	New Orleans Saints	80.18					
31	Dallas Cowboys	79.02					
32	Detroit Lions	77.79					
33	Carolina Panthers	76.05					
34	Buffalo Bills	75.48					

Remember that the actual values of the ratings are not as important as the *differences* between teams' ratings. For example, we predict that if Atlanta played Arizona at Arizona, Arizona would win by $2.01 + (80.84 - 80.31) \approx 2.5$ points. Of course, there is a considerable amount of uncertainty in any game. We might *predict* Arizona to win by 2.5 points, but the actual outcome could be much different.[10] ■

MODELING ISSUES

1. This model does not capture the effect of "intangibles," such as injuries to key players. If we were going to bet real money on NFL games, we might start with the ratings from the model and then modify them in a subjective fashion to capture any inside knowledge we might have.

2. We can improve the future predictive accuracy by giving more weight to more recent games. To do this, we could multiply the squared error for a game k weeks ago by a factor such as $(0.95)^k$. As an indication of how this "discounts" the importance of past games, this weighting gives a game from 5 weeks ago about 77% of the weight given to this week's game.

3. We can also use Solver to find the set of ratings that minimize the sum of *absolute* prediction errors. When we did this with the 2001 data, the ordering of the teams changed only slightly. ■

---

[10]If we were going to *simulate* NFL games based on these ratings, we would simulate a normally distributed point spread with the mean equal to the predicted point spread and standard deviation equal to about 14 points. Yes, there is this much variability in NFL games!

PROBLEMS

Skill-Building Problems

28. The file **P07_28.xls** lists the scores of all NFL games played during the 1996 season. Use this data set to rank the NFL teams from best to worst.

29. The file **P07_29.xls** lists the scores of all NFL games played during the 1997 season. Using all data except for the last game (which is the Super Bowl), rank the NFL teams from best to worst. Then make a forecast for this Super Bowl. (Note that the bookmakers favored Green Bay by 11 in this game, which Denver won, but you should find that our model is right on the money!)

30. Carry out the suggestion in Modeling Issue 3 on page 335. That is, find the ratings of the 2001 NFL teams using the sum of absolute prediction errors as the criterion to minimize. Discuss any differences in ratings from this method and the method used in Example 7.8.

31. The file **P07_31.xls** contains the same NFL 2001 data as we used in Example 7.8. However, it also includes the week (starting with week 1) in which the game was played. (We guessed a bit here, and because of byes, we might not have the timing exactly right, but it's close enough for this problem.) Carry out the suggestion in Modeling Issue 2 on page 335. That is, use a weighted sum of squared prediction errors, where the weight on any game played k weeks ago is 0.95^k. You can assume that the ratings are being made right after the final regular games of the season (in week 17), so for these final games, $k = 0$. Discuss how the ratings change when early-season games are discounted heavily.

32. The file **P07_32.xls** contains scores on all of the regular-season games in the NBA for the 2001–2002 basketball season. Use the same procedure as in Example 7.8 to rate the teams. Then sort the teams based on the ratings. Do these ratings appear to be approximately correct? (You might recall that the Lakers beat the Nets in the finals.) What does the model estimate the home court advantage to be?

33. The file **P07_33.xls** contains the scores of the 1994 Big Ten basketball season. Develop ratings for the 11 teams. Which was the best team? Which was the worst team? What is the estimated home court advantage? If you are an Indiana fan, try it again after deleting Indiana's huge loss to Minnesota. See how much this "outlier" affects the results.

Skill-Extending Problem

34. The method for rating teams in Example 7.8 is based on actual and predicted *point spreads*. This method can be biased if some teams "run up the score" in a few games. An alternative possibility is to base the ratings only on wins and losses. For each game, we observe whether the home team wins. Then from the proposed ratings, we predict whether the home team will win. (We predict the home team will win if the home team advantage plus the home team's rating is greater than the visitor team's rating.) We want the ratings such that the number of predictions that match the actual outcomes is maximized. Try modeling this. Do you run into difficulties? (Remember that Solver doesn't like IF functions.)

7.7 PORTFOLIO OPTIMIZATION MODELS

Given a set of investments, how do financial analysts determine the portfolio that has the lowest risk and yields a high expected return? This question was answered by Harry Markowitz in the 1950s. For his work on this and other investment topics, he received the Nobel Prize in economics in 1991. The ideas discussed in this section are the basis for most methods of *asset allocation* used by Wall Street firms. Asset allocation models are used, for example, to determine the percentage of assets to invest in stocks, gold, and Treasury bills. Before proceeding, however, we need to discuss some important formulas involving the expected value and variance of sums of random variables.

Weighted Sums of Random Variables

Let R_i be the (random) return earned during a year on a dollar invested in investment i. For example, if $R_i = 0.10$, a dollar invested at the beginning of the year grows to $1.10 at the end of the year, whereas if $R_i = -0.20$, a dollar invested at the beginning of the year decreases in value to $0.80. We assume that n investments are available. Let x_i be the fraction of our money invested in investment i. We assume that $x_1 + x_2 + \cdots + x_n = 1$, so that all of our money is invested. (To prevent shorting a stock—that is, selling shares we don't own—we will assume that $x_i \geq 0$.) Then the annual return on our investments is given by the random variable R_p, where

$$R_p = R_1 x_1 + R_2 x_2 + \cdots + R_n x_n$$

(The subscript p on R_p stands for "portfolio.")

Let μ_i be the expected value (also called the mean) of R_i, let σ_i^2 be the variance of R_i (so that σ_i is the standard deviation of R_i), and let ρ_{ij} be the correlation between R_i and R_j. To do any work with investments, you must understand how to use the following formulas, which relate the data for the individual investments to the expected return and the variance of return for a *portfolio* of investments.

$$\text{Expected value of } R_p = \mu_1 x_1 + \mu_2 x_2 + \cdots + \mu_n x_n \tag{7.5}$$

$$\text{Variance of } R_p = \sigma_1^2 x_1^2 + \sigma_2^2 x_2^2 + \cdots + \sigma_n^2 x_n^2 + \sum_{i \neq j} \rho_{ij} \sigma_i \sigma_j x_i x_j \tag{7.6}$$

The latter summation in the variance formula is over all pairs of investments. The quantities in equations (7.5) and (7.6) are extremely important in portfolio selection because of the risk–return trade-off investors need to make. All investors want to choose portfolios with high return, measured by the expected value in equation (7.5), but they also want portfolios with low risk, usually measured by the variance in equation (7.6).

Because we never actually know the true expected values (μ_i's), variances (σ_i^2's), and correlations (ρ_{ij}'s), we must estimate them. If historical data are available, we can proceed as follows:

1. Estimate μ_i by $\overline{X}_i$, the sample average of returns on investment i over several previous years. You can use Excel's AVERAGE function to calculate $\overline{X}_i$.

2. Estimate σ_i^2 by s_i^2, the sample variance of returns on investment i over several previous years. You can use Excel's VAR function to calculate s_i^2.

3. Estimate σ_i by s_i, the sample standard deviation of returns on investment i. You can calculate s_i with Excel's STDEV function. (Alternatively, you can calculate s_i as the square root of s_i^2.)

4. Estimate ρ_{ij} by r_{ij}, the sample correlation between past returns on investments i and j. You can calculate the r_{ij}'s by using Excel's CORREL function.

We now estimate the mean and variance of the return on a portfolio by replacing each parameter in equations (7.5) and (7.6) with its sample estimate. This yields

$$\text{Estimated expected value of } R_p = \overline{X}_1 x_1 + \overline{X}_2 x_2 + \cdots + \overline{X}_n x_n \tag{7.7}$$

$$\text{Estimated variance of } R_p = s_1^2 x_1^2 + s_2^2 x_2^2 + \cdots + s_n^2 x_n^2 + \sum_{i \neq j} r_{ij} s_i s_j x_i x_j \tag{7.8}$$

In keeping with common practice, we express the annual return on investments in decimal form. Thus, a return of 0.10 on a stock means that the stock has increased in value by 10%.

Covariances indicate relationships between variables, but unlike correlations, covariances are affected by the units in which the variables are measured.

We can rewrite equation (7.8) slightly by using *covariances* instead of correlations. The covariance between two stock returns is another measure of the relationship between the two returns, but unlike a correlation, it is *not* scaled to be between -1 and $+1$. This is because covariances are affected by the units in which the returns are measured.

Although a covariance is a somewhat less intuitive measure than a correlation, it is used so frequently by financial analysts that we will use it here as well. If c_{ij} is the estimated covariance between stocks i and j, then $c_{ij} = r_{ij} s_i s_j$. Using this equation and the fact that the correlation between any stock and itself is 1, we can also write $c_{ii} = s_i^2$ for each stock i. Therefore, an equivalent form of equation (7.8) is the following:

$$\text{Estimated variance of } R_p = \sum_{i,j} c_{ij} x_i x_j \qquad \textbf{(7.9)}$$

As we will see in the portfolio optimization example, this allows us to calculate the estimated portfolio variance very easily with Excel's matrix functions.

Matrix Functions in Excel

Equation (7.8) for the variance of portfolio return looks intimidating, particularly if there are many potential investments. Fortunately, we can take advantage of two built-in Excel matrix functions to simplify our work. In this subsection we illustrate how to use Excel's MMULT (matrix multiplication) and TRANSPOSE functions. Then in the next subsection we will put these to use in the portfolio selection model.

A **matrix** is a rectangular array of numbers. We say a matrix is an $i \times j$ matrix if it consists of i rows and j columns. For example,

$$A = \begin{pmatrix} 1 & 2 & 3 \\ 4 & 5 & 6 \end{pmatrix}$$

is a 2×3 matrix, and

$$B = \begin{pmatrix} 1 & 2 \\ 3 & 4 \\ 5 & 6 \end{pmatrix}$$

is a 3×2 matrix. If the matrix has only a single row, we call it a **row vector**. Similarly, if it has only a single column, we call it a **column vector**.

If matrix A has the same number of columns as matrix B has rows, then we can construct the **matrix product** of A and B, denoted AB. The entry in row i, column j of the product AB is obtained by summing the products of the elements in row i of A with the corresponding elements in column j of B. If A is an $i \times k$ matrix and B is a $k \times j$ matrix, then AB is an $i \times j$ matrix.

For example, if

$$A = \begin{pmatrix} 1 & 2 & 3 \\ 2 & 4 & 5 \end{pmatrix}$$

and

$$B = \begin{pmatrix} 1 & 2 \\ 3 & 4 \\ 5 & 6 \end{pmatrix}$$

then AB is the following 2×2 matrix:

$$AB = \begin{pmatrix} 1(1) + 2(3) + 3(5) & 1(2) + 2(4) + 3(6) \\ 2(1) + 4(3) + 5(5) & 2(2) + 4(4) + 5(6) \end{pmatrix} = \begin{pmatrix} 22 & 28 \\ 39 & 50 \end{pmatrix}$$

The Excel MMULT function performs matrix multiplication in a single step. The spreadsheet in Figure 7.33 indicates how to multiply matrices of different sizes. (See the file **MatrixMult.xls**.) For example, to multiply matrix 1 by matrix 2 (which is possible because matrix 1 has 3 columns and matrix 2 has 3 rows), we select the range B13:C14, type the formula

=MMULT(B4:D5,B7:C9)

and press Ctrl-Shift-Enter (all three keys at once). Note that we selected a range with 2 rows because matrix 1 has 2 rows, and we selected a range with 2 columns because matrix 2 has 2 columns.

Figure 7.33 Examples of Matrix Multiplication in Excel

	A	B	C	D	E	F	G	H	I	J	K	L	M	N
1	Matrix multiplication in Excel													
2														
3	Typical multiplication of two matrices													
4	Matrix 1	1	2	3				Multiplication of a matrix and a column						
5		2	4	5				Column 1	2					
6									3					
7	Matrix 2	1	2						4					
8		3	4											
9		5	6					Matrix 1 times Column 1, with formula =MMULT(B4:D5,I4:I6)						
10								Select range with 2 rows, 1 column, enter formula, press Ctrl-Shift-Enter						
11	Matrix 1 times Matrix 2, with formula =MMULT(B4:D5,B7:C9)								20					
12	Select range with 2 rows, 2 columns, enter formula, press Ctrl-Shift-Enter.								36					
13		22	28											
14		39	50					Multiplication of a row and a matrix						
15								Row 1		4	5			
16	Multiplication of a quadratic form (row times matrix times column)													
17	Matrix 3	2	1	3				Row 1 times Matrix 1, with formula =MMULT(I14:J14,B4:D5)						
18		1	-1	0				Select range with 1 row, 3 columns, enter formula, press Ctrl-Shift-Enter						
19		3	0	4					14	28	37			
20														
21	Transpose of Column 1 times Matrix 3 times Column 1							Multiplication of a row and a column						
22	Formula is =MMULT(TRANSPOSE(I4:I6),MMULT(B17:D19,I4:I6))							Row 2		1	6	3		
23	Select range with 1 row, 1 column, enter formula, press Ctrl-Shift-Enter													
24		123						Row 2 times Column 1, with formula =MMULT(I22:K22,I4:I6)						
25								Select range with 1 row, 1 column, enter formula, press Ctrl-Shift-Enter						
26	Notes on quadratic form example:								32					
27	Two MMULT's are required because MMULT works on only two ranges at a time.													
28	TRANSPOSE is needed to change a column into a row.													

The matrix multiplication in cell B24 indicates that (1) we can multiply three matrices together by using MMULT twice, and (2) we can use the TRANSPOSE function to convert a column vector to a row vector (or vice versa), if necessary. Here, we want to multiply Column 1 by the product of Matrix 3 and Column 1. However, Column 1 is 3×1, and Matrix 3 is 3×3, so Column 1 times Matrix 3 doesn't work. Instead, we must transpose Column 1 to make it 1×3. Then the result of multiplying all three together is a 1×1 matrix (a number). We calculate it by selecting cell B24, typing the formula

=MMULT(TRANSPOSE(I4:I6),MMULT(B17:D19,I4:I6))

and pressing Ctrl-Shift-Enter. We use MMULT twice in this formula because it can multiply only *two* matrices at a time.

→ EXCEL FUNCTION: *MMULT*

*The MMULT and TRANSPOSE functions are useful for matrix operations. They are called array functions because they return results to an entire range, not just a single cell. The MMULT function multiplies two matrices and has the syntax **=MMULT(range1,range2)**, where range1 must have as many columns as range2 has rows. To use this function, highlight a range that has as many rows as range1 and as many columns as range2, type the formula, and press Ctrl-Shift-Enter. The resulting formula will have curly brackets around it in the Excel formula bar. You should not type these curly brackets. Excel enters them automatically to remind you that this is an array formula.* ■

The Portfolio Selection Model

Most investors have two objectives in forming portfolios: to obtain a large expected return and to obtain a small variance (to minimize risk). The problem is inherently nonlinear because variance is nonlinear. The most common way of handling this two-objective problem is to specify a minimal expected return that we require and then minimize the variance subject to the constraint on the expected return. The following example illustrates how we can use Solver to do this.

| EXAMPLE | 7.9 PORTFOLIO OPTIMIZATION AT PERLMAN & BROTHERS |

Perlman & Brothers, an investment company, intends to invest a given amount of money in three stocks. From past data, the means and standard deviations of annual returns have been estimated as shown in Table 7.7. The correlations between the annual returns on the stocks are listed in Table 7.8. The company wants to find a minimum-variance portfolio that yields an expected annual return of at least 0.12.

Table 7.7 Estimated Means and Standard Deviations of Stock Returns

Stock	Mean	Standard Deviation
1	0.14	0.20
2	0.11	0.15
3	0.10	0.08

Table 7.8 Estimated Correlations Between Stock Returns

Combination	Correlation
Stocks 1 and 2	0.6
Stocks 1 and 3	0.4
Stocks 2 and 3	0.7

Objective To use NLP to find the portfolio of the three stocks that minimizes the risk, measured by portfolio variance, subject to achieving an expected return of at least 0.12.

WHERE DO THE NUMBERS COME FROM?

Financial analysts typically estimate the required means, standard deviations, and correlations for stock returns from historical data, as discussed at the beginning of this section. However, you should be aware that there is no guarantee that these estimates, based on *historical* return data, will be relevant for *future* returns. If the analysts have new information about the stocks, they should incorporate this new information into their estimates.

The optimal solution indicates the fractions to invest in the various securities, and these fractions are relevant regardless of the total dollar amount to be invested.

Solution

The variables and constraints for this model are listed in Table 7.9. One interesting aspect of this model is that we do *not* have to specify the amount of money invested—it could be $100, $1000, $1,000,000, or any other amount. The model determines the *fractions* of this amount to invest in the various stocks, and these fractions are then relevant for any investment amount. All we require is that the fractions sum to 1, so that all of the money is invested. Besides this, we require *nonnegative* fractions to prevent shorting stocks.[11] We also

---

[11]If you want to allow shorting, do not check the Assume Non-Negative box in Solver options.

require that the expected return from the portfolio be at least as large as the specified minimal required expected return.

Table 7.9 Variables and Constraints for Portfolio Optimization Model

Input variables	Estimates of means, standard deviations, and correlations for stock returns, minimum required expected portfolio return
Decision variables (changing cells)	Fractions invested in the various stocks
Objective (target cell)	Portfolio variance (minimize)
Other output variables	Covariances between stock returns, total fraction of money invested, expected portfolio return
Constraints	Total fraction invested = 1 Expected portfolio return ≥ Minimum required expected portfolio return

---

DEVELOPING THE SPREADSHEET MODEL

The individual steps are now listed. (See Figure 7.34 and the file **Portfolio.xls.**)

Figure 7.34 Portfolio Optimization Model

	A	B	C	D	E	F	G	H	I
1	Portfolio selection model								
2									
3	Stock input data								
4		Stock 1	Stock 2	Stock 3					
5	Mean return	0.14	0.11	0.1					
6	StDev of return	0.2	0.15	0.08					
7									
8	Correlations	Stock 1	Stock 2	Stock 3		Covariances	Stock 1	Stock 2	Stock 3
9	Stock 1	1	0.6	0.4		Stock 1	0.04	0.018	0.0064
10	Stock 2	0.6	1	0.7		Stock 2	0.018	0.0225	0.0084
11	Stock 3	0.4	0.7	1		Stock 3	0.0064	0.0084	0.0064
12									
13	Investment decisions								
14		Stock 1	Stock 2	Stock 3		Range names used:			
15	Fractions to invest	0.500	0.000	0.500		Actual_return	=Model!$B$23		
16						Fractions_to_invest	=Model!$B$15:$D$15		
17	Constraint on investing everything					Portfolio_variance	=Model!$B$25		
18		Total invested		Required value		Required_return	=Model!$D$23		
19		1.00	=	1		Total_invested	=Model!$B$19		
20									
21	Constraint on expected portfolio return								
22		Actual return		Required return					
23		0.12	>=	0.12					
24									
25	Portfolio variance	0.0148							
26	Portfolio stdev	0.1217							

---

1 Inputs. Enter the inputs in the shaded ranges. These include the estimates of means, standard deviations, and correlations, as well as the required expected return.

2 Fractions invested. Enter *any* trial values in the Fractions_to_invest range for the fractions of Perlman's money placed in the three investments. Then sum these with the SUM function in cell B19.

3 Expected annual return. Use equation (7.7) to compute the expected annual return in cell B23 with the formula

=SUMPRODUCT(B5:D5,Fractions_to_invest)

4 **Covariance matrix.** We want to use equation (7.9) to calculate the portfolio variance. To do this, we must first calculate a matrix of covariances. Using the general formula for covariance, $c_{ij} = r_{ij}s_i s_j$ (which holds even when $i = j$ since $r_{ii} = 1$), we can calculate these from the inputs, using lookups. Specifically, enter the formula

=HLOOKUP($F9,$B$4:$D$6,3)*B9*HLOOKUP(G$8,$B$4:$D$6,3)

in cell G9, and copy it to the range G9:I11. (This formula is a bit tricky, so take a close look at it. The term B9 captures the relevant correlation. The two HLOOKUP terms capture the appropriate standard deviations.)

5 **Portfolio variance.** Although we won't go into the mathematical details, it can be shown that the summation in equation (7.9) is really the product of three matrices: a row of fractions invested times the covariance matrix times a column of fractions invested. To calculate it, enter the formula

=MMULT(Fractions_to_invest,MMULT(G9:I11,TRANSPOSE(Fractions_to_invest)))

The MMULT function can multiply only two matrices at a time.

in cell B25 and press Ctrl-Shift-Enter. (Remember that Excel will put curly brackets around this formula. You should *not* type these curly brackets.) Note that this formula uses two MMULT functions. Again, this is because MMULT can multiply only two matrices at a time. Therefore, we first multiply the last two matrices and then multiply this product by the first matrix.

6 **Portfolio standard deviation.** Most financial analysts talk in terms of portfolio *variance*. However, it is probably more intuitive to talk about portfolio *standard deviation* because it is in the same units as the returns. We calculate the standard deviation in cell B26 with the formula

=SQRT(Portfolio_variance)

Actually, we could use either cell B25 or B26 as the target cell to minimize. Minimizing the square root of a function is equivalent to minimizing the function itself.

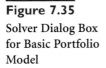

USING SOLVER

The completed Solver dialog box should appear as in Figure 7.35. The constraints specify that the expected return must be at least as large as the minimum required return, and all of the company's money must be invested. We constrain the changing cells to be nonnegative (to avoid short selling), but because of the squared terms in the variance formula, we do *not* check the Assume Linear Model option.

Figure 7.35
Solver Dialog Box
for Basic Portfolio
Model

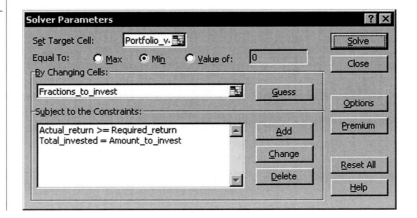

Discussion of the Solution

It is difficult to guess the best allocation in portfolio optimization models. It depends not only on expected returns and standard deviations of returns, but also on correlations between returns.

The solution in Figure 7.34 indicates that the company should put half of its money in each of stocks 1 and 3, and it should not invest in stock 2 at all. This might be somewhat surprising, given that the ranking of riskiness of the stocks is 1, 2, 3, with stock 1 being the most risky but also having the highest expected return. However, the correlations play an important role in portfolio selection, so we can usually not guess the optimal portfolio on the basis of the means and standard deviations of stock returns alone.

We can interpret the portfolio standard deviation of 0.1217 in a probabilistic sense. Specifically, if we believe that stock returns are approximately *normally* distributed, then the probability is about 0.68 that the actual portfolio return will be within 1 standard deviation of the expected return, and the probability is about 0.95 that the actual portfolio return will be within 2 standard deviations of the expected return. Given that the expected return is 0.12, this implies a lot of risk—2 standard deviations below this mean is a *negative* return (or loss) of slightly more than 0.12!

Is the Solver Solution Optimal?

The constraints for this model are linear, and it can be shown that the portfolio variance is a convex function of the investment fractions. Therefore, we are guaranteed that the Solver solution is optimal.

Sensitivity Analysis

This model begs for a sensitivity analysis on the minimum required return. When the company requires a larger expected return, it must assume a larger risk. We see how this occurs in Figure 7.36. We use SolverTable with cell D23 as the single input cell, allowing it to vary from 0.10 to 0.14 in increments of 0.005. Note that values outside this range are of little interest. Stock 3 has the minimum expected return, 0.10, and stock 1 has the highest expected return, 0.14, so no portfolio can have an expected return outside of this range.

Figure 7.36   The Efficient Frontier

	A	B	C	D	E	F	G
28	Sensitivity of optimal portfolio to minimum required returr						
29	Required	Stock 1	Stock 2	Stock 3	Port stdev	Exp return	
30		$B$15	$C$15	$D$15	$B$26	$B$23	
31	0.100	0.000	0.000	1.000	0.0800	0.10	
32	0.105	0.125	0.000	0.875	0.0832	0.11	
33	0.110	0.250	0.000	0.750	0.0922	0.11	
34	0.115	0.375	0.000	0.625	0.1055	0.12	
35	0.120	0.500	0.000	0.500	0.1217	0.12	
36	0.125	0.625	0.000	0.375	0.1397	0.13	
37	0.130	0.750	0.000	0.250	0.1591	0.13	
38	0.135	0.875	0.000	0.125	0.1792	0.14	
39	0.140	1.000	0.000	0.000	0.2000	0.14	
40							

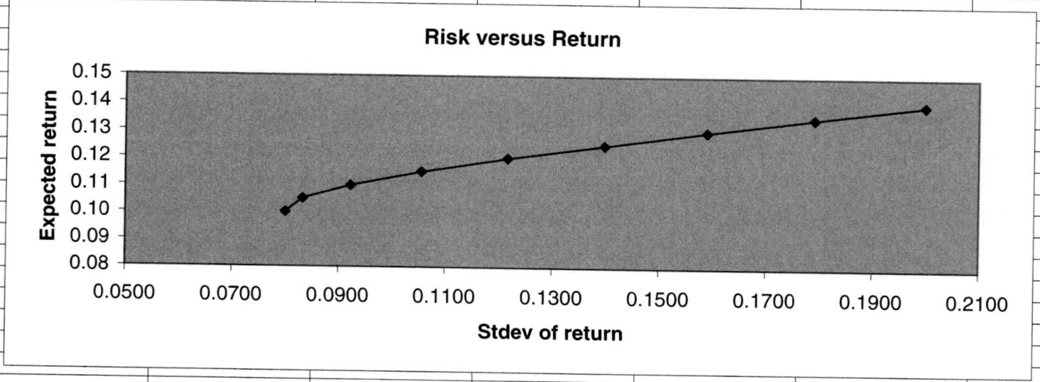

Risk versus Return chart (Expected return vs. Stdev of return)

The results indicate that the company should put more and more into risky stock 1 as the required return increases—and stock 2 continues to be unused. The accompanying X-Y chart (with the option to "connect the dots") shows the risk–return trade-off. As the company assumes more risk, as measured by portfolio standard deviation, the expected return increases, but at a decreasing rate.

Financial analysts typically put risk on the horizontal axis and expected return on the vertical axis in this type of risk–return chart.

The curve in this chart is called the **efficient frontier**. Points on the efficient frontier can be achieved by appropriate portfolios. Points below the efficient frontier can be achieved, but they are not as good as points on the efficient frontier because they have a lower expected return for a given level of risk. In contrast, points above the efficient frontier are unachievable—the company cannot achieve this high an expected return for a given level of risk. ■

MODELING ISSUES

1. Typical real-world portfolio selection problems involve a large number of potential investments, certainly many more than three. This admittedly requires more input data, particularly for the correlation matrix, but the basic model does not change at all. In particular, the matrix formula for portfolio variance is exactly the same. This shows the power of using Excel's matrix functions. Without them, the formula for portfolio variance would be a long involved sum.

2. If Perlman is allowed to short a stock, we simply allow the fraction invested in that stock to be negative. To implement this, we eliminate the nonnegativity constraints on the changing cells.

3. An alternative objective might be to minimize the probability that the portfolio loses money. We will illustrate this possibility in one of the problems. ■

PROBLEMS

Skill-Building Problems

35. For each of the following, answer whether it makes sense to multiply the matrices of the given sizes. In each case where it makes sense, demonstrate an example in Excel, where you can make up the numbers.
  a. AB, where A is 3×4 and B is 4×1
  b. AB, where A is 1×4 and B is 4×1
  c. AB, where A is 4×1 and B is 1×4
  d. AB, where A is 1×4 and B is 1×4
  e. ABC, where A is 1×4, B is 4×4, and C is 4×1
  f. ABC, where A is 3×3, B is 3×3, and C is 3×1
  g. $A^T B$, where A is 4×3 and B is 4×3, and A^T denotes the transpose of A

36. Add a new stock, stock 4, to the model in Example 7.9. Assume that the estimated mean and standard deviation of return for stock 4 are 0.125 and 0.175, respectively. Also, assume the correlations between stock 4 and the original three stocks are 0.3, 0.5, and 0.8. Run Solver on the modified model, where the required expected portfolio return is again 0.12. Is stock 4 in the optimal portfolio? Then run SolverTable as in the example. Is stock 4 in any of the optimal portfolios on the efficient frontier?

37. In the model in Example 7.9, stock 2 is not in the optimal portfolio. Use SolverTable to see whether it ever enters the optimal portfolio as its correlations with stocks 1 and 3 vary. Specifically, use a two-way SolverTable with two inputs, the correlations between stock 2 and stocks 1 and 3, each allowed to vary from 0.1 to 0.9 in increments of 0.1. Capture as outputs the three changing cells. Discuss the results. (*Note*: You'll have to change the model slightly. For example, if you use cells B10 and C11 as the two SolverTable input cells, you'll have to ensure that cells C9 and D10 change accordingly. This is easy. Just put formulas in these latter two cells.)

38. The stocks in Example 7. 9 are all *positively* correlated. What happens when they are *negatively* correlated? Answer for each of the following scenarios. In each case, two of the three correlations are the negatives of their original values. Discuss the differences between the optimal portfolios in these three scenarios.

a. Change the signs of the correlations between stocks 1 and 2 and between stocks 1 and 3. (Here, stock 1 tends to be going in a different direction from stocks 2 and 3.)

b. Change the signs of the correlations between stocks 1 and 2 and between stocks 2 and 3. (Here, stock 2 tends to be going in a different direction from stocks 1 and 3.)

c. Change the signs of the correlations between stocks 1 and 3 and between stocks 2 and 3. (Here, stock 3 tends to be going in a different direction from stocks 1 and 2.)

39. The file **P07_39.xls** contains historical monthly returns for 28 companies. For each company, calculate the estimated mean return and the estimated variance of return. Then calculate the estimated correlations between the companies' returns. Note that "return" here means *monthly* return. (*Hint:* Make life easy for yourself by using StatTools' Summary Statistics capabilities.)

40. This problem continues using the data from the previous problem. The file **P07_40.xls** includes all of the previous data. It also contains fractions in row 3 for creating a portfolio. These fractions are currently all equal to 1/28, but they can be changed to any values you like, so long as they continue to sum to 1. For any such fractions, find the estimated mean, variance, and standard deviation of the resulting portfolio return.

Skill-Extending Problems

41. Continuing the previous problem, find the portfolio that achieves an expected monthly return of at least 0.01% and minimizes portfolio variance. Then use SolverTable to sweep out the efficient frontier, as in Example 7.9. Create a chart of this efficient frontier from your SolverTable results. What are the relevant lower and upper limits on the required expected monthly return?

42. In many cases we can assume that the portfolio return is at least approximately *normally* distributed. Then we can use Excel's NORMDIST function to calculate the probability that the portfolio return is negative. The relevant formula is **=NORMDIST(0,*mean*,*stdev*,1)**, where *mean* and *stdev* are the expected portfolio return and standard deviation of portfolio return, respectively.

a. Modify the model in Example 7.9 slightly, and then run Solver, to find the portfolio that achieves at least a 0.12 expected return and minimizes the probability of a negative return. Do you get the same optimal portfolio as before? What is the probability that the return from this portfolio will be negative?

b. Using the model in part **a**, proceed as in Example 7.9 to use SolverTable and create a chart of the efficient frontier. However, this time put the probability of a negative return on the horizontal axis.

7.8 CONCLUSION

Although a large number of real-world problems can be approximated well by linear models, there are also many problems that are inherently nonlinear. We have analyzed several of these in this chapter, including the important class of portfolio selection models where the risk, usually measured by portfolio variance, is a nonlinear function of the decision variables. We have purposely neglected much of the mathematics behind nonlinear optimization because of its technical difficulty. However, it is important to realize that nonlinear models present many more hazards for spreadsheet Solvers (or any other optimization software) than linear models. Unless we can verify that the assumptions for a minimization or maximization problem are satisfied—and this can be very difficult to do—there is no guarantee that Solver will converge to the optimal solution (or even converge at all). The examples in this chapter were purposely kept small and "nice" so that Solver could handle them and produce optimal solutions. Larger and more complex nonlinear models are not always so accommodating and frequently require solution methods well beyond the scope of this book.

Summary of Key Management Science Terms

Term	Explanation	Page
Nonlinear programming models	Models where there are nonlinearities in the objective and/or the constraints	296
Global optimum	Solution that is guaranteed to be *the* optimal solution	297
Local optimum	Solution that is better than all nearby solutions, but might not be the best overall	297
Convex function	Function with a nondecreasing slope	298
Concave function	Function with a nonincreasing slope	298
Optimality guarantee for NLP models	No package, including Solver, can guarantee that the solution it stops at will be the global optimum unless certain convexity/concavity conditions are satisfied.	300
Demand function	A function that relates demand for a product to its price	302
Constant elasticity demand function	A demand function where elasticity (% change in demand for a 1% change in price) is constant for any price	302
Minimizing sum of squared errors	A popular method of fitting a curve of some form to a set of points; the "errors" are the differences between observed and predicted values	319
Unconstrained models	An optimization model with no constraints	320
Weighted sum of random variables	An important quantity in financial portfolio analysis; random variables are returns from investments, weights are fractions put in investments	336
Return, risk measures of portfolio models	Portfolio models try to maximize expected return and minimize variance of return (risk); formulas for these involve correlations or covariances among investment returns	337
Matrix	A rectangular array of numbers; often useful for simplifying complex summation formulas	338
Efficient frontier	Curve that shows the largest expected portfolio return possible for a given level of risk	344

Summary of Key Excel Terms

Term	Explanation	Excel	Page
SUMXMY2 function	Useful for calculating distance between two points	=SUMXMY2 (*xRange,yRange*)	328
MMULT function	An array function that multiplies two matrices stored in Excel ranges	Highlight result range, type =MMULT(*range1,range2*), press Ctrl-Shift-Enter	339

PROBLEMS

Skill-Building Problems

43. Suppose Ford currently sells 250,000 Ford Tauruses annually. The unit cost of a Taurus, including the delivery cost to a dealer, is $16,000. The current Taurus price is $20,000, and the current elasticity of demand for the Taurus is -1.5.
  a. Determine a profit-maximizing price for a Taurus. Do this when the demand function is of the constant elasticity type. Do it when the demand function is linear.
  b. Suppose Ford makes an average profit of $800 from servicing a Taurus purchased from a Ford dealer. (This is an average over the lifetime of the car.) How do your answers to part a change?

44. Suppose the current exchange rate is 100 yen per dollar. We currently sell 100 units of a product for 700 yen. The cost of producing and shipping the product to Japan is $5, and the current elasticity of demand is -3. Find the optimal price to charge for the product (in yen) for each of the following exchange rates: 60 yen/$, 80 yen/$, 100 yen/$, 120 yen/$, 140 yen/$, and 160 yen/$. Assume the demand function is linear.

45. Another way to derive a demand function is to break the market into segments and identify a low price, a medium price, and a high price. For each of these prices and market segments, we ask company experts to estimate product demand. Then we use Excel's trend curve fitting capabilities to fit a *quadratic* function that represents that segment's demand function. Finally, we add the segment demand curves to derive an aggregate demand curve. Try this procedure for pricing a candy bar. Assume the candy bar costs $0.55 to produce. The company plans to charge between $1.10 and $1.50 for this candy bar. Its marketing department estimates the demands shown in the file **P07_45.xls** (in thousands) in the three regions of the country where the candy bar will be sold. What is the profit-maximizing price, assuming that the *same* price will be charged in all three regions?

46. Widgetco produces widgets at plants 1 and 2. It costs $20\,x^{1/2}$ dollars to produce x units at plant 1 and $40\,x^{1/3}$ dollars to produce x units at plant 2. Each plant can produce up to 70 units. Each unit produced can be sold for $10. At most 120 widgets can be sold. Determine how Widgetco can maximize its profit.

47. If a monopolist produces q units, she can charge $100 - 4q$ dollars per unit. The fixed cost of production is $50 and the variable cost is $2 per unit.
  a. How can the monopolist maximize her profit?
  b. If the monopolist must pay a sales tax of $2 per unit, will she increase or decrease production (relative to the situation with no sales tax)?

  c. Continuing part **b**, use SolverTable to see how a change in the sales tax affects the optimal solution.
  d. Again continuing part **b**, use SolverTable to see how simultaneous changes in the fixed and variable costs of production affect the optimal output level. (Use a two-way table.)

48. It costs a company $12 to purchase an hour of labor and $15 to purchase an hour of capital. If L hours of labor and K units of capital are available, then $L^{2/3}K^{1/3}$ machines can be produced. Suppose the company has $10,000 to purchase labor and capital.
  a. What is the maximum number of machines it can produce?
  b. Use SolverTable to see how a change in the price of labor changes the optimal solution.
  c. Use SolverTable to see how a change in the price of capital changes the optimal solution.
  d. Use SolverTable to see how a change in the amount of money available changes the optimal solution.

49. In the previous problem what is the minimum-cost method of producing 100 machines? (Ignore the $10,000 budget constraint.)

50. The cost per day of running a hospital is $200,000 + 0.002x^2$ dollars, where x is the number of patients served per day. What number of patients served per day minimizes the cost per patient of running the hospital?

51. There are two firms producing widgets. It costs the first firm q_1^2 dollars to produce q_1 widgets and the second firm $0.5\,q_2^2$ dollars to produce q_2 widgets. If a total of q widgets are produced, consumers will pay $200 - q$ dollars for each widget. If the two manufacturers want to collude in an attempt to maximize the sum of their profits, how many widgets should each company produce? (The model for this type of problem is called a **collusive duopoly model**.)

52. A company manufactures two products. If it charges price p_i for product i, it can sell q_i units of product i, where $q_1 = 60 - 3p_1 + p_2$ and $q_2 = 80 - 2p_2 + p_1$. It costs $25 to produce a unit of product 1 and $72 to produce a unit of product 2. How many units of each product should the company produce, and what prices should it charge, to maximize its profit?

53. Q&H Company advertises during soap operas and football games. Each soap opera ad costs $50,000, and each football game ad costs $100,000. If S soap opera ads are purchased, they will be seen by $5S^{1/2}$ million men and $20S^{1/2}$ million women. If F football ads are purchased, they will be seen by $17F^{1/2}$ million men and $7F^{1/2}$ million women. The company wants at least 40 million men and at least 60 million women to see its ads.

  a. Determine how to minimize Q&H's cost of reaching the required number of viewers.

  b. How does this model violate the proportionality and additivity assumptions of LP?

  c. Suppose that the number of women (in millions) reached by F football ads and S soap opera ads is $7F^{1/2} + 20S^{1/2} - 0.2(FS)^{1/2}$. Why might this be a more realistic representation of the number of women viewers seeing Q&H's ads?

54. Beerco has $100,000 to spend on advertising in four markets. The sales revenue (in thousands of dollars) that can be created in each market by spending x_i thousand dollars in market i is given in the file **P07_54.xls**.

  a. To maximize its sales revenue, how much money should Beerco spend in each market?

  b. Use SolverTable to see how a change in the advertising budget affects the optimal sales revenue.

55. A beer company has divided Bloomington into two territories. If the company spends x_1 dollars on promotion in territory 1, it can sell $60\,x_1^{1/2}$ cases of beer there, and if it spends x_2 dollars on promotion in territory 2, it can sell $40\,x_2^{1/2}$ cases of beer there. Each case of beer sold in territory 1 sells for $10 and incurs $5 in shipping and production costs. Each case of beer sold in territory 2 sells for $9 and incurs $4 in shipping and production costs. A total of $5000 is available for promotion.

  a. How can the beer company maximize its profit?

  b. If an extra dollar could be spent on promotion, by approximately how much would the company's profit increase? By how much would its revenue increase?

  c. Use SolverTable to see how a change in the price of beer 1 affects the optimal solution. Do the same for a change in the price of beer 2.

56. A firm is planning to spend $10,000 on advertising. It costs $3000 per minute to advertise on television and $1000 per minute to advertise on radio. If the firm buys x minutes of television advertising and y minutes of radio advertising, its revenue in thousands of dollars is given by $-2x^2 - y^2 + xy + 8x + 3y$. How can the firm maximize its revenue?

57. Proctor and Ramble has given you $12 million to spend on advertising Huggys diapers during the next 12 months. At the beginning of January, Huggys has a 30% market share. During any month, 10% of the people who purchase Huggys defect to brand X, and a fraction $0.2\,a^{1/2}$ of customers who usually buy brand X switch to Huggys, where a is the amount spent on advertising in millions of dollars. For example, if you spend $4 million during a month, 40% of brand X's customers switch to Huggys. Your goal is to maximize

Proctor and Ramble's average market share during the next 12 months, where the average is computed from each month's ending share. Determine an appropriate advertising policy. (*Hint*: Make sure you enter a nonzero trial value for each month's advertising expense or Solver might give you an error message.)

58. Based on Kolesar and Blum (1973). Suppose that a company must service customers lying in an area of A square miles with n warehouses. Kolesar and Blum showed that when the warehouse(s) are located properly, the average distance between a warehouse and a customer is $(A/n)^{1/2}$. Assume that it costs the company $60,000 per year to maintain a warehouse and $400,000 to build a warehouse. Also, assume that a $400,000 cost is equivalent to incurring a cost of $40,000 per year indefinitely. The company fills 160,000 orders per year, and the shipping cost per order is $1 per mile. If the company serves an area of 100 square miles, how many warehouses should it have?

59. A company has five factories. The x- and y-coordinates of the location of each factory are given in the file **P07_59.xls**. The company wants to locate a warehouse at a point that minimizes the sum of the squared distances of the plants from the warehouse. Where should the warehouse be located?

60. Monroe County is trying to determine where to place the county fire station. The locations of the county's four major towns are as follows: (10, 20), (60, 20), (40, 30), and (80, 60). (See Figure 7.37.) Town 1 averages 20 fires per year; town 2, 30 fires; town 3, 40 fires; and town 4, 25 fires. The county wants to build the fire station in a location that minimizes the average distance that a fire engine must travel to respond to a fire. Since most roads run in either an east–west or a north–south direction, we assume that the fire engine must do the same. For example, if the fire station is located at (30, 40) and a fire occurs at town 4, the fire engine has to travel $|80 - 30| + |60 - 40| = 70$ miles to the fire.

Figure 7.37   Existing Locations for Fire Station Problem

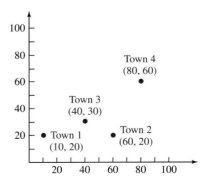

a. Determine where the fire station should be located.

b. Use SolverTable to see how the optimal location of the fire station changes as the number of fires at town 3 changes.

61. Consider three investments. You are given the following means, standard deviations, and correlations for the annual return on these three investments. The means are 0.12, 0.15, and 0.20. The standard deviations are 0.20, 0.30, and 0.40. The correlation between stocks 1 and 2 is 0.65, between stocks 1 and 3 is 0.75, and between stocks 2 and 3 is 0.41. You have $10,000 to invest and can invest no more than half of your money in any single stock. Determine the minimum-variance portfolio that yields an expected annual return of at least 0.14.

62. I have $1000 to invest in three stocks. Let R_i be the random variable representing the annual return on $1 invested in stock i. For example, if $R_i = 0.12$, then $1 invested in stock i at the beginning of a year is worth $1.12 at the end of the year. The means are $E(R_1) = 0.14$, $E(R_2) = 0.11$, and $E(R_3) = 0.10$. The variances are $Var\ R_1 = 0.20$, $Var\ R_2 = 0.08$, and $Var\ R_3 = 0.18$. The correlations are $r_{12} = 0.8$, $r_{13} = 0.7$, and $r_{23} = 0.9$. Determine the minimum-variance portfolio that attains an expected annual return of at least 0.12.

63. Oilco must determine how many barrels of oil to extract during each of the next 2 years. If Oilco extracts x_1 million barrels during year 1, each barrel can be sold for $30 - x_1$ dollars. If Oilco extracts x_2 million barrels during year 2, each barrel can be sold for $35 - x_2$ dollars. The cost of extracting x_1 million barrels during year 1 is x_1^2 million dollars, and the cost of extracting x_2 million barrels during year 2 is $2\ x_2^2$ million dollars. A total of 20 million barrels of oil are available, and at most $250 million can be spent on extraction. Determine how Oilco can maximize its profit (revenues less costs) for the next 2 years.

64. Suppose that we are hiring a weather forecaster to predict the probability that next summer will be rainy or sunny. The following suggests a method that can be used to ensure that the forecaster is accurate. Suppose that the actual probability of next summer being rainy is 0.6. (For simplicity, we assume that the summer can only be rainy or sunny.) If the forecaster announces a probability p that the summer will be rainy, he receives a payment of $1 - (1 - p)^2$ if the summer is rainy and a payment of $1 - p^2$ if the summer is sunny. Show that the forecaster will maximize his expected profit by announcing that the probability of a rainy summer is 0.6.

65. The cost of producing x units of a product during a month is $x^{1/2}$ dollars. Show that the minimum-cost method of producing 40 units during the next 2 months is to produce all 40 units during a single month.

66. A company uses raw material to produce two products. For $15, a unit of raw material can be purchased and processed into four units of product 1 and two units of product 2. If x_1 units of product 1 are produced, they can be sold at $25 - x_1$ dollars per unit. If x_2 units of product 2 are produced, they can be sold at $14 - x_2$ dollars per unit. (Negative prices are not permitted.) The company can choose the number of units of raw material that are purchased and processed. How can the company maximize its profit?

Skill-Extending Problems

67. Most economies have a goal of maximizing the average consumption per period. Assume that during each year, an economy saves the same (to be determined) percentage S of its production. During a year in which the beginning capital level is K, a quantity $K^{1/2}$ of capital is produced. If the economy saves a percentage S of its capital, then during the current year it consumes $(1 - S)K^{1/2}$ units of capital and, through savings, adds $S\ K^{1/2}$ units of capital. Also, during any year, 10% of all capital present at the beginning of the year depreciates or wears out.

a. What annual savings percentage S maximizes the long-run average consumption level? Assume that year 50 represents the long run.

b. Use SolverTable to see how the optimal value of S depends on the annual depreciation rate.

68. Each morning during rush hour, 10,000 people want to travel from New Jersey to New York City. If a person takes the commuter train, the trip lasts 40 minutes. If x thousand people per morning drive to New York, it takes $20 + 5x$ minutes to make the trip. This problem illustrates a basic fact of life: If people make their decisions individually, they will cause more congestion than need actually occur!

a. Show that if people make their decisions individually, an average of 4000 people will travel by road from New Jersey to New York. Here you should assume that people will divide up between the trains and roads in a way that makes the average travel time by road equal to the travel time by train. When this "equilibrium" occurs, nobody has an incentive to switch from the road to the train or vice versa.

b. Show that the average travel time per person is minimized if 2000 people travel by road.

69. Based on Grossman and Hart (1983). A salesperson for Fuller Brush has three options: quit, put forth a low effort level, or put forth a high effort level. Suppose for simplicity that each salesperson will sell $0, $5000, or $50,000 worth of brushes. The probability of each sales amount depends on the effort level as described in the file **P07_69.xls**. If a salesperson is paid w dollars, he or she earns a "benefit" of $w^{1/2}$

units. In addition, low effort costs the salesperson 0 benefit units, whereas high effort costs 50 benefit units. If a salesperson were to quit Fuller and work elsewhere, he or she could earn a benefit of 20 units. Fuller wants all salespeople to put forth a high effort level. The question is how to minimize the cost of encouraging them to do so. The company cannot observe the level of effort put forth by a salesperson, but it can observe the size of his or her sales. Thus, the wage paid to the salesperson is completely determined by the size of the sale. This means that Fuller must determine w_0, the wage paid for sales of \$0; w_{5000}, the wage paid for sales of \$5000; and $w_{50,000}$, the wage paid for sales of \$50,000. These wages must be set so that the salespeople value the expected benefit from high effort more than quitting and more than low effort. Determine how to minimize the expected cost of ensuring that all salespeople put forth high effort. (This problem is an example of **agency theory**.)

70. Kellpost Cereal Company sells four products: (1) Special L (a low-calorie, high-nutrition cereal); (2) Corn Bran (another low-calorie, high-nutrition cereal); (3) Admiral Smacks (a sugary cereal pitched at the children's market); and (4) Honey Pops (another sweet cereal pitched at the children's market). Kellpost has sufficient production capacity to produce a total of 10,000 boxes of cereal per month. For each of the last 16 months, Kellpost has kept track of the price and sales of each product. (These data are listed in the file **P07_70.xls**.) Market executives believe that Special L and Corn Bran might be substitutes for each other, as might be Admiral Smacks and Honey Pops. For example, this means that an increase in the price of Special L might raise the sales of Corn Bran. The variable cost of bringing a box of each cereal to market is as follows: Special L, \$2.00; Corn Bran, \$2.20; Admiral Smacks, \$2.30; Honey Pops, \$2.40.

   a. Use the given information to determine the price for each cereal that will enable Kellpost to maximize profits.

   b. Now suppose that Kellpost can increase its monthly production capacity. The cost (per year) of doing this is \$20,000 per thousand boxes of added monthly capacity. Can you determine an optimal capacity level?

Modeling Problems

71. For the product mix example (Example 3.2 in Chapter 3), discuss where you think the assumptions of a linear model are most likely to break down. How might an NLP formulation look in this situation?

72. For the Chandler Oil blending example (Example 4.4 in Chapter 4), discuss where you think the assumptions of a linear model are most likely to break down. How might an NLP formulation look in this situation?

73. For the SureStep aggregate planning example (Example 4.3 in Chapter 4), is it likely that the cost per worker of changing the size of the workforce during a month would be constant (as we assumed)? How could an NLP formulation account for a situation in which the cost per worker of changing the size of the workforce is not constant?

74. (This problem and the next problem refer to the sports ratings model in Section 7.6.) If you were going to give more recent games more weight, how might you determine whether the weight given to a game from k weeks ago should be, say, $(0.95)^k$ or $(0.9)^k$?

75. If you were going to use the approach from Section 7.6 to forecast future sports contests, what problems might you encounter early in the season? How might you resolve these problems?

76. UE is going to invest \$400 million dollars to acquire companies in the auto and/or electronics industry. How would you apply portfolio optimization to determine which companies should be purchased?

77. Your family owns a large farm that can grow wheat, corn, cotton, alfalfa, barley, pears, and apples. Each product requires a certain amount of labor each month and a certain number of hours of machine time. You have just studied portfolio optimization and want to help your family run its farm. What would you do?

78. Your company is about to market a new golf club. You have convened a focus group of 100 golfers and asked them to compare your club to the clubs produced by your competitors. You have found, for example, that 30 customers in the focus group would purchase your club if you charged \$20, 28 customers would purchase your club if you charged \$25, and so on. How could you use this information to determine the price at which your club should be sold?

Kate Torelli, a security analyst for Lion-Fund, has identified a gold mining stock (ticker symbol GMS) as a particularly attractive investment. Torelli believes that the company has invested wisely in new mining equipment. Furthermore, the company has recently purchased mining rights on land that has high potential for successful gold extraction. Torelli notes that gold has underperformed the stock market in the last decade and believes that the time is ripe for a large increase in gold prices. In addition, she reasons that conditions in the global monetary system make it likely that investors may once again turn to gold as a safe haven in which to park assets. Finally, supply and demand conditions have improved to the point where there could be significant upward pressure on gold prices.

GMS is a highly leveraged company, so it is quite a risky investment by itself. Torelli is mindful of a passage from the annual report of a competitor, Baupost, which has an extraordinarily successful investment record: "Baupost has managed a decade of consistently profitable results despite, and perhaps in some respect due to, consistent emphasis on the avoidance of downside risk. We have frequently carried both high cash balances and costly market hedges. Our results are particularly satisfying when considered in the light of this sustained risk aversion." She would therefore like to *hedge* the stock purchase—that is, reduce the risk of an investment in GMS stock.

Currently GMS is trading at $100 per share. Torelli has constructed seven scenarios for the price of GMS stock one month from now. These scenarios and corresponding probabilities are shown in Table 7.10.

To hedge an investment in GMS stock, Torelli can invest in other securities whose prices tend to move in the direction opposite to that of GMS stock. In particular, she is considering over-the-counter put options on GMS stock as potential hedging instruments. The value of a put option increases as the price of the underlying stock decreases. For example, consider a put option with a strike price of $100 and a time to expiration of one month. This means that the owner of the put has the right to sell GMS stock at $100 per share one month in the future. Suppose that the price of GMS falls to $80 at that time. Then the holder of the put option can exercise the option and receive $20 (= 100 − 80). If the price of GMS falls to $70, the option would be worth $30 (= 100 − 70). However, if the price of GMS rises to $100 or more, the option expires worthless.

Torelli called an options trader at a large investment bank for quotes. The prices for three (European-style) put options are shown in Table 7.11. Torelli wishes to invest $10 million in GMS stock and put options.

Table 7.11 Put Option Prices (Today) for GMS Case Study

	Put Option A	Put Option B	Put Option C
Strike price	90	100	110
Option price	$2.20	$6.40	$12.50

Questions

1. Based on Torelli's scenarios, what is the expected return of GMS stock? What is the standard deviation of the return of GMS stock?

2. After a cursory examination of the put option prices, Torelli suspects that a good strategy is to buy one put option A for each share of GMS stock purchased. What are the mean and standard deviation of return for this strategy?

Table 7.10 Scenarios and Probabilities for GMS Stock in One Month

	Scenario 1	Scenario 2	Scenario 3	Scenario 4	Scenario 5	Scenario 6	Scenario 7
Probability	0.05	0.10	0.20	0.30	0.20	0.10	0.05
GMS stock price	150	130	110	100	90	80	70

3. Assuming that Torelli's goal is to minimize the standard deviation of the portfolio return, what is the optimal portfolio that invests all $10 million? (For simplicity, assume that fractional numbers of stock shares and put options can be purchased. Assume that the amounts invested in each security must be nonnegative. However, the number of options purchased need *not* equal the number of shares of stock purchased.) What are the expected return and standard deviation of return of this portfolio? How many shares of GMS stock and how many of each put option does this portfolio correspond to?

4. Suppose that short selling is permitted—that is, the nonnegativity restrictions on the portfolio weights are removed. Now what portfolio minimizes the standard deviation of return? *Hint:* A good way to attack this problem is to create a table of security returns, as indicated in Table 7.12. Only a few of the table entries are shown. To correctly compute the standard deviation of portfolio return, you will need to incorporate the scenario probabilities. If r_i is the portfolio return in scenario i, and p_i is the probability of scenario i, then the standard deviation of portfolio return is

$$\sqrt{\sum_{i=1}^{7} p_i (r_i - \mu)^2}$$

where $\mu = \sum_{i=1}^{7} p_i r_i$ is the expected portfolio return.

Table 7.12 Table of Security Returns

	GMS Stock	Put Option A	Put Option B	Put Option C
Scenario 1			−100%	
2	30%			
⋮				
7				220%

CHAPTER

8

Decision Making under Uncertainty

© Photodisc

DECISION AND RISK ANALYSIS AT DU PONT

Formal decision analysis in the face of uncertainty frequently occurs at the most strategic levels of a company's planning process and typically involves teams of high-level managers from all areas of the company. This is certainly the case with Du Pont, as reported by two internal decision analysis experts, Krumm and Rolle (1992), in their article "Management and Application of Decision and Risk Analysis in Du Pont." Du Pont's formal use of decision analysis began in the 1960s, but because of a lack of computing power and distrust of the method by senior-level management, it never really got a foothold. However, by the mid-1980s things had changed considerably. The company was involved in a faster-moving, more uncertain environment, more people throughout the company were empowered to make decisions, and these decisions had to be made more quickly. In addition, the computing power had arrived to make large-scale quantitative analysis feasible. Since that time, Du Pont has embraced formal decision-making analysis in all its businesses, and the trend is almost certain to continue.

The article describes a typical example of decision analysis within the company. One of Du Pont's businesses, Business Z (so-called for reasons of confidentiality), was stagnating. It was not set up to respond quickly to changing customer demands, and its financial position was declining due to lower prices and market share. A decision board and a project team were empowered to turn things around. The project team developed a detailed timetable to accomplish three basic steps: frame the problem, assess uncertainties and perform the analysis, and implement the recommended decision. The first step involved setting up a "strategy table" to list the possible strategies and the factors that would affect or be affected by them. The three basic strategies were (1) a base-case strategy (continue operating as is), (2) a product differentiation strategy (develop new products), and (3) a cost leadership strategy (shut down the plant and streamline the product line).

In the second step, the team asked a variety of experts throughout the company for their assessments of the likelihood of key uncertain events. In the analysis step they then used all of the information gained to determine the strategy with the largest expected net present value. Two important aspects of this analysis step were the extensive use of sensitivity analysis (many what-if questions) and the emergence of new "hybrid" strategies that dominated the strategies that had been considered to that point. In particular, the team finally decided on a product differentiation strategy that also decreased costs by shutting down some facilities in each plant.

When it was time for the third step, implementation, the decision board needed little convincing. Since all of the key people had been given the opportunity to provide input to the process, everyone was convinced that the right strategy had been selected. All that was left was to put the plan in motion and monitor its results. The results were impressive. Business Z made a complete turnaround, and its net present value increased by close to $200 million. Besides this tangible benefit, there were definite intangible benefits from the overall process. As Du Pont's vice president for finance said, "The D&RA [decision and risk analysis] process improved communication within the business team as well as between the team and corporate management, resulting in rapid approval and execution. As a decision maker, I highly value such a clear and logical approach to making choices under uncertainty and will continue to use D&RA whenever possible." ■

8.1 INTRODUCTION

In this chapter we provide a formal framework for analyzing decision problems that involve uncertainty. We will discuss the following:

- criteria for choosing among alternative decisions
- how probabilities are used in the decision-making process
- how early decisions affect decisions made at a later stage
- how a decision maker can quantify the value of information
- how attitudes toward risk can affect the analysis

Throughout, we will employ a powerful graphical tool—a decision tree—to guide the analysis. A decision tree enables the decision maker to view all important aspects of the problem at once: the decision alternatives, the uncertain outcomes and their probabilities, the economic consequences, and the chronological order of events. We will show how to implement decision trees in Excel by taking advantage of a very powerful and flexible add-in from Palisade called PrecisionTree.

Many examples of decision making under uncertainty exist in the business world, including the following.

- Companies routinely place bids for contracts to complete a certain project within a fixed time frame. Often these are sealed bids, where each company presents a bid for completing the project in a sealed envelope. Then the envelopes are opened, and the low bidder is awarded the bid amount to complete the project. Any particular company in the bidding competition must deal with the uncertainty of the other companies' bids. The trade-off is between bidding low to win the bid and bidding high to make a bigger profit.

- Whenever a company contemplates introducing a new product into the market, there are a number of uncertainties that affect the decision, probably the most important being the customers' reaction to this product. If the product generates high customer demand, the company will make a large profit. But if demand is low—and, after all, the vast majority of new products do poorly—the company might not even recoup its development costs. Because the level of customer demand is critical, the company might try to gauge this level by test marketing the product in one region of the country. If this test market is a success, the company can then be more optimistic that a full-scale national marketing of the product will also be successful. But if the test market is a failure, the company can cut its losses by abandoning the product.

- Borison (1995) describes an application of formal decision analysis by Oglethorpe Power Corporation (OPC), a Georgia-based electricity supplier. The basic decision OPC faced was whether to build a new transmission line to supply large amounts of electricity to parts of Florida and, if the company decided to build it, how to finance this project. OPC had to deal with several sources of uncertainty: the cost of building new facilities, the demand for power in Florida, and various market conditions, such as the spot price of electricity.

- Utility companies must make many decisions that have significant environmental and economic consequences. [Balson et al. (1992) provide a good discussion of such consequences.] For these companies it is not necessarily enough to conform to federal or state environmental regulations. Recent court decisions have found companies liable—for huge settlements—when accidents occurred, even though the companies followed all existing regulations. Therefore, when utility companies decide, say, whether to replace equipment or mitigate the effects of environmental pollution, they must take into account the possible environmental consequences (such as injuries to people) as well as economic consequences (such as lawsuits). An aspect of these situations that makes decision analysis particularly difficult is that the potential "disasters" are often extremely improbable; hence, their likelihoods are difficult to assess accurately.

8.2 ELEMENTS OF A DECISION ANALYSIS

Although decision making under uncertainty occurs in a wide variety of contexts, all problems have three common elements: (1) the set of decisions (or strategies) available to the decision maker, (2) the set of possible outcomes and the probabilities of these outcomes, and (3) a value model that prescribes monetary values for the various decision–outcome combinations. Once these elements are known, the decision maker can find an "optimal" decision, depending on the optimality criterion chosen.

Before moving on to realistic business problems, we discuss the basic elements of any decision analysis for a very simple problem. We assume that a decision maker must choose among three decisions, labeled $D1$, $D2$, and $D3$. Each of these decisions has three possible outcomes, labeled $O1$, $O2$, and $O3$.

Payoff Tables

At the time the decision must be made, the decision maker does *not* know which outcome will occur. However, once the decision is made, the outcome will eventually be revealed, and a corresponding payoff will be received. This payoff might actually be a cost, in which case it is indicated as a negative value. The listing of payoffs for all decision–outcome pairs is called the **payoff table**.[1] For our simple decision problem, this payoff table appears in Table 8.1. For example, if the decision maker chooses decision $D2$ and outcome $O3$ then occurs, a payoff of $40 is received.

Table 8.1   Payoff Table for Simple Decision Problem

		Outcome		
		O1	*O2*	*O3*
Decision	*D1*	10	10	10
	D2	−10	20	40
	D3	−30	30	70

> A **payoff table** lists the payoff for each decision–outcome pair. Positive values correspond to "rewards" (or "gains") and negative values correspond to "costs" (or "losses").

A decision maker gets to decide which row of the payoff table she wants. However, she does not get to choose the column.

This table shows that the decision maker can play it safe by choosing decision $D1$. This provides a sure $10 payoff. With decision $D2$, rewards of $20 or $40 are possible, but a loss of $10 is also possible. Decision $D3$ is even riskier; the possible loss is greater, and the maximum gain is also greater. Which decision would you choose? Would your choice change if the values in the payoff table were really measured in *thousands* of dollars? The answers to these questions are what this chapter is all about. We need a criterion for making choices, and we need to evaluate this criterion so that we can identify the "best" decision. As we will see, it is customary to use one particular criterion for decisions involving "moderate" amounts of money.

Before proceeding, there is one very important point we need to emphasize. In any decision-making problem where there is uncertainty, the "best" decision can always have less than optimal results—that is, we can be unlucky. Regardless of which decision we choose, we might get an outcome that, in hindsight, makes us wish we had made a different decision. For example, if we make decision $D3$, hoping for a large reward, we might get outcome $O1$, in which case we will wish we had chosen decision $D1$ or $D2$. Or if we choose decision $D2$, hoping to limit possible losses, we might get outcome $O3$, in which case we will wish we had chosen decision $D3$. The point is that decision makers must make rational decisions, based on the information they have when the decisions must be made, and then live with the consequences. "Second guessing" these decisions, just because of bad luck with the outcomes, is not appropriate.

---

[1] In situations where all monetary consequences are costs, it is customary to list these costs in a **cost table**. In this case, all monetary values are shown as *positive* costs.

Possible Decision Criteria

What do we mean by a "best" decision? We will eventually settle on one particular criterion for making decisions, but we first explore some possibilities. With respect to Table 8.1, one possibility is to choose the decision that maximizes the *worst* payoff. This criterion, called the **maximin** criterion, is appropriate for a very conservative (or pessimistic) decision maker. The worst payoffs for the three decisions are the minimums in the three rows: 10, −10, and −30. The maximin decision maker chooses the decision corresponding to the best of these: decision $D1$ with payoff 10. Clearly, such a criterion tends to avoid large losses, but it fails to even consider large rewards. Hence, it is typically *too* conservative and is not commonly used.

> The **maximin** criterion finds the worst payoff in each row of the payoff table and chooses the decision corresponding to the maximum of these.

The maximin and maximax criteria make sense in some situations, but they are generally not used in real decision making problems.

At the other extreme, the decision maker might choose the decision that maximizes the *best* payoff. This criterion, called the **maximax** criterion, is appropriate for a risk taker (or optimist). The best payoffs for the three decisions are the maximums in the three rows: 10, 40, and 70. The maximax decision maker chooses the decision corresponding to the best of these: decision $D3$ with payoff 70. This criterion looks tempting, since it focuses on large gains, but its very serious downside is that it ignores possible losses. Because this type of decision making could eventually bankrupt a company, the maximax criterion is also seldom used.

> The **maximax** criterion finds the best payoff in each row of the payoff table and chooses the decision corresponding to the maximum of these.

Expected Monetary Value (EMV)

We have introduced the maximin and maximax criteria because (1) they are occasionally used to make decisions, and (2) they illustrate that there are several "reasonable" criteria for making decisions. In fact, there are a number of other possible criteria available that we will not discuss. Instead, we will now focus on a criterion that is generally regarded as the preferred criterion in most decision problems. It is called the **expected monetary value**, or **EMV**, criterion. To motivate the EMV criterion, we first note that the maximin and maximax criteria make no reference to how *likely* the various outcomes are. However, decision makers typically have at least some idea of these likelihoods, and they ought to use this information in the decision-making process. After all, if outcome $O1$ in our problem is extremely unlikely, then the pessimist who uses maximin is being overly conservative. Similarly, if outcome $O3$ is quite unlikely, then the optimist who uses maximax is taking an unnecessary risk.

The EMV approach assesses probabilities for each outcome of each decision and then calculates the *expected* payoff from each decision based on these probabilities. This expected payoff, or EMV, is a weighted average of the payoffs in any given row of the payoff table, weighted by the probabilities of the outcomes. We calculate the EMV for each decision, and we choose the decision with the largest EMV.

> The **expected monetary value**, or **EMV**, for any decision is a weighted average of the possible payoffs for this decision, weighted by the probabilities of the outcomes. Using the EMV criterion, we choose the decision with the largest EMV. This is sometimes called "playing the averages."

Where do the probabilities come from? This is a difficult question to answer in general because it depends on each specific problem. In some cases the current decision problem is similar to those a decision maker has faced many times in the past. Then the probabilities can be estimated from the knowledge of previous outcomes. If a certain type of outcome occurred, say, in about 30% of previous situations, we might estimate its current probability as 0.30.

There is almost always a subjective element in assessing the probabilities for real decision-making problems. There is almost never a single "correct" assessment.

However, there are many decision problems that have no parallels in the past. In such cases, a decision maker must use whatever information is available, plus some intuition, to assess the probabilities. For example, if the problem involves a new product decision, and one possible outcome is that a competitor will introduce a similar product in the coming year, the decision maker will have to rely on any knowledge of the market and the competitor's situation to assess the probability of this outcome. It is important to note that this assessment can be very subjective. Two decision makers could easily assess the probability of the *same* outcome as 0.30 and 0.45, depending on their information and feelings, and neither could be considered "wrong." This is the nature of assessing probabilities subjectively in real business situations.

With this general framework in mind, let's assume that our decision maker assesses the probabilities of the three outcomes in Table 8.1 as 0.4, 0.4, and 0.2.[2] Then it is simple to calculate the EMV for each decision as the sum of products of payoffs and probabilities:

$$\text{EMV for } D1: \quad 10(0.4) + 10(0.4) + 10(0.2) = 10$$
$$\text{EMV for } D2: \quad -10(0.4) + 20(0.4) + 40(0.2) = 12$$
$$\text{EMV for } D3: \quad -30(0.4) + 30(0.4) + 70(0.2) = 14$$

These calculations lead to the optimal decision: Choose decision $D3$ because it has the largest EMV.

The EMV is a weighted average of possible monetary values. It is usually not a monetary value that can actually occur.

It is important to understand what the EMV of a decision represents—and what it doesn't represent. For example, the EMV of 14 for decision $D3$ does *not* mean that we expect to gain $14 from this decision. The payoff table indicates that the result from $D3$ will be a loss of $30, a gain of $30, or a gain of $70; it will *never* be a gain of $14. The EMV is only a weighted average of the possible payoffs. As such, it can be interpreted in one of two ways. First, suppose we can imagine the problem occurring many times, not just once. If we use decision $D3$ each time, then *on average*, we will make a gain of about $14. About 40% of the time we will lose $30, about 40% of the time we will gain $30, and about 20% of the time we will gain $70. These average to $14. For this reason, using the EMV criterion is sometimes referred to as "playing the averages."

But what if the current problem is a "one-shot deal," which will *not* occur many times in the future? Then the second interpretation of EMV is still relevant. It states that the EMV is a "sensible" criterion for making decisions under uncertainty. This is actually a point that has been debated in intellectual circles for years—what is the best criterion for making decisions? However, researchers have generally concluded that EMV makes sense, even for one-shot deals, as long as the monetary values are not too large. For situations where the monetary values are extremely large, we will introduce an alternative criterion in the last section of this chapter. Until then, however, we will continue to use EMV.

This is the gist of decision making uncertainty. We develop a payoff table, we assess probabilities of outcomes, we calculate EMVs, and we choose the decision with the largest

---

[2]We always express probabilities as numbers between 0 and 1 that sum to 1. However, they are often expressed in more intuitive, but equivalent, ways. For example, we might assess that outcomes $O1$ and $O2$ are equally likely and that each of these is twice as likely as outcome $O3$. This assessment leads to the same probabilities: 0.4, 0.4, and 0.2.

EMV. However, before proceeding to examples, it is useful to introduce a few other concepts: sensitivity analysis, decision trees, and risk profiles.

Sensitivity Analysis

Some of the quantities in a decision analysis, particularly the probabilities, are often intelligent guesses at best. It is important, especially in real-world business problems, to accompany any decision analysis with a sensitivity analysis. Here we systematically vary inputs to the problem to see how (or if) the outputs—the EMVs and the best decision—change. For our simple decision problem, this is easy to do in a spreadsheet. We first develop the spreadsheet model shown in Figure 8.1. (See the file **SimpleDecisionProblem.xls**.)

Figure 8.1

Spreadsheet Model of Simple Decision Problem

	A	B	C	D	E	F
1	Simple decision problem under uncertainty					
2						
3			Outcome			
4			O1	O2	O3	EMV
5	Decision	D1	10	10	10	10
6		D2	-10	20	40	12
7		D3	-30	30	70	14
8	Probability		0.4	0.4	0.2	

Usually, the most important information from a sensitivity analysis is whether the optimal decision continues to be optimal as one or more inputs change.

After entering the payoff table and probabilities, we calculate the EMVs in column F as a sum of products, using the formula

=SUMPRODUCT(C5:E5,$C$8:$E$8)

in cell F5 and copying it down. Then it is easy to change any of the inputs and see whether the optimal decision continues to be D3. For example, you can check that if the probabilities change only "slightly" to 0.5, 0.4, and 0.1, the EMVs change to 10, 7, and 4. Now D3 is the worst decision and D1 is the best, so that it appears that the optimal decision is quite sensitive to the assessed probabilities. As another example, if the probabilities remain the same but the last payoff for D2 changes from 40 to 55, then its EMV changes to 16, and D2 becomes the best decision.

Given a simple spreadsheet model, it is easy to make a number of "ad hoc" changes to inputs, as we have done here, to answer specific sensitivity questions. However, it is often useful to conduct a more systematic sensitivity analysis, and we will see how to do this later in the chapter. The important thing to realize at this stage is that a sensitivity analysis is not an "afterthought" to the overall analysis; it is a key component of the analysis.

Decision Trees

The decision problem we have been analyzing is very basic. We make a decision, we then observe an outcome, we receive a payoff, and that is the end of it. Many decision problems are of this basic form, but many are more complex. In these more complex problems, we make a decision, an outcome is observed, we make a second decision, a second outcome is observed, and so on. A graphical tool called a **decision tree** has been developed to represent decision problems. Decision trees can be used for any decision problems, but they are particularly useful for the more complex types. They clearly show the sequence of events (decisions and outcomes), as well as probabilities and monetary values. The decision tree for our simple problem appears in Figure 8.2 (page 360). This tree is based on one we drew by hand and calculated with a hand calculator. We urge you to try this on your own, at least once. However, later in the chapter we will introduce an Excel add-in that automates the procedure.

Figure 8.2

Decision Tree for
Simple Decision
Problem

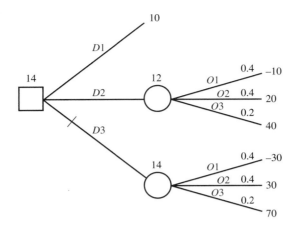

To understand this decision tree, we need to introduce a number of decision tree conventions that have become standard.

Decision tree conventions

1. Decision trees are composed of **nodes** (circles, squares, and triangles) and **branches** (lines).

2. The nodes represent points in time. A **decision node** (a square) represents a time when the decision maker makes a decision. A **probability node** (a circle) represents a time when the result of an uncertain outcome becomes known. An **end node** (a triangle) indicates that the problem is completed—all decisions have been made, all uncertainty has been resolved, and all payoffs and costs have been incurred. (When people draw decision trees by hand, they often omit the actual triangles, as we have done in Figure 8.2. However, we still refer to the right-hand tips of the branches as the end nodes.)

3. Time proceeds *from left to right*. This means that any branches leading into a node (from the left) have already occurred. Any branches leading out of a node (to the right) have not yet occurred.

4. Branches leading out of a decision node represent the possible decisions; the decision maker can choose the preferred branch. Branches leading out of probability nodes represent the possible outcomes of uncertain events; the decision maker has no control over which of these will occur.

5. Probabilities are listed on probability branches. These probabilities are *conditional* on the events that have already been observed (those to the left). Also, the probabilities on branches leading out of any probability node must sum to 1.

6. Monetary values are shown to the right of the end nodes. (As we will discuss shortly, some monetary values are also placed next to the branches where they occur in time.)

7. EMVs are calculated through a "folding back" process, discussed next. They are shown above the various nodes. It is then customary to mark the optimal decision branch(es) in some way. We have marked ours with a small notch.

The decision tree in Figure 8.2 follows these conventions. The decision node comes first (to the left) because the decision maker must make a decision *before* observing the uncertain outcome. The probability nodes then follow the decision branches, and the probabilities appear above their branches. (Actually, there is no need for a probability node after the $D1$ branch, because the monetary value is 10 for each outcome.) The ultimate payoffs appear next to the end nodes, to the right of the probability branches. The EMVs above the probability nodes are for the various decisions. For example, if we go along the $D2$ branch, the EMV is 12. The maximum of the EMVs is written above the decision node. Since it corresponds to $D3$, we put a notch on the $D3$ branch to indicate that this decision is optimal.

This decision tree is almost a direct translation of the spreadsheet model in Figure 8.1. Indeed, it might be argued that the decision tree is overkill for such a simple problem; the spreadsheet model provides all of the information we need—in a more compact form. However, decision trees are very useful in business problems. First, they provide a manager with a graphical view of the whole problem. This can be useful in its own right for the insights it provides, especially in more complex problems. Second, the decision tree provides a framework for doing all of the EMV calculations. Specifically, it allows us to use the following "folding back" procedure to find the EMVs and the optimal decision.

Folding back procedure

Starting from the right of the decision tree and working back to the left:

1. At each probability node, calculate an EMV—a sum of products of monetary values and probabilities.

2. At each decision node, take a maximum of EMVs to identify the optimal decision.

This is exactly what we did in Figure 8.2. At each probability node, we calculated EMVs in the usual way and wrote them above the nodes. Then at the decision node, we took the maximum of the three EMVs and wrote it above this node. Although this procedure entails more work for more complex decision trees, the same two steps—taking EMVs at probability nodes and taking maximums at decision nodes—are the only ones required. In addition, we will introduce an Excel add-in in the next section that does the calculations for us.

Risk Profiles

In our small example each decision leads to three possible monetary payoffs with various probabilities. In more complex problems, the number of outcomes could be larger, maybe considerably larger. It is then useful to represent the probability distribution of the monetary values for any decision graphically. Specifically, we show a bar chart, where the bars are located at the possible monetary values, and the heights of the bars correspond to the probabilities. In decision making contexts, this type of chart is called a **risk profile**. By looking at the risk profile for a particular decision, we see the risks and rewards involved. By comparing risk profiles for different decisions, we gain more insight into their relative strengths and weaknesses.

The **risk profile** for a decision is a bar chart that represents the probability distribution of monetary outcomes for this decision.

The risk profile for decision $D3$ appears in Figure 8.3 (page 362). It shows that a loss of $30 and a gain of $30 are equally likely with probability 0.4 each, and that a gain of $70 has probability 0.2. The risk profile for decision $D2$ would be similar, except that its bars would be over the values -10, 20, and 40, and the risk profile for decision $D1$ would be a single bar of height 1 over the value 10.

Figure 8.3

Risk Profile for
Decision *D3*

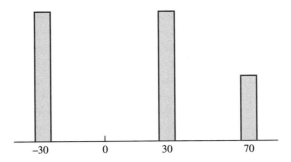

*A risk profile shows
the complete
probability distribution
of monetary
outcomes, but we
typically use only its
mean, the EMV, for
making decisions.*

Note that the EMV for any decision is a summary measure from the complete risk profile—it is the *mean* of the corresponding probability distribution. Therefore, when we use the EMV criterion for making decisions, we are not using *all* of the information in the risk profiles; we are comparing only their means. Nevertheless, risk profiles can be useful as extra information for making decisions. For example, a manager who sees too much risk in the risk profile of the EMV-maximizing decision might choose to override this decision and instead choose a somewhat less risky alternative.

We now apply all of these concepts to the following example.

EXAMPLE | **8.1 BIDDING FOR A GOVERNMENT CONTRACT AT SCITOOLS**

SciTools Incorporated, a company that specializes in scientific instruments, has been invited to make a bid on a government contract. The contract calls for a specific number of these instruments to be delivered during the coming year. The bids must be sealed (so that no company knows what the others are bidding), and the low bid wins the contract. SciTools estimates that it will cost $5000 to prepare a bid and $95,000 to supply the instruments if it wins the contract. On the basis of past contracts of this type, SciTools believes that the possible low bids from the competition, if there is any competition, and the associated probabilities are those shown in Table 8.2. In addition, SciTools believes there is a 30% chance that there will be *no* competing bids. What should SciTools bid to maximize its EMV?

Table 8.2 Data for Bidding Example

Low Bid	Probability
Less than $115,000	0.2
Between $115,000 and $120,000	0.4
Between $120,000 and $125,000	0.3
Greater than $125,000	0.1

Objective To develop a decision model that finds the EMV for various bidding strategies and indicates the best bidding strategy.

WHERE DO THE NUMBERS COME FROM?

The company has probably done a thorough cost analysis to estimate its cost to prepare a bid and its cost to manufacture the instruments if it wins the contract. Its estimates of whether, or how, the competition will bid are probably based on previous bidding experience and some subjectivity. This is discussed in more detail next.

Solution

Let's examine the three elements of SciTools' problem. First, SciTools has two basic strategies: submit a bid or do not submit a bid. If SciTools submits a bid, then it must decide how much to bid. Based on SciTools' cost to prepare the bid and its cost to supply the instruments, there is clearly no point in bidding less than $100,000—SciTools wouldn't make a profit even if it won the bid. Although any bid amount over $100,000 might be considered, the data in Table 8.2 suggest that SciTools might limit its choices to $115,000, $120,000, and $125,000.[3]

The next element of the problem involves the uncertain outcomes and their probabilities. We have assumed that SciTools knows exactly how much it will cost to prepare a bid and how much it will cost to supply the instruments if it wins the bid. (In reality, these are probably only estimates of the actual costs, and a follow-up study could treat these costs as additional uncertain quantities.) Therefore, the only source of uncertainty is the behavior of the competitors—will they bid, and if so, how much? From SciTools' standpoint, this is difficult information to obtain. The behavior of the competitors depends on (1) how many competitors are likely to bid and (2) how the competitors assess *their* costs of supplying the instruments. Nevertheless, we will assume that SciTools has been involved in similar bidding contests in the past and can, therefore, predict competitor behavior from past competitor behavior. The result of such prediction is the assessed probability distribution in Table 8.2 and the 30% estimate of the probability of no competing bids.

The last element of the problem is the value model that transforms decisions and outcomes into monetary values for SciTools. The value model is straightforward in this example. If SciTools decides not to bid, then its monetary value is $0—no gain, no loss. If it makes a bid and is underbid by a competitor, then it loses $5000, the cost of preparing the bid. If it bids B dollars and wins the contract, then it makes a profit of B minus $100,000— that is, B dollars for winning the bid, minus $5000 for preparing the bid and $95,000 for supplying the instruments. For example, if it bids $115,000 and the lowest competing bid, if any, is greater than $115,000, then SciTools wins the bid and makes a profit of $15,000.

Developing the Payoff Table

The corresponding payoff table, along with probabilities of outcomes, appears in Table 8.3. At the bottom of the table, we list the probabilities of the various outcomes. For example, the probability that the competitors' low bid is less than $115,000 is 0.7 (the probability of at least one competing bid) multiplied by 0.2 (the probability that the lowest competing bid is less than $115,000).

Table 8.3   Payoff Table for SciTools Bidding Example

		No bid	<115	>115, <120	>120, <125	>125
				Competitors' Low Bid ($1000s)		
SciTools' Bid ($1000s)	No bid	0	0	0	0	0
	115	15	−5	15	15	15
	120	20	−5	−5	20	20
	125	25	−5	−5	−5	25
Probability		0.3	0.7(0.2) = 0.14	0.7(0.4) = 0.28	0.7(0.3) = 0.21	0.7(0.1) = 0.07

---

[3]The problem with a bid such as $117,000 is that the data in Table 8.2 make it impossible to calculate the probability of SciTools winning the contract if it bids this amount. Other than this, however, there is nothing that rules out such "in-between" bids.

It is sometimes possible to simplify payoff tables to better understand the essence of the problem. In the present example, if SciTools bids, then the only necessary information about the competitors' bid is whether it is lower or higher than SciTools' bid. That is, SciTools really only cares whether it wins the contract. Therefore, an alternative way of presenting the payoff table is shown in Table 8.4. (See the file **SciTools1.xls** for these and other calculations. However, we urge you to work this problem on a piece of paper with hand calculator, just for practice with the concepts.)

Table 8.4 Alternative Payoff Table for SciTools Bidding Example

		Monetary Value		Probability That SciTools Wins
		SciTools Wins	SciTools Loses	
	No Bid	NA	0	0.00
SciTools' Bid ($1000s)	**115**	15	−5	0.86
	120	20	−5	0.58
	125	25	−5	0.37

The third and fourth columns of this table indicate the payoffs to SciTools, depending on whether it wins or loses the bid. The rightmost column shows the probability that SciTools wins the bid for each possible decision. For example, if SciTools bids $120,000, then it wins the bid if there are no competing bids (probability 0.3) *or* if there are competing bids but the lowest of these is greater than $120,000 [probability 0.7(0.3 + 0.1) = 0.28]. In this case the total probability that SciTools wins the bid is 0.3 + 0.28 = 0.58.

Developing the Risk Profiles

From Table 8.4 we can obtain risk profiles for each of SciTools' decisions. Again, this risk profile simply indicates all possible monetary values and their corresponding probabilities in a bar chart. For example, if SciTools bids $120,000, there are two monetary values possible, a profit of $20,000 and a loss of $5000, and their probabilities are 0.58 and 0.42, respectively. The corresponding risk profile, shown in Figure 8.4, is a bar chart with two bars, one above −$5000 with height 0.42 and one above $20,000 with height 0.58. On the other hand, if SciTools decides not to bid, there is a sure monetary value of $0—no profit, no loss. The risk profile for the "no bid" decision, not shown here, is even simpler. It has a single bar above $0 with height 1.

Figure 8.4

Risk Profile for a Bid of $120,000

Calculating EMVs

The EMVs for SciTools' problem are listed in Table 8.5. As always, each EMV (other than the EMV of $0 for not bidding) is a sum of products of monetary outcomes and probabilities. These EMVs indicate that if SciTools uses the EMV criterion for making its decision, it should bid $115,000. The EMV from this bid, $12,200, is the largest of the EMVs.

Table 8.5　EMVs for SciTools Bidding Example

Alternative	EMV Calculation	EMV
No bid	0(1)	$0
Bid $115,000	15,000(0.86) + (−5000)(0.14)	$12,200
Bid $120,000	20,000(0.58) + (−5000)(0.42)	$9,500
Bid $125,000	25,000(0.37) + (−5000)(0.63)	$6,100

As discussed previously, it is very important to understand what an EMV implies and what it does not imply. If SciTools bids $115,000, its EMV is $12,200. However, SciTools will definitely *not* earn a profit of $12,200. It will earn $15,000 or it will lose $5000. The EMV of $12,200 represents only a weighted average of these two possible values. Nevertheless, it is the value that we use as our decision criterion.

Developing the Decision Tree

The corresponding decision tree for this problem is shown in Figure 8.5. This is a direct translation of the payoff table and EMV calculations. The company first makes a bidding decision, it then observes what the competition bids, if anything, and it finally receives a payoff. The folding back process is equivalent to the calculations shown in Table 8.5.

Figure 8.5

Decision Tree for SciTools Bidding Example

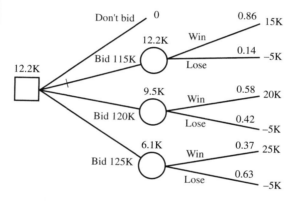

It is common to place monetary values below the branches where they occur in time.

As long as we follow the decision tree conventions, there are often equivalent ways to structure a decision tree. One alternative for this example that might be more intuitive appears in Figure 8.6 (page 366). This tree shows exactly how the problem unfolds. The company first decides whether to bid at all. If the company does not make a bid, the profit is a sure $0. Otherwise, the company then decides how much to bid. Note that if the company decides to bid, it incurs a sure cost of $5000, so we place this cost under the Bid branch. This is a common procedure, to place the monetary values on the branches where they occur in time, and it is followed by the PrecisionTree add-in we will examine in the next section. Once the company decides how much to bid, it then observes whether there is any competition. If there isn't any, the company wins the bid for sure and makes a corresponding profit. Otherwise, if there is competition, the company eventually discovers whether it wins or loses the bid, with the corresponding probabilities and payoffs. Note that we place these payoffs below the branches where they occur in time. Also, we place the *cumulative* payoffs at the ends of the branches. Each cumulative payoff is the sum of all payoffs on branches that lead to that end node.

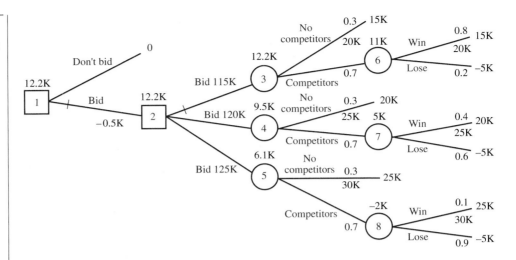

Figure 8.6

Equivalent Decision Tree for SciTools Bidding Example

Folding Back the Decision Tree

The folding back procedure is bit more complex than it was for the smaller tree in Figure 8.5. To illustrate, we have numbered the nodes in Figure 8.6 for reference. The EMVs above a selected few of these nodes are calculated as follows:

- Node 7: EMV = 20000(0.40) + (−5000)(0.60) = $5000 (uses monetary values from end nodes)
- Node 4: EMV = 20000(0.30) + (5000)(0.70) = $9500 (uses monetary value from an end node and the EMV from node 7)
- Node 2: EMV = max(12200, 9500, 6100) = $12,200 (uses EMVs from nodes 3, 4, and 5)
- Node 1: EMV = max(0, 12200) = $12,200 (uses monetary value from an end node and EMV from node 2)

The results are the same, regardless of whether we use the table of EMVs in Table 8.5, the decision tree in Figure 8.5, or the decision tree in Figure 8.6 because they all calculate the same EMVs in equivalent ways. In each case, we see that the company should bid $115,000, with a resulting EMV of $12,200. Of course, this decision is not *guaranteed* to produce a good outcome for the company. For example, the competition could bid less than $115,000, in which case SciTools would be out $5000. Alternately, the competition could bid over $120,000, in which case SciTools would be kicking itself for not bidding $120,000 and getting an extra $5000 in profit. Unfortunately, in problems with uncertainty, we can virtually never guarantee that the optimal decision will produce the best result. All we can guarantee is that the EMV-maximizing decision is the most rational decision, given what we know when we must make the decision.

Sensitivity Analysis

The next step in the SciTools decision analysis is to perform a sensitivity analysis. We will eventually see that PrecisionTree, an Excel add-in that helps automate the decision-making process, has some powerful sensitivity analysis tools. However, it is also possible to use Excel data tables. One example is shown in Figure 8.7. (See the file **SciTools1.xls**.) We first calculate the EMVs in column G, exactly as described previously. Then we find the maximum of these in cell B21, and we use the following nested IF formula in cell B22 to find the decision from column B that achieves this maximum:

=IF(G16=B21,B16,IF(G17=B21,B17,IF(G18=B21,B18,B19)))

This long formula simply checks which EMV in column G matches the maximum EMV in cell B21 and returns the corresponding decision from column B.

Figure 8.7 Sensitivity Analysis with a Data Table

	A	B	C	D	E	F	G
1	SciTools Bidding Example						
2							
3	Inputs						
4	Cost to prepare a bid	$5,000		Range names used:			
5	Cost to supply instruments	$95,000		BidCost	=Data!$B$4		
6				PrNoBid	=Data!$B$7		
7	Probability of no competing bid	0.3		ProdCost	=Data!$B$5		
8	Comp bid distribution (if they bid)						
9	<$115K	0.2					
10	$115K to $120K	0.4					
11	$120K to $125K	0.3					
12	>$125K	0.1					
13							
14	EMV analysis		Monetary outcomes		Probabilities		
15							
16		No bid	SciTools wins	SciTools loses	SciTools wins	SciTools loses	EMV
17	SciTools' Bid	$115,000	NA	0	0	1	$0
18		$120,000	$15,000	-$5,000	0.86	0.14	$12,200
19		$125,000	$20,000	-$5,000	0.58	0.42	$9,500
20			$25,000	-$5,000	0.37	0.63	$6,100
21	Maximum EMV	$12,200					
22	Best decision	$115,000					
23							
24	Data table for sensitivity analysis						
25	Probability of no competing bid	Maximum EMV	Best decision				
26		$12,200	$115,000				
27	0.2	$11,800	$115,000				
28	0.3	$12,200	$115,000				
29	0.4	$12,600	$115,000				
30	0.5	$13,000	$115,000				
31	0.6	$14,200	$125,000				
32	0.7	$16,900	$125,000				

Once we have the formulas in cells B21 and B22 set up, the data table is easy. In Figure 8.7 we have allowed the probability of no competing bid to vary from 0.2 to 0.7. The data table shows how the optimal EMV increases over this range. Also, its third column shows that the $115,000 bid is optimal for small values of the input, but that $125,000 becomes optimal for larger values. The main point here is that if we set up a spreadsheet model that links all of the EMV calculations to the inputs, it is easy to use data tables to perform sensitivity analyses on selected inputs. ■

PROBLEMS

Solutions for problems whose numbers appear within a color box can be found in the Student Solutions Manual. Order your copy today at http://e-catalog.thomsonlearning.com/110/ by using ISBN 0-534-39687-9.

Skill-Building Problems

1. In the simple 3-decision, 3-outcome example, we found that decision $D3$ is the EMV-maximizing decision for the probabilities we used. See whether you can find probabilities that make decision $D1$ the best. See if you can find probabilities that make decision $D2$ the best. Qualitatively, how can you explain the re-

sults? That is, which types of probabilities tend to favor the various decisions?

2. Using a data table in Excel, perform a sensitivity analysis on the simple 3-decision, 3-outcome example. Specifically, continue to assume that outcomes $O1$ and $O2$ are equally likely, each with probability p. Since the probabilities of all outcomes must sum to 1, the probability of outcome $O3$ must be $1 - 2p$. Let p vary from 0 to 0.5, in increments of 0.05. How does the optimal EMV vary? How does the optimal decision vary? Why can't p be greater than 0.5?

3. For the simple 3-decision, 3-outcome example, are there any probabilities that make the EMV criterion equivalent to the maximin criterion? Are there any probabilities that make the EMV criterion equivalent to the maximax criterion? Explain.

4. In the SciTools example, which decision would a maximin decision maker choose? Which decision would a maximax decision maker choose? Would you defend either of these criteria for this particular example? Explain.

5. In the SciTools example, suppose that we make two changes: all references to $115,000 change to $110,000, and all references to $125,000 change to $130,000. Rework the EMV calculations and the decision tree. What is the best decision and its corresponding EMV?

6. In the SciTools example, the probabilities for the low bid of competitors, given that there is at least one competing bid, are currently 0.2, 0.4, 0.3, and 0.1. Let the second of these be p, and let the others sum to 1 − p but keep the same ratios to one another: 2 to 3 to 1. Use a one-way data table to see how (or whether) the optimal decision changes as p varies from 0.1 to 0.7 in increments of 0.05. Explain your results.

7. In the SciTools example, use a two-way data table to see how (or whether) the optimal decision changes as the bid cost and the company's production cost change simultaneously. Let the bid cost vary from $2000 to $8000 in increments of $1000, and let the production cost vary from $90,000 to $105,000 in increments of $2500. Explain your results.

Skill-Extending Problems

8. A decision d is said to be **dominated** by another decision D if, for every outcome, the payoff from D is better than (or no worse than) the payoff from d.
   a. Explain why you would never choose a dominated decision, using the maximin criterion; using the maximax criterion; using the EMV criterion.
   b. Are any of the decisions in the simple 3-decision, 3-outcome example dominated by any others? What about in the SciTools example?

9. Besides the maximin, maximax, and EMV criteria, there are other possible criteria for making decisions.

One possibility involves "regret." The idea behind regret is that if we make any decision and then some outcome occurs, we look at that outcome's column in the payoff table to see how much more we could have made if we had chosen the *best* payoff in that column. For example, if the decision we make and the outcome we observe lead to a $50 payoff, and if the highest payoff in this outcome's column is $80, then our regret is $30. We don't want to look back and see how much more we *could* have made, if only we had made a different decision. Therefore, we calculate the regret for each cell in the payoff table (as the maximum payoff in that column minus the payoff in that cell), calculate the maximum regret in each row, and choose the row with the smallest maximum regret. This is called the **minimax regret** criterion.
   a. Apply this criterion to the simple 3-decision, 3-outcome example. Which decision do you choose?
   b. Repeat part **a** for the SciTools example.
   c. In general, discuss potential strengths and weaknesses of this decision criterion.

10. Referring to the previous problem, another possible criterion is called **expected regret**. Here we calculate the regret for each cell, take a weighted average of these regrets in each row, weighted by the probabilities of the outcomes, and choose the decision with the smallest expected regret.
   a. Apply this criterion to the simple 3-decision, 3-outcome example. Which decision do you choose?
   b. Repeat part **a** for the SciTools example.
   c. The expected regret criterion is actually *equivalent* to the EMV criterion, in that they always lead to the same decisions. Argue why this is true.

11. In the SciTools example, you might argue that there is a *continuum* of possible low competitor bids (given that there is at least one competing bid), not just 4 possibilities. In fact, assume the low competitor bid in this case is normally distributed with mean $118,000 and standard deviation $4,500. Also, assume that SciTools will still either not bid or bid $115,000, $120,000, or $125,000. Use Excel's NORMDIST function to find the EMV for each of SciTools' alternatives. Which is the best decision now? Why can't this be represented in a decision tree?

8.3 THE PRECISIONTREE ADD-IN

Decision trees present a challenge for Excel. We must somehow take advantage of Excel's calculating capabilities (to calculate EMVs, for example) and its graphical capabilities (to depict the decision tree). Fortunately, there is a powerful add-in, PrecisionTree, developed by Palisade Corporation, that makes the process relatively straightforward. This add-in not only enables us to draw and label a decision tree, but it performs the folding-back procedure automatically and then allows us to perform sensitivity analysis on key input parameters.

The first thing you must do to use PrecisionTree is to "add it in." You do this in two steps. First, you must install the Palisade Decision Tools suite (or at least the PrecisionTree program) with the Setup program on the CD-ROM that accompanies this book. Of course, you need to do this only once. Then to run PrecisionTree, there are three options (we usually use the first):

- If Excel is not currently running, you can launch Excel *and* PrecisionTree by clicking on the Windows Start button and selecting the PrecisionTree item from the Palisade Decision Tools group in the list of Programs.

- If Excel is currently running, the procedure in the previous bullet will launch PrecisionTree on top of Excel.

- If Excel is already running and the Decision Tools toolbar in Figure 8.8 is showing, you can start PrecisionTree by clicking on its icon (the third from the left).

Figure 8.8

Palisade Decision
Tools Toolbar

You will know that PrecisionTree is ready for use when you see its toolbar (shown in Figure 8.9) and a PrecisionTree menu to the left of the Help menu. By the way, if you want to unload PrecisionTree *without* closing Excel, you can use the PrecisionTree/Help/About menu item and click on Unload.

Figure 8.9

PrecisionTree
Toolbar

The Decision Tree Model

PrecisionTree is quite easy to use—at least its most basic items are. We will lead you through the steps for the SciTools example. Figure 8.10 (page 370) shows the results of this procedure, just so that you can see what you are working toward. (See the file **Sci-Tools2.xls**.) However, we recommend that you work through the steps on your own, starting with a blank spreadsheet.

Building the Decision Tree

1 **Inputs.** Enter the inputs shown in columns A and B of Figure 8.11.

2 **New tree.** Click on the new tree button (the far left button) on the PrecisionTree toolbar, and then click on cell A14 below the input section to start a new tree. Click on the name box of this new tree (it probably says "tree #1") to open a dialog box. Type in a descriptive name for the tree, such as SciTools Bidding, and click on OK. You should now see the beginnings of a tree, as in Figure 8.12.

3 **Decision nodes and branches.** From here on, keep the tree in Figure 8.10 in mind. This is the finished product we eventually want. To obtain decision nodes and branches, click on the (only) triangle end node to open the dialog box in Figure 8.13 (page 371). Click on the green square to indicate that we want a decision node, and fill in the dialog box as shown. We are calling this decision "Bid?" and specifying that there are two possible decisions. The tree expands as shown in Figure 8.14. The boxes that say "branch" show

Figure 8.10 Completed Tree from PrecisionTree

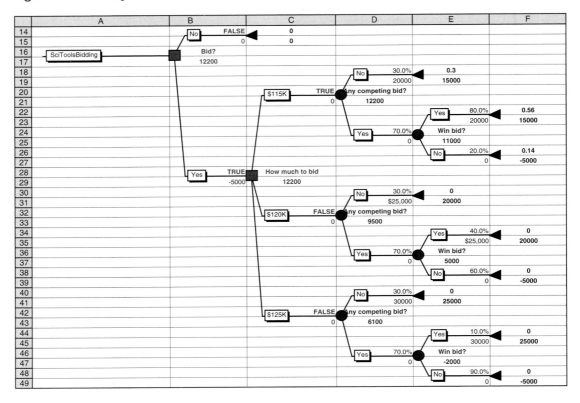

Figure 8.11

Inputs for SciTools
Bidding Example

	A	B	C	D	E
1	**SciTools Bidding Example**				
2					
3	**Inputs**				
4	Cost to prepare a bid	$5,000		**Range names used:**	
5	Cost to supply instruments	$95,000		BidCost	=Data!$B$4
6				PrNoBid	=Data!$B$7
7	Probability of no competing bid	0.3		ProdCost	=Data!$B$5
8	Comp bid distribution (if they bid)				
9	<$115K	0.2			
10	$115K to $120K	0.4			
11	$120K to $125K	0.3			
12	>$125K	0.1			

Figure 8.12

Beginnings of a New
Tree

	A	B
13		
14	SciTools Bidding	1
15		0

the default labels for these branches. Click on either of them to open another dialog box where you can provide a more descriptive name for the branch. Do this to label the two branches "No" and "Yes." Also, you can enter the immediate payoff or cost for either branch right below it. Since there is a $5000 cost of bidding, enter the formula

=-BidCost

right below the "Yes" branch in cell B19. (It is negative to reflect a *cost*.) The tree should now appear as in Figure 8.15.

Figure 8.13

Dialog Box for Adding a New Decision Node and Branches

Figure 8.14

Tree with Initial Decision Node and Branches

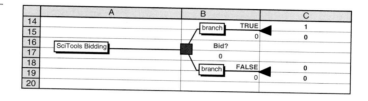

Figure 8.15

Decision Tree with Decision Branches Labeled

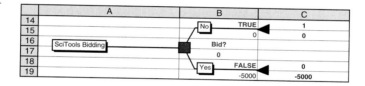

→ **PRECISIONTREE TIP:** *Allowable Entries*

On your computer screen, you will note the color-coding PrecisionTree uses. If you investigate any colored (nonblack) cells, you will see strange formulas that PrecisionTree uses for its own purposes. You should not mess with these formulas. You should enter your own probabilities and monetary values only in the black cells. ■

4 **More decision branches.** The top branch is completed; if SciTools does not bid, there is nothing left to do. So click on the bottom end node (the triangle), following Sci-Tools' decision to bid, and proceed as in the previous step to add and label the decision node and three decision branches for the amount to bid. (Again, refer to Figure 8.10.) The tree to this point should appear as in Figure 8.16 (page 372). Note that there are no monetary values below these decision branches because no *immediate* payoffs or costs are associated with the bid amount decision.

5 **Probability nodes and branches.** We now need a probability node and branches from the rightmost end nodes to capture whether the competition bids. Click on the top one of these end nodes to bring up the same dialog box as in Figure 8.13. Now, however, click on the red circle box to indicate that we want a probability node. Label it "Any competing bid?", specify two branches, and click on OK. Then label the two branches "No" and "Yes." Next, repeat this procedure to form another probability node (with two branches) following the "Yes" branch, call it "Win bid?", and label its branches as shown in Figure 8.17.

Figure 8.16

Tree with All
Decision Nodes and
Branches

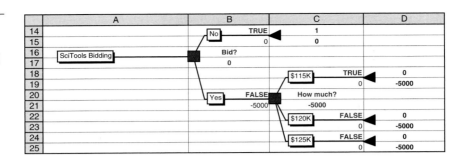

Figure 8.17   Decision Tree with One Set of Probability Nodes and Branches

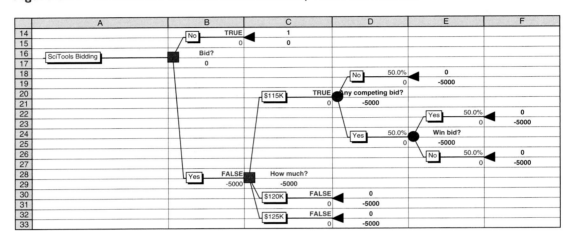

6 **Copying probability nodes and branches.** You could now repeat the same procedure from the previous step to build probability nodes and branches following the other bid amount decisions, but because they are structurally equivalent, you can save a lot of work by using PrecisionTree's copy and paste feature. Click on the leftmost probability node to open a dialog box and click on Copy. Then click on either end node below to bring up the same dialog box, and click on Paste. Do this again with the other end node. Decision trees can get very "bushy," but this copy and paste feature can make them much less tedious to construct.

7 **Labeling probability branches.** You should now have the decision tree shown in Figure 8.18. It is structurally the same as the completed tree in Figure 8.10, but the probabilities and monetary values on the probability branches are incorrect. Note that each probability branch has a value above and below the branch. The value above is the probability (the default values make the branches equally likely), and the value below is the monetary value (the default values are 0). We can enter any values or formulas in these cells, exactly as we do in typical Excel worksheets. As usual, it is a good practice to refer to input cells in these formulas whenever possible. In addition, range names can be used instead of cell addresses.

→ **PRECISIONTREE TIP:** *Sum of Probabilities*
PrecisionTree does not *enforce the rule that probabilities on branches leading out of a node must sum to* 1. *You must enforce this rule with appropriate formulas.* ■

Figure 8.18 Structure of Completed Tree

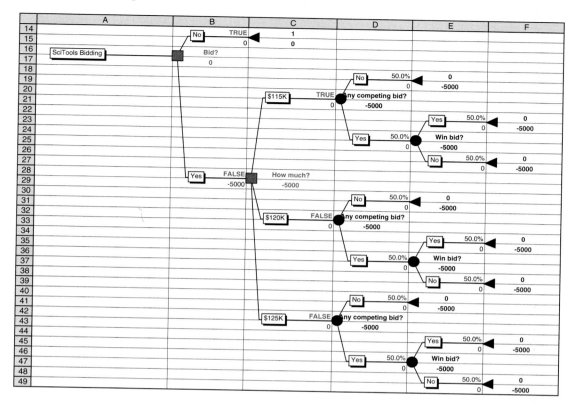

→ **PRECISIONTREE TIP:** *Entering Monetary Values, Probabilities*

A good practice is to calculate all of the monetary values and probabilities that will be needed in the decision tree in some other area of the spreadsheet. Then the values needed next to the tree branches can be created with simple "linking" formulas. ■

We will get you started with the probability branches following the decision to bid $115,000. First, enter the probability of no competing bid in cell D18 with the formula

=PrNoBid

and enter its complement in cell D24 with the formula

=1-D18

Next, enter the probability that SciTools wins the bid in cell E22 with the formula

=SUM(B10:B12)

and enter its complement in cell E26 with the formula

=1-E22

(Remember that SciTools wins the bid only if the competition bids higher, and in this part of the tree, SciTools is bidding $115,000.) For the monetary values, enter the formula

=115000-ProdCost

in the two cells, D19 and E23, where SciTools wins the contract. Note that we already subtracted the cost of the bid in cell B29, so we should *not* do so again. This would be double-counting, and you should always avoid it in decision trees.

⑧ Enter the other formulas on probability branches. Using the previous step and Figure 8.10 as a guide, enter formulas for the probabilities and monetary values on the other probability branches, those following the decision to bid $120,000 or $125,000.

→ PRECISIONTREE TIP: *Copying Subtrees*
Take advantage of PrecisionTree's copying ability to speed up the tree-building process. However, it is generally a good idea to fill the subtree as much as possible (with labels, probabilities, and monetary values) before copying. In that way, the copies will require less work. Note that formulas on the subtree are copied in the usual Excel way (with regard to relative and absolute references), so that the formulas on the copies often have to be adjusted slightly. In this example, we could have sped up the process slightly by completing step 7 before copying. Then step 8 would entail only a few formula adjustments on the copied subtrees. ∎

Interpreting the Decision Tree

To find the optimal decision strategy in any PrecisionTree tree, follow the TRUE labels.

We are finished! The completed tree in Figure 8.10 shows the best strategy and its associated EMV, as we discussed previously. In fact, a comparison of the decision tree in Figure 8.6 that we created manually and the tree from PrecisionTree in Figure 8.10 indicates virtually identical results. The best decision strategy is now indicated by the TRUE and FALSE labels above the decision branches (rather than the notches we entered by hand). Each TRUE corresponds to the optimal decision out of a decision node, whereas each FALSE corresponds to a suboptimal decision. Therefore, we simply follow the TRUE labels. In this case, the company should bid, and its bid amount should be $115,000.

Note that we never have to perform the folding-back procedure manually. PrecisionTree does it for us. Essentially, the tree is completed as soon as we finish entering the relevant inputs. In addition, if we change any of the inputs, the tree reacts automatically. For example, try changing the bid cost in cell B4 from $5000 to some large value such as $20,000. You'll see that the tree calculations update automatically, and the best decision is then *not* to bid, with an associated EMV of $0.

→ PRECISIONTREE TIP: *Values at End Nodes*
You will notice that there are two values following each triangle end node. The bottom value is the sum of all monetary values on branches leading to this end node. The top value is the probability of getting to this end node when the optimal strategy is used. This explains why many of these probabilities are 0; the optimal strategy would never lead to these end nodes. ∎

Policy Suggestion and Risk Profile for Optimal Strategy

The Policy Suggestion shows only the subtree corresponding to the optimal decision strategy.

Once the decision tree is completed, PrecisionTree has several tools we can use to gain more information about the decision analysis. First, we can see a risk profile and other information about the *optimal* decision. To do so, click on the fourth button from the left on the PrecisionTree toolbar (it looks like a staircase) and fill in the resulting dialog box as shown in Figure 8.19. (You can experiment with other options.) The Policy Suggestion option allows us to see only that part of the tree that corresponds to the best decision, as shown in Figure 8.20.

The Risk Profile option provides a graphical risk profile of the optimal decision. (If we checked the Statistics Report box, we would also see this information numerically.) As the risk profile in Figure 8.21 indicates, there are only two possible monetary outcomes if SciTools bids $115,000. It either wins $15,000 or loses $5000, and the former is much more likely. (The associated probabilities are 0.86 and 0.14, respectively.) This graphical information is even more useful when there are a larger number of possible monetary outcomes. We can see what they are and how likely they are.

Figure 8.19

Dialog Box for
Information About
Optimal Decision

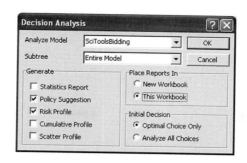

Figure 8.20

Subtree for Optimal
Decision

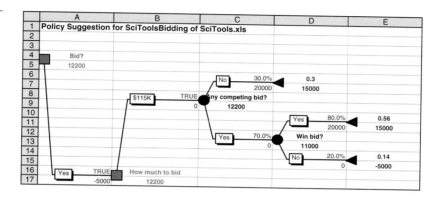

Figure 8.21

Risk Profile of
Optimal Decision

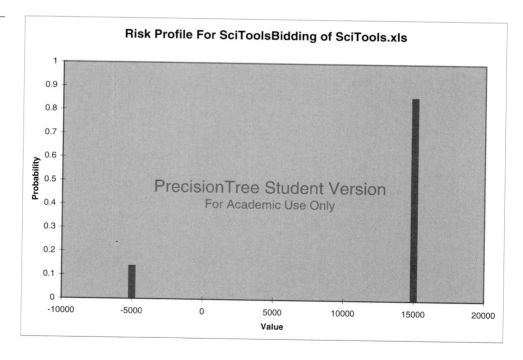

Sensitivity Analysis

We have already stressed the importance of a follow-up sensitivity analysis to any decision problem, and PrecisionTree makes this relatively easy to perform. First, we can enter any values into the input cells and watch how the tree changes. But we can obtain more systematic information by clicking on PrecisionTree's sensitivity button, the fifth from the left on the toolbar (it looks like a tornado). This brings up the dialog box in Figure 8.22. It requires an EMV cell to analyze (and an optional descriptive name) at the top and one or more input cells in the middle. You enter the specifications for these input cells in the bottom section of the dialog box.

Figure 8.22

Sensitivity Analysis Dialog Box

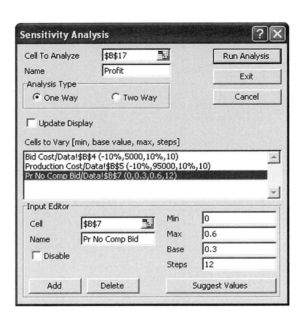

It takes some practice and experimenting to get used to PrecisionTree's sensitivity analysis tools. However, they are powerful and worth learning.

The cell to analyze (at the top) is usually the EMV cell at the far left of the decision tree—this is the cell shown in the figure—but it can be *any* EMV cell. For example, if we *assume* SciTools will prepare a bid and we want to see how sensitive the EMV from that point on is to inputs, we could select cell C29 (refer to Figure 8.10) to analyze. Next, for any input cell such as the production cost cell (B5), we enter a minimum value, a maximum value, a base value (probably the original value in the model), and a number of steps. For example, to specify these for the production cost, we clicked on the Suggest Values button. This default setting varies the production cost by as much as 10% from the original value in either direction in a series of 10 steps. We can also enter our own desired values. We did so for the probability of no competing bids, varying its value from 0 to 0.6 in a sequence of 12 steps.

After specifying the values we want to test in the Input Editor section, we need click on the Add button to make this input appear in the middle section. If there is an input in the middle section that we are not interested in, we can highlight it and click on the Delete button (to remove it completely) or the Disable box (to disable it temporarily).

When we click on Run Analysis, PrecisionTree varies each of the (enabled) inputs in the middle section, one at a time if we select the OneWay option, and presents the results in several ways in a *new* Excel workbook with Sensitivity, Tornado, and Spider Graph sheets.[4] (Actually, if only one input is specified, we get only the Sensitivity sheet. This makes sense, since the purpose of Tornado and Spider Graph sheets is to *compare* inputs.)

---

[4]It is easy to copy these new sheets to the original workbook with Excel's Edit/Move or Copy Sheet menu item. We suspect that in some future version, PrecisionTree will provide the option to place the sensitivity sheets in the original workbook automatically.

Sensitivity Chart

In the sensitivity charts, we are especially interested in where (or whether) lines cross. This is where decisions change.

The Sensitivity sheet includes several charts, of which Figure 8.23 is typical. This shows how the EMV varies with the production cost for *both* of the original decisions (bid or don't bid). This type of graph is useful for seeing whether the optimal decision *changes* over the range of the input variable. It does so only if the two lines cross. In this particular graph it is clear that the "Bid" decision dominates the "No bid" decision over the production cost range we selected.

Figure 8.23

EMV versus Production Cost for Each of Two Decisions

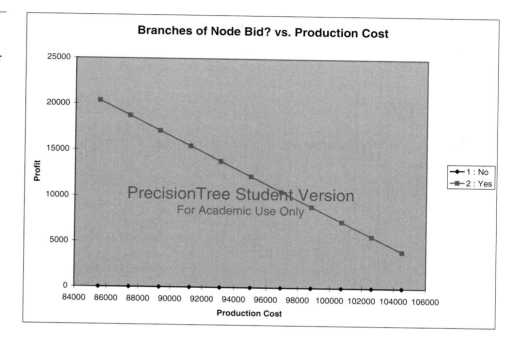

Tornado Chart

The Tornado sheet shows how sensitive the EMV of the *optimal* decision is to each of the selected inputs over the specified ranges. (See Figure 8.24 on page 378.) The length of each bar shows the percentage change in the EMV in either direction, so inputs with longer bars have a greater effect on the selected EMV. The bars are always arranged from longest on top to shortest on the bottom—hence the name *tornado* chart. Here we see that production cost has the largest effect on EMV, and bid cost has the smallest effect.

Spider Chart

Tornado charts and spider charts indicate which inputs the selected EMV is most sensitive to.

Finally, the Spider Chart sheet contains the graph in Figure 8.25. It shows how much the optimal EMV varies in magnitude for various percentage changes in the input variables. The steeper the slope of the line, the more the EMV is affected by a particular input. We again see that the production cost has a relatively great effect, whereas the other two inputs have relatively small effects.

Another Sensitivity Chart

Each time we click on the sensitivity button, we can run a different sensitivity analysis. For example, we might want to choose cell C29 as the cell to analyze. This is the optimal EMV for the problem, given that the company has decided to place a bid. One interesting chart from this analysis (from the Sensitivity sheet) is shown in Figure 8.26 (page 379). It indicates how the EMV varies with the probability of no competing bid for *each* of the three

Figure 8.24

Tornado Chart for
SciTools Example

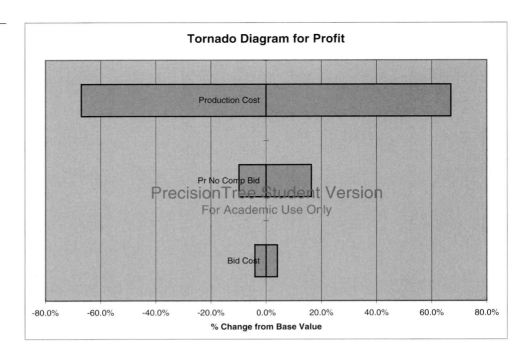

Figure 8.25

Spider Chart for
SciTools Example

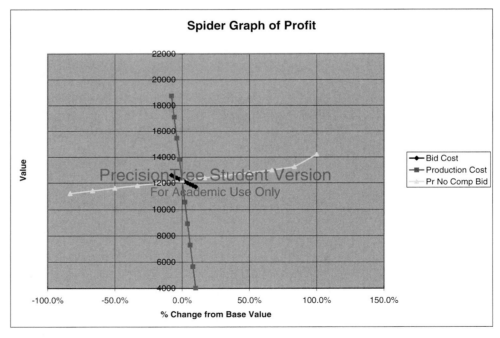

bid amount decisions. As we see, the $115,000 bid is best for most of the range, but when the probability of no competing bid is sufficiently large (about 0.55), the $120,000 bid becomes best.

A one-way sensitivity analysis varies only one input at a time. A two-way analysis varies two inputs simultaneously.

Two-Way Sensitivity Chart

Another interesting option is to run a two-way analysis (by clicking on the Two Way button in Figure 8.22). Then we see how the selected EMV varies as each *pair* of inputs vary simultaneously. We analyzed the EMV in cell C29 with this option, using the same inputs

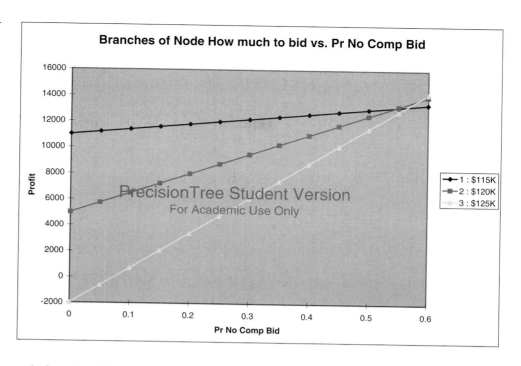

as before. A typical result is shown in Figure 8.27. For each of the possible values of production cost and the probability of no competitor bid, this chart indicates which bid amount is optimal. (By choosing cell C29, we are assuming SciTools will bid; the question is only how much.) As we see, the optimal bid amount remains $115,000 unless the production cost *and* the probability of no competing bid are both large. Then it becomes optimal to bid $120,000 or $125,000. This makes sense intuitively. As the chance of no competing bid increases and a larger production cost must be recovered, it seems reasonable that SciTools should increase its bid.

Figure 8.27

Two-Way Sensitivity
Analysis

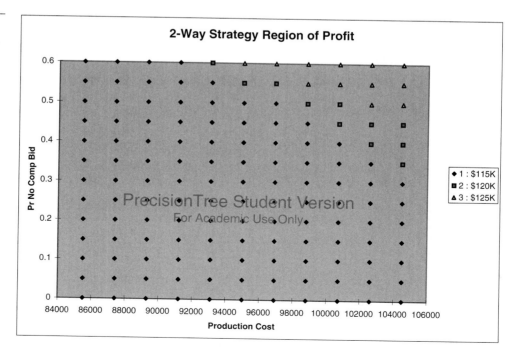

We reiterate that a sensitivity analysis is always an important component of any real-world decision analysis. If we had to construct decision trees by hand—with paper and pencil—a sensitivity analysis would be virtually out of the question. We would have to re-compute everything each time through. Therefore, one of the most valuable features of the PrecisionTree add-in is that it enables us to perform sensitivity analyses in a matter of seconds.

PROBLEMS

12. In a tree built with PrecisionTree, there are two blue values at each end node, the top one of which is a probability. Why are so many of these probabilities 0 in the finished tree in Figure 8.10? What do the remaining (positive) probabilities represent?

13. In the SciTools example, we saw that there are two equivalent decision tree structures, shown in Figures 8.5 and 8.6. Use PrecisionTree to create the first of these, and verify that it yields the same EMVs and the same optimal decision as the tree we developed in this section.

14. For the completed decision tree in Figure 8.10, the monetary values in black are those we enter. The monetary values in color are calculated automatically by PrecisionTree. For this particular example, explain exactly how these latter values are calculated (remember the folding back process) and what they represent. These include the blue values at the end nodes, the red values at the probability nodes, and the green values at the decision nodes.

15. For the SciTools example, once you build the tree as in Figure 8.10 and then run a one-way sensitivity analysis with the dialog box filled in as in Figure 8.22, you obtain six charts. (Try it.) Explain exactly what each of these charts represents. (These charts come in left/right pairs. We illustrated only those on the right in the text.)

16. The tornado chart in Figure 8.24 and the spider chart in Figure 8.25 show basically the same information in slightly different forms. Explain in words exactly what information they give.

17. Explain in words what information a two-way sensitivity chart, such as the one in Figure 8.27, provides. Demonstrate how you could provide this same information without PrecisionTree's sensitivity tools, using only data tables. (You can still utilize the tree built with PrecisionTree.)

8.4 BAYES' RULE

So far, the examples have required a single decision. We now examine multistage problems, where the decision maker must make at least two decisions that are separated in time, such as when a company must first decide whether to buy information that will help it make a second decision. In multistage decision problems we typically have alternating sets of decision nodes and probability nodes. The decision maker makes a decision, some uncertain outcomes are observed, the decision maker makes another decision, more uncertain outcomes are observed, and so on. Before we can analyze such problems, we must resolve one important probability issue.

The whole purpose of Bayes' rule is to revise probabilities as new information becomes available.

In a multistage decision tree, all probability branches at the *right* of the tree are conditional on outcomes that have occurred earlier, to their left. Therefore, the probabilities on these branches are of the form $P(A|B)$, read A given B, where A is an event corresponding to a current probability branch, and B is an event that occurs *before* event A in time. However, it is sometimes more natural to *assess* conditional probabilities in the opposite order, that is, $P(B|A)$. Whenever this is the case, we must use **Bayes' rule** to obtain the probabilities needed on the tree. Essentially, Bayes' rule is a mechanism for revising probabilities as new information becomes available.

To develop Bayes' rule, let A_1 through A_n be any outcomes. Without any further information, we believe the probabilities of the A's are $P(A_1)$ through $P(A_n)$. These are called **prior probabilities**. We then have the possibility of gaining some information. There are several information outcomes we might observe, a typical one of which is labeled B. We assume the probabilities of B, given that any of the A's will occur, are known. These probabilities, labeled $P(B|A_1)$ through $P(B|A_n)$, are often called **likelihoods**. Since an information outcome might influence our thinking about the probabilities of the A's, we need to find the conditional probability $P(A_i|B)$ for each outcome A_i. This is called the **posterior probability** of A_i. This is where Bayes' rule enters the picture. It states that we can calculate posterior probabilities using the following formula.

Bayes' rule

$$P(A_i|B) = \frac{P(B|A_i)P(A_i)}{P(B|A_1)P(A_1) + \cdots + P(B|A_n)P(A_n)} \tag{8.1}$$

In words, Bayes' rule says that the posterior is the likelihood times the prior, divided by a sum of likelihoods times priors. As a side benefit, the denominator in Bayes' rule is also useful in multistage decision trees. It is the probability $P(B)$ of the information outcome:

Denominator of Bayes' rule

$$P(B) = P(B|A_1)P(A_1) + \cdots + P(B|A_n)P(A_n) \tag{8.2}$$

In the case where there are only two A's, which we will relabel as A and Not A, Bayes' rules takes the following form:

Bayes' rule for two outcomes

$$P(A|B) = \frac{P(B|A)P(A)}{P(B|A)P(A) + P(B|\text{Not } A)P(\text{Not } A)} \tag{8.3}$$

We illustrate the mechanics of Bayes' rule in the following example. [See Feinstein (1990) for a real application of this example.]

EXAMPLE | 8.2 DRUG TESTING COLLEGE ATHLETES

If an athlete is tested for a certain type of drug usage (steroids, say), then the test result will be either positive or negative. However, these tests are never perfect. Some athletes who are drug free test positive, and some who are drug users test negative. The former are called **false positives**; the latter are called **false negatives**. We will assume that 5% of all athletes use drugs, 3% of all tests on drug-free athletes yield false positives, and 7% of all tests on drug users yield false negatives. Suppose a typical athlete is tested. If this athlete tests positive, are we sure that he is a drug user? If he tests negative, are we sure he does not use drugs?

Objective To use Bayes' rule to revise the probability of being a drug user, given the positive or negative results of the test.

The estimate that 5% of all athletes are drug users is probably based on a well-known national average. The error rates from the tests are undoubtedly known from extensive experience with the tests. (However, we are not claiming that the numbers used here match reality.)

Solution

Let D and ND denote that a randomly chosen athlete is or is not a drug user, and let $T+$ and $T-$ indicate a positive or negative test result. (The outcomes D and ND correspond to A and Not A in equation (8.3), where either $T+$ or $T-$ corresponds to B.) We are given the following probabilities. First, since 5% of all athletes are drug users, we know that $P(D)$ = 0.05 and $P(ND)$ = 0.95. These are the prior probabilities. They represent the chance that an athlete is or is not a drug user *prior* to the results of a drug test.

Second, from the information on the accuracy of the drug test, we know the conditional probabilities $P(T+|ND)$ = 0.03 and $P(T-|D)$ = 0.07. In addition, a drug-free athlete tests either positive or negative, and the same is true for a drug user. Therefore, we also have the probabilities $P(T-|ND)$ = 0.97 and $P(T+|D)$ = 0.93. These four conditional probabilities of test results given drug user status are the likelihoods of the test results.

Given these priors and likelihoods, we want posterior probabilities such as $P(D|T+)$, the probability that an athlete who tests positive is a drug user, and $P(ND|T-)$, the probability that an athlete who tests negative is drug free. They are called posterior probabilities because they are assessed *after* the drug test results.

Using Bayes' rule for two outcomes, equation (8.3), we find

$P(D|T+)$

$$= \frac{P(T+|D)P(D)}{P(T+|D)P(D) + P(T+|ND)P(ND)} = \frac{(0.93)(0.05)}{(0.93)(0.05) + (0.03)(0.95)} = 0.620$$

and

$P(ND|T-)$

$$= \frac{P(T-|ND)P(ND)}{P(T-|D)P(D) + P(T-|ND)P(ND)} = \frac{(0.97)(0.95)}{(0.07)(0.05) + (0.97)(0.95)} = 0.996$$

In words, if the athlete tests positive, there is still a 38% chance that he is *not* a drug user, but if he tests negative, we are virtually sure he is not a drug user. The denominators of these two formulas are the probabilities of the test results. We find them from equation (8.2):

$$P(T+) = 0.93(0.05) + 0.03(0.95) = 0.075$$

and

$$P(T-) = 0.07(0.05) + 0.97(0.95) = 0.925$$

The first Bayes' rule result might surprise you. After all, there is only a 3% chance of a false positive, so if you observe a positive test result, you should be pretty sure that the athlete is a drug user, right? The reason the first posterior probability is "only" 0.620 is that very few athletes in the population are drug users—only 5%. Therefore, we need a lot of evidence to convince us that a particular athlete is a drug user, and a positive test result from a somewhat inaccurate test is not enough evidence to be totally convincing. On the other hand, a negative test result simply adds confirmation to what we already suspected—that a typical athlete is *not* a drug user. This is why $P(ND|T-)$ is so close to 1.

A More Intuitive Calculation

If you have trouble understanding or implementing Bayes' rule, you are not alone. At least one study has shown that even trained medical specialists have trouble with this type of calculation. Most of us do not think intuitively about conditional probabilities. However, there is an equivalent and more intuitive way to obtain the same result.

Imagine that there are 100,000 athletes. Since 5% of all athletes are drug users, we assume 5000 of our athletes use drugs and the other 95,000 do not. Now we administer the test to all of them. We expect 3%, or 2850, of the nonusers to test positive (since the false positive rate is 3%), and we expect 93%, or 4650, of the drug users to test positive (since the false negative rate is 7%). Therefore, we observe a total of 2850 + 4650 = 7500 positives. If we choose one of these athletes at random, what is the probability that we choose a drug user? It is clearly

$$P(D|T+) = 4650/7500 = 0.620$$

This is the same result we got using Bayes' rule! So if you have trouble with Bayes' rule using probabilities, you can use this alternative method of using *counts*. (By the way, the 100,000 value is irrelevant. We could have used 10,000, 50,000, 1,000,000, or any other convenient value.)

This alternative procedure, using counts instead of probabilities, is equivalent to Bayes' rule and is probably more intuitive.

Spreadsheet Implementation of Bayes' Rule

It is fairly easy to implement Bayes' rule in a spreadsheet, as illustrated in Figure 8.28 for the drug example. (See the file **DrugBayes.xls**.[5])

Figure 8.28

Bayes' Rule for Drug-Testing Example

	A	B	C	D	E	F
1	Illustration of Bayes' rule using drug example					
2						
3	Prior probabilities of drug user status					
4		User	Non-user			
5		0.05	0.95	1		
6						
7	Likelihoods of test results, given drug user status					
8		User	Non-user			
9	Test positive	0.93	0.03			
10	Test negative	0.07	0.97			
11		1	1			
12						
13	Unconditional probabilities of test results (denominators of Bayes' rule)					
14	Test positive	0.075				
15	Test negative	0.925				
16		1				
17						
18	Posterior probabilities of drug user status (Bayes' rule)					
19		User	Non-user			
20	Test positive	0.620	0.380	1		
21	Test negative	0.004	0.996	1		

The given priors and likelihoods are listed in the ranges B5:C5 and B9:C10. We first use equation (8.2) to calculate the denominators for Bayes' rule, the unconditional probabilities of the two possible test results, in the range B14:C15. Since each of these is a sum of products of priors and likelihoods, the formula in cell B14 is

=SUMPRODUCT($B$5:$C$5,B9:C9)

[5]The Bayes2 sheet in this file illustrates how Bayes' rule can be used when there are more than two possible test results and/or drug user categories.

and this is copied to cell B15. Then we use equation (8.1) to calculate the posterior probabilities in the range B20:C21. Since each of these is a product of a prior and a likelihood, divided by a denominator, the formula in cell B20 is

=B$5*B9/$B14

and this is copied to the rest of the B20:C21 range. The various 1's in the margins of Figure 8.28 are row sums or column sums that must equal 1. We show them only as checks of our logic.

As we have noted, a positive drug test still leaves a 38% chance that the athlete is *not* a drug user. Is this a valid argument for not requiring drug testing of athletes? We will explore this question in a continuation of the drug-testing example in the next section. ■

PROBLEMS

Skill-Building Problems

18. For each of the following, use a one-way data table to see how the posterior probability of being a drug user, given a positive test, varies as the indicated input varies. Write a brief explanation of your results.
  a. Let the input be the prior probability of being a drug user, varied from 0.01 to 0.10 in increments of 0.01.
  b. Let the input be the probability of a false positive from the test, varied from 0 to 0.10 in increments of 0.01.
  c. Let the input be the probability of a false negative from the test, varied from 0 to 0.10 in increments of 0.01.

19. In the drug testing, assume there are three possible test results: positive, negative, and inconclusive. For a drug user, the probabilities of these outcomes are 0.65, 0.06, and 0.29. For a nonuser, they are 0.03, 0.72, and 0.25. Use Bayes' rule to find a table of all posterior probabilities. (The prior probability of being a drug user is still 0.05.) Then answer the following.
  a. What is the posterior probability that the athlete is a drug user, given that her test results are positive; given that her test results are negative; given that her drug results are inconclusive?
  b. What is the probability of observing a positive test result; a negative test result; an inconclusive test result?

20. Referring to the previous problem, find the same probabilities through the counting argument explained in this section. Start with 100,000 athletes and divide them into the various categories.

Skill-Extending Problem

21. The terms *prior* and *posterior* are relative. Assume that the drug test has been performed, and the outcome is positive, which leads to the posterior probabilities in row 20 of Figure 8.28. Now assume there is a *second* test, independent of the first, that can be used as a follow-up. We assume that its false positive and false negative rates are 0.02 and 0.06.
  a. Use the posterior probabilities from row 20 as *prior* probabilities in a second Bayes' rule calculation. (Now *prior* means prior to the second test.) If the athlete also tests positive in this second test, what is the posterior probability that he is a drug user?
  b. We assumed that the two tests are independent. Why might this not be realistic? If they are not independent, what kind of additional information would we need about the likelihoods of the test results?

8.5 MULTISTAGE DECISION PROBLEMS

In this section we investigate multistage decision problems. In many such problems the first stage decision is whether to purchase information that will help make a better second stage decision. In this case the information, if obtained, typically changes the probabilities of later outcomes. To revise the probabilities once the information is obtained, we often need to apply Bayes' rule, as discussed in the previous section. In addition, we typically want to learn how much the information is worth. After all, information usually comes at a price, so we want to know whether the information is worth its price. This leads to an investigation of the value of information, an important theme of this section.

We begin with a continuation of the drug-testing example from the previous section. If drug tests are not completely reliable, should they be used? As we will see, it all depends on the "costs."[6]

8.3 DRUG TESTING COLLEGE ATHLETES

The administrators at State University are trying to decide whether to institute mandatory drug testing for athletes. They have the same information about priors and likelihoods as in Example 8.2, but they now want to use a decision tree approach to see whether the benefits outweigh the costs.[7]

Objective To use a multistage decision framework to see whether mandatory drug testing can be justified, given a somewhat unreliable test and a set of "reasonable" monetary values.

WHERE DO THE NUMBERS COME FROM?

We already discussed the source of the probabilities in Example 8.2. The monetary values we will need are discussed in detail here.

Solution

We have already discussed the uncertain outcomes and their probabilities. Now we need to discuss the decision alternatives and the monetary values—the other two elements of a decision analysis. We will assume that there are only two alternatives: perform drug testing on all athletes or don't perform any drug testing. In the former case we assume that if an athlete tests positive, this athlete is then barred from athletics.

Assessing the Monetary Values

The "monetary" values are more difficult to assess. They include

- the benefit B from correctly identifying a drug user and barring this person from athletics
- the cost C_1 of the test itself for a single athlete (materials and labor)
- the cost C_2 of falsely accusing a nonuser (and barring this person from athletics)
- the cost C_3 of not identifying a drug user and allowing this person to participate in athletics
- the cost C_4 of violating a nonuser's privacy by performing the test

Real decision problems often involve nonmonetary benefits and costs. These must be assessed, relative to one another, before rational decisions can be made.

It is clear that only C_1 is a direct monetary cost that is easy to measure. However, the other "costs" and the benefit B are real, and they must be compared on some scale to enable administrators to make a rational decision. We will do so by comparing everything to the cost C_1, to which we will assign value 1. (This does not mean that the cost of testing an athlete is necessarily $1; it just means that we will express all other monetary values as

---

[6]It might also depend on whether there is a second type of test that could help confirm the findings of the first test. However, we will not consider such a test.
[7]Again, see Feinstein (1990) for an enlightening discussion of this drug-testing problem at a real university.

multiples of C_1.) Clearly, there is a lot of subjectivity involved in making these comparisons, so sensitivity analysis on the final decision tree is a must.

Developing a Benefit–Cost Table

Before developing this decision tree, it is useful to form a benefit–cost table for both alternatives and all possible outcomes. Because we will eventually maximize expected net *benefit*, all benefits in this table have a positive sign and all costs have a negative sign. These net benefits are listed in Table 8.6. The first two columns are relevant if no tests are performed; the last four are relevant when testing is performed. For example, if a positive test is obtained for a nonuser and this athlete is barred from athletics, there are three costs: the cost of the test (C_1), the cost of falsely accusing the athlete (C_2), and the cost of violating the athlete's privacy (C_4). The other entries are obtained similarly.

Table 8.6 Net Benefit for Drug-Testing Example

| Ultimate decision | Don't Test | | Perform Test | | | |
	D	ND	D and $T+$	ND and $T+$	D and $T-$	ND and $T-$
Bar from athletics	B	$-C_2$	$B-C_1$	$-(C_1+C_2+C_4)$	$B-C_1$	$-(C_1+C_2+C_4)$
Don't bar	$-C_3$	0	$-(C_1+C_3)$	$-(C_1+C_4)$	$-(C_1+C_3)$	$-(C_1+C_4)$

DEVELOPING THE DECISION TREE MODEL

The decision model, developed with PrecisionTree and shown in Figures 8.29 and 8.30, is now fairly straightforward. (See the file **DrugTesting.xls**.) We first enter all of the benefits and costs in an input section. These, together with the Bayes' rule calculations from Example 8.2, appear at the top of the spreadsheet in Figure 8.29. Then we use PrecisionTree in the usual way to build the tree in Figure 8.30 and enter the links to the values and probabilities.

Figure 8.29 Inputs and Bayes' Rule Calculations for Drug-Testing Example

	A	B	C	D	E	F
1	Drug testing decision					
2						
3	Benefits			Given probabilities		
4	Identifying user	25		Prior probabilities		
5					User	Non-user
6	Costs				0.05	0.95
7	Test cost	1				
8	Barring non-user	50		Conditional probabilities of test results		
9	Not identifying user	20			User	Non-user
10	Violation of privacy	2		Positive	0.93	0.03
11				Negative	0.07	0.97
12	Key probabilities					
13	PrUser	0.05		Bayesian revision		
14	PrFalseNegative	0.07		Unconditional probabilities of test results		
15	PrFalsePositive	0.03		Positive	0.075	
16				Negative	0.925	
17						
18				Posterior probabilities		
19					User	Non-user
20				Positive	0.620	0.380
21				Negative	0.004	0.996

It is important to understand the timing (from left to right) in this decision tree. If drug testing is performed, the result of the drug test is observed first (a probability node). Each test result leads to an action (bar from sports or don't), and then the eventual benefit or cost depends on whether the athlete uses drugs (again a probability node). You might argue that

Figure 8.30 Decision Tree for Drug-Testing Example

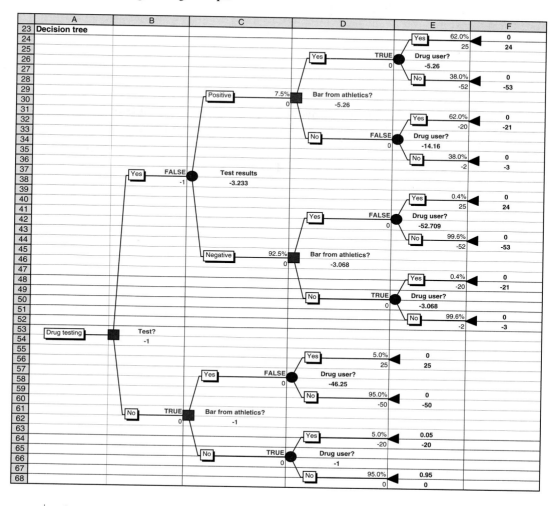

the university never knows for certain whether the athlete uses drugs, but we must include this information in the tree to get the correct benefits and costs. On the other hand, if no drug testing is performed, then there is no intermediate test result node or branches.

We require Bayes' rule because it yields exactly those probabilities that are needed in the decision tree.

Make sure you understand which probabilities are used in the tree. In the lower part, where we don't test, the probabilities are the prior probabilities. We have no test information in this case. In the upper part, where we test, the probabilities for the user and nonuser branches are posterior probabilities, given the results of the test. The reason is that by the time we get to these nodes, the results of the test have already been observed. However, the probabilities for the test results are *unconditional* probabilities, the denominators in Bayes' rule. They are not conditional probabilities such as $P(T+ \mid D)$ because we condition only on information to the *left* of any given branch. In other words, by the time we get to the test result branches, we do not yet know whether the athlete is a user.

Discussion of the Solution

Now we move on to the solution. First, we discuss the benefits and costs shown in Figure 8.29. These were chosen fairly arbitrarily, but with some hope of reflecting reality. The largest cost is falsely accusing (and then barring) a nonuser. This is 50 times as large as the cost of the test. The benefit of identifying a drug user is only half this large, and the cost of not identifying a user is 40% as large as barring a nonuser. The violation of the privacy of a nonuser is twice as large as the cost of the test. Based on these values, the decision tree implies that drug testing should *not* be performed (and no athletes should be barred). The EMVs for testing and for not testing are both negative, indicating that the costs outweigh the benefits for each, but the EMV for not testing is slightly *less* negative.[8]

Sensitivity Analysis

What would it take to change this decision? We begin with the assumption, probably accepted by most people in our society, that the cost of falsely accusing a nonuser (C_2) is the largest of the benefits and costs in the range B4:B10. In fact, because of possible legal costs, we might argue that C_2 is *more* than 50 times the cost of the test. But if we increase C_2, the scales are tipped even farther in the direction of not testing. On the other hand, if the benefit B from identifying a user and the cost C_3 for not identifying a user increase, then testing might be the preferred alternative. We tried this, keeping C_2 constant at 50. When B and C_3 both had value 45, no testing was still optimal, but when they both increased to 50—the same magnitude as C_2—then testing won out by a small margin. However, it would be difficult to argue that B and C_3 are of the same magnitude as C_2.

Other than the benefits and costs, the only other input we might vary is the accuracy of the test, measured by the error probabilities in cells B14 and B15. Presumably, if the test makes fewer false positives and false negatives, testing might be a more attractive alternative. We tried this, keeping the benefits and costs the same as those in Figure 8.29 but changing the error probabilities. Even when each error probability was decreased to 0.01, however, the no-testing alternative was still optimal—by a fairly wide margin.

In summary, based on a number of reasonable assumptions and parameter settings, this example has shown that it is difficult to make a case for mandatory drug testing. ■

The Value of Information

The drug-testing decision problem represents a typical multistage decision problem. We first decide whether to obtain some information that could be useful—the results of a drug test. If we decide not to obtain the information, we make a decision right away (bar the athlete or don't), based on prior probabilities. If we do decide to obtain the information, then we first observe the information and *then* make the final decision, based on posterior probabilities.

The questions we ask now are: How much is the information worth, and if it costs a given amount, should we purchase it? Presumably, information that will help us make our ultimate decision should be worth something, but it might not be clear how much the information is worth. In addition, even if the information is worth something, it might not be worth as much as its actual price. Fortunately, the answers to our questions are embedded in the decision tree itself.

We will find the values of two types of information: sample information and perfect information. Sample information is the information from the experiment itself. For example, it is the information from the (less than perfect) drug test. Perfect information, on the other hand, is information from a perfect test—that is, a test that will tell us with certainty which ultimate outcome will occur. In the drug example, this would correspond to a test that never makes mistakes. Admittedly, perfect information is almost never available at any price, but finding its value is still useful because it provides an upper bound on the value of *any* information. For example, if perfect information is valued at $2000, then *no* information can possibly be worth more than $2000.

---

[8]The university in the Feinstein (1990) study came to the same conclusion.

We will find the **expected value of sample information**, or **EVSI**, and the **expected values of perfect information**, or **EVPI**. They are defined as follows:

> The **EVSI** is the most we would be willing to pay for the sample information.

> *Formula for EVSI*
> EVSI = EMV with (free) sample information − EMV without information   **(8.4)**

> The **EVPI** is the most we would be willing to pay for the perfect information.

> *Formula for EVPI*
> EVPI = EMV with (free) perfect information − EMV without information   **(8.5)**

Information that has no effect on the ultimate decision is worthless.

We first make one important general point about the value of information. Suppose we have an ultimate decision to make. Before making this decision, we obtain information, supposedly to help us make the ultimate decision. But suppose we make the *same* ultimate decision, regardless of the information we obtain—the same decision we would have made in the absence of information. Can you guess the value of this information? It is zero! The information cannot be worth anything if it never leads to a different decision than we would have made without the information. The moral is that if you plan to pay something for information, you are wasting your money unless you use this information to influence your decision making.

We will see how the value of information can be evaluated in the following typical multistage decision problem.

EXAMPLE | **8.4 MARKETING A NEW PRODUCT AT ACME**

The Acme Company is trying to decide whether to market a new product. As in many new-product situations, there is considerable uncertainty about whether the new product will eventually "catch on." Acme believes that it might be wise to introduce the product in a regional test market before introducing it nationally. Therefore, the company's first decision is whether to conduct the test market.

Acme estimates that the net cost of the test market is $100,000. We assume this is mostly fixed costs, so that the same cost is incurred regardless of the test market results. If Acme decides to conduct the test market, it must then wait for the results. Based on the results of the test market, it can then decide whether to market the product nationally, in which case it will incur a fixed cost of $7 million. On the other hand, if the original decision is *not* to run a test market, then the final decision—whether to market the product nationally—can be made without further delay. Acme's unit margin, the difference between its selling price and its unit variable cost, is $18. We assume this is relevant only for the national market.

Acme classifies the results in either the test market or the national market as great, fair, or awful. Each of these results in the national market is accompanied by a forecast of total units sold. These sales volumes (in 1000s of units) are 600 (great), 300 (fair), and 90 (awful). In the absence of any test market information, Acme estimates that probabilities of the three national market outcomes are 0.45, 0.35, and 0.20, respectively.

In addition, Acme has the following historical data from products that were introduced into both test markets and national markets.

This is clearly an approximation of the real problem. In the real problem there would be a continuum of possible outcomes, not just three.

- Of the products that eventually did great in the national market, 64% did great in the test market, 26% did fair in the test market, and 10% did awful in the test market.

- Of the products that eventually did fair in the national market, 18% did great in the test market, 57% did fair in the test market, and 25% did awful in the test market.

- Of the products that eventually did awful in the national market, 9% did great in the test market, 48% did fair in the test market, and 43% did awful in the test market.[9]

The company wants to use a decision tree approach to find the best strategy. It also wants to find the expected value of the information provided by the test market.

Objective   To develop a decision tree to find the best strategy for Acme, to perform a sensitivity analysis on the results, and to find EVSI and EVPI.

WHERE DO THE NUMBERS COME FROM?

The fixed costs of the test market and the national market are probably accurate estimates, based on planned advertising and overhead expenses. The unit margin is just the difference between the anticipated selling price and the known unit cost of the product. The sales volume estimates are clearly an approximation to reality, since the sales from any new product would form a continuum of possible values. Here, the company has "discretized" the problem into three possible outcomes for the national market, and it has estimated the sales for each of these outcomes. As for the probabilities of national market results given test market results, these are probably based on results from previous products that went through test markets and then national markets.

Solution

We begin by discussing the three basic elements of this decision problem: the possible strategies, the possible outcomes and their probabilities, and the value model. The possible strategies are clear. Acme must first decide whether to run a test market. Then it must decide whether to introduce the product nationally. However, it is important to realize that if Acme decides to run a test market, it can base the national market decision on the results of the test market. In this case its final strategy will be a **contingency plan**, where it conducts the test market, then introduces the product nationally if it receives sufficiently positive test market results and abandons the product if it receives sufficiently negative test market results. The optimal strategies from many multistage decision problems involve similar contingency plans.

> In a **contingency plan**, later decisions can depend on earlier decisions and information received.

Bayes' rule is required whenever the probabilities in the statement of the problem are in the "wrong order" for what we need in the tree.

Regarding the uncertain outcomes and their probabilities, we note that the given prior probabilities of national market results in the absence of test market results will be needed in one part of the tree: where Acme decides not to run a test market. However, the historical percentages we quoted are really likelihoods of test market results, given national market results. For example, one of these is P(Great test market | Great national market) $= 0.64$. Such probabilities are the opposite of what we need in the tree. This is because the event to the right of the given sign, "great national market," occurs in time *after* the event

---

[9]You can question why the company ever marketed products nationally after awful test market results, but we will assume that, for whatever reason, the company made a few such decisions—and that a few even turned out to be winners.

to the left of the given sign, "great test market." This is a sure sign that Bayes' rule is required.

The required posterior probabilities of national market results, given test market results, are calculated directly from Bayes' rule, equation (8.1). For example, if *NG*, *NF*, and *NA* represent great, fair, and awful national market results, respectively, and if *TG*, *TF*, and *TA* represent similar events for the test market, than one typical example of a posterior probability calculation is

$$P(NG|TF) = \frac{P(TF|NG)P(NG)}{P(TF|NG)P(NG) + P(TF|NF)P(NF) + P(TF|NA)P(NA)}$$

$$= \frac{0.26(0.45)}{0.26(0.45) + 0.57(0.35) + 0.48(0.20)} = \frac{0.117}{0.4125} = 0.2836$$

This is a reasonable result. In the absence of test market information, we believe the probability of a great national market is 0.45. However, after a test market with only fair results, we revise the probability of a great national market down to 0.2836. The other posterior probabilities are calculated similarly. In addition, the denominator in this calculation, 0.4125, is the unconditional probability of a fair test market. We will need such test market probabilities in the tree.

Finally, the monetary values in the tree are straightforward. There are fixed costs of test marketing or marketing nationally, which are incurred as soon as these "go ahead" decisions are made. From that point, if we market nationally, we observe the sales volumes and multiply them by the unit margin to obtain the selling profits.

Implementing Bayes' Rule

The inputs and Bayes' rule calculations are shown in Figure 8.31. (See file **Acme.xls**.) We perform the Bayes' rule calculations exactly as in the drug example. To calculate the unconditional probabilities for test market results, the denominators for Bayes' rule from equation (8.2), enter the formula

=SUMPRODUCT($B$17:$D$17,B21:D21)

in cell G16 and copy it down to cell G18. To calculate the posterior probabilities from equation (8.1), enter the formula

=B$17*B21/$G16

in cell G22 and copy it to the range G22:I24.

Figure 8.31 Inputs and Bayes' Rule Calculations for Acme Marketing Example

	A	B	C	D	E	F	G	H	I	J	K	L
1	**Acme marketing example**											
2												
3	**Inputs**											
4	Fixed costs ($1000s)											
5	Test market	100										
6	National market	7000										
7												
8	Unit margin (either market)	$18										
9												
10	Possible quantities sold (1000s of units) in national market											
11	Great	600										
12	Fair	300										
13	Awful	90										
14						**Bayes' rule calculations**						
15	Prior probabilities of national market results					Unconditional probabilities of test mkt results (denominators of Bayes' rule)						
16		Great	Fair	Awful		Great	0.3690					
17		0.45	0.35	0.20		Fair	0.4125					
18						Awful	0.2185					
19	Likelihoods of test market results (along side), given national market results (along top) from historical data											
20		Great	Fair	Awful		Posterior probabilities of national mkt results (along top), given test mkt results (along side)						
21	Great	0.64	0.18	0.09			Great	Fair	Awful			
22	Fair	0.26	0.57	0.48		Great	0.7805	0.1707	0.0488			
23	Awful	0.10	0.25	0.43		Fair	0.2836	0.4836	0.2327			
24						Awful	0.2059	0.4005	0.3936			

DEVELOPING THE DECISION TREE MODEL

The tree is now straightforward to build and label, as shown in Figure 8.32. Note that the fixed costs of test marketing and marketing nationally appear on the decision branches where they occur in time, so that only the selling profits need to be placed on the probability branches. For example, the formula for the selling profit in cell D33 is **=B8*B11**.

Pay particular attention to the probabilities on the branches. The top group are the prior probabilities from the range B17:D17. In the bottom group, the probabilities on the left are unconditional probabilities of test market results from the range G16:G18, and those on the right are posterior probabilities of national market results from the range G22:I24. Again, this corresponds to the standard decision tree convention, where all probabilities on the tree are conditioned on any events that have occurred to the left of them.

Figure 8.32 Decision Tree for Acme Marketing Example

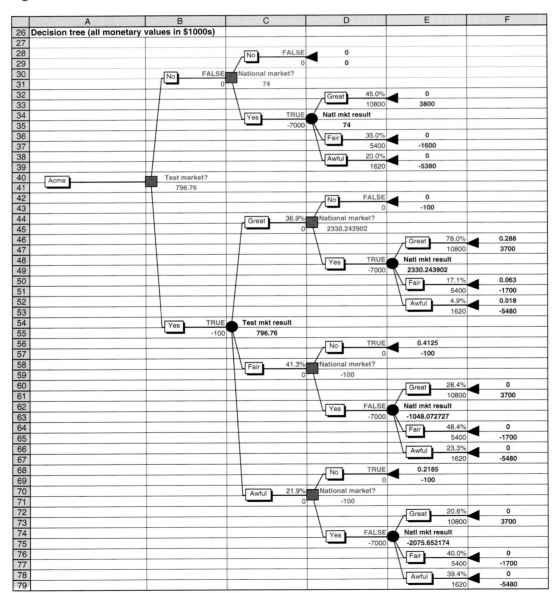

Discussion of the Solution

To interpret this tree, note that each value just below each node name is an EMV. (These are colored red or green in Excel.) For example, the 796.76 in cell B41 is the EMV for the entire decision problem. It means that Acme's best EMV from acting optimally is $796,760. As another example, the 74 in cell D35 means that if Acme ever gets to that point—there is no test market and the product is marketed nationally—then the EMV is $74,000. Actually, this is the expected selling profit minus the $7 million fixed cost, so the expected selling profit, given that no information from a test market has been obtained, is $7,074,000.

We can also see Acme's optimal strategy by following the TRUE branches from left to right. Acme should first run a test market. If the test market result is great, then the product should be marketed nationally. However, if the test market result is fair or awful, the product should be abandoned. In these cases the prospects from a national market look bleak, so Acme should cut its losses. (And there *are* losses. In these latter two cases, Acme has already spent $100,000 on the test market and has nothing to show for it.)

Once we have done the work to build the tree, we can reap the benefits of Precision-Tree's tools. For example, its policy suggestion and risk profile outputs are given in Figures 8.33 and 8.34 (page 394). (We obtain these by clicking on PrecisionTree's "staircase" button.) The policy suggestion shows only the part of the tree corresponding to the optimal strategy. Note that there are two values at each end node. The bottom number is the combined monetary value if we proceed along this sequence of branches, and the top number is the probability of this sequence of branches. This information leads directly to probability distribution in the risk profile. For this optimal strategy, the only possible monetary outcomes are a gain of $3,700,000 and losses of $100,000, $1,700,000, and $5,480,000. Their respective probabilities are 0.288, 0.631, 0.063, and 0.018. Fortunately, the large possible losses are unlikely enough that the EMV is still positive, $796,760.

Figure 8.33

Policy Suggestion (Optimal Strategy Branches)

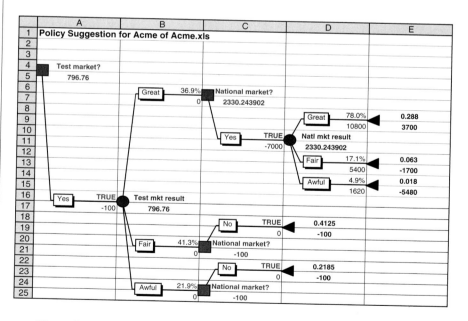

You might argue that the large potential losses and the slightly higher than 70% chance of *some* loss should persuade Acme to abandon the product right away—without a test market. However, this is what "playing the averages" with EMV is all about. Since the EMV of this optimal strategy is greater than 0, the EMV from abandoning the product right away, Acme should go ahead with this optimal strategy if the company is indeed an

Figure 8.34

Risk Profile of
Optimal Strategy

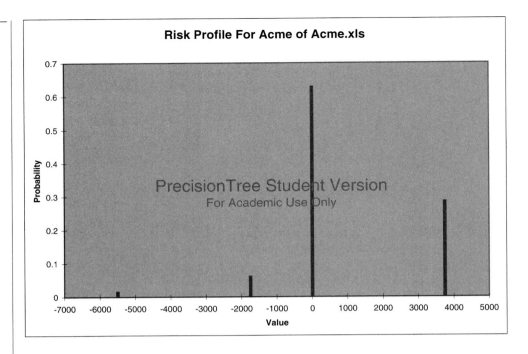

Risk Profile For Acme of Acme.xls

PrecisionTree Student Version
For Academic Use Only

EMV maximizer. In Section 8.6 we will see how this reasoning could change if Acme is a risk-averse decision maker—as it might be with multimillion dollar losses looming in the future!

Sensitivity Analysis

There are several sensitivity analyses we can perform on this model. We will investigate how things change when the unit margin, currently $18, varies from $8 to $28. This could change our decision about whether to run a test market or to market nationally.

Sensitivity analysis is often important for the insights it provides. It makes us ask, Why do these results occur?

We first analyze the overall EMV in cell B41, setting up the sensitivity dialog box as in Figure 8.35. The resulting graph is shown in Figure 8.36. The graph indicates that for small unit margins, it is better *not* to run a test market. The top line, at value 0, corresponds to abandoning the product altogether, whereas the bottom line, at value −100, corresponds to running a test market and then abandoning the product regardless of the results. Similarly, for large unit margins, it is also best not to run a test market. Again, the top line is 100 above the bottom line. However, the reasoning now is different. For large unit margins, the company should market nationally *regardless* of test market results, so there is no reason to spend money on a test market. Finally, for intermediate unit margins, as in our original model, the graph shows that it is best to test market. We hope you agree that this one single graph provides a lot of information and insight!

By changing the cell to analyze in Figure 8.35, we can gain additional insight. For example, if no test market is available, the EMV for deciding nationally right away, in cell C31, is relevant. The resulting graph is in Figure 8.37 (page 396). As we see, it is a contest between getting zero profit from abandoning the product, and getting a linearly increasing profit from marketing nationally. The breakpoint appears to be slightly below $18. If the unit margin is above this value, Acme should market nationally; otherwise, it should abandon the product.

We can also choose to analyze any of the EMVs in cells D45, D59, or D71. Each of these is relevant in the case where we have run the test market, we have observed the test market results, and we are about to decide whether to market nationally. For example, if we choose D71 as the cell to analyze, we obtain the graph in Figure 8.38. It indicates that there

Figure 8.35

Dialog Box for
Sensitivity Analysis

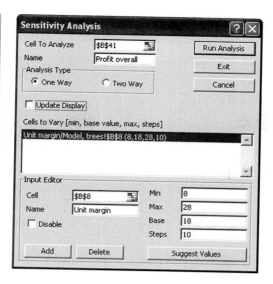

Figure 8.36

Sensitivity Analysis
on Overall Profit

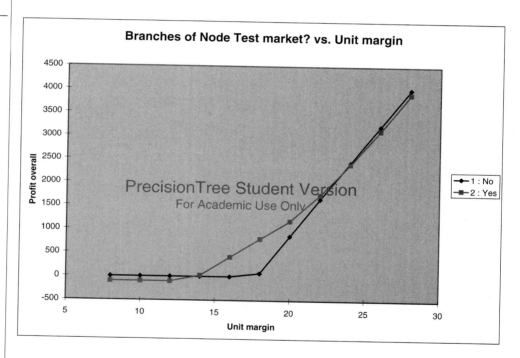

are indeed situations—where the unit margin is about $26 or more—when the company should market nationally, even though the test market is awful. In contrast, the graph in Figure 8.39, where we analyze cell D45, indicates the opposite behavior. It shows that if the unit margin is low enough—about $13.50 or less—the company should abandon the product nationally, even though the test market results are great. These are very useful insights.

Expected Value of Sample Information

The role of the test market in this example is to provide information in the form of more accurate probabilities of national market results. Information usually costs something, as it does in Acme's problem. Currently, the fixed cost of the test market is $100,000, which is evidently not too much to pay because Acme's best strategy is to run the test market.

Figure 8.37

Sensitivity Analysis
for Deciding
Nationally Right
Away

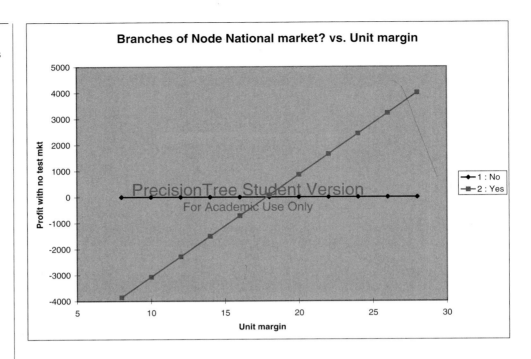

Branches of Node National market? vs. Unit margin

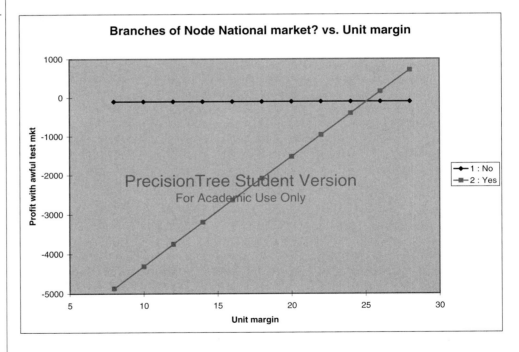

Branches of Node National market? vs. Unit margin

However, we might ask how much this test market is really worth. This is the expected value of sample information, or EVSI, and it is simple to obtain from the tree. From Figure 8.32, we see that the EMV from test marketing is $796,760, $100,000 of which is the cost of the test market. Therefore, if we could run this test market for free, the expected profit would be $896,760. On the other hand, the EMV from not running a test market is $74,000 (see cell C31 in the tree). From equation (8.4), the difference is EVSI:

$$\text{EVSI} = \$896,760 - \$74,000 = \$822,760$$

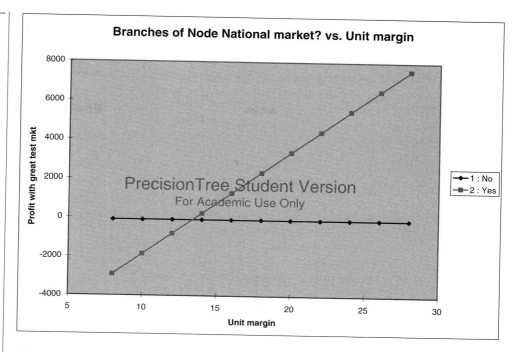

Branches of Node National market? vs. Unit margin

You can check that if you put any value less than 822.76 in cell B5, the test market fixed cost cell, the decision to test market will continue to be best.

Intuitively, this test market is worth something because it changes the optimal decision. With no test market information, the best decision is to market nationally. (See the top part of the tree in Figure 8.32.) However, with the test market information, the ultimate decision depends on the test market results. Specifically, Acme should market nationally only if the test market result is great. This is what makes information worth something—its outcome affects the optimal decision.

Expected Value of Perfect Information

We did a lot of work to find EVSI. We had to assess various conditional probabilities, use Bayes' rule, and then build a fairly complex decision tree. In general, Acme might have many sources of information it could obtain that would help it make its national decision; the test market we analyzed is just one of them. The question, then, is how much such information *could* be worth. This is answered by EVPI, the expected value of perfect information. It provides an upper bound on how much *any* information could be worth, and it is relatively easy to calculate.

Our perfect information envelope is obviously a fiction, but it helps to explain how perfect information works.

Imagine that Acme could purchase an envelope that has the true national market result—great, fair, or awful—written inside. Once opened, this envelope would remove all uncertainty, and Acme could make the correct decision. EVPI is what this envelope is worth. To calculate it, we build the tree in Figure 8.40 (page 398). The key here is that the nodes are reversed in time. We first open the envelope to discover what is inside. This corresponds to the probability node. Then we make the "easy" decision. Given the cost parameters, it is easy to see that Acme should market nationally only if the contents of the envelope reveal that the national market will be great. Otherwise, Acme should abandon the product right away.

The EVPI calculation is now straightforward. If we get the envelope (perfect information) for free, the tree in Figure 8.40 indicates that the EMV is $1,710,000. If we have no information, the EMV is, as before, $74,000. Therefore, from equation (8.5),

$$EVPI = \$1,710,000 - \$74,000 = \$1,636,000$$

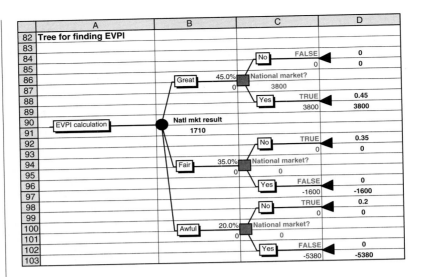

Figure 8.40

Decision Tree for Evaluating EVPI

No sample information, test market or otherwise, could possibly be worth more than this. So if some hotshot market analyst offers to provide "extremely reliable" market information to Acme for, say, $1.8 million, Acme knows this information cannot be worth the cost. ■

PROBLEMS

Skill-Building Problems

22. In deciding whether to perform mandatory drug testing, we claimed that it is difficult to justify such testing under reasonable conditions. Check this yourself in the following questions.

    a. Drug testing ought to be more attractive if the test is more reliable. Keeping the costs the same as in the example, use PrecisionTree's two-way sensitivity tool to see whether the optimal decision (test or not test) changes as the probability of a false positive and the probability of a false negative both change. You can let them vary through some reasonable ranges. How do you explain the results?

    b. Repeat part **a**, but first double the two monetary values that make the test more attractive: the benefit of identifying a user and the cost of not identifying a user. How do your results differ from those in part **a**?

    c. In this part, keep the probabilities of false positives and false negatives the same, but let the benefits and costs vary. Specifically, let the benefit of identifying a user and the cost of not identifying a user be of the form $25a$ and $20a$, where a is some factor that you will vary. Similarly, let the cost of barring a nonuser and the cost of violating privacy be of the form $50b$ and $2b$. The cost of the test is still 1. (The idea is that large values of a and/or small

values of b will make the testing more attractive.) Use PrecisionTree's two-way sensitivity tool to see whether the optimal decision (test or not test) changes for a reasonable range of values of a and b. Discuss your results.

23. In the drug testing decision, find and interpret EVSI and EVPI. Here, "sample" information refers to the information from the imperfect drug test, whereas "perfect" information refers to completely reliable information on whether the athlete uses drugs.

24. Explain in general why EVSI is independent of the actual cost of the information. For example, in the Acme problem EVSI is the same regardless of whether the actual cost of the test market is $100,000, $200,000, or any other value. Then explain how EVSI, together with the actual cost of the information, leads to the decision about whether to purchase the information.

25. Following up on the previous problem, the "expected net gain from information" is defined as the expected amount we gain by having access to the information, at its given cost, as opposed to not having access to the information. Explain how you would calculate this in general. What is its value for the Acme problem?

26. Prior probabilities are often educated guesses at best, so it is worth performing a sensitivity analysis on their values. However, we must make sure that we vary them so that all probabilities are nonnegative and sum to 1. For the Acme problem, perform the following sensitivity analyses on the three prior probabilities and comment on the results.

a. Vary the probability of great in a one-way sensitivity analysis from 0 to 0.6 in increments of 0.1. Do this in such a way that the probabilities of the two other outcomes, fair and awful, stay in the same ratio as they are currently, 7 to 4.

b. Vary the probabilities of great and fair independently in a two-way sensitivity analysis. You can choose the ranges over which these vary, but you must ensure that the three prior probabilities continue to be nonnegative and sum to 1. (For example, you couldn't choose ranges where the probabilities of great and fair could be 0.6 and 0.5.)

27. In the Acme problem, perform a sensitivity analysis on the quantity sold from a great national market (the value in cell B11). Let this value vary over a range of values *greater than* the current value of 600, so that a great national market is even more attractive than before. Does this ever change the optimal strategy? In what way?

28. Using trial and error on the prior probabilities in the Acme problem, find values of them that make EVSI equal to 0. These are values where Acme will make the same decision, regardless of the test market results it observes.

Skill-Extending Problems

29. We related EVPI to the value of an envelope that contains the true ultimate outcome. We can extend this concept to "less than" perfect information. For example, in the Acme problem suppose that we could purchase information that would tell us, with certainty, that one of the following two outcomes will occur: (1) the national market will be great, or (2) the national market will not be great. Notice that outcome (2) doesn't tell us whether the national market will be fair or awful; it just tells us that it won't be great. How much should Acme be willing to pay for such information?

30. The concept behind EVPI is that we purchase perfect information (the envelope), we then open the envelope to see which outcome occurs, and then we make an easy decision. We do *not*, however, get to choose what information the envelope contains. Sometimes a company can pay, not to obtain information, but to influence the outcome. Consider the following version of the Acme problem. There is no possibility of a test market, so that Acme must decide right away whether to market nationally. However, suppose Acme can pay to change the probabilities of the national market outcomes from their current values, 0.45, 0.35, and 0.20, to the new values p, $(7/11)(1 - p)$, and $(4/11)(1 - p)$, for some p. (In this way, the probabilities of fair and awful stay in the same ratio as before, 7 to 4, but by making p large, the probability of great increases.)

a. How much should Acme be willing to pay for the change if $p = 0.6$? If $p = 0.8$? If $p = 0.95$?

b. Are these types of changes realistic? Answer by speculating on the types of actions Acme might be able to take to make the probability of a great national market higher. Do you think such actions would cost more or less than what Acme should be willing to pay for them (from part **a**)?

8.6 INCORPORATING ATTITUDES TOWARD RISK[10]

Rational decision makers are sometimes willing to violate the EMV maximization criterion when large amounts of money are at stake. These decision makers are willing to sacrifice some EMV to reduce risk. Are you ever willing to do so personally? Consider the following scenarios.

■ You have a chance to enter a lottery where you will win $100,000 with probability 0.1 or win nothing with probability 0.9. Alternatively, you can receive $5000 for certain. How many of you—truthfully—would take the certain $5000, even though the EMV of the lottery is $10,000? Or change the $100,000 to $1,000,000 and the $5000 to $50,000 and ask yourself whether you'd prefer the sure $50,000!

■ You can either buy collision insurance on your expensive new car or not buy it, where the insurance costs a certain premium and carries some deductible provision. If you decide to pay the premium, then you are essentially paying a certain amount to avoid a gamble: the possibility of wrecking your car and not having it insured. You can be

[10]This section is somewhat advanced and can be omitted without any loss of continuity.

sure that the premium is greater than the expected cost of damage; otherwise, the insurance company would not stay in business. Therefore, from an EMV standpoint you should not purchase the insurance. But how many of you drive without this type of insurance?

These examples, the second of which is certainly realistic, illustrate situations where rational people do not behave as EMV maximizers. Then how do they act? This question has been studied extensively by many researchers, both mathematically and behaviorally. Although the answer is still not agreed upon universally, most researchers agree that if certain basic behavioral assumptions hold, people are **expected utility** maximizers—that is, they choose the alternative with the largest expected utility. Although we will not go deeply into the subject of expected utility maximization, the discussion in this section will acquaint you with the main ideas.

Utility Functions

We begin by discussing an individual's **utility function**. This is a mathematical function that transforms monetary values—payoffs and costs—into **utility values**. Essentially, an individual's utility function specifies the individual's preferences for various monetary payoffs and costs and, in doing so, it automatically encodes the individual's attitudes toward risk. Most individuals are **risk averse**, which means intuitively that they are willing to sacrifice some EMV to avoid risky gambles. In terms of the utility function, this means that every extra dollar of payoff is worth slightly less to the individual than the previous dollar, and every extra dollar of cost is considered slightly more costly (in terms of utility) than the previous dollar. The resulting utility functions are shaped as shown in Figure 8.41. Mathematically, these functions are said to be **increasing** and **concave**. The increasing part means that they go uphill—everyone prefers more money to less money. The concave part means that they increase at a decreasing rate. This is the risk-averse behavior.

Figure 8.41
Risk-Averse Utility
Function

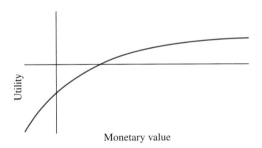

There are two aspects of implementing utility maximization in a real decision analysis. First, we must obtain an individual's (or company's) utility function. This is a time-consuming task that typically involves many trade-offs. It is usually carried out by experts in the field, and we will not discuss the details of the process here. Second, we must use the resulting utility function to find the best decision. This second step is relatively straightforward. We simply substitute utility values for monetary values in the decision tree and then fold back as usual. That is, we calculate expected *utilities* at probability branches and take maximums (of expected utilities) at decision branches. We will look at a numerical example later in this section.

Exponential Utility

As we have indicated, utility assessment is tedious. Even in the best of circumstances, when a trained consultant attempts to assess the utility function of a single person, the process requires the person to make a series of choices between hypothetical alternatives involving uncertain outcomes. Unless the person has some training in probability, these choices will probably be difficult to understand, let alone make, and it is unlikely that the person will answer *consistently* as the questioning proceeds. The process is even more difficult when a company's utility function is being assessed. Because the company executives involved typically have different attitudes toward risk, it is difficult for these people to reach a consensus on a common utility function.

For these reasons classes of "ready-made" utility functions have been developed. One important class is called **exponential utility** and has been used in many financial investment analyses. An exponential utility function has only one adjustable numerical parameter, called the **risk tolerance**, and there are straightforward ways to discover the most appropriate value of this parameter for a particular individual or company. So the advantage of using an exponential utility function is that it is relatively easy to assess. The drawback is that exponential utility functions do not capture all types of attitudes toward risk. Nevertheless, their ease of use has made them popular.

An exponential utility function has the following form:

Exponential utility

$$U(x) = 1 - e^{-x/R}$$

(8.6)

Here x is a monetary value (a payoff if positive, a cost if negative), $U(x)$ is the utility of this value, and $R > 0$ is the risk tolerance. As the name suggests, the risk tolerance measures how much risk the decision maker will accept. The larger the value of R, the less risk averse the decision maker is. That is, a person with a large value of R is more willing to take risks than a person with a small value of R.

> In terms of exponential utility, the **risk tolerance** is a single number that specifies an individual's aversion to risk. The higher the risk tolerance, the less risk averse the individual is.

To assess a person's (or company's) exponential utility function, we need only to assess the value of R. There are a couple of tips for doing this. First, it has been shown that the risk tolerance is approximately equal to that dollar amount R such that the decision maker is indifferent between the following two options:

- Option 1: Obtain no payoff at all.
- Option 2: Obtain a payoff of R dollars or a loss of $R/2$ dollars, depending on the flip of a fair coin.

For example, if you are indifferent between a bet where you win $1000 or lose $500, with probability 0.5 each, and not betting at all, then your R is approximately $1000. From this criterion it certainly makes intuitive sense that a wealthier person (or company) ought to have a larger value of R. This has been found in practice.

Finding the appropriate risk tolerance value for any company or individual is not necessarily easy, but it is easier than assessing an entire utility function from scratch.

A second tip for finding R is based on empirical evidence found by Ronald Howard, a prominent decision analyst. Through his consulting experience with large companies, he discovered tentative relationships between risk tolerance and several financial variables: net sales, net income, and equity. [See Howard (1988).] Specifically, he found that R was approximately 6.4% of net sales, 124% of net income, and 15.7% of equity for the companies he studied. For example, according to this prescription, a company with net sales of $30 million should have a risk tolerance of approximately $1.92 million. Howard admits that these percentages are only guidelines. However, they do indicate that larger and more profitable companies tend to have larger values of R, which means that they are more willing to take risks involving large dollar amounts.

We illustrate the use of the expected utility criterion, and exponential utility in particular, with the following example.

EXAMPLE | **8.5 DECIDING WHETHER TO ENTER RISKY VENTURES AT VENTURE LIMITED**

Venture Limited is a company with net sales of $30 million. The company currently must decide whether to enter one of two risky ventures or invest in a sure thing. The gain from the latter is a sure $125,000. The possible outcomes for the less risky venture are a $0.5 million loss, a $0.1 million gain, and a $1 million gain. The probabilities of these outcomes are 0.25, 0.50, and 0.25. The possible outcomes of the more risky venture are a $1 million loss, a $1 million gain, and a $3 million gain. The probabilities of these outcomes are 0.35, 0.60, and 0.05. If Venture Limited must decide on exactly one of these alternatives, what should it do?

Objective   To see how the company's risk averseness, determined by its risk tolerance in an exponential utility function, affects its decision.

WHERE DO THE NUMBERS COME FROM?

The outcomes for each of the risky alternatives probably form a continuum of possible values. However, as in Example 8.4, the company has "discretized" these into a few possibilities, and it has made intelligent estimates of the monetary consequences and probabilities of these discrete possibilities.

Solution

Don't worry about the actual utility values (for example, whether they are positive or negative). Only the relative magnitudes matter in terms of decision making.

We will assume that Venture Limited has an exponential utility function. Also, based on Howard's guidelines, we will assume that the company's risk tolerance is 6.4% of its net sales, or $1.92 million. (We will perform a sensitivity analysis on this parameter later on.) We can substitute into equation (8.6) to find the utility of any monetary outcome. For example, the gain from the riskless alternative (in $1000s) is 125, and its utility is

$$U(125) = 1 - e^{-125/1920} = 1 - 0.9370 = 0.0630$$

As another example, the utility of a $1 million loss is

$$U(-1000) = 1 - e^{-(-1000)/1920} = 1 - 1.6834 = -0.6834$$

These are the values we use (instead of monetary values) in the decision tree.

DEVELOPING THE DECISION TREE MODEL

Fortunately, PrecisionTree takes care of all the details. After we build a decision tree and label it (with monetary values) in the usual way, we click on the name of the tree (the box on the far left of the tree) to open the dialog box in Figure 8.42. We then fill in the utility function information as shown in the upper right section of the dialog box. This says to use an exponential utility function with risk tolerance 1920. (As indicated in the spreadsheet, we are measuring all monetary values in $1000s.) It also indicates that we want expected utilities (as opposed to EMVs) to appear in the decision tree.

Figure 8.42

Dialog Box for Specifying the Exponential Utility Criterion

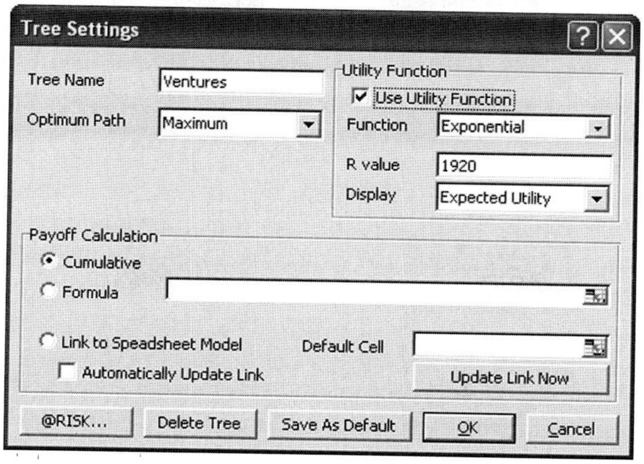

The completed tree for this example is shown in Figure 8.43. (See the file **Venture.xls**.) We build it in exactly the same way as usual and link probabilities and monetary values to its branches in the usual way. For example, there is a link in cell C22 to the monetary value in cell B12. However, the expected values shown in the tree (those shown in color on a computer screen) are expected *utilities*, and the optimal decision is the one with the largest expected utility. In this case the expected utilities for the riskless option, investing in the less risky venture, and investing in the more risky venture are 0.0630, 0.0525, and 0.0439, respectively. Therefore, the optimal decision is to take the riskless option.

The tree is built and labeled (with monetary values) exactly as before. PrecisionTree then takes care of calculating the expected utilities.

Figure 8.43

Decision Tree for Risky Venture Example

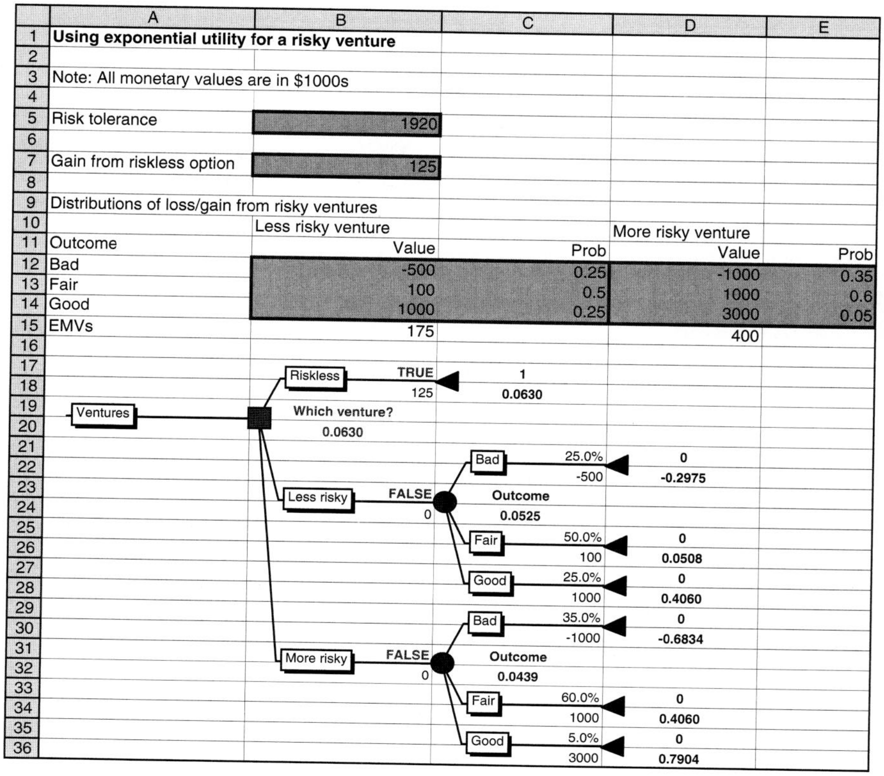

A risk averse decision
maker typically gives
up EMV to avoid
risk—when the stakes
are large enough.

Discussion of the Solution

As we see from the tree, the riskless option is best in terms of the expected utility criterion; it has the largest expected utility. However, note that the EMVs of the three decisions are $125,000, $175,000, and $400,000. (The latter two of these are calculated in row 15 as the usual "sumproduct" of monetary values and probabilities.) So from an EMV point of view, the more risky venture is definitely best. In fact, the ordering of the three alternatives using the EMV criterion is exactly the *opposite* of the ordering using expected utility. But Venture Limited is sufficiently risk averse, and the monetary values are sufficiently large, that the company is willing to sacrifice $275,000 of EMV to avoid risk.

Sensitivity Analysis

How sensitive is the optimal decision to the key parameter, the risk tolerance? We can answer this by changing the risk tolerance (through the dialog box in Figure 8.42) and watching how the decision tree changes.[11] You can check that when the company becomes *more* risk tolerant, the more risky venture eventually becomes optimal. In fact, this occurs when the risk tolerance increases to approximately $2.210 million. In the other direction, of course, when the company becomes *less* risk tolerant, the riskless decision continues to be optimal. (The "middle" decision, the less risky alternative, is evidently not optimal for *any* value of the risk tolerance.) The bottom line is that the "optimal" decision depends entirely on the attitudes toward risk of Venture Limited's top management. ■

Is Expected Utility Maximization Used?

The previous discussion indicates that utility maximization is a fairly involved task. The question, then, is whether the effort is justified. Theoretically, expected utility maximization might be interesting to researchers, but is it really used in the business world? The answer appears to be: not very often. For example, one recent article on the practice of decision making [see Kirkwood (1992)] quotes Ronald Howard—the same person we quoted previously—as having found risk aversion to be of practical concern in only 5% to 10% of business decision analyses. This same article quotes the president of a Fortune 500 company as saying, "Most of the decisions we analyze are for a few million dollars. It is adequate to use expected value (EMV) for these."

PROBLEMS

Skill-Building Problems

31. For the risky venture example, create a line chart that includes three series—that is, three lines (or curves). Each line should show the expected utility of a particular decision for a sequence of possible risk tolerance values. (You'll have to create the data for the chart "manually," by changing the risk tolerance, recording the three expected utilities somewhere on the spreadsheet, changing the risk tolerance again, and so on.) This chart should make it clear when the more risky option becomes optimal and whether the less risky option is ever optimal.

32. In the risky venture example, the more risky alternative, in spite of its dominating EMV, is not preferred by a decision maker with risk tolerance $1.92 million. Now suppose everything stays the same except for the best monetary outcome of the more risky alternative (the value in cell D14). How much larger must this value be for the decision maker to prefer the more risky alternative? What is the corresponding EMV at that point?

33. In the risky venture example, suppose there is no riskless alternative; the only two possible decisions are

---

[11]We show the risk tolerance in cell B5, but the values in the decision tree are not linked to this cell. We need to go through the dialog box to change the risk tolerance.

the less risky venture and the more risky venture. Explore which of these is the preferred alternative for a range of risk tolerances. Can you find a "cutoff point" for the risk tolerance such that the less risky venture is preferred for risk tolerances below the cutoff and the more risky venture is preferred otherwise?

Skill-Extending Problem

34. Do the absolute magnitudes of the monetary outcomes matter in the risky venture example? Consider the following two possibilities. In each case, multiply all monetary values in the example by a factor of A. (For example, double them if $A = 2$.) For each part, briefly explain your findings.
  a. Currently, an EMV-maximizer would choose the most risky venture. Would this continue to be the case for any factor A?
  b. Currently, an expected utility maximizer with risk tolerance $1.92 million prefers the riskless alterna-

tive. Would this continue to be the case for any factor A greater than 1? What about when A is less than 1? You can answer by using trial and error on A.
  c. Referring to the dialog box in Figure 8.42, there is a display dropdown with three options: expected value (EMV), expected utility, and certainty equivalent. The latter is defined for any gamble as the sure monetary amount a risk averse person would take as a trade for the risky gamble. For example, you can check that the certainty equivalent for the more risky alternative is 86.2017 (in thousands of dollars). Explain what this really means by calculating the utility of 86.2017 manually and comparing it to the *expected* utility from the more risky venture (as shown on the tree). How does this explain why the decision maker prefers the riskless alternative to the more risky venture?

8.7 CONCLUSION

In this chapter we have discussed methods that can be used in decision-making problems where uncertainty is a key element. Perhaps the most important skill you can gain from this chapter is the ability to approach decision problems with uncertainty in a systematic manner. This systematic approach requires you to list all possible decisions or strategies, list all possible uncertain outcomes, assess the probabilities of these outcomes (possibly with the aid of Bayes' rule), calculate all necessary monetary values, and finally do the necessary calculations to obtain the best decision. If large dollar amounts are at stake, you might also need to perform a utility analysis, where the decision maker's attitudes toward risk are taken into account. Once the basic analysis has been completed, using "best guesses" for the various parameters of the problem, you should perform a sensitivity analysis to see whether the best decision continues to be best within a range of problem parameters.

Summary of Key Management Science Terms

Term	Explanation	Page
Payoff (or cost) table	A table that lists the payoffs (or costs) for all combinations of decisions and uncertain outcomes	356
Maximin criterion	The pessimist's criterion; find the worst possible payoff for each decision, and choose the decision with the best of these	357
Maximax criterion	The optimist's criterion; find the best possible payoff for each decision, and choose the decision with the best of these	357
Expected monetary value (EMV)	The weighted average of the possible payoffs from a decision, weighted by their probabilities	357
EMV criterion	Choose the decision with the maximum EMV	357

(continued)

Term	Explanation	Page
Decision tree	A graphical device for illustrating all of the aspects of the decision problem and for finding the optimal decision (or decision strategy)	359
Folding back procedure	Calculation method for decision tree; starting at the right, take EMVs at probability nodes, maximums of EMVs at decision nodes	361
Risk profile	Bar chart that represents the probability distribution of monetary outcomes for any decision	361
Bayes' rule	Formula for updating probabilities as new information becomes available; prior probabilities are transformed into posterior probabilities	381
Expected value of sample information (EVSI)	The most the (imperfect) sample information (such as the results of a test market) would be worth	389
Expected value of perfect information (EVPI)	The most perfect information on some uncertain outcome would be worth; represents an upper bound on *any* EVSI	389
Contingency plan	A decision strategy where later decisions depend on earlier decisions and outcomes observed in the meantime	390
Utility function	A mathematical function that encodes an individual's (or company's) attitudes toward risk	400
Expected utility criterion	Choose the decision that maximizes the expected utility; typically sacrifices EMV to avoid risk when large monetary amounts are at stake	400
Exponential utility function, risk tolerance	A popular class of utility functions, where only a single parameter, the risk tolerance, has to be specified	401

Summary of Key Excel Terms

Term	Explanation	Excel	Page
PrecisionTree add-in	Useful Excel add-in developed by Palisade for building and analyzing decision trees in Excel	Has its own menu and toolbar	368
PrecisionTree sensitivity chart	Useful for seeing how the optimal decision changes as selected inputs vary	Use PrecisionTree/Analysis/ Sensitivity menu item (or Sensitivity Analysis toolbar button)	375
PrecisionTree tornado and spider charts	Useful for seeing which inputs affect a selected EMV the most	Use PrecisionTree/Analysis/ Sensitivity menu item (or Sensitivity Analysis toolbar button)	377

PROBLEMS

Skill-Building Problems

35. The SweetTooth Candy Company knows it will need 10 tons of sugar 6 months from now to implement its production plans. Jean Dobson, SweetTooth's purchasing manager, has essentially two options for acquiring the needed sugar. She can either buy the sugar at the going market price when she needs it, 6 months from now, or she can buy a futures contract now. The contract guarantees delivery of the sugar in 6 months but the cost of purchasing it will be based on today's market price. Assume that possible sugar futures contracts available for purchase are for 5 tons or 10 tons only. No futures contracts can be purchased or sold in the intervening months. Thus, SweetTooth's possible decisions are: (1) purchase a futures contract for 10 tons of sugar now, (2) purchase a futures contract for 5 tons of sugar now and purchase 5 tons of sugar in 6 months, or (3) purchase all 10 tons of needed sugar in 6 months. The price of sugar bought now for delivery in 6 months is $0.0851 per pound. The transaction costs for 5-ton and 10-ton futures contracts are $65 and $110, respectively. Finally, Ms. Dobson has assessed the probability distribution for the possible prices of sugar 6 months from now (in dollars per pound). The file **P08_35.xls** contains these possible prices and their corresponding probabilities.

   a. Given that SweetTooth wants to acquire the needed sugar in the least costly way, formulate a cost table that specifies the cost (in dollars) associated with each possible decision and possible sugar price in the future.

   b. Use PrecisionTree to identify the decision that minimizes SweetTooth's expected cost of meeting its sugar demand.

   c. Perform a sensitivity analysis on the optimal decision and summarize your findings. In response to which model inputs is the expected cost value most sensitive?

36. Carlisle Tire and Rubber, Inc., is considering expanding production to meet potential increases in the demand for one of its tire products. Carlisle's alternatives are to construct a new plant, expand the existing plant, or do nothing in the short run. The market for this particular tire product may expand, remain stable, or contract. Carlisle's marketing department estimates the probabilities of these market outcomes as 0.25, 0.35, and 0.40, respectively. The file **P08_36.xls** contains Carlisle's estimated payoff (in dollars) table.

   a. Use PrecisionTree to identify the strategy that maximizes this tire manufacturer's expected profit.

   b. Perform a sensitivity analysis on the optimal decision and summarize your findings. In response to which model inputs is the expected profit value most sensitive?

37. A local energy provider offers a landowner $180,000 for the exploration rights to natural gas on a certain site and the option for future development. This option, if exercised, is worth an additional $1,800,000 to the landowner, but this will occur only if natural gas is discovered during the exploration phase. The landowner, believing that the energy company's interest in the site is a good indication that gas is present, is tempted to develop the field herself. To do so, she must contract with local experts in natural gas exploration and development. The initial cost for such a contract is $300,000, which is lost forever if no gas is found on the site. If gas is discovered, however, the landowner expects to earn a net profit of $6,000,000. Finally, the landowner estimates the probability of finding gas on this site to be 60%.

   a. Formulate a payoff table that specifies the landowner's payoff (in dollars) associated with each possible decision and each outcome with respect to finding natural gas on the site.

   b. Use PrecisionTree to identify the strategy that maximizes the landowner's expected net earnings from this opportunity.

   c. Perform a sensitivity analysis on the optimal decision and summarize your findings. In response to which model inputs is the expected profit value most sensitive?

38. Techware Incorporated is considering the introduction of two new software products to the market. In particular, the company has four options regarding these two proposed products: introduce neither product, introduce product 1 only, introduce product 2 only, or introduce both products. Research and development costs for products 1 and 2 are $180,000 and $150,000, respectively. Note that the first option entails no costs because research and development efforts have not yet begun. The success of these software products depends on the trend of the national economy in the coming year and on the consumers' reaction to these products. The company's revenues earned by introducing product 1 only, product 2 only, or both products in various states of the national economy are given in the file **P08_38.xls**. The probabilities of observing a strong, fair, and weak trend in the national economy in the coming year are 0.30, 0.50, and 0.20, respectively.

   a. Formulate a payoff table that specifies Techware's net revenue (in dollars) for each possible decision and each outcome with respect to the trend in the national economy.

b. Use PrecisionTree to identify the strategy that maximizes Techware's expected net revenue from the given marketing opportunities.

c. Perform a sensitivity analysis on the optimal decision and summarize your findings. In response to which model inputs is the expected net revenue value most sensitive?

39. Consider an investor with $10,000 available to invest. He has the following options regarding the allocation of his available funds: (1) he can invest in a risk-free savings account with a guaranteed 3% annual rate of return; (2) he can invest in a fairly safe stock, where the possible annual rates of return are 6%, 8%, or 10%; or (3) he can invest in a more risky stock where the possible annual rates of return are 1%, 9%, or 17%. Note that the investor can place all of his available funds in any one of these options, or he can split his $10,000 into two $5000 investments in any two of these options. The joint probability distribution of the possible return rates for the two stocks is given in the file **P08_39.xls**.

    a. Formulate a payoff table that specifies this investor's return (in dollars) in one year for each possible decision and each outcome with respect to the two stock returns.

    b. Use PrecisionTree to identify the strategy that maximizes the investor's expected earnings in one year from the given investment opportunities.

    c. Perform a sensitivity analysis on the optimal decision and summarize your findings. In response to which model inputs is the expected earnings value most sensitive?

40. A buyer for a large department store chain must place orders with an athletic shoe manufacturer 6 months prior to the time the shoes will be sold in the department stores. In particular, the buyer must decide on November 1 how many pairs of the manufacturer's newest model of tennis shoes to order for sale during the upcoming summer season. Assume that each pair of this new brand of tennis shoes costs the department store chain $45 per pair. Furthermore, assume that each pair of these shoes can then be sold to the chain's customers for $70 per pair. Any pairs of these shoes remaining unsold at the end of the summer season will be sold in a closeout sale next fall for $35 each. The probability distribution of consumer demand for these tennis shoes (in hundreds of pairs) during the upcoming summer season has been assessed by market research specialists and is provided in the file **P08_40.xls**. Finally, assume that the department store chain must purchase these tennis shoes from the manufacturer in lots of 100 pairs.

    a. Formulate a payoff table that specifies the contribution to profit (in dollars) from the sale of the tennis shoes by this department store chain for each possible purchase decision (in hundreds of

pairs) and each outcome with respect to consumer demand.

    b. Use PrecisionTree to identify the strategy that maximizes the department store chain's expected profit earned by purchasing and subsequently selling pairs of the new tennis shoes.

    c. Perform a sensitivity analysis on the optimal decision and summarize your findings. In response to which model inputs is the expected earnings value most sensitive?

41. Each day the manager of a local bookstore must decide how many copies of the community newspaper to order for sale in her shop. She must pay the newspaper's publisher $0.40 for each copy, and she sells the newspapers to local residents for $0.50 each. Newspapers that are unsold at the end of day are considered worthless. The probability distribution of the number of copies of the newspaper purchased daily at her shop is provided in the file **P08_41.xls**. Employ a decision tree to find the bookstore manager's profit-maximizing daily order quantity.

42. Two construction companies are bidding against one another for the right to construct a new community center building in Lewisburg, Pennsylvania. The first construction company, Fine Line Homes, believes that its competitor, Buffalo Valley Construction, will place a bid for this project according to the distribution shown in the file **P08_42.xls.** Furthermore, Fine Line Homes estimates that it will cost $160,000 for its own company to construct this building. Given its fine reputation and long-standing service within the local community, Fine Line Homes believes that it will likely be awarded the project in the event that it and Buffalo Valley Construction submit exactly the same bids. Employ a decision tree to identify Fine Line Homes' profit-maximizing bid for the new community center building.

43. Suppose that you have sued your employer for damages suffered when you recently slipped and fell on an icy surface that should have been treated by your company's physical plant department. Specifically, your injury resulting from this accident was sufficiently serious that you, in consultation with your attorney, decided to sue your company for $500,000. Your company's insurance provider has offered to settle this suit with you out of court. If you decide to reject the settlement and go to court, your attorney is confident that you will win the case but is uncertain about the amount the court will award you in damages. He has provided his assessment of the probability distribution of the court's award to you in the file **P08_43.xls**. Let S be the insurance provider's proposed out-of-court settlement (in dollars). For which values of S will you decide to accept the settlement? For which values of S will you choose to take your

chances in court? Of course, you are seeking to maximize the expected payoff from this litigation.

44. Suppose that one of your colleagues has $2000 available to invest. Assume that all of this money must be placed in one of three investments: a particular money market fund, a stock, or gold. Each dollar your colleague invests in the money market fund earns a virtually guaranteed 12% annual return. Each dollar he invests in the stock earns an annual return characterized by the probability distribution provided in the file **P08_44.xls**. Finally, each dollar he invests in gold earns an annual return characterized by the probability distribution given in the file.

   a. If your colleague must place all of his available funds in a single investment, which investment should he choose to maximize his expected earnings over the next year?

   b. Suppose now that your colleague can place all of his available funds in one of these three investments as before, or he can invest $1000 in one alternative and $1000 in another. Assuming that he seeks to maximize his expected total earnings in one year, how should he allocate his $2000?

45. Consider a population of 2000 individuals, 800 of whom are women. Assume that 300 of the women in this population earn at least $60,000 per year, and 200 of the men earn at least $60,000 per year.

   a. What is the probability that a randomly selected individual from this population earns less than $60,000 per year?

   b. If a randomly selected individual is observed to earn less than $60,000 per year, what is the probability that this person is a man?

   c. If a randomly selected individual is observed to earn at least $60,000 per year, what is the probability that this person is a woman?

46. Yearly automobile inspections are required for residents of the state of Pennsylvania. Suppose that 18% of all inspected cars in Pennsylvania have problems that need to be corrected. Unfortunately, Pennsylvania state inspections fail to detect these problems 12% of the time. Consider a car that is inspected and is found to be free of problems. What is the probability that there is indeed something wrong that the inspection has failed to uncover?

47. Consider again the landowner's decision problem described in Problem 37. Suppose now that, at a cost of $90,000, the landowner can request that a soundings test be performed on the site where natural gas is believed to be present. The company that conducts the soundings concedes that 30% of the time the test will indicate that no gas is present when it actually is. When natural gas is not present in a particular site, the soundings test is accurate 90% of the time.

   a. Given that the landowner pays for the soundings test and the test indicates that gas is present, what is the landowner's revised estimate of the probability of finding gas on this site?

   b. Given that the landowner pays for the soundings test and the test indicates that gas is not present, what is the landowner's revised estimate of the probability of not finding gas on this site?

   c. Should the landowner request the given soundings test at a cost of $90,000? Explain why or why not. If not, when (if ever) would the landowner choose to obtain the soundings test?

48. The chief executive officer of a firm in a highly competitive industry believes that one of her key employees is providing confidential information to the competition. She is 90% certain that this informer is the vice president of finance, whose contacts have been extremely valuable in obtaining financing for the company. If she decides to fire this vice president and he is the informer, she estimates that the company will gain $500,000. If she decides to fire this vice president but he is not the informer, the company will lose his expertise and still have an informer within the staff; the CEO estimates that this outcome would cost her company about $2.5 million. If she decides not to fire this vice president, she estimates that the firm will lose $1.5 million regardless of whether he actually is the informer (since in either case the informer is still with the company). Before deciding whether to fire the vice president for finance, the CEO could order lie detector tests. To avoid possible lawsuits, the lie detector tests would have to be administered to all company employees, at a total cost of $150,000. Another problem she must consider is that the available lie detector tests are not perfectly reliable. In particular, if a person is lying, the test will reveal that the person is lying 95% of the time. Moreover, if a person is not lying, the test will indicate that the person is not lying 85% of the time.

   a. To minimize the expected total cost of managing this difficult situation, what strategy should the CEO adopt?

   b. Should the CEO order the lie detector tests for all of her employees? Explain why or why not.

   c. Determine the maximum amount of money that the CEO should be willing to pay to administer lie detector tests.

49. A customer has approached a bank for a $100,000 1-year loan at a 12% interest rate. If the bank does not approve this loan application, the $100,000 will be invested in bonds that earn a 6% annual return. Without additional information, the bank believes that there is a 4% chance that this customer will default on the loan, assuming that the loan is approved. If the customer defaults on the loan, the bank will lose

$100,000. At a cost of $1000, the bank can thoroughly investigate the customer's credit record and supply a favorable or unfavorable recommendation. Past experience indicates that in cases where the customer did not default on the approved loan, the probability of receiving a favorable recommendation on the basis of the credit investigation was 0.80. Furthermore, in cases where the customer defaulted on the approved loan, the probability of receiving a favorable recommendation on the basis of the credit investigation was 0.25.

a. What course of action should the bank take to maximize its expected profit?

b. Compute and interpret the expected value of sample information (EVSI) in this decision problem.

c. Compute and interpret the expected value of perfect information (EVPI) in this decision problem.

50. A company is considering whether to market a new product. Assume, for simplicity, that if this product is marketed, there are only two possible outcomes: success or failure. The company assesses that the probabilities of these two outcomes are p and $1 - p$, respectively. If the product is marketed and it proves to be a failure, the company will lose $450,000. If the product is marketed and it proves to be a success, the company will gain $750,000. Choosing not to market the product results in no gain or loss for the company. The company is also considering whether to survey prospective buyers of this new product. The results of the consumer survey can be classified as favorable, neutral, or unfavorable. In similar cases where proposed products proved to be market successes, the likelihoods that the survey results were favorable, neutral, and unfavorable were 0.6, 0.3, and 0.1, respectively. In similar cases where proposed products proved to be market failures, the likelihoods that the survey results were favorable, neutral, and unfavorable were 0.1, 0.2, and 0.7, respectively. The total cost of administering this survey is C dollars.

a. Let $p = 0.4$. For which values of C, if any, would this company choose to conduct the consumer survey?

b. Let $p = 0.4$. What is the largest amount that this company would be willing to pay for perfect information about the potential success or failure of the new product?

c. Let $p = 0.5$ and $C = \$15,000$. Find the strategy that maximizes the company's expected earnings in this situation. Does the optimal strategy involve conducting the consumer survey? Explain why or why not.

51. The U.S. government is attempting to determine whether immigrants should be tested for a contagious disease. Let's assume that the decision will be made on a financial basis. Furthermore, assume that each immigrant who is allowed to enter the United States and has the disease costs the country $100,000. Also,

each immigrant who is allowed to enter the United States and does not have the disease will contribute $10,000 to the national economy. Finally, assume that x percent of all potential immigrants have the disease. The U.S. government can choose to admit all immigrants, admit no immigrants, or test immigrants for the disease before determining whether they should be admitted. It costs T dollars to test a person for the disease; the test result is either positive or negative. A person who does not have the disease *always* tests negative. However, 20% of all people who *do* have the disease test negative. The government's goal is to maximize the expected net financial benefits per potential immigrant.

a. Let $x = 10$ (i.e., 10%). What is the largest value of T at which the U.S. government will choose to test potential immigrants for the disease?

b. How does your answer to the question in part **a** change when x increases to 15?

c. Let $x = 10$ and $T = \$100$. Find the government's optimal strategy in this case.

d. Let $x = 10$ and $T = \$100$. Compute and interpret the expected value of perfect information (EVPI) in this decision problem.

52. The senior executives of an oil company are trying to decide whether to drill for oil in a particular field in the Gulf of Mexico. It costs the company $300,000 to drill in the selected field. Company executives believe that if oil is found in this field its estimated value will be $1,800,000. At present, this oil company believes that there is a 48% chance that the selected field actually contains oil. Before drilling, the company can hire a geologist at a cost of $30,000 to prepare a report that contains a recommendation regarding drilling in the selected field. There is a 55% chance that the geologist will issue a favorable recommendation and a 45% chance that the geologist will issue an unfavorable recommendation. Given a favorable recommendation from the geologist, there is a 75% chance that the field actually contains oil. Given an unfavorable recommendation from the geologist, there is a 15% chance that the field actually contains oil.

a. Assuming that this oil company wishes to maximize its expected net earnings, determine its optimal strategy through the use of a decision tree.

b. Compute and interpret EVSI for this decision problem.

c. Compute and interpret EVPI for this decision problem.

53. A local certified public accountant must decide which of two copying machines to purchase for her expanding business. The cost of purchasing the first machine is $3100, and the cost of maintaining the first machine each year is uncertain. The CPA's office manager believes that the annual maintenance cost for the first machine will be $0, $150, or $300 with probabilities

0.325, 0.475, and 0.20, respectively. The cost of purchasing the second machine is $3000, and the cost of maintaining the second machine through a guaranteed maintenance agreement is $225 per year. Before the purchase decision is made, the CPA can hire an experienced copying machine repairperson to evaluate the quality of the first machine. Such an evaluation would cost the CPA $60. If the repairperson believes that the first machine is satisfactory, there is a 65% chance that its annual maintenance cost will be $0 and a 35% chance that its annual maintenance cost will be $150. If, however, the repairperson believes that the first machine is unsatisfactory, there is a 60% chance that its annual maintenance cost will be $150 and a 40% chance that its annual maintenance cost will be $300. The CPA's office manager believes that the repairperson will issue a satisfactory report on the first machine with probability 0.50.

a. Provided that the CPA wishes to minimize the expected total cost of purchasing and maintaining one of these two machines for a 1-year period, which machine should she purchase? When, if ever, would it be worthwhile for the CPA to obtain the repairperson's review of the first machine?

b. Compute and interpret EVSI for this decision problem.

c. Compute and interpret EVPI for this decision problem.

54. FineHair is developing a new product to promote hair growth in cases of male pattern baldness. If FineHair markets the new product and it is successful, the company will earn $500,000 in additional profit. If the marketing of this new product proves to be unsuccessful, the company will lose $350,000 in development and marketing costs. In the past, similar products have been successful 60% of the time. At a cost of $50,000, the effectiveness of the new restoration product can be thoroughly tested. If the results of such testing are favorable, there is an 80% chance that the marketing efforts of this new product will be successful. If the results of such testing are not favorable, there is a mere 30% chance that the marketing efforts of this new product will be successful. FineHair currently believes that the probability of receiving favorable test results is 0.60.

a. Identify the strategy that maximizes FineHair's expected net earnings in this situation.

b. Compute and interpret EVSI for this decision problem.

c. Compute and interpret EVPI for this decision problem.

55. Hank is considering placing a bet on the upcoming showdown between the Penn State and Michigan football teams in State College. The winner of this contest will represent the Big Ten Conference in the Rose Bowl on New Year's Day. Without any additional in-

formation, Hank believes that Penn State has a 0.475 chance of winning this big game. If he wins the bet, he will win $500; if he loses the bet, he will lose $550. Before placing his bet, he may decide to pay his friend Al, who happens to be a football sportswriter for the *Philadelphia Enquirer*, $50 for Al's expert prediction on the game. Assume that Al predicts that Penn State will win similar games 55% of the time, and that Michigan will win similar games 45% of the time. Furthermore, Hank knows that when Al predicts that Penn State will win, there is a 70% chance that Penn State will indeed win the football game. Finally, when Al predicts that Michigan will win, there is a 20% chance that Penn State will proceed to win the upcoming game.

a. To maximize his expected profit from this betting opportunity, how should Hank proceed?

b. Compute and interpret EVSI for this decision problem.

c. Compute and interpret EVPI for this decision problem.

56. A product manager at Clean & Brite (C&B) seeks to determine whether her company should market a new brand of toothpaste. If this new product succeeds in the marketplace, C&B estimates that it could earn $1,800,000 in future profits from the sale of the new toothpaste. If this new product fails, however, the company expects that it could lose approximately $750,000. If C&B chooses not to market this new brand, the product manager believes that there would be little, if any, impact on the profits earned through sales of C&B's other products. The manager has estimated that the new toothpaste brand will succeed with probability 0.50. Before making her decision regarding this toothpaste product, the manager can spend $75,000 on a market research study. Such a study of consumer preferences will yield either a positive recommendation with probability 0.50 or a negative recommendation with probability 0.50. Given a positive recommendation to market the new product, the new brand will eventually succeed in the marketplace with probability 0.75. Given a negative recommendation regarding the marketing of the new product, the new brand will eventually succeed in the marketplace with probability 0.25.

a. To maximize expected profit, what course of action should the C&B product manager take?

b. Compute and interpret EVSI for this decision problem.

c. Compute and interpret EVPI for this decision problem.

57. Ford is going to produce a new vehicle, the Pioneer, and wants to determine the amount of annual capacity it should build. Ford's goal is to maximize the profit from this vehicle over the next 10 years. Each vehicle will sell for $13,000 and incur a variable production

cost of $10,000. Building 1 unit of annual capacity will cost $3000. Each unit of capacity will also cost $1000 per year to maintain, even if the capacity is unused. Demand for the Pioneer is unknown but marketing estimates the distribution of annual demand to be as shown in the file **P08_57.xls**. Assume that the number of units sold during a year is the minimum of capacity and annual demand.

    a. Explain why a capacity of 1,300,000 is not a good choice.

    b. Which capacity level should Ford choose?

58. Pizza King (PK) and Noble Greek (NG) are competitive pizza chains. Pizza King believes there is a 25% chance that NG will charge $6 per pizza, a 50% chance NG will charge $8 per pizza, and a 25% chance that NG will charge $10 per pizza. If PK charges price p_1 and NG charges price p_2, PK will sell $100 + 25(p_2 - p_1)$ pizzas. It costs PK $4 to make a pizza. PK is considering charging $5, $6, $7, $8, or $9 per pizza. To maximize its expected profit, what price should PK charge for a pizza?

59. Many decision problems have the following simple structure. A decision maker has two possible decisions, 1 and 2. If decision 1 is made, a *sure* cost of c is incurred. If decision 2 is made, there are two possible outcomes, with costs c_1 and c_2 and probabilities p and $1 - p$. We assume that $c_1 < c < c_2$. The idea is that decision 1, the riskless decision, has a "moderate" cost, whereas decision 2, the risky decision, has a "low" cost c_1 or a "high" cost c_2.

    a. Find the decision maker's cost table, that is, the cost for each possible decision and each possible outcome.

    b. Calculate the expected cost from the risky decision.

    c. List as many scenarios as you can think of that have this structure. (Here's an example to get you started. Think of insurance, where you pay a sure premium to avoid a large possible loss.)

60. A nuclear power company is deciding whether to build a nuclear power plant at Diablo Canyon or at Roy Rogers City. The cost of building the power plant is $10 million at Diablo and $20 million at Roy Rogers City. If the company builds at Diablo, however, and an earthquake occurs at Diablo during the next 5 years, construction will be terminated and the company will lose $10 million (and will still have to build a power plant at Roy Rogers City). Without further expert information the company believes there is a 20% chance that an earthquake will occur at Diablo during the next 5 years. For $1 million, a geologist can be hired to analyze the fault structure at Diablo Canyon. She will predict either that an earthquake will occur or that an earthquake will not occur. The geologist's past record indicates that she will predict an earthquake on 95% of the occasions for which an

earthquake will occur and no earthquake on 90% of the occasions for which an earthquake will not occur. Should the power company hire the geologist? Also, calculate and interpret EVSI and EVPI.

61. Consider again Techware's decision problem described in Problem 38. Suppose now that Techware's utility function of net revenue x (measured in dollars), earned from the given marketing opportunities, is $U(x) = 1 - e^{-x/350000}$.

    a. Find the course of action that maximizes Techware's expected utility. How does this optimal decision compare to the optimal decision with an EMV criterion? Explain any difference in the two optimal decisions.

    b. Repeat part **a** when Techware's utility function is $U(x) = 1 - e^{-x/50000}$.

62. Consider again the bank's customer loan decision problem in Problem 49. Suppose now that the bank's utility function of profit x (in dollars) is $U(x) = 1 - e^{-x/150000}$. Find the strategy that maximizes the bank's expected utility in this case. How does this optimal strategy compare to the optimal decision with an EMV criterion? Explain any difference in two optimal strategies.

Skill-Extending Problems

63. Mr. Maloy has just bought a new $30,000 sport utility vehicle. As a reasonably safe driver, he believes that there is only about a 5% chance of being in an accident in the forthcoming year. If he is involved in an accident, the damage to his new vehicle depends on the severity of the accident. The probability distribution for the range of possible accidents and the corresponding damage amounts (in dollars) are given in the file **P08_63.xls**. Mr. Maloy is trying to decide whether he is willing to pay $170 each year for collision insurance with a $300 deductible. Note that with this type of insurance, he pays the *first* $300 in damages if he causes an accident and the insurance company pays the remainder.

    a. Formulate a payoff table that specifies the cost (in dollars) associated with each possible decision and type of accident.

    b. Use PrecisionTree to identify the strategy that minimizes Mr. Maloy's annual expected cost.

    c. Perform a sensitivity analysis on the optimal decision and summarize your findings. In response to which model inputs is the expected earnings value most sensitive?

64. The purchasing agent for a microcomputer manufacturer is currently negotiating a purchase agreement for a particular electronic component with a given supplier. This component is produced in lots of 1000, and the cost of purchasing a lot is $30,000. Unfortunately, past experience indicates that this supplier has occasionally shipped defective components to its customers. Specifically, the proportion of defective components supplied by this supplier is described by the probability distribution given in the file **P08_64.xls**. While the microcomputer manufacturer can repair a defective component at a cost of $20 each, the purchasing agent is intrigued to learn that this supplier will now assume the cost of replacing defective components in excess of the first 100 faulty items found in a given lot. This guarantee may be purchased by the microcomputer manufacturer prior to the receipt of a given lot at a cost of $1000 per lot. The purchasing agent is interested in determining whether it is worthwhile for her company to purchase the supplier's guarantee policy.

    a. Formulate a payoff table that specifies the microcomputer manufacturer's total cost (in dollars) of purchasing and repairing (if necessary) a complete lot of components for each possible decision and each outcome with respect to the proportion of defective items.

    b. Use PrecisionTree to identify the strategy that minimizes the expected total cost of achieving a complete lot of satisfactory microcomputer components.

    c. Perform a sensitivity analysis on the optimal decision and summarize your findings. In response to which model inputs is the expected earnings value most sensitive?

65. A home appliance company is interested in marketing an innovative new product. The company must decide whether to manufacture this product essentially on its own or employ a subcontractor to manufacture it. The file **P08_65.xls** contains the estimated probability distribution of the cost of manufacturing 1 unit of this new product (in dollars) under the alternative that the home appliance company produces the item on its own. This file also contains the estimated probability distribution of the cost of purchasing 1 unit of this new product (in dollars) under the alternative that the home appliance company commissions a subcontractor to produce the item.

    a. Assuming that the home appliance company seeks to minimize the expected unit cost of manufacturing or buying the new product, use PrecisionTree to see whether the company should make the new product or buy it from a subcontractor.

    b. Perform a sensitivity analysis on the optimal expected cost. Under what conditions, if any, would the home appliance company select an alternative different from the one you identified in part **a**?

66. A grapefruit farmer in central Florida is trying to decide whether to take protective action to limit damage to his crop in the event that the overnight temperature falls to a level well below freezing. He is concerned that if the temperature falls sufficiently low and he

fails to make an effort to protect his grapefruit trees, he runs the risk of losing his entire crop, which is worth approximately $75,000. Based on the latest forecast issued by the National Weather Service, the farmer estimates that there is a 60% chance that he will lose his entire crop if it is left unprotected. Alternatively, the farmer can insulate his fruit by spraying water on all of the trees in his orchards. This action, which would likely cost the farmer C dollars, would prevent total devastation but might not completely protect the grapefruit trees from incurring some damage as a result of the unusually cold overnight temperatures. The file **P08_66.xls** contains the assessed distribution of possible damages (in dollars) to the insulated fruit in light of the cold weather forecast. Of course, this farmer seeks to minimize the expected total cost of coping with the threatening weather.

    a. Find the maximum value of C below which the farmer will choose to insulate his crop in hopes of limiting damage as result of the unusually cold weather.

    b. Set C equal to the value identified in part **a**. Perform sensitivity analysis to determine under what conditions, if any, the farmer might be better off not spraying his grapefruit trees and taking his chances in spite of the threat to his crop.

67. A retired partner from Goldman Sachs has 1 million dollars available to invest in particular stocks or bonds. Each investment's annual rate of return depends on the state of the economy in the forthcoming year. The file **P08_67.xls** contains the distribution of returns for these stocks and bonds as a function of the economy's state in the coming year. This investor wants to allocate her $1 million to maximize her expected total return 1 year from now.

    a. If $X = Y = 15\%$, find the optimal investment strategy for this investor.

    b. For which values of X (where $10\% < X < 20\%$) and Y (where $12.5\% < Y < 17.5\%$), if any, will this investor prefer to place all of her available funds in the given stocks to maximize her expected total return one year from now?

    c. For which values of X (where $10\% < X < 20\%$) and Y (where $12.5\% < Y < 17.5\%$), if any, will this investor prefer to place all of her available funds in the given bonds to maximize her expected total return one year from now?

68. A city in Ohio is considering replacing its fleet of gasoline-powered automobiles with electric cars. The manufacturer of the electric cars claims that this municipality will experience significant cost savings over the life of the fleet if it chooses to pursue the conversion. If the manufacturer is correct, the city will save about $1.5 million dollars. If the new technology employed within the electric cars is faulty, as some critics suggest, the conversion to electric cars will cost the city $675,000. A third possibility is that less serious problems will arise and the city will break even with the conversion. A consultant hired by the city estimates that the probabilities of these three outcomes are 0.30, 0.30, and 0.40, respectively. The city has an opportunity to implement a pilot program that would indicate the potential cost or savings resulting from a switch to electric cars. The pilot program involves renting a small number of electric cars for 3 months and running them under typical conditions. This program would cost the city $75,000. The city's consultant believes that the results of the pilot program would be significant but not conclusive; she submits the values in the file **P08_68.xls**, a compilation of probabilities based on the experience of other cities, to support her contention. For example, the first row of her table indicates that given that a conversion to electric cars actually results in a savings of $1.5 million, the conditional probabilities that the pilot program will indicate that the city saves money, loses money, and breaks even are 0.6, 0.1, and 0.3, respectively.

a. What actions should this city take to maximize the expected savings?

b. Should the city implement the pilot program at a cost of $75,000?

c. Compute and interpret EVSI for this decision problem.

69. A manufacturer must decide whether to extend credit to a retailer who would like to open an account with the firm. Past experience with new accounts indicates that 45% are high-risk customers, 35% are moderate-risk customers, and 20% are low-risk customers. If credit is extended, the manufacturer can expect to lose $60,000 with a high-risk customer, make $50,000 with a moderate-risk customer, and make $100,000 with a low-risk customer. If the manufacturer decides not to extend credit to a customer, the manufacturer neither makes nor loses any money. Prior to making a credit extension decision, the manufacturer can obtain a credit rating report on the retailer at a cost of $2000. The credit agency concedes that its rating procedure is not completely reliable. In particular, the credit rating procedure will rate a low-risk customer as a moderate-risk customer with probability 0.10 and as a high-risk customer with probability 0.05. Furthermore, the given rating procedure will rate a moderate-risk customer as a low-risk customer with probability 0.06 and as a high-risk customer with probability 0.07. Finally, the rating procedure will rate a high-risk customer as a low-risk customer with probability 0.01 and as a moderate-risk customer with probability 0.05.

a. Find the strategy that maximizes the manufacturer's expected net earnings.

b. Should the manufacturer routinely obtain credit rating reports on those retailers who seek credit approval? Why or why not?

c. Compute and interpret EVSI for this decision problem.

70. A television network earns an average of $1.6 million each season from a hit program and loses an average of $400,000 each season on a program that turns out to be a flop. Of all programs picked up by this network in recent years, 25% turn out to be hits and 75% turn out to be flops. At a cost of C dollars, a market research firm will analyze a pilot episode of a prospective program and issue a report predicting whether the given program will end up being a hit. If the program is actually going to be a hit, there is a 90% chance that the market researchers will predict the program to be a hit. If the program is actually going to be a flop, there is a 20% chance that the market researchers will predict the program to be a hit.

a. Assuming that $C = \$160,000$, identify the strategy that maximizes this television network's expected profit in responding to a newly proposed television program.

b. What is the maximum value of C that this television network should be willing to incur in choosing to hire the market research firm?

c. Compute and interpret EVPI for this decision problem.

71. A publishing company is trying to decide whether to publish a new business law textbook. Based on a careful reading of the latest draft of the manuscript, the publisher's senior editor in the business textbook division assesses the distribution of possible payoffs earned by publishing this new book. The file **P08_71.xls** contains this probability distribution. Before making a final decision regarding the publication of the book, the editor can learn more about the text's potential for success by thoroughly surveying business law instructors teaching at universities across the country. Historical frequencies based on similar surveys administered in the past are also provided in this file.

a. Find the strategy that maximizes the publisher's expected payoff (in dollars).

b. What is the most (in dollars) that the publisher should be willing to pay to conduct a new survey of business law instructors?

c. If the actual cost of conducting the given survey is less than the amount identified in part **a**, what should the publisher do?

d. Assuming that a survey could be constructed that provides "perfect information" to the publisher, how much should the company be willing to pay to acquire and implement such a survey?

72. Sharp Outfits is trying to decide whether to ship some customer orders now via UPS or wait until after the threat of another UPS strike is over. If Sharp Outfits decides to ship the requested merchandise now and the UPS strike takes place, the company will incur

$60,000 in delay and shipping costs. If Sharp Outfits decides to ship the customer orders via UPS and no strike occurs, the company will incur $4000 in shipping costs. If Sharp Outfits decides to postpone shipping its customer orders via UPS, the company will incur $10,000 in delay costs regardless of whether UPS goes on strike. Let p represent the probability that UPS will go on strike and impact Sharp Outfits's shipments.

a. For which values of p, if any, does Sharp Outfits minimize its expected total cost by choosing to postpone shipping its customer orders via UPS?

b. Suppose now that, at a cost of $1000, Sharp Outfits can purchase information regarding the likelihood of a UPS strike in the near future. Based on similar strike threats in the past, the probability that this information indicates the occurrence of a UPS strike is 27.5%. If the purchased information indicates the occurrence of a UPS strike, the chance of a strike actually occurring is 0.105/0.275. If the purchased information does not indicate the occurrence of a UPS strike, the chance of a strike actually occurring is 0.680/0.725. Provided that $p = 0.15$, what strategy should Sharp Outfits pursue to minimize its expected total cost?

c. Continuing part b, compute and interpret EVSI when $p = 0.15$.

d. Continuing part b, compute and interpret the EVPI when $p = 0.15$.

73. An investor has $10,000 in assets and can choose between two different investments. If she invests in the first investment opportunity, there is an 80% chance that she will increase her assets by $590,000 and a 20% chance that she will increase her assets by $190,000. If she invests in the second investment opportunity, there is a 50% chance that she will increase her assets by $1.19 million and a 50% chance that she will increase her assets by $1000. This investor has an exponential utility function for final assets with a risk tolerance parameter equal to $600,000. Which investment opportunity will she prefer?

74. City officials in Fort Lauderdale, Florida, are trying to decide whether to evacuate coastal residents in anticipation of a major hurricane that may make landfall near their city within the next 48 hours. Based on previous studies, it is estimated that it will cost approximately $1 million to evacuate the residents living along the coast of this major metropolitan area. However, if city officials choose not to evacuate their residents and the storm strikes Fort Lauderdale, there would likely be some deaths as a result of the hurricane's storm surge along the coast. Although city officials are reluctant to place an economic value on the loss of human life resulting from such a storm, they realize that it may ultimately be necessary to do so to make a sound judgment in this situation. Prior to

making the evacuation decision, city officials consult hurricane experts at the National Hurricane Center in Coral Gables regarding the accuracy of past predictions. They learn that in similar past cases, hurricanes that were *predicted* to make landfall near a particular coastal location actually did so 60% of the time. Moreover, they learn that in past similar cases hurricanes that were predicted *not* to make landfall near a particular coastal location actually did so 20% of the time. Finally, in response to similar threats in the past, weather forecasters have issued predictions of a major hurricane making landfall near a particular coastal location 40% of the time.

a. Let L be the economic valuation of the loss of human life resulting from a coastal strike by the hurricane. Employ a decision tree to help these city officials make a decision that minimizes the expected cost of responding to the threat of the impending storm as a function of L. To proceed, you might begin by choosing an initial value of L and then perform sensitivity analysis on the optimal decision by varying this model parameter. Summarize your findings.

b. For which values of L will these city officials *always* choose to evacuate the coastal residents, regardless of the Hurricane Center's prediction?

75. A homeowner wants to decide whether he should install an electronic heat pump in his home. Given that the cost of installing a new heat pump is fairly large, the homeowner would like to do so only if he can count on being able to recover the initial expense over *five* consecutive years of cold winter weather. After reviewing historical data on the operation of heat pumps in various kinds of winter weather, he computes the expected annual costs of heating his home during the winter months with and without a heat pump in operation. These cost figures are shown in the file **P08_75.xls**. The probabilities of experiencing a mild, normal, colder than normal, and severe winter are $0.2(1 - x)$, $0.5(1 - x)$, $0.3(1 - x)$, and x, respectively.

a. Given that $x = 0.1$, what is the most that the homeowner is willing to pay for the heat pump?

b. If the heat pump costs $500, how large must x be before the homeowner decides it is economically worthwhile to install the heat pump?

c. Given that $x = 0.1$, compute and interpret EVPI when the heat pump costs $500.

d. Repeat part c when $x = 0.15$.

76. Many men over 50 take the PSA blood test. The purpose of the PSA test is to detect prostate cancer early. Dr. Rene Labrie of Quebec conducted a study to determine whether the PSA test can actually prevent cancer deaths. In 1989, Dr. Labrie randomly divided all male registered voters between 45 and 80 in Quebec City into two groups. Two-thirds of the men were

asked to be tested for prostate cancer and one-third were not asked. Eventually, 8137 men were screened for prostate cancer (PSA plus digital rectal exam) in 1989; 38,056 men were not screened. By 1997 only 5 of the screened men had died of prostate cancer whereas 137 of the men who were not screened had died of prostate cancer (*Source*: *New York Times*, May 19, 1998).

   a. Discuss why this study seems to indicate that screening for prostate cancer saves lives.

   b. Despite the results of this study, many doctors are not convinced that early screening for prostate cancer saves lives. Can you see why they doubt the conclusions of the study?

77. Sarah Chang is the owner of a small electronics company. In 6 months a proposal is due for an electronic timing system for the 2008 Olympic Games. For several years, Chang's company has been developing a new microprocessor, a critical component in a timing system that would be superior to any product currently on the market. However, progress in research and development has been slow, and Chang is unsure about whether her staff can produce the microprocessor in time. If they succeed in developing the microprocessor (probability p_1), there is an excellent chance (probability p_2) that Chang's company will win the $1 million Olympic contract. If they do not, there is a small chance (probability p_3) that she will still be able to win the same contract with an alternative, inferior timing system that has already been developed. If she continues the project, Chang must invest $200,000 in research and development. In addition, making a proposal (which she will decide whether to do after seeing whether the R&D is successful or not) requires developing a prototype timing system at an additional cost of $50,000. Finally, if Chang wins the contract, the finished product will cost an additional $150,000 to produce.

   a. Develop a decision tree that can be used to solve Chang's problem. You can assume in this part of the problem that she is using EMV (of her net profit) as a decision criterion. Build the tree so that she can enter any values for p_1, p_2, and p_3 (in input cells) and automatically see her optimal EMV and optimal strategy from the tree.

   b. If $p_2 = 0.8$ and $p_3 = 0.1$, what value of p_1 makes Chang indifferent between abandoning the project and going ahead with it?

   c. How much would Chang be willing to pay the Olympic organization (now) to guarantee her the contract in the case where her company is successful in developing the contract? (This guarantee is in force only if she is successful in developing the product.) Assume $p_1 = 0.4$, $p_2 = 0.8$, and $p_3 = 0.1$.

   d. Suppose now that this a "big" project for Chang. Therefore, she decides to use expected utility as

her criterion, with an exponential utility function. Using some trial and error, see which risk tolerance changes her initial decision from "go ahead" to "abandon" when $p_1 = 0.4$, $p_2 = 0.8$, and $p_3 = 0.1$.

78. Suppose an investor has the opportunity to buy the following contract, a stock call option, on March 1. The contract allows him to buy 100 shares of ABC stock at the end of March, April, or May at a guaranteed price of $50 per share. He can "exercise" this option at most once. For example, if he purchases the stock at the end of March, he can't purchase more in April or May at the guaranteed price. The current price of the stock is $50. Each month, we assume the stock price either goes up by a dollar (with probability 0.6) or goes down by a dollar (with probability 0.4). If the investor buys the contract, he is hoping that the stock price will go up. The reasoning is that if he buys the contract, the price goes up to $51, and he buys the stock (that is, he exercises his option) for $50, then he can turn around and sell the stock for $51 and make a profit of $1 per share. On the other hand, if the stock price goes down, he doesn't have to exercise his option; he can just throw the contract away.

   a. Use a decision tree to find the investor's optimal strategy (that is, when he should exercise the option), *assuming* he purchases the contract.

   b. How much should he be willing to pay for such a contract?

79. The Ventron Engineering Company has just been awarded a $2 million development contract by the U.S. Army Aviation Systems Command to develop a blade spar for its Heavy Lift Helicopter program. The blade spar is a metal tube that runs the length of and provides strength to the helicopter blade. Due to the unusual length and size of the Heavy Lift Helicopter blade, Ventron is unable to produce a single-piece blade spar of the required dimensions, using existing extrusion equipment and material. The engineering department has prepared two alternatives for developing the blade spar: (1) sectioning or (2) an improved extrusion process. Ventron must decide which process to use. (Backing out of the contract at any point is not an option.) The risk report has been prepared by the engineering department. The information from it is explained next.

    The sectioning option involves joining several shorter lengths of extruded metal into a blade spar of sufficient length. This work will require extensive testing and rework over a 12-month period at a total cost of $1.8 million. Although this process will definitely produce an adequate blade spar, it merely represents an extension of existing technology.

    To improve the extrusion process, on the other hand, it will be necessary to perform two steps: (1) improve the material used, at a cost of $300,000, and

(2) modify the extrusion press, at a cost of $960,000. The first step will require 6 months of work, and if this first step is successful, the second step will require another 6 months of work. If both steps are successful, the blade spar will be available at that time, that is, a year from now. The engineers estimate that the probabilities of succeeding in steps 1 and 2 are 0.9 and 0.75, respectively. However, if either step is unsuccessful (which will be known only in 6 months for step 1 and in a year for step 2), Ventron will have no alternative but to switch to the sectioning process—and incur the sectioning cost on top of any costs already incurred.

Development of the blade spar must be completed within 18 months to avoid holding up the rest of the contract. If necessary, the sectioning work can be done on an accelerated basis in a 6-month period, but the cost of sectioning will then increase from $1.8 million to $2.4 million. Frankly, the Director of Engineering, Dr. Smith, wants to try developing the improved extrusion process. This is not only cheaper (if successful) for the current project, but its expected side benefits for future projects could be sizable. Although these side benefits are difficult to gauge, Dr. Smith's best guess is an additional $2 million. (Of course, these side benefits are obtained only if both steps of the modified extrusion process are completed successfully.)

a. Develop a decision tree to maximize Ventron's EMV. This includes the revenue from this project, the side benefits (if applicable) from an improved extrusion process, and relevant costs. You don't need to worry about the time value of money; that is, no discounting or NPVs are required. Summarize your findings in words in the spreadsheet.

b. What value of side benefits would make Ventron indifferent between the two alternatives?

c. How much would Ventron be willing to pay, right now, for perfect information about both steps of the improved extrusion process? (This information would tell Ventron, right now, the ultimate success and failure outcomes of both steps.)

80. Based on Balson et al. (1992). An electric utility company is trying to decide whether to replace its PCB transformer in a generating station with a new and safer transformer. To evaluate this decision, the utility needs information about the likelihood of an incident, such as a fire, the cost of such an incident, and the cost of replacing the unit. Suppose that the total cost of replacement as a present value is $75,000. If the transformer is replaced, there is virtually no chance of a fire. However, if the current transformer is retained, the probability of a fire is assessed to be 0.0025. If a fire occurs, then the cleanup cost could be high ($80 million) or low ($20 million). The probability of a high cleanup cost, given that a fire occurs, is assessed at 0.2.

a. If the company uses EMV as its decision criterion, should it replace the transformer?

b. Perform a sensitivity analysis on the key parameters of the problem that are difficult to assess, namely, the probability of a fire, the probability of a high cleanup cost, and the high and low cleanup costs. Does the optimal decision from part **a** remain optimal for a "wide" range of these parameters?

c. Do you believe EMV is the correct criterion to use in this type of problem involving environmental accidents?

The Jogger Shoe Company is trying to decide whether to make a change in its most popular brand of running shoes. The new style would cost the same to produce, and it would be priced the same, but it would incorporate a new kind of lacing system that (according to its marketing research people) would make it more popular.

There is a fixed cost of $300,000 of changing over to the new style. The unit contribution to before-tax profit for either style is $8. The tax rate is 35%. Also, because the fixed cost can be depreciated and will therefore affect the after-tax cash flow, we need a depreciation method. We assume it is straight-line depreciation.

The current demand for these shoes is 190,000 pairs annually. The company assumes this demand will continue for the next 3 years if the current style is retained. However, there is uncertainty about demand for the new style, if it is introduced. The company models this uncertainty by assuming a normal distribution in year 1, with mean 220,000 and standard deviation 20,000. The company also assumes that this demand, whatever it is, will remain constant for the next 3 years. However, if demand in year 1 for the new style is sufficiently low, the company can always switch back to the current style and realize an annual demand of 190,000. The company wants a strategy that will maximize the expected net present value (NPV) of total cash flow for the next 3 years, where a 15% interest rate is used for the purpose of calculating NPV. ■

The Westhouser Paper Company in the state of Washington currently has an option to purchase a piece of land with good timber forest on it. It is now May 1, and the current price of the land is $2.2 million. Westhouser does not actually need the timber from this land until the beginning of July, but its top executives fear that another company might buy the land between now and the beginning of July. They assess that there is 1 chance out of 20 that a competitor will buy the land during May. If this does not occur, they assess that there is 1 chance out of 10 that the competitor will buy the land during June. If Westhouser does not take advantage of its current option, it can attempt to buy the land at the beginning of June or the beginning of July, provided that it is still available.

Westhouser's incentive for delaying the purchase is that its financial experts believe there is a good chance that the price of the land will fall significantly in one or both of the next 2 months. They assess the possible price decreases and their probabilities in Table 8.7 and Table 8.8. Table 8.7 shows the probabilities of the possible price decreases during May. Table 8.8 lists the *conditional* probabilities of the possible price decreases in June, *given* the price decrease in May. For example, it indicates that if the price decrease in May is $60,000, then the possible price decreases in June are $0, $30,000, and $60,000 with respective probabilities 0.6, 0.2, and 0.2.

If Westhouser purchases the land, it believes that it can gross $3 million. (This does not count the cost of purchasing the land.) But if it does not purchase the land, Westhouser believes that it can make $650,000 from alternative investments. What should the company do?

Table 8.7 Distribution of Price Decrease in May

Price Decrease	Probability
$0	0.5
$60,000	0.3
$120,000	0.2

Table 8.8 Distribution of Price Decrease in June

Price Decrease in May					
$0		**$60,000**		**$120,000**	
June Decrease	**Probability**	**June Decrease**	**Probability**	**June Decrease**	**Probability**
$0	0.3	$0	0.6	$0	0.7
$60,000	0.6	$30,000	0.2	$20,000	0.2
$120,000	0.1	$60,000	0.2	$40,000	0.1

Biotechnical Engineering specializes in developing new chemicals for agricultural applications. The company is a pioneer in using the sterile-male procedure to control insect infestations. It operates several laboratories around the world where insects are raised and then exposed to extra-large doses of radiation, making them sterile. As an alternative to chlorinated hydrocarbon pesticides, such as DDT, the sterile-male procedure has been used more frequently with a good track record of success, most notably with the Mediterranean Fruitfly (or Medfly).

That pest was controlled in California through the release of treated flies on the premise that the sterile male flies would compete with fertile wild males for mating opportunities. Any female that has mated with a sterile fly will lay eggs that do not hatch. The California Medfly campaigns required about five successive releases of sterile males—at intervals timed to coincide with the time for newly hatched flies to reach adulthood—before the Medfly was virtually eliminated. (Only sterile flies were subsequently caught in survey traps.) The effectiveness of the sterile-male procedure was enhanced by the release of malathion poisonous bait just a few days before each release, cutting down on the number of viable wild adults.

More recently, Biotechnical Engineering has had particular success in using genetic engineering to duplicate various insect hormones and pheromones (scent attractants). Of particular interest is the application of such methods against the Gypsy Moth, a notorious pest that attacks trees. The company has developed synthetic versions of both hormones and pheromones for that moth. It has a synthetic sexual attractant that male moths can detect at great distances. Most promising is the synthetic juvenile hormone.

The juvenile hormone controls moth metamorphosis, determining the timing for the transformation of a caterpillar into a chrysalis and then into an adult. Too much juvenile hormone wreaks havoc with this process, causing caterpillars to turn into freak adults that cannot reproduce.

Biotechnical Engineering has received a government contract to test its new technology in an actual eradication campaign. The company will participate in a small-scale campaign against the Gypsy Moth in the state of Oregon. Since the pest is so damaging, Dr. June Scribner, the administrator in charge, is considering using DDT as an alternative procedure. Of course, that banned substance is only available for government emergency use because of the environmental damage it may cause. In addition to spraying with DDT, two other procedures may be employed: (1) using Biotechnical's scent lure, followed by release of sterile males, and (2) spraying with the company's juvenile hormone to prevent larvae from developing into adults. Dr. Scribner wants to select the method that yields the best expected payoff, described below.

Although both of the newer procedures are known to work under laboratory conditions, there is some uncertainty about successful propagation of the chemicals in the wild and about the efficacy of the sterile-male procedure with moths.

If the scent-lure program is launched at a cost of $5 million, Biotechnical claims that it will have a 50–50 chance of leaving a low number of native males versus a high number. Once the results of that phase are known, a later choice must be made to spray with DDT or to release sterile males; the cost of the sterilization and delivery of the insects to the countryside is an additional $5 million. But if this two-phase program is successful, the net present value of the worth of trees saved is $30 million, including the benefit of avoiding all other forms of environmental damage. The indigenous moth population would be destroyed, and a new infestation could occur only from migrants. Biotechnical's experience with other eradication programs indicates that if the scent lure leaves a small native male population, there is a 90% chance for a successful eradication by using sterile males; otherwise, there is only a 10% chance for success by using sterile males. A failure results in no savings.

[12]This case was written by Lawrence L. Lapin, San Jose State University.

The cost of synthesizing enough juvenile hormone is $3 million. Biotechnical maintains that the probability that the hormone can be effectively disseminated is only 0.20. If it works, the worth of the trees saved and environmental damage avoided will be $50 million. This greater level of savings is possible because of the permanent nature of the solution, since a successful juvenile hormone can then be applied wherever the moths are known to exist, virtually eliminating the pest from the environment. But if the hormone does not work, the DDT must still be used to save the trees.

DDT constitutes only a temporary solution, and the worth of its savings in trees is far less than the worth of either of the esoteric eradication procedures—if they prove successful. To compare alternatives, Dr. Scribner proposes using the net advantage (crop and environmental savings, minus cost) relative to where she would be were she to decide to use DDT at the outset or were she to be forced to spray with it later. (Regardless of the outcome, Biotechnical will be reimbursed for all expenditures. The decision is hers, not the company's.)

Questions

1. Under Biotechnical's proposal, the selection of DDT without even trying the other procedures would lead to a neutral outcome for the government, having zero payoff. Discuss the benefits of Dr. Scribner's proposed payoff measure.

2. Construct Dr. Scribner's decision tree diagram, using the proposed payoff measure.

3. What action will maximize Dr. Scribner's expected payoff?

4. Dr. Scribner is concerned about the assumed 50–50 probability for the two levels of surviving native males following the scent-lure program.
   a. Redo the decision tree analysis to find what action will maximize Dr. Scribner's expected payoff when the probability of low native males is, successively, (1) 0.40 or (2) 0.60 instead.
   b. How is the optimal action affected by the probability level assumed for the low native male outcome?

5. Dr. Scribner is concerned about the assumed 0.20 probability for the dissemination success of the juvenile hormone.
   a. Keeping all other probabilities and cash flows at their original levels, redo the decision tree analysis to find what action will maximize Dr. Scribner's expected payoff when the probability of juvenile hormone success is, successively, (1) 0.15 or (2) 0.25 instead.
   b. How is the optimal action affected by the probability level assumed for the juvenile hormone's success?

6. Dr. Scribner is concerned about the assumed probability levels for the success of the sterile-male procedure.
   a. Keeping all other probabilities and cash flows at their original levels, redo the decision tree analysis to find what action will maximize Dr. Scribner's expected payoff when the sterile-male success probabilities are instead as follows:
      (1) 80% for low native males and 5% for high native males
      (2) 70% for low native males and 15% for high native males
   b. How is the optimal action affected by the probability level assumed for the success of the sterile-male procedure?

7. Dr. Scribner is concerned about the assumed levels for the net present value of the worth of trees saved and damage avoided. She believes these amounts are only accurate within a range of ±10%.
   a. Keeping all other probabilities and cash flows at their original levels, redo the decision tree analysis to find what action will maximize Dr. Scribner's expected payoff when the two net present values are instead, successively, (1) 10% lower or (2) 10% higher than originally assumed.
   b. How is the optimal action affected by the level assumed for the net present values of the savings from using one of the two esoteric Gypsy Moth eradication procedures? ■

Introduction to Simulation Modeling

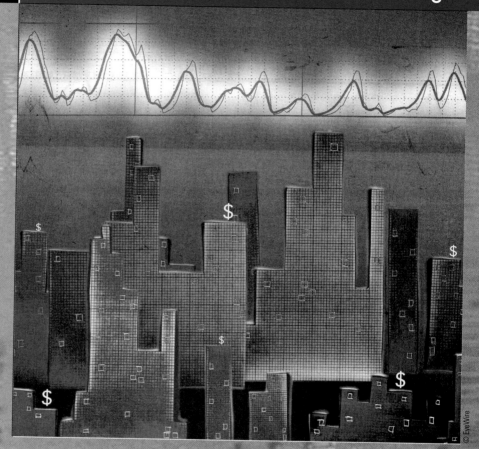

© EyeWire

CALL PROCESSING SIMULATION AT AT&T

Simulation is a versatile tool that allows companies to ask many what-if questions about changes in their systems without actually changing the systems themselves. As reported in the article "AT&T's Call Processing Simulator (CAPS) Operational Design for Inbound Call Centers" by Brigandi et al. (1994), AT&T has used a simulation model called CAPS to help its corporate customers design and operate their call centers. These call centers are the locations into which customers phone, usually using 800 numbers, for customer service, telephone shopping, and other services. The system that is used to handle these calls—the way calls are routed to agents, the number of lines open, the prerecorded messages given to customers, the way customer queues are handled, and so on—can be extremely complex and difficult to understand, let alone optimize. Therefore, AT&T developed the CAPS simulation tool to simulate a variety of operating policies for its corporate customers. AT&T reports that it has used this tool to regain more than $1 billion from a customer base of approximately 2000 corporate customers per year. The CAPS tool has improved the customers' call-center operations dramatically and has helped sell these customers on further AT&T services.

As an example, a major airline's reservation system was supported by 19 separate call centers located near domestic and international airports. In 1992, the airline decided to consolidate its reservations centers. AT&T helped the airline by running a series of CAPS studies to determine the characteristics of efficient, load-balanced call centers that would accomplish the airline's goals. The airline was particularly interested in reducing its 10% blocked-call rate while using its resources more efficiently. The result of the CAPS studies was a $25 million savings in the airline's reservations call-center operations costs and an ability to handle approximately 3000 more reservation sales calls per day. At the same time, AT&T strengthened its position as the 800-number service communications carrier of choice with the airline. Its annual billed network services for the airline increased by 5% on a base of $49 million. ■

9.1 INTRODUCTION

A simulation model is a computer model that imitates a real-life situation. It is like other mathematical models, but it explicitly incorporates uncertainty in one or more input variables. When we run a simulation, we allow these random input variables to take on various values, and we keep track of any resulting output variables of interest. In this way, we are able to see how the outputs vary as a function of the varying inputs.

The fundamental advantage of a simulation model is that it shows us an entire distribution of results, not simply a single bottom-line result. As an example, suppose an automobile manufacturer is planning to develop and market a new model car. The company is ultimately interested in the net present value (NPV) of the profits from this car over the next 10 years. However, there are many uncertainties surrounding this car, including the yearly customer demands for it, the cost of developing it, and others. We could develop a spreadsheet model for the 10-year NPV, using our *best guesses* for these uncertain quantities. We could then report the NPV based on these best guesses, with the implicit understanding that this best-guess NPV is going to occur. However, this analysis would be incomplete and probably misleading—after all, how can we be certain that any *specific* value of NPV will occur? It is much better to treat the uncertainty explicitly with a simulation model. This involves entering probability distributions for the uncertain quantities and seeing how the NPV varies as the uncertain quantities vary.

Each different set of values for the uncertain quantities can be considered a scenario. Simulation allows us to generate many scenarios, each leading to a particular NPV. In the end, we see a whole distribution of NPVs, not a single best guess. We can see what the NPV will be on average, and we can also see worst-case and best-case results.

Simulation models are also useful for determining how sensitive a system is to changes in operating conditions. For example, we might simulate the operations of a supermarket. Once the simulation model has been developed, we can then run it (with suitable modifications) to ask a number of what-if questions. For example, if the supermarket experiences a 20% increase in business, what will happen to the average time customers must wait for service?

A great benefit of computer simulation is that it enables us to answer these types of what-if questions without actually changing (or building) a physical system. For example, the supermarket might want to experiment with the number of open registers to see the effect on customer waiting times. The only way it can *physically* experiment with more registers than it currently owns is to purchase more equipment. Then if it determines that this equipment is not a good investment—customer waiting times do not decrease appreciably—the company is stuck with expensive equipment it doesn't need. Computer simulation is a much less expensive alternative. It provides the company with an electronic replica of what would happen *if* the new equipment were purchased. Then, if the simulation indicates that the new equipment is worth the cost, the company can be confident that purchasing it is the right decision. Otherwise, it can abandon the idea of the new equipment *before* the equipment has been purchased.

Spreadsheet simulation modeling is quite similar to the other modeling applications in this book. We begin with input variables and then relate these with appropriate Excel formulas to produce output variables of interest. The main difference is that simulation uses *random* numbers to drive the whole process. These random numbers are generated with special functions that we will discuss in detail. Each time the spreadsheet recalculates, all of the random numbers change. This gives us the ability to model the logical process once and then use Excel's recalculation ability to generate many different scenarios. By collecting the data from these scenarios, we see which values of the outputs are most likely and we see the best-case and worst-case scenarios.

In this chapter we will illustrate spreadsheet models that can be developed with the basic Excel package. However, because simulation is becoming such an important tool for analyzing real problems, add-ins to Excel have been developed to streamline the process of developing and analyzing simulation models. Therefore, we also introduce @RISK, one of the most popular simulation add-ins. This add-in not only augments the simulation capabilities of Excel, but it also enables users to analyze models much more quickly and easily.

The purpose of this chapter is to introduce basic simulation concepts, show how simulation models can be developed in Excel, and demonstrate the capabilities of the @RISK add-in. Then in the next chapter, armed with the necessary simulation tools, we will explore a number of interesting and useful simulation models.

9.2 REAL APPLICATIONS OF SIMULATION

There are many published applications of simulation. These cover a wide variety of topics, as we discuss briefly in this section.

Burger King developed a simulation model for its restaurants [see Swart and Donno (1981)]. This model was used to answer business questions such as whether the restaurant should open a second drive-through window, and how much customer waiting times would increase if a new sandwich were added to the menu.

Many companies (Cummins Engine, Merck, Procter & Gamble, Kodak, and United Airlines, to name a few) have used simulation to determine which of several possible investment projects they should choose. This is often referred to as **risk analysis**. As an example, consider a situation where a company must choose a single investment. If the future cash flows for each investment project are known with certainty, then most companies advocate choosing the investment with the largest net present value (NPV). However, if future cash flows are not known with certainty, then it is not clear how to choose between competing projects. Using simulation, we can obtain a distribution of the NPV for a project. Then we can answer such questions as:

- Which project is the riskiest?
- What is the probability that an investment will yield at least a 20% return?
- What is the probability that the NPV of an investment will be less than −$1 billion—that is, a loss of more than $1 billion?

To illustrate the use of simulation in corporate finance, we refer to Norton (1994). This article describes a simulation model that was used by Merck, the world's largest drug company, to determine whether Merck should pay $6.6 billion to acquire Medco, a mail-order drug company. The model's inputs included the following:

- possible scenarios for the future of the U.S. health-care system, such as a single-payer system, universal coverage, and so forth
- possible future changes in the mix of generic and brand-name drugs
- probability distributions of profit margins for each product
- assumptions about competitors' reactions to a merger with Medco

A simulation of the Merck model was performed to see how the merger would perform under various possible scenarios. As Merck's CFO, Judy Lewent, says, "Monte Carlo techniques are a very, very powerful tool to get a more intelligent look at a range of outcomes. It's almost never useful in this kind of environment to build a single bullet forecast." The simulation results indicated that the merger with Medco would benefit Merck regardless of the type of health insurance plan (if any) the federal government enacted.

Other applications of simulation include the following:

- Companies must constantly make inventory-ordering decisions in the face of unknown demand. In special cases, analytic (nonsimulation) models can be used to help make decisions. However, when the problems become more complex, simulation often provides the only feasible solution method. We will consider a typical ordering model in this chapter.

- Firms must often bid against competitors to win a contract. If a firm's bid is too low, it will probably win the contract, but it will make very little profit on the contract. On the other hand, if the firm bids too high, it will probably not win the contract at all. The firm must decide how much to bid, although the competitors' bids are uncertain. In the next chapter we will develop a simulation model that can help a firm choose the bid amount that maximizes its expected profit. This provides a different approach to the bidding problem than the one we discussed in Example 8.1 of the previous chapter.

- Large corporate projects can frequently be divided into smaller activities. (A prime example is the Apollo space mission.) To create the project's schedule, the company must estimate the length of time required to finish the project. It might also wish to expedite activities most critical to finishing the project to speed up the schedule. We discussed a version of this problem in Chapter 5, where all of the activity times were assumed to be known with certainty. It is much more realistic to assume that these times can only be estimated with probability distributions. In this case simulation is required. We will examine this topic in the next chapter.

9.3 PROBABILITY DISTRIBUTIONS FOR INPUT VARIABLES

In spreadsheet simulation models, input cells can contain random numbers. Any output cells then vary as these random inputs change.

In this section we discuss the "building blocks" of spreadsheet simulation models. All spreadsheet simulation models are similar to the spreadsheet models we have developed in previous chapters. They have a number of cells that contain values of input variables. The other cells then contain formulas that embed the logic of the model and eventually lead to the output variable(s) of interest. The primary difference between the spreadsheet models we have developed so far and simulation models is that at least one of the input variable cells in a simulation model contains *random numbers*. We can make these random numbers change by recalculating the spreadsheet. Each time the spreadsheet recalculates, the new random values of the inputs produce new values of the outputs. This is the essence of simulation—seeing how outputs vary as random inputs change.

→ EXCEL TIP: *Recalculation Key*

The easiest way to make a spreadsheet recalculate is to press the F9 key. This is often called the "recalc" key. ■

Technically speaking, we do not actually enter random numbers in input cells; we enter *probability distributions*. In general, a probability distribution indicates the possible values of a variable and the probabilities of these values. As a very simple example, we might indicate by an appropriate formula (to be described later) that we want a probability distribution with possible values 50 and 100, and corresponding probabilities 0.7 and 0.3. The effect of this is that if we then press the F9 key repeatedly and watch this input cell, we will see the value 50 about 70% of the time and the value 100 about 30% of the time. No other values besides 50 and 100 will appear.

When we enter a given probability distribution in a random input cell, we are describing the possible values and the probabilities of these values that we believe mirror reality. There are many probability distributions to choose from, and we should always attempt to choose an appropriate distribution for each specific problem. This is not necessarily an easy task. Therefore, we will address it in this section by answering several key questions:

■ What types of probability distributions are available, and why do we choose one probability distribution rather than another in an actual simulation model?

■ Which probability distributions can we use in simulation models, and how do we invoke them with Excel formulas?

In later sections we will address one additional question: Does the choice of input probability distribution really matter—that is, does it have a large effect on the *outputs* from the simulation?

Types of Probability Distributions

It is useful to think of a toolbox that contains the probability distributions you know and understand. As you obtain more experience in simulation modeling, you will naturally add probability distributions to this toolbox that you can then use in *future* simulation models. We will begin by adding a few useful probability distributions to this toolbox. However, before adding any specific distributions, we look at some important characteristics of probability distributions in general. These include the following distinctions:

■ Discrete versus continuous
■ Symmetric versus skewed
■ Bounded versus unbounded
■ Positive versus not necessarily positive

Discrete versus Continuous

A probability distribution is **discrete** if it has a finite number of possible values.[1] For example, if we throw two dice and look at the sum of the faces showing, there are only 11 discrete possibilities: the integers 2 through 12. In contrast, a probability distribution is

---

[1]Actually, it is possible for a discrete variable to have a "countably infinite" number of possible values, such as all the nonnegative integers 0, 1, 2, and so on. However, this is not an important distinction for practical applications.

continuous if its possible values are essentially some continuum. An example is the amount of rain that falls during a month in Indiana. It could be any decimal value from 0 to, say, 15 inches.

The graph of a discrete distribution is a series of spikes, as shown in Figure 9.1.[2] The height of each spike is the probability of the corresponding value. That's all there is to it. You can have as many possible values as you like, and their probabilities can be any positive numbers that sum to 1.

Figure 9.1

A Typical Discrete Probability Distribution

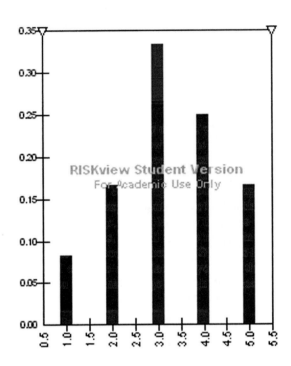

The heights above a density function are not probabilities, but they still indicate relative likelihoods of the possible values.

In contrast, a continuous distribution is characterized by a **density function**, a smooth curve as shown in Figure 9.2. There are two important properties of density functions. First, the height of the density curve above any point is not actually a probability—that is, it is not necessarily between 0 and 1. However, the heights still indicate relative likelihoods. For example, the height of the density above 12 is about 5 times as large as the height above 6 in the figure. Therefore, a random number from this distribution is about 5 times as likely to be near 12 as to be near 6.

Second, probabilities for continuous distributions are found as areas under the density curve. Specifically, the probability of being between 6 and 12 in Figure 9.2 is the shaded area between the vertical lines at 6 and 12. Density functions are always scaled so that the *entire* area under the density is 1. This means that any particular area, such as the area between 6 and 12, is always a value between 0 and 1—that is, a probability. We will not actually calculate areas under particular density functions because this typically requires integral calculus. However, it is important that you understand conceptually that probabilities are areas under the density.

[2]This figure and several later figures have been captured from Palisade's RISKview program. This program, which is included on the CD-ROM with this book, is discussed later in the chapter.

Figure 9.2

A Typical
Continuous
Probability
Distribution

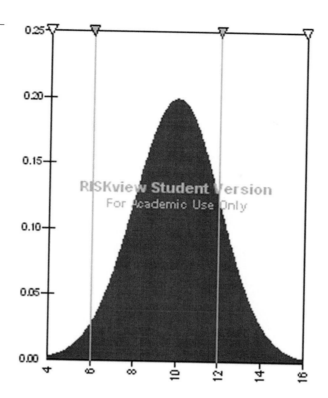

A continuous distribution is described by a **density function**. Heights above the density function indicate relative likelihoods but are not necessarily values between 0 and 1. Probabilities are found as areas under the density function.

Sometimes it is convenient to treat a discrete probability distribution as continuous, and vice versa. For example, consider a student's random score on an exam that has 1000 possible points. If the grader scores each exam to the nearest integer, then even though the score is really discrete with many possible integer values, it is probably more convenient to model its distribution as a continuum. Continuous probability distributions are typically more intuitive and easier to work with than discrete distributions in cases such as this, where there are many possible values. In contrast, we sometimes "discretize" continuous distributions for simplicity. As an example, consider a random interest rate with possible values in the continuum from 5% to 15%. We might model this with a discrete probability distribution with possible values 5%, 7.5%, 10%, 12.5%, and 15%. Although this is not as common as going the other way—from discrete to continuous—it is often done by simulation modelers.

Symmetric versus Skewed

A probability distribution is **symmetric** (around some point) if the distribution to the left of the point is a mirror image of the distribution to the right of the point. Otherwise, the distribution is **skewed**. If a distribution is skewed, then we say it is **skewed to the right** (or **positively skewed**) if the "longer tail" is the right tail. Otherwise, we say the distribution is **skewed to the left** (or **negatively skewed**). The distribution in Figure 9.2 is symmetric, the distribution in Figure 9.3 (page 430) is skewed to the right, and the distribution in Figure 9.4 is skewed to the left.

Figure 9.3

A Positively Skewed Probability Distribution

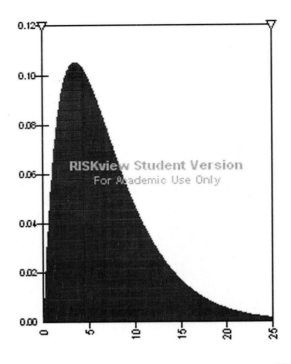

Figure 9.4

A Negatively Skewed Probability Distribution

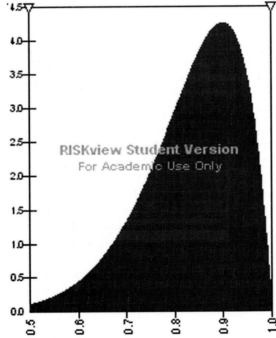

We typically choose between a symmetric and skewed distribution on the basis of realism. For example, if we want to model a student's score on a 100-point exam, we will probably choose a left-skewed distribution. This is because a few poorly prepared students typically "pull down the curve." On the other hand, if we want to model the time it takes to serve a customer at a bank, we will probably choose a right-skewed distribution. This is because most customers take only a minute or two, but a few customers take a long time. Finally, if we want to model the monthly return on a stock, we might choose a distribution symmetric around 0, reasoning that the stock return is just as likely to be positive as negative and there is no obvious reason for skewness one way or the other.

Bounded versus Unbounded

A probability distribution is **bounded** if there are values A and B such that no possible value can be less than A or greater than B. The value A is then the *minimum* possible value, and the value B is the *maximum* possible value. The distribution is **unbounded** if there are no such bounds. Actually, it is possible for a distribution to be bounded in one direction but not the other. As an example, the distribution of scores on a 100-point exam is bounded between 0 and 100. In contrast, the distribution of the amount of damages Mr. Jones submits to his insurance company in a year is bounded on the left by 0, but there is no natural upper bound. Therefore, we might model this amount with a distribution that is bounded by 0 on the left but is unbounded on the right. Alternatively, if we believe there is no possibility of a damage amount over, say, $20,000, then we would model this amount with a distribution that is bounded in both directions.

Positive (or Nonnegative) versus Unrestricted

One important special case of bounded distributions occurs with variables that are inherently *positive* (or possibly *nonnegative*). For example, if we want to model the random cost of manufacturing a new product, we know for sure that this cost must be positive. There are many other such examples. In each case, we should model the randomness with a probability distribution that is bounded below by 0. We do not want to allow negative values because they make no practical sense.

Common Probability Distributions

Think of the *ProbabilityDistributions. xls* file as a "dictionary" of the most commonly used distributions. Keep it handy for reference.

Now that we know the *types* of probability distributions available, we will add some common probability distributions to our toolbox. To help you learn and explore these, we developed the file **ProbabilityDistributions.xls**. Each sheet in this file illustrates a particular probability distribution. It describes the general characteristics of the distribution, it indicates how you can generate random numbers from the distribution, either with Excel's built-in functions or with @RISK functions, and it includes histograms of these distributions from simulated data to illustrate their shapes.[3]

A family of distributions has a common name, such as "normal." Each member of the family is specified by one or more numerical parameters.

It is important to realize that each of the following distributions is really a *family* of distributions. Each member of the family is specified by one or more parameters. For example, there is not a *single* normal distribution; there is a normal distribution for each possible mean and standard deviation we specify. Therefore, when you try to find the most appropriate input probability distribution in a simulation model, you first have to choose the most appropriate family, and then you have to select the most appropriate member of that family.

Uniform Distribution

The uniform distribution is the flat "equally likely" distribution.

The uniform distribution is the "flat" distribution illustrated in Figure 9.5 (page 432). It is bounded by a minimum and a maximum, and all values between these two extremes are equally likely. You can think of this as the "I have no idea" distribution. For example, a manager might realize that a building cost is uncertain. If she can state only that, "I know the cost will be between $20,000 and $30,000, but other than this, I have no idea what the

---

[3]In later sections of this chapter, and all through the next chapter, we will discuss much of @RISK's functionality. For this section, the only functionality we will use is @RISK's collection of functions, such as RISKNORMAL and RISKTRIANG, for generating random numbers from various probability distributions. You can skim the details of these functions for now and refer back to them as necessary in later sections.

cost will be," then a uniform distribution from \$20,000 to \$30,000 is a natural choice. However, even though some people do use the uniform distribution in such cases, we don't believe these situations are very common or realistic. If the manager really thinks about it, she can probably provide more information about the uncertain cost, such as, "The cost is more likely to be close to \$25,000 than to either of the extremes." Then some distribution other than the uniform will be more appropriate.

Figure 9.5

The Uniform Distribution

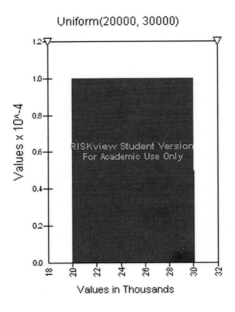

Uniform(20000, 30000)

Regardless of whether the uniform distribution is an appropriate candidate as an input distribution, it is important for another reason. All spreadsheet packages are capable of generating random numbers uniformly distributed between 0 and 1. These are the "building blocks" of all simulated random numbers, in that random numbers from all other probability distributions are generated from these building blocks.

The RAND function is Excel's "building block" function for generating random numbers.

In Excel, we can generate a random number between 0 and 1 by entering the formula

=RAND()

in any cell. (The parentheses to the right of RAND indicate that this is an Excel function with no arguments. These parentheses *must* be included.)

→ **EXCELFUNCTION: *RAND***
*To generate a random number equally likely to be anywhere between 0 and 1, enter the formula =**RAND()** into any cell. Press the F9 key to make it change randomly.* ■

In addition to being between 0 and 1, the numbers created by this function have two properties that we would expect "random" numbers to have.

- **Uniform property.** Each time we enter the RAND function in a cell, all numbers between 0 and 1 have the same chance of occurring. This means that approximately 10% of the numbers generated by the RAND function will be between 0.0 and 0.1; 10% of the numbers will be between 0.65 and 0.75; 60% of the numbers will be between 0.20 and 0.80; and so on. This property explains why we say the random numbers are *uniformly distributed* between 0 and 1.

- **Independence property.** Different random numbers generated by the computer are *probabilistically independent.* This implies that when we generate a random number in cell A5, say, it has no effect on the values of any other random numbers generated in the spreadsheet. For example, if one call to the RAND function yields a large random number such as 0.98, there is no reason to suspect that the *next* call to RAND will yield an abnormally small (or large) random number; it is unaffected by the value of the first random number.

To illustrate the RAND function, open a new workbook, enter the formula **=RAND()** in cell A1, and copy it to the range A1:A500. This generates 500 random numbers. Figure 9.6 displays the values we obtained. However, when you try this on your PC, you will undoubtedly obtain *different* random numbers. This is an inherent characteristic of simulation—no two answers are ever exactly alike. Now press the "recalc" (F9) key. All of the random numbers will change. In fact, each time you press the F9 key or do anything to make your spreadsheet recalculate, all of the cells containing the RAND function will change.

Figure 9.6

Uniformly
Distributed Random
Numbers Generated
by the RAND
Function

	A	B	C	D
1	500 random numbers from RAND() function			
2				
3	Random #			
4	0.1732			
5	0.7545			
6	0.2249			
7	0.0991			
8	0.0406			
9	0.1207			
10	0.4203			
501	0.0048			
502	0.5366			
503	0.7806			

A histogram of the 500 random numbers for our illustration is shown in Figure 9.7. (Again, If you try this on your PC, the shape of your histogram will not be identical to the one shown in Figure 9.7 because it will be based on *different* random numbers.) From property 1, we would expect *equal* numbers of observations in the 10 categories. Although the heights of the bars are not exactly equal, the differences are due to chance—not to a faulty random number generator.

Figure 9.7

Histogram of the
500 Random
Numbers Generated
by the RAND
Function

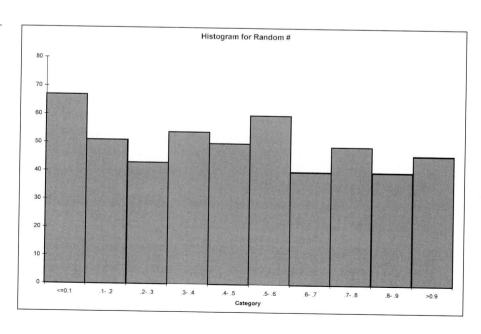

→ **EXCELTOOL:** *Creating a Histogram*

A histogram, also called a frequency chart, indicates the number of observations in each of several user-defined categories. It is possible to create a histogram similar to the one in Figure 9.7 with Excel's Frequency function and the Chart Wizard. We explain the somewhat involved procedure in the appendix to this chapter. However, it is considerably easier to create histograms with an Excel add-in such as @RISK (or the statistical StatTools add-in that accompanies this book). We will explain how to create histograms in @RISK in Section 9.5. ■

→ **TECHNICAL EXCEL NOTE:** *Pseudo-random Numbers*

*The "random" numbers generated by the RAND function (or by any other package's random number generator) are not really random. They are sometimes called **pseudo-random numbers**. Each successive random number follows the previous random number by a complex arithmetic operation. If you happen to know the details of this arithmetic operation, you can predict ahead of time exactly which random numbers will be generated by the RAND function. This is quite different from using a "true" random mechanism, such as spinning a wheel, to get the next random number—a mechanism that would be impractical to implement on a computer. Mathematicians and computer analysts have studied many ways to produce random numbers that have the two properties we just discussed, and they have developed many competing random number generators such as the RAND function in Excel. The technical details need not concern us. The important point is that these random number generators produce numbers that are useful for simulation modeling.* ■

It is simple to generate a uniformly distributed random number with a minimum and maximum other than 0 and 1. For example, the formula

=200+100*RAND()

generates a number uniformly distributed between 200 and 300. (Make sure you see why.) Alternatively, you could use the @RISK formula[4]

=RISKUNIFORM(200,300)

You can take a look at this and other properties of the uniform distribution on the Uniform sheet in the **ProbabilityDistributions.xls** file. (See Figure 9.8.)

Figure 9.8

Properties of Uniform Distribution

	A	B	C	D	E
1	Uniform distribution				
2					
3	Characteristics				
4	Continuous				
5	Symmetric				
6	Bounded in both directions				
7	Not necessarily positive (depends on bounds)				
8					
9	This is a flat distribution between two values, labeled here MinVal and MaxVal.				
10	Note that if MinVal=0 and MaxVal=1, then we can just use Excel's RAND function.				
11					
12	Parameters				
13	MinVal	50			
14	MaxVal	100			
15					
16	Excel		Example		
17	=MinVal + (MaxVal-MinVal)*RAND()		95.14617966		
18					
19	@Risk				
20	=RiskUniform(MinVal,MaxVal)		54.36082371		

---

[4]As we have done with other Excel functions, we will capitalize the @RISK functions, such as RISKUNIFORM, in the text. However, this is not necessary when you enter the formulas in Excel.

→ **@RISK FUNCTION:** *RISKUNIFORM*

To generate a random number from any uniform distribution, enter the formula =**RISKUNI-FORM(MinVal,MaxVal)** *in any cell. Here,* MinVal *and* MaxVal *are the minimum and maximum possible values. Note that if* MinVal *is 0 and* MaxVal *is 1, this function is equivalent to Excel's RAND function.* ■

Freezing Random Numbers

The automatic recalculation of random numbers can be useful sometimes and annoying other times. There are situations when we want the random numbers to stay fixed—that is, we want to "freeze" them at their current values. The following three-step method will do this.

1. **Select the range.** Select the range that you want to freeze, such as A4:A503 in Figure 9.6.

2. **Copy.** Use the Copy command to copy this range.

Random numbers that have been frozen do not change when you press the F9 key.

3. **Paste Special with Values.** With the same range still selected, select Paste Special from the Edit menu and choose the Values option. This procedure pastes a copy of the range onto itself, except that the entries are now *numbers*, not formulas. Therefore, whenever the spreadsheet recalculates, these numbers do not change.

Each sheet in the **ProbabilityDistributions.xls** file has a list of 500 random numbers that have been frozen. We created the histograms in the sheets based on the frozen random numbers. However, we encourage you to enter "live" random numbers in column C and create a new histogram from these. Once the histogram is created, you can press F9 to watch the random numbers—and the histogram—change. (Again, see the appendix to this chapter for instructions on how to create histograms.)

USING RISKVIEW

RISKview is a separate software package—not an Excel add-in—that can be used to analyze probability distributions.

The **ProbabilityDistributions.xls** file illustrates a few frequently used probability distributions, and it shows the formulas required to generate random numbers from these distributions. There is also a package called RISKview in the Palisade DecisionTools suite that you can use to experiment with probability distributions. RISKview is actually not connected to Excel at all; it is a stand-alone application, and it is extremely easy to use. Essentially, it allows us to see the shapes of various distributions and to calculate probabilities for them, all in a graphical, user-friendly interface.[5]

To run RISKview, click on the Windows Start button, go to the Programs tab, locate the Palisades DecisionTools suite, and select the RISKview item. There will probably be a Distribution Window open within RISKview, as shown in Figure 9.9 (page 436). (If no such window is open, use the Insert/Distribution Window menu item.) From this window, select a distribution from the Dist. . . dropdown list. (We chose Uniform in Figure 9.9.) Then in the boxes below, enter the parameters of this distribution. (We entered a minimum of 75 and a maximum of 150 for illustration.) Now you see the shape of the distribution in the middle, and you see a number of summary measures to the right. For example, you see that the mean and standard deviation of this uniform distribution are 112.5 and 21.651.

From here, everything is interactive. Suppose you want to find the probability that a value from this distribution is less than 95. You have two options. First, you can drag the left-hand "slider" in the diagram (the vertical line with the triangle at the top) to the position 95, as shown in Figure 9.9. We see immediately that the left-hand probability is 0.267.

---

[5]The functionality of RISKview is also included in the much more encompassing @RISK program, through its Model Window, but we believe the stand-alone RISKview is somewhat easier to learn and use.

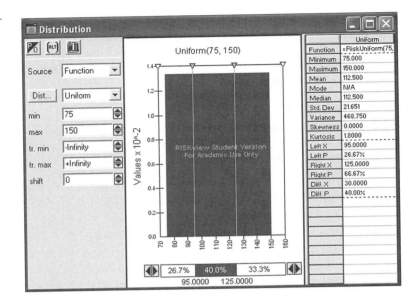

Alternatively, you can enter the value 95 as the "Left X" value in the table to the right to see that the "Left P" value is 0.267. Similarly, if you want the probability that a value from this distribution is greater than 125, you can drag the right-hand slider to the position 125, or you can enter 125 as the "Right X" value in the table. In either case, you see that the required probability (the "Right P") is 0.6667.

You can also enter probabilities instead of values. For example, if you want the value such that there is probability 0.10 to the left of it—the 10th percentile—enter 10% as the "Left P" in the table. You will see that the corresponding value (the "Left X") is 82.5. Similarly, if you want the value such that there is probability 0.10 to the right of it, enter 90% as the "Right P" value in the table, and you will see that the corresponding value is 142.5.

We like RISKview because it is quick and easy. We urge you to use it and experiment with some of its options.

Discrete Distribution

A discrete distribution is useful for many situations, either when the uncertain quantity is not really continuous (the number of televisions demanded, for example) or when you want a discrete approximation to a continuous variable. All you need to do is specify the possible values and their probabilities, making sure that the probabilities sum to 1. Because of this flexibility in specifying values and probabilities, discrete distributions can have practically any shape.

As an example, suppose a manager estimates that the demand for a particular brand of television during the coming month will be 10, 15, 20, or 25 with respective probabilities 0.1, 0.3, 0.4, and 0.2. This is a typical discrete distribution, and it is illustrated in Figure 9.10.

The Discrete sheet of the **ProbabilityDistributions.xls** file indicates how to work with a discrete distribution. (See Figure 9.11.) As we see, there are two quite different ways to generate a random number from this distribution in Excel. We will discuss the "Excel" way in detail in Section 9.4. For now, we simply mention that this is one case (of many) where it is much easier to generate random numbers with @RISK functions than with built-in Excel functions. Assuming that @RISK is loaded, all you need to do is enter the

Figure 9.10

Discrete
Distribution (from
RISKview)

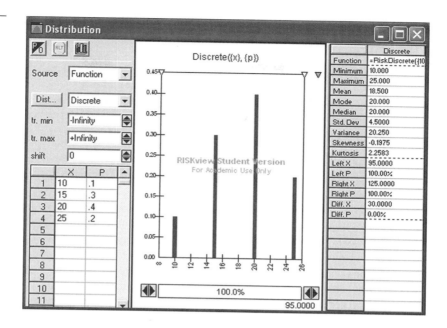

function RISKDISCRETE with two arguments, a list of possible values and a list of their probabilities, as in

=RISKDISCRETE(B13:B16,C13:C16)

The Excel way, which requires cumulative probabilities and a lookup table, requires more work and is harder to remember.

→ @RISK Function: *RISKDISCRETE*

To generate a random number from any discrete probability distribution, enter the formula **=RISKDISCRETE(valRange,probRange)** *into any cell. Here* valRange *is the range where the possible values are stored, and* probRange *is the range where their probabilities are stored.* ∎

Figure 9.11

Properties of a
Discrete
Distribution

	A	B	C	D	E	F	G	H
1	General discrete distribution							
2								
3	Characteristics							
4	Discrete							
5	Can be symmetric or skewed (or bumpy, i.e., basically any shape)							
6	Bounded in both directions							
7	Not necessarily positive (depends on possible values)							
8								
9	This can have any shape, depending on the list of possible values and their probabilities.							
10								
11	Parameters				Lookup table required for Excel method			
12		Values	Probabilities		CumProb	Value		
13		10	0.1		0	10		
14		15	0.3		0.1	15		
15		20	0.4		0.4	20		
16		25	0.2		0.8	25		
17								
18	Excel		Example					
19	=VLOOKUP(RAND(),LookupTable,2)		25					
20								
21	@Risk							
22	=RiskDiscrete(Values,Probs)		15					

At this point, a relevant question is, Why would a manager choose this particular discrete distribution? First, it is clearly an approximation. After all, if it is possible to have demands of 20 and 25, why aren't demands of 22 or 24 possible? Here, the manager approximates a discrete distribution with *many* possible values—all integers from 0 to 50, say—with a discrete distribution with a few well-chosen values. This is common in simulation modeling. Second, where do the probabilities come from? They are probably a blend of historical data (perhaps demand was near 15 in 30% of previous months) and the manager's subjective feelings about demand *next* month.

Normal Distribution

The normal distribution is the familiar bell-shaped curve that is the hallmark of statistics. (See Figure 9.12.) It is also useful in simulation modeling as a continuous input distribution. However, it is not always the most appropriate distribution. It is symmetric, which can be a drawback when a skewed distribution is more realistic. Also, it allows negative values, which are not appropriate in many situations. For example, the demand for televisions cannot be negative. Fortunately, this possibility of negative values is often not a problem. The two parameters of a normal distribution are its mean and standard deviation. Suppose you generate a normally distributed random number with mean 100 and standard deviation 20. Then as you probably recall from statistics, there is almost no chance of having values more than 3 standard deviations to the left of the mean. Therefore, negative values will virtually never occur in this situation.

Figure 9.12

Normal Distribution (from RISKview)

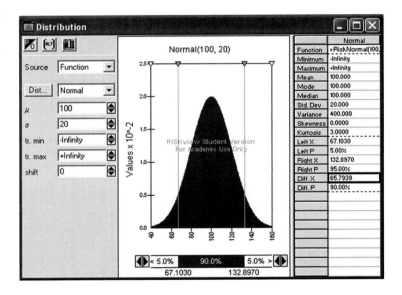

A tip-off that a normal distribution might be an appropriate candidate for an input variable is a statement such as, "We believe the most likely value of demand is 100, the chances are about 95% that demand will be no more than 40 units on either of side of this most likely value, and the shape of the distribution is symmetric around this most likely value." Because a normally distributed value is within 2 standard deviations of its mean with probability 0.95, this statement translates easily to a mean of 100 and a standard deviation of 20. We do not imply that a normal distribution is the *only* candidate for distribution of demand, but the statement naturally leads us to this distribution.

The Normal sheet in the **ProbabilityDistributions.xls** file indicates how we can generate normally distributed random numbers in Excel, either with or without @RISK. (See Figure 9.13.) This is one case where an add-in is not really necessary—the formula

=NORMINV(RAND(),*Mean,Stdev*)

will always work. Still, it is not nearly so easy to remember as @RISK's

=RISKNORMAL(*Mean,Stdev*)

formula.

Figure 9.13

Properties of the Normal Distribution

	A	B	C	D
1	**Normal distribution**			
2				
3	**Characteristics**			
4	Continuous			
5	Symmetric (bell-shaped)			
6	Unbounded in both directions			
7	Is both positive and negative			
8				
9	This is the familiar bell-shaped curve, defined by two parameters:			
10	the mean and the standard deviation			
11				
12	**Parameters**			
13	Mean	100		
14	Stdev	10		
15				
16	**Excel**		**Example**	
17	=NORMINV(RAND(),Mean,Stdev)		96.90464811	
18				
19	**@Risk**			
20	=RISKNORMAL(Mean,Stdev)		103.0232281	

→ **@RISK Function:** *RISKNORMAL*

To generate a normally distributed random number, enter the formula
*=RISKNORMAL(**Mean,Stdev**) in any cell. Here,* Mean *and* Stdev *are the mean and standard deviation of the normal distribution.* ■

Triangular Distribution

A triangular distribution is a good choice in many simulation models because it is flexible and its parameters are easy to understand.

The triangular distribution is somewhat similar to the normal distribution in that its density function rises to some point and then falls, but it is more flexible and intuitive than the normal distribution. Therefore, it is an excellent candidate for many continuous input variables. The shape of a triangular density function is literally a triangle, as shown in Figure 9.14 (page 440). It is specified by three easy-to-understand parameters: the minimum possible value, the most likely value, and the maximum possible value. The high point of the triangle is above the most likely value. Therefore, if a manager states that, "We believe the most likely development cost is $1.5 million, and we don't believe the development cost could possibly be less than $1.2 million or greater than $2.1 million," the triangular distribution with these three parameters is a natural choice. Note that, as in this numerical example, the triangular distribution can be skewed if the mostly likely value is closer to one extreme than another. Of course, it can also be symmetric if the most likely value is right in the middle.

The Triangular sheet of the **ProbabilityDistributions.xls** file indicates how to generate random values from this distribution. (See Figure 9.15.) As we see, there is no way to do it with native Excel (at least not without a lot of trickery). However, it is easy with @RISK, using the RISKTRIANG function, as in

=RISKTRIANG(B15,B16,B17)

Figure 9.14

Triangular
Distribution (from
RISKview)

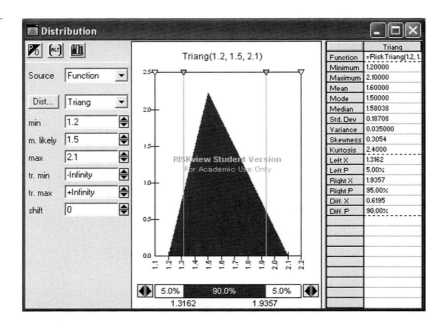

All we need to feed this function are the minimum value, the most likely value, and the maximum value—in this order and separated by commas. You will see this function in many of our examples. Just remember that it has an "abbreviated" spelling: **RISKTRI-ANG**, not RISKTRIANGULAR.

Figure 9.15

Properties of the
Triangular
Distribution

	A	B	C	D	E
1	Triangular distribution				
2					
3	Characteristics				
4	Continuous				
5	Can be symmetric or skewed in either direction				
6	Bounded in both directions				
7	Not necessarily positive (depends on bounds)				
8					
9	The density of this distribution is literally a triangle. The "top" of the triangle				
10	is above the most likely value, and the base of the triangle extends from the				
11	minimum value to the maximum value. It is intuitive for non-technical people				
12	because the three parameters are meaningful.				
13					
14	Parameters				
15	Min	50			
16	MostLikely	85			
17	Max	100			
18					
19	Excel				
20	There is no easy way to do it. This is a case where we need an add-in.				
21					
22	@Risk		Example		
23	=RiskTriang(Min,MostLikely,Max)		64.68390057		

→ @RISK FUNCTION: *RISKTRIANG*

*To generate a random number from a triangular distribution, enter the formula =**RISKTRI-ANG(MinVal,MLVal,MaxVal)** in any cell. Here,* MinVal *is the minimum possible value,* MLVal *is the most likely value, and* MaxVal *is the maximum value.* ∎

Binomial Distribution

A random number from a binomial distribution indicates the number of "successes" in a certain number of identical "trials."

The binomial distribution is a discrete distribution, but unlike the "general" discrete distribution we discussed previously, the binomial distribution applies to a very specific situation. This is when a number of independent and identical "trials" occur, where each trial results in a "success" or "failure," and we want to generate the random number of successes in these trials. There are two parameters of this distribution, usually labeled n and p. Here, n is the number of trials and p is the probability of success on each trial.

As an example, suppose an airline company sells 170 tickets for a flight and estimates that 80% of the people with tickets will actually show up for the flight. How many people will actually show up? We could state that *exactly* 80% of 170, or 136 people, will show up, but this neglects the inherent randomness. A more realistic way to model this situation is to say that each of the 170 people, independently of one another, will show up with probability 0.8. Then the number of people who actually show up is binomially distributed with $n = 170$ and $p = 0.8$. This distribution is illustrated in Figure 9.16. (Although this distribution appears to be continuous, it is really a sequence of very thin bars above integer values.)

Figure 9.16

Binomial Distribution (from RISKview)

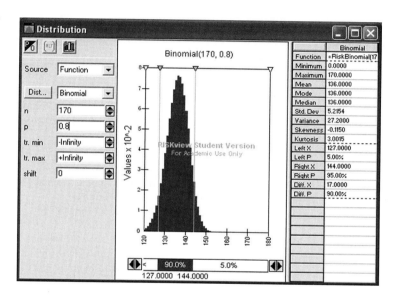

The Binomial sheet of the **ProbabilityDistributions.xls** file indicates how to generate random numbers from this distribution. (See Figure 9.17.) Although it is possible to do this with native Excel, using the built-in CRITBINOM function and the RAND function, it is not very intuitive or easy to remember. Clearly, the @RISK way is preferable. In the airline example, we would generate the number who show up with the formula

=**RISKBINOM(170,0.8)**

Note that the histogram in this figure is approximately bell-shaped. This is no accident. When the number of trials n is reasonably large and p isn't too close to 0 or 1, the binomial distribution can be well approximated by the normal distribution.

➔ @RISK FUNCTION: *RISKBINOM*

*To generate a random number from a binomial distribution, enter the formula =**RISKBINOM(NTrials,PrSuc)** in any cell. Here, NTrials is the number of trials, and PrSuc is the probability of a "success" on each trial.* ∎

Figure 9.17

Properties of the
Binomial
Distribution

	A	B	C	D	E	F	G
1	**Binomial distribution**						
2							
3	**Characteristics**						
4	Discrete						
5	Can be symmetric or skewed						
6	Bounded below by 0, bounded above by Ntrials						
7	Nonnegative						
8							
9	This distribution is of the number of "successes" in a given number of identical,						
10	independent trials, when the probability of success is constant on each trial.						
11							
12	**Parameters**						
13	NTrials	170					
14	PSuccess	0.8					
15							
16	**Excel**		**Example**				
17	=CRITBINOM(NTrials,PSuccess,RAND())		131				
18	This will generate the number of successes in NTrials, with PSuccess as the probability of success on each trial						
19							
20	**@Risk**						
21	=RISKBINOMIAL(NTrials,PSuccess)		142				

PROBLEMS

*Solutions for problems whose numbers appear within a color box
can be found in the Student Solutions Manual. Order your copy
today at http://e-catalog.thomsonlearning.com/110/ by using
ISBN 0-534-39687-9.*

Skill-Building Problems

1. Use the RAND function and the Copy command to
   generate a set of 100 random numbers.
   a. What fraction of the random numbers are smaller
      than 0.5?
   b. What fraction of the time is a random number less
      than 0.5 followed by a random number greater
      than 0.5?
   c. What fraction of the random numbers are larger
      than 0.8?
   d. Freeze these random numbers. However, instead of
      pasting them over the original random numbers,
      paste them onto a new range. Then press the F9 re-
      calculate key. The original random numbers should
      change, but the pasted copy should remain the
      same.

2. Use Excel's functions (not @RISK) to generate 1000
   random numbers from a normal distribution with
   mean 100 and standard deviation 10. Then freeze
   these random numbers.
   a. Calculate the mean and standard deviation of these
      random numbers. Are they approximately what
      you would expect?
   b. What fraction of these random numbers are with k
      standard deviations of the mean? Answer for $k =$
      1; for $k = 2$; for $k = 3$. Are the answers close to
      what they should be (as you learned in your statis-
      tics course)?

   c. Create a histogram of the random numbers using
      10–15 categories of your choice. Does this his-
      togram have approximately the shape you would
      expect?

3. Use RISKview to draw a uniform distribution from
   400 to 750. Then answer the following questions.
   a. What are the mean and standard deviation of this
      distribution?
   b. What are the 5th and 95th percentiles of this
      distribution?
   c. What is the probability that a random number from
      this distribution is less than 450?
   d. What is the probability that a random number from
      this distribution is greater than 650?
   e. What is the probability that a random number from
      this distribution is between 500 and 700?

4. Use RISKview to draw a normal distribution with
   mean 500 and standard deviation 100. Then answer
   the following questions.
   a. What is the probability that a random number from
      this distribution is less than 450?
   b. What is the probability that a random number from
      this distribution is greater than 650?
   c. What is the probability that a random number from
      this distribution is between 500 and 700?

5. Use RISKview to draw a triangular distribution with
   parameters 300, 500, and 900. Then answer the following questions.
   a. What are the mean and standard deviation of this
      distribution?

b. What are the 5th and 95th percentiles of this distribution?

c. What is the probability that a random number from this distribution is less than 450?

d. What is the probability that a random number from this distribution is greater than 650?

e. What is the probability that a random number from this distribution is between 500 and 700?

6. Use RISKview to draw a binomial distribution that results from 50 trials with probability of success 0.3 on each trial, and use it to answer the following questions.

a. What are the mean and standard deviation of this distribution?

b. You have to be more careful in interpreting RISKview probabilities with a discrete distribution such as this binomial. For example, if you move the left slider to 11, you find a probability of 0.139 to the left of it. But is this the probability of "less than 11" or "less than or equal to 11"? One way to check is to use Excel's BINOMDIST function. The formula **=BINOMDIST($k,n,p,$1)** calculates the probability that a binomial random number with parameters n and p is less than or equal to k. (The last argument, 1, ensures that you get a *cumulative* probability.) Use this function to interpret the 0.139 value from RISKview.

c. Using part **b** to guide you, use RISKview to find the probability that a random number from this distribution will be greater than 17. Check your answer by using the BINOMDIST function appropriately in Excel.

7. Use RISKview to draw a triangular distribution with parameters 200, 300, and 600. Then superimpose a normal distribution on this drawing, choosing the mean and standard deviation to match those from the triangular distribution.

a. What are the 5th and 95th percentiles for these two distributions?

b. What is the probability that a random number from the triangular distribution is less than 400? What is this probability for the normal distribution?

c. Experiment with the sliders to answer other questions like in part **b**. Would you conclude that these two distributions differ most in the extremes (right or left) or in the middle? Explain.

8. We all hate to bring change to a store. By using random numbers, we could eliminate the need for change and give the store and the customer a fair deal. This problem indicates how it could be done.

a. Suppose that you buy something for $0.20. How could you use random numbers (built into the cash register system) to decide whether you should pay

$1.00 or nothing? This would eliminate the need for change!

b. If you bought something for $9.60, how would you use random numbers to eliminate the need for change?

c. In the long run, why is this method fair to both the store and the customers? Would you personally (as a customer) be willing to abide by such a system?

Skill-Extending Problems

9. A company is about to develop and then market a new product. It wants to build a simulation model for the entire process, and one key uncertain input is the development cost. For each of the following scenarios, choose an "appropriate" distribution, together with its parameters, justify your choice in words, and use RISKview to draw your chosen distribution.

a. Company experts have no idea what the distribution of the development cost is. All they can state is that "we are 95% sure it will be at least $450,000," and "we are 95% sure it will be no more than $650,000."

b. Company experts can still make the same two statements as in part **a**, but now they can also state that "we believe the distribution is symmetric, reasonably bell-shaped, and its most likely value is about $550,000."

c. Company experts can still make the same two statements as in part **a**, but now they can also state that "we believe the distribution is skewed to the right, and its most likely value is about $500,000."

10. Continuing the preceding problem, suppose that another key uncertain input is the development time, which is measured in an *integer* number of months. For each of the following scenarios, choose an "appropriate" distribution, together with its parameters, justify your choice in words, and use RISKview to draw your chosen distribution.

a. Company experts believe the development time will be from 6 to 10 months, but they have absolutely no idea which of these will result.

b. Company experts believe the development time will be from 6 to 10 months. They believe the probabilities of these five possible values will increase linearly to a most likely value at 8 months and will then decrease linearly.

c. Company experts believe the development time will be from 6 to 10 months. They believe that 8 months is twice as likely as either 7 months or 9 months and that either of these latter possibilities is three times as likely as either 6 months or 10 months.

9.4 SIMULATION WITH BUILT-IN EXCEL TOOLS

In this section we will show how spreadsheet simulation models can be developed and analyzed with Excel's built-in tools without using add-ins. As we will see, this is certainly possible, but it presents two problems. First, the @RISK functions illustrated in the **ProbabilityDistributions.xls** file are not available. We are able to use only Excel's RAND function and transformations of it to generate random numbers from various probability distributions. Second, there is a bookkeeping problem. Once we build an Excel model with output cells linked to appropriate random input cells, we can press the F9 key as often as we like to see how the outputs vary. However, how do we keep track of these output values and summarize them? This bookkeeping feature is the real strength of a simulation add-in such as @RISK. We will see that it can be done with Excel, usually with data tables, but the summarization of the resulting data is completely up to the user—you!

To illustrate the procedure, we will analyze a simple "news vendor" problem. This problem occurs when a company (such as a news vendor) must make a one-time purchase of a product (such as a newspaper) to meet customer demands for a certain period of time. If the company orders too few newspapers, it will lose potential profit by not having enough on hand to satisfy its customers. If it orders too many, it will have newspapers left over at the end of the day that, at best, can be sold at a loss. The following example illustrates this basic problem in a slightly different context.

| EXAMPLE | 9.1 ORDERING CALENDARS AT WALTON BOOKSTORE |

In August, Walton Bookstore must decide how many of next year's nature calendars to order. Each calendar costs the bookstore $7.50 and sells for $10. After February 1, all unsold calendars will be returned to the publisher for a refund of $2.50 per calendar. Walton believes that the number of calendars it can sell by February 1 follows the probability distribution shown in Table 9.1. Walton wants to develop a simulation model to help it decide how many calendars to order.

Table 9.1 Probability Distribution of Demand for Walton Example

Demand	Probability
100	0.30
150	0.20
200	0.30
250	0.15
300	0.05

Objective To use built-in Excel tools—including the RAND function and data tables, but no add-ins—to simulate profit for several order quantities and ultimately choose the "best" order quantity.

WHERE DO THE NUMBERS COME FROM?

The monetary values are straightforward. The numbers in Table 9.1 are the key to the simulation model. They are discussed in more detail next.

Solution

We first discuss the probability distribution in Table 9.1. It is a discrete distribution with only five possible values: 100, 150, 200, 250, and 300. In reality, it is clear that other values of demand are possible. For example, there could be demand for exactly 187 calendars. In spite of its apparent lack of realism, we use this discrete distribution for two reasons. First, its simplicity is a nice feature to get us started with simulation modeling. Second, discrete distributions are often used in real business simulation models. Even though the discrete distribution is only an *approximation* to reality, it can still give us important insights into the actual problem.

As for the probabilities listed in Table 9.1, they are typically drawn from historical data or (if historical data are lacking) educated guesses. In this case, the manager of Walton Bookstore has presumably looked at demands for calendars in previous years, and he has used any information he has about the market for next year's calendars to estimate, for example, that the probability of a demand for 200 calendars is 0.30. The five probabilities in this table *must* sum to 1. Beyond this requirement, we want them to be as reasonable and consistent with reality as possible.

Another important point to realize is that this is really a decision problem under uncertainty. Walton must choose an order quantity *before* knowing the demand for calendars. Unfortunately, we cannot use Solver because of the uncertainty.[6] Therefore, we will develop a simulation model for any *fixed* order quantity. Then we will run this simulation model with various order quantities to see which one appears to be best.

DEVELOPING THE SIMULATION MODEL

Now we discuss the ordering model. For any fixed order quantity, we will show how Excel can be used to simulate 1000 replications (or any other number of replications). Each replication is an independent replay of the events that occur. To illustrate, suppose we want to simulate profit if Walton orders 200 calendars. Figure 9.18 (page 446) illustrates the results obtained by simulating 1000 independent replications for this order quantity. (See the file **Walton1.xls**.) Note that there are a number of hidden rows in Figure 9.18. This will be the case for several of the spreadsheet figures in this chapter. To develop this model, use the following steps.

❶ Inputs. Enter the cost data in the range B4:B6, the probability distribution of demand in the range E5:F9, and the proposed order quantity, 200, in cell B9. Pay particular attention to the way the probability distribution is entered (and compare to the Discrete sheet in the **ProbabilityDistributions.xls** file). Columns E and F contain the possible demand values and the probabilities from Table 9.1. It is also necessary (see step 3 for the reasoning) to have the cumulative probabilities in column D. To obtain these, first enter the value 0 in cell D5. Then enter the formula

=F5+D5

in cell D6 and copy it to the range D7:D9.

❷ Generate random numbers. Enter a random number in cell B19 with the formula

=RAND()

and copy this to the range B20:B1018.

---

[6]Palisade Corporation has another Excel add-in called RiskOptimizer that can be used for optimization in a simulation model. However, we will not discuss this software here. It is *not* included on the CD-ROM.

Figure 9.18 Walton Bookstore Simulation Model

	A	B	C	D	E	F	G	H	I	J	K
1	Simulation of Walton's bookstore										
2											
3	Cost data			Demand distribution				Range names used:			
4	Unit cost	$7.50		Cum Prob	Demand	Probability		LookupTable	=Model!$D$5:$F$9		
5	Unit price	$10.00		0.00	100	0.30		Order_quantity	=Model!$B$9		
6	Unit refund	$2.50		0.30	150	0.20		Profit	=Model!$G$19:$G$1018		
7				0.50	200	0.30		Unit_cost	=Model!$B$4		
8	Decision variable			0.80	250	0.15		Unit_price	=Model!$B$5		
9	Order quantity	200		0.95	300	0.05		Unit_refund	=Model!$B$6		
10											
11	Summary measures for simulation below										
12	Average profit	$204.13		95% confidence interval for expected profit							
13	Stdev of profit	$328.04		Lower limit	$183.79						
14	Minimum profit	-$250.00		Upper limit	$224.46						
15	Maximum profit	$500.00									
16											
17	Simulation								Distribution of profit		
18	Replication	Random #	Demand	Revenue	Cost	Refund	Profit			Value	Frequency
19	1	0.2249	100	$1,000	$1,500	$250	-$250			-250	299
20	2	0.6693	200	$2,000	$1,500	$0	$500			125	191
21	3	0.4164	150	$1,500	$1,500	$125	$125			500	510
22	4	0.7562	200	$2,000	$1,500	$0	$500				
23	5	0.1581	100	$1,000	$1,500	$250	-$250				
24	6	0.0579	100	$1,000	$1,500	$250	-$250				
25	7	0.7452	200	$2,000	$1,500	$0	$500				
26	8	0.3717	150	$1,500	$1,500	$125	$125				
27	9	0.5077	200	$2,000	$1,500	$0	$500				
28	10	0.6669	200	$2,000	$1,500	$0	$500				
1012	994	0.7689	200	$2,000	$1,500	$0	$500				
1013	995	0.8861	250	$2,000	$1,500	$0	$500				
1014	996	0.4036	150	$1,500	$1,500	$125	$125				
1015	997	0.4092	150	$1,500	$1,500	$125	$125				
1016	998	0.5055	200	$2,000	$1,500	$0	$500				
1017	999	0.2457	100	$1,000	$1,500	$250	-$250				
1018	1000	0.3484	150	$1,500	$1,500	$125	$125				

③ Generate demands. The key to the simulation is the generation of the customer demands in the range C19:C1018 from the random numbers in column B and the probability distribution of demand. Here is how it works. We divide the interval from 0 to 1 into five segments: 0.0 to 0.3 (length 0.3), 0.3 to 0.5 (length 0.2), 0.5 to 0.8 (length 0.3), 0.8 to 0.95 (length 0.15), and 0.95 to 1.0 (length 0.05). Note that these lengths are the probabilities of the various demands. Then we associate a demand with each random number, depending on which interval the random number falls in. For example, if a random number is 0.5279, this falls in the third interval, so we associate the third possible demand value, 200, with this random number.

The easiest way to implement this procedure is to use a VLOOKUP function. To do this, we create a "lookup table" in the range D5:E9 (range-named LookupTable). This table has the cumulative probabilities in column D and the possible demand values in column E. In fact, the whole purpose of the cumulative probabilities in column D is to allow us to use the VLOOKUP function. To generate the simulated demands, enter the formula

This rather cumbersome procedure for generating a discrete random number is greatly simplified when we use @RISK.

=VLOOKUP(B19,LookupTable,2)

in cell C19 and copy it to the range C20:C1018. For each random number in column B, this function compares the random number to the values in D5:D9 and returns the appropriate demand from E5:E9.

This step is the key to the simulation, so make sure you understand exactly what it entails. The rest is "bookkeeping," as we illustrate in the following steps. First, however, we note that a separate column for the random numbers in column B is not really necessary. They could be included in the VLOOKUP function directly, as in

=VLOOKUP(RAND(),LookupTable,2)

4 Revenue. Once the demand is known, the number of calendars sold is the smaller of the demand and the order quantity. For example, if 150 calendars are demanded, 150 will be sold. But if 250 are demanded, only 200 can be sold (because Walton orders only 200). Therefore, to calculate the revenue in cell D19, enter the formula

=Unit_price*MIN(C19,Order_quantity)

5 Ordering cost. The cost of ordering the calendars does not depend on the demand; it is the unit cost multiplied by the number ordered. Calculate this cost in cell E19 with the formula

=Unit_cost*Order_quantity

6 Refund. If the order quantity is greater than the demand, there is a refund of $2.50 for each calendar left over; otherwise, there is no refund. Therefore, enter the refund in cell F19 with the formula

=Unit_refund*MAX(Order_quantity-C19,0)

For example, if demand is 150, then 50 calendars are left over, and this MAX is 50, the larger of 50 and 0. However, if demand is 250, then no calendars are left over, and this MAX is 0, the larger of −50 and 0. (This calculation could also be accomplished with an IF function instead of a MAX function.)

7 Profit. Calculate the profit in cell G19 with the formula

=D19-E19+F19

8 Copy to other rows. Do the same bookkeeping for the other 999 replications by copying the range D19:G19 to the range D20:G1018.

9 Summary measures. Each profit value in column G corresponds to one randomly generated demand. We usually want to see how these vary from one replication to another. First, calculate the average and standard deviation of the 1000 profits in cells B12 and B13 with the formulas

=AVERAGE(Profit)

and

=STDEV(Profit)

Similarly, calculate the smallest and largest of the 1000 profits in cells B14 and B15 with the MIN and MAX functions.

10 Confidence interval for expected profit. Calculate a 95% confidence interval for the expected profit in cells E13 and E14 with the formulas

=B12-1.96*B13/SQRT(1000)

and

=B12+1.96*B13/SQRT(1000)

(See the section on confidence intervals on page 448 for details.)

11 Distribution of simulated profits. There are only three possible profits, −$250, $125, or $500 (depending on whether demand is 100, 150, or at least 200—see the following discussion). We can use the COUNTIF function to count the number of times each of these possible profits is obtained. To do so, enter the formula

=COUNTIF(Profit,I19)

in cell J19 and copy it down to cell J21.

At this point, it is a good idea to stand back and see what we have accomplished. First, in the body of the simulation, rows 19–1018, we randomly generated 1000 possible demands and the corresponding profits. Because there are only five possible demand values (100, 150, 200, 250, and 300), there are only five possible profit values: −$250, $125, $500, $500, and $500. Also, note that for the order quantity 200, the profit is $500 regardless of whether demand is 200, 250, or 300. (Make sure you understand why.) A tally of the profit values in these rows, including the hidden rows, indicates that there are 299 rows with profit equal to −$250 (demand 100), 191 rows with profit equal to $125 (demand 150), and 510 rows with profit equal to $500 (demand 200, 250, or 300). The average of these 1000 profits is $204.13, and their standard deviation is $328.04. (Again, remember that your answers will differ from these because your random numbers will differ from those shown in Figure 9.18.)

Typically, we want a simulation model to capture one or more output variables, such as profit. These output variables depend on random inputs, such as demand. Our goal is to estimate the probability distributions of the outputs. In the Walton simulation we estimate the probability distribution of profit to be

$$P(\text{Profit} = -\$250) = 299/1000 = 0.299$$

$$P(\text{Profit} = \$125) = 191/1000 = 0.191$$

$$P(\text{Profit} = \$500) = 510/1000 = 0.510$$

We also estimate the mean of this distribution to be $204.13 and its standard deviation to be $328.04. It is important to realize that if the entire simulation were run again with *different* random numbers (such as the ones you might have generated on your PC), the answers would be slightly different. This is the primary reason for the confidence interval in cells E13 and E14. This interval expresses our uncertainty about the *mean* of the profit distribution. Our best guess for this mean is the average of the 1000 profits we happened to observe. However, because the corresponding confidence interval is somewhat wide, from $183.79 to $224.46, we are not at all sure of the *true* mean of the profit distribution. We are only 95% confident that the true mean is within this interval. If we run this simulation again with different random numbers, the average profit might be quite different from the average profit we observed, $204.13, and the other summary statistics would probably also be different.

Notes about Confidence Intervals

It is common in computer simulations to estimate the mean of some distribution by the average of the simulated observations, just as we estimated the mean of the profit distribution by the average of 1000 profits. The usual practice is then to accompany this estimate with a **confidence interval**, which indicates the accuracy of the estimate. You might recall from statistics that to obtain a confidence interval for the mean, you start with the estimated mean and then add and subtract a multiple of the **standard error** of the estimated mean. If we denote the estimated mean (that is, the average) by $\bar{X}$, we have the following formula.

> ***Confidence interval for the mean***
>
> $$\bar{X} \pm (\text{Multiple} \times \text{Standard Error of } \bar{X})$$

The standard error of $\bar{X}$ is the standard deviation of the observations divided by the square root of n, the number of observations:

> **Standard error of $\overline{X}$**
>
> $$s/\sqrt{n}$$

Here, s is the symbol for the standard deviation of the observations. We obtain it with the STDEV function in Excel.

The "multiple" in the confidence interval formula depends on the confidence level and the number of observations. If the confidence level is 95%, for example, then the multiple is usually very close to 2, so a good guideline is to go out 2 standard errors on either side of the average to obtain an approximate 95% confidence interval for the mean.

> **Approximate 95% confidence interval for the mean**
>
> $$\overline{X} \pm 2s/\sqrt{n}$$

To be more precise, if n is reasonably large, which is almost always the case in simulations, the central limit theorem from statistics implies that the correct multiple is the number from the standard normal distribution that cuts off probability 0.025 in each tail. This is a famous number in statistics: 1.96. Because 1.96 is very close to 2, it is acceptable for all practical purposes to use 2 instead of 1.96 when forming the confidence interval.

Analysts often plan a simulation so that the confidence interval for the mean of some important output will be sufficiently narrow. The reasoning is that narrow confidence intervals imply more precision about the estimated mean of the output variable. If the confidence level is fixed at some value such as 95%, then the only way to narrow the confidence interval is to simulate more replications. Assuming that the confidence level is 95%, the following value of n is required to ensure that the resulting confidence interval will have length approximately equal to some specified value L:

The idea is to choose the number of iterations large enough so that the resulting confidence interval will be sufficiently narrow.

> **Sample size determination**
>
> $$n = \frac{16 \times (\text{Estimated standard deviation})^2}{L^2}$$

To use this formula, we must have an estimate of the standard deviation of the output variable. For example, in the Walton simulation we saw that with $n = 1000$, the resulting 95% confidence interval for the mean profit has length $224.46 - \$183.79 = \$40.66$. Suppose that we want to reduce this length to 25—that is, we want $L = \$25$. We do not know the exact standard deviation of the profit distribution, but we can estimate it from the simulation as 328.04. Therefore, to obtain the required confidence interval length L, we need to simulate n replications, where

$$n = \frac{16(328.04)^2}{25^2} \approx 2755$$

(When this formula produces a noninteger, it is common to round upward.) The claim, then, is that if we rerun the simulation with 2755 replications rather than 1000 replications, the length of the 95% confidence interval for the mean profit will be close to 25.

Finding the Best Order Quantity

We are not yet finished with the Walton example. So far, we have run the simulation for only a single order quantity, 200. Walton's ultimate goal is to find the best order quantity. Even this statement must be clarified. What do we mean by "best?" As in Chapter 8, we will use the *expected* profit as our optimality criterion—that is, EMV—but we will see that other characteristics of the profit distribution could influence our decision. We can obtain the required outputs with a data table. Specifically, we use a data table to rerun the simulation for other order quantities. We show this data table in Figure 9.19. (This is still part of the **Walton1.xls** file.)

Figure 9.19

Data Table for
Walton Bookstore
Simulation

	A	B	C	D	E
1020	Data table for average profit versus order quantity				
1021	Order quantity	AvgProfit			
1022		$204.13			
1023	100	$250.00			
1024	125	$256.44			
1025	150	$262.88			
1026	175	$233.50			
1027	200	$204.13			
1028	225	$120.19			
1029	250	$36.25			
1030	275	($76.00)			
1031	300	($188.25)			

To optimize in simulation models, try various values of the decision variable(s) and run the simulation for each of them.

To create this table, enter the trial order quantities shown in the range A1023:A1031, enter the link **=B12** to the average profit in cell B1022, and select the data table range, A1022: B1031. Then use the Data/Table command, specifying that the column input cell is B9 (see Figure 9.18). Finally, construct a bar chart of the average profits in the data table, as in Figure 9.20. Note that an order quantity of 150 appears to maximize the average profit. Its average profit of $262.88 is slightly higher than the average profits from nearby order quantities and much higher than the profit gained from an order of 200 or more calendars. However, again keep in mind that this is a simulation, so that all of these average profits depend on the particular random numbers we generated. If we rerun the simulation with different random numbers, it is conceivable that some other order quantity could be best.

Figure 9.20   Average Profit versus Order Quantity

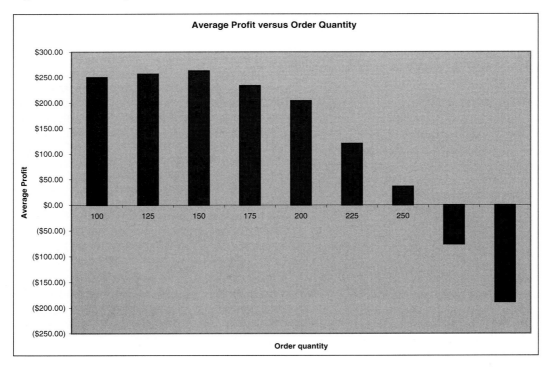

To Freeze or Not to Freeze

In developing this simulation model, we didn't instruct you to freeze the random numbers in column B. The effect is that every time you press the F9 key or make any change to your spreadsheet model, a new set of simulated answers (including those in the data table) will appear. Depending on the speed of your computer, this recalculation can take a few seconds, even for a relatively small simulation. For larger simulations, the recalculation time can be quite lengthy, which is one of the primary reasons you might want to freeze your random numbers.

However, the drawback is that once the random numbers are frozen, you are stuck with that particular set of random numbers. We will typically *not* freeze the random numbers. This way we will be able to generate many different scenarios simply by pressing the F9 key.

Using a Data Table to Repeat Simulations

The Walton simulation is a particularly simple "one-line" simulation model. We are able to capture all of the logic—generating a demand and calculating the corresponding profit—in a single row. Then to replicate the simulation, we simply copy this row down as far as we like. Many simulation models are significantly more complex and require more than one row to capture the logic. Nevertheless, they still result in one or more output quantities (such as profit) that we want to replicate. We now illustrate another method that is more general (still using the Walton example). It uses a *data table* to generate the replications. Refer to Figure 9.21 and the file **Walton2.xls**.

Figure 9.21 Using a Data Table to Simulate Replications

	A	B	C	D	E	F	G	H	I	J	K
1	Simulation of Walton's bookstore										
2											
3	Cost data			Demand distribution				Range names used:			
4	Unit cost	$7.50		CumProb	Demand	Probability		LookupTable	=Model!$D$5:$F$9		
5	Unit price	$10.00		0.00	100	0.30		Order_quantity	=Model!$B$9		
6	Unit refund	$2.50		0.30	150	0.20		Profit	=Model!$B$24:$B$1023		
7				0.50	200	0.30		Unit_cost	=Model!$B$4		
8	Decision variable			0.80	250	0.15		Unit_price	=Model!$B$5		
9	Order quantity	200		0.95	300	0.05		Unit_refund	=Model!$B$6		
10											
11	Summary measures from simulation below										
12	Average	$206.38		95% confidence interval for expected profit							
13	StDev	$323.17		Lower limit	$186.35						
14	Minimum	-$250.00		Upper limit	$226.40						
15	Maximum	$500.00									
16											
17	Simulation										
18		Demand	Revenue	Cost	Refund	Profit					
19		250	$2,000	$1,500	$0	$500					
20											
21	Data table for replications, each shows profit from that replication										
22	Replication	Profit									
23		$500									
24	1	-$250									
25	2	-$250									
26	3	$500									
27	4	$500									
28	5	$500									
29	6	-$250									
30	7	$500									
31	8	$500									
32	9	$500									
33	10	$500									
1017	994	$125									
1018	995	$125									
1019	996	-$250									
1020	997	-$250									
1021	998	$500									
1022	999	-$250									
1023	1000	$500									

Through row 19, this model is exactly like the previous model. That is, we use the given data at the top of the spreadsheet to construct a typical "prototype" of the simulation in row 19. Actually, we use our earlier suggestion. We eliminate an explicit random number cell and enter the formula

=VLOOKUP(RAND(),LookupTable,2)

for demand in cell B19. Also, we use a convention introduced in Chapter 2: We enclose any random quantity, in this case demand, in a dashed green border. This is totally optional. We do it only for readability.

Note that we no longer copy this row 19 down—and we definitely do *not* freeze the cell with the random number, cell B19. Instead, we form a data table in the range A23:B1023 to replicate the basic simulation 1000 times. In column A we list the replication numbers, 1–1000. The formula for the data table in cell B23 is **=F19**. This forms a link to the profit from the prototype row for use in the data table. Then we select the Data/Table menu item and enter *any blank cell* (such as C23) as the column input cell. (No row input cell is necessary, so its box should be left empty.) This tricks Excel into repeating the row 19 calculations 1000 times, each time with a new random number, and reporting the profits in column B of the data table. (If we wanted to see other simulated quantities, such as revenue, for each replication, we could add extra output columns to the data table.)

The key to simulating many replications in Excel (without an add-in) is to use a data table with any blank cell as the column input cell.

→ **EXCEL TIP:** *How Data Tables Work*
To understand this procedure, you must understand exactly how data tables work. When we create a data table, Excel takes each value in the left column of the data table (here column A), substitutes it into the cell we designate as the column input cell, recalculates the spreadsheet, and returns the "bottom line" value (or values) we have requested in the top row of the data table (such as profit). It might seem silly to substitute each replication number from column A into a blank cell such as cell C23, but this part is really irrelevant. The important part is the recalculation. Each recalculation leads to a new random demand and the corresponding profit, and these profits are the quantities we want. Of course, this means that we should not freeze the quantity in cell B19 before forming the data table. The whole point of the data table is to use a different random number for each replication, and this will occur only if the random demand in row 19 is left unfrozen. ■

→ **EXCEL TIP:** *Recalculation Mode*
Here is a useful Excel tip for speeding up recalculation. Select the Tools/Options menu item, click on the Calculation tab, click on the Automatic Except Tables option, and click on OK. Now when you change anything in your spreadsheet, everything will recalculate in the usual way except data tables. Data tables will not recalculate until you intentionally press the F9 key. Data tables can require a lot of computing time, so this option can be very useful. However, be aware that if you set this option and then form a data table, you will have to press F9 to make the data table recalculate the first time. Otherwise, you will see the same output value the whole way down the data table. ■

Using a Two-Way Data Table

We can carry this method one step further to see how the profit depends on the order quantity. Here we use a two-way data table with the replication number along the side and possible order quantities along the top. See Figure 9.22 and the file **Walton3.xls**. Now the data table range is A23:F1023, and the driving formula, entered in cell A23, is again the link **=F19**. The column input cell should again be *any blank cell*, and the row input cell should be B9 (the order quantity). Each cell in the body of the data table shows a simulated profit for a particular replication and a particular order quantity, and each is based on a *different* random demand.

Figure 9.22   Using a Two-Way Data Table for the Simulation Model

	A	B	C	D	E	F	G	H	I	J	K
1	Simulation of Walton's bookstore										
2											
3	Cost data			Demand distribution				Range names used:			
4	Unit cost	$7.50			CumProb	Demand	Probability	LookupTable	=Model!$D$5:$F$9		
5	Unit price	$10.00			0.00	100	0.30	Order_quantity	=Model!$B$9		
6	Unit refund	$2.50			0.30	150	0.20	Unit_cost	=Model!$B$4		
7					0.50	200	0.30	Unit_price	=Model!$B$5		
8	Decision variable				0.80	250	0.15	Unit_refund	=Model!$B$6		
9	Order quantity	200			0.95	300	0.05				
10											
11	Summary measures of simulated profits for each order quantity										
12				Order quantity							
13		100	125	150	175	200	225	250	275	300	
14	Average profit	$250.00	$260.00	$285.00	$246.25	$140.00	$131.25	-$20.00	$31.25	-$210.00	
15	Stdev profit	$0.00	$85.04	$161.78	$244.00	$338.48	$363.83	$393.96	$435.63	$455.58	
16											
17	Simulation										
18			Demand	Revenue	Cost	Refund	Profit				
19			250	$2,000	$1,500	$0	$500				
20											
21	Data table showing profit for replications with various order quantities										
22	Replication			Order quantity							
23	$500.00	100	125	150	175	200	225	250	275	300	
24	1	$250	$313	$375	$250	$500	-375	250	687.5	-750	
25	2	$250	$125	$375	-$125	$125	375	250	125	0	
26	3	$250	$313	$0	$438	-$250	-375	250	-625	0	
27	4	$250	$313	$375	-$125	-$250	-375	-500	-250	0	
28	5	$250	$313	$375	$438	-$250	-375	-125	125	0	
29	6	$250	$313	$375	$438	$500	375	-125	-625	375	
30	7	$250	$313	$375	$438	$500	0	625	-250	375	
31	8	$250	$313	$375	-$125	$125	0	250	500	375	
32	9	$250	$313	$0	-$125	$500	375	-125	-625	375	
1019	996	$250	$313	$375	$438	$500	-375	625	125	-750	
1020	997	$250	$313	$375	$438	-$250	562.5	625	-250	375	
1021	998	$250	$125	$375	$250	$500	-375	250	-625	-750	
1022	999	$250	$313	$0	$438	$125	562.5	625	125	0	
1023	1000	$250	$125	$375	$438	$500	562.5	-125	125	-750	

Figure 9.23

Bar Chart of Average Profits for Different Order Quantities

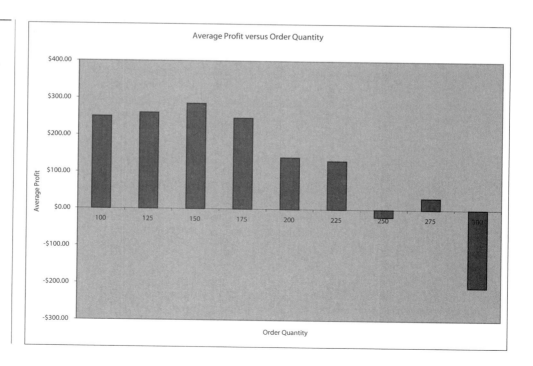

By averaging the numbers in each column of the data table (see row 14), we again see that 150 appears to be the best order quantity. It is also helpful to construct a bar chart of these averages, as in Figure 9.23. Now, however, assuming you have not frozen anything, the data table and the corresponding chart will change each time you press the F9 key. To see whether 150 is always the best order quantity, you can press the F9 key and see whether the bar above 150 continues to be the highest. ■

By now you should appreciate the usefulness of data tables in spreadsheet simulations. They allow us to take a "prototype" simulation and replicate its key results as often as we like. This method makes summary statistics (over the entire group of replications) and corresponding charts fairly easy to obtain. Nevertheless, it takes some work to create the data tables and charts. In the next section we will see how the @RISK add-in does a lot of this work for us.

PROBLEMS

Skill-Building Problems

11. Suppose you own an expensive car and purchase auto insurance. This insurance has a $1000 deductible, so that if you have an accident and the damage is less than $1000, you pay for it out of your pocket. However, if the damage is greater than $1000, you pay the first $1000 and the insurance pays the rest. In the current year there is probability 0.025 of your having an accident. If you have an accident, the damage amount is normally distributed with mean $3000 and standard deviation $750.

    a. Use Excel and a one-way data table to simulate the amount you have to pay for damages to your car. Run 5000 iterations. Then find the average amount you pay, the standard deviation of the amounts you pay, and a 95% confidence interval for the average amount you pay. (Note that many of the amounts you pay will be 0 because you have no accident.)

    b. Continue the simulation in part **a** by creating a two-way data table, where the row input is the deductible amount, varied from $500 to $2000 in multiples of $500. Now find the average amount you pay, the standard deviation of the amounts you pay, and a 95% confidence interval for the average amount you pay for *each* deductible amount.

    c. Do you think it is reasonable to assume that damage amounts are *normally* distributed? What would you criticize about this assumption? What might you suggest instead?

12. In August 2003, a car dealer is trying to determine how many 2004 cars to order. Each car ordered in August 2003 costs $10,000. The demand for the dealer's 2004 models has the probability distribution shown in

the file **P09_12.xls**. Each car sells for $15,000. If demand for 2004 cars exceeds the number of cars ordered in August, the dealer must reorder at a cost of $12,000 per car. Excess cars can be disposed of at $9000 per car. Use simulation to determine how many cars to order in August. For your optimal order quantity, find a 95% confidence interval for the expected profit.

13. In the Walton Bookstore example, suppose that Walton receives no money for the first 50 excess calendars returned but receives $2.50 for every calendar after the first 50 returned. Does this change the optimal order quantity?

14. A sweatshirt supplier is trying to decide how many sweatshirts to print for the upcoming NCAA basketball championships. The final four teams have emerged from the quarterfinal round, and there is now a week left until the semifinals, which are then followed in a couple of days by the finals. Each sweatshirt costs $10 to produce and sells for $25. However, in 3 weeks, any leftover sweatshirts will be put on sale for half price, $12.50. The supplier assumes that the demand for his sweatshirts during the next 3 weeks (when interest is at its highest) has the distribution shown in the file **P09_14.xls**. The residual demand, after the sweatshirts have been put on sale, has the distribution also shown in this file. The supplier, being a profit maximizer, realizes that every sweatshirt sold, even at the sale price, yields a profit. However, he also realizes that any sweatshirts produced but not sold (even at the sale price) must be thrown away, resulting in a $10 loss per sweatshirt. Analyze the supplier's problem with a simulation model.

Skill-Extending Problem

15. In the Walton Bookstore example with a discrete demand distribution, explain why an order quantity other than one of the possible demands cannot maximize the expected profit. (*Hint*: Consider an order of 190 calendars. If this maximizes expected profit, then it must yield a higher expected profit than an order of 150 or 100. But then an order of 200 calendars must also yield a larger expected profit than 190 calendars. Why?)

9.5 INTRODUCTION TO @RISK

@RISK provides a number of functions for simulating from various distributions, and it takes care of all the bookkeeping in spreadsheet simulations. Simulating without @RISK in Excel requires much more work for the user.

Spreadsheet simulation modeling has become extremely popular in recent years, both in the academic and corporate communities. Much of the reason for this popularity is due to simulation add-ins such as @RISK. There are two primary advantages to using such an add-in. First, an add-in gives us easy access to many probability distributions we might want to use in our simulation models. We already saw in Section 9.3 how the RISKDISCRETE, RISKNORMAL, and RISKTRIANG functions, among others, are easy to use and remember. Second, an add-in allows us to perform simulations much more easily than is possible with Excel alone. To replicate a simulation in Excel, we typically need to build a data table. Then we have to calculate summary statistics, such as averages, standard deviations, and percentiles, with built-in Excel functions. If we want graphs to enhance the analysis, we have to create them. In short, we have to perform a number of time-consuming steps for each simulation. Simulation add-ins such as @RISK perform much of this work for us automatically.

Although we will focus on @RISK in this book, it is not the only available simulation add-in for Excel. A worthy competitor is Crystal Ball, developed by Decisioneering (www.decisioneering.com). Crystal Ball has much of the same functionality as @RISK. In addition, because of the relative ease of developing "home-grown" applications in Excel with Excel's built-in macro language Visual Basic for Applications (VBA), some individuals are developing their own simulation add-ins for Excel. However, we have a natural bias for @RISK—we have been permitted by its developer, Palisade Corporation (www.palisade.com), to include it in the CD-ROM that accompanies this book. If it were not included, you would have to purchase it from Palisade at a fairly steep price. Indeed, Microsoft Office does not include @RISK, Crystal Ball, or any other simulation add-in—you must purchase them separately.

@RISK Features

Here is an overview of some of @RISK's features. We will discuss all of these in more detail later in this section.

1. @RISK contains a number of functions such as RISKNORMAL and RISKDISCRETE that make it easy to generate observations from the most important probability distributions. We discussed these in Section 9.3.

2. You can specify any cell or range of cells in your simulation model as **output cells**. When you run the simulation, @RISK automatically keeps summary measures (averages, standard deviations, percentiles, and others) from the values generated in these output cells across the replications. It can also create graphs such as histograms based on these values. In other words, @RISK takes care of tedious bookkeeping operations for you.

3. @RISK has a special function, RISKSIMTABLE, that allows you to run the same simulation several times, using a different value of some key input variable each time. This input variable is typically a decision variable. For example, suppose that you

would like to simulate an inventory ordering policy (as in the Walton Bookstore example). Your ultimate purpose is to compare simulation outputs across a number of possible order quantities such as 100, 150, 200, 250, and 300. If you use an appropriate formula involving the RISKSIMTABLE function, the entire simulation will be performed for each of these order quantities separately—with one click of a button. You can then compare the outputs to choose the "best" order quantity.

Loading @RISK

To build simulation models with @RISK, you need to have Excel open with @RISK added in. The first step, if you have not already done so, is to install the PalisadeDecision Tools suite with the Setup program on the CD-ROM that accompanies this book. Then you can load @RISK by clicking on the Windows Start button, selecting the Programs group, selecting the Palisade Decision Tools group, and finally selecting the @RISK item. If Excel is already open, this will load @RISK inside Excel. If Excel is not yet open, this will launch Excel and @RISK simultaneously.[7] (When you are asked whether you want to load the macros, click on Yes.) Once @RISK is loaded, you will see two new toolbars, the Decision Tools toolbar in Figure 9.24, and the @RISK toolbar in Figure 9.25.[8] You will also have a new @RISK menu added to the usual Excel menu bar.

Figure 9.24
Decision Tools Toolbar

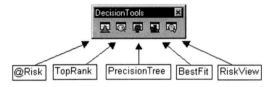

Figure 9.25
@RISK Toolbar

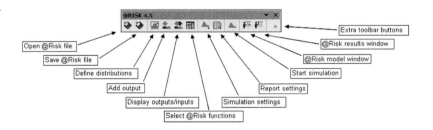

@RISK Models with a Single Random Input Variable

The majority of the work (and thinking) goes into developing the model. Setting up @RISK and then running it are relatively easy.

In the remainder of this section we will illustrate some of @RISK's functionality by revisiting the Walton Bookstore example. Then in the next chapter, we will use @RISK to help develop a number of interesting simulation models. Throughout our discussion, you should keep one very important idea in mind. The development of a simulation model is basically a two-step procedure. The first step is to build the model itself. This step requires you to build in all of the logic that transforms inputs (including @RISK functions such as RISKDISCRETE) into outputs (such as profit). This is where most of the work and thinking go, exactly as in models from previous chapters, and @RISK cannot do this for you. It is *your* job to enter the formulas that link inputs to outputs appropriately. However, once

---

[7]We have had the best luck when we (1) close other applications we are not currently using, and (2) launch Excel and @RISK together by starting @RISK (rather than starting @RISK *after* Excel is already running).
[8]The Decision Tools toolbar lets you open other programs in the suite, such as the PrecisionTree add-in used in Chapter 8.

this logic has been incorporated, @RISK takes over in the second step. It automatically replicates your model, with different random numbers on each replication, and it reports any summary measures that you request in tabular or graphical form. Therefore, @RISK can greatly decrease the amount of "busy work" you need to do, but it is not a magic bullet!

We begin by analyzing an example with a single random input variable.

EXAMPLE	9.2 Using @RISK at Walton Bookstore

This is the same Walton bookstore model as before, except that we now use a triangular distribution for demand.

Recall that Walton Bookstore buys calendars for $7.50, sells them at the regular price of $10, and gets a refund of $2.50 for all calendars that cannot be sold. In contrast to Example 9.1, we will now assume that Walton estimates a triangular probability distribution for demand, where the minimum, most likely, and maximum values of demand are 100, 175, and 300, respectively. The company wants to use this probability distribution, together with @RISK, to simulate the profit for any particular order quantity. It eventually wants to find the "best" order quantity.

Objective   To learn about @RISK's basic functionality by revisiting the Walton bookstore problem.

Where Do the Numbers Come From?

The monetary values are the same as before. The parameters of the triangular distribution of demand are probably Walton's best subjective estimates, possibly guided by its experience with previous calendars.

Solution

We will use this example to illustrate many (but certainly not all) of @RISK's features. We first see how it helps us to choose an appropriate input probability distribution for demand. Then we will use it to build a simulation model for a specific order quantity and generate outputs from this model. Finally, we will see how the RISKSIMTABLE function enables us to simultaneously generate outputs from several order quantities so that we can choose a "best" order quantity.

Developing the Simulation Model

The spreadsheet model for profit is essentially the same as we developed previously *without @RISK*, as shown in Figure 9.26 (page 458). (See the file **Walton4.xls**.) The only new things to be aware of are the following.

❶ Input distribution.   To generate a random demand, enter the formula

=ROUND(RISKTRIANG(E4,E5,E6),0)

in cell B13 for the random demand. This uses the RISKTRIANG function to generate a demand from the given input distribution. (As before, we continue to put a dashed green border around random input cells.) We also use Excel's ROUND function to round demand to the nearest integer. Recall from our discussion in Section 9.3 that Excel has no built-in functions to generate random numbers from a triangular distribution, but it is easy with @RISK.

Figure 9.26

Simulation Model with a Fixed Order Quantity

	A	B	C	D	E	F
1	Simulation of Walton's Bookstore using @RISK					
2						
3	Cost data			Demand distribution - triangular		
4	Unit cost	$7.50		Minimum	100	
5	Unit price	$10.00		Most likely	175	
6	Unit refund	$2.50		Maximum	300	
7						
8	Decision variable					
9	Order quantity	200				
10						
11	Simulated quantities					
12		Demand	Revenue	Cost	Refund	Profit
13		203	$2,000	$1,500	$0	$500
14						
15	Summary measures of profit from @Risk - based on 1000 iterations					
16	Minimum	-$1,307.50				
17	Maximum	$500.00				
18	Average	$164.11				
19	Standard deviation	$335.05				

② **Output cell.** When we run the simulation, we want @RISK to keep track of profit. In @RISK's terminology, we need to designate the Profit cell, F13, as an **output cell**. There are two ways to designate a cell as an output cell. One way is to highlight it and then click on the Add Output Cell button on the @RISK toolbar. (See Figure 9.25.) An equivalent way is to add **RISKOUTPUT(*"label"*)+** to the cell's formula. (Here, "label" is a label that will be used for @RISK's reports. In this case it makes sense to use "Profit" as the label.) Either way, the formula in cell F13 changes from

=C13+E13-D13

to

=RISKOUTPUT("Profit")+C13+E13-E13

The plus sign following RISKOUTPUT does *not* indicate addition. It is simply @RISK's way of indicating that we want to keep track of the value in this cell (for reporting reasons) as the simulation progresses. Any number of cells can be designated in this way as output cells. They are typically the "bottom line" values of primary interest. We will enclose such cells with a double-black border for emphasis.

③ **Inputs and outputs.** @RISK keeps a list of all input cells (cells with @RISK random functions) and output cells. If you want to check the list at any time, click on the Display Inputs, Outputs button on the @RISK toolbar (see Figure 9.25). It provides an Explorer-like list, as shown in Figure 9.27.

Figure 9.27

List of @RISK Inputs and Outputs

④ **Model Window and RISKview.** As indicated in Figure 9.27, when you ask for a list of @RISK inputs and outputs, you see them in the @RISK Model window. (You can also open this Model window directly from the @RISK toolbar. See the third from right button in Figure 9.25.) This Model window provides a lot of advanced tools. We just mention that if you select its Insert/Distribution Window menu item, you get all of the same functionality of RISKview discussed previously. By the way, once the @RISK Model window has been opened, you cannot close it without closing @RISK entirely; you can only minimize it. (The same goes for the @RISK Results window, to be discussed shortly.)

5 **Summary functions.** @RISK provides several functions for summarizing output values. We illustrate these in the range B16:B19 of Figure 9.26. They contain the formulas

=RISKMIN(F13)

=RISKMAX(F13)

=RISKMEAN(F13)

and

=RISKSTDDEV(F13)

These @RISK summary functions allow you to show simulation results on the same sheet as the model. They are totally optional.

The values in these cells are not of any use until we run the simulation. However, once the simulation runs, these formulas capture summary statistics of profit. For example, the RISKMEAN function calculates the average of the profits generated during the simulation. Although these same summary statistics also appear in @RISK output reports, it is sometimes handy to have them in the same worksheet as the model.

Running the Simulation

Now that we have developed the model for Walton, the rest is straightforward. The procedure is always the same. We specify the simulation settings and the report settings and then run the simulation.

Checking the Monte Carlo option has no effect on the ultimate simulation results, but it allows us to see "random" numbers in the model sheet.

1 **Simulation settings.** We must first tell @RISK how we want the simulation to be run. To do so, click on the Simulation Settings button on the @RISK toolbar. Click on the Iterations tab and fill out the dialog box as in Figure 9.28. This says that we want to replicate the simulation 1000 times, each time with a new random demand. (@RISK uses the term *iteration* instead of *replication*. We actually prefer the latter, but we will use both terms interchangeably.) Then click on the Sampling tab and fill out the dialog box as in Figure 9.29. For technical reasons, it is *always* best to use Latin Hypercube sampling—it is more efficient. We also recommend checking the Monte Carlo button in the Standard Recalc group. Although this has *no* effect on the ultimate results, it means that you will see *random* numbers in the spreadsheet—that is, values that change when you press the F9 key. Otherwise, if you select the default Expected Value option, the values in the spreadsheet will not appear to be random—they will not change when you press the F9 key. We find this disconcerting.

Figure 9.28

Setting the Number of Iterations (Replications)

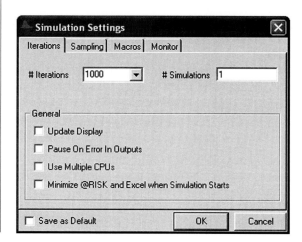

Figure 9.29

Other Simulation
Settings

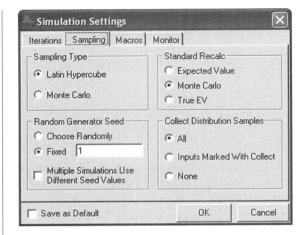

*The Report Settings
option allows us to
receive selected
@RISK results in new
Excel worksheets.*

② Report Settings. By default, when @RISK runs a simulation model, it shows its results in a "Results window" that is seemingly outside of Excel. Often you will prefer to have the results in an Excel worksheet, probably in the same workbook as your model. This is easy to accomplish. Click on the Report Settings button on the @RISK toolbar to obtain the dialog box in Figure 9.30. We suggest that you use the settings shown here, although you can experiment with other settings. We are asking for a simulation summary and output graphs, to be placed in the *same* workbook as the model. By checking both of the top two boxes, we will see the results in our workbook *and* in @RISK's Results window. This is a good idea because @RISK's Results window provides more flexibility that you will come to appreciate. (If you like these settings, check the Save as Default box. Then you won't have to go through this procedure again on future models.)

Figure 9.30

@RISK Report
Settings

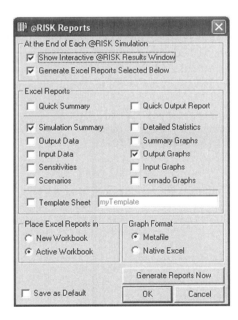

③ Run the simulation. We are now ready to run the simulation. To do so, simply click on the Start Simulation button on the @RISK toolbar. (We think of this as the "red piano" button.) At this point, @RISK repeatedly generates a random number for each random input cell, recalculates the worksheet, and keeps track of all output cell values. You can watch the progress at the bottom left of the screen.

Discussion of the Simulation Results

@RISK generates a large number of output measures. We discuss the most important of these now.

1. **Summary Report.** Assuming that the top box in Figure 9.30 is checked (which we recommend), we are immediately transferred to the @RISK Results window. This window contains the summary results in Figure 9.31. The top line summarizes the 1000 profits generated during the simulation. The smallest of these was −$235, the largest was $500, they averaged $337.50, 5% of them were less than or equal to −$47.50, and 95% of them were below $500. (Actually, there were many iterations with a profit of $500, so the 95th percentile shown is the same as the maximum profit.) Note that the summary measures reported here match those from the RISKMIN, RISKMAX, and RISKMEAN functions in Figure 9.26. Also, note in Figure 9.31 that @RISK also summarizes the random input cells, in this case the random demand cell.

Figure 9.31   @RISK Summary Report

	Name	Cell	Minimum	Mean	Maximum	x1	p1	x2	p2	x2-x1	p2-p1	Errors
Output 1	Profit	F13	-235	337.4975	500	-47.5	5%	500	95%	547.5	90%	0
Input 1	Demand	B13	101.8832	191.66	295.0232	127.2914	5%	264.4886	95%	137.1971	90%	0

Leave Latin Hypercube sampling on. It produces more accurate results.

→ **@RISK Technical Issue:** *Latin Hypercube Sampling*

In the dialog box in Figure 9.29, you should keep the Sampling Type at the default Latin Hypercube setting. This is a much more efficient option than the other (Monte Carlo) option because it produces a more accurate estimate of the mean profit. In fact, we were surprised how accurate it is. In repeated runs of this model, always using different random numbers, we virtually always got a mean profit within a few pennies of $337.50. It turns out that this is the true mean profit for this input distribution of demand. Amazingly, simulation estimates it correctly—almost right on the button—on virtually every run! Unfortunately, this means that a confidence interval for the mean, based on @RISK's outputs and the usual confidence interval formula (which assumes Monte Carlo sampling), will be much wider (more pessimistic) than it should be. Therefore, we will not even calculate such confidence intervals from here on. ■

2. **Detailed Statistics.** We can also request more detailed statistics within the @RISK Results window with the Insert/Detailed Statistics menu item. (There is also a toolbar button for doing this.) These detailed statistics are shown in Figure 9.32 (page 462). All of the information from Figure 9.31 is here, plus more. (A few other measures extend below this figure.) For example, the 25th percentile indicates that 25% of the 1000 profits generated were below $207.50. Also, because the 10th percentile for profit is positive, we estimate that the probability of breaking even, with an order quantity of 200, is somewhere between 0.05 and 0.10.

The Detailed Statistics window shows many summary measures, including percentiles and "target" values.

3. **Target values.** By scrolling to the bottom of the detailed statistics list in Figure 9.32, you can enter any target value or target percentage. If you enter a target value, @RISK calculates the corresponding percentage, and vice versa. Here we entered a target profit of $0, and @RISK calculated the corresponding percentage as 7.5%. (See Figure 9.33 on page 462.) This means that 7.5% of the 1000 profits were $0 or negative. We can also enter a percentage. For the second target we enter 12%. We see that 12% of the simulated profits were less than or equal to $65. @RISK provides room for up to 10 target value/percentage pairs.

Figure 9.32

Detailed Statistics
Window

Detailed Statistics

Name	Profit	Demand
Description	Output	RiskTriang(E4,E5,E6)
Cell	F13	B13
Minimum	-235	101.8832
Maximum	500	295.0232
Mean	337.4975	191.66
Std Deviation	189.0535	41.26522
Variance	35741.22	1702.818
Skewness	-0.9485486	0.234637
Kurtosis	2.796431	2.401627
Errors Calculated	0	0
Mode	500	175.013
5% Perc	-47.5	127.2914
10% Perc	42.5	138.6778
15% Perc	102.5	147.3879
20% Perc	162.5	154.7688
25% Perc	207.5	161.1534
30% Perc	252.5	167.0146
35% Perc	290	172.4418
40% Perc	327.5	177.4952
45% Perc	372.5	182.6519
50% Perc	410	188.1791
55% Perc	455	193.8298
60% Perc	500	199.9946
65% Perc	500	206.3709
70% Perc	500	213.2889
75% Perc	500	220.8136
80% Perc	500	229.1767
85% Perc	500	238.5924
90% Perc	500	249.9173
95% Perc	500	264.4886

Figure 9.33

Target Values and
Percentiles

Detailed Statistics

Name	Profit	Demand
Description	Output	RiskTriang(E4,E5,E6)
Cell	F13	B13
95% Perc	500	264.4886
Filter Minimum		
Filter Maximum		
Filter Type		
# Values Filtered	0	0
Scenario #1	>75%	
Scenario #2	<25%	
Scenario #3	>90%	
Target #1 (Value)	0	
Target #1 (Perc%)	7.5%	
Target #2 (Value)	65	
Target #2 (Perc%)	12%	
Target #3 (Value)		
Target #3 (Perc%)		

Use @RISK charts, particularly histograms, to get an immediate and intuitive view of the distributions of outputs.

4. **Simulation data.** The results to this point *summarize* the simulation. It is also possible to see the full results—the data, demands and profits, from all 1000 replications. To do this, select the Insert/Data menu item in @RISK's Results Window. A portion of the data for this simulation is shown in Figure 9.34.

5. **Charts.** To see the results graphically, click on the Profit item in the left pane (the Explorer-like list) of the Results Window and then select the Insert/Graph/Histogram menu item. This creates a histogram of the 1000 profits from the simulation, as shown in Figure 9.35. You can move the "sliders" at the top of the chart to the left or right to see various probabilities. For example, after moving the sliders, we see in the figure that 7.5% of the simulated profits are below $0 and 67.8% are above $270. Also, we see that the distribution of profit is very skewed to the left when the order quantity is 200. Evidently, triangularly distributed inputs do not always lead to triangularly distributed outputs! Why does this skewness occur? If demand is greater than 200, the or-

Figure 9.34
Simulation Data
Window

Name	Profit	Demand
Description	Output	RiskTriang(E4,E5,E6)
Iteration# / Cell	F13	B13
1	500	271.31909
2	252.50000	167.31625
3	500	248.32030
4	500	203.35899
5	500	221.70041
6	500	207.22614
7	500	260.43826
8	500	240.70154
9	335	177.58284
10	500	210.15402
11	500	208.80281
12	290	171.54398
13	500	235.61909
14	335	178.16908

der quantity level, then 200 calendars will be sold and profit will be $500, regardless of the *exact* demand. Therefore, there is a reasonably good chance (about 40%) that profit will be exactly $500. On the other side, when demand is less than 200, profit gradually decreases as demand decreases. This leads to the negative skewness.

Figure 9.35
Histogram of
Simulated Profits

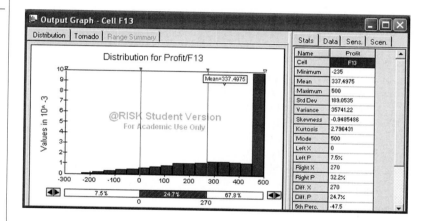

6. **Outputs in Excel.** Often we will want the simulation outputs, including charts, in an Excel workbook. The easiest way to get the results in Figures 9.31 and 9.35, say, into an Excel workbook is to fill out the Report Settings dialog box as we did in Figure 9.30. In this case, separate worksheets are created to hold the reports. For example, a worksheet named Summary Report (see Figure 9.36 on page 464, which shows most of the report) is created to hold virtually the same information as in Figure 9.31.

It is also possible to get selected summary measures of outputs in the same worksheet as the simulation model by using @RISK's summary functions. For example, if we want to see the average of the simulated profits, we can enter the formula **=RISKMEAN(F13)** in some blank cell, as we did in Figure 9.26. Then once the simulation has been run, this cell will indicate the average of the simulated profits. (Until the simulation is run, this cell won't contain any useful information.) To learn about other @RISK summary functions, check out @RISK's online help for "statistics functions." We will illustrate a few more of these in the next chapter.

Figure 9.36 @RISK Summary Report in Excel Worksheet

	A	B	C	D	E	F	G	H
1		@RISK Summary Report						
2								
3		General Information						
4								
5		**Workbook Name**	Walton4.xls					
6		**Number of Simulations**	1					
7		**Number of Iterations**	1000					
8		**Number of Inputs**	1					
9		**Number of Outputs**	1					
10		**Sampling Type**	Latin Hypercube					
11		**Simulation Start Time**	6/30/03 13:18:05					
12		**Simulation Stop Time**	6/30/03 13:18:07					
13		**Simulation Duration**	0:00:02					
14		**Random Seed**	1					
15		**Total Errors**	0					
16								
17		Output and Input Summary Statistics						
18								
19		**Output Name**	**Output Cell**	**Simulation**	**Minimum**	**Maximum**	**Mean**	**Std Dev**
20		Profit	$F$13	1	-$235	$500	$337	$189
21								
22		**Input Name**	**Input Cell**	**Simulation**	**Minimum**	**Maximum**	**Mean**	**Std Dev**
23		Demand	$B$13	1	101.8831787	295.0231934	191.6600563	41.26522056

USING RISKSIMTABLE

Walton's ultimate goal is to choose an order quantity that provides a large average profit. We could rerun the simulation model several times, each time with a different order quantity in the order quantity cell, and compare the results. However, this has two drawbacks. First, it takes a lot of time and work. The second drawback is more subtle. Each time we run the simulation, we get a *different* set of random demands. Therefore, one of the order quantities could win the contest just by luck. For a fairer comparison, it is better to test each order quantity on the *same* set of random demands.

The RISKSIMTABLE function in @RISK enables us to obtain a fair comparison quickly and easily. We illustrate this function in Figure 9.37. (See the file **Walton5.xls**.) There are two modifications to the previous model. The first is that we have listed order quantities we want to test in row 9. (We chose these as representative order quantities. You could change, or add to, this list.) Second, instead of entering a *number* in cell B9, we enter the *formula*

=RISKSIMTABLE(D9:H9)

Note that the list does not need to be entered in the spreadsheet (although we believe this is a good idea). We could instead enter the formula

=RISKSIMTABLE({150,175,200,225,250})

where the list of numbers must be enclosed in curly brackets. In either case, the worksheet displays the first member of the list, 150, and the corresponding calculations for this first order quantity. However, the model is now set up to run the simulation for *all* order quantities in the list.

To do this, click on the Simulation Settings button on the @RISK toolbar and fill out the Iterations dialog box as shown in Figure 9.38. Specifically, enter 1000 for the number of iterations and 5 for the number of simulations. @RISK will then run 5 simulations of 1000 iterations each, one simulation for each order quantity in the list, and it will use the *same* 1000 random demands for each simulation.

The RISKSIMTABLE function allows us to run several simulations at once— one for each value of some variable (usually a decision variable).

Figure 9.37

Model with a RISKSIMTABLE Function

	A	B	C	D	E	F	G	H
1	Simulation of Walton's Bookstore using @RISK							
2								
3	Cost data			Demand distribution - triangular				
4	Unit cost	$7.50		Minimum	100			
5	Unit price	$10.00		Most likely	175			
6	Unit refund	$2.50		Maximum	300			
7								
8	Decision variable			Possible order quantities				
9	Order quantity	150		150	175	200	225	250
10								
11	Simulated quantities							
12		Demand	Revenue	Cost	Refund	Profit		
13		254	$1,500	$1,125	$0	$375		

Figure 9.38

Simulation Settings for Multiple Simulations

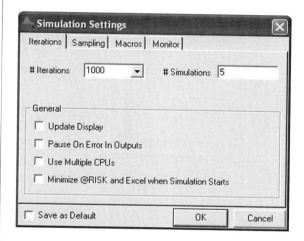

→ @RISK FUNCTION: *RISKSIMTABLE*

*To run several simulations all at once, enter the formula =**RISKSIMTABLE(InputRange)** in any cell. Here,* InputRange *refers to a list of the values to be simulated, such as various order quantities. Before running the simulation, make sure the Simulation Settings has the number of simulations set to the number of values in the* InputRange *list.* ■

After running the simulations, @RISK's Report Window shows the results for all 5 simulations. For example, the basic summary report is shown in Figure 9.39. (A list of detailed statistics for all simulations is also available.) The first five lines show summary statistics of profit for the five order quantities in the list. It is clear that order quantities of 225 or 250 (simulations #4 and #5) are not very good, and an order quantity of 175 (simulation #2) leads to the largest average profit. However, the decision is still not completely clear. The top three average profits are fairly close, but there is more potential of large losses and large gains if we use an order quantity of, say, 175 rather than 150.

Figure 9.39 Summary Statistics from Five Simulations

	Name	Cell	Sim#	Minimum	Mean	Maximum	x1	p1	x2	p2	x2-x1	p2-p1	Errors
Output 1	Profit	F13	1	15	354.165	375	202.5	5%	375	95%	172.5	90%	0
Output 1	Profit	F13	2	-110	367.2025	437.5	77.5	5%	437.5	95%	360	90%	0
Output 1	Profit	F13	3	-235	337.505	500	-47.5	5%	500	95%	547.5	90%	0
Output 1	Profit	F13	4	-360	270.3225	562.5	-172.5	5%	562.5	95%	735	90%	0
Output 1	Profit	F13	5	-485	175	625	-297.5	5%	625	95%	922.5	90%	0

Comparing summary measures doesn't always tell the whole story. Comparing histograms often provides more insight.

Separate histograms of profit from each simulation shed light on this decision, and they are easy to obtain. In fact, we get these histograms in an Output Graphs worksheet for free if we use the same Report Settings as in Figure 9.32. The histograms for order quantities of 150, 175, and 200 are shown in Figure 9.40. These histograms indicate that the profit distribution is extremely skewed for each of these order quantities, and that it is slightly more spread out as the order quantity increases. If the Walton manager decides to go entirely according to *mean* profit, he will choose an order quantity of 175. However, the information in these histograms—and his feelings toward risk—could conceivably make him choose another order quantity.

Figure 9.40 Histograms of Profit from Best Three Order Quantities

@RISK Output Graphs

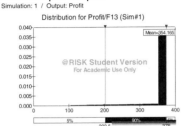
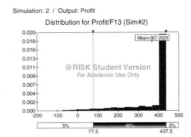
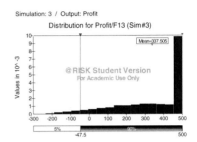

@RISK Models with Several Random Input Variables

We conclude this section with one final modification of the Walton Bookstore example. To this point, there has been a single random variable, demand. Often there are several random variables, each reflecting some uncertainty, and we want to include each of these in the simulation model. The following example illustrates how this can be done, and it also illustrates a very useful feature of @RISK, its sensitivity analysis.

EXAMPLE **9.3 ADDITIONAL UNCERTAINTY AT WALTON BOOKSTORE**

As in the previous Walton Bookstore example, Walton needs to place an order for next year's calendar. We continue to assume that the calendars will sell for $10 and customer demand for the calendars at this price is triangularly distributed with minimum value, most likely value, and maximum value equal to 100, 175, and 300. However, there are now two other sources of uncertainty. First, the maximum number of calendars Walton's supplier can supply is uncertain and is modeled with a triangular distribution. Its parameters are 125 (minimum), 200 (most likely), and 250 (maximum). Once Walton places an order, the supplier will charge $7.50 per calendar *if* he can supply the entire Walton order. Otherwise, he will charge only $7.25 per calendar. Second, unsold calendars can no longer be returned to the supplier for a refund. Instead, Walton will put them on sale for $5 apiece after February 1. At that price, Walton believes the demand for leftover calendars is triangularly distributed with parameters 0, 50, and 75. Any calendars *still* left over, say, after March 1, will be thrown away. Walton plans to order 200 calendars and wants to use simulation to analyze the resulting profit.

Objective To develop and analyze a simulation model with multiple sources of uncertainty, using @RISK, and to introduce @RISK's sensitivity analysis features.

WHERE DO THE NUMBERS COME FROM?

As in Example 9.2, the monetary values are straightforward, and the parameters of the triangular distributions would probably be educated guesses, possibly based on experience with previous calendars.

Solution

As always, we first need to develop the model. Then we can run the simulation with @RISK and examine the results.

DEVELOPING THE SIMULATION MODEL

The completed model is in Figure 9.41. (See the file **Walton6.xls**.) The model itself requires a bit more logic than the previous Walton model. It can be developed with the following steps.

Figure 9.41

@RISK Simulation Model with Three Random Inputs

	A	B	C	D	E	F	G	H	I
1	Simulation of Walton's Bookstore using @RISK								
2									
3	Cost data			Demand distribution: triangular					
4	Unit cost 1	$7.50			Regular price	Sale price			
5	Unit cost 2	$7.25		Minimum	100	0			
6	Regular price	$10.00		Most likely	175	50			
7	Sale price	$5.00		Maximum	300	75			
8									
9	Decision variable			Supply distribution: triangular					
10	Order quantity	200		Minimum	125				
11				Most likely	200				
12				Maximum	250				
13									
14	Simulated quantities				At regular price		At sale price		
15	Maximum supply	Actual supply	Cost	Demand	Revenue	Left over	Demand	Revenue	Profit
16	151	151	$1,095	190	$1,510	0	57	$0	$415

1 Random inputs. There are three random inputs in this model: the most the supplier can supply Walton, the customer demand when the selling price is $10, and the customer demand for sale-price calendars. Generate these in cells A16, D16, and G16 (using the ROUND function to obtain integers) with the RISKTRIANG function. Specifically, the formulas in cells A16, D16, and G16 are

=ROUND(RISKTRIANG(E10,E11,E12),0)

=ROUND(RISKTRIANG (E5,E6,E7),0)

and

=ROUND(RISKTRIANG (F5,F6,F7),0)

Note that in cell G16, we generate the random *potential* demand for calendars at the sale price even though there might not be any calendars left to put on sale.

2 Actual supply. The number of calendars supplied to Walton is the smaller of the number ordered and the maximum the supplier is able to supply. Calculate this value in cell B16 with the formula

=MIN(A16,Order_quantity)

3 Order cost. Walton gets the reduced price, $7.25, if the supplier cannot supply the entire order. Otherwise, Walton must pay $7.50 per calendar. Therefore, calculate the total order cost in cell C16 with the formula (using the obvious range names)

=IF(A16>=Order_quantity,Unit_cost_1,Unit_cost_2)*B16

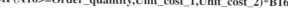

④ Other quantities. The rest of the model is straightforward. Calculate the revenue from regular-price sales in cell E16 with the formula

=Regular_price*MIN(B16,D16)

Calculate the number left over after regular-price sales in cell F16 with the formula

=MAX(B16-D16,0)

Calculate the revenue from sale-price sales in cell H16 with the formula

=Sale_price*MIN(F16,G16)

Finally, calculate profit and designate it as an output cell for @RISK in cell I16 with the formula

=RISKOUTPUT("Profit")+E16+H16-C16

We could also designate other cells (the revenue cells, for example) as output cells, but we have chosen to have a single output cell, Profit.

Running the Simulation

On each iteration, @RISK generates a new set of random inputs and calculates the corresponding output(s).

As always, the next steps are to specify the simulation settings (we chose 1000 iterations and 1 simulation), specify the report settings (we used the same as in the previous example), and run the simulation. It is important to realize what @RISK does when it runs a simulation, especially when there are several random input cells. For each iteration, @RISK generates a random value for each input variable *independently*. In this example, it generates a maximum supply in cell A16 from one triangular distribution, it generates a regular-price demand in cell D16 from another triangular distribution, and it generates a sale-price demand in cell G16 from a third triangular distribution. With these input values, it then calculates profit. It then iterates this procedure 1000 times and keeps track of the corresponding profits.[9]

Discussion of the Simulation Results

Selected results are given in Figures 9.42 and 9.43. They indicate an average profit of $396, a 5th percentile of $56, a 95th percentile of $528, and a distribution of profits that is again skewed to the left.

Figure 9.42
@RISK Summary Report

	Name	Cell	Minimum	Mean	Maximum	x1	p1	x2	p2	x2-x1	p2-p1	Errors
Output 1	Profit	I16	-230	396.291	547.25	55.75	5%	528	95%	472.25	90%	0
Input 1	Maximum supply	A16	126.652	191.6645	247.5416	146.4764	5%	232.2443	95%	85.76784	90%	0
Input 2	Demand	D16	101.8832	191.6617	295.0232	127.2089	5%	264.356	95%	137.147	90%	0
Input 3	Demand	G16	1.245575	41.66713	74.81119	13.5884	5%	65.2654	95%	51.677	90%	0

Sensitivity Analysis

We now demonstrate a feature of @RISK that is particularly useful when there are several random input cells. This feature lets us see which of these inputs is most related to, or *correlated* with, an output cell. To perform this analysis, select the Insert/Graph/Tornado Graph menu item from the @RISK Results window. In the resulting dialog box, select Correlation from the dropdown list on the right. This produces the results in Figure 9.44.

---

[9]It is also possible to *correlate* the inputs, as we will demonstrate in the next section.

Figure 9.43

Histogram of
Simulated Profits

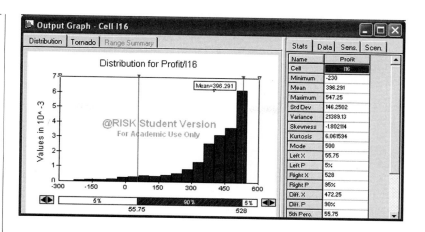

Figure 9.44

Tornado Graph for
Sensitivity Analysis

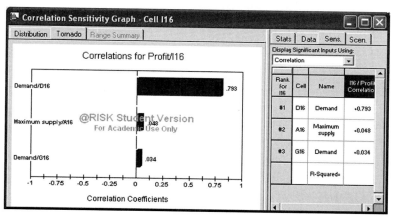

*A tornado chart
allows us to see which
of the random inputs
have the most effect
on an output.*

(The Regression option produces similar results, but we believe the Correlation option is easier to understand.)

This figure shows graphically and numerically how each of the random inputs correlates with profit: the higher the (magnitude of the) correlation, the stronger the relationship between that input and profit. In this sense, we see that the regular-price demand has by far the largest effect on profit. The other two inputs, maximum supply and sale-price demand, are nearly uncorrelated with profit, so they are much less important. Identifying important input variables is important for real applications. If a random input is highly correlated with an important output, then it might be worth the time and money to learn more about this input and possibly reduce the amount of uncertainty involving it. ∎

PROBLEMS

Skill-Building Problems

16. If you add several normally distributed random numbers, the result is normally distributed, where the mean of the sum is the sum of the individual means, and the variance of the sum is the sum of the individual variances. (Remember that variance is the square of standard deviation.) This is a difficult result to prove mathematically, but it is easy to demonstrate with simulation. To do so, run a simulation where you add three normally distributed random numbers, each with mean 100 and standard deviation 10. Your single output variable should be the sum of these three numbers. Verify with @RISK that the distribution of this output is approximately normal with mean 300 and variance 300 (hence, standard deviation $\sqrt{300} = 17.32$).

17. In Problem 11, suppose that the damage amount is triangularly distributed with parameters 500, 1500, and 7000. That is, the damage in an accident can be as low as $500 or as high as $7000, the most likely value is $1500, and there is definite skewness to the right. (It turns out, as you can verify in RISKview, that the mean of this distribution is $3000, the same as in Problem 11.) Use @RISK to simulate the amount you pay for damage. Run 5000 iterations. Then answer the following questions. In each case, explain how the indicated event would occur.

   a. What is the probability that you pay a positive amount but less than $250?

   b. What is the probability that you pay more than $500?

   c. What is the probability that you pay exactly $1000 (the deductible)?

18. Continuing the previous problem, assume as in Problem 11 that the damage amount is *normally* distributed with mean $3000 and standard deviation $750. Run @RISK with 5000 iterations to simulate the amount you pay for damage. Compare your results with those in the previous problem. Does it appear to matter whether you assume a triangular distribution or a normal distribution for damage amounts? Why isn't this a totally fair comparison? (*Hint*: Use RISKview to find the standard deviation for the triangular distribution.)

19. In Problem 12, suppose that the demand for cars is normally distributed with mean 100 and standard deviation 15. Use @RISK to determine the "best" order quantity—that is, the one with the largest mean profit. Using the statistics and/or graphs from @RISK, discuss whether this order quantity would be considered best by the car dealer. (The point is that a decision maker can use more than just *mean* profit in making a decision.)

20. Use @RISK to analyze the sweatshirt situation in Problem 14. Do this for the discrete distributions given in the problem. Then do it for normal distributions. For the normal case, assume that the regular demand is normally distributed with mean 9800 and standard deviation 1300 and that the demand at the reduced price is normally distributed with mean 3800 and standard deviation 1400.

Skill-Extending Problem

21. Although the normal distribution is a reasonable input distribution in many situations, it does have two potential drawbacks: (1) it allows negative values, even though they may be extremely improbable, and (2) it is a symmetric distribution. Many situations are modeled better with a distribution that allows only positive values and is skewed to the right. Two of these are the gamma and lognormal distributions, and @RISK enables you to generate observations from each of these distributions. The @RISK function for the gamma distribution is RISKGAMMA, and it takes two arguments, as in =**RISKGAMMA(3,10)**. The first argument, which must be positive, determines the shape. The smaller it is, the more skewed the distribution is to the right; the larger it is, the more symmetric the distribution is. The second argument determines the scale, in the sense that the product of it and the first argument equals the mean of the distribution. (The mean above is 30.) Also, the product of the second argument and the square root of the first argument is the standard deviation of the distribution. (Above, it is $\sqrt{3}(10) = 17.32$.) The @RISK function for the lognormal distribution is RISKLOGNORM. It has two arguments, as in =**RISKLOGNORM(40,10)**. These arguments are the mean and standard deviation of the distribution. Rework Example 9.2 for the following demand distributions. Do the simulated outputs have any different qualitative properties with these skewed distributions than with the normal distribution used in the example?

   a. Gamma distribution with parameters 2 and 85

   b. Gamma distribution with parameters 5 and 35

   c. Lognormal distribution with mean 170 and standard deviation 60

9.6 THE EFFECTS OF INPUT DISTRIBUTIONS ON RESULTS

In Section 9.3 we discussed input distributions. The randomness in input variables causes the variability in the output variables. We now briefly explore whether the choice of input distribution(s) makes much difference in the distribution of an output variable such as profit. This is an important question. If the choice of input distribution doesn't matter much, then we do not need to agonize over this choice. However, if it *does* make a difference, then we have to be more careful about choosing the most appropriate input distribution for any particular problem. Unfortunately, it is impossible to answer the question definitively. The best we can say in general is, "It depends." Some models are more sensitive to changes in the shape or parameters of input distributions than others. Still, the issue is worth exploring.

We discuss two types of sensitivity analysis in this section. First, we see whether the shape of the input distribution matters. In the Walton bookstore example, we have been assuming a triangularly distributed demand with some skewness. Do we get basically the same results if we try another input distribution such as the normal distribution? Second, we see whether the *independence* of input variables that we have implicitly assumed to this point is crucial to the output results. Many random quantities in real situations are not independent; they are positively or negatively correlated. Fortunately, @RISK enables us to build correlation into a model. We will analyze the effect of this correlation.

Effect of the Shape of the Input Distribution(s)

We first explore the effect of the shape of the input distribution(s). As the following example indicates, if we make a "fair" comparison, the shape can have a relatively minor effect.

EXAMPLE | **9.4 EFFECT OF DEMAND DISTRIBUTION AT WALTON'S**

We will continue to explore the demand for calendars at Walton Bookstore. We keep the same unit cost, unit price, and unit refund for leftovers as in Example 9.2. However, in that example we assumed a triangular distribution for demand with parameters 100, 175, and 300. Assuming that Walton orders 200 calendars, is the distribution of profit affected if we instead assume a *normal* distribution of demand?

Objective   To see whether a triangular distribution with some skewness gives the same profit distribution as a normal distribution for demand.

WHERE DO THE NUMBERS COME FROM?

The numbers here are the same as in Example 9.2. However, as discussed next, we will choose the parameters of the normal distribution to provide a "fair" comparison with the triangular distribution we used earlier.

Solution

For a fair comparison of alternative input distributions, the distributions should have (at least approximately) equal means and standard deviations.

Before diving in, it is important in this type of analysis to make a fair comparison. When we select a normal distribution for demand, we must choose a mean and standard deviation for this distribution. Which values should we choose? It seems only fair to choose the *same* mean and standard deviation that the triangular distribution has. To find the mean and standard deviation for a triangular distribution with given minimum, most likely, and maximum values, we can take advantage of RISKview. Open RISKview, select the triangular distribution, and enter the parameters 100, 175, and 300. We see that the mean and standard deviation are 191.67 and 41.248, respectively. Therefore, for a fair comparison we will use the normal distribution with mean 191.67 and standard deviation 41.248. In fact, RISKview allows you to see a comparison of these two distributions, as in Figure 9.45 (page 472). To get this chart, click on the "P/O" button in RISKview, select the normal distribution from the gallery, and enter 191.67 and 41.248 as its mean and standard deviation.

Figure 9.45

Triangular and
Normal
Distributions for
Demand

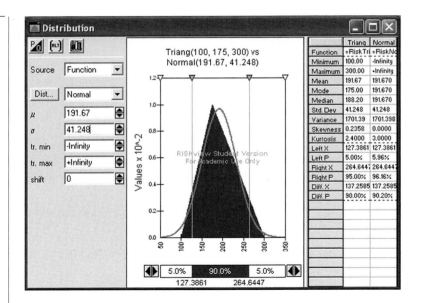

DEVELOPING THE SIMULATION MODEL

The logic in this model is almost exactly the same as we have seen before. (See Figure 9.46 and the file **Walton7.xls**.) However, a clever use of the RISKSIMTABLE function allows us to run two simulations at once, one for the triangular distribution and one for the corresponding normal distribution. The two steps required are as follows.

Figure 9.46   @RISK Model for Comparing Two Input Distributions

	A	B	C	D	E	F	G	H	I	J
1	Simulation of Walton's Bookstore using @RISK - two possible demand distributions									
2										
3	Cost data			Demand distribution 1 - triangular				Demand distribution 2 - normal		
4	Unit cost	$7.50		Minimum	100			Mean	191.67	
5	Unit price	$10.00		Most likely	175			Stdev	41.248	
6	Unit refund	$2.50		Maximum	300					
7										
8	Decision variable									
9	Order quantity	200								
10										
11	Demand distribution to use	1	←	Formula is =RiskSimtable({1,2})						
12										
13	Simulated quantities									
14		Demand	Revenue	Cost	Refund	Profit				
15		174	$1,740	$1,500	$65	$305				

As you continue to use @RISK, look for ways to use the RISKSIMTABLE function. It can really improve your efficiency because it allows you to run several simulations at once.

❶ RISKSIMTABLE function. We index the two distributions as 1 and 2. To indicate that we want to run the simulation with both of them, enter the formula

=RISKSIMTABLE({1,2})

in cell B11. Note that when we enter actual numbers in this function, rather than cell references, @RISK requires us to put curly brackets around the list of numbers.

❷ Demand. When the value in cell B11 is 1, we want the demand distribution to be triangular. When it is 2, we want the distribution to be normal. Therefore, enter the formula

=ROUND(IF(B11=1,RISKTRIANG(E4,E5,E6),RISKNORMAL(I4,I5)),0)

in cell B15. Again, the effect is that the first simulation will use the triangular distribution; the second will use the normal distribution.

Figure 9.49 Simulation Model with Correlations

	A	B	C	D	E	F	G	H	I	J	K	L
1	Simulation of Walton's Bookstore using @RISK - correlated demands											
2												
3	Cost data - same for each product			Demand distribution for each product- triangular					Correlation matrix between demands			
4	Unit cost	$7.50		Minimum	100						Product 1	Product 2
5	Unit price	$10.00		Most likely	175				Product 1	1	-0.9	
6	Unit refund	$2.50		Maximum	300				Product 2	-0.9	1	
7												
8	Decision variables								Possible correlations to try			
9	Order quantity 1	200							-0.9	0	0.9	
10	Order quantity 2	200										
11												
12	Simulated quantities											
13		Demand	Revenue	Cost	Refund	Profit			Note RISKSIMTABLE function in cell J6.			
14	Product 1	123	$1,230	$1,500	$193	-$78						
15	Product 2	284	$2,000	$1,500	$0	$500						
16	Totals	407	$3,230	$3,000	$193	$423						

To enter random values in any cells that are correlated, we start with a typical @RISK formula, such as

=RISKTRIANG(E4,E5,E6).

Then we add an extra argument, the RISKCORRMAT function, as follows:

=RISKTRIANG(E4,E5,E6,RISKCORRMAT(J5:K5,1))

The RISKCORRMAT function is "tacked on" as an extra argument to a typical random @RISK function.

The first argument of the RISKCORRMAT function is the correlation matrix range. The second is an index of the variable. In our case, the first calendar demand will have index 1, and the second will have index 2.

→ **@RISK Function: RISKCORRMAT**

This function enables us to correlate two or more input variables in an @RISK model. The function has the form RISKCORRMAT(CorrMat,Index), where CorrMat is a matrix of correlations and Index is an index of the variable being correlated to others. For example, if there are three correlated variables, Index is 1 for the first variable, 2 for the second, and 3 for the third. The RISKCORRMAT function is not entered by itself. Rather, it is entered as the last argument of a random @RISK function, such as =RISKTRIANG(10,15,30,RISKCOR-RMAT(CorrMat,2)). ■

DEVELOPING THE SIMULATION MODEL

Armed with this knowledge, the simulation model in Figure 9.49 is straightforward. It can be developed as follows.

1 Inputs. Enter the inputs in the shaded ranges in columns B and D.

2 Correlation matrix. For the correlation matrix in the range J5:H6, enter 1's on the diagonal, and enter the formula

=J6

in cell K5. Then, because we want to compare the results for several correlations (those in the range I9:K9), enter the formula

=RISKSIMTABLE(I9:K9)

in cell J6. This will allow us to simultaneously simulate negatively correlated demands, uncorrelated demands, and positively correlated demands.

3 **Order quantities.** We will assume the company orders the *same* number of each calendar, 200, so enter this value in cells B9 and B10. However, the simulation is set up so that you can experiment with any order quantities in these cells, including unequal values.

4 **Correlated demands.** Generate correlated demands by entering the formula

=ROUND(RISKTRIANG(E4,E5,E6,RISKCORRMAT(J5:K6,1)),0)

in cell B14 for demand 1 and the formula

=ROUND(RISKTRIANG(E4,E5,E6, RISKCORRMAT (J5:K6,2)),0)

in cell B15 for demand 2. The only difference between these is the index of the variable being generated. The first has index 1; the second has index 2.

5 **Other formulas.** The other formulas in rows 14 and 15 are identical to ones we developed in previous examples, so we won't discuss them again here. The quantities in row 16 are simply sums of rows 14 and 15. Also, the only @RISK output we specified is the total profit in cell F16.

Running the Simulation

We set up and run @RISK exactly as before. For this example, we set the number of iterations to 1000 and the number of simulations to 3 (because we are trying three different correlations).

Discussion of the Simulation Results

Selected numerical and graphical results are shown in Figures 9.50 and 9.51. You will probably be surprised to see that the *mean* total profit is the same, regardless of the correlation. This is no coincidence. In each of the three simulations, @RISK uses the *same* random numbers, but it "shuffles" them in different orders to get the correct correlations. This means that averages are unaffected. (The idea is that the average of the numbers 30, 26, and 48 is the same as the average of the numbers 48, 30, and 26.)

Figure 9.50

Summary Results for Correlated Model

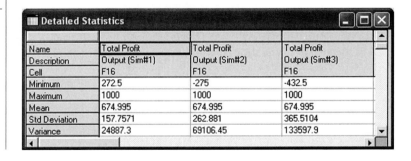

Name	Total Profit	Total Profit	Total Profit
Description	Output (Sim#1)	Output (Sim#2)	Output (Sim#3)
Cell	F16	F16	F16
Minimum	272.5	-275	-432.5
Maximum	1000	1000	1000
Mean	674.995	674.995	674.995
Std Deviation	157.7571	262.881	365.5104
Variance	24887.3	69106.45	133597.9

Figure 9.51 Graphical Results for Correlated Model

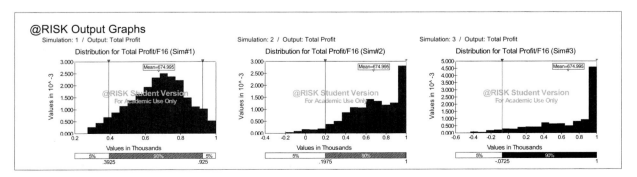

However, the correlation has a definite effect on the *distribution* of total profit. We can see this in Figure 9.50, for example, where the standard deviation of total profit increases as the correlation goes from negative to zero to positive. This same increase in variability is apparent in the histograms in Figure 9.51. Do you see intuitively why this increase in variability occurs? It is basically the "Don't put all of your eggs in one basket" effect. When the correlation is negative, high demands for one product tend to cancel low demands for the other product, so extremes in profit are rare. However, when the correlation is positive, high demands for the two products tend to go together, as do low demands. These make extreme profits on either end much more likely.

This same phenomenon would occur if we simulated an investment portfolio containing two stocks. When the stocks are positively correlated, the portfolio is much riskier (more variability) than when they are negatively correlated. Of course, this is the idea behind the advice that investors should diversify their portfolios. ■

MODELING ISSUES

We illustrated the RISKCORRMAT function for *triangularly* distributed values. However, it can be used with any of @RISK's distributions by tacking on RISKCORRMAT as a last argument. We can even mix them. For example, assuming CMat is the range name for a 2 × 2 correlation matrix, we could enter the formulas

=RISKNORMAL(10,2,RISKCORRMAT(CMat,1))

and

=RISKUNIFORM(100,200,RISKCORRMAT(CMat,2))

With the RISKCORRMAT function, we can correlate random numbers from any distributions.

into cells A4 and B4, say, and then copy them down. In this case @RISK generates a sequence of normally distributed random numbers in column A and another sequence of uniformly distributed random numbers in column B. Then it shuffles them in some complex way until their correlation is approximately equal to the specified correlation in the correlation matrix. ■

PROBLEMS

Skill-Building Problems

22. Bottleco produces six-packs of soda cans. Each can is supposed to contain at least 12 ounces of soda. If the total weight in a six-pack is under 72 ounces, Bottleco is fined $100 and receives no sales revenue for the six-pack. Each six-pack sells for $3.00. It costs Bottleco $0.02 per ounce of soda put in the cans. Bottleco can control the mean fill rate of its soda-filling machines. The amount put in each can by a machine is normally distributed with standard deviation 0.10 ounce.

  a. Assume that the weight of each can in a six-pack has a 0.8 correlation with the weight of the other cans in the six-pack. What mean fill quantity (within 0.05 ounce) maximizes expected profit per six-pack?

  b. If the weights of the cans in the six-pack are probabilistically independent, what mean fill quantity (within 0.05 ounce) will maximize expected profit per six-pack?

  c. How can you explain the difference in the answers to parts **a** and **b**?

23. When you use @RISK's correlation feature to generate correlated random numbers, how can you verify that they are correlated? Try the following. Use the RISKCORRMAT function to generate two normally distributed random numbers, each with mean 100 and standard deviation 10, and with correlation 0.7. To run a simulation, you need an output variable, so sum these two numbers and designate the sum as an output variable. Now run @RISK with 500 iterations. In the @RISK Results window, select the Insert/Data menu item to see the actual simulated data.

a. Copy these data into Excel and then use Excel's CORREL function to calculate the correlation between the two input variables. It should be close to 0.7. Then draw a scatterplot (X-Y chart) of these two input variables. The plot should indicate a definite positive relationship.

b. Are the two input variables correlated with the output? Use Excel's CORREL function to find out. Interpret your results intuitively.

24. Repeat the previous problem, but make the correlation between the two inputs equal to -0.7. Explain how the results change.

25. Repeat Problem 23, but now make the second input variable triangularly distributed with parameters 50, 100, and 500. This time, verify not only that the correlation between the two inputs is approximately 0.7, but also that the shapes of the two input distributions are approximately what they should be: normal for the first and triangular for the second. Do this by creating histograms in Excel. The point is that you can use @RISK's RISKCORRMAT function to correlate random numbers from *different* distributions.

26. Suppose you are going to invest equal amounts in three stocks. The annual return from each stock is normally distributed with mean 0.01 (1%) and standard deviation 0.06. The annual return on your portfolio, the output variable of interest, is the average of the three stock returns. Run @RISK, using 1000 iterations, on each of the following scenarios.

a. The three stock returns are highly correlated. The correlation between each pair is 0.9.

b. The three stock returns are practically independent. The correlation between each pair is 0.1.

c. The first two stocks are moderately correlated. The correlation between their returns is 0.4. The third stock's return is negatively correlated with the other two. The correlation between its return and each of the first two is -0.8.

d. Compare the portfolio distributions from @RISK for these three scenarios. What do you conclude?

e. You might think of a fourth scenario, where the correlation between *each* pair of returns is a large negative number such as -0.8. But explain intuitively why this makes no sense. Try running the simulation with these negative correlations to see what happens.

27. The effect of the shapes of input distributions on the distribution of an output can depend on the output function. For this problem, assume there are 10 input variables. We want to compare the case where these 10 inputs each have a normal distribution with mean 1000 and standard deviation 250 to the case where they each have a triangular distribution with parameters 600, 700, and 1700. (You can check with RISKview that even though this triangular distribution is very skewed, it has the same mean and approximately the same standard deviation as the normal distribution.) For each of the following outputs, run @RISK twice, once with the normally distributed inputs and once with the triangularly distributed inputs, and comment on the differences between the resulting output distributions. For each simulation run 10,000 iterations.

a. Let the output be the *average* of the inputs.

b. Let the output be the *maximum* of the inputs.

c. Calculate the average of the inputs. Let the output be the minimum of the inputs if this average is less than 1000; otherwise, let the output be the maximum of the inputs.

Skill-Extending Problem

28. The Business School at State University currently has three parking lots, each containing 155 spaces. Two hundred faculty members have been assigned to each lot. On a peak day, an average of 70% of all lot 1 parking sticker holders show up, an average of 72% of all lot 2 parking sticker holders show up, and an average of 74% of all lot 3 parking sticker holders show up.

a. Given the current situation, estimate the probability that on a peak day, at least one faculty member with a sticker will be unable to find a spot. Assume that the number who show up at each lot is independent of the number who show up at the other two lots. (*Hint*: Use the RISKBINOMIAL function.)

b. Now suppose the numbers of people who show up at the three lots are correlated (correlation 0.9). Does your solution work as well? Why or why not?

9.7 CONCLUSION

Simulation has traditionally not received the attention it deserves in management science courses. The primary reason for this has been the lack of easy-to-use simulation software. Now with Excel's built-in simulation capabilities, plus powerful and affordable add-ins such as @RISK and Crystal Ball, simulation is receiving its rightful emphasis. The world is full of uncertainty, which is what makes simulation so valuable. Simulation models provide important insights that are missing in models that do not incorporate uncertainty explicitly. In addition, simulation models are relatively easy to understand and develop. Therefore, we suspect that simulation models (together with optimization models) will soon be the primary emphasis of many management science courses—if they are not already. In this chapter we have illustrated the basic ideas of simulation, how to perform simulation with Excel built-in tools, and how @RISK greatly enhances Excel's basic capabilities. In the next chapter we will build on this knowledge to develop and analyze simulation models in a variety of business areas.

Summary of Key Management Science Terms

Term	Explanation	Page
Simulation models	Models with random inputs that affect one or more outputs where the randomness is modeled explicitly	424
Probability distributions for input variables	Specification of the possible values and their likelihoods for random input variables; these must be specified in any simulation model	427
Density function	Function that indicates the probability distribution of a continuous random variable; probabilities are areas under the density	429
Uniform distribution	The flat distribution, where all values in a bounded continuum are equally likely	431
Histogram	A bar chart that shows the numbers of observations in specified categories	434
Discrete distribution	A general distribution where a discrete number of possible values and their probabilities are specified	436
Normal distribution	The familiar bell-shaped distribution, specified by a mean and a standard deviation	438
Triangular distribution	Literally a triangular-shaped distribution, specified by a minimum value, a most likely value, and a maximum value	439
Binomial distribution	The random number of "successes" in a given number of independent "trials," where each trial has the same probability of success	441
Confidence interval	An interval around an estimate of some parameter, such that we are very confident the true value of the parameter is within the interval	448
Latin hypercube sampling	An efficient way of simulating random numbers for a simulation model, where the results are more accurate than with other sampling methods	461
Correlated inputs	Random quantities, such as returns from stocks in the same industry, that tend to go together (or possibly go in opposite directions from one another)	474

Summary of Key Excel Terms

Term	Explanation	Excel	Page
F9 key	The "recalc" key, used to make the spreadsheet recalculate	Press the F9 key	427
RAND function	Excel's built-in random number generator; generates uniform random number between 0 and 1	=RAND()	432
Freezing random numbers	Changing "volatile" random numbers into "fixed" numbers	Copy range, paste it onto itself with the Paste Special/Values option	435
RISKview	A stand-alone package (not really an Excel add-in) for exploring potential probability distributions		435
@RISK random functions	A set of functions, including RISKNORMAL and RISKTRIANG, for generating random numbers from various distributions	=RISKNORMAL (*mean,stdev*) or =RISKTRIANG (*min,mostlikely,max*), for example	435–441
Replicating with Excel only	Useful when an add-in such as @RISK is not available	Develop simulation model, use a data table with any blank Column Input cell to replicate one or more outputs	451
@RISK	A useful simulation add-in developed by Palisade	Has its own toolbar in Excel	455
RISKSIMTABLE function	Used to run an @RISK simulation model for several values of some variable, often a decision variable	=RISKSIMTABLE(*list*)	455, 464
RISKOUTPUT function	Used to indicate that a cell contains an output that will be tracked by @RISK	=RISKOUTPUT ("Profit")+Revenue-Cost, for example	458
RISKCORRMAT function	Used to correlate two or more random input variables	=RISKNORMAL(100,10, RISKCORRMAT (*CorrMat*,2)), for example	475
Creating histograms in Excel	Method for specifying categories (bins) and using Excel's FREQUENCY function as basis for a bar chart	See appendix for details	485

PROBLEMS

Skill-Building Problems

29. Six months before its annual convention, the American Medical Association must determine how many rooms to reserve. At this time, the AMA can reserve rooms at a cost of $50 per room. The AMA believes the number of doctors attending the convention will be normally distributed with a mean of 5000 and a standard deviation of 1000. If the number of people attending the convention exceeds the number of rooms reserved, extra rooms must be reserved at a cost of $80 per room.

    a. Use simulation with @RISK to determine the number of rooms that should be reserved to minimize the expected cost to the AMA.

    b. Rework part **a** for the case where the number attending has a triangular distribution with minimum value 2000, maximum value 7000, and most likely value 5000. Does this change the substantive results from part **a**?

30. You have made it to the final round of "Let's Make a Deal." You know that there is $1 million prize behind either door 1, door 2, or door 3. It is equally likely that the prize is behind any of the three doors. The two doors without a prize have nothing behind them. You randomly choose door 2. Before you see whether the prize is behind door 2, host Monty Hall opens a door that has no prize behind it. To be specific, suppose that before door 2 is opened, Monty reveals that there is no prize behind door 3. You now have the opportunity to switch and choose door 1. Should you switch? Use a spreadsheet to simulate this situation 1000 times. For each replication use an @RISK function to generate the door behind which the prize sits. Then use another @RISK function to generate the door that Monty will open. Assume that Monty plays as follows: Monty knows where the prize is and will open an empty door, but he cannot open door 2. If the prize is really behind door 2, Monty is equally likely to open door 1 or door 3. If the prize is really behind door 1, Monty must open door 3. If the prize is really behind door 3, Monty must open door 1.

31. A new edition of our management science textbook will be published 1 year from now. Our publisher currently has 2000 copies on hand and is deciding whether to do another printing before the new edition comes out. The publisher estimates that demand for the book during the next year is governed by the probability distribution in the file **P09_31.xls**. A production run incurs a fixed cost of $62,000 plus a variable cost of $10 per book printed. Books are sold for $30 per book. Any demand that cannot be met incurs a penalty cost of $2 per book, due to loss of goodwill.

Half of any leftover books can be sold to Barnes and Noble for $3 per book. Out publisher is interested in maximizing expected profit. The following print run sizes are under consideration: 0 (no production run), 1000, 2000, 4000, 6000, and 8000. What decision would you recommend? Use simulation with at least 100 replications. For your optimal decision, our publisher can be 90% certain that the actual profit associated with remaining sales of the current edition will be between what two values?

32. It is equally likely that annual unit sales for Widgetco's widgets will be low or high. If sales are low (60,000), the company can sell the product for $10 per unit. If sales are high (100,000), a competitor will enter and Widgetco can sell the product for only $8 per unit. The variable cost per unit has a 25% chance of being $6, a 50% chance of being $7.50, and a 25% chance of being $9. Annual fixed costs are $30,000.

    a. Use simulation, with at least 400 replications, to estimate Widgetco's expected annual profit.

    b. Construct a 95% confidence interval for Widgetco's annual expected profit.

    c. Now suppose that annual unit sales, variable cost, and unit price are equal to their respective expected values—that is, there is no uncertainty. Determine Widgetco's annual profit for this scenario.

    d. Can you conclude from the results in parts **a** and **c** that the expected profit from a simulation is equal to the profit from the scenario where each input assumes its expected value? Explain.

33. W. L. Brown, a direct marketer of women's clothing, must determine how many telephone operators to schedule during each part of the day. W. L. Brown estimates that the number of phone calls received each hour of a typical 8-hour shift can be described by the probability distribution in the file **P09_33.xls**. Each operator can handle 15 calls per hour and costs the company $20 per hour. Each phone call that is not handled is assumed to cost the company $6 in lost profit. Considering the options of employing 6, 8, 10, 11, 13, 14, or 20 operators, use simulation to determine the number of operators that minimizes the expected hourly cost (labor costs plus lost profits).

34. Assume that all of your job applicants must take a test, and that the scores on this test are normally distributed. The "selection ratio" is the cutoff point you use in your hiring process. For example, a selection ratio of 20% means that you will accept applicants for jobs who rank in the top 20% of all applicants. If you choose a selection ratio of 20%, the average test score of those selected will be 1.40 standard deviations above average. Use simulation to verify this fact, proceeding as follows.

    a. Show that if you want to accept only the top 20% of all applicants, you should accept applicants whose test scores are at least 0.84 standard deviation above average. (No simulation is required here. Just use the appropriate Excel normal function.)

    b. Now generate 400 test scores from a normal distribution with mean 0 and standard deviation 1. The average test score of those selected is the average of the scores that are at least 0.84. To determine this, use Excel's DAVERAGE function. To do so, put the heading Score in cell A3, generate the 400 test scores in the range A4:A403, and name the range A3:A403 Data. In cells C3 and C4, enter the *labels* Score and >0.84. (The range C3:C4 is called the *criterion* range.) Then calculate the average of all applicants who will be hired by entering the formula =DAVERAGE(Data,"Score",C3:C4) in any cell. This average should be close to the theoretical average, 1.40. [This formula works as follows. Excel finds all observations in the Data range that satisfy the criterion described in the range C3:C4 (Score>0.84). Then it averages the values in the Score column (the second argument of DAVERAGE) corresponding to these entries. Look in online help for more about Excel's database functions.]

    c. What information would you need to determine an "optimal" selection ratio? How could you determine an optimal selection ratio?

35. Lemington's is trying to determine how many Jean Hudson dresses to order for the spring season. Demand for the dresses is assumed to follow a normal distribution with mean 400 and standard deviation 100. The contract between Jean Hudson and Lemington's works as follows. At the beginning of the season, Lemington's reserves x units of capacity. Lemington's must take delivery for at least $0.8x$ dresses and can, if desired, take delivery on up to x dresses. Each dress sells for $160 and Jean charges $50 per dress. If Lemington's does not take delivery on all x dresses, it owes Jean a $5 penalty for each unit of reserved capacity that was unused. For example, if Lemington's orders 450 dresses and demand is for 400 dresses, then Lemington's will receive 400 dresses and owe Jean 400($50) + 50($5). How many units of capacity should Lemington's reserve to maximize its expected profit?

36. Dilbert's Department Store is trying to determine how many Hanson T-shirts to order. Currently the shirts are sold for $21.00, but at later dates the shirts will be offered at a 10% discount, then a 20% discount, then a 40% discount, then a 50% discount, and finally a 60% discount. Demand at the full price of $21.00 is be-

lieved to be normally distributed with mean 1800 and standard deviation 360. Demand at various discounts is assumed to be a multiple of full price demand. These multiples, for discounts of 10%, 20%, 40%, 50%, and 60% are, respectively, 0.4, 0.7, 1.1, 2, and 50. For example, if full-price demand were 2500, then at a 10% discount, customers would be willing to buy 1000 T-shirts. The unit cost of purchasing T-shirts depends on the number of T-shirts ordered, as shown in the file **P09_36.xls**. Use simulation to see how many T-shirts Dilbert's should order. Model the problem so that Dilbert's first orders some quantity of T-shirts, then discounts deeper and deeper, as necessary, to sell all of the shirts.

Skill-Extending Problems

37. The annual return on each of four stocks for each of the next 5 years is assumed to follow a normal distribution, with the mean and standard deviation for each stock, as well as the correlations between stocks, listed in the file **P09_37.xls**. We believe that the stock returns for these stocks in a given year are correlated, according to the correlation matrix given, but we believe the returns in different years are uncorrelated. For example, the returns for stocks 1 and 2 in year 1 have correlation 0.55, but the correlation between the return of stock 1 in year 1 and the return of stock 1 in year 2 is 0, and the correlation between the return of stock 1 in year 1 and the return of stock 2 in year 2 is also 0. The file has the formulas you might expect for this situation entered in the range C20:G23. You can check how the RISKCORRMAT function has been used in these formulas. Just so that we have an @RISK output cell, we calculate the average of all returns in cell B25 and designate it as an @RISK output. (This cell is not really important for the problem, but we include it because @RISK requires at least one output cell.)

    a. Using the model exactly as it stands, run @RISK with 1000 iterations. The question is whether the correlations in the simulated data are close to what we expect. To find out, go to @RISK's Report Settings and check the Input Data option before you run the simulation. This will show you all of the simulated returns on a new sheet. Then use Excel's CORREL function to calculate correlations for all pairs of columns in the resulting Inputs Data Report sheet. (This is tedious. We recommend instead that you use the StatTools add-in included with this book or the Analysis ToolPak that ships with Excel to create a matrix of all correlations.) Comment on whether the correlations are different from what you expect.

    b. Recognizing that this is a common situation (correlation within years, no correlation across years), @RISK allows you to model it by adding a *third* argument to the RISKCORRMAT function: the year index in row 19 of the **P09_37.xls** file. For example, the RISKCORRMAT part of the formula in cell C20 becomes =RiskNormal($B5,$C5, RiskCorrmat($B$12:$E$15,$B20,C$19)). Make this change to the formulas in the range C20:G23, rerun the simulation, and redo the correlation analysis in part **a**. Verify that the correlations between inputs are now more in line with what you expect.

38. It is surprising (but true) that if 23 people are in the same room, there is about a 50% chance that at least two people will have the same birthday. Suppose you want to estimate the probability that if 30 people are in the same room, at least two of them will have the same birthday. You can proceed as follows.
    a. Generate the "birthdays" of 30 different people. Ignoring the possibility of a leap year, each person has a 1/365 chance of having a given birthday (call the days of the year 1, 2, . . . , 365). You can use a formula involving the INT and RAND functions to generate birthdays.
    b. Once you have generated 30 people's birthdays, how can you tell whether at least two people have the same birthday? The key here is to use Excel's RANK function. (You can learn how to use this function with Excel's Function Wizard.) This function returns the rank of a number relative to a given group of numbers. In the case of a tie, two numbers are given the same rank. For example, if the set of numbers is 4, 3, 2, 5, the RANK function will return 2, 3, 4, 1. If the set of numbers is 4, 3, 2, 4, the RANK function will return 1, 3, 4, 1.
    c. After using the RANK function, you should be able to determine whether at least two of the 30 people have the same birthday.

39. United Electric (UE) sells refrigerators for $400 with a 1-year warranty. The warranty works as follows. If any part of the refrigerator fails during the first year after purchase, UE replaces the refrigerator for an average cost of $100. As soon as a replacement is made, another 1-year warranty period begins for the customer. If a refrigerator fails outside the warranty period, we assume that the customer immediately purchases another UE refrigerator. Suppose that the amount of time a refrigerator lasts follows a normal distribution with a mean of 1.8 years and a standard deviation of 0.3 year.
    a. Estimate the average profit per year UE earns from a customer.
    b. How could the approach of this problem be used to determine the optimal warranty period?

40. A Tax Saver Benefit (TSB) plan allows you to put money into an account at the beginning of the calendar year that can be used for medical expenses. This amount is not subject to federal tax—hence the phrase TSB. As you pay medical expenses during the year, you are reimbursed by the administrator of the TSB until the TSB account is exhausted. From that point on, you must pay your medical expenses out of your own pocket. On the other hand, if you put more money into your TSB than the medical expenses you incur, this extra money is lost to you. Your annual salary is $50,000 and your federal income tax rate is 30%.
    a. Assume that your medical expenses in a year are normally distributed with mean $2000 and standard deviation $500. Build an @RISK model in which the output is the amount of money left to you after paying taxes, putting money in a TSB, and paying any extra medical expenses. Experiment with the amount of money put in the TSB, using a RISKSIMTABLE function.
    b. Rework part **a**, but this time assume a gamma distribution for your annual medical expenses. Use $\alpha = 16$ and $\beta = 125$ as the two parameters of this distribution. These imply the same mean and standard deviation as in part **a**, but the distribution of medical expenses is now skewed to the right, which is probably more realistic. Using simulation, see whether you should now put more or less money in a TSB than in the symmetric case in part **a**.

41. At the beginning of each week, a machine is in one of four conditions: 1 = excellent; 2 = good; 3 = average; 4 = bad. The weekly revenue earned by a machine in state 1, 2, 3, or 4 is $100, $90, $50, or $10, respectively. After observing the condition of the machine at the beginning of the week, the company has the option, for a cost of $200, of instantaneously replacing the machine with an excellent machine. The quality of the machine deteriorates over time, as shown in the file **P09_41.xls**. Four maintenance policies are under consideration:
    ■ Policy 1: Never replace a machine.
    ■ Policy 2: Immediately replace a bad machine.
    ■ Policy 3: Immediately replace a bad or average machine.
    ■ Policy 4: Immediately replace a bad, average, or good machine.
    Simulate each of these policies for 50 weeks (using 250 iterations each) to determine the policy that maximizes expected weekly profit. Assume that the machine at the beginning of week 1 is excellent.

42. Simulation can be used to illustrate a number of results from statistics that are difficult to understand with nonsimulation arguments. One is the famous central limit theorem, which says that if you sample enough values from *any* population distribution and then average these values, the resulting average will be approximately normally distributed. Confirm this

by using @RISK with the following population distributions (run a separate simulation for each): (a) discrete with possible values 1 and 2 and probabilities 0.2 and 0.8; (b) exponential with mean 1 (use the RISKEXPON function with the single argument 1); (c) triangular with minimum, most likely, and maximum values equal to 1, 9, and 10. (Note that each of these distributions is very nonnormal.) Run each simulation with 10 values in each average, and run 1000 iterations to simulate 1000 averages. Create a histogram of the averages to see that it is indeed bell-shaped. Then repeat, using 30 values in each average. Are the histograms based on 10 values qualitatively different from those based on 30?

43. In statistics we often use observed data to test a hypothesis about a population or populations. The basic method uses the observed data to calculate a test statistic (a single number). If the magnitude of this test statistic is sufficiently large, we reject the "null" hypothesis in favor of the "research" hypothesis. As an example, consider a researcher who believes teenage girls sleep longer than teenage boys on average. She collects observations on $n = 40$ randomly selected girls and $n = 40$ randomly selected boys. (We assume that each observation is the average sleep time over several nights for a given person.) The averages are $\bar{X}_1 = 7.9$ hours for the girls and $\bar{X}_2 = 7.6$ hours for the boys. The standard deviation of the 40 observations for girls is $s_1 = 0.5$ hour; for the boys it is $s_2 = 0.7$ hour. The researcher, consulting her statistics textbook, then calculates the test statistic

$$\frac{\bar{X}_1 - \bar{X}_2}{\sqrt{s_1^2/40 + s_2^2/40}} = \frac{7.9 - 7.6}{\sqrt{0.25/40 + 0.49/40}} = 2.206$$

Based on the fact that 2.206 is "large," she claims that her research hypothesis is confirmed—girls *do* sleep longer than boys.

You are skeptical of this claim, so you check it out by running a simulation. In your simulation you assume that girls and boys have the *same* mean and standard deviation of sleep times in the entire population, say, 7.7 and 0.6. You also assume that the distribution of sleep times is normal. Then you repeatedly simulate observations of 40 girls and 40 boys from this distribution and calculate the test statistic. The question is whether the observed test statistic, 2.206, is "extreme." If it is larger than most or all of the test statistics you simulate, then the researcher is justified in her claim; otherwise, this large a statistic could have happened just by chance, even if the girls and boys have identical population means. Use @RISK to see which is the case.

Modeling Problems

44. Big Hit Video must determine how many copies of a new video to purchase. Assume that the company's goal is to purchase a number of copies that will maximize its expected profit from the video during the next year. Describe how you would use simulation to solve this problem. To simplify matters, assume that each time a tape is rented, it is rented for one day.

45. Many people who are involved in a small auto accident do not file a claim because they are afraid their insurance premiums will be raised. Suppose that City Farm Insurance has three rates. If you file a claim, you are moved to the next higher rate. How might you use simulation to determine whether a particular claim should be filed?

46. A building contains 1000 lightbulbs. Each bulb lasts at most 5 months. The company maintaining the building is trying to decide whether it is worthwhile to practice a "group replacement" policy. Under a group replacement policy, all bulbs are replaced every T months (where T is to be determined). Also, bulbs are replaced when they burn out. Assume that it costs $0.05 to replace each bulb during a group replacement and $0.20 to replace each burned-out bulb if it is replaced individually. How would you use simulation to determine whether a group replacement policy is worthwhile?

47. We are constantly hearing reports on the nightly news about natural disasters—droughts in Texas, hurricanes in Florida, floods in California, and so on. We often hear that one of these was the "worst in over 30 years," or some such statement. Are natural disasters getting worse these days, or does it just appear so? How might you use simulation to answer this question? Here is one possible approach. Imagine that there are N areas of the country (or the world) that tend to have, to some extent, various types of weather phenomena each year. For example, hurricanes are always a potential problem for Florida. You might model the severity of the problem for any area in any year by a normally distributed random number with mean 0 and standard deviation 1, where negative values are interpreted as mild years and positive values are interpreted as severe years. (We suggest the normal distribution, but there is no reason other distributions couldn't be used instead.) Then you could simulate such values for all areas over a period of many years and keep track, say, of whether any of the areas have worse conditions in the current year than they have had in the past 30 years. What might you keep track of? How might you interpret your results?

APPENDIX CREATING HISTOGRAMS WITH EXCEL TOOLS

When we deal with probability distributions of input or output variables, it is useful to create histograms. A histogram, really just a bar chart, lets us see how the data are distributed. We divide the data range into a number of categories, usually called **bins**, count the number of observations in each bin, and then use these counts as the basis for the histogram.

Simulation and statistical software packages, including @RISK, typically have the ability to create a histogram (with automatically chosen bins) with the click of a button. It is also possible to create a histogram with native Excel tools, but you have to do most of the work manually. We lead you through the steps of this process here.

The ingredients for a histogram and the finished product are shown in Figure 9.52. (See the file **Histogram.xls**.) It is based on the given data in column A (which really extends down to row 203—that is, 200 observations). We then build the histogram with the following steps.

Figure 9.52

Creation of Histogram

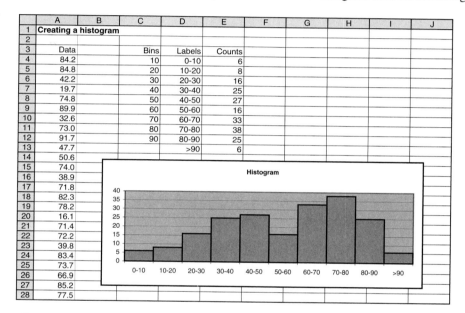

① Bins. We have to choose the bins. This choice typically depends on the range of the data and the number of observations. A scan of these data indicates that they are all in the range 0 to 100. Therefore, we conveniently choose 10 equal-length bins: 0–10, 10–20, and so on, up to 90–100. We designate the first 9 of these by their right-hand endpoints, as shown in column C. The first bin is really "<=10", the second is ">10 and <=20", and so on. We only need to specify the first 9 bins in column C. The 10th is then automatically ">90".

② Bin Labels. Although this step is not entirely necessary, it is nice to have meaningful labels for the bins on the horizontal axis of the histogram. We enter these labels manually in column D. (Prefix each label with an apostrophe, as in '10–20, to make sure it is interpreted as a label.)

③ Counts. To get the counts of observations in the various bins in column E, we use Excel's FREQUENCY function. This is an "array" function that fills up an entire range at once. It takes two arguments, the data range and the bins range. To use it, highlight the range D4:D13, type the formula

=FREQUENCY(A4:A203,C4:C12)

and press Ctrl-Shift-Enter (all three keys at once). As with all array functions in Excel, you will see curly brackets around the formula in the formula bar. However, you should *not* type these curly brackets.

④ Chart. To create the histogram, use the Chart Wizard. In step 1, choose the default type of column chart. The key is step 2, where the dialog box under the Series tab should be filled out as in Figure 9.53. Here you can see how we use the labels and counts in columns D and E.

Figure 9.53

Settings for
Histogram Chart

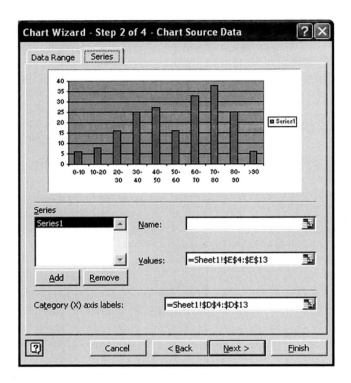

⑤ Gaps. As indicated in Figure 9.53, the default column chart has gaps between the columns. It is customary to have no gaps in a histogram. To get rid of the gaps, right-click on any bar in the histogram, select the Format Data Series menu item, click on the Options tab, and set the gap width to 0, as shown in Figure 9.54.

Figure 9.54

Setting Gap Width

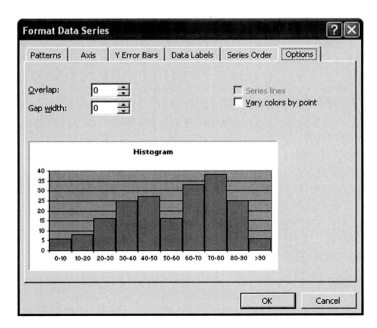

9.1 SKI JACKET PRODUCTION

Egress, Inc., is a small company that designs, produces, and sells ski jackets and other coats. The creative design team has labored for weeks over its new design for the coming winter season. It is now time to decide how many ski jackets to produce in this production run. Because of the lead times involved, no other production runs will be possible during the season. Predicting ski jacket sales months in advance of the selling season can be quite tricky. Egress has been in operation for only 3 years, and its ski jacket designs were quite successful in two of those years. Based on realized sales from the last 3 years, current economic conditions, and professional judgment, twelve Egress employees have independently estimated demand for their new design for the upcoming season. Their estimates are listed in Table 9.2.

Table 9.2 Estimated Demands

14,000	16,000
13,000	8,000
14,000	5,000
14,000	11,000
15,500	8,000
10,500	15,000

To assist in the decision on the number of units for the production run, management has gathered the data in Table 9.3. Note that S is the price Egress charges retailers. Any ski jackets that do not sell during the season can be sold by Egress to discounters for V per jacket. The fixed cost of plant and equipment is F. This cost is incurred irrespective of the size of the production run.

Table 9.3 Monetary Values

Variable production cost per unit (C):	$80
Selling price per unit (S):	$100
Salvage value per unit (V):	$30
Fixed production cost (F):	$100,000

Questions

1. Egress management believes that a normal distribution is a reasonable model for the unknown demand in the coming year. What mean and standard deviation should Egress use for the demand distribution?

2. Use a spreadsheet model to simulate 1000 possible outcomes for demand in the coming year. Based on these scenarios, what is the expected profit if Egress produces $Q = 7800$ ski jackets? What is the expected profit if Egress produces $Q = 12,000$ ski jackets? What is the standard deviation of profit in these two cases?

3. Based on the same 1000 scenarios, how many ski jackets should Egress produce to maximize expected profit? Call this quantity Q.

4. Should Q equal mean demand or not? Explain.

5. Create a histogram of profit at the production level Q. Create a histogram of profit when the production level Q equals mean demand. What is the probability of a loss greater than $100,000 in each case? ■

CASE 9.2 EBONY BATH SOAP

Management of Ebony, a leading manufacturer of bath soap, is trying to control its inventory costs. The weekly cost of holding one unit of soap in inventory is $30 (one unit is 1000 cases of soap). The marketing department estimates that weekly demand averages 120 units, with a standard deviation of 15 units, and is reasonably well modeled by a normal distribution. If demand exceeds the amount of soap on hand, those sales are *lost*—that is, there is no backlogging of demand. The production department can produce at one of three levels: 110, 120, or 130 units per week. The cost of changing production from one week to the next is $3000.

Management would like to evaluate the following production policy. If the current inventory is less than $L = 30$ units, then produce 130 units in the next week. If the current inventory is greater than $U = 80$ units, then produce 110 units in the next week. Otherwise, continue at the previous week's production level.

Ebony currently has 60 units of inventory on hand. Last week's production level was 120.

Questions

1. Create a spreadsheet to simulate 52 weeks of operation at Ebony. Graph the inventory of soap over time. What is the total cost (inventory cost plus production change cost) for the 52 weeks?

2. Use a simulation of 500 iterations to estimate the average 52-week cost with values of U ranging from 30 to 80 in increments of 10. Keep $L = 30$ for every trial.

3. Calculate the sample mean and standard deviation of the 52-week cost under each policy. Using those results, construct 95% confidence intervals for the average 52-week cost for each value of U. Graph the average 52-week cost versus U. What is the best value of U for $L = 30$?

4. What other production policies might be useful to investigate? ∎

Simulation Models

© Photodisc

AUTOMATING OPERATIONS AT THE UNITED STATES POSTAL SERVICE

One of the key benefits of simulation methodology is that it allows a company to see how important outputs respond to various scenarios. Each scenario, which is determined by certain inputs and operating policies, can be simulated, and statistics can be collected. By running enough scenarios, the company obtains useful information about which inputs and policies tend to produce the best outputs. This methodology was used in the 1980s by the United States Postal Service (USPS), as described in the article "Management Science in Automating Postal Operations: Facility and Equipment Planning in the United States Postal Service" by Cebry et al. (1992). At the time, the USPS was faced with increasing competitive pressure from a variety of competitors, including other advertising media, alternative retail and delivery companies, and electronic mail. Automation technology was identified as the only way to handle an increase in mail volume, to maintain cost competitiveness, and to provide adequate service.

The process of getting mail from the sender to the receiver is an extremely complex one. Mail enters the process as a mixed product—many types of mail addressed in various ways to many geographical regions—and it must be sorted in several stages before it can eventually reach the proper destination. The USPS recognized the need for automated equipment to speed up this process and to save on labor costs. In fact, by the early 1980s it had purchased optical character recognition (OCR) machines that could identify the destination (at least on some mail) and attach a bar code corresponding to the ZIP code to the mail. It had also purchased bar code sensing machines that could read these bar codes and automatically help sort the mail. Part of the cost-effectiveness of these new machines relied on heavy use by businesses of the new nine-digit ZIP codes. Unfortunately, businesses were somewhat slow to use the nine-digit codes.

At about this time, the USPS realized that it needed to use management science methods to utilize its existing automation equipment most effectively and to plan appropriately for the future. It hired a consulting company, Kenan Systems Corporation, to help compare automation alternatives. The result was META, a simulation model that quantifies the impacts of changes in mail processing and delivery operations. The META model is very complex, but it can be described briefly as follows.

Mail of various types and of various volumes enters the system and progresses through a number of "links." Each of the links is one step in the overall sorting process that gets the mail from its origin to its final destination. The META model takes as its inputs various mail streams (types of mail with similar characteristics) and routes these streams through the links of the sorting process according to user-specified rules. For example, a rule might specify which mail streams receive highest priority on certain automation equipment at each link. Each set of mail streams and each set of rules corresponds to a single scenario in the simulation model. Given a typical scenario, the model simulates the throughput of the system, the number of errors made, the amount of labor required, and the total cost. These outputs are then compared to identify the best policies for the USPS to implement.

The META model, first developed in 1985, has proved to be extremely useful and versatile. Using this simulation tool, the USPS formulated a corporate automation plan (CAP), which was first released in 1989. By the time CAP was to be fully implemented in 1995, the postal service expected it to save 100,000 work years annually, which translates to over $4 billion. Just as important, by using the model as part of an ongoing planning process, the USPS ensured that it would implement future technologies in a timely and cost-effective manner. ■

10.1 INTRODUCTION

In the previous chapter we introduced most of the important concepts for developing and analyzing spreadsheet simulation models. We also discussed many of the available features in the powerful simulation add-in, @RISK, that accompanies this book. Now we apply the tools to a wide variety of problems that can be analyzed by simulation. For convenience, we group the applications into four general areas: (1) operations models, (2) financial models, (3) marketing models, and (4) games of chance. The only overriding theme in this chapter is that simulation models can yield important insights in all of these areas. You do not need to cover all of the models in this chapter or cover them in the order in which they are presented. Rather, you can cover the ones of most interest to you and in practically any order.

10.2 OPERATIONS MODELS

Whether we are discussing the operations of a manufacturing or a service company, there is likely to be uncertainty that can be modeled by simulation. In this section we look at examples of bidding for a government contract (uncertainty in the bids by competitors), warranty costs (uncertainty in the time until failure of an appliance), drug production (uncertainty in the yield), and project scheduling (uncertainty in the duration of activities).[1]

Bidding for Contracts

In situations where a company must bid against competitors, simulation can often be used to determine the company's optimal bid. Usually the company does not know what its competitors will bid, but it might have an idea about the *range* of the bids its competitors will choose. In this section we show how to use simulation to determine a bid that maximizes the company's expected profit.[2]

EXAMPLE | **10.1 BIDDING FOR A GOVERNMENT CONTRACT**

The Miller Construction Company is trying to decide whether to make a bid on a construction project. Miller believes it will cost the company $10,000 to complete the project (if it wins the contract), and it will cost $350 to prepare a bid. Four potential competitors are going to bid against Miller. The lowest bid will win the contract, and the winner will then be given the winning bid amount to complete the project. Based on past history, Miller believes that each competitor's bid will be a multiple of its (Miller's) cost to complete the project, where this multiple has a triangular distribution with minimum, most likely, and maximum values 0.9, 1.3, and 2.5, respectively. These four competitors' bids are also assumed to be independent of one another. If Miller decides to prepare a bid, its bid amount will be a multiple of $500 in the range $10,500 to $15,000. The company wants to use simulation to determine which strategy to use to maximize its expected profit.

Objective   To simulate the profit to Miller from any particular bid, and to see which bid amount is best.

WHERE DO THE NUMBERS COME FROM?

We already discussed this type of bidding problem in Chapter 8. The new data required here are the distributions of competitors' bids. A triangular distribution is chosen for simplicity, although Miller could try other types of distributions. The parameters of this distribution are probably educated guesses, possibly based on previous bidding experience against these same competitors.

Solution

The logic is straightforward. We first simulate the competitors' bids. Then for any bid Miller makes, we see whether Miller wins the contract, and if so, what its profit is.

---

[1]Additional simulation models in the operations area will be examined in the next chapter, where we develop queueing simulations with uncertainty in customer arrival times and service times.
[2]You can compare this to the bidding example, Example 8.1, in Chapter 8.

DEVELOPING THE SIMULATION MODEL

The simulation model appears in Figure 10.1. (See the file **Bidding.xls**.) It can be developed with the following steps. (Note that this model does not check the possibility of Miller not bidding at all. But this case is easy. If Miller opts not to bid, the profit is a certain $0.)

Figure 10.1   Bidding Simulation Model

	A	B	C	D	E	F	G	H	I	J	K	L	M
1	**Bidding Problem**												
2													
3	**Inputs**												
4	Our cost to prepare a bid	$350											
5	Our cost to complete project	$10,000											
6													
7	Parameters of triangular distributions for each competitor's bid (expressed as multiple of Miller's cost to complete project)												
8	Min	0.9											
9	Most likely	1.3											
10	Max	2.5											
11					Possible bids for Miller								
12	Miller's bid	$10,500		$10,500	$11,000	$11,500	$12,000	$12,500	$13,000	$13,500	$14,000	$14,500	$15,000
13													
14	**Simulation**												
15	Competitors' bids	$16,092	$17,295	$15,082	$14,144								
16	Minimum competitor bid	$14,144											
17													
18	Miller wins bid? (1 if yes, 0 if no)	1											
19	Miller's profit	$150											

---

1 Inputs. Enter the inputs in the shaded cells. These include Miller's costs, Miller's possible bids, and the parameters of the triangular distribution for the competing bids.

2 Miller's bid. We can test all of Miller's possible bids simultaneously with the RISKSIMTABLE function. To set up for this, enter the formula

=RISKSIMTABLE(D12:M12)

Recall that the RISKSIMTABLE function allows you to run a separate simulation for each value in its list.

in cell B12. As with all uses of this function, the spreadsheet shows the simulated values for the *first* bid, $10,500. However, when we run the simulation, we will see outputs for all of the bids.

3 Competitors' bids. Generate random bids for the four competitors in row 15 by entering the formula

=RISKTRIANG($B$8,$B$9,$B$10)*$B$5

in cell B15 and copying across. (Remember that the random value is the *multiple* of Miller's cost to complete the project.) Calculate the smallest of these in cell B16 with the formula

=MIN(B15:E15)

Of course, Miller will not see these other bids until it has submitted its own bid.

4 Win contract? See whether Miller wins the bid by entering the formula

=IF(B12<B16,1,0)

in cell B18. Here, 1 means that Miller wins the bid, and 0 means a competitor wins the bid. Then designate this cell as an @RISK output cell. Recall that to designate a cell as an @RISK output cell, you select the cell and then click on the Add Output button on @RISK's toolbar. You can then "name" this output appropriately. We used the name "Win bid."

5 **Miller's profit.** If Miller submits a bid, the bid cost is lost for sure. Beyond that, the profit to Miller is the bid amount minus the cost of completing the project if the bid is won. Otherwise, Miller makes nothing. So enter the formula

=IF(B18=1,B12-B5,0)-B4

in cell B19. Then designate this cell as an additional @RISK output cell. (We named it "Profit".)

Running the Simulation

We set the number of iterations to 1000, and we set the number of simulations to 10 because there are 10 bid amounts Miller wants to test. As in the previous chapter, we also continue to set the Report Settings in @RISK so that summary output and output graphs appear as worksheets in the Excel file. This is optional, but we believe it is a good practice.

Discussion of the Simulation Results

The summary results appear in Figure 10.2. For each simulation—that is, each bid amount—there are two outputs: 1 or 0 to indicate whether Miller wins the contract and Miller's profit. A little thought should convince you that each of these can have only two possible values for any bid amount. For example, if Miller bids $12,000, it will either win or lose the contract, and its profit will be either $1650 or -350. This is reflected in the histogram of profit for this bid amount in Figure 10.3 (page 494), where there are only two bars. The two possible values of the outputs appear in the Minimum and Maximum columns of Figure 10.2.

Figure 10.2 Summary Results from @RISK

	Name	Cell	Sim#	Minimum	Mean	Maximum	x1	p1	x2	p2	x2-x1	p2-p1
Output 1	Wins Bid	B18	1	0	0.866	1	0	5%	1	95%	1	90%
Output 1	Wins Bid	B18	2	0	0.77	1	0	5%	1	95%	1	90%
Output 1	Wins Bid	B18	3	0	0.665	1	0	5%	1	95%	1	90%
Output 1	Wins Bid	B18	4	0	0.545	1	0	5%	1	95%	1	90%
Output 1	Wins Bid	B18	5	0	0.415	1	0	5%	1	95%	1	90%
Output 1	Wins Bid	B18	6	0	0.307	1	0	5%	1	95%	1	90%
Output 1	Wins Bid	B18	7	0	0.212	1	0	5%	1	95%	1	90%
Output 1	Wins Bid	B18	8	0	0.15	1	0	5%	1	95%	1	90%
Output 1	Wins Bid	B18	9	0	0.095	1	0	5%	1	95%	1	90%
Output 1	Wins Bid	B18	10	0	0.064	1	0	5%	1	95%	1	90%
Output 2	Profit	B19	1	-350	83	150	-350	5%	150	95%	500	90%
Output 2	Profit	B19	2	-350	420	650	-350	5%	650	95%	1000	90%
Output 2	Profit	B19	3	-350	647.5	1150	-350	5%	1150	95%	1500	90%
Output 2	Profit	B19	4	-350	740	1650	-350	5%	1650	95%	2000	90%
Output 2	Profit	B19	5	-350	687.5	2150	-350	5%	2150	95%	2500	90%
Output 2	Profit	B19	6	-350	571	2650	-350	5%	2650	95%	3000	90%
Output 2	Profit	B19	7	-350	392	3150	-350	5%	3150	95%	3500	90%
Output 2	Profit	B19	8	-350	250	3650	-350	5%	3650	95%	4000	90%
Output 2	Profit	B19	9	-350	77.5	4150	-350	5%	4150	95%	4500	90%

The Mean column, on the other hand, indicates the *average* of these values over the 1000 iterations. For example, the mean of 0.545 for the "Wins Bid" output for simulation 4 indicates that Miller wins the contract on 54.5% of the iterations when bidding $12,000. The mean profit of $740 for this bid amount is simply a weighted average of the two possible profits, $1650 and -350. Specifically, you can check that it is $0.545(1650) + 0.455(-350) = 740$. The other means in the output can be interpreted similarly.

Figure 10.3

Histogram of Profit
for a $12,000 Bid

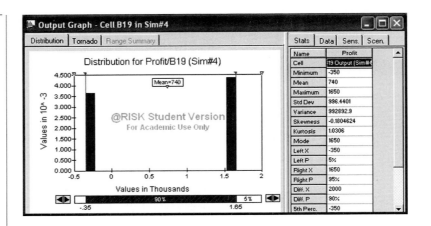

@RISK, or any other
simulation package,
can show only the
output distribution for
any particular
decision. It is then up
to us to make the
"best" decision.

What should Miller bid? First, it is clear that Miller *should* bid. Not bidding means no profit, whereas all of the possible bids except for the last one lead to a positive expected profit with at most a $350 loss. If Miller is an EMV maximizer, as discussed in Chapter 8, then the $12,000 bid should be chosen because it has the highest mean profit. However, if Miller is risk averse, a smaller bid amount might be attractive. As the bid amounts increase, the upside potential is greater, but the chance of not winning the bid and losing $350 increases. ■

Warranty Costs

When you buy a new product, it usually carries a warranty. A typical warranty might state that if the product fails within a certain period such as 1 year, then you will receive a new product at no cost, and it will carry the *same* warranty. However, if the product fails after the warranty period, then you have to bear the cost of replacing the product. Due to random lifetimes of products, we need a way to estimate the warranty costs (to the company) of a product. We see how simulation can accomplish this in the next example.

EXAMPLE | **10.2 WARRANTY COSTS FOR A CAMERA**

The Yakkon Company sells a popular camera for $250. This camera carries a warranty such that if the camera fails within 1.5 years, the company gives the customer a new camera for free. If the camera fails after 1.5 years, the warranty is no longer in effect. Every replacement camera carries exactly the same warranty as the original camera, and the cost to the company of supplying a new camera is always $185. Use simulation to estimate, for a given sale, the number of replacements under warranty and the NPV of profit from the sale, using a discount rate of 12%.

Objective To use simulation to estimate the number of replacements under warranty and the total NPV of profit from a given sale.

WHERE DO THE NUMBERS COME FROM?

The warranty information is a policy decision made by the company. The hardest input to estimate is the probability distribution of the lifetime of the product. We discuss this next.

Solution

The gamma
distribution is a
popular distribution,
especially when we
want a right-skewed
distribution of a
nonnegative quantity.

The only randomness in this problem concerns the time until failure of a new camera. Yakkon could estimate the distribution of time until failure from historical data. This would probably indicate a right-skewed distribution, as shown in Figure 10.4. If you look through the list of distributions available in @RISK (or, equivalently, in RISKview), you will see several with this same basic shape. The one shown in Figure 10.4 is a commonly used distribution called the **gamma** distribution. For variety, we will use this distribution in this example, although other choices (such as the triangular) are certainly possible.

Selecting a Gamma Distribution

You can learn about
distributions from
RISKview or from the
@RISK Model window
by selecting its
Insert/Distribution
Window menu item.

The gamma distribution is characterized by two parameters, α and β. These determine its exact shape and location. It can be shown that the mean and standard deviation are $\mu = \alpha\beta$ and $\sigma = \sqrt{\alpha\beta}$. Alternatively, if we have desired values of the mean and standard deviation, we can solve these equations for α and β to give us the desired mean and standard deviation. Specifically, this leads to $\alpha = \mu^2/\sigma^2$ and $\beta = \sigma^2/\mu$. So, for example, if we want a gamma distribution with mean 2.5 and standard deviation 1 (which in this example would be based on camera lifetime data from the past), we should choose $\alpha = 2.5^2/1^2 = 6.25$ and $\beta = 1^2/2.5 = 0.4$. These are the values shown in Figure 10.4 and the ones we will use for this example. The values in the figure (from RISKview or the @RISK Model window) imply that the probability of failure before 1.5 years is about 0.15, so that the probability of failure out of warranty is about 0.85.

Figure 10.4

Right-Skewed Gamma Distribution

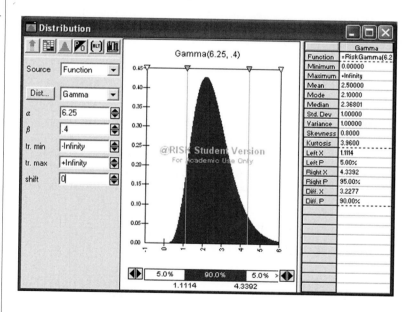

DEVELOPING THE SIMULATION MODEL

The simulation model appears in Figure 10.5 (page 496). (See the file **Warranty.xls**.) The particular random numbers in this figure indicate an example (a rather unusual one) where there are two failures within warranty. However, because the lifetime of the second replacement (cell D17) is greater than 1.5, the company incurs only two replacement costs, as shown in cells B19 and C19. The model can be developed with the following steps.

Figure 10.5

Warranty
Simulation Model

	A	B	C	D	E	F
1	**Warranty costs for camera**					
2						
3	**Inputs**					
4	Parameters of time to failure distribution of any new camera (Gamma)					
5	Desired mean	2.5				
6	Desired stdev	1				
7	Implied alpha	6.250				
8	Implied beta	0.400				
9						
10	Warranty period	1.5				
11	Cost of new camera (to customer)	$250				
12	Replacement cost (to company)	$185				
13	Discount rate	12%				
14						
15	**Simulation of new camera and its replacements (if any)**					
16	Camera	1	2	3	4	5
17	Lifetime	1.285	0.750	2.926	NA	NA
18	Time of failure	1.285	2.035	4.961	NA	NA
19	Cost to company	185	185	0	0	0
20	Discounted cost	159.93	146.90	0.00	0.00	0.00
21						
22	Failures within warranty	2				
23	NPV of profit from customer	($241.83)				

1 **Inputs.** Enter the inputs in the shaded cells.

2 **Parameters of gamma distribution.** As we discussed previously, if we enter a desired mean and standard deviation (in cells B5 and B6), then we have to calculate the parameters of the gamma distribution. Do this by entering the formulas

=B5^2/B6^2

and

=B6^2/B5

in cells B7 and B8.

3 **Lifetimes and times of failures.** We will generate at most 5 lifetimes and corresponding times of failures. Why only 5? We could generate more, but it is extremely unlikely that this same customer would experience more than 5 failures within warranty, so 5 suffices. As soon as a lifetime is greater than 1.5, the warranty period, we do not generate any further lifetimes, since "the game is over"; instead, we record "NA" in row 17. With this in mind, enter the formulas

=RISKGAMMA(B7,B8)

=IF(B17<B10,RISKGAMMA(B7,B8),"NA")

and

=IF(C17="NA","NA",IF(C17<$B$10,RISKGAMMA($B$7,$B$8),"NA"))

in cells B17, C17, and D17, and copy the latter formula to cells E17 and F17. These formulas guarantee that once "NA" is recorded in a cell, all cells to its right will also contain "NA." To get the actual times of failures, relative to time 0 when the customer originally purchases the camera, enter the formulas

=B17

and

=IF(C17="NA","NA",B18+C17)

in cells B18 and C18, and copy the latter across row 18. These values will be used for the NPV calculation, since for NPV we need to know exactly when cash flows occur.

→@RISK Function: *RISKGAMMA*

To generate a random number from the gamma distribution, use the RISKGAMMA function in the form =**RISKGAMMA(Alpha,Beta)**. The mean and standard deviation of this distribution are $\mu = \alpha\beta$ and $\sigma = \sqrt{\alpha\beta}$. Equivalently, we have $\alpha = \mu^2/\sigma^2$ and $\beta = \sigma^2/\mu$. ∎

4 **Costs and discounted costs.** In row 19 we enter the replacement cost ($185) or 0, depending on whether a failure occurs within warranty, and in row 20 we discount these costs back to time 0, using the failure times in row 18. To do this, enter the formulas

=IF(B17<B10,B12,0)

and

=IF(C17="NA",0,IF(C17<$B$10,$B$12,0))

in cells B19 and C19, and copy this latter formula across row 19. Then enter the formula

=IF(B19>0,B19/(1+$B$13)^B18,0)

in cell B20 and copy it across row 20. This formula uses that well-known fact that the present value of a cash flow at time t is the cash flow multiplied by $1/(1 + r)^t$, where r is the discount rate.

5 **Outputs.** Calculate two outputs, the number of failures within warranty and the NPV of profit, with the formulas

=COUNTIF(B19:F19,">0")

and

=B11-B12-SUM(B20:F20)

in cells B22 and B23. Then designate these two cells as @RISK output cells. Note that the NPV is the margin from the sale (undiscounted) minus the sum of the discounted costs from replacements under warranty.

Running the Simulation

The @RISK setup is typical. We run 1000 iterations of a *single* simulation (since there is no RISKSIMTABLE function).

Discussion of the Simulation Results

The @RISK summary statistics and histograms for the two outputs appear in Figures 10.6, 10.7, and 10.8 (page 498). They show a pretty clear picture. About 85% of the time, there are no failures under warranty and the company makes a profit of $65, the margin from the camera sale. However, there is about a 12.4% chance of exactly 1 failure under warranty, in which case the company's NPV of profit will be an approximate $100 loss. Additionally, there is about a 2.6% chance that there will be even more failures under warranty, in which case the loss will be even greater. Note that in our 1000 iterations, the maximum number of failures under warranty was 3, and the maximum net loss was $392.95. On average, the NPV of profit was $36.40.

These results indicate that Yakkon is not suffering terribly from warranty costs. However, there are several ways the company could decrease the effects of warranty costs. First, it could increase the price of the camera. Second, it could decrease the warranty period, say, from 1.5 years to 1 year. Third, it could change the terms of the warranty. For example, it could stipulate that if the camera fails within a year, the customer gets a new camera for free, whereas if the time to failure is between 1 and 1.5 years, the customer pays some pro rata share of the replacement cost. Finally, it could try to sell the customer an

Excel's NPV function can be used only for cash flows that occur at the ends of the respective years. Otherwise, we have to discount cash flows "manually."

Figure 10.6 @RISK Summary Statistics for Warranty Model

	Name	Cell	Minimum	Mean	Maximum	x1	p1	x2	p2	x2-x1	p2-p1
Output 1	Failures	B22	0	0.181	3	0	5%	1	95%	1	90%
Output 2	NPV of profit	B23	-392.9472	36.40486	65	-100.3102	5%	65	95%	165.3102	90%
Input 1	Lifetime	B17	0.4611222	2.499405	6.749623	1.109532	5%	4.334471	95%	3.224939	90%
Input 2	NA / NA	C17	0.6380706	2.497259	6.55201	1.129459	5%	4.30687	95%	3.177411	90%
Input 3	NA / NA	D17	0.9474899	2.464315	5.349961	1.033511	5%	4.658089	95%	3.624578	90%

Figure 10.7

Histogram of Number of Failures

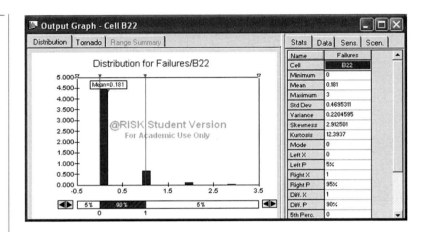

Figure 10.8

Histogram of NPV of Profit

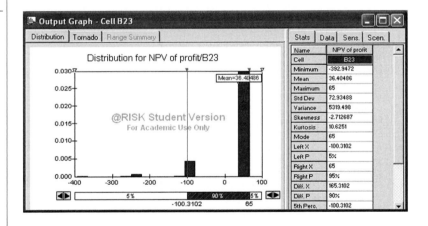

extended warranty—at a hefty price. We ask you to explore these possibilities in the problems. ∎

Drug Production with Uncertain Yield

In many manufacturing settings, products are produced in batches, and the usable *yields* from these batches are uncertain. This is particularly true in the drug industry. The following example illustrates how a drug manufacturer can take this uncertainty into account when planning production.

EXAMPLE | **10.3 Trying to Meet an Order Due Date at Wozac**

The Wozac Company is a drug manufacturing company. Wozac has recently accepted an order from its best customer for 8000 ounces of a new miracle drug, and Wozac wants to plan its production schedule to meet the customer's promised delivery date of December 1, 2004. There are three sources of uncertainty that make planning difficult. First, the drug must be produced in batches, and there is uncertainty in the time required to produce a batch, which could be anywhere from 5 to 11 days. This uncertainty is described by the discrete distribution in Table 10.1. Second, the yield (usable quantity) from any batch is uncertain. Based on historical data, Wozac believes the yield can be modeled by a triangular distribution with minimum, most likely, and maximum values equal to 600, 1000, and 1100 ounces, respectively. Third, all batches must go through a rigorous inspection once they are completed. The probability that a typical batch passes inspection is only 0.8. With probability 0.2, the batch fails inspection, and *none* of it can be used to help fill the order. Wozac wants to use simulation to help decide how many days prior to the due date it should begin production.

Table 10.1   Distribution of Days to Complete a Batch

Days	Probability
5	0.05
6	0.10
7	0.20
8	0.30
9	0.20
10	0.10
11	0.05

Objective   To use simulation to learn when Wozac should begin production for this order so that there is a high probability of completing it by the due date.

Where Do the Numbers Come From?

The important inputs here are the probability distributions of the time to produce a batch, the yield from a batch, and the inspection result. The probabilities we have assumed would undoubtedly be based on previous production data. For example, the company might have observed that about 80% of all batches in the past passed inspection. Of course, a *discrete* distribution is natural for the number of days to produce a batch, and a *continuous* distribution is appropriate for the yield from a batch.

Solution

The idea is to simulate successive batches—their days to complete, their yields, and whether they pass inspection—and keep a running total of the usable ounces obtained so far. We then use IF functions to check whether the order is complete or another batch is required. We simulate only as many as batches as are required to meet the order, and we keep track of the days required to produce all of these batches. In this way we can "back up" to see when production must begin to meet the due date. For example, if the simulation indicates that the order takes 96 days to complete, then production must begin on August 27, 2004, 96 days before the due date.

The completed model appears in Figure 10.9. (See the file **DrugProduction.xls**.) It can be developed as follows.

Figure 10.9 Drug Production Simulation Model

	A	B	C	D	E	F	G	H	I	J	K	L
1	Planning production of a drug											
2												
3	Assumptions:											
4	The drug is produced in similar-sized batches, although the yield in each batch is random. Also, the number of days to											
5	produce a batch is random. Each batch is inspected, and if it doesn't pass inspection, none of that batch can be used.											
6												
7	Input section											
8	Amount required (ounces)	8000										
9	Promised delivery date	12/01/04										
10												
11	Distribution of days needed to produce a batch (discrete)											
12		Days	Probability									
13		5	0.05									
14		6	0.10									
15		7	0.20									
16		8	0.30									
17		9	0.20									
18		10	0.10									
19		11	0.05									
20												
21	Distribution of yield (ounces) from each batch (triangular)											
22		Min	Most likely		Max							
23		600	1000		1100							
24												
25	Probability of passing inspection	0.8										
26												
27	Simulation model							Summary measures				
28	Batch	Days	Yield	Pass?	CumYield	Enough?		Batches required	12			
29	1	8	807.0	No	0.0	Not yet		Days to complete	100			
30	2	8	935.9	Yes	935.9	Not yet		Day to start	8/23/04			
31	3	9	1021.3	Yes	1957.2	Not yet						
32	4	8	998.9	Yes	2956.1	Not yet		@Risk summary outputs				
33	5	8	825.0	Yes	3781.1	Not yet		Max batches reqd	18			
34	6	8	782.9	No	3781.1	Not yet						
35	7	9	850.1	Yes	4631.2	Not yet		Avg days reqd	93	8/30/04		
36	8	8	781.6	No	4631.2	Not yet		Min days reqd	62	9/30/04		
37	9	8	842.0	Yes	5473.2	Not yet		Max days reqd	157	6/27/04		
38	10	9	698.5	Yes	6171.7	Not yet		5th perc days reqd	72	9/20/04		
39	11	10	1030.1	Yes	7201.8	Not yet		95th perc days reqd	122	8/1/04		
40	12	7	976.9	Yes	8178.7	Yes						
41	13							Probability of meeting due date for several starting dates				
42	14								7/15/04	0.995		
43	15								8/1/04	0.953		
44	16								8/15/04	0.837		
45	17								9/1/04	0.477		
46	18								9/15/04	0.127		
47	19											
48	20											
49	21											
50	22											
51	23											
52	24											
53	25											

1 **Inputs.** Enter all of the inputs in the shaded cells.

2 **Batch indexes.** We do not know ahead of time how many batches will be required to fill the order. We want to have enough rows in the simulation to cover the worst case that is likely to occur. After some experimentation we found that 25 batches are almost surely enough. Therefore, enter the batch indexes 1–25 in column A of the simulation section. (If 25 were not enough, we could always add more rows.) The idea, then, is to fill the *entire* range B29:F53 with formulas. However, we will use IF functions in these formulas so that if enough has already been produced to fill the order, blanks are inserted in the remaining cells. For example, the scenario shown in Figure 10.9 is one where 12 batches were required, so blanks appear below row 40.

3 **Days for batches.** Simulate the days required for batches in column B. To do this, enter the formulas

=RISKDISCRETE(B13:B19,C13:C19)

and

=IF(OR(F29="Yes",F29=""),"",RISKDISCRETE($B$13:$B$19,$C$13:$C$19))

in cell B29 and B30, and copy the latter formula down to cell B53. Note how the IF function enters a blank in this cell if either of two conditions is true: the order was just completed in the previous batch or it has been completed for some time. Similar logic will appear in later formulas.

4 **Batch yields.** Simulate the batch yields in column C. To do this, enter the formulas

=RISKTRIANG(B23,C23,D23)

and

=IF(OR(F29="Yes",F29=""),"",RISKTRIANG($B$23,$C$23,$D$23))

in cells C29 and C30, and copy the latter formula down to cell C53.

5 **Pass inspection?** Check whether each batch passes inspection with the formulas

We can use Excel's RAND function inside an IF function to simulate whether some event occurs or does not occur.

=IF(RAND()<B25, "Yes","No")

and

=IF(OR(F29="Yes",F29=""),"",IF(RAND()<$B$25, "Yes","No"))

in cells D29 and D30, and copy the latter formula down to cell D53. Note that we could use @RISK's RISKUNIFORM(0,1) function instead of RAND(), but there is no real advantage to doing so. They are essentially equivalent.

6 **Order filled?** We keep track of the cumulative usable production and whether the order has been filled in columns E and F. First, enter the formulas

=IF(D29="Yes",C29,0)

and

=IF(E29>=B8, "Yes","Not yet")

in cells E29 and F29 for batch 1. Then enter the general formulas

=IF(OR(F29="Yes",F29=""),"",IF(D30="Yes",C30+E29,E29))

and

=IF(OR(F29="Yes",F29=""),"",IF(E30>=$B$8,"Yes","Not yet"))

in cells E30 and F30, and copy them down to row 53. Note that the entry in column F is "Not enough" if the order is not yet complete. In the row that completes the order, it changes to "Yes," and then it is blank in succeeding rows.

7 **Summary measures.** Calculate the batches and days required in cells I28 and I29 with the formulas

=COUNT(B29:B53)

and

=SUM(B29:B53)

These are the two cells we use as output cells for @RISK, so designate them as such. Also, calculate the day the order should be started to just meet the due date in cell I30 with the formula

=B9-I29

Date subtraction in Excel allows us to calculate the number of days between two given dates.

This formula uses "date subtraction" to find an elapsed time. (We assume for simplicity that production occurs every day of the week.)

This completes the simulation model development. The other entries in columns H–J will be explained shortly.

Running the Simulation

We set the number of iterations to 1000 and the number of simulations to 1, and then run the simulation as usual.

Discussion of the Simulation Results

After running the simulation, we obtain the histograms of the number of batches required and the number of days required in Figures 10.10 and 10.11.

Figure 10.10

Histogram of Batches Required

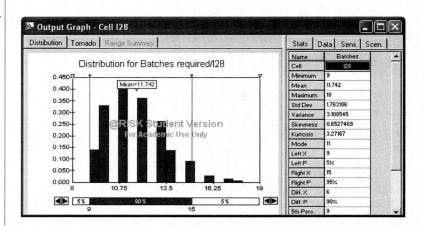

Figure 10.11

Histogram of Days Required

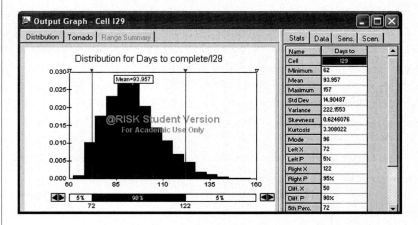

How should Wozac use this information? The key questions are, How many batches will be required? and When should we start production? To answer these questions, it is helpful to use several of @RISK's statistical functions. These functions, which we have not yet discussed, can be entered directly into the Excel model worksheet. (They provide useful information *after* the simulation has been run.) These functions provide no new information we didn't already have from the @RISK Results window, but they allow us to see (and manipulate) this information directly in our spreadsheet.

For the first question, we enter the formula

=RISKMAX(I28)

in cell I33. (Refer to Figure 10.9.) It shows that the worst case from the 1000 iterations, in terms of batches required, is 18 batches. (If this maximum were 25, we would add more rows to the simulation model and run the simulation again!)

We can answer the second question in two ways. First, we can calculate summary measures for days required and then back up from the due date. We do this in the range I35:J39. The formulas in column I are

=INT(RISKMEAN(I29))

=RISKMIN(I29)

=RISKMAX(I29)

=RISKPERCENTILE(I29,0.05)

and

=RISKPERCENTILE(I29,0.95)

Using @RISK summary functions such as RISKMEAN, RISKPERCENTILE, and others allows us to capture simulation results in the same worksheet as the simulation model. These functions do not provide useful results until the simulation is run.

(The first uses the INT function to produce an integer.) We then subtract each of these from the due date to obtain the potential starting dates in column J. Wozac should realize the pros and cons of these starting dates. For example, if the company wants to be 95% sure of meeting the due date, it should start production on August 1. In contrast, if Wozac starts production on September 20, there is only a 5% chance of meeting the due date.

Alternatively, we can get a more direct answer to our question by using @RISK's RISKTARGET function. This allows us to find the probability of meeting the due date for *any* starting date, such as the trial dates in the range H42:H46. We enter the formula

=RISKTARGET(I29,$B$8-H42)

in cell I42 and copy it down. This function returns the fraction of iterations where the (random) value in the first argument is less than or equal to the (fixed) value in the second argument. For example, we see that 83.7% of the iterations have a value of DaysReqd less than or equal to 108, the number of days from August 15 to the due date.

What is our recommendation to Wozac? We suggest going with the 95th percentile—begin production on August 1. Then there is only a 5% chance of failing to meet the due date. But the table in the range H42:I46 also provides useful information. For each potential starting date, Wozac can see the probability of meeting the due date. ∎

Project Scheduling Models

When activity times are random, we typically cannot say for certain whether a given activity will be on the critical path.

In Chapter 5 we learned how to calculate the required time to complete a project that consists of several activities. We also saw that the critical path consists of the "bottleneck" activities, those activities that cannot be delayed without delaying the project as a whole. In that chapter we assumed that the individual activity times are known with certainty. We now make the more realistic assumption that the activity times are random with given probability distributions, and we find the distribution of the time needed to complete the project. Because of randomness, we can no longer identify *the* critical path. We can only determine the *probability* that any activity is critical.

To illustrate this latter statement, suppose that activities A and B can begin immediately. Activity C can then begin as soon as activities A and B are both completed, and the project is completed as soon as activity C is completed. (See Figure 10.12.) Activity C is clearly on the critical path, but what about A and B? Let's say that the *expected* activity times of A and B are 10 and 12. If we use these expected times and ignore any uncertainty about the actual times—that is, if we proceed as in Chapter 5—then activity B is definitely a critical activity because its duration is definitely longer than activity A's duration. However, suppose there is some positive probability that A can have duration 12 and B can have duration 11. Under this scenario, A is a critical activity. Therefore, we cannot say in advance which of the activities, A or B, will be critical. However, we can use simulation to see how *likely* it is that each of these activities is critical. We can also see how long the entire project is likely to take.

Figure 10.12

A Simple Project Network

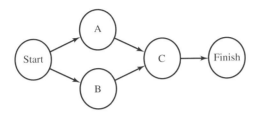

We illustrate the procedure in the following example. It is the same example as in Chapter 5 (without crashing). We repeat the "story" here for your convenience.

EXAMPLE 10.4 A ROOM CONSTRUCTION PROJECT WITH UNCERTAIN ACTIVITY TIMES

Tom Lingley, an independent contractor, has agreed to build a new room on an existing house. He plans to begin work on Monday morning, June 1. The main question is when he will complete his work, given that he works only on weekdays. The owner of the house is particularly hopeful that the room will be ready by the end of Friday, June 26, that is, in 20 or fewer working days. The work proceeds in stages, labeled A through J, as summarized in Table 10.2. Three of these activities, E, F, and G, will be done by separate independent subcontractors. The *expected* durations of the activities (in days) are shown in the table. (These are the same activity times that were used in Example 5.7 of Chapter 5.) However, these are only best guesses. Lingley knows that the *actual* activity times can vary because of unexpected delays, worker illnesses, and so on. He would like to use simulation to see (1) how long the project is likely to take, (2) how likely it is that the project will be completed by the deadline, and (3) which activities are likely to be critical.

Table 10.2 Activity Time Data

Description	Index	Predecessor(s)	Expected Duration (Days)
Prepare foundation	A	None	4
Put up frame	B	A	4
Order custom windows	C	None	11
Erect outside walls	D	B	3
Do electrical wiring	E	D	4
Do plumbing	F	D	3
Put in duct work	G	D	4
Hang dry wall	H	E, F, G	3
Install windows	I	B, C	1
Paint and clean up	J	H	2

Objective To simulate the time to complete the room-building project, and to estimate the probability that any given activity will be part of the critical path.

WHERE DO THE NUMBERS COME FROM?

All of the data are the same as in Chapter 5 except for the probability distributions for activity times. We discuss these in some detail here.

Solution

We first need to choose distributions for the uncertain activity times. Then, given any randomly generated activity times, we will illustrate a method for calculating the length of the project and identifying the activities on the critical path.

The PERT Distribution

As always, there are several reasonable candidate probability distributions we could use for the random activity times. Here we illustrate a distribution that is popular in project scheduling, called the PERT distribution. As shown in Figure 10.13 (page 506), it is a "curved" version of the triangular distribution. Like the triangular distribution, the PERT distribution is specified by three parameters that Tom should be able to estimate from past experience: a minimum value, a most likely value, and a maximum value. The distribution in the figure uses the values 7, 10, and 19 for these three values, which implies a mean of 11.[3] We will use this distribution for activity C. Its random activity time can be generated with @RISK using the formula

=RISKPERT(7,10,19)

Similarly, for the other activities, we will choose parameters for the PERT distribution that lead to the means in Table 10.2. (In reality, it would be done the other way around. The contractor would estimate the minimum, most likely, and maximum parameters for the various activities, and the means would then follow from these. We want to keep the means the same as the activity times in Chapter 5 for comparison.)

→ **@RISK FUNCTION: RISKPERT**
To generate a random number with @RISK from the PERT distribution, a "curved" version of the triangular distribution, enter the formula **=RISKPERT(Min,Most likely,Max).** ■

DEVELOPING THE SIMULATION MODEL

The key to the model is representing the project network in activity-on-node (AON) form, as in Figure 10.14, and then finding the earliest start and finish times, the latest start and finish times, and the slacks for each of the activities, exactly as we did in Chapter 5.[4] (We refer to Section 5.6 for explanations and formulas for these quantities.) These formulas allow us to calculate the total project time for any *fixed* values of the activity times—that is, for any iteration of the simulation. By looking at the slacks for any iteration, we are able to see which activities are critical for that iteration (since an activity is critical only if its slack is 0).

---

[3]This distribution is named after the acronym PERT (Program Review and Evaluation Technique) that is synonymous with project scheduling in an uncertain environment. Its mean is always a weighted average of its three parameters, with the most likely value getting 4 times as much weight as the other two. In this case, the mean is $[(1)7 + 4(10) + (1)19]/(1 + 4 + 1) = 11$.
[4]We continue to show activity times next to the nodes, but these are now *mean* activity times.

Figure 10.13
Pert Distribution

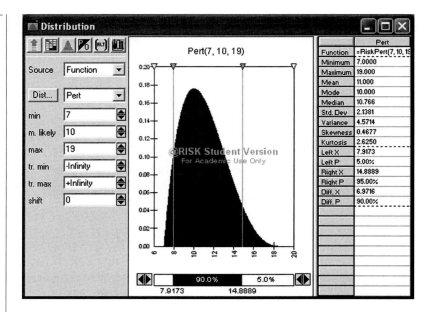

Figure 10.14
AON Network for
Room-Building
Project

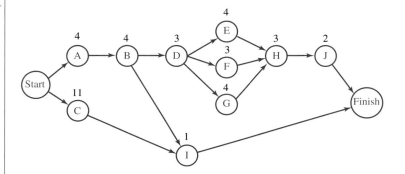

The model is a direct extension of the model in Chapter 5, as shown in Figure 10.15. (See the **ProjectSchedulingSim.xls** file.) For completeness, we will go through all of the steps, including those we covered in Chapter 5.

1 Inputs. Enter the information about precedence relationships and the parameters of the PERT activity time distributions in the shaded cells. As discussed previously, we actually chose the minimum, most likely, and maximum values to achieve the means in Table 10.2. Note that some of these distributions are symmetric about the most likely value, whereas others are skewed.

2 Activity times. Generate random activity times in column I by entering the formula

=RISKPERT(E6,F6,G6)

in cell I6 and copying it down. Of course, the durations for the fictitious Start and Finish nodes, in cells I5 and I16, are nonrandom and are equal to 0.

3 Earliest start and finish times. The earliest start time for any activity in column B is the maximum of the earliest finish times of each of this activity's immediate predecessors. For example, to get the earliest start time for activities B and H, enter the formulas

The logic behind steps 3–6 is exactly the same as for the nonrandom project networks in Chapter 5.

=C21

Figure 10.15 Project Scheduling Simulation Model

	A	B	C	D	E	F	G	H	I
1	Room construction project with random durations								
2									
3	Data on activity network				Parameters of PERT distributions				
4	Activity	Label	Predecessors	Successors	Min	Most likely	Max	Implied mean	Duration
5	Dummy Start node	Start	None	A,C					0
6	Prepare foundation	A	Start	B	1.5	3.5	8.5	4	2.698
7	Put up frame	B	A	D,I	3	4	5	4	3.723
8	Order custom windows	C	Start	I	7	10	19	11	12.841
9	Erect outside walls	D	B	E,F,G	2	2.5	6	3	3.826
10	Do electrical wiring	E	D	H	3	3.5	7	4	4.001
11	Do plumbing	F	D	H	2	2.5	6	3	2.425
12	Put in duct work	G	D	H	2	4	6	4	4.385
13	Hang dry wall	H	E ,F,G	J	2.5	3	3.5	3	3.025
14	Install windows	I	B,C	Finish	0.5	1	1.5	1	0.760
15	Paint and clean up	J	H	Finish	1.5	2	2.5	2	1.788
16	Dummy Finish node	Finish	I,J	None					0
17									
18	Activity start and finish times								
19	Activity	Earliest start time	Earliest finish time	Latest finish time	Latest start time	Slack	On critical path?	Prob(critical)	
20	Start	0.00	0.00	0.00	0.00				
21	A	0.00	2.70	2.70	0.00	0.00	1	0.967	
22	B	2.70	6.42	6.42	2.70	0.00	1	0.967	
23	C	0.00	12.84	18.68	5.84	5.84	0	0.001	
24	D	6.42	10.25	10.25	6.42	0.00	1	0.999	
25	E	10.25	14.25	14.63	10.63	0.38	0	0.451	
26	F	10.25	12.67	14.63	12.21	1.96	0	0.072	
27	G	10.25	14.63	14.63	10.25	0.00	1	0.476	
28	H	14.63	17.66	17.66	14.63	0.00	1	0.999	
29	I	12.84	13.60	19.44	18.68	5.84	0	0.001	
30	J	17.66	19.44	19.44	17.66	0.00	1	0.999	
31	Finish	19.44	19.44	19.44	19.44				
32									
33	Project completion time	19.44							

and

=MAX(C25:C27)

in cells B22 and B28. Enter similar formulas for the other activities. (As we discussed in Chapter 5, there is no simple way to enter a single formula and then copy it to calculate these earliest start time formulas. They must be entered individually, with reference to the AON diagram.) Then, since the earliest finish time for any activity is its earliest start time plus its duration, enter the formula

=B20+I5

in cell C20, and copy it down to cell C31.

4 **Project time.** The project time is the earliest start time of the Finish node, so enter a link to it in cell B33 with the formula

=RISKOUTPUT("Project_time")+B31

Note that we have designated this as an @RISK output cell.

5 **Latest start and finish times.** The latest the Finish node can finish without delaying the project is the project time itself, so enter the link

=B33

in cell D31. Each other latest finish time is the minimum of the latest start times, where the minimum is over all of the activity's immediate successors. As in step 3, there is no easy way to enter one formula and copy it; each formula depends on the activity's successors. For example, the formulas for activities D and H, in cells D24 and D28, are

=MIN(E25:E27)

and

=E30

The other latest finish times are similar. The latest start times are then the latest finish times minus the durations, so enter the formula

=D20-I5

in cell E20 and copy it down.

6 **Slacks.** The slack for any activity is the difference between the activity's latest start and earliest start times, so enter the formula

=E21-B21

in cell F21 and copy it down. Note that we do not need these slacks for the Start and Finish nodes.

7 **Critical activities.** To see whether an activity is critical, enter the formula

=IF(F21=0,1,0)

in cell G21 and copy it down. This records a 1 for any activity with 0 slack—that is, for any critical activity. However, if you press the F9 key to generate new random durations, you will see that the critical activities can change from one iteration to another. It is convenient to calculate averages of these 0's and 1's in column H. To do so, enter the formula

=RISKMEAN(G21)

in cell H21 and copy it down. Initially, the values in this column will be meaningless. However, after running the simulation, they will indicate the fraction of iterations that result in 1. This fraction is easily interpreted as the probability that the activity is critical.

Running the Simulation

We set the number of iterations to 1000 and the number of simulations to 1, and then run the simulation in the usual way.

Discussion of the Simulation Results

After running the simulation, we request the histogram of project times shown in Figure 10.16. Recall from Chapter 5 that when the activity times are not random, the project time is 20 days. Now it varies from a low of 16.49 days to a high of 26.74 days, with an average of 20.42 days.[5] Because Tom Lingley is interested in the probability of finishing the project within 20 days, we moved the left slider in the graph to 20. This indicates that there is only about a 38.6% chance of achieving his target. In fact, we see that there is about a 5% chance that the project will take longer than 23 days. This is certainly not good news for Lingley, and he might have to resort to the crashing we discussed in Chapter 5.

The @RISK averages of 0's and 1's in the range H21:H30 of Figure 10.15 indicate the fraction of iterations where each activity was critical. Five of these fractions, for activities A, B, D, H, and J, are very close to 1. This means that these activities are almost always critical. Evidently, only very unusual values for the random durations can make these activities noncritical. Similarly, activities C and I are almost never critical; their fractions are nearly 0. The fractions for the other activities, E, F, and G, are less extreme. Any one of them could easily be on the critical path. Therefore, we see that there is no *single* critical path. It depends completely on the random durations we happen to observe.

---

[5]It can be shown mathematically that the expected project time is *always* greater than when the expected activity times are used to calculate the project time (as in Chapter 5). In other words, an assumption of certainty always leads to an underestimation of the true expected project time.

Figure 10.16

Histogram of
Project Completion
Time

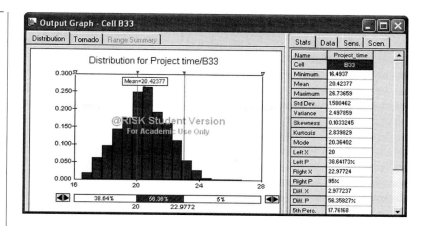

One last observation is that the 0's and 1's in column G are "all or nothing." That is, if the slack changes from 0 to a very small positive number such as 0.00023, then the 0–1 variable in column G changes from 0 to 1 and indicates that the corresponding activity is noncritical. We suspect that this happened in the few iterations where activities A, B, D, H, and J were not critical. They were probably still very *close* to being critical. ∎

PROBLEMS

Solutions for problems whose numbers appear within a color box can be found in the Student Solutions Manual. Order your copy today at http://e-catalog.thomsonlearning.com/110/ by using ISBN 0-534-39687-9.

Skill-Building Problems

1. In Example 10.1, the possible profits vary from negative to positive for each of the 10 possible bids examined.
   a. For each of these, use @RISK's Target feature to find the probability that Miller's profit is positive. Do you believe these results should have any bearing on Miller's choice of bid?
   b. Again, use @RISK's Target feature to find the 10th percentile for each of these bids. Can you explain why the percentiles have the values you obtain?

2. If the number of competitors in Example 10.1 doubles, how does the optimal bid change?

3. Referring to Example 10.1, if the average bid for each competitor stays the same, but their bids exhibit less variability, does Miller's optimal bid increase or decrease? To study this question assume that each competitor's bid, expressed as a multiple of Miller's cost to complete the project, follows each of the following distributions.
   a. Triangular with parameters 1.0, 1.3, and 2.4
   b. Triangular with parameters 1.2, 1.3, and 2.2

   c. Check (in RISKview or @RISK's Model window) to see that the distributions in parts **a** and **b** have the same mean as the original triangular distribution in the example, but smaller standard deviations. What is the common mean? Why is it not the same as the most likely value, 1.3?

4. In the warranty example, Example 10.2, we introduced the gamma distribution to model the right skewness of the lifetime distribution. Experiment to see whether we could have used the triangular distribution instead. Let its minimum value be 0, and choose its most likely and maximum values so that this triangular distribution has approximately the same mean and standard deviation as the gamma distribution in the example. (Use RISKview and trial and error to do this.) Then run the simulation and comment on similarities or differences between your outputs and the outputs in the example.

5. See how sensitive the results in the warranty example, Example 10.2, are to the following changes. For each part, make the change indicated, run the simulation, and comment on any differences between your outputs and the outputs in the example.
   a. The cost of a new camera is increased to $300.
   b. The warranty period is decreased to 1 year.
   c. The terms of the warranty are changed. If the camera fails within 1 year, the customer gets a new

camera for free. However, if the camera fails between 1 year and 1.5 years, the customer pays a pro rata share of the new camera, going linearly from 0 to full price. For example, if it fails at 1.2 years, which is 40% of the way from 1 to 1.5, the customer pays 40% of the full price.

    d. The customer pays $50 up front for an extended warranty. This extends the warranty to 3 years. This extended warranty is just like the original, so that if the camera fails within 3 years, the customer gets a new camera for free.

6. In the drug production example, Example 10.3, we commented on the 95th percentile on days required in cell I39 and the corresponding date in cell J39. If the company begins production on this date, then it is 95% sure to complete the order by the due date. We found this date to be August 1. Do you always get this answer? Find out by (1) running the simulation 10 more times, each with 1000 iterations, and finding the 95th percentile and corresponding date in each, and (2) running the simulation once more, but with 10,000 iterations. Comment on the difference between simulations 1 and 2 in terms of accuracy. Given these results, when would you recommend that production should begin?

7. In the drug production example, Example 10.3, suppose we want to run 5 simulations, where we vary the probability of passing inspection from 0.6 to 1.0 in increments of 0.1. Use the RISKSIMTABLE function appropriately to do this. Comment on the effect of this parameter on the key outputs. In particular, does the probability of passing inspection have a big effect on when production should start? (*Note*: When this probability is low, it might be necessary to produce more than 25 batches, the maximum we built into our model. Check whether this maximum should be increased.)

8. The city of Bloomington is about to build a new water treatment plant. Once the plant is designed (D), we can select the site (S), the building contractor (C), and the operating personnel (P). Once the site is selected, we can erect the building (B). We can order the water treatment machine (W) and prepare the operations

manual (M) only after the contractor is selected. We can begin training (T) the operators when both the operations manual and operating personnel selection are completed. When the treatment plant and the building are finished, we can install the treatment machine (I). Once the treatment machine is installed and operators are trained, we can obtain an operating license (L). The distribution of the time (in months) needed to complete each activity is given in the file **P10_08.xls**. Use simulation to estimate the probability that the project will be completed in (a) under 50 days and (b) more than 55 days. Also estimate the probabilities that B, I, and T are critical activities.

9. To complete an addition to the Business Building, the activities in the file **P10_09.xls** must be completed (all times are in months). The project is completed once Room 111 has been destroyed and the main structure has been built.

    a. Estimate the probability that it will take at least 3 years to complete the addition.

    b. For each activity, estimate the probability that it will be a critical activity.

10. To build Indiana University's new law building, the activities in the file **P10_10.xls** must be completed (all times are in months).

    a. Estimate the probability that the project will take less than 30 months to complete.

    b. Estimate the probability that the project will take more than 3 years to complete.

    c. For each of the activities A, B, C, and G, estimate the probability that it is a critical activity.

Skill-Extending Problem

11. In Tom Lingley's room construction in Example 10.4, we see that activities C and I are almost never on the critical path. Therefore, we might expect that the durations of these activities are not highly correlated with the total project time. Use @RISK's sensitivity analysis, with the correlation option, to see whether this is the case. What correlations between the inputs and the output do you find? Can you explain why they turn out as they do?

10.3 FINANCIAL MODELS

There are many financial applications where simulation can be applied. Future cash flows, future stock prices, and future interest rates are some of the many uncertain variables financial analysts must deal with. In every direction they turn, they see uncertainty. In this section we will analyze a few typical financial applications that can benefit from simulation modeling.

Financial Planning Models

Many companies, such as GM, Eli Lilly, Procter & Gamble, and Pfizer, use simulation in their capital budgeting and financial planning processes. Simulation can be used to model the uncertainty associated with future cash flows. In particular, simulation can be used to answer questions such as the following:

- What are the mean and variance of a project's net present value (NPV)?
- What is the probability that a project will have a negative NPV?
- What are the mean and variance of a company's profit during the next fiscal year?
- What is the probability that a company will have to borrow more than $2 million during the next year?

The following example illustrates how simulation can be used to evaluate an investment opportunity.

EXAMPLE 10.5 DEVELOPING A NEW CAR AT GF AUTO

General Ford (GF) Auto Corporation is developing a new model of compact car. This car is assumed to generate sales for the next 5 years. GF has gathered information about the following quantities through focus groups with the marketing and engineering departments.

- **Fixed cost of developing car.** This cost is assumed to $1.4 billion. The fixed cost is incurred at the beginning of year 1, before any sales are recorded.
- **Margin per car.** This is the unit selling price minus the variable cost of producing a car. GF assumes that in year 1, the margin will be $5000. Every other year, GF assumes the margin will decrease by 4%.[6]
- **Sales.** The demand for the car is the uncertain quantity. In its first year, GF assumes sales—number of cars sold—will be triangularly distributed with parameters 100,000, 150,000, and 170,000. Every year after that, the company assumes that sales will decrease by some percentage, where this percentage is triangularly distributed with parameters 5%, 8%, and 10%. GF also assumes that the percentage decreases in successive years are independent of one another.
- **Depreciation and taxes.** The company will depreciate its development cost on a straight-line basis over the lifetime of the car. The corporate tax rate is 40%.
- **Discount rate.** GF figures its cost of capital at 15%.

Given these assumptions, GF wants to develop a simulation model that will evaluate its NPV of after-tax cash flows for this new car over the 5-year time horizon.

Objective To simulate the cash flows from the new car model, from the development time to the end of its life cycle, so that GF can estimate the NPV of after-tax cash flows from this car.

WHERE DO THE NUMBERS COME FROM?

There are many inputs to this problem. As we indicated, they are probably obtained from experts within the company and from focus groups of potential customers.

---

[6]The margin decreases because variable costs tend to increase through time, whereas selling prices tend to remain fairly constant through time.

Solution

This model is like most financial multiyear spreadsheet models. The completed model extends several years to the right, but most of the work is for the first year or two. From that point, we simply copy to the other years to complete the model.

DEVELOPING THE SIMULATION MODEL

The simulation model for GF appears in Figure 10.17. (See the file **NewCar.xls**) It can be formed as follows.

Figure 10.17 GF Auto Simulation Model

	A	B	C	D	E	F	G
1	New car simulation						
2							
3	Inputs			Parameters of triangular distributions			
4	Fixed development cost	$1,400,000,000			Min	Most likely	Max
5	Year 1 contribution	$5,000		Year 1 sales	100000	150000	170000
6	Annual decrease in contribution	4%		Annual decay rate	5%	8%	10%
7	Tax rate	40%					
8	Discount rate	15%					
9							
10	Simulation						
11	End of year	1	2	3	4	5	
12	Unit sales	119934	111660	102046	93875	86188	
13	Unit contribution	$5,000	$4,800	$4,608	$4,424	$4,247	
14	Revenue minus variable cost	$599,667,932	$535,969,415	$470,227,891	$415,272,121	$366,016,207	
15	Depreciation	$280,000,000	$280,000,000	$280,000,000	$280,000,000	$280,000,000	
16	Before tax profit	$319,667,932	$255,969,415	$190,227,891	$135,272,121	$86,016,207	
17	After tax profit	$191,800,759	$153,581,649	$114,136,735	$81,163,273	$51,609,724	
18	Cash flow	$471,800,759	$433,581,649	$394,136,735	$361,163,273	$331,609,724	
19							
20	NPV of cash flows	($31,372,238)					

① **Inputs.** Enter the various inputs in the shaded cells.

② **Unit sales.** Generate first year sales in cell B12 with the formula

=RISKTRIANG(E5,F5,G5)

Then generate the reduced sales in later years by entering the formula

=B12*(1-RISKTRIANG($E$6,$F$6,$G$6))

in cell C12 and copying it across row 12. Note that each sales figure is a random fraction of the *previous* sales figure.

③ **Contributions.** Calculate the unit contributions in row 13 by entering the formulas

=B5

and

=B13*(1-$B$6)

in cells B13 and C13, and copying the latter across. Then calculate the contributions in row 14 as the product of the corresponding values in rows 12 and 13.

④ **Depreciation.** Calculate the depreciation each year in row 15 as the development cost in cell B4 divided by 5. This is exactly what "straight-line depreciation" means.

⑤ **Before-tax and after-tax profits.** To calculate the before-tax profit in any year, we subtract the depreciation from total contribution, so each value in row 16 is the difference between the corresponding values in rows 14 and 15. The reason is that depreciation isn't

We subtract depreciation to get before-tax profit, but we then add it back after taxes have been deducted.

taxed. To calculate the after-tax profits in row 17, we multiply each before-tax profit by 1 minus the tax rate in cell B7. Finally, each cash flow in row 18 is the sum of the corresponding values in rows 15 and 17. Here we add depreciation back to get the cash flow.

6 **NPV.** Calculate the NPV of cash flows in cell B20 with the formula

=-B4+NPV(B8,B18:F18)

and designate it as an @RISK output cell (the only output cell). Here, we are assuming that the development cost is incurred right now, so that it isn't discounted, and that all other cash flows occur at the ends of the respective years. This allows us to use the NPV function directly.

Running the Simulation

We set the number of iterations to 1000 and the number of simulations to 1, and then run the simulation as usual.

Discussion of the Simulation Results

Financial analysts typically look at VAR to see how bad—or more precisely, almost how bad—things could get.

After running @RISK, we obtain the summary measures for total NPV in Figure 10.18 and the histogram in Figure 10.19. These results are somewhat comforting, but also a cause of concern, for GF. On the bright side, the mean NPV is about $135 million, and there is some chance that the NPV could go well above that figure, even up to almost $400 million. However, there is also a dark side as shown by the two sliders in the histogram. We placed one slider over an NPV of 0. As the histogram indicates, there is about an 84% chance of a positive NPV, but there is about a 16% chance of losing money. The second slider is positioned at its default 5 percentile setting. Financial analysts often call this percentile the **value at risk**, or **VAR**, because it indicates nearly the worst possible outcome. From this simulation, we see that GF's VAR is approximately an $86 million loss.

> The **value at risk**, or **VAR**, is the 5th percentile of a distribution, and it is used primarily in financial models. It indicates nearly the worst possible outcome.

Figure 10.18 Summary Measures for Total NPV

	Name	Cell	Minimum	Mean	Maximum	x1	p1	x2	p2	x2-x1	p2-p1
Output 1	NPV	B20	-1.81457E+0	1.352617E+0	3.978437E+0	-8.655371E+	5%	3.182785E+0	95%	4.048322E+0	90%
Input 1	Unit sales	B12	101659.9	139998.4	168822.3	113183.3	5%	161605.2	95%	48421.97	90%
Input 2	Unit sales	C12	5.081735E-0	7.666666E-0	9.922638E-0	0.0586586	5%	9.289388E-0	95%	3.423527E-0	90%

Figure 10.19

Histogram of Total NPV

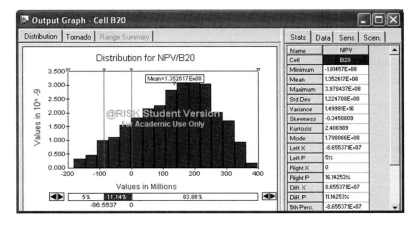

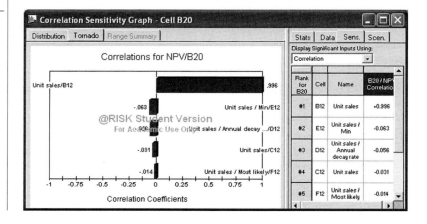

What is most responsible for this huge variability in NPV, the variability in first-year sales or the variability in annual sales decreases? We can answer this with @RISK's tornado chart. (See Figure 10.20.) To get this chart, go to the @RISK Results window, and in the left-hand "explorer" pane, right-click on the NPV output and select a tornado chart. If necessary, we suggest that you click on the drop-down list to the right of the chart and select the Correlation option. This chart answers our question emphatically. Variability in first-year sales is by far the largest influence on NPV. It correlates almost perfectly with NPV. The annual decreases in sales are not unimportant, but they have much less effect on NPV. If GF wants to get a more favorable NPV distribution, it should do all it can to boost first-year sales—and make the first-year sales distribution less variable.

Figure 10.20
Tornado Chart
for NPV

Cash Balance Models

All companies track their cash balance through time. As specific payments come due, companies might need to take out short-term loans to keep a minimal cash balance. The following example illustrates one such application.

EXAMPLE | **10.6 MAINTAINING A MINIMAL CASH BALANCE AT ENTSON**

The Entson Company believes that its monthly sales during the period from November 2003 to July 2004 are normally distributed with the means and standard deviations given in Table 10.3. Each month Entson incurs fixed costs of $250,000. In March taxes of $150,000 and in June taxes of $50,000 must be paid. Dividends of $50,000 must also be paid in June. Entson estimates that its receipts in a given month are a weighted sum of sales from the current month, the previous month, and two months ago with weights 0.2, 0.6, and 0.2. In symbols, if R_t and S_t represent receipts and sales in month t, then

$$R_t = 0.2S_{t-2} + 0.6S_{t-1} + 0.2S_t \qquad (10.1)$$

The materials and labor needed to produce a month's sales must be purchased one month in advance, and the cost of these averages to 80% of the product's sales. For example, if sales in February are $1,500,000, then the February materials and labor costs are $1,200,000, but these must be paid in January.

Table 10.3 Monthly Sales (in Thousands of Dollars) for Entson

	Nov.	Dec.	Jan.	Feb.	Mar.	Apr.	May	Jun.	Jul.
Mean	1500	1600	1800	1500	1900	2600	2400	1900	1300
St Dev	70	75	80	80	100	125	120	90	70

At the beginning of January 2004, Entson has $250,000 in cash. The company wants to ensure that each month's ending cash balance never dips below $250,000. This means that Entson might have to take out short-term (one-month) loans. For example, if the ending cash balance at the end of March is $200,000, Entson will take out a loan for $50,000, which it will then pay back (with interest) one month later. The interest rate on a short-term loan is 1% per month. At the beginning of each month, Entson earns interest of 0.5% on its cash balance. The company wants to use simulation to estimate the maximum loan it will need to take out to meet its desired minimum cash balance. Entson also wants to analyze how its loans vary through time, as well as to estimate the total interest paid on these loans.

Objective To simulate Entson's cash flows and the loans the company must take out to meet a minimum cash balance.

WHERE DO THE NUMBERS COME FROM?

Although there are many monetary inputs in the problem statement, they should all be easily accessible. Of course, Entson chooses the minimum cash balance of $250,000 as a matter of company policy.

Solution

There is a considerable amount of bookkeeping in this simulation, so it is a good idea to list the events in chronological order that occur each month. We assume the following:

- Entson observes its beginning cash balance.
- Entson receives interest on its beginning cash balance.
- Receipts arrive and expenses are paid (including payback of the previous month's loan, if any, with interest).
- If necessary, Entson takes out a short-term loan.
- The final cash balance is observed, which becomes next month's beginning cash balance.

DEVELOPING THE SIMULATION MODEL

The completed simulation model appears in Figure 10.21 (page 516). (See the file **CashBalance.xls.**) It requires the following steps.

1 Inputs. Enter the inputs in the shaded cells. Note that we simulate loans (in row 42) only for the period from January 2004 to June 2004. However, we need sales figures (in row 28) in November and December from the previous year to generate receipts for January and February. Also, we need July 2004 sales to generate the material and labor costs paid in June 2004.

Figure 10.21

Cash Balance Simulation Model

	A	B	C	D	E	F	G	H	I	J
1	Entson cash balance simulation									
2				All monetary values are in $1000s.						
3	Inputs									
4	Distribution of monthly sales (normal)									
5		Nov	Dec	Jan	Feb	Mar	Apr	May	Jun	Jul
6	Mean	1500	1600	1800	1500	1900	2600	2400	1900	1300
7	St Dev	70	75	80	80	100	125	120	90	70
8										
9	Monthly fixed cost			250	250	250	250	250	250	
10	Tax, dividend expense:			0	0	150	0	0	100	
11										
12	Receipts in any month are of form: A*(sales from 2 months ago)+B*(previous month's sales)+C*(current month's sales), where:									
13		A	B	C						
14		0.2	0.6	0.2						
15										
16	Cost of materials and labor for next month, spent this month, is a percentage of product's sales from next month, where the percent									
17		80%								
18										
19	Initial cash in January	250								
20	Minimum cash balance	250								
21										
22	Monthly interest rates									
23	Interest rate on loan	1.0%								
24	Interest rate on cash	0.5%								
25										
26	Simulation									
27		Nov	Dec	Jan	Feb	Mar	Apr	May	Jun	Jul
28	Actual sales	1456.854	1680.379	1821.380	1414.494	1761.048	2487.289	2585.647	1802.452	1227.222
29										
30	Cash, receipts									
31	Beginning cash balance			250.000	533.529	589.161	250.000	250.000	250.000	
32	Interest on cash balance			1.250	2.668	2.946	1.250	1.250	1.250	
33	Receipts			1663.874	1711.803	1565.182	1836.985	2361.712	2409.336	
34	Costs									
35	Fixed costs			250	250	250	250	250	250	
36	Tax, dividend expenses			0	0	150	0	0	100	
37	Material, labor expenses			1131.595	1408.838	1989.831	2068.517	1441.962	981.778	
38	Loan payback (principal)				0.000	0.000	482.543	962.825	291.824	0.000
39	Loan payback (interest)				0.000	0.000	4.825	9.628	2.918	0.000
40										
41	Cash balance before loan			533.529	589.161	-232.543	-712.825	-41.824	1036.984	
42	Loan amount (if any)			0.000	0.000	482.543	962.825	291.824	0.000	
43	Final cash balance			533.529	589.161	250.000	250.000	250.000	1036.984	
44										
45	Maximum loan	962.825								
46	Total intest on loans	17.372								

2 **Actual sales.** Generate the sales in row 28 by entering the formula

=RISKNORMAL(B6,B7)

in cell B28 and copying across.

3 **Beginning cash balance.** For January 2004 enter the cash balance with the formula

=B19

in cell D31. Then for the other months enter the formula

=D43

in cell E31 and copy it across row 31. This reflects that the beginning cash balance for one month is the final cash balance from the previous month.

4 **Incomes.** Entson's incomes (interest on cash balance and receipts) are entered in rows 32 and 33. To calculate these, enter the formulas

=$B$24*D31

and

=SUMPRODUCT($B$14:$D$14,B28:D28)

in cells D32 and D33 and copy them across rows 32 and 33. This latter formula, which is based on equation (10.1), multiplies the fixed weights in row 14 by the relevant sales and adds these products to calculate receipts.

⑤ Expenses. Entson's expenses (fixed costs, taxes and dividends, material and labor costs, and payback of the previous month's loan) are entered in rows 35–39. Calculate these by entering the formulas

=D9

=D10

=$B$17*E28

=D42

and

=D42*$B$23

in cells D35, D36, D37, E38, and E39 and copying these across rows 35–39. (For the loan payback, we are assuming that no loan payback is due in January.)

⑥ Cash balance before loan. Calculate the cash balance before the loan (if any) by entering the formula

=SUM(D31:D33)-SUM(D35:D38)

in cell D41 and copying it across row 41.

The loan amounts are determined by the random cash inflows and outflows and the fact that Entson's policy is to maintain a minimum cash balance.

⑦ Amount of loan. If the value in row 41 is below the minimum cash balance ($250,000), Entson must borrow enough to bring the cash balance up to this minimum. Otherwise, no loan is necessary. Therefore, enter the formula

=MAX($B$20-D41,0)

in cell D42 and copy it across row 42. (We could use an IF function, rather the MAX function, to accomplish the same result.)

⑧ Final cash balance. Calculate the final cash balance by entering the formula

=D41+D42

in cell D43 and copying it across row 43.

⑨ Maximum loan, total interest. Calculate the maximum loan from January to June in cell B45 with the formula

=MAX(D42:I42)

Then calculate the total interest paid on all loans in cell B46 with the formula

=SUM(E39:J39)

An @RISK output range, as opposed to a single output cell, allows us to obtain a summary chart that shows the whole simulated range at once. This range is typically a time series.

⑩ Output range. In the usual way, designate cells B45 and B46 as output cells. Also, designate the entire range of loans, D42:I42, as an output range. To do this, highlight this range and click on the @RISK Add Output toolbar button. It will ask you for a name of the output. We suggest "Loans." Then a typical formula in this range, such as the formula for cell E42, will be

=RISKOUTPUT("Loans",2) + MAX($B$20-E41,0)

This indicates that cell E42 is the second cell in the Loans output range.

Running the Simulation

We set the number of iterations to 1000 and the number of simulations to 1. For the Report Settings, we check the usual Simulation Summary and Output Graphs options, but we also check the Summary Graphs option. We then run the simulation in the usual way.

Discussion of the Simulation Results

After running the simulation, we obtain the summary results in Figure 10.22. They indicate that the maximum loan varies considerably, from a low of $429,929 to a high of $1,459,396. The average is $945,440. We also see that Entson is spending close to $20,000 on average in interest on the loans, although the actual amounts vary considerably from one iteration to another.

Figure 10.22   Summary Measures for Simulation

Summary Statistics

	Name	Cell	Minimum	Mean	Maximum	x1	p1	x2	p2	x2-x1	p2-p1
Output 1	Loan amount (if any) / Jan	D42	0	0.7442349	64.46103	0	5%	0	95%	0	90%
Output 2	Loan amount (if any) / Feb	E42	0	15.41051	288.0704	0	5%	99.2227	95%	99.2227	90%
Output 3	Loan amount (if any) / Mar	F42	215.0196	734.7674	1236.705	470.9106	5%	988.1519	95%	517.2413	90%
Output 4	Loan amount (if any) / Apr	G42	429.9293	943.5331	1459.396	681.2911	5%	1201.029	95%	519.7381	90%
Output 5	Loan amount (if any) / May	H42	0	293.5412	784.7014	48.02259	5%	517.3	95%	469.2775	90%
Output 6	Loan amount (if any) / Jun	I42	0	0	0	0	5%	0	95%	0	90%
Output 7	Maximum loan	B45	429.9293	945.4401	1459.396	683.0499	5%	1201.029	95%	517.9792	90%
Output 8	Total interest	B46	9.115582	19.87996	32.79556	13.14942	5%	27.00764	95%	13.85822	90%

We can also gain insights from the summary chart of the series of loans, shown in Figure 10.23. To get this chart, go to the @RISK Results window, right-click on the Loans output in the left pane, and select Summary Graph. Actually, when we designate an output *range* and then ask, in the Report Settings dialog box, for Output Graphs, we get a separate histogram for *each* cell in the range. However, the summary chart is probably more revealing. This chart clearly shows how the loans vary through time. The middle line is the expected loan amount. The inner bands extend to 1 standard deviation on each side of the mean, and the outer bands extend to the 5th and 95th percentiles. We see that the largest loans will be required in March and April.

Figure 10.23

Summary Chart of Loans Through Time

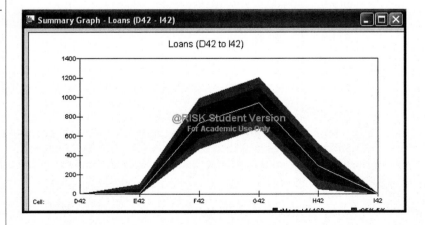

Is it intuitively clear why the required loans peak in March and April? After all, why should Entson need money in months when its sales tend to be relatively high? There are two factors working here. First, Entson has to pay its costs early. For example, it has to pay

80% of its April sales for labor and material expenses in March. Second, most of its receipts arrive late. For example, 80% of its receipts from sales in March are not received until *after* March. Therefore, the answer to our question is that the timing and amounts of loans is fairly complex. Of course, this is why Entson goes to the trouble of building a simulation model! ∎

Investment Models

Individual investors typically want to choose investment strategies that meet some pre-specified goal. The following example is typical. Here, a person wants to meet a retirement goal, starting at an early age.

EXAMPLE

10.7 INVESTING FOR RETIREMENT

Attorney Sally Evans has just begun her career. At age 25, she has 40 years until retirement, but she realizes that now is the time to start investing. She plans to invest $1000 at the beginning of each of the next 40 years. Each year, she plans to put fixed percentages—the same each year—of this $1000 into stocks, Treasury bonds (T-bonds), and Treasury bills (T-bills). However, she is not sure which percentages to use. (We will call these percentages investment weights.) She does have historical annual returns from stocks, T-bonds, and T-bills from 1946 to 2001. These are listed in the file **Retirement.xls**. This file also includes inflation rates for these years. For example, for 1993 the annual returns for stocks, T-bonds, and T-bills were 9.99%, 18.24%, and 2.90%, respectively, and the inflation rate was 2.75%. Sally would like to use simulation to help decide what investment weights to use, with the objective of achieving a large investment value, in *today's* dollars, at the end of 40 years.

Objective To use simulation to estimate the value of Sally's future investments, in today's dollars, from several investment strategies in T-bills, T-bonds, and stocks.

WHERE DO THE NUMBERS COME FROM?

Historical returns and inflation rates, such as those quoted here, are widely available on the Web.

Solution

We will simulate future scenarios by randomly choosing past scenarios, giving higher probabilities to more recent scenarios. This is sometimes called a "bootstrap" approach.

The most difficult modeling aspect is settling on a way to use historical returns and inflation factors to generate *future* values of these quantities. We will use a "scenario" approach. We think of each historical year as a possible scenario, where the scenario specifies the returns and inflation factor for that year. Then for any future year, we randomly choose one of these scenarios. It seems intuitive that more recent scenarios ought to have a greater chance of being chosen. To implement this idea, we give a weight (not to be confused with the investment weights) to each scenario, starting with weight 1 for 2001. Then the weight for any year is a "damping factor" multiplied by the weight from the next year. For example, the weight for 1996 is the damping factor multiplied by the weight for 1997. To change these weights to probabilities, we divide each weight by the sum of all the weights. The damping factor we will illustrate is 0.98. Others could be used instead, and we are frankly not sure which will produce the most realistic results. (This is an important question for financial research!)

Without a package like RiskOptimizer, we cannot find the "best" set of investment weights, but the simulation model lets us experiment with various sets of weights.

The other difficult part of the solution is knowing which investment weights to try. This is really an optimization problem—find three weights that add to 1 and produce the largest mean final cash. Palisade has another software package, RiskOptimizer, that solves this type of optimization–simulation problem. However, we will simply try several sets of weights, where some percentage is put into stocks and the remainder is split evenly between T-bonds and T-bills, and see which does best. You can try other sets if you like.

DEVELOPING THE SIMULATION MODEL

The historical data and the simulation model (each with some rows hidden) appear in Figures 10.24 and 10.25. (Again, see the **Retirement.xls** file.) It can be developed as follows.

Figure 10.24

Historical Data, Inputs, and Probabilities

	A	B	C	D	E	F	G
18	Historical data and probabilities						
19	Year	T-Bills	T-Bonds	Stocks	Inflation	ProbWts	Probability
20	1946	0.0035	-0.0010	-0.0807	0.1817	0.3292	0.0097
21	1947	0.0050	-0.0263	0.0571	0.0901	0.3359	0.0099
22	1948	0.0081	0.0340	0.0550	0.0271	0.3428	0.0101
23	1949	0.0110	0.0645	0.1879	-0.0180	0.3497	0.0103
24	1950	0.0120	0.0006	0.3171	0.0579	0.3569	0.0105
52	1978	0.0718	-0.0116	0.0656	0.0903	0.6283	0.0186
53	1979	0.1038	-0.0122	0.1844	0.1331	0.6412	0.0189
54	1980	0.1124	-0.0395	0.3242	0.1240	0.6543	0.0193
55	1981	0.1471	0.0185	-0.0491	0.0894	0.6676	0.0197
56	1982	0.1054	0.4035	0.2141	0.0387	0.6812	0.0201
57	1983	0.0880	0.0068	0.2251	0.0380	0.6951	0.0205
58	1984	0.0985	0.1543	0.0627	0.0395	0.7093	0.0209
59	1985	0.0772	0.3097	0.3216	0.0377	0.7238	0.0214
60	1986	0.0616	0.2444	0.1847	0.0113	0.7386	0.0218
61	1987	0.0547	-0.0269	0.0523	0.0441	0.7536	0.0223
62	1988	0.0635	0.0967	0.1681	0.0442	0.7690	0.0227
63	1989	0.0837	0.1811	0.3149	0.0465	0.7847	0.0232
64	1990	0.0781	0.0618	-0.0317	0.0611	0.8007	0.0236
65	1991	0.0560	0.1930	0.3055	0.0306	0.8171	0.0241
66	1992	0.0351	0.0805	0.0767	0.0290	0.8337	0.0246
67	1993	0.0290	0.1824	0.0999	0.0275	0.8508	0.0251
68	1994	0.0390	-0.0777	0.0131	0.0267	0.8681	0.0256
69	1995	0.0560	0.2348	0.3720	0.0250	0.8858	0.0262
70	1996	0.0514	0.0143	0.2382	0.0330	0.9039	0.0267
71	1997	0.0491	0.0994	0.3186	0.0170	0.9224	0.0272
72	1998	0.0516	0.1492	0.2834	0.0160	0.9412	0.0278
73	1999	0.0439	-0.0825	0.2089	0.0270	0.9604	0.0284
74	2000	0.0537	0.1666	-0.0903	0.0340	0.9800	0.0289
75	2001	0.0573	0.0557	-0.1185	0.0160	1.0000	0.0295
76					Sums -->	33.8702	1.0000

1 **Inputs.** Enter the data in the shaded regions of Figures 10.24 and 10.25. These include the historical returns and inflation factors (shown as decimals), the alternative sets of investment weights we plan to test, and other inputs.

2 **Weights.** The investment weights we will use for the model are in rows 10–12. (For example, the first set puts 80% in stocks and 10% in each of T-bonds and T-bills.) We can simulate all three sets of weights simultaneously with a RISKSIMTABLE and VLOOKUP combination as follows. First, enter the formula

=RISKSIMTABLE({1,2,3})

in cell A16. Then enter the formula

=VLOOKUP($A$16,LTable1,2)

Figure 10.25   Simulation Model

	A	B	C	D	E	F	G
1	Planning for retirement						
2							
3	Inputs						
4	Damping factor	0.98					
5	Yearly investment	$1,000					
6	Planning horizon	40	years				
7							
8	Alternative sets of weights to test						
9	Index	T-Bills	T-Bonds	Stocks			
10	1	0.10	0.10	0.80			
11	2	0.20	0.20	0.60			
12	3	0.30	0.30	0.40			
13							
14	Weights used						
15	Index	T-Bills	T-Bonds	Stocks			
16	1	0.10	0.10	0.80			
17							
18	Historical data and probabilities						
19	Year	T-Bills	T-Bonds	Stocks	Inflation	ProbWts	Probability
20	1946	0.0035	-0.0010	-0.0807	0.1817	0.3292	0.0097
21	1947	0.0050	-0.0263	0.0571	0.0901	0.3359	0.0099
22	1948	0.0081	0.0340	0.0550	0.0271	0.3428	0.0101
23	1949	0.0110	0.0645	0.1879	-0.0180	0.3497	0.0103
24	1950	0.0120	0.0006	0.3171	0.0579	0.3569	0.0105
25	1951	0.0149	-0.0394	0.2402	0.0587	0.3642	0.0108
52	1978	0.0718	-0.0116	0.0656	0.0903	0.6283	0.0186
53	1979	0.1038	-0.0122	0.1844	0.1331	0.6412	0.0189
54	1980	0.1124	-0.0395	0.3242	0.1240	0.6543	0.0193
55	1981	0.1471	0.0185	-0.0491	0.0894	0.6676	0.0197
56	1982	0.1054	0.4035	0.2141	0.0387	0.6812	0.0201
57	1983	0.0880	0.0068	0.2251	0.0380	0.6951	0.0205
58	1984	0.0985	0.1543	0.0627	0.0395	0.7093	0.0209
59	1985	0.0772	0.3097	0.3216	0.0377	0.7238	0.0214

Range names used

LTable1	=Model!$A$10:$D$12
LTable2	=Model!$A$20:$E$75
Weights	=Model!$B$16:$D$16

Output from simulation below

Final cash (today's dollars)	$14,915

Simulation model — Column offset for lookup2

Future year	Beginning cash	Scenario	T-Bills (2)	T-Bonds (3)	Stocks (4)	Inflation (5)	Ending cash	Deflator
1	$1,000	1984	1.0985	1.1543	1.0627	1.0395	1075	0.962
2	2075	1972	1.0384	1.0568	1.1898	1.0341	2410	0.930
3	3410	1996	1.0514	1.0143	1.2382	1.0330	4083	0.901
4	5083	1977	1.0512	0.9933	0.9282	1.0677	4813	0.843
5	5813	1996	1.0514	1.0143	1.2382	1.0330	6959	0.817
6	7959	1994	1.0390	0.9223	1.0131	1.0267	8012	0.795
33	112982	1988	1.0635	1.0967	1.1681	1.0442	129986	0.190
34	130986	1946	1.0035	0.9990	0.9193	1.1817	122562	0.161
35	123562	1955	1.0157	0.9870	1.3156	1.0037	154793	0.161
36	155793	1987	1.0547	0.9731	1.0523	1.0441	162744	0.154
37	163744	1977	1.0512	0.9933	0.9282	1.0677	155068	0.144
38	156068	1974	1.0800	1.0435	0.7353	1.1220	124946	0.128
39	125946	1979	1.1038	0.9878	1.1844	1.1331	145679	0.113
40	146679	1966	1.0476	1.0365	0.8994	1.0335	136108	0.110

in cell B16 and copy it to cells C16 and D16. Then modify the formulas in these latter two cells, changing the last argument of the VLOOKUP to 3 and 4, respectively. For example, the formula in cell D16 should end up as

=VLOOKUP($A$16,LTable1,4)

The effect is that we will run three simulations, one for each set of weights in rows 10–12.

3 Probabilities. Enter value 1 in cell F75. Then enter the formula

=$B$4*F75

in cell F74 and copy it *up* to cell F20. Sum these values with the SUM function in cell F76. Then to convert them to probabilities (numbers that add to 1), enter the formula

=F20/$F$76

in cell G20 and copy it down to cell G75. Note how the probabilities for more recent years are considerably larger. When we randomly select scenarios, the recent years will have a greater chance of being chosen. (The SUM formula in cell G76 simply confirms that the probabilities sum to 1.)

4 Scenarios. Moving to the model in Figure 10.25, we want to simulate 40 scenarios in columns K–O, one for each year of Sally's investing. To do this, enter the formulas

=RISKDISCRETE($A$20:$A$75,$G$20:$G$75)

and

=1+VLOOKUP($K20,LTable2,L$18)

in cells K20 and L20, and then copy this latter formula to the range M20:O20. Make sure you understand how the RISKDISCRETE and VLOOKUP functions combine to achieve our goal. (Also, check the list of range names we have used at the top of Figure 10.25.)The RISKDISCRETE randomly generates a year from column A, using the probabilities in column G. Then the VLOOKUP captures the data from this year. (We add 1 to the VLOOKUP to get a value such as 1.08, rather than 0.08.) This is the key to the simulation.

5 **Beginning, ending cash.** The bookkeeping part is straightforward. Begin by entering the formula

=B5

in cell J20 for the initial investment. Then enter the formulas

=J20*SUMPRODUCT(Weights,L20:N20)

and

=$B$5+P20

in cells P20 and J21 for ending cash in the first year and beginning cash in the second year. The former shows how the beginning cash grows in a given year. You should think through it carefully. The latter implies that Sally reinvests her previous money, plus she invests an additional $1000. Copy these formulas down columns J and P.

6 **Deflators.** We eventually want to deflate future dollars to today's dollars. The proper way to do this is to calculate deflators (also called deflation factors). Do this by entering the formula

=1/O20

in cell Q20. Then enter the formula

=Q20/O21

in cell Q21 and copy it down. The effect is that the deflator for future year 20, say, in cell Q39, is 1 divided by the product of all 20 inflation factors up through that year.

7 **Final cash.** Calculate the final value *in today's dollars* in cell K15 with the formula

=P59*Q59

Then designate this cell as an @RISK output cell. Note that multiplying by the deflator for year 40 is similar to taking an NPV. The only difference is that the inflation rates differ through the 40 years, whereas NPV calculations typically involve the *same* discount rate each year.

Running the Simulation

Set the number of iterations to 1000 and the number of simulations to 3 (one for each set of investment weights we want to test). Then run the simulation as usual.

Discussion of the Simulation Results

Summary results appear in Figure 10.26. The first simulation, which invests the most heavily in stocks, is easily the winner. Its mean final cash, slightly above $176,000 in today's dollars, is much greater than the means for the other two sets of weights. The first simulation also has a *much* larger upside potential (its 95th percentile is over $400,000), and even its downside is slightly better than the others: its 5th percentile is the best, and its minimum is only slightly worse than the minimum for the other two sets of weights.

Nevertheless, the histogram for simulation 1 (put 80% in stocks), shown in Figure 10.27, indicates a lot of variability—and skewness—in the distribution of final cash.[7] As

---

[7]Interestingly, these results are much better than in the same model in the second edition of our *Practical Management Science* book. There we used historical data only through 1994. With the bull market that lasted through most of the late 1990s, and with the most recent years being most likely to be chosen in the simulation, we are now likely to generate better investment outcomes. With more of the bear market years we are currently experiencing, however, this could easily turn around in our next edition!

Figure 10.26 Summary Results from @RISK

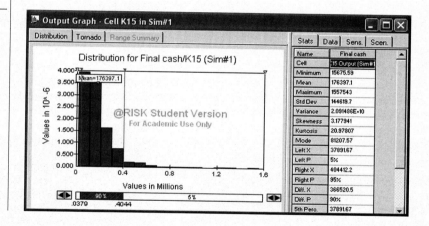

	Name	Cell	Sim#	Minimum	Mean	Maximum	x1	p1	x2	p2	x2-x1	
Output 1	Final cash	K15	1	15675.59	176397.1	1557543	37891.67	5%	404412.2	95%	366520.5	9(
Output 1	Final cash	K15	2	18231.91	116082.4	690959	35362.4	5%	240140.4	95%	204778	9(
Output 1	Final cash	K15	3	18815.06	76878.3	367171	31067.61	5%	140558.9	95%	109491.3	9(
Input 1	Index	A16	1	1	1	1	1	5%	1	95%	0	9(

in Example 10.5, the concept of value at risk (VAR) is useful. Recall that VAR is defined as the 5th percentile of a distribution and is often the value investors worry about. Perhaps Sally should rerun the simulation with different investment weights, with an eye on the weights that increase her VAR. Right now it is close to $38,000—not too good considering that she invested $40,000 total. She might not like the prospect of a 5% chance of ending up with no more than this! We also encourage you to try running this simulation with other investment weights, both for the 40-year horizon and (after modifying the spreadsheet model slightly) for shorter time horizons such as 10 or 15 years. Even though the stock strategy appears to be best for a long horizon, it is not necessarily guaranteed to dominate for a shorter time horizon.

Figure 10.27

Histogram of Final Cash with 80% in Stocks

PROBLEMS

Skill-Building Problems

12. Rerun the new car simulation from Example 10.5, but now introduce uncertainty into the fixed development cost. Let it be triangularly distributed with parameters $1.2 billion, $1.3 billion, and $1.7 billion. (You can check that the mean of this distribution is $1.4 billion, the same as the cost given in the example.) Comment on the differences between your output and those in the example. Would you say these differences are "important" for the company?

13. Rerun the new car simulation from Example 10.5, but now use the RISKSIMTABLE function appropriately

to simulate discount rates of 7.5%, 10%, 12.5%, and 15%. Comment on how the outputs change as the discount rate decreases from the value we used, 15%.

14. In the cash balance model from Example 10.6, the timing is such that some receipts are delayed by 1 or 2 months, and the payments for materials and labor must be made a month in advance. Change the model so that all receipts are received immediately, and payments made this month for materials and labor are 80% of sales *this* month (not next month). The period of interest is again January–June. Rerun the simulation, and comment on any differences between your outputs and those from the example.

15. In the cash balance model from Example 10.6, is the $250,000 minimum cash balance requirement really "costing" the company very much? Find out by rerunning the simulation with minimum required cash balances of $50,000, $100,000, $150,000, and $200,000. Use the RISKSIMTABLE function to run all simulations at once. Comment on the outputs from these simulations. In particular, comment on whether the company appears to be "better off" with a lower minimum cash balance.

16. Run the retirement model from Example 10.7 with a damping factor of 1.0 (instead of 0.98), again using the same three sets of investment weights. Explain in words what it means, in terms of the simulation, to have a damping factor of 1. Then comment on the differences, if any, between your simulation results and those in the example.

17. The simulation output from Example 10.7 indicates that an investment heavy in stocks produces the best results. Would it be better to invest *entirely* in stocks? Find out by rerunning the simulation. Is there any apparent downside to this strategy?

18. Modify the model from Example 10.7 so that you use only the years 1970–2001 of historical data. Run the simulation for the same three sets of investment weights. Comment on whether your results differ in any important way from those in the example.

19. Referring to the retirement example in Example 10.7, rerun the model for a planning horizon of 10 years; 15 years; 25 years. For each, try to find the set of investment weights that maximize the VAR (the 5th percentile) of final cash in today's dollars. Does it appear that a portfolio heavy in stocks is better for long horizons but not for shorter horizons?

Skill-Extending Problems

20. Change the new car simulation from Example 10.5 as follows. It is the same as before for years 1–5, including depreciation through year 5. However, the car might sell through year 10. Each year *after* year 5, the company examines sales. If fewer than 90,000 cars were sold that year, there is a 50% chance the car won't be sold after that year. Modify the model and run the simulation. Keep track of two outputs: NPV (through year 10) and the number of years of sales.

21. Based on Kelly (1956). You currently have $100. Each week you can invest any amount of money you currently have in a risky investment. With probability 0.4, the amount you invest is tripled (e.g., if you invest $100, you increase your asset position by $300), and, with probability 0.6, the amount you invest is lost. Consider the following investment strategies:
- Each week invest 10% of your money.
- Each week invest 30% of your money.
- Each week invest 50% of your money.

Use @RISK to simulate 100 weeks of each strategy 1000 times. Which strategy appears to be best? (In general, if you can multiply your investment by M with probability p and lose your investment with probability q, you should invest a fraction $[p(M - 1) - q]/(M - 1)$ of your money each week. This strategy maximizes the expected growth rate of your fortune and is known as the **Kelly criterion**.) [*Hint*: If an initial wealth of I dollars grows to F dollars in 100 weeks, then the weekly growth rate, labeled r, satisfies $F = (1 + r)^{100} I$, so that $r = (F/I)^{1/100} - 1$.]

22. Amanda has 30 years to save for her retirement. At the beginning of each year, she puts $5000 into her retirement account. At any point in time, all of Amanda's retirement funds are tied up in the stock market. Suppose the annual return on stocks follows a normal distribution with mean 12% and standard deviation 25%. What is the probability that at the end of 30 years, Amanda will have reached her goal of having $1,000,000 for retirement? Assume that if Amanda reaches her goal *before* 30 years, she will stop investing. (*Hint*: Each year you should keep track of Amanda's beginning cash position—for year 1, this is $5000—and Amanda's ending cash position. Of course, Amanda's ending cash position for a given year is a function of her beginning cash position and the return on stocks for that year. To estimate the probability that Amanda will meet her goal, use an IF statement that returns 1 if she meets her goal and 0 otherwise.)

10.4 MARKETING MODELS

There are plenty of opportunities for marketing departments to use simulation. They face uncertainty in the brand-switching behavior of customers, the entry of new brands into the market, customer preferences for different attributes of products, the effects of advertising on sales, and so on. We will examine some interesting marketing applications of simulation in this section.

Models of Customer Loyalty

Churn occurs when customers leave one company and go to another company.

What is a loyal customer worth to a company? This is an extremely important question for companies. (It is an important part of customer relationship management, or CRM, currently one of the hottest topics in marketing.) Companies know that if customers become dissatisfied with the company's product, they are likely to switch and never return. Marketers refer to this customer loss as **churn**. The loss in profit from churn can be large, particularly since long-standing customers tend to be more profitable in any given year than new customers. The following example uses a reasonable model of customer loyalty and simulation to estimate the worth of a customer to a company. It is based on the excellent discussion of customer loyalty in Reichheld (1996).

EXAMPLE	10.8 THE LONG-TERM VALUE OF A CUSTOMER AT CCAMERICA

CCAmerica is a credit card company that does its best to gain customers and keep their business in a highly competitive industry. The first year a customer signs up for service typically results in a loss to the company because of various administrative expenses. However, after the first year, the profit from a customer is typically positive, and this profit tends to increase through the years. The company has estimated the mean profit from a typical customer to be as shown in column B of Figure 10.28 (page 526). For example, the company expects to lose $40 in the customer's first year but to gain $87 in the fifth year—provided that the customer stays loyal that long. For modeling purposes, we will assume that the *actual* profit from a customer in the customer's nth year of service is normally distributed with mean shown in Figure 10.28 and standard deviation equal to 10% of the mean. At the end of each year, the customer leaves the company, never to return, with probability 0.15, the **churn rate**. Alternatively, the customer stays with probability 0.85, the **retention rate**. The company wants to estimate the NPV of the net profit from any such customer who has just signed up for service at the beginning of year 1, at a discount rate of 15%, assuming that the cash flow occurs in the middle of the year.[8] It also wants to see how sensitive this NPV is to the retention rate.

Objective   To use simulation to find the NPV of a customer and to see how this varies with the retention rate.

WHERE DO THE NUMBERS COME FROM?

The numbers in Figure 10.28 are undoubtedly averages, based on historical records of many customers. To build in randomness for any *particular* customer, we need a probability distribution around the numbers in this figure. We arbitrarily chose a normal distribution centered on the historical average and a standard deviation of 10% of the average. These are educated guesses. Finally, the churn rate is a number very familiar to marketing people, and it can also be estimated from historical customer data.

Solution

The idea is to keep simulating profits (or a loss in the first year) for the customer until the customer churns. We will simulate 30 years of potential profits.

---

[8]This will make the NPV calculation slightly more complex, but it is probably more realistic than our usual assumption that cash flows occur at the *ends* of the years.

Figure 10.28

Mean Profit as a
Function of Years as
Customer

	A	B
9	Estimated means	
10	Year	Mean Profit(if still here)
11	1	($40.00)
12	2	$66.00
13	3	$72.00
14	4	$79.00
15	5	$87.00
16	6	$92.00
17	7	$96.00
18	8	$99.00
19	9	$103.00
20	10	$106.00
21	11	$111.00
22	12	$116.00
23	13	$120.00
24	14	$124.00
25	15	$130.00
26	16	$137.00
27	17	$142.00
28	18	$148.00
29	19	$155.00
30	20	$161.00
31	21	$161.00
32	22	$161.00
33	23	$161.00
34	24	$161.00
35	25	$161.00
36	26	$161.00
37	27	$161.00
38	28	$161.00
39	29	$161.00
40	30	$161.00

DEVELOPING THE SIMULATION MODEL

The simulation model appears in Figure 10.29. (See the file **CustomerLoyalty.xls**.) It can be developed with the following steps.

❶ Inputs. Enter the inputs in the shaded cells.

❷ Retention rate. Although an 85% retention rate was given in the statement of the problem, we will investigate retention rates from 75% to 95%, as shown in column D. To run a separate simulation for each of these, enter the formula

=RISKSIMTABLE(D4:D8)

in cell B4.

❸ Timing of churn. In column C, we want to use simulation to discover when the customer churns. This column will contain a sequence of No's, followed by a Yes, and then a sequence of blanks. To generate these, enter the formulas

=IF(RAND()<1-B4,"Yes","No")

and

=IF(OR(C11="",C11="Yes"),"",IF(RAND()<1-$B$4,"Yes","No"))

in cells C11 and C12, and copy the latter formula down column C. Study these formulas carefully to see how the logic works. Note that they do not rely on @RISK functions. Excel's RAND function can be used any time we want to simulate whether an event occurs.

❹ Actual and discounted profits. Profits (or a loss in the first year) occur as long as there is not a blank in column C. Therefore, simulate the actual profits by entering the formula

=IF(C11<>"",RISKNORMAL(B11,$B$6*ABS(B11)),0)

As usual, Excel's RAND function can be used inside an IF statement to determine whether a given event occurs.

Figure 10.29 Customer Loyalty Model

	A	B	C	D	E	F	G	H	I
1	Customer loyalty model in the credit card industry								
2									
3	Inputs			Retention rates to try					
4	Retention rate	0.75		0.75					
5	Discount rate	0.15		0.80					
6	Stdev % of mean	10%		0.85					
7				0.90					
8				0.95					
9	Estimated means		Simulation				Outputs		
10	Year	Mean Profit(if still here)	Quits at end of year?	Actual profit	Discounted profit		NPV	$24.08	
11	1	($40.00)	No	($33.87)	($31.58)		Years loyal	2	
12	2	$66.00	Yes	$68.65	$55.66				
13	3	$72.00		$0.00	$0.00		@RISK means (copied)		
14	4	$79.00		$0.00	$0.00		Churn rate	NPV	Years loyal
15	5	$87.00		$0.00	$0.00		0.25	$93.42	3.92
16	6	$92.00		$0.00	$0.00		0.20	$130.46	4.95
17	7	$96.00		$0.00	$0.00		0.15	$178.16	6.52
18	8	$99.00		$0.00	$0.00		0.10	$253.37	9.54
19	9	$103.00		$0.00	$0.00		0.05	$367.02	16.09
20	10	$106.00		$0.00	$0.00				
21	11	$111.00		$0.00	$0.00				
22	12	$116.00		$0.00	$0.00				
23	13	$120.00		$0.00	$0.00				
24	14	$124.00		$0.00	$0.00				
25	15	$130.00		$0.00	$0.00				
26	16	$137.00		$0.00	$0.00				
27	17	$142.00		$0.00	$0.00				
28	18	$148.00		$0.00	$0.00				
29	19	$155.00		$0.00	$0.00				
30	20	$161.00		$0.00	$0.00				
31	21	$161.00		$0.00	$0.00				
32	22	$161.00		$0.00	$0.00				
33	23	$161.00		$0.00	$0.00				
34	24	$161.00		$0.00	$0.00				
35	25	$161.00		$0.00	$0.00				
36	26	$161.00		$0.00	$0.00				
37	27	$161.00		$0.00	$0.00				
38	28	$161.00		$0.00	$0.00				
39	29	$161.00		$0.00	$0.00				
40	30	$161.00		$0.00	$0.00				

in cell D11 and copying it down. (The absolute value function, ABS, is required in case any of the cash flows are negative. A normal distribution cannot have a *negative* standard deviation.) Then discount these appropriately in column E by entering the formula

=D11/(1+$B$5)^(A11-0.5)

Careful discounting is required if cash flows occur in the middle of a year.

in cell E11 and copying it down. Note how the exponent of the denominator accounts for the cash flow in the *middle* of the year.

5 **Outputs.** We will actually keep track of two outputs, the total NPV and the number of years the customer stays with the company. Calculate the NPV in cell H10 by summing the discounted values in column E. (They have already been discounted, so the NPV function is not needed.) To find the number of years the customer is loyal, note that it will always be the number of No's in column C, plus 1. Therefore, calculate it in cell H11 with the formula

=COUNTIF(C11:C40,"No")+1

Finally, designate both of cells H10 and H11 as @RISK output cells.

Running the Simulation

Set the number of iterations to 1000 and the number of simulations to 5 (one for each potential retention rate). Then run the simulation as usual.

Discussion of the Simulation Results

Selected summary results and the histogram for an 85% retention rate appear in Figures 10.30 and 10.31. The histogram indicates that there is almost a 15% chance that the NPV will be negative, whereas the chance that it will be above $300 is about 25%. We also see from the summary measures that the mean NPV and the mean number of years loyal are quite sensitive to the retention rate.

Figure 10.30   Summary Results for Customer Loyalty Model

Name		Cell	Sim#	Minimum	Mean	Maximum	x1	p1	x2	p2	x2-x1	p2-p
Output 1	NPV	H10	1	-47.65872	106.2579	555.7654	-40.18921	5%	368.772	95%	408.9612	90%
Output 1	NPV	H10	2	-52.39644	136.6262	576.4826	-39.68343	5%	416.9794	95%	456.6628	90%
Output 1	NPV	H10	3	-48.43272	185.492	583.8674	-39.13831	5%	504.3708	95%	543.509	90%
Output 1	NPV	H10	4	-45.04898	251.2639	608.9139	-36.73272	5%	549.9857	95%	586.7184	90%
Output 1	NPV	H10	5	-43.8304	359.4091	594.9365	-29.11508	5%	573.6893	95%	602.8044	90%
Output 2	Years loyal	H11	1	1	4.216	27	1	5%	11	95%	10	90%
Output 2	Years loyal	H11	2	1	5.1	31	1	5%	14	95%	13	90%
Output 2	Years loyal	H11	3	1	6.845	31	1	5%	20	95%	19	90%
Output 2	Years loyal	H11	4	1	9.449	31	1	5%	27	95%	26	90%
Output 2	Years loyal	H11	5	1	15.862	31	1	5%	31	95%	30	90%

Figure 10.31

Histogram of NPV for an 85% Retention Rate

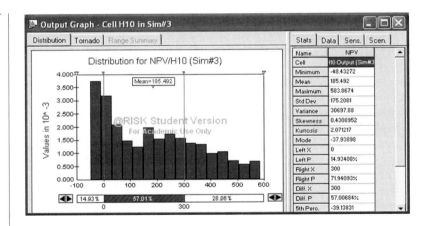

Varying the churn rate can have a large impact on the value of a customer.

To follow up on this observation, we copied the means to the model sheet and then created a line chart of them as a function of the churn rate, which is 1 minus the retention rate. (See Figure 10.32.) This line chart shows the rather dramatic effect the churn rate can have on the value of a customer. For example, if it decreases from the current 15% to 10%, the mean NPV increases by about 42%. If it decreases from 15% to 5%, the mean NPV increases by about 106%. In the other direction, if the churn rate increases from 15% to 20%, the mean NPV decreases by about 27%. This is why credit card companies are so anxious to keep their customers.

Figure 10.32

Sensitivity of
Outputs to the
Churn Rate

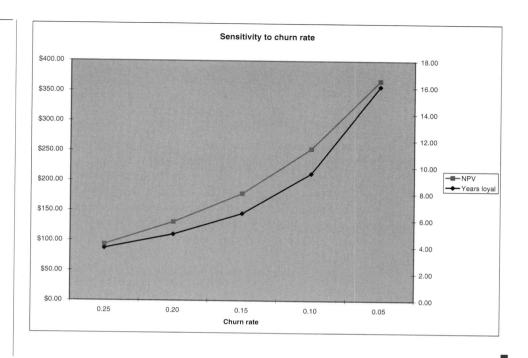

The following example is a variation of the previous example. We now investigate the effect of offering a customer an incentive to remain loyal. We also change the model to allow previous customers to rejoin our company.

| EXAMPLE | 10.9 REDUCING CHURN AT AOSN |

We are all aware of the fierce competition by Internet Service Providers (ISPs) to get our business. For example, MSN is always trying to attract AOL's customers, and vice versa. Some are even giving away prizes to entice us to sign up for a guaranteed length of time. This example is based on one such offer. We assume that an ISP named AOSN is willing to give a customer a free PC, at a cost of $700 to AOSN, if the customer will sign up for a guaranteed 3 years of service. During that time, the cost of service to the customer is a constant $21.95 per month, or $263.40 annually. After 3 years, we assume the cost of service will increase by 3% annually. We assume that in any year after the guaranteed 3 years, the probability is 0.7 that the customer will stay with AOSN. As in the previous example, this is the retention rate. We also assume that if a customer has switched to another ISP, there is always a probability of 0.1 that the customer will (without any free PC offer) willingly join AOSN. AOSN wants to see whether, in terms of NPV with a 10% discount rate, this offer makes financial sense. It also wants to see how the NPV varies with the retention rate.

Objective To use simulation to estimate whether it makes sense for an ISP to give away a free PC for a promise of at least 3 years of customer loyalty, and to see how the answer varies with the retention rate.

WHERE DO THE NUMBERS COME FROM?

In the previous example we discussed the switching rates, which would be estimated from extensive customer data. The other data in the problem statement are straightforward to obtain.

Solution

The solution strategy is fairly similar to the previous example. We use IF functions to check whether a customer is currently getting service from AOSN. There are two differences, however. First, we need to modify the logic so that a customer can leave AOSN *or* return. Second, we will run two side-by-side simulations: one for a customer who has just accepted a free PC for a guaranteed 3-year subscription and the other for a customer who is not currently an AOSN customer and does *not* accept such an offer. By comparing these, we can see whether the free PC is worth its cost to AOSN.

DEVELOPING THE SIMULATION MODEL

The completed simulation model appears in Figure 10.33. (See the file **FreePCValue.xls**.) It can be developed with the following steps.

Figure 10.33 Simulation Model of Free PC

	A	B	C	D	E	F	G	H	I	J	K	L	M
1	Estimating value of giving away free PC to get loyal customer												
2													
3	**Inputs**				Retention rates to try								
4	Retention rate	0.5			0.5								
5	Switchback rate	0.1			0.6								
6	Cost of PC	$700			0.7								
7	Yearly subscription cost	$263.40			0.8								
8	Annual cost increase	3%			0.9								
9	Discount rate	10%											
10													
11	Outputs from simulation below				Probability of difference being positive (copied from @RISK detailed statistics window)								
12	NPV with PC	$495.54			Retention rate	0.5	0.6	0.7	0.8	0.9			
13	NPV without PC	$355.20			Pr(positive)	0.354	0.428	0.457	0.555	0.607			
14	Difference	$140.34											
15													
16	Simulation		With Free PC				Without free PC						
17		End of year	Subscription cost	With us?	Quit?	Switch to us?	Revenue	With us?	Quit?	Switch to us?	Revenue		Random numbers for:
18		0					($700)						Quitting	Switching
19		1	$263.40	Yes	No	No	$263.40	No	No	No	$0.00		0.246469	0.782796
20		2	$263.40	Yes	No	No	$263.40	No	No	No	$0.00		0.053972	0.270932
21		3	$263.40	Yes	No	No	$263.40	No	No	No	$0.00		0.036452	0.206767
22		4	$271.30	Yes	Yes	No	$271.30	No	No	No	$0.00		0.868272	0.510256
23		5	$279.44	No	No	No	$0.00	No	No	No	$0.00		0.433793	0.489472
24		6	$287.82	No	No	No	$0.00	No	No	No	$0.00		0.318538	0.57638
25		7	$296.46	No	No	No	$0.00	No	No	No	$0.00		0.841844	0.966008
26		8	$305.35	No	No	No	$0.00	No	No	No	$0.00		0.375969	0.603462
27		9	$314.51	No	No	No	$0.00	No	No	No	$0.00		0.811538	0.324793
28		10	$323.95	No	No	No	$0.00	No	No	No	$0.00		0.006247	0.559018
29		11	$333.67	No	No	No	$0.00	No	No	No	$0.00		0.325493	0.874102
30		12	$343.68	No	No	No	$0.00	No	No	No	$0.00		0.764695	0.277527
31		13	$353.99	No	No	Yes	$0.00	No	No	Yes	$0.00		0.799397	0.092868
32		14	$364.61	Yes	No	No	$364.61	Yes	No	No	$364.61		0.26553	0.977769
33		15	$375.55	Yes	Yes	No	$375.55	Yes	Yes	No	$375.55		0.883594	0.992644
34		16	$386.81	No	No	No	$0.00	No	No	No	$0.00		0.970427	0.774233
35		17	$398.42	No	No	No	$0.00	No	No	No	$0.00		0.949285	0.137358
36		18	$410.37	No	No	No	$0.00	No	No	No	$0.00		0.20267	0.631057
37		19	$422.68	No	No	No	$0.00	No	No	No	$0.00		0.819029	0.89038
38		20	$435.36	No	No	No	$0.00	No	No	No	$0.00		0.631376	0.959077
39		21	$448.42	No	No	No	$0.00	No	No	No	$0.00		0.311376	0.233544
40		22	$461.87	No	No	No	$0.00	No	No	No	$0.00		0.850048	0.530678
41		23	$475.73	No	No	No	$0.00	No	No	No	$0.00		0.999792	0.171483
42		24	$490.00	No	No	Yes	$0.00	No	No	Yes	$0.00		0.344351	0.086882
43		25	$504.70	Yes	No	No	$504.70	Yes	No	No	$504.70		0.480088	0.15577
44		26	$519.84	Yes	No	No	$519.84	Yes	No	No	$519.84		0.024463	0.467051
45		27	$535.44	Yes	No	No	$535.44	Yes	No	No	$535.44		0.118411	0.121752
46		28	$551.50	Yes	Yes	No	$551.50	Yes	Yes	No	$551.50		0.938051	0.812733
47		29	$568.05	No	No	No	$0.00	No	No	No	$0.00		0.066749	0.749773
48		30	$585.09	No	No	No	$0.00	No	No	No	$0.00		0.729013	0.845488

1 **Inputs.** Enter the given data in the shaded cells.

2 **Retention rate.** We will test the retention rates in column D with 5 separate simulations, so enter the formula

=RISKSIMTABLE(D4:D8)

in cell B4.

3 **Subscription prices.** Enter a link to the current subscription price from cell B6 in cells B19–B21. Then calculate the increasing subscription costs with the formula

=B21*(1+$B$8)

in cell B22, copied down column B. For these latter years, the subscription is increasing by 3% annually.

Using common random numbers for two side-by-side simulations is a good practice. It results in a fairer comparison.

4 **Random numbers.** Columns C–F are for a customer who accepts a free PC, whereas columns G–J are for a customer who does not accept such an offer. To compare these fairly, they should use the *same* random numbers for generating switching behavior. Therefore, enter two columns of random numbers with the RAND function in columns L and M. The first set in column L will be used to see whether the customer quits AOSN in any year, whereas the second set in column M will be used to see whether the customers switches back to AOSN in any given year.

5 **Switching with free PC.** To understand columns C–E, each cell in column C indicates whether the customer is with AOSN during that year. If "Yes," then a "Yes" is possible in column D, meaning that the customer quits AOSN at the end of the year. If "No," then a "Yes" is possible in column E, meaning that the customer switches back to AOSN at the end of the year. (The meaning is the same in columns G–I.) For a customer who accepts a free PC, fill in columns C, D, and E as follows. Enter "Yes" in cells C19–C21 and "No" in cells D19–D20 and E19–E21. (This customer is not *allowed* to switch during the first 3 years.) Then enter the formulas

=IF(D21="Yes","No",IF(E21="Yes","Yes",C21))

=IF(L21<B4,"No","Yes")

and

=IF(C22="Yes","No",IF(M22<$B$5,"Yes","No"))

in cells C22, D21, and E22, and copy these down their respective columns. These formulas allow the customer to switch back and forth after 3 years.

6 **Switching with no free PC.** The logic for the customer in columns G–I is almost the same. Now we assume that the customer is not with AOSN in year 0, so enter the formula

=IF(RAND()<B5,"Yes","No")

in cell G19 to see whether she might join AOSN of her own accord in year 1. Then enter the same logic for the other cells in columns G–I as in the previous step, referring to the *same* random numbers in columns L and M.

7 **Revenue.** Enter a link to the cost of the PC in cell F18, but make it negative. Then enter the formula

=IF(C19="Yes",$B19,0)

in cell F19, and copy it to the ranges F19:F48 and J19:J48—the logic is equivalent for both customers.

8 **NPV.** We will assume that all cash flows are at the *ends* of the respective years, so enter the formulas

=F18+NPV(B9,F19:F48)

=NPV(B9,J19:J48)

and

=B12-B13

in cells B12, B13, and B14, and designate each of these as @RISK output cells. Note that the first includes the cost (to AOSN) of the PC, whereas the second does not. We are particularly interested in the difference, in cell B14. If it tends to be positive, then the free PC is worth the cost to AOSN.

Running the Simulation

Set up @RISK to run 1000 iterations and 5 simulations, one for each retention rate to be tested. Then run the simulation as usual.

Discussion of the Simulation Results

Selected results appear in Figures 10.34 and 10.35. The summary statistics indicate that the mean difference between the two NPVs is positive except for the lowest retention rate, 0.5. However, in all cases, this difference in NPV varies from more than $1000 negative to more than $1000 positive. This indicates that for some customers, the free PC offer will make money, whereas for others it will lose money. Another way to view the results is by the probabilities of positive differences in NPV, shown in the range E13:I13 of Figure 10.33. (We found these as target values in @RISK and then copied them to the model sheet.) With retention rates of 0.5, 0.6, and 0.7, there is actually less than a 50–50 chance that the difference will be positive. If the actual retention rate is 0.7, perhaps AOSN ought to rethink its free PC strategy. In a purely financial sense, it is not a clear winner.

Figure 10.34 Summary Statistics from @RISK

	Name	Cell	Sim#	Minimum	Mean	Maximum	x1	p1	x2	p2	x2-x1	p2-p
Output 1	NPV with PC	B12	1	-44.96318	450.129	1643.729	1.618756	5%	1040.449	95%	1038.83	90%
Output 1	NPV with PC	B12	2	-44.96318	557.7255	1881.721	28.84522	5%	1221.994	95%	1193.149	90%
Output 1	NPV with PC	B12	3	-44.96318	747.1815	2143.345	97.48615	5%	1557.061	95%	1459.575	90%
Output 1	NPV with PC	B12	4	-44.96318	1016.109	2373.562	176.149	5%	1914.727	95%	1738.578	90%
Output 1	NPV with PC	B12	5	-44.96318	1474.431	2373.562	387.6591	5%	2373.562	95%	1985.903	90%
Output 2	NPV without PC	B13	1	0	477.45	2343.729	33.53052	5%	1133.009	95%	1099.479	90%
Output 2	NPV without PC	B13	2	0	556.4101	2342.267	43.61764	5%	1340.08	95%	1296.463	90%
Output 2	NPV without PC	B13	3	0	681.3512	2407.564	43.61764	5%	1588.937	95%	1545.319	90%
Output 2	NPV without PC	B13	4	0	868.9688	2737.582	35.80929	5%	1979.308	95%	1943.499	90%
Output 2	NPV without PC	B13	5	0	1163.419	3073.562	38.24294	5%	2459.019	95%	2420.776	90%
Output 3	Difference	B14	1	-1119.107	-27.32102	1146.129	-482.3141	5%	476.3199	95%	958.634	90%
Output 3	Difference	B14	2	-1002.158	1.315424	1255.635	-700	5%	628.4503	95%	1328.45	90%
Output 3	Difference	B14	3	-1687.553	65.83024	1975.322	-700	5%	904.284	95%	1604.284	90%
Output 3	Difference	B14	4	-1797.02	147.1404	2304.222	-700	5%	1146.129	95%	1846.129	90%
Output 3	Difference	B14	5	-1985.3	311.0119	2373.562	-700	5%	1628.269	95%	2328.269	90%

Figure 10.35
Histogram of the
Difference in NPV
for a 70% Retention
Rate

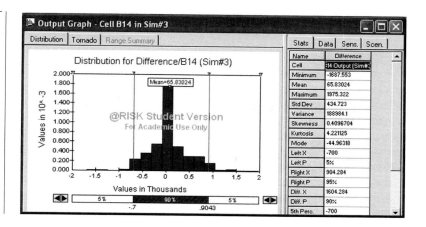

Market Share Models

We conclude this marketing section with a fairly simple model of market share behavior. This model is based on the type of competition faced by two dominant brands in an industry, such as Coca-Cola and Pepsi. We will ignore all other brands. Each quarter, one of the companies wins market share from the other in a random manner, although this behavior depends largely on how much each company promotes its product. The timing of promotions is the key to the model.

EXAMPLE | 10.10 ESTIMATING DYNAMIC MARKET SHARE WITH TWO DOMINANT BRANDS

We assume that there are two dominant companies in the soft drink industry, "us" and "them." For this example, we will view everything from the point of view of "us." We start with a 45% market share. During each of the next 20 quarters, each company promotes its product to some extent. To make the model simple, we will assume that each company each quarter either promotes at a "regular" level or at a "blitz" level. Depending on each company's promotional behavior in a given month, the change in our market share from this month to the next is triangularly distributed, with parameters given in Table 10.4. For example, if we blitz and they don't, then we could lose as much as 1% market share, we could gain as much as 6% market share, and our most likely outcome is an increase of 2% market share. We want to develop a simulation model that allows us to gauge the long-term change in our market share for any pattern of blitzing employed by us and them.

Table 10.4   Parameters of Market Share Change Distributions

Blitzer	Minimum	Most Likely	Maximum
Neither	−0.03	0	0.03
Both	−0.05	0	0.05
Only us	−0.01	0.02	0.06
Only them	−0.06	−0.02	0.01

Objective   To develop a simulation model that allows us to see how our market share will change through time for any pattern of blitzing by the two companies.

WHERE DO THE NUMBERS COME FROM?

Even if there are only two levels of advertising—and this is itself an obvious approximation to reality—the numbers in Table 10.4 are probably educated guesses at best. It is difficult to gauge the effects of advertising on market share, and many management science models have been developed to do so. However, marketers can use such models, along with their intuition, to make the required estimates.

Solution

The real purpose of the model is to allow us to test various patterns of blitzing by us and them.

The idea is that we will enter *any* pattern of blitzing, indicated by 0's and 1's, of the two companies, simulate the corresponding changes in market shares, and then track our market share through the 20-quarter period. Once the simulation has been developed, we can then use it as a tool to analyze various blitzing patterns.

DEVELOPING THE SIMULATION MODEL

The completed simulation model (with several hidden columns) appears in Figure 10.36. (See the file **MarketShare.xls**.) The following steps are required to develop it.

Figure 10.36 Market Share Simulation Model

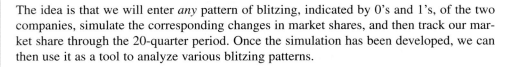

	A	B	C	D	E	F	G	H	S	T	U
1	Market share model										
2											
3	Inputs										
4	Our current market share	45%									
5											
6	Parameters of triangular distribution of change in our market share - depends on who has a big promotional campaign										
7		Minimum	Most likely	Maximum							
8	Neither	-0.03	0	0.03							
9	Both	0.05	0	0.05							
10	Only us	-0.01	0.02	0.06							
11	Only them	-0.06	-0.02	0.01							
12											
13	Promotional campaigns (1 if promote, 0 if not) - enter any patterns you want to test in the following two rows										
14	Quarter	1	2	3	4	5	6	7	18	19	20
15	Us	0	1	0	1	0	1	0	1	0	1
16	Them	1	0	1	0	1	0	1	0	1	0
17											
18	Simulation										
19	Possible changes in our market share										
20	Quarter	1	2	3	4	5	6	7	18	19	20
21	Neither promote	-0.17%	-0.37%	-0.93%	-1.38%	-0.86%	2.00%	-1.55%	0.58%	-1.34%	2.14%
22	Both promote	1.65%	-1.25%	-0.92%	-2.21%	2.05%	1.12%	1.83%	0.70%	3.57%	-4.08%
23	Only we promote	3.65%	0.28%	5.37%	3.35%	2.87%	2.92%	4.69%	-0.12%	1.33%	-0.01%
24	Only they promote	-3.67%	0.60%	-0.21%	-5.25%	-1.98%	-1.53%	-0.63%	-3.25%	-2.67%	0.13%
25											
26	Tracking our market share										
27	Beginning market share	45.00%	41.33%	41.61%	41.40%	44.74%	42.76%	45.68%	51.30%	51.18%	48.51%
28	Change in our market share	-3.67%	0.28%	-0.21%	3.35%	-1.98%	2.92%	-0.63%	-0.12%	-2.67%	-0.01%
29	Ending market share	41.33%	41.61%	41.40%	44.74%	42.76%	45.68%	45.06%	51.18%	48.51%	48.50%

1 **Inputs.** Enter the inputs in the shaded ranges.

2 **Blitz pattern.** Enter any sequence of 0's and 1's in rows 15 and 16. The 1's indicate blitz promotions. In reality, our company has no control over the pattern in row 16, and although we can choose the pattern in row 15, we probably have to choose it *before* observing their pattern in row 16. We arbitrarily entered a pattern where the 1's and 0's alternate for each company, and the two companies are "out of step" with one another. However, this is just for illustration.

3 **Possible market share changes.** It will simplify matters to generate the *possible* market share changes in rows 21–24. These will then be used as needed in row 28. To generate these random changes, enter the formula

=RISKTRIANG($B8,$C8,$D8)

in cell B21, and copy it to the range B21:U24.

4 **Our market share.** We track our market share in rows 27–29. There are really only two ideas here. First, our beginning market share in any quarter is our ending market share from the previous quarter. Second, the change in our market share in any quarter is one of the values in rows 21–24, depending on who blitzes that quarter. This will require a nested IF formula. Start by entering a link to our current market share (from cell B4) in cell B27. Then enter the formulas

=IF(AND(B16=0,B15=0),B21,IF(AND(B16=1,B15=1),B22,IF(AND(B16=0,B15=1),B23,B24)))

=B27+B28

and

=B29

in cells B28, B29, and C27, and copy all of these across. Again, the nested IF simply records the appropriate market share change for that quarter from rows 21–24.

5 **Output range.** We will designate the entire 20-quarter range in row 29 as an output range, so highlight this range and click on the @RISK Add Output button. We suggest that you name this output range "Market share."

Running the Simulation

We set @RISK to run 1000 iterations for a single simulation. However, unlike previous examples, the point here is not so much to see results for any particular simulation run, but rather to use the simulation model as a tool for analysis. That is, we can play any "game" we want by seeing how a blitzing strategy for "us" does against a given blitzing strategy for "them." For example, in the file **MarketShare_Random10.xls**, we entered formulas in their row 16 that guarantee exactly 10 randomly placed 1's.[9] This would be relevant if we believe they are going to blitz half of the time, but we have no idea when. Now we can try any strategy we want and run the resulting simulation.

Discussion of the Simulation Results

These results represent only one possibility. Other patterns of blitzes will certainly lead to different results.

Figure 10.37 (page 536) shows the summary graph of our market share through time when we react to their "random 10" strategy by blitzing in the middle 12 quarters, Q5–Q16. That is, we blitz two more quarters than they do, and we do our blitzing consecutively. The results are not unexpected. Because we blitz two more quarters than they do, we tend to gain market share—our average market share after 20 quarters is close to 50%, up from the initial 45%. However, the shape of this summary graph clearly shows what happens to our market share when we do not blitz and there is a chance that they do.

This example indicates quite clearly how a simulation model can be used as a tool to analyze all sorts of scenarios. In this case, the purpose is not to run a simulation once and then report these specific results. Rather, it is to run the simulation many times, tweaking various parameters on each run, to see what insights we can gain.

---

[9]These formulas are interesting in their own right. How can we randomly enter 0's and 1's and guarantee that exactly half are 1's? The idea is that if there is a 1 in Q1, then the probability of a 1 in Q2 should be 9/19. However, if there is a 0 in Q1, then the probability of a 1 in Q2 should be 10/19.

Figure 10.37

Summary Chart for Our "Middle 12" Strategy Versus Their "Random 10" Strategy

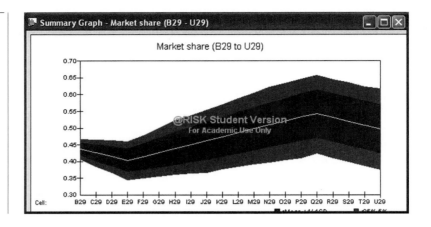

PROBLEMS

Skill-Building Problems

23. Suppose that Coke and Pepsi are fighting for the cola market. Each week each person in the market buys one case of Coke or Pepsi. If the person's last purchase was Coke, there is a 0.90 probability that this person's next purchase will be Coke; otherwise, it will be Pepsi. (We are considering only two brands in the market.) Similarly, if the person's last purchase was Pepsi, there is a 0.80 probability that this person's next purchase will be Pepsi; otherwise, it will be Coke. Currently half of all people purchase Coke, and the other half purchase Pepsi. Simulate one year of sales in the cola market and estimate each company's average weekly market share. Do this by assuming that the total market size is fixed at 100 customers. (*Hint:* Use the RISKBINOMIAL function.)

24. Seas Beginning sells clothing by mail order. An important question is when to strike a customer from their mailing list. At present, they strike a customer from their mailing list if a customer fails to order from six consecutive catalogs. They want to know whether striking a customer from their list after a customer fails to order from four consecutive catalogs will result in a higher profit per customer. The following data are available:

- If a customer placed an order the last time she received a catalog, then there is a 20% chance she will order from the next catalog.
- If a customer last placed an order one catalog ago, there is a 16% chance she will order from the next catalog she receives.
- If a customer last placed an order two catalogs ago, there is a 12% chance she will order from the next catalog she receives.

- If a customer last placed an order three catalogs ago, there is an 8% chance she will order from the next catalog she receives.
- If a customer last placed an order four catalogs ago, there is a 4% chance she will order from the next catalog she receives.
- If a customer last placed an order five catalogs ago, there is a 2% chance she will order from the next catalog she receives.

It costs $1 to send a catalog, and the average profit per order is $15. Assume a customer has just placed an order. To maximize expected profit per customer, would Seas Beginning make more money canceling such a customer after six nonorders or four nonorders?

25. Based on Babich (1992). Suppose that each week each of 300 families buys a gallon of orange juice from company A, B, or C. Let p_A denote the probability that a gallon produced by company A is of unsatisfactory quality, and define p_B and p_C similarly for companies B and C. If the last gallon of juice purchased by a family is satisfactory, then the next week they will purchase a gallon of juice from the same company. If the last gallon of juice purchased by a family is not satisfactory, then the family will purchase a gallon from a competitor. Consider a week in which A families have purchased juice A, B families have purchased juice B, and C families have purchased juice C. Assume that families that switch brands during a period are allocated to the remaining brands in a manner that is proportional to the current market shares of the other brands. Thus, if a customer switches from brand A, there is probability $B/(B + C)$ that he will switch to brand B and probability $C/(B + C)$ that he will switch to brand C. Suppose

that the market is currently divided equally: 100 families for each of the three brands.

a. After a year, what will the market share for each firm be? Assume $p_A = 0.10$, $p_B = 0.15$, and $p_C = 0.20$. (*Hint*: You will need to use the RISKBINOMIAL function to see how many people switch from A and then use the RISKBINOMIAL function again to see how many switch from A to B and from A to C.)

b. Suppose a 1% increase in market share is worth $10,000 per week to company A. Company A believes that for a cost of $1 million per year it can cut the percentage of unsatisfactory juice cartons in half. Is this worthwhile? (Use the same values of p_A, p_B, and p_C as in part **a**.)

Skill-Extending Problems

26. Suppose that GLC earns a $4000 profit each time a person buys a car. We want to determine how the expected profit earned from a customer depends on the quality of GLC's cars. We assume a typical customer will purchase 10 cars during her lifetime. She will purchase a car now (year 1) and then purchase a car every 5 years—during year 6, year 11, and so on. For simplicity, we assume that Hundo is GLC's only competitor. We also assume that if the consumer is satisfied with the car she purchases, she will buy her next car from the same company, but if she is not satisfied, she will buy her next car from the other company. Hundo produces cars that satisfy 80% of its customers. Currently, GLC produces cars that also satisfy 80% of its customers. Consider a customer whose first car is a GLC car. If profits are discounted at 10% annually, use simulation to estimate the value of this customer to GLC. Also estimate the value of a customer to GLC if it can raise its customer satisfaction rating to 85%; to 90%; to 95%.

27. The Mutron Company is thinking of marketing a new drug used to make pigs healthier. At the beginning of the current year, there are 1,000,000 pigs that might use the product. Each pig will use Mutron's drug or a competitor's drug once a year. The number of pigs is forecasted to grow by an average of 5% per year. However, this growth rate is not a sure thing. Mutron assumes that each year's growth rate is an independent draw from a normal distribution, with probability 0.95 that the growth rate will be between 3% and 7%. Assuming it enters the market, Mutron is not sure what its share of the market will be during year 1, so it models this with a triangular distribution. Its worst-case share is 20%, its most likely share is 40%, and its best-case share is 70%. In the absence of any *new* competitors entering this market (in addition to itself), Mutron believes its market share will remain the same in succeeding years. However, there are three potential entrants (in addition to Mutron). At the beginning of each year, each entrant that has not already entered the market has a 40% chance of entering the market. The year after a competitor enters, Mutron's market share will drop by 20% for each *new* competitor who entered. For example, if two competitors enter the market in year 1, Mutron's market share in year 2 will be reduced by 40% from what it would have been with no entrants. Note that if all three entrants have entered, there will be no more entrants. Each unit of the drug sells for $2.20 and incurs a variable cost of $0.40. Profits are discounted by 10% annually.

a. Assuming that Mutron enters the market, use simulation to find its net present value (NPV) for the next 10 years from the drug.

b. Again assuming that Mutron enters the market, it can be 95% certain that its *actual* NPV from the drug is between what two values?

10.5 SIMULATING GAMES OF CHANCE

We realize that this is a book about "business" applications. However, it is instructive (and fun) to see how simulation can be used to analyze games of chance, including sports contests. Indeed, many analysts refer to "Monte Carlo" simulation, and you can guess where that name comes from—the gambling casinos of Monte Carlo.

Simulating the Game of Craps

Most games of chance are great candidates for simulation since they are, by their very nature, driven by randomness. In this section we examine one such game that is extremely popular in the gambling casinos: the game of craps. In its most basic form, the game of craps is played as follows. A player rolls two dice and observes the sum of the two sides turned up. If this sum is 7 or 11, the player wins immediately. If the sum is 2, 3, or 12, the player loses immediately. Otherwise, if this sum is any other number (4, 5, 6, 8, 9, or 10), that number becomes the player's "point." Then the dice are thrown repeatedly until the sum is the player's point or 7. In case the player's point occurs before a 7, the player wins. But if a 7 occurs before the point, the player loses. The following example uses simulation to determine the properties of this game.

| EXAMPLE | **10.11 ESTIMATING THE PROBABILITY OF WINNING AT CRAPS** |

Joe Gamble loves to play craps at the casinos. He suspects that his chances of winning are less than 50–50, but he wants to find the probability that he wins a single game of craps.

Objective To use simulation to find the probability of winning a single game of craps.

WHERE DO THE NUMBERS COME FROM?

There are no input numbers here, only the rules of the game.

Solution

We will simulate a single game. By running this simulation for many iterations, we will find the probability that Joe wins a single game of craps. If his intuition is correct (and surely it must be, or the casino could not stay in business), this probability will be less than 0.5.

DEVELOPING THE SIMULATION MODEL

The simulation model is for a single game. (See Figure 10.38 and the file **Craps1.xls.**) There is a subtle problem here: We do not know how many tosses of the dice are necessary to determine the outcome of a single game. Theoretically, the game could continue forever, with the player waiting for his point or a 7. However, it is extremely unlikely that more than, say, 40 tosses are necessary in a single game. (This can be shown by a probability argument, but we will not present it here.) Therefore, we will simulate 40 tosses and use only those that are necessary to determine the outcome of a single game. The steps required to simulate a single game are as follows.

Figure 10.38 Simulation of Craps Game

	A	B	C	D	E	F	G	H	I	J
1	Craps Simulation									
2										
3	Simulated tosses									
4	Toss	Die 1	Die 2	Sum	Win on this toss?	Lose on this toss?	Continue?		Summary results from simulation	
5	1	1	3	4	0	0	Yes		Win? (1 if yes, 0 if no)	0
6	2	1	4	5	0	0	Yes		Number of tosses	3
7	3	6	1	7	0	1	No			
8	4	6	4	10					Pr(winning)	0.000
9	5	4	2	6					Expected number of tosses	3.000
10	6	6	5	11						
11	7	1	1	2						
12	8	3	5	8						
13	9	4	1	5						
14	10	2	4	6						
15	11	5	2	7						
16	12	2	2	4						
42	38	5	4	9						
43	39	5	2	7						
44	40	3	1	4						

1 Simulate tosses. Simulate the results of 40 tosses in the range B5:D44 by entering the formula

=RISKDUNIFORM({1, 2, 3, 4, 5, 6})

in cells B5 and C5 and the formula

=SUM(B5:C5)

in cell D5. Then copy these to the range B6:D44. The @RISK function RISKDUNIFORM takes a list of numbers and randomly selects one of the numbers from this list, where each number has equal probability (in this case 1/6). Note that the "D" in DUNIFORM stands for discrete.

→ **@RISK Function: *RISKDUNIFORM***
*The @RISK function RISKDUNIFORM in the form =**RISKDUNIFORM({List})** generates a random member of a given list, so that each member of the list has the same chance of being chosen. Here List is a list of values separated by commas.* ■

2 First toss outcome. Determine the outcome of the first toss with the formulas

=IF(OR(D5=7,D5=11),1,0)

=IF(OR(D5=2,D5=3,D5=12),1,0)

and

=IF(AND(E5=0,F5=0),"Yes","No")

in cells G5, H5, and I5. Note that we use the OR condition to check whether Joe wins right away (in which case a 1 is recorded in cell G5). Similarly, the OR condition in cell H5 checks whether he loses right away. In cell I5, we use the AND condition to check whether both cells G5 and H5 are 0, in which case the game continues. Otherwise, the game is over.

3 Outcomes of other tosses. Assuming the game continues beyond the first toss, Joe's point is the value in cell D5. Then we are waiting for a toss to have the value in cell D5 or 7, whichever occurs first. To implement this logic, enter the formulas

=IF(OR(G5="No",G5=""),"",IF(D6=$D$5,1,0))

=IF(OR(G5="No",G5=""),"",IF(D6=7,1,0))

and

=IF(OR(G5="No",G5=""),"",IF(AND(E6=0,F6=0),"Yes","No"))

in cells G6, H6, and I6, and copy these to the range G7:I44. The OR condition in each formula checks whether the game just ended on the previous toss or has been over for some time, in which case blanks are entered. Otherwise, the first two formulas check whether Joe wins or loses on this toss. If both of these return 0, the third formula returns "Yes" (and the game has just ended). Otherwise, it returns "No" (and the game continues).

4 Game outcomes. We keep track of two aspects of the game in @RISK output cells: whether Joe wins or loses and how many tosses are required. To find these, enter the formulas

=SUM(E5:E44)

and

=COUNT(E5:E44)

in cells J5 and J6, and designate each of these as an @RISK output cell. Note that both functions, SUM and COUNT, ignore blank cells.

As in many spreadsheet simulation models, the concepts in this model are simple. The key is careful bookkeeping.

Recall that the mean (or average) of a sequence of 0's and 1's is the fraction of 1's in the sequence. This can typically be interpreted as a probability.

5 Simulation summary. Although we will get various summary measures in the @RISK Results window when we run the simulation, it is useful to see some key summary measures right on the model sheet. To get these, enter the formula

=RISKMEAN(J5)

in cell J8 and copy it to cell J9. As the labels indicate, the RISKMEAN in cell J8, being an average of 0's and 1's, is just the fraction of iterations where Joe wins. The average in cell J9 is the average number of tosses until the game's outcome is determined.

Running the Simulation

We set the number of iterations to 10,000 (partly for variety and partly to obtain a very accurate answer) and the number of simulations to 1. Then we run the simulation as usual.

Discussion of the Simulation Results

Perhaps surprisingly, the probability of winning in craps is 0.493, only slightly less than 0.5.

After running @RISK, we obtain the summary results in cells J8 and J9 of Figure 10.38 (among others). Our main interest is in the average in cell J8. It represents our best estimate of the probability of winning, 0.494. (It can be shown with a probability argument that the exact probability of winning in craps is 0.493.) We also see that the average number of tosses needed to determine the outcome of a game was 3.395. (The maximum number of tosses ever needed was 29.) ■

Simulating the NCAA Basketball Tournament

Each year the suspense reaches new levels as "March Madness" approaches, the time of the NCAA Basketball Tournament. Which of the 64 teams in the tournament will reach the "Sweet Sixteen," which will go on to the prestigious "Final Four," and which team will be crowned champion? The excitement at Indiana University is particularly high, given the strong basketball tradition here, so it has become a yearly tradition at IU (at least for the authors) to simulate the NCAA Tournament right after the 64-team field has been announced. We share that simulation in the following example.

EXAMPLE	10.12 MARCH MADNESS

As of press time for this book, the most recent NCAA Basketball Tournament was the 2003 tournament. You might recall that Syracuse beat Kansas in the final game. Of course, on the Sunday evening when the 64-team field was announced, we did not know which team would win. All we knew were the pairings (which teams would play which other teams) and the team ratings, based on Jeff Sagarin's nationally syndicated rating system. We show how to simulate the tournament and keep a tally of the winners.

Objective To simulate the 64-team NCAA basketball tournament and keep a tally on how often each team wins the tournament.

WHERE DO THE NUMBERS COME FROM?

As soon as you learn the pairings for the *next* NCAA tournament, you can visit Sagarin's site at http://www.usatoday.com/sports/sagarin.htm#hoop for the latest ratings.

We model the point spread as normally distributed, with mean equal to the difference between the Sagarin ratings and standard deviation 10.

Solution

We need to make one probabilistic assumption. From that point, it is a matter of "playing out" the games and doing the required bookkeeping. To understand this probabilistic assumption, suppose team A plays team B and Sagarin's ratings for these teams are, say, 85 and 78. Then Sagarin predicts that the actual point differential in the game (team A's score minus team B's score) will be the difference between the ratings, 7.[10] We take this one step further. We assume the *actual* point differential is normally distributed with mean equal to Sagarin's prediction, 7, and standard deviation 10. (Why 10? This is an estimate based on an extensive analysis of historical data.) Then if the actual point differential is positive, team A wins. If it is negative, team B wins.

DEVELOPING THE SIMULATION MODEL

We will only outline the simulation model. You can see the full details in the file **March-Madness.xls**. (It includes the data for the 2003 tournament, but you can easily modify it for future tournaments by following the directions on the sheet.) The entire simulation is on a single Model sheet. Columns A–C list team indexes, team names, and Sagarin ratings. If two teams are paired in the first round, they are placed next to one another in the list. Also, all teams in a given region are listed together. (The regions are color-coded.) Columns K–Q contains the simulation. The first round results are at the top, the second round results are below these, and so on. Winners from one round are automatically carried over to the next round with appropriate formulas. Selected portions of the Model sheet appear in Figures 10.39 and 10.40 (page 542). We now describe the essential features of the model.

Figure 10.39

Teams and Sagarin Ratings

	A	B	C	D	E	F	G	H	I	J
1	Simulation of NCAA tournament, using Sagarin ratings (2003 data shown)									
2										
3	Final Sagarin ratings of teams									
4	Index	Team	Rating							
5	1	Texas	90.66							
6	2	UNCA	67.53							
7	3	LSU	84.62							
8	4	Purdue	84.95							
9	5	UConn	87.01							
10	6	BYU	84.69							
11	7	Stanford	84.82							
12	8	San Diego	78.48			Put teams (and their Sagarin ratings) in the				
13	9	Maryland	87.03			South regional here, in the order they're posted				
14	10	UNCW	81.77			on the pairings Web site (i.e., seed 1, then 16,				
15	11	Xavier	87.48			then 8, then 9, etc.)				
16	12	Troy State	79.36							
17	13	Michigan State	85.88							
18	14	Colorado	83.87			Assumption: The actual point spread for each				
19	15	Florida	88.96			game is normally distributed with mean equal				
20	16	Sam Houston St.	74.72			to difference between Sagarin ratings, standard				
21	17	Oklahoma	89.84			deviation 10.				
22	18	S.C. State	68.65							
23	19	Cal	83.92							
24	20	N.C. State	82.66							

❶ Teams and ratings. We first enter the teams and their ratings, as shown in Figure 10.39. Most of the teams shown here were in the South region in the 2003 tournament. Texas played UNC at Asheville in the first round, LSU played Purdue, and so on.

❷ Simulate rounds. Jumping ahead to the fourth-round simulation in Figure 10.40, we capture the winners from the previous round 3 and then simulate the games in round 4. The key formulas are in columns N and O. For example, the formulas in cells N126 and O126 are

=VLOOKUP(L126,LTable,3)-VLOOKUP(L127,LTable,3)

---

[10]In general, there is also a home-court advantage, but we assume all games in the tournament are on "neutral" courts, so that there is no advantage to either team.

Figure 10.40

NCAA Basketball
Simulation Model
(Last 3 Rounds
Only)

	K	L	M	N	O	P	Q
124	**Results of Round 4**						
125	Game	Indexes	Teams	Predicted	Simulated	Index of winner	Winner
126	1	1	Texas	1.7	4.88	1	Texas
127		15	Florida				
128	1	23	Louisville	5.38	-5.53	30	Auburn
129		30	Auburn				
130	1	33	Arizona	6.65	13.86	33	Arizona
131		41	Creighton				
132	1	49	Kentucky	11.98	37.96	49	Kentucky
133		58	S. Illinois				
134							
135	**Semifinals**						
136	Game	Indexes	Teams	Predicted	Simulated	Index of winner	Winner
137	1	1	Texas	6.83	23.17	1	Texas
138		30	Auburn				
139	2	33	Arizona	-0.98	-2.99	49	Kentucky
140		49	Kentucky				
141							
142	**Finals**						
143	Game	Indexes	Teams	Predicted	Simulated	Index of winner	Winner
144	1	1	Texas	-3.37	0.76	1	Texas
145		49	Kentucky				
146							
147	**Winner**	1					

and

=RISKNORMAL(N126,10)

The first of these looks up the ratings of the two teams involved (in this case, Texas and Florida) and subtracts them to get the predicted point spread. The second formula simulates a point spread with the predicted point spread as its mean. The rest of the formulas do the appropriate bookkeeping. You can view the details in the file.

3 **Outputs.** As shown by the boxed-in cells in Figure 10.40, we designate seven cells as @RISK output cells: the index of the winner, the indexes of the two finalists, and the indexes of the four semifinalists (the Final Four teams). However, the results we really want are tallies, such as the number of iterations where Duke (or any other team) wins the tournament. This takes some planning. In the @RISK Reports dialog box, if we check the Output Data option, we get a sheet called Outputs Data Report that lists the values of all @RISK output cells for *each* of the iterations. (We used 5000 iterations.) Once we have these, we can use COUNTIF functions to tally the number of wins (or finalist or semifinalist appearances) for each team, right in the original Model sheet.

The Output Data option in @RISK lists the outputs from each iteration of the simulation, which allows us to tally the winners.

Some of these tallies appear in Figure 10.41. For example, the formula in cell U5 is

=COUNTIF('Outputs Data Report'!$I$8:$I$5007,S5)

In this case, the range I8:I5007 of the Outputs Data Report contains the indexes of the 5000 winners, so this formula simply counts the number of these that are index 1.[11] As you can see, the top-rated team in the South region, Texas, won the tournament in 402 of the 5000 iterations and reached the Final Four almost a third of the time. (In fact, Texas *did* make it to the Final Four, but lost to Syracuse in the semifinals.) In contrast, the lowly rated Sam Houston State did not make the Final Four in any of the 5000 iterations.

[11]Unfortunately, each time we rerun the simulation, the Outputs Data Report is deleted and then recreated, which messes up the references in the tally formulas. Therefore, we created a macro to update these formulas. You can run the macro by clicking on the button at the top of Figure 10.41.

Figure 10.41

Tally of Winners

	S	T	U	V	W
1		Update formulas for tallies			
2					
3	Tally of winners, finalists, and semifinalists				
4	Index	Team	Winner	Finalist	Semifinalist
5	1	Texas	402	890	1552
6	2	UNCA	0	0	0
7	3	LSU	15	68	182
8	4	Purdue	13	40	120
9	5	UConn	50	141	355
10	6	BYU	14	64	178
11	7	Stanford	25	98	239
12	8	San Diego	0	0	3
13	9	Maryland	62	183	423
14	10	UNCW	1	9	34
15	11	Xavier	80	253	579
16	12	Troy State	0	1	13
17	13	Michigan State	25	93	258
18	14	Colorado	5	23	111
19	15	Florida	180	481	953
20	16	Sam Houston St.	0	0	0

PROBLEMS

Skill-Building Problems

28. The game of Chuck-a-Luck is played as follows: You pick a number between 1 and 6 and toss three dice. If your number does not appear, you lose $1. If your number appears *x* times, you win $*x*. On the average, how much money will you win or lose on each play of the game? Use simulation to find out.

29. A **martingale** betting strategy works as follows. We begin with a certain amount of money and repeatedly play a game in which we have a 40% chance of winning any bet. In the first game, we bet $1. From then on, every time we win a bet, we bet $1 the next time. Each time we lose, we double our previous bet. Currently we have $63. Assume we have unlimited credit, so that we can bet more money than we have. Use simulation to estimate the profit we will have earned after playing the game 50 times.

Skill-Extending Problems

30. Based on Morrison and Wheat (1984). When his team is behind late in the game, a hockey coach usually waits until there is one minute left before pulling the goalie. Actually, coaches should pull their goalies much sooner. Suppose that if both teams are at full strength, each team scores an average of 0.05 goal per minute. Also, suppose that if you pull your goalie you score an average of 0.08 goal per minute while your opponent scores an average of 0.12 goal per minute.

Suppose you are one goal behind with 5 minutes left in the game. Consider the following two strategies:
- Pull your goalie if you are behind at any point in the last 5 minutes of the game; put him back in if you tie the score.
- Pull your goalie if you are behind at any point in the last minute of the game; put him back in if you tie the score.

Which strategy maximizes your chance of winning or tying the game? Simulate the game using 10-second increments of time. Use the @RISKBINOMIAL function to determine whether a team scores a goal in a given 10-second segment. This is reasonable because the probability of scoring two or more goals in a 10-second period is near 0.

31. You are playing Pete Sampras in tennis, and you have a 42% chance of winning each point. (You are *good*!)
   a. Use simulation to estimate the probability you will win a particular game. Note that the first player to score at least 4 points and have at least 2 more points than his or her opponent wins the game.
   b. Use simulation to determine your probability of winning a set. Assume that the first player to win 6 games wins the set if he or she is at least 2 games ahead; otherwise, the first player to win 7 games wins the set.
   c. Use simulation to determine your probability of winning a match. Assume that the first player to win 3 sets wins the match.

10.6 CONCLUSION

We claimed in the previous chapter that spreadsheet simulation, especially together with an add-in like @RISK, is a very powerful tool. After seeing the examples in this chapter, you should now appreciate how powerful and flexible simulation can be. Unlike Solver optimization models, where we often make simplifying assumptions to achieve linearity, say, we allow virtually anything in simulation models. All we need to do is relate output cells to input cells with appropriate formulas, where any of the input cells can contain probability distributions to reflect uncertainty. The results of the simulation then show how bad things can get, how good they can get, and what we might expect on average. It is no wonder that companies like GM, Eli Lilly, and many others are increasingly relying on simulation models to analyze their corporate operations.

Summary of Key Management Science Terms

Term	Explanation	Page
Gamma distribution	Right-skewed distribution of nonnegative values useful for many quantities such as the lifetime of an appliance	495
PERT distribution	Distribution often used for random activity times in a project network	505
Value at risk (VAR)	Fifth percentile of distribution of some output, usually a monetary output; indicates nearly how bad the output could be	513
Churn	When customers stop buying our product or service and switch to a competitor	525

Summary of Key Excel Terms

Term	Explanation	Excel	Page
RISKGAMMA function	Implements the gamma gamma distribution in @RISK	=RISKGAMMA(*alpha*,*beta*)	497
RISKPERT function	Implements the PERT distribution in @RISK	=RISKPERT (*min*,*mostlikely*,*max*)	505
RISKDUNIFORM function	Generates a random number from a discrete set of possible values, where each has the same probability	=RISKDUNIFORM({1,2,3,4}), for example	539

PROBLEMS

Skill-Building Problems

32. You now have $3. You will toss a fair coin four times. Before each toss you can bet any amount of your money (including none) on the outcome of the toss. If heads comes up, you win the amount you bet. If tails comes up, you lose the amount you bet. Your goal is to reach $6. It turns out that you can maximize your chance of reaching $6 by betting either the money you have on hand or $6 minus the money you have on hand, whichever is smaller. Use simulation to estimate the probability that you will reach your goal.

33. You now have $1000, all of which is invested in a sports team. Each year there is a 60% chance that the value of the team will increase by 60% and a 40% chance that the value of the team will decrease by 60%. Estimate the mean and median value of your investment after 100 years. Explain the large difference between the estimated mean and median.

34. Suppose you have invested 25% of your portfolio in four different stocks. The mean and standard deviation of the annual return on each stock are as shown in the file **P10_34.xls**. The correlations between the annual returns on the four stocks are also shown in this file.
    a. What is the probability that your portfolio's annual return will exceed 20%?
    b. What is the probability that your portfolio will lose money during the course of a year?

35. A ticket from Indianapolis to Orlando on Deleast Airlines sells for $150. The plane can hold 100 people. It costs Deleast $8000 to fly an empty plane. Each person on the plane incurs variable costs of $30 (for food and fuel). If the flight is overbooked, anyone who cannot get a seat receives $300 in compensation. On average, 95% of all people who have a reservation show up for the flight. To maximize expected profit, how many reservations for the flight should Deleast book? (*Hint:* The function RISKBINOMIAL can be used to simulate the number who show up. It takes two arguments: the number of reservations booked and the probability that any ticketed person shows up.)

36. Based on Marcus (1990). The Balboa mutual fund has beaten the Standard and Poor's 500 during 11 of the last 13 years. People use this as an argument that you can "beat the market." Here is another way to look at it that shows that Balboa's beating the market 11 out of 13 times is not unusual. Consider 50 mutual funds, each of which has a 50% chance of beating the market during a given year. Use simulation to estimate the probability that over a 13-year period the "best" of the 50 mutual funds will beat the market for at least 11 out of 13 years. This probability turns out to exceed 40%, which means that the best mutual fund beating the market 11 out of 13 years is not an unusual occurrence!

37. You have been asked to simulate the cash inflows to a toy company for the next year. Monthly sales are independent random variables. Mean sales for the months January–March and October–December are $80,000, and mean sales for the months April–September are $120,000. The standard deviation for each month's sales is 20% of the month's mean sales. We model the method used to collect monthly sales as follows:
    ■ During each month a certain fraction of new sales will be collected. All new sales not collected become 1 month overdue.

■ During each month a certain fraction of 1-month overdue sales is collected. The remainder becomes 2 months overdue.
■ During each month a certain fraction of 2-month overdue sales is collected. The remainder are written off as bad debts.
You are given the information in the file **P10_36.xls** from some past months. Using this information, build a simulation model that generates the total cash inflow for each month. Develop a simple forecasting model and build the error of your forecasting model into the simulation. Assuming that there are $120,000 of 1-month-old sales outstanding and $140,000 of 2-month-old sales outstanding during January, you are 95% sure that total cash inflow for the year will be between what two values?

38. Consider a device that requires two batteries to function. If either of these batteries dies, the device will not work. Currently there are two brand new batteries in the device, and there are three extra brand new batteries. Each battery, once it is placed in the device, lasts a random amount of time that is triangularly distributed with parameters 15, 18, and 25 (all expressed in hours). When any of the batteries in the device dies, it is immediately replaced by an extra (if an extra is still available). Use @RISK to simulate the time the device can last with the batteries currently available.

39. Consider a drill press containing three drill bits. The current policy (called **individual replacement**) is to replace a drill bit when it fails. The firm is considering changing to a **block replacement** policy in which all three drill bits are replaced whenever a single drill bit fails. Each time the drill press is shut down, the cost is $100. A drill bit costs $50, and the variable cost of replacing a drill bit is $10. Assume that the time to replace a drill bit is negligible. Also, assume that the time until failure for a drill bit follows an exponential distribution with a mean of 100 hours. This can be modeled in @RISK with the formula **=RISKEXPON(100)**. Determine which replacement policy (block or individual replacement) should be implemented.

40. Freezco sells refrigerators. Any refrigerator that fails before it is 3 years old is replaced for free. Of all refrigerators, 3% fail during their first year of operation; 5% of all 1-year-old refrigerators fail during their second year of operation; and 7% of all 2-year-old refrigerators fail during their third year of operation.
    a. Estimate the fraction of all refrigerators that will have to be replaced.
    b. It costs $500 to replace a refrigerator, and Freezco sells 10,000 refrigerators per year. If the warranty period were reduced to 2 years, how much per year in replacement costs would be saved?

41. The annual demand for Prizdol, a prescription drug manufactured and marketed by the NuFeel Company, is normally distributed with mean 50,000 and standard deviation 12,000. We assume that demand during each of the next 10 years is an independent random draw from this distribution. NuFeel needs to determine how large a Prizdol plant to build to maximize its expected profit over the next 10 years. If the company builds a plant that can produce x units of Prizdol per year, it will cost $16 for each of these x units. NuFeel will produce only the amount demanded each year, and each unit of Prizdol produced will sell for $3.70. Each unit of Prizdol produced incurs a variable production cost of $0.20. It costs $0.40 per year to operate a unit of capacity.

   a. Among the capacity levels of 30,000, 35,000, 40,000, 45,000, 50,000, 55,000, and 60,000 units per year, which level maximizes expected profit? Use simulation to answer this question.

   b. Using the capacity from your answer to part **a**, NuFeel can be 95% certain that *actual* profit for the 10-year period will be between what two values?

42. We are trying to determine the proper capacity level for a new electric car. A unit of capacity gives us the potential to produce one car per year. It costs $10,000 to build a unit of capacity and the cost is charged equally over the next 5 years. It also costs $400 per year to maintain a unit of capacity (whether or not it is used). Each car sells for $14,000 and incurs a variable production cost of $10,000. The annual demand for the electric car during each of the next 5 years is believed to be normally distributed with mean 500,000 and standard deviation 100,000. The demands during different years are assumed to be independent. Profits are discounted at a 10% annual interest rate. We are working with a 5-year planning horizon. Capacity levels of 300,000, 400,000, 500,000, 600,000 and 700,000 are under consideration.

   a. Assuming we are risk neutral, use simulation to find the optimal capacity level.

   b. Using the answer to part **a**, there is a 5% chance that the *actual* discounted profit will exceed what value?

   c. Using the answer to part **a**, there is a 5% chance that the *actual* discounted profit will be less than what value?

   d. If we are risk averse, how might the optimal capacity level change?

Skill-Extending Problems

43. Consider an oil company that bids for the rights to drill in offshore areas. The value of the right to drill in a given offshore area is highly uncertain, as are the bids of the competitors. This problem will demonstrate the "winner's curse." The winner's curse states that the optimal bidding strategy entails bidding a substantial amount below your assumed value of the product for which you are bidding. The idea is that if you do not bid under your assumed value, your uncertainty about the actual value of the product will often lead you to win bids for products on which you (after paying your high bid) lose money. Suppose Royal Conch Oil (RCO) is trying to determine a profit-maximizing bid for the right to drill on an offshore oil site. The actual value of the right to drill is unknown, but it is equally likely to be any value between $10 million and $110 million. Seven competitors will bid against RCO. Each bidder's (including RCO's) estimate of the value of the drilling rights is equally likely to assume any number between 50% and 150% of the actual value. Based on past history, RCO believes that each competitor is equally likely to bid between 40% and 60% of its value estimate. Given this information, what fraction (within 0.05) of RCO's estimated value should it bid to maximize its expected profit? (*Note*: Use the RISKUNIFORM function to model the actual value of the field and the competitors' bids.)

44. We begin year 1 with $500. At the beginning of each year, we put half of our money under our mattress and invest the other half in Whitewater stock. During each year, there is a 50% chance that the Whitewater stock will double, and there is a 50% chance that we will lose half of our investment. To illustrate, if the stock doubles during the first year, we will have $375 under the mattress and $375 invested in Whitewater during year 2. We want to estimate our annual return over a 50-year period. If we end with F dollars, then our annual return is $(F/500)^{1/50} - 1$. For example, if we end with $10,000, our annual return is $20^{1/50} - 1 = 0.062$, or 6.2%. Run 1000 replications of an appropriate simulation. Based on the results, we can be 95% certain that our annual return will be between what two values?

45. Mary Higgins is a freelance writer with enough spare time on her hands to play the stock market fairly seriously. Each morning she observes the change in stock price of a particular stock and decides whether to buy or sell, and if so, how many shares to buy or sell. We will assume that on day 1, she has $100,000 cash to invest and that she spends part of this to buy her first 500 shares of the stock at the current price of $50 per share. From that point on, she follows a fairly simple "buy low, sell high" strategy. Specifically, if the price has increased three days in a row, she sells 25% of her shares of the stock. If the price has increased two days in a row (but not three), she sells 10% of her shares. In the other direction, if the price has decreased three days in a row, she buys 25% more shares, whereas if the price has decreased only two days in a row, she buys 10% more shares. We will assume a fairly simple model of stock price changes, as described in the file **P10_45.xls**. Each day the price can change by as much as $2 in either direction, and the probabilities depend on the previous price change: decrease, increase, or no change. Build a simulation model of this strategy for a period of 75 trading days. (You can assume that the stock price on each of the previous two days was $49.) Decide on interesting @RISK output cells, and then run @RISK for 500 iterations and report your findings.

46. You are considering a 10-year investment project. At present, the expected cash flow each year is $1000. Suppose, however, that each year's cash flow is normally distributed with mean equal to *last* year's actual cash flow and standard deviation $100. For example, suppose that the actual cash flow in year 1 is $1200. Then year 2 cash flow is normal with mean $1200 and standard deviation $100. Also, at the end of year 1, your best guess is that each later year's expected cash flow will be $1200.

    a. Estimate the mean and standard deviation of the NPV of this project. Assume that cash flows are discounted at a rate of 10% per year.

    b. Now assume that the project has an abandonment option. At the end of each year you can abandon the project for the value given in the file **P10_46.xls**. For example, suppose that year 1 cash flow is $400. Then at the end of year 1, you expect cash flow for each remaining year to be $400. This has an NPV of less than $6200, so you should abandon the project and collect $6200 at the end of year 1. Estimate the mean and standard deviation of the project with the abandonment option. How much would you pay for the abandonment option? (*Hint*: You can abandon a project at most once. Thus in year 5, for example, you abandon only if the sum of future expected NPVs is less than the year 5 abandonment value *and* the project has not yet been abandoned. Also, once you abandon the project, the actual cash flows for future years will be 0. So the future cash flows after abandonment should disappear.)

47. Toys For U is developing a new Madonna doll. The company has made the following assumptions:

    ■ It is equally likely that the doll will sell for 2, 4, 6, 8, or 10 years.
    ■ At the beginning of year 1, the potential market for the doll is 1 million. The potential market grows by an average of 5% per year. Toys For U is 95% sure that the growth in the potential market during any year will be between 3% and 7%. If uses a normal distribution to model this.
    ■ The company believes its share of the potential market during year 1 will be at worst 20%, most likely 40%, and at best 50%. It uses a triangular distribution to model this.

    ■ The variable cost of producing a doll during year 1 is equally likely to be $4 or $6.
    ■ Each year the selling price and variable cost of producing the doll will increase by 5%. The current selling price is $10.
    ■ The fixed cost of developing the doll (which is incurred right away, at time 0) is equally likely to be $4, $8, or $12 million.
    ■ Right now there is one competitor in the market. During each year that begins with 4 or fewer competitors, there is a 20% chance that a new competitor will enter the market.
    ■ We determine year t sales (for $t > 1$) as follows. Suppose that at the end of year $t - 1$, n competitors are present. Then we assume that during year t, a fraction $0.9 - 0.1n$ of the company's loyal customers (last year's purchasers) will buy a doll during the next year, and a fraction $0.2 - 0.4n$ of customers currently in the market who did not purchase a doll last year will purchase a doll from the company this year. We can now generate a prediction for year t sales. Of course, this prediction will not be exactly correct. We assume that it is sure to be accurate within 15%, however. (There are different ways to model this. You can choose any method that is reasonable.)

    a. @RISK to estimate the expected NPV of this project.

    b. Use the percentiles in @RISK's output to find an interval such that you are 95% certain that the company's *actual* NPV will be within this interval.

48. Dord Motors is considering whether to introduce a new model called the Racer. The profitability of the Racer will depend on the following factors:

    ■ The fixed cost of developing the Racer is equally likely to be $3 or $5 billion.
    ■ Year 1 sales are normally distributed with mean 200,000 and standard deviation 50,000. Year 2 sales are normally distributed with mean equal to actual year 1 sales and standard deviation 50,000. Year 3 sales are normally distributed with mean equal to actual year 2 sales and standard deviation 50,000.
    ■ The selling price in year 1 is $13,000. The year 2 selling price will be

    $$1.05[\text{year 1 price} + \$30(\% \text{ diff1})]$$

    where % diff1 is the percentage by which actual year 1 sales differ from expected year 1 sales. The 1.05 factor accounts for inflation. For example, if the year 1 sales figure is 180,000, which is 10% below the expected year 1 sales, then the year 2 price will be

    $$1.05[13,000 + 30(-10)] = \$13,335$$

    Similarly, the year 3 price will be

    $$1.05[\text{year 2 price} + \$30(\% \text{ diff2})]$$

where % diff2 is the percentage by which actual year 2 sales differ from expected year 2 sales.

- The variable cost is equally likely to be $5000, $6000, $7000, or $8000 during year 1 and is assumed to increase by 5% each year.

Your goal is to estimate the NPV of the new car during its first 3 years. Assume that cash flows are discounted at 10%. Simulate 1000 trials and estimate the mean and standard deviation of the NPV for the first 3 years of sales. Also, determine an interval such that you are 95% certain that the NPV of the Racer during its first 3 years of operation will be within this interval.

49. Rerun the simulation from the previous problem, but now assume that the fixed cost of developing the Racer is triangularly distributed with minimum, most likely, and maximum values $3, $4, and $5 billion. Also, assume that the variable cost per car in year 1 is triangularly distributed with minimum, most likely, and maximum values $5000, $7000, and $8000.

50. Truckco produces the OffRoad truck. The company wants to gain information about the discounted profits earned during the next 3 years. During a given year, the total number of trucks sold in the United States is

$$500,000 + 50,000G - 40,000I$$

where G is the percentage increase in gross domestic product during the year and I is the percentage increase in the consumer price index during the year. During the next 3 years, Value Line has made the predictions listed in the file **P10_50.xls**. In the past, 95% of Value Line's G predictions have been accurate within 6%, and 95% of Value Line's I predictions have been accurate within 5%. We assume that the actual G and I values are normally distributed each year.

At the beginning of each year, a number of competitors might enter the trucking business. The probability distribution of the number of competitors that will enter the trucking business is also given in the file **P10_50.xls**. Before competitors join the industry at the beginning of year 1, there are two competitors. During a year that begins with n competitors (after competitors have entered the business, but before any have left), OffRoad will have a market share given by $0.5(0.9)^n$. At the end of each year, there is a 20% chance that any competitor will leave the industry. The selling price of the truck and the production cost per truck are also given in the file **P10_50.xls**. Simulate 1000 replications of Truckco's profit for the next 3 years. Estimate the mean and standard deviation of the discounted 3-year profits, using a discount rate of 10%. You can use Excel's NPV function here. Do the same if there is a 50% chance during each year that any competitor will leave the industry.

51. Suppose you buy an electronic device that you operate continuously. The device costs you $100 and carries a 1-year warranty. The warranty states that if the device fails during its first year of use, you get a new device for no cost, and this new device carries exactly the same warranty. However, if it fails after the first year of use, the warranty is of no value. You need this device for the next 6 years. Therefore, any time the device fails outside its warranty period, you must pay $100 for another device of the same kind. (We assume the price does not increase during the 6-year period.) The time until failure for a device is gamma distributed with parameters $\alpha = 2$ and $\beta = 0.5$. (This implies a mean of 1 year.) Use @RISK to simulate the 6-year period. Include as outputs (1) your total cost, (2) the number of failures during the warranty period, and (3) the number of devices owned during the 6-year period.

52. Rework the previous problem for a case in which the 1-year warranty requires you to pay for the new device even if failure occurs during the warranty period. Specifically, if the device fails at time t, measured relative to the time it went into use, you must pay $100t$ for a new device. For example, if the device goes into use at the beginning of April and fails 9 months later, at the beginning of January, you must pay $75. The reasoning is that you got 9/12 of the warranty period for use, so you should pay that fraction of the total cost for the next device. As before, however, if the device fails outside the warranty period, you must pay the full $100 cost for a new device.

53. Based on Hoppensteadt and Peskin (1992). The following model (the Reed–Frost model) is often used to model the spread of an infectious disease. Suppose that at the beginning of period 1, the population consists of 5 diseased people (called infectives) and 95 healthy people (called susceptibles). During any period there is a 0.05 probability that a given infective person will encounter a particular susceptible. If an infective encounters a susceptible, there is a 0.5 probability that the susceptible will contract the disease. An infective lives an average of 10 periods with the disease. To model this, we assume that there is a 0.10 probability that an infective dies during any given period. Use @RISK to model the evolution of the population over 100 periods. Use your results to answer the following questions. [*Hint:* During any period there is a probability $0.05(0.50) = 0.025$ that an infective will infect a particular susceptible. Thus the probability that a particular susceptible is not infected during a period is $(1 - 0.025)^n$, where n is the number of infectives present at the end of the previous period.]

a. What is the probability that the population will die out?

b. What is the probability that the disease will die out?

c. On the average, what percentage of the population becomes infected by the end of period 100?

d. Suppose that people use infection "protection" during encounters. The use of protection reduces the probability that a susceptible will contract the disease during a single encounter with an infective from 0.50 to 0.10. Now answer parts **a–c** under the assumption that everyone uses protection.

54. Chemcon has taken over the production of Nasacure from a rival drug company. Chemcon must build a plant to produce Nasacure by the beginning of 2004. Once the plant is built, the plant's capacity cannot be changed. Each unit sold brings in $10 in revenue. The fixed cost (in dollars) of producing a plant that can produce x units per year of the drug is 5,000,000 + 10x. This cost is assumed to be incurred at the end of 2004. In fact, we assume that all cost and sales cash flows are incurred at the ends of the respective years. If a plant of capacity x is built, the variable cost of producing a unit of Nasacure is $6 - 0.1(x - 1,000,000)/100,000$. For example, a plant capacity of 1,100,000 units has a variable cost of $5.90. Each year a plant operating cost of $1 per unit of capacity is also incurred. Based on a forecasting sales model from the previous 10 years, Chemcon forecasts that demand in year t, D_t, is related to the demand in the previous year, D_{t-1}, by the equation

$$D_t = 67,430 + 0.985D_{t-1} + e_t$$

where e_t is a random term that is normally distributed with mean 0 and standard deviation 29,320. The demand in 2003 was 1,011,000 units. If demand for a year exceeds production capacity, all demand in excess of plant capacity is lost. Chemcon wants to determine a capacity level that will maximize expected discounted profits (using an interest rate of 10%) for the time period 2004–2013. Use simulation to help it do so.

55. The Tinkan Company produces 1-pound cans for the Canadian salmon industry. Each year the salmon spawn during a 24-hour period and must be canned immediately. Tinkan has the following agreement with the salmon industry. The company can deliver as many cans as it chooses. Then the salmon are caught. For each can by which Tinkan falls short of the salmon industry's needs, the company pays the industry a $2 penalty. Cans cost Tinkan $1 to produce and are purchased for $2 per can. If any cans are left over, they are returned to Tinkan and the company reim-

burses the industry $2 for each extra can. These extra cans are put in storage for next year. Each year a can is held in storage, a carrying cost equal to 20% of the can's production cost is incurred. It is well known that the number of salmon harvested during a year is strongly related to the number of salmon harvested the previous year. In fact, using past data, Tinkan estimates that the harvest size in year t, H_t (measured in the number of cans required), is related to the harvest size in the previous year, H_{t-1}, by the equation

$$H_t = H_{t-1}e_t$$

where e_t is normally distributed with mean 1.02 and standard deviation 0.10.

Tinkan plans to use the following production strategy. For some value of x, it will produce enough cans at the beginning of year t to bring its inventory up to $x + \hat{H}_t$, where $\hat{H}_t$ is the predicted harvest size in year t. Then it will deliver these cans to the salmon industry. For example, if it uses $x = 100,000$, the predicted harvest size is 500,000 cans, and 80,000 cans are already in inventory, then Tinkan will produce and deliver 520,000 cans. Given that the harvest size for the previous year was 550,000 cans, use simulation to help Tinkan develop a production strategy that will maximize its expected profit over the next 20 years.

56. You are unemployed and 21 years old and searching for a job. Until you accept a job offer, the following situation occurs. At the beginning of each year, you receive a job offer. The annual salary associated with the job offer is equally likely to be any number between $20,000 and $100,000. You must immediately choose whether to accept the job offer. If you accept an offer with salary x, you receive x per year while you work (we assume you retire at age 70), including the current year. Assume that cash flows are discounted so that a cash flow received 1 year from now has a present value of 0.9. You have adopted the following policy. You will accept the first job offer that exceeds w dollars.

a. Use simulation to determine the value of w (within $10,000) that maximizes the expected NPV of earnings you will receive the rest of your working life?

b. Repeat part **a**, assuming now that you get a 3% raise in salary every year after the first year you accept the job.

CASE | 10.1 College Fund Investment

Your next-door neighbor, Scott Jansen, has a 12-year-old daughter, and he wants to pay the tuition for her first year of college 6 years from now. The tuition for the first year will be $17,500. Scott has gone through his budget and finds that he can invest $200 per month for the next 6 years. Scott has opened accounts at two mutual funds. The first fund follows an investment strategy designed to match the return of the S&P 500. The second fund invests in short-term Treasury bills. Both funds have very low fees.

Scott has decided to follow a strategy in which he contributes a fixed fraction of the $200 to each fund. An adviser from the first fund suggested that each month he invest 80% of the $200 in the S&P 500 fund and the other 20% in the T-bill fund. The adviser explained that the S&P 500 has averaged much larger returns than the T-bill fund. Even though stock returns are risky investments in the short run, the risk would be fairly minimal over the longer 6-year period. An adviser from the second fund recommended just the opposite: invest 20% in the S&P 500 fund and 80% in T-bills, he said. Treasury bills are backed by the United States government. If you follow this allocation, he said, your average return will be lower, but at least you will have enough to reach your $17,500 target in 6 years.

Not knowing which adviser to believe, Scott has come to you for help.

Questions

1. The file **College.xls** contains 261 monthly returns of the S&P 500 and Treasury bills from January 1970 through September 1991. (If you can find more recent data on the Web, feel free to use it.) Suppose that in each of the next 72 months (6 years), it is equally likely that any of the historical returns will occur. Develop a spreadsheet model to simulate the two suggested investment strategies over the 6-year period. Plot the value of each strategy over time for a single iteration of the simulation. What is the total value of each strategy after 6 years? Do either of the strategies reach the target?

2. Simulate 1000 iterations of the two strategies over the 6-year period. Create a histogram of the final fund values. Based on your simulation results, which of the two strategies would you recommend? Why?

3. Suppose that Scott needs to have $19,500 to pay for the first year's tuition. Based on the same simulation results, which of the two strategies would you recommend now? Why?

4. What other real-world factors might be important to consider in designing the simulation and making a recommendation? ∎

An investor is considering the purchase of zero-coupon U.S. Treasury bonds. A 30-year zero-coupon bond yielding 8% can be purchased today for $9.94. At the end of 30 years, the owner of the bond will receive $100. The yield of the bond is related to its price by the following equation:

$$P = \frac{100}{(1 + y)^t}$$

Here, P is the price of the bond, y is the yield of the bond, and t is the maturity of the bond measured in years. Evaluating this equation for $t = 30$ and $y = 0.08$ gives $P = 9.94$.

The investor is planning to purchase a bond today and sell it one year from now. The investor is interested in evaluating the *return* on the investment in the bond. Suppose, for example, that the yield of the bond one year from now is 8.5%. Then the price of the bond one year later will be $9.39 [$= 100/(1 + 0.085)^{29}$]. The time remaining to maturity is $t = 29$, since one year has passed. The return for the year is -5.54% [$= (9.39 - 9.94)/9.94$].

In addition to the 30-year-maturity zero-coupon bond, the investor is considering the purchase of zero-coupon bonds with maturities of 2, 5, 10, or 20

years. All of the bonds are currently yielding 8.0%. (Bond investors describe this as a *flat yield curve*.) The investor cannot predict the future yields of the bonds with certainty. However, the investor believes that the yield of each bond one year from now can be modeled by a normal distribution with a mean of 8% and a standard deviation of 1%.

Questions

1. Suppose that the yields of the five zero-coupon bonds are all 8.5% one year from today. What are the returns of each bond over the period?

2. Using a simulation with 1000 iterations, estimate the expected return of each bond over the year. Estimate the standard deviations of the returns.

3. Comment on the following statement: "The expected yield of the 30-year bond one year from today is 8%. At that yield, its price would be $10.73. The return for the year would be 8% [$= (10.73 - 9.94)/9.94$]. Hence, the average return for the bond should be 8% as well. A simulation isn't really necessary. Any difference between 8% and the answer in Question 2 must be due to simulation error." ■

WAITING LINES AT LOURDES HOSPITAL AND L. L. BEAN

Long waiting lines in service organizations can be bad for business, and the money spent to reduce these lines is often money well spent. This is the conclusion of two studies reported in *Interfaces*, one relating to the mail-order company L. L. Bean and the other to Lourdes Hospital in New York State. Each study employed a queueing model to determine the staffing levels necessary to reduce congestion to an acceptable level.

The article "Staffing a Centralized Appointment Scheduling Department in Lourdes Hospital," by Agnihothri and Taylor (1991), describes how Lourdes Hospital decided to use a centralized system to schedule, by phone, appointments for outpatients and inpatients and ambulatory services requested by physicians, their staff, hospital personnel, and patients. The decision to centralize was certainly a sensible one. Instead of having doctors and patients call many different departments for appointments and information, the system allowed them to call a well-trained and centrally located staff. However, one disadvantage quickly became obvious: The staff were not able to handle the large numbers of calls, particularly at peak periods during the day. Their goal of being able to answer 90% of all arriving calls was not being met, and all parties involved—doctors, patients, and staff—were frustrated with long waits and busy signals.

The authors collected data on the rates of incoming calls and the times required to "service" these calls. They found, among other things, that the pattern of calls was approximately the same each day of the week but the rate of calls differed during various times of the day. Therefore, they solved several queueing models, each for a different time of day, to determine staffing levels that would eliminate much of the congestion and many of the complaints. The study was a big success. As the authors state, "Prior to the study, three to four formal complaints were made each week about the busy phone lines. They fell to less than one per week immediately after the staffing changes, and since July 1988, complaints have been very infrequent and can usually be attributed to a known factor, such as an unexpected absence of a staff member."

The L. L. Bean study reported in the article "Establishing Telephone-Agent Staffing Levels through Economic Optimization," by Andrews and Parsons (1993), is similar to the hospital study in that L. L. Bean also experienced high levels of telephone congestion. Too many customers calling to order merchandise got a busy signal or had to wait a long time on the line for an operator. The company had not ignored the problem in the past. In fact, it set a goal of having no more than 15% of the calls wait more than 20 seconds before reaching an operator, and it attempted to meet this goal with its rule-of-14: employ enough operators so that each handles about 14 calls per hour.

The problem was that there was little scientific basis for this rule-of-14; it was essentially an intuitive guideline. Worse yet, there was no guarantee that the company's goal of answering at least 85% of the calls within 20 seconds was a good one from an *economic* point of view. Before the study, L. L. Bean had never really analyzed the relevant costs, particularly the cost of lost business from fed-up customers who took their business elsewhere. After all, it was difficult to track customers who got busy signals or hung up after waiting a few minutes. Would they call L. L. Bean again or not? This study gathered data on lost business due to impatient customers, analyzed these data statistically, and then used a queueing model to determine the number of operators to employ (at various times of the day) to maximize expected profit. The authors report that for the first year it was used (1988) their new system resulted in an annualized profit gain of over $200,000. ∎

11.1 INTRODUCTION

A basic fact of life is that we all spend a great deal of time waiting in queues. We wait in line at a bank, at a supermarket, at a fast food restaurant, at a stoplight, and so on. Of course, people are not the only entities that wait in queues. Televisions at a television repair shop, other than the one(s) being repaired, are essentially waiting in line to be repaired. Also, when people submit computer jobs to a mainframe computer via remote terminals, these jobs typically wait in a queue (according to some priority system) until the computer has time to run them.

Mathematically, it does not really matter whether the entities waiting are people or televisions or computer jobs. The same type of analysis applies to all of these. The purpose of such an analysis is generally twofold. First, we want to examine an *existing* system to quantify its operating characteristics. For example, if a fast-food restaurant currently employs 12 people in various jobs, we might be interested in determining the amount of time a typical customer must wait in line or how many customers are typically waiting in line. Second, we want to learn how to make a system better. We might find, for example, that the fast-food restaurant would do better, from an economic standpoint, by employing only 10 workers and deploying them in a different manner.

The first objective, analyzing the characteristics of a given system, is quite difficult from a mathematical point of view. There are two basic modeling approaches: **analytical** and **simulation**. With the analytical approach, we search for mathematical *formulas* that describe the operating characteristics of the system, usually in "steady state." With this approach, the mathematical models are typically too complex to solve unless we make simplifying (and possibly unrealistic) assumptions. For example, at a supermarket customers typically join one of several lines (probably the shortest), possibly switch lines if they see that another line is moving faster, and eventually get served by one of the checkout people. Although this behavior is common—and is simple to describe in words—it is *very* difficult to analyze analytically. The second approach, simulation, allows us to analyze much more complex systems, *without* making many simplifying assumptions. However, the drawback to queueing simulation is that it usually requires specialized software packages or trained computer programmers to implement.

In this chapter we will employ both the analytical approach and simulation. For the former, we will discuss several well-known queueing models that describe some—but certainly not all—queueing situations in the real world. For these we will see how to calculate such operating characteristics as the average waiting time per customer, the average number of customers in line, and the fraction of time servers are busy. These analytical models generally require simplifying assumptions, and even then they can be difficult to understand. Therefore, we will also discuss queueing simulations. Unfortunately, queueing simulations are not nearly as straightforward as the simulations we developed in the previous two chapters. We typically need to generate random times between customer arrivals and random service times and then "play out" the events, and this playing out of events is far from easy in a spreadsheet. We will give only a taste of what can be done—and why commercial software packages are usually used instead of spreadsheets.

The second objective in many queueing studies is optimization, where we attempt to find the "best" system. Of course, to find the best system, we need to be able to analyze each of several competing systems, either analytically or by simulation. But beyond this, we must make difficult choices. For example, if the fast-food restaurant wants to decide how many employees to hire for various times of day, it must analyze the trade-off between more employees (better service, higher wages) and fewer employees (worse service, lower wages). The cost of extra employees is easy to quantify—the marginal cost of one extra employee is the wage rate. However, it is difficult to estimate the "cost" of making a customer wait an extra two minutes in line, say. In terms of immediate out-of-pocket costs, it costs the restaurant nothing. But it can have long-range implications: Fewer customers will bring their business to this restaurant. To find the optimal number of employees, the restaurant must estimate the dollar cost of having customers wait in line. Only by estimating this cost can it make an economic choice between the cost of waiting and the cost of more efficient service.

The formulas that relate queueing inputs to queueing outputs are quite difficult to derive mathematically. We will present a few of these formulas, but we will not derive them.

The examples in this chapter will highlight these two objectives. We will learn how to find important characteristics, such as expected waiting times, of specific systems, and we will also illustrate how to search for economically optimal systems.

This chapter is quite different from earlier chapters because of the nature of queueing systems. The models in previous chapters could almost always be developed from "first principles." By using relatively simple formulas involving functions like SUM, SUMPRODUCT, IF, and so on, we were able to convert inputs into outputs. This is no longer possible with queueing models. The inputs are typically mean customer arrival rates and mean service times. The required outputs are typically mean waiting times in queues, mean queue lengths, the fraction of time servers are busy, and possibly others. Deriving the formulas that relate the inputs to the outputs is mathematically *very difficult*, well beyond the level of this book. Therefore, there are many times in this chapter when you will have to "take our word for it." Nevertheless, the models we will illustrate are very valuable for the important insights they provide.

11.2 ELEMENTS OF QUEUEING MODELS

We begin by listing some of the features of queueing systems that distinguish one system from another. Almost all queueing systems are alike in that customers enter a system, possibly wait in one or more queues, get served, and then depart.[1] This general description of a queueing system—customers entering, waiting in line, and being served—hardly suggests the variety of queueing systems that exist. We now discuss some of the key features and their variations.

Characteristics of Arrivals

Interarrival times are the times between successive customer arrivals.

First, we must specify the customer arrival process. This includes the timing of arrivals as well as the types of arrivals. Regarding timing, it is most common to specify **interarrival times**, the times between successive customer arrivals. It is possible that these interarrival times are known—that is, nonrandom. For example, the arrivals at some doctors' offices are scheduled fairly precisely. However, it is much more common that interarrival times are random with a probability distribution. In real applications, this probability distribution must be estimated from observed customer arrival times. Also, it is very possible that this distribution varies through time. For example, the rate of arrivals to McDonald's is certainly higher around noon than in the middle of the afternoon.

We will assume customers arrive one at a time and all have the same priority.

Regarding the types of arrivals, there are at least two issues. First, do customers arrive one at a time or in batches—carloads, for example? The simplest system is when customers arrive one at a time, as we will assume in all of the models in this chapter. Second, are all customers essentially alike, or can they be separated into priority classes? At a computer center, for example, certain jobs might receive higher priority and run first, whereas the lower-priority jobs are sent to the back of the line and run only after midnight. We will assume throughout this chapter that all customers have the same priority.

We will assume there is no balking or reneging.

Another issue is whether (or how long) customers will wait in line. A customer might arrive at the system, see that too many customers are waiting in line, and decide not to enter the system at all. This is called **balking**. A variation of this is where the choice is made by the system, not the customer. In this case, we assume there is a waiting room size such that if the number of customers in the system equals the waiting room size, newly arriving customers are not allowed to enter the system. We call this a **limited waiting room** system. Another type of behavior is called **reneging**. This is when a customer already in line becomes impatient and leaves the system before starting service.

Service Discipline

We will always assume a first-come-first-served service discipline.

When customers enter the system, they might have to wait in line until a server becomes available. In this case we must specify the **service discipline**. The service discipline is the rule that states which customer, from all who are waiting, goes into service next. The most

---

[1]From here on, we will refer to the entities requesting service as "customers," regardless of whether they are actually people. Also, we will refer to "servers" performing service on these customers, regardless of the type of work being performed and whether the "servers" are people or machines.

common service discipline is **first-come-first-served** (FCFS), where customers are served in the order of their arrival. All of the models we will discuss will use the FCFS discipline. However, other service disciplines are possible, including **service-in-random-order** (SRO), **last-come-first-served** (LCFS), and various priority disciplines (if there are customer classes with different priorities). For example, a type of priority discipline used in some manufacturing plants is called the **shortest-processing-time** (SPT) discipline. In this case the jobs that are waiting to be processed are ranked according to their eventual processing (service) times, which are assumed to be known. Then the job with the shortest processing time is processed next.

One other aspect of the waiting process is whether there is a *single* line or *multiple* lines. For example, most banks now have a single line. An arriving customer joins the end of the line. When any teller finishes service, the customer at the head of the line then goes to that teller. In contrast, most supermarkets have multiple lines. When a customer goes to a checkout counter, she must choose which of several lines to enter. Presumably, she will choose the shortest line, but she might use other criteria in her decision. Once she joins a line—inevitably the slowest-moving one, from our experience!—she might decide to move to another line that seems to be moving faster.

Service Characteristics

Now we discuss the service itself. In the simplest systems, each customer is served by exactly one server, even though there might be multiple servers. For example, when you enter a bank, you are eventually served by a single teller, even though several tellers are working. The service times typically vary in some random manner, although constant (nonrandom) service times are sometimes possible. When service times are random, we must specify the probability distribution of a typical service time. This probability distribution can be the same for all customers and servers, or it can depend on the server and/or the customer. As with interarrival times, service time distributions must typically be estimated from service time data in real applications.

In a situation like the typical bank, where customers join a single line and are then served by the first available teller, we say the servers (tellers) are in **parallel**. (See Figure 11.1.) A different type of service process is found in many manufacturing settings. For example, various types of parts (the "customers") might enter a system with several types of machines (the "servers"). Each part type then follows a certain machine routing, such as machine 1, then machine 4, and then machine 2. Each machine has its own service time distribution, and a typical part might have to wait in line behind any or all of the machines on its routing. This type of system is called a **queueing network**. The simplest type of queueing network is a **series system**, where all parts go through the machines in numerical order: first machine 1, then machine 2, then machine 3, and so on. (See Figure 11.2 on page 558.) We will examine only parallel systems in this chapter.

Figure 11.1

Queueing System with Servers in Parallel

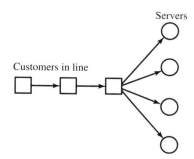

Figure 11.2

Queueing System
with Servers in
Series

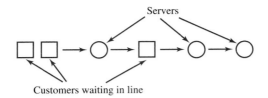

Short-Run Versus Steady-State Behavior

If you run a fast-food restaurant, you might be particularly interested in the queueing behavior during your peak lunchtime period. The customer arrival rate during this period increases sharply, and you might employ more workers to meet the increased customer load. In this case your primary interest is in the "short-run" behavior of the system—the next hour or two. Unfortunately, short-run behavior is the most difficult to analyze, at least with analytical models. This is one reason, among others, for using simulation.

But how do we draw the line between the "short run" and the "long run"? The answer depends on how long the effects of "initial conditions" last. In the restaurant example, the initial conditions are determined by the number of customers already in line at the beginning of the lunch period—say, at 11:30. Suppose the restaurant manager is interested in the average number of customers waiting in line over a 2-hour peak period. The question then is whether this average is strongly affected by the number of customers in line at 11:30. In other words, do the effects of the initial conditions get "washed out" in a period as long as 2 hours, or do they persist?

Ultimately, the only way to answer this question is with empirical evidence. We might compare a lunch period starting with no people in line at 11:30 to one where 10 people are already in line at 11:30. If the average levels of congestion over the entire 2-hour lunch period are approximately the same in each case, then the initial conditions at 11:30 evidently make little difference, and a *long-run* analysis is permitted. However, if the lunch period that starts with many people in line is never quite able to overcome this initial load—that is, it tends to stay crowded—then the initial conditions are important, and a *short-run* analysis is required.

Steady-state analysis is relevant for the long run, but the "long run" can sometimes be as short as an hour or two.

Analytical models are best suited for studying long-run behavior. This type of analysis is called **steady-state analysis** and is the focus of the first part of this chapter. One requirement for any steady-state analysis is that the parameters of the system remain constant for the entire time period. In particular, the arrival rate must remain constant. In the restaurant example, if the objective is to study a 2-hour peak lunchtime period where the arrival rate is significantly larger than normal, and if we decide to employ steady-state analysis, then the results of this 2-hour analysis do *not* apply to the rest of the day, when the arrival rate is much lower. If the parameters of the system change from one time period to another, a separate steady-state analysis is required for each time period. Alternatively, we can use simulation, where constant parameters such as the arrival rate are *not* required.

Unless a system is stable, queue lengths will eventually increase without bound.

Another requirement for steady-state analysis is that the system must be **stable**. This means that the servers must serve fast enough to keep up with arrivals—otherwise, the queue could theoretically grow without limit. For example, in a single-server system where all arriving customers join the system, the requirement for system stability is that the arrival rate must be less than the service rate. If the system is not stable, the analytical models discussed in this chapter cannot be used. Again, however, we can use simulation, which does not require system stability.

11.3 THE EXPONENTIAL DISTRIBUTION

Queueing systems generally contain uncertainty. Specifically, times between customer arrivals (interarrival times) and customer service times are generally modeled as random variables. The most common probability distribution used to model these uncertain quantities is the **exponential** distribution. Many queueing models can be analyzed in a fairly straightforward manner, even on a spreadsheet, if we assume exponentially distributed interarrival times and service times. This exponential assumption buys us a lot in terms of simplified analysis, but it is quite strong. Therefore, it is important to understand the exponential distribution and some of its ramifications for queueing applications.

The random variable X has an exponential distribution with parameter λ (with $\lambda > 0$) if the density function for X has the form

$$f(x) = \lambda e^{-\lambda x} \qquad \text{for } x > 0$$

(λ is the Greek letter "lambda." Its use is standard in the queueing literature.) The graph of this function appears in Figure 11.3. (We obtained this graph from RISKview, as in the previous two chapters.) You might want to compare this density to the more familiar bell-shaped, symmetric normal curve. In contrast to the normal distribution, the exponential distribution is not bell-shaped, and it is heavily skewed to the right. Because this density decreases continually from left to right, its most likely value is at 0. This means that X is more likely to be near 0 than any other value. Equivalently, if we collect many observations from an exponential distribution and draw a histogram of the observed values, then we expect it to resemble the smooth curve in Figure 11.3, with the tallest bars to the left.

Figure 11.3

Typical Exponential Distribution

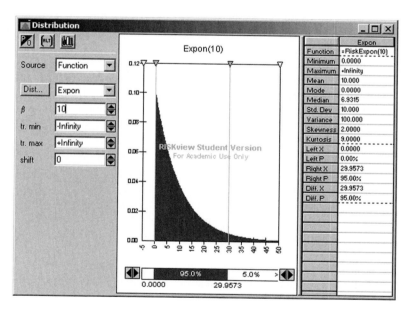

The mean and standard deviation of an exponential distribution are both equal to the reciprocal of the parameter λ.

The mean and standard deviation of this distribution are easy to remember. They are both equal to the *reciprocal* of the parameter λ. For example, an exponential distribution with parameter $\lambda = 0.1$ has both mean and standard deviation equal to 10.

The random variable X will always be expressed in some time unit, such as minutes. For example, X might be the number of minutes it takes to serve a customer. Now, suppose that the mean service time is 3 minutes. Then $1/\lambda = 3$, so that $\lambda = 1/3$. For this reason, λ can be interpreted as a *rate*—in this case, 1 customer every 3 minutes (on average). Of course, the value of λ depends on the unit of time. If we switch from minutes to hours, say,

λ changes from 1/3 (1 every 3 minutes) to 60(1/3) = 20 (20 every hour). The corresponding mean is then $1/\lambda = 1/20$ hour.

The Memoryless Property

The property that makes the exponential distribution so useful in queueing models (and in other management science models) is called the **memoryless property**. It can be stated as follows. Let x and h be any positive numbers that represent amounts of time. Then if X is exponentially distributed, the following equation holds:

$$P(X > x + h \mid X > x) = P(X > h) \tag{11.1}$$

The probability on the left is a conditional probability, the probability that X is greater than $x + h$, *given* that it is greater than x. The memoryless property states that this conditional probability is the same as the unconditional probability that X is greater than h. We now interpret this important property in several contexts.

First, suppose that X is the time, measured in hours, until failure of some item such as a lightbulb. Now consider two lightbulbs with the same exponential distribution of time to failure. The only difference is that the first lightbulb has already survived $x = 20$ hours, whereas the second lightbulb is brand new. Suppose we want the probabilities that lightbulbs 1 and 2 will survive at least $h = 5$ additional hours. The memoryless property says that these probabilities are the *same* for the two lightbulbs! This means that the lightbulb that has been in use for 20 hours has the same chance of surviving at least 5 more hours as the brand new lightbulb. For this reason, the memoryless property is sometimes called the "no wear-out" property.

As a second example, suppose that X is the time, measured in minutes, until the next customer arrival. Suppose it is currently 3:00 P.M., and the previous arrival occurred at 2:57 P.M. Then we know that X is greater than 3 minutes. Given this information, what is the probability that the *next* arrival will occur after 3:05 P.M.? (Here $x = 3$ and $h = 5$, measured in minutes.) This is the same as the probability that the next arrival would occur after 3:05 P.M. if there were an arrival right now, at 3:00 P.M. That is, as far as the future (after 3:00 P.M.) is concerned, we can forget how long it has been since the last arrival and assume that an arrival just occurred, at 3:00 P.M. This example illustrates why the property is called the *memoryless* property.

These examples indicate why the exponential distribution is attractive from a mathematical point of view. If we observe a process at any time, all exponential times (interarrival times and service times, say) essentially "start over" probabilistically—we do not have to know how long it has been since various events (the last arrival or the beginning of service) occurred. The exponential distribution is the only continuous probability distribution with this property. On the negative side, however, this strong memoryless property makes the exponential distribution inappropriate for many real applications. In the lightbulb example, we might dismiss the exponential assumption immediately on the grounds that lightbulbs *do* wear out—a bulb that has been in continuous use for 20 hours is *not* as good as a brand new one. The ultimate test of appropriateness is whether sample data fit an exponential curve. We illustrate how to check this in the following example.

EXAMPLE | **11.1 ESTIMATING INTERARRIVAL AND SERVICE TIME DISTRIBUTIONS AT A BANK**

A bank manager would like to use an analytical queueing model to study the congestion at the bank's automatic teller machines (ATMs). A simple model of this system requires that the interarrival times (times between customer arrivals to the machines) and service times (times customers spend with the machines) are exponentially distributed. During a period of time when business is fairly steady, several employees use stopwatches to gather data on interarrival times and service times. The data are listed in Figure 11.4 (with several rows hidden). The bank manager wants to know, based on these data, whether it is reasonable to assume exponentially distributed interarrival times and service times. In each case he also wants to know the appropriate value of λ.

Figure 11.4

Interarrival and Service Times for ATM Example

	A	B	C	D	E
1	Interarrival times and service times at a bank (in seconds)				
2					
3	Averages of data below				
4		InterArrivalTime	ServiceTime		
5		25.3	22.3		
6					
7	Customer	InterArrivalTime	ServiceTime		
8	1	8	11		
9	2	33	20		
10	3	9	16		
11	4	11	8		
12	5	5	12		
13	6	24	17		
14	7	4	41		
15	8	46	7		
16	9	25	19		
17	10	10	43		
101	94	3	11		
102	95	14	16		
103	96	17	30		
104	97	17	24		
105	98	3	31		
106	99	42	59		
107	100	112	22		
108	101	17	40		
109	102	5	11		

Objective   To test the appropriateness of the exponential distribution for interarrival time and service time data at ATMs.

WHERE DO THE NUMBERS COME FROM?

We already mentioned employees with stopwatches. Unless the bank has some electronic tracking device, manual recording of the data is necessary.

Solution

Exponentially distributed interarrival times are often more realistic than exponentially distributed service times.

To see whether these times are consistent with the exponential distribution, we plot histograms of the interarrival times and the service times. (See the file **ExponentialFit.xls**. Also, see the appendix to Chapter 9 for directions on creating histograms.) The histograms appear in Figures 11.5 and 11.6 (page 562). The histogram of interarrival times appears to be quite consistent with the exponential density in Figure 11.3. Its highest bar is at the left, and the remaining bars fall off gradually from left to right. On the other hand, the histogram of the service times is not shaped like the exponential density. Its highest bar is *not* the one farthest to the left but instead corresponds to the category from 15 to 30 seconds. Considering the way automatic teller machines operate, this is not surprising. There is some minimum time required to process any customer, regardless of the task, so that the most likely times are *not* close to 0. Therefore, the exponential assumption for interarrival times is reasonable, but it is questionable for service times.[2]

---

[2]There are formal statistical procedures for testing whether an exponential fit is reasonable, but this "eye-balling" method often suffices.

Figure 11.5   Histogram of Interarrival Times for ATM Example

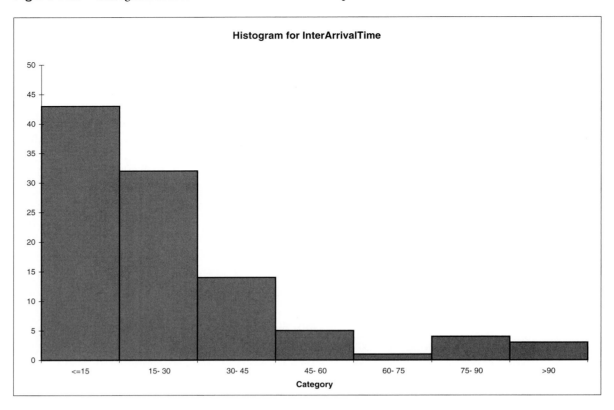

Figure 11.6   Histogram of Service Times for ATM Example

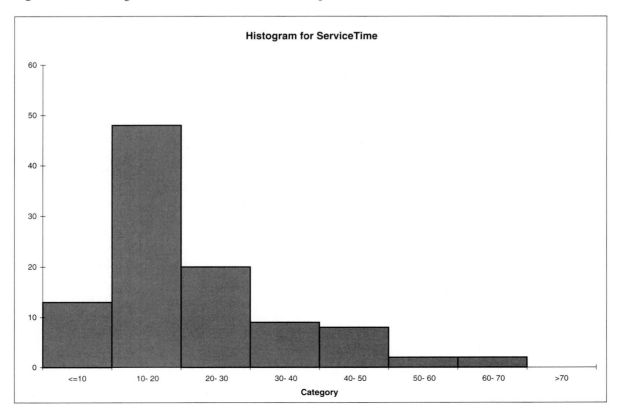

In either case, if the manager decides to accept the exponential assumption, the parameter λ is the rate of arrivals (or services) and is estimated by the reciprocal of the average of the observed times. For interarrival times, this estimate of λ is the reciprocal of the average in cell B5 of Figure 11.4: $1/25.3 = 0.0395$—that is, 1 arrival every 25.3 seconds. For service times, the estimated λ is the reciprocal of the average in cell C5: $1/22.3 = 0.0448$—that is, 1 service every 22.3 seconds. ∎

The Poisson Process Model

If we say arrivals occur according to a Poisson process, this means the interarrival times are exponentially distributed.

When the interarrival times are exponentially distributed, we often state that "arrivals occur according to a Poisson process." There is a close relationship between the exponential distribution, which measures *times* between events such as arrivals, and the **Poisson distribution**, which counts the *number* of events in a certain length of time. The details of this relationship are beyond the level of this book, so we will not explore this topic any further here. However, if we say that customers arrive at a bank according to a Poisson process with rate 1 every 3 minutes, this means that the interarrival times are exponentially distributed with parameter $\lambda = 1/3$.

PROBLEMS

Skill-Building Problems

1. An extremely important concept in queueing models is the difference between rates and times. If λ represents a rate (customers per hour, say), then argue why $1/\lambda$ is a time and vice versa.

2. Explain the basic relationship between the exponential distribution and a Poisson process. Also, explain how the exponential distribution and the Poisson distribution are fundamentally different. (*Hint*: What type of data does each describe?)

3. It is possible to generate random numbers in a spreadsheet that have an exponential distribution with a given mean. For example, to generate 200 such numbers from an exponential distribution with $\lambda = 1/3$, enter the formula **=−3*LN(RAND())** in cell A4 and copy it to the range A5:A203. Then select the A4:A203 range, choose the Edit/Copy command, and choose the Edit/Paste Special command with the Values option. (This "freezes" the random numbers, so that they don't change each time the spreadsheet recalculates.) Explore the properties of these numbers as follows.
   a. Find the average of the 200 numbers with the AVERAGE function. What theoretical value should this average be close to?
   b. Find the standard deviation of the 200 numbers with the STDEV function. What theoretical value should this standard deviation be close to?

c. Create a histogram of the random numbers, using about 15 categories, each of length 1, where the first category extends from 0 to 1. Does the histogram have the shape you would expect?
   d. Suppose that you collected the data in column A by timing arrivals at a store. The value in cell A4 is the time (in minutes) until the first arrival, the value in cell A5 is the time between the first and second arrivals, the value in cell A6 is the time between the second and third arrivals, and so on. How might you convince yourself that the interarrival times for this store are indeed exponentially distributed? What is your best guess for the arrival rate (customers per minute)?

Skill-Extending Problem

4. Do exponentially distributed random numbers have the memoryless property? Here is one way to find out. Generate many exponentially distributed random numbers with mean 3, using the formula in the previous problem. Find the fraction of them that are greater than 1. This estimates the probability $P(X > 1)$. Now find all random numbers that are greater than 4. Among these, find the fraction that are greater than 5. This estimates the probability $P(X > 4 + 1|X > 4)$. According to the memoryless property, these two estimates should be nearly equal. Are they? Try to do this *without* freezing the random numbers, so that you can get repeated estimates of the two probabilities by pressing the F9 key.

11.4 IMPORTANT QUEUEING RELATIONSHIPS

As we stated, the calculations required in queueing models are neither simple nor obvious. Fortunately, however, there are several very useful and general relationships that hold for a wide variety of queueing models. We briefly discuss them here so that we can use them in the queueing models in later sections.

There are two general types of outputs we typically calculate in a queueing model: **time averages** and **customer averages**. Typical time averages are[3]

- L, the expected number of customers in the system
- L_Q, the expected number of customers in the queue
- L_S, the expected number of customers in service
- P(all idle), the probability that all servers are idle
- P(all busy), the probability that all servers are busy

If you were going to estimate the quantity L_Q, for example, you might observe the system at many time points, record the number of customers in the queue at each time point, and then average these numbers. In other words, you would average this measure over *time*. Similarly, to estimate a probability such as P(all busy), you would observe the system at many time points, record a 1 each time all servers are busy and a 0 each time at least one server is idle, and then average these 0's and 1's.

In contrast, typical customer averages are

- W, the expected time spent in the system (waiting in line or being served)
- W_Q, the expected time a customer waits in the queue
- W_S, the expected time spent in service

To estimate the quantity W_Q, for example, you would observe many customers, record the time in queue for each customer, and then average these times over the number of customers observed. Now you are averaging over *customers*.

Little's Formula

Little's formula relates time averages, such as L, to customer averages, such as W. If we can find one of these, then Little's formula gives us the value of the other one.

There is a famous formula that relates time averages and customer averages in steady state. This formula was first discovered by Little, and it is still called **Little's formula**.[4] The formula is easy to state. Consider any queueing system. Let λ be the average rate at which customers enter this system, let L be the expected number of customers in the system, and let W be the expected time a typical customer spends in the system. Then Little's formula can be expressed as

$$L = \lambda W \qquad (11.2)$$

It can also be stated in terms of L_Q and W_Q or in terms of L_S and W_S. That is, two alternative versions of Little's formula are

$$L_Q = \lambda W_Q \qquad (11.3)$$

---

[3]These quantities will appear several times throughout this chapter, and we will continue to use this notation.
[4]The original result was published in Little (1961). Numerous extensions of the basic result have been published since, including Brumelle (1971), Stidham (1974), and Heyman and Stidham (1980). It is now known that Little's formula holds in an amazingly wide variety of queueing systems.

and

$$L_S = \lambda W_S \qquad \textbf{(11.4)}$$

The reasoning behind Little's formula is actually very simple. For example, to see why equation (11.3) is true, consider a long time period of length T. During this period, we expect about λT customers to arrive (from the definition of λ as a rate), and each of these waits in queue for an expected time W_Q. Therefore, the expected total number of customer-minutes spent in queue is $\lambda T W_Q$. On the other hand, the expected number of customers in the queue at any time during this period is L_Q, so the total number of customer-minutes spent in the queue can also be calculated as $L_Q T$. Setting $\lambda T W_Q$ equal to $L_Q T$ and canceling T, we get equation (11.3). Strictly speaking, this argument is valid only for an extremely large time T, which is why Little's formula is a *steady-state* result. When we use simulation for relatively small values of time T, we will see that Little's formula is only an approximation.

Typically, we use analytical methods to find one of the L's and then appeal to Little's formula to find the corresponding W. Alternatively, we can find L from W. For example, suppose the arrival rate to a single-server queueing system is 30 customers per hour ($\lambda = 30$). Also, suppose we know (probably from an analytical model) that the expected number of customers in the system is $L = 2.5$. Then equation (11.2) implies that a typical customer spends an expected time $W = L/\lambda = 2.5/30 = 0.0833$ hour $= 5$ minutes in the system. If we also know that the average number of customers in the queue is $L_Q = 1.8$, then equation (11.3) implies that a typical customer's expected time in the queue is $W_Q = L_Q/\lambda = 1.8/30 = 0.06$ hour $= 3.6$ minutes.

Other Relationships

There are two other formulas that relate these quantities. First, all customers are either in service or in the queue, so we have

$$L = L_Q + L_S \qquad \textbf{(11.5)}$$

In the example from the previous paragraph, equation (11.5) implies that $L_S = 2.5 - 1.8 = 0.7$. (For a single-server system this means that exactly one customer is in service 70% of the time and no customers are in service 30% of the time.)

Second, we have

$$W = W_Q + W_S \qquad \textbf{(11.6)}$$

Equation (11.6) follows because the time spent in the system is the time spent in the queue plus the time spent in service, and W_S is the expected time in service. In our numerical example, equation (11.6) implies that the expected time a typical customer spends in service is $5.0 - 3.6 = 1.4$ minutes.

One final important queueing measure is called the **server utilization**. The server utilization, denoted by U, is defined as the long-run fraction of time a typical server is busy. In a multiple-server system, where there are s identical servers in parallel, server utilization is defined as

$$U = L_S/s$$

Server utilization is the fraction of time a typical server is busy.

That is, it is the expected number of busy servers divided by the number of servers. For example, if $s = 3$ and $L_S = 2.55$, then $U = 0.85$. In this case the expected number of busy servers is 2.55, and each of the 3 servers is busy about 85% of the time.

Skill-Building Problems

5. Assume that parts arrive at a machining center at a rate of 60 parts per hour. The machining center is capable of processing 75 parts per hour—that is, the mean time to machine a part is 0.8 minute. If you are watching these parts *exiting* the machine center, what exit rate do you observe, 60 or 75 per hour? Explain.

6. Little's formula applies to an entire queueing system or to a subsystem of a larger system. For example, consider a single-server system composed of two "subsystems." The first subsystem is the waiting line, and the second is the service area, where service actually takes place. Let λ be the rate that customers enter the system and assume that $\lambda = 60$ per hour.
   a. If the expected number of customers waiting in line is 2.5, what does Little's formula applied to the first subsystem tell us?
   b. Let μ be the service rate of the server (in customers per hour). Assuming that $\lambda < \mu$ (so that the server can serve customers faster than they arrive), argue why the rate into the second subsystem must be λ. Then, letting $\mu = 80$ per hour, what does Little's formula applied to the second subsystem

tell us about the expected number of customers in service?

7. Consider a bank where potential customers arrive at rate of 60 customers per hour. However, because of limited space, 1 out of every 4 arriving customers finds the bank full and leaves immediately (without entering the bank). Suppose that the average number of customers waiting in line in the bank is 3.5. How long will a typical *entering* customer have to wait in line? (*Hint*: In Little's formula, λ refers only to customers who join the system.)

Skill-Extending Problem

8. Consider a fast-food restaurant where customers enter at rate 75 per hour. There are 3 servers. Customers wait in a single line and go, in first-come-first-served fashion, to the first of the 3 servers who is available. Each server can serve 1 customer every 2 minutes on average. If you are standing at the exit, counting customers as they leave the restaurant, at what rate will you see them leave? On average, how many of the servers are busy?

11.5 ANALYTICAL QUEUEING MODELS

In this section we discuss several analytical models for queueing systems. As we stated, these models cannot be developed without a fair amount of mathematical background—more than we assume in this book. Therefore, we must rely on the queueing models that have been developed in the management science literature—and there are literally hundreds or even thousands of these. We will illustrate only the most basic models, and even for these, we will provide only the key formulas. In some cases, we even automate these formulas with behind-the-scenes macros. This will enable you to focus on the aspects of practical concern: (1) the meaning of the assumptions and whether they are realistic, (2) the relevant input parameters, (3) interpretation of the outputs, and possibly (4) how to use the models for economic optimization.

The Basic Single-Server Model

Kendall's notation, such as M/M/1, allows us to describe a variety of queueing systems with a few well-chosen symbols.

We begin by discussing the most basic single-server model, labeled the $M/M/1$ model. This shorthand notation, developed by Kendall, implies three things. The first M implies that the distribution of interarrival times is exponential.[5] The second M implies that the distribution of service times is also exponential. Finally, the "1" implies that there is a *single* server. It is customary to let λ denote the arrival rate and μ denote the service rate. (Here, μ is the Greek letter "mu.") This means that $1/\lambda$ is the mean time between arrivals and $1/\mu$

---

[5]The M actually stands for "Markov," a technical term that is synonymous with the exponential distribution. You can also think of it as an acronym for "memoryless."

is the mean service time per customer. The model in this section is sometimes called the "classical" $M/M/1$ queueing model, which means that *all* customer arrivals join the system and stay until they are eventually served.

The mathematical derivation of the steady-state results for an $M/M/1$ queueing system is rather involved, so we will simply list the results, which are surprisingly simple. First, define ρ (the Greek letter "rho") by $\rho = \lambda/\mu$. This is called the **traffic intensity**, and it is a very useful measure of the congestion of the system. In fact, the system is stable only if $\rho < 1$. If $\rho \geq 1$, so that $\lambda \geq \mu$, then arrivals occur at least as fast as the server can handle them, and in the long run the queue will become infinitely large—that is, it will be unstable. Therefore, we must assume that $\rho < 1$ to obtain steady-state results.

The formulas presented here are not necessarily intuitive, and it takes a fair amount of mathematics to derive them rigorously. However, you can still use them!

Assuming that the system is stable, let p_n be the steady-state probability that there are exactly n customer in the system (waiting in line or being served) at any point in time. This probability can be interpreted as the long-run *fraction* of time when there are n customers in the system. For example, p_0 is the long-run fraction of time when there are no customers in the system, p_1 is the long-run fraction of time when there is exactly one customer is in the system, and so on. These steady-state probabilities can be found from the following steady-state equation:

$$p_n = (1 - \rho)\rho^n \qquad n \geq 0 \tag{11.7}$$

From the definition of expected value, the expected number of customers in the system, L, is the sum over all n of n multiplied by p_n. It can be shown that this sum reduces to

$$L = \frac{\rho}{1 - \rho} = \frac{\lambda}{\mu - \lambda} \tag{11.8}$$

where the last two expressions are equivalent. Then we can find W, W_Q, and L_Q from Little's formula and the fact that $1/\mu$ is the expected time in service:

$$W = L/\lambda \qquad W_Q = W - 1/\mu \qquad L_Q = \lambda W_Q \tag{11.9}$$

Two other results are worth noting. First, the server utilization U is the fraction of time the server is busy. This fraction is $1 - p_0 = \rho$, so that the server utilization is equal to the traffic intensity:

$$U = \rho \tag{11.10}$$

For example, if $\lambda = 40$ per hour and $\mu = 60$ per hour, then $U = \rho = 2/3$, so that the server is busy 2/3 of the time and is idle 1/3 of the time. Second, it is possible to derive the following explicit expression for the distribution of time spent by a typical customer in the queue:

$$P(\text{Time in queue} > t) = \rho e^{-\mu(1-\rho)t} \qquad \text{for any } t > 0 \tag{11.11}$$

The following example illustrates these results.

EXAMPLE | 11.2 QUEUEING AT A POSTAL BRANCH

The Smalltown postal branch employs a single clerk. Customers arrive at this postal branch according to a Poisson process at rate 30 customers per hour, and the average service time is exponentially distributed with mean 1.5 minutes. All arriving customers enter the branch, regardless of the number already waiting in line. The manager of the postal branch would ultimately like to decide whether to improve the system. To do this, she first needs to develop a queueing model that describes the steady-state characteristics of the current system.

Objective To model the postal branch's system as an $M/M/1$ queue and then use the analytical formulas in equations (11.7)–(11.11) to find the system's steady-state characteristics.

WHERE DO THE NUMBERS COME FROM?

The bank manager would need to proceed as in Example 11.1 to estimate the arrival rate and the mean service rate (and verify that the resulting distributions are at least approximately exponential).

Solution

To begin, we must choose a common unit of time and then express the arrival and service rates (λ and μ) in this unit. We could measure time in seconds, minutes, hours, or any other convenient time unit, as long as we are consistent. Here we will choose minutes. Then, because 1 customer arrives every 2 minutes, $\lambda = 1/2$. Also, because the mean service *time* is 1.5 minutes, the service *rate* is its reciprocal—that is, $\mu = 1/1.5 = 0.667$. Then the traffic intensity is

$$\rho = \lambda/\mu = (1/2)/(2/3) = 0.75$$

Because this is less than 1, we know that the system is stable and steady state will occur.

Using the Spreadsheet Model Template

To implement the formulas for the $M/M/1$ model, we have developed an $M/M/1$ "template" file. (See Figure 11.7 and the file **MM1_Template.xls**.) We will not provide step-by-step instructions because we expect that you will use this as a template rather than enter the formulas yourself. However, we make the following points.

Figure 11.7 Template for the $M/M/1$ Queue

	A	B	C	D	E	F	G	H	I
1	M/M/1 queue								
2									
3	Inputs				Just enter desired inputs in blue cells and				
4	Unit of time	minute			everything recalculates automatically.				
5	Arrival rate	0.500	customers/minute						
6	Service rate	0.667	customers/minute						
7									
8	Outputs								
9	Direct outputs from inputs				Distribution of number in system			Distribution of time in queue	
10	Mean time between arrivals	2.000	minutes		n (customers)	P(n in system)		t (in minutes)	P(wait > t)
11	Mean time per service	1.500	minutes		0	0.250		2.000	0.537
12	Traffic intensity	0.750			1	0.188			
13					2	0.141			
14	Summary measures				3	0.105			
15	Expected number in system	3.000	customers		4	0.079			
16	Expected number in queue	2.250	customers		5	0.059			
17	Expected time in system	6.000	minutes		6	0.044			
18	Expected time in queue	4.500	minutes		7	0.033			
19	Server utilization	75.0%			8	0.025			
20					9	0.019			
21					10	0.014			
22					11	0.011			
23					12	0.008			
24					13	0.006			
25					14	0.004			
26					15	0.003			
27					16	0.003			
28					17	0.002			
29					18	0.001			
30					19	0.001			
31					20	0.001			
32					21	0.001			
33					22	0.000			

1. All you need to enter are the inputs in cells B4 through B6. Note that the rates in cells B5 and B6 are relative to the time unit you specify in cell B4.

2. You can enter *numbers* for the rates in cells B5 and B6, or you can base these on observed data. (Example 11.1 illustrated the estimation of arrival and service rates from observed data.)

3. The value of L in cell B15 is calculated from equation (11.8). Then the values in cells B5, B15, and B17 are related by the equation (11.2) version of Little's formula, $L = \lambda W$, the values in cells B5, B16, and B18 are related by equation (11.3), $L_Q = \lambda W_Q$, and the value in cell B18 is calculated from $W_Q = W - 1/\mu$. From equation (11.10), the server utilization in cell B19 is the same as the traffic intensity in cell B12.

4. The steady-state probabilities in column F are based on equation (11.7). You can copy these down as far as you like, until the probabilities are negligible.

5. The waiting time probability in cell I11 is calculated from equation (11.11). You can enter any time t in cell H11 to obtain the probability that a typical customer will wait in the queue at least this amount of time. Alternatively, you can enter other values of t in cells H12, H13, and so on, and then copy the formula in cell I11 down to calculate other waiting time probabilities.

Discussion of the Results

From Figure 11.7, we see, for example, that when the arrival rate is 0.5 and the service rate is 0.667, the expected number of customers in the queue is 2.25 and the expected time a typical customer spends in the queue is 4.5 minutes. However, cells F11 and I11 indicate that 25% of all customers spend no time in the queue, and 53.7% spend more than 2 minutes in the queue. Also, just for illustration, cell F15 indicates that the steady-state probability of having exactly 4 customers in the system is 0.079. Equivalently, there are exactly 4 customers in the system 7.9% of the time.

The traffic intensity is the key determinant of the amount of congestion in the system.

The bank manager can experiment with other arrival rates or service rates in cells B5 and B6 to see how the various output measures are affected. One particularly important insight can be obtained through a data table, as shown in Figure 11.8. The current server utilization is 0.75, and the system is behaving fairly well, with short waits in queue on average. The data table, however, shows how bad things can get when the service rate is just

Figure 11.8 Effect of Varying Service Rate

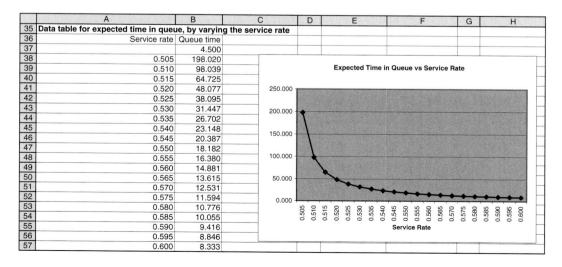

	A	B	C	D	E	F	G	H
35	Data table for expected time in queue, by varying the service rate							
36	Service rate	Queue time						
37		4.500						
38	0.505	198.020						
39	0.510	98.039						
40	0.515	64.725						
41	0.520	48.077						
42	0.525	38.095						
43	0.530	31.447						
44	0.535	26.702						
45	0.540	23.148						
46	0.545	20.387						
47	0.550	18.182						
48	0.555	16.380						
49	0.560	14.881						
50	0.565	13.615						
51	0.570	12.531						
52	0.575	11.594						
53	0.580	10.776						
54	0.585	10.055						
55	0.590	9.416						
56	0.595	8.846						
57	0.600	8.333						

barely above the arrival rate, so that the traffic intensity is just barely below 1. (The single output for this data table is the expected time in queue, from cell B18, and the column input cell is the service rate cell, B6.) The corresponding line chart shows that the expected time in queue increases extremely rapidly as the service rate gets closer to the arrival rate. Whatever else the bank manager learns from this model, she now knows that she does not want a service rate close to the arrival rate, at least not for extended periods of time.

We make one other important comment about this system. Our entire analysis depends on the fact that the arrival rate remains constant at 1 every 2 minutes, on average. Therefore, the results in Figure 11.7 are valid only for the period of time when this arrival rate is in effect. If the arrival rate suddenly changes, as it might during the lunch period or the 5:00 P.M. rush, then a new steady-state analysis must be performed with the new arrival rate. ■

The Basic Multiple-Server Model

Many service facilities such as banks and postal branches employ multiple servers. Usually, these servers work in parallel, so that each customer goes to exactly one server for service and then departs. In this section we will analyze the simplest version of this multiple-server parallel system, labeled the $M/M/s$ model. Again, the first M means that interarrival times are exponentially distributed. The second M means that the service times for *each* server are exponentially distributed. (We also assume that each server is identical to the others, in the sense that each has the same mean service time.) Finally, the s in $M/M/s$ denotes the number of servers. (If $s = 1$, the $M/M/s$ and $M/M/1$ models are identical.)

If you think about the multiple-server facilities you typically enter, such as banks, post offices, and supermarkets, you recognize that there are two types of waiting line configurations. The first, usually seen at supermarkets, is where each server has a separate line. Each customer must decide which line to join (and then either stay in that line or switch later on). The second, seen at most banks and post offices, is where there is a *single* waiting line, from which customers are served in FCFS (first-come-first-served) fashion. We will examine the second type only. It is arguably the more common system seen in real situations, and it is much easier to analyze mathematically.

There are three inputs to this system: the arrival rate λ, the service rate (per server) μ, and the number of servers s. To ensure that the system is stable, we must also assume that the traffic intensity, now given by $\rho = \lambda/(s\mu)$, is less than 1. In words, we require that the arrival rate λ be less than the *maximum* service rate $s\mu$ (which is achieved when all s servers are busy). If the traffic intensity is not less than 1, the length of the queue will eventually increase without bound.

$$\text{Stability in } M/M/s \text{ model:} \quad \rho = \lambda/(s\mu) < 1$$

The steady-state analysis for the $M/M/s$ system is more complex than for the $M/M/1$ system. As before, let p_n be the probability that there are exactly n customers in the system, waiting or in service. Then it turns out that all of the steady-state quantities depend on p_0, which can be calculated from a rather complex formula that we will not present here. Given p_0, other quantities can be calculated from the following formulas:

$$p_n = \begin{cases} \dfrac{(s\rho)^n p_0}{n!} & \text{if } 1 \le n \le s \\[2ex] \dfrac{(s\rho)^n p_0}{s! s^{n-s}} & \text{if } n > s \end{cases} \tag{11.12}$$

$$P(\text{All servers busy}) = \frac{(s\rho)^s p_0}{s!(1 - \rho)} \tag{11.13}$$

$$L_Q = P(\text{All servers busy}) \frac{\rho}{1 - \rho} \qquad\qquad \textbf{(11.14)}$$

$$W_Q = L_Q/\lambda \qquad W = W_Q + 1/\mu \qquad L = \lambda W \qquad \textbf{(11.15)}$$

$$P(\text{Wait in queue} > t) = P(\text{All servers busy})e^{-s\mu(1-\rho)t} \quad \text{for any } t > 0 \qquad \textbf{(11.16)}$$

These formulas are admittedly complex, so we have implemented them, with the use of a VBA macro, in a template file. The following example illustrates the process.

EXAMPLE | **11.3 QUEUEING AT COUNTY BANK**

County Bank has several branch locations. At one of these locations, customers arrive at a Poisson rate of 150 per hour. The branch employs 6 tellers. Each teller takes, on average, 2 minutes to serve a customer, and service times are exponentially distributed. Also, all tellers perform all tasks, so that customers can go to any of the 6 tellers. Customers who arrive and find all 6 servers busy join a single queue and are then served in FCFS fashion. As a first step, the bank manager wants to develop a queueing model of the current system. Then he wants to find the "best" number of tellers, given that tellers are paid $8 per hour.

Objective　To develop an $M/M/s$ queueing model for the bank and examine its steady-state properties, and then to find the number of servers that is best from an economic point of view.

WHERE DO THE NUMBERS COME FROM?

The same comments as in Example 11.2 apply here. Of course, the $8 figure is just the current hourly wage rate.

Solution

As with the $M/M/1$ system, we have created a template file that calculates p_0 (using a behind-the-scenes VBA macro) and implements the formulas in equations (11.12)–(11.16). (See the file **MMs_Template.xls** and Figure 11.9 on page 572.)

Using the Spreadsheet Model Template

The template file uses a macro to calculate the probability that the system is empty. Built-in formulas then calculate all other steady-state measures.

All you need to do is enter the inputs in cells B4–B7 and then click on the button. This button runs the macro that calculates p_0 in cell B16, and then the formulas in the other cells all recalculate automatically. For this example the necessary inputs are the unit of time (we have chosen "hour"), the arrival rate (150), the service rate per server (30), and the number of servers (6). We invite you to look at the formulas in the various cells to check that they do indeed implement equations (11.12)–(11.16). As with the $M/M/1$ template, you can copy the probability distribution in columns E and F as far down as you like, until the probabilities are negligible, and you can enter any time t in cell H12 to get the corresponding waiting time probability in cell I12.

Discussion of the Results

From Figure 11.9 we see that when there are 6 tellers and the traffic intensity is 0.833, the expected number of customers in the system is 7.94, and the expected time a typical customer spends in the system is 0.053 hour (about 3.2 minutes). Also, about 41% of all arriving customers can go immediately into service, whereas about 32% of all customers must wait more than 0.02 hour (about 1.2 minutes) in the queue. Finally, we can find the

Figure 11.9 Template for the $M/M/s$ Queue

	A	B	C	D	E	F	G	H	I
1	M/M/s Queue								
2					After entering inputs in blue cells, click on the button below				
3	Inputs				to run the macro that calculates P(0), the value in cell B16.				
4	Unit of time	hour			Everything else recalculates automatically. Do *not*				
5	Arrival rate	150	customers/hour		rearrange cells in this template -- this might cause the				
6	Service rate per server	30	customers/hour		macro to stop behaving correctly.				
7	Number of servers	6							
8						Click here.			
9	Outputs								
10	Direct outputs from inputs				Distribution of number in system			Distribution of time in queue	
11	Mean time between arrivals	0.007	hours		n (customers)	P(n in system)		t (in hours)	P(wait > t)
12	Mean time per service	0.033	hours		0	0.0045		0.020	0.322
13	Traffic intensity	0.833			1	0.0226			
14					2	0.0564			
15	Summary measures				3	0.0940			
16	P(system empty)	0.005			4	0.1175			
17	P(all servers busy)	58.8%			5	0.1175			
18	Expected number in system	7.938	customers		6	0.0979			
19	Expected number in queue	2.938	customers		7	0.0816			
20	Expected time in system	0.053	hours		8	0.0680			
21	Expected time in queue	0.020	hours		9	0.0567			
22	Percentage who don't wait in queue	41.2%			10	0.0472			
23					11	0.0394			
24					12	0.0328			
25					13	0.0273			
26					14	0.0228			
27					15	0.0190			
28					16	0.0158			
29					17	0.0132			
30					18	0.0110			
31					19	0.0092			
32					20	0.0076			
33					21	0.0064			
34					22	0.0053			
35					23	0.0044			
36					24	0.0037			
37					25	0.0031			
38					26	0.0026			
39					27	0.0021			
40					28	0.0018			
41					29	0.0015			
42					30	0.0012			

The server utilization in an M/M/s system—the fraction of time each server is busy—is identical to the traffic intensity.

expected fraction of time each teller is busy as L_S/s. We find L_S, the expected number of busy tellers, from $L_S = L - L_Q = 7.938 - 2.938 = 5$. Then the expected fraction of time each teller is busy is $L_S/s = 5/6 = 0.833$. If this number doesn't ring a bell, it should—it is the server utilization in cell B13. This is no coincidence. The server utilization in an $M/M/s$ system, calculated as the arrival rate divided by the maximum service rate, is always the expected fraction of time a typical server is busy.

Economic Analysis

We now turn to the economic analysis. There is a cost and a benefit from adding a teller. The cost is the wage rate paid to the extra teller, $8 per hour. The benefit is that customers wait less time in the bank. Note that adding an extra teller makes both W and W_Q decrease by the *same* amount. This is because W is W_Q plus the expected service time per customer, and the latter does not change with extra tellers. This means that extra tellers decrease only the expected time in line, not the time in service. (The latter would decrease only if we made each teller *faster*, rather than adding tellers.) To see how W_Q changes, try entering 7 and then 8 for the number of tellers in cell B7 of Figure 11.9 and clicking on the button for each change. You should observe that the value of W_Q changes from 0.0196 hour (with 6 tellers) to 0.0054 hour (with 7 tellers) to 0.0019 hour (with 8 tellers). Because the arrival rate is 150 customers per hour, these waiting times translate to 2.94, 0.81, and 0.285 customer-hours spent waiting in line each hour.

The real problem is to evaluate the *cost* of waiting in line. This is not an "out-of-pocket" cost for the bank, but it is an indirect cost since customers who experience long waits might take their business elsewhere. In any case, the key to the trade-off is assessing a unit cost, c_Q, per customer-hour spent waiting in the queue. If the manager can assess this unit cost, then the total expected cost per hour of customer waiting is $c_Q \lambda W_Q$. The reasoning is that λ customers arrive per hour and each waits an expected time W_Q in the queue. Then we can trade off this waiting cost against the cost of hiring extra tellers.

We provide another template in the file **MMs_Opt_Template.xls** that helps solve the problem. See Figure 11.10. You now need to provide the arrival rate, the service rate per server, the wage rate per server, and the unit waiting cost per customer per unit time in line. You should *not* enter the number of servers as an input. Instead, the macro—run by clicking on the button—calculates selected summary measures of the system for several choices of the number of servers. Specifically, for each number of servers, the macro does the same calculations we did in the *M/M/s* template to calculate the value of W_Q in row 17. Then the cost of wages in row 18 is the wage rate multiplied by the number of servers, the queueing cost in row 19 is $c_Q \lambda W_Q$, and the total cost in row 20 is the sum of these two costs.

Figure 11.10 A Template for Queueing Optimization

	A	B	C	D	E	F	G	H	I	J
1	M/M/s Queue - A "Template" for Optimizing				Directions:					
2					1. Enter the inputs in cells B4 through B8					
3	Inputs				2. Click on the button below to perform the calculations					
4	Unit of time	hour								
5	Arrival rate	150	custs/hour							
6	Service rate per server	30	custs/hour							
7	Wage rate per server	$8.00	$/hour			Perform the calculations				
8	Cost per customer for time in queue	$5.50	$/hour							
9										
10	Minimum number of servers	6								
11										
12	Outputs									
13	Number of servers	6	7	8						
14	Server utilization	0.833	0.714	0.625						
15	P(system empty)	0.005	0.006	0.006						
16	Percentage who wait in queue	0.588	0.324	0.167						
17	Expected time in queue	0.0196	0.0054	0.0019						
18	Wages paid per hour	$48.00	$56.00	$64.00						
19	Queueing cost per hour	$16.16	$4.46	$1.53						
20	Total cost per hour	$64.16	$60.46	$65.53						
21										
22		Starting with the minimum number of servers in column B, the macro								
23		keeps increasing the number of servers until the total cost in row 20								
24		increases. Then the next to last total cost must be the minimum.								
25										

To optimize, the macro begins by using the smallest number of servers required to keep the system stable. In this case, 6 servers are required, as seen in cell B10. Then it keeps adding a server and calculating the total expected cost for that number of servers— total wages plus total expected waiting cost—until the total expected cost starts to increase. Given the inputs in Figure 11.10, where the manager assesses customer waiting time at $5.50 per hour, the total expected cost when there are 6 tellers is $64.16. It then decreases to $60.46 with 7 tellers, and then it increases to $65.53 with 8 tellers. Because the total expected cost would only continue to increase with more than 8 tellers, the macro quits with 8, implying that 7 tellers is best.

One of the most difficult aspects of an economic analysis of a queueing system is assessing the unit cost of making a customer wait in line.

This procedure requires a value for c_Q in cell B8. Because this value is probably very difficult for a bank manager to assess, we can instead use an indirect approach. We can find ranges for c_Q where a specific number of servers is economically optimal. To do this, first enter the largest reasonable value of c_Q in cell B8 and run the macro. For example, if the manager knows he would never value customer waiting time at more than $20 per hour, enter $20 in cell B8. Running the macro with this c_Q gives the results in Figure 11.11. They imply that a choice of 8 tellers is optimal when $c_Q = 20$. They also imply that no more than 8 tellers would ever be optimal for any *smaller* value of c_Q. Given the output in Figure 11.11, we now ask, When is 6 tellers better than 7? The total cost comparison, using the values of W_Q in row 17, shows that 6 tellers is better than 7 when

$$6(8) + c_Q(150)(0.0196) < 7(8) + c_Q(150)(0.0054)$$

This reduces to $c_Q < 3.76$. Similarly, 7 tellers is better than 8 when

$$7(8) + c_Q(150)(0.0054) < 8(8) + c_Q(150)(0.0019)$$

This reduces to $c_Q < 15.24$. These results imply that it is best to use 6 tellers when $c_Q <$ \$3.76. Otherwise, if $c_Q <$ \$15.24, it is best to use 7 tellers. Finally, for c_Q between \$15.24 and \$20, it is best to use 8 tellers.

Figure 11.11 Output Useful for Sensitivity Analysis on the Unit Waiting Cost

		C	D	E	F	G	H	I	J
1	M/M/s Queue - A "Template" for Optimizing			Directions:					
2				1. Enter the inputs in cells B4 through B8					
3	Inputs			2. Click on the button below to perform the calculations					
4	Unit of time	hour							
5	Arrival rate	150	custs/hour						
6	Service rate per server	30	custs/hour						
7	Wage rate per server	$8.00	$/hour		Perform the calculations				
8	Cost per customer for time in queue	$20.00	$/hour						
9									
10	Minimum number of servers	6							
11									
12	Outputs								
13	Number of servers	6	7	8	9				
14	Server utilization	0.833	0.714	0.625	0.556				
15	P(system empty)	0.005	0.006	0.006	0.007				
16	Percentage who wait in queue	0.588	0.324	0.167	0.081				
17	Expected time in queue	0.0196	0.0054	0.0019	0.0007				
18	Wages paid per hour	$48.00	$56.00	$64.00	$72.00				
19	Queueing cost per hour	$58.75	$16.21	$5.58	$2.01				
20	Total cost per hour	$106.75	$72.21	$69.58	$74.01				
21									
22	Starting with the minimum number of servers in column B, the macro								
23	keeps increasing the number of servers until the total cost in row 20								
24	increases. Then the next to last total cost must be the minimum.								
25									

A Comparison of Models

Here is a question many of you have probably pondered while waiting in line. Would you rather go to a system with one fast server or a system with several slow servers? In the latter case, we will assume that only one waiting line forms, so that you can't get unlucky by joining the "wrong" line. The solution to the question is fairly straightforward, now that we know how to obtain outputs for $M/M/1$ and $M/M/s$ models. In the following example we will make the comparison numerically. For a fair comparison, we will assume that (1) the arrival rate is the same for both systems and (2) the service rate μ_{fast} for the single fast server is equal to $s\mu_{slow}$, where μ_{slow} is the service rate for *each* of the s slow servers.

EXAMPLE | **11.4 COMPARING ONE FAST SERVER TO SEVERAL SLOW SERVERS**

Which system has the better steady-state characteristics such as L, W, L_Q, and W_Q: a single-server system where the single server can serve 30 customers per hour, or a

5-server system where each of the servers can serve 6 customers per hour? For each system we will assume that customers arrive according to a Poisson process at rate 25 per hour.

Objective To see whether customers would prefer a system with one fast server or a system with several slower servers.

WHERE DO THE NUMBERS COME FROM?

We can use any representative inputs for the comparison. In fact, it would be useful to try others, just to see whether the qualitative results we discuss next continue to hold.

Solution

Perhaps surprisingly, the choice between these two systems is not entirely clear-cut.

First, note that the two models are comparable in the sense that $\mu_{\text{fast}} = s\mu_{\text{slow}}$ because $\mu_{\text{fast}} = 30$, $s = 5$, and $\mu_{\text{slow}} = 6$. Equivalently, the traffic intensity is 5/6 for each. The spreadsheets in Figures 11.12 and 11.13 answer our question. (They were formed from the **MM1_Template.xls** and **MMs_Template.xls** files simply by changing the inputs.) As you

Figure 11.12   *M/M/1 System with a Fast Server*

	A	B	C	D	E	F	G	H	I
1	M/M/1 queue								
2									
3	Inputs								
4	Unit of time	hour			Just enter desired inputs in blue cells and				
5	Arrival rate	25.000	customers/hour		everything recalculates automatically.				
6	Service rate	30.000	customers/hour						
7									
8	Outputs								
9	Direct outputs from inputs				Distribution of number in system			Distribution of time in queue	
10	Mean time between arrivals	0.040	hours		n (customers)	P(n in system)		t (in hours)	P(wait > t)
11	Mean time per service	0.033	hours		0	0.167		0.250	0.239
12	Traffic intensity	0.833			1	0.139			
13					2	0.116			
14	Summary measures				3	0.096			
15	Expected number in system	5.000	customers		4	0.080			
16	Expected number in queue	4.167	customers		5	0.067			
17	Expected time in system	0.200	hours		6	0.056			
18	Expected time in queue	0.167	hours		7	0.047			
19	Server utilization	83.3%			8	0.039			

Figure 11.13   *M/M/s System with Slow Servers*

	A	B	C	D	E	F	G	H	I
1	M/M/s Queue								
2					After entering inputs in blue cells, click on the button below				
3	Inputs				to run the macro that calculates P(0), the value in cell B16.				
4	Unit of time	hour			Everything else recalculates automatically. Do *not*				
5	Arrival rate	25	customers/hour		rearrange cells in this template -- this might cause the				
6	Service rate per server	6	customers/hour		macro to stop behaving correctly.				
7	Number of servers	5							
8						Click here.			
9	Outputs								
10	Direct outputs from inputs				Distribution of number in system			Distribution of time in queue	
11	Mean time between arrivals	0.040	hours		n (customers)	P(n in system)		t (in hours)	P(wait > t)
12	Mean time per service	0.167	hours		0	0.0099		0.250	0.178
13	Traffic intensity	0.833			1	0.0411			
14					2	0.0857			
15	Summary measures				3	0.1191			
16	P(system empty)	0.010			4	0.1240			
17	P(all servers busy)	62.0%			5	0.1034			
18	Expected number in system	7.267	customers		6	0.0861			
19	Expected number in queue	3.101	customers		7	0.0718			
20	Expected time in system	0.291	hours		8	0.0598			
21	Expected time in queue	0.124	hours		9	0.0498			
22	Percentage who don't wait in queue	38.0%			10	0.0415			

can see, the comparison is not entirely clear-cut. The $M/M/1$ system has a smaller L but a larger L_Q. Similarly, it has a smaller W but a larger W_Q. In addition, the $M/M/1$ system is worse in that it has a smaller percentage of customers who experience no waiting in line (16.7% versus 38.0%) and a larger percentage who must wait in line at least 0.25 hour (23.9% versus 17.8%). The basic conclusion is that if you hate to wait in a queue, you will prefer the system with multiple slow servers. However, once it is your turn to be served, you will clearly prefer the system with the single fast server. In this latter system you will spend less *total* time in the system, but more of it will be spent waiting in line. Take your choice! ■

The Effect of the Traffic Intensity

We have mentioned that for an $M/M/1$ or $M/M/s$ system to be stable, the traffic intensity must be less than 1. In words, the system must be able to service the customers faster than they arrive—otherwise, the queue length will eventually grow without limit. It is interesting to see what happens to a system when the traffic intensity gets closer and closer to 1 but stays less than 1. As the following continuation of the County Bank example shows, the effects can be disastrous. (We already saw this phenomenon for a single-server system in Example 11.2. It is worth seeing again, this time in a multiple-server setting.)

EXAMPLE	**11.5 INCREASINGLY LONG LINES AT COUNTY BANK**

Over a period of time, the County Bank branch office from Example 11.3 has been experiencing a steady increase in the customer arrival rate. This rate has increased from the previous value of 150 customers per hour to 160, then to 170, and it is still increasing. During this time, the number of tellers has remained constant at 6, and the mean service time per teller has remained constant at 2 minutes. The bank manager has seen an obvious increase in bank congestion. Is this reinforced by the $M/M/s$ model? What will happen if the arrival rate continues to increase?

Objective To see what happens to congestion in a multiple-server system when the traffic intensity gets close to 1.

WHERE DO THE NUMBERS COME FROM?

The numbers here are all hypothetical, just to illustrate an effect.

Solution

A multiple-server system with a traffic intensity just barely below 1 behaves very badly—customers must wait long times in line.

Because $s\mu$ has stayed constant at value $6(30) = 180$, the traffic intensity, $\lambda/(s\mu)$, has climbed from $150/180 = 0.833$ to $160/180 = 0.889$ to $170/180 = 0.944$—and it is still climbing. We know that λ must stay below 180 or the system will become unstable, but what about values of λ slightly below 180? We recalculated the spreadsheet in Figure 11.13 for several values of λ and obtained the results in Table 11.1. (W and W_Q are expressed in minutes.) Although each column of this table represents a stable system, the congestion is becoming unbearable. When $\lambda = 178$, the expected line length is over 80 customers, and a typical customer must wait about a half hour in line. Things are twice as bad when $\lambda = 179$.

Table 11.1 Effects of Increasing Arrival Rate

	Customer Arrival Rate (λ)					
	150	160	170	175	178	179
Traffic intensity	0.833	0.889	0.944	0.972	0.989	0.994
L	7.94	11.04	20.14	38.18	92.21	182.22
L_Q	2.94	5.71	14.47	32.35	86.28	176.25
W	3.18	4.14	7.11	13.09	31.08	61.08
W_Q	1.18	2.14	5.11	11.09	29.08	59.08

The conclusion should be clear to the bank manager. Something must be done to alleviate the congestion—probably adding extra tellers—and the bank will no doubt take such measures if it wants to stay in business. However, the point of the example is that systems moving toward the borderline of stability become extremely congested. As the results in the table indicate, there is a huge difference between a system with a traffic intensity of 0.9 and a system with a traffic intensity of 0.99! ■

Other Exponential Models

The basic $M/M/s$ model and its special case, the $M/M/1$ model, represent only two of the hundreds or even thousands of analytical queueing models researchers have studied. Some of these are relatively simple extensions of the models we have discussed, and others are much more complex. Two of the relatively simple extensions are the **limited waiting room** and **limited source** models. Both of these continue to assume exponential interarrival times and service times. In the limited waiting room model, we start with the basic $M/M/s$ (or $M/M/1$) model but assume that arrivals are turned away when the number already in the queue is at some maximum level. For example, we might prescribe that at most 10 customers can wait in line. If a customer arrives and there are already 10 customers in line, then this new customer must go elsewhere (to another bank branch, say).

In the limited source model we assume that there are only a finite (fairly small) number of customers in the entire population. The context is usually that the customers are machines. Then an "arrival" means that a machine breaks down and arrives to a repair center. A "service" means a machine repair. The unique aspect of this type of system is that the arrival rate to the repair center depends on the number of machines already there. When most of the machines are in repair, the arrival rate to the repair center is necessarily low—there are not very many machines left to break down because most of them are already broken down. Conversely, when the number in the repair shop is low, the arrival rate to the repair shop is higher because most machines are candidates for breakdowns.

Stability is not an issue when the number of customers allowed in the system is finite.

One interesting aspect of both of these systems is that stability is not an issue. That is, there is no need to require that a traffic intensity be less than 1 to ensure steady state. The reason is that there are only a finite number of customers (or machines) allowed in the system. Therefore, it is impossible for the congestion in the system to grow without bound. As a result, steady state always occurs, regardless of the relationship between the arrival rate and the service rate.

We will not give examples of these two systems. However, we have included templates for them in the files **Limited_Q_Template.xls** and **Limited_Source_Template.xls**, and several of the problems allow you to explore these templates.

Erlang Loss Model

All of the results so far have been made possible because of the exponential distribution and its memoryless property. If we drop the exponential assumption, for either interarrival times or service times, the mathematical derivations become much more difficult, and "nice" results are scarce. In this section we discuss one of the better-known results for non-exponential systems. Actually, we continue to assume a Poisson arrival process—that is, exponentially distributed interarrival times—but we relax the exponential service time requirement. This is important because many real-world service time distributions are definitely *not* exponential.

The model in this section is called the **Erlang loss model**.[6] The reason for the term *loss* is that there is no waiting room at all, so that customers who arrive when all servers are busy are lost to the system. As usual, we let λ be the arrival rate, μ be the service rate per server (so that $1/\mu$ is the mean service time), and s be the number of servers. Then the steady-state distribution is specified by p_n, $0 \leq n \leq s$, where p_n is again the probability of exactly n customers in the system, and n cannot be greater than s because no queueing is allowed.

The probability p_s is of particular interest. It is the probability that all s servers are busy, so it represents the fraction of arrivals who are lost to the system. Therefore, the effective arrival rate—the rate at which customers actually *enter* the system—is $\lambda(1 - p_s)$, the usual arrival rate multiplied by the probability that an arrival is able to enter the system. This is the arrival rate we need to use in Little's formula to relate L and W. To do this, first note that all time spent in the system is *service* time (no queueing), so $W = 1/\mu$. Then Little's formula reduces to

$$L = \lambda(1 - p_s)W = \lambda(1 - p_s)/\mu$$

Of course, L_Q and W_Q are irrelevant for this system because no customers are allowed to wait in a queue.

In the Erlang loss model, the steady-state distribution depends on the service time distribution only through its mean.

A rather remarkable mathematical result states that the steady-state probabilities for this system depend on the service time distribution only through the *mean* service time, $1/\mu$. That is, the *form* of the service time distribution does not matter; it could be exponential or anything else, as long as it has mean $1/\mu$. This allows us to calculate the steady-state distribution as if the service times were exponential. We illustrate the procedure in the following example.

EXAMPLE | **11.6 Requests for Fire Engines**

Suppose that a fire deparment receives an average of 24 requests for fire engines each hour, and that these requests occur according to a Poisson process. Each request causes a fire engine to be unavailable for an average of 20 minutes. To have at least a 99% chance of being able to respond to a request, how many fire engines should the fire department have?

Objective   To use the Erlang loss model to find an appropriate number of fire engines so that one is almost always available.

---

[6]It is named after Erlang, one of the pioneer researchers in queueing theory. Erlang studied queueing in telephone systems in the early 1900s.

The arrival rate and the mean service time would be available from historical data. Note that for the service time distribution, we need only the mean, 20 minutes. The Erlang loss model is then relevant, regardless of how the actual service times vary around this mean—they could all be close to 20 minutes or they could vary wildly around 20 minutes.

Solution

Luckily, we do not need to assume that service times are exponential to get results. This would probably be an unrealistic assumption for this example.

To model this as a queueing problem, we identify the requests for fire engines as customers and the fire engines as servers. Then the key aspect of the problem is that there is no queueing for service. If a request occurs when at least one fire engine is available, an available fire engine serves this request. (We assume that each request is serviced by a *single* fire engine.) However, if no fire engine is available, then this request is not serviced at all—it is lost. Therefore, this problem is essentially like the $M/M/s$ model with a waiting room size of 0, where s is the number of fire engines (a value to be determined). The only difference is that we are *not* assuming exponentially distributed service times. All we are told is that the mean service time is 20 minutes. Since there is probably some minimum time that all service times must exceed, the exponential assumption probably does not apply, so it is more realistic to assume nonexponentially distributed service times. However, the mathematical result mentioned previously makes this a moot point; only the *mean* service time matters.

Using the Spreadsheet Model Template

The main focus here is on p_s, the fraction of arriving requests that see no available fire engines. We want this fraction to be no greater than 0.01. We have developed a template to calculate this and other steady-state quantities. (See the file **ErlangLoss_Template.xls** and Figure 11.14.) As usual, all you need to do is enter the inputs in the shaded range and then click on a macro button to calculate the various quantities. We make the following comments about this template.

Figure 11.14 Erlang Loss Model

	A	B	C	D	E	F	G	H	I
1	Erlang Loss Model				Directions				
2									
3	Inputs				1. Enter the inputs in cells B4 through B7.				
4	Unit of time	hour			2. Press the "Do Calculations" button.				
5	Arrival rate	24	customers/hour						
6	Service rate	3	customers/hour			Do Calculations			
7	Number of servers	15							
8									
9									
10	Outputs								
11	Summary measures				Steady-state probabilities				
12	Percentage of requests lost	0.91%			n	P(n)			
13	Entering arrival rate	23.782	customers/hour		0	0.000			
14	Expected number in system	7.927	customers		1	0.003			
15	Expected time in system	0.333	hours		2	0.011			
16					3	0.029			
17					4	0.058			
18					5	0.092			
19					6	0.123			
20					7	0.141			
21					8	0.141			
22					9	0.125			
23					10	0.100			
24					11	0.073			
25					12	0.049			
26					13	0.030			
27					14	0.017			
28					15	0.009			

1. The service rate is entered as an input as usual. For this example, it is 3 per hour because each service request requires 20 minutes on average. Again, there is no requirement that the service times be *exponential* with this rate; all we need to know is the rate itself.

2. The macro calculates the steady-state distribution in columns E and F (using rather complex formulas) and reports the last of these in cell B12. This is the fraction of arrivals lost. We can then get the effective arrival rate, L, and W with simple formulas in cells B13:B15, as discussed earlier.

Discussion of the Results

To ensure that the fire department achieves its goal of meeting at least 99% of all requests, we need to vary the number of fire engines in cell B7 until the percentage of lost requests in cell B12 is no more than 1%. We did this by trial and error; the results appear in Table 11.2. As these results show, the required number of fire engines is 15. Using this value, which appears in Figure 11.14, the arrival rate of requests that can be serviced is 23.782, and the expected number of requests that are being serviced at any time, L, is 7.927.

Table 11.2 Outputs for Fire Engine Example

Number of Fire Engines	Percentage of Requests Lost
12	5.1%
13	3.1
14	1.7
15	0.9
16	0.5

General Multiple-Server Model[7]

A final interesting variation of the $M/M/s$ model is to allow nonexponential interarrival and/or service times. Then we use the letter G (for general) instead of M. Specifically, the $G/G/s$ model allows *any* interarrival time distribution and *any* service time distribution. This more general model is important for two reasons. First, data on interarrival times or service times often indicate that the exponential distribution represents a poor approximation to reality. (This is especially true for service times in real applications.) Second, summary measures such as W or W_Q can be quite sensitive to the *form* of the interarrival time and/or service time distributions. Therefore, $M/M/s$ models, even those that use the appropriate *mean* interarrival time and *mean* service time, can give very misleading results when the actual distributions are not exponential.

Unfortunately, it is extremely difficult to obtain exact analytical results for the $G/G/s$ model. This is the bad news. The good news is that there is an approximation to this model that gives quite accurate results. In addition, it can be implemented fairly easily in a spreadsheet. This approximation is attributed to two researchers, Allen and Cunneen, and is referred to as the Allen–Cunneen approximation. [See page 218 of Tanner (1995).] We illustrate it in the following example.

EXAMPLE | **11.7 REVISITING COUNTY BANK WITH NONEXPONENTIAL TIMES**

The bank manager in Example 11.3 doubts that the exponential distribution provides a good approximation to the actual interarrival times and service times. Therefore, he

---

[7]This subsection is somewhat more advanced and can be omitted without any loss in continuity.

collects data on successive interarrival times and service times on 127 consecutive customers. He then calculates the means and standard deviations of these, with the results shown in rows 5 and 6 of Figure 11.15. (See the Data sheet of the file **GGs_Template.xls**.) Are these data consistent with exponential interarrival times and service times? If not, how much do summary measures such as W_Q and L_Q change if we use the Allen–Cunneen approximation instead of the $M/M/s$ model? We again assume that there are 6 tellers at the bank.

Figure 11.15

Data for Estimating Parameters of Distributions

	A	B	C
1	Data (in minutes) during peak periods		
2			
3	Summary of data below		
4		Times between arrivals	Service times
5	Mean	0.0064	0.0364
6	Stdev	0.0069	0.0543
7	SqCV	1.1364	2.2243
8			
9	Data		
10	Customer	Times between arrivals	Service times
11	1	0.0028	0.0037
12	2	0.0043	0.0096
13	3	0.0015	0.0330
14	4	0.0098	0.0012
15	5	0.0235	0.0376
16	6	0.0090	0.0127
17	7	0.0025	0.0521
18	8	0.0021	0.0156
134	124	0.0048	0.0267
135	125	0.0046	0.0395
136	126	0.0051	0.0058
137	127	0.0039	0.0181

Objective To see how an approximation to the general multiple-server model can be implemented, and to see how sensitive steady-state measures are to the forms of the interarrival and service time distributions.

WHERE DO THE NUMBERS COME FROM?

As in Example 11.1, the manager probably needs to get employees with stopwatches to collect the data.

Solution

First, note that the estimated arrival rate from the data is the reciprocal of the average interarrival time. Taking the reciprocal of the value in cell B5, we obtain an arrival rate of about 155 customers per hour. Similarly, taking the reciprocal of the average service time in cell C5, we obtain a service rate (per server) of about 27 customers per hour. These are nearly the same rates we used in Example 11.3. But are these times *exponentially* distributed?

One useful measure for a distribution of positive quantities is the **squared coefficient of variation**, defined as the squared ratio of the standard deviation to the mean and denoted by *scv*.

> *Squared coefficient of variation*
> $$scv = (\text{standard deviation}/\text{mean})^2$$

You might recall that the standard deviation of the exponential distribution equals the mean, so that $scv = 1$ for the exponential distribution. Analysts often characterize a distribution as being more or less variable than an exponential distribution by seeing whether its *scv* is greater than or less than 1. Intuitively, the reason is that if we fix the mean at some value, then *scv* increases as the standard deviation increases. So if we compare a nonexponential distribution to an exponential distribution, both of which have the same mean, then the nonexponential will exhibit more variability than the exponential if its *scv* is greater than 1, and it will be less variable if its *scv* is less than 1. As we will see, this *scv* measure is critical. It is not only required by the Allen–Cunneen approximation, but it also has a big impact on the behavior of the queueing system.

Using the Spreadsheet Model Templates

The *scv* values for the bank data appear in row 7 of Figure 11.15. For example, the formula in cell B7 is **=(B6/B5)^2**. We see that the interarrival times are slightly more variable, and the service times are considerably more variable, than they would be for exponentially distributed times. This indicates that the $M/M/s$ model might give misleading results. We check this by comparing the $M/M/s$ results with the $G/G/s$ results. To obtain the $M/M/s$ results, we enter the reciprocals of the averages in row 4 of Figure 11.15 as inputs to the **MMs_Template.xls** file to obtain Figure 11.16. In particular, we see that $L_Q = 13.793$ and $W_Q = 0.089$ (about 5.3 minutes per customer).

Figure 11.16   Results from $M/M/s$ Model

	A	B	C	D	E	F	G	H	I
1	M/M/s Queue								
2					After entering inputs in blue cells, click on the button below				
3	Inputs				to run the macro that calculates P(0), the value in cell B16.				
4	Unit of time	hour			Everything else recalculates automatically. Do *not*				
5	Arrival rate	155.4169	customers/hour		rearrange cells in this template -- this might cause the				
6	Service rate per server	27.49069	customers/hour		macro to stop behaving correctly.				
7	Number of servers	6							
8						Click here.			
9	Outputs								
10	Direct outputs from inputs				Distribution of number in system			Distribution of time in queue	
11	Mean time between arrivals	0.006	hours		n (customers)	P(n in system)		t (in hours)	P(wait > t)
12	Mean time per service	0.036	hours		0	0.0011		0.020	0.699
13	Traffic intensity	0.942			1	0.0061			
14					2	0.0172			
15	Summary measures				3	0.0324			
16	P(system empty)	0.001			4	0.0458			
17	P(all servers busy)	84.6%			5	0.0518			
18	Expected number in system	19.446	customers		6	0.0488			
19	Expected number in queue	13.793	customers		7	0.0460			
20	Expected time in system	0.125	hours		8	0.0434			
21	Expected time in queue	0.089	hours		9	0.0409			
22	Percentage who don't wait in queue	15.4%			10	0.0385			

In contrast, the Allen–Cunneen approximation appears in Figure 11.17. This is from another template file, **GGs_Template.xls**, that implements this approximation. Its inputs include not only the arrival and service rates (the reciprocals of the mean times), but also the *scv* values for indicating variability. As we indicate in the figure, these inputs in the shaded cells can be entered as numbers or as links to summary measures from data, as we have done here. (Compare cells B7 and B8 of Figure 11.17 to row 7 of Figure 11.15, for example.) Then the approximation uses rather complex formulas in rows 11 through 20, which we will not list here, to obtain the approximate summary measures in cells B17 through B20. (Note that no macro is required.)

Discussion of the Results

Comparing the $M/M/s$ results in Figure 11.16 to the $G/G/s$ approximation in Figure 11.17, we note that the values of L_Q and W_Q have changed considerably from the $M/M/s$ model. They are now $L_Q = 23.177$ and $W_Q = 0.149$ (or about 8.9 minutes per customer). The reason is that congestion in a queueing system typically *increases* as the interarrival time and service time distributions exhibit more variability, even if they retain the same means. In particular, the large value of scv for the service time distribution causes considerably longer queue lengths and waiting times in the queue than in a comparable exponential system. In short, if the bank manager used the $M/M/s$ model in this situation, he would obtain overly optimistic results with respect to congestion.

Figure 11.17

Allen–Cunneen Approximation

	A	B	C	D	E	F	G
1	G/G/s template using the Allen-Cunneen approximation						
2							
3	**Inputs**						
4	Arrival rate	155.417					
5	Service rate per server	27.491					
6	Number of servers	6	Enter numbers here, or (as in this file) enter links to summary data from observed interarrival and service times on another sheet.				
7	scv for interarrival times	1.136					
8	scv for service times	2.224					
9							
10	**Calculations of intermediate quantities**						
11	Ratio of arrival rate to service rate	5.653	The approximation is valid only when the utilization in cell B12 is less than 1. Otherwise, it gives nonsensical outputs.				
12	Server utilization	0.942					
13	A Poisson quantity	0.760					
14	Erlang C-function	0.846					
15							
16	**Important outputs**						
17	Expected wait in queue	0.149					
18	Expected queue length	23.177					
19	Expected wait in system	0.186					
20	Expected number in system	28.830					

The Allen–Cunneen approximation is evidently not well known, but it is important for the insights it can provide. We saw in the example that, as the variability increases in the interarrival times or the service times, the congestion tends to increase. On the other side, this approximation allows us to see how much better a system might behave if we could *reduce* the variability. For example, suppose the bank has the same means as in the example, but it is somehow able to schedule the arrivals at exactly 1 customer every 1/155.417 hour—no uncertainty whatsoever. The results appear in Figure 11.18. (The only change we had to make was to enter 0 in cell B7.) The change in the outputs is rather dramatic. The values of W_Q and L_Q were 0.149 and 23.177 in the example. Now they have decreased to 0.099 and 15.340. This is one more example of how variability is the enemy in queueing systems.

Figure 11.18

Queueing System with No Variability in the Arrival Times

	A	B	C	D	E	F
1	G/G/s template using the Allen-Cunneen approximation					
2						
3	**Inputs**					
4	Arrival rate	155.417				
5	Service rate per server	27.491				
6	Number of servers	6	Enter numbers here, or (as in this file) enter links to summary data from observed interarrival and service times on another sheet.			
7	scv for interarrival times	0.000				
8	scv for service times	2.224				
9						
10	**Calculations of intermediate quantities**					
11	Ratio of arrival rate to service rate	5.653	The approximation is valid only when the utilization in cell B12 is less than 1. Otherwise, it gives nonsensical outputs.			
12	Server utilization	0.942				
13	A Poisson quantity	0.760				
14	Erlang C-function	0.846				
15						
16	**Important outputs**					
17	Expected wait in queue	0.099				
18	Expected queue length	15.340				
19	Expected wait in system	0.135				
20	Expected number in system	20.993				

PROBLEMS

Skill-Building Problems

9. A fast-food restaurant has one drive-through window. On average, 40 customers arrive per hour at the window. It takes an average of 1 minute to serve a customer. Assume that interarrival and service times are exponentially distributed.

    a. On average, how many customers are waiting in line?

    b. On average, how long does a customer spend at the restaurant (from time of arrival to time service is completed)?

    c. What fraction of the time are more than 3 cars in line? (Here, the line includes the car, if any, being serviced.)

10. The Decision Sciences Department is trying to determine whether to rent a slow or a fast copier. The department believes that an employee's time is worth $15 per hour. The slow copier rents for $4 per hour, and it takes an employee an average of 10 minutes to complete copying. The fast copier rents for $15 per hour, and it takes an employee an average of 6 minutes to complete copying. On average, 4 employees per hour need to use the copying machine. (Assume the copying times and interarrival times to the copying machine are exponentially distributed.) Which machine should the department rent to minimize expected total cost per hour?

11. The **MM1_Template.xls** file is now set up so that you can enter any integer in cell E11 and the corresponding probability of that many in the system appears in cell F11. Change this setup so that columns E and F specify the distribution of the number in the *queue* rather than the system. That is, set it up so that if you enter an integer in cell E11, the formula in cell F11 gives the probability of that many customers in the queue. (*Hint:* You don't even need to understand the current formula in cell F11. You only need to understand the relationship between the number in the queue and the number in the system. If there are n in the system, how many are in the queue?)

12. The **MM1_Template.xls** file is now set up so that when you enter any time value in cell H11, the formula in cell I11 gives the probability that the wait in queue will be greater than this amount of time. Suppose that you would like the information to go the other direction. That is, you would like to specify a probability, such as 0.05, in cell I11 and obtain the corresponding time in cell H11. Try doing this as follows with Excel's Goal Seek tool. Use the Tools/Goal Seek menu items to get to a dialog box. Then in this dialog box, enter I11 as the Set cell, enter the desired probability such as 0.05 in the By Value box, and en-

ter H11 as the changing cell. Use this procedure to answer the following. In an $M/M/1$ queue where customers are entering at rate 50 per hour and the mean service time is 1 minute, find the number of minutes t such that there is a 5% chance of having to wait in the queue more than t minutes.

13. Expand the **MM1_Template.xls** file so that the steady-state probability distribution of the number in the system is shown in tabular form and graphically. That is, enter values 0, 1, and so on (up to some upper limit you can choose) in the range from cell E11 down and copy the formula in cell F11 down accordingly. Then create a column chart using the data in columns E and F.

14. For an $M/M/1$ queueing system, we know that $L = \lambda/(\mu - \lambda)$. Suppose that λ and μ are both doubled. How does L change? How does W change? How does W_Q change? How does L_Q change? (Remember the basic queueing relationships, including Little's formula.)

15. Suppose that you observe a sequence of interarrival times, such as 1.2, 3.7, 4.2, 0.5, 8.2, 3.1, 1.7, 4.2, 0.7, 0.3, and 2.0. For example, 4.2 is the time between the arrivals of customers 2 and 3. If you average these, what parameter of the $M/M/s$ model are you estimating? Use these numbers to estimate the arrival rate λ. If instead these numbers were observed service times, what would their average be an estimate of, and what would the corresponding estimate of μ be?

16. In the $M/M/s$ model, where μ is the service rate per server, explain why $\lambda < \mu$ is *not* the appropriate condition for steady state, but $\lambda < s\mu$ is.

17. Expand the **MMs_Template.xls** file so that the steady-state probability distribution of the number in the system is shown in tabular form and graphically. That is, enter values 0, 1, and so on (up to some upper limit you can choose) in the range from cell E12 down and copy the formula in cell F12 down accordingly. Then create a column chart using the data in columns E and F.

18. Each airline passenger and his or her luggage must be checked to determine whether he or she is carrying weapons onto the airplane. Suppose that at Gotham City Airport, 10 passengers per minute arrive, on average. Also, assume that interarrival times are exponentially distributed. To check passengers for weapons, the airport must have a checkpoint consisting of a metal detector and baggage X-ray machine. Whenever a checkpoint is in operation, two employees are required. These two employees work simultaneously to check a *single* passenger. A checkpoint can check an average of 12 passengers per minute, where the time to check a passenger is also exponentially distributed. Under the assumption that the airport has only one checkpoint, answer the following questions.

a. Why is an $M/M/1$, not an $M/M/2$, model relevant here?

b. What is the probability that a passenger will have to wait before being checked for weapons?

c. On average, how many passengers are waiting in line to enter the checkpoint?

d. On average, how long will a passenger spend at the checkpoint (including waiting time in line)?

19. A supermarket is trying to decide how many cash registers to keep open. Suppose an average of 18 customers arrive each hour, and the average checkout time for a customer is 4 minutes. Interarrival times and service times are exponentially distributed, and the system can be modeled as an $M/M/s$ system. (In contrast to the situation at most supermarkets, we assume that all customers wait in a *single* line.) It costs $20 per hour to operate a cash register, and a cost of $0.25 is assessed for each minute the customer spends in the cash register area (in line or being served). How many registers should the store open to minimize the expected hourly cost?

20. A small bank is trying to determine how many tellers to employ. The total cost of employing a teller is $100 per day, and a teller can serve an average of 60 customers per day. On average, 50 customers arrive per day at the bank, and both service times and interarrival times are exponentially distributed. If the delay cost per customer-day is $100, how many tellers should the bank hire?

21. In this problem, all interarrival and service times are exponentially distributed.

a. At present, the finance department and the marketing department each has its own typists. Each typist can type 25 letters per day. Finance requires that an average of 20 letters per day be typed, and marketing requires that an average of 15 letters per day be typed. For each department, determine the average length of time that elapses between a request for a letter and completion of the letter.

b. Suppose that the two typists are grouped into a typing pool; that is, each typist is now available to type letters for either department. For this arrangement, calculate the average length of time between a request for a letter and completion of the letter.

c. Comment on the results of parts **a** and **b**.

d. Under the pooled arrangement, what is the probability that more than 0.2 day will elapse between a request for a letter and start of the letter?

22. MacBurger's is attempting to determine how many servers to have available during the breakfast shift. On average, 100 customers arrive per hour at the restau-

rant. Each server can handle an average of 50 customers per hour. A server costs $5 per hour, and the cost of a customer waiting in line for one hour is $20. Assuming that an $M/M/s$ model is applicable, determine the number of servers that minimizes the sum of hourly delay and service costs.

23. On average, 100 customers arrive per hour at the Gotham City Bank. The average service time for each customer is 1 minute. Service times and interarrival times are exponentially distributed. The manager wants to ensure that no more than 1% of all customers will have to wait in line for more than 5 minutes. If the bank follows the policy of having all customers join a single line, how many tellers must the bank hire?

The following four problems are optional. They are based on the limited queue and limited source models in the Limited_Q_Template.xls and Limited_Source_Template.xls files.

24. A service facility consists of one server who can serve an average of two customers per hour (service times are exponential). An average of three customers per hour arrive at the facility (interarrival times are assumed to be exponential). The system capacity is three customers: two waiting and one being served.

a. On average, how many potential customers enter the system each hour?

b. What is the probability that the server is busy at a typical point in time?

25. On average, 40 cars per hour are tempted to use the drive-through window at the Hot Dog King Restaurant. (We assume that interarrival times are exponentially distributed.) If a total of more than four cars are in line (including the car at the window), a car will not enter the line. It takes an average of 4 minutes (exponentially distributed) to serve a car.

a. What is the average number of cars waiting for the drive-through window (not including the car at the window)?

b. On average, how many cars will be served per hour?

c. I have just joined the line at the drive-through window. On average, how long will it be before I receive my food?

26. A laundromat has five washing machines. A typical machine breaks down once every 5 days. A repairer can repair a machine in an average of 2.5 days. Currently, three repairers are on duty. The owner of the laundromat has the option of replacing them with a superworker, who can repair a machine in an average of 5/6 of a day. The salary of the superworker equals the pay of the three regular employees. Breakdown and service times are exponential. Should the laundromat replace the three repairers with the superworker?

27. The limited source model can often be used to approximate the behavior of a computer's CPU (central processing unit). Suppose that 20 terminals (assumed to always be busy) feed the CPU. After the CPU responds to a user, he or she takes an average of 80 seconds before sending another request to the CPU (this is called the "think time"). The CPU takes an average of 2 seconds to respond to any request. On average, how long will a user have to wait before the CPU acts on his or her request? How will your answer change if there are 30 terminals? What if there are 40 terminals? Of course, you must make appropriate assumptions about the exponential distribution to answer this question.

Skill-Extending Problems

28. Consider an airport where taxis and customers arrive (exponential interarrival times) with respective rates of 1 and 2 per minute. No matter how many other taxis are present, a taxi will wait. If an arriving customer does not find a taxi, the customer immediately leaves.
  a. Model this system as an $M/M/1$ queue. (*Hint*: Think of the taxis as the "customers.")
  b. Find the average number of taxis that are waiting for a customer.
  c. Suppose all customers who use a taxi pay a $2 fare. During a typical hour, how much revenue will the taxis receive?

29. A bank is trying to determine which of two machines to rent for check processing. Machine 1 rents for $10,000 per year and processes 1000 checks per hour. Machine 2 rents for $15,000 per year and processes 1600 checks per hour. Assume that machines work 8 hours a day, 5 days a week, 50 weeks a year. The bank must process an average of 800 checks per hour, and the average check processed is for $100. Assume an annual interest rate of 20%. Then determine the cost to the bank (in lost interest) for each hour that a check spends waiting for and undergoing processing. Assuming that interarrival times and service times are exponentially distributed, which machine should the bank rent?

30. A worker at the State Unemployment Office is responsible for processing a company's forms when it opens for business. The worker can process an average of 4 forms per week. In 2002 an average of 1.8 companies per week submitted forms for processing, and the worker had a backlog of 0.45 week. In 2003 an average of 3.9 companies per week submitted forms for processing, and the worker had a 5-week backlog. The poor worker was fired but later sued to get her job back. The court said that because the amount of work submitted to the worker had approximately doubled, the worker's backlog should also have doubled. Because her backlog increased by more than a factor of 10, she must have been slacking off, so the state was justified in firing her. Use queueing theory to defend the worker. (This is based on an actual case!)

31. For the $M/M/1$ queueing model, why do the following results hold? (*Hint*: Remember that $1/\mu$ is the mean service time. Then think how long a typical arrival must wait in the system or in the queue.)
  a. $W = (L + 1)/\mu$
  b. $W_Q = L/\mu$

32. Referring to Problem 18, suppose the airline wants to determine how many checkpoints to operate to minimize operating costs and delay costs over a 10-year period. Assume that the cost of delaying a passenger for one hour is $10 and that the airport is open every day for 16 hours per day. It costs $1 million to purchase, staff, and maintain a metal detector and baggage X-ray machine for a 10-year period. Finally, assume that each passenger is equally likely to enter a given checkpoint, so that the "effective" arrival rate to any checkpoint is the total arrival rate divided by the number of checkpoints. (Assume that each checkpoint has its own waiting line.)

33. The manager of a bank wants to use an $M/M/s$ queueing model to weigh the costs of extra tellers against the cost of having customers wait in line. The arrival rate is 60 customers per hour, and the average service time is 4 minutes. The cost of each teller is easy to gauge: It is the $8.50 per hour wage rate. However, because it is difficult to estimate the cost per minute of waiting time, the bank manager decides to hire the minimum number of tellers so that a typical customer has probability 0.05 of waiting more than 5 minutes in line.
  a. How many tellers will the manager use, given this criterion?
  b. By deciding on this many tellers as "optimal," the manager is *implicitly* using some value (or some range of values) for the cost per minute of waiting time. That is, a certain cost (or cost range) would lead to the same number of tellers as suggested in part **a**. What is this implied cost (or cost range)?

34. On average, 100 customers arrive per hour at Gotham City Bank. It takes a teller an average of 2 minutes to serve a customer. Interarrival and service times are exponentially distributed. The bank currently has 4 tellers working. The bank manager wants to compare the following two systems with regard to the average number of customers present in the bank and the probability that a customer will spend more than 8 minutes in line.

■ **System 1:** Each teller has his or her own line (and no moving between lines is permitted). Arriving customers are equally likely to choose any teller.

■ **System 2:** All customers wait in a single line for the first available teller.

If you were the bank manager, which system would you prefer?

35. Consider the following two queueing systems.
   ■ **System 1:** An $M/M/1$ system with arrival rate λ and service rate 3μ
   ■ **System 2:** An $M/M/3$ system with arrival rate λ and each server working at rate μ

Which system will have the smaller W and L?

The following problems are optional. They are based on the limited queue model in the Limited_Q_Template.xls file.

36. Two one-barber shops sit side by side in Dunkirk Square. Each shop can hold a maximum of 4 people, and any potential customer who finds a shop full will not wait for a haircut. Barber 1 charges $11 per haircut and takes an average of 15 minutes to complete a haircut. Barber 2 charges $7 per haircut and takes an average of 10 minutes to complete a haircut. On average, 10 potential customers arrive per hour at each barber shop. Of course, a potential customer becomes an actual customer only if he or she finds that the shop is not full. Assuming that interarrival times and haircut times are exponential, which barber will earn more money?

37. The small mail-order firm Sea's Beginning has one phone line. An average of 60 people per hour call in orders, and it takes an average of 1 minute to handle a call. Time between calls and time to handle calls are exponentially distributed. If the phone line is busy, Sea's Beginning can put up to $c - 1$ people on hold. If $c - 1$ people are on hold, a caller gets a busy signal and calls a competitor (Air's End). Sea's Beginning wants only 1% of all callers to get a busy signal. How many people should it be able to put on hold, that is, what is the required value of c?

11.6 QUEUEING SIMULATION MODELS

A popular alternative to using the analytical models from the previous section is to develop queueing simulations. There are several advantages to using simulation. Probably the most important advantage is that we are not restricted to the assumptions required by the standard analytical queueing models. These models typically require that interarrival times and service times are exponentially distributed, customers wait in a single queue and are served in FCFS fashion, all servers are identical in terms of their service time distributions, there are no customer types with higher priority than others, and so on.[8] When we use simulation, anything goes. If we want nonexponential service times, they are easy to build in. If we want customers to wait in several lines, one behind each server, and we even want to allow them to switch queues (as you might in a supermarket), simulation can handle it. If we want higher-priority customers to be able to "bump" lower-priority customers out of service, this is no problem with simulation. Just about any queueing situation can be simulated.

A second advantage of queueing simulation is that we get to *see* the action through time. Simulation outputs typically include not only summary measures such as the average queue length for some period of time, but they can also include time series graphs of important quantities such as the number of servers busy or the number of customers waiting in line. In this way, we can see how queues build from time to time. In addition, we can run a simulation many times, each time using different random numbers, to see how one day might differ from another.

The downside of queueing simulation is that it has traditionally required a clever computer programmer, a specialized software package, or both. It is easy to generate all the random quantities (interarrival times and service times, say) required by a simulation. The difficult part is essentially a bookkeeping problem. Imagine that you are given a list of

---

[8]There are indeed analytical models for many "nonstandard" queueing situations, but they are mathematically too complex for most users to understand.

customer arrival times and their corresponding service times. The question is whether you can "play out" the events as they would then occur through time. Say customer 17 arrives at 9:47, sees that 4 customers are ahead of her in line, and all 3 of the servers in the system are currently busy with customers. How do you know when customer 17 will enter service, and with which server? This is the biggest challenge in a queueing simulation—keeping track of the timing of events as they occur. Special queueing software packages are available to do all of the bookkeeping for you, but this software is often expensive and far from trivial to master. Therefore, some people write their own programs, in C, Visual Basic, or FORTRAN, say, to keep track of the events. Unfortunately, even good programmers sometimes struggle when writing queueing simulations. There are numerous details to get straight. One "small" error can make a queueing simulation behave very differently than intended.

We know that most of you are not programmers. You want the insights that a simulation can provide, but you do not want to develop the simulations yourself. Therefore, we have developed a fairly general simulation model that you can run. It is based on a program, written in Excel's VBA programming language, that runs in the background and does all of the simulation bookkeeping. All you need to do is enter the appropriate input parameters and click a button. The outputs will appear automatically.

The simulation model we examine is a variation of the $M/M/s$ queueing model we discussed in the previous section. (It is in the file **MultServerSim.xls**.) Customers arrive at a service center according to a Poisson process (exponential interarrival times), they wait (if necessary) in a single queue, and then they are served by the first available server. The simulation model is different in the following respects from the analytical $M/M/s$ model.

- The service times are not necessarily exponentially distributed. We allow three options: (1) constant (nonrandom) service times, (2) exponentially distributed service times, and (3) gamma distributed service times. This latter option uses the gamma distribution, which is typically shaped as in Figure 11.19. Because its mode is *not* necessarily 0, as with the exponential distribution, it is often more realistic for service times. By allowing three different service time distributions, we can see how different amounts of variability in the service times affect outputs such as waiting times.

Figure 11.19
Typical Gamma Distribution

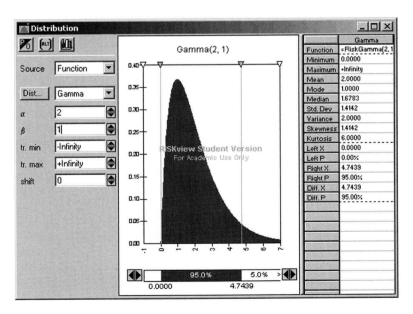

- The waiting room is of limited size, where this size is an input parameter. If the queue is already this long and another customer arrives, this new customer is not allowed to enter the system.

- The simulated run time is another user input. We might want to run a simulation for 100 hours (of *simulated* time) or only 10 minutes. By varying the run time, we can see how long-run behavior differs from short-run behavior. In addition, there is a "warm-up time" input. The simulation always starts empty and idle—no customers in the system—which might not be very realistic if we want to simulate a peak period, say, that starts with some customers already in the system. Therefore, the purpose of the warm-up period is to allow the system to get to a "typical" busy state. No statistics are collected during the warm-up period. Statistics are collected only during the run-time period. As an example, suppose a bank opens at 9:00 A.M., empty and idle, and we are interested in the period from 11:30 A.M. until 1:30 P.M. Then the warm-up period would be of length 2.5 hours, and the run-time period would be of length 2 hours.

- Every time you run the simulation, you are asked for a "random number seed." The actual number you enter is not important. The important part is that if you enter the *same* seed for two different runs, you get the same stream of random numbers. This is often useful for comparing different systems under "like" conditions (the same inter-arrival times and the same service times, say). Alternatively, if you enter *different* seeds for two different runs, you get a different stream of random numbers on each run. This is useful for seeing how much the system behavior can vary from one run to the next.

These last two points enable some very important insights into queueing systems in general. An analytical model such as the $M/M/s$ model provides summary measures, typically means, in steady state. It might say, for example, that the mean time in queue per customer is 4.85 minutes. But if we simulate such a system for 2 hours, say, and average the times in queue for the simulated customers, will the average be 4.85 minutes? The answer is a very definite "no." First, the average might not be the steady-state value because 2 hours might not be long enough to approximate steady state. Second, different runs using different random numbers will typically provide different averages. You might be surprised to see how much they can vary.

We now illustrate how the simulation works by revisiting the County Bank queueing situation (see Examples 11.3 and 11.7) with simulation.

EXAMPLE | **11.8 SIMULATING QUEUEING AT COUNTY BANK**

County Bank has already used analytical models to obtain steady-state measures of queueing behavior. However, it wonders whether these provide very realistic estimates of what occurs during a 2-hour peak period at the bank. During this peak period, arrivals occur according to a Poisson process of 2 per minute, there are 6 tellers employed, and each service time has a mean length of 2.7 minutes. The standard deviation of service times is estimated at 1.5 minutes, and a histogram of historical service times has a shape much like the shape in Figure 11.19, so that a gamma distribution is reasonable. What insights can the bank manager obtain from simulation?

Objective To simulate the bank's queueing system for a 2-hour peak period so that we can compare its actual behavior to the steady-state behavior predicted by $M/M/s$ and $G/G/s$ analytical models.

The only new input here is the standard deviation of service times. As with the rest of the inputs, it would be estimated from observed data on arrival times and service times.

Solution

For comparison, we first show results from the analytical models of the previous section. If we use the analytical $M/M/s$ model from the previous section (ignoring the fact that service times are not really exponentially distributed), we obtain the results in Figure 11.20. (The value in cell B6 is 1/2.7, the reciprocal of the mean service time.) For example, the mean wait in queue is $W_Q = 3.33$ minutes. If we use the analytical $G/G/s$ model with the Allen–Cunneen approximation, we obtain the results in Figure 11.21. [The values in cells B5 and B8 are 1/2.7 and $(1.5/2.7)^2$. The value in cell B7 is 1 because the exponential distribution has coefficient of variation 1.] The value of W_Q is now 2.18. Evidently, the gamma distribution, which has a much lower coefficient of variation, results in less time in the queue.

Figure 11.20

Results from the $M/M/s$ Model

	A	B	C
1	**M/M/s Queue**		
2			
3	**Inputs**		
4	Unit of time	hour	
5	Arrival rate	2	customers/hour
6	Service rate per server	0.37037	customers/hour
7	Number of servers	6	
8			
9	**Outputs**		
10	**Direct outputs from inputs**		
11	Mean time between arrivals	0.500	hours
12	Mean time per service	2.700	hours
13	Traffic intensity	0.900	
14			
15	**Summary measures**		
16	P(system empty)	0.002	
17	P(all servers busy)	74.0%	
18	Expected number in system	12.061	customers
19	Expected number in queue	6.661	customers
20	Expected time in system	6.031	hours
21	Expected time in queue	3.331	hours
22	Percentage who don't wait in queue	26.0%	

Figure 11.21

Results from the $G/G/s$ Model

	A	B	C	D	E	F
1	**G/G/s template using the Allen-Cunneen approximation**					
2						
3	**Inputs**					
4	Arrival rate	2.000		Enter numbers here, or (as in this		
5	Service rate per server	0.370		file) enter links to summary data		
6	Number of servers	6		from observed interarrival and		
7	scv for interarrival times	1.000		service times on another sheet.		
8	scv for service times	0.309				
9						
10	**Calculations of intermediate quantities**					
11	Ratio of arrival rate to service rate	5.400		The approximation is valid only		
12	Server utilization	0.900		when the utilization in cell B12 is		
13	A Poisson quantity	0.778		less than 1. Otherwise, it gives		
14	Erlang C-function	0.740		nonsensical outputs.		
15						
16	**Important outputs**					
17	Expected wait in queue	2.179				
18	Expected queue length	4.359				
19	Expected wait in system	4.879				
20	Expected number in system	9.759				

Using the Spreadsheet Simulation Model

When you open the file, you see the Explanation sheet in Figure 11.22. By clicking on the button, you see a couple of dialog boxes where you can enter the required inputs. These appear in Figures 11.23 and 11.24 (page 592). Note that the first of these asks you for a random number seed.

Figure 11.22   Explanation Sheet

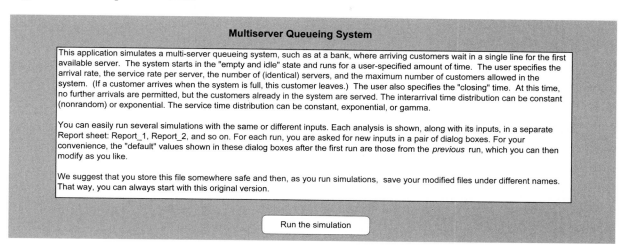

Multiserver Queueing System

This application simulates a multi-server queueing system, such as at a bank, where arriving customers wait in a single line for the first available server. The system starts in the "empty and idle" state and runs for a user-specified amount of time. The user specifies the arrival rate, the service rate per server, the number of (identical) servers, and the maximum number of customers allowed in the system. (If a customer arrives when the system is full, this customer leaves.) The user also specifies the "closing" time. At this time, no further arrivals are permitted, but the customers already in the system are served. The interarrival time distribution can be constant (nonrandom) or exponential. The service time distribution can be constant, exponential, or gamma.

You can easily run several simulations with the same or different inputs. Each analysis is shown, along with its inputs, in a separate Report sheet: Report_1, Report_2, and so on. For each run, you are asked for new inputs in a pair of dialog boxes. For your convenience, the "default" values shown in these dialog boxes after the first run are those from the *previous* run, which you can then modify as you like.

We suggest that you store this file somewhere safe and then, as you run simulations, save your modified files under different names. That way, you can always start with this original version.

Run the simulation

Figure 11.23
First Input Dialog Box

Inputs to queueing system

Enter all inputs:

OK

Cancel

Time unit
- Second
- ⦿ Minute
- Hour

Arrival Rate   2

Max allowed in queue   10

Simulation warmup time   120

Simulation run time   120

Random number seed:
(an integer from 1 to   111
2147483646)

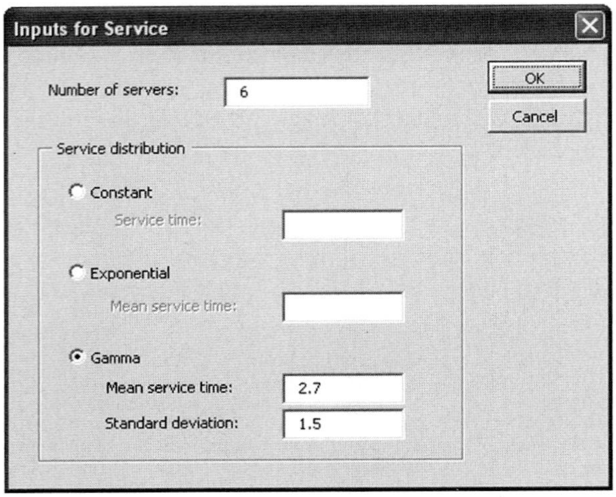

Figure 11.24

Second Input Dialog
Box

Inputs for Service

Number of servers: `6`

OK
Cancel

─ Service distribution ─

○ Constant

Service time: `          `

○ Exponential

Mean service time: `          `

◉ Gamma

Mean service time: `2.7`

Standard deviation: `1.5`

Figure 11.25

Simulation Results

	A	B	C
1	**Multiple Server Queueing Simulation**		
2			
3	**Inputs**		
4			
5	Time unit	minute	
6	Customer arrival rate	2.000	customers/minute
7	Mean time between arrivals	0.500	minute
8	Number of servers	6	
9	Service time distribution	Gamma	
10	Mean service time	2.700	minutes
11	Stdev of service times	1.500	minutes
12	Service rate for system	2.222	customers/minute
13	Maximum allowed in queue	10	customers
14	Simulation warmup time	120	minutes
15	Simulation run time	120	minutes
16	Random number seed	111	
17			
18	**Simulation Outputs**		
19			
20	Average time in queue per customer	1.06	minutes
21	Maximum time a customer was in queue	4.23	minutes
22	Average number of customers in queue	1.86	
23	Maximum number in queue	10	
24			
25	Average time in system per customer	3.86	minutes
26	Maximum time a customer was in system	9.45	minutes
27	Average number of customers in system	6.88	
28	Maximum number in system	16	
29			
30	Fraction of time each server is busy	83.4%	
31			
32	Number of customers processed	223	
33	Number of customers turned away	2	
34	Fraction of customers turned away	0.9%	

The simulation results appear in Figure 11.25. Again, we will not discuss all of the details, but when the simulation runs it does the following:

■ It starts with an empty and idle system—no customers are in the bank.

■ It keeps simulating customer arrivals and service times, and it keeps playing out the events, but it doesn't keep track of any customer statistics for the first 120 minutes, the warmup period. It keeps track of statistics only for the next 120 minutes, the runtime period.

■ If a customer arrives and there are already 10 customers in line, this customer is turned away (or, if you like, the customer decides not to bother waiting). If we want to ensure that no one is turned away, we can choose a large value for this input.

■ It reports the summary measures for this run, as shown in Figure 11.25.

Figure 11.26 Queue Length Distribution

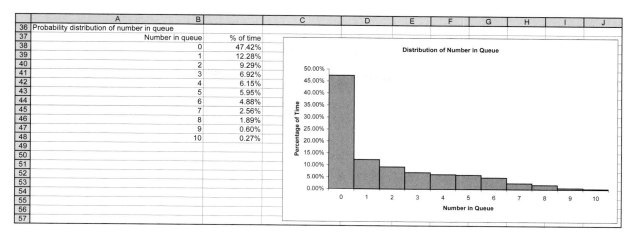

	A	B
36	Probability distribution of number in queue	
37	Number in queue	% of time
38	0	47.42%
39	1	12.28%
40	2	9.29%
41	3	6.92%
42	4	6.15%
43	5	5.95%
44	6	4.88%
45	7	2.56%
46	8	1.89%
47	9	0.60%
48	10	0.27%

Discussion of the Results

The outputs in Figure 11.25 should be self-explanatory. During the 2-hour period, 223 customers entered the bank, and 2 were turned away. Each teller was busy, on average, 83.4% of the time, the average customer waited in the queue for 1.06 minutes, the average length of the queue was 1.86, the maximum queue length was 10, and so on. We also obtain a graph of the queue length distribution, as shown in Figure 11.26. Each bar represents the percentage of simulated time the queue length was equal to any particular value. For example, the bar on the left shows that there was no queue at all about 48% of the time.

The simulation results can vary widely from one run to the next, due to different random numbers. This often reflects accurately what occurs in the real world.

Clearly, the average time in queue, 1.06 minutes, is much smaller than W_Q from the $M/M/s$ and $G/G/s$ models. Which is the "correct" value for County Bank's 2-hour peak period? This is not an easy question to answer. The 1.06 value from the simulation depends to a great extent on the random numbers we happened to simulate. To illustrate this, we ran the simulation several more times, each with a different random number seed, and we obtained values ranging from slightly under 0.7 to slightly over 2.1. This shows the bank manager that the average time in queue during any day's 2-hour peak period *depends on the day*. Some days she will get lucky and other days she won't. This variability from day to day—that is, from run to run—is one of the most important insights we can gain from simulation.

Besides the variability from day to day, the simulation results can depend on the length of the run-time period, and they can be affected by the limited queue size. For example, we ran the simulation for 10,000 minutes. The average time in queue did not change much, but hundreds of customers were turned away. Then we changed the maximum queue size to 100 and ran the simulation again for 10,000 minutes. The average time in queue was now much larger (over 2 minutes) and no customers were turned away. This illustrates that if all customers are allowed to enter the system, the average time in queue increases, whereas if many are turned away, the average time in queue, *for those who enter*, is much smaller. ■

The next example uses the same simulation model (still the **MultServerSim.xls** file) but with different inputs. Specifically, we will see the effect on waiting for different service time distributions, all with the same mean. For a given mean, the exponential distribution has the most variability, the constant distribution has the least (none), and the gamma distribution is typically in the middle. We will see whether this ordering carries over to average times in the queue.

EXAMPLE 11.9 QUEUEING FOR HELP AT HYTEX

HyTex is a software company that offers technical support for its customers over the phone. The demand for help is fairly constant throughout the day, with calls arriving at a rate of approximately 10 per minute. HyTex keeps 35 technical support lines open at all times, and it takes 3.5 minutes, on average, to answer a customer's question. Customers who call when all technical support people are busy face two possible situations. If there are fewer than 20 customers already on hold (the phone version of waiting in line), then a new caller is also put on hold. But if 20 customers are already on hold, a new caller gets a busy signal and must hang up. The service times—the times to answer customers' questions—are highly variable. HyTex wants to know how much it is suffering because of this variability.

Objective   To use simulation to analyze the effect of the shape of the service time distribution on customer waiting times.

WHERE DO THE NUMBERS COME FROM?

These inputs would be estimated from the extensive call data available. However, a subtle issue concerns the arrival rate of 10 per minute. It is not easy to estimate the arrival rate of *all* calls because it is difficult to track calls that receive a busy signal and are therefore lost.

Solution

This example is important because it illustrates how we can use a simulation model as a tool to study system behavior with various input parameters.

Selection of Inputs

If the service times are "highly variable," then a histogram of them might resemble an exponential distribution—that is, a lot of short calls but a few really long ones. Therefore, we first simulate the system with exponential service times. The arrival rate is 10, the mean service time is 3.5, the number of servers is 35, and the maximum allowable queue size is 20. With these parameters, we used a warm-up period of 1000 minutes and a run-time period of 2000 minutes for each simulation (you can think of this as several days "strung together"), and we made 5 runs with different random number seeds. We then changed the service time distribution to the gamma distribution with mean 3.5 and standard deviation 2.8. (This distribution has a squared coefficient of variation of 0.64, so it is not as variable as the exponential distribution, which has squared coefficient of variation 1.) Finally, we changed the service time distribution to be constant with value 3.5. For both the gamma and constant distributions, we made 5 runs, using the same seeds as in the exponential runs. (If you want to mimic our results, you should use the seeds 111, 222, 333, 444, and 555.)

Discussion of the Results

Selected results appear in Table 11.3. For each simulation run, we list two quantities: the average time in queue for the customers who did not receive busy signals, and the fraction of callers who received busy signals and were therefore lost. If we look only at the average times in queue, the results sometimes go in the *opposite* direction than what we predicted. The most variable distribution, the exponential, sometimes has the smallest times, whereas the least variable distribution, the constant, always has the largest times. However, there is a reason for this. These averages are only for the customers who were able to enter the system. As the percentages of lost callers show, many more callers were lost with the exponential than with the constant distribution, with the gamma distribution in the middle. (Over a period of 2000 minutes, with an arrival rate of 10 per minute, the system sees about 20,000 callers. An extra 1 percent lost therefore translates to about 200 callers—not an insignificant number.) With highly variable service times, customers do not wait quite as long in the queue because there are not as many customers to wait—many of them cannot get through at all!

Table 11.3 Comparison of Models

	Average Time in Queue			Percentage of Callers Lost		
Seed	Exponential	Gamma	Constant	Exponential	Gamma	Constant
111	0.92	0.84	0.92	4.8	3.6	3.0
222	0.81	0.80	0.85	4.1	3.1	2.3
333	0.81	0.81	0.87	4.0	3.4	2.8
444	0.80	0.82	0.88	4.7	3.5	2.8
555	0.77	0.75	0.82	3.8	2.9	2.4

So we again see that variability is the enemy. HyTex hates to have unhappy customers, and customers who receive busy signals are probably the unhappiest. The company should try to reduce the variability of service times, even if it cannot reduce the *mean* service time. If this is not possible, there are two other possible remedies: (1) hire more technical support people, and/or (2) rent more trunk lines, so that more customers can be put on hold. ■

PROBLEMS

Skill-Building Problems

38. The Smalltown Credit Union experiences its greatest congestion on paydays from 11:30 A.M. until 1:00 P.M. During these rush periods, customers arrive according to a Poisson process at rate 2.1 per minute. The credit union employs 10 tellers for these rush periods, and each takes 4.7 minutes to service a customer. Customers who arrive to the credit union wait in a single queue, if necessary, unless there are already 15 customers in the queue. In this latter case, arriving customers are too impatient to wait, and they leave the system. Simulate this system to find the average wait in queue for the customers who enter, the average number in queue, the percentage of time a typical teller is busy, and the percentage of arrivals who do not enter the system. Try this simulation under the following conditions and comment on your results. For each condition, make five separate runs, using a different random number seed on each run.

  a. Try a warm-up time of 2 hours. Then try no warm-up time. Use exponentially distributed service times for each.

  b. Try exponentially distributed service times. Then try gamma-distributed service times, where the standard deviation of a service time is 2.4 minutes. Use a warm-up period of 1 hour for each.

  c. Try 10 tellers, as in the statement of the problem. Then try 11, then 12. Use exponentially distributed

service times and a warm-up period of 1 hour for each.

  d. Why might the use of a long warm-up time bias the results toward *worse* system behavior than would actually be experienced? If you could ask the programmer of the simulation to provide another option concerning the warm-up period, what would it be? (*Hint*: The real rush doesn't begin until 11:30.)

39. How long does it take to reach "steady state"? Use simulation, with the **MultServerSim.xls** file, to experiment with the effect of warm-up time and run time on the key outputs. For each of the following, assume a five-server system with a Poisson arrival rate of 1 per minute and gamma-distributed service times with mean 4.0 minutes and standard deviation 3.1 minutes. For each part, make five separate runs, using a different random number seed on each run.

  a. Use a warm-up time of 0 and a run time of 30 minutes.

  b. Use a warm-up time of 0 and a run time of 180 minutes.

  c. Use a warm-up time of 120 minutes and a run time of 30 minutes.

  d. Use a warm-up time of 120 minutes and a run time of 180 minutes.

  e. Repeat parts **a–d** when the mean and standard deviation of service times are 4.8 and 4.2 minutes, respectively. (This should produce considerably more congestion.)

40. Given the model in the **MultServerSim.xls** file, what unit cost parameters should be used if we are interested in "optimizing" the system? Choose representative inputs and unit costs, and then illustrate how to use the simulation outputs to estimate total system costs.

41. Simulate the system in Problem 10. Make any assumptions about the warm-up time and run time you believe are appropriate. Try solving the problem with exponentially distributed copying times. Then try it with gamma-distributed copying times, where the standard deviation is 3.2 minutes. Do you get the same recommendation on which machine to purchase?

42. In Example 11.4 of Section 11.5, we examined whether an $M/M/1$ system with a single fast server is better or worse than an $M/M/s$ system with several slow servers. Keeping the same inputs as in the example, use simulation to see whether you obtain the same type of results as with the analytical models. Then repeat, using gamma-distributed service times with standard deviation 6 minutes.

43. A telephone-order sales company must determine how many telephone operators are needed to staff the phones during the 9-to-5 shift. It is estimated that an average of 480 calls are received during this time period and that the average call lasts for 6 minutes. There is no "queueing." If a customer calls and all operators are busy, this customer receives a busy signal and must hang up. If the company wants to have at most 1 chance in 100 of a caller receiving a busy signal, how many operators should be hired for the 9-to-5 shift? Base your answer on an appropriate simulation.

Does it matter whether the service times are exponentially distributed or gamma distributed? Experiment to find out.

44. US Airlines receives an average of 500 calls per hour from customers who want to make reservations, where the times between calls follow an exponential distribution. It takes an average of 3 minutes to handle each call. Each customer who buys a ticket contributes $100 to US Airlines profit. It costs $15 per hour to staff a telephone line. Any customer who receives a busy signal will purchase a ticket from another airline. How many telephone lines should US Airlines have? Base your answer on an appropriate simulation. Does it matter whether the service times are exponentially distributed or gamma distributed? Experiment to find out.

Skill-Extending Problem

45. A company's warehouse can store up to 4 units of a good. Each month, an average of 10 orders for the good are received. The times between the receipts of successive orders are exponentially distributed. When an item is used to fill an order, a replacement item is immediately ordered, and it takes an average of 1 month for a replacement item to arrive. If no items are on hand when an order is received, the order is lost. Use simulation to estimate the fraction of all orders that will be lost due to shortage. (*Hint*: Let the storage space for each item be a "server" and think about what it means for a server to be busy. Then decide on an appropriate definition of "service" time.)

11.7 CONCLUSION

We have seen that there are two basic approaches for analyzing queueing systems. The first is the analytical approach, where we attempt to find formulas (or possibly algorithms, implemented with macros) to calculate steady-state performance measures of the system. The second is the simulation approach, where we simulate the random elements of the system and then keep track of the events as they occur through time. The advantage of the analytical approach is that, at least for the simplest models, it provides summary measures such as L_Q and W_Q that are relatively simple to interpret. Also, if we have template files for these systems, we can easily vary the inputs to see how the outputs change. The main disadvantage of the analytical approach is that the mathematics becomes extremely complex unless we are willing to make simplifying assumptions, some of which can be unrealistic. For example, we must typically assume that service times are exponentially distributed, an unrealistic assumption in many real applications. Also, we must typically assume that the arrival rate remains constant through time and that we are concerned only with "steady state."

The simulation approach provides much more flexibility. Also, simulation lets us "see" how the system behaves and how queues can build up through time. The disadvantage of queueing simulation is that it is not well suited to spreadsheets. We have two basic choices: buy (and learn) specialized queueing software packages, or write our own queueing simulation in procedural languages such as VBA. Neither is an attractive possibility. However, the general queueing simulation model we have provided in the **MultServerSim.xls** file allows us to experiment with many system configurations to see how inputs and inherent randomness affect system outputs. The insights gained can be extremely valuable.

Summary of Key Management Science Terms

Term	Explanation	Page
Analytical queueing models	Models where outputs such as expected waiting time in queue can be calculated directly from inputs such as arrival rate and service rate	555
Queueing simulation models	Models where the events in a queueing process are "played out" through time, using simulated random numbers and careful bookkeeping	555
Interarrival times	Times between successive arrivals	556
Parallel system	Queueing system, such as at a bank, where each customer must be served by exactly one of (typically equivalent) servers	557
Steady-state analysis	Analysis of the "long run," where the effects of initial conditions have been washed out	558
Stable system	A system where the queue doesn't grow infinitely large in the long run	558
Exponential distribution, memoryless property	A popular distribution for queueing systems, characterized by the memoryless property where the future, given the current state, is independent of the past	559
Poisson process model	Series of events, such as customer arrivals, where times between events are exponentially distributed	563
Time averages	Averages, such as average queue length, taken over time	564
Customer averages	Averages, such as average waiting time, taken over customers	564
Little's formula	Important formula that relates time averages to customer averages	564
Server utilization	Average fraction of time a typical server is busy	565
$M/M/1$ and $M/M/s$ models	Simplest and most common analytical queueing models, where interarrival times and service times are exponentially distributed, and there is either a single server or multiple servers in parallel	566, 570
Traffic intensity	A measure of congestion; typically, the arrival rate divided by the maximum service rate	567
Limited waiting room models	Models where customers are turned away if the number of customers in the system is already at some maximum level	577
Limited source models	Models where there are a finite number of customers in the population, so that the arrival rate depends on how many of them are currently in the system	577

Term	Explanation	Page
Erlang loss model	Model where no customer arrivals are allowed when all servers are busy	578
$G/G/s$ model	General multiserver model, where interarrival times and service times are allowed to have *any* probability distributions	580
Squared coefficient of variation	Measure of variability: squared ratio of standard deviation to mean	581

Summary of Key Excel Terms

Term	Explanation	Excel	Page
Queueing templates	Ready-made spreadsheet files that implement complex queueing models, often with behind-the-scenes macros	See the **MM1_Template.xls** file, for example	568, 571, 573, 577, 579, 582

PROBLEMS

Skill-Building Problems

46. On average, 50 customers arrive per hour at a small post office. Interarrival times are exponentially distributed. Each window can serve an average of 25 customers per hour. Service times are exponentially distributed. It costs $25 per hour to open a window, and the post office values the time a customer spends waiting in line at $15 per customer-hour. To minimize expected hourly costs, how many postal windows should be opened?

47. On average, 300 customers arrive per hour at a huge branch of Bank 2. It takes an average of 2 minutes to serve each customer. It costs $10 per hour to keep a teller window open, and the bank estimates that it will lose $50 in future profits for each hour that a customer waits in line. How many teller windows should Bank 2 open?

48. Ships arrive at a port facility at an average rate of two ships every 3 days. On average, it takes a single crew 1 day to unload a ship. Assume that interarrival and service times are exponential. The shipping company owns the port facility as well as the ships using that facility. The company estimates that it costs $1000 per day for each day that a ship spends in port. The crew servicing the ships consists of 100 workers, each of whom is paid an average of $30 per day. A consultant has recommended that the shipping company hire an additional 40 workers and split the employees into two equal-size crews of 70 each. This would give each crew an average unloading or loading time of 1.5

days. Which crew arrangement would you recommend to the company?

49. On average, 40 jobs arrive per day at a factory. The time between arrivals of jobs is exponentially distributed. The factory can process an average of 42 jobs per day, and the time to process a job is exponentially distributed.
   a. On average, how long does it take before a job is completed (measured from the time the job arrives at the factory)?
   b. What fraction of the time is the factory idle?
   c. What is the probability that work on a job will begin within 2 days of its arrival at the factory?

50. A printing shop receives an average of one order per day. The average length of time required to complete an order is half a day. At any given time, the print shop can work on at most one job. Interarrival times and service times are exponentially distributed.
   a. On average, how many jobs are present in the print shop?
   b. On average, how long will a person who places an order have to wait until it is finished?
   c. What is the probability that an order will begin work within 2 days of its arrival?

51. At the Franklin Post Office, patrons wait in a single line for the first open window. On average, 100 patrons enter the post office per hour, and each window can serve an average of 45 patrons per hour. The post office estimates a cost of $0.10 for each minute a patron waits in line and believes that it costs $20 per hour to keep a window open. Interarrival times and service times are exponential.

a. To minimize the total expected hourly cost, how many windows should be open?

b. If the post office's goal is to ensure that at most 5% of all patrons will spend more than 5 minutes in line, how many windows should be open?

52. The manager of a large group of employees must decide whether she needs another photocopying machine. The cost of a machine is $40 per 8-hour day regardless of whether the machine is in use. On average, 4 people need to use the copying machine per hour. Each person uses the copier for an average of 10 minutes. Interarrival times and copying times are exponentially distributed. Employees are paid $8 per hour, and we assume that a waiting cost is incurred when a worker is waiting in line or is using the copying machine. How many copying machines should be rented?

53. The Newcoat Painting Company has for some time been experiencing high demand for its automobile repainting service. Because it has had to turn away business, management is concerned that the limited space available to store cars awaiting painting has cost them in lost revenue. A small vacant lot next to the painting facility has recently been made available for rental on a long-term basis at a cost of $10 per day. Management believes that each lost customer costs $20 in profit. Current demand is estimated to be 21 cars per day with exponential interarrival times (including those turned away), and the facility can service at an exponential rate of 24 cars per day. Cars are processed on a FCFS basis. Waiting space is now limited to 9 cars but can be increased to 20 cars with the lease of the vacant lot. Newcoat wants to determine whether the vacant lot should be leased. Management also wants to know the expected daily lost profit due to turning away customers if the lot is leased. Only one car can be painted at a time. (Try using the **Limited_Q_Template.xls** file for an analytical solution and the **MultServerSim.xls** file for a simulation solution.)

54. On average, 90 patrons arrive per hour at a hotel lobby (interarrival times are exponential) waiting to check in. At present there are 5 clerks, and patrons wait in a single line for the first available clerk. The average time for a clerk to service a patron is 3 minutes (exponentially distributed). Clerks earn $10 per hour, and the hotel assesses a waiting time cost of $20 for each hour that a patron waits in line.

a. Compute the expected cost per hour of the current system.

b. The hotel is considering replacing one clerk with an Automatic Clerk Machine (ACM). Management estimates that 20% of all patrons will use an ACM. An ACM takes an average of 1 minute to service a patron. It costs $48 per day (1 day equals 8 hours) to operate an ACM. Should the hotel install the ACM? Assume that all customers who are willing to use the ACM wait in a separate queue.

Skill-Extending Problem

55. The mail order firm of L. L. Pea receives an average of 200 calls per hour, where times between calls are exponentially distributed. It takes an L. L. Pea operator an average of 3 minutes to handle a call. If a caller gets a busy signal, L. L. Pea assumes that he or she will call a competing mail-order company, and L. L. Pea will lose an average of $30 in profit. The cost of keeping a phone line open is $9 per hour. How many operators should L. L. Pea have on duty? Use simulation to answer this question. Does the answer depend on whether the service times are exponentially distributed?

Modeling Problems

56. Bloomington Hospital knows that insurance companies are going to reduce the average length of stay of many types of patients. How can queueing models be used to determine how changes in insurance policies will influence the hospital?

57. Excessive delays have recently been noted on New York City's 911 system. Discuss how you would use queueing models to improve the performance of the 911 system.

58. Suppose that annually an average of λ library patrons want to borrow a book. A patron borrows the book for an average of $1/\mu$ years. Suppose we observe that the book is actually borrowed an average of R times per year. Explain how we can estimate λ, which is an unobservable quantity. (*Hint*: Let U be the expected number of times per year a patron wants to borrow the book and the book is out. Note that $\lambda = R + U$.)

59. Based on Quinn et al. (1991). Winter Riggers handles approximately $400 million in telephone orders per year. Winter Riggers' system works as follows. Callers are connected to an agent if one is available. Otherwise, they are put on hold (if a "trunk" or line is available). A customer can hang up at any time and leave the system. Winter Riggers would like to efficiently manage the telephone system (lines and agents) used to process these orders. Of course, orders are very seasonal and depend on the time of day.

a. What decisions must Winter Riggers make?

b. What would be an appropriate objective for Winter Riggers to minimize (or maximize)? What difficulties do you see in specifying the objective?

c. What data would Winter Riggers need to keep track of to improve its efficiency?

60. Zerox has 16 service centers throughout the United States. Zerox is trying to determine how many technicians it should assign to each service center. How would you approach this problem?

61. Based on Kolesar et al. (1974). Metropolis PD Precinct 88 must determine the minimum number of police cars required to meet its needs for the next 24 hours. An average call for service requires 30 minutes. The number of calls the police department expects to receive during each hour is shown in the file **P11_61.xls**. The Metropolis PD standard of service is that there should be a 90% chance that a car is available to respond to a call. For each of the following, discuss how you might find a solution.

a. Suppose that patrol officer teams assigned to a car work an 8-hour shift beginning at 12 A.M., 8 A.M., or 4 P.M. Officers get an hour off for a meal. This hour can be anytime between the second and fifth hour of their shift. The precinct wants to know how many teams are needed to meet daily demand.

b. Suppose that patrol officer teams assigned to a car begin their 8-hour shifts at 12 A.M., 8 A.M., 12 P.M., 4 P.M., and 8 P.M. An hour off for meals may be taken anytime during a shift. The precinct again wants to know how many teams are needed to meet daily demand.

The Catalog Company is a mail- and phone-order company that sells generic brands of houseware items and clothing. Approximately 95% of customer orders are received by phone; the remaining 5% are received in the mail. Phone orders are accepted at Catalog Company's toll-free 800 number, 800-SAVE-NOW. The number is available 9 hours per day (8 A.M. to 5 P.M.), 5 days a week.

Sarah Walters, a recent graduate of Columbia Business School, has just been hired by Catalog to improve its operations. Sarah would like to impress her boss, Ben Gleason, the president of Catalog Company, with some ideas that would quickly improve the company's bottom line. After spending a week learning about Catalog's operations, Sarah feels that a substantial impact can be made by a closer evaluation of the phone order system.

Currently, Catalog employs a single full-time operator to take orders over the phone. Sarah wonders whether additional operators should be hired to take phone orders. Ben feels that Sarah's time might be better spent studying the catalog mailing lists. Ben reasons that the mailing lists are where customers are generated, and improving the list will bring in more revenue. And besides, Ben says, "Catalog's phone operator, Betty Wrangle, seems to be doing nothing more than half of the time that I walk by. Hiring more operators to do nothing will just waste more money." Although Sarah knows the mailing lists are important, she thinks that a study of the mailing lists will take far more time than a quick evaluation of the phone order system.

Forging ahead, Sarah discovered the following information about the phone order system. The phone operator, Betty Wrangle, is paid $9 per hour in wages and benefits. The average cost to Catalog for a completed 800 number call is $1.50. With only one phone line, any incoming calls that arrive when Betty is on the phone to another customer get a busy signal. The cost of the phone line is $40 per month. The phone company can immediately add up to four additional phone lines using the same 800 number, each at a cost of $40 per month per line. Catalog's phone system is such that it cannot be upgraded in the near future to allow incoming calls to be placed on hold. The average profit on an order (not including the cost of the operator or phone call) is 40% of the amount of the order. For example, an order of $100 brings a profit of $40 to Catalog.

Sarah decided that additional information needed to be collected about the frequency of incoming calls, the length of the calls, and so on. After talking to the phone company, Sarah learned that she could borrow equipment for one day that could detect when a call was coming in, even when Betty was on the phone. The caller would still get a busy signal and be lost, but Sarah would know that a call had been attempted. Sarah collected almost 9 hours of data the next day; these data are presented in the file **Catalog.xls**. Sarah believes that most of the callers who receive a busy signal take their business elsewhere and are totally lost to Catalog. Sarah does not feel that extending the hours of operation of the 800 number would be beneficial because the hours of operation are printed prominently in all of the catalogs.

The first call arrives 0.036 hour into the day. It takes Betty 0.054 hour to process the call and record the order for $65.21 worth of merchandise. Callers 5 and 6 get busy signals when they call, because Betty was still processing caller 4. Because calls 5 and 6 were lost, no call length information was available and no orders were placed. Data collection was stopped at call number 80.

Questions

Use the complete information in the file **Catalog.xls** to answer the following questions.

1. Approximately what fraction of the time is Betty idle? Is Ben's estimate correct?

2. Approximately how many calls are lost in an average hour due to a busy signal?

3. Use the data to estimate the average arrival rate of all attempted calls to Catalog. Give an approximate 95% confidence interval for the estimate. Plot a frequency histogram of interarrival times. Does the distribution of interarrival times appear to be exponential?

4. Use the data to estimate the average service rate of all completed calls. Give an approximate 95% confidence interval for the estimate. Plot a frequency histogram of service times. Does the service time distribution appear to be exponential? Give an approximate 95% confidence interval for the average revenue per call.

5. Would you recommend that Catalog acquire additional phone lines and operators? If so, how many? If not, why not? Justify your answer in enough detail so that Ben Gleason would be convinced of your recommendation. ■

Pacific National Bank is a medium-size bank with 21 branches in the San Francisco Bay Area. Until very recently, Pacific did not operate its own automatic teller machines (ATMs); instead, it relied on an outside vendor to operate these. Ninety percent of the ATM customers obtained cash advances with non-Pacific credit cards, so the ATMs did little to directly improve Pacific's own banking business. Operations Vice President Nancy Meisterhaus wants to change that, by having Pacific offer a broader mix of banking services with its own machines tied into its own data-processing network.

The industry consensus is that the ATM appeals to customers in much the same way as the supermarket express line: It minimizes the amount of waiting. But for Pacific, the 24-hour ATM would also have the broader appeal of providing essential banking services at all hours, reaching a segment of the market not currently served. Historically, customers who find standard banking hours inconvenient have been lost to Pacific, so the ATM will increase the bank's market share.

Besides attracting more customers and servicing existing customers better, the ATM operation should offer substantial cost advantages. Fewer human tellers would be required for the same volume of transactions as before. The per transaction cost of the machine, which does need some human attention for restocking and maintenance, should be substantially less. But even if that were not so, its 24-hour readiness would be extremely expensive to duplicate with human tellers, who would have to be given extra protection for dangerous late-night work.

Ms. Meisterhaus selected the Walnut Creek office as the test branch for a captive ATM. Customers from that branch were recruited to sign up for a Pacific ATM card. All residents within the neighboring zip codes were offered an incentive to open free checking accounts at Pacific when they also signed up for the card. Once a critical mass of ATM card holders was established—but before the

banking ATM was installed—statistics were kept. The arrival times in Table 11.4 were determined for various times of the week.

Table 11.4   Customer Arrivals at the Walnut Creek Office—Before ATM Installation

Period	Daily Average Number of Arrivals
(1) Monday–Friday 10 A.M.–12 P.M.	155
(2) Monday–Friday 12–1 P.M.	242
(3) Monday–Friday 1–3 P.M.	290
(4) Friday 3–6 P.M.	554

The bank opens at 10 A.M. and closes at 3 P.M., except on Friday, when it closes at 6 P.M. Past study shows that, over each period, customers arrive randomly at a stable mean rate, so the assumption of a Poisson process is valid. The mean time required to complete customer transactions is 2 minutes, and the individual service times have a frequency distribution with a pronounced positive skew, so an exponential distribution is a reasonable approximation to reality.

Tellers all work part-time and cost $10 per bank hour. Pacific's experience has established that there will be a significant drop-off in clientele soon after a bout during which customers suffer lengthy delays in getting teller access. The supplier of the ATM equipment claims that other banks of comparable size have experienced a 30% diversion of regular business away from human tellers to the ATM, which produced a further 20% expansion beyond the previous level of overall client transactions—all absorbed by the ATM, half of it outside regular banking hours. The supplier also maintains that ATM traffic is fairly uniform, except between 11 P.M. and 6 A.M., when it is negligible. Ms. Meisterhaus believes that the ATM busy-period arrivals will constitute a single Poisson process.

Industry experience is that the mean service time at an ATM is one-half minute, with an exponential distribution serving as an adequate approximation to the unknown positively skewed unimodal distribution that actually applies. Ms.

[10]This case was written by Lawrence L. Lapin, San Jose State University.

Meisterhaus believes that, once the ATM is installed, the Walnut Creek human tellers will be left with a greater proportion of the more involved and lengthy transactions, raising their mean service time to 2.5 minutes.

Ms. Meisterhaus knows that much of the evaluation of the ATM operations will be a queueing exercise. Her knowledge of this subject is a bit rusty, so she has retained you to assist her.

Questions

1. Assume that Pacific National Bank remains with human tellers only.
   a. For each time period in Table 11.4, determine the minimum number of tellers needed on station to service the customer stream.
   b. Assume that the number of tellers found in part **a** is used. For each time period, determine the mean customer waiting time.
   c. For each time period, determine the mean customer waiting time when the number of tellers is one more than found in part **a**.

2. Past experience shows that the drop-off in clientele due to waiting translates into an expected net present value in lost future profits of $0.10 per minute. For each time period in Table 11.4, determine the average hourly queueing system cost (server cost + waiting cost), assuming that the bank uses the following service arrangement:
   a. The minimum number of human tellers necessary to service the arriving customers
   b. One teller more than was found in part **a** of Question 1

3. Suppose that the ATM is installed and that customers themselves decide whether to use human tellers or to use the ATM, and that two queues form independently for each. Finally, assume that a 10% traffic increase is generated by the ATM within each open time period and that all of it is for the ATM.
   a. For each period in Table 11.4, determine the mean arrival rate at the human teller windows.
   b. Do the same with regard to the mean arrival rate at the ATM.
   c. Find the minimum number of human tellers required to be on station during each time period.

4. Assume that the number of human tellers used is one more than that found in part **c** of Question 3. Determine for Ms. Meisterhaus the mean customer waiting time during each open period in Table 11.4 for those customers who seek the following:
   a. Human tellers
   b. Access to the ATM

5. The hourly cost of maintaining and operating the ATM is $5. Increased customer traffic results in additional bank profit estimated to be $0.20 per transaction. Determine for Ms. Meisterhaus the net hourly queueing system cost, reflecting any profit increase, for operating with the ATM for each of the four periods identified in Table 11.4. Use the mean waiting times from Question 4.

6. Consider the complete 24-hour, 7-day picture. Incorporate whatever information you need from Questions 1 through 5 and your solutions, plus any additional information in the case and any necessary assumptions, to compare the net cost of operation with and without the ATM. Then give your overall recommendation to Ms. Meisterhaus.

Regression and Forecasting Models

© Brand X Pictures/Photodisc

FORECASTING AT TACO BELL

How much quantitative analysis occurs at fast-food restaurants? At Taco Bell, a lot! This is described in an article by Huerter and Swart (1998), who explain the approach to labor management that has occurred at Taco Bell restaurants over the past decade. Labor is a large component of costs at Taco Bell. Approximately 30% of every sales dollar goes to labor. However, the unique characteristics of fast-food restaurants make it difficult to plan labor utilization efficiently. In particular, the Taco Bell product—food—cannot be inventoried; it must be made fresh at the time the customer orders it. Because of shifting demand throughout any given day, where the lunch period accounts for approximately 52% of a day's sales and as much as 25% of a day's sales can occur during the busiest hour, labor requirements vary greatly throughout the day. If too many workers are on hand during slack times, they are paid for doing practically nothing. Worse than that, however, are the lost sales (and unhappy customers) that occur if too few workers are on hand during peak times. Prior to 1988, Taco Bell made very little effort to manage the labor problem in an efficient, centralized manner. It simply allocated about 30% of each store's sales to the store managers and let them allocate it as best they could—not always with good results.

In 1988 Taco Bell initiated its "value meal" deals, where certain meals were priced as low as 59 cents. This increased demand to the point where management could no longer ignore the labor allocation problem. Therefore, in-store computers were installed, data from all stores were collected, and a team of analysts was assigned the task of developing a cost-efficient labor allocation system. This system, which has been fully integrated into all Taco Bell stores since 1993, is composed of three subsystems: (1) a forecasting subsystem that, for each store, forecasts the arrival rate of customers by 15-minute interval by day of week; (2) a simulation subsystem that, for each store, simulates the congestion and number of lost customers that will occur for any customer arrival rate, given a specific number (and deployment) of workers; and (3) an optimization subsystem that, for each store, indicates the minimum cost allocation of workers, subject to various constraints, such as a minimum service level and a minimum shift length for workers. Although all three of these subsystems are important, the forecasting subsystem is where it all starts. Each store must have a reasonably accurate forecast of future customer arrival rates, broken down by small time intervals (such as 11:15 A.M. to 11:30 A.M. on Friday), before labor requirements can be predicted and labor allocations can be made in an intelligent manner. Like many real-world forecasting systems, Taco Bell's system has two important characteristics: (1) it requires extensive data, which have been made available by the in-store computer systems, and (2) the eventual forecasting method used is mathematically a fairly simple one, namely, 6-week moving averages, which we will study in this chapter.

Simple or not, the forecasts, as well as the other system components, have enabled Taco Bell to cut costs and increase profits considerably. In its first 4 years, 1993–1996, the labor management system is estimated to have saved Taco Bell approximately $40.34 million in labor costs. Because the number of Taco Bell stores is constantly increasing, the annual companywide savings from the system will certainly grow in the future. In addition, the focus on quantitative analysis has produced other side benefits for Taco Bell. Its service is now better and more consistent across stores, with many fewer customers leaving because of slow service. Also, the quantitative models developed have enabled Taco Bell to evaluate the effectiveness of various potential productivity enhancements, including self-service drink islands, customer-activated touch screens for ordering, and smaller kitchen areas. So the next time you order food from Taco Bell, you can be assured that there is definitely a method to the madness! ■

12.1 INTRODUCTION

Many decision-making applications depend on a forecast of some quantity. Here are several examples.

- When a service organization, such as a fast-food restaurant, plans its staffing over some time period, it must forecast the customer demand as a function of time. This might be done at a very detailed level, such as the demand in successive half-hour periods, or at a more aggregate level, such as the demand in successive weeks.

- When a company plans its ordering or production schedule for a product, it must forecast the customer demand for this product so that it can stock appropriate quantities—neither too much nor too little.

- When an organization plans to invest in stocks, bonds, or other financial instruments, it typically attempts to forecast movements in stock prices and interest rates.

- When government representatives plan policy, they attempt to forecast movements in macroeconomic variables such as inflation, interest rates, and unemployment.

There are many forecasting methods available, and all practitioners have their favorites. To say the least, there is little agreement among practitioners or theoreticians as to the *best* forecasting method. The methods can generally be divided into three groups: (1) **judgmental** methods, (2) **regression** methods, and (3) **extrapolation** methods. The first of these is basically nonquantitative and will not be discussed here.

Regression models, also called **causal** models, forecast a variable by estimating its relationship with other variables. For example, a company might use a regression model to estimate the relationship between its sales and its advertising level, the population income level, the interest rate, and possibly others. The technique of regression is extremely popular, due to its flexibility and power. Regression can estimate relationships between time series variables or cross-sectional variables (those that are observed at a single point in time), and it can discover linear or nonlinear relationships.

Extrapolation methods, also called **time series methods**, use past data of a time series variable—and nothing else—to forecast future values of the variable. Many extrapolation methods are available, including the two we will discuss here: moving averages and exponential smoothing. All extrapolation methods search for *patterns* in the historical series and then attempt to extrapolate these patterns into the future. Some try to track long-term upward or downward trends and then project these. Some try to track the seasonal patterns (sales up in November and December, down in other months, for example) and then project these.

Regression analysis and time series analysis are both very broad topics, with many entire books and thousands of research articles devoted to them. We can only scratch the surface of these topics in a single chapter. However, a little can go a long way. By the time you have read this chapter, you will be able to apply some very powerful techniques.

12.2 OVERVIEW OF REGRESSION MODELS

Regression analysis is the study of relationships between variables. It is one of the most useful tools for a business analyst because it applies to so many situations. Some potential uses of regression analysis in business address the following questions:

- How do wages of employees depend on years of experience, years of education, and gender?

- How does the current price of a stock depend on its own past values, as well as the current and past values of a market index?

- How does a company's current sales level depend on its current and past advertising levels, the advertising levels of its competitors, the company's own past sales levels, and the general level of the market?

- How does the unit cost of producing an item depend on the total quantity of items that have been produced?

- How does the selling price of a house depend on such factors as the appraised value of the house, the square footage of the house, the number of bedrooms in the house, and perhaps others?

Each of these questions asks how a single variable, such as selling price or employee wages, depends on other relevant variables. If we can estimate this relationship, we can not only better understand how the world operates, but we can also do a better job of predicting the variable in question. For example, we can not only understand how a company's sales are affected by its advertising, but we can also use the company's records of current and past advertising levels to predict future sales.

Regression is capable of dealing with cross-sectional data and time series data.

There are several ways to categorize regression analysis. One categorization is based on the type of data being analyzed. There are two basic types: cross-sectional data and time series data. Cross-sectional data are usually data gathered from approximately the same period of time from a cross section of a population. The housing and wage examples mentioned previously are typical cross-sectional studies. The first concerns a sample of houses, presumably sold during a short period of time, such as houses sold in Bloomington, Indiana, during the first quarter of 2003. The second concerns a sample of employees observed at a particular point in time, such as a sample of automobile workers observed at the beginning of 2004. In contrast, time series studies involve one or more variables that are observed at several, usually equally spaced, points in time. The stock price example mentioned previously fits this description. We observe the price of a particular stock and possibly the price of a market index at the beginning of every week, say, and then try to explain the movement of the stock's price through time.

Regression uses one or more independent variables to explain a single dependent variable.

A second categorization of regression analysis involves the number of explanatory variables in the analysis. First, we must introduce some terms. In every regression study there is a single variable that we are trying to explain or predict. This is called the **dependent** variable (or the **response** variable) and is often denoted generically as *Y*. To help explain or predict the dependent variable, we use one or more **independent** variables. These variables are also called **explanatory** variables or **predictor** variables, and they are often denoted generically as *X*'s. If there is a single independent variable, the analysis is called **simple regression**. If there are several independent variables, it is called **multiple regression**.

There are important differences between simple and multiple regression. The primary difference, as the name implies, is that simple regression is simpler. The calculations are simpler, the interpretation of output is somewhat simpler, and fewer complications can occur. We will begin with a simple regression example to introduce the ideas of regression. Then we will move on to the more general topic of multiple regression.

We will show how to estimate regression equations that describe relationships between variables. We will also discuss the interpretation of these equations, explain numerical measures that indicate the goodness of fit of the equations we estimate, and describe how to use the regression equations for prediction.[1]

The Least-Squares Line

The basis for regression is a rather simple idea. If we create a scatterplot of one variable *Y* versus another variable *X*, we obtain a swarm of points that indicates any possible relationship between these two variables. To quantify this relationship, we try to find the "best-fitting" line (or curve) through the points in the graph. But what do we mean by "best-fitting"?

Consider the scatterplot in Figure 12.1. The line shown is one possible fit. It appears to be a reasonably good fit, but we need a numerical measure of the goodness-of-fit so that we can compare this fit with the fits of other possible lines.

The measure commonly used is the **sum of squared residuals**. Here, a **residual** is defined as the vertical distance from a point to the line, as illustrated for points A and B. If the point is above the line (point A), the residual is positive; if the point is below the line (point B), the residual is negative. To measure the goodness-of-fit, we square all of the

---

[1]The terms *prediction* and *forecasting* are practically synonyms. Some analysts reserve the term *forecasting* for future values of a time series variable, whereas they use the term *prediction* for any type of variable, time series or otherwise. However, we will not make this distinction.

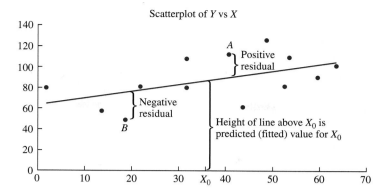

Figure 12.1

Scatterplot with Proposed Regression Line

residuals and sum them. Intuitively, a good fit should have a small sum of squared residuals. In fact, the line we want is the line with the *minimum* sum of squared residuals, where the minimum is over all possible lines. We call this the line the **least-squares line**. This is the line that is found by regression. (Why do we *square* the residuals? One reason is to make them all positive. Another is to severely penalize large residuals. The most compelling reason, though, is that this is the way it has been done by statisticians for many years.)

> A **residual** is a prediction error. It is the difference between an observed Y and the predicted Y from the regression line.

> The **least-squares regression line** is the line that minimizes the sum of squared residuals.

The details of the procedure used to find the least-squares line are beyond the scope of this book. The procedure is basically a calculus problem. Fortunately, it is done automatically by regression software, including software built into Excel. We will rely on this software to find the least-squares line, and we will then interpret the results.

Prediction and Fitted Values

Once we find the least-squares line, we can use it for prediction. Geometrically, this is easy. Given any value of X, we predict the corresponding value of Y to be the height of the line above this X. This is shown in Figure 12.1 for the value X_0. The predicted Y value is called the **fitted value**.

> A **fitted value** is a predicted value of Y found by substituting given X's into the regression equation.

In contrast, the height of any point is the **actual value** of Y for this point. Therefore, we have the following important relationship. It states that the residual for any point is the difference between the observed value of Y and the predicted value of Y.

> *Relationship between residuals and fitted values*
> $$\text{Residual} = \text{Actual value} - \text{Fitted value} \qquad \textbf{(12.1)}$$

In general, we will estimate the least-squares line as a regression equation relating Y to one or more X's. For example, this equation might be $Y = 5 + 3X$. To predict Y for any given value of X, we simply substitute this value of X into the regression equation. This gives the fitted value of Y. For example, with the proposed equation, if $X = 2$, the fitted (predicted) value of Y is $5 + 3(2) = 11$. If we happen to know that the actual value of Y for this point is 13, say, then the residual is positive: $13 - 11 = 2$. On the other hand, if the actual value is 8, then the residual is negative: $8 - 11 = -3$.

Measures of Goodness-of-Fit

Besides the sum of squared residuals, other measures of goodness-of-fit typically are quoted in regression analyses. We briefly describe these here and discuss them in more detail in subsequent sections.

Standard Error of Estimate

The sum of squared residuals is measured in *squared* units of the Y variable. For example, if Y is sales in dollars, then the sum of squared residuals is in squared dollars. It is more meaningful to obtain a related measure in dollars. The resulting measure is called the **standard error of estimate**. It is obtained by averaging and then taking the square root, as shown in the following formula. In this formula, n is the number of observations and k is the number of independent variables in the regression equation.

> *Formula for standard error of estimate*
> $$\text{Standard error of estimate} = \sqrt{\text{Sum of squared residuals}/(n - k - 1)} \quad \textbf{(12.2)}$$

The standard error of estimate is a measure of the magnitude of the prediction errors we are likely to make, based on the regression equation.

The standard error of estimate is useful because it provides an estimate of the magnitude of the prediction errors we are likely to make. For example, if the standard error of estimate is $150, then as a ballpark estimate, we expect our predictions to be off by about $150. More precisely, the standard error of estimate behaves like a standard deviation. Therefore, from the well-known empirical rule of statistics, we expect about 2/3 of our predictions to be no greater than $150 (one standard error) in magnitude, and we expect about 95% of our predictions to be no greater than $300 (2 standard errors) in magnitude.

Multiple R and R-Square

Another goodness-of-fit measure is called the **multiple R**. It is defined as the correlation between the actual Y values and the fitted Y values. In general, a correlation is a number between -1 and $+1$ that measures the goodness-of-fit of the linear relationship between two variables. A correlation close to -1 or $+1$ indicates a tight linear fit, whereas a correlation close to 0 tends to indicate no linear fit—usually a shapeless swarm of points. In regression, we want the fitted Y values to be close to the actual Y values, so we want a scatterplot of the actual versus the fitted values to be close to a 45° line, with the multiple R close to $+1$.

> *Formula for multiple R*
> $$\text{Multiple } R = \text{Correlation between actual } Y\text{'s and fitted } Y\text{'s} \quad \textbf{(12.3)}$$

How large should multiple R be to indicate a "good" fit? This is difficult to answer directly, other than to say "the larger, the better." However, if we square the multiple R, we get a measure that has a more direct interpretation. This measure is known simply as **R-square**. It represents *the percentage of the variation of the Y values explained by the X's included in the regression equation*. For example, if multiple R is 0.8, then R-square is 0.64, so we say that 64% of the variation of Y has been explained by the regression. The idea is that the X's included in the regression are presumably related to Y, so that they help explain why the Y values vary as they do. Naturally, we want the X's to explain as much of this variation as possible, so we want R-square values as close to 1 as possible.

> **Formula for R-square**
>
> R-square $=$ (multiple R)^2 $=$ Percentage of variation of Y explained by regression (12.4)

The R-square value can never decrease as more independent variables are added to the regression equation.

Although R-square is probably the most frequently quoted measure in regression analyses, some caution is necessary. First, R-square values are often disappointingly low. Some variables in business are simply not easy to explain, particularly those in behavioral areas. Regressions in these areas sometimes have R-squares in the 10% to 20% range. This does not necessarily mean that these regressions are useless. After all, explaining 20% of the variation in some variable is better than not explaining anything at all. Second, R-squares can sometimes be inflated by adding X's to the equation that do not really belong. This is due to the mathematical property that R-square can only *increase*, never decrease, when extra X's are added to an equation. In general, we have to avoid the temptation to build large equations with many X's just to pump up R-square. It is usually preferable to include only a few "important" X's and omit those that yield only marginal increases in R-square. Finding the "right set" of X's, however, is not easy. In fact, it is probably the biggest challenge to the analyst and takes a good deal of experience.

12.3 SIMPLE REGRESSION MODELS

In this section we discuss how to estimate the regression equation for a dependent variable Y based on a single independent variable X. (The common terminology is that we "regress Y on X.") This equation is the equation of the least-squares line passing through the scatterplot of Y versus X. Since we are estimating a *straight* line, the regression equation will be of the form $Y = a + bX$, where, as in basic algebra, a is called the **intercept** and b is called the **slope**.

> **Equation for simple regression**
> $$Y = a + bX$$ (12.5)

Regression-Based Trend Models

A special case of simple regression is when the only independent variable is time, usually labeled t (rather than X). In this case the dependent variable Y is some time series variable, such as a company's monthly sales, and the purpose of the regression is to see whether this dependent variable follows a trend through time. If there is a *linear* trend, then the equation for Y has the form $Y = a + bt$. If $b > 0$, then Y increases by b units every time period, whereas if $b < 0$, then Y decreases by b units every time period. Alternatively, if there is an *exponential* trend, the equation for Y has the form $Y = ae^{bt}$. In this case, the variable Y changes by a constant *percentage* each time period, and this percentage is approximately equal to the coefficient in the exponent, b. For example, if $b = 0.025$, then Y increases by about 2.5% per period, whereas if $b = -0.025$, then Y decreases by about 2.5% per period.

> With a **linear** trendline, the variable changes by a constant *amount* each period.
>
> With an **exponential** trendline, the variable changes by a constant *percentage* each period.

The following example illustrates how easily trends can be estimated with Excel.

EXAMPLE	12.1 FORECASTING SALES AT BEST CHIPS

It is customary to index time from 1 to the number of time periods.

The Best Chips Company produces and sells potato chips throughout the country. Its sales have been growing steadily over the past 10 years, as shown in Figure 12.2 and the file **ExponentialGrowth.xls**.[2] (Note that we have indexed the years so that year 1 corresponds to 1993.) The company would like to predict its sales for the next couple of years, assuming that the upward trend it has observed in the past 10 years will continue in the future. How should it proceed?

Figure 12.2

Historical Sales at Best Chips

	A	B
1	Sales at Best Chips	
2		
3	Historical data	
4	Year (1=1993)	Sales ($ millions)
5	1	1.345
6	2	1.352
7	3	1.463
8	4	1.511
9	5	1.610
10	6	1.649
11	7	1.713
12	8	1.850
13	9	2.051
14	10	2.203

Objective To fit linear and exponential trendlines to the company's historical sales data and to use the better of these trendlines to predict future sales.

Solution

We begin by using the Chart Wizard to create the X-Y plot of Sales versus Year shown in Figure 12.3. It is clear that sales are increasing through time, but it is not absolutely clear whether they are increasing at a constant rate, which would favor a linear trendline, or at an increasing rate, which would favor an exponential trendline. Therefore, we will try fitting both of these.

→ EXCEL TOOL: *Creating a Scatterplot with the Chart Wizard*
To create a scatterplot in Excel, click on the Chart Wizard and select the X-Y (Scatter) option. Then in the second step of the wizard, click on the Series tab and select the ranges for the X values (those on the horizontal axis) and the Y values (those on the vertical axis). This is the key step. You can experiment with other options, but they are mainly for formatting the chart. ■

Fitting a Linear Trendline

To superimpose a linear trendline on any scatterplot, we select the chart and then select the Chart/Add Trendline menu item. This brings up the dialog box in Figure 12.4. You can select any of six types of trendlines. For now, select the default Linear option. Also, click on the Options tab and check the Display equation box. (You can also elect to show the *R*-square value if you like.) The result appears in Figure 12.5 (page 614).

---

[2]We will omit the "Where Do the Numbers Come From?" sections in this chapter because the data sources should be obvious.

Figure 12.3

Time Series Plot of
Sales

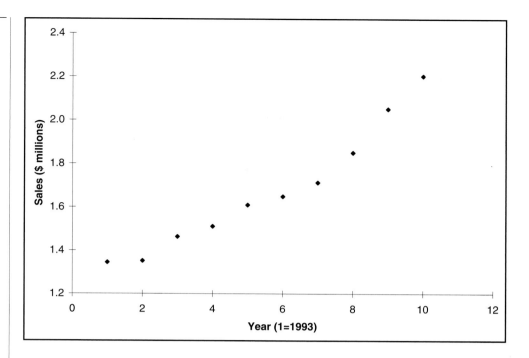

Figure 12.4

Dialog Box for
Adding a Trendline

→ **EXCEL TOOL:** *Inserting Trendlines*

It is easy to fit any of several types of trendlines to an X-Y plot of some variable versus time. To do so, select the chart and then select the Chart/Add Trendline menu item. This brings up a dialog box where you can select one of several types of trendlines. In addition, under the Options tab you can elect to display an equation of the trendline and/or the R-square value on the chart. This equation and/or the R-square value appear in a textbox. You can select this textbox and move it or change its font size as you like. ∎

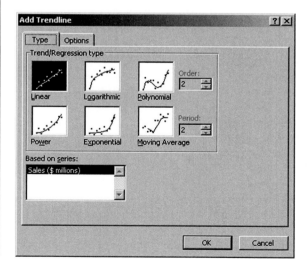

Figure 12.5

Plot with
Superimposed
Linear Trendline

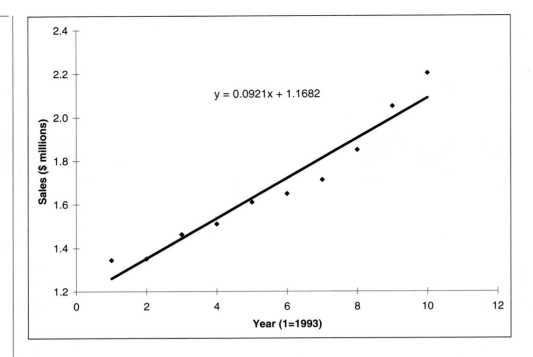

*The coefficient of time
in the linear trendline
equation represents
the change in the
variable per time
period.*

This figure shows the best-fitting straight line to the points, and it indicates that the equation of this straight line is $y = 0.0921x + 1.1682$. Here, y corresponds to sales and x corresponds to year.[3] The most important part of this equation is the coefficient of x, 0.0921. It implies that sales are increasing by $0.0921 million per year—*if* we believe that the linear trendline provides a good fit.

Fitting an Exponential Trendline

*The coefficient of time
in the exponent of the
exponential trendline
equation represents
the (approximate)
percentage change in
the variable per time
period.*

To obtain an exponential trendline, we go through the same procedure except that we select the Exponential option in Figure 12.4. The resulting *curve* appears in Figure 12.6. The equation for the curve is $y = 1.2278e^{0.0541x}$. The most important part of this equation is the coefficient in the exponent, 0.0541. It implies that sales are increasing by approximately 5.4% per year. In general, the coefficient in the exponent of an exponential trendline equation, when expressed as a percentage, indicates the approximate percentage by which the series is changing each period. Note that if this coefficient were negative, such as -0.0325, then the series would be *decreasing* by approximately 3.25% each period (and the plot would be trending downward). (We say "approximate" because the exact rate is $e^b - 1$ when the coefficient in the exponent is b. For example, when $b = 0.0541$, the exact rate is $e^{0.0541} - 1 = 0.0556$, or 5.56%.)

Measuring the Goodness-of-Fit

Which of these trendlines provides the better fit? We can proceed in two ways. First, we can "eyeball" it. Looking at the superimposed trendlines in Figures 12.5 and 12.6, it appears that the exponential fit is slightly better. However, the typical way to measure fits to a trendline through time is to calculate the historical predictions from each curve and the corresponding absolute percentage errors (APEs). We find the predictions by plugging the

---

[3]Although we like to use the variable t to denote time, Excel uses the variable x in its trendline equations.

Figure 12.6

Plot with
Superimposed
Exponential
Trendline

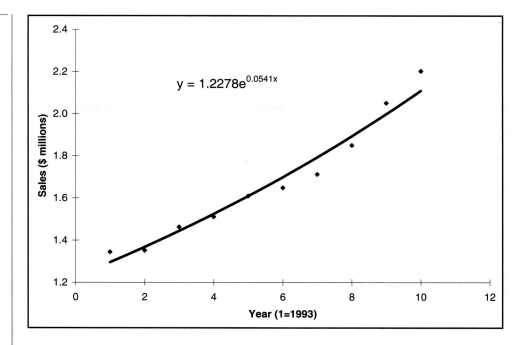

$y = 1.2278e^{0.0541x}$

year indexes (1 to 10) into the trendline equations. We then calculate the APE for each year from the following equation.

Absolute percentage error

$$\text{APE} = \frac{\left| \text{Actual sales} - \text{Predicted sales} \right|}{\text{Actual sales}}$$

(12.6)

A measure of goodness-of-fit is then the average of these APE values, denoted by MAPE (mean absolute percentage error).[4] This measure is quite intuitive. For example, if it is 2.1%, then we know that the predicted values for the historical period are off—too low or too high—by 2.1% on average.

A useful measure of the goodness-of-fit of any trendline through time is **MAPE**, the mean absolute percentage error. It is the average of the APE values calculated from equation (12.6).

All of this is implemented in Figure 12.7 (page 616). To create the predictions, APEs, and MAPEs, proceed as follows.

1 **Predictions.** Calculate the predictions from the linear trendline by entering the formula

=1.1682+0.0921*A5

---

[4]We will see this measure and two other measures of forecast errors when we study time series forecasting in more detail in Sections 12.5–12.7.

Figure 12.7

Evaluating the
Goodness-of-Fit of
Each Trendline

	A	B	C	D	E	F	G	H
1	Sales at Best Chips							
2								
3	Historical data			Predictions		Absolute percentage errors		
4	Year (1=1993)	Sales ($ millions)		Linear	Exponential	Linear	Exponential	
5	1	1.345		1.260	1.295	0.0630	0.0370	
6	2	1.352		1.352	1.367	0.0003	0.0112	
7	3	1.463		1.445	1.443	0.0126	0.0135	
8	4	1.511		1.537	1.523	0.0169	0.0082	
9	5	1.610		1.629	1.608	0.0116	0.0012	
10	6	1.649		1.721	1.698	0.0435	0.0294	
11	7	1.713		1.813	1.792	0.0583	0.0461	
12	8	1.850		1.905	1.892	0.0297	0.0224	
13	9	2.051		1.997	1.997	0.0263	0.0265	
14	10	2.203		2.089	2.108	0.0517	0.0433	
15	11			2.181	2.225			
16	12			2.273	2.348			
17								
18					MAPE	0.0314	0.0239	

in cell D5 and copying it down to cell D16. (Note that cells D15 and D16 then contain the predictions for 2003 and 2004. There is no way to know how good these future predictions are until we observe actual sales in 2003 and 2004.) Similarly, calculate the predictions from the exponential trendline by entering the formula

=1.2278*EXP(0.0541*A5)

in cell E5 and copying it down to cell E16. Note that we calculate e to some power in Excel with Excel's EXP function.

→ **EXCEL FUNCTION: EXP**
The formula =EXP(value) is equivalent to the special number e raised to the power value. (Here, e is approximately equal to 2.718.) For example, $e^{2.5}$ can be calculated in Excel with the formula =EXP(2.5), which evaluates to 12.1825. The EXP function is often called the "antilog" function. ■

2 **APE values.** Calculate all of the APE values at once by entering the formula

=ABS($B5-D5)/$B5

in cell F5 and copying it to the range F5:G14. This follows directly from equation (12.6) and Excel's ABS (absolute value) function.

3 **MAPE values.** Calculate the MAPE for each trendline by entering the formula

=AVERAGE(F5:F14)

in cell F18 and copying it to cell G18.

Discussion of the Results

The MAPE values confirm that the exponential trendline is slightly better than the linear trendline. The exponential trendline is off, on average, by 2.39%, whereas the similar figure for the linear trendline is 3.14%. Using the exponential trendline, we estimate that sales are increasing by slightly more than 5% per year. The predictions in cells E15 and E16 essentially project this 5% increase to the years 2003 and 2004. Again, however, we can't tell how good these future predictions are until we observe *actual* sales in 2003 and 2004.

→ **TECHNICAL NOTE: Estimating an Exponential Trendline with Regression**
Excel actually uses regression to estimate the exponential trendline. However, regression always estimates linear equations of the form Y = a + bX. Therefore, to estimate an equation of the form Y = ae^{bt}, a logarithmic transformation is required. By taking logarithms of both sides and using the rules of logarithms, we obtain ln(Y) = ln(a) + bt, which is linear in time t.

[The dependent variable is now ln(Y).] Excel actually makes this transformation behind the scenes when it estimates the exponential trendline, but it hides the details from us. ∎

Caution about Exponential Trendlines

Exponential trendlines are often used in predicting sales and other economic quantities. However, we urge caution with such predictions. It is difficult for *any* company to sustain a given percentage increase year after year. For example, we used this same procedure on quarterly sales at the computer chip giant Intel, starting in 1986. Through 1996, Intel sales rose at a staggering rate of approximately 27% per year, and the corresponding exponential fit was quite good. However, since that time, Intel sales have gone up much more slowly, and in some quarters they have actually decreased. If we had used the exponential trendline through 1996 to forecast sales after 1996, we would have overpredicted by huge amounts! ∎

Using an Independent Variable Other Than Time

We are not restricted to using time as the independent variable in simple regression. Any variable X that is related to the dependent variable Y is a candidate. The following example illustrates one such possibility. It shows how we can still take advantage of Excel's Add Trendline option, even though the resulting trendline is not what we usually think of with trend—a trend through *time*.

EXAMPLE | 12.2 ESTIMATING TOTAL COST FOR A SINGLE PRODUCT

Consider a company that produces a single product. For each of the past 16 months, the company has kept track of the number of units produced as well as the total cost of production. These data appear in Figure 12.8 and the file **CostRegression1.xls**. What can simple regression tell us about the relationship between these two variables? How can it be used to predict future production costs?

Figure 12.8

Cost and Production Data for a Single Product

	A	B	C
1	Cost Regression Example		
2			
3	Month	Units Produced	Total Cost
4	1	500	131000
5	2	600	135000
6	3	400	104000
7	4	300	76000
8	5	800	186000
9	6	900	190100
10	7	600	150000
11	8	400	98000
12	9	300	78000
13	10	200	60000
14	11	400	108000
15	12	600	152000
16	13	700	158000
17	14	500	134380
18	15	300	86000
19	16	200	60000

Objective To use simple regression to estimate the relationship between Units Produced and Total Cost, and to use this relationship to predict future total costs.

Solution

A scatterplot of Y versus X is always a good place to start in any regression analysis.

When we try to relate two variables with regression, it is always a good idea to create a scatterplot of the two variables first, just to see whether there is any relationship worth pursuing. This can be done with Excel's Chart Wizard in the usual way, which leads to the scatterplot in Figure 12.9. This plot indicates a clear linear relationship, where Total Cost increases linearly as Units Produced increases.

Figure 12.9 Scatterplot of Total Cost versus Units Produced

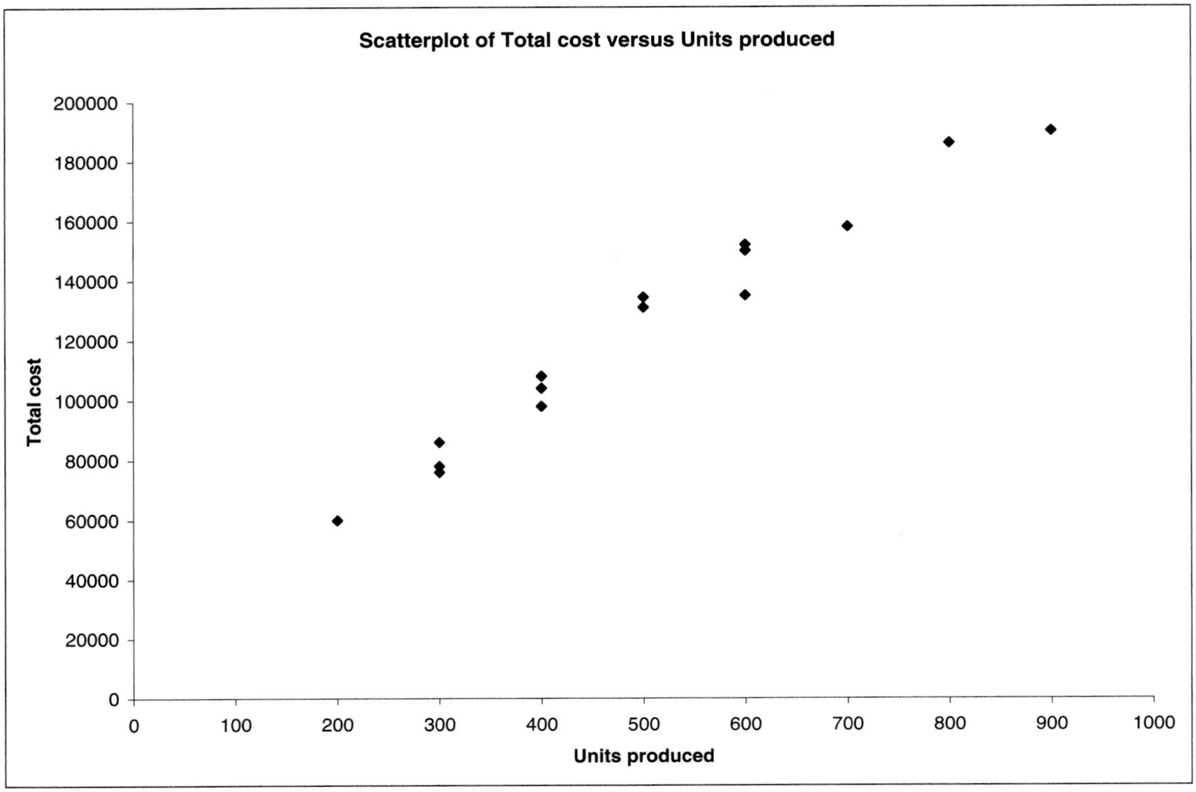

Fitting a Linear Trendline

Excel's Trendline tool can be used even when the independent variable X does not represent time.

We can now fit a straight line to this plot using Excel's Trendline tool. To do so, select the chart and then select the Chart/Add Trendline menu item. In the resulting dialog box, click on the Type tab and select the Linear option. Then click on the Options tab and check the Display equation and Display R-squared boxes. The results appear in Figure 12.10.

Discussion of the Results

The equation of the straight line has a slope, 198.47, and an intercept, 23,643. For this example both numbers have a natural interpretation. The slope corresponds to the unit variable cost of production. We estimate that each extra unit produced contributes $198.47 to total cost. The intercept corresponds to the fixed cost of production. We estimate that the fixed cost is $23,643, regardless of the production level.

As discussed previously, the R-square value is the percentage of variation of Total Cost explained by Units Produced. In this case, Units Produced explains slightly more than 97% of the variation in Total Cost; only about 3% of this variation is left unexplained. Alternatively, multiple R, the square root of R-square, is the correlation between the actual Total Cost values and the fitted Total Cost values, as predicted by the regression equation. In this case, multiple R is $\sqrt{0.9717} = 0.9858$.

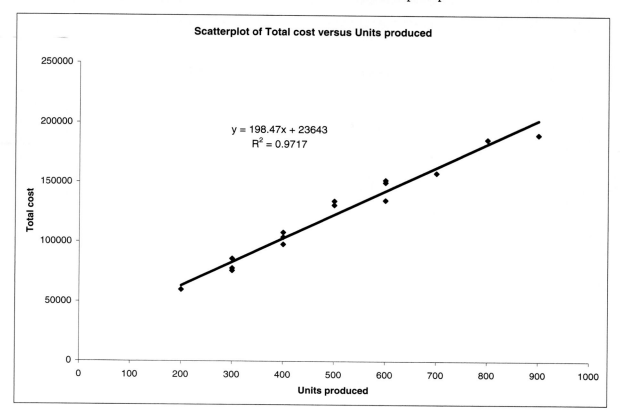

We can now find the fitted values, the residuals, and the standard error of estimate. The results appear in Figure 12.11 (page 620). (Rows 4–19 contain the historical data for the first 16 months. Rows 20 and 21 are used for prediction in the next 2 months.) We first insert the intercept and slope values from the chart in cells F4 and F5. To get the fitted values for any months, we substitute into the regression equation. To do this, enter the formula

=$F$4+$F$5*B4

in cell H4 and copy it down to cell H21. Note that the last two of these are actually predictions of future months, given the proposed values of Units Produced in cells B20 and B21.

To calculate the residuals as differences between actual and fitted values, enter the formula

=C4-H4

in cell I4 and copy it down to cell H19. (Note that no residuals are available for months 17 and 18 because their *actual* total costs are not yet known.) Then calculate the standard error of estimate in cell F8 with the formula

=SQRT(SUMSQ(I4:I19)/(16-1-1))

This formula, based on equation (12.2), uses Excel's SUMSQ function to sum the squares of the residuals, and then it divides by the number of observations minus the number of independent variables minus 1.

Figure 12.11

Simple Regression Output

	A	B	C	D	E	F	G	H	I
1	Cost Regression Example								
2									
3	Month	Units Produced	Total Cost		Regression parameters from chart			Fitted Values	Residuals
4	1	500	131000		Intercept	23643		122878	8122
5	2	600	135000		Slope	198.47		142725	-7725
6	3	400	104000					103031	969
7	4	300	76000		Standard error of estimate			83184	-7184
8	5	800	186000			7262		182419	3581
9	6	900	190100					202266	-12166
10	7	600	150000					142725	7275
11	8	400	98000					103031	-5031
12	9	300	78000					83184	-5184
13	10	200	60000					63337	-3337
14	11	400	108000					103031	4969
15	12	600	152000					142725	9275
16	13	700	158000					162572	-4572
17	14	500	134380					122878	11502
18	15	300	86000					83184	2816
19	16	200	60000					63337	-3337
20	17	400						103031	
21	18	800						182419	
22									
23						Future predictions			
24									

→ **EXCEL FUNCTION: SUMSQ**
The SUMSQ function, in the form **=SUMSQ(range)**, returns the sum of the squares of the values in the specified range. ∎

The most important aspects of the output are the following:

- We estimate that each additional unit produced adds about $198 to total cost.

- The large *R*-square and multiple *R* values confirm exactly what the scatterplot indicates—that there is a very strong linear relationship between Total Cost and Units Produced.

- The standard error of estimate indicates that the prediction errors based on this regression equation will be in the neighborhood of $7000—many prediction errors will be less than this value and a few will be more. This large an error might sound like a lot, but it is not all that large compared to the magnitudes of total costs, which are often well over $100,000. ∎

PROBLEMS

Solutions for problems whose numbers appear within a color box can be found in the Student Solutions Manual. Order your copy today at http://e-catalog.thomsonlearning.com/110/ by using ISBN 0-534-39687-9.

Skill-Building Problems

1. The file **P12_01.xls** contains quarterly sales at Johnson & Johnson from 1991 through the first quarter of 2001. Chart these sales and fit both a linear trendline and an exponential trendline through the points. Then calculate the MAPE for each. Does either provide a good fit? Which of the two provides the better fit? Interpret the better-fitting trendline.

2. The file **P12_02.xls** contains quarterly sales at Intel from 1986 through the first quarter of 2001. Chart these sales through the end of 1996 only, and fit an exponential trendline to these points. Interpret the growth rate you find. (Is it annual or quarterly?) Calculate the MAPE for these years. Then use this exponential trendline to predict the quarterly sales from 1997 on, and calculate the MAPE for this period. Describe your results in a concise memo to Intel management.

3. The file **P12_03.xls** gives the annual sales for Microsoft (in millions of dollars) for a 10-year period.
a. Fit an exponential trendline to these data.

b. By what percentage do you estimate that Microsoft will grow each year?

c. Why can't a high rate of exponential growth continue for a long time?

d. Rather than an exponential curve, what type of curve might better represent the growth of a new technology?

e. If you can find Microsoft sales data since the period shown in the file, check whether its sales continued at the exponential rate from part **b**.

4. The file **P12_04.xls** contains monthly data on production levels and production costs during a 4-year period for a company that produces a single product. Use simple regression on all of the data to see how Total Cost is related to Units Produced. Use the resulting equation to predict total cost in month 49, given that the proposed production level for that month is 450 units. Do you see anything "wrong" with the analysis? How should you modify your analysis if your main task is to find an equation useful for predicting *future* costs, and you know that the company installed new machinery at the end of month 18? Write a concise memo to management that describes your findings.

5. Management of a home appliance store in Charlotte would like to understand the growth pattern of the monthly sales of VCR units over the past 2 years. The managers have recorded the relevant data in the file **P12_05.xls**. Have the sales of VCR units been growing linearly over the past 24 months? By examining the results of a linear trendline, explain why or why not.

6. Do the sales prices of houses in a given community vary systematically with their sizes (as measured in square feet)? Attempt to answer this question by estimating a simple regression model where the sales price of the house is the dependent variable and the size of the house is the independent variable. Use the sample data given in **P12_06.xls**. Interpret your estimated model, the associated *R*-square value, and the associated standard error of estimate.

7. The file **P12_07.xls** contains observations of the American minimum wage during each of the years from 1950 through 1994. Has the minimum wage been growing at roughly a *constant* rate over this period? Use simple linear regression analysis to address this question. Explain your results.

8. Based on the data in the file **P12_08.xls** from the U.S. Department of Agriculture, explore the relationship between the number of farms (*X*) and the average size of a farm (*Y*) in the United States between 1950 and 1997. Specifically, generate a simple linear regression model and interpret it.

Skill-Extending Problems

9. We discussed linear and exponential trendlines. Another popular choice is a *power* trendline, also called a *constant elasticity* trendline. This trendline has the form $y = ax^b$, and it has the property that when *x* increases by 1%, *y* changes by a *constant* percentage. In fact, this constant percentage is approximately equal to the exponent *b* (which could be positive or negative). The power trendline is often cited in the economics literature, where, for example, *x* might be price and *y* might be demand. Fortunately, it can be found through Excel's Trendline tool; the power trendline is just another option. Estimate and interpret a power trendline for the data on demand and price of some commodity listed in the file **P12_09.xls**. In particular, if price increases by 1%, what do you expect to happen to demand? Calculate the MAPE for this power trendline. Would you say it provides a good fit?

10. Sometimes curvature in a scatterplot can be fit adequately (especially to the naked eye) by several trendlines. We discussed the exponential trendline, and the power trendline is discussed in the previous problem. Still another fairly simple trendline is the *parabola*, a polynomial of order 2 (also called a *quadratic*). For the demand-price data in the file **P12_10.xls**, fit all three of these types of trendlines to the data, and calculate the MAPE for each. Which provides the best fit? (*Hint*: Note that a polynomial of order 2 is still another of Excel's Trendline options.)

11. The management of Beta Technologies, Inc., is trying to determine the variable that best explains the variation of employee salaries using a sample of 52 full-time employees; see the file **P12_11.xls**. Estimate simple linear regression models to identify which of the following has the *strongest* linear relationship with annual salary: the employee's gender, age, number of years of relevant work experience prior to employment at Beta, number of years of employment at Beta, or number of years of post-secondary education. Provide support for your conclusion.

12.4 MULTIPLE REGRESSION MODELS

When we try to explain a dependent variable Y with regression, there are often a multitude of independent variables to choose from. In this section we explore multiple regression, where the regression equation for Y includes a number of independent variables, the X's. The general form of this equation is shown in the box. Geometrically, this equation represents a "hyperplane" through a scatter of points in $(k + 1)$-dimensional space (k X's and 1 Y). However, unless $k = 1$ or $k = 2$, this hyperplane is impossible to draw. Nevertheless, it is helpful to keep the image of a plane passing through a set of points in mind as you study multiple regression.

> **Multiple regression equation**
> $$Y = a + b_1X_1 + b_2X_2 + \cdots + b_kX_k \qquad (12.7)$$

In equation (12.7), a is again the Y-intercept, and b_1 through b_k are the slopes. Collectively, we refer to a and the b's as the **regression coefficients**. Each slope coefficient is the expected change in Y when that particular X increases by 1 unit and the other X's in the equation remain constant. For example, b_1 is the expected change in Y when X_1 increases by 1 unit and the other X's in the equation, X_2 through X_k, remain constant. The intercept a is typically less important. Literally, it is the expected value of Y when all of the X's equal 0. However, this makes sense only if it is practical for all of the X's to equal 0, and this is rarely the case.

> The **regression coefficients** are the intercept and slopes of the regression equation.

We illustrate these ideas in the following extension of Example 12.2.

EXAMPLE | 12.3 ESTIMATING TOTAL COST FOR SEVERAL PRODUCTS

Suppose the company from Example 12.2 now produces three different products, A, B, and C. The company has kept track of the number of units produced of each product and the total production cost for the past 15 months. These data appear in Figure 12.12 and in the file **CostRegression2.xls**. What can multiple regression tell us about the relationship between these variables? How can multiple regression be used to predict future production costs?

Figure 12.12

Cost and Production Data for Multiple Products

	A	B	C	D	E
1	Multiple regression example				
2					
3	Month	Units A	Units B	Units C	Total Cost
4	1	696	819	895	58789
5	2	627	512	925	50276
6	3	122	323	814	43703
7	4	313	981	670	50857
8	5	340	884	356	46397
9	6	462	599	673	46731
10	7	269	302	737	40328
11	8	343	495	878	42368
12	9	986	191	592	44617
13	10	555	314	467	40515
14	11	908	593	749	55546
15	12	595	115	458	36856
16	13	557	369	160	35697
17	14	271	550	457	40130
18	15	878	750	983	59929

Objective To use multiple regression to estimate the relationship between units produced of three products and the total production cost, and to use this relationship to predict future total costs.

Solution

A useful first step in multiple regression is to create a scatterplot of Y versus each of the X's.

The dependent variable Y is again Total Cost, but there are now three potential X's, Units A, Units B, and Units C. We are not required to use all three of these, but we will do so here. In fact, it is again a good idea to begin with scatterplots of Y versus each X to see which X's are indeed related to Y. We did this, obtaining three scatterplots, a typical one of which appears in Figure 12.13. This scatterplot—and the ones for products A and C are similar—indicates a fairly strong linear relationship between Total Cost and Units B.

Figure 12.13 Scatterplot of Total Cost versus Units B

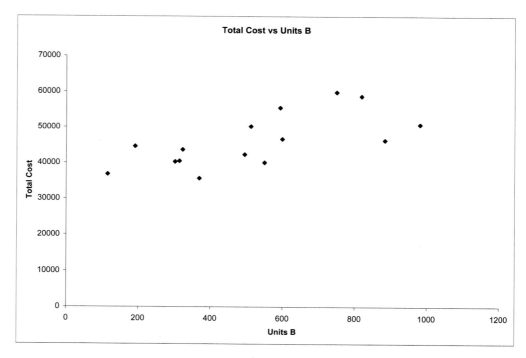

USING ANALYSIS TOOLPAK

When there are multiple independent variables, Excel's Trendline option cannot be used to find the regression equation.

Unfortunately, when there are multiple X's, we cannot estimate the multiple regression equation by using Excel's Trendline option as we did with simple regression. Instead, we must use a statistical software package or an Excel add-in. Fortunately, Excel includes such an add-in, called Analysis ToolPak. (See the following paragraph about loading this add-in.)

→ **EXCEL TOOL:** *The Analysis ToolPak Add-In*
The Analysis ToolPak add-in is part of Excel. It performs a number of statistical analyses, including regression. To use it, you must first make sure it is loaded in memory. To do this, select the Tool/Add-Ins menu item, and if necessary, check the Analysis ToolPak item. (You do not need to check the Analysis ToolPak–VBA item. We will not be using it.) You will know the Analysis ToolPak is loaded because there will now be a Data Analysis menu item under the Tools menu. ■

To run the regression analysis with Analysis ToolPak, select the Tools/Data Analysis menu item, select Regression from the list of Analysis Tools, and fill out the resulting dialog box as shown in Figure 12.14. The following options are the most important; you can experiment with the other settings.

- The range for the X's must be contiguous. In other words, the data for the independent variables must be in adjacent columns. You might have to move the data around to get the X's next to each other.

- It is useful for reporting purposes to include the variable names (row 3 in our case) in the Y and X's ranges. If you do this, you should check the Labels box.

- There are a number of options on where to put the output. We chose cell G3 (of the same worksheet as the data) as the upper left corner of our output range.

- If you check the Residuals box, you automatically get the fitted (predicted) values of the Y's and the corresponding residuals.

Figure 12.14

Regression Dialog Box from Analysis ToolPak

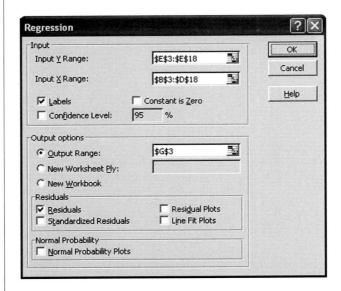

Discussion of the Results

The resulting output appears in Figure 12.15. We will not explain *all* of this output, but we will focus on the highlights. The most important part is the regression equation itself, which is implied by the values in the H19:H22 range:

Predicted Total Cost = 20,261 + 12.802Units A + 17.691Units B + 15.230Units C

The interpretation is much like that in simple regression. Each coefficient of a Units variable can be interpreted as a variable cost. For example, we estimate that each extra unit of product B contributes about $17.69 to total cost. The constant term, 20,261, is again the estimated fixed cost of production. This cost is incurred regardless of the level of production.

The other important outputs are R-square, multiple R, the standard error of estimate, the fitted values, and the residuals.

- The R-square value is the percentage of variation of Total Cost explained by the *combination* of all three independent variables. We see that these three Units variables explain about 94.6% of the variation in Total Cost—a fairly high percentage.

- The multiple R, the square root of R-square, is the correlation between the actual Y's and fitted values. Because R-square is large, the multiple R is also large: 0.973. This

Figure 12.15 Regression Output for Multiple Products

	G	H	I	J	K	L	M	N	O
3	SUMMARY OUTPUT								
4									
5	*Regression Statistics*								
6	Multiple R	0.972577248							
7	R Square	0.945906504							
8	Adjusted R Square	0.931153733							
9	Standard Error	1980.505375							
10	Observations	15							
11									
12	ANOVA								
13		*df*	*SS*	*MS*	*F*	*Significance F*			
14	Regression	3	754480290.6	251493430	64.11721	2.96954E-07			
15	Residual	11	43146416.96	3922401.54					
16	Total	14	797626707.6						
17									
18		*Coefficients*	*Standard Error*	*t Stat*	*P-value*	*Lower 95%*	*Upper 95%*	*Lower 95.0%*	*Upper 95.0%*
19	Intercept	20261.27255	1968.132719	10.2946678	5.53E-07	15929.43945	24593.10565	15929.43945	24593.10565
20	Units A	12.80187952	2.082756581	6.1466038	7.24E-05	8.217760879	17.38599817	8.217760879	17.38599817
21	Units B	17.69116546	2.137036333	8.27836438	4.71E-06	12.98757783	22.3947531	12.98757783	22.3947531
22	Units C	15.22981506	2.346388351	6.49074781	4.48E-05	10.06544651	20.39418361	10.06544651	20.39418361
23									
24									
25									
26	RESIDUAL OUTPUT								
27									
28	*Observation*	*Predicted Total Cost*	*Residuals*						
29	1	57291.12969	1497.870306						
30	2	51433.50666	-1157.506662						
31	3	39934.41776	3768.582241						
32	4	51827.27025	-970.2702529						
33	5	45674.71602	722.2839786						
34	6	47022.41454	-291.4145408						
35	7	40272.08381	55.91618561						
36	8	46781.22176	-4413.221757						
37	9	45278.98888	-661.9888833						
38	10	40033.66528	481.3347223						
39	11	53783.37176	1762.62824						
40	12	36888.1302	-32.13019623						
41	13	36356.72991	-659.7299137						
42	14	40420.74839	-290.7483911						
43	15	59740.60508	188.3949238						
44									
45			95% prediction interval						
46	16	45922.388	41961.377	49883.398					
47	17	44906.803	40945.793	48867.814					
48									
49	Future predictions								
50									

The interpretation of regression output for multiple regression is similar to that for simple regression. In particular, R-square, multiple R, the standard error of estimate, the fitted values, and the residuals mean exactly the same thing in either case.

high value implies that the points in a scatterplot (not shown) of actual *Y* values versus fitted values will be close to a 45° line.

■ The standard error of estimate has exactly the same interpretation as before. It is a ballpark estimate of the magnitude of the prediction errors we are likely to make, based on the regression equation. Here, this value is about $1981—not too bad considering that the total costs vary around $50,000.

■ The fitted values are found by substituting each set of *X*'s into the regression equation, and the residuals are the differences between actual total costs and fitted values. Analysis ToolPak calculates these automatically for us in the range H28:G43 (if we check the Residuals box in Figure 12.14). As indicated by the standard error of estimate, most of the residuals are no more than about $2000 in magnitude, and quite a few are considerably less than this.

A Note about Adjusted R-square

If adjusted R-square decreases when extra independent variables are added to a regression equation, these variables are not useful and should probably be deleted.

You are probably wondering what the *adjusted* R-square value means in the multiple regression output. Although it has no simple interpretation like R-square (percentage of variation explained), it is useful for comparing regression equations. The problem with R-square is that it can *never* decrease when we add extra independent variables to a regression equation. However, there ought to be some "penalty" for adding variables that don't really belong. This is the purpose of adjusted R-square. It acts as a monitor. If we add one or more extra independent variables to an already existing equation, adjusted R-square *can* decrease. If this occurs, then we have evidence that the extra independent variables don't really belong in the equation and should probably be deleted.

Prediction of Future Costs

If we conclude that the fit is good enough to provide useful *future* predictions, we can then substitute future estimates of production levels into the regression equation. We did this for the proposed values of the X's for months 16 and 17 in rows 19 and 20. (These do not appear in Figure 12.15.) Specifically, we enter the formula

=$H$19+$H$20*B19+$H$21*C19+$H$22*D19

in cell H46 and copy it to cell H47. Of course, this could be done for *any* assumed production levels in these two months, not just the ones we chose. In each case the predicted total cost is approximately in the $45,000 to $46,000 range, and the standard error of estimate implies that these predictions are probably not off by more than about $2000.

In real business situations, regression analysis provides only guidelines, not exact numbers to 10 decimal places. Therefore, don't be afraid to round output values when you present your analysis.

More specifically, it is common to quote a **95% prediction interval** for each future prediction. This is an interval such that we are 95% sure that the actual future value will be inside this interval. Although the exact calculation of a 95% prediction interval is somewhat complex, a good and easy approximation is to go out 2 standard errors of estimate on either side of the predicted value. For example, an approximate 95% prediction interval for the total cost in month 16 extends (aside from rounding) from $45,922 - 2(1981) = 41,960$ to $45,922 + 2(1981) = 49,884$. We show these prediction intervals in the range I46:J47. Their relatively large widths indicate that even with an excellent fit—an R-square of 94.6% is quite large—we cannot ensure accurate future predictions. ■

Incorporating Categorical Variables

In regression analysis we are always searching for good independent variables to explain some dependent variable Y. Often these independent variables are quantitative, such as the Units Produced variables in the two previous examples. However, there are often useful, qualitative categorical variables that help explain Y, such as gender (male or female), region of country (east, south, west, or north), quarter of year (Q1, Q2, Q3, or Q4), and so on. Because regression works entirely with numbers, we need a way to transform these categorical variables into numeric variables that can be used in a regression equation. The solution is to use **dummy** variables, also called **0–1** variables or **indicator** variables. For any categorical variable, we create a dummy variable for each possible category. Its value is 1 for each observation in that category, and it is 0 otherwise.

> A **dummy** variable for any category equals 1 for all observations in that category and 0 for all observations not in that category.

For example, the variable Gender has two possible values, Male and Female, so we can create two dummy variables, Male and Female. Male equals 1 for all males and 0 for all females, whereas Female equals 1 for all females and 0 for all males. As another example, if the variable Quarter has possible values Q1, Q2, Q3, and Q4, we can create four dummy variables, one for each quarter. For example, the dummy variable Quarter1 equals 1 for all quarter 1 observations and 0 for all other observations.

For a categorical variable with m categories, include only m − 1 of the corresponding dummy variables in the regression equation. Any one of them can be omitted.

There is one technical rule we must follow when using dummy variables in regression. If a categorical variable has m categories, we should use only $m - 1$ of the m possible dummy variables in the regression equation. We can omit *any* one of the dummies, which becomes the **reference** category. We then interpret the regression coefficients of the included dummies with respect to the reference category. For example, if Y is salary, and if we include the dummy variable Male in the equation, then the reference category is female. If the coefficient of Male turns out to be, say, $2000, then the interpretation is that, all else being equal, males average $2000 more in salary than females. If we had included Female instead of Male in the equation, then the coefficient of Female would be −$2000, meaning again that females average $2000 less than males. The point is that one dummy must be omitted, and it doesn't matter which one we omit.

The following example, another extension of Example 12.2, illustrates the use of dummy variables.

| EXAMPLE | 12.4 Estimating Production Costs at Three Company Plants |

Suppose the company in Example 12.2 produces a single product at three different manufacturing plants. As in that example, the company wants to regress total cost on units produced, but it suspects that the relationship between these variables might differ across plants. It has monthly data from the past 16 months for each of the plants, some of which appear in Figure 12.16. (See the file **CostRegression3.xls**.) How can the company use dummy variables to estimate the relationship between total cost and units produced for all three plants simultaneously?

Figure 12.16

Cost Data for Three Plants

	A	B	C	D
1	Cost regression example at three plants			
2				
3	Month	Plant	Units Produced	Total Cost
4	1	1	800	190600
5	1	2	500	142200
6	1	3	200	46400
7	2	1	400	99700
8	2	2	800	194300
9	2	3	300	74400
10	3	1	300	82800
11	3	2	700	171100
12	3	3	200	50100
13	4	1	400	104300
14	4	2	600	158600
15	4	3	200	52100
16	5	1	600	148800
17	5	2	800	201500
18	5	3	600	132000
19	6	1	300	81500
20	6	2	600	155900
21	6	3	200	45300

Objective   To use dummy variables for plants to estimate a single regression equation relating total cost to units produced for all three plants.

Solution

Once we get the data set up properly, we can use Analysis ToolPak to run the regression in the usual way. However, we must first create the dummy variables.

Creating the Dummy Variables

The simplest way to create dummy variables for the plants is with IF formulas. The results are shown in Figure 12.17. The formulas for the dummies in cells C4, D4, and E4 are

=IF(B4=1,1,0)

=IF(B4=2,1,0)

and

=IF(B4=3,1,0)

which are then copied down their respective columns. Actually, we need only two of these dummies in the regression equation. Since Analysis ToolPak requires the independent variables to be in adjacent columns, we will include the Plant2 and Plant3 dummies, along with the quantitative variable Units Produced, as the independent variables. This means that plant 1 is the reference category.

Figure 12.17

Original Data with Dummy Variables Added

	A	B	C	D	E	F	G
1	Cost regression example at three plants						
2							
3	Month	Plant	Plant1	Plant2	Plant3	Units Produced	Total Cost
4	1	1	1	0	0	800	190600
5	1	2	0	1	0	500	142200
6	1	3	0	0	1	200	46400
7	2	1	1	0	0	400	99700
8	2	2	0	1	0	800	194300
9	2	3	0	0	1	300	74400
10	3	1	1	0	0	300	82800
11	3	2	0	1	0	700	171100
12	3	3	0	0	1	200	50100
13	4	1	1	0	0	400	104300
14	4	2	0	1	0	600	158600
15	4	3	0	0	1	200	52100
16	5	1	1	0	0	600	148800
17	5	2	0	1	0	800	201500
18	5	3	0	0	1	600	132000
19	6	1	1	0	0	300	81500
20	6	2	0	1	0	600	155900
21	6	3	0	0	1	200	45300

Discussion of the Results

The regression output from the Analysis ToolPak appears in Figure 12.18. It literally implies the following regression equation for predicting total cost:

Predicted Total Cost = 22,852 + 12,972Plant2 − 15,045Plant3 + 204.15Units Produced

However, it is more intuitive to think of this as three separate equations, one for each plant. For plant 1, the reference category, the dummies Plant2 and Plant3 are 0, so the equation reduces to

Predicted Total Cost (plant 1) = 22,852 + 204.15Units Produced

For plant 2, the dummy Plant2 is 1 and the dummy Plant3 is 0, so the equation reduces to

Predicted Total Cost (plant 2) = (22,852 + 12,972) + 204.15Units Produced

Finally, for plant 3, the dummy Plant2 is 0 and the dummy Plant3 is 1, so the equation reduces to

Predicted Total Cost (plant 3) = (22,852 − 15,045) + 204.15Units Produced

Figure 12.18

Regression Output
with Dummy
Variables Included

	I	J	K	L	M	N	O
3	SUMMARY OUTPUT						
4							
5	*Regression Statistics*						
6	Multiple R	0.997419428					
7	R Square	0.994845516					
8	Adjusted R Square	0.994494074					
9	Standard Error	3525.056931					
10	Observations	48					
11							
12	ANOVA						
13		*df*	*SS*	*MS*	*F*	*Significance F*	
14	Regression	3	1.05525E+11	35175003210	2830.75234	2.50011E-50	
15	Residual	44	546745160.2	12426026.37			
16	Total	47	1.06072E+11				
17							
18		*Coefficients*	*Standard Error*	*t Stat*	*P-value*	*Lower 95%*	*Upper 95%*
19	Intercept	22851.93566	1607.293271	14.21765154	4.65979E-18	19612.64904	26091.22
20	Plant2	12971.97383	1278.60863	10.14538266	4.27256E-13	10395.10755	15548.84
21	Plant3	-15045.29035	1262.499706	-11.9170644	2.2872E-15	-17589.69123	-12500.89
22	Units Produced	204.1461287	2.688319186	75.93820322	2.64487E-48	198.7281776	209.5641

We see from these equations that the coefficient of Units Produced is 204.15 for each plant. Therefore, if any of the plants produces an extra unit, we expect its total cost to increase by about $204. The only difference between the equations is in their intercepts. Specifically, if plants 1 and 2 produce the same numbers of units, we expect plant 2's total cost to be $12,972 *higher* than plant 1's. Similarly, if plants 1 and 3 produce the same numbers of units, we expect plant 3's total cost to be $15,045 *lower* than plant 1's. In this sense, the coefficients of the dummy variables allow us to compare each plant to the reference plant. Of course, we can also compare *nonreference* plants to one another. If plants 2 and 3 produce the same numbers of units, we expect plant 2's total cost to be ($12,972 + $15,045) higher than plant 3's.

Geometrically, the regression analysis produces three parallel lines for the three plants, as shown in Figure 12.19. Each of the lines has the same slope, 204.15, but they have different intercepts. By including the dummy variables as we have done, we are forcing the regression to estimate parallel lines, so that the effect of Units Produced on Total Cost is the *same* for each plant. If we believe this effect *differs* across plants—that is, we believe the variable costs for the three plants might not be the same—we must include extra independent variables, called *interaction* variables, to the regression equation. However, we will not pursue this topic here.

Figure 12.19

Estimation of Three
Parallel Regression
Lines

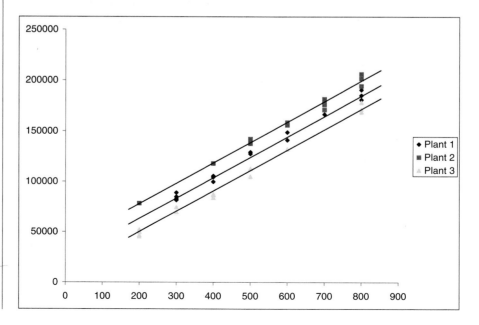

A Caution about Regression Assumptions

In this brief introduction to regression, we have discussed only the basic elements of regression analysis, and we have omitted many of the technical details that can be found in more complete statistics books. In particular, we have not discussed what can go wrong if various statistical assumptions behind regression analysis are violated. Although there is not room here for a complete discussion of these assumptions and their ramifications, we briefly state a few cautions you should be aware of.

Multicollinearity

In the best of worlds, we would like the independent variables, the X's, to provide nonoverlapping information about the dependent variable Y. We do not want them to provide redundant information. However, there are times when redundancy is difficult to avoid. For example, in trying to explain employee salaries, three potential independent variables are age, years of seniority with this company, and years of experience with this type of job. These three variables are likely to be highly correlated with one another (as well as with salary), and it is not clear whether we should include all three in a regression equation for salary.

Multicollinearity makes it difficult to interpret individual regression coefficients, but it does not have a negative effect on predictions.

When we do include X's that are highly correlated with one another, we introduce a problem called **multicollinearity**. The problem is that when X's are highly correlated, it is virtually impossible to sort out their separate influences on Y. This inability to sort out separate effects can even lead to "wrong" signs on the regression coefficients. For example, if age, years of seniority, and years of experience are all entered in an equation for salary, it is quite possible that one of the three regression coefficients will be *negative*, even though all three variables are positively correlated to salary. Therefore, the presence of multicollinearity makes regression equations difficult to interpret. Fortunately, however, multicollinearity is not a problem if we are concerned only with *prediction* of new Y's.

Nonlinear Relationships

If scatterplots of Y versus the various X's indicate any nonlinear relationships, then the linear relationship we have been estimating will almost certainly lead to a poor fit and poor predictions. Fortunately, as with the exponential trendline, there are often nonlinear transformations of Y and/or the X's that "straighten out" the scatterplots and allow us to use *linear* regression. We will not discuss such transformations. We simply warn you that if the scatterplots of the original variables do not appear to be linear, you should not blindly proceed to estimate linear relationships.

Nonconstant Error Variance

One assumption of regression is that the variation of the Y's above any values of the X's should be the same, regardless of the particular values of the X's chosen. Sometimes this assumption is clearly violated. For example, if Y is a household's annual amount spent on vacations and X is the household's annual income, it is very possible that the variation of the Y's for low-income households is considerably less than that for high-income households. The low-income households don't have much to spend on vacations, so their vacation spending is likely to be tightly bunched at low values. In contrast, the high-income households have a lot to spend, but they might or might not elect to spend it on vacations. Typically, nonconstant error variance appears in a scatterplot as a "fan-shape" swarm of points. We simply alert you to this possibility and suggest that you obtain expert help if you spot an obvious fan shape.

Autocorrelation of Residuals

Autocorrelation means that a variable's values are correlated to its own previous values. This typically occurs in time series variables. For example, we might be using regression to forecast monthly sales. If the residuals are autocorrelated, then an overprediction in January is likely to be followed by an overprediction in February, and an underprediction in June is likely to be followed by an underprediction in July. It is not difficult to detect autocorrelation of residuals (although we will not discuss the measures for doing so), but it is much more difficult to deal with autocorrelation appropriately. Again, you should consult an expert if you believe your time series analysis is subject to autocorrelation.

PROBLEMS

Skill-Building Problems

12. Suppose you are an analyst for a company that produces four products, and you are trying to decide how much of each product to produce next month. To model this decision problem, it turns out that you need the unit variable production cost for each product. After some digging, you find the historical data on production levels and costs in the file **P12_12.xls**. Use these data to find estimates of the unit costs you need. You should also find an estimate of the fixed cost of production. Will this be of any use to you in deciding how much of each product to produce? Why or why not?

13. A trucking company wants to predict the yearly maintenance expense (Y) for a truck using the number of miles driven during the year (X_1) and the age of the truck (X_2, in years) at the beginning of the year. The company has gathered the data given in the file **P12_13.xls**. Note that each observation corresponds to a particular truck. Estimate a multiple regression model using the given data. Interpret each of the estimated regression coefficients. Also, interpret the standard error of estimate and the R-square value for these data.

14. An antique collector believes that the price received for a particular item increases with its age and with the number of bidders. The file **P12_14.xls** contains data on these three variables for 32 recently auctioned comparable items. Estimate a multiple regression model using the given data. Interpret each of the estimated regression coefficients. Is the antique collector correct in believing that the price received for the item increases with its age and with the number of bidders? Interpret the standard error of estimate and the R-square value for these data.

15. Stock market analysts are continually looking for reliable predictors of stock prices. Consider the problem of modeling the price per share of electric utility stocks (Y). Two variables thought to influence this stock price are return on average equity (X_1) and annual dividend rate (X_2). The stock price, returns on equity, and dividend rates on a randomly selected day

for 16 electric utility stocks are provided in the file **P12_15.xls**. Estimate a multiple regression model using the given data. Interpret each of the estimated regression coefficients. Also, interpret the standard error of estimate and the R-square value for these data.

16. Consider the enrollment data for *Business Week*'s top 50 U.S. graduate business programs in the file **P12_16.xls**. Use these data to estimate a multiple regression model to assess whether there is a systematic relationship between the total number of full-time students and the following explanatory variables: the proportion of female students, the proportion of minority students, and the proportion of international students enrolled at these distinguished business schools.
   a. Interpret the coefficients of your estimated regression model. Do any of these results surprise you? Explain.
   b. How well does your estimated regression model fit the given data?

17. David Savageau and Geoffrey Loftus, the authors of *Places Rated Almanac* (published in 1997 by Macmillan), have ranked 325 metropolitan areas in the United States with consideration of the following aspects of life in each area: cost of living, transportation, jobs, education, climate, crime, arts, health, and recreation. The data are in the file **P12_17.xls**. The last column lists the city's overall score, which is the average of the other scores. (You can check this with Excel's AVERAGE function.)
   a. Use multiple regression analysis to explore the relationship between the metropolitan area's overall score and the set of potential explanatory variables.
   b. Does the given set of explanatory variables do a good job of explaining changes in the overall score? Explain why or why not.

18. Suppose that a regional express delivery service company wants to estimate the cost of shipping a package (Y) as a function of cargo type, where cargo type includes the following possibilities: fragile, semifragile, and durable. Costs for 15 randomly chosen packages of approximately the same weight and same distance shipped, but of different cargo types, are provided in the file **P12_18.xls**.

a. Formulate an appropriate multiple regression model to predict the cost of shipping a given package.

b. Estimate the formulated model using the given sample data, and interpret the estimated regression coefficients.

c. According to the estimated regression model, which cargo type is the *most* costly to ship? Which cargo type is the *least* costly to ship?

d. How well does the estimated model fit the given sample data? How might the model be improved?

e. Given the estimated regression model, predict the cost of shipping a package with semifragile cargo.

Skill-Extending Problems

19. The owner of a restaurant in Bloomington, Indiana, has recorded sales data for the past 19 years. He has also recorded data on potentially relevant variables. The data are listed in the file **P12_19.xls**.

a. Estimate a simple regression model involving annual sales (the dependent variable) and the size of the population residing within 10 miles of the restaurant (the independent variable). Interpret R-square for this regression.

b. Add another independent variable—annual advertising expenditures—to the regression model in part **a**. Estimate and interpret this expanded model. How does the R-square value for this multiple regression model compare to that of the simple regression model estimated in part **a**? Explain any difference between the two R-square values. How can you use the adjusted R-squares for a comparison of the two models?

c. Add one more explanatory variable to the multiple regression model estimated in part **b**. In particular, estimate and interpret the coefficients of a multiple regression model that includes the *previous* year's advertising expenditure. How does the inclusion of this third explanatory variable affect the R-square, compared to the corresponding values for the model of part **b**? Explain any changes in this value. What does the adjusted R-square for the new model tell you?

20. A regional express delivery service company recently conducted a study to investigate the relationship between the cost of shipping a package (Y), the package weight (X_1), and the distance shipped (X_2). Twenty packages were randomly selected from among the large number received for shipment, and a detailed analysis of the shipping cost was conducted for each package. These sample observations are given in the file **P12_20.xls**.

a. Estimate a simple linear regression model involving shipping cost and package weight. Interpret the slope coefficient of the least squares line as well as the value of R-square.

b. Add another explanatory variable—distance shipped—to the regression model in part **a**. Estimate and interpret this expanded model. How does the R-square value for this multiple regression model compare to that of the simple regression model estimated in part **a**? Explain any difference between the two R-square values. How can you use the adjusted R-squares for a comparison of the two models?

21. Suppose that you are interested in predicting the price of a laptop computer based on its various features. The file **P12_21.xls** contains observations on the sales price and a number of potentially relevant variables for a randomly chosen sample of laptop computers.

a. Formulate a multiple regression model that includes all potential explanatory variables and estimate it with the given sample data.

b. Interpret the estimated regression equation. Indicate the impact of each attribute on the computer's sales price. For example, what impact does the monitor type have on the average sales price of a laptop computer?

c. How well does the estimated regression model fit the data given in the file?

d. Use the estimated regression equation to predict the price of a laptop computer with the following features: a 60-megahertz processor, a battery that holds its charge for 240 minutes, 32 megabytes of RAM, a DX chip, a color monitor, a mouse pointing device, and a 24-hour, toll-free customer service hotline.

12.5 OVERVIEW OF TIME SERIES MODELS

To this point, we have discussed regression as a method of forecasting. Because of its flexibility, regression can be used equally well for time series variables and for non–time series variables. From here on, however, we will focus exclusively on time series variables, and we will discuss nonregression approaches to forecasting. All of these approaches fall under the general umbrella of **extrapolation** methods.

With an extrapolation method, we form a time series plot of the variable Y that we want to forecast, we analyze any patterns inherent in this time series plot, and we extrapolate these patterns into the future. We do *not* use any other variables—the X's from regression—to forecast Y; we use only past values of Y to forecast future values of Y. The idea is that history will repeat itself. Therefore, if we can discover the patterns in the historical data, we ought to obtain reasonably good forecasts by projecting these historical patterns into the future.

Before examining specific extrapolation techniques, we discuss the types of patterns we are likely to see in time series data. We also briefly discuss the measures that are typically used to judge how well our methods "track" the historical data.

Components of Time Series

A time series variable Y typically contains one or more components. These components are called the *trend* component, the *seasonal* component, the *cyclic* component, and the *random* (or *noise*) component. We provide a brief discussion of these components here.

We start with a very simple time series. This is a series where every observation is the same, as shown in Figure 12.20. The graph in this figure shows time t on the horizontal axis and the observation value Y on the vertical axis. It is assumed that Y is measured at regularly spaced intervals, usually days, weeks, months, quarters, or years. We will denote the value of Y in period t as Y_t. As indicated in the figure, the individual points are usually joined by straight lines to make any patterns in the time series more apparent. Since all observations in this series are equal, the resulting plot is a horizontal line. We will refer to this series as the *base* series. Then we will build more interesting times series from this base series.

Figure 12.20
The Base Series

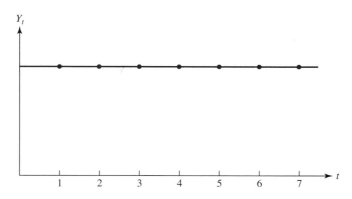

Trend Component

A trend implies a consistent upward or downward movement of the series through time.

If the observations increase or decrease regularly through time, we say that the time series has a **trend**. The graphs in Figure 12.21 (page 634) illustrate several possible trends. We already discussed the linear trend in Figure 12.21a and the exponential trend in Figure 12.21b in Section 12.3. The curve in Figure 12.21c is an *S-shaped* trend. As an example, this type of trend curve is appropriate for a new product that takes a while to catch on, then exhibits a rapid increase in sales as the public becomes aware of it, and finally tapers off to a fairly constant level. The curves in Figure 12.21 all represent *upward* trends. Of course, we could just as well have *downward* trends of the same types.

→ **Excel Tool:** *Creating a Time Series Plot*
There are (at least) two ways to create a time series plot in Excel. One way is to create a scatterplot of the time series variable versus time, choosing the X-Y subtype where the dots are connected. A more flexible way is to create a line chart with the Chart Wizard. Then in

step 2 of the wizard, if you click on the Series tab, you can select one or more series to plot. This allows you, for example, to plot an original series with a series of forecasts superimposed on it. We use this method to create the plots in the next two sections of this chapter. ■

Figure 12.21   Series with Trends

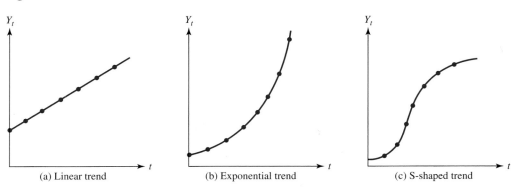

(a) Linear trend   (b) Exponential trend   (c) S-shaped trend

Seasonal Component

A seasonal pattern is a pattern where some seasons are regularly higher than others each year.

Many time series have a **seasonal** component. For example, a company's sales of swimming pool equipment increase every spring, then stay relatively high during the summer, and then drop off until next spring, at which time the yearly pattern repeats itself. An important aspect of the seasonal component is that it tends to be predictable from one year to the next. That is, the *same* seasonal pattern tends to repeat itself every year.

In Figure 12.22 we show two possible seasonal patterns. In Figure 12.22a there is nothing but the seasonal component. That is, if there were no seasonal variation, we would have the base series from Figure 12.20. In Figure 12.22b we show a seasonal pattern superimposed on an upward-sloping trend line.

Figure 12.22

Series with
Seasonality

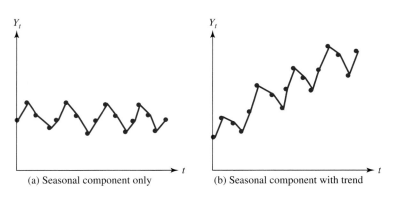

(a) Seasonal component only   (b) Seasonal component with trend

Cyclic Component

The third component of a time series is the **cyclic** component. By studying past movements of many business and economic variables, it becomes apparent that there are business cycles that affect many variables in similar ways. For example, during a recession housing starts generally go down, unemployment goes up, stock prices go down, and so on. But when the recession is over, all of these variables tend to move in the opposite direction.

We know that the cyclic component exists for many time series because we are able to see it as periodic swings in the levels of the time series plots. However, the cyclic component is harder to predict than the seasonal component. The reason is that seasonal variation is much more regular. For example, swimming pool supplies sales *always* start to increase during the spring. Cyclic variation, on the other hand, is more irregular because the "business cycle" does not always have the same length. A further distinction is that the length of a seasonal cycle is generally one year, whereas the length of a business cycle is generally much longer than one year.

The graphs in Figure 12.23 illustrate the cyclic component of a time series. In Figure 12.23a cyclic variation is superimposed on the base series from Figure 12.20. In Figure 12.23b this same cyclic variation is superimposed on the series from Figure 12.22b. The resulting graph has trend, seasonal variation, and cyclic variation.

Figure 12.23

Series with Cyclic Component

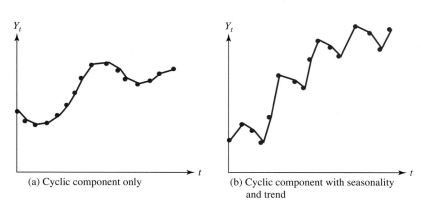

(a) Cyclic component only

(b) Cyclic component with seasonality and trend

Random (Noise) Component

By definition, noise is unpredictable. It often makes trends and seasonal patterns more difficult to recognize.

The final component in a time series is called the **random** component, or simply **noise**. This unpredictable component gives most time series plots their irregular, zigzag appearance. Usually, a time series can be determined only to a certain extent by its trend, seasonal, and cyclic components. Then other factors determine the rest. These other factors might be inherent randomness, unpredictable "shocks" to the system, the unpredictable behavior of human beings who interact with the system, and others.

Figures 12.24 and 12.25 (page 636) show the effect that noise can have on a time series graph. The graph on the left of each figure shows the random component only, superimposed on the base series. Then on the right of each figure, the random component is superimposed on the graph of trend with seasonal component from Figure 12.22b. The difference between Figure 12.24 and Figure 12.25 is the relative magnitude of the noise. When it is small, as in Figure 12.24, the other components emerge fairly clearly; they are not disguised by the noise. But if the noise is large in magnitude, as in Figure 12.25, the noise can make it difficult to distinguish the other components.

Figure 12.24

Series with Noise

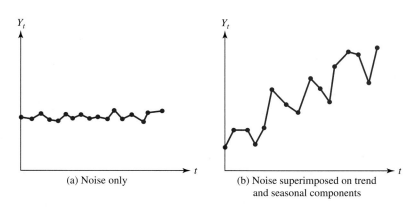

(a) Noise only

(b) Noise superimposed on trend and seasonal components

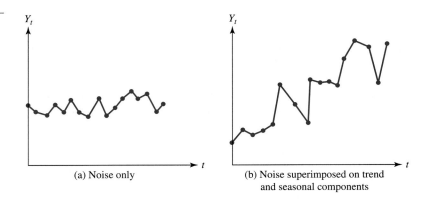

Figure 12.25

Series with More Noise

(a) Noise only

(b) Noise superimposed on trend and seasonal components

Measures of Forecast Error

When we use any extrapolation method, we build a model to track the observed historical data, and then we use this model to forecast future values of the data. The only way we can judge whether the future forecasts are likely to be any good is to measure how well the model tracks the historical data. There are several measures that time series analysts typically use. We present three of the most popular measures in the section.

As before, let Y_t be the observed value in time period t. Given any forecasting model, let F_t be the "one-period-ahead" forecast of Y_t made at time $t - 1$. For example, for monthly data, if t corresponds to August, then F_t is the forecast of August's value made one month before, in July. Also, let E_t be the corresponding forecast error, $E_t = Y_t - F_t$. If E_t is positive, our forecast is too low, whereas if E_t is negative, our forecast is too high. We want the E_t's to be small, so that our "forecasts" of the historical data track the actual data closely.

The three measures of forecasting accuracy we propose are MAE (mean absolute error), RMSE (root mean square error), and MAPE (mean absolute percentage error). These are given by the following formulas, where N is the number of historical periods for which our model provides forecasts.

Formula for mean absolute error

$$\text{MAE} = \frac{\sum_{t=1}^{N} |E_t|}{N} \tag{12.8}$$

Formula for RMSE

$$\text{RMSE} = \sqrt{\frac{\sum_{t=1}^{N} E_t^2}{N}} \tag{12.9}$$

Formula for MAPE

$$\text{MAPE} = \frac{\sum_{t=1}^{N} |E_t/Y_t|}{N} \tag{12.10}$$

RMSE is similar to a standard deviation in that the errors are squared; because of the square root, its units are the same as those of the original variable. The MAE is similar to the RMSE, except that absolute values of errors are used instead of squared errors. The

MAPE (the same measure we introduced in Section 12.3) is probably the easiest measure to understand because it does not depend on the units of the original variable; it is always stated as a percentage. For example, the statement that the forecasts are off on average by 2% has a clear meaning, even if you do not know the units of the variable being forecasted.

A good forecasting model will typically make all three measures of forecast errors small.

Depending on the forecasting software package used, one or more of these measures will typically be reported. Fortunately, models that make any one of these measures small tend to make the others small as well, so that we can choose whichever measure we want to focus on. Also, once we have calculated the E_t's (which follow from the particular forecasting technique being used), we can calculate MAE, RMSE, and MAPE quite easily from Excel's built-in functions, as we discuss subsequently.

One caution is in order, however. We calculate MAE, RMSE, or MAPE to see how well our forecasting model tracks *historical* data. But even if these measures are small, there is no guarantee that *future* forecasts will be accurate. As we stated previously, extrapolation methods all make the implicit assumption that history will repeat itself. Unfortunately, history does not always repeat itself. When this is the case, a model that closely tracks historical data might yield poor forecasts of the future. In addition, there is a danger of tracking a historical series *too* closely. There is no point in tracking every little up and down if these movements represent random noise that will not repeat in the future.

12.6 MOVING AVERAGES MODELS

Perhaps the simplest and one of the most frequently used extrapolation methods is the method of **moving averages**. Very simply, the forecast for any period with this method is the average of the observations from the past few periods. To implement the moving averages method, we first choose a **span**, the number of terms in each moving average. Let's say the data are monthly and we choose a span of 6 months. Then the forecast of next month's value is the average of the previous 6 months' values. For example, we average the January–June values to forecast July, we average the February–July values to forecast August, and so on. This is the reason for the term *moving* averages.

> The **span** in the moving averages method is the number of observations in each average.

The larger the span, the smoother the forecast series will be.

The role of the span is important. If the span is large—say, 12 months—then many observations go into each average, and extreme values have relatively little effect on the averages. The resulting series of forecasts will be much smoother than the original series. (For this reason, the moving average method is called a **smoothing** method.) In contrast, if the span is small—say, 3 months—then extreme observations have a larger effect on the averages, and the forecast series will be much less smooth. In the extreme, if the span is 1, there is no smoothing effect at all. The method simply forecasts next month's value to be the same as this month's value.

What span should we use? This requires some judgment. If we believe the ups and downs in the series are random noise, then we do not want future forecasts to react too quickly to these ups and downs, and we should use a relatively large span. But if we want to track most of the ups and downs—under the belief that these ups and downs are predictable—then we should use a smaller span. We should not be fooled, however, by a plot of the forecast series—that is, a plot of the averages—superimposed on the original series. This graph will almost always look better when a small span is used, because the forecast series will appear to track the original series better. But this does not mean it will provide better future forecasts. Again, there is little point in tracking random ups and downs closely if they represent unpredictable noise.

The following example illustrates the use of moving averages on a series of weekly sales.

EXAMPLE | **12.5 FORECASTING WEEKLY SALES OF HARDWARE AT LEE'S**

Lee's is a local discount store that sells a variety of merchandise, much like Kmart, Wal-Mart, and Target. In particular, it sells a full line of hardware. The company has kept track of weekly total dollar sales of hardware items for the past 104 weeks. These data appear in the file **HardwareSales1.xls**. Lee's is planning to use moving averages, with an appropriate span, to forecast future weekly hardware sales. Does this appear to be a good idea?

Objective To judge the effectiveness of the moving averages method, with different spans, to forecast weekly hardware sales at Lee's.

Solution

A series that meanders, with no obvious trend or seasonality, is a good candidate for moving averages.

A time series plot of weekly sales appears in Figure 12.26. This series appears to "meander," with no obvious trend or seasonality. Evidently, sales of hardware at Lee's are relatively constant throughout each year. This type of series is a good candidate for moving averages. However, it is not clear which span to use. We tried spans of 3, 6, and 12 weeks. Spans of 3 and 6 gave similar results, whereas a span of 12 gave less good results. We illustrate the calculations for a span of 3; you can check the calculations for the other spans in the file **HardwareSales1.xls**.

Figure 12.26

Time Series Plot of Hardware Sales

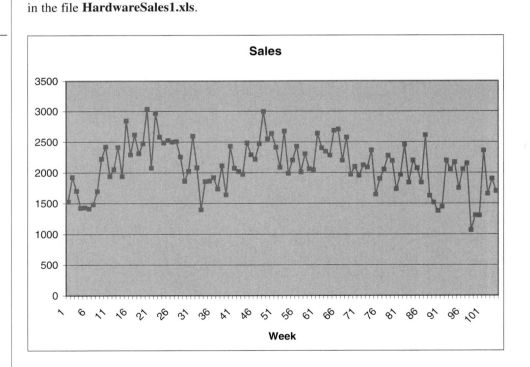

DEVELOPING THE SPREADSHEET MODEL

Using a span of 3, the forecast for week 4 is the average of the observed sales in weeks 1–3, the forecast for week 5 is the average of the observed sales in weeks 2–4, and so on. The calculations are straightforward in Excel, as shown in Figure 12.27 (with many hidden rows).[5] There are no forecasts for weeks 1–3 because we do not have the sales values before week 1 that would be required for the moving averages. Therefore, we start in week 4 with the formula

=AVERAGE(B10:B12)

in cell C13. Then we copy this formula down to cell C114 for the other months.

Figure 12.27
Moving Average Forecasts with Span 3

	A	B	C	D	E	F
9	Week	Sales	Forecast_3	Error_3	AE_3	APE_3
10	1	1526				
11	2	1929				
12	3	1704				
13	4	1423	1719.7	-296.7	296.7	20.8%
14	5	1430	1685.3	-255.3	255.3	17.9%
15	6	1410	1519.0	-109.0	109.0	7.7%
16	7	1478	1421.0	57.0	57.0	3.9%
17	8	1698	1439.3	258.7	258.7	15.2%
18	9	2223	1528.7	694.3	694.3	31.2%
19	10	2420	1799.7	620.3	620.3	25.6%
106	97	2152	1993.7	158.3	158.3	7.4%
107	98	1069	1987.7	-918.7	918.7	85.9%
108	99	1306	1759.0	-453.0	453.0	34.7%
109	100	1302	1509.0	-207.0	207.0	15.9%
110	101	2361	1225.7	1135.3	1135.3	48.1%
111	102	1658	1656.3	1.7	1.7	0.1%
112	103	1903	1773.7	129.3	129.3	6.8%
113	104	1702	1974.0	-272.0	272.0	16.0%
114	105		1754.3			
115	106		1786.4			
116	107		1747.6			
117	108		1762.8			

To forecast future values with moving averages, use previous forecasts when actual values are not available.

Note that the forecast in cell C114 is for the *future* week 105, where there is no corresponding sales value. It is a bit trickier to calculate forecasts for weeks farther into the future. For example, to forecast sales for week 106, we would like to average sales for weeks 103–105, but we have no sales value for week 105. In this case, the rule is to use a *forecast* instead of a sales value whenever a sales value is not available. Therefore, the formula in cell C115 for the week 106 forecast is

=AVERAGE(B112:B113,C114)

The forecasts for weeks 107 and 108 are similar. Each is an average of 3 values, using forecasts instead of sales values when sales values are not available.

Once we have the forecasts, we can calculate the forecast errors—for weeks where both sales and forecast values are available—by subtraction. The values in column D are sales values in column B minus forecasts in column C. For later use, we also calculate the absolute errors in column E with the ABS function, and the absolute percentage errors in column F. Each value in column F is the absolute error in column E divided by the sales value in column B.

Discussion of the Results

Two useful graphs are shown in Figures 12.28 and 12.29 (page 640). The superimposed series of forecasts in Figure 12.28 indicates that the forecasts track the general ups and downs of the sales series fairly well, although the forecast series is smoother than the sales series. This is exactly what we want. The difference between these two series is probably unpredictable noise, which is impossible (and undesirable) to track exactly.

---

[5]Analysis ToolPak includes an implementation of the moving averages forecasting method. It calls the span the "interval." However, its forecasts are (mistakenly, in our opinion) shifted one row up from ours. In any case, the method is simple enough to implement in Excel without an add-in.

Figure 12.28

Sales with Forecasts
(Span 3)
Superimposed

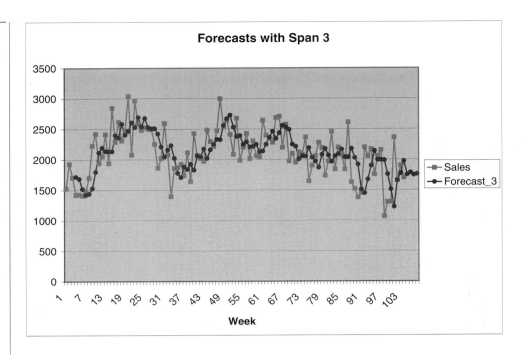

Figure 12.29

Forecast Errors with
Span 3

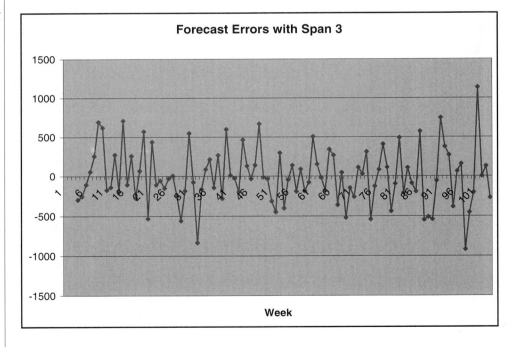

It is also useful to examine the series of forecast errors in Figure 12.29. This series appears to be a random series of ups and downs—again exactly what we want. If the series of forecast errors indicated some sort of pattern, such as an upward trend or a spike every fourth week, then our forecasting method would be missing something, and we would need to try another forecasting method to "pick up" this pattern. The current series of forecast errors shows no such pattern, so our moving averages method is evidently doing about as good a job as possible in tracking the sales series.

To obtain more evidence on how well the moving averages forecasts are doing, we calculate the summary measures MAE, RMSE, and MAPE. These appear in Figure 12.30 for all three spans we tried. The formulas for span 3 in cells B5–B7 are

=AVERAGE(E13:E113)

=SQRT(SUMSQ(D13:D113)/COUNT(D13:D113))

and

=AVERAGE(F13:F113)

As we see, the forecasts with span 3 are off, on average, by about $278 (from MAE) or about 13.9% (from MAPE), and the errors are only worse with spans of 6 or 12. These errors are fairly sizable, and it isn't certain whether the forecasts will be of much help to Lee's management. However, it is very possible that more accurate forecasts are not available. There might simply be too much noise in the sales series to permit better forecasts.

Figure 12.30

Summary Measures of Forecast Errors

	A	B	C	D
3	Summary measures from forecasts below			
4	Span	3	6	12
5	MAE	278.1	284.4	314.8
6	RMSE	358.3	360.8	387.4
7	MAPE	13.9%	14.3%	15.7%

PROBLEMS

Skill-Building Problems

22. The file **P12_22.xls** contains the daily closing prices of American Express stock for a 1-year period.
    a. Using a span of 3 days, forecast the price of this stock for the next trading day with the method of moving averages. How well does the moving average method with span 3 forecast the known observations in this data set?
    b. Repeat part **a** with a span of 10.
    c. Which of these two spans appears to be more appropriate? Explain your choice.

23. The closing value of the AMEX Airline Index for each trading day during a 1-year period is given in the file **P12_23.xls**.
    a. How well does the moving average method track this series when the span is 4 days? When the span is 12 days?
    b. Using the more appropriate span, forecast the closing value of this index on the next 15 trading days.

24. The closing value of the Dow Jones Industrial Index for each trading day for a 1-year period is provided in the file **P12_24.xls**.
    a. Using a span of 2 days, forecast the price of this index for the next trading day with the method of moving averages. How well does the moving average method with span 2 forecast the known observations in this data set?

    b. Repeat part **a** with a span of 5 days; with a span of 15 days.
    c. Which of these three spans appears to be most appropriate? Explain your choice.

25. The file **P12_25.xls** contains the daily closing prices of Wal-Mart stock during a 1-year period. Use the method of moving averages with a carefully chosen span to forecast this time series for the next 3 trading days. Defend your choice of the span used.

Skill-Extending Problems

26. Consider the file **P12_26.xls**, which contains total monthly U.S. retail sales data. Use the method of moving averages with a carefully chosen span to forecast U.S. retail sales for the following 12 months. What makes this time series more challenging to forecast?

27. The file **P12_27.xls** contains quarterly sales of Johnson & Johnson. A time series plot of this series indicates a clear upward trend. Use moving averages to forecast this series, experimenting with the span. What do you conclude about the effectiveness of using moving averages on an upward-trending time series?

12.7 EXPONENTIAL SMOOTHING MODELS

Exponential smoothing forecasts put more weight on recent observations.

The one main criticism of the moving averages method is that it puts equal weight on each value in a typical moving average. Many people would argue that if next month's forecast is to be based on the previous 12 months' observations, say, then more weight ought to be placed on the more recent observations. Exponential smoothing is a method that addresses this criticism. It bases its forecasts on a *weighted* average of past observations, with more weight put on the more recent observations. In addition, it is not difficult for most business people to understand, at least conceptually. Therefore, this method finds widespread use in the business world, particularly when frequent and automatic forecasts of many items are required.

There are several versions of exponential smoothing. The simplest is called, naturally enough, **simple** exponential smoothing. It is relevant when there is no pronounced trend or seasonality in the series. If there is a trend but no seasonality, then **Holt's** method is applicable. If, in addition, there is seasonality, then **Winters'** method can be used. This does not exhaust the list of exponential smoothing models—researchers have invented many other variations—but these are the most common models. We will discuss simple exponential smoothing in some detail. Then we will provide a brief account of Holt's and Winters' methods.

> **Simple** exponential smoothing is appropriate when there is no trend or seasonality. **Holt's** method is appropriate when there is trend but no seasonality. **Winters'** method is appropriate when there is seasonality (and possibly trend as well).

Simple Exponential Smoothing

Simple exponential smoothing is appropriate for a series with no obvious trend or seasonal component. An example is the hardware sales data from Example 12.5 that meanders through time but doesn't really have any consistent upward or downward trend. In fact, we will reexamine this series in this section.

We first introduce two new terms. Every exponential model has at least one **smoothing constant**, which is always a number between 0 and 1. Simple exponential smoothing has a single smoothing constant denoted by α (alpha). Its role will be discussed shortly. The second new term is L_t, called the **level** of the series at time t. Essentially, the level is where we think the series would be at time t if there were no random noise. It is not observable but can only be estimated.

> The **level** of the series is an estimate of where the series would be if it were not for random noise.

The simple exponential smoothing method is defined by the following equation. It states that the estimated level at time t, right after observing Y_t, is a weighted average of the current observation Y_t and the *previous* estimated level, L_{t-1}. The current observation gets weight α and the previous level gets weight $1 - \alpha$.

> *Formula for simple exponential smoothing*
> $$L_t = \alpha Y_t + (1 - \alpha)L_{t-1} \qquad (12.11)$$

To forecast, we use the most recently calculated level and project it into all future periods. For example, for monthly data, if the most recently observed value is for June, we calculate the level for June from equation (12.11) and then use this level as a forecast for July, August, and so on. In a month, after we have observed July's value, we calculate the level for July, again using equation (12.11), and then use this updated level as a forecast for August, September, and so on. The idea in simple exponential smoothing is that we believe the series is not really going anywhere. So as soon as we estimate where the series ought to be in period t (if it were not for random noise), we forecast that this is where it will also be in any future period.

The smoothing constant α is analogous to the span in moving averages. There are two ways to see this. The first way is to rewrite equation (12.11) using the fact that the forecast error, E_t, made in forecasting Y_t at time $t - 1$ is $E_t = Y_t - F_t = Y_t - L_{t-1}$. A bit of algebra then gives the following formula.

Equivalent formula for simple exponential smoothing

$$L_t = L_{t-1} + \alpha E_t \qquad \textbf{(12.12)}$$

Equation (12.12) states that the next estimate of the level is adjusted from the previous estimate by adding a multiple of the most recent forecast error. This makes intuitive sense. If our previous forecast was too high, then E_t is negative, so we adjust the estimate of the level downward. The opposite is true if our previous forecast was too low. However, equation (12.12) says that we do not adjust by the *entire* magnitude of E_t, but only by a fraction of it. If α is small, say, $\alpha = 0.1$, then the adjustment is minor; if α is close to 1, the adjustment is large. Therefore, if we want to react quickly to movements in the series, we choose a large α; otherwise, we choose a small α.

Another way to see the effect of α is to substitute recursively into equation (12.11) for L_t. After some algebra, it is possible to verify that L_t satisfies the following formula, where the sum in this formula extends back to the first observation at time $t = 1$.

Another equivalent formula for simple exponential smoothing

$$L_t = \alpha Y_t + \alpha(1 - \alpha)Y_{t-1} + \alpha(1 - \alpha)^2 Y_{t-2} + \alpha(1 - \alpha)^3 Y_{t-3} + \cdots \qquad \textbf{(12.13)}$$

Equation (12.13) indicates that the exponentially smoothed forecast is a weighted average of previous observations, just as we promised. Furthermore, because $1 - \alpha$ is less than 1, the weights on the Y's decrease from time t backward. Therefore, if α is close to 0, so that $1 - \alpha$ is close to 1, the weights decrease very slowly. In this case, observations from the distant past continue to have a large influence on the next forecast. This means that the graph of the forecasts will be relatively smooth, just as with a large span in the moving averages method. But when α is close to 1, the weights decrease rapidly, and only very recent observations have much influence on the next forecast. In this case forecasts react quickly to sudden changes in the series, and the forecast series isn't much smoother than the original series.

The smaller the smoothing constant, the smoother the forecast series will be. Typically, a smoothing constant from 0.1 to 0.2 is used.

Which value of α should you use? There is no universally accepted answer to this question. However, many practitioners recommend a value around 0.1 or 0.2. Others recommend experimenting with different values of α until a measure such as RMSE or MAPE is minimized. Some software packages even have an optimization feature that finds this optimal value of α. But as we discussed in general for extrapolation methods, the value of α that tracks the historical series most closely does not necessarily guarantee the most accurate *future* forecasts.

The following example uses the same hardware sales series as in Example 12.5 to see whether simple exponential smoothing can improve on the forecasts made by moving averages.

EXAMPLE | **12.6 FORECASTING HARDWARE SALES AT LEE'S**

In the previous example, we saw that the moving averages method was able to provide only fair forecasts of weekly hardware sales at Lee's. Using the best of three potential spans, its forecasts were still off by about 13.9% on average. The company would now like to try simple exponential smoothing to see whether this method, with an appropriate smoothing constant, can outperform the moving averages method. How should the company proceed?

Objective To see whether simple exponential smoothing with an appropriate smoothing constant can provide more accurate forecasts of weekly hardware sales than the moving averages forecasts.

Solution

We already saw in Example 12.5 that the hardware sales series meanders through time, with no apparent trends or seasonality. Therefore, this series is a good candidate for simple exponential smoothing. This is no guarantee that the method will provide accurate forecasts, but at least we cannot rule it out as a promising forecasting method.

DEVELOPING THE SPREADSHEET MODEL

To implement simple exponential smoothing, we must use equation (12.11) repeatedly.[6] You can think of this procedure as climbing a ladder. Equation (12.11) shows how to move from one step to the next step (from time period $t - 1$ to time period t). However, just as in climbing a ladder, we have to get to the *first* step before we can continue. Note that the equation for L_1 requires a value for L_0, and no such value is given automatically. Choosing a value for L_0 is called *initializing the procedure*. One popular initialization technique is to set L_0 equal to Y_1, the first observation, so that from equation (12.11), we have

$$L_1 = \alpha Y_1 + (1 - \alpha)Y_1 = Y_1$$

This gets us started, and then equation (12.11) can be used to "climb the rest of the ladder."

The calculations for a smoothing constant of $\alpha = 0.1$ appear in Figure 12.31. (See the file **HardwareSales2.xls**.) The first level, L_1, using our initialization procedure, is the same as the first observation, so we enter it in cell C10 with the formula **=B10**. From then on, we calculate each level from equation (12.11). The typical formula, entered in cell C11, is

=$B$4*B11+(1-$B$4)*C10

We then copy this formula down to cell C113. Next, since each forecast is the previous level, we enter the formula **=C10** in cell D11 and copy it down to cell D114. Finally, the calculations of forecast errors in columns E–G use exactly the same formulas as with moving averages, so we will not repeat these formulas here.

Discussion of the Results

Note that cell D114 contains the forecast for the first *future* week, week 105. In fact, this same forecast is used for *all* future weeks, at least until week 105's sales value is observed. This accounts for the forecasts in cells D115:D117. However, once week 105's sales value

---

[6]Analysis ToolPak implements simple exponential smoothing, although it refers to a "damping factor." This damping factor corresponds to our $1 - \alpha$. We believe it is more instructive to implement this method without the help of an add-in.

Figure 12.31

Simple Exponential Smoothing Forecasts with Smoothing Constant 0.1

	A	B	C	D	E	F	G
1	Weekly sales of hardware at Lee's						
2							
3	Summary measures from forecasts below						
4	Smoothing constant	0.1					
5	MAE	307.9					
6	RMSE	381.6					
7	MAPE	15.4%					
8							
9	Week	Sales	Level	Forecast	Error	AE	APE
10	1	1526	1526				
11	2	1929	1566.3	1526	403.0	403.0	20.9%
12	3	1704	1580.1	1566.3	137.7	137.7	8.1%
13	4	1423	1564.4	1580.1	-157.1	157.1	11.0%
14	5	1430	1550.9	1564.4	-134.4	134.4	9.4%
15	6	1410	1536.8	1550.9	-140.9	140.9	10.0%
16	7	1478	1531.0	1536.8	-58.8	58.8	4.0%
17	8	1698	1547.7	1531.0	167.0	167.0	9.8%
18	9	2223	1615.2	1547.7	675.3	675.3	30.4%
19	10	2420	1695.7	1615.2	804.8	804.8	33.3%
106	97	2152	1983.1	1964.4	187.6	187.6	8.7%
107	98	1069	1891.7	1983.1	-914.1	914.1	85.5%
108	99	1306	1833.1	1891.7	-585.7	585.7	44.8%
109	100	1302	1780.0	1833.1	-531.1	531.1	40.8%
110	101	2361	1838.1	1780.0	581.0	581.0	24.6%
111	102	1658	1820.1	1838.1	-180.1	180.1	10.9%
112	103	1903	1828.4	1820.1	82.9	82.9	4.4%
113	104	1702	1815.8	1828.4	-126.4	126.4	7.4%
114	105			1815.8			
115	106			1815.8			
116	107			1815.8			
117	108			1815.8			

is observed, equation (12.11) will be used once more to estimate the level for week 105, and this value will then be used as a forecast for all future weeks. The procedure continues in this way as future sales values are observed.

As with moving averages, it is useful to create plots of the sales series with the forecast series superimposed. Figure 12.32 shows this plot with $\alpha = 0.1$; Figure 12.33 (page 646) shows it with $\alpha = 0.3$. As we see, the forecast series is *smoother* with the smaller smoothing constant. In this sense, a small value of α in exponential smoothing corresponds to a large span in moving averages. If we want the forecasts to react less to random ups and downs of the series, we choose a smaller value of α. This is the reasoning behind the common practice of choosing a small smoothing constant such as 0.1 or 0.2.

A small smoothing constant α corresponds to a large span in moving averages. Each produces a relatively smooth forecast series.

Figure 12.32

Forecast Series with Smoothing Constant 0.1

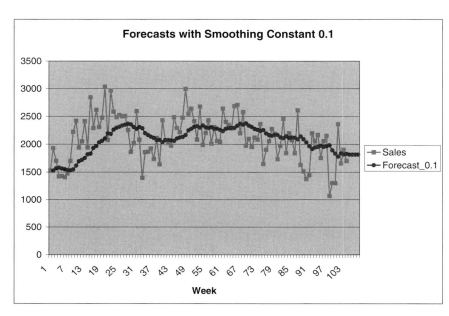

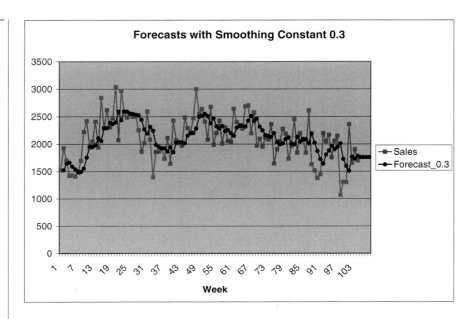

Figure 12.33

Forecast Series with Smoothing Constant 0.3

We show the summary measures of the forecast errors for three potential smoothing constants, 0.1, 0.2, and 0.3, in Figure 12.34. These are calculated exactly as in the moving averages method. From these summary measures we can make two conclusions. First, the summary measures decrease slightly as the smoothing constant increases. We tried making the smoothing constant even larger, but virtually no improvement was possible with smoothing constants larger than 0.3. Second, the best of these results is virtually the same as the best moving averages results. The best forecasts with each method have errors in the 13%–14% range. Again, this is due to the relatively large amount of noise inherent in the sales series. In cases like this, it is conceivable that we could track the ups and downs of the historical series more closely with a larger smoothing constant, but this would almost surely not result in better *future* forecasts. The bottom line is that noise, by definition, is not predictable.

Figure 12.34

Summary Measures of Forecast Errors

	A	B	C	D
3	Summary measures from forecasts below			
4	Smoothing constant	0.1	0.2	0.3
5	MAE	307.9	279.3	268.4
6	RMSE	381.6	353.5	346.3
7	MAPE	15.4%	14.1%	13.5%

■

Holt's Method for Trend[7]

The simple exponential smoothing model generally works well if there is no obvious trend in the series. But if there is a trend, then this method consistently lags behind it. For example, if the series is constantly increasing, simple exponential smoothing forecasts will be consistently low. Holt's method rectifies this by dealing explicitly with trend. In addition to the level of the series L_t and its smoothing constant α, Holt's method includes a trend term, T_t, and a corresponding smoothing constant β (beta). The interpretation of L_t is exactly as before. The interpretation of T_t is that it represents an estimate of the *change* in the series from one period to the next.

After observing all of the data through time period t and calculating the most recent estimates of level and trend, L_t and T_t, we then forecast the next value of the series, at time

[7]This subsection, which uses an add-in, can be omitted without any loss in continuity.

$t + 1$, to be $L_t + T_t$. Similarly, we forecast the value at time $t + 2$ to be $L_t + 2T_t$, the value at $t + 3$ to be $L_t + 3T_t$, and so on. Each future forecast tacks on an additional T_t to the previous forecast.

There are two defining equations for Holt's method, one for L_t and one for T_t. These are similar to equation (12.11) and are as follows.

Formulas for Holt's exponential smoothing method

$$L_t = \alpha Y_t + (1 - \alpha)(L_{t-1} + T_{t-1}) \tag{12.14}$$

$$T_t = \beta(L_t - L_{t-1}) + (1 - \beta)T_{t-1} \tag{12.15}$$

Equation (12.14) is reasonable because $L_{t-1} + T_{t-1}$ is where we think the series should be at time t, based on information up to period $t - 1$. Similarly, equation (12.15) is reasonable because $L_t - L_{t-1}$ is an estimate of the most recent trend.

Although we could plug into these equations in Excel, the procedure is somewhat tedious. In addition, we have another initialization problem to deal with: how to determine appropriate values of L_0 and T_0. Unfortunately, Analysis ToolPak does not implement Holt's method. Therefore, we believe this is a good time to rely on another add-in to help us out. We have included such an add-in, StatTools, on the CD-ROM that accompanies this book. StatTools was developed by Palisade Corporation. It implements Holt's method and many other statistical procedures in Excel.

→ EXCEL ADD-IN: *StatTools from Palisade*

*The StatTools add-in implements many statistical procedures. To use StatTools, you must first install it by running the **Setup.exe** program on the CD-ROM that accompanies this book. Then you must load StatTools. The easiest way to do this is to go to the Windows Start button, select All Programs, select Palisade, and finally select StatTools. If Excel is not already running, this will launch Excel.* ■

The following example briefly describes how StatTools can be used to implement Holt's method on a time series with obvious trend.

EXAMPLE | 12.7 FORECASTING QUARTERLY SALES AT JOHNSON & JOHNSON

The file **Johnson&Johnson.xls** contains quarterly sales data for Johnson & Johnson from second quarter 1991 through first quarter 2001 (in millions of dollars). A time series plot appears in Figure 12.35 (page 648). It indicates a fairly consistent upward trend, with a relatively small amount of noise. Can Holt's method be used to provide reasonably accurate forecasts of this series?

Objective   To use Holt's exponential smoothing model to track the trend in the Johnson & Johnson quarterly sales data.

Solution

We will illustrate how StatTools can be used to implement Holt's method on the sales data. This requires two steps: identifying the data set and then doing the forecasting.

Identifying the Data Set

StatTools works with "data sets," which you have to specify before performing any statistical analysis. The data in this file, shown in Figure 12.36 (with some hidden rows), are in

Figure 12.35   Quarterly Johnson & Johnson Sales

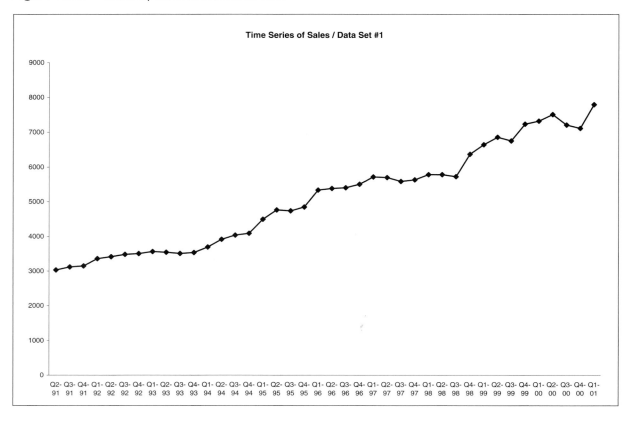

Figure 12.36

Data Set for Time
Series Data

	A	B
3	Quarter	Sales
4	Q2-91	3031
5	Q3-91	3119
6	Q4-91	3148
7	Q1-92	3357
8	Q2-92	3413
9	Q3-92	3480
10	Q4-92	3503
11	Q1-93	3560
12	Q2-93	3541
13	Q3-93	3506
14	Q4-93	3531
39	Q1-00	7319
40	Q2-00	7508
41	Q3-00	7204
42	Q4-00	7108
43	Q1-01	7791

the range A3:B43. To specify the data set, select the StatTools/Data Set Manager menu item, fill out the resulting dialog box as shown in Figure 12.37, and click on OK. Now you are ready to perform a statistical analysis on this data set.

Applying Holt's Method

To apply Holt's method, select the StatTools/Time Series & Forecasting/Forecast menu item. There are three tabs on the resulting dialog box. The most important is the Forecast Settings tab, which you should fill in as shown in Figure 12.38. This indicates that (1) Sales is the time series variable of interest, (2) we want 8 quarters of future forecasts,

Figure 12.37
Data Set Manager

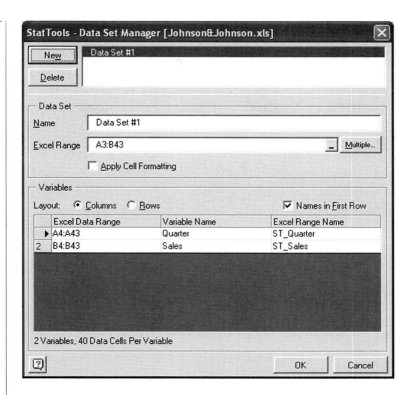

(3) we are using Holt's method, and (4) we want to optimize the smoothing constants (to give the smallest possible RMSE). The other two tabs are straightforward and are not shown here. The Time Scale tab lets you indicate that these are quarterly data, beginning with quarter 2 of 1991, and the Graphs to Display tab lets you choose which of three graphs you want StatTools to create.

Figure 12.38
Forecast Settings

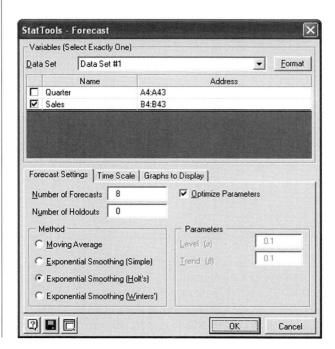

Discussion of the Results

The StatTools output for Holt's method consists of three sections: summary data, detailed data, and charts. The summary data appear in Figure 12.39. They indicate that the best smoothing constants are 0.821 (for level) and 0.0 (for trend). These produce the error measures shown. For example, MAPE is 2.83%. Although the smoothing constants shown here minimize RMSE, you can experiment with other smoothing constants in cells B9 and B10. For example, if you set both smoothing constants equal to 0.2, you will see that RMSE increases to 277.6 and MAPE increases to 4.59%. Clearly, the choice of smoothing constants *does* make a difference.

Figure 12.39

Summary Data

	A	B
8	*Forecasting Constants (Optimized)*	
9	Level (Alpha)	0.821
10	Trend (Beta)	0.000
11		
12		
13	*Holt's Exponential*	
14	Mean Abs Err	151.38
15	Root Mean Sq Err	198.36
16	Mean Abs Per% Err	2.83%

The detailed data section, shown in Figure 12.40 (with some hidden rows), is where equations (12.14) and (12.15) are implemented. You can look at the formulas in this section to gain a better technical understanding of Holt's method. In particular, note how the future forecasts in rows 103–110 project the ending level and trend in row 102 into the future.

Figure 12.40 Detailed Data

	A	B	C	D	E	F
62	*Forecasting Data*	Sales	Level	Trend	Forecast	Error
63	Q2-1991	3031.0000	3031.00	119.00		
64	Q3-1991	3119.0000	3124.55	119.00	3150.00	-31.00
65	Q4-1991	3148.0000	3165.09	119.00	3243.55	-95.55
66	Q1-1992	3357.0000	3343.96	119.00	3284.09	72.91
67	Q2-1992	3413.0000	3421.94	119.00	3462.96	-49.96
68	Q3-1992	3480.0000	3490.90	119.00	3540.94	-60.94
69	Q4-1992	3503.0000	3522.13	119.00	3609.90	-106.90
70	Q1-1993	3560.0000	3574.51	119.00	3641.13	-81.13
71	Q2-1993	3541.0000	3568.29	119.00	3693.51	-152.51
72	Q3-1993	3506.0000	3538.43	119.00	3687.29	-181.29
98	Q1-2000	7319.0000	7313.92	119.00	7290.60	28.40
99	Q2-2000	7508.0000	7494.57	119.00	7432.92	75.08
100	Q3-2000	7204.0000	7277.27	119.00	7613.57	-409.57
101	Q4-2000	7108.0000	7159.57	119.00	7396.27	-288.27
102	Q1-2001	7791.0000	7699.32	119.00	7278.57	512.43
103	Q2-2001				7818.32	
104	Q3-2001				7937.32	
105	Q4-2001				8056.32	
106	Q1-2002				8175.32	
107	Q2-2002				8294.32	
108	Q3-2002				8413.32	
109	Q4-2002				8532.32	
110	Q1-2003				8651.32	

Two useful charts produced by StatTools appear in Figures 12.41 and 12.42. The first of these superimposes the forecasts onto the original series. It also shows the projected forecasts at the right. We see that the forecasts track the series quite well and the future projections follow the clear upward trend. The chart in Figure 12.42 shows the series of forecast errors. If the forecast method is working well, this chart should be "random," with no apparent patterns. The only suspicious pattern evident here is that the zigzags appear to be increasing in magnitude through time. Perhaps a more sophisticated forecasting method

Figure 12.41   Time Series with Forecasts Superimposed

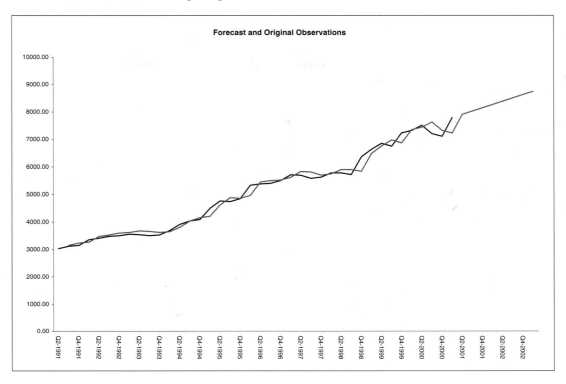

Figure 12.42   Series of Forecast Errors

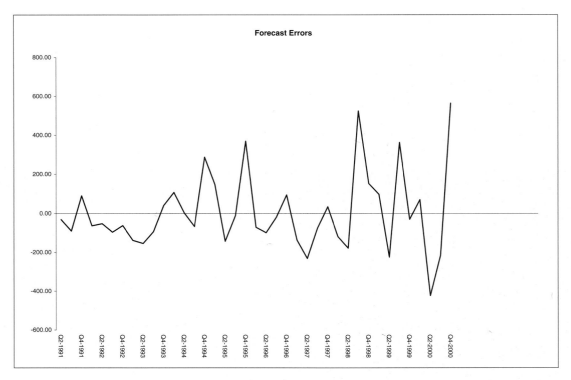

could deal with this pattern, but we will not pursue it here. For our purposes, Holt's method seems to be doing quite well with this data set. It tracks the historical data closely, and it accurately projects the upward trend. ■

Winters' Method for Seasonality[8]

Winters' exponential smoothing method is only one of several popular methods for dealing with seasonality.

When a time series exhibits obvious seasonality, such as swimming pool supply sales that are always higher in the spring and summer than in the rest of the year, none of the extrapolation methods discussed to this point will do a good job. They will all miss the seasonal ups and downs. Various methods have been proposed to deal with seasonality. One possibility is to use regression with dummy variables for the seasons. Another possibility is to "deseasonalize" the series first, then use one of the methods we have discussed to forecast the deseasonalized series, and finally "reseasonalize" the forecasts. We will not discuss these possibilities here, but we do mention that many time series listed in newspapers, magazines, and government reports actually list deseasonalized data—that is, they have already manipulated the data to remove any seasonality, presumably so that we can identify trends more clearly.

In addition to the level and trend terms, Winters' method requires a whole series of seasonal factors, one for each season.

The method we briefly discuss here is a direct extension of Holt's exponential smoothing model. It is called Winters' method. Like Holt's method, Winters' method estimates a level L_t and a trend T_t, using smoothing constants α and β. These have the same interpretation as before. In addition, there is a seasonal factor S_t for each season, where a "season" is usually a month or a quarter. Each seasonal factor represents the percentage by which that season is typically above or below the average for all seasons. For example, if the seasonal factor for June is 1.35, then a typical June value is 35% higher than the average for *all* months. Or if the seasonal factor for February is 0.75, then a typical February value is 25% lower than the average for all months. With Winters' method, these seasonal factors are continually updated as we observe more values of the time series, using still another smoothing constant γ (gamma) and another smoothing equation similar to equations (12.11), (12.14), and (12.15). Due to their complexity, we will not present the smoothing equations for Winters' method here.

To see how forecasting works with Winters' method, suppose we have observed data up through June of some year, and we have used these data to calculate the most recent level L_t, the most recent trend T_t, and the updated seasonal factors. Then the forecast for July is $(L_t + T_t)S_{\text{July}}$, the forecast for August is $(L_t + 2T_t)S_{\text{August}}$, and so on. In other words, we proceed exactly as with Holt's method, except that we multiply each forecast by the relevant seasonal factor.

Fortunately, we can rely on the StatTools add-in to make the calculations, as illustrated in the following example.

EXAMPLE	12.8 FORECASTING QUARTERLY SALES AT COCA-COLA

The data in the **CocaCola.xls** file represent quarterly sales (in millions of dollars) for Coca-Cola from quarter 1 of 1986 through quarter 1 of 2001. As we might expect, there has been an upward trend in sales during this period, and there is also a fairly regular seasonal pattern, as shown in Figure 12.43. Sales in the warmer quarters, 2 and 3, are consistently higher than in the colder quarters, 1 and 4. How well can Winters' method track this upward trend and seasonal pattern?

[8]This subsection, which uses an add-in, can be omitted without any loss in continuity.

Figure 12.43 Quarterly Coca-Cola Sales

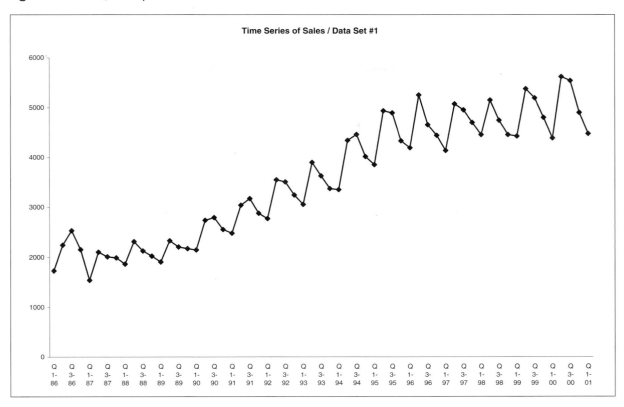

Time Series of Sales / Data Set #1

Objective To use Winters' exponential smoothing method to track the upward trend and regular seasonal pattern in Coca-Cola's quarterly sales.

Solution

We will keep this discussion brief since the procedure required for Winters' method is practically the same as for Holt's method. We again create a data set with StatTools, and then we fill in the dialog box for forecast settings as shown in Figure 12.44 (page 654). The only difference is that when we check the Winters' option, an extra smoothing constant (for seasonality) appears.

Discussion of the Results

The StatTools output for Winters' method is very similar to the Holt's method output. The summary section in Figure 12.45 shows the optimal smoothing constants, which produce a MAPE of 3.57%. Again, you can manually try other smoothing constants in the range B9:B11 to see how sensitive the summary measures are to the smoothing constants.

The detailed data section in Figure 12.46 implements the exponential smoothing equations for Winters' method. Note in particular the seasonality factors in column E. They remain constant from year to year (because gamma is 0), and they indicate a clear pattern, where sales in quarters 1 and 4 are always below average, and sales in quarters 2 and 3 are always above average. Also, the trends in column D indicate that, aside from the seasonality, sales tend to increase through time by about $50 million per quarter.

Figure 12.44

Forecast Settings for Winters' Method

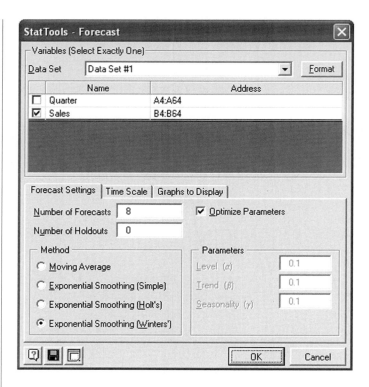

Figure 12.45

Summary Data

	A	B
8	*Forecasting Constants (Optimized)*	
9	Level (Alpha)	0.873
10	Trend (Beta)	0.000
11	Season (Gamma)	0.000
12		
13		
14	*Winters' Exponential*	
15	Mean Abs Err	115.26
16	Root Mean Sq Err	156.52
17	Mean Abs Per% Err	3.57%

Figure 12.46 Detailed Data

	A	B	C	D	E	F	G
63	*Forecasting Data*	Sales	Level	Trend	Season	Forecast	Error
64	Q1-1986	1734.8270	1955.06	50.70	0.89		
65	Q2-1986	2244.9610	2041.15	50.70	1.10	2200.50	44.47
66	Q3-1986	2533.8050	2362.95	50.70	1.05	2206.37	327.44
67	Q4-1986	2154.9630	2264.50	50.70	0.96	2319.06	-164.10
68	Q1-1987	1547.8190	1816.65	50.70	0.89	2054.40	-506.58
69	Q2-1987	2104.4120	1911.74	50.70	1.10	2048.65	55.76
70	Q3-1987	2014.3630	1916.48	50.70	1.05	2069.87	-55.51
71	Q4-1987	1991.7470	2059.58	50.70	0.96	1890.08	101.66
120	Q1-2000	4391.0000	4960.96	50.70	0.89	4478.79	-87.79
121	Q2-2000	5621.0000	5109.38	50.70	1.10	5498.24	122.76
122	Q3-2000	5543.0000	5243.23	50.70	1.05	5442.57	100.43
123	Q4-2000	4903.0000	5127.18	50.70	0.96	5086.46	-183.46
124	Q1-2001	4479.0000	5064.11	50.70	0.89	4594.60	-115.60
125	Q2-2001					5611.40	
126	Q3-2001					5448.29	
127	Q4-2001					5011.78	
128	Q1-2002					4673.59	
129	Q2-2002					5833.88	
130	Q3-2002					5662.18	
131	Q4-2002					5206.63	
132	Q1-2003					4853.54	

Figure 12.47 Time Series with Forecasts Superimposed

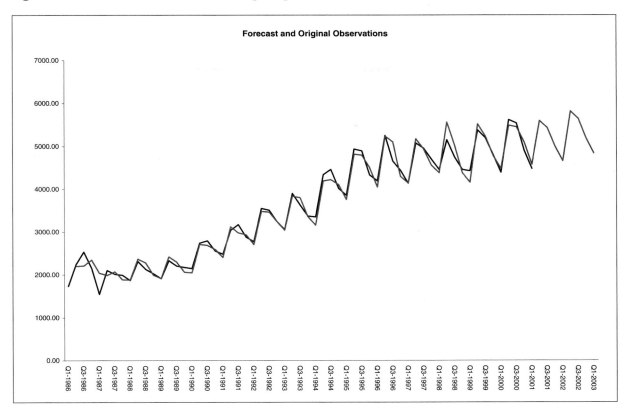

> The chart in Figure 12.47 indicates how well Winters' method (with these smoothing constants) tracks the sales pattern through time. It even picks up the slight decrease in the upward trend in more recent years and projects this pattern into the future. If we had used Holt's method on this data set, it would have identified the upward trend, but it would have completely missed the seasonality pattern. ■

PROBLEMS

Skill-Building Problems

28. You have been assigned to forecast the number of aircraft engines ordered each month by Commins Engine Company. At the end of February, the forecast is that 100 engines will be ordered during April. During March, 120 engines are ordered. Using $\alpha = 0.3$, determine a forecast (at the end of March) for the number of orders placed during April. Answer the same question for May. Use simple exponential smoothing.

29. Simple exponential smoothing with $\alpha = 0.3$ is being used to forecast sales of radios at Lowland Appliance. Forecasts are made on a monthly basis. After August

radio sales are observed, the forecast for September is 100 radios.

  a. During September, 120 radios are sold. After observing September sales, what do we forecast for October radio sales? For November radio sales?

  b. It turns out that June sales were recorded as 10 radios. Actually, however, 100 radios were sold in June. After correcting for this error, develop a forecast for October radio sales.

30. The file **P12_30.xls** contains the quarterly numbers of applications for home mortgage loans at a branch office of Northern Central Bank.

a. Create a time series chart of the data. Based on what you see, which of the exponential smoothing models do you think will provide the best forecasting model? Why?

b. Use simple exponential smoothing to forecast these data, using a smoothing constant of 0.1.

c. Repeat part **b**, but search for the smoothing constant that makes RMSE as small as possible. Does it make much of an improvement over the model in part **b**?

31. The file **P12_31.xls** contains the monthly number of airline tickets sold by the CareFree Travel Agency.

a. Create a time series chart of the data. Based on what you see, which of the exponential smoothing models do you think will provide the best forecasting model? Why?

b. Use simple exponential smoothing to forecast these data, using a smoothing constant of 0.1.

c. Repeat part **b**, but search for the smoothing constant that makes RMSE as small as possible. Does it make much of an improvement over the model in part **b**?

32. The file **P12_32.xls** contains yearly data on the proportion of Americans under the age of 18 living below the poverty level.

a. Create a time series chart of the data. Based on what you see, which of the exponential smoothing models do you think will provide the best forecasting model? Why?

b. Use simple exponential smoothing to forecast these data, using a smoothing constant of 0.1.

c. Repeat part **b**, but search for the smoothing constant that makes RMSE as small as possible. Create a chart of the series with the forecasts superimposed from this optimal smoothing constant. Does it make much of an improvement over the model in part **b**?

d. Write a short report to summarize your results. Considering the chart in part **c**, would you say the forecasts are "good"?

33. The file **P12_33.xls** contains weekly data for the S&P 500 stock index from the beginning of 2002 to mid-2003. (It was downloaded from the Yahoo site. You can follow the hyperlink in the file to obtain more recent data if you like.) In particular, the file lists closing prices in column H, adjusted for dividends and stock splits.

a. Create a time series plot of the adjusted closing prices. Does it look like moving averages and/or simple exponential smoothing will perform well on this series?

b. Run moving averages on the adjusted closing prices, experimenting with the span. Which span appears to work best? Report the MAE, RMSE, and MAPE values, and show a graph of the series with the forecasts superimposed, for the best span.

c. Run simple exponential smoothing on the adjusted closing prices, experimenting with the smoothing constant. Which smoothing constant appears to work best? Report the MAE, RMSE, and MAPE values, and show a graph of the series with the forecasts superimposed, for the best smoothing constant.

34. TOD Chevy is using Holt's method to forecast weekly car sales. Currently, the level of the series is estimated to be 50 cars per week, and the trend is estimated to be 6 cars per week. During the current week, 30 cars are sold. After observing the current week's sales, forecast the number of cars sold 1 week from now; 2 weeks from now; 3 weeks from now. Use $\alpha = \beta = 0.3$.

35. Consider the American Express closing price data from Problem 22 in the file **P12_22.xls**.

a. Create a time series chart of the data. Based on what you see, which of the exponential smoothing models do you think will provide the best forecasting model? Why?

b. Use Holt's exponential smoothing to forecast these data, using the smoothing constants $\alpha = \beta = 0.1$.

c. Repeat part **b**, searching for the smoothing constants that make RMSE as small as possible. Does it make much of an improvement over the result in part **b**?

36. The University Credit Union is open Monday through Saturday. Winters' method is being used to predict the number of customers entering the bank each day. (The six days of the week are considered the "seasons.") After observing the number of arrivals on Monday, the updated estimates of level and trend of the series are 200 and 1, respectively, and the estimated seasonal factors for Monday through Saturday are 0.90, 0.70, 0.80, 1.10, 1.20, and 1.30. Provide forecasts for Tuesday through Saturday of the current week.

37. The file **P12_37.xls** contains monthly retail sales of U.S. liquor stores.

a. Is seasonality present in these data? If so, characterize the seasonality pattern.

b. Use Winters' method to forecast this series with smoothing constants $\alpha = \beta = 0.1$ and $\gamma = 0.3$. Does the forecast series seem to track the seasonal pattern well? What are your forecasts for the next 12 months?

38. The file **P12_38.xls** contains monthly time series data for total U.S. retail sales of building materials (which includes retail sales of building materials hardware and garden supply stores, and mobile home dealers).

a. Is seasonality present in these data? If so, characterize the seasonality pattern.

b. Use Winters' method to forecast this series with smoothing constants $\alpha = \beta = 0.1$ and $\gamma = 0.3$. Does the forecast series seem to track the seasonal pattern well? What are your forecasts for the next 12 months?

Skill-Extending Problems

39. A version of simple exponential smoothing can be used to predict the outcome of sporting events. To illustrate, consider pro football. We first assume that all games are played on a neutral field. Before each day of play, we assume that each team has a rating. For example, if the rating for the Bears is $+10$ and the rating for the Bengals is $+6$, we would predict the Bears to beat the Bengals by $10 - 6 = 4$ points. Suppose that the Bears play the Bengals and win by 20 points. For this game, we "underpredicted" the Bears' performance by $20 - 4 = 16$ points. The best α for pro football is $\alpha = 0.10$. After the game, we therefore increase the Bears' rating by $16(0.1) = 1.6$ and decrease the Bengals's rating by 1.6 points. In a rematch, the Bears would be favored by $(10 + 1.6) - (6 - 1.6) = 7.2$ points.

  a. How does this approach relate to the equation $L_t = L_{t-1} + \alpha E_t$?

  b. Suppose that the home field advantage in pro football is 3 points; that is, home teams tend to outscore visiting teams by an average of 3 points a game. How could the home field advantage be incorporated into this system?

  c. How could we determine the best α for pro football?

  d. How might we determine ratings for each team at the beginning of the season?

  e. Suppose we tried to apply the previous method to predict pro football (16-game schedule), college football (11-game schedule), college basketball (30-game schedule), and pro basketball (82-game schedule). Which sport would probably have the smallest optimal α? Which sport would probably have the largest optimal α?

  f. Why would this approach probably yield poor forecasts for major league baseball?

40. Holt's method assumes an *additive* trend. For example, a trend of 5 means that the level will increase by 5 units per period. Suppose there is actually a *multiplicative* trend. This means that if the current estimate of the level is 50 and the current estimate of the trend is 1.2, we would predict demand to increase by 20% per period. So we would forecast the next period's demand to be $50(1.2)$ and forecast the demand two periods in the future to be $50(1.2)^2$. If we want to use a multiplicative trend in Holt's method, we should use the following equations:

$$L_t = \alpha Y_t + (1 - \alpha)U$$
$$T_t = \beta V + (1 - \beta)T_{t-1}$$

  a. Determine what U and V should be to make this a sensible forecasting method.

  b. Suppose we are working with monthly data and month 12 is December, month 13 is January, and so on. Also suppose that the level and trend, right after observing December's value, are $L_{12} = 100$ and $T_{12} = 1.2$, respectively. Then we observe $Y_{13} = 200$. At the end of month 13, what is the forecast for month 14? For month 15? Assume $\alpha = \beta = 0.5$.

12.8 CONCLUSION

We have seen numerous examples in this book where numeric input data for a spreadsheet model are required. In real situations, these data are often obtained through regression or an extrapolation forecasting method. In this chapter we have discussed regression and some of the more popular extrapolation methods for time series forecasting. These are important tools in any management scientist's tool kit. In fact, they are becoming required tools for just about any business analyst, because virtually all business analysts need to relate variables, discover trends and seasonal patterns, and make forecasts. Fortunately, the basic tools we have presented are reasonably easy to understand and use, especially given the built-in capabilities of Excel and the available statistical add-ins for Excel. These tools are extremely widespread, flexible, and powerful. We suspect that most of you will use them at some point in your careers.

Summary of Key Management Science Terms

Term	Explanation	Page
Regression models	Statistical models that estimate an equation to relate one variable to one or more "explanatory" variables	607
Extrapolation (time series) models	Statistical models that relate a time series variable to previous values of that same variable	607, 632

Term	Explanation	Page
Dependent variable	The variable being explained in a regression model, typically denoted by Y	608
Independent variables	The variables used to explain the dependent variable in a regression model, typically denoted by X's	608
Simple regression	A regression model with a single independent variable	608
Multiple regression	A regression model with multiple independent variables	608
Least-squares line	The regression line that minimizes the sum of squared residuals; the resulting line from a typical regression analysis	609
Residual	The difference between an actual Y value and the value predicted by the regression equation	609
Fitted value	A predicted value of Y, as predicted by the regression equation	609
Standard error of estimate	Essentially, the standard deviation of the residuals; an estimate of the magnitude of prediction errors made from the regression equation	610
Multiple R	The correlation between the actual Y's and the fitted Y's	610
R-square	The percentage of variation of the Y's explained by the regression	611
Linear trend	A trend, usually through time, where a variable changes by a constant *amount* each time period	611
Exponential trend	A trend, usually through time, where a variable changes by a constant *percentage* each time period	611
Dummy variables	0–1 variables that are used in regression equations to encode a categorical variable such as Gender or Quarter	626
Time series components	The items, including trend, seasonality, cyclic behavior, and noise, that produce the patterns observed in most time series variables	633
MAE, RMSE, MAPE	Three popular measures of forecast errors in time series analysis	615, 636
Moving averages method	A forecasting method where the forecast for any period is the average of the several most recent periods	637
Span	The number of terms in each average in moving averages; larger spans produce a smoother forecast series	637
Exponential smoothing methods	A forecasting method where the forecast for any period is a weighted average of previous periods, with more recent periods getting more weight	642
Smoothing constants	One or more constants, all between 0 and 1, that drive the exponential smoothing equation(s); lower values produce a smoother forecast series	642
Simple exponential smoothing	Version of exponential smoothing appropriate when there is no obvious trend or seasonality	642
Holt's method	Version of exponential smoothing appropriate when there is a trend but no obvious seasonality	646
Winters' method	Version of exponential smoothing appropriate when there is seasonality and possibly a trend	652

Summary of Key Excel Terms

Term	Explanation	Excel	Page
Creating scatterplot	Useful for identifying a relationship between two variables	Use the Chart Wizard, with an X-Y chart	612
Superimposing trendline	Useful for identifying a linear or exponential trend through a scatterplot	Create scatterplot, then use the Chart/Add Trendline menu item	613
EXP function	Used to raise the special number e to a power; also called the "antilog" function	=EXP(*value*)	616
SUMSQ function	Used to sum the squares of values in a range	=SUMSQ(*range*)	620
Analysis ToolPak	A statistical add-in that ships with Excel; useful for regression and several other statistical procedures	Use Tools/Data Analysis menu item	623
Creating time series plot	Useful for seeing how a time series variable behaves through time	Use the Chart Wizard, with a Line chart	633
StatTools add-in	A statistical add-in developed by Palisade that is considerably more powerful than Analysis ToolPak	Has its own menu, toolbar	647

PROBLEMS

Skill-Building Problems

41. The file **P12_41.xls** lists sales (in millions of dollars) of Dell Computer during the period 1987–1997 (where year 1 corresponds to 1987).
    a. Fit an exponential trendline to these data.
    b. Use your part **a** answer to predict 1999 sales for Dell.
    c. Use your part **a** answer to describe how the sales of Dell have grown from year to year.

42. The file **P12_42.xls** contains the sales (in millions of dollars) for Sun Microsystems.
    a. Use these data to predict the company's sales for the next 2 years. You need consider only a linear and exponential trend, but you should justify the equation you choose.
    b. In words, how do your predictions of sales increase from year to year?

43. The file **P12_43.xls** contains the sales in (millions of dollars) for Procter and Gamble.
    a. Use these data to predict Procter & Gamble sales for the next 2 years. You need consider only a lin-
    ear and exponential trend, but you should justify the equation you choose.
    b. Use your part **a** answer to explain in words how your predictions of Procter & Gamble sales will increase from year to year.

44. Management of a home appliance store in Charlotte would like to understand the growth pattern of the monthly sales of VCR units over the past 2 years. Managers have recorded the relevant data in the file **P12_44.xls**. The question is whether the sales of VCR units have been growing *linearly* over the past 24 months.
    a. Generate a scatterplot for sales versus time. Comment on the observed behavior of monthly VCR sales at this store.
    b. Estimate a simple regression model to explain the variation of monthly VCR sales over the given time period. Interpret the estimated regression coefficients.

45. The "beta" of a stock is found by running a regression with the monthly return on a market index as the independent variable and the monthly return on the stock

as the dependent variable. The beta of the stock is then the slope of this regression.

a. Explain why most stocks have a positive beta.

b. Explain why a stock with a beta with absolute value greater than 1 is more volatile than the market and a stock with a beta with absolute value less than 1 is less volatile than the market.

c. Use the data in the file **P12_45.xls** to estimate the beta for Ford Motor Company.

d. What percentage of the variation in Ford's return is explained by market variation? What percentage is unexplained by market variation?

46. The file **P12_46.xls** contains the amount of money spent advertising a product (in thousands of dollars) and the number of units sold (in millions) for 8 months.

a. Assume that the only factor influencing monthly sales is advertising. Fit the following two curves to these data: linear ($Y = a + bX$) and power ($Y = aX^b$). Which equation best fits the data?

b. Interpret the best-fitting equation. (See Problem 9, page 621.)

c. Using the best-fitting equation, predict sales during a month in which $60,000 is spent on advertising.

47. Callaway Golf is trying to determine how the price of a set of clubs affects the demand for clubs. The file **P12_47.xls** contains the price of a set of clubs (in dollars) and the monthly sales (in millions of sets sold).

a. Assume the only factor influencing monthly sales is price. Fit the following two curves to these data: linear ($Y = a + bX$) and exponential ($Y = ae^{bX}$). Which equation best fits the data?

b. Interpret your best-fitting equation. (See Problem 9, page 621.)

c. Using the best-fitting equation, predict sales during a month in which the price is $470.

48. When potential workers apply for a job that requires extensive manual assembly of small intricate parts, they are initially given three different tests to measure their manual dexterity. The ones who are hired are then periodically given a performance rating on a 0–100 scale that combines their speed and accuracy in performing the required assembly operations. The file **P12_48.xls** lists the test scores and performance ratings for a randomly selected group of employees. It also lists their seniority (months with the company) at the time of the performance rating.

a. Run the regression of JobPerf versus all four independent variables. List the equation, the R-square value, and the standard error of estimate. Do all of the regression coefficients have the signs you would expect? Briefly explain.

b. Referring to the equation in part **a**, if a worker (outside of the 80 in the sample) has 15 months of seniority and test scores of 57, 71, and 63, give a prediction and an approximate 95% prediction in-

terval for this worker's JobPerf score.

c. Arguably, the three test measures provide overlapping (or redundant) information. It might be sensible to regress JobPerf versus only two explanatory variables, Sen and AvgTest, where AvgTest is the average of the three test scores, that is, AvgTest = (Test1 + Test2 + Test3)/3. Run this regression and report the same measures as in part **a**: the equation itself, R-square, and the standard error of estimate. Can you argue that this equation is "just as good as" the equation in part **a**? Explain briefly.

49. The file **P12_49.xls** contains quarterly revenues of Toys 'R Us. Discuss the seasonal and trend components of the growth of Toys 'R Us revenues. Also, use any reasonable forecasting method to forecast quarterly revenues for the next year. Explain your choice of forecasting method.

50. Let Y_t be the sales during month t (in thousands of dollars) for a photography studio, and let P_t be the price charged for portraits during month t. The data are in the file **P12_50.xls**.

a. Use regression to fit the following model to these data: $Y_t = a + b_1 P_t + b_2 Y_{t-1}$. This says that current sales are related to current price and sales in the previous month. (*Hint*: You won't be able to use the first month's data because there is no value for the previous month's sales.)

b. If the price of a portrait during month 21 is $10, what would we predict for sales in month 21?

51. The file **P12_51.xls** contains data on monthly U.S. housing sales (in thousands of houses).

a. Use Winters' method with $\alpha = \beta = 0.1$ and $\gamma = 0.3$ to forecast this series. Ask for 12 months of future forecasts. Then use Winters' method a second time with the values of the smoothing constants that minimize RMSE.

b. Compare the two sets of outputs. How do they track the historical data? How do their future forecasts differ? Which of the two do you believe?

Skill-Extending Problems

52. The auditor of Kiely Manufacturing is concerned about the number and magnitude of year-end adjustments that are made annually when the financial statements of Kiely Manufacturing are prepared. Specifically, the auditor suspects that the management of Kiely Manufacturing is using discretionary write-offs to manipulate the reported net income. To check this, the auditor has collected data from 25 firms that are similar to Kiely Manufacturing in terms of manufacturing facilities and product lines. The cumulative reported third quarter income and the final net income reported are listed in the file **P12_52.xls** for each of these 25 firms. If Kiely Manufacturing reported a cumulative third quarter income of $2,500,000 and a

preliminary net income of $4,900,000, should the auditor conclude that the relationship between cumulative third quarter income and the annual income for Kiely Manufacturing differs from that of the 25 firms in this sample? Why or why not?

53. The file **P12_53.xls** contains data on pork sales. Price is in dollars per hundred pounds, quantity sold is in billions of pounds, per capita income is in dollars, U.S. population is in millions, and GNP is in billions of dollars.

   a. Use the data on all potential explanatory variables to develop a regression equation that could be used to predict the quantity of pork sold during future periods.

   b. Find the correlations between all pairs of variables. (We recommend StatTools.) What evidence do you see of multicollinearity? How could this cause a problem with the regression? Run another regression without potentially redundant variables. How does this new regression compare to the one in part **a**?

   c. Suppose that during each of the next two quarters, price is 45, U.S. population is 240, GNP is 2620, and per capita income is 10,000. (These are in the units described above.) Predict the quantity of pork sold during each of the next 2 quarters using the equations from parts **a** and **b**. How do they compare?

54. The belief that larger majorities for an incumbent president in a presidential election help the incumbent's party increase its representation in the House and Senate is called the "coattail" effect. The file **P12_54.xls** gives the percent by which each president since 1948 won the election and the number of seats in the House and Senate gained (or lost) during each election. Are these data consistent with the idea of presidential coattails? (*Source: Wall Street Journal,* September 10, 1996)

55. The auditor of Kaefer Manufacturing uses regression analysis during the analytical review stage of the firm's annual audit. The regression analysis attempts to uncover relationships that exist between various account balances. Any such relationship is subsequently used as a preliminary test of the reasonableness of the reported account balances. The auditor wants to determine whether a relationship exists between the balance of accounts receivable at the end of the month and that month's sales. The file **P12_55.xls** contains data on these two accounts for the last 36 months. It also shows the sales levels 2 months prior to month 1.

   a. Is there any statistical evidence to suggest a relationship between the monthly sales level and accounts receivable?

   b. Referring to part **a**, would the relationship be described any better by including this month's sales

and the previous month's sales (called lagged sales) in the equation for accounts receivable? What about adding the sales from more than a month ago to the equation? For this problem, why might it make accounting sense to include lagged sales variables in the equation? How do you interpret their coefficients?

   c. During month 37, which is a fiscal year-end month, the sales were $1,800,000. The reported accounts receivable balance was $3,000,000. Does this reported amount seem consistent with past experience? Explain.

56. (Based on an actual court case in Philadelphia) In the 1994 congressional election, the Republican candidate outpolled the Democratic candidate by 400 votes (excluding absentee ballots). The Democratic candidate outpolled the Republican candidate by 500 absentee votes. The Republican candidate sued (and won), claiming that vote fraud must have played a role in the absentee ballot count. The Republican's lawyer ran a regression to predict (based on past elections) how the absentee ballot margin could be predicted from the votes tabulated on voting machines. Selected results are given in the file **P12_56.xls**. Show how this regression could be used by the Republican to support his claim of vote fraud. (*Hint*: Does the 1994 observation fall outside the general pattern? That is, in statistical terms, is it an *outlier*?)

57. The file **P12_57.xls** contains data on the price of new and used Taurus sedans. All used prices are from 1995. For example, a new Taurus bought in 1985 cost $11,790, and the wholesale used price of that car in 1995 was $1700. A new Taurus bought in 1994 cost $18,680, and it could be sold used in 1995 for $12,600.

   a. You want to predict the resale value (as a percentage of the original price of the vehicle) as a function of the vehicle's age. Find an equation to do this. (You should try at least two different equations and choose the one that fits best.)

   b. Suppose all police cars are Ford Tauruses. If you were the business manager for the New York Police Department, what use would you make of your findings from part **a**?

58. Confederate Express is attempting to determine how its monthly shipping costs depend on the number of units shipped during a month. The file **P12_58.xls** contains the number of units shipped and total shipping costs for the last 15 months.

   a. Use regression to determine a relationship between units shipped and monthly shipping costs.

   b. Plot the errors for the predictions in order of time sequence. Is there any unusual pattern?

   c. Suppose there was a trucking strike during months 11–15, and we believe that this might have influenced shipping costs. How could the answer to part **a** be modified to account for the effects of the strike? After accounting for the effects of the strike, does the unusual pattern in part **b** disappear? (*Hint*: Use a dummy variable.)

59. You are trying to determine the effects of three packaging displays (A, B, and C) on sales of toothpaste. The file **P12_59.xls** contains the number of cases of toothpaste sold for 9 consecutive weeks. The type of store (GR = grocery, DI = discount, and DE = department store) and the store location (U = urban, S = suburban, and R = rural) are also listed.
    a. Run a multiple regression to determine how the type of store, display, and store location influence sales. Which potential explanatory variables should be included in the equation? Be sure to explain your rationale for including or excluding variables.
    b. What type of store, store location, and display appears to maximize sales?

60. Pernavik Dairy produces and sells a wide range of dairy products. Because most of the dairy's costs and prices are set by a government regulatory board, most of the competition between the dairy and its competitors takes place through advertising. The controller of Pernavik has developed the sales and advertising levels for the last 52 weeks. These appear in the file **P12_60.xls**. Note that the advertising levels for the three weeks prior to week 1 are also listed. The controller wonders whether Pernavik is spending too much money on advertising. He argues that the company's contribution-margin ratio is about 10%. That is, 10% of each sales dollar goes toward covering fixed costs. This means that each advertising dollar has to generate at least $10 of sales or the advertising is not cost-effective. Use regression to determine whether advertising dollars are generating this type of sales response. (*Hint*: It is very possible that the sales value in any week is affected not only by advertising this week, but also by advertising levels in the past one, two, or three weeks. These are called "lagged" values of advertising. Try regression models with lagged values of advertising included, and see whether you get better results.)

61. The file **P12_61.xls** contains data on a motel chain's revenue and advertising.
    a. Use these data and multiple regression to make predictions of the motel chain's revenues during the next four quarters. Assume that advertising during each of the next four quarters is $50,000. (*Hint*: Try using advertising, lagged by one period, as an independent variable. See the previous problem for an explanation of a "lagged" variable. Also, use dummy variables for the quarters to account for possible seasonality.)
    b. Use simple exponential smoothing to make predictions for the motel chain's revenues during the next four quarters. Experiment with the smoothing constant.
    c. Use Holt's method to make forecasts for the motel chain's revenues during the next four quarters. Experiment with the smoothing constants.
    d. Use Winters' method to determine predictions for the motel chain's revenues during the next four quarters. Experiment with the smoothing constants.
    e. Which forecasts would you expect to be the most reliable?

62. The file **P12_62.xls** contains 5 years of monthly data for a company. The first variable is Time (1–60). The second variable, Sales1, has data on sales of a product. Note that Sales1 increases linearly throughout the period, with only a minor amount of noise. (The third variable, Sales2, will be used in the next problem.) For this problem use the Sales1 variable to see how the following forecasting methods are able to track a linear trend.
    a. Forecast this series with the moving averages method with various spans such as 3, 6, and 12. What can you conclude?
    b. Forecast this series with simple exponential smoothing with various smoothing constants such as 0.1, 0.3, 0.5, and 0.7. What can you conclude?
    c. Repeat part **b** with Holt's method, again for various smoothing constants. Can you do much better than in parts **a** and **b**?

63. The Sales2 variable in the file from the previous problem was created from the Sales1 variable by multiplying by monthly seasonal factors. Basically, the summer months are high and the winter months are low. This might represent the sales of a product that has a linear trend and seasonality.
    a. Repeat parts **a–c** from the previous problem to see how well these forecasting methods can deal with trend *and* seasonality.
    b. Use Winters' method, with various values of the three smoothing constants, to forecast the series. Can you do much better? Which smoothing constants work well?
    c. What can you conclude from your findings in parts **a** and **b** about forecasting this type of series?

Howie's Bakery is one of the most popular bakeries in town, and the favorite at Howie's is French bread. Each day of the week, Howie's bakes a number of loaves of French bread, more or less according to a daily schedule. To maintain its fine reputation, Howie's gives to charity any loaves not sold on the day they are baked. Although this occurs frequently, it is also common for Howie's to run out of French bread on any given day—more demand than supply. In this case, no extra loaves are baked that day; the customers have to go elsewhere (or come back to Howie's the next day) for their French bread. Although French bread at Howie's is always popular, Howie's stimulates demand by running occasional 10% off sales.

Howie's has collected data for 20 consecutive weeks, 140 days in all. These data are listed in the file

Howies.xls. The variables are Day (Monday–Sunday), Supply (number of loaves baked that day), OnSale (whether French bread is on sale that day), and Demand (loaves actually sold that day). Howie's would like you to see whether regression can be used successfully to estimate Demand from the other data in the file. Howie reasons that if these other variables can be used to predict Demand, then he might be able to determine his daily supply (number of loaves to bake) in a more cost-effective way.

How successful is regression with these data? Is Howie correct that regression can help him determine his daily supply? Is any information "missing" that would be useful? How would you obtain it? How would you use it? Is this extra information *really* necessary? ■

Wagner Printers performs all types of printing including custom work, such as advertising displays, and standard work, such as business cards. Market prices exist for standard work, and Wagner Printers must match or better these prices to get the business. The key issue is whether the existing market price covers the cost associated with doing the work. On the other hand, most of the custom work must be priced individually. Because all custom work is done on a job-order basis, Wagner routinely keeps track of all the direct labor and direct materials costs associated with each job. However, the overhead for each job must be estimated. The overhead is applied to each job using a predetermined (normalized) rate based on estimated overhead and labor hours. Once the cost of the prospective job is determined, the sales manager develops a bid that reflects both the existing market conditions and the estimated price of completing the job.

In the past the normalized rate for overhead has been computed by using the historical average of overhead per direct labor hour. Wagner has become increasingly concerned about this practice for two reasons. First, it hasn't produced accurate forecasts of overhead in the past. Second, technology has changed the printing process, so that the labor content of jobs has been decreasing, and the normalized rate of overhead per direct labor hour has steadily been increasing. The file **Wagner.xls** shows the overhead data that Wagner has collected for its shop for the past 52 weeks. The average weekly overhead for the last 52 weeks is $54,208, and the average weekly number of labor hours worked is 716. Therefore, the normalized rate for overhead that will be used in the upcoming week is about $76 (= 54,208/716) per direct labor hour.

Questions

1. Determine whether you can develop a more accurate estimate of overhead costs.

2. Wagner is now preparing a bid for an important order that may involve a considerable amount of repeat business. The estimated requirements for this project are 15 labor hours, 8 machine hours, $150 direct labor cost, and $750 direct material cost. Using the existing approach to cost estimation, Wagner has estimated the cost for this job as $2040 (= 150 + 750 + (76 × 15)). Given the existing data, what cost would you estimate for this job? ■

The Indiana University Credit Union Eastland Plaza branch was having trouble getting the correct staffing levels to match customer arrival patterns. On some days, the number of tellers was too high relative to the customer traffic, so that tellers were often idle. On other days, the opposite occurred; long customer waiting lines formed because the relatively few tellers could not keep up with the number of customers. The credit union manager, James Chilton, knew that there was a problem, but he had little of the quantitative training he believed would be necessary to find a better staffing solution. James figured that the problem could be broken down into three parts. First, he needed a reliable forecast of each day's number of customer arrivals. Second, he needed to translate these forecasts into staffing levels that would make an adequate trade-off between teller idleness and customer waiting. Third, he needed to translate these staffing levels into individual teller work assignments—who should come to work when.

The last two parts of the problem require analysis tools (queueing and scheduling) that we will not pursue here. However, you can help James with the first part—forecasting. The file **CreditUnion.xls** lists the number of customers entering this credit union branch each day of the past year. It also lists other information: the day of the week, whether the day was a staff or faculty payday, and whether the day was the day before or after a holiday. Use this data set to develop one or more forecasting models that James could use to help solve his problem. Based on your model(s), make any recommendations about staffing that appear reasonable. ■

REFERENCES

Agnihothri, R., and P. Taylor. "Staffing a Centralized Appointment Scheduling Department in Lourdes Hospital." *Interfaces* 21, no. 5 (1991): 1–15.

Andrews, B., and H. Parsons. "Establishing Telephone-Agent Staffing Levels through Economic Optimization." *Interfaces* 23, no. 2 (1993): 14–20.

Arntzen, B., G. Brown, T. Harrison, and L. Trafton. "Global Supply Chain Management at Digital Equipment Corporation." *Interfaces* 25, no. 1 (1995): 69–93.

Babich, P. "Customer Satisfaction: How Good Is Good Enough?" *Quality Progress* 25 (Dec. 1992): 65–68.

Balson, W., J. Welsh, and D. Wilson. "Using Decision Analysis and Risk Analysis to Manage Utility Environmental Risk." *Interfaces* 22, no. 6 (1992): 126–139.

Bean, J., C. Noon, S. Ryan, and G. Salton. "Selecting Tenants in a Shopping Mall." *Interfaces* 18, no. 2 (1988): 1–10.

Bean, J., C. Noon, and G. Salton. "Asset Divestiture at Homart Development Company." *Interfaces* 17, no. 1 (1987): 48–65.

Borison, A. "Oglethorpe Power Corporation Decides about Investing in a Major Transmission System." *Interfaces* 25, no. 2 (1995): 25–36.

Boykin, R. "Optimizing Chemical Production at Monsanto." *Interfaces* 15, no. 1 (1985): 88–95.

Brigandi, A., D. Dargon, M. Sheehan, and T. Spencer. "AT&T's Call Processing Simulator (CAPS) Operational Design for Inbound Call Centers." *Interfaces* 24, no. 1 (1994): 6–28.

Brumelle, S. "On the Relation between Customer and Time Averages in Queues." *J. of Applied Probability* 8 (1971): 508–520.

Caulkins, J., E. Kaplan, P. Lurie, T. O'Connor, and S. Ahn. "Can Difficult-to-Reuse Syringes Reduce the Spread of HIV Among Injection Drug Users?" *Interfaces* 28, no. 3 (1998): 23–33.

Cebry, M., A. DeSilva, and F. DiLisio. "Management Science in Automating Postal Operations: Facility and Equipment Planning in the United States Postal Service." *Interfaces* 22, no. 1 (1992): 110–130.

Charnes, A., and L. Cooper. "Generalization of the Warehousing Model." *Operational Research Quarterly* 6 (1955): 131–172.

Dantzig, G. "The Diet Problem." *Interfaces* 20, no. 4 (1990): 43–47.

Denardo, E., U. Rothblum, and A. Swersey. "Transportation Problem in Which Costs Depend on Order of Arrival." *Management Science* 34 (1988): 774–784.

DeWitt, C., L. Lasdon, A. Waren, D. Brenner, and S. Melhem. "OMEGA: An Improved Gasoline Blending System for Texaco." *Interfaces* 19, no. 1 (1989): 85–101.

Dijkstra, M., L. Kroon, M. Salomon, J. van Nunen, and L. Wassenhove. "Planning the Size and Organization of KLM's Aircraft Maintenance Personnel." *Interfaces* 24, no. 6 (1994): 47–65.

Dolan, Robert J. & Simon, Hermann, *Power Pricing*. The Free Press, New York, 1996.

Eaton, D., et al. "Determining Emergency Medical Service Vehicle Deployment in Austin, Texas." *Interfaces* 15, no. 1 (1985): 96–108.

Efroymson, M., and T. Ray. "A Branch-Bound Algorithm for Plant Location." *Operations Research* 14 (1966): 361–368.

Evans, J. "The Factored Transportation Problem." *Management Science* 30 (1984): 1021–1024.

Feinstein, C. "Deciding Whether to Test Student Athletes for Drug Use." *Interfaces* 20, no. 3 (1990): 80–87.

Fitzsimmons, J., and L. Allen. "A Warehouse Location Model Helps Texas Comptroller Select Out-of-State Audit Offices." *Interfaces* 13, no. 5 (1983): 40–46.

Gigerenzer, G. *Calculated Risks: How to Know When Numbers Deceive You.* New York: Simon & Schuster, 2002.

Glover, F., and D. Klingman. "Network Applications in Industry and Government." *AIIE Transactions* 9 (1977): 363–376.

Grossman, S., and O. Hart. "An Analysis of the Principal Agent Problem." *Econometrica* 51 (1983): 7–45.

Hansen, P., and R. Wendell. "A Note on Airline Commuting." *Interfaces* 11, no. 12 (1982): 85–87.

Heady, E., and A. Egbert. "Regional Planning of Efficient Agricultural Patterns." *Econometrica* 32 (1964): 374–386.

Heyman, D. and S. Stidham. "The Relation between Customer and Time Averages in Queues." *Operations Research* 28 (1980): 983–984.

Hoppensteadt, F., and C. Peskin. *Mathematics in Medicine and the Life Sciences.* New York: Springer-Verlag, 1992.

Howard, R. "Heathens, Heretics, and Cults: The Religious Spectrum of Decision Aiding." *Interfaces* 22, no. 6 (1992): 15–27.

Howard, R. "Decision Analysis: Practice and Promise." *Management Science* 34, no. 6 (1988): 679–695.

Huerter, J., and W. Swart. "An Integrated Labor-Management System for Taco Bell." *Interfaces* 28, no. 1 (1998): 75–91.

Jacobs, W. "The Caterer Problem." *Naval Logistics Research Quarterly* 1 (1954): 154–165.

Kahn, J., M. Brandeau, and J. Dunn-Mortimer. "OR Modeling and AIDS Policy: From Theory to Practice." *Interfaces* 28, no. 3 (1998): 3–22.

Kelly, J. "A New Interpretation of Information Rate." *Bell System Technical Journal* 35 (1956): 917–926.

Kirkwood, C. "An Overview of Methods for Applied Decision Analysis." *Interfaces* 22, no. 6 (1992): 28–39.

Kolesar, P., and E. Blum. "Square Root Laws for Fire Engine Response Distances." *Management Science* 19 (1973): 1368–1378.

Kolesar, P., T. Crabill, K. Rider, and W. Walker. "A Queueing Linear Programming Approach to Scheduling Police Patrol Cars." *Operations Research* 23 (1974): 1045–1062.

Krajewski, L., L. Ritzman, and P. McKenzie. "Shift Scheduling in Banking Operations: A Case Application." *Interfaces* 10, no. 2 (1980): 1–8.

Krumm, F., and C. Rolle. "Management and Application of Decision and Risk Analysis in Du Pont." *Interfaces* 22, no. 6 (1992): 84–93.

Lancaster, L. "The Evolution of the Diet Model in Managing Food Systems." *Interfaces* 22, no. 5 (1992): 59–68.

Lanzenauer, C., E. Harbauer, B. Johnston, and D. Shuttleworth. "RRSP Flood: LP to the Rescue." *Interfaces* 17, no. 4 (1987): 27–40.

LeBlanc, L.J., J.A. Hill, Jr., G.W. Greenwell, and A.O. Czesnat. "Nu-kote's Spreadsheet Linear Programming Models for Supply-Chain Optimization." Working paper, Owen Graduate School of Management, Vanderbilt University, June 20, 2002.

LeBlanc, L.J., D. Randels, Jr., and T.K. Swann. "Heery International's Spreadsheet Optimization Model for Assigning Managers to Construction Projects." *Interfaces* 30, no. 6 (2000): 95–106.

Liggett, R. "The Application of an Implicit Enumeration Algorithm to the School Desegregation Problem." *Management Science* 20 (1973): 159–168.

Little, J.D.C. "A Proof for the Queuing Formula $L = \lambda W$." *Operations Research* 9 (1961): 383–387.

Love, R., and J. Hoey. "Management Science Improves Fast-Food Operations." *Interfaces* 20, no. 2 (1990): 21–29.

Machol, R. "An Application of the Assignment Problem." *Operations Research* 18 (1970): 745–746.

Magoulas, K., and D. Marinos-Kouris. "Gasoline Blending LP." *Oil and Gas Journal* (July 1988): 44–48.

Makuch, W., J. Dodge, J. Ecker, D. Granfors, and G. Hahn. "Managing Consumer Credit Delinquency in the US Economy: A Multi-Billion Dollar Management Scienc4e Application." *Interfaces* 22, no. 1 (1992): 90–109.

Marcus, A. "The Magellan Fund and Market Efficiency." *Journal of Portfolio Management* (Fall 1990): 85–88.

Martin, C., D. Dent, and J. Eckhart. "Integrated Production, Distribution, and Inventory Planning at Libbey-Owens-Ford." *Interfaces* 23, no. 3 (1993): 68–78.

Miser, H. "Avoiding the Corrupting Lie of a Poorly Stated Problem." *Interfaces* 23, no. 6 (1993): 114–119.

Morrison, D., and R. Wheat. "Pulling the Goalie Revisited." *Interfaces* 16, no. 6 (1984): 28–34.

Muckstadt, J., and R. Wilson. "An Application of Mixed Integer Programming Duality to Scheduling Thermal Generating Systems." *IEEE Transactions on Power Apparatus and Systems* (1968): 1968–1978.

Norton, R. "Which Offices or Stores Perform Best? A New Tool Tells." *Fortune* October 31 (1994).

Oliff, M., and E. Burch. "Multiproduct Production Scheduling at Owens-Corning Fiberglass." *Interfaces* 15, no. 5 (1985): 25–34.

Owens, D., M. Brandeau, and C. Sox. "Effect of Relapse to High-Risk Behavior on the Costs and Benefits of a Program to Screen Women for Human Immunodeficiency Virus." *Interfaces* 28, no. 3 (1998): 52–74.

Paltiel, A., and K. Freedberg. "The Cost-Effectiveness of Preventing Cytomegalovirus Disease in AIDS Patients." *Interfaces* 28, no. 3 (1998): 34–51.

Quinn, P., B. Andrews, and H. Parsons. "Allocating Telecommunications Resources at L. L. Bean, Inc." *Interfaces* 21, no. 1 (1991): 75–91.

Ravindran, A. "On Compact Book Storage in Libraries." *Opsearch* 8 (1971): 245–252.

Reichheld, F. *The Loyalty Effect.* Harvard Business School Press (1996).

Robichek, A., D. Teichroew, and M. Jones. "Optimal Short-Term Financing Decisions." *Management Science* 12 (1965): 1–36.

Robinson, P., L. Gao, and S. Muggenborg. "Designing an Integrated Distribution System at DowBrands, Inc." *Interfaces* 23, no. 3 (1993): 107–117.

Rohn, E. "A New LP Approach to Bond Portfolio Management." *Journal of Financial and Quantitative Analysis* 22 (1987): 439–467.

Rothstein, M. "Hospital Manpower Shift Scheduling by Mathematical Programming." *Health Services Research* (1973).

Schindler, S., and T. Semmel. "Station Staffing at Pan American World Airways." *Interfaces* 23, no. 3 (1993): 91–106.

Silver, E., D. Pyke, and R. Peterson, *Inventory Management and Production Planning and Scheduling,* 3rd ed., New York: Wiley, 1998.

Smith, S. "Planning Transistor Production by Linear Programming." *Operations Research* 13 (1965): 132–139.

Sonderman, D., and P. Abrahamson. "Radiotherapy Design Using Mathematical Programming." *Operations Research* 33, no. 4 (1985): 705–725.

Spencer, T., A. Brigandi, D. Dargon, and M. Sheehan. "AT&T's Telemarketing Site Selection System Offers Customer Support. *Interfaces* 20, no. 1 (1990).

Stidham, S. A Last Word on $L = \lambda W$." *Operations Research* 22 (1974): 417–421.

Sullivan, R., and S. Secrest. "A Simple Optimization DSS for Production Planning at Dairyman's Cooperative Creamery Association." *Interfaces* 15, no. 5 (1985): 46–54.

Swart, W., and L. Donno. "Simulation Modeling Improves Operations, Planning and Productivity of Fast-Food Restaurants." *Interfaces* 11, no. 6 (1981): 35–47.

Tanner, Mike. *Practical Queueing Analysis.* Berkshire, England: McGraw-Hill International (UK) Ltd., 1995.

Volkema, R. "Managing the Process of Formulating the Problem." *Interfaces* 25, no. 3 (1995): 81–87.

Waddell, R. "A Model for Equipment Replacement Decisions and Policies." *Interfaces* 13, no. 4 (1983): 1–8.

Walker, W. "Using the Set Covering Problem to Assign Five Companies to Firehouses." *Operations Research* 22 (1974): 275–277.

Westerberg, C., B. Bjorklund, and E. Hultman. "An Application of Mixed Integer Programming in a Swedish Steel Mill." *Interfaces* 7, no. 2 (1977): 39–43.

Winston, W. L. *Operations Research: Applications and Algorithms.* 4th ed. Belmont, California: Duxbury Press, 2003.

Zangwill, W. "The Limits of Japanese Production Theory." *Interfaces* 22, no. 5 (1992): 14–25.